BOURNEMOUTH TROLLEYBUSES

Second revised and greatly expanded edition published
to mark the 50th anniversary of the Abandonment of the
Bournemouth Trolleybus System on 26 April 1969.

David R.H. Bowler

Published by Adam Gordon

(Front Cover) Using the Five Ways turning circle amongst the pine trees at the junction of Queens Park Avenue with Charminster Road on a service 28 short-working is Sunbeam MS2 no. 213 (ALJ975) built in 1935 and still in all-day operation in summer 1963. In the background is the Five Ways Hotel built in the mid-1920s and an Eldridge, Pope house for much of the trolleybus era.

Roger G. Funnell (courtesy Mrs D. Funnell and Rodney Funnell)

(Rear Cover, Top) On 5 July 1965, Sunbeam MF2B no. 287 (YLJ287) scoots across Wimborne Road, Winton Banks, from Talbot Road into Crimea Road at the end of an interworking service 31 and 30 journey through Ensbury Park, Wallisdown and Talbot Village.

David Pearson

(Rear Cover, Bottom) BUT9641T no. 237 (KLJ337) speeds west across the junction of Holdenhurst Road with St. Paul's Road and Waverley Road heading for the Lansdowne, the Square and Westbourne on 4 July 1965. The wiring that led up St. Paul's Road past the Railway Hotel towards Cemetery Junction has already been removed to enable work on the Town Centre By-pass (today's Wessex Way) to start. This was the first trolleybus route closure in Bournemouth.

Robin Helliar-Symons

This publication is in no way to be considered an official publication of Bournemouth Christchurch Poole Council or Bournemouth Transport Ltd. (trading as Yellow Buses), although due acknowledgement is made of the Council and the Company, and their predecessor organisations as sources of official information contained therein. Acknowledgement is also made to the erstwhile Bournemouth Borough Council for permission to use the County Borough coat of arms (old version) in the cover design.

ISBN 978-1-910654-24-8

Publication no.126

Published in 2019 by Adam Gordon, Kintradwell Farmhouse, Brora, Sutherland, KW9 6LU
Tel: 01408 622660   E-mail: adam@ahg-books.com

Designed and typeset by Barnabas Gordon
Tel: 07795 201 502   Email: Barney@ahgbooks.com

Printed by Henry Ling, 90 Prince of Wales Rd, Dorchester DT1 1HD

CONTENTS

HISTORY OF THE SYSTEM

APPENDICES

MAPS

System

Network Development

FOREWORD

I am delighted to have been asked to write the foreword for this wonderful publication celebrating the history of trolleybuses in Bournemouth.

This book is published at an opportune moment as 2019 marks the 50th anniversary of the cessation of Bournemouth's once extensive trolleybus network.

As the successor operator, we celebrate 117 years of continuous service to the town in 2019. Bournemouth has always had a fascinating and flourishing transport scene, having operated both trams and trolleybuses prior to motorbuses becoming the norm. A word often overused is "iconic", however, I feel safe in applying that in this context, as Bournemouth's trolleybuses were indeed iconic and serve as a reminder of times past when public transport was owned and operated in a very different way to today.

Whilst this book will undoubtedly appeal to trolleybus enthusiasts, it is also a useful source of history for today's residents and students of public transport. Just look at the rich vein of history that flows through this book and compare photographs of locations from the past to what we encounter today. Some locations are barely recognisable whilst others have barely altered.

Yellow Buses have embraced the theme of the 50-year anniversary, and for our part, we have added some appropriate vinyls to our fleet number 30, which is our 'history bus'. The inside features numerous photos of public transport through the years including trolleybuses, whilst we have added some trolleybus images to the exterior of the bus to commemorate this important milestone.

I sincerely hope that you enjoy reading this superb publication. I commend the author, David Bowler, for this remarkable book, and hope that those readers who do not live locally are inspired to visit our wonderful town.

David Squire FCILT
Managing Director
Bournemouth Transport Ltd. t/a Yellow Buses
January 2019

It was a bright sunny morning on 2 August 1964 as open-top Sunbeam MS2 no. 201 (BRU11) rolls down Bath Road past H+D's Pavilion Garage to terminate at the Pier on a service 38 journey from Carbery Avenue, Tuckton. Service 38 last operated on 23 August 1964 and open-top trolleybus no. 201, despite its smart and shiny appearance, was withdrawn.
Tim Runnacles

INTRODUCTION

Throughout the trolleybus era, Bournemouth was probably the most genteel and refined resort of all the United Kingdom's coastal holiday destinations. Every corner and traffic island had carefully planted and tended flower beds, colourful public gardens could be found throughout the town and the ubiquitous pine trees left an all-pervading scent in the streets. Beautifully clean beaches, aided by the phenomenon of a "double high water", and a broad entertainment offer made the town an ideal location for both holiday and residence. The primrose-painted and smartly turned-out "Silent Service" of Bournemouth Corporation Transport fitted perfectly into this environment and provided a reliable scheduled service that was second to none.

It is now fifty years since the last trolleybus ran on the streets of Bournemouth; could they have survived those years and still be operating today? The town has changed considerably since then, perhaps reflecting the changes in British society. Those who use public transport are almost sneered upon as the community blindly follows American norms, such as out-of-town shopping malls and motorways, but in a country that is about a fortieth of its size. Few families now take an annual seaside holiday at home: prices are lower and the weather more reliable on the other side of the world. Britain is no longer a global power and has faded on the world stage. As in every other town today, cars, lorries and vans, block the streets emitting unhealthy and unpleasant exhaust fumes, whilst one cannot but fail to notice that slowly parts of the fabric of Bournemouth have begun to deteriorate.

Accepting that the currently prevailing situation in Britain would have occurred anyway, then the late Ian Cunningham was correct when he wrote in 2001 that *"neither the Bournemouth Council nor Ronald Cox and I in management had any inherent desire to remove the trolleybuses, but the fact remains that so many factors were stacked up against them – Government policy, economics, the demise of trolleybus manufacturing in Britain, one-person-operation and relative inflexibility – that there was little choice"*.

In the mid-1930s much was made of the unpleasantness of smoke and fumes from motor vehicles, but at the same time advertisements encouraged smoking a noted make of cigarettes "for your throats' sake". Times have changed and today, we know that exhaust emissions jeopardise human life on this planet, yet central government makes little effort to dissuade the public from using, primarily imported, fossil fuels and limiting their personal mobility.

As far as urban transport is concerned the trolleybus offers the ideal solution with full manoeuvrability whether using traction power from the overhead line or li-ion batteries and super-capacitors for offline running, and the energy required is electricity from renewable sources such as biomass, hydro, solar, wave or wind power, with completely emission-free and noiseless operation. Having been resident abroad for well over forty years and having had the opportunity to travel widely in my professional career, I have seen how cities and towns as far apart as Castellón and Guangzhou, Valparaiso and Yalta, and Vancouver and Zürich, have moved forward and developed trolleybuses as a valid mode of urban transport for the future. British trolleybus development came to a halt with the outbreak of the Second World War and never restarted, whilst political dogma since then has not furthered public transport in general. The story of the Leeds trolleybus project (2005-2016) speaks volumes.

Bournemouth trolleybuses in their heyday still command my affections as the finest system in the world at that time. The town could still have trolleybuses and Britain could be a greener, more pleasant land, but it would require a total re-think, the like of which my generation will sadly never see.

On Sunday 20 April 1969, Sunbeam MS2 no. 212 (ALJ973) by now owned by the RTS and full of its members, passed the Riverside Inn, between Tuckton roundabout and Tuckton Bridge, for the final time. The author was privileged to ride in the cab for the majority of the journey.
Robin Helliar-Symons

AUTHOR'S ACKNOWLEDGMENTS

Almost forty years after first encountering and being fired with enthusiasm for Bournemouth's trolleybuses, my first attempt at preparing a detailed history of trolleybus operations in a town was published by Trolleybooks in 2001. Since then continuing enquiries and research have shown that there was considerably more to write about the erstwhile system, so it seems only right and proper that to commemorate the fiftieth anniversary of Bournemouth's last trolleybus an entirely new and expanded volume should appear.

Over the intervening eighteen years and in particular over the last few years, there has been a regular exchange of enquiries and information between myself and two other dedicated Bournemouth trolleybus enthusiasts, both of whom were instrumental in my first book. David Chalk, who joined Bournemouth Corporation Transport in 1956 and who stayed with the undertaking and its successor organisation, Yellow Buses, for his entire career in various Head Office and managerial positions, has provided a huge amount of background information together with his professional experiences. John Mawson, with whom I have been in regular contact since the early 1980s, grew up in Bournemouth and carefully researched the trolleybus system in the peak years of trolleybus operation. He too has proved a fountain of knowledge throughout, particularly on electrical and overhead wiring issues. Both gentlemen have willingly given of their time and opened their personal archives to me. Thank you both!

In respect of photographs, David Chalk kindly placed his entire collection at my disposal, whilst Diane and Rod Funnell generously loaned me that of Husband and Father the late Roger Funnell; and Malcolm Pearce that of his Father (G.O.P. Pearce) together with his personal archive. Paul Creswell,

Robin Helliar-Symons, Malcolm Keeley and David Pearson have also made large numbers of their photographs available to me. Deb Ball, niece of the late Stanley King, obligingly placed his Bournemouth photographs at my disposal. Information, sometimes related to minutiae, and photographs have also been freely given by Keith Baynton, Tony Belton, Gavin Booth, Gordon Casely, Richard Delahoy, Bob Hall, Dave Hall, Fred Ivey, David Janes, Barry Moore, Colin Page, Tim Runnacles, Michael Russell and Peter Smith. Many thanks to you all.

My special thanks go to John Stainforth for painstakingly and patiently digitising my hand-drawn maps to produce a crystal-clear insight to the development of the trolleybus system, and to Rod Funnell for his initial thoughts and preparations on how this might be achieved.

The staff of the Heritage Zone at Bournemouth Library, Robert Morris and Laura Waters at the John Price Memorial Library of the National Tramway Museum, and Alan Oxley of the Omnibus Society all deserve my sincere gratitude.

At Yellow Buses, David Squire, Managing Director, has been most supportive, whilst David Symes, who cares for the company's archives, has gone to great pains to assist me in my research.

It would be impossible for me to mention every person who has helped me in the preparation of this homage to Bournemouth trolleybuses individually, but to every single one of them I am sincerely grateful.

Finally I wish to extend my thanks to my publisher Adam Gordon, his son Barnabas and their team for ensuring that this book, completed to their customary high standard, appears in the 50th anniversary year of the closure of the Bournemouth trolleybus system.

In summer 1962 Sunbeam MS2 no. 213 (ALJ975) turns out of Gladstone Road, the northern leg of the Boscombe terminal loop, back into Ashley Road prior to running back to the Square by way of Holdenhurst Road and Old Christchurch Road. Fred Ivey

NOTES FOR GUIDANCE

Terms and expressions

For the benefit of non-enthusiasts the more obscure terms used in connection with trolleybuses, and in particular the trolleybus overhead line installations, are explained:

Bracket Arm
: A tubular steel support bolted to the upper section of the traction pole at right angles and projecting over the road, from which to suspend the trolley wire as an alternative to a span wire. Usually employed where the length of span wire between traction poles would be unduly long or along straight stretches on narrow roads to reduce the number of traction poles. Also referred to as a single bracket arm to differentiate from a gantry or double bracket arm.

Cantrail
: The horizontal length of metal or wood above the upper saloon windows on a double-deck vehicle that supported the roof.

Converter
: Rotating electromechanical device, like a motor or a generator, used to convert alternating current (AC) into direct current (DC).

Composite (body)
: In this form of bodywork, the main framework is constructed from hardwood, reinforced as necessary with steel flitches, supports and brackets, and panelled in metal.

Dress Ring
: See wheel trim.

Drop Light
: A type of opening side window employed in the main side bays of the lower and upper saloons of bus bodies whereby the entire pane of glass dropped downwards into a recess within the side panels below.

Frog
: The overhead line equipment equating to railway points where one pair of running wires left or joined another, known as facing frogs where the lines diverged or trailing frogs where the lines converged. Facing frogs were operated either by hand (the conductor leaving the vehicle and pulling an operating handle, connected by cable to the frog mechanism, on an adjacent traction pole) or automatically by the trolley heads of a trolleybus energising a solenoid through a contact fitted to the overhead line a short distance before the frog. The direction of the frog could be changed by the trolleybus drawing power as the trolley heads passed beneath the contact. Trailing frogs were spring loaded.

Gantry
: A tubular steel support joining the upper section of two traction poles on opposite sides of the roadway, from which to suspend the trolley wire as an alternative to span wire.

Half-drop
: A type of opening side window employed in the main side bays of the lower and upper saloons of bus bodies whereby the window was divided horizontally into two; the upper pane of glass dropped downwards outside the fixed lower pane.

Hanger
: The attachment which, by use of a mechanical grip or "ear" and a porcelain insulator, supported the trolley wire beneath a bracket arm or span wire.

Interworking
: An operational policy of connecting two advertised services at a terminal point using a single vehicle.

Metal framed (body)
: In this form of bodywork, a steel or aluminium frame was built with timber packers and wooden inserts to accept the many screws needed to hold the interior finishers and exterior panels. Also referred to as an "all metal" body.

Motor Generator
: An electric motor using the traction power supply as its source of energy, driving a generator to produce power for a vehicle's low tension lighting.

Pull-off
: A span wire or wires providing additional support or securing a correct alignment of the trolley wires on bends under the correct tension, creating a curve consisting of a series of short straight sections.

Quarter Light
: A separate, roughly triangular, side window situated between the driver's cab door or main cab side window(s) and the front pillar.

Railless
: See trolleybus.

Rectifier
: A device for converting alternating current (AC) into direct current (DC).

Regional Traffic Commissioner
: During the Second World War, Traffic Commissioners received wider powers from the Ministry of War Transport to determine and coordinate the use of road vehicles, and administer fuel rationing for commercial vehicles.

Registration Mark
: The individual alphanumeric reference compulsorily displayed at front and rear of all mechanically-propelled vehicles and their trailers in the UK. The alpha code identifying the place of issue (County or County Borough) was followed or preceded by a number between 1 and 9999.

Reversing Triangle
: An arrangement in the overhead line to enable vehicles to turn by means of a three-point reversing procedure into and out of a side turning. Also referred to as a reverser.

Rosette
: An anchor fitting, rag-bolted or otherwise fixed to the face of a building, used instead of a traction pole, to which a span wire or wires was attached.

Route	The way or series of roads and streets between two points.
Running Wire	See trolley wire.
Section Insulator	An overhead line assembly containing a short length of non-conductive material of the same profile as the trolley wire to break the route up into electrically isolated half-mile sections as required by law in the United Kingdom.
Service	The timetabled frequency of vehicles identified by a service number along a stipulated route.
Span Wire	The load-bearing wire erected across the width of the roadway (usually between opposite or diagonally opposite traction poles, but sometimes anchored to buildings by a wall rosette) from which the trolley wires were suspended.
T-pole	A bamboo pole of the same length as a trolley retrieval pole with two hooks at one end. One hook was placed over the negative trolley head and the other over the positive head. An insulated cable to each hook was connected to a power source (which could be a second T-pole with its hooks placed over energised overhead wires) thus providing traction current to a trolleybus for manoeuvring purposes.
Top Light	A type of opening window employed in the main side bays of the lower and upper saloons of bus bodies whereby the upper portion of the window was divided vertically into two, one or both sections sliding horizontally. On earlier vehicles top lights could be found above other windows, including the driver's cab windscreen and rear platform, some being fixed and others opening inwards by use of bottom-mounted hinges.
Trackless	See trolleybus.
Traction Pole	A steel tubular pole used to support bracket arms, gantries and span wires, usually about 31ft long, set 6ft into the ground at the roadside at a 5° rake away from the road (to compensate for the weight supported) and embedded in concrete. There were four grades of pole—light, medium, heavy and extra heavy, varying in girth and used according to the weight and/or strain they were expected to carry.
Traffic Area	The Road Traffic Act, 1930 divided the United Kingdom for regulatory purposes into Traffic Areas, each administered by Traffic Commissioners. Initially part of the Southern Traffic Area, from 1933 Bournemouth and Poole became part of the South Eastern Traffic Area.
Traffic Commissioners	Throughout the trolleybus era in Bournemouth, motorbus services in the United Kingdom were administered within a specified Traffic Area by Commissioners who were responsible for approving the route to be followed, the time table to apply, the fares to be charged, etc., as well as licencing the vehicle crews. Traffic Commissioners had no jurisdiction over trolley vehicle operation. During the Second Word War, their responsibilities increased and they became known as Regional Traffic Commissioners.
Trolleybase	The point at which the trolley poles were attached to the roof or a roof-mounted gantry of the vehicle. The trolleybase enabled the trolley poles to move laterally and vertically, whilst large inclined springs more or less parallel to the trolley poles provided the tension necessary to keep the under-running skid or wheel in contact with running wires.
Trolley Booms	See trolley poles.
Trolleybus	A public passenger transport vehicle with rubber tyres which travels along ordinary roads and is powered by electricity that is collected, by means of under-running wheels or skids attached to sprung trolleypoles, from a pair of conductor wires hung above the road. Contrary to a tramcar, a trolleybus does not require tracks laid in the road surface and was accordingly initially known as a railless or trackless.
Trolley Head:	The retention and swivel device at the extreme end of each trolleypole which held the under-running current collecting skid or wheel.
Trolley Pole	The roof mounted tubular boom which, by means of a sprung base permitting lateral and vertical movement, kept the under-running skid or wheel in contact with the running wires in order to draw current to propel the vehicle.
Trolley Vehicle	The official term used in legislative documents for a trolleybus.
Trolley Wire:	The conductor wire along which the under-running wheels or skids ran. The pair of wires were kept laterally apart and suspended about 20ft above the surface of the road. The wire nearest the centre of the road had positive polarity and that nearest the edge of the road had negative polarity.
Turning Crcle	An arrangement in the overhead line to turn vehicles back along the route by means of a U-turn.

Twin Line Hanger:	A spacer assembly designed to clamp the two trolley wires the correct distance apart (generally 2ft in the Bournemouth trolleybus era) when supported by bracket arm or span wire. The trolley wire itself was held by "ears" bolted to and insulated from the hanger assembly.
Vent Panel:	The panels immediately above the lower saloon windows but below the upper deck floor-line which could contain ventilators or ventilation louvres.
Weekday	Monday-Saturday inclusive throughout Bournemouth's tram and trolleybus era.
Wheel Trim	An ornamental pressed steel ring, normally chromium plated, fitted over the exterior face of the wheel hub. Also referred to as dress rings.

Abbreviations

The following abbreviations are used in the text:

AA	Anti-Attrition Metal Co.
AC	Alternating Current
AEC	Associated Equipment Company
Ald	Alderman
ARP	Air Raid Precautions
ATS	Auxiliary Territorial Service
BCT	Bournemouth Corporation Transport (Tramways)
BH&D	Brighton, Hove & District Omnibus Co. Ltd.
BIC	British Insulated Cables Ltd.
BICC	British Insulated Callender's Cables Ltd.
BoT	Board of Trade
BPES	Bournemouth & Poole Electricity Supply Co. Ltd.
BPTA	Bournemouth Passenger Transport Association
BTH	British Thomson-Houston
BTS	British Trolleybus Society (Reading Transport Society until April 1971)
BUT	British United Traction
DC	Direct Current
FMPTE	Federation of Municipal Passenger Transport Employers
FP	Feeder Pillar
HCC	Hampshire County Council
H&D	Hants & Dorset Motor Services Ltd.
hp	Horsepower
LGOC	London General Omnibus Company
LSWR	London & South Western Railway Co.
LUT	London United Tramways
MCW	Metropolitan-Cammell-Weymann Ltd.

MEXE	Military Experimental Engineering Establishment (later Military Experimental Establishment)
MoL	Ministry of Labour and National Service
MoT	Ministry of Transport (known as the Ministry of War Transport between 1941 and 1946, and the Ministry of Transport and Civil Aviation between 1946 and 1959)
MoWT	Ministry of War Transport
MMC	Motor Manufacturing Co.
MP	Mains Pillar
MPTA	Municipal Passenger Transport Association
NJIC	National Joint Industrial Council (for the Road Passenger Transport Industry unless otherwise stated)
NTA	National Trolleybus Association
OAP	Old Age Pensioner
OCB	Oil-filled Circuit Breaker
O/T	Open top
pa.	per annum
PCC	Paper Control Commission
PO	Post Office
PSV	Public Service Vehicle
REME	Royal Electrical and Mechanical Engineers
RPI	Retail Price Index
RTC	Regional Traffic Commissioner
RTS	Reading Transport Society (British Trolleybus Society from May 1971)
SB	Switch Box
SEB	Southern Electricity Board
SETC	Traffic Commissioner for the South-Eastern Area
S&D	Somerset & Dorset Joint Railway
SR	Southern Railway Co.
TGWU	Transport & General Workers' Union
UDC	Urban District Council
UK	United Kingdom
WAAF	Women's Auxiliary Air Force
W&D	Wilts and Dorset Motor Services Ltd.

At various points in the text use has been made of a standard code (which will be familiar to enthusiasts) when referring to the type of body and seating capacity of a particular type of trolleybus. The code usually consists of two figures separated by an oblique stroke to indicate, respectively, the upper- and lower-deck seating capacity. Letters are prefixed to indicate body type and suffixed to indicate doorway positions. The elements of this code used in connection with Bournemouth's trolleybuses are as follows:

Prefix letter(s)	B	Single-deck bus
	H	Highbridge double-deck layout, i.e. with centre as opposed to side gangway in upper saloon.
Figures		Indicate the number of seats in the upper and lower saloons respectively.
Suffix letter(s)	C	Centre doorway position.
	D	Dual-doorway vehicle; the Bournemouth standard design for new vehicles 1929-1963 featured an open-platform entry at the rear and exit through the forward doorway (fitted with folding doors).
	R	Rear doorway with open platform.

For example, Sunbeam MS2s 150-173 (BRU1-24) were H31/25D, i.e. highbridge bodywork with 31 seats upstairs, 25 seats downstairs and dual doorways.

Conversion Factors: Units and Currency

During the period in which the trolleybuses operated, Britain used Imperial units of measure and pre-decimal currency. These traditional units are used throughout this book as no useful purpose would be served in providing conversions in the text.

Length	1 inch (in) = 25.4 centimetres (cm)
	1 foot (ft) = 12 inches = 30.5 centimetres (cm)
	1 yard (yd) = 3 feet = 91.4 centimetres (cm)
	1 chain = 22 yards = 20.1 metres (mt)
	1 furlong = 10 chains = 22 yards = 201 metres
	1 mile = 8 furlongs = 1.61 kilometres (km)
Area	1 acre = 4,840 square yards = 4,046.86 square metres
Weight	1 quarter (qtr) = 127 kilogrammes (kgs)
	1 hundredweight (cwt) = 4 quarters = 50.8 kilogrammes (kgs)
	1 imperial ton = 20 hundredweights (cwt) = 1.02 metric tonnes
Currency	1 penny (d) = 0.4166 pence (p) thus 2.4d = 1p
	1 shilling (s) = 12d = 5 pence (p)
	1 pound (£) = 20 shillings (s) = 240d = 100p

The following table will be of use to readers wishing to convert any figures quoted to metric units and decimal currency.

The arms of Bournemouth were granted on 24 March 1891 and are made up of features (the cross, birds and the basic colours of gold and blue) originating from those of Edward the Confessor, Bournemouth standing in his former royal estate, and Hampshire (the roses in the lion's paws), Bournemouth's historical county. The four salmon represent the River Stour, which provides the boundary with Christchurch, whilst the rampant English lions indicate the importance of defence along the South Coast. The wreath of roses on the knight's helmet surmounted by one of Bournemouth's ubiquitous pine trees points to the town's natural beauty, this being emphasised by the apt motto Pulchritudo et Salubritas—Beauty and Health.

On service 25, BUT9641T no. 236 (KLJ336), rebuilt in October 1962 without a front staircase, eases to a halt at the northbound Boscombe Hospital stop on Ashley Road as the road starts to rise up to cross above the railway line at Boscombe Station. In the background can be seen the Ashley Road positive feeder. Both the hospital and the station have been demolished since the photograph was taken.
Roger G. Funnell (courtesy Mrs D. Funnell and Rodney Funnell)

This book is dedicated to my late Mother and Father with my sincerest thanks for their generosity, kindness and understanding in respect to my interest in Bournemouth's trolleybuses.

CHAPTER ONE

SETTING THE SCENE

"*This fashionable watering place, with its eastern and its western stations, its piers, its groves of pines, its promenades, and its Covered gardens, was...like a fairy place suddenly created by the stroke of a wand, and allowed to get a little dusty. An outlying eastern tract of the enormous Egdon Waste was close at hand, yet on the very verge of that tawny piece of antiquity such a glittering novelty as this pleasure city had chosen to spring up. Within the space of a mile from its outskirts every irregularity of soil was prehistoric, every channel an undisturbed British trackway; not a sod having been turned there since the days of the Caesars. Yet the exotic had grown here, suddenly as the prophet's gourd*"

Tess of the d'Urbervilles', Thomas Hardy, Chapter 55

The physical geography of lowland Britain is dominated by a line of chalk hills running from Flamborough Head in the north to the Dorset coast in the south. Tens of thousands of years ago the soft chalk cliffs stretching from Durlston Head to the Needles were breached by the sea which flooded into the valley made by the present day rivers Avon, Corfe, Frome, Piddle and Stour, creating today's Poole Bay. The chalk also runs some 400ft beneath the town of Bournemouth, and below that lies clay and then sand containing pockets of pipe clay which come to the surface beyond the Bourne Stream at Branksome and once fed potteries there. Bournemouth's sour soil and gravelled uplands, covered by an urban blanket today, have been terraced by changing river levels, whilst the beds of dried-up streams are now the town's valleys and tree-lined chines, some still having traces of streams in them, the largest being the Bourne Valley. A few farms and market gardens still exist at the former and Holdenhurst and Muscliffe, the only areas not yet completely covered with urban sprawl.

Bournemouth benefits from warm sunny summers, the average temperature in July being 18°C, and a light average rainfall of 31in. Seven miles of beaches are particularly clean due to the phenomenon of a second half-tide which follows each main tide, having made its way around the Isle of Wight and along the Solent. In short, Bournemouth remains the perfect site for a seaside holiday resort.

In 1914 the Mayor wrote *"Bournemouth is a town unhampered by a past"* and a century and half ago there were only a few large houses, a pier and sand. Yet Bournemouth does have a past—Iron Age man set up a trading post at Double Dykes and a harbour at Hengistbury; Neolithic man left a burial ground at Holdenhurst; and the Roman Colonists left their spade marks in the clay too. The Danes landed nearby and Leland, the Tudor chronicler, mentioned "Bowurnemouth". The modern town was born at Holdenhurst, recorded in Domesday as "Holeest", but the sparse population ensured that the area remained popular for smuggling into the late 1700s. On the site of today's Square, a settlement sprang up around the first bridge across the Bourne Stream at Holdenhurst Bottom, the crossing still being known as Holdenhurst Bridge in 1856. The high ground between the Bourne Stream and Holdenhurst was named Littledown and, until the 1920s, it was grazed by sheep, driven through Sheepwash to the west of Iford Bridge, and Broadway Lane was still a narrow track. Moordown, a mile south, was described in 1853 as *"a tract of heathland on which many poor families are settled"*.

The 1805 Enclosure Award provided the catalyst for the town's growth. Speculators invested in estates and extensive sites for later development. In 1810 Lewis Tregonwell was captivated by Bourne Chine, bought 8½ acres, planted more pine trees and built a new home, now part of the Royal Exeter Hotel. But it was Dr Augustus Granville who really influenced the development as a health resort: in 1841 he made a brief visit and then went on to publish details of *"a perfect discovery among sea-nooks"* and *"a place suitable for the resort of the better classes"* in his book "The Spas of England".

The first guide book in 1840 spoke of *"an air of tranquil repose"*, others of the health-giving properties of the sea water and the ubiquitous pines. Sanatoria came, then residences and gardens, followed by hotels and businesses. By 1856 the population had reached some 7,000 and an Act of Parliament established a Board of Commissioners who controlled a semi-circular district radiating one mile from the Belle Vue, an early hotel situated almost on the site of today's Pavilion. The Lansdowne, named after the circus in Bath, was the point where the long climb of Old Christchurch Road was joined by the road which crossed the Bourne Stream near the Belle Vue Hotel. Tracks to Holdenhurst and Winton radiated from the junction. By 1882, with Boscombe and part of Springbourne added to the Commissioner's District in 1876, the population had reached 17,000. In 1888 a Charter was granted and Bournemouth became an urban district of Hampshire. It was elevated to become a Borough from 23 July 1890 and County Borough from 1 April 1900. Gold and blue armorial bearings with the motto "Pulchritudo et Salubritas" (beautiful and healthy) were received from the College of Arms in 1891. Throughout the period covered by this book Bournemouth remained a part of Hampshire, but local government reorganisation saw the town, together with Christchurch, annexed by Dorset on 1 April 1974. As a result of further changes Bournemouth became a unitary authority in 1997 and in April 2019, Bournemouth was merged with Christchurch and Poole to create a single unitary authority.

Between 1890 and 1900 Bournemouth acquired the rest of Boscombe, Malmesbury Park and Westbourne, reaching a population of almost 60,000 and growing to 67,000 by 1910.

The town's administrative area grew in stages from the original 1,140 acre Commissioner's District of 1856 as follows:

1876	Boscombe and Springbourne (503 acres)
1884	Malmesbury Park, Westbourne and further areas of Boscombe (771 acres)
1895	remainder of Malmesbury Park (179 acres)
1901	Pokesdown, Southbourne, Winton and remainder of Boscombe (3,527 acres)
1914	Charminster, Queen's Park and Strouden (793 acres)
1931	Ensbury, Holdenhurst, Kinson, Howe, Wallisdown (4,627 acres)
1932	Hengistbury Head (357 acres)

As the surrounding districts were absorbed so churches

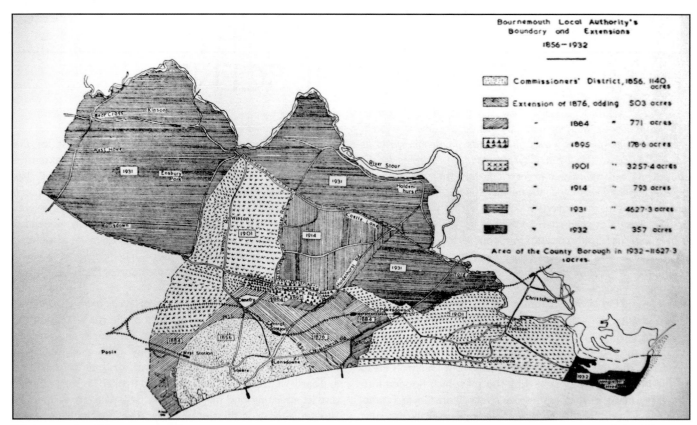

Bournemouth Local Authority's
Boundary and Extensions
1856-1932

	Commissioners' District, 1856.	1140 acres
	Extension of 1876, adding	503 acres
	" 1884 "	771 acres
	" 1895 "	178·6 acres
	" 1901 "	3257·4 acres
	" 1914 "	793 acres
	" 1931 "	4627·3 acres
	" 1932 "	357 acres

Area of the County Borough in 1932 – 11627·3 acres.

The growth of Bournemouth   **John Mawson**

were built, and parks, band stands and theatres proliferated. By 1939 the Bournemouth Guide listed over 500 hotels and guest houses, with bed and breakfast from 21s weekly. However, later that year some 40 hotels were requisitioned for military purposes. During the trolleybus era the population grew from 116,803 in 1931, to 144,451 in 1939, to 154,926 in 1951 and finally to 155,620 in 1961. Housing almost filled the heathland south of Kinson in the 1950s and large areas to the north of Castle Lane have been built upon since then.

The Southampton and Dorchester Railway linking the two towns by way of Brockenhurst, Lymington Junction, Christchurch Road, Ringwood, West Moors, Wimborne, Wareham and Wool opened in 1847, plans for a direct route from West Moors to Holdenhurst having been defeated by the Earl of Malmesbury. The line was worked from the outset by the London & South Western Railway (LSWR), the two companies amalgamating in 1848. There was a branch to Lower Hamworthy, opposite Poole across Quay Channel, and in 1851 Francis Butler introduced a twice-daily horse omnibus service between Lower Hamworthy (Poole) station and the Bath Hotel, Bournemouth. That same year a service between the LSWR Christchurch Road Station (renamed Holmsley in 1888), and the Bath Hotel, 12 miles away, was opened by the owner of the King's Arms Hotel in Christchurch, the journey taking 40 minutes via Christchurch at a fare of 10s 6d. He soon had competitors, for example Francis Graham (grandfather of the founder of Hants & Dorset Motor Services Ltd.) and Thomas Elliott of Royal Blue Coaches fame.

A branch line was built from Ringwood to Christchurch via Hurn in 1862 and a horse bus linked Christchurch with Bournemouth. This line was extended across the River Stour into Bournemouth in 1870, initially ending at a station to the east of Holdenhurst Road (which was later incorporated into the railway goods station facilities) known as Bournemouth East. On 20 July 1885 a further extension was opened to the west side of Holdenhurst Road where a new, larger station, retaining

the name Bournemouth East but renamed Bournemouth Central on 1 May 1899, had been built. In 1888 the LSWR opened a direct line from Lymington Junction through Sway, New Milton and Hinton Admiral to Christchurch and the bus services between Holmsley and Bournemouth lost their passengers.

However, the first main line trains had reached the town from the west. The Poole & Bournemouth Railway end-on extension to the LSWR Broadstone Junction-Poole line reached Bournemouth West on 15 June 1874 and, from 20 July 1874, the Somerset & Dorset Railway from Bath and thence the Midlands also began working through to Bournemouth West. A link between East and West Stations through Meyrick Park opened in 1884. Further stations opened in Pokesdown in 1886 and Boscombe in 1897, whilst a halt was in operation at Meyrick Park Bridge for Winton between 1906 and 1917.

The first horse bus service to operate wholly within Bournemouth was opened by Henry Laidlaw on 14 March 1870 between the new Bournemouth East Station and the Square, the route being extended to Bournemouth West Station on 15 June 1874. Primarily a jobmaster and operator of excursions, Laidlaw became the predominant bus operator, but far from the only one, in the town until the Bournemouth, Boscombe and Westbourne Omnibus Co. was formed in 1889. The Hackney Carriage Inspector reported in 1897 that there were 97 licensed omnibuses in the town. By the end of the century there were three main Companies licensed to operate within the Borough:

The Bournemouth, Boscombe and Westbourne Omnibus Ltd. with services Pokesdown-County Gates, Westbourne; Richmond Hill (top)-Richmond Park; The Arcade (Old Christchurch Road)-Richmond Park; Bournemouth Square-Winton Banks; Southbourne Winter Gardens (near Southbourne Cross Roads)-Bournemouth.

On 28 October 1901 the Company amalgamated with the

An early 1890s view of a Bournemouth, Boscombe & Westbourne Omnibus Ltd. horse bus in Old Christchurch Road, passing the entrance to Bournemouth Arcade. Note the additional trace horse on the offside assisting up the gradient from the Square. **David Chalk collection**

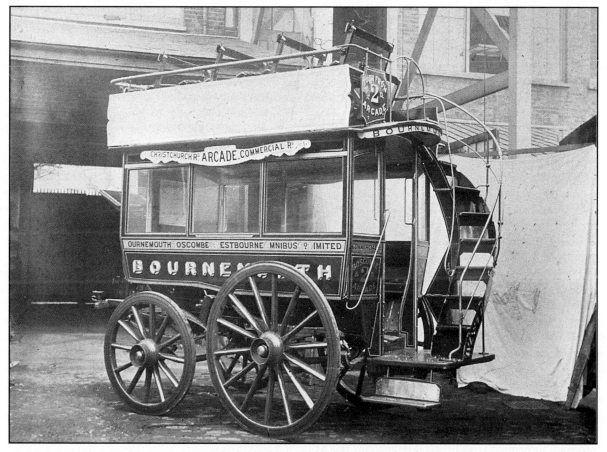

A new double-deck horse bus for the Bournemouth, Boscombe & Westbourne Omnibus Co. Ltd. following completion by its builder, Alex Dodson, Harmood Grove, Chalk Farm Road, London NW1. **David Chalk collection**

Bournemouth General Penny Omnibus.

Operations ceased on 23 July 1902 when Bournemouth Corporation's Lansdowne-Warwick Road, Pokesdown electric tram service started.

The Bournemouth General Penny Omnibus Co. Ltd. with services Pokesdown-County Gates, Westbourne; Boscombe-Bournemouth Square via Ashley Road and Holdenhurst Road; Springbourne-Bournemouth Square via Richmond Park. The Company had its offices at 5 (later 6) Wootton Gardens, subsequently to become the tramways offices from 1920 to 1940.

The Boscombe Park, Pokesdown and Southbourne Omnibus Syndicate Ltd. with services Southbourne-Bournemouth Square; Parkwood Road, Boscombe-Seamoor Road, Westbourne. It, too, was wound-up on 1 August 1902 when the tramways were introduced.

The horse buses did not run to any timetable and a rather lax licensing system resulted in aggressive competition along the several parallel routes. In December 1898, a common timetable was suggested and the Corporation's Horse Committee appointed a full-time Omnibus Timekeeper in September 1899.

Another mode of public transport to appear on Bournemouth's streets at the end of the 19th century was the so-called motor wagonettes—large cars seating 8-10 passengers made by the Motor Manufacturing Co. (MMC) of Coventry—used predominantly for excursions, although 16 were licensed by the Council for local services. The first such service commenced on 28 September 1899 between Bournemouth and Canford Cliffs via County Gates, operated by the Canford Cliffs Motor Omnibus Co. using three MMC vehicles with tiller steering. Three other firms operated wholly within Bournemouth competing with the horse buses. Although successful, their small capacity ensured that they were put out of business by the coming of the trams.

The first reference to the possibility of tramways in Bournemouth was in 1881 when the Provincial Tramways Co. Ltd., a group operating tramways in Cardiff, Plymouth and Portsmouth, proposed a line, potentially using electric traction despite this still being in its infancy, from Bournemouth East Station to Poole, but they were unable to obtain operating powers. In 1897 the British Electric Traction Co. (BET), another tramway operating group, suggested a Bournemouth-Poole service but, following Bournemouth Town Council's objections, application was only made for that portion of the route outside the borough, from County Gates, Branksome (the other side of the Dorset/Hampshire border at County Gates being Westbourne, Bournemouth) through Upper Parkstone to Poole Station. Having gained the support of Poole Corporation and Branksome UDC, a Light Railway Order was granted in 1899 and work started on the 3.76-mile-long Poole and District Electric Traction Co. (PDET) line on 4 May 1900. It was built as a single line with passing loops to 3ft 6in gauge using the overhead trolley system for the supply of traction current to the electric trams and with a depot at Ashley Road, Upper Parkstone. Services commenced on 6 April 1901 at a through fare of 3d. There were initially eleven cars, joined by six more in late 1901 and early 1902, all double-deck open-top on two-axle trucks, finished in a livery of Cambridge blue and white. In late 1899 the BET applied for an extension of their light railway through Bournemouth to Christchurch and Purewell, as well as a line to Winton (Pokesdown, Southbourne and Winton not yet being parts of Bournemouth) which was subsequently

deleted by a House of Lords Select Committee. This prompted Bournemouth Corporation to apply for its own Tramways Act, primarily as a blocking measure and the following year to propose its own Lansdowne-Christchurch tramway.

More or less compromised into building their own tramways, a Bournemouth Council deputation visited Brussels and Paris in the summer of 1901 and recommended that the more expensive, but less obtrusive, underground conduit system of current collection be used in the town centre and overhead trolleys elsewhere. The Bournemouth Corporation Tramways Act, 1901, granted the Corporation powers to construct and operate tramways within the borough. However, should construction not commence within two-years, the powers would lapse and the BET be granted authority to construct and work the tramways. The 1901 Act also required that reciprocal through running powers be granted between the BET's Poole and Christchurch lines with the Corporation's town lines.

The Corporation soon realised that their proposed single track with passing loops tramway County Gates, Westbourne-Bournemouth Square-Lansdowne-Boscombe-Warwick Road, Pokesdown hardly offered a comprehensive public transport solution for the growing town. A revised scheme foresaw double track on the originally-proposed route and additional single track with passing loop lines to Charminster along both Capstone Road and Charminster Road; to Springbourne along Holdenhurst Road; and to Winton along Wimborne Road. The Poole Hill-Lansdowne section of the "Main Line" was to be equipped with the conduit system.

Whilst all this was being discussed, the BET decided to make a legal challenge. The resultant wrangling would have implications on the development of the trolleybus system some thirty years later and indeed on public transport in the area until the results of the radical Transport Act 1985 were felt. In 1902 they applied for an injunction restraining the Corporation from constructing the tramways as their powers had, in principle, already lapsed. They pointed out that no substantial progress had been made in implementing the Corporation's original scheme and that construction was unlikely to start within the stipulated two-year period. Judgement was given in favour of the Corporation but, on 15 July 1902, the Court of Appeal overturned this decision and granted the injunction.

When the Corporation threatened to take the matter to the House of Lords, the BET suggested that negotiations should take place to sell their tramway interests in Poole and Christchurch to Bournemouth Corporation. This was agreed to and an independent tribunal appointed to decide the price. To complicate matters, in January 1903 the Poole Tramways Committee wrote to Bournemouth Corporation offering to purchase the PDET at the same price as Bournemouth Corporation agreed to pay, with running powers to Bournemouth Square to be included in the agreement. In April 1903 the local authorities reached an understanding that the Borough of Poole and Branksome Urban District Council (UDC) would buy the PDET which would then be leased to Bournemouth Corporation for thirty years and worked as a part of their tramway system. Bournemouth would pay Poole an annual fee which would represent the whole of the capital borrowed by Poole to purchase the PDET and at the end of the thirty-year period Poole and Branksome would jointly own the light railway.

Arbitration began on 27 May 1903 but continued until December 1904. Compared to Bournemouth Corporation's

Poole and District Electric Traction Company (PDET) car 4 was built in 1901 by G.F. Milnes on a Brill 21E 2-axle truck and became Bournemouth no. 58 after acquistion in 1905. **David Bowler collection**

Until the town centre portion of the tramways which used the the side-slot underground conduit system of power collection, trams from Pokesdown temporarily terminated in Christchurch Road at the Lansdowne. Car no. 6 built by G.F. Milnes on Brill 22E maximum traction bogies is seen at the Lansdowne in summer 1902 shortly after operations commnced. The balcony on the right is that of the Metropole Hotel in the apex of the junction of Christchurch Road and Holdenhurst Road where they enter the Lansdowne, whilst behind the hut in the middle of the road can be seen the buildings along Old Christchurch Road.

Bournemouth Transport Ltd.

Bournemouth Corporation Tramways bought only a single batch of 2-axle cars, nos. 21-48, built, like their early bogie cars, by **G.F. Milnes & Co. Ltd.** on Peckham Cantilever trucks and equipped with two **Westinghouse 49B** 30hp traction motors. Although further 2-axle cars entered the fleet with the **PDET** acquisition, the undertaking standardised on bogie cars for all subsequent purchases. **Bournemouth Transport Ltd.**

In addition to its own two-axle trams, others were subsequently acquired from the **PDET**, and used primarily on the Side Routes. No. 35 is seen in Holdenhurst Road approaching the junction with Cotlands Road opposite the (then) Fire Station on its way to Winton in about 1905. **David Bowler collection**

estimate of £60,000-£70,000, the BET claimed £430,000. The PDET, including the Upper Parkstone depot, together with the BET's rights in Bournemouth and Christchurch, were finally valued at £112,000. The terms were only agreed in early 1905: Bournemouth Corporation bought the PDET, retained the tramcars and took on most of the employees, but sold the fixed assets (track, overhead equipment and depot) to Poole Corporation, who then leased them back to Bournemouth for thirty years.

On 20 May 1905, Bournemouth Corporation enquired whether the PDET would accept payment without waiting for the terms of the conveyances to be agreed. The company agreed to this request and the PDET Board arranged to accept the money from the Bournemouth Town Clerk and his London agent, and complete the purchase at the London offices of their solicitors on the morning of 15 June 1905. Including legal costs, etc., Bournemouth Corporation had to pay a total of £117,850. The operational take-over was in the early hours of 16 June 1905 following arrival of the last tram at Parkstone depot and the subsequent ticket checking! Just after midnight the Chairman of the Bournemouth Tramways Committee, the Borough Engineer, the Town Clerk, the Bournemouth Traffic Manager and three Corporation clerks arrived and the PDET was formally handed over to the Town Clerk by the Company Secretary.

In the meantime Bournemouth Corporation had started construction of their own 3ft 6in gauge tramways and sections were opened as soon as they were complete. The initial Lansdowne-Warwick Road, Pokesdown section, mainly double-track and equipped on the overhead trolley wire system, together with the southern access line to Southcote Road depot, along Palmerston Road and St. Clement's Road, opened on 23 July 1902, followed by the Lansdowne-Holdenhurst Road-Ashley Road, Boscombe route and northern depot access line along St. Swithun's Road and Southcote Road on 16 October 1902. Services were extended through the town centre to Westbourne on 18 December 1902, using the side-slot underground conduit system of power collection for the first time from the Lansdowne as far west as St. Michael's Church, Poole Hill.

Additional tramway routes opened as follows:

Holdenhurst Road - Capstone Road - Charminster Road Cemetery Junction - Bodorgan Road (top of Richmond Hill), 22 December 1902

Holdenhurst Road (Central Station) - St. Paul's Road - Cemetery Junction, 3 January 1903

Cemetery Junction - Winton Banks, 17 January 1903

Winton Banks - Moordown, 22 January 1903

Bodorgan Road (top of Richmond Hill) - Richmond Hill, Bournemouth Square, 16 April 1903

Warwick Road, Pokesdown - Southbourne - Christchurch Priory, 17 October 1905

Branksome Station - Lower Parkstone - Poole Park, 3 August 1906

Of the above additional routes, solely the Bodorgan Road - Square line was built with the conduit system of power collection; all other lines employed the overhead trolley system. The Lower Parkstone line was built by Poole Corporation and, like the other light railways in Poole, leased and operated by Bournemouth Corporation Tramways (BCT).

Adjoining Central Depot, Southcote Road, workshops and an electricity generating station were built. Traction current at 550 volts DC was supplied to the lines in Bournemouth, whilst those in Christchurch and Poole were supplied by the Bournemouth and Poole Electricity Supply Co. Ltd. (BPES).

On 3 July 1905 a 650yd link with the erstwhile PDET line at County Gates was installed. Additional depots opened at Moordown and Pokesdown in spring 1906, both being used later by the trolleybuses. The undertaking's head office was at 5 Lansdowne Crescent. As the Pokesdown line had, by then, been extended to Christchurch, through services between Poole and Christchurch were immediately introduced over the 11-mile route, with a running time of some 90 minutes. Bournemouth thereby became the first municipality to operate tramways in two other municipal areas.

The first tram deliveries comprised 19 double-deck open-top bogie cars (fleet numbers 2-20), a luxury single-deck car (No. 1) for use by the Tramways Committee, other Council organisations and for private hire, and displayed on the manufacturer's stand at the 1902 Tramways & Light Railways Exhibition, and 28 double-deck open-top cars (21-48) on two-axle trucks. The two classes were virtually identical except in length and built by G. F. Milnes & Co. Ltd., Hadley, Shropshire. Six more Milnes bogie cars (49-54), identical to the initial deliveries, followed in 1904, with a further ten (72-81), this time from Brush rather than Milnes, in 1907. All the above were equipped with both a conduit power collector or "plough", which was secured to a carrier beneath the centre of the tramcar and lowered or raised through trap doors at specified points in the road surface to make or break contact with the conduit conductor rails, and trolley poles. The PDET cars were also acquired in 1905 and were progressively overhauled and repainted into BCT livery, being given fleet numbers 55-71.

Bournemouth's tramways were now complete and, apart from the progressive doubling of single track with passing loop sections and the abandonment of the conduit system of current collection, it remained little changed until 1929. The conduit system soon proved unreliable and expensive in operation. For the sake of appearances, the conduit containing the positive and negative conductor rails was laid immediately below the offside running rail rather than centrally as on the London County Council Tramways network. Strengthened by underground yokes every 3ft 9in, a concrete-walled conduit some 2ft wide and 2ft deep lay beneath the road surface. The 1in-wide offside running rail groove accommodated the tramcar's wheel flange and also served as a slot for the plough's access to the conductor rails. Mechanical restraints required that the conduit be transferred to a central position at junctions and turnouts, although two Connett-patent side-slot turnouts were installed at the Square in 1906.

The tramway extension to Christchurch required construction of a purpose-built reinforced concrete bridge at Tuckton over the River Stour, replacing a privately-owned narrow wooden structure. The new bridge opened on 17 October 1905, tolls being levied on all traffic, including an additional ½d for all tram (and later trolleybus) passengers, receipted with a separate ticket.

The tramway system's early days were characterised by the lack of a professional tramways manager with overall responsibility for the undertaking. Initially, the task was divided between Mr F.W. Lacey, who in addition to being the Borough Engineer and Surveyor took on the tramway engineering; Mr I.M. Bulfin, the Borough Electrical Engineer, looked after electrical matters; and Mr C. Barber (who at least had an appropriate background, having come from Blackburn Corporation Tramways) was the Traffic Manager. These divided responsibilities probably led to the Bournemouth undertaking's high operating costs in relation to similarly-sized systems, as well as poor staff training and low standards of efficiency.

A runaway accident on 1 May 1908, when the motorman lost control of car 72 as it descended the gradient of Avenue Road from the Triangle to Bournemouth Square, brought matters to a head. The car derailed on the curve near Fairlight Glen, which had a 6mph speed limit, at some 25mph and plunged over a wall into the garden of a private house below, killing seven passengers. The Board of Trade (BoT) Enquiry identified faulty magnetic brakes, compounded by poor supervision, as the cause and exonerated the motorman. Shortly thereafter Mr J.B. Hamilton, Manager of Leeds Corporation Tramways, was invited to prepare a report on the undertaking, leading in April 1909 to the combination of managerial responsibilities in a single position and the appointment of the undertaking's first General Manager, Mr Charles Hill, formerly of Birmingham Corporation Tramways. In 1911, Ignatius Mary Bulfin, previously Borough Electrical Engineer and since 1909 Chief Assistant to the General Manager and Tramways Electrical Engineer,

succeeded Mr Hill. He remained General Manager throughout the remaining tramway era in the town and the conversion to trolleybus operation.

Mr Hill, having reviewed tramway operation during his first year in post, concluded that the side-slot conduit system was a drain on resources and uneconomic to operate. Frequent renewals of the underground conductor rails and running rails were necessary as any latitudinal or longitudinal unevenness increased wear and broadened the slot. The conduit required regular cleaning and constant drainage, whilst rubbish or metal objects touching the underground conductor rails frequently led to short circuits. He calculated that conversion to the overhead system would save £3,000 pa. and recommended this to the Tramways & Parliamentary Committee, which accepted the proposal. In June 1910, the full Council however, having seen a model of the Square equipped for overhead trolley operation, deferred a decision and recommended an approach to Mr A.L.C. Fell, Chief Officer to the London County Council Tramways, the largest and by now only other surviving conduit tramway operator in Britain, to evaluate the Bournemouth system.

Mr Fell's responses indicated expensive corrective action and thus Mr Hill repeated that although he could continue to maintain the conduit section of the tramways, both the conductor rails and running rails now needed replacement. The Tramways & Parliamentary Committee again recommended conversion to the Council, which agreed at its meeting of 28 October 1910. Work was carried out in early 1911 and, following a BoT inspection, conduit operation in Bournemouth ceased on 12 May 1911, and the overhead trolley system was

Following acquisition of the Poole and District Electric Traction Company (PDET) their cars were absorbed into the Bournemouth fleet, overhauled, renumbered and repainted into BCT livery. Bournemouth 56, formerly PDET 2, was built by G.F. Milnes in 1901 on a Brill 21E 2-axle truck. **Bournemouth Transport Ltd.**

used throughout from the next day.

Services varied over the years, but during the peak years of the tramways (mid-1920s-1932) the following regular services and short-workings operated:

Poole Railway Station-Poole Park - Constitution Hill - Upper Parkstone - Branksome Station - County Gates - Bournemouth Square - Lansdowne - Boscombe - Pokesdown-Fisherman's Walk-Southbourne - Tuckton Bridge - Christchurch Priory (every 16 minutes winter, 8 minutes summer)

Upper Parkstone (Albert Road) - Branksome Station - County Gates - Bournemouth Square - Lansdowne - Boscombe - Pokesdown - Fisherman's Walk - Southbourne, Cross Roads (every 8 minutes summer only)

Poole Railway Station - Poole Park - Constitution Hill - Upper Parkstone - Branksome Station - County Gates - Bournemouth Square - Lansdowne - Boscombe - Pokesdown - Fisherman's Walk - Southbourne, Cross Roads (every 16 minutes, winter only)

County Gates - Bournemouth Square - Lansdowne - Boscombe - Pokesdown - Fisherman's Walk (every 8 minutes, winter only)

Poole Railway Station - Poole Park - Lower Parkstone - Branksome Station - County Gates - Bournemouth Square (every 16 minutes)

Bournemouth Square - Lansdowne - Central Station -

Boscombe Station - Ashley Road, Boscombe (every 5 minutes winter, 4 minutes summer)

Richmond Hill, Bournemouth Square (Albert Road) - Cemetery Junction - Wimborne Road - Alma Road, Winton - Peter's Hill - Moordown (every 8 minutes)

Richmond Hill, Bournemouth Square (Albert Road) - Cemetery Junction - Wimborne Road - Alma Road, Winton Banks (every 8 minutes, summer only)

Holdenhurst Road, Lansdowne - St. Paul's Road - Cemetery Junction - Wimborne Road - Alma Road, Winton - Peter's Hill - Moordown (every 8 minutes)

Richmond Hill, Bournemouth Square (Albert Road) - Cemetery Junction - Charminster Road - King's Road (every 8 minutes, summer only)

Richmond Hill, Bournemouth Square (Albert Road) - Cemetery Junction - Charminster Road - King's Road - Capstone Road, Holdenhurst Road (every 8 minutes)

East-west services traversing Christchurch Road, Holdenhurst Road or Poole Road were known as the "Main Road" services; those serving inland locations by way of Capstone Road, St Paul's Road or Wimborne Road were known as the "Side Route" services. This terminology continued until the end of trolleybus operation in the town. Richmond Hill services did not enter the Square (there was a connecting track but no overhead wire), but commenced and terminated at the foot of Richmond Hill.

The typical appearance of a Bournemouth bogie tramcar once driver's platform vestibules were fitted. This is potentially no. 92, the first car to be equipped with vestibules, as subsequent reconstructions and deliveries had indicator boxes in the bottom of the two window panes behind the staircase. **David Bowler collection**

Increasing traffic and improved frequencies led to the purchase of ten more double-deck open-top bogie cars (fleet numbers 83-92) in 1914 to the same basic design as the original deliveries, followed by batches of twenty in 1921 (93-112) and 1924-6 (113-132) which were equipped with driver's platform vestibules and permitted further increases in frequency following further track doubling in the 1920s as well as replacing the low-capacity ex-PDET cars.

At its greatest extent Bournemouth Corporation Tramways operated a network of 21.95 route miles and 30 track miles (including the Poole Light Railways). By 1922 the trams were carrying 24.27 million passengers annually. There was a maximum of 131 double-deck open-top tramcars, of which 28 were mounted on four-wheel trucks and the remainder on bogies; one single-deck luxury saloon also mounted on bogie trucks and a four-wheel works cars at any one time. Some 17 open-top four-wheel cars were acquired with the takeover of the PDET fleet but, with the exception of three cars retained for permanent way maintenance purposes; these were withdrawn progressively in the period 1921-6 and replaced by additional bogie cars. However, all tramcars remained in stock until final closure. Apart from changed destination equipment and, in the case of the bogie cars, the addition of driver's vestibules, they remained unchanged in appearance throughout their entire operating lives.

The tramcars were painted in a maroon and primrose livery ornately lined out in gold, and comprised the following cars:

1 Single-deck private hire car built in 1902 by G.F. Milnes mounted on Brill 22E maximum traction bogie trucks.

2-20 Open-top cars built in 1902 by G.F. Milnes mounted on Brill 22E maximum traction bogie trucks.

21-48 Open-top cars built in 1902 by G.F. Milnes mounted on Peckham cantilever 4-wheel trucks.

49-54 Open-top cars built in 1902 by G.F. Milnes mounted on Brill 22E maximum traction bogie trucks.

55-58 Open-top cars ex-PDET 1-4 built in 1901 by G.F. Miles mounted on Brill 21E 4-wheel trucks and acquired in 1905.

59-65 Uncanopied open-top cars ex-PDET 5-11 built in 1905 by the Electric Railway & Tramway Carriage Works mounted on Brill 21E 4-wheel trucks and acquired in 1905.

66-71 Open-top cars ex-PDET 12-17 built in 1901/2 by Brush mounted on Brush A-type 4-wheel trucks and acquired in 1905.

72-81 Open-top cars built in 1906 by Brush mounted on Brill 22E maximum traction bogie trucks.

82 Open-top car formerly numbered 71 (ex-PDET 17) built in 1901/2 by Brush mounted on Brush A-type 4-wheel trucks.

83-92 Open-top cars built in 1902 by United Electric Car Co. mounted on Brill 22E maximum traction bogie trucks.

93-112 Open-top cars built in 1921 by Brush mounted on Brill 22E maximum traction bogie trucks.

113-132 Open-top cars built in 1924/6 by Brush mounted on Brill 22E maximum traction bogie trucks.

B Breakdown and stores car built in 1903 by G.F. Milnes mounted on Peckham cantilever 4-wheel truck.

All cars except 1 and B were of double-deck open top construction with direct stairs.

Nos. 1-54, 72-81 were equipped for conduit operation.

Cars 93-132 were delivered with driver's vestibules; cars 83-92 were subsequently fitted with driver's vestibules.

Cars 55 (as a works car), 85, 95, 103, 108, 112, 114-16, 121, 128 were sold to the Llandudno and Colwyn Bay Electric Railway Limited in 1936 for further service, all surviving until 1956.

Competing Hants & Dorset Motor Services Ltd. (H&D) motorbuses between Bournemouth and Poole along the route of the Lower Parkstone line, and the need to renew the permanent way, led to the abandonment of this section on 5 January 1929. Although still operating at the peak of their efficiency, tramway operations were constrained by the number of single-track sections on the network, primarily on the lines in Poole and between Pokesdown and Christchurch; increasing road traffic; and the need to extend lines into newly built-up areas. It is understood that the Corporation was not permitted to operate closed-top cars, as on many other 3ft 6in gauge systems, and the necessity to run only open-top double-deck trams made the vehicles seem increasingly unattractive, although maintained in spotlessly-clean condition, in a national anti-tramway environment. The expiry of the 30-year lease of the Poole Light Railways was beginning to loom on the horizon, whilst the ongoing need for track renewals and general modernisation "stacked the cards" increasingly against continued tramway operations in Bournemouth.

A busy scene in the Square towards the end of the tramway era. No. 84 built in 1914 by the United Electric Car Co., Preston, and vestibuled later, and another unvestibuled bogie car wait in the siding on the west side of the Square whilst no. 112 reverses before heading east.

National Tramway Museum (Photographer's name not recorded)

Vestibuled car 98 of 1921 and an earlier unvestibuled bogie car from the 1907 Brush-built batch 72-81 (as evidenced by the vertical ventilators) wait in the siding to the west of the Square. Note the five white slip boards along the upper-deck side railings which were used to indicate those sections of the Main Road and Ashley Road routes being covered by a particular journey. When not in use, i.e. when a journey was not covering the entire route between Poole Station and Christchurch or the Square and Boscombe, the boards were reversed to show a blank black side.

National Tramway Museum (Photographer's name not recorded)

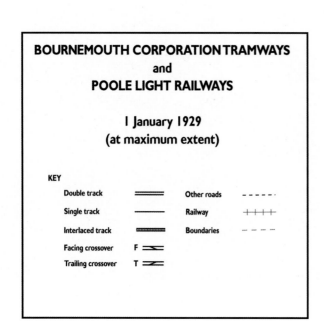

BOURNEMOUTH CORPORATION TRAMWAYS
and
POOLE LIGHT RAILWAYS

1 January 1929
(at maximum extent)

KEY

Double track	═══════	Other roads	— — — —
Single track	───────	Railway	++++++
Interlaced track	▬▬▬▬▬▬	Boundaries	– – – –
Facing crossover	F ═◄══		
Trailing crossover	T ══►═		

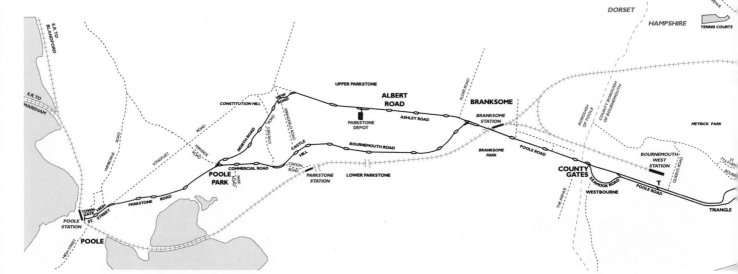

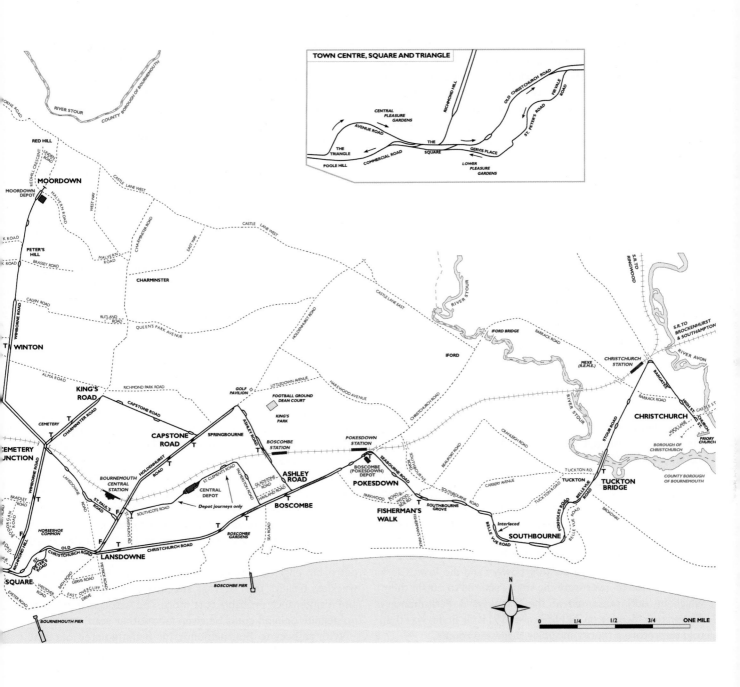

TOWN CENTRE, SQUARE AND TRIANGLE

RICHMOND HILL

OLD CHRISTCHURCH ROAD

FIR VALE ROAD

CENTRAL PLEASURE GARDENS

AVENUE ROAD

ST. PETER'S ROAD

GERVIS PLACE

THE SQUARE

THE TRIANGLE

POOLE HILL

COMMERCIAL ROAD

LOWER PLEASURE GARDENS

RIVER STOUR

COUNTY BOROUGH OF BOURNEMOUTH

OSBORNE ROAD

RED HILL

REDHILL CRESCENT

LINDEN ROAD

CASTLE LANE WEST

MOORDOWN

MOORDOWN DEPOT

WEST WAY

MALVERN ROAD

CHARMINSTER ROAD

EAST WAY

CASTLE LANE WEST

CASTLE LANE EAST

S.R. TO RINGWOOD

K ROAD

PETER'S HILL

BRASSEY ROAD

MALVERN ROAD

CHARMINSTER

RIVER STOUR

S.R. TO BROCKENHURST & SOUTHAMPTON

K ROAD

WIMBORNE ROAD

CALVIN ROAD

RUTLAND ROAD

QUEEN'S PARK AVENUE

MOORDOWN EAST ROAD

IFORD BRIDGE

BARRACK ROAD

RIVER AVON

WINTON

ALMA ROAD

IFORD

MEXE (R.E.M.E.)

CHRISTCHURCH STATION

RAMGATE

KING'S ROAD

RICHMOND PARK ROAD

GOLF PAVILION

LITTLEDOWN AVENUE

HARLEWOOD AVENUE

BARRACK ROAD

CAPSTONE ROAD

FOOTBALL GROUND DEAN COURT

KING'S PARK

CHRISTCHURCH ROAD

ANGLE ST. CASTLE ST.

CHRISTCHURCH

CEMETERY

CHARMINSTER ROAD

CAPSTONE ROAD

SPRINGBOURNE

ASHLEY ROAD

BOSCOMBE STATION

POKESDOWN STATION

WOOL LANE

BOROUGH OF CHRISTCHURCH

PRIORY CHURCH

CEMETERY JUNCTION

HOLDENHURST ROAD

BOURNEMOUTH CENTRAL STATION

ST. CLEMENT'S ROAD

PALMERSTON ROAD

CRANLEIGH ROAD

SOUTHBOURNE ROAD

BEAUFORT ROAD

COUNTY BOROUGH OF BOURNEMOUTH

LANDSDOWNE ROAD

CENTRAL DEPOT

ASHLEY ROAD

BOSCOMBE (POKESDOWN) DEPOT

SEABOURNE ROAD

TUCKTON RD.

TUCKTON

TUCKTON BRIDGE

BRADLEY ROAD

ST. PAUL'S ROAD

GLADSTONE ROAD

HAVILAND ROAD

Depot journeys only

BOSCOMBE

CARBERY AVENUE

TUCKTON ROAD

SOUTHCOTE ROAD

POKESDOWN

SOUTHBOURNE GROVE

BROADWAY

RICHMOND HILL

HORSESHOE COMMON

SEA ROAD

FISHERMAN'S WALK

PARKWOOD ROAD

WOOD ROAD

SIDE RD.

SOUTHBOURNE ROAD

Interlaced

SOUTHBOURNE

BELLE VUE ROAD

CRANLEIGH ROAD

OLD CHRISTCHURCH ROAD

LANSDOWNE

CHRISTCHURCH ROAD

BOSCOMBE GARDENS

FISHERMAN'S WALK ROAD

BELLE VUE ROAD

ST. PETER'S ROAD

GERVIS ROAD

WESTOVER ROAD

BOSCOMBE PIER

SQUARE

EXETER ROAD

EAST OVERCLIFF DRIVE

N

BOURNEMOUTH PIER

0 1/4 1/2 3/4 ONE MILE

13

CHAPTER TWO

EARLY DAYS

The first reference to railless electric street traction in Bournemouth can be found in the Tramways & Parliamentary Committee's Minutes to its 21 October 1910 meeting in which a report from the Annual Conference of the Municipal Tramways Association, held in Bradford in September 1910, was presented. At this conference it had been announced by Mr C.J. Spencer, the Association President and General Manager of Bradford City Tramways, that Bradford had obtained powers to run a line of trackless or railless trolley cars as a feeder to their tramway system. The Bournemouth participants noted that "Such a system has now become practical and has been in use for some time on the Continent. Where the population is thin it is impossible to run a tramway proper with any chance of success financially. The average cost of constructing and equipping a tramway system is from £14,000 to £15,000 per mile, whereas the trackless system can be installed for possibly one-fifth of that sum. In our own case, providing we were given the necessary powers, the lines from Sea Road to Boscombe Pier and from the Lansdowne to Bournemouth Pier seem particularly suitable for such an extension of our system." In the meantime, a letter had been received from Mr Spencer offering to show a deputation the trackless trolley line when it opened towards the end of January 1911 (in fact the opening was delayed until 20 June 1911).

The Tramways & Parliamentary Committee instructed Bournemouth's then General Manager, Charles Hill, to thank Mr Spencer, but further consideration was deferred. Subsequently, Mr Hill was instructed to keep himself informed of trackless car progress with particular reference to a possible route along Sea Road between Boscombe and Boscombe Pier. On 26 June 1911, Mr Hill's newly-appointed successor, Ignatius Bulfin, reported that the trackless trolley systems in Bradford and Leeds had opened six days earlier and that he expected valuable background information on their operation would soon be available. He suggested that it would be advisable to acquire trackless trolley operating powers and the Town Clerk was instructed to investigate the steps required to obtain them, which he duly presented at the Tramways & Parliamentary Committee Meeting on 24 November 1911. Mr Bulfin was then told to prepare a report, including suggested routes.

There was no immediate progress but at the Tramways & Parliamentary Committee Meeting on 24 May 1912 a letter from Mr Spencer as Secretary of the Municipal Tramways Association was read with respect to the trackless trolley vehicles content of the forthcoming Light Railways Bill and seeking the Council's support. The Committee asked the Town Clerk to write to Bournemouth's MPs as suggested and instructed the General Manager to report on trackless trolley developments.

On 21 June 1912 Mr Bulfin briefed the Committee on his visit to the Municipal Tramways Association conference at Cardiff on 6-7 June 1912 at which a paper entitled "The relative merits of Petrol Buses and Railless Trolley Vehicles" by Mr E. Hatton, General Manager of Newcastle upon Tyne Corporation Tramways, had provoked discussion and mixed opinion as to which was preferable. Mr J.B. Hamilton, General Manager at Leeds, operated and favoured trackless trolleys. Overhead equipment cost £1,250 per mile, practically the same as at Bradford, working expenses averaged 4.01d per car mile and capital charges 1d per car mile, making a total cost of 5.01d per car mile. Mr Spencer of Bradford (who moved to the London United Tramways six years later and subsequently introduced trolleybuses to the capital) was not quite so sanguine, his working expenses being 6.6d per car mile and capital charges 1d per car mile, making a total of 7.6d per car mile, but the electricity price was 1d per unit compared to 0.43d in Leeds. Mr W. Luntley of Wolverhampton reported that the total running costs of his Albion petrol buses were 7.25d per car mile. Rotherham was reported as about to open a trackless trolley route incorporating several novel improvements and the Association looked forward to the results of their experience with interest.

Mr Bulfin made a résumé of the presentation. Arguments in favour of trackless trolleys had been that they used the same traction motors and gearing as electric tramcars, and that the motive power was inexpensive; they were faster and more reliable than petrol buses; and maintenance of the electric motors was much cheaper than for petrol engines. However, if traffic did not develop on an experimental trackless trolley route, expensive infrastructure had to be dismantled and potentially scrapped. Other disadvantages were the additional initial cost of £1,250 per mile for overhead equipment and the lack of flexibility, in that trackless trolley vehicles could only work a suitably equipped route. Petrol buses needed no expensive fixed infrastructure, nor were they restricted to suitably equipped streets; in the event of one route not paying, the buses could be moved to another one. Such buses cost about the same as trackless trolley vehicles; there was a good second-hand market value for modern motor buses if it was found necessary to dispose of them and their reliability had much improved in the preceding five years. On the other hand, petrol bus engines were not as reliable as the electric motors of trackless trolleys, their average speed was lower, whilst repairs and maintenance probably cost more. The Association felt that no definite opinion could be given for another year.

With respect to Bournemouth, Mr Bulfin pointed out that the Board of Trade (BoT) had submitted a general Bill to Parliament to amend the Light Railways Act to include trackless trolley routes. If approved, Light Railway Commissioners appointed by the BoT would be authorised to grant Provisional Orders empowering tramway authorities to equip and work trackless trolley systems, instead of having to embark on the complicated and expensive procedures of a Parliamentary Bill. He anticipated that, by the time the BoT proposals had become law, more reliable figures as to the advantages and economics of each system of traction would have become available. However, when the Light Railways Bill 1912 was enacted it concentrated on financial matters and did not include the hoped-for authorisation; indeed apart from the years of the Second World War, a local Act of Parliament remained necessary for the construction of any trolley vehicle route. From 1945 there was an option for trolleybus operators to adopt a simpler procedure with a Ministerial Order subject to Parliamentary confirmation, and this was imposed upon all remaining operators in 1962.

The Secretary of the Boscombe Progress Association wrote to the Tramways and Parliamentary Committee on 11 October 1912 calling attention to "the necessity of providing some suitable vehicle for passenger conveyance to and from the Boscombe sea-front", and suggesting a trackless car. The Town Clerk replied that the Council was not in a position to adopt the suggestion. This request was repeated on 13 January 1913 and the General Manager was accordingly instructed on 24 January 1913 to consider the matter.

Mr Bulfin reported on 17 March 1913 on the relative merits of Trackless Trolleys and Petrol Omnibuses for use in Boscombe. *"On the suggested route for the system, namely, Boscombe Arcade to the Boscombe Pier, I have been in correspondence with those using the latest type of petrol-electric bus, and the opinion is that the gradients are such as almost to make it prohibitive for petrol buses to be used. This bears out our own experience with petrol and petrol-electric vehicles on the same route in past years.*

"In regard to Trackless Trolleys no such difficulty is entertained, as at the present time long grades of 1 in 15 are in daily use and in the present Session of Parliament a Bill is being promoted for a route, the grades on which are as high as 1 in 7. The brakes are capable of stopping the cars on a grade of 1 in 15 at a speed of 20 mph in a distance of 25 yards. The cost of the vehicles under either system is practically the same, £700 to £800, each capable of accommodating 28-30 passengers.

"In the event of the Committee agreeing to a system of public vehicles on this route, I would suggest that a larger scheme be adopted namely from Boscombe Arcade to Boscombe Pier and thence along the Undercliff Drive to Bournemouth Pier and Bournemouth Pier Approach, with a terminus in the Square. Should such a scheme be approved I recommend trackless trolleys with the use of trailers[1] on the seafront from Boscombe Pier to Bournemouth Pier Approach. The poles for the overhead equipment would be planted at the foot of the cliffs thereby causing as little obstruction and unsightliness as possible, at the same time removed from storms and erosion. The poles could also be used for lighting on Undercliff Drive."

The estimated total cost for such a scheme was given as:

Promotion of Bill	£ 1,500
2½ miles overhead at £1,350 per mile	£ 3,125 (sic)
8 cars and 4 trailers	£ 7,600
Cables and connection	£ 1,000
Sundries	£ 375
Total	£13,600

Mr Bulfin estimated working expenses at 6.75d per car mile and capital charges at 2.25d; receipts at 11.5d; giving a profit of 2.5d per car mile. Based on a five-minute service from 10am to 10pm, March to September inclusive, an estimated 150,000 miles pa. would be run at an annual profit of £1,500. A 15-year loan would have been used to finance the project.

Meanwhile, on 28 February 1913, a film and talk on trackless trolleys was given at the Electric Theatre in Commercial Road, Bournemouth, at which representatives of both Bournemouth and Poole Corporations were present, the evening being chaired by the Mayor of Poole.

On the following day, 1 March 1913, The Bournemouth Visitors' Directory included suggestions for a railless traction scheme for the Branksome Park, Canford Cliffs, Lilliput and Sandbanks area, as an extension of Bournemouth Corporation

Tramways was felt impracticable and uneconomic. Behind the scheme were Messrs Clough, Smith and Co. Ltd., tramway and trolleybus overhead wiring contractors. The routes proposed were:

1. County Gates, junction of Poole Road with The Avenue via The Avenue, Western Road, Haven Road, Flaghead Road, West Road, Shore Road, Banks Road to Sandbanks (6.56 miles)
(At this time West Road ran from halfway along Flaghead Road, to the north of it, and Shore Road. Subsequently West Road was renamed as an extension of Haven Road and the western part of Flaghead Road became Haven Road and Chaddesley Glen. The route was similar to the first section of the Branksome Park and Swanage Light Railway proposal of 1906)

1a. From a junction with Haven Road along Ravine Road (3.78 chains)
(Understood to be for depot purposes)

2. Poole (Park Gates East), crossroads with Parkstone Road and Alverton Avenue via Sandbanks Road and Lilliput Hill Road to a junction with West Road (2.4 miles)
(Lilliput Hill Road was the northern continuation of Shore Road between Brudennel Road and Critchell Mount Road, and was subsequently renamed as a continuation of Sandbanks Road)

2a. From Shore Road to West Road
(Creating a junction between routes 1 and 2)

A local company was formed to promote the scheme, known variously as The Poole, Sandbanks and Westbourne Electric Car Co. Ltd.; The Poole, Sandbanks and Westbourne Rail-less Traction Co.; and also as The Sandbanks Railless Electric Car Co. Ltd..

Clough, Smith had been founded in 1910 by two electrical engineers, Norman Clough and Sidney Smith, already experienced in tramway electrification, who saw a business opportunity as contractors in the design and installation of overhead line equipment and traction current supplies for tramways and early trolleybus systems, as well as trolley vehicle chassis and complete vehicles. Their activities included the overhead wiring installations at Aberdare and Hove (1914, both Cedes-Stoll systems)[2]; vehicle suppliers for Tees-side (1919, in association with Straker-Squire); and the complete installations at Chesterfield (1926) and Darlington (1927). Despite their Sandbanks endeavours, there is no evidence of them ever operating a railless trolley system although their overhead wiring contracting continued until the 1960s.

At its meeting of 18 April 1913 the Town Clerk reported to the Tramways Committee that the matter of trackless trolley cars and petrol omnibuses had also been before the Beach Committee, which had recommended that a subcommittee be formed for full consideration with a subsequent report to the Joint Tramways, Roads and Beach Committees. At the same meeting a letter was read from a Committee appointed to improve transport in Branksome Park, Canford Cliffs, Lilliput and Sandbanks, together with the district lying between Lilliput and Parks Gates East. Its Secretary asked for Bournemouth Council's co-operation and support in a proposed application for Parliamentary powers to construct a trackless trolley system in Poole from County Gates to the Haven (the area

---

[1] The mention of trailers is interesting. No British system ever used trailers, although they were already common-place in Austria and Germany.

[2] The Cedes-Stoll system used two closely-spaced trolley wires, the current being collected by a small four-wheeled carriage running on top of these wires and connected to the vehicle via a flexible cable.

around the Haven Hotel at the end of the Sandbanks spit). This was referred to the new subcommittee.

The subcommittee presented its report on the proposed Undercliff Drive Trackless Trolley route to the Tramways Committee Meeting on 23 May 1913. They considered it inadvisable to proceed further until construction of the Undercliff Drive was complete. It was suggested that Bournemouth Council take no action on the Branksome Park proposals as the area was in Poole, Dorset, and outside their jurisdiction. However, the Town Clerk should monitor the Council's interests during the progress of the proposed application for Parliamentary powers by the Poole, Sandbanks & Westbourne Rail-less Traction Co. The Tramways Committee adopted these recommendations.

Mr Bulfin reported to the Tramways Committee Meeting of 20 June 1913 on his attendance at the Municipal Tramways Association, Managers' Section Meeting, 5-6 June 1913 in Sunderland. *"I took the opportunity of my visit to the North to inspect the different systems of trackless trolley at Bradford, Leeds and Keighley in order to see the latest developments and to test the ease of running and convenience to passengers on such a system after they have been running some considerable time. In each case I find that the original vehicles are being withdrawn and are to be superseded by vehicles of a stronger and more efficient type, the new designs being based on the experience gained from running the chain-driven original types. Bradford and Leeds have adopted the RET system with chain and gear driven vehicles, the chain in each case being a weak point and a great source of trouble.*

"The trackless trolleys in each of these towns ply over every class of road surface—wood paving, sett paving, tar macadam and ordinary granite and from the point of view of comfort to passengers,

it becomes absolutely necessary that the roads traversed should be thoroughly well maintained. No trouble has been experienced in these systems, either with the trolleys or the motors.

"In Keighley, which has only just been opened, they are experimenting with the 'Cedes-Stoll' system, in which there are no gears or chain-drive, the motors being in the hub of the rear wheels. The system, if it proves satisfactory in practice, should be the ideal one, but I have great doubts myself as to the practicality of the motors."

On 28 October 1913 Bournemouth Council approved that application be made in the 1914 Parliamentary Session for powers to extend the tramways half a mile along Charminster Road, from the Capstone Road turn as far north as the junction with Green Road. It also asked that the Tramways Committee consider the question of tramway extensions in general together with alternative modes of transport as feeders to the tramways.

Also in 1913, local residents proposed that a tramway or, failing Parliamentary approval, a tangential trackless trolley route, be built between Wimborne Road, Moordown and Kings Road. Nothing further was heard about the tramway extension, but a notice in the *Bournemouth Daily Echo* appeared shortly afterwards, stating the intention of The Bournemouth and District Railless Traction Co. to apply for a Parliamentary Bill to operate trackless trolleys in that part of Bournemouth. At the 19 December 1913 Tramways Committee Meeting a copy of the Railless Traction Co.'s Bill proposing "a system of electrically propelled trolley vehicles" along Charminster Road, Charminster Avenue and Malvern Road was presented. Fearing competition, the Tramways Committee recommended that the Bill be opposed. At the same meeting it was agreed to make an

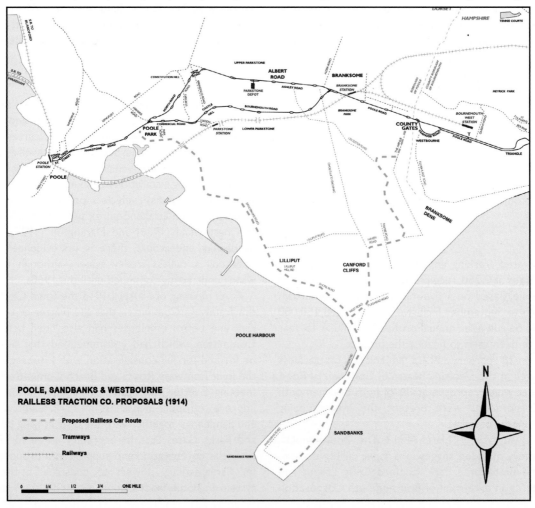

application to the BoT for a loan to operate motor omnibuses between Alumhurst Road and Westbourne Arcade; Boscombe Arcade and Boscombe Pier; and Charminster Road (Queen's Park Avenue) and Cemetery Junction.

On 3 January 1914, the Poole, Sandbanks and Westbourne Railless Traction Co. and the Bournemouth District Railless Traction Co. both formally deposited their Bills in the House of Commons. Both Bills were passed to the House of Lords but subsequently withdrawn.

The Poole, Sandbanks and Westbourne Railless Traction Co. (Clough Smith) had sought powers to construct and operate railless cars along three routes:

County Gates - The Avenue - Western Road - Canford Cliffs - Haven Road-Shore Road, to the Haven Hotel at Sandbanks

Poole Park East Gates (Parkstone tramway junction)-Sandbanks Road-Lilliput Hill Road-Shore Road-Sandbanks

Ravine Road, Canford Cliffs to a depot at Westlands
(A location approximating to today's Westlands Drive which runs parallel to, and about 50 yards to the north of, Haven Road)

Poole Council had already indicated that it was willing to grant all permissions, subject to BoT approval, with the proviso "that the company be prepared to sell the undertaking as a going concern after a period of 15 years". This could have made Poole a trolleybus operator in its own right by 1929 but the outbreak of the First World War and the Bill's withdrawal sealed its fate and nothing further was heard of the scheme.

In February 1914, Clough, Smith & Co. Ltd. wrote on behalf of the promoters of the Poole, Sandbanks and Westbourne Railless Traction Bill, to ask if Bournemouth Council would permit them to take their current supply from the tramway feeder cable in Parkstone Road. The Tramways Committee was not in favour, whilst the Town Clerk reported that he had lodged a Petition against the Bill. Following a meeting with the Company, clauses for the protection of Bournemouth Corporation were incorporated in the draft Bill. Agreement

was reached on 20 March 1914 and Bournemouth Corporation withdrew its Petition.

Following a meeting between a deputation of the promoters and the Council's subcommittee, the promoters' solicitors, Messrs Mooring Aldridge & Haydon, wrote on 12 February 1914 to state that their clients had decided to withdraw the Bournemouth District Railless Traction Bill. In September 1914 they enquired why the Charminster Road motor bus service had been withdrawn. The Council responded that there had been few passengers and that the service had been loss-making. Motor bus services between County Gates and Sandbanks began in 1916 operated by Bournemouth & District Motor Services Ltd., trading as the "Silver Fleet" and to be known later as Hants & Dorset Motor Services Ltd. (H&D).

A seemingly unconnected public meeting held in November 1914, suggested that trolleybuses should be used to extend public transport the short distance from the Queen's Park Hotel, at the junction of Ashley Road with Holdenhurst Road, to the Queen's Park Golf Pavilion to serve the football ground in King's Park nearby. Nothing further was done until a trolleybus branch was built in 1934.

Trackless Cars Ltd. of Leeds demonstrated an advanced, front-wheel drive, two-axle with dropped rear axle, double-deck trackless trolley vehicle using a General Licence (the predecessor of trade plates) at the Tramways and Light Railways Congress held in Bournemouth on 22 and 23 June 1922. The vehicle was equipped with an almost streamlined centre entrance body having a central staircase and platform doors, seating 30 passengers in the lower and 34 in the upper saloon, built by the Blackburn Aeroplane and Motor Co. Ltd. (one of the shareholders of Trackless Cars Ltd.) at their Olympia Works, Roundhay Road, Leeds.

Whilst at Bournemouth it was housed at the Central Tram Depot in Southcote Road. No additional trolley wires were erected, a skate trailing in the tram rails being employed for the return current.

After the Congress, it was taken to the London United Tramways' Fulwell Depot for inspection and demonstration purposes prior to being purchased by Leeds Corporation

The Trackless Cars Ltd. Demostrator at the Leeds works of the Blackburn Aeroplane & Motor Co. Ltd. in June 1922, being prepared for its journey to Bournemouth.
Blackburn Aeroplane & Motor Co. Ltd.

Tramways in December 1923. In Leeds it was registered NW5550, given fleet number 513 and entered service on 10 January 1924. Further details about this vehicle can be found in Appendix B.

The topic of trackless trolley vehicles was not mentioned in the Tramways Committee Minutes again until 20 February 1925, when, in response to criticism of tramways and their apparent obsolescence, and road congestion, Mr Bulfin referred to the financial burden on tramway operators from which all road users benefited. Certain of his observations remain accurate today and illustrate the first signs of Britain's obsession with the private car:

"On either side of the road private motor cars and delivery vans are drawn up alongside the shops. The carriageway is reduced to half its capacity by these standing vehicles. The only space on the roadway for through traffic is the centre of the road, and it is here that the tramway lines are laid. The motorist coming along any of these roads finds his brother motorist occupying each side of the road. He therefore gets to the centre of the road himself and comes across a tramcar coming in the opposite direction. He considers he should have entirely the right of way, that the tramcar should get to one side to allow him to pass, but the tramcar runs on lines and cannot get out of the way and maintains its position.

"The tramways have been in the present position in the town for over 20 years. No trouble ever existed until six years ago in connection with the running, but now the number of private motor cars has increased so considerably that the people who had and hold the right of the road are to be done away with and the newcomer to take first place. The motorist, having sounded his horn, imagines he has complied with all the requisites in connection with the Law and he can go ahead. Should anything block his way it must be removed at once."

Reference was made to the looming necessity to relay the track of the two tram routes in Poole and their possible substitution by trackless trolley vehicles. Bournemouth's trams carried 60-70 passengers within an extreme width of 6ft 6in. Trackless trolley vehicles and motor buses carried half that figure, but were 12in wider, indicating that twice the number of vehicles would be required to carry the same number of passengers. Comfort required perfect road conditions and only small towns had given up their tramways, e.g. Chesterfield (carrying 3.5 million passengers pa. with 17 cars), Ipswich (5.5 million passengers with 36 cars), Keighley (4 million passengers with 12 cars).

Mr Bulfin considered that the sole reason these towns had given up their tramways was because the track had worn out. Capital charges for renewing permanent way seemed so high that these undertakings had preferred to spend their money on new rolling stock as a substitute for the trams. If sufficient finance had been available to renew their permanent way, they would have undoubtedly retained their trams. Although Birmingham, Bradford and Leeds operated trackless trolleys, they were in small numbers compared to the trams, e.g. Birmingham had 12 trackless trolleys compared to 658 tramcars, Bradford 19 compared to 250, and Leeds 14 compared to 362. None of these towns intended to abandon their tramways. He made the further point that the maximum permitted speed of trackless trolleys was 12mph whereas trams were allowed to travel at up to 20mph. In his opinion trackless trolley vehicles were suitable for taking over a service which had been built up by motor omnibuses, but they required turning circles and

regular attention to their steering. He added that since the end of the First World War, Bournemouth had spent £250,000 reconstructing its tramways, and gave some interesting financial statistics:

Bournemouth tramways, assessed on rails, cables, etc., paid almost £4,000 pa. in rates, equal to a 1d rate.

Road maintenance cost £15,000 pa., equal to a 4d rate

Annual capital charges on an outstanding amount in excess of £500,000 were £60,000, equal to a 1s 5d rate.

Note: In the tramway and trolleybus era, rates were a tax on property ownership based on the nominal value in the case of residential property, reassessed periodically in revaluations and assessed as X pence (d) in the pound (240d).

Bournemouth's tramways had never received financial support from the rates but, if they were abandoned, all these charges would have to be met by the ratepayer.

	Trams	Motor Buses	Trackless Trolleys
Seats	70	30-40	30-40
Cost	£2,500-£3,000	£1,200-£1,800	£1,800-£2,000
Life	20 years	5 years	5-10 years
Max speed	20mph	12mph	12mph
Width	6ft 6in	7ft 6in	7ft 6in-7ft 10in
Cost per mile	15.52d	12-18d	16.57d Aberdare 17.49d Halifax 17.65d Keighley 12.15d Birmingham

Note: the table refers to trackless trolleys having a width of 7ft 10in, although road vehicles at that time were limited to a maximum width of 7ft 6in.

Mr Bulfin estimated that to convert the Poole tram routes to trackless trolley operation instead of relaying the track, entirely new overhead equipment, costing between £10,000 and £15,000, would be required as the existing traction poles would be unable to take the additional strain. Some 30-35 vehicles would be needed to meet existing traffic demands, costing £60,000-£70,000. Road surface improvements would cost £25,000. The annual charge of £6,930 on the Poole Light Railways would be payable until 1934. There was also no assurance that an application to Parliament for an Act or Order for the installation would be approved. In May 1925 the Ministry of Transport (MoT) sanctioned a 20-year loan of £30,000 for track reconstruction on the original Upper Parkstone portion of the Poole Corporation Light Railways and work commenced in October 1925.

On 18 March 1927 the Joint Bournemouth and Poole Tramway Committee agreed that the Lower Parkstone tram route, which ran between Pottery Junction and Poole Park, be abandoned and that Poole Corporation would promote a Parliamentary Bill to operate motor buses in its own right. In the meantime the Lower Parkstone tram track was patched up

Looking west towards Commercial Road, tramcars load at the shelter which incorporated waiting rooms, an inspector's office and messroom, in the Square in 1927. The shelter was built in 1924 as a gift to the town by Captain H.B. Norton, JP, a former member of the Town Council; passengers boarded trams at the driving end from beneath the roofed area but alighted on to the strips of pavement in the conventional manner. Trolleybuses never used these boarding points. The track and overhead wire branching off towards the right of the photograph lead towards the bottom of Richmond Hill and were not used by service cars. When the shelter was demolished prior to the construction of the Square roundabout in 1947, the roof-mounted clock was placed on a tower in the middle of the roundabout. David Bowler collection

to enable trams to continue operating safely until buses could be substituted. Towards the end of December 1927, the MoT sanctioned a £20,000 loan for the proposed abandonment, road reinstatement and the purchase of replacing motor buses.

A year later it was learned that Poole had decided not to exercise omnibus powers itself but that it planned to delegate them to Hants and Dorset Motor Services (H&D). By mid-June 1928 concessions to protect the revenue of Bournemouth's trams, which would continue to run between Poole and Bournemouth via Upper Parkstone, were secured. Trams ceased to run along the Lower Parkstone line from 5 January 1929.

Passengers travelling solely within the Bournemouth boundaries were not permitted to use the H&D services, although passengers travelling beyond the County Borough boundary could be picked up at stops in Bournemouth, and those travelling into Bournemouth from Dorset could be set down. The motor bus fare between Bournemouth Square and County Gates (the first stop in Dorset) was 2d, whilst the tram fare for the same journey was 1d thereby setting a precedent for a 50% surcharge to fares for motor buses operating along any Bournemouth tram route.

Mr Bulfin briefed the Tramways Committee on 18 October 1929 about adding a clause to the proposed Borough Boundary Extension Bill for the provision of a trackless trolley system. Committee Members were taken by Corporation motor bus to Hastings and Maidstone to inspect the trackless trolley

systems in those towns on 24 October and 25 October 1929 respectively. Whilst in Maidstone, and as a direct result of what they had seen, the Tramways Committee held a meeting at which it was unanimously agreed to recommend that powers be sought in the Boundary Extension Bill to operate trackless trolleys on all existing tram routes in Bournemouth. Appropriate notices were subsequently posted on all routes in the town. This eventually became the Bournemouth Corporation Act, 1930, which also encompassed both motor bus operation and the necessary relationships with competing bus companies.

The Tramways Committee considered a scheme for running express motor buses on routes paralleling the trams system at its 20 December 1929 meeting. This led to the introduction, on 17 April 1930, of limited-stop express motor bus services between the Square and County Gates, Queen's Park Hotel, Moordown and Tuckton, and between the Lansdowne and King's Road. The motor buses only stopped at fare stages, ran every 15 minutes and charged fares 50% higher than those applicable on the trams.

The express motor buses proved unremunerative and by 30 July 1930 only the Tuckton and Moordown services remained. In winter 1930 the former was extended across Tuckton Bridge to Christchurch via Christchurch Railway Station, and the Moordown service was extended along Wimborne Road as far as the junction with New Road, Northbourne, both ceasing to be express services.

An unidentified 2-axle car from the 21-48 batch and early bogie car 7 are seen at the north end of Lansdowne Road, Cemetery Junction in the early 1930s. The structure behind the 2-axle car is the public conveniences.

Bournemouth Transport Ltd.

During the Tramways Committee Meeting of 10 March 1930, the Town Clerk submitted the MoT's report on Part IV of the Bournemouth Corporation Bill (Tramways, Trolley Vehicles and Omnibuses) and referred to the petitions against this part of the Bill.

The independent advisor to Bournemouth County Borough Council, Mr Arthur R. Fearnley, General Manager of Sheffield Corporation Tramways since 1904, recommended the purchase of H&D's motor bus operations in Bournemouth, the areas to be added to the Borough, and between Bournemouth and Christchurch, if suitable terms could be arranged. Council representatives and Mr Fearnley negotiated with H&D and reached agreement on 24 March 1930 at a cost of £9,000 plus legal fees. This, it turned out, was well timed, as it was only a few months before the Road Traffic Act, 1930—the Act which strictly regulated the operation of motor bus services for the next 56 years—reached the statute book.

The Bournemouth Corporation Act 1930 (20 & 21 Geo.5) (Chapter clxxxi), received Royal Assent on 1 August 1930. Amongst other things the Act extended the Boundaries of the Borough of Bournemouth and, in Part IV, empowered the Mayor, Aldermen and Burgesses of the Borough to run trolley vehicles and omnibuses within and beyond the Borough, and to abandon and discontinue the Corporation's tramways. The County Boundary between Hampshire and Dorset was also adjusted to include the parishes of Kinson and Holdenhurst in the County Borough of Bournemouth, on the Hampshire side.

Under the provisions of the Act the estimated cost of the provision of trolley vehicle and motor bus services were as follows:

a.   Provision of trolley vehicles   £300,000

b.   Provision and adaption of electrical   £157,000
     equipment and the construction of other
     works necessary for working such trolley
     vehicles

c.   Provision of omnibuses   £300,000

d.   Erection and adaption of buildings for use by   £80,000
     trolley vehicles and omnibuses

e.   Reconstruction of the roads upon   £63,000
     which tramways are to be removed and
     discontinued under this Act

Loan financing over several years was foreseen for this expenditure. Powers were also given to work trolley vehicles along a further 14 new routes, the total authorised mileage being 30. (See Appendix O).

Another opportunity was offered to the Tramways Committee, together with those Council members who wished to accompany them, to see a trackless trolley system in operation, with a visit to Wolverhampton on 27-28 November 1930. In total, 31 councillors travelled by train to Wolverhampton, where they were received by Mr C. Owen Silvers, Engineer and General Manager of the Corporation Transport undertaking and immediately conducted on a tour of the town's system accompanied by Wolverhampton Town Council. The trip included a journey along the Tettenhall route, negotiating one of the few hills in the town, aboard a three-axle double-deck trackless trolley vehicle. The journey was then repeated on a three-axle double-deck motor bus. A stop was made on the steepest part of the hill and the party observed and listened to both types of vehicles ascending and descending the gradient. The consensus was that the trackless trolley was more silent, there was less vibration and more even acceleration compared to the motor bus and a complete absence of smell and fumes. They also noticed the ease with which the trackless trolley vehicle could negotiate and pass other vehicles in the road and draw into the kerb, and several emergency stops were made, proving the capacity of the vehicle to pull up in an emergency. Mr Silvers subsequently spent several hours at the party's hotel answering questions.

Tram 100, built in 1921 to a twenty year old design but for the driver's platform vestibules, loads at the east end of Seamoor Road, Westbourne, in August 1933. The destination Albert Road refers to a turning point on Ashley Road, Upper Parkstone. Bournemouth was the first municipality to operate tramways in two other Boroughs (Christchurch and Poole), the route between Christchurch, Church Street, and Poole, Railway Station (Towngate Street level crossing) being some 11 miles long - the longest tram route in South England.

M.J. O'Connor (Tramway Museum Society collection)

The Bournemouth delegation was given to understand that the universal opinion in Wolverhampton was that the comfort and ease of travelling by trackless trolley vehicle was very much better than that on a motor bus and furthermore, following a petition of residents along the route, a six mile motorbus service was shortly to be replaced by trolley vehicles. In general, any service having a frequency of 20 minutes or better was best served by trolley vehicle.

Discussion extended to the cost of converting a tram route with overhead trolley power supply to trackless trolley operation. It was estimated that road reinstatement could cost between £3,000 and £4,000 per mile, but that the traction poles supporting the overhead equipment could be reused with concrete reinforcement where necessary to bear the extra strain. Additional feeder cables were needed every half mile to serve both positive and negative wires. The cost of converting the existing overhead system for trolley vehicles was thus between £800 and £2,000 per mile. It was noted that Wolverhampton anticipated being able to repay the entire outstanding tramway debt of £150,000 by 31 March 1931, just 7½ years after commencing the replacement of its tramways by trolley vehicles.

The Council was cautious as to how best to replace the tramway system which still had an outstanding debt of £311,000.

In 1931 the Royal Commission on Transport stated an opinion that:

"it will be to the advantage of the towns where they (the tramcars)

exist to get rid of them by degrees, and to substitute trackless trolley vehicles or motor omnibuses, as some authorities have done already. The substitution of the trackless trolley vehicles may ultimately prove to be the best solution in certain cases (or at all events it may form an economic transition from the tramcar to the motor omnibus), as already observed, the use of generating plant which supplied power for the trams can be continued, and the only serious cost involved consists in adapting the overhead equipment for trackless trolleys... and the provision of new vehicles."

From 22 May 1931 the Tramways Committee was renamed the Transport Committee.

As a result of the economic depression, from 22 October 1932 the Main Road tram frequencies were reduced with winter frequencies of 20 and 10 minutes operating throughout the year, whilst the Side Route frequencies were similarly reduced to 10 minutes.

It was to be a further two years before the Transport Committee, at its 20 January 1933 meeting, recommended that a short section of trolleybus wiring be strung along a tram route and a public service be operated as an experiment. It selected the Poole Road route between Bournemouth Square and County Gates, Westbourne, where the existing one-way traffic scheme around Seamoor Road already followed by the tramways provided a ready-made terminal loop. It also encompassed Commercial Road and Poole Hill, the steepest gradient on the tramway system, excluding Richmond Hill. The additional overhead wiring was erected by the Transport

Tram 30, built by G.F. Milnes on a Peckham Cantilever truck in 1902, has reached the Square terminus of the Side Routes at the bottom of Richmond Hill at its junction with Albert Road. The girder work in the background will be the basis of the new Bournemouth Echo newspaper offices constructed in 1932-1933 by Seal & Hardy and now a Grade II Art Deco listed building.

David Chalk collection

Department; indeed it subsequently carried out all the overhead wiring work for the entire trolleybus system. It was arranged that four different prototype trolleybuses would be hired in an effort to identify the type best suited to Bournemouth's needs.

The *Bournemouth Daily Echo* eagerly awaited the arrival of the trolleybuses. Its 5 May 1933 issue quoted Mr W. Craven Ellis, MP for Southampton, speaking at a luncheon in Bournemouth the day before *"We all look upon Bournemouth as the Queen of Watering Places. You have a very high reputation, and that requires a great deal of maintaining. There is one thing that I look upon as a serious handicap, and that is for a modern, up-to-date town you have an evident sign of antiquity. That is your trams."* Replying to the taunt, the Mayor, Councillor J.R. Edgecombe, said *"We must put up with them a little bit longer yet"*.

On 8 May 1933, under the heading *"Bournemouth's trolley-bus transport experiment is likely to start this week"*, Ald. F. B. Summerbee was quoted *"The trolley-bus service will in all probability be instituted on the Square-County Gates route next Saturday. Before the public use it tests will have to be carried out by the Ministry of Transport. The experiment may last to the end of June.*

"Bournemouth's trolleybus experiment is one which has attracted attention in many parts of the country. The cost to the town is only about £500, and that is principally for the erection of the overhead wires on the route. This installation is now practically complete. The object of the experiment is to give the public the opportunity of judging what form of transport is suitable in the event of a decision being taken to replace the tramways system by some other means of transport. It is expected that two trolleybuses will launch the service, but that four will be used at some time or another during the course of the experiment".

The experimental trolleybus fleet was made up of a Sunbeam-BTH MS2 three-axle trolleybus fitted with Weymann double-deck bodywork; an AEC 661T two-axle and an AEC 663T three-axle trolleybus, both with English Electric double-deck bodywork; and a Thornycroft two-axle trolleybus with Brush single-deck bodywork. They carried Bournemouth registration marks LJ7701-4 respectively, issued at the start of the hire. The three double-deckers were delivered with conventional rear open platform entrance and exit, and finished in the then standard Bournemouth motor bus livery of primrose with two maroon bands and a white roof. The single-deck Thornycroft, however, had a central sliding doorway and was painted two-tone blue which, coupled with its speed of up to 40mph, earned it the nickname "Bluebird".

The Sunbeam MS2 arrived during the morning of Wednesday 10 May 1933, having been towed by the manufacturer's three-axle lorry. They set out from the factory on the previous day at about noon. Mr Alan Butler of Wolverhampton Corporation Transport sat at the wheel of the trolleybus and recalled in May 1969 that *"The journey was uneventful until we were in the area of Sutton Scotney at about 2am next morning when it began to rain very heavily. As the lighting system was direct from the overhead wiring, the bus had two horse lamps on the front lit by candles and a red one on the back. For some reason which to this day I cannot*

One of the final batch of tramcars built for Bournemouth in 1924-1926, no. 126 built by Brush on Brill 22E maximum traction bogies is seen in Poole Road, Westbourne, at the Methodist Church stop opposite the east end of Seamoor Road, destined for Christchurch in the early 1930s. Note that the wording along the rocker panels (the base of the side panels) was progressively changed from **BOURNEMOUTH CORPORATION TRAMWAYS** to simply **BOURNEMOUTH CORPORATION** in the late 1920s.

G.N. Southerden (Tramway Museum Society collection)

explain, I made an emergency stop and the tow rope broke. The lorry went into a ditch and the front of the trolleybus was within inches of a low bridge. No damage was done and the AA from Southampton rerouted and guided us along a safe route, reaching Bournemouth about 6am after a rather strenuous time". The next to arrive was the single-deck Brush-Thornycroft, which came on an LMS low-loader wagon by rail from Loughborough and arrived in the morning of 11 May, and the third to arrive was the two-axle double-decker AEC-English Electric 661T, which was towed by road from Preston, Lancashire and arrived at noon on 11 May 1933. The fourth, the AEC-English Electric 663T, only arrived a week later on 20 May 1933. All four vehicles were garaged at the Central Tramway Depot in Southcote Road, which was reached by using one trolley arm on the tram (positive) wire and a trailing skate (negative) in one of the tram rails. As the trolleybus followed the alignment of the tram track it was accompanied by spectacular flashing, much to the amusement of children in the street, as the skate made erratic electrical contact.

An initial inspection of the route and vehicles by the MoT was scheduled for Friday 12 May 1933 with an enquiry on the Saturday following which the certificate for public service would be issued. For the duration of the tests marks were painted on the road surface as a guidance to the unfamiliar trolleybus

drivers, e.g. "on" and "off" at Seamoor Road with respect to the traction power supply.

The *Bournemouth Daily Echo* of 12 May 1933 recorded: *"Crowds gathered in Bournemouth Square and at Westbourne today to watch the MoT tests of the two electrical trolley-bus vehicles which are being put into an experimental service between the Square and County Gates. The trolley-buses, both double deckers, were subject to searching tests by Col. E. Woodhouse the Ministry Inspector, who also closely examined the overhead installation.*

"On his round of inspection of the overhead gear (he walked over the route) Col. Woodhouse was accompanied by Ignatius Bulfin and Police Superintendent W. Deacon of Bournemouth division, Hampshire Constabulary. The Mayor of Bournemouth, Ald. Summerbee and members of the Transport Committee together with Mr Herbert Vickers, AMIEE, the Chief Assistant and Electrical Engineer BCT rode in the AEC-EE trolleybus which was the first one to go round the route for testing purposes".

The newspaper report went on to note that, including the party from the MoT, there were twenty passengers on board whilst some 50cwt of tramcar brake blocks had been added in small bags to simulate the weight of a laden vehicle. Brake tests were carried out on Poole Road and descending Avenue Road where just one, the electrical, of the three combinations of brakes was used.

Sunbeam MS2 LJ7701 operating on the experimental trolleybus service to County Gates, Westbourne, photographed at the boarding point on the south side of the Square in 1933. The vehicles were not allocated fleet numbers during the period that they were on hire. Note the destination COUNTY GATES and the blank service number display. Old Christchurch Road is visible in the background.

Bournemouth Transport Ltd. (David Chalk collection)

Wolverhampton Corporation Transport loaned three drivers for the initial operation of the experimental vehicles and to train Bournemouth tram motormen as trolleybus drivers. Reportedly, the vehicle tester who accompanied the Brush-Thornycroft single-decker had also never driven a trolleybus before!

On Saturday 13 May 1933, Bournemouth's experimental trolleybus route was formally approved by Col. Woodhouse of the MoT, public service being inaugurated at 12 noon at a fare of 1d between Bournemouth Square and Westbourne. The Sunbeam MS2 and the two-axle AEC661T entered service

first, driven by Wolverhampton men although the conductors were BCT employees. The first public journey was run by Sunbeam MS 2 (LJ7701) driven by Mr Butler, who went on to become Traffic Superintendent at Wolverhampton. The first local trolleybus driver was Mr W. (Bill) Biddlecombe. The Thornycroft single-decker started running on 15 May 1933 and the three-axle AEC663T trolleybus on 23 May 1933. There is no evidence that any of the vehicles carried fleet numbers during the experimental period; indeed, there was no reason to believe at this stage that these vehicles would be purchased should a trolleybus system be permanently established. The

Two-axle AEC-EE 661T trolleybus LJ7703 also seen at the loading island on the south side of the Square on 13 May 1933. Further details about this vehicle and the other 1933 demonstrators, all of which were acquired later by Bournemouth Corporation Transport, can be found in Appendix A.

Bournemouth Transport Ltd. (David Chalk collection)

stops were similar to those used by the trams. Passengers in the first trolleybuses away commented on the absence of noise and fumes, and the advantages of kerbside loading.

Public appreciation was soon forthcoming. In a letter published in the 14 May 1933 edition of the *Bournemouth Daily Echo*, Mr J.P.P. Coote wrote:

"I have seen trolley buses working in other towns, and now I have seen them in Bournemouth. I consider there is little comparison between the places. In Bournemouth we are a hilly town; they were working on the flat. If any town was made for trolley buses it is Bournemouth - I stood in the middle of Poole Hill, Commercial Road and watched one go up the hill. There was not a sound as it went by. Shortly after a tram car went roaring up, shaking the foundations of the houses; followed by a very noisy motor bus. I then went on a 'circular tour' in a trolley bus to County Gates and back, a soundless and most comfortable trip. Trolley buses can go much faster than the tram cars, and if wished as fast as the motor buses. I cannot understand any reason against them. Upright standards are already up, and one (and often two) overhead wires, requiring then only one additional wire. I believe the running is cheaper!"

At a time when electrical interference to radio reception by trolleybuses was a "hot topic", much was made of the use of "choke-coil" equipment on the vehicles. On 13 May 1933, the newspaper commented *"This morning an Echo reporter listened-in to a three-valve screen-grid radio gramophone at a wireless dealer's shop on Poole Hill to compare the measure of interference between the tramcar and the trolley-bus. The set was operated alternately on the short and long wave bands, and contrary to experience reported*

from other towns, where a trolleybus system is in operation, the new type of vehicle scored heavily. Poole Hill was the ideal spot for the test, because it is here that the vehicles are on their full electrical load when they are climbing. The loud speaker of the set used reproduced an irritating tearing sound as every Westbourne bound tramcar passed. This interference began before the tramcar arrived, and it continued until the vehicle came to a standstill outside St. Michael's Church. Interference caused by the passing trolley-bus was infinitesimal as compared with the passage of the tramcar. All that could be discerned was just a momentary 'swish', and the programme which was being transmitted was then received normally."

Nonetheless, there were letters to the newspaper expressing concerns about trolleybuses being unable to overtake each other, the benefits of express motor buses to outlying suburbs, the unsightliness of overhead wiring and the risk of reducing tram fares when trolleybuses were introduced thereby creating a loss-making service.

In the local newspaper of 10 June 1933, the following Editorial appeared:

"It was, of course, not to be expected that after only a month's experiment with trolley-buses, the Transport Committee would be able to give any definite indication as to the bearing the trials might have on the framing of future policy. There were put before the Council, however, some quite enlightening facts which are likely to stimulate public interest in the problem that is gradually hardening into definite form; the question as to what will be the best substitute when the time comes for scrapping the trams. It was shown that within the first 24 days of the running of these trolley-buses on the experimental

Few views exist of the two experimental AEC vehicles and rear views are especially rare. This one shows the two-axle AEC661T, registration number LJ7703, on the experimental Square - County Gates service in 1933.
S.E. Harrison
(D.A.P. Janes collection)

London United tramways no. 61 (AHX801) an experimental AEC-EE691T with London General Omnibus Co. Ltd. 30ft long bodywork on demonstration on the experimental Bournemouth trolleybus route in June 1933. It is seen here at the eastern end of Seamoor Road, Westbourne, just prior to the junction with Alum Chine Road.
Martin Nimmo collection

route between Bournemouth Square and County Gates as many as 104,568 passengers were carried. Nor were the alternative modes of transport adversely affected. Even making allowances for the fact that the novelty of the system must have attracted many folk, the impression gained by those making a first acquaintance with the 'rail-less tram' has been, on the whole, quite favourable. Many other aspects of the problem have, of course, yet to come under review, such as the reconstruction of the overhead equipment; what routes will be most suitable; the cost of maintenance. Then, if the petrol bus should, after detailed examination of running costs, prove to be the preferable form of transport, there remains the question of the disposal of the generating station. Amongst other matters calling for the exercise of resourcefulness is the question as to whether island sites - such as those lying to north and south of the central tramway shelter, which not infrequently involve setting down and taking up of passengers from the roadway, instead of from a 'refuge' pavement - whether such methods as these cannot be improved upon. A trolley-bus service over the whole of the present tramway system means devising convenient turning points at different existing tramway termini - like those at Christchurch and Moordown. From present indications, however, it would appear that when, in perhaps a year's time, the Council can really get to grips with the pros and cons of the whole transport question, there will be disclosed very good grounds for advocating the gradual substitution on certain selected tram routes of trolley-buses for the fixed-rail cars. But in a growing town this lateral freedom seems also to need an elasticity of route that only the motor bus can offer."

Two trolleybuses were on show at the 38th annual convention of the Incorporated Municipal Electrical Association held in Bournemouth, 12-17 June 1933, namely the AEC663T (LJ7702) hired to BCT and London United Tramways (LUT) 61 (AHX801), an experimental AEC 691T trolleybus fitted with a London General Omnibus Co. centre-entrance 74-seat body built at Chiswick. The press recorded that LUT 61 was the largest electrical trolley-bus in the world and that it arrived in Bournemouth on 12 June 1933. Further vehicle details can be found in Appendix B.

The Mayor, Councillor J.R. Edgecombe, welcoming the 1,100 delegates, commented "I hope that the day is not far distant when some means will be found of storing electricity so that we may get electric buses on the roads. During the last few months we in Bournemouth have been much interested in transport, and we have been trying trolley buses as an experiment, and they have been very much appreciated, but personally I think that the day is not far distant - and there may be some inventors amongst you - when we shall get electric omnibuses".

Mr Bulfin reported to the Transport Committee meeting of 19 June 1933 on his initial and very positive experiences of operating trolleybuses and recommended that the vehicles be licensed for a further three months' service (at a cost of £92 8s 1d). Trolleybuses had at last arrived in Bournemouth!

Towards the end of this further three months Mr Bulfin submitted the following statement to the Transport Committee: "In considering the question as to what form of transport should

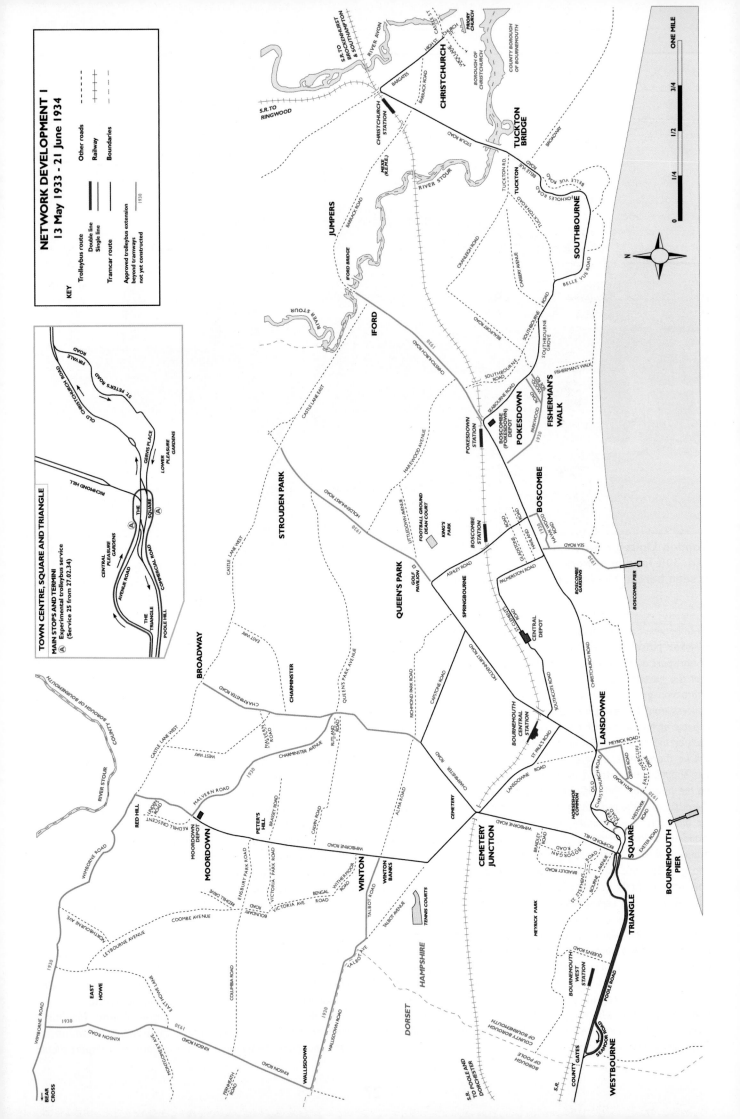

NETWORK DEVELOPMENT I
13 May 1933 - 21 June 1934

KEY

Trolleybus route
Double line
Single line

Tramcar route

Approved trolleybus extension
beyond tramways
not yet constructed — 1930

Other roads
Railway
Boundaries

TOWN CENTRE, SQUARE AND TRIANGLE

MAIN STOPS AND TERMINI
Ⓐ Experimental trolleybus service
(Service 25 from 27.02.34)

RICHMOND HILL
FIR VALE ROAD
ST. PETER'S ROAD
OLD CHRISTCHURCH ROAD
GERVIS PLACE
THE SQUARE
LOWER PLEASURE GARDENS
CENTRAL PLEASURE GARDENS
AVENUE ROAD
COMMERCIAL ROAD
THE TRIANGLE
POOLE HILL

ONE MILE
0   1/4   1/2   3/4

N

BEAR CROSS

WALLISDOWN
EAST HOWE
MOORDOWN
WINTON
WINTON BANKS
BROADWAY
CHARMINSTER
STROUDEN PARK
QUEEN'S PARK
SPRINGBOURNE
CEMETERY JUNCTION
BOURNEMOUTH CENTRAL STATION
LANSDOWNE
HORSESHOE COMMON
SQUARE
TRIANGLE
WESTBOURNE
BOURNEMOUTH PIER
BOURNEMOUTH WEST STATION
BOSCOMBE
BOSCOMBE PIER
POKESDOWN
FISHERMAN'S WALK
SOUTHBOURNE
IFORD
JUMPERS
CHRISTCHURCH
TUCKTON BRIDGE
TUCKTON

S.R. TO RINGWOOD
S.R. TO BROCKENHURST & SOUTHAMPTON
RIVER AVON
RIVER STOUR

S.R. TO POOLE AND TO DORCHESTER

DORSET
HAMPSHIRE

COUNTY BOROUGH OF BOURNEMOUTH
COUNTY BOROUGH OF CHRISTCHURCH
BOROUGH OF POOLE

take the place of the existing Tramways, certain facts should be borne in mind:

i.   No matter what form of transport is decided on, the cost of removing or covering up the existing tramway tracks will apply equally to each.

ii. The number of vehicles to take the place of the existing tramways will be the same in each case, and the costs of these vehicles will be practically the same under each form of transport, but the maintenance and repair costs are the lowest in the case of the Trackless Trolley and the life of the Trackless Trolley Vehicle is the longest.

iii. The motive power in the case of petrol at five miles to the gallon, and petrol costing 11⁹/₁₆d per gallon works out at 2.3d per mile, while in the case of the Trackless Trolley Vehicles using 1.65 units to the mile at 0.72d per unit, works out at 1.2d per mile, i.e. 1.1d per mile cheaper than petrol, and this on the 1,847,606 miles required to be run, represents a saving of some £8,500 per annum.

"The Wolverhampton Corporation operate a fleet of 51 D.D. Petrol Omnibuses and a fleet of 95 Trolley Vehicles, and the cost of operating these different types of vehicles works out at 11.069d per mile for Petrol Vehicles, and 9.516d per mile for Trolley Vehicles, a saving of 1.553d per mile in favour of Trolley Vehicles over petrol, and this on a mileage of 1,847,606, as would be run in Bournemouth by the vehicles in the Corporation area represents a saving per annum of £11,955, and the saving per annum on capital charges by the adoption of T.T. is £1,694. The total saving per annum by the use of T.T. is therefore £13,649.

"The present working costs in Bournemouth of the Tramway system is 13.33d per mile, and taking the working costs of the T.T. system of Wolverhampton, 9.516d, the adoption of the T.T. system in place of trams would show a saving of 3.814d per mile, and this on the 1,847,606 miles to be run, would show a saving of some £29,361 per annum of the T.T. system over the trams.

"The present contribution of Capital Charges on the Tramway system per annum (interest and sinking fund) in Bournemouth is some £56,800. The Capital Charges if T.T. system is installed would be some £33,000, a saving of £23,800 and the saving in working expenses of T.T. over trams, as shown above, is £29,361. The total saving, therefore, per annum on the installation of T.T. in place of trams would be some £53,161."

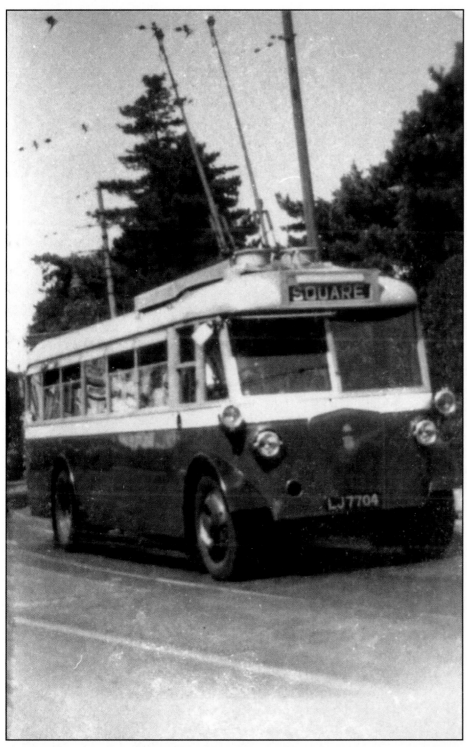

Brush-Thornycroft LJ7704 enters the Square from Avenue Road during the experimental period of trolleybus operation.
Travel Lens (photographer's name not recorded)

TRANSPORT COMMITTEE, 22nd September, 1933.

14.—Transport Services (see **Clause 3 above**).

(i) **Private and Confidential.**

Resolved—That a copy of the following statement, prepared by the Engineer and General Manager, be sent to each member of the Council a week prior to the next meeting of the Council :—

BOURNEMOUTH CORPORATION TRANSPORT SERVICES.

In considering the question as to what form of transport should take the place of the existing Tramways, certain facts should be borne in mind :—

I.   No matter what form of transport is decided on, the cost of removing or covering up the existing tramway tracks will apply equally to each.

II.   The number of vehicles to take the place of the existing tramways will be the same in each case, and the costs of these vehicles will be practically the same under each form of transport, but the maintenance and repairs costs are the lowest in the case of the Trackless Trolley and the life of the Trackless Trolley Vehicle is the longest.

III. The motive power in the case of petrol at five miles to the gallon, and petrol costing 11-9/16d. per gallon works out at 2.3d. per mile, while in the case of the Trackless Trolley Vehicle using 1.65 units to the mile at .72d. per unit, works out at 1.2d. per mile, i.e., 1.1d. per mile cheaper than petrol, and this, on the 1,847,606 miles required to be run, represents a saving of some £8,500 per annum.

The Wolverhampton Corporation operate a fleet of 51 D.D. Petrol Omnibuses and a fleet of 95 Trolley Vehicles, and the cost of operating these different types of vehicles works out at 11.069d. per mile for Petrol Vehicles, and 9.516d. per mile for Trolley Vehicles, a saving of 1.553d. per mile in favour of Trolley Vehicles over petrol, and this on a mileage of 1,847,606, as would be run in Bournemouth by the vehicles in the Corporation area represents a saving per annum of £11,955, and the saving per annum on capital charges by the adoption of T.T. is £1,694. The total saving per annum by the use of T.T. is therefore £13,649.

The present working costs in Bournemouth of the Tramway system is 13.33d. per mile, and taking the working costs of the T.T. system of Wolverhampton, 9.516d., the adoption of the T.T. system in place of trams would show a saving of 3.814d. per mile, and this on the 1,847,606 miles to be run, would show a saving of some £29,361 per annum of the T.T. system over the trams.

The present contribution of Capital Charges on the Tramway system per annum (interest and sinking fund) in Bournemouth is some £56,800. The Capital Charges if T.T. system is installed would be some £33,000, a saving of £23,800 and the saving in working expenses of T.T. over trams, as shown above, is £29,361. The total saving, therefore, per annum on the installation of T.T. in place of trams would be some £53,161.

1379

BOURNEMOUTH CORPORATION TRANSPORT SERVICES.

TROLLEY 'BUS SYSTEM.

COMPARATIVE WORKING COSTS, BOURNEMOUTH AND WOLVERHAMPTON.

BOURNEMOUTH EXPERIMENTAL SERVICE in Operation for 15 Weeks.

	Bournemouth. Average Running Cost per mile	Wolverhampton. Average Running Cost per mile.
Traffic Expenses—	d.	s.
Superintendence	.052	.104
Wages of Drivers and Conductors	3.591	3.519
Wages of Regulators and Depot Clerks		
Cleaning	.517	—
Oiling	.020	.542
Fuel, Light, Water and Cleaning Sheds	—	.137
Tickets. Punches, Cash Bags, etc.	.116	.276
Uniforms	.050	.035
Traffic Equipment on Routes ...	—	.011
Licences	.840	.529
Miscellaneous	.017	.007
	5.203	5.160
General Expenses—		
Salaries and Wages of General Office Staff	.200	.267
Rents, Rates and Taxes ...	.100	.568
Printing and Stationery ...	.050	.054
Law Charges, etc.	—	—
Accident Insurance, Superannuation, etc.	.526	.320
Miscellaneous	—	.070
	.876	1.279
Maintenance and Repairs		
Electrical Equipment of Line ...	.127	.390
Buildings and Fixtures ...	—	.022
Workshop Tools and Sundry Plant	.000	.016
* ⎰ Trolley 'Bus Tyres	.013 ⎱	
,, Chassis ...	.036 ⎬	1.398
⎱ ,, Bodies ...	.027 ⎰	
Other Rolling Stock	—	.048
	.203	1.874
Power : 60,907 units at .72 ...	1.248	1.203
	7.530	9.516

Hire of 'Buses for Experimental Service works out at 3.921d. per mile.

Total miles run in Bournemouth	35,135
Traffic Receipts	£2,176 12s.
Average Receipts per mile run	14.870d.
Wolverhampton—	
Average Receipts per mile run	14.924d.

*The Cost for Tyres, Chassis and Bodies is very low in connection with Bournemouth due to those items being in absolutely new condition.

CHAIRMAN.

BOURNEMOUTH CORPORATION TRANSPORT SERVICES.

1380

	CAPITAL CHARGES	ANNUAL CAPITAL CHARGES (Interest and Sinking Fund) on CAPITAL OUTLAY.		
		Trackless Trolley.	Petrol 'Buses.	Heavy Oil Engine.
(I.) Taking up Permanent Way and making good roadway or covering up rails and tramway area with asphalte, 16 miles—28,160 yards run, 5 yards wide—140,800 square yards at 7/6, repayable 20 years	£53,000			
(II.) No. 100 D.D. Vehicles at £2,000 each, repayable in 10 years ... ... Trackless Trolley ... ... repayable in eight years Petrol	£200,000	£4,042 £25,500	£4,042 £30,625	£4,042 £30,625
(III.) Overhead Equipment, Cables, extra Poles, reinforcing poles, labour in erecting and filling, 20 years	£45,000	£3,431	—	—
	£298,000	£32,973	£34,667	£34,667

REPLACING THE TRAMS

The trolleybus experiment proved a complete success, revenue covering both running and hire costs. Accordingly, on 22 September 1933, the Transport Committee accepted Mr Bulfin's recommendations that:

a. The policy to be adopted in connection with the transport of the town shall be the substitution of an electric trolley bus system in place of the present tramways; such replacement to be undertaken as and when general circumstances and track renewals demand.

b. After full consideration of the different routes, that the first to be taken in hand to be the Ashley and Holdenhurst Roads route to the Square.

c. The experimental service of electric trolley buses from the Square to County Gates be made permanent, and the necessary licences renewed.

The Council adopted these recommendations on 7 October 1933 and decided to replace the trams with trolleybuses over a three-year period.

A month later the Committee instructed Mr Bulfin to purchase the four hired trolleybuses being used on the 1¼-mile-long experimental route and, in December 1933, it recommended that £7,345 be borrowed for this purpose under the provisions of the 1930 Act (see Appendix O). The purchase prices negotiated were: Sunbeam MS2 £2,000; AEC 663T £2,042; AEC 661T £1,853 and the Thornycroft £1,450. The vehicles were added to the BCT fleet as numbers 68-71, 67 being until then the highest-numbered motor bus. The hire costs had been 3.921d per mile with receipts of 14.87d per mile.

Despite the tram track having been re-laid and partially doubled since 1915, the Ashley Road and Holdenhurst Road route was the logical initial tram-to-trolleybus conversion as it passed the St. Swithun's Road access line to the Central Depot, Southcote Road, and also terminated close to the other access line along Palmerston Road, Boscombe. In November 1933 there was correspondence with the MoT about plans for the route, and work started on preparing specifications and inviting tenders for twelve three-axle double-deck trolleybuses.

On 22 December 1933, the tenders of W.T. Glover & Co. Ltd., one of seven received, at £2,580 9s 4d, for the Ashley Road traction power feeder cables, and that of the Sunbeam Motor Car Co. for twelve 56-seater three-axle double-deck trolleybuses at £2,135 each, were accepted by the Transport Committee. The vehicles were to be fitted with composite

No. 72 (AEL400) was the first of the production Park Royal bodied Sunbeam MS2s to be delivered, reaching Bournemouth on 8 June 1934 and entering service on 13 June 1934, nine days prior to the opening of the first tram to trolleybus conversion, to Boscombe by way of Holdenhurst Road and Ashley Road on 22 June 1934. This publicity photograph, taken to demonstrate use of the separate rear entrance and front exit, was made shortly after delivery at the junction of St. Swithun's Road and Southcote Road. Bournemouth Transport Ltd.

Sunbeam MS2 trolleybuses 72, 73 and four others, together with **AEC-EE 663T 69** bringing up the rear, in Southcote Road on 21 June 1934 (the day before the Ashley Road, Boscombe extension opened). The generating station and its cooling towers are visible in the background.   **Bournemouth Transport Ltd.**

Bournemouth's pre-war standard trolleybus was the three-axle Sunbeam MS2 equipped with composite bodywork by either Park Royal Vehicles Ltd. or English Electric Co. Ltd. to the Corporation's own specification. This publicity view shows the first of the town's "production" trolleybuses, Park Royal bodied no. 72 (AEL400) posed at the junction of Southcote Road with St. Swithun's Road on 21 June 1934. Note the rails of the tramway reversing triangle in the roadway in front of the trolleybus.   **Bournemouth Transport Ltd. (David Chalk collection)**

bodywork having a separate rear entrance and front exit, and the bodywork order was shared equally between Park Royal Vehicles Ltd. and English Electric Co. Ltd.

Preliminary arrangements for the start of the Bournemouth Square-Ashley Road trolleybus service included recommendations that the fares should be the same as those prevailing on the trams with some reductions of the higher fares and the discontinuance of certain stops.

On the Bournemouth Square-Westbourne trolleybus route, the trial of a self-printing Verometer ticket machine began on 27 February 1934. Interestingly, the service number 25 appeared on the tickets, although it was not displayed on the trolleybuses. This suggests that the service number series 21-28, at least, had been earmarked for future trolleybus services. It is understood that a TIM ticket machine was also tested about this time, but BCT preferred to remain with the tested Bell Punch form of ticket and issuance.

At the Transport Committee meeting of 20 April 1934, the General Manager was instructed to prepare plans for the introduction of trolleybuses on the routes between a) Moordown and Bournemouth Square via Richmond Hill and Cemetery Junction; b) Moordown and the Lansdowne via Cemetery Junction; and c) Cemetery Junction and Castle Lane via Charminster Road (in principle a continuation of the Capstone Road tram route). This led to a Transport Committee Resolution in May 1934 that trolleybuses should replace trams

on these routes and that tenders be invited at once, to include 36 additional double-deck trolleybuses but excluding tram track removal, at an estimated cost of £123,493. On streets in which both trams and trolleybuses were expected to operate for any length of time, trolleybus wiring was to be hung between the tram wires and the kerb, using bracket arms instead of the tramway span wires wherever necessary.

Rather than seek an additional town centre terminus, it was felt that the turning circle at Bournemouth Square, which had been provided for the experimental County Gates, Westbourne route, could be modified for use by trolleybuses from Moordown and Charminster Road (although, to provide trolleybus parking space, kerbside parking of other vehicles in Avenue Road might have to cease). The Superintendent of Police asked that the number of trolleybuses waiting at the Avenue Road bus stop at any one time be limited to five and this was agreed. In the event, the Richmond Hill trolleybuses were provided with their own circle of wiring independent of the Main Road routes. The question of the Moordown terminus was referred to a subcommittee.

The Transport Committee meeting of 19 June 1934 heard that the vehicles and overhead equipment for the Square-Ashley Road route had been inspected and passed by the MoT. The Parliamentary Secretary to the Minister of Transport, Lt. Col. C.M. Headlam, DSO, MP, accepted the invitation to attend the trolleybus inauguration ceremony. Invitations were also sent to

Lt. Col. C.M. Headlam, DSO, OBE, MP, Parliamentary Secretary to the Minister of Transport (in the single-breasted light-coloured suit) with the Mayors of Bournemouth, Alderman J.R. Edgecombe; Wolverhampton, Councillor Bertram Kidson JP; Christchurch, Alderman N. Barnes and Poole, Councillor Walter C.J. Shortt at the Square prior to the inaugural journey along Holdenhurst Road to Ashley Road, Boscombe on 22 June 1934. Also amongst the guests were Lt. Gen. Sir Travers Clarke, Chairman of the STD Group and the Sunbeam Motor Car Co. Ltd., Mr Charles Owen Silvers, General Manager and Engineer of the Wolverhampton Transport Department, and Mr James Calder, General Manager Reading Corporation Transport. This was Bournemouth's initial tram to trolleybus conversion and signalled the start of a programme that would be completed in just 22 months when trams ceased to run to Christchurch on 8 April 1936.   **Bournemouth Transport Ltd.**

the Mayor of Wolverhampton; Municipal Tramways & Transport Association, Incorporated Municipal Electrical Association, Tramway, Light Railways and Transport Association; the Editors of the Electrical Railway Bus & Tram Journal, Transport World; Motor Transport; the local press; and senior management of the Sunbeam Motor Car Co. Ltd., Park Royal Coachworks, English Electric and The British Thomson-Houston Co. Ltd.. The Mayor of Bournemouth invited guests to lunch at the Royal Bath Hotel to meet the Parliamentary Secretary, after which the guests were taken to the Town Hall to join those attending the ceremony.

Thus, on the afternoon of Friday 22 June 1934, the Westbourne-Bournemouth Square trolleybus service was extended under the new wiring along Old Christchurch Road, Holdenhurst Road and Ashley Road to Boscombe, the new service being designated:

25 Westbourne, Seamoor Road - West Station - Bournemouth Square - Lansdowne - CentralStation - Springbourne - Boscombe Station - Boscombe, Portman Road

At the Square, westbound trolleybuses loaded and unloaded at the island in the junction with Exeter Road previously used by the experimental service to Westbourne. This stop was also used by journeys commencing at the Square (a turning circle for vehicles from the east having been installed on the west side of the tramway shelter). Eastbound vehicles used a stop located immediately to the west of the entrance to the Central Pleasure Gardens where Avenue Road entered the Square. The twelve Sunbeam MS2s, fleet numbers 72-83, costing £25,250, with which to serve the new route arrived between 8 June

and 27 July 1934. The new portion of trolleybus route was 2.7 miles long and led to the withdrawal of 12 trams, a total of 18 trams being sold in November 1934 to A.F. Newell & Co. Ltd., who scrapped them at the Council dump which then existed in King's Park.

Like the trams before them, the trolleybuses followed separate routes between the Square and Horseshoe Common: the eastbound wiring was along Old Christchurch Road whereas the westbound wiring turned south from Old Christchurch Road opposite Horseshoe Common into Fir Vale Road, reaching the Square via St. Peter's Road and Gervis (pronounced 'Jarvis') Place. The route continued along Old Christchurch Road to the Lansdowne and eastwards along Holdenhurst Road, with a junction about 100yd south of Central Station into St. Swithun's Road giving access to Southcote Road and thence the Central Depot. A reversing triangle was installed at Capstone Road although there is no evidence of journeys regularly turning there, but no trolleybus wiring equivalents of the tramway crossovers at Lowther Road or Boscombe Station were added. Further along Holdenhurst Road, at the Queen's Park Hotel, the wiring turned south into Ashley Road, which it followed for its entire length, towards Boscombe Station and the centre of Boscombe where an anti-clockwise terminal loop was constructed. At the south end of Ashley Road the wiring turned east into Christchurch Road (paralleling the Lansdowne-Pokesdown tram route), then north into Portman Road and finally into Gladstone Road (two roads which had not previously been served by trams), before rejoining Ashley Road. The service was advertised as originating and terminating at the junction of Ashley Road with Christchurch Road, Boscombe.

Central Depot was accessible both from Holdenhurst Road, by

On the opening day of Bournemouth's first trolleybus route converted from tramway operation, 22 June 1934, no. 73 (AEL401) bedecked with flags leaves the Square heading west up Commercial Road towards Westbourne. Note the line of decorated trolleybuses waiting in Avenue Road. The clock tower on the roof of the tramway passenger waiting room is visible to the rear of 73. Bournemouth Transport Ltd. (David Chalk collection)

Four beflagged Sunbeam MS2s wait where Avenue Road joins the Square on 22 June 1934. Bournemouth Town Hall is visible in the backgound beyond Central Pleasure Gardens.
Malcolm Pearce (G.O.P. Pearce)

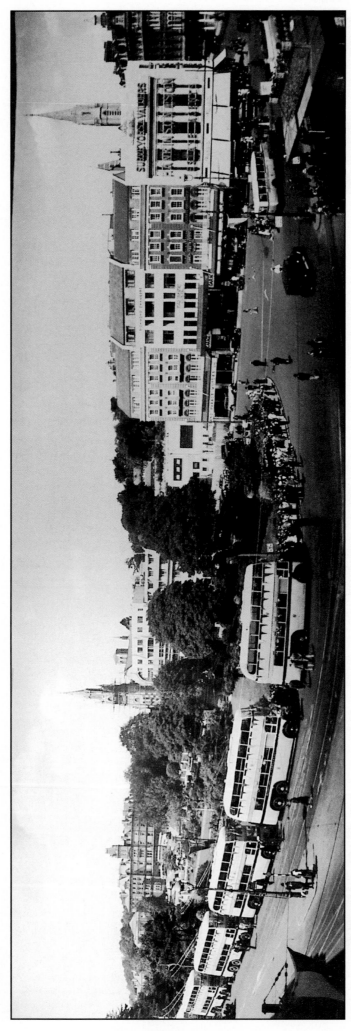

The line of new, beflagged trolleybuses extended along the north side of Avenue Road to where it entered the Square by the entrance to the Central Pleasure Gardens. The Town Hall is visible in the left background. Note the queue of would-be passengers hoping to make an inaugural trip. Bournemouth Transport Ltd.

Three-axle AEC-EE 663T trolleybus LJ7702 seen at the stop on the south side of the Square prior to turning back into Old Christchurch Road by means of the new turning circle on the west side of the tramways waiting room. The destination Holdenhurst Road and 25 service number displays indicate that this photograph was taken after the Boscombe extension opened on 22 June 1934 although it is not clear to which terminal point the vehicle was running. A.N. Porter (David Chalk collection)

means of the north end of St. Swithun's Road and then the length of Southcote Road to the depot complex entrance opposite the junction with Carlton Road, and also from Boscombe, with wiring erected in Christchurch Road, Boscombe from Ashley Road as far as the junction with Palmerston Road, then along Palmerston Road and St. Clement's Road to the eastern depot entrance. This paralleled the tramway access in both directions but, following the tramway abandonment, was unusual in having a three-wire layout (see Appendix I) along Southcote Road and a short section at the south end of Palmerston Road.

Tram services along the length of Holdenhurst Road and Ashley Road ceased, but trams to and from Moordown continued to run along Holdenhurst Road between St. Paul's Road and the Lansdowne until 28 June 1935, whilst tramway equipment remained in place as far north as Capstone Road until 23 August 1935 and between the Lansdowne and St. Swithun's Road until December 1935 for depot access purposes. The tender of A.F. Newell & Co. Ltd. to remove two tramcars per week from the depot was accepted. Surplus stocks of tram rail were sold to Leicester Corporation and various tramcar spares to Coventry.

Trolleybuses were high on the agenda of the 20 July 1934 Transport Committee meeting. Mr Bulfin was instructed to prepare plans for the conversion of the tram route from the Lansdowne along Christchurch Road through Boscombe to Pokesdown Station and thence by way of Fisherman's Walk, Southbourne and Tuckton Bridge to Christchurch, as well as an entirely new trolleybus route eastwards along Christchurch Road beyond Pokesdown Station as far as Iford Bridge. It was also recommended that six more trolleybuses be ordered as

a follow-on to the initial Sunbeam contract. These were again Park Royal-bodied Sunbeam MS2 vehicles which became fleet numbers 84-89. They were delivered in October 1934, bringing the trolleybus fleet up to 22.

On 26 July 1934, the Committee inspected one of the new trolleybuses at Central Depot, Southcote Road and suggested some modifications. They decided that for all future trolleybus orders the bench seat over the rear wheel arch would be lowered as on the vehicle inspected. Modifications to the upper-deck ventilation were also requested, namely that two half-strip windows or quarter lights were to be used one on either side of the front windows, instead of fixed ones; two additional half-drop side windows, "Hit and Miss" ventilators and an additional Flettner Extractor ventilator in the front dome. They approved the new grab handles to the front exit on the vehicle inspected and instructed that all trolleybuses be so equipped.

The thirty-year lease of the Poole Light Railways between County Gates and Poole Station through Upper Parkstone was now approaching its expiry date. By the early 1930s major track renewals and doubling were becoming necessary; thus, in line with their plans for the rest of their tramways, Bournemouth Corporation duly applied for powers under a Provisional Order to substitute the tramways in Poole with trolleybuses. Objections were received from Poole Corporation, Dorset County Council and H&D. On 1 August 1934 the Poole Town Clerk wrote to inform the Bournemouth Transport Committee that the Poole Transport Committee was unable to recommend that its Council should agree to the replacement of the tramways with trolleybuses. At the same time H&D made an offer to take over the Poole tramways, pay off the

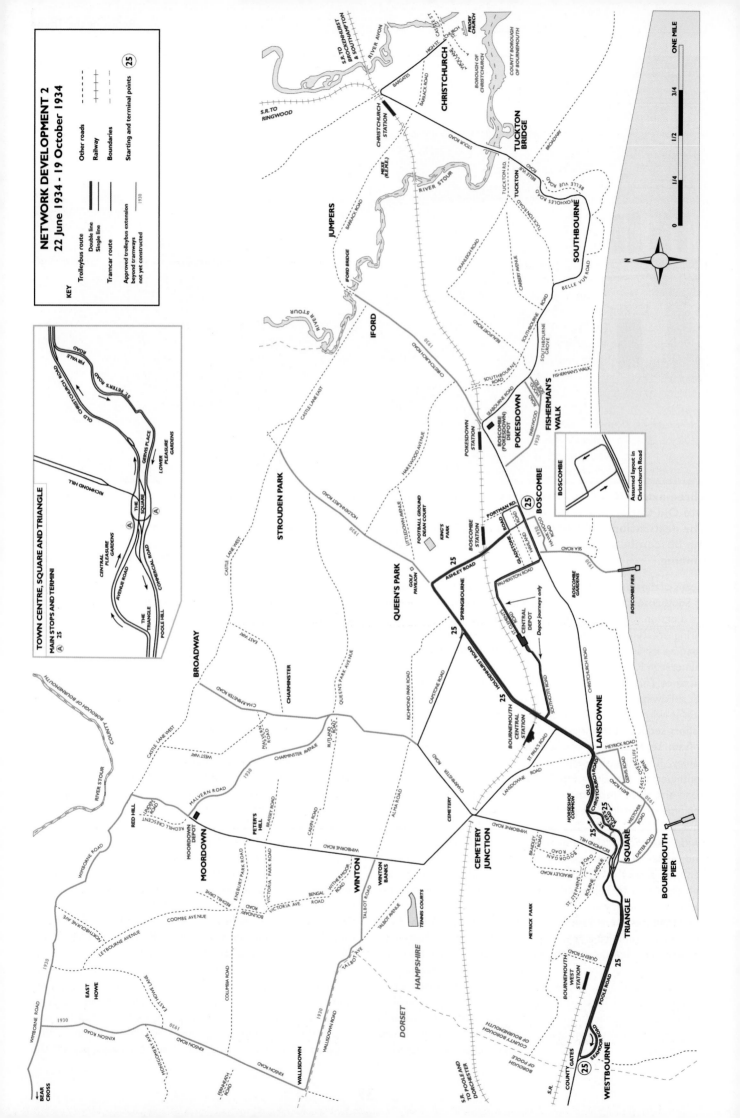

NETWORK DEVELOPMENT 2
22 June 1934 - 19 October 1934

KEY

Trolleybus route
Double line
Single line

Tramcar route
Double line
Single line

Approved trolleybus extension beyond tramways not yet constructed — 1930

Other roads
Railway
Boundaries
Starting and terminal points — (25)

TOWN CENTRE, SQUARE AND TRIANGLE
MAIN STOPS AND TERMINI — (A) 25

PIR VALE ROAD
ST PETER'S ROAD
OLD CHRISTCHURCH ROAD
RICHMOND HILL
GERVIS PLACE
LOWER PLEASURE GARDENS
THE SQUARE
CENTRAL PLEASURE GARDENS
AVENUE ROAD
COMMERCIAL ROAD
POOLE HILL
THE TRIANGLE

BEAR CROSS

EAST HOWE

WIMBORNE ROAD
KINSON ROAD 1930
MONTAGU ROAD
FERNHEATH ROAD
WALLISDOWN ROAD 1930
COOMBE AVENUE
LETBOURNE AVENUE
COLUMBIA ROAD
NORTHBOURNE AVE
RIVER STOUR
BOROUGH OF BOURNEMOUTH

WALLISDOWN
MOORDOWN
MOORDOWN DEPOT
RED HILL
REDHILL ROAD
REDHILL CRESCENT
PETER'S HILL
MALVERN ROAD 1930
ENSBURY PARK ROAD
BRASSEY ROAD
CABIN ROAD
REDHILL DRIVE
VICTORIA PARK ROAD
VICTORIA AVE
BENGAL ROAD
WITHERMOOR ROAD

WINTON
WINTON BANKS
TALBOT ROAD
TALBOT AVENUE
TENNIS COURTS

BROADWAY
CASTLE LANE WEST
CHARMINSTER ROAD
CHARMINSTER
CHARMINSTER AVENUE
MALVERN ROAD
RUTLAND ROAD
WEST WAY
EAST WAY
QUEEN'S PARK AVENUE

STROUDEN PARK
CASTLE LANE WEST
CASTLE LANE EAST

RICHMOND PARK ROAD
CAPSTONE ROAD
QUEEN'S PARK
GOLF PAVILION
LITTLEDOWN AVENUE
HAREWOOD AVENUE
HOLDENHURST ROAD 1930

ASHLEY ROAD
SPRINGBOURNE

CEMETERY JUNCTION
CEMETERY
WIMBORNE ROAD
ALMA ROAD
LANSDOWNE ROAD

DORSET
HAMPSHIRE

BOURNEMOUTH WEST STATION
QUEENS ROAD
BRADFORD ROAD
STEPHEN'S RD
MEYRICK PARK
BODORGAN RD
BRADLEY ROAD
BODORGAN ROAD
BOURNE AVENUE
RICHMOND HILL

TRIANGLE
POOLE ROAD
SEAMOOR ROAD
WESTBOURNE
(25)
COUNTY GATES
BOROUGH OF POOLE
BOROUGH OF BOURNEMOUTH
S.R. POOLE AND TO DORCHESTER
S.R. TO POOLE

BOURNEMOUTH PIER
EXETER ROAD
BATH ROAD
EAST OVERCLIFF DRIVE
GERVIS ROAD
WESTOVER ROAD
MEYRICK ROAD
OLD CHRISTCHURCH ROAD
CHRISTCHURCH ROAD
HORSESHOE COMMON

LANSDOWNE
BOURNEMOUTH CENTRAL STATION
ST PAUL'S ROAD
HOLDENHURST ROAD
SOUTHCOTE ROAD
CENTRAL DEPOT
Depot journeys only

BOSCOMBE
BOSCOMBE STATION
PORTMAN RD.
GLADSTONE ROAD
SEA ROAD
HAWKWOOD ROAD
PALMERSTON ROAD
BOSCOMBE GARDENS
BOSCOMBE PIER
CHRISTCHURCH ROAD 1930

FISHERMAN'S WALK
FISHERMAN'S WALK
SOUTHBOURNE ROAD
SOUTHBOURNE GROVE

POKESDOWN
POKESDOWN STATION
BOSCOMBE (POKESDOWN) DEPOT
SEABOURNE ROAD

SOUTHBOURNE
BELLE VUE ROAD
CARBERY AVENUE
BEAUFORT ROAD
SOUTHBOURNE ROAD

IFORD
CHRISTCHURCH ROAD 1930
CASTLE LANE EAST

JUMPERS
FORD BRIDGE
RIVER STOUR
BARRACK ROAD
CRANLEIGH ROAD
PARKWOOD ROAD

CHRISTCHURCH
CHRISTCHURCH STATION
BARGATES
HIGH ST
CASTLE ST
CHURCH ST
PRIORY CHURCH
RIVER AVON
S.R. TO BROCKENHURST & SOUTHAMPTON
S.R. TO RINGWOOD
BOROUGH OF CHRISTCHURCH

TUCKTON BRIDGE
TUCKTON
TUCKTON ROAD
STOUR ROAD
BELLE VUE ROAD
FOXHOLES ROAD
BROADWAY
COUNTY BOROUGH OF BOURNEMOUTH

MEXE (KEME)

BOSCOMBE
Assumed layout in Christchurch Road

N

ONE MILE
0   1/4   1/2   3/4

outstanding loan and replace the trams with motor buses. Somewhat daunted, the Committee instructed the Town Clerk to find out Christchurch Council's views on a trolley vehicle service from Iford Bridge to Christchurch via Barrack Road.

H&D subsequently applied to the South Eastern Traffic Commissioners (SETC), the licensing authority for the area following the Road Traffic Act, 1930 as amended by the Road and Rail Traffic Act, 1933, to operate replacement motor bus services in Poole, whereupon the Bournemouth Transport Committee authorised the Town Clerk and Mr Bulfin to oppose these applications. As a result, the MoT wrote, at the end of September 1934, to invite Bournemouth Council to discussions about the proposed sale of Poole Council's light railway interests to H&D. The Committee recommended powers be sought for Bournemouth Corporation to operate transport services in the Borough of Poole.

In August 1934, the Town Clerk drew Mr Bulfin's attention to a number of legal points in connection with the planned Iford Bridge trolleybus extension. In his response, the General Manager interestingly asked that permission be sought for a trolleybus extension from Iford Bridge over the River Stour and along Barrack Road, Stour Road and Bargates, Christchurch with a turning circle in front of Christchurch Town Hall. This led to an informal contact with Wolverhampton Corporation Transport, which was already operating trolleybuses in the areas of other authorities, e.g. Bilston, Coseley and Walsall.

The tramways terminated in Christchurch with two sidings in Church Street, an impossible terminal location for replacement trolleybuses. Following discussions, Christchurch Council gave their approval on 21 September 1934 to the construction of a trolleybus turning circle in Christchurch High Street in the width of the road outside the Town Hall when the tram service ceased. However, it did not agree to trolleybuses being extended from Iford Bridge along Barrack Road. Accordingly when, in October 1934, Christchurch Council asked for a fare reduction on motor bus service 1 (Bournemouth Square-Purewell via Iford and Christchurch) it was told that this would be impossible—although the introduction of trolleybuses would have permitted a substantial reduction! In the meantime, BPES announced that it was prepared to supply traction power to a Christchurch trolleybus route and, if required, the Poole line at 1d per unit.

It was announced that in the period 1 January-21 September 1934 the number of passengers carried by trolleybus between Westbourne and Ashley Road, Boscombe had increased by 250,000 compared to the same period in 1933 when there was a mixture of tram and trolleybus operation.

On 3 September 1934 the Transport Committee inspected the site of the proposed Moordown trolleybus terminus and recommended that application be made to the MoT to use "Old Wimborne Road", now Lawford Road, as part of an anti-clockwise turning loop comprising Castle Lane West and Wimborne Road. They also decided that trolleybus overhead wiring from the Lansdowne to Iford Bridge should be supported

An evocative view of one of Bournemouth's earlier trolleybuses, 79 (AEL407), a 1934 Sunbeam MS2 with English Electric bodywork built to a Park Royal design. It is pictured here waiting in Holdenhurst Road, Springbourne, just to the north of the Queen's Park Hotel and the junction with Ashley Road. It carries the original livery of primrose with white roof, maroon bands beneath the upper and lower deck windows, yellow vent panels above the lower deck windows and red lining-out on the main primrose-painted body panels (20 March 1935).

Malcolm Pearce (G.O.P. Pearce)

Queen's Park Corner on a cold 21 February 1935. Sunbeam MS2 78 (AEL406) stands at the north end of Ashley Road displaying **RESERVED CAR** whilst 87 (ALJ63) heads down Holdenhurst Road towards the Lansdowne and County Gates on a service 25 working. Note the police emergency telephone on the corner

David Bowler collection

An unidentified English Electric bodied Sunbeam MS2 (probably 78 - see the preceding view) stands at the Queen's Park Golf Pavilion terminus at the junction of Littledown Avenue (on the right) with Holdenhurst Road on 21 February 1935. The side indicator box, apparently only fitted on the nearside of the lower deck saloon, shows **RESERVED CAR**.

David Bowler collection

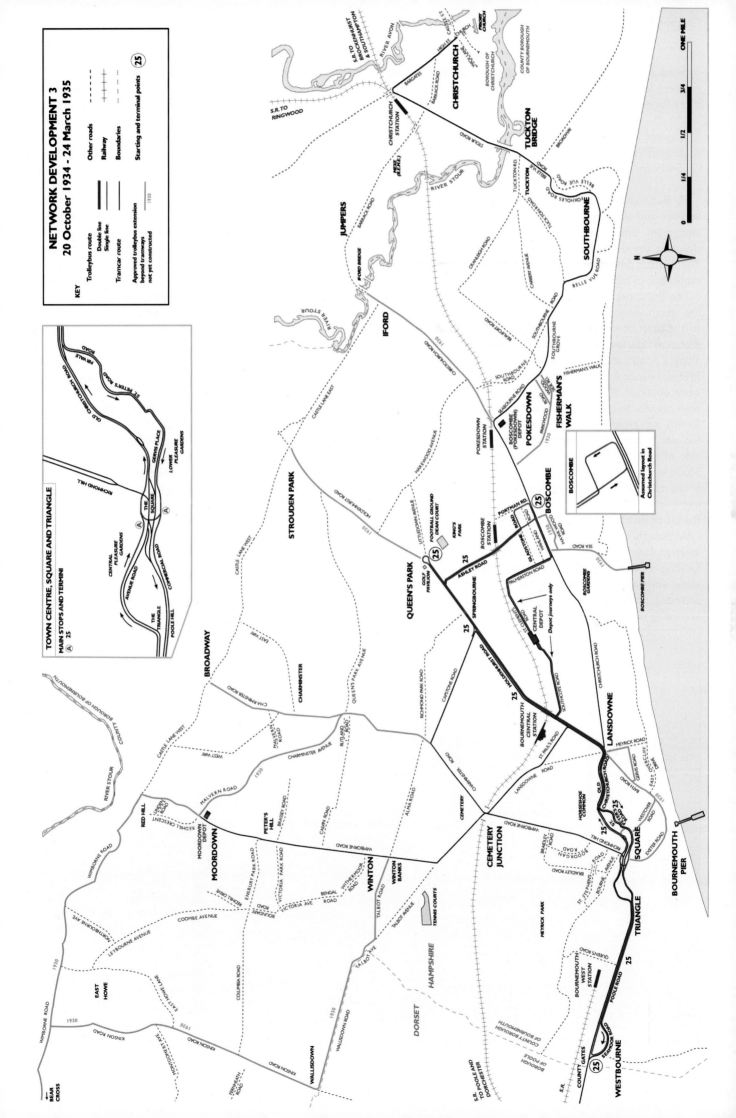

by bracket arms instead of span wire. Seven tenders had been received for the supply of 36 more trolleybuses, of which the three lowest were:

Leyland Motors Ltd.	£72,360
English Electric Co.	£79,020
Sunbeam Motor Car Co.	£79,128

Mr Bulfin stressed the advantages of having a fleet of standard vehicles and equipment, whilst commenting on the electrical equipment offered by the tendering firms. Accordingly, on the next day the full Council accepted Sunbeam's tender for double-deck 56-seat trolleybuses, to be fitted with Park Royal bodywork to basically the same design as before.

The Transport Committee also adopted his suggestion that the extension of trolleybuses from a) Bournemouth Square to the junction of Castle Lane West and Wimborne Road via Richmond Hill and Wimborne Road, and b) from the Lansdowne along Christchurch Road to the Borough boundary at Iford Bridge, be put in hand immediately the necessary approvals were obtained. Mr Bulfin reported that he was in negotiation with respect to a turning point at Iford Bridge. The following month, agreement was reached to purchase Council land on the north side of Christchurch Road on the Bournemouth side of Iford Bridge, between Bridle Crescent and the River Stour, formerly Clingan's Farm, for £2,250. In due course, the actual turning circle was laid out on the site of the former farmhouse. The Committee also went on to seek authority for the purchase of a further 48 trolleybuses as and when required.

Within three weeks Sunbeam offered to supply the 48 additional vehicles for £101,304, as a "follow-on" to the existing order, some £4,200 less than they would cost at the same unit price as in the current contract for 36 vehicles, provided that the Council was prepared to accept delivery, according to a mutually agreed programme, over a nine-month period commencing immediately following completion of the 36-vehicle contract. The Transport Committee accepted this clause, which was intended to retain jobs at Sunbeam during the prevailing difficult economic climate, on condition that Park Royal bodywork was supplied.

A short branch, serving Dean Court football ground 200yd south of the terminus in addition to the Queen's Park municipal golf course to the north, opened on 20 October 1934. Where the trolleybuses turned south off Holdenhurst Road at the Queen's Park Hotel into Ashley Road and towards Boscombe, parallel wiring (but not a turnout frog) was installed for some distance to permit vehicles to continue the 350yd north-eastwards along Holdenhurst Road as far as its junction with Littledown Avenue, where a turning circle in the width of the road was erected. This terminus was referred to as the Queen's Park Golf Pavilion, the building (demolished in 1966 for the construction of Wessex Way) being on the north side of Holdenhurst Road. Trolleybuses had to re-pole in Holdenhurst Road until a junction was installed at an unknown later date, possibly in June 1938 when regular services, rather than just football specials, began to run along the branch. On 19 October 1934 (and again on 13 November 1934) instructions were issued to conductors that, on service 25 trolleybuses operating to Queen's Park Golf Pavilion, any passenger wishing to travel to the terminus be allowed to do so at the same fare as that to Queen's Park Hotel, and also that passengers might be picked up at the same point again without additional charge. Trolleybuses 84-89 were purchased specifically for this extension; in addition to special journeys for football matches at Dean Court (when six or more vehicles were used), the line was used for all kinds of events in King's Park, such as circus or funfair visits, flower shows and various sporting fixtures. With police approval, the trolleybus waiting area on the west side of Holdenhurst Road at Queen's Park Golf Pavilion turning circle was moved to the opposite side of the road in late 1935.

Brand new Sunbeam MS2 103 is seen at Queen's Park Golf Pavilion turning circle on 23 March 1935 two days before it entered revenue-earning service.
Malcolm Pearce (G.O.P. Pearce)

Six Sunbeam MS2s led by 82 equipped with English Electrc bodywork built to a Park Royal design lined up along the south side of Holdenhurst Road, immediately to the north of the Queen's Park Hotel (junction with Ashley Road) on football special duties (23 March 1935). Malcolm Pearce (G.O.P. Pearce)

Tenders for feeder cables, conduits, section boxes, etc., for the mile-long Iford Bridge extension were invited. There were 17 replies, that of Messrs W.T. Glover & Co., Trafford Park, Manchester, at £14,774 6s 1d being accepted by the Council at its 30 October 1934 meeting, notwithstanding that Glover's past work had provoked a number of insurance claims relating to unprotected work, implements and unlit manhole covers, etc. To minimise the number of lay-offs in the difficult economic climate, Mr Bulfin was able to arrange with Glover's that 63 seasonal conductors and cleaners not engaged in winter could be employed on cable-laying work.

The Negotiating Committee met with Poole Council again on 7 November 1934. Poole requested an annual minimum amount in respect of the capitation fee in connection with the proposal to run trolleybuses instead of trams on the Upper Parkstone route. Bournemouth Transport Committee recommended that the Bournemouth offer be amended to include a guaranteed minimum of £3,500 pa. but, at the end of the month, the Town Clerk reported that Poole Council had not responded to the revised offer, nor to its proposal that the MoT suggestion—to submit the matter to an independent expert—be taken up.

As H&D's proposals for a working agreement with Poole had not been sanctioned by the MoT, the Company promoted a Parliamentary Bill to gain its approval. On 21 December 1934 the Town Clerk further reported that H&D had deposited the Poole Road Transport Bill for the operation of motor bus services in that town. The Bournemouth Transport Committee resolved that the Town Clerk should lodge an objection to this Bill and that H&D's applications to the SETC also be opposed.

On 31 December 1934 the Christchurch Town Clerk wrote to the Transport Committee with respect to the proposed turning circle in High Street, Christchurch, and asked that an alternative site be considered. At the same time, the Christchurch Ratepayers' Association wrote to support any application to operate trolleybuses in their Borough, as they were convinced that this would lead to lower fares in and out of Christchurch. The Boscombe Ratepayers' Association, meanwhile, supported Bournemouth Council in its promotion of a Bill to unify transport services in the Boroughs of Bournemouth, Christchurch and Poole, noting that the trolleybus was the recognised transport system of the future in Bournemouth's view. In January 1935 the Bournemouth Corporation (Trolley Vehicles) Provisional Order, relating to the Upper Parkstone tram route in Poole and with exactly this latter intent, was duly deposited and all requisite notices served. The Town Clerk subsequently advised that six objections had been received.

At its meeting on 22 February 1935, the Bournemouth Transport Committee recommended that the Council promote a "late" Parliamentary Bill to operate trolleybuses in the Borough of Poole over the existing light railway route between County Gates and Poole Station, with installation of a reversing triangle proposed at Serpentine Road, just short of the railway crossing, i.e. exactly as the Provisional Order already applied for.

A public meeting at Bournemouth Town Hall on 8 March 1935 decided by 102 to 65 votes to support this recommendation, whilst there is also evidence that many Poole residents would have welcomed trolleybuses.

Alderman (Ald.) F.B. Summerbee, Chairman of Bournemouth's Transport Committee, commented to the Bournemouth Daily Echo of 5 March 1935 that: "Poole seeks to secure powers to run into Bournemouth Square and to pick up and set down on the route which is within the Borough of Bournemouth.

"Under the respective Acts of Poole and Bournemouth neither authority has the right to run into the area of the other authority without that area's consent.

"On two occasions in the past we have desired to extend our services in the Poole area, largely at the instigation of people living in those areas, but on each occasion the Poole Corporation have

Bournemouth's trams were kept in immaculate condition until the end of tramway operation. No. 108, on Brill 22E maximum traction bogies, was built by Brush, Loughborough, in 1921 and, although delivered with driver's vestibules, is basically identical to the design of cars delivered in 1902 presumably due to a prohibition of running top-covered cars on 3ft 6in gauge track. This view, believed to have been made for road safety purposes in February 1935, was taken in Upper Parkstone. Bournemouth Transport Ltd. (David Chalk collection)

notified us of their objection to such applications and we have promptly withdrawn our applications having regard to the objections.

"The latest development has been that we were perfectly willing that the issue should be largely settled in the Houses of Parliament and approached the bus company and the Poole Council that they should allow orders to be made pro forma and sent to Parliament in a Confirmation Bill.

"This both the company and Poole declined to agree to. Our only reason for this course was that the whole problem should be put before one tribunal and on the definite understanding that neither the position of the company nor Poole Council should be prejudiced by the making of the order.

"The authorities themselves consider that it is in the interests of all parties that the whole matter should come before the same tribunal. Thus instead of the matter coming before the Minister of Transport it will be thrashed out by the Parliamentary Committee. The only way to secure this was by the promotion of a Late Bill and this has been promoted".

This postponed the hearing of the Provisional Order pending the hearing by the Parliamentary Committee of the petitions for the Bills. Poole Town Council, however, retaliated by promoting their own (Poole Road Transport) Bill seeking powers to abandon the tramways and replace them with H&D motor buses.

Meanwhile, on 21 May 1935, the SETC heard H&D's application to run services between Bournemouth and Poole via Upper Parkstone in place of BCT trams, and gave dispensation for replacement motor bus services to commence prior to the Bill receiving Royal Assent. A provisional agreement covering these services granted Bournemouth Corporation protection from H&D as follows:

a. Passengers picked up and set down within 150yd of County Gates were also to be considered Corporation passengers; at all other points surrounding Bournemouth an imaginary line was drawn 440yd outside the boundary and passengers picked up between this line and the actual boundary were also considered Corporation passengers unless a supplementary 1d fare was paid.

b. Corporation Inspectors could board H&D buses within the Corporation area and the 440yd extension referred to above.

c. H&D would not introduce any fare concessions in addition to those already issued by the Corporation.

d, H&D vehicles travelling to/from the west would not stop in the Square without Corporation approval.

H&D tramway-replacement motor buses began to run without ceremony between Bournemouth Square Bus Station and Poole on Saturday 8 June 1935, the day after the tramway lease expired. The company paid £75,000 for the tramways and contributed £7,500 towards the cost of removing the rails. It also took over the depot at Albert Road, Upper Parkstone.

Whilst the Poole Road Transport Bill was progressing through Parliament, Bournemouth Corporation and H&D had formulated a provisional agreement covering their relationship and all H&D services crossing the Borough Boundary:

1. H&D fares within the Corporation area could not be less than on Corporation services;

2. The Corporation was to receive the revenue from all H&D passengers both taken up and set down on any one journey within the Corporation area less the cost of carrying such passengers. The Transport Department and H&D would serve the same stops in the Corporation area;

3. H&D passengers who were picked up outside the Corporation area and changed buses at the Square (including the H&D Bus Station) to continue their journeys and alight in the Corporation area were to be considered as passengers travelling totally within the Corporation area, both picked up and set down in the BCT area on the same journey as between the Square and the point where they were set down.
Passengers who were picked up in the Corporation area and who changed buses at the Square to continue their

journeys to points outside the Corporation area were to be considered as passengers both picked up and set down in the Corporation area on the same journey as between the points where they were picked up and the Square.

The Square was deemed to be the commencing or terminal point (as the case may be) of all H&D services which entered or left Bournemouth;

4. H&D would pay £1,000 pa. in quarterly payments for raising no objections to the abandonment of the light railways in the Borough of Poole and the relinquishment by Bournemouth Corporation of its rights therein after 7 June 1935 when the lease to the Bournemouth Corporation of the light railways terminates;

5. H&D would not oppose any new routes for trolley vehicles or PSVs proposed by the Corporation within the Corporation area;

6. H&D would not apply for any new or additional routes within the Corporation area without the Corporation's consent;

7. The Corporation would not apply for any routes outside their area over which H&D were already operating without the Company's consent;

8. H&D agreed to employ men displaced on the Poole Light Railways who could not be found employment by Bournemouth Corporation.

The Poole Road Transport Act 1935 gained Royal Assent on 2 August 1935, resulting in the following legislative consequences: the Bill for a Bournemouth Corporation Act (25 & 26 Geo.5 1934-5) was not enacted and Bournemouth Corporation withdrew its application for a Provisional Order, in both cases for permission to operate trolleybuses along the Upper Parkstone tram route in Poole. The withdrawal of the trams made 70 men surplus to requirements and BCT submitted to H&D lists of men suggesting their employment if satisfactory.

The Bournemouth Corporation Act 1930 contained an agreement that H&D buses running over BCT routes would charge 50% higher fares between the Square and Bear Cross and Purewell. The Poole Road Transport Act 1935 contained a different agreement, whereby all revenue taken on H&D buses from passengers travelling wholly within the BCT area would pass to BCT, less the cost of carrying those passengers. BCT continued to provide H&D with special H&D tickets which were over-stamped BCT and BCT Inspectors had the right to board H&D buses to make occasional checks. The revenue from H&D was shown in the Transport Department's accounts and apportioned between motor buses and trolleybuses. The agreement lasted for 40 years. Certain H&D journeys were exempt from this agreement and therefore carried a maroon-painted board or special maroon destination blind showing "NOT ON SERVICE FOR BOURNEMOUTH CORPORATION PASSENGERS".

Noting plans to operate trolleybuses on Richmond Hill, the MoT instructed that vehicles must be equipped with a coasting brake to limit their downhill speed and emergency run-back brakes to offer more safety when travelling uphill. The coasting brake was a specialised form of rheostatic braking (not to be confused with the conventional rheostatic brake with which the undertaking's post-war deliveries and most other trolleybuses were equipped) which limited the speed to a pre-set figure (8mph in Bournemouth) when coasting down a gradient. The brake was compulsorily selected on the controller, known as the "reverser" in Bournemouth, by the driver at the start of the descent (for practical purposes the stop at Richmond Gardens opposite Bodorgan Road) and disengaged at the bottom (the Albert Road stop at the Catholic Church of the Sacred Heart). There were no special signs or indications to drivers. Once selected, the brake was independent of the power supply and no further action was needed by the driver. Once the mechanical brake had been released, the trolleybus was allowed to coast away, speed increasing up to 8mph when a smooth check would be felt as the brake came into operation. This speed would then be maintained until the driver applied a mechanical brake to bring the vehicle to a halt. The heat produced was dissipated throughout the descent rather than confining it to a period of heavy braking at the bottom of the hill.

The run-back brake prevented a trolleybus running backwards out of control on a gradient and was automatic in operation. A special contactor was energised and held open during normal running but, if there was a dewirement, power failure or voltage overload, the contactor closed and completed the braking circuit, limiting backwards speed to 2mph, and giving the driver an opportunity to steer into the kerb or even chock the wheels. Under normal circumstances no action was required; however, if traction power was still available at the trolleys, on Bournemouth's vehicles it was necessary for the driver to switch off a circuit breaker manually to permit the run-back brake to operate—an important point in potentially a moment of panic!

Although the MoT later stipulated the use of a coasting brake for trolleybuses whenever descending prescribed steep gradients in Bournemouth, Brighton, Hastings, Huddersfield and London, its earliest use of such regulatory power was in relation to the 1 in 8 (12.5%) gradient of Richmond Hill, Bournemouth.

Additional trolleybuses for the Richmond Hill routes were already on order when, in November 1934, Mr Bulfin reported to the Transport Committee that "additional equipment was required to comply with the instructions of the MoT for limiting the speed of trolleybuses when running downhill, and to prevent them running back". On 4 December 1934, the Council approved the purchase of British Thomson-Houston coasting and run-back brake equipment at a cost of £18 10s per vehicle and its attachment to the 84 trolleybuses then on order. Then, on 21 December 1934, the Transport Committee approved Sunbeam's offer to supply and retrospectively install the additional coasting and run-back equipment to those trolleybuses already in service for £25 each. In all, Bournemouth purchased 166 trolleybuses equipped with coasting and run-back brakes as well as a further seven acquired many years later second-hand from Brighton and already so equipped.

The next stage in the system's development was the introduction of services to Iford. Trolleybus overhead wiring paralleling the tram route was erected along Christchurch Road between the Lansdowne and Palmerston Road, Boscombe, where the existing connection to the Central Depot in Southcote Road branched off, and then further eastwards as far as Pokesdown Station. Where the tram lines swung south into Seabourne Road, the trolleybus wires continued over the railway bridge and down the hill through new housing developments in

Christchurch Road, past the junction with Castle Lane East, to a turning circle on the north side of Christchurch Road just west of Iford Bridge over the River Stour and the borough boundary with Christchurch. Following withdrawal, the body of tram No.1, Bournemouth's sole single-deck passenger car, was placed there as a waiting room. The trolleybuses did not directly replace a tram or motor bus service, although motor bus service 1 Bournemouth Square-Purewell also operated along Christchurch Road.

Ald. Summerbee stated that the Corporation hoped to have the Square-Moordown route open by Whitsun 1935, with the Square-Castle Lane West, and Lansdowne-Moordown routes opened by the end of June 1935. Dealing with trolleybus fares he went on to say that, taking them as a whole, the average distance for a penny would work out at 1.06 miles, as against the tramway distance of 0.98 miles. Southbourne Ratepayers' Association asked if it would be possible, when the trolleybus service to Southbourne had been introduced, to offer a through service to and from Central Station. It was considered too early to respond to this request.

Mr Bulfin reported very satisfactory traffic returns for the Ashley Road-County Gates, Westbourne trolleybus service. From its inauguration on 22 June 1934 until 20 September 1934 a quarter of a million more passengers had been carried than in the 1933 period of mixed trolleybus and tram operation. Comparative traffic returns showed continuing passenger growth:

From 22 June 1934 until:	Trolleybus and tram	Trolleybus	Increase	Increase per week
21 Nov 1934	3,298,801	2,848,555	450,346	20,470
12 Dec 1934	3,647,009	3,105,188	541,821	21,672
16 Jan 1935	4,266,866	3,562,592	704,274	23,476
13 Mar 1935	5,178,618	4,246,627	931,991	24,526
15 May 1935	6,272,461	5,145,899	1,126,562	23,969

In preparation for the Iford Bridge extension, it was essential that trolleybus driver training was completed within seven weeks and this necessitated training on rest days too. On their normal working days drivers were paid half wages but normal rates on rest days. Retrospective payments were made to men who had already been trained.

The inspection of the Lansdowne-Iford Bridge trolleybus route by Lt. Col. E. Woodhouse was scheduled for Friday 22 March 1935, commencing at the Lansdowne at 10.15am. Members of the Council were invited to accompany the Transport Committee. Subject to the line being passed for traffic, a formal opening was planned for 3pm on Wednesday 27 March 1935, some three weeks earlier than planned. The MoT Inspector's Report, dated 28 March 1935, makes interesting reading:

"The new route, which is 3 miles in length, lies wholly within the Borough, and connects, at the Lansdowne, with the existing trolley vehicle route from The Square to Ashley Road, whence it follows Christchurch Road to a turning circle at Iford which has been constructed off the highway on land acquired by the Corporation. For about 2 miles from The Lansdowne the route follows the line of the existing tramway to Christchurch, which leaves it at Seabourne Road, Pokesdown. This tramway will continue in operation for the present. From Seabourne Road to the Iford terminus the route forms Route No. 9, authorised by the Bournemouth Corporation Act, 1930."

"The carriageway is of ample width throughout, and its surface, which is partly of wood blocks and partly of tar macadam, is in good condition. Lighting is by gas, the fittings being carried on the poles supporting the overhead work; the lamp brackets have been raised where necessary to give sufficient clearance for double-decked vehicles. There are no severe gradients, the steepest being one of 1 in 14 [between Pokesdown and Holdenhurst Avenue] for a length of about 5 chains. The route crosses the Southern Railway near Pokesdown Station; I was informed that the Company have raised no objection to trolley vehicles crossing the bridge in question."

"The Iford turning circle is concrete surfaced and its dimensions are such that there is room for 1 or 2 trolley vehicles to stand there, without interference with those turning. A disused tramcar body has been adapted as a shelter for waiting passengers. The lighting of the turning circle appeared to be inadequate and the Transport Manager undertook to install extra lamps before operation over the route commences."

"On the section traversed by the tramway the overhead work is partly of span wire type; elsewhere double [sic] brackets with poles on both sides of the road, are used. The latter form of construction is employed almost exclusively between Seabourne Road and the Iford terminus; none of the brackets exceeds 16ft in length. [considered the acceptable maximum nationally] All new poles are of BS section, reinforced as a rule. The existing poles, of the heavy tubular section with unwelded joint which have been in use for many years, have been carefully examined and reinforced internally; they appear to be standing the additional load satisfactorily."

"The overhead contact wire is 4/0 grooved, mainly of copper, though some cadmium copper has been installed as an experiment. Triple insulation, positive to earth, is provided throughout. Current is supplied from the Corporation's tramway generating station, the positive and negative feeding points being as shown on plans 5, 6 and 7 which accompanied the Transport Manager's letter of 26 February 1935. Section switching arrangements comply with Requirements and all feeder pillars and poles carrying section switches are earthed to copper earth plates."

"Guard wiring, of which there are a few spans near Pokesdown Station, is carried on full sized insulators and complies with Requirements. Elsewhere telephone crossings (which are few in number) are run in insulated wire, and hooks have been provided where a P.O. line runs alongside the route. The Post Office representative expressed his satisfaction with the arrangements which have been made."

"The service over this route will be carried out by double-decked 6-wheeled vehicles at intervals of about 8 minutes."

"At the request of the Transport Manager, I also inspected a short branch which has been made from the existing Holdenhurst Road-Ashley Road route, forming part of Route No. 10 authorised by the Bournemouth Corporation Act, 1930. This is about 350 yards in length and follows Holdenhurst Road, from Ashley Road as far as its junction with Littledown Avenue and Thistlebarrow Road, where a turning circle has been constructed. The carriageway width is ample and its surface, of the tarmac type, is in good condition. Span wire construction has been adopted, with triple insulation, the poles being of BS section, and the overhead contact wire 4/0 copper."

"This extension, and the intermediate turning point which it provides, will only be used occasionally, during daylight, to deal with traffic to and from football matches, etc., in Queen's Park [sic, the football ground being at Dean Court in King's Park], to which it is adjacent. To avoid the necessity for facing points and crossings in the overhead work at the junction with the Ashley Road route, the contact wires leading to the extension have been run parallel over one span with those previously existing; it is the intention to transfer the trolley booms from one set of wires to the other during a stop at this point.

"Both on the Iford route and on the above-mentioned extension the work of equipment for trolley vehicle operation appeared to have been well carried out and I recommend that both be approved.

"No [BoT] compulsory stops [for safety purposes] are recommended but Superintendent Deacon [Hampshire Constabulary] asked that request stops should not be fixed too close to traffic light signals, of which there are 3 sets on the Iford route. The Transport Manager agreed to fix such stops in consultation with the Police.

I recommend the following speeds be authorised:

25 MPH
1. In Christchurch Road between the Lansdowne and the Iford Terminus

2. In Holdenhurst Road between Ashley Road and the Queen's Park turning circle.

5 MPH
1. When passing below all overhead points and crossings
2. When rounding all turning circles.

E. Woodhouse"

A through trolleybus service numbered 24, operating between Westbourne and Iford Bridge, via Bournemouth Square, the Lansdowne and Christchurch Road, was introduced at 3pm on Monday 25 March 1935. In addition to the service 24 trolleybuses, the main Poole-Christchurch tram route, which continued to operate as before, ran in parallel as far as Pokesdown Station, although tram short workings to Boscombe ceased. There were now two trolleybus services in operation:

24 Westbourne, Seamoor Road - West Station - Bournemouth Square - Lansdowne - Boscombe Gardens- Boscombe Arcade - Pokesdown - Iford Bridge

25 Westbourne, Seamoor Road-West Station-Bournemouth Square-Lansdowne-Central Station-Springbourne-Queen's Park Corner-Boscombe Station- Boscombe, Portman Road

Internal advertising spaces on the cove panels of each deck were contracted to Messrs Frank Mason & Co. for ten years less four spaces per vehicles which were offered to other Committees for a minimum period of three years at 10s per bus.

Mr Bulfin's service as General Manager and Engineer was

Its driver having just received instructions from an Inspector, Sunbeam MS2 90 (ALJ964) stands in Christchurch Road, Iford, on its first day in service, 25 March 1935. Note the bracket arm suspension with traction poles on both sides of the road, a feature of the Iford extension until replaced by conventional span wires. The overhead wiring can be seen branching off to the left and the turning circle whilst Iford Bridge over the River Stour is but a hundred yards behind the trolleybus.
Malcolm Pearce (G.O.P. Pearce)

An unidentified Park Royal bodies Sunbeam MS2 at Iford turning circle.   **David Chalk collection**

Westbound trolleybus 84, heading for County Gates, Westbourne, and tram 119 with its indicator blinds already changed for the next journey to Christchurch, traverse Gervis Place past the Plummer Roddis store on 8 June 1935. The gentleman standing next to the traction pole is Herbert Vickers, Chief Assistant and Electrical Engineer.

Bournemouth Transport Ltd. (David Chalk collection)

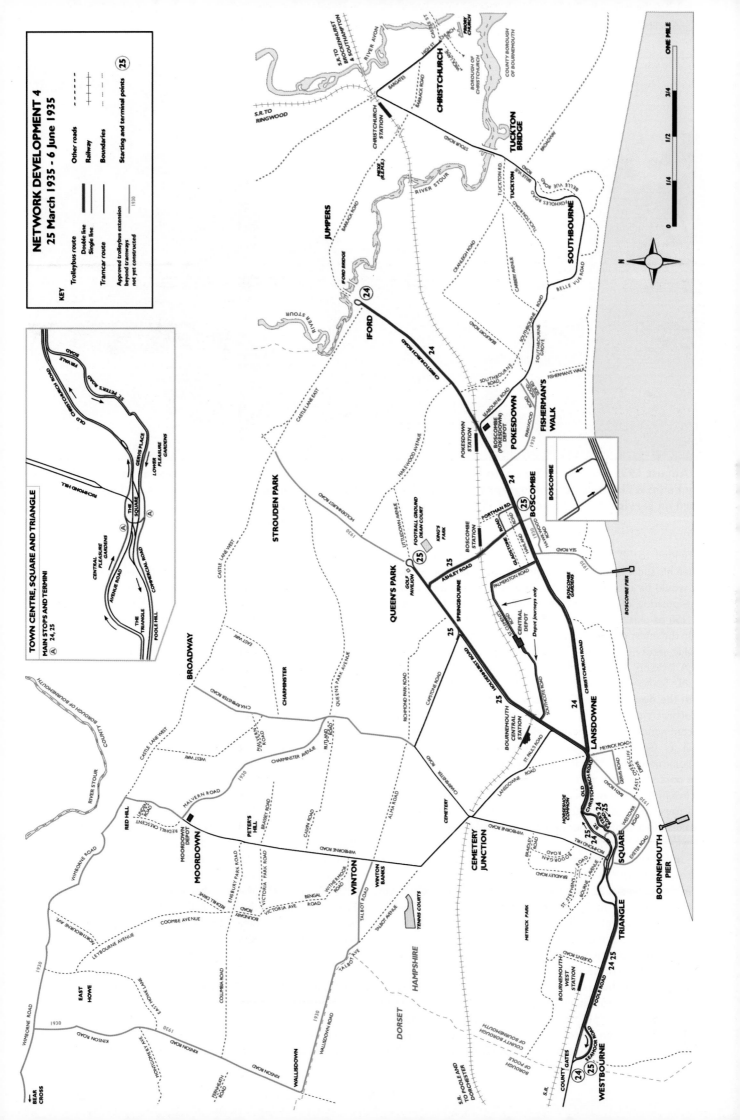

In August 1935 brand new Sunbeam MS2 trolleybus 134, posing in the westbound carriageway of Poole Road for Sunbeam BTH publicity photographs, is passed by trolleybus 73, delivered fourteen months earlier, heading for Iford on service 24 and tram 83 of 1914 destined for Fisherman's Walk.

Bournemouth Transport Ltd. (Sunbeam BTH)

extended to 30 September 1935 on the understanding that when his successor had been appointed and taken up his duties he would be retained until this date in a consultative capacity. The position of General Manager was advertised at salary of £1,250 pa plus a motor car allowance of £100.

In the midst of preparations for King George V's Silver Jubilee, having interviewed the General Managers of the St. Helens (A.A. Jackson), Blackpool (W. Luff) and Burnley, Colne & Nelson (C.H. Stafford) municipal transport undertakings, together with the Bournemouth Chief Assistant and Electrical Engineer (Herbert Vickers), on 3 May 1935 the Transport Committee recommended Mr Duncan P. Morrison from Kingston upon Hull as General Manager. Bournemouth Council made the appointment on 7 May 1935. Mr Ignatius Bulfin, who had held the post since 1911, retired in September 1935. He continued to live in Bournemouth until his death on 19 February 1954.

Later in the year, on 20 September 1935, Mr Wilfred Douglas Reakes, Area Traffic Superintendent of the United Automobile Services Ltd., Darlington, who was eventually to succeed Mr Morrison as General Manager, was appointed Traffic Superintendent.

In the 43 weeks 22 June 1934-17 April 1935 the trolleybuses carried almost a million more passengers between County Gates and Boscombe 5,745,153 compared to 4,747,079 in the equivalent period of the previous year.

Wooden "slip-boards" indicating the principal intermediate points, similar to those already used on BCT motor buses, were mounted above the lower maroon band at lower saloon waist-rail level on the trolleybuses from the end of May 1935. Their use was discontinued in 1938 possibly because the introduction of 4-line destination screens and auxiliary "in town" indicators at front and rear had made them redundant, although there

were also rumours that they led to vehicles so equipped exceeding the then maximum permissible width of 7ft 6in.

Also in May 1935, notice was given to use part of the north side of Avenue Road above the Central Pleasure Gardens as a trolleybus parking space. Later in the month it was recommended that work to convert the Pokesdown Station-Fisherman's Walk-Southbourne-Tuckton Bridge-Christchurch tram route to trolleybus operation should start in early September 1935. It was suggested that Christchurch Corporation should be again approached for consent to extend trolleybuses from Iford Bridge along Barrack Road to Stour Road, Christchurch. As a preliminary, motor bus shuttle service 2A began to operate on Monday 8 July 1935 between Pokesdown Station, Parkwood Road and Southbourne Cross Roads.

The last trams between Bournemouth Square and Moordown ran late in the evening of 6 June 1935 and early in the morning of Friday 7 June 1935 trolleybuses with pennants flying took over the service. At 11.30pm that same day the last tram from Bournemouth Square reached Upper Parkstone Depot: through services were henceforth provided by H&D whilst trolleybuses provided the service as far as County Gates.

On 7 June 1935, the day that Ramsay Madonald resigned as Prime Minister of the National Government (a coalition) and was replaced by Stanley Baldwin, trolleybuses replaced trams between Bournemouth Square and Moordown Depot via Richmond Hill and Wimborne Road:

26 Bournemouth Square-Cemetery Junction-Winton-Moordown Depot

The Wimborne Road trams had never run into the Square itself, passengers boarding from waiting shelters, "stepped"

The crew of Sunbeam MS2 128 proudly pose for the photographer prior to departure from Iford Bridge turning circle for County Gates, Westbourne on a service 24 working in autumn 1935. The trolleybus sports the new slip-boards indicating the principal intermediate points whilst, in the background, the body of tramcar no. 1 still carries its ornate livery.   Omnibus Society (C.F. Klapper)

A Sunbeam MS2 leaves the Square and surges up Richmond Hill on Side Route service 26 to Moordown.
Wolverhampton Archives (Sunbeam BTH)

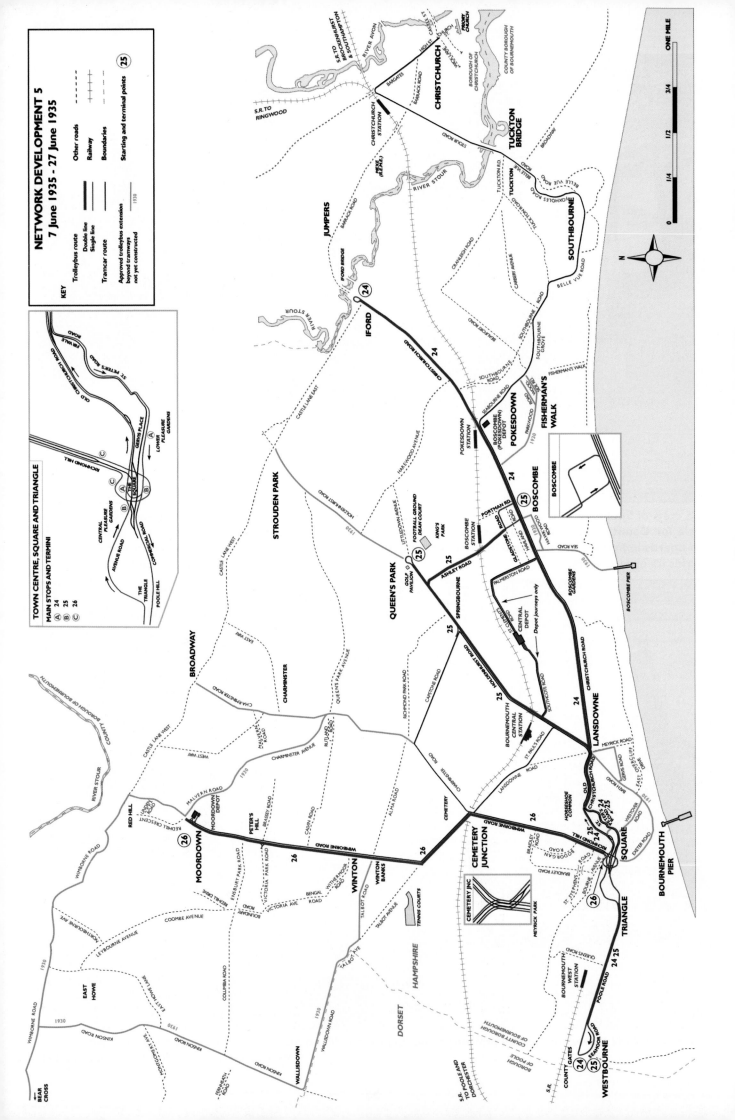

NETWORK DEVELOPMENT 5
7 June 1935 - 27 June 1935

KEY

Trolleybus route

| | Double line | Other roads |
| | Single line | Railway |
Tramcar route | | Boundaries |

Approved trolleybus extension
beyond tramways
not yet constructed

(25) Starting and terminal points

TOWN CENTRE, SQUARE AND TRIANGLE

MAIN STOPS AND TERMINI
- Ⓐ 24
- Ⓑ 25
- Ⓒ 26

ONE MILE

0   1/4   1/2   3/4

N

to allow for the gradient, at the base of Richmond Hill. The new trolleybus service and subsequently all other Wimborne Road services commenced on the north side of the Square, between Bourne Avenue and Richmond Hill outside Henlys' car showrooms and Burton the tailors, the terminal point being the Albert Road stop at the bottom of Richmond Hill although, no doubt, some passengers alighted on the south side of the Square at the triangular traffic island outside Bobbys. White lines were painted on the road surface at the sharp corner out of the Square into Richmond Hill to aid the new drivers in negotiating the optimum route to be followed around the corner followed by the immediate ascent of the hill.

At Moordown trolleybuses turned by driving into the depot forecourt and then reversing into Wimborne Road although there were already active plans to extend the service to the junction with Castle Lane West. The trams had continued to Redhill Crescent, 30yd past the depot, but to avoid unnecessarily complex overhead work, the tramway overhead wiring was cut back to the depot entrance for the three-week period that both trams and trolleybuses operated along Wimborne Road. During the work to modify the overhead wiring at the crossroads of Holdenhurst Road with St. Paul's Road and Waverley Road, a horse-drawn tower wagon toppled sideways as it was being manoeuvred, leaving the two linesmen hanging from the overhead. One fell and was slightly injured, while the other was brought down with a ladder.

White lines also marked the route to be taken at Cemetery Junction for vehicles heading towards the Square and it was noted by passengers that great care was taken in negotiating this turn. After leaving the traffic signals in Wimborne Road it was reported that one had the impression that the vehicle was going to turn into Charminster Road as there was a decided half left turn. This was followed by a turn to the right and another to the left giving the impression that the trolleybus was going along Lansdowne Road. Finally, following a half turn to the right, the trolleybus pulled up opposite St. Augustin's Church.

The fare between the Square and Moordown Post Office was 2½d, a half penny cheaper than the former tram fare and 2d less than the BCT motorbus fare. Workmen's fares and returns were also available.

The *Bournemouth Daily Echo* of Friday 7 June 1935 commented *"Early morning passengers expressed their keen appreciation of the new trolley bus service; for comfort, cheapness and speed they found it a great improvement on the former service. In silence alone there is a big advantage over the trams, which is already a boon to those living or working on the route".*

Some passengers commented that they felt that the trolleybuses reduced the journey time by up to 50%! There were certainly substantial timing reductions due to the trolleybuses' superior acceleration and the fact that the tramway was not double-track throughout, a number of passing loops surviving in Winton and Moordown until abandonment.

"Many intending passengers failed to realise that trolley buses pull into the side of the road to pick up and set down. Several people went to the centre of the road at several stopping places to board the vehicle. They ran back to the security of the pavement, however,

The old and the new. Open top tram 112 dating from 1921 and Sunbeam MS2 no. 98 (ALJ972) new in March 1935 pass in Wimborne Road, Winton, during the short period in June 1935 (7 - 27 June) when the Square - Richmond Hill - Moordown service had already been converted to trolleybus operation (service 26) but the Square - Lansdowne - Moordown service continued to be operated by tram. Note the single bracket arms planted on both sides of the road supporting the trolleybus overhead wiring and, on a short section of span wire, the tram overhead wiring too. In the late 1930s the bracket arms were removed and conventional span wires supporting the trolleybus overhead wiring substituted.
Bournemouth Transport Ltd.

On 21 June 1935, looking southwards in Wimborne Road at Peters Hill, Winton, an unidentified trolleybus heading for the Square on service 26 waits for a lady passenger to board tramcar no. 93 destined for the Lansdowne. Peters Hill is a rise in Wimborne Road to the north of Kemp and Wycliffe Roads, the origin of the name possibly being due to the ability to see the spire of St. Peter's Church in Bournemouth from the top of the hill. Bournemouth Transport Ltd.

when the vehicle swerved in and came to rest by the kerb".

Trams continued to operate between the Lansdowne and Moordown for another three weeks, running alongside the trolleybuses from Cemetery Junction.

The connecting line between Holdenhurst Road and Cemetery Junction along St. Paul's Road and Lansdowne Road past Central Station opened on 28 June 1935. A further Moordown service, the 27, was introduced that day, both the 26 and 27 being extended beyond Moordown Depot to a reversing triangle at the junction of Redhill Crescent with Wimborne Road.

26 Bournemouth Square - Cemetery Junction - Winton - Moordown, Wimborne Road, Redhill Crescent

27 Bournemouth Square, Gervis Place - Lansdowne - Central Station - Cemetery Junction - Winton - Moordown, Wimborne Road, Redhill Crescent

The trams which had continued to run along Wimborne Road between Cemetery Junction and Moordown Depot since 7 June 1935 last ran at the close of service on the evening of 27 June 1935.

On the first day of trolleybus operation along Lansdowne Road branches from overhanging trees were still being lopped away. Apparently the destination Lansdowne was displayed as the Sunbeam MS2s in service only had single-line destination boxes, the blinds being changed at the Lansdowne to read Square thus avoiding any confusion north of Cemetery Junction with service 26 vehicles taking a more direct route. It was reported that once negotiations with certain frontagers had been completed, the roadway at the Castle Lane West end of Wimborne Road would be widened and overhead wiring strung beyond Redhill Crescent to Lawford Road.

The Capstone Road tram service, Square, foot of Richmond Hill-Wimborne Road-Cemetery Junction-Charminster Road-Capstone Road, junction with Holdenhurst Road, last operated

on 22 August 1935. It had been agreed in January 1935 that those portions of the road occupied by tram lines in Holdenhurst Road, from Central Station to the Queen's Park Hotel, and onwards in Ashley Road to Christchurch Road, Boscombe, would be handed over to the Roads Committee. Nonetheless, the tramcars used on Capstone Road continued to follow St. Swithun's Road and Holdenhurst Road when entering or leaving service until the route was abandoned. The Transport Committee contributed £4,326 towards the reinstatement of the above-mentioned roads.

At the beginning of June 1935 the first National Electrical Convention was held in Bournemouth. Ald. Summerbee, wrote a front page article in the Convention number of the *"Trolley-Bus Gazette"*. Headed *"Why Bournemouth Chose Trolley-Buses"* he wrote *"Naturally, since Bournemouth is a health resort, noise, smell and vibration were factors which could not be lightly passed over, as so many of our visitors and residents come to Bournemouth to get away from the rush and turmoil of city life".*

From 8 June 1935, as a result of the tramway abandonment in Poole, the service frequency of the Main Road tram route changed to every 20 minutes between the Square and Christchurch, with a superimposed 20-minute service between the Square and Southbourne Cross Roads and a 10-minute service between the Square and Fisherman's Walk. The Fisherman's Walk tram service ceased on 20 November 1935 and the Southbourne service last ran on 22 December 1935. The Christchurch service continued unchanged until 8 April 1936.

The reader's letter published in the *Bournemouth Daily Echo* on 8 June 1935 gives an accurate impression of the anti-tramway public sentiment of the time although there is nothing to suggest that the tramcars and the majority of the track were not well maintained:

Sir, reluctantly I have left Bournemouth, as the noise of the trams was unbearable, nerve-shattering and most depressing and I had gone there for peace and quiet.

An authority on this subject has just declared that noise is

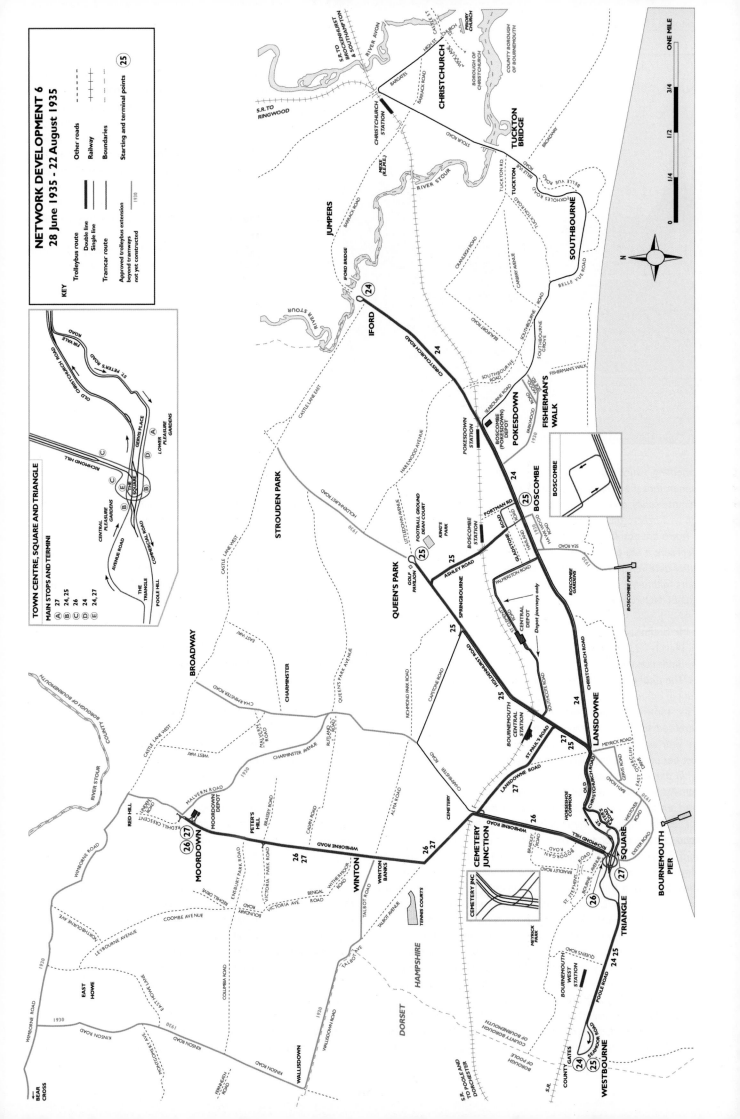

NETWORK DEVELOPMENT 6
28 June 1935 - 22 August 1935

KEY

Trolleybus route		Other roads
Double line		Railway
Single line		Boundaries
Tramcar route		Starting and terminal points
Approved trolleybus extension beyond tramways not yet constructed	1930	25

TOWN CENTRE, SQUARE AND TRIANGLE

MAIN STOPS AND TERMINI

A 27
B 24, 25
C 26
D 24
E 24, 27

Shortly after the introduction of trolleybuses on the Moordown route (7 June 1935) and with the tramway overhead equipment still in place trolleybus no. 106 commences the descent of Richmond Hill. The tramway trackwork clearly shows that the original single line down Richmond Hill was doubled at a later date. Thornycroft motorbus no. 50 (LJ3002) on service 5 from Malvern Road overtakes Sunbeam MS2 no. 106 (ALJ980) on its way to the Square from Moordown. Richmond Hill positive feeder, for both the former trams and the new trolleybuses, is evident in the foreground.

National Tramway Museum
(Photographer's name not recorded)

something which ought not to be tolerated by decent men and women, that the nerves of the nation were a tremendous factor in its ultimate sanity, and that a nervy nation could be easily stampeded. I can well believe this.

Trams are obsolete and a menace to the public in many ways, and I feel sure it will be a great relief to many of the visitors when these out-of-date vehicles are abolished altogether.
Yours faithfully
PRO BONO PUBLICO

Mr Bulfin's 24th and final Annual Report, for the year ending 31 March 1935, contained a number of interesting facts about the undertaking:

"The total output of current (from the Southcote Road generating station) amounted to 4,548,390 units, as compared with 4,362,110 units, some 186,280 more units than last year. This is due to increased trolleybus mileage being run. The coal consumed during the year was 5,629 tons, as against 5,335 tons last year. The total cost per unit, including all capital charges, worked out at 0.70d.

"In the year in question, on June 22nd, 1934, the trolleybus route from Ashley Road terminus along Ashley Road, Holdenhurst Road to the Lansdowne and via Old Christchurch Road to the Square, was opened for traffic, the trams being taken off both the Holdenhurst Road and Ashley Road. On March 28th of this year the route from Iford Bridge to the Lansdowne was opened up for traffic, while on May 13th, 1933, the section from the Square to County Gates was opened up as a trolleybus route. The opening of these two routes, with the existing one, meant that a through service of trolleybuses was obtained between Iford Bridge and County Gates, and between the Christchurch Road at its junction with Ashley Road, along Holdenhurst Road to County Gates, and, although it did not occur in the present financial year, a further section from Moordown to the Square was opened for traffic on June 7th. The receipts and running of these different systems have been very satisfactory".

In a valedictory message, he reviewed his years in post:

"During this period, not only has the Transport System not received any aid from the rates but they have contributed over £30,000 in

relief on the rates. They have in the same period paid in rates to Bournemouth £83,182, to Poole £16,231, and to Christchurch £4,124. They have laid, maintained and kept in repair over one-third of the main road from Christchurch to Poole, and some miles of side routes in Bournemouth at an approximate cost of £18,000 per annum, and in this period they have run 55,885,657 miles, carried 632,490,720 passengers and taken in receipts £4,420,493. They have maintained a staff of over 700 and paid in wages in the period £1,895,360, and repaid capital to the extent of £710,150."

The £14,449 8s 4d deficit, due to increased capital charges, income tax and the restoration of staff wages cut in the recession, was reduced to £5,999 15s 2d by a transfer from the reserves and this amount was carried forward to the net revenue account for settlement at a later date.

It should be borne in mind that the American stock market crash in 1929 provoked a global economic depression and although the UK had still not recovered from the effects of the First World War, the nation did not suffer as badly as many other countries. The effects of the depression in the first half of the 1930s were uneven, with Bournemouth and Southern England avoiding mass unemployment although visitor numbers stagnated and public transport usage declined. In the second half of the decade the region became more prosperous with the arrival of new light industries and an increase in visitors as the nation's economy recovered whilst low interest rates fuelled a growth in the resident population.

Nonetheless, as in every other trolleybus-operating town, there were letters to the press about radio interference. One resident on Charminster Road wrote: "I would like to express my emphatic protest against having the trolley bus introduced into my drawing room, via the wireless set". An official responded that "Every trolley bus is equipped with a choke and condenser, as fitted by the Sunbeam Company, which practically eliminates interference".

The Bournemouth Daily Echo reported on 2 July 1935 that:

"A start has been made with the work of constructing the overhead equipment for the trolleybus extension between the Cemetery Junction and Castle Lane. The popularity of the trolleybus has been

Sunbeam MS2 no. 133, delivered on 26 August 1935, and another MS2 stand in the southbound carriageway of Wimborne Road outside Moordown Depot. The Overhead Department had been forced to set itself a list of priorities during the conversion programme and it will be noticed that although the reversing triangle at Redhill Crescent is visible in the background the frogs for entry to the depot building have not yet been inserted.

Omnibus Society (R.T. Wilson)

further demonstrated by the decision of Brighton Corporation to apply for powers to run trolleybuses in place of trams. The overhead tram wires have disappeared in Winton where the substituted wires for the trolleybuses are now in use. As in the bad old days of the tramcar a boy still has to operate a "points system" at Cemetery Junction, but they are now overhead and he now does it from a safer position on the pavement. The 'narrow squeaks' that lad must have had while doing his job in the middle of a rushing stream of traffic must be 'legion'."

For the 1935 summer season, Southern Railway expresses were accelerated to bring Bournemouth within two hours of London, further encouraging tourism.

A reader's letter in the *Bournemouth Daily Echo* of 6 July 1935 commented:

"As a resident in the Lansdowne Road I wish to express my relief at the advent of the trolley-bus. The absence of the noisy trams has made my life now bearable. We find that the trolley-bus is the quietest of all the vehicles, much less noisy than the motorbus or an ordinary trade lorry. It seems to me that the trolley-bus is the very best mode of transit that can at present be devised; it is cooler, no heat from the engines (how the drivers of the motorbuses stand in this hot weather, I cannot imagine), no smell of petrol or fumes of the exhaust, the slight hiss made overhead is not at all bothersome."

On 9 July 1935 the Negotiating Subcommittee met Christchurch Corporation, which was concerned about pending BCT fare increases which included motor bus service 1 through the town and who asked for the reduction of a number of single fares and that return tickets booked before 8.45am should be available from any main fare stage along the route at the ordinary single fare. Bournemouth replied that, if Christchurch Council consented to and supported an application by Bournemouth Corporation to run trolley vehicles along Barrack Road from Iford Bridge to Stour Road

(and, if desired, along the continuation of Barrack Road to the High Street), they would be prepared to grant more or less all the concessions requested. The letter went on to suggest that the trolleybus service from Iford Bridge to Christchurch would be every eight minutes. It concluded by indicating that Bournemouth Council would be prepared to purchase property in Wick Lane and install a turntable and small depot there to house three vehicles, thus enabling the proposed turning circle at the Town Hall to be dispensed with.

Christchurch Transport Committee could not agree to trolleybuses operating along Barrack Road. However, a letter from a member of the public suggesting a turning point at Fisherman's Walk when trolleybuses to Christchurch were introduced received a sympathetic hearing. Bournemouth's Transport Committee recommended that, subject to there being no objection from the MoT, a turning point should be installed there at once.

The *Bournemouth Daily Echo* on 2nd August 1935 reported that a trolleybus had visited Christchurch High Street in the dead of night, using a single trolley arm on the tramway overhead wiring and a return skate in the rail, to test clearances.

During the year London Transport loaned four trolleybus drivers from its Fulwell Depot to train additional Bournemouth crews.

Traction poles along Charminster Road had been planted some months prior and as soon as the Moordown route had been completed the Overhead Department started work on the wiring required between Cemetery Junction and Castle Lane West. Where the trams turned east into Capstone Road, they continued along the full length of Charminster Road to its junction with Castle Lane West at the Broadway Hotel. Good weather aided progress but the intense heat made the men's work aloft arduous. Work was completed by 7 August 1935 but

The terminus of service 26 at Moordown Post Office, Wimborne Road, Moordown, in 1936. Sunbeam MS2 no. 104 is about to reverse into Redhill Crescent - the spring trail frog of the reverser is visible in the overhead wiring behind the trolleybus - prior to returning to the Square. **Bournemouth Transport Ltd.**

road resurfacing between Alma Road and Castle Lane, and the correction of camber and elevations at road junctions before the route could be regarded as satisfactory, continued until 14 August 1935. Immediately thereafter, the invitation to the MoT Inspector, Major Wilson, was sent and the inspection took place on the afternoon of Thursday, 22 August 1935 in excellent weather. Major Wilson was accompanied on his inspection by Ald. F.B. Summerbee, Chairman of the Transport Committee, the recently-retired General Manager Ignatius Bulfin and his successor Duncan Morrison, and Police Superintendent Deacon. He complimented all concerned in the planning and conversion work, and gave provisional approval to operate trolleybuses along Charminster Road from the next day.

In the meantime, the warm, sunny weather saw joy-riders on the last open-top trams up Richmond Hill and Wimborne Road to Cemetery Junction, Capstone Road and Holdenhurst Road, which had paralleled the trolleybuses between the Square and Cemetery Junction since 7 June 1935. The only remaining tram route was now between the Square and Christchurch via Fisherman's Walk and Southbourne, although trolleybuses were already serving the route as far as Pokesdown Station.

Trolleybus services started first thing on Friday 23 August 1935, with capacity loads on the morning journeys:

28 Bournemouth Square - Cemetery Junction - Five Ways - Castle Lane West, Broadway Hotel, Luckham Road

The 1¾-mile extension included a turning circle around the pine tree wooded island at Five Ways, at the junction with Queen's Park Avenue, and a terminal reversing triangle at the junction of Charminster Road with the northern end of Luckham Road, a few yards south of Castle Lane West and the Broadway Hotel. The town centre terminus was the Albert Road stop. The boarding point for the 28 and subsequently all Charminster Road services was on the west side of the Square by the entrance to the Central Pleasure Gardens. The first departure from the Square was at 6.30am to Five Ways and

7.35am to Luckham Road. The first return journeys were at 6.16am and 7.50 respectively.

Sadly the long-lasting excellent weather, with temperatures into the mid-eighties Fahrenheit, came to an end, the rain and additional terminating trolleybuses leading to severe traffic jams in the Square.

In early September 1935 the MoT gave retrospective consent to the introduction of trolleybuses between the junction of Holdenhurst Road with St. Paul's Road and Cemetery Junction, and the extension beyond Moordown Depot to the reversing triangle at the junction of Wimborne Road with Redhill Cresent (services to these points had commenced on 28 June 1935), as well as sending their formal approval of the new line between Cemetery Junction and Castle Lane West, Broadway Hotel, which had opened on 23 August 1935.

The passenger appeal of the new trolleybuses can be shown by the following statistics from the Bournemouth Square-Moordown (service 26) and Square-Moordown via Lansdowne (service 27) traffic returns compared to the 1934/5 tram figures:

From 7 June 1935 until:	Trolleybus	Tram	Increase	Increase per week
17 Jul 1935	685,051	481,566	203,485	33,914
17 Sept 1935	2,021,247	1,505,171	516,076	36,863
9 Oct 1935	2,496,330	1,873,685	622,645	34,591
13 Nov 1935	3,007,250	2,267,410	739,840	32,167
11 Dec 1935	3,401,059	2,558,813	842,246	3,194
15 Jan 1936	3,914,890	2,959,257	955,633	29,864
15 Apr 1936	5,171,719	3,884,200	1,287,519	28,611

The Roads Committee accepted responsibility for 41,502 square yards of road space previously occupied by Side Route tram lines (as defined in the Tramways Act, 1870) for an agreed payment of £15,540 15s.

Attention now turned to the Pokesdown-Fisherman's Walk-

In late 1935, at the bottom of Richmond Hill with the Punshon Memorial Church and, beyond, the Central Hotel on the left, no. 130 (BEL815) with its indicator blinds already correctly changed to show its next destination, Moordown, passes 97 (ALJ971) on its ascent to Cemetery Junction, Charminster Road and Castle Lane (at Broadway Hotel, Luckham Road). In the background the former Hants & Dorset bus and Royal Blue coach station, and the spire of St. Andrew's Presbyterian Church, both at the north end of Exeter Road where it enters the Square, can be seen. The bus station was built in 1931, enlarged in 1959, severely damaged by fire in 1976 and demolished in the early 1980s, whilst the church had its spire removed following damage in the Second World War and is no longer used as a church. Bournemouth was the first trolleybus operator to equip its vehicles with a coasting brake (in 1935).

Bournemouth Transport Ltd.

Southbourne-Tuckton Bridge-Christchurch portion of the Main Road tram route, by now truncated to operate between the Square and Christchurch. Lt. Col. Woodhouse of the MoT inspected the Pokesdown Station-Fisherman's Walk trolleybus extension, just under half a mile in length, on 20 November 1935 and an additional trolleybus service was introduced the next day:

23 Bournemouth Square, Gervis Place - Lansdowne - Boscombe Gardens - Boscombe Arcade - Pokesdown Station - Fisherman's Walk, Wentworth Avenue

A terminal loop was installed at the north end of Fisherman's Walk in the width of the road at the junction of Wentworth Avenue with Fisherman's Avenue, and thus about 30yd south of the tram route in Seabourne Road. At Pokesdown Station the eastbound trolleybus stop for Fisherman's Walk was outside the Fire Station in Seabourne Road, whilst the westbound one remained outside the depot in Christchurch Road as for the trams.

The journey time between the Square and Fisherman's Walk was reduced by 7-8 minutes, not least due to the trams having to wait in passing loops south of Pokesdown Station when the single track was already occupied by a tram from the opposite direction. The first trolleybus left the Square at 6.58am on weekdays and the last at 11.20pm.

The editorial in the 22 November 1935 edition of the *Bournemouth Daily Echo* commented *"With the introduction of the Fisherman's Walk trolley-buses tradesmen and residents along the main road have noticed a marked decrease in traffic noise. There are only 6-8 trams left running in the borough, now operating the service to Christchurch, and as these pass only at twenty minute intervals*

the old familiar clatter is conspicuous by its absence. No one regrets the departure of the noise, least of all those who happen to live near points and loops".

The Fisherman's Walk extension and thus increased trolleybus services along Christchurch Road prompted a reorganisation of stops between the Lansdowne and Pokesdown Station, unifying stops for all types of vehicles. Some stops were moved a short distance; the majority, such as at Boscombe Gardens, Boscombe Arcade and Portman Road were moved just a few yards. In all cases the aim was to avoid the stops for both inward and outward vehicles being exactly opposite each other as this had caused congestion in the past. Until now service 25 vehicles had set down and picked up passengers in Christchurch Road, Boscombe; from Monday 16 December 1935 the stop was moved to Ashley Road where the trams had terminated. This left the Christchurch Road wiring clear for Fisherman's Walk and Iford trolleybuses, which, until now, had been delayed by waiting Ashley Road vehicles.

The introduction of trolleybus service 23 replaced the Square-Fisherman's Walk short-working tram service but the 20-minute tram service between the Square and Southbourne Cross Roads continued to run. Express motor bus service 2 also continued to operate every 15 minutes Bournemouth Square-Southbourne - Christchurch (parallel to the trams) until 10 May 1936, when it was curtailed to Square-Tuckton Bridge only every 20 minutes, but by way of Beaufort Road and Cranleigh Road which did not parallel the trolleybuses. It was withdrawn entirely on 30 June 1936. When trolleybuses subsequently reached Southbourne Cross Roads on 23 December 1935, both the short-working tram service to that point and motor bus service 2A, which by then was shuttling between Fisherman's Walk and Southbourne Cross Roads (it

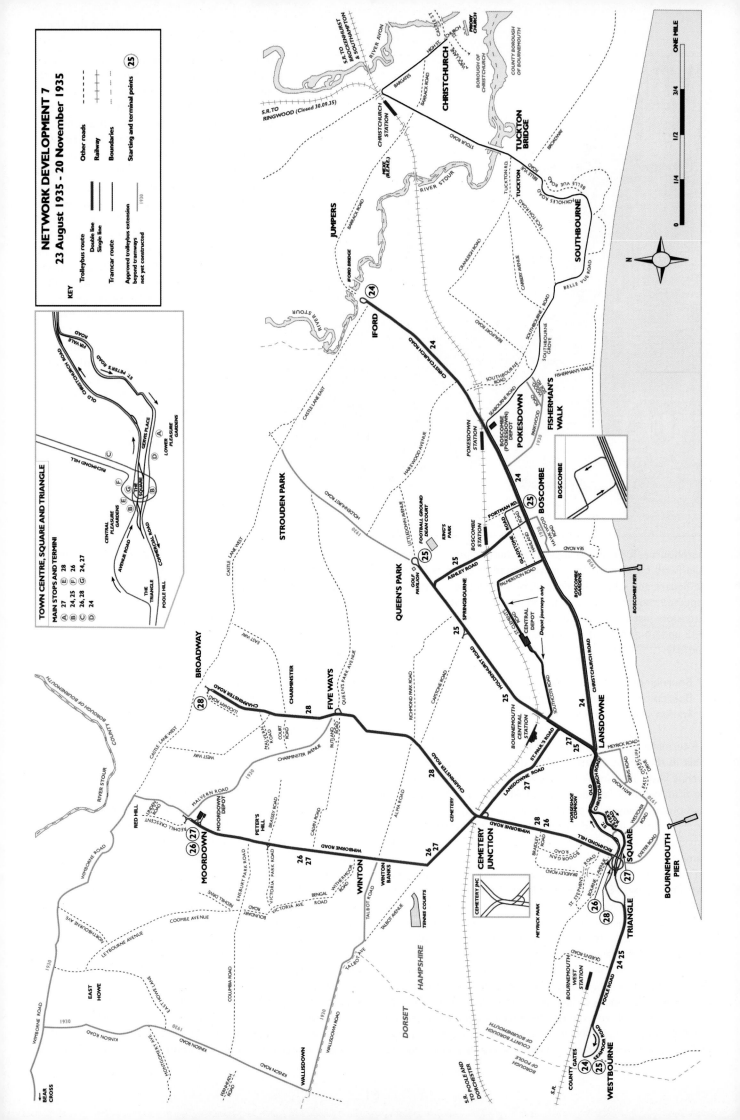

A busy scene in the Square in late summer 1935 following the introduction of service 28. In the foreground a trolleybus circumnavigates the Square to one of the loading points before departing on a service 28 working to Castle Lane (Broadway Hotel). Two trolleybuses head across the Square from Avenue Road into Old Christchurch Road whilst one of Bournemouth's surviving trams makes its way west to the crossover where it will reverse and head back towards Christchurch. Bournemouth Transport Ltd. (David Chalk collection)

had commenced operating on 8 July 1935 between Pokesdown Station, Parkwood Road-Southbourne Cross Roads to offer a fast connection to trolleybus service 24), were withdrawn. A full tram service Bournemouth Square-Christchurch every 20 minutes continued to operate at Christchurch Council's insistence.

MoT approval to operate trolleybuses between Fisherman's Walk and Southbourne Cross Roads was received in mid-December 1935 and a further trolleybus service commenced on Monday 23 December 1935.

22 Bournemouth Square, Gervis Place - Lansdowne - Boscombe Gardens - Boscombe Arcade - Pokesdown Station - Fisherman's Walk - Southbourne Cross Roads

A terminal loop was constructed at Southbourne Cross Roads around the public conveniences at the junction of Southbourne Overcliff Drive and St. Catherine's Road.

Henceforth the six trams required to operate the remaining tram service between the Square and Christchurch were based at Boscombe (Pokesdown) Depot, although a total of 12 cars, to allow for any contingencies, and breakdown car B were housed there. As the ten cars sold to the Llandudno & Colwyn Bay Electric Railway after the final tramway abandonment were amongst these 12, there cannot have been any major problems. It is assumed that the tram tracks providing access to Central Depot, Southcote Road, now ceased to be used and that the tracks were progressively lifted.

The new service and other tram and trolleybus routes immediately suffered from the winter weather conditions with heavy hoar frosts and ice coating the conductor wires leading to interruptions in the power supply and thus erratic running, as well as increased radio reception interference. This was particularly noticeable between Fisherman's Walk and Southbourne Cross Roads as there had been no passing trolleybuses to remove the ice that had accumulated in the, until then, three days of cold weather.

It was announced that a cross-town service to Westbourne would commence in the New Year and on 1 January 1936 services were augmented by the introduction of:

22A Westbourne, Seamoor Road - Bournemouth Square - Lansdowne-Boscombe Gardens - Boscombe Arcade -

Pokesdown Station - Fisherman's Walk - Southbourne - Southbourne Cross Roads (junction with St Catherine's Road and Southbourne Overcliff Drive)

23A Westbourne, Seamoor Road-West Station - Bournemouth Square - Lansdowne - Boscombe Gardens - Boscombe Arcade - Pokesdown Station - Fisherman's Walk, Wentworth Avenue

24A Westbourne, Seamoor Road - Bournemouth Square - Lansdowne - Boscombe Gardens - Boscombe Arcade - Pokesdown Station - Iford Bridge

It will be seen that the Transport Department took this opportunity to refine its service numbering system whereby basic services carried a number whilst extensions and variations were given an alphabetical suffix. With the introduction of service 24A, service 24 was curtailed from the same date to operate Bournemouth Square-Iford Bridge only. The same approach was followed from 1 March 1936 when service 25 was curtailed to run Bournemouth Square-Boscombe, Portman Road or Queen's Park Golf Pavilion, Holdenhurst Road, and the Westbourne, Seamoor Road-Boscombe, Portman Road or Queen's Park Golf Pavilion, Holdenhurst Road service was renumbered 25A.

25 Bournemouth Square - Lansdowne - Central Station - Springbourne - Boscombe Station - Boscombe, Portman Road or Queen's Park Golf Pavilion, Holdenhurst Road

25A Westbourne, Seamoor Road -West Station - Bournemouth Square - Lansdowne - Central Station - Springbourne - Boscombe Station - Boscombe, Portman Road

Mr Morrison, the new General Manager, adopted an improved destination layout on the undertaking's vehicles, and trolleybuses already in service were altered retrospectively. From November 1935, whenever the biennial repaint took place, the single-line final destination indicator boxes with service number box immediately above, at front and rear, were converted to the larger style, introduced with the 126-149 series then being delivered. All further deliveries were built to this new style by Park Royal. The screens, able to accommodate

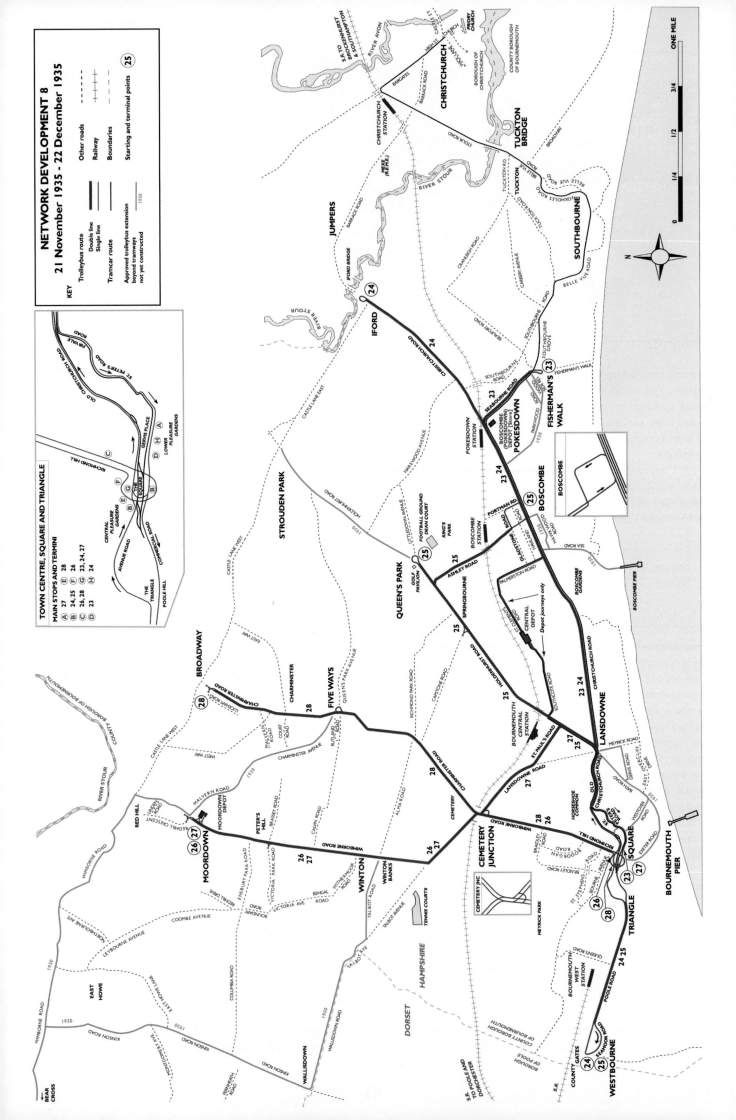

NETWORK DEVELOPMENT 8
21 November 1935 - 22 December 1935

KEY

Trolleybus route
Double line
Single line

Tramcar route

Approved trolleybus extension
beyond tramways
not yet constructed

Other roads
Railway
Boundaries

Starting and terminal points (25)

TOWN CENTRE, SQUARE AND TRIANGLE

MAIN STOPS AND TERMINI

(A) 27   (E) 28
(B) 24,25   (F) 26
(C) 26,28   (G) 23,24,27
(D) 23   (H) 24

ONE MILE

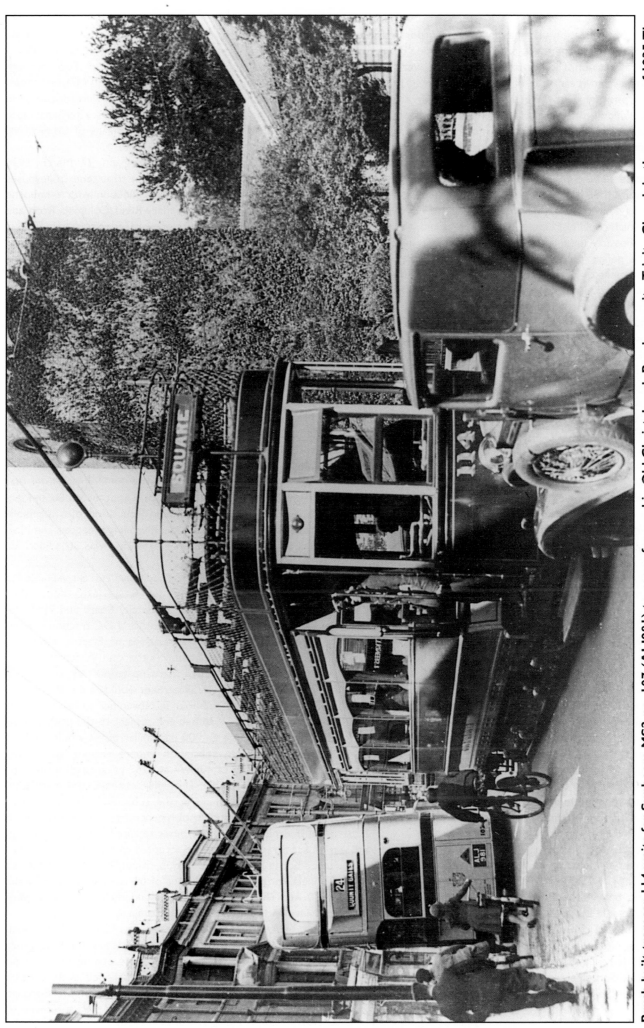

Brush-built tramcar 114 waits for Sunbeam MS2 no. 107 (ALJ981) to move forward in Old Christchurch Road opposite Trinity Church in the summer of 1935. The trolleybus is on a service 24 working to County Gates, Westbourne. Upon withdrawal, tram 114 was sold to the Llandudno & Colwyn Bay Electric Railway Co. Ltd. Bournemouth Transport Ltd. (David Chalk collection)

four lines of destination information, were incorporated into the front and rear upper-deck panels of the earlier deliveries, in a central position. The service number boxes were moved to the right-hand (near) side of the new displays at the front and to a position below the display immediately above the platform window on the nearside at the rear. The single-line ultimate destination boxes internally-mounted in the rearmost side windows on both sides of the lower deck saloon were retained unchanged. More mundanely, work also started on fitting heaters in the driving cabs of the trolleybuses.

In January 1936 it was announced that the undertaking had recorded a deficit for the year ending 31 March 1935 of £5,999 15s 2d, which could not be met from reserves and was carried forward. Possibly looking for means of increasing income to offset the deficit, the Lighting Committee was asked for an annual payment of 2s for each lighting bracket attached to a trolleybus traction pole. As at 21 February 1936 there were 529 such attachments which, together with the poles, required a repaint every 2 years for a payment of 2s 6d each.

Following receipt of a letter regarding overlapping fare stages on trolleybuses returning to the Central Depot, Southcote Road, 1d fares were introduced between Lansdowne and Central Depot via Southcote Road, and between Boscombe Arcade and Central Depot via Palmerston Road.

On 21 February 1936, the Transport Committee rejected the MoT proposals for a new road layout at Cemetery Junction. Following a meeting between the Borough Engineer and General Manager, they recommended on 20 March 1936 that vehicle-actuated traffic lights be installed there and that the trolleybus turning circle there be removed to ease straight through running. Although the traffic lights were installed, the turning circle remained in regular use until 26 March 1956 and was only cut down in 1960.

One month's notice was given in February 1936 to Christchurch (as required by the 1930 Act) of intent to abandon the tramways in its Borough. To operate the replacement services more vehicles had been delivered. Trolleybuses 90-125 (ALJ 964-ALJ999) entered service between 25 March 1935 and 7 July 1935; 126-137 (BEL811-BEL822) between 10 August 1935 and 14 September 1935; 138-149 (BEL823-BEL834) on 1 June 1936; 150-159 (BRU1-BRU10) between 7 April 1936 and 9 April 1936; and, finally, 160-173 (BRU11-BRU24) between 1 and 2 June 1936. All were Sunbeam MS2 three-axle vehicles with Park Royal bodywork. The trolleybus fleet now comprised 106 vehicles, namely the four experimental vehicles (two AEC prototypes, the Thornycroft single decker and one Sunbeam MS2), and 102 Sunbeam MS2 three-axle standard type 56-seat vehicles having rear entrance and front exit, twin staircases and driver-operated folding doors at the front exit. This was to remain the largest provincial fleet of trolleybuses of the same type in the country.

With standardisation in mind, the Weymann-bodied Sunbeam MS2 former demonstrator, by now numbered 68, was rebuilt with a front entrance and front staircase to match the standard trolleybus bodywork design in September 1936. The AEC 663T three-axle and AEC 661T two-axle prototypes, numbers 69 and 70, were converted to petrol-engined motor buses in September-November 1936 and March-June 1936 respectively. Each vehicle required an AEC engine, gearbox, propeller shaft, radiator, exhaust pipe, silencer, 40-gallon fuel tank with Autovac equipment, brake gear including vacuum tank, Lockheed reservoir, new front springs to take the additional weight,

lighting dynamo and a complete rewiring. Number 71, the single deck Thornycroft/Brush trolleybus, was retained until 1942.

Pending the complete reconstruction of Bournemouth Square (which was actually only carried out in 1947), temporary measures for the coming summer season were discussed in March 1936, including running all trolleybuses terminating in the Square through to the Triangle by means of Commercial Road with the return along Avenue Road.

The Transport Committee Meeting on 27 March 1936 recommended that powers be sought to extend trolleybuses along Ensbury Park Road, from its junction with Wimborne Road to its junction with Boundary Road, Columbia Road and Redhill Drive, the construction of overhead to start immediately powers had been obtained.

The first move towards a possible alternative to terminating trolleybuses in the width of High Street, Christchurch, in front of the Town Hall, was in November 1935 when the Bournemouth Town Clerk approached the brewers, Strong & Co. of Romsey, Ltd., to ask under what terms they might be prepared to grant a lease of the coach yard, off Church Street, adjoining their Dolphin Hotel public house and adjacent to the tramways' passenger waiting shelter. Bournemouth suggested a rent of £150 pa for a term of twenty years with a penalty of £200 should the company terminate the lease prematurely. Mr Morrison had discussed the cost of the works likely to be required and received an estimate of £930 12s 11d. He was instructed to approach Christchurch Council. At the Transport Committee Meeting of 20 March 1936 the lowest of five tenders for building work in the coach yard of the Dolphin Hotel, that of Bryant & Trowbridge, at £197 10s, was accepted. Six tenders were received for the supply and installation of a turntable, that of Sanderson Bros. Ltd., at £380, being accepted. The MoT inspection of the Christchurch extension was scheduled for Wednesday 8 April 1936.

It had become apparent that additional current was needed for the summer season and for future expansions. After negotiations with the Central Electricity Board and BPES, the latter offered a ten-year agreement for a DC traction current supply delivered at their substations at Electric House in Yelverton Road; Green Road, Winton; and Watcombe Road, Southbourne; for maximum loads up to 500kW at point of supply. Charges under the agreement would be £4 10s for each kilowatt used in any half-hour in November to February, plus a running charge of 0.3d per unit subject to the price of coal and a service charge £1,000 pa. Similar terms would apply at BPES's Christchurch Substation (where existing agreements for agreed capacity of 400kW at £267 pa. applied) if the total package was acceptable. The offer assumed the installation of mercury arc rectifiers at the substations, but no special provisions for the handling of regenerative braking, with which all of Bournemouth's trolleybuses to date had been fitted.

These arrangements were accepted with capital expenditure to be borne by the Corporation, namely £3,500 for cables to connect to the supply paid out of the loan authorised by the 1930 Act. The three substations and their equipment were provided and maintained by the Company.

On 24 April 1936 Mr Morrison was instructed to obtain information on trolleybus traction batteries for emergency manoeuvring purposes. The findings are not minuted but no Bournemouth trolleybus was ever equipped with traction batteries. He was also told to establish with the Borough Engineer the future traffic arrangements at the Lansdowne so

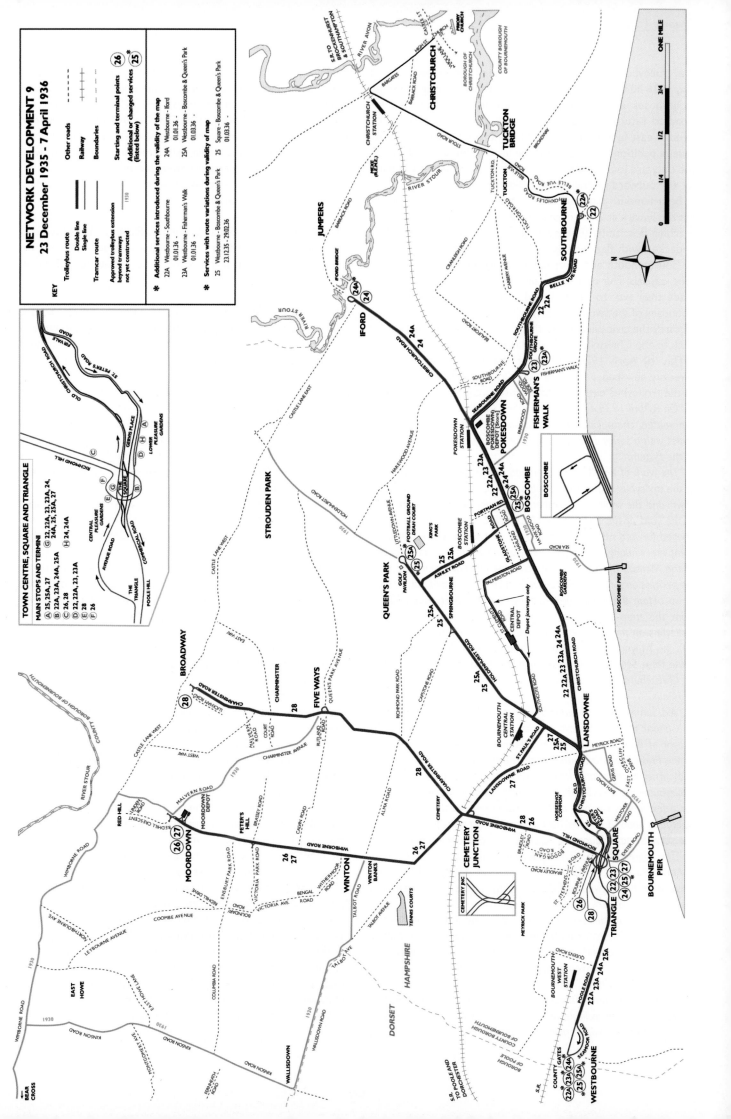

NETWORK DEVELOPMENT 9
23 December 1935 - 7 April 1936

that trolleybus turning facilities could be provided there. On 22 May 1936 he was instructed to erect overhead wiring to enable trolleybuses arriving at the Lansdowne along Holdenhurst Road to return over the same route, i.e. a turning circle, or to turn east by the Metropole Hotel into Christchurch Road. Queue positions were to be made at the Metropole Hotel on the outward journey along Christchurch Road and at the Bank for the outward journey along Holdenhurst Road.

Bournemouth Corporation's last service tram, car No.108, left the Square at 2.15 pm on 8 April 1936 for Christchurch. On reaching Boscombe (Pokesdown) Depot it was joined by 115, bedecked with flags and special placards, carrying the Mayors of Bournemouth and Christchurch, together with a group of civic officials. The two trams, picking up passengers en route, made their way to Tuckton Bridge over the River Stour (the boundary of the two boroughs), where a trolleybus was waiting to carry the civic party on to the terminus at Christchurch and back to the Christchurch Town Hall for tea.

The 10 April 1936 edition of the *Bournemouth Times & Directory* newspaper included the following article in its review of the trolleybus extension to Christchurch:

"On 8 April 1936 Ald. F.B. Summerbee, Chairman of the Transport Committee, championed the trolleybus installation and replied to critics with a series of figures which he felt championed the efficacy of the system.

"The work of installing the overhead equipment for the extension of the trolleybus system from Southbourne Cross Roads to the Priory Town and the making of temporary arrangements for a terminus in the yard of the Dolphin Hotel, Church Street, Christchurch was pushed forward rapidly of late in order that the service might be in complete working for Easter. Only yesterday morning an Inspector of the Ministry of Transport inspected the extended route. He gave his permission for the trolley buses [sic] to be operated but an hour or so before the inaugural ceremony. The civic party disembarked from the tram at Tuckton Bridge where they boarded the first trolleybus on the extended route back to Christchurch. Before they left, the Mayor of Bournemouth declared open the section of the route from Southbourne Cross Roads to the Bridge and the Mayor of Christchurch that section from the Bridge to the Christchurch terminus.

"Ald. Summerbee handed to the Mayor of Christchurch (Councillor D. Galton) the first trolleybus ticket into Christchurch and to the Mayor of Bournemouth (Ald. H.G. Harris) the last tram ticket out of the Priory Town to Bournemouth. The trolleybuses were instituted in Bournemouth in June 1934 by Ald. Edgecombe, then Mayor. The trolleybus route from Southbourne Cross Roads to the Square (which for a few weeks ran only as far as Fisherman's Walk) had been in operation about 3 months. Taking the running costs of 10d per mile, the service had produced £2,222 over and above the running costs.

"The aggregate of trolleybus passengers from all services between 1 April 1935 and 1 March 1936 had been 19,111,838 and yet there were people who said the trolleybuses were not popular. They were getting a return of 14.61d per car mile.

"In respect of the service opened that day it was intended to operate from Christchurch a 12-minute service but whether it would remain would depend on the support received. The new service would allow for a minimum saving of 11 minutes on the journey Bournemouth to Christchurch.

"On route 26 from Moordown to the Square from June 1935 to March 1936 with trolleybuses as compared with the same period the year previous with trams there had been an increase in the number of passengers of 597,829. The gross profit after allowing for the costs of running at 10d a mile for the trolleybuses was £6,768 against a gross profit on the trams of £2,799. Thus the trolleybus showed an increased profit of £3,969. The trolleybuses showed in addition a saving in running expenses of £909. Also on that route they had run 68,878 more miles, which meant that the public were getting a very much better service than before".

On 8 April 1936, two trolleybus services were introduced on the Christchurch extension:

21   Bournemouth Square, Gervis Place - Lansdowne - Boscombe Gardens - Boscombe Arcade - Pokesdown Station - Fisherman's Walk - Southbourne - Tuckton Bridge - Christchurch, Church Street

21A Westbourne, Seamoor Road - Bournemouth Square - Lansdowne - Boscombe Gardens - Boscombe - Pokesdown - Fisherman's Walk - Southbourne - Tuckton Bridge - Christchurch, Church Street

Pending completion of work on a turntable in the former coach yard of the Dolphin Hotel, trolleybuses terminated at Christchurch by making a "three-point turn" from Church Street into the yard using a T-pole and connecting cables. One newspaper suggested that the turntable might be electrically operated later but there is no evidence that such equipment was ever installed.

Service 22 to Tuckton Bridge and 22A to Southbourne Cross Roads were suspended from the same date as the through running trolleybuses to and from Christchurch offered sufficient capacity.

Trolleybus fares Southbourne Cross Roads-Christchurch were held at the same level as those used on motor bus service 2 Bournemouth Square-Christchurch (re-routed away from Christchurch Road along Manor Road and Beechwood Avenue), which had commenced as express service 2 between the Square and Tuckton along the tram route.

The new route crossed the River Stour over Tuckton Bridge, a reinforced concrete structure built in 1905 for the tramway extension to Christchurch. A toll was levied on all traffic over the bridge, including tramway and subsequently trolleybus passengers who received a separate ½d ticket. The overhead wiring on Tuckton Bridge was held by bracket gantries spanning the road, whilst the traction poles mounted in the deck of the bridge received extra support from metal buttresses across the footpath to the metal railings. Trolleybuses were prohibited to pass on the narrow bridge, the roadway being just 19ft 6in wide, and subject to a maximum speed limit of 10mph. The 1930 Act granted Christchurch Corporation the right to buy that part of the trolleybus system in its borough on the last day of 1955 or on the last day of every subsequent seventh year, if it so wished.

The changeover from tramway to trolleybus operation, originally planned for three years, was thus completed in just 22 months. Yet despite having operated costly duplicate services during this period, the enormous growth in traffic promoted by the trolleybuses (service 26 passenger figures increased by 31% in its first year of operation), albeit at lower fares, ensured a net profit of £10,000 on trolleybus operations after paying all interest charges on capital expenditure in the financial year ending 31 March 1936. The trolleybuses were a major success!

The first trolleybus to Christchurch, Sunbeam MS2 no. 97 (ALJ971), stands in Church Street ready for its return journey to Bournemouth having turned by use of T-poles in the entrance to the yard that would, some months later, house the turntable. The two gentlemen in raincoats standing on the disused tramlines are Mr Herbert Vickers, Chief Assistant and Electrical Engineer and Mr Duncan P. Morrison, Engineer and General Manager.
Wolverhampton Archives (Sunbeam Collection)

A number of BCT personalities lined up along the side of the first trolleybus to leave Christchurch. Looking from the front to the rear of the vehicle, the gentleman in the light coloured raincoat and hat is Mr H. Vickers, Chief Assistant and Electrical Engineer, the short gentleman to the rear of the front exit with a dark bowler hat is Alderman F.B. Summerbee, Chairman of the Transport Committee. Further along the trolleybus in front of the route slipboard stands W.D. Reakes, then Traffic Superintendent, wearing a suit and dark bowler hat, whilst further to the rear are William Baxendale, Works Superintendent and Albert Lodge, Accountant and later Commercial Assistant.
Wolverhampton Archives (Sunbeam Collection)

The last days of the trams.

David Packer

The main shopping area of Christchurch Road, Boscombe, in the mid-1930s.

David Bowler collection

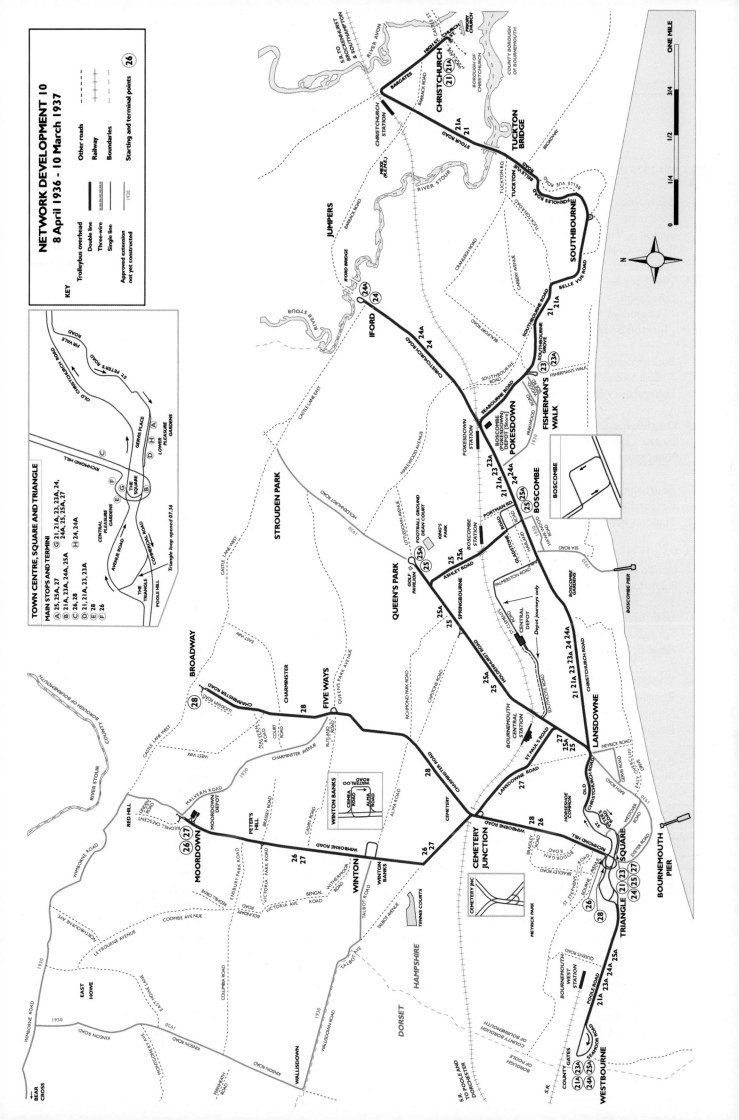

KEY

Trolleybus overhead
Double line
Three-wire
Single line

Approved extension
not yet constructed

Other roads
Railway
Boundaries

1930

Starting and terminal points ㉖

TOWN CENTRE, SQUARE AND TRIANGLE

MAIN STOPS AND TERMINI

A 25, 25A, 27
B 21A, 23A, 24A, 25A
C 26, 28
D 21, 21A, 23, 23A
E 28
F 26
G 21, 21A, 23, 23A, 24, 24A, 25, 25A, 27
H 24, 24A

Triangle loop opened 07.36

ONE MILE

0   1/4   1/2   3/4

N

Places labelled on map:
BEAR CROSS, WALLISDOWN, EAST HOWE, RED HILL, MOORDOWN, WINTON, WINTON BANKS, BROADWAY, FIVE WAYS, CHARMINSTER, STROUDEN PARK, QUEEN'S PARK, CEMETERY JUNCTION, LANSDOWNE, TRIANGLE, BOURNEMOUTH PIER, BOSCOMBE, BOSCOMBE PIER, POKESDOWN, FISHERMAN'S WALK, SOUTHBOURNE, IFORD, JUMPERS, CHRISTCHURCH, TUCKTON BRIDGE, WESTBOURNE

COUNTY BOROUGH OF BOURNEMOUTH
COUNTY BOROUGH OF CHRISTCHURCH
BOROUGH OF POOLE
HAMPSHIRE / DORSET

RIVER AVON, RIVER STOUR

CHAPTER FOUR
THE SYSTEM DEVELOPS

By mid-1936 the following trolleybus services were operated:

21 Bournemouth Square, Gervis Place - Lansdowne - Boscombe Gardens - Boscombe Arcade - Pokesdown Station - Fisherman's Walk - Southbourne - Tuckton Bridge - Christchurch, Church Street

21A Westbourne, Seamoor Road - Bournemouth Square - Lansdowne - Boscombe Gardens - Boscombe Arcade - Pokesdown Station - Fisherman's Walk - Southbourne - Tuckton Bridge - Christchurch, Church Street

23 Bournemouth Square, Gervis Place - Lansdowne - Boscombe Gardens - Boscombe - Pokesdown - Fisherman's Walk, Wentworth Avenue

23A Westbourne, Seamoor Road - West Station - Bournemouth Square - Lansdowne - Boscombe Gardens - Boscombe - Pokesdown - Fisherman's Walk, Wentworth Avenue

24 Bournemouth Square, Gervis Place - Lansdowne - Boscombe Gardens - Boscombe Arcade - Pokesdown Station - Iford Bridge

24A Westbourne, Seamoor Road - Bournemouth Square - Lansdowne - Boscombe Gardens - Boscombe Arcade - Pokesdown Station - Iford Bridge

25 Bournemouth Square - Lansdowne - Central Station - Springbourne - Boscombe Station - Boscombe, Portman Road or Queen's Park Golf Pavilion, Holdenhurst Road

25A Westbourne, Seamoor Road - West Station - Bournemouth Square - Lansdowne - Central Station - Springbourne - Boscombe Station - Boscombe, Portman Road or Queen's Park Golf Pavilion, Holdenhurst Road

26 Bournemouth Square - Cemetery Junction - Winton - Moordown, Wimborne Road, Redhill Crescent

27 Bournemouth Square, Gervis Place - Lansdowne - Central Station - Cemetery Junction - Winton - Moordown, Wimborne Road, Redhill Crescent

28 Bournemouth Square - Cemetery Junction - Five Ways - Broadway Hotel, Luckham Road

The Transport Committee Meeting of 19 June 1936 considered a report from its subcommittee suggesting eight further trolleybus routes:

1. Kinson - Wimborne Road, Moordown: from the junction of Columbia Road and Kinson Road, proceeding along Columbia Road and Ensbury Park Road to the junction of Ensbury Park Road with Wimborne Road, Moordown.
2. Ensbury Park Hotel - Ensbury: from the junction of Ensbury Park Road and Redhill Drive, proceeding along Coombe Avenue, Leybourne Avenue, and Northbourne Avenue to the junction of Northbourne Avenue with Wimborne Road, Ensbury.

3. Moordown - Iford: from the junction of Wimborne Road and Castle Lane West, south-eastwards along Castle Lane to the junction of Castle Lane East with Christchurch Road, Iford.

4. Wimborne Road - Holdenhurst Road: from the junction of Alma Road and Wimborne Road, proceeding along Alma Road and Richmond Park Road to the junction of Richmond Park Road with Holdenhurst Road, Springbourne.

5. Tuckton - Seabourne Road, Fisherman's Walk: from the junction of Tuckton Road and Stour Road, proceeding along Tuckton Road, Cranleigh Road, Beaufort Road and Beresford Road to its junction with Seabourne Road, Fisherman's Walk.

6. Fisherman's Walk: Parkwood Road, Southbourne Road terminal loop

7. Iford - Christchurch: from the junction of Iford Lane and Christchurch Road, proceeding along Christchurch Road, Barrack Road, across Stour Road to the junction of Barrack Road with High Street, Christchurch.

8. Bear Cross - Wallisdown: from the junction of Wimborne Road with Ringwood Road, Bear Cross, proceeding along Ringwood Road to the junction of Wallisdown Road and Ringwood Road, along Wallisdown Road to the junction of Wallisdown Road with Kinson Road.

It was resolved to apply to the MoT for a Provisional Order authorising trolley vehicle operation on Routes 1-6 and 8 with, in the meantime, the Town Clerk seeking the consent of Poole Council, in respect of Route 8. This was necessary as, following the 1930 boundary changes, about 200yd west of the junction of Wallisdown Road with Kinson Road at Canford Road, Highmoor, the boundary between the Boroughs of Bournemouth and Poole changed from the south side to the north side of Wallisdown Road. A mile-long section at the western end of Wallisdown Road was accordingly in Poole. The Negotiating Subcommittee was authorised to reopen negotiations with Christchurch Council in respect of Route 7.

By the third week of January 1937, objections had been received to the grant of a Provisional Order as follows:

Route 1, Ensbury Park Road, from residents.

Route 4, Richmond Park Road, from residents in the road and neighbouring roads.

Route 7, Barrack Road, Christchurch, from Hampshire County Council, Christchurch Council and residents in the road.

Route 8, Wallisdown Road, from Dorset County Council, Poole Corporation, H&D.

and generally, surprisingly, from BPES.

At the same meeting, Mr Morrison presented his first Annual Report in Bournemouth, namely for the year ending 31 March 1936, which despite the trolleybuses' financial success, showed a £21,307 deficit. Indeed, in most pre-war years, although trolleybuses made a surplus, the undertaking's overall net result was a loss, requiring support from the rates in the years ending March 1936 to March 1939.

The following tram routes had been converted to trolleybus operation:

Bournemouth Square - Moordown Depot	7 June 1935
Lansdowne-Moordown, Redhill Crescent	28 June 1935
Bournemouth Square - Charminster Road junction with Capstone Road (and extended to Broadway Hotel, Castle Lane West)	23 August 1935
Bournemouth Square-Fisherman's Walk	21 November 1935
Fisherman's Walk-Southbourne Cross Roads	23 December 1935

Mr Morrison considered that the financial results had been influenced by the almost complete tram to trolleybus change-over, together with the following factors:

- the withdrawal of operations in Poole;
- service co-ordination with other operators, leading to a fall in motorbus fares;
- the introduction of trolleybuses at lower fares than on the trams;

while expenditure had increased due to:

- operation of duplicate services during the change-over;
- staff changes to suit the new conditions;
- the cost of staff retraining.

The Municipal Tramways & Transport Association again held their annual conference in Bournemouth in 1936, between 24 and 26 June, and, as a background for participants, the 18 June 1936 edition of *Transport World* magazine contained a review

English Electric bodied Sunbeam MS2 no. 81 (AEL409) pauses on the south side of the Square running on a short-lived service 24A journey from Iford Bridge to County Gates, Westbourne, in September 1936. The front indicator boxes have already been rebuilt to the new standard adopted in November 1935.

David Chalk collection (R.T. Wilson)

of the undertaking, concentrating on the "great success of the trolleybus". It was recorded that the tram-to-trolleybus conversion programme had been completed and that the trolleybus network now extended to 15½ route miles. A further 30 miles of trolleybus route were authorised and the next extension would be of 1¾ miles from Wimborne Road, Moordown, along Ensbury Park Road, Coombe Avenue, Leybourne Avenue (subject to a Provisional Order for Route 2, above, being granted) to Ensbury, where building development was taking place.

The magazine reported that in the 51 weeks ending 27 May 1936, the number of passengers carried on the Square-Moordown service had increased from 4,417,452, when trams operated, to 5,805,830. A commensurate increase had been recorded on all converted routes. The changeover from trams had been fully justified both for technical reasons and public popularity. Motorbuses were seen as no more than trolleybus feeders.

It continued that early problems with the overhead equipment had been corrected and, in an effort to speed-up services, the new lines would be equipped with non-fouling fittings so that the slipper form of current collector could be tested (rather than the trolley wheels used hitherto). Negotiations were under way with the appropriate authorities to rearrange stopping places to better suit the changed traffic conditions. Once this had been completed, overhead equipment, such as section insulators, would be repositioned optimally to meet the new traffic conditions. A recommendation that all stopping places be set back 150ft from cross roads or junctions, as well as a "staggered" gap of 300ft between the stops for opposite directions, would be introduced as far as possible. Principal stops, it had been decided, would be equipped with queuing barriers and yellow road markings.

The *Transport World* review concluded with the news that, to overcome the problem of voltage drop on the more distant parts of the network and to cope with planned extensions, the feeder and distribution system was being remodelled with the introduction of three substations (Electric House; Watcombe Road, Southbourne (known as Carbery); and Green Road, Winton) taking power from the grid. At that time power was being supplied wholly by the Corporation's Southcote Road generating station and the grid-supplied Christchurch substation.

On 24 July 1936, a subcommittee considered an additional trolleybus route from the Lansdowne to the Square along Bath Road, continuing either via the Pier Approach, Bournemouth Pier and Exeter Road, with a turning point at the Pier Approach, or along Westover Road to Gervis Place. There was some disagreement and only the latter route was recommended, with construction to start as soon as possible. On 18 September 1936, the Transport Committee learned that the Council had declined to adopt this resolution, but they repeated their recommendation that installation be carried out as soon as possible, for revenue reasons and in order to complete the system.

Although the public were keen to see a regular trolleybus service to the Queen's Park Golf Pavilion, the Transport Committee recommended that no change was necessary and the branch remained served solely by football specials on the days that the Cherries (the name by which Bournemouth AFC is known) were playing at Dean Court.

Special destination boards "TO AND FROM TENNIS" were placed in the nearside driver's cab windscreen in trolleybuses travelling between the Square and Moordown or Winton during the Bournemouth (Open) Lawn Tennis Tournament at Melville Park, which took place between 27 July and 8 August 1936.

To avoid internal corrosion, it was agreed to fit finials to the tops of traction poles and at bracket arm ends. In the same meeting it was recommended that tramway traction poles and overhead equipment remaining in Capstone Road be removed as soon as possible.

On 3 July 1936 a special Transport Committee Meeting had instructed the General Manager to consider fare increases in the light of his Annual Report. This led to the proposal, on 9 October 1936, that the 1½d fares introduced on all services when trolleybus operations started should be abolished and the previous tram fares reintroduced. On 26 November 1936, the Transport Committee approved the General Manager's suggestions (see Appendix K). With effect from 25 January 1937, the SETC approved the revised motorbus fares (trolleybus fares not being under their jurisdiction), excluding those between the Square and County Gates which were still under discussion between Bournemouth and Poole Councils. Thus the 17-month "holiday" of reduced fares was over. As H&D was unable to adjust its fares at such short notice, the fares were actually increased from 1 February 1937.

At the Transport Committee meeting on 18 December 1936, Mr Morrison reported that plans for the Charminster Avenue extension were being prepared and would soon be submitted to the MoT, and that the Post Office Telephone and Telegraph Authorities had been informed in respect of telephone wires above the road.

On 27 November 1936, a deputation from Belfast which, despite the purchase of a fleet of 50 streamlined tramcars the year before was considering the experimental conversion of its Falls Road route to trolleybus operation, visited the undertaking and was entertained to lunch.

A petition was received asking for a public transport connection from Central Station via Southcote Road, Drummond Road and Christchurch Road to the Lansdowne and the Pavilion. The Transport Committee replied that this was currently impossible but further consideration would be given when trolleybuses operated along Bath Road and Westover Road. Only in October 1937 was it recommended that a half-hourly motorbus service be introduced from Ashley Road to the Square via Drummond Road, Southcote Road, the Lansdowne, and Bath Road (Drummond Road was never wired for trolleybuses).

During the course of 1936, with the conversion programme complete, Mr Morrison started a modernisation of BCT's ancillary fleet which, until then, had consisted of three Tilling-Stevens TS3 petrol-electric tower wagons, the chassis of which dated from 1914-15, and a Shelvoke & Drewry motor lorry, delivered in 1924 as an office van. Two of the tower wagons were withdrawn and their telescopic towers transferred to the chassis of two Tilling-Stevens TS6 petrol-electric buses (RU2012-3). In December 1936 he recommended that the remaining tower wagon and lorry be scrapped, and that two suitable 25cwt chassis, one to be equipped with a tipping wagon body and the other with a telescopic tower, be purchased. The work was put in hand and tenders invited. By February 1937, the tender of Lee Motor Works (Bournemouth) Ltd. for a Bedford tipping wagon and a Bedford chassis for a tower wagon at a total cost of £440 8s 6d had been accepted. In the meantime,

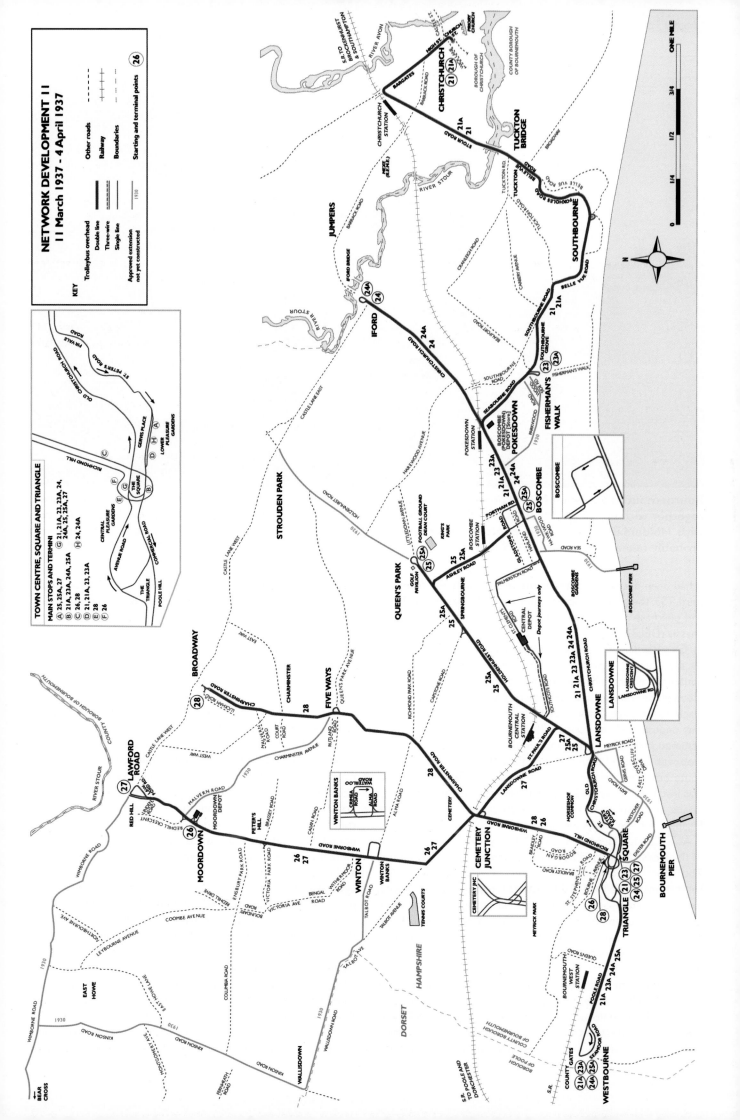

TOWN CENTRE, SQUARE AND TRIANGLE

MAIN STOPS AND TERMINI

Ⓐ 25, 25A, 27   Ⓖ 21, 21A, 23, 23A, 24,
Ⓑ 21A, 23A, 24A, 25A   24A, 25, 25A, 27
Ⓒ 26, 28   Ⓗ 24, 24A
Ⓓ 21, 21A, 23, 23A
Ⓔ 28
Ⓕ 26

ONE MILE

0   1/4   1/2   3/4

CHRISTCHURCH
㉑ ㉑Ⓐ

TUCKTON
BRIDGE

SOUTHBOURNE

JUMPERS

IFORD
㉔Ⓐ ㉔

POKESDOWN
FISHERMAN'S
WALK ㉓ ㉓Ⓐ

BOSCOMBE
㉕Ⓐ ㉕

QUEEN'S PARK
㉕Ⓐ ㉕

STROUDEN PARK

BOSCOMBE PIER

LANSDOWNE

BROADWAY
㉘

FIVE WAYS

LAWFORD ROAD
㉗

MOORDOWN
㉖

WINTON

CEMETERY
JUNCTION

BOURNEMOUTH
PIER

SQUARE
㉑ ㉓
㉔ ㉕ ㉗
㉖

TRIANGLE
㉘

WESTBOURNE
㉑ ㉓Ⓐ
㉔ ㉕Ⓐ

EAST
HOWE

BEAR
CROSS

Bournemouth's Sunbeam MS2 prototype no. 68 (LJ7701) is seen parked with its trolley booms down and secured, together with no. 98 (ALJ972), at the Queen's Park Golf Pavilion terminus at the junction of Littledown Avenue with Holdenhurst Road. This photograph shows no. 68 after its reconstruction in September 1936 and was probably taken in the winter of 1936-37. Malcolm Pearce (G.O.P. Pearce)

it had been decided to transfer the telescopic tower from the third TS3 tower wagon on to another TS6 chassis (RU2014) and purchase a new Rawlins tower to mount on the Bedford chassis (DEL37).

Taxis standing at the service 28 boarding point at the entrance to the Central Pleasure Gardens on the west side of the Square were becoming a problem and at its 18 December 1936 meeting the Transport Committee resolved that the Horse and Hackney Carriage Committee be informed that their presence was undesirable. The construction of a trolleybus "loop way", assumed to be the passing loop in the overhead wiring at the stop, was approved. In preparation for the alternative trolleybus route between the Lansdowne and the Square, Mr Morrison was instructed to erect 25 traction poles in Bath and Westover Roads in consultation with the Electrical and Public Lighting Engineer for use as lighting standards.

At a Council Meeting in early January 1937, a joint report of the Horse, Road, and Transport Committees was presented. The Borough Engineer presented a plan showing the suggestions of the MoT, the Transport Department and himself, for a changed layout at the Square, including amongst other things, construction of an island at the entrance of Exeter Road as a trolleybus stop, removal of the taxi rank and a widened pavement on the north side between Bourne Avenue and Richmond Hill.

The tram track fan leading into Boscombe (Pokesdown) Depot as well as street track as far as just west of Parkwood Road had been removed by the first week of March 1937, and the redundant tramcars which had been stored in the building had been dismantled and removed. No trolleybus overhead

equipment leading into the depot had yet been installed and trolleybuses were driven in and out using "T"-poles hooked over running lines and over hooked-down trolley heads. It was announced that the depot would be used solely to store spare trolleybuses and that no service vehicles would be housed there until proper overhead wiring was installed.

At its meeting on 11 January 1937 the Town Clerk reported to the Transport Committee on negotiations with H&D on the Council's application to operate trolleybuses along Wallisdown Road (and thence along Ringwood Road to Bear Cross), i.e. Route 8 of the Provisional Order application. H&D were making application to the SETC to operate motorbuses on a circular route through Wallisdown and another service along Ringwood Road between Bear Cross and Upton (to the northwest of Poole). The Transport Committee resolved to oppose H&D running such services within the Bournemouth Borough boundaries, and advised the Company of the terms whereby mutual running over Wallisdown Road between Kinson Road and Ringwood Road would be acceptable. Poole Council was again asked for its consent to BCT operating along those portions of Wallisdown Road within the Borough of Poole

Subsequently, on 15 February 1937, a meeting of the Bournemouth Town Clerk, Poole Corporation and H&D addressed the topic, resulting in the proposal to operate trolleybuses along the western part of Wallisdown Road being dropped. Since 1 December 1930 BCT motorbus service 9 had replaced an H&D service between Winton Banks and Columbia Road via Wallisdown Road and Kinson Road. Acknowledging this service would be replaced by trolleybuses, Poole consented to an hourly BCT motorbus service, which commenced on

26 June 1937 as the 9A (Bournemouth Square-Bear Cross), running the entire length of Wallisdown Road and thence along Ringwood Road.

MoT approval to the following extensions and turning points was received in January 1937:

a)   New curve at the Lansdowne enabling southbound vehicles to turn left (east) out of Holdenhurst Road into Christchurch Road,

b)   Turning point at the Lansdowne anti-clockwise around the island made up by Lansdowne Crescent between Holdenhurst Road and Lansdowne Road (installed in the 1936-7 financial year),

c)   Turning loop along Alma Road, Waterloo Road, and Crimea Road, Winton (the area known as Winton Banks),

d)   Turntable at Christchurch (brought into use 19 June 1936),

e)   Extension from Moordown, Redhill Crescent to Castle Lane West via Wimborne Road, and a single line terminal loop along Lawford Road, Castle Lane West and Wimborne Road (Redhill) (opened 11 March 1937).

Despite exhaustive research it has proved impossible to establish when a)-c) above were first available for use.

The Transport Committee agreed at its 22 January 1937 meeting that trolleybus services to Fisherman's Walk be extended to Southbourne Cross Roads from 9.30am to 12 noon daily. It is assumed that these journeys simply became 22 and 22A although it has proved impossible to establish the date of the change. It is likely that the extension, if action was taken, was introduced with the summer timetable and became permanent on 1 October 1937.

The Committee also learned that the MoT had approved erection of trolleybus overhead equipment in Charminster Avenue and work proceeded apace. The MoT advised that, due to other commitments, it would grant authority for the Corporation to operate trolleybuses on its own responsibility and subject to any requirements subsequently deemed necessary by the official inspection. With the completion of road resurfacing, services commenced on 5 April 1937, thus:

29   Bournemouth Square - Richmond Hill - Cemetery Junction - Five Ways - Malvern Road.

A reversing triangle was strung at the north end of Charminster Avenue at its junction with Malvern Road. The

This Sunbeam BTH publicity photograph was taken in 1937 and show six trolleybuses including a 21, 23 and 26. The queue in front of the Central Pleasure Gardens (behind the tall lamp post) is for CharminsterRoad (services 28 and 29). A service 26 departure, operated by no. 114, can be seen in the bottom right of the photograph prior to turning sharp left on to Richmond Hill. The loading island outside the erstwhile tramway waiting rooms now serves motorbus services as evidenced by AEC Regent no. 67 loading for Bear Cross whilst hordes of would-be passengers besiege a diminutive Du Cros single-decker.   **Wolverhampton Archives (Sunbeam BTH)**

Borough Engineer then turned his attention to removing the remaining tram track in Christchurch Road from the Lansdowne to Parkwood Road.

Simultaneously, wiring was extended along Wimborne Road to the junction with Castle Lane West at Redhill, an anti-clockwise single line turning loop being built northbound along Lawford Road, west along Castle Lane West and then back into Wimborne Road. The terminal arrangements were built with a further extension along Wimborne Road westwards to Bear Cross (as authorised) in mind, a junction frog being placed in the northbound wiring which continued some distance past Lawford Road towards the junction between Wimborne Road and Castle Lane. Service 27 was extended under the new wiring to Castle Lane West from 11 March 1937, but it was subsequently decided to extend service 26 instead and the 27 ceased to run beyond Redhill Crescent on 14 April 1937. From 15 April 1937 services operated as follows:

26   Bournemouth Square - Richmond Hill - Cemetery Junction - Wimborne Road - Winton - Moordown - Castle Lane West, Lawford Road

27   Bournemouth Square, Gervis Place - Lansdowne - Central Station - St Paul's Road - Cemetery Junction - Wimborne Road - Winton - Moordown, Wimborne Road, Redhill Crescent

Meanwhile, on 19 February 1937, the Transport Committee recommended that construction should start on a route extension commencing in Talbot Road at its junction with Wimborne Road (commonly known as Winton Banks, as there was a branch of the major High Street banks on each corner), along Talbot Road and Wallisdown Road, to its junction with Kinson Road, East Howe. The island near the junction of Kinson Road with Columbia Road, East Howe, was deemed a more suitable location for the turning circle than that originally proposed at the Liberal Club some 300yd south thereof. In November 1937, the Borough Engineer was able to acquire the land required for road widening at the junction of Kinson, Fernheath and Acres Road (Fernheath Road extended to Kinson Road at that time and only later was the east end of it absorbed into Turbary Park Avenue) and recommended that the Transport Committee contribute £85, half the estimated cost of the street works.

The Transport Committee recommended that the Council's resolution of 30 October 1936 not to extend trolleybuses along Bath and Westover Roads for a one-year period from that date be rescinded. An inbound service along these roads to the Square was urgently needed because of congestion on Old Christchurch Road and, in particular, traffic delays from the Quadrant on Hinton Road through Gervis Place to Westover Road. The diversion of some westbound journeys along Bath Road would alleviate this problem. Furthermore, there was an absence of direct transport facilities from the eastern and northern parts of the borough direct to the amusement centres, including the new Pier Approach Baths, whilst H&D was always aggressively looking for opportunities to capture BCT's business. An alternative route would accordingly increase revenue. In the ensuing discussion some councillors sought assurances that trolleybuses would never run to the

Congestion in the Square looking west to Commercial Road and the Central Pleasure Gardens photographed from the roof of the former tramways waiting rooms in about 1937 as evidenced by the mixture of revised and original indicator boxes on the front upper deck panels of the trolleybuses. No. 75, having pulled out of Avenue Road, is heading for Iford but displaying service number 24; it can be assumed that this was, in fact, a 24A jouney from Westbourne to Iford Bridge, this service only operating between 1 January 1936 and 31 October 1937. It already displays its fleet number on the lower-deck side panels although clearly still retaining a white roof.

David Chalk collection

Pier or along the sea front but the Mayor pointed out that the Corporation already had powers to run to the Pier Approach and along Exeter Road to the Square. Ald. Summerbee stressed that trolleybuses were profitable whereas motorbuses were not. The Town Council adopted the recommendation by 33 votes to 19 on 6 April 1937.

Working fast, one-way westbound (inbound) wiring from the Lansdowne along Bath Road as far as the Royal Bath Hotel and then along Westover Road past the Pavilion to a junction with the existing inbound wiring at Gervis Place was erected. After test runs on 7 May 1937, the first vehicle on Saturday 8 May 1937 to make the journey carried members of the Transport Committee and Departmental officials. Public services followed immediately at 10.30 am. Alternate westbound vehicles on services 21, 23, 24, 25 and 27 were rerouted along Bath and Westover Roads to the Square. Once again, MoT authority to operate trolleybuses along the extension on the Corporation's own responsibility until the subsequent official inspection could be made was received. Through fares to the Square were unaffected.

Initially, paper stickers, affixed at the top of the driver's cab nearside windscreen, displayed:

VIA **BATH** & WESTOVER ROAD
for BOURNEMOUTH PIER and PAVILION

These were subsequently replaced by special boards with white lettering on a red background in the base of the nearside windscreen indicating those journeys traversing Bath and Westover Roads until vehicles were fitted with auxiliary destination screens at the top of the windscreen and immediately above the rear platform window.

The number of trolleybuses on service 27 running to Bournemouth Square via Bath Road was soon questioned, and the General Manager carried out a census of the number of passengers on this service travelling to stops in Old Christchurch Road. By July 1937, the Transport Committee recommended that the practice of running service 27 trolleybuses alternately over the two lines to the Square should continue.

In the autumn of 1936 Great Britain had undergone a constitutional crisis culminating in the abdication of King Edward VIII. Officialdom was eager to "paper over the cracks" and restore faith in the monarchy and thus the foreseen date of his Coronation was retained following the accession of his brother Prince Albert, Duke of York. Accordingly, public spectacle, intended to emphasise the British Empire, was encouraged. Thus, on 19 February 1937, the Transport Committee had approved, at an estimated £300, designs for the decoration and illumination of a trolleybus, upon which premium fares would be charged, for King George VI's Coronation.

Asked if there was any reason for having an illuminated trolleybus, Councillor Langton, Chairman, said the decorations would not be limited to the Coronation festivities. It was proposed to have a decorative scheme which could be fitted to any trolleybus and it was suggested that the vehicle should be used on every suitable occasion, such as during conferences and carnivals or anything that needed a little brightening up. The vehicle would generate revenue and would be run over any route deemed worthwhile. Consequently, trolleybus 152 was decorated with nearly 1,200 Mazda red, white and blue lamps (having a nominal candle power in excess of 12,000); various illuminated symbols supplied by British Thomson-Houston and illuminated borough arms on the front upper-deck panel. It was used on service 21 for the rest of the summer, double fares being charged.

Many buildings and streets, particularly Old Christchurch Road and Westover Road were decorated with flags, garlands and photographs of the royal couple. The *Bournemouth Daily Echo* suggested *"An excellent view of the decorated shops is obtainable from the top of a trolleybus, especially during a rush hour when the speed of traffic is reduced in Old Christchurch Road"*. King George VI was crowned at Westminster Abbey on 12 May 1937 and that afternoon some 36 motorbuses and trolleybuses transported 4,000 school children from all parts of Bournemouth to Dean Court football ground for open-air entertainment and a picnic. Although many of the Coronation festivities in South East England were interrupted by heavy rain storms, Bournemouth was spared and the clouds had gone by 2.45pm. Public transport continued until after 2am the next morning. In addition to illuminated 152,

No. 144 (BEL829) poses with members of the Transport Committee and Department officials following the inaugural journey from the Lansdowne to Gervis Place via Bath Road and Westover Road on 8 May 1937.
Bournemouth Daily Echo

the entire BCT fleet was decorated with streamer flags and bunting. During the course of summer 1937 other trolleybuses were decorated for the Boscombe Carnival, the Hospital Fete and the Bournemouth Regatta, indeed vehicles were frequently decorated for special events until the outbreak of war.

In June 1937 the MoT approved the Bournemouth Corporation (Trolley Vehicles) Provisional Order, excluding the Bear Cross-Wallisdown via Ringwood Road and Wallisdown Road application (Route 8), thereby granting powers for a further ten miles of trolleybus routes, namely:

1. Kinson-Wimborne Road, Moordown.

2. Ensbury Park Hotel-Ensbury.

3. Moordown (Redhill)-Iford via Castle Lane.

4. Wimborne Road (Winton Banks)-Holdenhurst Road (Springbourne) via Richmond Park Road.

5. Tuckton-Seabourne Road, Fisherman's Walk via Cranleigh Road.

6. Fisherman's Walk: Parkwood Road, Southbourne Road terminal loop.

The *Bournemouth Daily Echo* wrote "Making it quite clear - now that there is an alternative route from Lansdowne to the Square by the trolleybuses, special indicators are being fixed to vehicles to prevent confusion among passengers". No. 123 displays the paper sticker indicating that on its westbound service 24 journey it would operate via Bath and Westover Roads. It was also carrying a Union Flag shield at the front of the upper-deck in preparation for the Coronation celebrations later in the month.

Bournemouth Daily Echo

7. Iford-High Street, Christchurch via Barrack Road (for its entire length).

However, Parliamentary Approval to the Provisional Order was withheld in July 1937 due to the stance of Christchurch Council, which was steadfastly defended by the local MP, Major J. D. Mills. Whilst acknowledging that the western end of Christchurch was practically a dormitory of Bournemouth, the Christchurch Chamber of Commerce objected to another trolleybus route into their Borough whilst there were concerns about trolleybuses turning at the busy junction of Barrack Road with Stour Road (creating a circular route via Iford and Southbourne). Christchurch would not agree to trolleybus operation along the eastern portion of Barrack Road between the cross roads with Stour Road and its junction with High Street at Fountain Corner (Route 7) despite the offer of various incentives. The matter was referred to a Select Committee in the next parliamentary session. This meant that although the MoT had agreed to its inclusion, the Provisional Order could not be confirmed in Parliament and that, for the time being, BCT could not proceed with the equipment of any of the other six routes.

On 15 November 1937 the Bournemouth Transport Committee visited an alternative route proposed by Christchurch Council, along Portfield Road and the south end of Fairmile joining Bargates at its junction with Stour Road, but found it unacceptable.

On 30 March 1938 the House of Commons Select Committee decided that trolleybuses would not be allowed to operate on that part of Barrack Road between Stour Road and Fountain Corner, High Street (formerly a gravel pit and known as the Pit Site) in Christchurch. The Bournemouth Corporation (Trolley Vehicles) Order Confirmation Act, 1938 (see Appendix O) reflected this change, and the Barrack Road trolleybuses, when finally introduced, had to operate via Christchurch Station under the existing wiring along Stour Road and Bargates. In preparation for the extension, which necessitated use of Barrack Road bridge over the Southern Railway (SR), there was correspondence in autumn 1938 with the County Surveyor. Bournemouth and Hampshire County Council were asked to share the cost of constructing a temporary footbridge on the west side of the bridge, after deducting a MoT grant. The Council agreed to offer one third without liability.

The outbreak of war in 1939 necessitated several renewals of these powers. Authorised Route 1 of the 1937 Order was completed in April 1938, Route 2 in April 1939, Route 7 in July 1943, Routes 5 and 6 in August 1948, and Routes 2 and 4 were never equipped for trolleybus operation at all.

In April 1937 the Transport Committee had estimated that there would be a loss of £26,504 for the year 1936-7 yet, on 18 June 1937, Mr Morrison was able to report a gross surplus of £49,728 on the undertaking as a whole for the year ending 31 March 1937, an increase of £12,676. Income had decreased by £2,206, but working expenses had fallen by £14,882. There had been a £15,956 19s increase in capital charges between 1935-6 and 1936-7 reflecting what had practically amounted to a new fleet of rolling stock and overhead equipment, as well as considerable investment in the underground feeder system. After paying all capital charges, there was a surplus of £14,058 19s 9d on trolleybus operations whereas motorbuses had lost £15,393 3s 9d. By financial wizardry, the final eight days of tramway operation in the borough made a loss of £18,910

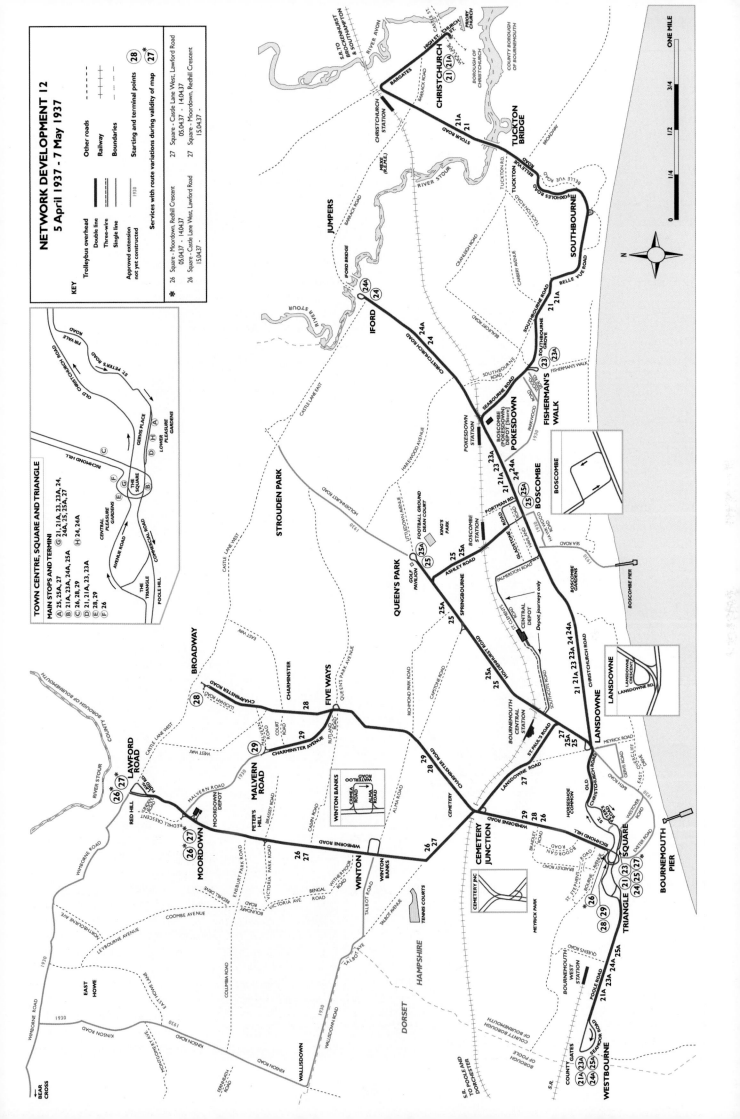

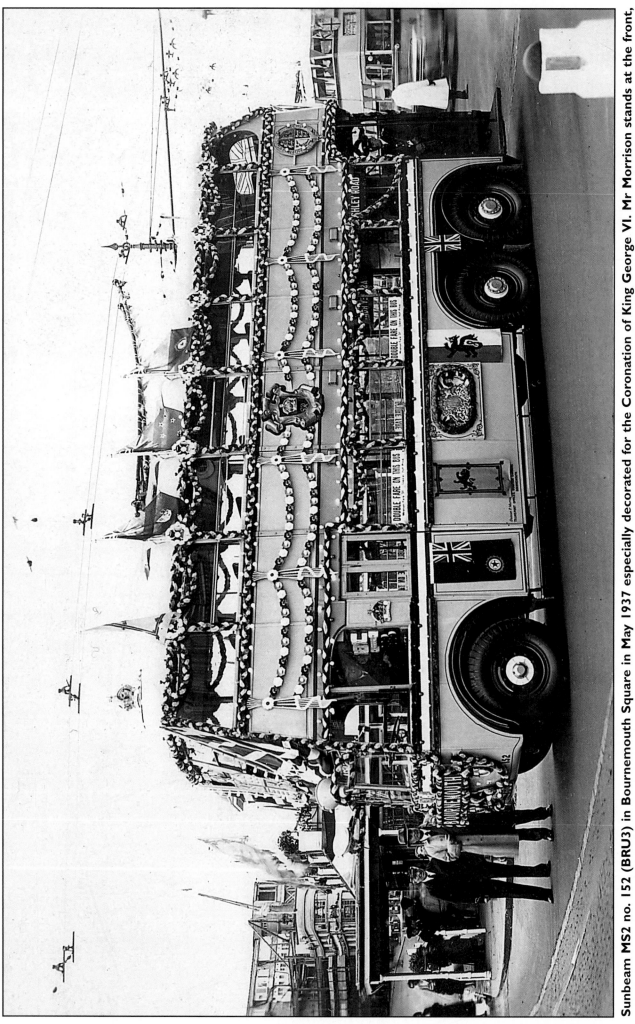

Sunbeam MS2 no. 152 (BRU3) in Bournemouth Square in May 1937 especially decorated for the Coronation of King George VI. Mr Morrison stands at the front, wearing a raincoat and trilby hat. Behind him can be seen the former tramway passenger shelter and the buildings in the apex between Old Christchurch Road and Gervis Place. The scaffolding in the background surrounds the Plummer Roddis department store then under construction (opened 1938). Note the window bills declaring double the normal fares payable on this bus. Another, lesser decorated MS2 is visible to the rear of 152.

David Chalk collection

An evening view of illuminated Sunbeam MS2 no. 152 decorated for the Coronation of King George VI. The decorations included nearly 1,200 Mazda red, white and blue lamps, and various illuminated symbols supplied by British Thomson-Houston. Note the huge spotlights at the front, illuminating the Borough coat of arms framed by a pair of Union flags. The crown at the front of the roof contained a rotating flashing unit which gave a variety of changing effects.

David Chalk collection

Decorated and illuminated trolleybus no. 152 is seen here on Coronation Day, 12 May 1937, at the traffic island on the north side of the Square on its way to Christchurch. In the background a service 26 trolleybus, bedecked with flags, pulls on to the Wimborne Road stop between Bourne Avenue and the bottom of Richmond Hill.

Malcolm Pearce (G.O.P. Pearce)

Decorated Sunbeam MS2 no. 152 (BRU3) is seen heading east in Christchurch Road, Pokesdown, immediately outside the railway station. In the background can be seen the pillars at the entrance to Boscombe (Pokesdown) Depot to the left of the receding H&D double-deck motorbus.

Malcolm Pearce (G.O.P. Pearce)

19s 11d, despite having operated just 4,460 miles. Nonetheless, there was still a large tramways debt outstanding, the charges in respect of which, at that time, were foreseen to continue until 1945, reducing each year, with the largest reduction in 1939.

Total energy output from the generating station had been 5,337,300 units compared to 6,021,470 in 1936, the reduced output being due to the introduction of the three additional substations taking current from BPES. Coal consumption in the year fell from 7,286 to 6,734 tons although the cost had increased by 2s per ton (petrol by 1d per gallon, and materials by 10-20%) in relation to the preceding year. The total cost of electrical energy per unit including all capital charges was 0.71d. BPES delivered 1,389,530 units at the four substations they supplied during the year. Service changes reduced the mileage run by 361,458, but the number of passengers carried had increased by 75,222. The National Joint Industrial Council (NJIC) for the Road Passenger Transport Industry, of which the Corporation was a member, also increased wage scales, with drivers and conductors gaining 2s 6d per week and cleaners, labourers, etc., 1s per week. Finally, the undertaking would have been £70 11s 4d worse off if it had not been for the introduction of uncollected fare boxes in August 1936.

The main items of capital expenditure on the trolleybus system had been:

- completion of Christchurch route,
- installation of a turntable at the Christchurch terminus,
- turning circle at the Triangle,
- turning circle at the Lansdowne (Holdenhurst Road),
- the Moordown-Castle Lane West, Lawford Road extension
- Malvern Road extension (Charminster Avenue)

A member of the public wrote to the Transport Committee in June 1937 asking if, when trolleybuses replaced the motorbus shuttle between Fisherman's Walk and Tuckton (service 8), a through service could be operated between the Square and Tuckton via Cranleigh Road. The Committee replied that favourable consideration would be given when this was carried out, yet in September 1937 when a petition protesting against trolleybuses operating along Parkwood Road was received, it

A special souvenir ticket was issued to those passengers fortunate enough to travel on decorated and illuminated trolleybus no. 152 on 12 May 1937, the day of King George VI's Coronation, although they paid double fare for the privilege.

David Chalk collection

replied that there was no intention to operate such a service. The petition, however, may have been related to fears that plans for the alternative route between Christchurch Road and Seabourne Road, along the entire length of Parkwood Road avoiding Pokesdown Station (route 7 of the 1930 Act), were being revived.

At its meeting on 23 July 1937 the Transport Committee recommended that installation of overhead equipment along Castle Lane West from Wimborne Road, Lawford Road, to Charminster Road, Broadway Hotel, should start as soon as powers were granted under the pending Provisional Order. At the same meeting, permission was granted to Bournemouth Boy Scouts to use the barn at Iford Bridge turning circle as their headquarters as long as they kept it in repair. At about the same time, the Lighting Committee complained of the damage to street lamps by trolleybuses.

It was felt that Poole Road and Westbourne passengers were overprovided for and thus on 30 September 1937 services 23 and 23A ceased to operate, services 22 Square-Southbourne and 22A Westbourne-Southbourne being reintroduced in their place the next day. Then, on 31 October 1937, services 24A Westbourne-Iford Bridge and 25 Square-Boscombe, Portman Road or Queen's Park Golf Pavilion were also withdrawn, the latter being replaced by an enhanced service 25A Westbourne-Boscombe, Portman Road with football specials to/from Queen's Park Golf Pavilion.

In December 1937 a letter was received suggesting that, to avoid congestion in Bournemouth Square at peak periods, trolleybuses be extended down Bath Road to the Pier but consideration was deferred pending a report by the General Manager.

Mr Morrison reported to the 28 January 1938 Transport Committee meeting that MoT approval had been received for trolleybus operation over certain routes, extensions and turning points, authorised by the 1930 Act and recently inspected by a Ministry official, and in respect of which a provisional authority had been issued subject to that inspection. On 16 February 1938 the Bournemouth Corporation (Trolley Vehicles) Provisional Order Confirming Bill was read a second time in the House of Commons, but a petition against the Order was made by Christchurch Corporation.

During March 1938 a complaint was received about the compulsory MoT stop on the inward journey at the top of Bath Hill (which, being less steep than Richmond Hill, did not require use of the coasting brake). The Transport Department investigated the conversion of the compulsory into a request stop although its position could not be altered; nevertheless it remained signed "All Bus Stop" throughout the trolleybus era.

The 22 April 1938 Transport Committee meeting recommended that, subject to approval being obtained, work on the trolleybus extensions along Ensbury Park Road (Route 1, Kinson-Wimborne Road, Moordown), Barrack Road (Route 7, Iford to Christchurch), and Castle Lane West (Route 3, Moordown to Iford) start as soon as possible.

The 1937 Provisional Order became the Bournemouth Corporation (Trolley Vehicles) Order Confirmation Act of 26 May 1938; Route 7 of the Provisional Order became Route 8 in the Confirmation Act, and Route 8 of the Provisional Order was deleted, thus the Confirmation Act contained no Route 7. Construction work started on Route 3 immediately. Solely the north-westerly end of Castle Lane West, i.e. Wimborne Road to Charminster Road, was wired before priority was given to the

Ensbury Park Road and Columbia Road route. In the meantime the Wallisdown extension had been completed and a turning circle built in front of a row of shops (Wonderholme Parade) at the junction of Columbia Road and Kinson Road. Despite concerns that shortages of equipment due to the rearmament drive could delay the opening until after Easter, trolleybuses replaced motorbus service 9, which ran between Winton and Wallisdown, on 15 April 1938 (Good Friday) as service 30, as follows:

30   Bournemouth Square - Richmond Hill - Cemetery Junction - Winton - Talbot Village - Wallisdown - Columbia Road

As foreseen, trolleybuses operating on this service were experimentally equipped with slipper trolley heads and carbon inserts in place of wheel collectors.

The Minutes of the 22 April 1938 Transport Committee Meeting referred to the General Manager's Annual Report on 1937-8:

"Referring to trolleybus operation it will be seen that after meeting capital charges there is a surplus on the year's working of £14,407 15s 4d while on the motorbus side there is a deficit of £4,825 9s 9d. Total consumption of electrical energy was 7,093,600 units of which 5,233,360 units were generated at the Department's Southcote Road station at a cost of 0.81d per unit including capital charges while the remaining 1,860,240 units were taken at the four substations from the Company at a cost of 0.78d per unit. Compared with the previous year, the figures show a decrease of generation at the Department's station of 103,940 units while there was an increase of 470,710 units taken from the Company, the more economic distribution of energy being responsible for the adjustment.

During the financial year under review the following extensions opened:

- Five Ways - Malvern Road (service 29) 0.43 miles, constructed in the previous year but opened for service on 5 April 1937
- Bath and Westover Roads, 0.63 miles, opened 8 May 1937
- Talbot Road, Wallisdown, Kinson Road (service 30) 1.92 miles constructed and practically completed by 31 March 1938

Total mileage of trolleybus services was now 30.77 miles".

Mr Morrison added that 51 trolleybuses had been repainted during the year, whilst nine miles of trolley wire had been renewed. The carbon insert slipper shoe current collector experiment had proved successful and a complete changeover was planned, thus removing trolley wheel noise. Finally, the Transport Department were working closely with Post Office engineering staff with respect to alleged radio interference.

The number of passengers carried had increased by almost 670,000 and despite an increase in working expenses of over £9,000 it had proved possible to increase the surplus by some £345 on 1936-7 after all net revenue charges had been met (see Appendix Q for details).

In early June 1938, the Royal Counties Show was held at Talbot Village and 152 was once again decorated and illuminated for use on the new service 30. Normal fares applied.

The General Manager reported on 27 June 1938 on a proposal to reroute some trolleybuses on the Christchurch-Bournemouth Square service via Ashley Road and Holdenhurst

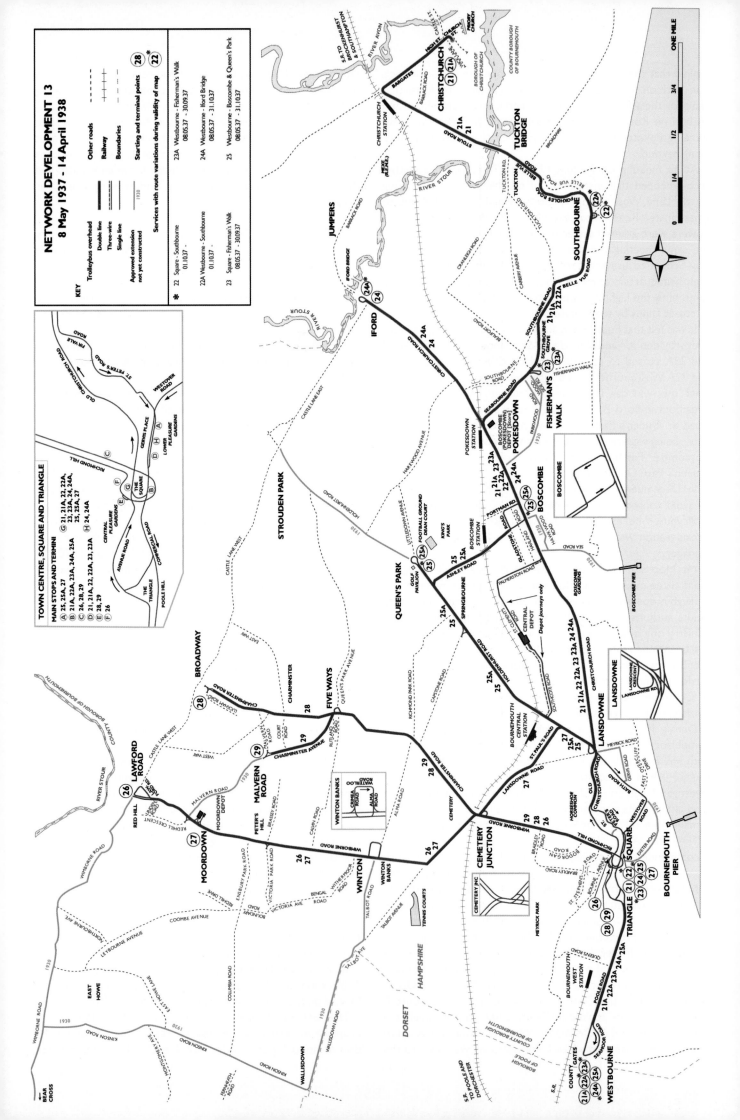

In May 1937 a Sunbeam MS2 negotiates the awkward bend at the Quadrant, where St. Peter's Road, Hinton Road and Gervis Place meet, with road resurfacing underway following the removal of the tram track. Beales department store with its glass panelling above the pavement outside received a direct hit in the air raid on the town centre on 23 May 1943 and the building subsequently collapsed being replaced by a new store in the 1950s.   **Bournemouth Daily Echo**

A trolleybus picks its way through the road works at Boscombe Arcade where rubber-covered operating strips for vehicle actuation of the traffic lights at the junction of Christchurch Road with Sea Road were being laid in the road surface. This system superseded the fixed time interval operation at a number of locations on the trolleybus network. **Bournemouth Daily Echo**

Road to provide a direct link from Southbourne and Fisherman's Walk to Central Station. Instead, he recommended that a link be introduced by extending every third vehicle on service 25 along Christchurch Road and Seabourne Road to Fisherman's Walk thus providing a vehicle every 15 minutes between Fisherman's Walk and Central Station. On 28 July 1938, a new service along Holdenhurst Road was introduced:

25B Westbourne - Bournemouth Square - Lansdowne - Central Station - Ashley Road, Boscombe - Pokesdown Station - Fisherman's Walk

In the same meeting a petition concerning the frequency of the Queen's Park trolleybus service was reviewed. The General Manager commented that a special summer season service between Bournemouth Square and Queen's Park Golf Pavilion could be operated from 25 July 1938 and, if a demand was proved, one vehicle an hour on the Ashley Road service could be diverted to Queen's Park during the winter months. The timetable for service 25A was therefore drawn up in this manner.

By July 1938 the first war scares began to circulate. Mr Morrison asked for instructions as to staff wishing to receive Air Raid Precautions (ARP) training.

The 20 September 1938 edition of *Passenger Transport Journal* reported that work on the new route along Castle Lane West, permitting the introduction of a circular trolleybus service Bournemouth Square-Cemetery Junction-Winton-Moordown-Charminster-Cemetery Junction-Square, was almost complete following delays caused by armament work which had made it difficult to obtain the necessary junction castings. Thus, from 19 October 1938, without any ceremony, Wimborne Road services to Lawford Road and Charminster Road services to the Broadway Hotel were linked along Castle Lane West, operating as two unidirectional circular services every 30 minutes:

26A Bournemouth Square - Cemetery Junction - Winton - Moordown - Castle Lane West - Broadway Hotel - Five Ways - Cemetery Junction - Bournemouth Square
Unidirectional service (clockwise) worked in conjunction with service 28A.

28A Bournemouth Square - Cemetery Junction - Five Ways - Broadway Hotel - Castle Lane West - Moordown - Winton - Cemetery Junction - Bournemouth Square
Unidirectional circular service (anti-clockwise) worked in conjunction with service 26A.

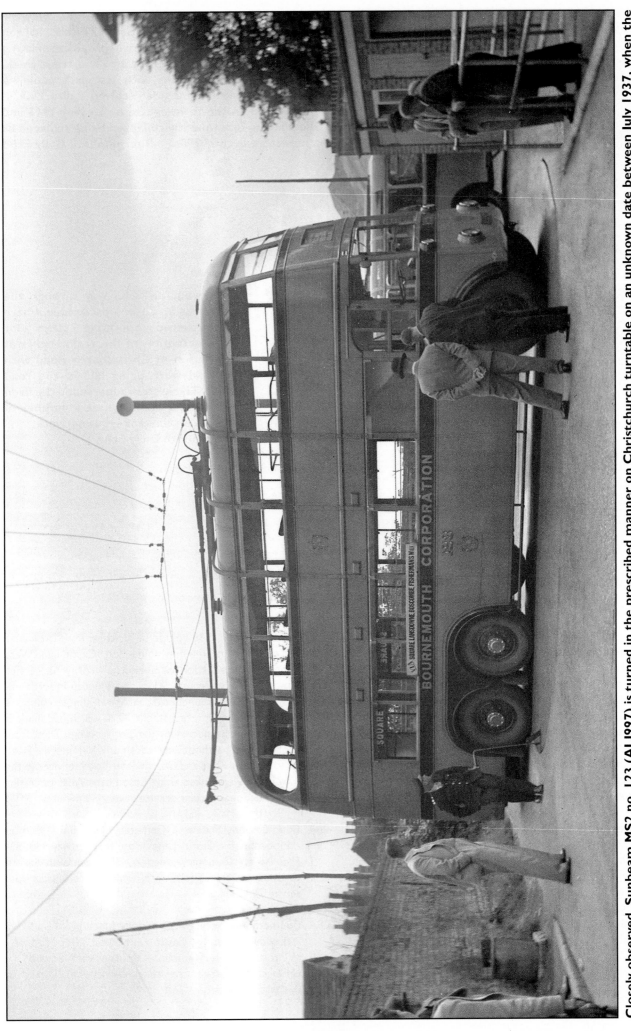

Closely observed, Sunbeam MS2 no. 123 (ALJ997) is turned in the prescribed manner on Christchurch turntable on an unknown date between July 1937, when the first single deck Bedford WTB motorbuses with "sun saloon" bodies (in the background) were delivered, and the outbreak of the Second World War. The presence of the motorbus and the groups of male observers suggest that this could have been a Transport Committee inspection. No. 123 was on a normal 21 service journey. Omnibus Society (C.F. Klapper)

Having completed the turn and placed the trolley heads on the westbound pair of overhead wires, the driver climbs back into the cab of no. 123 prior to driving it off the turntable to load passengers. The trolleybus will then follow the length of High Street, Christchurch, before continuing over Tuckton Bridge, through Southbourne and Bostombe to the Square.   Omnibus Society (C.F. Klapper)

On 15 April 1938, the first day of trolleybus services through Wallisdown, Park Royal bodied Sunbeam MS2 no. 102 (ALJ976) of 1935 turns out of Columbia Road turning circle at Wonderholme Parade across the east end of Acres Road into Kinson Road. No. 102 will then follow Kinson Road south to its junction with Wallisdown Road where it will turn east towards Winton and thence Wimborne Road to the Square. Note the short-lived pre-war side slip-boards introduced in 1935.   Malcolm Pearce (G.O.P. Pearce)

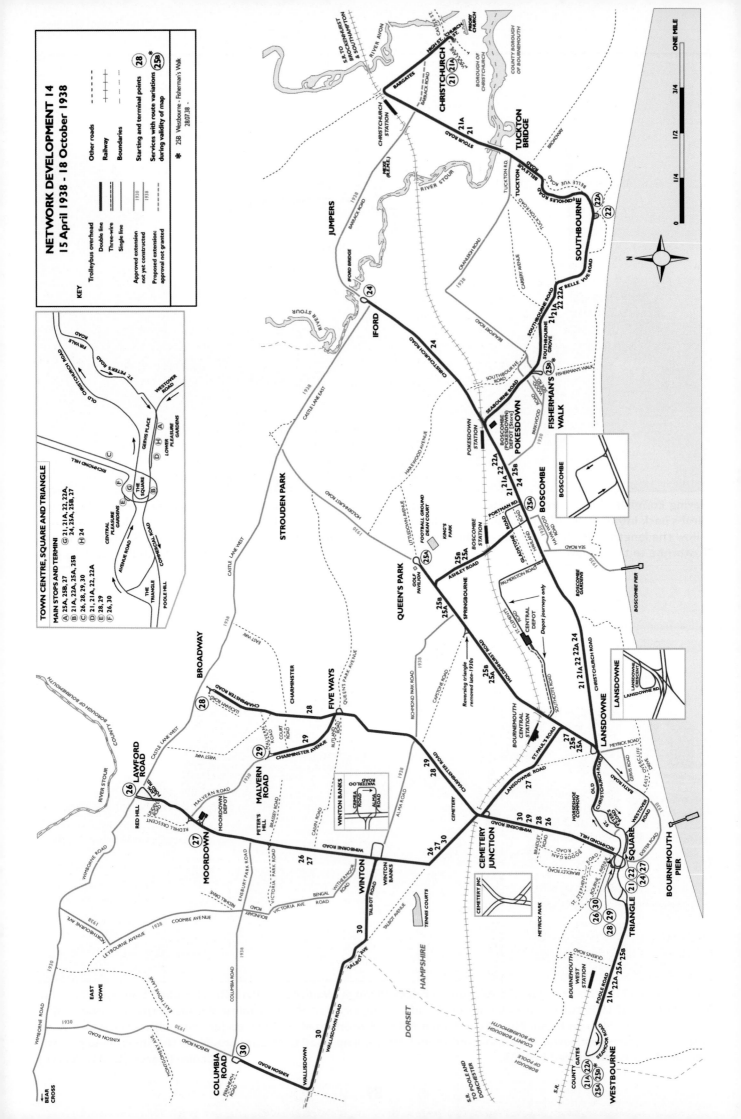

The extension reportedly cost about £2,000. The nominal terminus was West Way, the maximum fare to this point whether via Charminster Road or Wimborne Road being 3½d. On the same date the northern terminus of service 26 Bournemouth Square-Castle Lane West, Lawford Road, was cut back to Moordown, Wimborne Road, Redhill Crescent except at weekday morning peak hours, and even these ceased to run beyond Redhill Crescent on 1 October 1939.

As the further extension of trolleybus wiring along the remainder of Castle Lane, providing a link with the Christchurch Road line at Iford, was then not expected for two years, it was proposed to improve the motorbus service to develop the traffic. The length of Castle Lane had been served by service 14, Moordown to Iford (with an extension to Tuckton between 1 April 1935 and 30 September 1936), every two hours since 12 October 1931, but this basic frequency remained unchanged, apart from a few extra journeys towards the end of the Second World War, until the introduction of trolleybuses on 15 October 1951.

The Lighting Committee was informed on 26 November 1938 that the Transport Committee was prepared to erect traction poles for the street lighting of certain portions of Castle Lane West on condition that the Lighting Committee bear the loan charges until the poles are used for transport purposes. It is understood that some poles were actually planted before war broke out.

In mid-October 1938 a letter in the *Bournemouth Daily Echo* remarked upon the start of work to extend trolleybuses along Ensbury Park Road and made reference to the Town Hall

enquiry at which a number of local residents had objected, due to the road being unsuitable and too narrow. The Roads Committee had pointed out that "the camber of the road could be reduced to give additional width". Road work was now in progress but the correspondent considered that this means of widening the road was farcical as several residents had been approached for consent to plant traction poles in their front garden. This, he felt, gave every justification for the objections.

On 25 November 1938 the General Manager was authorised to advertise for tenders for cables for the trolleybus service along Ensbury Park Road and Moordown Depot roof repairs. Eight tenders for cables were received and the lowest, that of Messrs W.T. Glover, Ltd. at £2,742 18s 5d, was accepted.

By now many employees were applying for releases to attend special courses of Territorial Army training.

In April 1939, the MoT advised that it was unable to inspect the Ensbury Park Road trolleybus route at that time, but had no objection to it being brought into use prior to an inspection, subject to compliance with any requirements that may subsequently be made. Trolleybus services therefore started on 8 April 1939, when a circular operation with service 30 was introduced:

30   Bournemouth Square - Cemetery Junction - Winton - Wallisdown - Columbia Road - Ensbury Park - Winton - Cemetery Junction - Bournemouth Square
Unidirectional circular service (clockwise) worked in conjunction with service 30A

Now decorated for the Royal Counties Show, decorated and illuminated trolleybus no. 152 is seen outside Wonderholme Parade, the terminus of service 30 at the junction of Kinson Road with Columbia Road. Note the new tourist advertising boards along the side of the roof. Standing between the Inspector (on the left) and the Conductor, is Driver Biddlecombe.

Malcolm Pearce (G.O.P. Pearce)

30A Bournemouth Square - Cemetery Junction - Winton - Ensbury Park - Columbia Road - Wallisdown - Winton - Cemetery Junction - Bournemouth Square
Unidirectional circular service (anti-clockwise) worked in conjunction with service 30

Mr Herbert Vickers, Chief Assistant and Electrical Engineer, retired on 30 April 1939, after 27½ years' service. He had arrived in Bournemouth shortly after conduit tramway operation ceased, having started his career in Wolverhampton, where he had worked with the Lorain surface contact system of power collection. In Bournemouth he had been responsible for the post-First World War re-equipment programme, the installation of additional generating plant at Southcote Road, and, latterly, the tram to trolleybus conversion and trolleybus route extensions.

Although the 1939 summer timetable map showed a service 24 running as far as Stour Road, Christchurch, construction work had not commenced before the outbreak, in September 1939, of the Second World War which deferred the extension until 1943. All other development of the trolleybus system, excluding the addition of emergency terminal points, ceased until the war was over. Meanwhile tram track was still being removed in Wimborne Road.

Mr Morrison presented his Annual Report for 1938 to the Transport Committee meeting held on 23 June 1939:
"Extensions to trolleybus system
- *Talbot Road, Wallisdown and Kinson Road, Service 30, 1.94 miles, construction of route was almost completed in the previous year. Put into service 15 April 1938.*
- *Circular Services 26A and 28A, 0.64 miles, Castle Lane from Charminster Road to Wimborne Road. Constructed and put into service 19 October 1938.*

- *Ensbury Park and Columbia Roads, Circular Services 30 and 30A, 1.24 miles. This route was constructed and partially completed by 31 March 1939.*

"Trolleybus route mileage now totals 33.35 miles.

"Two of the extensions referred to, which have been carried out during the year, have enabled the Department to operate the first two circular services which the Transport Committee had as their objective when trolleybus services were inaugurated in 1934.
"Fleet
The trolleybuses are now five years old but are in sound mechanical condition and compare favourably in appearance with more modern types now available. 49 trolleybuses have been repainted and 18 miles of trolley wire renewed during the year. A complete changeover from wheel collector to slipper shoe collector had taken place at a high initial cost but it has proved a sound change. The irritating hissing noise of the wheel has been eliminated, while wear on the overhead line and fittings has been considerably reduced. The only cause for anxiety will be operation in severe damp frost but provision has been made for a special type of shoe to be fitted to remove ice from the overhead line. Overhead equipment of better design is now available and when renewals are carried out, every opportunity is taken to use the most modern types of fittings, while as far as possible we are replacing the heavy and perhaps objectionable-looking bracket arms by span wire construction.
"Generating Station
Major repairs have been necessary to the steam drums and superheaters of the Babcock and Wilcox water-tube boilers, while overhaul and certain replacements have been executed on the two turbines. It will be necessary to carry out extensive repairs to both the artesian well and the chimney stack".

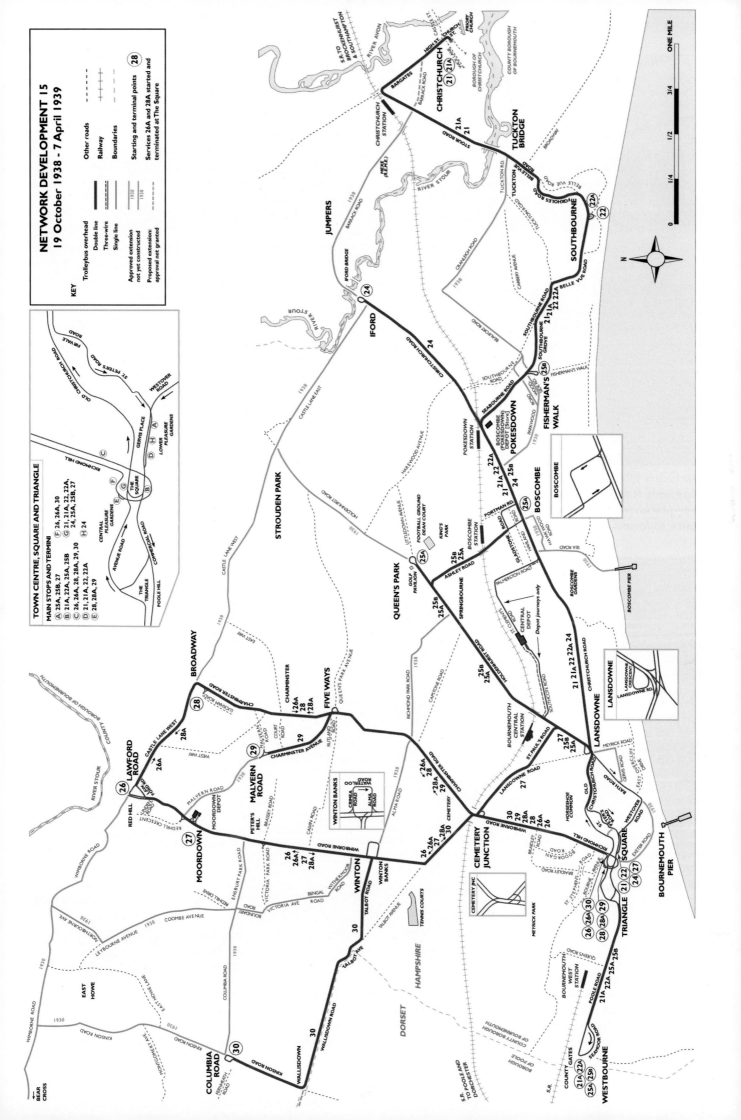

Sunbeam MS2 no. 74 (AEL402) ascends Old Christchurch Road past the Guinea Dress Shop and the rebuilt Plummer Roddis department store on a service 27 journey to Moordown via the Lansdowne. The notice in the rear platform window is indistinct but is potentially a temporary solution for the auxiliary indicator showing the route followed westbound between the Lansdowne and the Square or the name of an event served by the 27.
D.A.P. Janes collection

The driver of no.91 (ALJ965) makes his way to the rear of the trolleybus to assist in the turning procedure on the Christchurch timetable prior to returning to Westbourne as a 21A on 29 May 1939. The last summer holiday season before the tribulations of war was approaching and the paper exhortation in the nearside window of the driver's cab for travel to and from the Christchurch Fire Brigade Display was appropriate in more ways than one. Note that by now, the roof of no. 91 is painted primrose yellow.
Malcolm Pearce (G.O.P. Pearce)

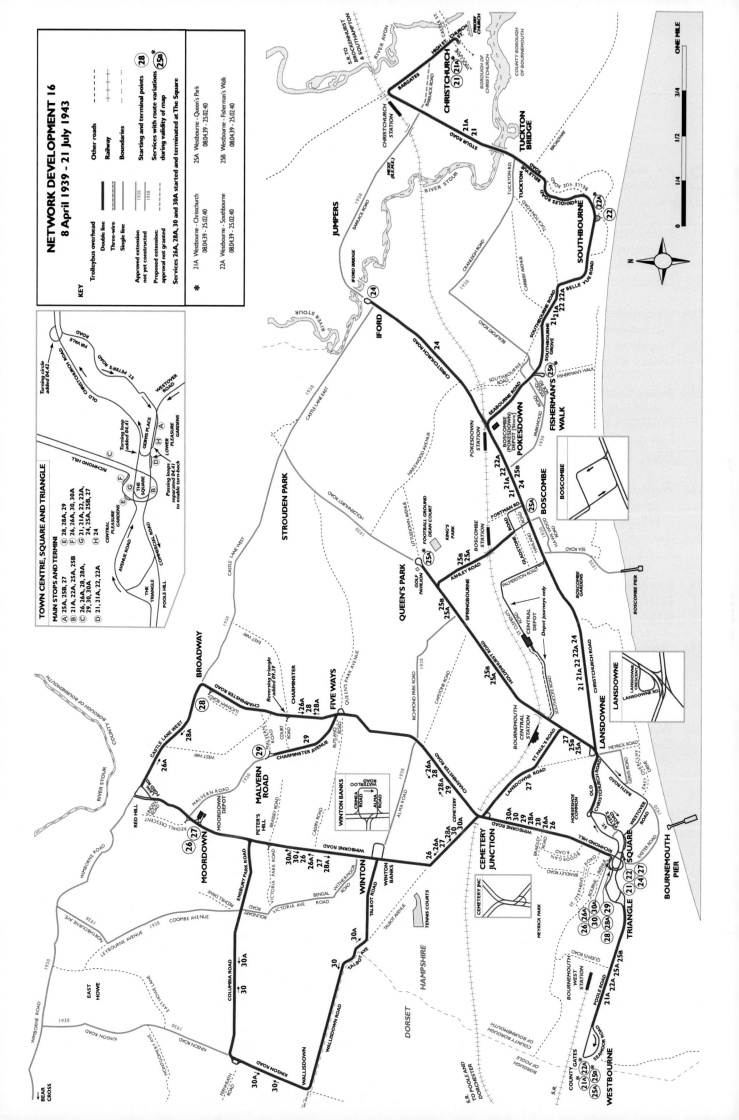

NETWORK DEVELOPMENT 16
8 April 1939 - 21 July 1943

KEY

Trolleybus overhead
Double line
Three-wire
Single line

Other roads
Railway
Boundaries

1930
1938

Approved extension
not yet constructed

Proposed extension
approval not granted

Starting and terminal points   28

Services with route variations
during validity of map   25B

*   21A Westbourne - Christchurch   25A Westbourne - Queen's Park
         08.04.39 - 25.02.40   08.04.39 - 25.02.40

     22A Westbourne - Southbourne   25B Westbourne - Fisherman's Walk
         08.04.39 - 25.02.40   08.04.39 - 25.02.40

Services 26A, 28A, 30 and 30A started and terminated at The Square

TOWN CENTRE, SQUARE AND TRIANGLE

MAIN STOPS AND TERMINI

A   25A, 25B, 27   E   28, 28A, 29
B   21A, 22A, 25A, 25B   F   26, 26A, 30, 30A
C   26, 26A, 28, 28A,   G   21, 21A, 22, 22A,
     29, 30, 30A   24, 25A, 25B, 27
D   21, 21A, 22, 22A   H   24

ONE MILE

CHAPTER FIVE

THE SECOND WORLD WAR

By the time the Second World War was declared on 3 September 1939 the following trolleybus services were in operation:

21 Bournemouth Square, Gervis Place - Lansdowne - Boscombe Gardens - Boscombe - Pokesdown - Fisherman's Walk - Southbourne - Tuckton Bridge - Christchurch, Church Street

21A Westbourne, Seamoor Road - Bournemouth Square - Lansdowne - Boscombe Gardens - Boscombe - Pokesdown - Fisherman's Walk - Southbourne - Tuckton Bridge - Christchurch, Church Street

22 Bournemouth Square, Gervis Place - Lansdowne - Boscombe Gardens - Boscombe - Pokesdown - Fisherman's Walk - Southbourne Cross Roads (junction with St Catherine's Road and Southbourne Overcliff Drive)

22A Westbourne, Seamoor Road - Bournemouth Square - Lansdowne - Boscombe Gardens - Boscombe - Pokesdown - Fisherman's Walk - Southbourne - Southbourne Crossroads (junction with St Catherine's Road and Southbourne Overcliff Drive)

24 Bournemouth Square, Gervis Place - Lansdowne - Boscombe Gardens - Boscombe - Pokesdown - Iford Bridge

25A Westbourne - Bournemouth Square - Lansdowne - Central Station - Holdenhurst Road - Springbourne - Ashley Road - Portman Road, Boscombe or Queen's Park Golf Pavilion, Holdenhurst Road

25B Westbourne - Bournemouth Square - Lansdowne - Central Station - Springbourne - Ashley Road, Boscombe - Pokesdown - Fisherman's Walk, Wentworth Avenue

26 Bournemouth Square - Richmond Hill - Cemetery Junction - Wimborne Road - Winton - Moordown Wimborne Road, Redhill Crescent (Castle Lane West, Lawford Road during weekday morning peak hours)

26A Bournemouth Square - Cemetery Junction - Winton - Moordown - Castle Lane West - Broadway Hotel - Five Ways - Cemetery Junction - Bournemouth Square
Unidirectional circular service (clockwise) worked in conjunction with service 28A.

27 Bournemouth Square, Gervis Place - Lansdowne - Central Station - St Paul's Road - Cemetery Junction - Wimborne Road - Winton - Moordown, Wimborne Road, Redhill Crescent

28 Bournemouth Square - Richmond Hill - Cemetery Junction - Charminster Road - Five Ways - Broadway Hotel, Luckham Road

28A Bournemouth Square - Cemetery Junction - Five Ways - Broadway Hotel - Castle Lane West - Moordown - Winton - Cemetery Junction - Bournemouth Square
Unidirectional circular service (anti-clockwise) worked in conjunction with service 26A.

29 Bournemouth Square - Richmond Hill - Cemetery Junction - Five Ways - Malvern Road, junction with Charminster Avenue

30 Bournemouth Square - Richmond Hill - Cemetery Junction - Winton - Wallisdown - Columbia Road - Winton - Cemetery Junction - Richmond Hill - Bournemouth Square
Unidirectional circular service (clockwise) worked in conjunction with service 30A

30A Bournemouth Square - Cemetery Junction - Winton - Ensbury Park - Columbia Road - Wallisdown - Winton - Cemetery Junction - Bournemouth Square
Unidirectional circular service (anti-clockwise) worked in conjunction with service 30

The motorbus fleet soon became involved in moving evacuees and troops about the area, whilst the streets were generally quiet with people greatly limiting their movements. Out of the 78 motorbuses in the BCT fleet, six were allocated to the fire brigade and six to the ARP with a further 21 requisitioned by the MoT in July 1940. Initially, trains and long-distance coaches continued to run normally. During 1938 a Government Evacuation Scheme had been developed which divided the country into zones, classified as "evacuation", "neutral", or "reception", Bournemouth being considered to be sufficiently safe for use as a reception zone. Evacuation from the perceived danger areas, in principle major urban centres and places of military significance, began on 1 September 1939. Throughout the country, some three million people, primarily children, young and expectant mothers, and the disabled were evacuated. Bournemouth initially agreed to take 20,000 people, primarily from London, Portsmouth and Southampton, half being scheduled to arrive on 1 September 1939, with Christchurch taking a further 2,500. However, only 2,700 arrived in Bournemouth on 2 September 1939.

ARP Wardens were called-up for duty and the construction of trenches and air raid shelters expedited. Public shelters were already in place in the vicinity of the Square (with a capacity of 2,400 people), Charminster and Winton (1,200), Boscombe (700), Southbourne (600), Westbourne (600), West Station area (200), and Poole Hill (180). In the meantime it was considered that the safest place was the sea front although coastal defence work had been underway since July 1939.

From 3 September 1939 all motorbus, whether BCT or H&D, and trolleybus services ceased at lighting-up time (then

As the last peacetime summer came to an end, a schoolgirl admires no. 132 (BEL817) as it drives off the turntable to the passenger loading point at Christchurch. Note the bamboo trolley boom retrieval pole hanging from the insulated terminal span wire, rather than from the hook provided. **Omnibus Society (E.G.P. Masterman)**

one hour after sunset), which, of course, was slightly earlier each evening, e.g. 8.40pm on 4 September 1939, due to the difficulties in maintaining services with many staff having been called-up for military service and concerns about vehicles complying with "black-out" regulations. Until then the last departures from Bournemouth Square and other main termini had been at 11.30pm. There were also many fewer potential passengers on the streets in the evenings. Mr Morrison stated *"This is by no means an alarmist action. We are trying to set an example to the public by keeping off the roads after dark. It really is not safe, and there will be no demand for services. Entertainment houses are closed and people have been advised to keep indoors. We feel that we shall be serving the interests of everybody best by keeping off the roads and leaving them clear for those who have to use them in the event of an emergency. It is probable that the matter will be reviewed in the light of experience at the end of the week".* Appropriate notices were posted in the trolleybuses.

The imposition of "black-out" restrictions on 1 September 1939 brought severe lighting restrictions; in addition to having masked headlamps, all saloon windows were painted with blue lacquer and only one internal light was retained in each saloon. Virtually all street lighting was switched off until the "dim-out" was introduced in 1944, traffic lights were fitted with masked lenses with shielding above or switched off in the hours of darkness, and white paint was applied liberally to kerbstones, the base of traction poles and any exposed corners or edges. The number of accidents in the hours of darkness soared. Would-be passengers complained that with darkened indicator displays at night it was impossible to see where buses were going to and suggested that conductors shout out the destination.

As far as BCT was concerned, from October 1940 everything on motorbuses and trolleybuses above the upper deck waistband vehicle roof was painted a matt chocolate brown

colour as a camouflage measure (although this does not seem to have applied to single-deck motorbuses). Front and rear portions of the mudguards, the base of the offside rear corner panel and the lifeguard rails were painted white. From 1943, some motorbuses operated in grey undercoat or in brown with maroon bands, but all trolleybuses retained the reduced primrose livery. The legend "Bournemouth Corporation" along the maroon band below the lower deck saloon windows was also gradually removed from about 1941 as a security precaution, although some of the vehicles that remained in Bournemouth retained it for several years whilst those loaned to other undertakings seem to have deliberately displayed the Bournemouth legend throughout, it is rumoured to confuse any invaders. Vehicle windows were masked, initially by painting with blue lacquer or by pasting brown paper on to each pane. To avoid mass vehicle damage or destruction in air raids, some of the fleet were left parked overnight in quiet side roads such as St. Clement's Road and Southcote Road, rather than in the depot buildings.

Upon the declaration of war, all cinemas, theatres and other places of entertainment were closed. No bands performed on the bandstands, the circus at the Winter Gardens was cancelled and the Concert Party on Boscombe Pier disbanded. The train service to and from London was reduced from 14 to six trains per day from 11 September 1939.

Evening entertainments recommenced after about a week and on 11 September 1939 the normal timetable was reintroduced until 8pm with half-hourly services thereafter until 10pm, initially maintained by single-deck motorbuses with suitably masked lighting. Additional vehicles were available for the closure of cinemas and theatres at 10pm. From 18 September 1939 trolleybuses appeared on the half-hourly skeleton service (not least to conserve fuel supplies) and last services were again

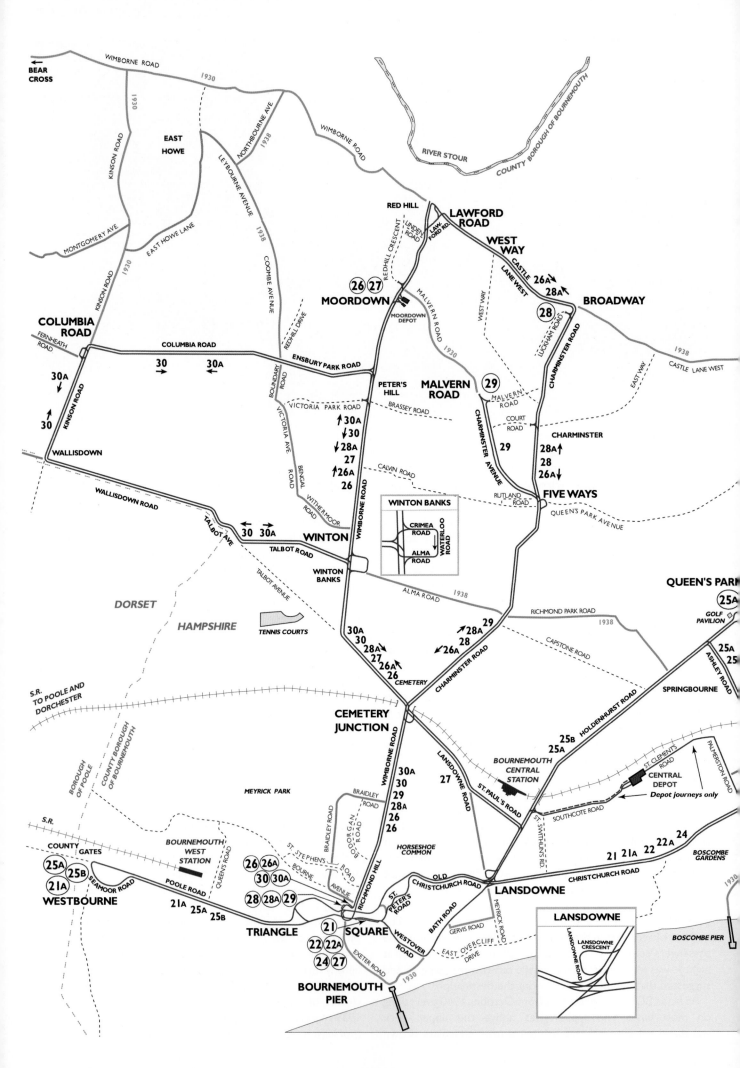

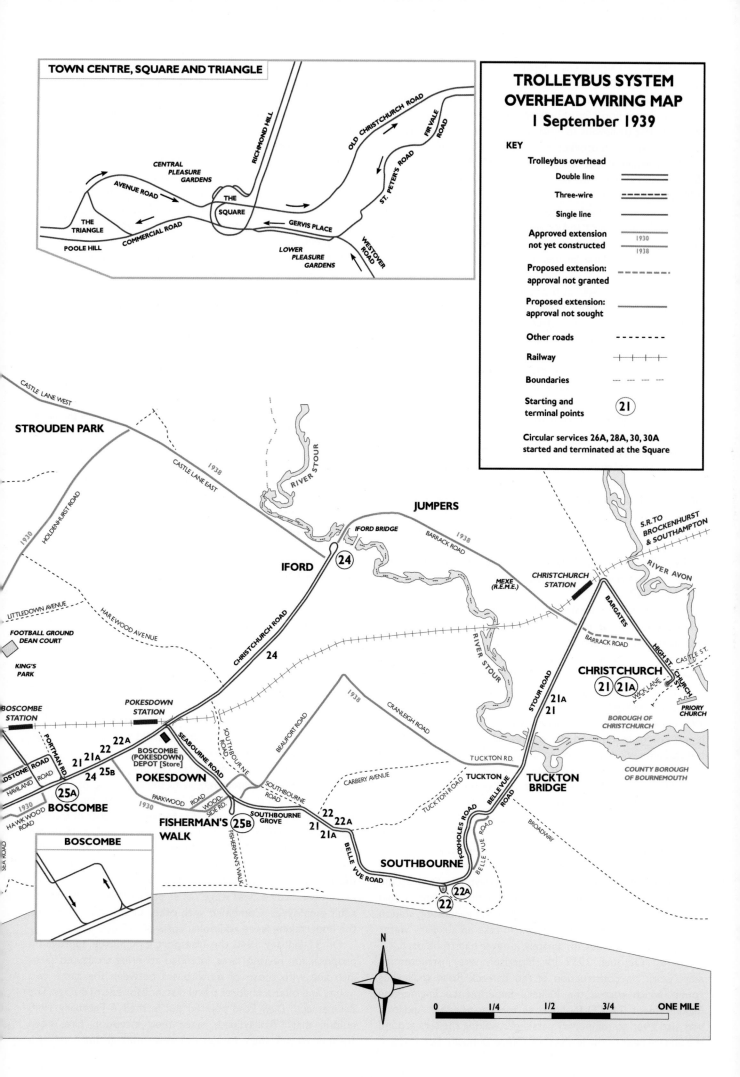

TOWN CENTRE, SQUARE AND TRIANGLE

TROLLEYBUS SYSTEM
OVERHEAD WIRING MAP
1 September 1939

KEY

Trolleybus overhead

Double line

Three-wire

Single line

Approved extension
not yet constructed

1930

1938

Proposed extension:
approval not granted

Proposed extension:
approval not sought

Other roads

Railway

Boundaries

Starting and
terminal points

21

Circular services 26A, 28A, 30, 30A
started and terminated at the Square

extended to 10.30pm. Last departures from Bournemouth Square were at 10.30 for Castle Lane West, Lawford Road via both the Lansdowne and via Richmond Hill; Broadway Hotel, Luckham Road; Iford; Southbourne and Wallisdown via Talbot Road. The last trolleybus to Christchurch was at 9.45pm (there being a service 1 motorbus to Purewell via Christchurch at 10.30); to Ashley Road, Boscombe at 10.40pm, Westbourne at 10.20pm, and Wallisdown via Ensbury Park Road at 10pm.

Mr Morrison commented: *"Should it be decided eventually to make the lighting restrictions less stringent, the question of a later and more frequent night service would be reconsidered"*. He paid tribute to the crews. Modifications to the darkening of windows were carried out, blue lacquer being the preferred solution. One window in each bus would be left unlacquered allowing in more natural light as well as the rear platform window to assist drivers reversing but both would be fitted with blinds. In order to avoid any scratching of the lacquer when the windows were opened and shut it was applied to the inside of the bottom pane and on the outside of the top pane. A notice warned passengers "After sunset the drop windows and blinds must not be adjusted or interfered with". However, within a few days it was decided to leave two windows on the nearside and one on the offside in each saloon without lacquer but fitted with blinds.

Increasingly people went out again in the evenings and by Saturday 16 September 1939, 24 trolleybuses were running on late evening services. This was also the date that petrol rationing came into force. From 1 October 1939 motorbus services were reduced and the morning peak hour extension of trolleybus service 26 was cut back from Lawford Road to Moordown, Redhill Crescent.

The official finishing time for buses leaving Bournemouth Square on Sundays was brought forward to 10.15pm from 28 October 1939.

By now, two horizontal white bands, one at eye level and the other about 1ft from the ground, had been painted around some traction poles and trees on the pavement to aid pedestrians and vehicles in the "black-out". A third band was added later. White lines appeared across the road at pedestrian crossings, which until then had only been marked by square metal studs in the road surface (black and white "zebra" stripes first appeared in 1951). The blue lacquer on saloon windows proved unpopular; it was gradually removed and window blinds were fitted to all buses. Some windows were covered with netting glued to the pane to reduce the risk of flying glass during air-raids. By the end of October 1939, a uniform national system of interior and exterior lighting was recommended to comply with "black-out" regulations.

The Southcote Road generating station plant had been rebuilt after the General Strike to burn either coal or oil and there were still oil stocks remaining. It generated about 80% of the traction power required for the trolleybuses at this time and it was felt that in an emergency the entire network could be supplied. In 1940 the artesian well at the generating station was connected to the town's mains in case an auxiliary water supply was needed but, fortunately, it never had to be used.

On 20 October 1939 Mr Morrison was instructed to start work on construction of the Barrack Road trolleybus route (which passed the Military Experimental Engineering Establishment (MEXE) facilities) as soon as possible. Approval was also given to temporary passenger waiting shelters around the Square next to the Inspectors' Office, opposite Burtons and

Bobby's premises, and at the approach to the Central Gardens. The bus shelter in the middle of the Square was remodelled in November 1939 to include a passenger waiting room and an enlarged canteen for crews, all without altering the appearance of the building.

Victor Mitchell, a trolleybus driver, appealed in a letter published in the *Bournemouth Daily Echo* on 21 October 1939: *"Please allow me space in your ever popular journal so that I may appeal to the users of electric torches at night to spare a moment's thought and consideration to the drivers of public service transport. In so doing they will be rendering yeoman service to a cause that I have greatly at heart, i.e. 'Safety First'.*

"It has become a common thing along our roads, as soon as a driver endeavours in the inky blackness of nights to draw his vehicle towards the kerb, to have maybe half a dozen torches flashed upwards at him. But I am sure people would not do so if they only knew the danger.

As the driver of a trolleybus, I claim to speak with experience. The lights which are flashed into my cabin after dark are in the main many times brighter than I am allowed to get a huge vehicle safely through our town. When they start flashing on and off, one loses at once guidance while endeavouring to make the kerb. I do not doubt for one moment that if people could sit for an hour beside the driver, they would alight full of admiration for the way he has driven. They would realise the strain involved during 'black-out' driving, a strain such as has never been experienced before.

"I therefore, on behalf of all who, to earn their daily bread, have to drive public transport through the hours of darkness, appeal to the great army of torch users, to keep their rays of light directed to the pavement of roadway."

The Pavilion and cinemas had reopened after a fortnight, and, by the end of November 1939, audiences were up to pre-war levels. Last buses from the main termini were extended to 11pm on 13 November 1939. Four large air raid shelters had been constructed in the gardens opposite the Palace Court Hotel just to the east of the Pavilion (they still exist under the rhododendrons, and are used to store Parks Department equipment).

Drivers of trolleybuses coming out of service from Boscombe to the Central Depot, Southcote Road were instructed to return via Portman Road, Ashley Road, Holdenhurst Road and Central Station rather than via Palmerston Road with effect from 7 December 1939, probably to avoid having to turn them in the depot yard in the "black-out".

Wartime inflation rapidly began. The price of coal increased by 6d per ton retrospectively from the beginning of October 1939 with a further increase of 1s 4d from 3 November 1939 which together were estimated to increase the cost of traction current generation by £700 pa. Also in November 1939 the Municipal Passenger Transport Association (MPTA) advised that the NJIC had received an application for increased wages from the Transport and General Workers' Union (TGWU). From 7 December 1939 a "war wage" of 4s per week was awarded to adult employees. Combined with other unavoidable increases, the undertaking faced additional costs of £25,000 pa.

On 31 January 1940 the Transport Committee approved a proposal for revised fares intended to bring trolleybus fares into line with those of motorbuses between the same two points and offer a uniform travel distance for each 1d stage. The *Bournemouth Daily Echo* pointed out in their 6 February 1940 edition that: "Trolleybuses, since their inception, have been cheaper to ride than the petrol buses, although they are, by a consensus of opinion more comfortable than the petrol buses". It was planned to introduce the revised fares on 1 March 1940 but consent from the MoT and the SETC was still outstanding at that date. Indeed, there is no evidence that the increases or the changes to return fares were ever implemented.

In the same meeting, the Transport Committee recorded its appreciation of the traffic staff's effort in "black-out" conditions. Noting that from 1 February 1940 a "black-out" speed limit of 20mph in built-up areas applied to all vehicles, it was felt that the prevailing timetables could accommodate this reduced speed. From 1 April 1940 the undertaking's headquarters moved from 6 Wootton Gardens, off Old Christchurch Road, to 99 Southcote Road, next to the generating station and Central Depot complex. The move was prompted by the increasingly dilapidated state of the Wootton Gardens property, the sagging ceilings of which were already supported by disused tram rails. The new headquarters was created by knocking two semi-detached houses built for senior employees at the generating station and already owned by the Department into one.

All piers around the British coastline were rendered unusable to any potential seaborne invader and explosives were used to blow gaps in both Boscombe and Bournemouth Piers whilst much of the decking on what remained was removed. Beaches became prohibited areas, mines were laid and various other defences were installed. Holiday-making virtually ceased and Bournemouth, as a seaside resort, suffered a major decline in the volume of passenger traffic, particularly in summer. Accordingly,

trolleybus services 21A, 22A and 25B ceased operation on 24 February 1940. On the other hand, evacuees moved into the area.

The initial "phoney war" period had developed into something more serious in the late spring of 1940 with the German invasion of the Low Countries, then the ignominy of the evacuation of the British Expeditionary Force from Dunkirk as France, too, fell under German occupation. Fearing an imminent invasion, a schedule of Defence Areas, access to which was limited to residents and those with a genuine need, was hurriedly prepared; from 11 July 1940 a coastal strip roughly 20 miles deep, stretching along the South Coast of England from Bexhill to Portland, was declared such an area. Holiday and pleasure trips to Bournemouth came to an end, and foreign residents were required to leave.

In June 1940, the Military Authorities expressed their dissatisfaction with the dispersion of the fleet at night and suggested that it be housed under cover in the depots. Mr Morrison reported that Boscombe (Pokesdown) Depot could no longer be used for this purpose due to the air raid shelter in the building. The ARP Committee was asked to find or construct an alternative shelter, so that the depot could be used to house vehicles, although this was not done until later in the year. The depot could be used again for storage purposes by April 1941.

The first enemy air raid on Bournemouth took place just after midnight on 3 July 1940: properties were damaged and a house destroyed in Southbourne, but without casualties. The

No. 171 (BRU22) heads a line of seven trolleybuses parked along the north side of St. Clement's Road as part of the wartime effort to disperse the fleet away from the depot building and thus avoid catastrophic loss in the case of a direct hit in a bombing raid. In the background, towards the left, can be seen the carshed of Central Depot, Southcote Road, and beyond that the chimney and cooling towers of the generating station.

David Chalk collection

quip "Two to the bomb hole" began to be heard on trolleybuses. Later, in July 1940, BCT announced that if an air raid warning should sound in the evening and the "All Clear" not be given until after public transport would normally have ceased, buses would wait until after the "All Clear" so that they could take passengers home whatever the time. Drivers were instructed to stop their vehicles when the "Alert" sounded, and their conductors were to direct passengers to the nearest air-raid shelters. Towards the end of August 1940, revised regulations from the Ministry of Home Security permitted vehicular traffic to circulate after an air raid warning (the so-called "Alert") had sounded. Traffic was required to halt if an air raid was actually in progress in the vicinity whilst trolleybuses were to proceed to the nearest public air raid shelter on their route with sufficient accommodation for their passengers and park nearby. After the "All Clear", trolleybuses had to wait for a reasonable time for the passengers to re-board before continuing their journey.

A BCT Home Guard detachment, a platoon of the 7th Battalion Hampshire Home Guard, was raised, their principal use being to guard the Southcote Road generating station. Office and maintenance staff worked overtime to crew essential services but the trolleybus fleet was not fully employed. At the end of July 1940 over a dozen trolleybuses, including three out of service with accident damage, were placed in store. A number of others were also withdrawn at the end of September 1940

for overhaul, but were replaced by some of the others taken out of service in July.

Elsewhere in the UK, transport undertakings in industrial towns were experiencing major growths in traffic demand and in summer 1940 Mr Morrison received enquiries about the possibility of hiring some of the stored trolleybuses. The Bournemouth Transport Committee agreed to release twelve to Wolverhampton whilst on 23 August 1940 it agreed to loan a further 18 trolleybuses if required. In October 1940, twelve recently overhauled Sunbeam MS2s (76, 84, 105, 107, 129, 130, 131, 132, 137, 156, 161 and 168) were loaned to Wolverhampton Corporation which operated a fleet of virtually identical (but for the front staircase and exit) Park Royal-bodied MS2s dating from 1935-6. Between 4 September 1940 and 24 October 1940, each of the twelve vehicles was towed from Bournemouth to Wolverhampton by the Sunbeam company, which had its factory in the town. Some equipment, such as indicator blinds, run-back brake apparatus and trolley heads (not least as Wolverhampton still used wheel collectors), was removed prior to departure. The hire fee was £20 per month for each trolleybus and 22 Bournemouth drivers and conductors were temporarily transferred to crew them. The men received their normal wages plus an allowance of 3s 6d per night to cover their lodging expenses; however, a lack of suitable accommodation coupled with the reluctance of the

No. 132 (BEL817) returned to its place of birth on 27 September 1940 and was to remain with the hard-pressed Wolverhampton system almost 8 years. Here, the 22 Bournemouth crew members also transferred are being addressed by Chief Inspector Reed of Wolverhampton Corporation Transport Department outside the "Municipal Tramways Car Depot" in Cleveland Road. It will be noticed that no. 132 is in full pre-war livery, complete with fleet name, but for the white paint on the mudguards and lifeguard rail as an aid to visibility in the "black-out". Would a potential foreign invader having reached Wolverhampton wonder if he had inadvertently arrived in Bournemouth? **Transport World**

Ministry of Labour and National Service (MoL) to cover this lodging allowance saw a number of the crews subsequently return to Bournemouth.

Five Bournemouth trolleybuses remained in Wolverhampton until 1946 and the remainder until 1948. As part of the wartime salvage drive, Wolverhampton Corporation was also loaned a number of surplus traction poles (to be replaced on a like for like basis at the end of hostilities) and purchased some items of tramway overhead equipment deemed surplus to Bournemouth's needs.

By April 1941 more than a dozen surplus trolleybuses were placed in store at Boscombe (Pokesdown) Depot although there was still an air raid shelter in the building. The vehicles themselves were exchanged periodically with others as these became due for overhaul.

Bournemouth did have some strategic value during the war. Early in 1940 it became a principal training area for RAF recruits, whilst a number of army regiments also came to the town. Progressively, an assortment of government ministries and War Department offices moved to Bournemouth, whilst leave centres, military hospitals and munitions factories were scattered about the town. A considerable number of hotels were requisitioned, for example the Palace Court Hotel was used as accommodation for American troops, and the Royal Bath Hotel was used variously as a Canadian billet and WAAF Officers' Mess, whilst the Linden Hall was used by the Ministry of Agriculture.

From Monday 23 September 1940, on the MPTA's recommendation, vehicles continued to operate during the period of air raid warnings until the time of the last bus. Last buses were retimed to leave Bournemouth Square at 10.30pm until 27 October 1940. The 18 October 1940 Transport Committee Meeting recommended that last buses from the main termini be cut back once again, to 10.15pm, from 28 October 1940, with the exception of Saturdays when the last bus from the Square remained at 10.30pm. In that year British Summer Time (GMT +1 hour) continued throughout the year and the clocks were not put back by an hour at the end of the summer, indeed this situation continued throughout the war and clocks continued to be advanced by a further one hour each spring (British Double Summer Time) and put back by an hour each autumn until July 1945. The clocks were brought back in line with GMT at the end of summer in 1945.

At 3.30am on 16 November 1940, the Luftwaffe paid Bournemouth another visit. Six parachute mines were dropped over Bournemouth, killing 53 people and damaging 2,321 properties.

In consultation with the Regional Transport Commissioner (RTC), the wartime equivalent of the SETC but with considerably more powers, an agreement to loan the further 18 surplus trolleybuses, as previously approved, to London Transport was negotiated in November 1940. Accordingly in December 1940, Sunbeam MS2s 72-75, 77-83, 85-87, 89, 117, 123 and 145 were despatched for service in the east of London where they were based at Ilford Depot, operating exclusively on services 691 (Barking-Barkingside) and 693 (Barking-Chadwell Heath). These were the only Sunbeam trolleybuses to have operated in London and some of them, having suffered war damage, were repaired in London Transport's Charlton Works. London released them between November 1941 and September 1942. Some returned to Bournemouth and others passed on to Newcastle upon Tyne, from where they were subsequently passed to either Llanelly & District Traction Co. Ltd. or South Shields Corporation Transport. Some then went on to Walsall

Bournemouth Sunbeam MS2 72 (AEL400) is seen in Horns Road, just south of the junction with Birkbeck Road, whilst on loan to London Transport on its way to Barking Broadway February 1941.

Stephen Lockwood collection

Corporation. All 18 vehicles returned to Bournemouth by August 1945. These loans appear to have been coordinated by the MoT/MoWT at a hire charge of £25 per vehicle per month. Further details can be found in Appendix C.

An inexorable rise in the cost of oil-based fuels and tyres, both dependent on increasingly uncertain imports from abroad, as well as coal, continued.

The General Manager reported to the 2 December 1940 Transport Committee meeting that it was impossible to meet traffic demands with the number of staff available. He was therefore given permission to employ conductresses and locate a supplier of female uniforms. Mr Morrison added that the Department was trying to put additional services into operation where required. In both 1940 and 1941 there was a revision of bus stops and several request stops became compulsory, whilst others were abolished as a fuel and tyre economy. The first conductresses started work on 25 January 1941, some being trained later as trolleybus drivers, with the first of these taking up their duties in April 1942.

Early in 1941 the undertaking's Transport Engineer, Mr W. Baxendale, gave notice of his appointment as Deputy General Manager with Wallasey Transport. The vacant position was immediately advertised and seven applicants were invited for interview, including Mr F.J. Cunuder of Hastings and two BCT employees. Following a special meeting on 28 February 1941, Mr H.W. Ashby, then Chief Engineer at Kingston upon Hull Corporation Transport, was recommended for appointment as Engineer at £600 pa. He took up the position soon afterwards, remaining with the Bournemouth undertaking until his retirement in October 1955. It will be recalled that his new superior, Mr Morrison, had also come from Hull.

In February 1941, the Transport Committee discussed the case of a driver who had stopped his trolleybus during an "Alert" in frosty conditions which were causing *"terrific and continuous flashing of the overhead wires"*. Many passengers had asked him to stop in case the flashing had been seen by enemy aircraft. Councillors were told that a Departmental lorry converted from 1930 Thornycroft motorbus 44 (LJ1608) in August 1940 had been equipped with trolley booms in January 1941 fitted with special cutters, used to disperse ice around the wire when necessary. They were also informed that the Ministry of Home Security, following tests by the Air Ministry, had recently stated that flashes from trolleybuses, trams or electric trains offered no guidance to enemy aircraft, and *"that the wheels of public transport must be kept turning"*.

Circular shades were fitted to the internal lights of trolleybuses during the year; three downstairs and three upstairs, together with an additional three on each deck for use when there was no "Alert". On the platform there was a shaded spotlight, illuminating both the platform and the kerb, enabling passengers to board and alight safely. To help drivers in the "black-out", oil lamps were placed at night on traffic islands. As the Sunbeam MS2s were equipped with motor generator sets it can be assumed that they had limited emergency lighting.

During another air raid, at around midnight on 10-11 April 1941, four flats in St. Stephen's Road, between Richmond Hill and the Town Hall, and F.W. Woolworth's store in Commercial Road near the Square, were destroyed with eight fatalities and Richmond Hill Congregational church damaged.

On Saturday, 12 April 1941, a bomb was dropped immediately outside the premises of W.H. Smith in the Square, blocking access eastwards into Old Christchurch Road. An overhead wiring link from Gervis Place into Old Christchurch Road, in front of the apex of buildings between these two thoroughfares, was immediately installed, enabling trolleybus services 21-24 and 27 to terminate in Gervis Place and start their outward journey with an immediate turn to the right into Old Christchurch Road. Service 25A was split in two; the eastern section operated between Ashley Road, Boscombe and Gervis Place, whilst the western section was presumably covered by motorbuses as there was no overhead wiring enabling trolleybuses from the west to turn back at the Square. These terminal arrangements continued until gas and water main damage were repaired, but the overhead wiring remained in place until May 1953, although in latter days a line of traffic bollards would have prevented its use.

On 1 May 1941 the Ministry of Shipping and the MoT were merged into the Ministry of War Transport (MoWT) with the aim of improved coordination of transport for the duration of the war. As far as Bournemouth's trolleybus operations were concerned, the responsible government department was now the MoWT.

During the course of May 1941 the MoL applied for the release for military service of three of the five electricians employed by the Transport Department. The General Manager was already operating with a skeleton staff and had so far refused to release them but notification had now been received that action would be taken to enforce compliance with the Ministry's application. The Transport Committee recommended that all possible steps be taken by the Council with a view to the retention of the men by the Corporation as, if the "call-up" came into effect, it would be impossible to operate trolleybuses. As a result, the MoL notified the Transport Department that it had been classified as a "Protected" undertaking in connection with the revised Schedule of Reserved Occupations.

In the autumn of 1941, the local newspapers reported that the Transport Department wanted the thirty trolleybuses on loan to other undertakings returned, but that the prospects were remote. An arrangement was reached in mid-October 1941 for the return of some of the trolleybuses from London and it was hoped that these would be back by 6 November 1941. A visit to Wolverhampton in connection with the trolleybuses and staff on loan there was also made.

During the summer of 1941, last trolleybuses from Bournemouth Square were temporarily extended until 11pm but, on the instructions of the RTC, these were brought forward again to 10.15pm from 6 October 1941 and curtailed again to 9.30pm from 17 November 1941.

The Department tried to reduce dust emissions from the generating station chimneys in Southcote Road caused by the enforced use of inferior quality coal. The coal position had become progressively more difficult. Supplies of high quality coal became limited and the only alternative offered by the Mines Department was screenings - practically coal dust. It had proved impossible to burn the latter in the Babcock & Wilcox boilers and, to raise steam satisfactorily in the Lancashire boilers, it was necessary to fit turbine-type fire bars as well as installing a more modern form of forced draught. The cost exceeded £1,000. At the same time, a 1,500kW Daniel Adamson/Mather & Platt turbo-generator was acquired from the blitzed Bristol tramways and installed at Southcote Road. The quality of coal continued to deteriorate and it proved necessary to use a greater proportion of screenings. A dust extractor, again costing more than £1,000, was fitted to the

In 1941 Thornycroft no. 71 (LJ7704) Bluebird, in fleet livery since December 1936 but by now with alterations to comply with "black-out" regulations, was photographed, probably to promote its sale, near Queen's Park Golf Pavilion teminus.   **David Chalk collection**

Pictured outside the east end of the Central Depot, Southcote Road main shed, is single-deck Thornycroft BD no. 71 (LJ7704) in wartime livery.
                                                                                                        David Chalk collection

Winton Banks junction during the Second World War looking north along Wimborne Road. Note that only a portion of the green lens on the traffic lights remains, the base of each traction pole is painted with rings of white and the approaching trolleybus, no. 74, recently returned from its loan to London Transport, is in wartime garb with headlamp masks.

Bournemouth
Transport Ltd.

base of the chimney flue in an effort to reduce the quantity of coal dust being emitted from the chimney. This reduced the nuisance (50-70 cubic feet per day of dust was extracted) of which neighbours had complained.

At the Transport Committee's request, the General Manager investigated the possible operation of eastbound trolleybuses from Old Christchurch Road to the Lansdowne via Hinton Road, Gervis Place, Westover Road and Bath Road. On 19 September 1941 they recommended that the necessary overhead equipment should be installed as soon as possible, but nothing further was heard. At the same meeting Mr Morrison was instructed to investigate the possibility of constructing a trolleybus turning point at Horseshoe Common for use as a terminus for services from the east in case of serious war damage at the Square. On this basis, he was instructed on 24 October 1941 to provide it as soon as possible. A rather tight emergency turning circle was laid out by Horseshoe Common at the junction of Dean Park Road with Old Christchurch Road, where the Lansdowne-Square westbound wiring turned south into Fir Vale Road. The overhead wiring was strung in late March or early April 1942.

In November 1941 the Beach and Pavilion Committee asked that trolleybus services be extended to 10.15pm in order to preserve some kind of social life, and it was decided that, until further notice, the current "autumn" services would continue to be operated, the last trolleybus leaving the Square at 10.15pm.

On 19 December 1941 the Transport Committee approved the sale of the single-deck Thornycroft demonstrator trolleybus, 71, to South Shields Corporation for £300. The vehicle passed through a dealer, Derry & Co., and was quickly licensed for service in South Shields in January 1942.

As a general rule, most buses were running in service largely full for most of the day, and it became difficult to keep time. Conductors were under extreme pressure collecting fares. As a result, volunteer auxiliary conductors were engaged to take over the regular conductors' platform duties, including announcing stops, supervising loading and unloading, giving bell signals to the driver and generally aiding passengers. They were provided with blue and gold identifying arm bands, travelling free when on duty, and special insurance cover was

arranged. In view of the long hours being worked by crews under difficult conditions, 21B Avenue Road, known as Fairlight Glen, was rented for £78 pa. to provide canteen facilities close to the Square. The increased number of passengers carried and excellent traffic returns permitted the redemption of all outstanding debts and loans on the former tramways from the Reserve Fund at the end of the 1941 financial year.

Double summertime (GMT +2 hours) was introduced on Easter Sunday 5 April 1942 in an effort to secure the maximum benefit from natural lighting and thereby reduce energy consumption. On the same date services were extended from 10.15pm until 10.30pm (11pm on Saturdays).

In the first minutes of 28 May 1942, a bomb that had fallen three nights earlier, just 30 yards from the War Memorial in the Central Pleasure Gardens and close to Avenue Road and the Square, exploded. Avenue Road was closed to traffic until 11am on 29 May 1942 as further unexploded bombs were suspected, but none was found. Enemy-occupied territory lay just 67 miles south of the town and "tip and run" raids were frequent.

Appreciating that there was a national need for new motorbuses and trolleybuses to carry vastly increased numbers of passengers, and to replace war-damaged, commandeered and worn-out vehicles, the Ministry of Supply and the MoWT had sanctioned the manufacture of a limited number of new vehicles annually which they allocated to undertakings who applied. Some double-deck "utility" trolleybuses were available under the programme planned for 1943, and the MoWT was prepared to allocate four such vehicles to Bournemouth, if required. Mr Morrison suggested that operators which had hired Bournemouth vehicles should consider purchasing these new trolleybuses so that the hired ones could be returned.

One of the Bournemouth drivers transferred to Wolverhampton had written to the Transport Committee asking that employees might be allowed to return home, perhaps two at a time, for a month. Mr Morrison wrote to his opposite number at Wolverhampton enquiring if it might be possible to arrange for the Bournemouth men to be returned either permanently or temporarily. It is not known how many crew members returned as a result of this request, but all had returned before the end of the war due to staff shortages

On 6 April 1942, Sunbeam MS2 no. 119 waits to be turned on the Christchurch turntable before returning to the Square on a service 21 working.
David Chalk collection

in Bournemouth. In September 1942, the MoL notified the Bournemouth undertaking that they would be carrying out a further review of the department's staff with a view to "calling-up" more men for military service. By now there were 200 women conductors in BCT and others were under training.

The temporary transfer of nine Bournemouth trolleybuses operating in London to Newcastle upon Tyne, which was awaiting delivery of utility vehicles, was approved in August 1942.

With effect from Sunday 4 October 1942, the time of the last trolleybuses from the Square and other main terminal points was brought forward again to 10pm daily (the last motorbuses continued to be at 9.30pm). Until then it had been 11pm on Saturdays and 10.30pm on other days of the week. The end of cinema performances was advanced accordingly, although many already finished at 9.45pm. The MoWT had instructed that the number of bus stops must be reduced in the interest of fuel and rubber economies. They suggested a stopping place every 440 yards but acknowledged that half that distance was the basis generally worked on in the provinces, especially in populated areas. Thus, from the same date, some 49 individual stops on trolleybus routes were discontinued and four relocated, yet in mid-November 1942 the RTC wrote requesting further reductions to the number of stops.

There were public protests at the last bus "curfew" on the Tuesday and Wednesday thereafter whilst members of the public also endeavoured to board special late journeys reserved for night workers. BCT commented: *"Five trolleybuses leave the Square after the conclusion of public passenger services at 10pm. And they are reserved for war workers who hold green passes (signed by both the employer and BCT) which permit them to board the vehicles. Though the buses may leave the Square with some vacant places many war workers are picked up at intermediate*

points, and the general public cannot, therefore, be permitted to use these special services".

Here it should be mentioned that from 1940 onwards many additional journeys were introduced on Sunday mornings prior to the start of normal trolleybus services primarily to deal with the traffic created by the opening of new factories or the expansion of existing ones contributing to the war effort. All these journeys were motorbus-operated over a combination of trolleybus and motorbus routes, i.e. special journeys that differed from standard routes and in some cases operated over roads not used by normal services. By the end of the war there were eleven of these special journeys plus about a dozen journeys which followed standard routes. They continued to run, for as long as required, throughout the rest of the trolleybus era.

In the meantime Christchurch Town Council had been considering Bournemouth's application of the Barrack Road extension to create a circular route as far as the Stour Road cross roads. The *Bournemouth Daily Echo* reported that *"one of the reasons why Mr Morrison felt it necessary to make application to the Council was that there was an understanding that before trolleybuses should run along Barrack Road a footpath would be constructed along the side of the Barrack Road railway bridge nearer Southbourne.*

"The Council felt that the introduction of the service would be dangerous if the footpath was not constructed, and decided not to grant consent. There is a footpath on the other side of the bridge.

"Bournemouth Corporation has powers under an Act of Parliament to construct the trolleybus overhead, but it was subject to an understanding arrived at the time of the Act. It was more or less a Gentleman's agreement. The footpath cannot be made owing to war conditions".

Bournemouth Councillors were astounded at Christchurch's

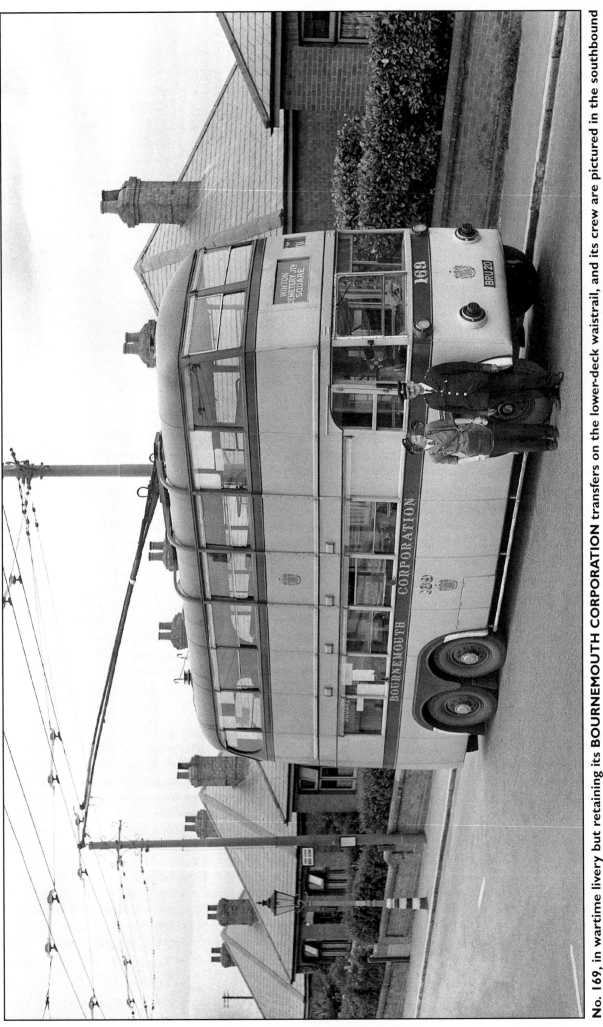

No. 169, in wartime livery but retaining its **BOURNEMOUTH CORPORATION** transfers on the lower-deck waistrail, and its crew are pictured in the southbound carriageway of Kinson Road, opposite the Columbia Road, Wonderholme Parade, turning circle on a 30A, the unidirectional circular service (anti-clockwise) to and from the Square around the Columbia Road, Kinson Road and Wallisdown Road loop. The crew offer something of a commentary on wartime difficulties: the young lady conductor has her cap at a jaunty angle and her dust jacket sleeves rolled up to to be as fashionable as the uniform permits, the elderly driver has probably agreed to continue work after the normal retirement age. The presence of a conductress indicates that this photograph was taken after late January 1941.

Omnibus Society (C.F. Klapper)

stance and the newspaper felt it would just be a matter of time before Whitehall looked into the matter.

Mr Morrison reported to the Transport Committee Meeting of 18 September 1942 as to the potential for extending trolleybus operation from Iford Bridge along Barrack Road into Christchurch. In respect of the railway bridge, there was now 75% less road traffic than pre-war when Bournemouth had agreed to pay for a footbridge. As Christchurch had considered the matter twice and refused permission until the footpath over the railway had been provided, Mr Morrison was instructed to approach the MoWT for permission and to proceed with the work as soon as possible.

On 9 November 1942 Christchurch Town Council learned that they had been overruled by a MoWT decision although they had secured their requirement that trolleybuses should turn left at Stour Road cross roads into Christchurch, although with the option of turning right towards Southbourne and operating a circular service.

The undertaking was invited to a conference of local operators, hosted by the RTC on 10 November 1942, to address the subject of a general curtailment of transport services. Mr Morrison stated that people were delaying their journeys home until the times of the final departure. "We have had to put on 25-30 extra vehicles some nights to get the people away. It cannot continue". Further reductions in the number of bus stops were also requested. Accordingly, from Sunday 15 November 1942, times of last journeys were once again adjusted, last trolleybuses leaving the Square and other terminal points at 9.30pm on weekdays and 9pm on Sundays (as did the motorbuses). It was announced that there would be no further mass duplication of last services

On Sunday 6 December 1942 last journeys were brought forward to 9pm throughout the week, indeed some last departures from outlying termini were earlier. From the same date Sunday morning services were withdrawn, the first buses operating at 1pm.

The supplementary toll for all trolleybus passengers crossing Tuckton Bridge was withdrawn concurrent with the abolition of pedestrian tolls from 1 December 1942. Vehicle tolls were not withdrawn until 1 October 1943 when MoWT approval was granted.

The Acting Town Clerk applied to the MoWT for an extension of the time for the commencement of trolley vehicle services authorised by the 1938 Order Confirmation Act. As the war moved into a critical phase, the Ministry replied that an application under the Special Enactments (Extension of Time) Act, 1940, extending the time for carrying out these powers by three years, would be more appropriate. On 18 June 1943 the Transport Committee learned that the MoWT had indeed granted a three-year extension.

As the four reciprocating generator sets used at Southcote Road power station for peak loads and emergency purposes required extensive overhaul, an order for new turbo-generator sets was placed. Installation was under way by September 1943. Two of the four Bellis & Morcom reciprocating engines proved to be worn-out and a tender for their disposal had been received from three leading contractors and that of Messrs T.W. Ward, Ltd., of £187 accepted. An electric pump was also required for the turbo-generator set, and the General Manager recommended the purchase of a suitable pump, at an estimated cost of £390-£400.

Just before 1pm on Sunday 23 May 1943, a fine spring day,

twelve Focke-Wulf 190 fighter-bombers accompanied by twelve Messerschmitt 109s suddenly roared over the cliffs at Southbourne. Flying low they had only been picked up by naval radar at St. Boniface Down, Isle of Wight, and although Fighter Command had been alerted, the air-raid sirens in Bournemouth had not been sounded as the aircraft attacked. During the next four minutes 21 bombs exploded in ten areas of the town, completely destroying 59 buildings and damaging 3,422 other properties. Later on several unexploded bombs were found. People relaxing in the Pleasure Gardens were raked by machine gun fire.

The Central Hotel, on the Square at the bottom of Richmond Hill, and the Punshon Memorial Church next door received direct hits, the hotel being destroyed and the church so seriously damaged that it had to be demolished and replaced with a new building in Exeter Road. Beales' department store on the corner of Hinton Road and Old Christchurch Road received a direct hit from a 500lb bomb and a ruptured gas main in the store caught fire. The blaze was contained by 5pm but not before much of the building had collapsed. The Metropole Hotel, in the apex of Holdenhurst Road and Christchurch Road at the Lansdowne, a billet for Canadian airmen, was also hit by a 500lb bomb causing walls and floors to collapse. The Holdenhurst Road Fire Station almost next door was able to offer prompt assistance. Several trolleybuses suffered damaged panelling and blown-in windows, whilst others were raked with machine-gun fire.

In total 77 civilians were killed and 196 injured, and the military death toll, announced only after the war, totalled 131. Trolleybus Driver H.E. Rodgers was killed and Driver W. Sackley seriously injured. The Transport Committee gave sympathetic consideration to augmenting the usual grant of 13 weeks' pay to Mrs Rogers whilst Driver Sackley's Government Injury Allowance was not deducted from his pay in view of his long service.

Several roads in the town centre were closed for some time due to dangerous buildings. Trolleybuses from the east could not use their normal route via Fir Vale Road, St. Peter's Road and Gervis Place to the Square and were turned at Horseshoe Common. Only during the afternoon of Saturday 29 May 1943, six days after the raid, had rubble been sufficiently cleared away to permit the extension of trolleybuses down Richmond Hill to the Square, whilst by 4pm those from the east, which had been terminating at Horseshoe Common, also reached the Square. It is assumed that no trolleybuses operated along Bath Road and Westover Road during this period. Although reopened for public transport, the roads concerned only opened again to normal traffic on 29 July 1943. Trolleybuses entering service from Central Depot, Southcote Road, and heading for Boscombe by way of Holdenhurst Road and the Lansdowne, could no longer do so until the Metropole Hotel had been demolished and the site levelled, and they too used Horseshoe Common. Side Route services terminated at the top of Richmond Hill and reversed by use of T-poles.

Following the 23 May 1943 "incident", the Transport Committee again recommended that overhead equipment should be erected above Hinton Road, Westover Road and Bath Road to enable eastbound trolleybuses to travel from the Square to the Lansdowne and thus permit a trolleybus service along these roads in both directions. They also recommended the installation of a trolleybus turning point at the top of Richmond Hill (the subsequent Bodorgan Road reversing triangle). In their quest to identify alternative trolleybus termini in the case of

No. 113 pulls away from the Jumpers Corner westbound stop on the then new Barrack Road extension on service 20 to the Square as the alighted passengers swarm across the road. Malcolm Pearce (G.O.P. Pearce)

further bombing, the Town Clerk was asked to report on the route from the junction of Bath Road with Westover Road via the Pier Approach and Exeter Road to the Square, for which authority was already held, and seeking MoWT approval to operate trolleybuses along Lansdowne Road from its junction with St. Paul's Road to the Lansdowne.

Having obtained the necessary authorities and, more importantly, materials, the Barrack Road extension between Iford Bridge and Stour Road, Christchurch, past various military installations, was now complete. The MoWT raised no objection to services commencing on the Corporation's own responsibility before an official inspection. The route was inaugurated with a new service 20 on Thursday 22 July 1943:

20　Bournemouth Square, Gervis Place - Lansdowne - Boscombe Gardens - Boscombe - Pokesdown - Iford - Jumpers - Christchurch, Church Street

The frequency of service 21, which also operated between Bournemouth Square and Christchurch but via Fisherman's Walk, Southbourne Cross Roads and Tuckton Bridge, was slightly reduced (although the details are not known) as a result, more trolleybuses terminating at Southbourne Cross Roads. This reduction was no doubt influenced by the reduction in passenger numbers—a fall of some five million—during the year ending 31 March 1944. From 8 November 1943 some peak-hour unadvertised journeys terminating at Southbourne Cross Roads were extended to the west (Bournemouth) side of Tuckton Bridge, a reversing triangle having been installed at the crossroads of Belle Vue Road with Tuckton Road and Wick Lane. Trolleybuses reversed into the east end of Tuckton Road:

22　Bournemouth Square, Gervis Place - Lansdowne - Boscombe Gardens - Boscombe - Pokesdown - Fisherman's Walk - Southbourne Cross Roads - Tuckton, Tuckton Road

The Transport Committee, at its 23 July 1943 meeting, recommended that the General Manager be authorised to start overhead construction from the junction of Bath Road with Westover Road along Bath Road, the Pier Approach and Exeter Road to the Square. They also recommended an application to the MoWT for authority to operate trolleybuses in Lansdowne Road from its junction with St. Paul's Road to the Lansdowne for the purpose of connecting two existing trolley vehicle routes. At the same meeting, in response to an enquiry, Mr Morrison was instructed to reply that the Transport Committee was prepared to introduce a service along The Grove and Fairmile (to the north and northeast of Barrack Road) in Christchurch providing it has the support of Christchurch Corporation, but nothing further was heard.

In October 1943 plans to loan two trolleybuses to Llanelly District Traction in South Wales were announced. These proved to be 77, which had been with Newcastle upon Tyne Corporation Transport and Electricity Department until 5 February 1943, and 123, which had been with South Shields Corporation Transport until 31 May 1943. It is likely that the vehicles were overhauled prior to being towed by BCT, apparently via Reading, to Llanelly.

Following negotiations in November 1943 with BPES regarding the Department's increased maximum traction current demand for the year 1941-2, the General Manager completed a report on the undertaking's electricity supplies. Technical considerations and the prevailing circumstances made

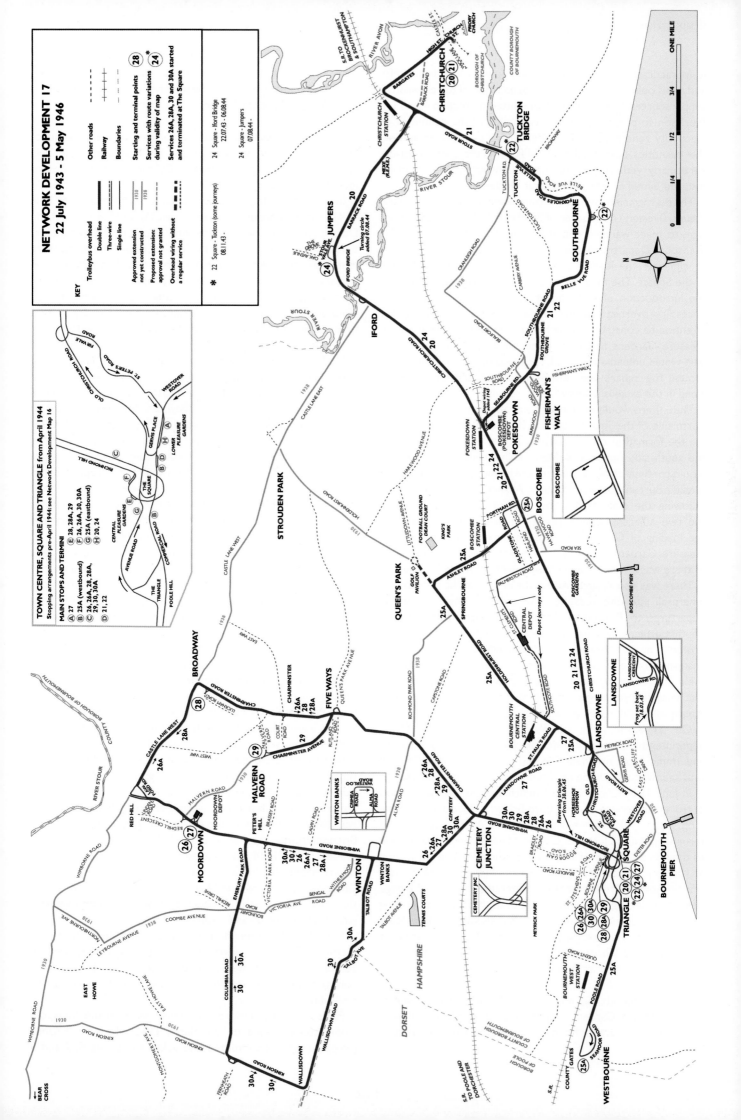

NETWORK DEVELOPMENT 17
22 July 1943 - 5 May 1946

it impracticable to source all traction power needs from BPES and in his opinion, proper use had been made of the alternative supply sources. The Transport Committee thereupon asked Mr Morrison to prepare periodic statements of the quantities of electricity generated at the undertaking's own power station, the quantities purchased from BPES, and the costs involved, particularly with respect to the plant which was then being installed, aimed at achieving greater efficiency.

The *Bournemouth Times & Directory* (formerly the *Bournemouth Visitors' Directory*) newspaper of 28 March 1944 carried a report that, to meet wartime conditions, the Council had given the Transport Department permission to experiment with a plan to eliminate the loading and unloading of vehicles at islands in the Square. The matter had been under consideration since the introduction of trolleybuses. Work would start once the necessary overhead fittings could be obtained, it being the intention to construct queue bays in the vicinity of the Lower Pleasure Gardens in Gervis Place, where all buses from the east would unload and reload. They would then continue right around the Square and return east along Old Christchurch Road in the established way.

Thus, there would no longer be a stop at the island on the north side of the Square opposite Burton's (it being unsuitable for the formation of a queue) or at the equivalent island on the south side opposite Bobby's. Trolleybuses for Moordown would continue straight round to the loading point immediately outside Burton's between Bourne Avenue and Richmond Hill, following the main traffic flow, instead of passing between the two adjacent islands. There would be no alteration to the loading of Charminster Road departures in front of the Pleasure Gardens between Avenue Road and Bourne Avenue as there was a wide pavement with plenty of room for queuing.

There was also a plan to relieve the muddle at the Lansdowne, where all intending passengers waited in a single queue for departures to Boscombe, Christchurch, Iford, Purewell and Southbourne. It was planned to form three separate queue positions at this location and, in an effort to avoid people changing from one queue to another as an alternative bus to their destination approached, the queues would be designed so that intending passengers moved in the opposite direction to that in which the buses were travelling.

On 21 April 1944, Mr W.D. Reakes, AMInstT, Traffic Superintendent, was promoted to Deputy General Manager and Traffic Superintendent. He had joined BCT in 1935, and thus seen virtually all the replacement of trams by trolleybuses.

In June 1944, Christchurch Council approved the extension of trolleybus service 24 over Iford Bridge and around a turning loop along Oak Avenue and Stourvale Avenue (the actual terminal point) at Jumpers Corner. Matters were delayed due to the non-availability of a turnout for the overhead wiring but, at 10am on Monday, 7 August 1944, the Jumpers turning circle was pronounced ready for traffic. The rather tight Iford Bridge turning circle, together with its tramcar (No. 1) body waiting room, was retained for use by motorbus service 14, Moordown to Iford, and short-working trolleybuses. Trolleybus services operating along Christchurch Road beyond Pokesdown were amended to operate as follows:

20   Bournemouth Square, Gervis Place - Lansdowne - Boscombe Gardens - Boscombe - Pokesdown - Iford - Jumpers - Barrack Road - Christchurch, Church Street

24   Bournemouth Square, Gervis Place - Lansdowne - Boscombe Gardens - Boscombe - Pokesdown - Iford Bridge - Jumpers Corner

Iford Bridge residents soon complained of the infrequency and unreliability of service 24 but Mr Morrison could only refer to staff shortages and make H&D aware regarding inward journeys from Iford.

In preparation for the D-Day landings in Normandy (6 June 1944), the area around Bournemouth, Poole Harbour and the Dorset coast was used as an assembly point for equipment and troops. Security precautions made it necessary to ban pleasure visitors and train services were further reduced; nonetheless, the military authorities still feared traffic bottlenecks could hamper their activities. The restriction on visitors to Bournemouth was lifted on 12 July 1944 and on the August Bank Holiday (at that time the first Monday in August) the town was crowded.

Continuing service cutbacks enforced by MoWT edict had led to long queues at key bus stops, particularly at peak periods. A Workers' Priority Travel Scheme, whereby key workers were issued with identifying permits giving them priority over other passengers queuing to board trolleybuses for their journeys to and from work, came into force on 6 September 1944. Over 20,000 priority passes (pink coloured for men and buff for women) were issued to such regular daily travellers for use Monday-Friday 12.30pm-2.15pm and Saturdays 5.15pm-6.30pm and 12 noon-1.30pm. The pattern of working hours then prevailing probably made it unnecessary to operate the scheme during the less pronounced morning peak. Priority passengers queued on one side of the bus stop flag and boarded first, whilst non-priority passengers queued on the other side and only boarded after the queue of priority passengers had been cleared. Stop signs indicated which side the priority pass holders had to stand. Priority was also given to fire watchers, war workers on shift work, etc., on the last service each evening and on the special Sunday morning services before 1pm. Passes for school children were also approved on 24 November 1944 and came into effect shortly afterwards. The auxiliary conductors were responsible for enforcing the scheme, leaving the regular conductors free to get on with collecting fares. All these Priority Pass arrangements, which were apparently often abused, were discontinued with effect from 20 October 1945.

Permission was sought from the RTC to schedule the departure of last buses half an hour later, at 9.30pm, during August and early September. This was granted and took effect from 5 August 1944. However, from 18 September 1944 to 5 November 1944 last buses were again curtailed to 9pm but, with the main theatre of the war in Europe moving away from Britain's shores, they were extended to 9.30pm on Monday 6 November 1944 and skeleton Sunday morning services reintroduced despite a shortage of conductors. The Home Guard was stood down in November 1944 and a visitor wrote that there was already evidence that Bournemouth's vehicles were being tidied up and cleaned.

Ten-year-old Derek Thornton was killed instantly on 11 October 1944 when, watching a train depart from Boscombe Station, he jumped over a safety fence on the brow of the railway bridge in Ashley Road into the path of an oncoming trolleybus.

Plans to enlarge Moordown Depot were on the Transport Committee's agenda on 23 March 1945 when the Finance (Negotiating) Subcommittee was asked to acquire 5, 7 and 9

Rose Gardens, a cul-de-sac at the rear of the depot building, together with the allotments at the rear of these properties and the rear of 13, 15 and 17 Rose Gardens, for an extension and the provision of an exit for vehicles into Rose Gardens and Malvern Road. Ultimately, houses 13, 15 and 17 Rose Gardens would also be required. The General Manager was asked to report further with a development in the vicinity of Castle Lane.

At the end of March 1945, the erection of passenger waiting shelters was approved at the Square for services 25, 28 and 29, and at Cemetery Junction a) southbound, on the east side of the road at the north end of Lansdowne Road near the existing shelter, b) northbound, along the cemetery wall in Charminster Road, c) southbound in Wimborne Road on the opposite side to St. Augustin's Church, and d) southbound in Wimborne Road prior to the junction, on the opposite side of the road to numbers 34, 26 and the then air-raid shelter.

Due to the growing shortage of labour, BCT employees were only permitted six days' holiday during the period 1 April 1945-31 October 1945, the remaining six days to which they were entitled having to be taken off-season if possible (or payment in lieu). The NJIC Emergency Committee considered that road passenger transport services should operate on Victory in Europe (VE) Day and on the two days thereafter, and that employees should receive special rates of overtime pay. Victory in Europe was declared on 8 May 1945 and most trolleybuses were decorated with flags. Unfortunately, however, there was a serious breakdown of the turbo-generator at the Southcote Road generating station shortly afterwards.

In July 1945 a subcommittee considered the General Manager's plan to improve accommodation at Central Depot, Southcote Road, but recommended only temporary improvements until a scheme for the ultimate rebuilding and development of the Central Depot and site had been completed. The full Transport Committee confirmed that special overtime rates would apply on Victory in Japan (VJ) Day, 14th August 1945, and it was recommended that times of last services be extended to 10.30pm as soon as practicable with representations to be made to the MoL once again with regard to recruiting additional conductors.

Bournemouth now prepared itself for the post-war boom, whilst looking back on the years from 1939 to 1944 which saw 219 persons killed, 507 injured and 13,590 buildings damaged or destroyed.

Wartime inflation: development of tyre mileage agreement prices in the Second World War

Throughout the trolleybus era, tyres were supplied to the undertaking under a mileage agreement and the tender divided between well-known manufactures such as Dunlop, Goodyear and later Firestone. The manufacture of artificial rubber was in its infancy when the war broke out thus prices soared as demand increased; the sea journey from the natural rubber latex growing areas of South East Asia became increasingly dangerous and finally the plantations fell into the hands of the Japanese

Date	Increase	Tyre Cost (pence per vehicle mile)
		0.24d
1 March 1940	5%	0.25d
1 January 1941	10%	0.275d
1 July 1941	7.5%	0.295d
1 January 1942	5%	0.31d
1 April 1942	12.5%	0.35d
1 July 1942	20%	0.42d
1 April 1943	9.5%	0.46d
1 January 1944	8.5%	0.50d
1 April 1944	16%	0.58d
1 July 1944	19%	0.69d
1 January 1945	14.5%	0.79d
1 April 1945	5%	0.83d
1 July 1945	10%	0.91d
1 October 1945	11%	1.01d
1 January 1946	9%	1.10d

Thereafter, commencing 1 April 1946, the rate per mile began to fall again somewhat.

CHAPTER SIX
POST-WAR RECOVERY

The end of the war in 1945 saw the following Bournemouth trolleybus services operating:

20   Bournemouth Square, Gervis Place - Lansdowne - Christchurch Road - Boscombe - Pokesdown - Iford - Jumpers - Barrack Road - Christchurch, Church Street

21   Bournemouth Square, Gervis Place - Lansdowne - Christchurch Road - Boscombe - Pokesdown - Fisherman's Walk - Southbourne Cross Roads - Tuckton Bridge - Christchurch, Church Street

22   Bournemouth Square, Gervis Place - Lansdowne - Christchurch Road - Boscombe - Pokesdown - Fisherman's Walk - Southbourne Cross Roads - Tuckton, Tuckton Road

24   Bournemouth Square, Gervis Place - Lansdowne - Christchurch Road - Boscombe - Pokesdown - Iford - Jumpers Corner

25A Westbourne - Bournemouth Square - Lansdowne - Central Station - Holdenhurst Road - Springbourne - Boscombe, Portman Road

26   Bournemouth Square - Richmond Hill - Cemetery Junction - Wimborne Road - Winton - Moordown, Wimborne Road, Redhill Crescent

26A Bournemouth Square - Cemetery Junction - Winton - Moordown - Castle Lane West - Broadway Hotel - Five Ways - Cemetery Junction - Bournemouth Square
Unidirectional circular service (clockwise) worked in conjunction with service 28A

27   Bournemouth Square - Lansdowne - Central Station-St Paul's Road - Cemetery Junction - Wimborne Road - Winton - Moordown, Wimborne Road, Redhill Crescent

28   Bournemouth Square - Richmond Hill - Cemetery Junction - Charminster Road - Five Ways - Broadway Hotel, Luckham Road

28A Bournemouth Square - Cemetery Junction - Five Ways - Broadway Hotel - Castle Lane West - Moordown - Winton - Cemetery Junction - Bournemouth Square
Unidirectional circular service (anti-clockwise) worked in conjunction with service 26A

29   Bournemouth Square - Richmond Hill - Cemetery Junction - Five Ways - Malvern Road

30   Bournemouth Square - Richmond Hill - Cemetery Junction - Winton - Wallisdown - Columbia Road - Winton - Cemetery Junction - Richmond Hill - Bournemouth Square
Unidirectional circular service (clockwise) worked in conjunction with service 30A

30A Bournemouth Square - Cemetery Junction - Winton - Ensbury Park - Columbia Road - Wallisdown - Winton - Cemetery Junction - Bournemouth Square
Unidirectional circular service (anti-clockwise) worked in conjunction with service 30

Evening services were extended from 9.30pm to about 10.30pm from 5 November 1945 and a skeleton service reintroduced on Sunday mornings from 11 November 1945. The frequencies in this additional hour of evening services were remarkable: as illustrations services 20 & 24 every 15 minutes

Although no. 115 (ALJ989) has lost its headlamp masks, the white paint around the mudguards and the matt chocolate colored paintwork above the upper-deck waistband remain. This is the tired look presented by immediate post-war Britain.
Bournemouth Transport Ltd.

Bournemouth Square photographed from the west in 1946. Particularly noticeable is the gaping absence of the Central Hotel and the Punshon Memorial Church at the bottom of Richmond Hill. Trolleybus no. 141 makes its way across the egress from Gervis Place before rounding the Square to the Side Route loading points as no. 88, already with post-war primrose yellow upper-deck window surrounds, turns out of the Square to climb Richmond Hill destined for Wallisdown (service 30). David Chalk collection (Bournemouth Transport)

Bournemouth Square, photographed from the east in 1946. No. 117 is loading for Christchurch at the 21, 22 and 23 stop directly opposite W.H. Smith's shop and lending library with the 25A stop just beyond opposite the National Provincial Bank. Tram rails are still evident in the road surface but even in these hard times at least one trolleybus has lost its wartime livery and been repainted with a primrose yellow coloured upper-deck window surround.
David Chalk collection

to Iford, every 30 minutes to Christchurch; services 21 & 22 every 15 minutes to
Southbourne, every 30 minutes to Christchurch; service 25 every 10 minutes; service 26 every 10 minutes with journeys to Winton Banks every 7½ minutes; services 28 & 29 every 15 minutes.

Also in November 1945, a Transport Committee subcommittee visited two potential sites for a proposed depot on Castle Lane and asked Mr Reakes (in the absence of Mr Morrison, who was ill) to make further enquiries. Having considered the option of extending Moordown Depot by acquiring land at the rear and side, the proposal to construct an entirely new depot and staff recreation ground on a ten-acre site on the Corporation's Strouden Farm, just off Castle Lane West, was approved on 18 January 1946.

At its meeting on 21 December 1945, the Transport Committee recommended that work on the trolleybus extension from the Royal Bath Hotel to Bournemouth Square via Bath Road, the Pier and Exeter Road, already approved by the Council, should start as soon as possible. The Highways & Works Committee was asked to install a roundabout, on trial, at the Lansdowne. By June 1946 Mr Morrison was able to report that the Lansdowne roundabout proposals created no overhead wiring difficulties and added that the police had no objections.

It was recommended that, as soon as alternative arrangements could be made, the parking of out-of-service trolleybuses in Gervis Place and Avenue Road cease, and that the Highways & Works Committee permit the use of St. Peter's Road car park or vacant land in Fir Vale Road instead. Suitable parking west of the Square was also needed.

A generating station breakdown had led to an exceptional maximum electricity demand on 10 November 1945 but, under the circumstances, BPES agreed not to increase the maximum demand charge. The stoker gear for the Lancashire boilers at the Southcote Road generating station was considered life-expired and in need of urgent replacement. On 22 March 1946 the Committee recommended that two sets, at £220 each, be purchased from Messrs J. Proctor, Ltd.

Despite inflation, the undertaking's accounts for the year ending 31 March 1946 saw a record net surplus of some £84,000 before tax, of which £75,037 was due to trolleybus operations. A contribution of £30,000 relieved the rates. A further proposal for external vehicle advertising from Henbest Publicity Services Ltd. was rejected.

Rather than buy a new overhead tower wagon, it was decided to recondition the chassis of one of the six AEC Regent 661 petrol-engined motorbuses bought from Huddersfield Joint Omnibus Committee (a consortium consisting of Huddersfield Corporation and the London, Midland and Scottish Railway Co.), in January 1945, mount extendible towers and purchase appropriate bodywork from an outside firm at a cost of £500-£600. Thus ex-Huddersfield VH6218 re-entered service as tower wagon 10 in the BCT Overhead Department fleet on 1 February 1947.

To prepare Bournemouth for its post-war holidaymakers some traction poles were repainted in early 1946. In March 1946 BPES was granted permission to attach street lighting equipment to overhead equipment and traction poles in Christchurch whilst, in April 1946, it was authorised to attach lighting cables to traction poles at Iford Bridge, Barrack Road Railway Bridge, and Stour Road, Christchurch.

In preparation for a scheme to re-develop Bournemouth Square, it was decided at a meeting of the Transport Committee on 23 March 1946 that bus stops should be revised as follows:
Gervis Place: from the junction of Gervis Place with Old Christchurch Road eastwards to Westover Road, the stops, in sequence from east to west, to be:

a) services 21, 22, 23 (the latter to be re-introduced on 6 May 1946)
b) services 20 and 24
c) service 27

Opposite the island on the west side of the Square, but beyond the pedestrian crossing, to be the location of the stop for service 25A (to Westbourne).

Avenue Road: from the existing service 25A stop, westwards to Fairlight Glen or possibly Avenue Road car park, the stops, in sequence from east to west, to be:

a) service 25A (to Boscombe)
b) services 26 and 26A
c) services 30 and 30A
d) services 28 and 29

It will be noted that this scheme would effectively remove the terminal point of the Side Route trolleybuses from the Square to Avenue Road which, due to the absence of any alternative roads, would have to be reached via the Triangle. Those motorbus services still using the stops in the middle of the Square at the former tramway waiting room would be moved to Bourne Avenue and Gervis Place.

Responding to a letter from the MoT (the MoWT reverted to its previous title in April 1946) regarding the 1943 Extension of Time Order, on 26 April 1946 Transport Committee recommended that further application be made under the Special Enactments (Extension of Time) Act 1940 to provide an extension of time for the introduction of trolleybus services on Routes Nos. 2, 4, 5, 6 and 8 (this latter being an error, as the 1938 Order Confirmation Act had no Route 8) and part of Route 3 (Broadway Hotel-Iford via Castle Lane) authorised by the 1937 Order and confirmed by the 1938 Order Confirmation Act. This was done, ministerial approval for a further three-year extension being granted in September 1946.

No sooner was the £2,000 account for the repair and overhaul of the No. 2 Allen Turbo Set settled than the General Manager reported that the No. 1 Set also needed a thorough overhaul. This was estimated to cost some £1,500 and Messrs W.H. Allen was recommended for the work.

On 5 May 1946 unidirectional circular operation of trolleybus services 26A and 28A ceased and on 6 May 1946 services serving Castle Lane West were rearranged as follows:

26 Bournemouth Square - Richmond Hill - Cemetery Junction - Wimborne Road - Winton - Moordown, Wimborne Road, Redhill Crescent

26A Bournemouth Square - Cemetery Junction - Winton - Moordown - Castle Lane West, junction with West Way

27 Bournemouth Square, Gervis Place - Lansdowne - Cemetery Junction - Winton - Moordown - Castle Lane West, junction with Lawford Road

28   Bournemouth Square - Cemetery Junction - Five Ways - Broadway Hotel, Luckham Road (weekday peak hours only)

28A   Bournemouth Square - Cemetery Junction - Five Ways - Broadway Hotel - Castle Lane West, junction with West Way

There was no trolleybus turning facility on Castle Lane West at its junction with West Way and interworking of services 26A and 28A here began, effectively creating a circular routing. Interworking at various points became a feature of the post-war trolleybus system (see Appendix E) although not all were advertised or offered through fares.

Also on 6 May 1946 service 23 was reintroduced at peak hours only with a limited number of irregular journeys during the weekday morning peak hours extended beyond the Square to Westbourne although they continued to display service number 23 (not 23A). That same day, having received RTC permission, weekday and Sunday services returned to pre-war standards with last trolleybuses from the Square being rescheduled to 11.30pm.

The 24 May 1946 meeting of the Transport Committee studied the architects' (Messrs Jackson and Greenen) plan for a proposed new depot on Castle Lane West. Although their remit had been to prepare reports and plans for extensions and alterations to various depots, the architects felt that the best

solution would be to transfer all repair activities to Castle Lane, thereby relieving the shortage of space in the other depots.

As passenger figures continued to increase, Mr Morrison was instructed at the same meeting to report on the undertaking's requirements for new trolleybuses to meet future developments, bearing in mind the time lag between order and delivery. A programme of equipping principal bus stops with passenger waiting shelters began.

Several letters were received in May 1946 from the public suggesting improved services, including a Square-Cemetery Junction shuttle service which the General Manager countered with plans for a service between the top of Richmond Hill and Winton Banks, but neither was ever introduced. A sub-committee considered a Moordown-Bear Cross trolleybus extension, which would permit a through service Bournemouth Square-Bear Cross. A further suggestion was that some service 22 journeys should be extended to turn at Tuckton Bridge, instead of Southbourne Cross Roads. Mr Morrison stated that the position would improve when motorbus service 8 (Fisherman's Walk-Cranleigh Road-Tuckton) was converted to trolleybus operation but, in the meantime, some peak hour journeys would be extended to Tuckton Bridge.

A Bell Punch "Ultimate" Ticket Machine was demonstrated on the Ashley Road-Westbourne route during the Public Transport Association Conference, which took place 28-30 May 1946.

In March 1946 Mr Morrison had been instructed by the

Amongst the first passenger waiting shelters from Light Steelwork Ltd. were these two examples for service 27 and 25 respectively on the north side of Holdenhurst Road at the Lansdowne, erected in 1946. Mr W.D. Reakes, then Deputy General Manager and Traffic Superintendent, is standing next to the cab of no. 164 (BRU15)

David Chalk collection (Bournemouth Transport)

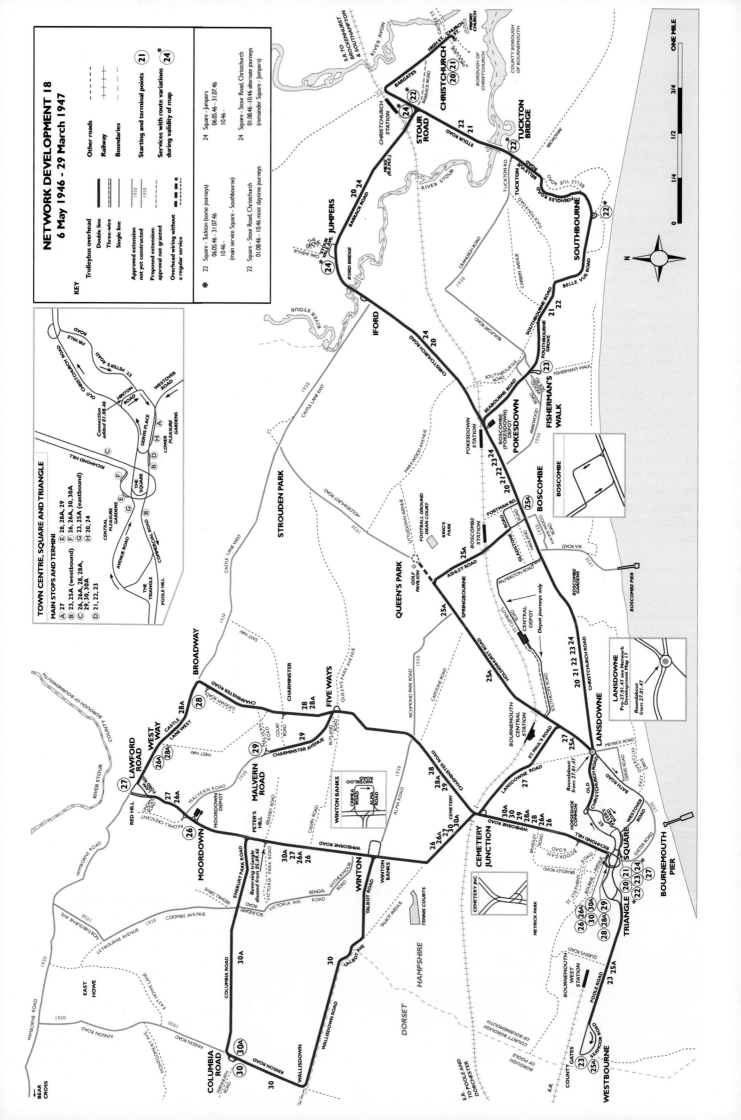

NETWORK DEVELOPMENT 18
6 May 1946 - 29 March 1947

KEY

Trolleybus overhead		Other roads
Double line		Railway
Three-wire		Boundaries
Single line		1930
		1938
Approved extension not yet constructed		Starting and terminal points (21)
Proposed extension: approval not granted		Services with route variations during validity of map * (24)
Overhead wiring without a regular service		

22 Square - Tuckton (some journeys) 06.05.46 - 31.07.46 10.46 -

24 Square - Jumpers 06.05.46 - 31.07.46 10.46 -

(main service Square - Southbourne)

22 Square - Stour Road, Christchurch 01.08.46 - 10.46 alternate journeys

24 Square - Stour Road Christchurch 01.08.46 -10.46 most daytime journeys (remainder Square - Jumpers)

TOWN CENTRE, SQUARE AND TRIANGLE

MAIN STOPS AND TERMINI

(A) 27
(B) 23, 25A (westbound)
(C) 26, 26A, 28, 28A, 29, 30, 30A
(D) 21, 22, 23

(E) 28, 28A, 29
(F) 26, 26A, 30, 30A
(G) 23, 25A (eastbound)
(H) 20, 24

Connection added 01.08.46

ONE MILE

0   1/4   1/2   3/4

Transport Committee to convert motorbus service 8 to trolleybus operation as soon as possible. This was reiterated at the Transport Committee's meeting on 21 June 1946 which, having considered his proposals for trolleybus route extensions, recommended that they be carried out in the sequence shown below and that the Highways and Works Committee evaluate any road improvements necessary:

1) Fisherman's Walk-Cranleigh Road-Tuckton (motorbus service 8)
2) Malvern Road extension to Moordown Depot
3) Holdenhurst Road and Castle Lane (from Charminster Road to Queen's Park)
4) Leybourne Avenue, Coombe Avenue to Wimborne Road
5) Wimborne Road, between Moordown and Bear Cross
6) Kinson Road from the junction with Columbia Road to the Dolphin Hotel, Kinson (on the south side of Wimborne Road between Kinson Road and Poole Lane)
7) Alma Road and Richmond Park Road

At the 21 June 1946 meeting Mr Morrison also presented his minimum needs to enlarge and modernise the undertaking's fleet, namely 24 three-axle double-deck front-exit trolleybuses, and 30 double-deck and 15 single-deck motorbuses. He added that it was unlikely that the trolleybuses would be delivered in less than two to three years. No decision was made at this time. Subject to the necessary consents, in September 1946 the Transport Committee recommended that any future vehicles be constructed to the newly-permitted 8ft maximum width rather than the previously prevailing 7ft 6in.

On 19 July 1946 the Transport Committee received a deputation from the Southbourne Ratepayers' Association which pointed out that residents east of Southbourne Cross Roads found it difficult to board vehicles heading towards Bournemouth. In particular, service 21 trolleybuses were already full to capacity. It was suggested that the Tuckton Bridge-Square service be improved between 12 noon and 7pm. The

Committee regretted that a lack of platform staff made this impossible, but hoped that the situation would improve when motorbus service 8 was converted to trolleybus operation. The increasing number of passengers on all services required more supervisory staff: accordingly three Regulators were promoted to Inspector and seven Drivers promoted to Regulator.

From 1 July 1946 coal prices rose due to increased railway rates whilst in mid-September 1946 there was a general reduction in coal supplies, the undertaking's generating station receiving an allocation of 170 tons per week from the Midlands instead of South Wales, this being 3 tons less than the previous allocation. This set-back was accompanied by an increase in the price of furnace coke. It was decided to investigate use of an auxiliary oil-burning plant and other boiler equipment as an economy and to reduce the dependency on coal. In spite of all the tribulations during the war regarding the times of last departures on trolleybus and motorbus services, the number of passengers wishing to travel in the late evening had fallen, making it possible to conserve fuel supplies by cutting back all services from a daily 11.30pm finish to 11pm on weekdays and 10pm on Sundays from 1 December 1946.

Following immediate complaints an analysis of the reduced late evening services showed:

Date	Traffic receipts after 10.30pm
Monday 2 December 1946 (first day of curtailment)	8.22d per vehicle mile
Wednesday 4 December 1946	10.09d per vehicle mile
Saturday 7 December 1946	15.25d per vehicle mile

The operating costs (excluding overhead expenditure) at that time were 18.56d per vehicle mile.

The proposal to build a Transport Department traffic office

No. 122 (ALJ996) loads at the westbound stop in Talbot Road with Winton Banks junction in the background on its way to Columbia Road, junction with Kinson Road (despite the indicator blind showing simply Wallisdown). Note the milk churns on the rear of the lorry stopped at the traffic lights in front of Lloyds Bank.

Malcolm Pearce
(G.O.P. Pearce)

on the west side of the Square above the Central Pleasure Gardens was approved by the Parks and Town Planning Department but by late November 1946 the tenders had been amended to a smaller, temporary structure.

It was decided to cease using Brassey Road reversing triangle, which was actually in Victoria Park Road opposite Brassey Road, from 5 September 1946 due to increasing road traffic. The reverser was irregularly used and was dismantled on 29 May 1948.

A request for a direct through service between those parts of Boscombe along Christchurch Road and Westbourne had been received. The 20 September 1946 Transport Committee meeting deferred consideration until the roundabouts planned for the Lansdowne and the Square were completed. On 7 January 1947 a promise was given to Cllr. Thomson that, unless the Council thought differently, such services would be introduced upon completion of the Square roundabout. In October 1946, the General Manager made the unusual observation that, when vehicle trials at the new Lansdowne roundabout were carried out, it might be found that hand-operated frogs controlled from the centre of the roundabout, rather than electrically-operated automatic frogs, would ease the flow of traffic. Meanwhile the MoT approved plans for a trolleybus route extension along Lansdowne Road from its junction with St. Paul's Road to the Lansdowne for the purpose of connecting trolley vehicle routes, under the conditions of the Bournemouth Corporation Act, 1930.

As the post-war Britain increasingly returned to normality, on 7 October 1946 the "Bournemouth Belle" Pullman train made its first post-war trip from London Waterloo. Work began to reconstruct the Pier.

The 18 October 1946 Transport Committee meeting considered Christchurch Council's proposals to build a new road across the Pit Site, Christchurch from Bargates to Barrack Road, and to introduce a one-way system from the traffic lights by the Fountain Inn in a clockwise direction round the triangle formed by Barrack Road, the new road and Bargates. This was approved subject to Bournemouth Corporation not being responsible for the cost of overhead wiring changes. The work, in mid-January 1947, disrupted traffic, trolleybuses having to use a one-way system temporarily using the eastbound wiring in both directions. Hampshire County Council responded in February 1947 that they considered that trolleybus services would greatly benefit from the planned one-way system and that it was reasonable to ask the Corporation to make a contribution towards the estimated cost of £550 for changing the overhead layout. Bournemouth Corporation then enquired what proportion the County Council would be prepared to contribute!

It was also agreed to improve the layout of the reversing arrangements at Tuckton off Belle Vue Road at the east end of Tuckton Road, about 100yd west of Tuckton Bridge, which had been in use since 8 November 1943, to avoid the necessity of having to re-pole trolleybuses. This would have involved the installation of a frog on the "siding" in Tuckton Road to create a reversing triangle, but it is not known if this alteration was ever carried out.

On 22 November 1946 the MoT authorised the equipment for trolleybuses of Routes 5 and 6 (motorbus service 8, Fisherman's Walk-Tuckton) of the 1938 Order Confirmation Act. It was agreed to proceed as and when equipment was available. The Ministry wrote again on 19 December 1946

to confirm that they had no objection to the equipment of Routes 1, 2 and 4 authorised by the 1930 Act for trolleybuses. Route 1 and 2 referred to the Bath Road and Westover Road extensions opened on 8 May 1937, and Route 4 to Hinton Road. On 1 August 1946 a single pair of wires had been strung above Hinton Road enabling trolleybuses to leave Old Christchurch Road just east of the Arcade and join the westbound wiring leading out of St. Peter's Road into Gervis Place.

At the Bournemouth Council meeting of 7 January 1947, Councillor Owen Ellum asked, in view of the Government's request for coal and electricity economies, for an assurance that no new trolleybus routes would be introduced at present, but that motorbuses be used instead. Ald. Arthur Langton could not give that assurance. It was Council policy to institute trolleybus services, and the anxiety of the Transport Committee at present was to introduce one in Southbourne to provide a better service in the Beaufort and Cranleigh Roads area, so that motorbuses could be released for use in areas not served by trolley vehicles. "Is it not a fact", asked Councillor Ellum, "that trolleybuses are costing 18.77d per mile, plus overhead equipment and a very expensive power station, against a cost of 17.61d per mile inclusive for motorbuses?" Ald. Langton responded that "Bournemouth has every reason to be thankful, in the light of events, for our trolleybus services". The 18.77d was inclusive of everything. The figure for trolleybuses was for 56-seater double-decker vehicles, carrying eight standing passengers, whereas the figure for the motorbuses was an average for the whole fleet, many of which were single-deck 25-seaters, whilst most of the double-

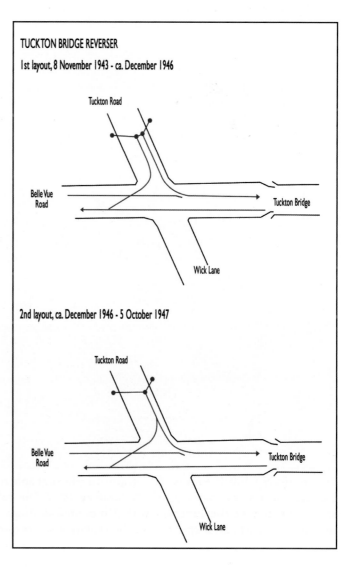

TUCKTON BRIDGE REVERSER

1st layout, 8 November 1943 - ca. December 1946

Tuckton Road

Belle Vue Road

Tuckton Bridge

Wick Lane

2nd layout, ca. December 1946 - 5 October 1947

Tuckton Road

Belle Vue Road

Tuckton Bridge

Wick Lane

deckers were only 48-seaters carrying up to five standing passengers.

At its meeting on 24 January 1947 the Transport Committee meeting recommended that a second tower wagon be constructed by adapting the chassis of another ex-Huddersfield AEC Regent 661 motorbus and adding an extending tower thereon. The shortening of the chassis, by Lee Motors Ltd., Bournemouth, was estimated to cost £425 and the tower equipment, to be fitted by the Transport Department, some £780. Tower wagon 12 (VH6217) entered service on 1 November 1948.

Mr Morrison had unsuccessfully endeavoured for some months to obtain a quotation for an oil-burning plant to be installed at Southcote Road Generating Station. Thus, on 24 January 1947 the Transport Committee was forced to recommend that the existing boiler be reconditioned. It was felt that the first and second rings of both furnaces on the No. 1 Lancashire boiler should be renewed at an estimated £1,000. Attempts to find a firm prepared to carry out the renovations proved difficult, and only in March 1947 was one identified able to carry out the repairs to the insurance company's satisfaction. The Committee also approved the re-blading of the 1,500 kW turbine at a cost of ca. £1,500.

Preliminary work on the new Lansdowne layout started on 21 October 1946; within three days BCT had planted some traction poles and within a week work to remove the former tram track junction was underway, with some labouring being carried out by German prisoners of war. Initial plans for the Lansdowne roundabout overhead wiring included frogs for access to and from Lansdowne Road, presumably to offer alternative

terminal arrangements for Side Route trolleybuses, although this may have been related to the earlier idea of a Square-Cemetery Junction shuttle service. However, no trolleybuses ever operated in the southern end of Lansdowne Road, and they retained their route along St. Paul's Road, passing close to Bournemouth Central Station. The Department's "Instructions to Trolleybus Drivers", dated 22 January 1947, referred to frogs and some yards of overhead wiring extending into Lansdowne Road, but this was all removed again shortly thereafter to avoid the risk of dewirements circling the Lansdowne. Prior to the construction of the roundabout, there was an anti-clockwise turning circle following Lansdowne Crescent between the west end of Holdenhurst Road and the south end of Lansdowne Road, in front of the Post Office, for vehicles coming out of Central Depot, Southcote Road, to take up eastbound duties on services 25A or any unscheduled short workings.

The Lansdowne was closed to traffic from Saturday evening, 25 January until Monday morning, 27 January 1947, for the necessary road layout changes and trolleybus overhead installation (in principle a circle with branches into five roads). Work started at midnight, and it took just 3½ hours to cut down the old wiring and connect the new layout, which had been strung above the existing wiring during the preceding weeks. Four tower wagons were used, one having presumably been borrowed from the Borough Engineer. The clear weather soon became atrocious and snow began to fall. The *Bournemouth Daily Echo* of 27 January 1947 reported: *"Soon the rattle of shackles and the swish of falling wires broke the silence as the workmen commenced the big task of disconnecting the old trolley bus wires and connecting up the new overhead gear that*

Not entirely what it seems! A composite photograph made up of shots of the western and eastern side of the Lansdowne on the morning of 27 January 1947. The join in the two photographs can be seen just in front of the trolleybus at the junction with Holdenhurst Road. Note that with the exception of one vehicle receiving instructions from an Inspector, all the trolleybuses retain their matt paint above the upper deck waistrail.

David Chalk collection

encircles the central roundabout". Ordinary traffic to and from the Square was diverted via Stafford Road, Oxford Road, St. Paul's Road and St. Swithun's Road, or via Bath Road and Gervis Road East. A shuttle service of motorbuses operated to and from the Square and Westbourne via Bath Road or Madeira Road. Trolleybuses from the east (services 20-25A and 27) reversed, using T-poles, prior to the Lansdowne at the junction with Gervis Road when following Christchurch Road or at the junction with St. Swithun's Road when following Holdenhurst Road.

Only one-third of kerbing was in place by the Monday morning when trolleybuses started to use the roundabout. The *Bournemouth Daily Echo* reported some dewirements at the Holdenhurst Road frog but no major hold-ups resulted. However, problems were soon experienced as trolleybuses made their way around the new roundabout, with passengers alighting from the rear platform into the road at the Lansdowne then being confronted by other traffic as the kerbs were surrounded by guard rails.

Soon after, Britain descended into the sub-arctic winter of 1947 and much snow fell in Bournemouth, with some 15,000 tons of snow being cleared from the main thoroughfares. At lunchtime on 29 January 1947 a trolleybus skidded when descending Richmond Hill and came to rest broadside across the road halfway down with its front resting against the wall on the east side of the road. It was freed after about an hour by persuasion and road grit. The temperature remained below freezing point for some five days, making both Bath Road and Richmond Hill impassable on occasion due to the slippery state of the road surface. BCT employees were widely praised for their efforts in keeping services running.

A number of pre-war bus stops, deleted as an economy measure during the war, were reintroduced.

In preparation for the construction of a roundabout at Bournemouth Square, on 15 February 1947 work began marking out the new layout with kerbstones and on planting traction poles, with the bottom 7ft painted white, in new locations. On 28 February 1947 the *Bournemouth Daily Echo*

reported that: "*Preparatory work now being done in the Square affords by the positions in which the kerbstones are being laid and new traction poles erected an indication of the route traffic will take on the southern side to make the journey round the new central island on a 30-foot carriageway*". By 21 March 1947 all traffic, other than trolleybuses, was making use of the new circular route around the Square dictated by the circle of kerbstones. Four gaps in this kerbing allowed the trolleybuses to follow the existing overhead equipment in the Square.

On Friday 18 March 1947 in the *Bournemouth Daily Echo*, a BCT official was quoted as saying in respect of the forthcoming changes "*The change-over will not be nearly such a big job as we were faced with when the Lansdowne roundabout alteration was made. We anticipate everything being completed by noon*". On Monday 31 March 1947 a detailed report recorded that "*Operation Square, Bournemouth's biggest traffic switch since the advent of petrol and trolleybuses, was carried into effect on Saturday after most people had retired for the night.*

"*The switch effects sweeping changes in the hub of the borough:*

(1) *It has created a bigger Square traffic circus and an island centre,*

(2) *All vehicles move in one circular route, the central lanes having been wiped out,*

(3) *All Corporation transport stops have been removed from the Square to adjacent points, Avenue Road having four stops*".

Work on the switch-over began at 11pm on Saturday 29 March 1947, when buses had set off on their final journey. Gangs of workers, each with their special mission, moved on to the scene. At 7am on Sunday, squads of men got to work with ladders and spanners to fix the outrigger notice boards to stanchions. Other workers with white paint and brushes marked the new bus stops on the highway. By 9.30am the new overhead wiring installation was ready for testing and by 9.43am the first trolleybus operated beneath it. Normal services began at 10am. Prior to that, the trolleybuses were substituted by motorbuses. Trolleybus drivers and conductors had been issued with printed instructions regarding the route change and the new frogs. "*It is working remarkably well*" remarked Mr Morrison,

As an indication of the attrocious road conditions in the winter of 1947, on 29 January 1947 a Side Routes trolleybus skidded whilst descending Richmond Hill.

Bournemouth Daily Echo

to the newspaper's reporter as he watched the traffic swinging round on the new route, whilst Mr Reakes commented "It is surprising how quickly the passengers are getting used to the new stops".

On Sunday 30 March 1947 the new overhead layout at the Square roundabout came into operation. The terminal arrangements in Gervis Place for trolleybuses on services 20-24 and 27 were changed, the existing long loop in the overhead wiring that ran from just west of the junction with Westover Road almost as far as the emergency link into Old Christchurch Road, i.e. behind the Plummer Roddis department store, being modified to become three individual loops. That nearest the Square served as the terminus for services 21, 22 and 23 via Fisherman's Walk, the middle loop served services 20 and 24 via Iford, and that nearest to Westover Road was used by the 25A, 27 and for spare vehicles. The loop further west virtually opposite the bottom of Richmond Hill where Gervis Place and Old Christchurch Road join the Square, which had served the 21, 22, 23 and 25A stop until now, was removed (only to be reinstated on 28 June 1953 to serve as a new terminus for service 27).

The Richmond Hill services, which had terminated and loaded outside the entrance to the Central Pleasure Gardens on the west side of the Square between Avenue Road and Bourne Avenue, or on the north side of the Square between Bourne Avenue and Richmond Hill, were extended west up Commercial Road to the Triangle, inbound vehicles offloading their passengers either at Albert Road at the bottom of the hill or immediately outside Woolworths at the east end of Commercial Road. Outbound vehicles picked up in Avenue Road between the Fairlight Glen enquiry office and the Square. Three passing loops were added to the single line overhead in Avenue Road, that nearest Fairlight Glen serving services 28, 28A and 29 via Charminster Road; the middle loop serving services 30 and 30A via Winton; whilst that nearest the Square served services 26 and 26A via Winton. The Triangle was now considered the official terminus of the Side Routes, although most departures waited five or more minutes in Avenue Road before continuing to their suburban termini. Passengers were carried between the Square and the Triangle at an additional fare of ½d. "Double track" overhead wiring westbound up Commercial Road between the Square and the Triangle, with a facing frog at the east end of Commercial Road, was installed enabling trolleybuses heading for Westbourne to use the left hand lane whereas those heading for the Triangle used the right hand, this layout coming into use on Sunday 6 April 1947.

The tramway passenger waiting shelter in the middle of the Square was demolished, leaving its clock as a free-standing clock tower in the middle of the new roundabout. The lost property office, which had also been housed in the shelter, was moved to two Nissen huts which were built on a strip of the Central Pleasure Gardens on Avenue Road. One hut handled enquiries and housed an inspectors' office. It was linked to the other hut, which provided conductors with individual spaces for checking tickets and cashing-up, as well as a staff mess room.

The remaining tram rails and wooden block road surface in Charminster Road between Capstone Road and Iddesleigh Road were removed, and the traction power feeder cable from Tuckton Bridge to Bargates, Christchurch, was relaid in a deep trench (often in the middle of the road, necessitating great care for traffic particularly trolleybuses). Whilst all this was going on, on 24 March 1947 Admiral Viscount Louis Mountbatten was

sworn in as 30th and final Viceroy of India, whilst interestingly the SR announced long-term plans to electrify the railway line to Bournemouth and potentially beyond (something that was actually only achieved in 1967).

With the extension of all Side Route trolleybus services (except the 27) from the Square to the Triangle, operations on this part of the network thus became:

26   Triangle - Bournemouth Square - Richmond Hill - Cemetery Junction - Wimborne Road - Winton - Moordown, Wimborne Road, Redhill Crescent

26A   Triangle - Bournemouth Square - Richmond Hill - Cemetery Junction - Winton - Moordown - Castle Lane West, junction with West Way

27   Bournemouth Square, Gervis Place - Lansdowne - Central Station - St Paul's Road - Cemetery Junction - Wimborne Road - Winton - Moordown - Castle Lane West, junction with Lawford Road

28   Triangle - Bournemouth Square - Cemetery Junction - Charminster Road - Five Ways - Broadway Hotel, Luckham Road

28A   Triangle - Bournemouth Square - Cemetery Junction - Five Ways - Broadway Hotel - Castle Lane West, junction with West Way

29   Triangle - Bournemouth Square - Cemetery Junction - Five Ways - Malvern Road, junction with Charminster Avenue

30   Triangle - Bournemouth Square - Richmond Hill - Cemetery Junction - Winton - Wallisdown - Columbia Road, junction with Kinson Road

30A   Triangle - Bournemouth Square - Richmond Hill - Cemetery Junction - Winton - Ensbury Park - Columbia Road, junction with Kinson Road

In November 1946, the Town Clerk had been instructed to investigate options for a proposed parking place for spare vehicles at the Triangle. He reported in February 1947 on the terms upon which the Durrant Estate would sell part of the grassed area at the Triangle and tenders were invited for the construction of a parking place. That of £982 from F.S. Loader Ltd. was accepted.

New Conditions of Service formulated by the NJIC, covering a guaranteed week for platform staff, hours of work, overtime and holidays, and relating to all operating and maintenance employees, were introduced in March 1947. The undertaking's costs were estimated to increase by £25,000 pa. Nonetheless, at the end of the 1946-47 financial year, the Transport Committee was able to contribute £50,000 to the rates.

As requested by the public, from 10 April 1947 some journeys on services 21 and 22 were extended beyond the Square to Westbourne showing service numbers 21A and 22A respectively. The 21A and 22A had been suspended due to wartime conditions on 25 February 1940. The 21A journeys to and from Westbourne operated a limited number of irregular journeys during the weekday morning peak hours only; however,

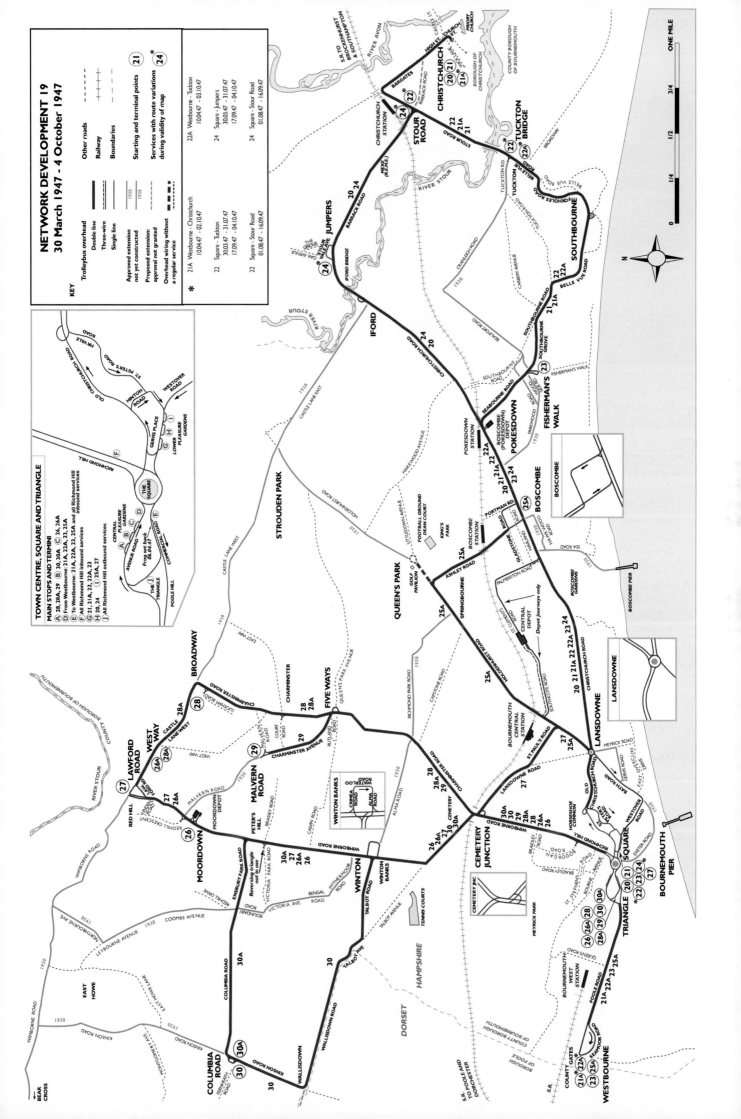

NETWORK DEVELOPMENT 19
30 March 1947 - 4 October 1947

KEY

Trolleybus overhead
- Double line
- Three-wire
- Single line

Approved extension: not yet constructed

Proposed extension: approval not granted

* Overhead wiring without a regular service

Other roads
- Other roads
- Railway
- Boundaries

1930
1938

Starting and terminal points — (21)

Services with route variations during validity of map — (24) *

21A	Westbourne - Christchurch	10.04.47 - 02.10.47
22	Square - Tuckton	30.03.47 - 31.07.47
		17.09.47 - 04.10.47
22	Square - Stour Road	01.08.47 - 16.09.47

22A	Westbourne - Tuckton	10.04.47 - 03.10.47
24	Square - Jumpers	30.03.47 - 31.07.47
		17.09.47 - 04.10.47
24	Square - Stour Road	01.08.47 - 16.09.47

TOWN CENTRE, SQUARE AND TERMINI

MAIN STOPS AND TERMINI

(A) 28, 28A, 29 (B) 30, 30A (C) 26, 26A
(D) To Westbourne: 21A, 22A, 23, 25A
(E) From Westbourne: 21A, 22A, 23, 25A
(F) All Richmond Hill inbound services
(G) 21, 21A, 22, 22A, 23
(H) 20, 24
(I) 25A, 27
(J) All Richmond Hill outbound services

Frog set back 06.04.47

Reversing triangle not in use

ONE MILE

N

The new Square roundabout from the east, seen from the buildings in the apex of the junction of Gervis Place (to the left) and Old Christchurch Road (to the right). One of BCT's classic 1939 Leyland TD5 petrol-engined motorbuses with sliding opening roof circles the roundabout in parallel with a Sunbeam MS2 on service 25A. The loading points for the Side Route trolleybus service are evident in Avenue Road by The Fifty Shilling Tailor's shop. Commercial Post Card

the 22A provided a through service between Southbourne and Westbourne every 20 minutes during the daytime from about 8am.

The changed pattern of services serving the Southbourne and Tuckton Bridge areas was accordingly:

21 Bournemouth Square, Gervis Place - Lansdowne - Boscombe Gardens - Boscombe Arcade - Pokesdown Station - Fisherman's Walk - Southbourne - Tuckton Bridge - Christchurch, Church Street

21A Westbourne, Seamoor Road - Bournemouth Square - Lansdowne - Boscombe Gardens - Boscombe Arcade - Pokesdown Station - Fisherman's Walk - Southbourne - Tuckton Bridge - Christchurch, Church Street

22 Bournemouth Square, Gervis Place - Lansdowne - Boscombe Gardens - Boscombe Arcade - Pokesdown Station - Fisherman's Walk - Southbourne Cross Roads (some peak-hour unadvertised journeys extended to Tuckton, Tuckton Road, junction with Belle Vue Road)

22A Westbourne, Seamoor Road - Bournemouth Square - Lansdowne - Boscombe Gardens - Boscombe Arcade - Pokesdown Station - Fisherman's Walk - Southbourne - Southbourne Cross Roads - Tuckton, Tuckton Road, junction with Belle Vue Road

23 Westbourne, Seamoor Road - Bournemouth Square - Lansdowne - Boscombe Gardens - Boscombe Arcade - Pokesdown Station - Fisherman's Walk, Wentworth Avenue

During the summer months of 1947, Sunday evening services were extended to 10.30pm from Easter Sunday 6 April 1947 and to 11pm from Whit Sunday 26 May 1947 (instead of 10pm). From 1 August 1947 most daytime service 22 journeys were extended across Tuckton Bridge and along Stour Road to its junction with Barrack Road, Christchurch. At this point they interworked with service 24, turned left and headed along Barrack Road through Jumpers and Iford back to the Square, and vice versa. The circular operation was shown as operating

every few minutes 10am-5pm but was discontinued in October 1946. The same interworking was reinstated for the summer season 1947.

The police asked when trolleybuses would be extended to Bournemouth Pier, stressing the importance of this to the new traffic system at the Square. They were advised that this would be carried out as soon as possible, subject to equipment being available, once motorbus service 8 Fisherman's Walk-Cranleigh Road-Tuckton had been converted to trolleybus operation. However, by late June 1947, no overhead equipment had been erected in Beaufort or Cranleigh Roads due to a shortage of traction poles. Reversal at the already busy crossroads of Bellevue Road, Tuckton Road and Wick Lane, Tuckton, had proved unsatisfactory and this provoked the suggestion that trolleybuses terminating there be extended westwards about 600yd along Tuckton Road to its junction with Carbery Avenue, the traffic island then at the junction of Cranleigh Road with Carbery Avenue offering a suitable turning circle. The Committee approved this and at 4.30pm on 5 October 1947, the first service trolleybus travelled up Tuckton Road and turned at the new Carbery Avenue turning circle. All vehicles on service 22 previously terminating at Tuckton were extended thus, as the new overhead wiring layout above the junction of Tuckton Road with Belle Vue Road had absorbed the reversing triangle. The journeys beyond Tuckton crossroads and back did not appear in the timetables, although this was considered in the layover time, the whole purpose of the extension being to avoid the difficult reversing manoeuvre.

The Department was represented at the 19 September 1947 Transport Committee Meeting by Mr Reakes, the Deputy General Manager, as Mr Morrison was seriously ill. He reported that the replacement of the indicator blind display "County Gates" by "Westbourne" in the side destination boxes was underway (trolleybuses never reached County Gates, a hundred yards west of the Seamoor Road terminus). Further consideration was given to winter services and, with effect from 12 October 1947, Sunday services terminated at 10.30pm instead of 11pm.

In November 1947, the Transport Committee agreed to buy stoker gear costing £265 from Messrs J. Proctor Ltd. It also recommended the purchase of 24 three-axle double-deck

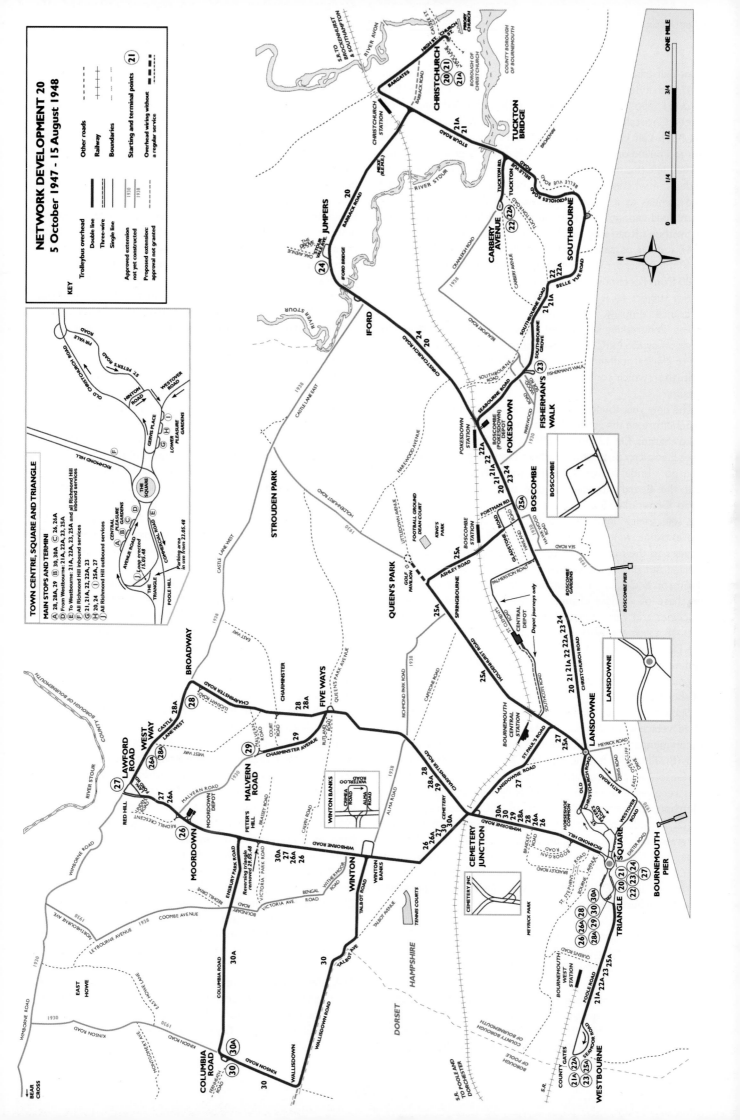

NETWORK DEVELOPMENT 20
5 October 1947 - 15 August 1948

KEY

Trolleybus overhead
- Double line
- Three-wire
- Single line

Other roads
Railway
Boundaries

1930
1938

Starting and terminal points

Overhead wiring without a regular service

21

Approved extension not yet constructed

Proposed extension: approval not granted

TOWN CENTRE, SQUARE AND TRIANGLE

MAIN STOPS AND TERMINI

(A) 28, 28A, 29 (B) 30, 30A (C) 26, 26A
From Westbourne: 21A, 22A, 23, 25A
(D) To Westbourne: 21A, 22A, 23, 25A and all Richmond Hill inbound services
(E) All Richmond Hill outbound services
(F) All Richmond Hill inbound services
(G) 21, 21A, 22, 22A, 23
(H) 20, 24 (I) 25A, 27
(J) All Richmond outbound services

Loop erected 15.05.48

Parking area in use from 23.05.48

THE SQUARE

CENTRAL PLEASURE GARDENS

LOWER PLEASURE GARDENS

GERVIS PLACE

RICHMOND HILL

AVENUE ROAD

COMMERCIAL ROAD

THE TRIANGLE

POOLE HILL

HINTON ROAD

WESTOVER ROAD

OLD CHRISTCHURCH ROAD

ST. PETER'S ROAD

FIR VALE ROAD

ONE MILE

0   1/4   1/2   3/4

N

front-exit trolleybuses. These went out to tender in December 1947 with a deadline for the return of tenders of 1 March 1948.

On 11 September 1947 an empty trolleybus rolled away in High Street, Christchurch, and mounted a traffic island, demolishing the Keep Left bollard, before a Mr E. Hiscock jumped into the cab and pulled on the handbrake. The driver later admitted that he had left the trolleybus unattended without placing a chock under the wheels, as instructed. Mr Hiscock was forwarded two guineas as a token of appreciation. A trolleybus coming from Iford ran into the rear of one from Southbourne at the St. Swithun's Road stop in Christchurch Road on 18 November 1947 and five passengers were slightly injured. On 20 February 1948 the Transport Committee approved the estimate of £250-£300 from Portsmouth Aviation Co. for repairs to the accident victim subject to it not exceeding the £300 covered by the insurance company.

The Undertaking introduced the 44-hour week, following its sanction by the NJIC, with effect from 29 December 1947. This led to clerical staff helping as auxiliary Drivers and Conductors, a situation which continued into the 1960s during the summer season.

The new year found the Department plagued with additional expenditure on the generating station, not least a rise in coal and coke charges. On 13 January 1948 a meeting between the new Area Electricity Board, the Southern Electricity Board (SEB), and transport undertakings in its area took place. It was disclosed that the Board intended to take over the BCT Southcote Road Generating Station as a part of the nationalisation of the electricity industry. Electricity "load-shedding" during the extreme winter normally did not affect the trolleybuses. Repairs to the turbo-generator diaphragms costing £685 were carried out during the course of the winter by Messrs Daniel Adamson & Co., Ltd. The General Manager reported as to the purchase of a phase changer in order to install three-phase machines and was instructed to obtain quotations. Repairs to the ash conveyor were needed, but could be carried out by the Department's own staff for £150-£200. A turbine overhaul and new shunt coils were required, one coil being faulty. It was suggested that a complete replacement set be bought at a cost of about £216.

Subject to the MoT approving the operation of 8ft-wide vehicles, on 24 March 1948 the Transport Committee recommended acceptance of the British United Traction Co. Ltd. (BUT) tender for the supply of 24 chassis, with Crompton Parkinson electrical equipment, at £62,856. One lower tender was received. The recommended bodywork tender was from Metropolitan-Cammell-Weymann Ltd. (MCW), to supply 24 all-metal 8ft-wide bodies at £75,000. Should width permission not be granted, BUT would supply 24 chassis to a width of 7ft 6in, again with Crompton Parkinson electrical equipment, at a cost of £62,136, while MCW would supply 7ft 6in-wide all-metal bodywork at £73,800. In addition, spare parts for the proposed new trolleybuses were approved:

a) electrical spares by Crompton Parkinson (8ft or 7ft 6in-wide trolleybuses) £2,264 17s.
b) chassis spares by BUT £2,005 9s.

Sanction was therefore sought for a loan of £142,726 to cover vehicles and spares. This was to be covered from three sources, namely an MoT loan of £30,621 for the vehicles; a loan of £58,105 under the 1930 Act; and a loan of £54,000 under the

1938 Order Confirmation Act. Over nine months later, on 8 January 1949, the MoT gave formal approval to operate 8ft-wide trolley vehicles on services 24 and 25A, which subsequently became a general approval covering all routes on the system.

The Standing Passengers Order, 1948, permitted the carriage (with restrictions) of up to eight standing passengers on trolleybuses, with effect from 10 May 1948. A census was taken between 11 and 18 May 1948 at the Triangle and Avenue Road stops due to the prohibition on carrying standing passengers up Richmond Hill. Only during the evening peaks were a substantial number of passengers left behind at the Avenue Road stop and in very few cases during the week was a trolleybus already full when reaching Avenue Road. The census showed that at peak periods the waiting time was not more than ten minutes. It was accordingly recommended that the Avenue Road stops be given priority for the provision of passenger waiting shelters.

On 15 May 1948, a single pair of trolley wires was erected above the Triangle parking area, which had been used by motorbuses since the beginning of the month. Trolleybuses started to use the park on 23 May 1948 instead of running empty to and from Central Depot, Southcote Road, after the morning rush hour and prior to the evening peak. There was space for twelve vehicles.

No doubt influenced by the proposals for a new depot on Castle Lane, the 23 July 1948 Transport Committee meeting recommended that the Strouden Park trolleybus route extension should have priority and requested a report as to suggested turning points. The Borough Engineer confirmed that a service road near the Strouden Park shopping centre would be suitable, although this was never followed-up. The introduction of trolleybuses along Castle Lane to Strouden Park was accordingly recommended.

A request from Messrs Frank Mason & Co. Ltd., for advertising on bus shelters and, once again, on the exterior of the undertaking's vehicles was rejected. Interior advertising for turf accountants was also considered unacceptable.

Material shortages had delayed the erection of overhead equipment along the route extension from Fisherman's Walk, by way of Beaufort Road and Cranleigh Road, to Tuckton, but on 16 August 1948 trolleybuses replaced motorbus service 8, which had shuttled between Fisherman's Walk and Tuckton only. Trolleybuses on the replacement service continuing past Fisherman's Walk to and from Bournemouth Square displayed service number 22B and Tuckton Bridge as destination. As there was no trolleybus turning point at Tuckton Bridge at this time, services 22 and 22B interworked at the junction of Belle Vue Road with Tuckton Road, Tuckton (see Appendix E). Carbery Avenue turning circle was therefore only used on a regular basis as the Tuckton trolleybus terminus from 5 October 1947 until 15 August 1948. The trolleybus service offer to the Southbourne and Tuckton areas now appeared as follows:

21 Bournemouth Square, Gervis Place - Lansdowne - Boscombe Gardens - Boscombe Arcade - Pokesdown Station - Fisherman's Walk - Southbourne - Tuckton Bridge - Christchurch, Church Street

21A Westbourne, Seamoor Road - Bournemouth Square - Lansdowne - Boscombe Gardens - Boscombe Arcade - Pokesdown Station - Fisherman's Walk - Southbourne - Tuckton Bridge - Christchurch, Church Street

Shortly after the Triangle parking area opened to trolleybuses, no.80 (AEL408) with English Electric body prepares to depart. This was one of just six Sunbeam MS2s bodied by English Electric to the Park Royal design. The English Electric bodies were readily identifiable from those built by Park Royal: the smaller side ventilators, the single "Y"-shaped stanchion supporting the two trolley boom retaining hooks at the rear of the roof, the step in the off side bay 1 side panel and the generally more angular appearance. The arcade of shops in the background has since been replaced by Bournemouth's Central Library which opened in 2002.

D.A.P. Janes collection (photographer's name not recorded)

22　Bournemouth Square, Gervis Place - Lansdowne - Boscombe Gardens - Boscombe Arcade - Pokesdown Station - Fisherman's Walk - Southbourne Cross Roads - Tuckton, Tuckton Road, junction with Belle Vue Road

22A　Westbourne, Seamoor Road - Bournemouth Square - Lansdowne - Boscombe Gardens - Boscombe Arcade - Pokesdown Station - Fisherman's Walk - Southbourne Cross Roads - Tuckton, Tuckton Road, junction with Belle Vue Road

22B　Bournemouth Square, Gervis Place - Lansdowne - Boscombe Gardens - Boscombe Arcade - Pokesdown Station - Fisherman's Walk - Beaufort Road - Cranleigh Road - Tuckton, Tuckton Road, junction with Belle Vue Road

23　Bournemouth Square, Gervis Place - Lansdowne - Boscombe Gardens - Boscombe Arcade - Pokesdown Station - Fisherman's Walk, Wentworth Avenue
(peak hours only, with some journeys to Westbourne, Seamoor Road)

On 3 October 1948 services 21A and 22A operated for the last time and on 4 October 1948 service 22B was extended

beyond the Square to Westbourne in their place.

It will be noted that when first introduced all journeys on the 22B operated between the Square and Tuckton, running every ten minutes all day Monday-Sundays. From 4 October 1948 the daytime service was every 20 minutes between Westbourne and Tuckton, plus an additional service every 20 minutes between Fisherman's Walk and Tuckton only, thus giving a 10 minutes frequency between these two points. Evening services Monday-Saturday were every 30 minutes between the Square and Tuckton, plus every 30 minutes between Fisherman's Walk and Tuckton, giving a 15-minute frequency between the latter two points. On Sundays, the weekday service applied from approximately 2pm, but on Sunday mornings there was only a 30 minutes frequency between Fisherman's Walk and Tuckton, with no through journeys to the Square.

At some stage shortly after the October timetable came into force, the through trolleybus service between the Square and Tuckton via Beaufort Road and Cranleigh Road in the evenings must have been withdrawn as the Transport Committee Meeting of 22 October 1948 discussed a request from the public that a through service be reintroduced after 8pm. The Committee recommended that it should be reintroduced for a period of one month, and that loading figures should be recorded. This census showed no demand existed and the through service

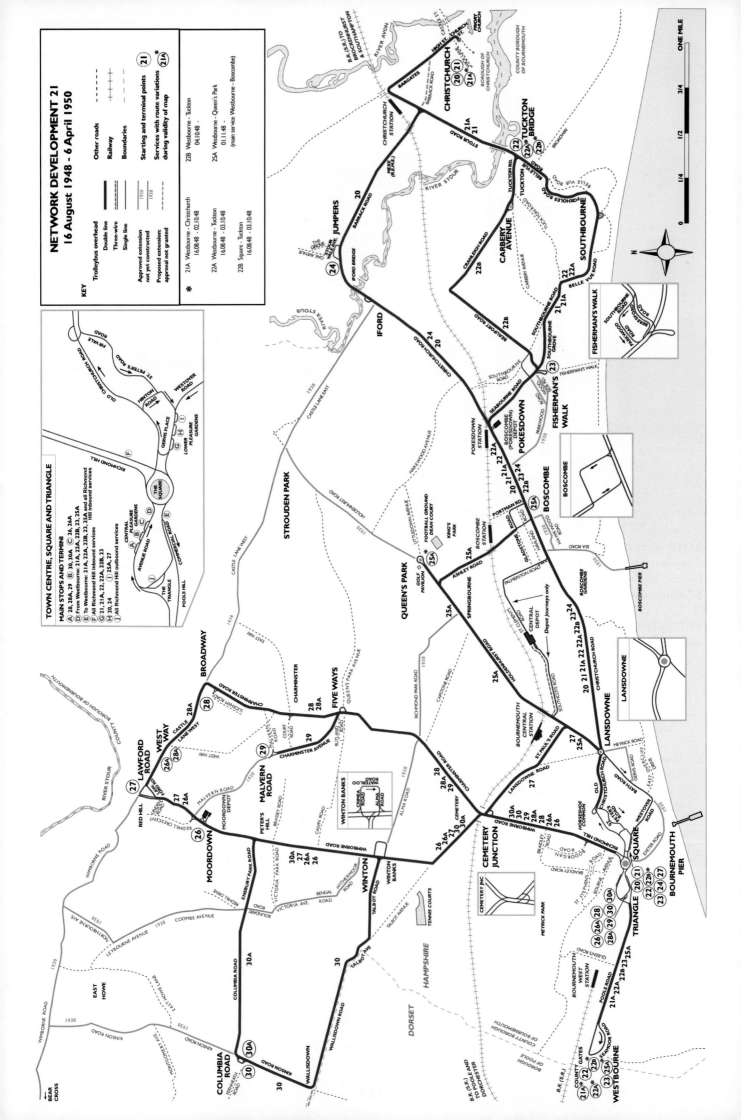

Trolleybus service 22B Square - Tuckton via Beaufort Road and Cranleigh Road commenced on 11 August 1948. Early in the morning of the first day Sunbeam MS2 no. 128 (BEL813) poses for the photographer beneath the eastbound wiring in Beresford Road with the crossover of the Fisherman's Walk, Parkwood Road loop line into Southbourne Road above the vehicle's front dome.

Malcolm Pearce (G.O.P. Pearce)

No. 91 (ALJ965) turns out of the north end of Beaufort Road into Cranleigh Road on 16 August 1948 on a 22B service to Tuckton, Tuckton Road, junction with Belle Vue Road, known simply as Tuckton Bridge on the main indicator blinds. The building on the corner containing the Beaufort Shoe Stores still stands but is now a domestic residence.

Malcolm Pearce (G.O.P. Pearce)

after 8pm was discontinued and the Fisherman's Walk-Tuckton shuttle service reintroduced. In general, however, ever-increasing passenger loads led to notices being displayed in trolleybuses from the end of September 1948 encouraging young persons to give up their seats to older passengers. Nonetheless, the March 1949 timetable saw a reintroduction of the schedules applicable from 4 October 1948.

The September 1948 quotation of ca. £290 from W.H. Allen for overhaul and repair of the turbine rotor, etc., was accepted, but their quotation for a phase changer proved to be for unsuitable equipment. An alternative offer from the Westinghouse Brake & Signal Co. costing £189 4s was thus approved. Messrs Green & Son Ltd. replaced the worn-out economiser at the generating station for £3,521, with the Transport Department carrying out the installation at an estimated cost of £400, the costs being met from the renewal fund.

After several months of ill health and a number of absences, the General Manager, Mr D.P. Morrison, died on 1 November 1948, aged 61. He had seen the number of passengers carried by the undertaking increase from 19,111,838 pa. when he was appointed in 1935, to 60 million in 1947. It was Mr Morrison who had devised the "wee red box" honesty boxes placed on each deck, which were then yielding £300 pa. in uncollected fares.

Mr Wilfred Douglas Reakes, then Deputy General Manager and Traffic Superintendent, who had taken on much of Mr Morrison's work during his illness, was appointed General Manager (without having advertised the position) at a salary of £1,350 pa., rising by annual increments of £50 to a maximum of £1,500 pa., plus travelling allowance for a private car.

On 10 December 1948 the last trolleybus on loan to Wolverhampton (129) returned to Bournemouth, while the use of Auxiliary Conductors in Bournemouth ceased on 31 December 1948.

On 21 November 1948, Col C.A. Langley carried out a number of MoT inspections, namely:

a) A preliminary inspection as to the suitability of Castle Lane from Charminster Road to Christchurch Road for trolleybuses. This line was subsequently constructed and opened on 15 October 1951.

b) A preliminary inspection of a proposed triangular layout in the overhead line at the junction of Tuckton Road and Belle Vue Road, Tuckton, to permit a turn from Tuckton Road into Belle Vue Road towards Christchurch and in the reverse direction (in addition to the existing turn from Belle Vue Road eastbound into Tuckton Road and vice versa). Permission was granted and, after erection of the new wiring, the new layout subsequently approved on 15 December 1950.

c) Retrospective inspection of the one-way Hinton Road (The Quadrant) connecting line between Old Christchurch Road and Gervis Place, originally authorised by the 1930 Act, and in service, on the Corporation's own responsibility, since 1 August 1946. Official approval was granted on 19 December 1946.

On 26 November 1948 negotiations for the acquisition of land at the rear of Moordown Depot were halted pending the result of the Council's negotiations with the MoT about a suggested depot on Castle Lane. The District Valuer had made a valuation for the Transport Committee's appropriation of

7.567 acres of land from the Highways and Works Committee and 9.72 acres of land from the Housing Committee for the proposed Castle Lane Depot. Following receipt of a letter from the MoT suggesting that the planned extension of trolleybus overhead wiring along Castle Lane be reconsidered due to the state of the nation's economy, it was recommended that further consideration be deferred until the result of a meeting with the Ministry was known. In the meantime, the proposed extension was changed from first to second priority. Sufficient equipment was, however, already available for the extension along Bath Road to the Pier Approach and onwards along Exeter Road to Bournemouth Square. Thus, on 21 January 1949, the Transport Committee recommended that this extension, which had already received Council approval, should become first priority and that the MoT should be approached for their approval of the extension and of a turning circle at the Pier. Application was made for loan sanction for trolley vehicle equipment to the amount of £7,500 for this extension, exercising the borrowing powers conferred by the Bournemouth Corporation Act, 1930.

Application for a further extension of time in respect of those trolley vehicle routes authorised by the 1937 Provisional Order but which had not yet been introduced had been made in December 1948. Immediately after the war, published plans had included the routes to Bear Cross authorised under the 1930 Act as well as the extension from Malvern Road to Moordown, but despite several discussions and proposals through the 1950s no further routes, apart from that along Castle Lane, were constructed. Until 1957 periodic renewals were made of the powers to construct routes along Richmond Park Road and Alma Road and from the Ensbury Park Hotel to Kinson (Wimborne Road) via Coombe Avenue, Leybourne Avenue and Northbourne Avenue, whilst other proposals remained under discussion until 1962-3. The MoT gave their consent in May 1949 to an extension of time for a further period of three years for the start of trolleybus services on Routes 2 and 4 and part of Route 3.

On 20 May 1949 the Transport Committee gave up any idea of acquiring land to extend Moordown Depot and approved the construction of a new depot on Castle Lane. They recommended that the opening of the Castle Lane (Mallard Road) Depot and the inauguration of the Strouden Park trolleybus route extension along Castle Lane West should coincide. On 18 July 1949 motorbus service 31 started to operate three times a day between Strouden Park (junction of Castle Lane East and Holdenhurst Road) and the Square via Charminster Road.

An invitation to tender for the Castle Lane site clearance appeared in the press on 5 August 1949, while the highest tender for the purchase and removal of a 320-tube cast iron Green's economiser and related site clearance at the Generating Station, Southcote Road - that of George Cohen Sons and Co. Ltd. at £80 - was accepted.

The same Transport Committee meeting agreed with the Highways & Works Committee that, if road widening for the Bournemouth Pier trolleybus extension could not be completed before mid-July 1949, then work should not start until after September. The estimated cost of the first portion of the extension was £4,500 and the total £7,500.

At the 24 June 1949 Transport Committee meeting, Mr Reakes reported on the anticipated electrical distribution needs for the planned Castle Lane Depot and trolleybus route. It was estimated that the cost of rectifier equipment, additional switchgear at the existing SEB substation at the junction of

Throop Road with Holdenhurst Road near to the latter's junction with Castle Lane and the laying of a 0.5 sq.in. armoured cable from that substation to the junction of Castle Lane West and Charminster Road would total an estimated £16,000. The SEB had quoted approximately £3,000 for a 500kW rectifier with an eleven-month delivery time.

The start of site works for Castle Lane Depot was delayed when Trevor Construction withdrew its tender. The next lowest tender of £16,392 8s 7d, from Messrs Grounds & Newton Ltd., was therefore accepted and, on 29 August 1949, the Transport Committee requested the Finance Committee to approve an estimated £151,216 for the first section of the scheme, which included road works, garage overhead and ancillary equipment. In September 1949 it was recommended that the widening and reconstruction of part of Mallard Road for access purposes, at an estimated £2,885, also be included in the cost of the new depot. By October 1949, fourteen tenders had been received for the construction of the new maintenance works and garage. The lowest, from Messrs James Drewitt & Son Ltd. for £97,948, was accepted subject to Finance Committee and MoT approval, and satisfactory sureties being submitted.

In September 1949 the MoT approved the trolleybus route extension to Bournemouth Pier along the western part of Bath Road (beyond its junction with Westover Road), the Pier Approach and Exeter Road. Rather belatedly, the Highways and Works Committee recommended that no services ran down Bath Road between Westover Road and the Pier Approach until the road had been widened. The Transport Committee would not agree to this as the Council had already sanctioned the introduction of services and the MoT had also approved trolleybus operation over the road in its present state.

In September 1949 the Department received a letter of complaint about grit and smoke emissions from Southcote Road Generating Station, and the Transport Committee received a memo from the Health Subcommittee on the same matter. Mr Reakes acknowledged difficulties with the grit extractor and wrote to the coal suppliers for a higher quality coal in an effort to achieve improvements.

On 23 September 1949 the Transport Committee granted permission for street lights to be fixed on certain traction poles requested by the Borough Engineer.

During spring and summer 1949 Wolverhampton withdrew its own fleet of Sunbeam MS2 trolleybuses and in October 1949 it offered to sell Bournemouth a quantity of MS2 spare parts for £450.

Plans for a reversing triangle at the junction of Castle Lane East and Holdenhurst Road, then foreseen as the terminus of the Strouden Park extension rather than Iford, were felt unsuitable by both the MoT and the police. The Borough Engineer suggested that a piece of land in the Meyrick Estate to the north-east of the junction be purchased and that a turning circle could be erected upon it using direct labour at an estimated total cost of £500. This was indeed subsequently built and brought into use on 23 May 1953, although the through service to Iford opened on 15 October 1951.

There had been a slight reduction in the total cost of the

At the west end of Christchurch Road where it joins the Lansdowne, Sunbeam MS2 no. 117, heading for Tuckton on a 22B, passes westbound no. 140 making its way to the Square and with its indictor blinds already changed for the next trip. On the right hand side of the road are the overgrown remains of the bombed-out Metropole Hotel and in the distance behind no. 140 the building with a cupola at the top of Old Christchurch Road was once the headquarters of Butlin's Holidays. Note the Positive Feeder on traction pole P60 above no. 117.

Omnibus Society (R.T. Wilson)

Castle Lane Depot scheme based on estimates for the following equipment which included:

Electric Mains
Laying traction mains along Castle Lane   £14,000
3-phase mains for workshop machinery   £ 2,000

Overhead equipment
Extension in Castle Lane West to Holdenhurst Road £10,770
Depot   £ 4,400
The Finance Committee was requested to sanction £34,880

The Transport Committee meeting on 18 November 1949 heard that two passenger waiting shelters had been erected in Avenue Road for services 28, 29, 30 and 30A; that work on a similar shelter for service 26 would start shortly; and that a suitable site for a service 25 shelter had been identified immediately opposite the emergency vehicular access to the Central Pleasure Gardens. However, by 23 December 1949 it had been decided to move this latter entrance some thirty feet closer to the Square and install an additional fire-fighting sump for emergency use in the gardens near the taxi-drivers' shelter in Bourne Avenue. The cost was shared jointly by the Fire Brigade and Transport Department.

Yet more expense was being incurred at Southcote Road Generating Station. The turbo-generator velocity wheel needed re-blading and a new guide ring was required. The manufacturers, Messrs D. Adamson & Co. Ltd., submitted quotations of £687 and £320 respectively, which were accepted. However, an emergency Transport Committee Meeting was convened on 11 January 1950 to consider further repairs to the turbo-generator. Adamson's had requested that the Council's Standing Orders on the giving of sureties should be waived with respect to the turbo-generator repairs contract into which they proposed to enter. As the repairs were urgently needed, the firm reputable and the only one able to carry out the necessary work, the Committee resolved that the surety be waived. In March 1950, an estimate of £126 from Messrs V.G. Morris Ltd. was accepted for repairs to the generating station chimney.

The immediate post-war period was greatly influenced by the Labour Government's policy of nationalising major industries and utilities, including public transport. The Area Managers' Committee of the MPTA wrote to the Transport Committee about the proposed creation of a nationalised Northern Passenger Transport Area, asking them (amongst other local authorities) to examine the scheme and give their views with respect to the Bournemouth area. It was recommended that the Council protest against any suggestion that BCT be nationalised. The Council supported the policy of the National Union of Ratepayers' Associations and Local Government League passed at their November 1949 conference: "This Conference having considered the published scheme of the Transport Commission for the transfer of Road Passenger Transport to the said Commission, expresses its opinion that such proposals are contrary to the public interest. It further expresses its determination to resist any proposals involving the confiscation of valuable Municipal assets, and the complete abolition of local control regarding fares, provision of services, finance and administration of a service so essential to the welfare and convenience of the community".

Following a meeting at Town Hall on 31 January 1950, the Southbourne Ratepayers' Association warned of the threat of nationalisation without compensation of the town's million-pound transport system that had contributed £113,000 in rate relief in the last four years. Ald. Langton, Chairman of the Transport Committee, reminded the meeting that London Transport, in principle state-owned, had increased fares three times since its formation in 1933 and a fourth was pending. He hinted that an un-nationalised transport system in Bournemouth might still be able to avoid an increase in fares, and retain the penny fare. "We can do it by other adjustments. Our bus service is the poor man's Rolls-Royce", he added. In the meantime, a general election on 23 February 1950 had seen the Labour Party returned to power but with only a slim majority and the fear of imminent nationalisation of municipal transport receded somewhat into the background.

Amongst other items in connection with the Castle Lane Depot scheme, the Transport Committee meeting of 24 February 1950 recommended acceptance of the SEB's tender of £17,397 for feeder cables, including their installation and jointing for the extension of trolleybus services along Castle Lane. It was estimated that overhead equipment, including pillars and panels, would cost £15,899.

By now 12 Sunbeam MS2s required a thorough bodywork overhaul and, following an inspection by the bus bodybuilder Weymann, this was estimated to cost £284 per vehicle. Later in the year their reconditioning was entrusted to Reading & Co. Ltd., Portsmouth, who had presumably submitted a lower quotation.

In March 1950, the MoT wrote to the undertaking approving the scheme to equip Castle Lane West from its junction with Charminster Road at the Broadway Hotel to its junction with Holdenhurst Road (Strouden Park) for trolleybus operation under the provisions of the 1938 Order Confirmation Act. Faced with difficulties in identifying a suitable location for a terminus at Strouden Park, the Transport Committee recommended at its meeting on 24 March 1950 that application be made immediately for the equipment of Castle Lane East beyond the junction with Holdenhurst Road as far as Christchurch Road, Iford for trolleybuses.

Traction poles were planted along the western end of Bath Road and in Exeter Road in the first half of February 1950. Overhead wiring was completed from the junction of Bath and Westover Roads, outside the Royal Bath Hotel, down to the Pier Approach with a passing loop in Bath Road at the side of the Pier Approach indoor baths in early March 1950. At the hotel's request traction poles outside the hotel were painted white to match the building's colour, whilst white-painted poling was continued down Bath Road to the Pier itself. Trolleybuses turned around an island of gardens immediately outside the Pier, known as the Pier Approach, and returned up Bath Road to the Royal Bath Hotel and under new eastbound wiring to the Lansdowne. A single pair of wires continued from a frog in front of the kiosks at the west side of the Pier Approach in a north-westerly direction along Exeter Road to Bournemouth Square, wiring in the opposite direction never being installed. The MoT inspection took place in April 1950, the Inspector congratulating the department on the standard of workmanship although a Rotarian complained at the disfigurement of the fine panorama when approaching the seafront.

Trial runs had reached the Pier on 14 March 1950. According to an interview which Ald. Langton gave to the Bournemouth Daily Echo, published on 4 April 1950, the Transport Committee had still not decided which service(s) would operate to the

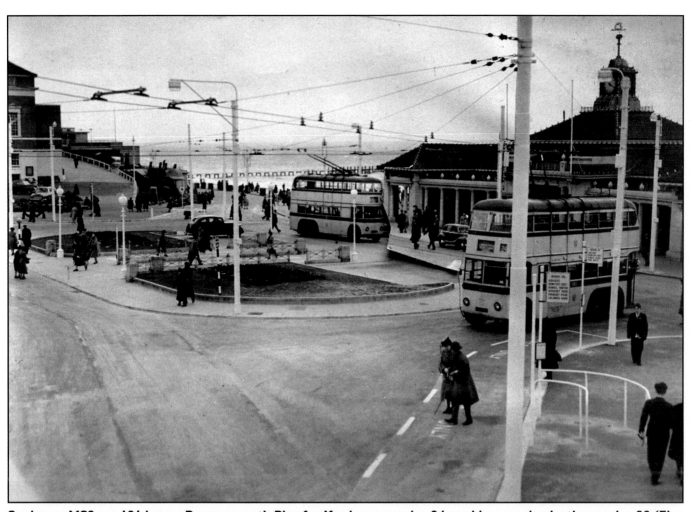

Sunbeam MS2 no. 121 leaves Bournemouth Pier for Iford on a service 24 working, passing by the service 28 (Five Ways) and 30A (Columbia Road) stops on the western side of the Pier Approach. Another unidentified MS2 follows no. 121 around the terminal loop. The dull weather and the fashions of the pedestrians' warm clothing suggests that this composite photograph was taken at Easter 1950, when trolleybuses reached Bournemouth Pier for the first time.   Southern Newspapers plc

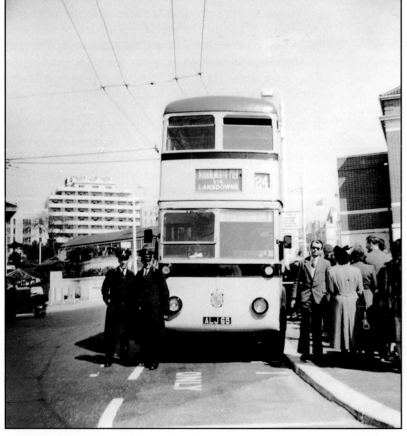

Deputy Chief Inspector Biddlecombe and another Inspector stand in front of Sunbeam MS2 no. 89 (ALJ65) at the Bournemouth Pier stop shortly after its arrival from Iford Bridge on the opening day of the Pier extension, 7 April 1950. Behind the two Inspectors can be seen the roof of H+D's Pavilion Garage and beyond that the luxurious Palace Court Hotel on Westover Road.

Malcolm Pearce (G.O.P. Pearce)

The seasonal supplementary service 25 between Bournemouth Pier and the Queen's Park Golf Pavilion only operated in 1950 (for both the Easter weekend and the summer holiday season). No. 131 (BEL816) is seen loading for Queen's Park outside the Pier Approach Baths. David Chalk collection

Pier at Easter. However, regular services were introduced on Good Friday 7 April 1950 and operated until Easter Tuesday 11 April 1950. This conveniently coincided with the completion of the reconstruction of the buildings at the pier head, the pier itself having reopened following reconstruction from wartime damage and partial demolition in November 1947.

They then ceased until the summer timetable commenced on 27 May 1950 and continued until 1 October 1950. Extra journeys on five services, each at 20-minute intervals, were made to and from the Pier:

23   Bournemouth Pier - Lansdowne - Christchurch Road - Boscombe Gardens - Boscombe Arcade - Pokesdown Station - Fisherman's Walk, Wentworth Avenue

24   Bournemouth Pier - Lansdowne - Christchurch Road - Boscombe Gardens - Boscombe Arcade - Pokesdown Station - Iford Bridge

25   Bournemouth Pier - Lansdowne - Central Station - Holdenhurst Road - Springbourne - Queen's Park Corner-Queen's Park Golf Pavilion, Holdenhurst Road

28   Bournemouth Pier - Cemetery Junction - Charminster Road - Five Ways

30A   Bournemouth Pier - Cemetery Junction - Winton - Moordown - Ensbury Park - Columbia Road, junction with Kinson Road

Services 28 and 30A operated northbound between Bournemouth Pier and Cemetery Junction by way of Exeter Road and Richmond Hill, and southbound journeys followed Lansdowne Road, St. Paul's Road, Holdenhurst Road and Bath Road. The route followed by trolleybus services from Bournemouth Pier and their use of the single northbound line along Exeter Road to the Square varied over the years (see Appendix E). In addition to providing a source of additional traffic, it should be remembered that the Pier was also foreseen as an alternative town centre terminus capable of reducing the number of trolleybuses at the Square, hence the eastbound wiring along the length of Bath Road providing a direct route back to the Lansdowne.

Despite gales, scudding clouds and showers, Good Friday 1950 brought Bournemouth the heaviest Easter tourist invasion since the war, with 50,000 visitors. Some 13,000 deck-chairs were occupied by lunch-time! There were half-mile-long traffic jams at the Lansdowne and the Square.

The Transport Committee meeting on 21 April 1950 deferred consideration of the site of a proposed substation near Bournemouth Pavilion to supply additional power needed for the trolleybus system. In fact, this substation was never built.

Earlier in May 1950, the MoT approved the scheme to equip Castle Lane East from Holdenhurst Road to Christchurch Road, Iford, for trolleybus operation under the provisions of the 1937 Order confirmed by the 1938 Order Confirmation Act. The estimated cost of the extension was £6,634 10s 3d and the Finance Committee was asked to apply for the necessary loan sanction. A suggestion the following month that the Holdenhurst Road trolleybus route be extended from Queen's Park to Castle Lane East was considered premature.

From 27 May 1950, service 22B was cut back from

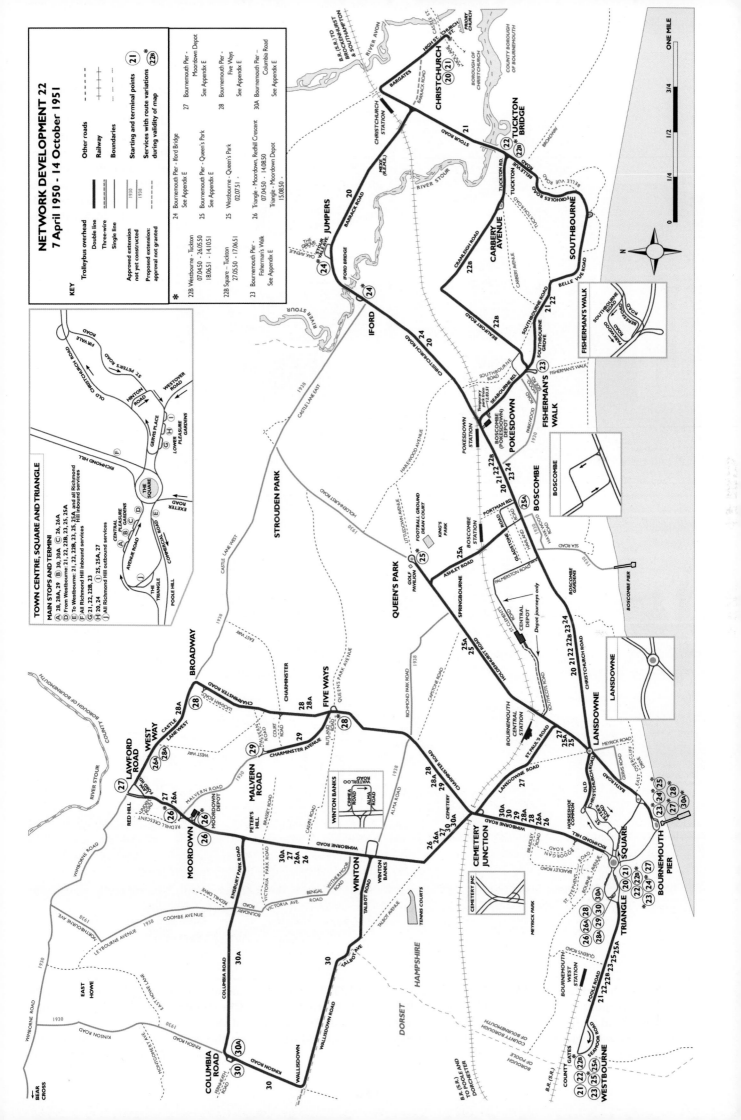

NETWORK DEVELOPMENT 22
7 April 1950 - 14 October 1951

KEY

Trolleybus overhead

Double line	━━━━━
Three-wire	┼┼┼┼┼
Single line	─────

Approved extension not yet constructed — 1930

Proposed extension: approval not granted — 1938

Other roads	
Railway	
Boundaries	

(21) Starting and terminal points

(22B) * Services with route variations during validity of map

22B Westbourne - Tuckton
07.04.50 - 26.05.50
18.06.51 - 14.10.51

22B Square - Tuckton
27.05.50 - 17.06.51

23 Bournemouth Pier - Fisherman's Walk
See Appendix E

24 Bournemouth Pier - Iford Bridge
See Appendix E

25 Bournemouth Pier - Queen's Park
See Appendix E

25 Westbourne - Queen's Park
02.07.51 -

26 Triangle - Moordown, Redhill Crescent
07.04.50 - 14.08.50
Triangle - Moordown Depot
15.08.50

27 Bournemouth Pier - Moordown Depot
See Appendix E

28 Bournemouth Pier - Five Ways
See Appendix E

30A Bournemouth Pier - Columbia Road
See Appendix E

TOWN CENTRE, SQUARE AND TRIANGLE

MAIN STOPS AND TERMINI

(A) 28, 28A, 29   (B) 30, 30A   (C) 26, 16A
(D) To Westbourne: 21, 22, 22B, 23, 25, 25A
(E) To Westbourne: 21, 22, 22B, 23, 25, 25A and all Richmond Hill inbound services
(F) All Richmond Hill inbound services
(G) 21, 22, 22B, 23
(H) 20, 24   (I) 25, 25A, 27
(J) All Richmond Hill outbound services

ONE MILE

0   1/4   1/2   3/4

No. 142 (BEL827) is seen at the loading point at the west end of Bath Road outside the Pier Approach Baths on Good Friday 7 April 1950, the first day of scheduled service trolleybus operation to and from Bournemouth Pier. *Malcolm Pearce (G.O.P. Pearce)*

Having towed brand-new BUT9641T trolleybus no. 203 (KLJ337) from Weymann's Addlestone factory on 8 July 1950, the Transport Department's Thornycroft BC/FC LJ1608 turns out of Christchurch Road, Boscombe into Palmerston Road on its way to Central Depot, Southcote Road. The remains of the trolley bases, used to support trolley booms with which to lubricate the overhead wires, can still be seen on the roof of the workshop behind the lorry's cab.
Malcolm Pearce (G.O.P. Pearce)

BUT9641T no. 203 (KLJ337) has just reached Central Depot, Southcote Road, and been parked on the south side of the facilities close to the St. Clement's Road entrance (8 July 1950). Malcolm Pearce (G.O.P.Pearce)

Another view of BUT9641T no. 203 (KLJ337) "resting" on the disused tramway track fan of Central Depot, Southcote Road on 8 July 1950 following its tow from Weymann's in Addlestone. Malcolm Pearce (G.O.P. Pearce)

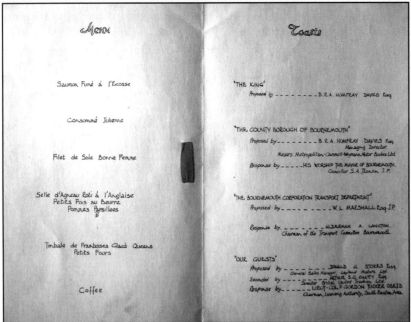

Wimborne Road. The Redhill Crescent reverser was dismantled on 11 November 1950, although it was reinstated in July 1953, coming back into use on 26 July 1953 due to the closure of Moordown Depot.

In May 1950, the Transport Committee agreed to pay increased costs of £36 2s due to rises in labour rates and materials for the first two BUT9641T chassis. The first of the BUTs to arrive at Central Depot, Southcote Road was 203 (KLJ337) on 8 July 1950 after being towed from Weymann's body building works at Addlestone, Surrey by the Department's Thornycroft LJ1608. The 16 August 1950 edition of *Passenger Transport* recorded that "*On Thursday 20 July 1950, the Transport Committee, accompanied by senior Transport Department staff, Lieut. Col. F. Gordon Tucker, Chairman of the South Eastern Area Licensing Authority, and representatives of the manufacturers, inspected KLJ337, the first of the BUT9641T trolleybuses to arrive in Bournemouth. To acquaint drivers with the first 8ft wide vehicle in the fleet and the new electrical equipment, the vehicle was used for training purposes only until more of the batch arrived in August*". For this purpose, 203 benefited from a particularly large RESERVED display on its main destination box indicator blinds.

In September 1950, BUT notified a further increase to the chassis cost of £147 4s 0d due to additional equipment and price increases for other equipment covered by the "rise and fall" clause in the agreement amounting to £664 4s 0d.

The first eleven BUT9641Ts delivered (200-210) entered traffic on the 25A Westbourne-Boscombe, Portman Road service from 1 October 1950. Before being delivered to Bournemouth, 212 was an exhibit on Weymann's stand at the Commercial Motor Transport Exhibition, held at London's Earls Court 22-30 September 1950. Eight more (211-217, 219) entered service on 1 November 1950 and the final five (218, 220-223) on 1 January 1951. In December 1950 Weymann notified further price increases caused by alterations and amendments to the original design and increased costs for certain equipment. The Transport Committee was obliged to accept an increased charge of £4,315 for the 24 all-metal trolleybus bodies. Mr Reakes commented that each new vehicle cost 2½ times that of a pre-war trolleybus. When all 24 new trolleybuses were in service, first priority was given to using them on service 25A, then the 24 and then the Side Routes 26-32.

Confronted with a lack of suitable overnight parking accommodation for the enlarged fleet following the BUT9641T deliveries (Hurn Airport had already been considered), in October 1950 the Transport Department asked the Baths and Health Committees (subject to approval by the Planning Department) if a parcel of land on the west side of Seabourne Road near its junction with Christchurch Road, Pokesdown, adjacent to Boscombe (Pokesdown) Depot, could be used for the overnight storage of 16 trolleybuses between 10.30pm and 8.30am until Castle Lane Depot was ready. The land, which had been occupied by a military strong point, cottages making up the British Restaurant and advertisement hoardings, had been reserved for a new public baths and health centre. This was approved, subject to there being no new entry from Christchurch Road and the plot being cleaned of rubbish daily before 8.30am. The temporary parking space came into

Westbourne to operate Bournemouth Square-Tuckton only, leaving Poole Road and Westbourne served solely by the 25A.

Bournemouth Trades Council felt that increased road traffic had made it dangerous to continue to turn trolleybuses using the reversing triangle at Wimborne Road, Redhill Crescent, opposite Moordown Post Office. The alternative of extending all journeys terminating there to Castle Lane West, Lawford Road would have been uneconomic. Mr Reakes therefore investigated using the inside of Moordown Depot instead. On 14 August 1950, Redhill Crescent reversing triangle was locked out of use and replaced by a new anti-clockwise turning circle at Moordown Depot strung across the entrance to the depot extension, through an opening made in the side wall of the main shed and back out of the front of the depot building into

On its first day in revenue service, 1 October 1950, BUT9641T no. 206 (KLJ 340) pauses at the Lansdowne stop at the west end of Holdenhurst Road on a 25A journey to Westbourne.　　　　**Malcolm Pearce (G.O.P. Pearce)**

Also on its first day in passenger-carrying service, 1 October 1950, no. 207 loads for Springbourne, Ashley Road and Boscombe at the west end of Holdenhurst Road. The 25A, and later the 25, was very much a "trunk" service passing Bournemouth West, Bournemouth Central and Boscombe railway stations, as well as the shopping streets in the middle of the town, Boscombe and Westbourne.　　　　**Malcolm Pearce (G.O.P. Pearce)**

Sixteen BUT9641Ts entered service for the first time on 1 October 1950. No. 210 (KLJ344) pulls away from the Lansdowne stop in Holdenhurst Road on its way to the Square from Queen's Park Golf Pavilion.

Malcolm Pearce (G.O.P. Pearce)

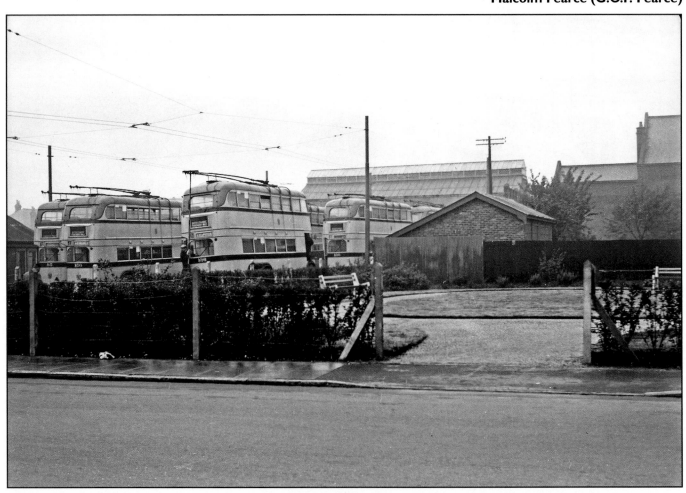

The temporary parking space, adjacent to Boscombe (Pokesdown) Depot viewed from Seabourne Road.

Omnibus Society (R.T. Wilson)

No. 148 and another Sunbeam MS2 wait, with chocks under their front offside wheels, beneath the eastbound wiring in Seabourne Road, Pokesdown, whilst another trolleybus manoeuvres out of the temporary parking space into the roadway. the building visible behind the trolleybuses is Pokesdown Fire Station. See Appendix G for plan.

Omnibus Society (R.T. Wilson)

The overcrowded nature of BCT's depots at this time is evidenced by this view of the east end of Central Depot, Southcote Road taken on 18 February 1951. To the left no. 98 (ALJ972), still in wartime livery, and no. 107 (ALJ981), together with the vehicle behind it, are already stored out of service although only officially withdrawn at the end of the year. Nos. 161 (BRU12) and 144 (BEL829) survived to end of the summer season in 1959 and 1960 respectively. The inside the depot building is clearly packed with trolleybuses.

Malcolm Pearce (G.O.P. Pearce)

use in November 1950, trolleybuses using T-poles for access from Seabourne Road, until a hand-operated frog was inserted in the westbound wiring, connected to a single line which led into another frog that provided two sidings above the space, and these were first used on 12 March 1951. It is understood that all vehicles entering or leaving the parking area came from or went to the Fisherman's Walk direction. It is likely that overhead was not initially erected as it was thought that the new Castle Lane Depot would be ready for occupation in early 1951, but delays in construction meant that it could not be used until October 1951 and then only for parking purposes and not for operational use until July 1953. Accordingly, the parking space only remained in use until 1 October 1951, the wiring being dismantled in March 1952.

The Transport Department recorded a deficit in the financial year 1949-50, despite carrying what turned out to be its maximum number of passengers, and anticipated a deficit for 1950-51. The 103 trolleybuses in service at the time, however, had earned £342,816 in revenue, covered some 3.4 million miles and carried 47.25 million passengers. No part of the trolleybus network had less than a 15-minute frequency and the majority had a trolleybus every five minutes. Having considered the General Manager's report, the Transport Committee meeting of 21 July 1950 recommended that application be made for a general fares revision based on a mileage rate. In his calculations the costs of replacing five miles of 50-year-old high tension feeder cables (£8,800), a new feeder cable from Yelverton Road to the Pier (£4,000) and the wiring of Alma Road (£6,000) and Castle Lane East (£6,634), all based on 20-year loan periods, in addition to the ongoing increased expenses, were assumed. The Deputy Town Clerk appeared at a public enquiry into the proposals on

23 November 1950 and reported to the Transport Committee the next day on the Chairman of the Licensing Authority's remarks on rate relief from Transport Department profits. As a clarification, it must be pointed out that the Licensing Authority, namely the SETC, only had jurisdiction over motorbus and not trolleybus fares at this time; however, the Transport Committee had to consider the undertaking as a whole whilst ensuring that the fare between any two points was identical whether the journey was made by motorbus or trolleybus. The Chairman had felt that every opportunity should be taken to build up a reasonable reserve to meet contingencies and, if such a reserve was accumulated, the Authority would like an undertaking from the Corporation that no further rate relief from Transport Department profits would be made without the SETC and the MoT being consulted. The Finance Committee recommended that this undertaking be given. The SETC and the MoT granted increases in both motorbus and trolleybus fares with effect from 1 March 1951.

The traction supply cable over Tuckton Bridge developed faults in August 1950 and was replaced at a cost of £375.

By September 1950 the department's 30cwt crane was considered life-expired and a Jones "Super 20" crane mounted on a Leyland SQ2 chassis (TF447) was hired from Brighton Corporation to plant traction poles along Castle Lane. As there was an option to buy the crane, the Transport Committee recommended that an offer of £500 (including £50 hire charge) be made. This was accepted and the crane, built in 1929, was used until September 1962 before being remounted on a Guy Arab FD motorbus chassis (FRU224) in December 1962.

The SEB advised that the existing traction current tariffs would apply at the proposed new intake point at the Holdenhurst

Still in regular service, Sunbeam MS2 no. 68 (LJ7701) loads at the Square stop for services 25 and 25A at the east end of Avenue Road prior to departure for Boscombe.   **Omnibus Society (R.T. Wilson)**

Road substation, subject to an annual service charge of £500. It added that the entire matter of traction supplies would be reviewed soon.

In order to ensure sufficient space for longer-distance passengers, it was suggested that either minimum fares be introduced on trolleybuses travelling to Christchurch, or express buses be operated, as trolleybuses left Gervis Place full of passengers travelling only as far as Boscombe or the Lansdowne. Another alternative would have been to extend more trolleybuses from Iford to Christchurch, but Ald. Langton stated that Christchurch turntable was already operating at full capacity, handling a trolleybus every five minutes. Soon afterwards, negotiations began with Messrs Strong (Romsey) Ltd., the brewers, with a view to purchase or lease the turntable site upon expiry of the existing agreement in 1956. This led to an offer to extend the lease by 20 years, the rent to be increased from £150 to £200 pa, with an agreement to break after 14 years.

At the end of October 1950, eleven motorbuses including the two converted trolleybuses 69 and 70, together with the last 1925-vintage Tilling Stevens TS6 petrol-electric vehicle (RU 2013) which had been used as a tower wagon by the Overhead Department, were offered for sale. A single tender, from Sherwood Car Sales, Parkstone, at £150 per vehicle, was received and accepted.

Passengers received cuts and bruises when two trolleybuses collided in Wimborne Road on Monday 18 December 1950. A trolleybus on service 30 heading for the Square skidded across the road on the icy surface and hit the offside front of BUT9641T 212, a 27 heading in the opposite direction, which was stationary at the Stokeswood Road stop. No trolleybuses could pass the spot in either direction from about 8.20am when the crash occurred until a breakdown vehicle pulled the trolleybuses off the road shortly before 9am. The drivers were lucky to escape injury. No. 212 suffered considerable damage to its offside front corner and was returned to Weymann from 5 February 1951 to 11 April 1951, not returning to service until 1 August 1951.

The summer extension of trolleybus services to Bournemouth Pier had not developed the traffic hoped for in summer 1950; accordingly, for the 1951 season, only certain vehicles on services 23, 24 and 27 were rerouted from Bournemouth Square. The diverted services operated from Good Friday to Easter Tuesday, from 12-15 May (Whitsun) and then during the summer season from 4 June to 30 September 1951. The 22B was again extended to Westbourne from 18 June until 14 October 1951.

The Town Clerk reported to the 20 April 1951 Transport Committee meeting that the Tramways Act 1870 required the publication of the proposed revision to the trolleybus byelaws in the *London Gazette* and in a local newspaper. The same meeting deferred consideration of the 1949 Extension of Time Order, until its September 1951 meeting. They also authorised the department to strip 18 trolleybuses and to use the salvaged electrical equipment, etc., as spares. In May 1952 their remains, the first Sunbeam MS2s to be withdrawn, were sold to James Thompson & Co., Cardiff, for scrap. These comprised: 68, 74, 78, 94, 98, 102, 103, 104, 107, 108, 110, 113, 120, 124, 126, 133, 151, 169. Scrap copper trolley wire was sold to Thomas Bolton and Sons Ltd. at the controlled price.

Traction poles in Bournemouth Square and the Lansdowne were decorated in 1951 for the Festival of Britain. By now

Although still incomplete, Castle Lane (Mallard Road) Depot was made available for vehicle storage purposes on 15 October 1951. In this view, taken on that day, work on the overhead wiring continues whilst two lines of vehicles, Sunbeam MS2s to the left and BUT9641Ts to the right, can be seen. At the time of its construction, the garage had the longest span of pre-stressed concrete in the country and for this reason is now a listed building.

Malcolm Pearce (G.O.P. Pearce)

Pictured at the north end of Charminster Road at its junction with Castle Lane West on 15 October 1951, no. 216 (KLJ350) is operating on the anti-clockwise unidirectional circular service 32, but erroneously displaying 31 (the clockwise service) on its number blind!   Malcolm Pearce (G.O.P. Pearce)

Heading east along Castle Lane on a warm spring day, BUT9641T 208 (KLJ342) is on clockwise unidirectional circular service 31 heading for Iford and then along Christchurch Road back to the Square. The Castle referred to in the name of the road is that of Christchurch whilst, although already having a wide carriageway by the early 1950s, it was still somewhat a lane passing through open fields between Strouden Park and Iford. Today, Castle Lane is an extremely busy road with traffic jams for several hours of the day.   Omnibus Society (S.E. Letts)

the population of Bournemouth had reached 144,726 (28,000 more than in 1931) whilst Christchurch had almost doubled in size to reach 20,506 people.

With effect from 11 June 1951, the 48-hour week was reintroduced for traffic staff in place of the normal 44-hour week due to an acute shortage of personnel.

On 20 July 1951 it was announced that there had been a deficit in the 1950-51 financial year due to the reduced number of passengers and increased costs. In the preceding three months alone, i.e. April-June 1951, there had been a fall of 1,345,170 journeys on trolleybuses, with commensurate falls on motorbus services. More than half of all motorbus services ran at a loss all the year round. Having reached a peak of passengers in 1949, trolleybus services had been reduced by 10,000 miles in the preceding winter. A 33.3% increase in revenue had been budgeted for as a result of the March 1951 fare increases, but revenues had only increased by 21.4% due to the continuing fall in passenger numbers. The increasing costs were underlined that same day when the NJIC announced a new wage award with effect from 16 July 1951, resulting in estimated additional costs of £25,000 pa. Mr Reakes was instructed to recommend further route and service economies, and a new increased fare structure, potentially with a 2d minimum fare. His recommendations were presented on 18 September 1951 and adopted immediately for introduction as soon as possible. It was anticipated that the economies would permit traffic staff to revert to a 44-hour week.

During the late summer of 1951 there was considerable correspondence with the MoT. The revised Trolley Vehicle Byelaws submitted on 3 April 1951 received Ministerial approval, with effect from 1 August 1951, whilst on 27 August 1951 use of the Castle Lane East trolleybus extension was approved, pending official inspection, which actually took place on 21 November

1951. Then, on 21 September 1951, the Transport Committee decided to apply for an Order for a further extension of time in respect of those trolley vehicle routes authorised by the 1937 Order and included in the 1949 Extension of Time Order but which had not yet been put into operation.

On 15 October 1951, what proved to be Bournemouth's final trolleybus route extension, along Castle Lane from the Broadway Hotel, past the Mallard Road entrance to the Castle Lane depot site, to Christchurch Road, Iford, came into service. As a consequence, motorbus services 14 and 31 were replaced by two circular trolleybus services:

31   Triangle - Bournemouth Square - Richmond Hill - Cemetery Junction - Charminster Road - Five Ways - Broadway Hotel - Castle Lane - Strouden Park - Iford - Boscombe - Pokesdown - Christchurch Road - Lansdowne - Bournemouth Square
Unidirectional circular service (clockwise) worked in conjunction with service 32

32   Bournemouth Square - Lansdowne - Christchurch Road - Boscombe - Pokesdown - Iford - Strouden Park - Castle Lane - Broadway Hotel - Five Ways - Charminster Road - Cemetery Junction - Richmond Hill - Bournemouth Square - Triangle
Unidirectional circular service (anti-clockwise) worked in conjunction with service 31

A petition from 518 ratepayers suggesting improvements to service 30, which had been reduced from a 15-minute to a 20-minute frequency as part of the undertaking's economy measures, and public transport along Columbia Road in general was received. In a letter to the *Bournemouth Daily Echo* it was

As the summer season draws to a close, no. 205 (KLJ339) turns south at Queen's Park Corner out of Holdenhurst Road, Springbourne, into Ashley Road on a 25A journey to Boscombe, Portman Road (25 September 1951).
Malcolm Pearce (G.O.P. Pearce)

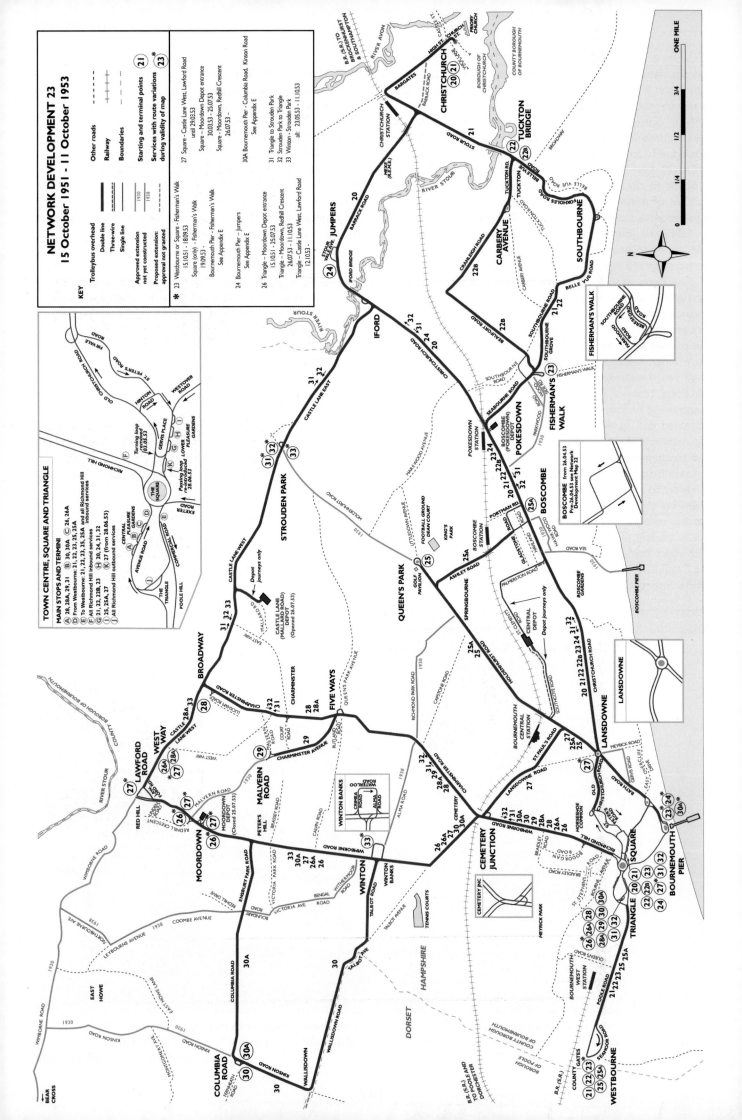

NETWORK DEVELOPMENT 23
15 October 1951 - 11 October 1953

KEY

Trolleybus overhead
- Double line
- Three-wire
- Single line

Other roads
Railway
Boundaries

1930
1938

Approved extension not yet constructed

Proposed extension: approval not granted

Starting and terminal points ㉑

Services with route variations during validity of map ㉓ *

23 Westbourne or Square - Fisherman's Walk 15.10.51 - 18.09.53
Square (only) - Fisherman's Walk 19.09.53 -
Bournemouth Pier - Fisherman's Walk See Appendix E

24 Bournemouth Pier - Jumpers See Appendix E

26 Triangle - Moordown Depot entrance 15.10.51 - 25.07.53
Triangle - Moordown, Redhill Crescent 26.07.53 - 11.10.53
Triangle - Castle Lane West, Lawford Road 12.10.53 -

27 Square - Castle Lane West, Lawford Road until 29.03.53
Square - Moordown Depot entrance 30.03.53 - 25.07.53
Square - Moordown, Redhill Crescent 26.07.53 -

30A Bournemouth Pier - Columbia Road, Kinson Road See Appendix E

31 Triangle to Strouden Park
32 Strouden Park to Triangle
33 Winton - Strouden Park all: 23.05.53 - 11.10.53

TOWN CENTRE, SQUARE AND TRIANGLE

MAIN STOPS AND TERMINI
(A) 28, 28A, 29, 31
(B) 30, 30A
(C) 26, 26A
(D) From Westbourne: 21, 22, 23, 25, 25A
(E) To Westbourne: 21, 22, 23, 25, 25A and all Richmond Hill inbound services
(F) All Richmond Hill inbound services
(G) 21, 22, 22B, 23
(H) 30, 24, 31, 32
(I) 25, 25A, 27
(J) All Richmond Hill outbound services
(K) 27 (from 28.06.53)

BOSCOMBE from 26.04.53 see Network Development Map 22
Pre-26.04.53 see Network Development Map 22

FISHERMAN'S WALK

LANDSOWNE

CEMETERY JNC

WINTON BANKS

In **Belle Vue Road, Southbourne**, a few yards to the west of Southbourne Cross Roads, Sunbeam MS2 no. 115 (ALJ989) pauses outside the 4-star Southbourne Cliffs Hotel on its way to Tuckton Bridge and Christchurch. The hotel, which opened as the South Cliff Hotel in 1881, was an integral part of the Southbourne-on-Sea Freehold Land Company's investment in the development of the area as a beautiful place to live and a health resort in the 1870s and 1880s. This land company, headed by Dr. Thomas Compton, endeavoured to emulate the success of Louis Tregonwell in Bournemouth at the beginning of the 19th century. Following its closure, the hotel was converted into flats and finally demolished in 1988.

NTA Collection (photographer R.F. Mack)

pointed out that, although there was a parallel motorbus service (the 7) it ran at almost the same times as service 30 whilst although there was a total of seven buses an hour, those for West Howe were always full.

In September 1951, tenders were invited for a new coal elevator plant for the generating station at an estimated £500. In addition, from 1 October 1951 increased coal prices put extra costs of £5,945 pa on the undertaking and influenced the SEB's traction power charges under the sliding scale.

Early in 1952 a petition was received asking that the Strouden Park circular trolleybus services along Castle Lane operate to and from Bournemouth Square via Moordown, rather than via Charminster Road. The department therefore carried out a census over the period 14 January 1952-7 February 1952 which showed that only about 5% of passengers transferred at the Broadway Hotel on to services going to Moordown. The existing routing and time table had been prepared in consultation with the Strouden Park Local Government Association and there was accordingly no change.

The flood of additional costs and the financial position of the undertaking provoked the Transport Committee on 21 March 1952 to authorise another application for a general fares revision as soon as possible. There were also thoughts about introducing books of tickets and offering them for sale at a discount; however, rather than have books, weekly tickets were introduced on 1 December 1952. In view of the need to economise, there was no special celebration of the undertaking's Golden Jubilee on 23 July 1952.

Supplementary journeys on trolleybus services 23, 24 and 30A were operated to and from Bournemouth Pier over the Easter weekend 1952 and in the summer season (which that year encompassed the Whitsun holiday).

On 16 May 1952 the MoT consented to a further three-year extension of the 1937 Order, for the commencement of Routes 2 (Junction Redhill Drive with Ensbury Park Road along Redhill Drive to and along Coombe Avenue, along Leybourne Avenue and Northbourne Avenue to Wimborne Road) and 4 (along Alma and Richmond Park Roads from Wimborne Road to Holdenhurst Road). The Transport Committee asked Mr Reakes for an estimate of the cost of equipping these routes.

On 19 May 1952 it was learned that increased labour rates and material charges had again raised the costs of the 24 BUT9641Ts by £866 3s 0d. The Transport Committee accepted the increase and asked that the Finance Committee provide an additional loan sanction.

The SETC appointed Deputy Chief Inspector W. Biddlecombe, the undertaking's Trolleybus Driving Test Examiner, as the MoT's delegated Motorbus Driving Test Examiner in September 1952.

Bournemouth Chamber of Trade complained of television interference, allegedly caused by trolleybuses. Mr Reakes stated that the matter was under discussion with the MPTA and the Joint Electricity Distribution & Collection Committee, whose findings would be reported in due course. On 24 October 1952, permission to span private telephone lines above the trolleybus wires in Columbia Road was refused.

In October 1952 it was learned that the NJIC

for the Road Passenger Transport Industry had made a further award to platform staff and unskilled workers which would lead to additional costs of £17,000-£18,000 pa and that no provision had been made for this in the increased fares application then pending before the SETC and the MoT. It was agreed that, if approved, the new fares would be introduced on Monday 1 December 1952. The Transport Committee decided that the undertaking's financial position ruled out decorating vehicles for the pending Coronation of Queen Elizabeth scheduled for 2 June 1953.

The *Bournemouth Times & Directory* recorded in their 28 November 1952 issue that:

"From next Monday the one penny fare will go on all motor and trolleybus routes. The daily return ticket will be replaced by five- or six-day weekly tickets of which a million and half have already been printed. Each day's return journey will cost about one and one-third times the single fare based on the new fares. That is the same proportion as the daily return. These tickets will be issued on Mondays and Tuesdays only before 8.45am; on each remaining day of the week the first journey must be commenced before the same hour.

"Bournemouth has been one of the last towns in the country to retain the one penny fare. The new minimum will be 1½d for 1,500 yards instead of 1d for 1,200 yards. A number of fare stages have been abolished mainly where stages are too close together. Another change is the abolition of ½d changes in fares higher than 2d. Special factory bus passengers will be charged one and a half times the single fare for a return instead of one and a third as now. Children's tickets will be reckoned to the nearest 1d instead of the nearest ½d".

The new fares were reckoned to the nearest penny above, e.g. half of a 5d fare was considered 3d. Although halfpenny fares above 1½d, i.e. 2½d, 3½d, 4½d, 5½d, 6½d, 7½d, 8½d disappeared, halfpenny fare units were retained outside the Corporation area in H&D territory on motorbus services 1 and 19 for a few more years, whilst a special 1½d ticket existed in the Ultimate ticket machine range between 1953 and 1956 for use as a schoolchildren's return.

The *Bournemouth Times & Directory* reported:

"When the South Eastern Traffic Commissioners heard the Corporation's application last month it was stated that the transport accounts would be down £52,000 by next March if it was not granted. A year's extra revenue from increased fares from 58 million passengers would yield £66,161 [sic] (£46,000 from trolleybuses, £19,200 from motorbuses) it was then said. Since the last application for fare increases in November 1950, ordinary wages have gone up 17.2%, skilled workers' wages 21.2%, coal 24%, petrol 49% and diesel fuel 48%. But since the present fare increase applications went in there had been another wage increase which averages about 7s per week. Thus even with the benefit of the new fares the undertaking will still be £18,000 in the red a year".

In addition, All-Day tickets were available in 1953 (only). They cost 2s for adults and 1s for children, and were valid on all services except the motorbus summer pleasure services, but were obviously not a success.

CHAPTER SEVEN
DECLINING LOADS AND STAFF SHORTAGES

At the beginning of 1953 BCT was operating the following year-round trolleybus services

20 Bournemouth Square, Gervis Place - Lansdowne - Christchurch Road - Boscombe Gardens - Boscombe Arcade - Pokesdown Station - Iford - Jumpers Corner - Barrack Road - Christchurch, Church Street (5¾ miles)

21 Bournemouth Square, Gervis Place - Lansdowne - Boscombe Gardens - Boscombe Arcade - Pokesdown Station - Fisherman's Walk - Southbourne - Tuckton Bridge - Christchurch, Church Street (6 miles)

22 Bournemouth Square, Gervis Place - Lansdowne - Boscombe Gardens - Boscombe Arcade - Pokesdown Station - Fisherman's Walk - Southbourne Cross Roads - Tuckton, Tuckton Road, junction with Belle Vue Road (5 miles)
(some weekday morning peak hour extensions to/from Westbourne, Seamoor Road)

22B Bournemouth Square, Gervis Place - Lansdowne- Boscombe Gardens - Boscombe Arcade - Pokesdown Station - Fisherman's Walk - Beaufort Road - Cranleigh Road - Tuckton, Tuckton Road, junction with Belle Vue Road (5 miles)

23 Bournemouth Square, Gervis Place - Lansdowne - Boscombe Gardens - Boscombe Arcade - Pokesdown Station - Fisherman's Walk, Wentworth Avenue (3 miles) (peak hours only, with some journeys to/from Westbourne, Seamoor Road) (4½ miles)

24 Bournemouth Square, Gervis Place - Lansdowne - Boscombe Gardens - Boscombe Arcade - Pokesdown Station - Iford - Jumpers Corner (4 miles)

25 Westbourne, Seamoor Road - West Station - Bournemouth Square - Lansdowne - Central Station - Holdenhurst Road - Springbourne - Queen's Park Corner - Queen's Park Golf Pavilion, Holdenhurst Road (3½ miles)

25A Westbourne, Seamoor Road - West Station - Bournemouth Square - Lansdowne - Central Station - Holdenhurst Road - Springbourne - Queen's Park Corner - Boscombe Station - Boscombe, Portman Road (3¾ miles)

26 Triangle - Bournemouth Square - Richmond Hill - Cemetery Junction - Winton - Moordown Depot (3 miles)

26A Triangle - Bournemouth Square - Richmond Hill - Cemetery Junction - Winton - Moordown - Castle Lane West, junction with West Way (3¾ miles)

Pictured in Bath Road at St. Peter's Road and Gervis Road, Sunbeam MS2 no. 92 is about to descend the hill to the Royal Bath Hotel prior to turning into Westover Road on its way to the Square. In the background is Bournemouth's new GPO telephone exchange.
David Chalk collection

27 Bournemouth Square, Gervis Place - Lansdowne - Central Station - St Paul's Road - Cemetery Junction - Winton - Moordown - Castle Lane West, junction with Lawford Road (4 miles)

28 Triangle - Bournemouth Square - Richmond Hill - Cemetery Junction - Charminster Road - Five Ways - Broadway Hotel, Luckham Road (3 miles)

28A Triangle - Bournemouth Square - Richmond Hill - Cemetery Junction - Charminster Road - Five Ways - Broadway Hotel - Castle Lane West, junction with West Way (3½ miles)

29 Triangle - Bournemouth Square - Richmond Hill - Cemetery Junction - Charminster Road - Five Ways - Malvern Road, junction with Charminster Avenue (2¾ miles)

30 Triangle - Bournemouth Square - Richmond Hill - Cemetery Junction - Winton - Wallisdown - Columbia Road, junction with Kinson Road (3¾ miles)

30A Triangle - Bournemouth Square - Richmond Hill - Cemetery Junction - Winton - Ensbury Park - Columbia Road, junction with Kinson Road (3¾ miles)

31 Triangle - Bournemouth Square - Richmond Hill - Cemetery Junction - Broadway Hotel - Strouden Park - Iford - Pokesdown Station - Boscombe Arcade - Boscombe Gardens - Lansdowne - Bournemouth Square, Gervis Place (9½ miles)
Unidirectional circular service (clockwise) worked in conjunction with service 32

32 Bournemouth Square, Gervis Place - Lansdowne - Boscombe Gardens - Boscombe Arcade - Pokesdown Station - Iford - Strouden Park - Broadway Hotel - Cemetery Junction - Richmond Hill - Bournemouth Square - Triangle (9½ miles)
Unidirectional circular service (anti-clockwise) worked in conjunction with service 31.

In an effort to cut costs and avoid major new investment, in February 1953 the Council agreed in principle to discontinue power generation at Southcote Road; Bournemouth and Glasgow (at Pinkston) being the last two municipal transport undertakings in the UK to generate their own traction power. An electrical consultant, Mr W.L. Marshall of Preston, was engaged to review the retention or otherwise of the BCT generating station. He submitted his report in April 1953 in which he expressed the view that the existing equipment was old and the cost of generation uneconomic. It had a maximum capacity of 3,000 kW and in the year ending 31 March 1952 it had provided 6,900,860 units of which 6,038,105 were used for traction purposes. The combined output of the five SEB substations was stated to be 2,100kW and in the same year they had provided 2,826,600 units—32% of the total traction load.

Consideration was given to replacing the plant with three diesel-driven 1,000kW generators, requiring approximately 16 new outgoing feeder panels at an estimated cost of £100,000. Together with oil storage tanks, etc., the total cost was expected to be £120,000.

In July 1953, Mr Reakes reported on his negotiations for special bulk tariffs using solely an SEB supply whilst in the meantime tenders for a further year's supply of coal were invited. The SEB proposed to substitute 2,500kW of converting capacity for the BCT's own 3,000kW generating capacity. This was deemed adequate as some of the existing converter substations were somewhat under-loaded and the new scheme would permit a transfer of some of the load. A further 500kW substation would be housed in a new building at Iddesleigh Road and the remaining 500kW inside Boscombe (Pokesdown) Depot. The SEB would own and maintain all AC distribution gear up to, but not including, the main AC circuit breakers which fed the rectifier transformer or transformers. All converting plant comprising switchgear on the AC side of the rectifier transformers, rectifiers, auxiliary plant, DC switchgear, protective gear, and DC feeder cables would be supplied and owned by BCT.

Heading for the Square on a 22B working, Sunbeam MS2 117 (ALJ991) prepares to pull away from the Seafield Road stop on Cranleigh Road (13 August 1954).
Malcolm Pearce (G.O.P. Pearce)

Resting at the loading point in Stourvale Avenue, Jumpers, no. 125 (ALJ999) awaits departure time for its trip back to the Square on a service 24 working.
David Chalk collection

The SEB proposed the following tariff:
Maximum demand charge: 105s per kVA in respect of the highest simultaneous half-hour maximum demand during the months November-February. For each and every kVA of demand on a half-hourly basis recorded at other times of the year of supply in excess of the highest registered during the four winter months there would be a charge of 42s 6d per kVA.
Unit charge: 5d per unit
Fuel cost variation: at the rate of 0.00075d per unit for each 1d variation from 38s per ton related to a calorific value of 11,000 BTUs per lb.

The additional equipment needed was estimated to cost £37,500 with a further £1,000 for additions and variations to DC feeder cables (see Appendix H for details of the building and equipment) plus the cost of buildings.

Some alterations would be needed to the trolleybuses' electrical equipment as the pre-war vehicles were equipped with regenerative braking. If other trolleybuses were in the vicinity absorbing power then this energy was readily absorbed, however, if the line was unreceptive then the energy was absorbed by the DC generators at the power station. Rectifiers would not absorb such regenerated energy and special load-absorbing resistance and associated switchgear in the substations would be required. It was recommended that the regenerative braking be disconnected and only rheostatic electrical braking be used, the changes costing £30 per vehicle.

An additional positive feeder of 0.5 sq.in. cross-section about ¾ mile long between the positive feeder pillar on Richmond Hill and the positive feeder pillar at St. Augustin's would be required. The existing 0.183 sq.in. feeders supplying Derby Road, Southcote Road, Holdenhurst Road, Cleveland Road, Ashley Road, Palmerston Road would be regrouped. There would be substitution of a reduced number of 0.5 sq.in. cables with a consequent smaller number of outgoing feeders from the new substation. Subsequently, there were negotiations with the SEB about its use of one of the Department's underground cable ducts between the Lansdowne and Cotlands Road.

The total cost was to be offset by the sale of existing equipment and the disposal of the Southcote Road Generating Station site and buildings. The cost per unit of the proposed SEB bulk supply would be lower than the alternative of installing diesel-driven generators. It was estimated that the SEB solution would save £14,273 pa.

In February 1953 it was suggested that an experimental trolleybus shuttle service between Iford and Moordown Depot be introduced. Although it was decided to take no action, interestingly just three months later a Winton-Strouden Park service was introduced and this was extended to run between the Triangle and Iford Bridge in the autumn. A traction pole outside Beale's store in Old Christchurch Road was removed, at the firm's expense, and a rosette attached to the building.

On 12 March 1953 experiments started with two Bell Punch "Ultimate" ticket-issuing machines, instead of the traditional Bell Punch system using a ticket rack and punch (see Appendix K). As a result, it was decided to standardise on the "Ultimate" system, estimated to save £550 or more after the first year, the changeover being completed by 22 March 1954.

Commencing on Monday 30 March 1953, trolleybus service 27 was curtailed during weekday daytime to Moordown Depot but continued to operate to Castle Lane West, junction with

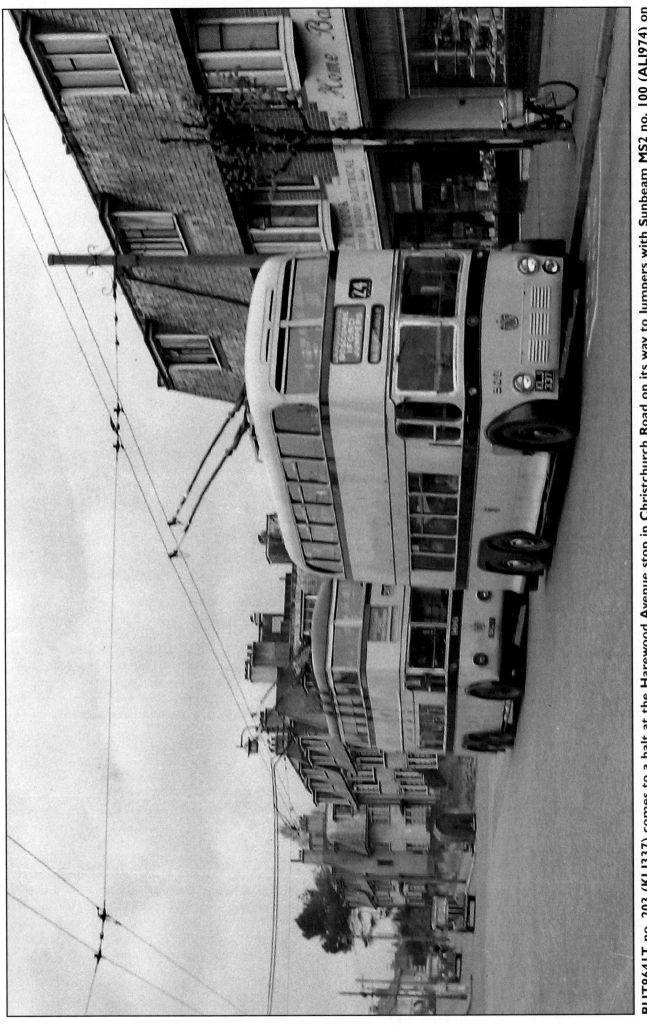

BUT9641T no. 203 (KLJ337) comes to a halt at the Harewood Avenue stop in Christchurch Road on its way to Jumpers with Sunbeam MS2 no. 100 (ALJ974) on service 20 immediately behind. Just by the bus stop at 1066 Christchurch Road was a confectionary and sweet shop which amusingly traded as "The Hastings". Omnibus Society (R.T. Wilson)

Lawford Road during peak hours. The frequency of motorbus service 3, which paralleled service 27 as far as Castle Lane West, was increased in compensation. From the same date the evening and Sunday morning service was curtailed to Lansdowne-Moordown Depot only (except in the peak summer period) and from 28 June 1953 the Square terminus of the 27 was moved from the eastern to the western end of Gervis Place, using a stop previously used by motorbus services 3 and 3A. Motorbus service 3 and trolleybus service 27 now shared this stop, while motorbus service 3A now used the former 27 stop. An additional passing loop in the overhead wiring was installed here on 3 May 1953 at the same time as the wartime emergency link from Gervis Place directly into Old Christchurch Road was removed.

Construction of a new turning circle at the junction of Holdenhurst Road with Castle Lane, Strouden Park (close to where the Cooper Dean roundabout was later built), started on 20 March 1953. On 23 May 1953, an hourly service 33 was introduced between Winton Banks and the new turning circle, a tar and chippings track through the gorse bushes. The MoT Inspection of the installation took place on 24 July 1953. In addition, throughout the summer, the hourly circular services 31 and 32 were enhanced by an hourly short-working via Charminster Road to Strouden Park turning circle, together offering two journeys an hour between the Triangle and Strouden Park.

31   Triangle - Bournemouth Square - Cemetery Junction - Broadway Hotel - Strouden Park - Iford - Pokesdown Station - Boscombe Arcade - Boscombe Gardens - Lansdowne - Bournemouth Square, Gervis Place
Unidirectional circular service (clockwise) worked in conjunction with service 32.

32   Bournemouth Square, Gervis Place - Lansdowne, Boscombe Gardens - Boscombe Arcade - Pokesdown Station - Iford - Strouden Park - Broadway Hotel - Cemetery Junction - Bournemouth Square - Triangle
Unidirectional circular service (anti-clockwise) worked in conjunction with service 31.

33   Winton, Crimea Road - Moordown - Broadway Hotel - Strouden Park, Castle Lane East, junction with Holdenhurst Road

The future of Moordown Depot was discussed at the 24 April 1953 Transport Committee Meeting. It was agreed that the premises would be vacated and tenders issued for their sale or lease by the end of July 1953. It also considered and agreed to the employment of students as temporary conductors in the summer period. Student conductors first appeared in June 1953, working on all services. On 26 April 1953 a new eastbound overhead wiring layout was introduced in Christchurch Road, Boscombe, permitting 25A trolleybuses turning out of Ashley Road to overtake Main Road services at their Ashley Road stop prior to turning north to reach the 25A terminal point in Portman Road.

Only two trolleybus services reached Bournemouth Pier in summer 1953; services 23 from Fisherman's Walk and 30A from Columbia Road. These operated as required, the public timetable simply including the note under these services that "a frequent service of buses" would operate to the Pier.

The Coronation Festivities for HM Queen Elizabeth II led to services operating until midnight on 2 June 1953, and until 11pm on all other weekdays in the period 30 May-6 June 1953 inclusive. Traction poles in Christchurch, Old Christchurch and Wimborne Roads were decorated for the occasion with flags and bunting. Staff working on Coronation Day were given a day's holiday in lieu or two days' pay.

In July 1953, six Sunbeam MS2s dating from 1934 (72, 73, 75-77, 79) were sold for scrap to Messrs James Thompson & Co. (Cardiff) Ltd. for £300. From 5 July 1953 the last buses on Sundays were rescheduled to leave Bournemouth Square at 11pm instead of 10.30pm.

Following an official opening by the Mayor, Councillor H.P.E. Mears, OBE, JP, on 23 July 1953, the new £500,000 Castle Lane (Mallard Road) Depot came into operational use the next day and Moordown Depot, together with its turnround loop, ceased to be used. By 26 July 1953 the building at Moordown was vacated and, having considered three tenders the premises were leased from 1 August 1954 to Post Office Telephones for

Rounding the south side of the Square roundabout, Sunbeam MS2 no. 152 (BRU3) already (correctly) displays indicator blinds for its next trip - to Malvern Road on service 29.
NTA Collection (photographer R.F. Mack)

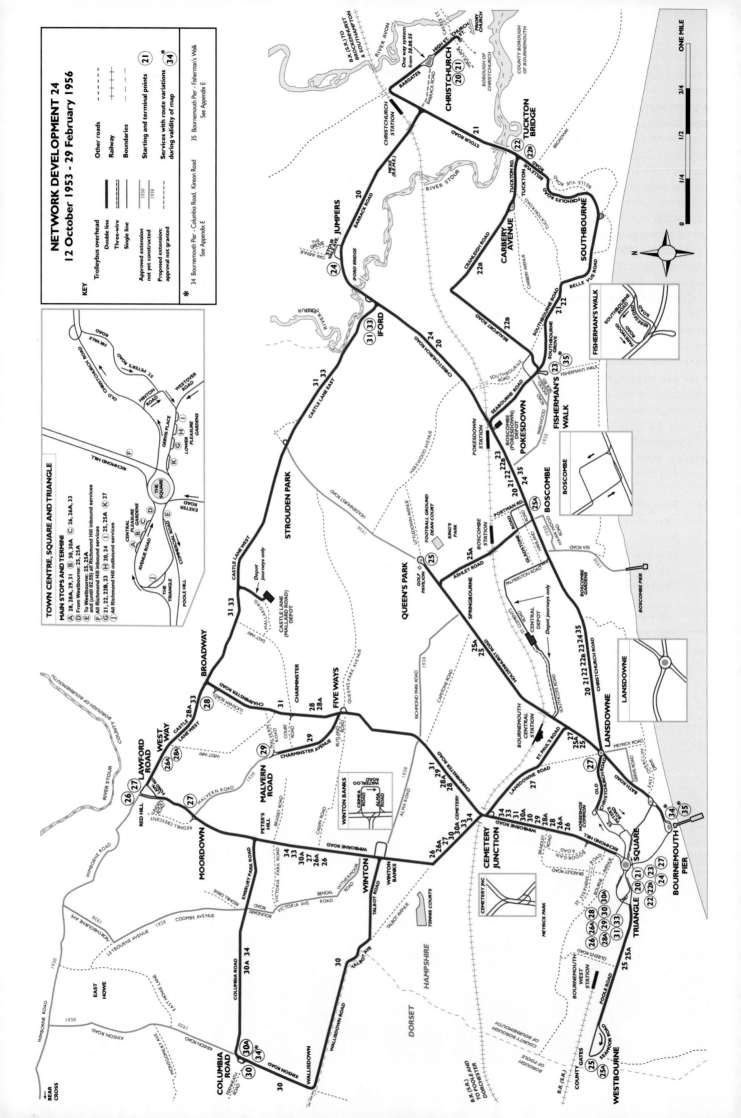

21 years as a vehicle depot, at an annual rent of £1,900 (in fact, they continued to use the building until it was demolished in 1984). The Redhill Crescent reversing triangle was reinstated for use by services 26 and 27 although from 12 October 1953 all service 26 trolleybuses were extended to Lawford Road.

26   Triangle - Bournemouth Square - Cemetery Junction - Winton - Moordown - Castle Lane West, Lawford Road

27   Bournemouth Square, Gervis Place - Lansdowne - Cemetery Junction - Winton - Moordown, Wimborne Road, junction with Redhill Crescent

The reversing triangle remained intact until the withdrawal of trolleybuses to Moordown on 25 September 1966, but was last used by service vehicles on off-peak 34 journeys (service 27 having been renumbered 34 in the meantime) on 25 March 1956.

On 11 October 1953 unidirectional services 31 and 32 were withdrawn to be replaced by a new bidirectional service 31 operating hourly between the Triangle and Iford Bridge via Charminster Road. Service 33 was similarly extended to run between the Triangle and Iford Bridge via Winton and Moordown, again operating hourly, thus providing two journeys an hour along Castle Lane between the Broadway Hotel and Iford:

31   Triangle - Bournemouth Square - Cemetery Junction - Five Ways - Broadway Hotel - Strouden Park - Iford Bridge

33   Triangle - Bournemouth Square - Cemetery Junction - Winton - Moordown - Broadway Hotel - Castle Lane - Strouden Park - Iford Bridge

The *Bournemouth Times & Directory* for 7 August 1953 recorded that: "*The April 1953 report of the Consulting Transport Engineer on power supply for Corporation Trolleybuses, together with the General Manager's report dated 21 July 1953, were submitted to the Transport Committee at the end of July. They recommended that an alternative source of power should be implemented.*

"*Last February the council agreed to discontinue the use and dispose of the Southcote Road generating station. It was decided to approach an electrical consultant with a view to negotiating with the Southern Electricity Board for supply of electric power. Councillor O. E. Ellum (Conservative) warned that this investment needed careful consideration because many towns were discarding their trolleybuses in favour of diesel driven vehicles. In 1932-33 it had been argued in favour of trolleybuses that the Corporation had its own generating station. They had a good service from the trolleybuses but they had found great difficulty in making things pay. In 1936 there was a loss of £25,000, in 1937 a deficit of £26,604 [sic, these figures are not substantiated by the Department's own records]. During the war they did very well and transport made a profit. Other towns were making profits with motor buses. Now in 1953 the Borough Treasurer had stated they were going to lose £35,000 on transport. They would be entirely in the hands of the Southern Electricity Board.*

"*The Transport Committee Chairman, Ald. A. Langton, said that this was all part of the long going trolley versus motor bus arguments which Mr Ellum had been preaching 23 years ago in Southbourne. Any sensible interpretation of the consultant's report would prove without doubt that what was proposed was going to put the undertaking in a*

very much better position within 18 months. Transport finance would benefit from about £14,000 (a conservative figure as only £2,000 had been included for the disposal of the generating station plant)".

The 23 October 1953 Transport Committee meeting recommended that the Finance Committee apply to borrow £42,450 for the new buildings and equipment required for an alternative power supply to the existing distribution board. The consultant was retained to handle the machinery disposal. He was awarded fees representing 5% of all capital expenditure on the traction power supply conversion (excluding buildings) plus the amount raised by the disposal of redundant power station plant and equipment.

The 4 November 1953 *Bournemouth Daily Echo* noted "*Ald. Langton told the Council that Bournemouth Corporation are losing £1,000 per month by continuing to operate the Southcote Road generating station for trolleybus power. The Finance Committee considered that the application to borrow £44,325 for an alternative electricity source, including £1,875 consultant's fee, was excessive*".

The Parks Committee was in agreement to release a portion of the Wimborne Road Cemetery grounds for the construction of a substation off Charminster Road on Iddesleigh Road but recommended that it be set back and that the Parks Superintendent be made responsible for removal of trees. Consent was given by the Ministry of Housing and Local Government in mid-April 1954 for the appropriation for transport purposes of 0.0235 acres of cemetery land. Pokesdown substation was constructed in Boscombe Depot at the same time, reducing the depot's capacity from 16 vehicles to 12.

In December 1953 negotiations started with the SEB about the rent for those portions of the substation buildings which it needed. The Board's request that the portion of land to be leased for 99 years for the proposed substation behind Central Depot, Southcote Road, be slightly enlarged was granted.

On 16 January 1954 the MoT approved the Council's proposals for an alternative traction power supply. Five tenders had been received for the electrical work at the proposed new substations, that of the Hackbridge and Hewittic Electric Co. Ltd. at £41,135 for electrical equipment (12-phase working) plus £7,198 19s 0d for cables being accepted, and loan sanctions requested. In the meantime essential maintenance work at the generating station had to continue, the No. 2 turbine set was repaired in September 1953 whilst the superheater tubes (£220) and the cooling towers were made good soon thereafter.

By 1 January 1954 the fleet had fallen to 103 trolleybuses:

Sunbeam MS2	80-93, 95-97, 99-101, 105, 106, 109, 111, 112, 114-119, 121-123, 125, 127-132, 134-150, 152-168, 170-173 (Total 79)
BUT9641T	200-223 (Total 24)

of which the following 86 vehicles were licensed for service:

Sunbeam	MS2 80-83, 85-89, 91, 93, 95-97, 99, 100, 105, 106, 109, 111, 112, 115-118, 121, 122, 125, 127, 128, 130-132, 134-138, 140-142, 144-146, 148-150, 152-154, 157, 158, 160, 162, 164-166, 168, 170-173 (Total 62)
BUT9641T	200-223 (Total 24)

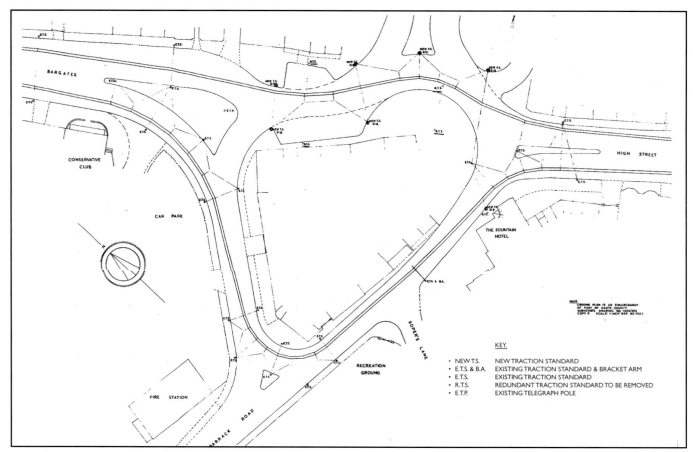

KEY.

- NEW T.S. — NEW TRACTION STANDARD
- E.T.S. & B.A. — EXISTING TRACTION STANDARD & BRACKET ARM
- E.T.S. — EXISTING TRACTION STANDARD
- R.T.S. — REDUNDANT TRACTION STANDARD TO BE REMOVED
- E.T.P. — EXISTING TELEGRAPH POLE

The revised overhead wiring layout at the Pit Site, Christchurch around the one-way system at the junction of Bargates, Barrack Road, Christchurch by-pass and High Street came into use on 28 August 1955. Large scale detailed plans, prepared for the Overhead Department, showed the precise position of each traction pole, span wire and hangar. This plan has been substantially reduced in size but the key has been enlarged for clarity.

Bournemouth Transport Ltd.

Defying the **NO ENTRY** sign at the Pit Site, Sunbeam MS2 125 (ALJ999) leaves High Street, Christchurch and heads north into Bargates whilst all other traffic is obliged to turn left and follow the new one-way system.

David Chalk collection

The 17 unlicensed vehicles were all stored at Castle Lane (Mallard Road) Depot.

At the end of February 1954, having considered an anticipated deficit for the year 1954-5, an application was made to the SETC for a 2d minimum fare on all services, an increase of 1d per day in the cost of weekly tickets where the daily rate was 3d, and by 2d per day in all other cases, and a general reduction in frequencies after 7.30pm during the winter months. Approval for the fare increases was granted and the changes took place on 13 December 1954, the minimum fare becoming 2d, although the 1d and 1½d values were retained for children's fares. In the meantime, there had been further wage rises totalling almost £15,000 pa.

With regard to the power supply, the *Bournemouth Daily Echo* reported that: *"The changeover to power from the grid will be completed by the end of September 1955. When the Corporation decided in February 1954 to apply to the Ministry of Transport for sanction to borrow £50,702 to effect the changeover it was said that electrical equipment would cost £41,135, cables £7,198 and a consultants fee 5% on £47,500 but that the alternative supply would save £14,000 pa. The current will come from the grid through eight substations, three—which Bournemouth Corporation have built at Southcote Road, Iddesleigh Road, and Pokesdown (inside Boscombe Depot)—and the remainder belonging to the Southern Electricity Board at Green Road, Winton; Electric House, Southbourne; Holdenhurst Road and Christchurch".*

The Christchurch Town Clerk had first asked for the undertaking's support of the Hampshire County Council (HCC) application to the MoT for the replacement of the traffic lights at the junction of Barrack Road with Bargates and Christchurch High Street by a roundabout in January 1953. Bournemouth Council had no objection to the proposed roundabout, on the understanding that the HCC reimbursed them their expenses in adopting the scheme and that their existing operating and turning rights in Christchurch were retained.

Based on a letter from the MoT, it was recommended on 23 July 1954 that an application for trolleybus operating powers be made for roads in the vicinity of Fountain Corner as required by the HCC and the Christchurch Borough Council for their proposed scheme. At the beginning of September 1954 the HCC asked if Bournemouth Corporation would bear the cost of obtaining the necessary Provisional Order for trolleybus operation around the roundabout. This was refused and, on 14 September 1954, the County Council agreed to accept these costs.

Christchurch Corporation started work on the construction of the Pit Site roundabout in the summer of 1954, together with the related short one-way system at what later became (in 1958) the western end of the Christchurch By-Pass on the then main Bournemouth - Southampton A35 road. When Bournemouth Corporation was notified of the expected date of completion, in order that the trolleybus overhead wiring could be modified to comply with the new road arrangements, it was realised that the additional Parliamentary Powers would not be granted in time. From 13 November 1954, all traffic except the trolleybuses began to use the new one-way system around what was subsequently to be the southern half of the roundabout. The trolleybuses continued to operate over their original course, those proceeding westbound actuating traffic lights by means of a contact skate on the overhead wire. The enactment of the Bournemouth Corporation (Trolley Vehicles) Order Confirmation Act, 1955, approved the erection of 9.1

chains of a diversion to the overhead wiring and trolleybuses started to comply with the route taken by all other traffic from 28 August 1955.

Operation of trolleybuses to and from Bournemouth Pier on seasonal supplementary services to Fisherman's Walk (service 23 in 1953) and Columbia Road (30A) recommenced on 16 April 1954 for the period Good Friday-Easter Monday and again on 5 June 1954 for the summer, but the journeys were redesignated with their own separate service numbers:

34   Bournemouth Pier - Lansdowne - St Paul's Road - Cemetery Junction - Winton - Moordown - Ensbury Park Road - Columbia Road, junction with Kinson Road *(formerly service 30A)*

35   Bournemouth Pier - Lansdowne - Christchurch Road - Boscombe - Fisherman's Walk, Wentworth Avenue *(formerly service 23)*

The Bournemouth Trades Council wrote on 12 June 1954 suggesting that trolleybuses should cease to turn at Redhill Crescent reversing triangle. Service 26 had last used it on 11 October 1953 although service 27, later renumbered 34, continued to use it off-peak up to and including 25 March 1956.

By mutual agreement with the TGWU the 48-hour week was reintroduced from 7 June 1954 in an effort to cope with staff shortages. Severe traffic congestion in the 1954 summer season caused considerable service dislocation and the Transport Committee placed on record their appreciation of the traffic staff's work.

The Transport Committee, at its meeting on 18 June 1954, recommended that two-section passenger waiting shelters already in stock be erected at Westbourne, Lloyds Bank (services 25, 25A) and Brassey Road, inward (services 30A, 34).

In July 1954, 147 was recorded as having been rebuilt in the body shop and 90 stripped for rebuilding. Also in 1954, 97 and 129 were rebuilt

In contravention of Section 15 of the Bournemouth Corporation Act, 1901, as extended by Section 99 of the 1930 Act, Mr Nigel Ponsford was prosecuted on 13th June 1954 for wilfully interfering with trolleybus frog-operating equipment. Subsequently, on 31st October 1954, the police reported a similar interference, but on this occasion a warning was given.

In June 1954 the revised tender from the Hackbridge and Hewittic Electric Co. Ltd. for equipment at the proposed substations, based on the electrical consultant's suggestions and thereby saving £2,100, was accepted. Two tenders were received for the construction of the Iddesleigh Road and Boscombe (Pokesdown) Depot substations, that of Messrs Cooper & Rowe (Contractors) Ltd. at £3,795 being accepted. The Finance Committee was asked to apply for loan sanction for this amount and the estimated cost of the Central Depot, Southcote Road, substation. In October 1954, the sole tender received, that from Messrs Willis Bros. & Jackson Ltd. for this latter substation, for £3,060, was accepted.

At its 22 October 1954 meeting the Transport Committee learned that Christchurch had decided not to exercise its powers to purchase that portion of the trolleybus network in their Borough in 1955. However, Christchurch Council's request that a preferential fare be introduced within its area was rejected.

At lunchtime on Monday 31 October 1954, a trolley wire

Gordon Pearce stood in the forecourt of Boscombe (Pokesdown) Depot to photograph no. 134 (BEL819) pausing to take on more passengers on its journey to Bournemouth Pier on seasonal supplementary service 35 from Fisherman's Walk (16 August 1954).   **Malcolm Pearce (G.O.P. Pearce)**

The summer season of 1954 saw the Bournemouth Pier - Columbia Road supplementary service renumbered from 30A to 34. Here, Sunbeam MS2 116 (ALJ990), exemplifying Livery 5 is seen resting at the Pier boarding point with the Pavilion to the rear. Note the semaphore arm illuminated traffic indicators in black protective boxes on the leading side pillar to the driver's cab and that the auxiliary single-line indicator box is still located at the top of the driver's nearside windscreen.   **David Chalk collection (Roy Marshall)**

broke in Holdenhurst Road near the Lansdowne, causing short hold-ups.

The SEB's proposals of 12 July 1954 for the supply of traction current, subject to an excess maximum demand tariff of £2 12s 6d per kW, instead of £2 17s 6d, from March to October inclusive, were accepted. Substation equipment, including ballast resistances, to handle power regenerated by the Sunbeam MS2s, was ordered at an estimated £573 18s. In mid-March 1955 it was agreed that, subject to Ministry of Housing and Local Government approval, 0.178 acres of land at Central Depot, Southcote Road, be leased to the SEB for 99 years at a rent of £100 pa. However, due to continuing delays in arranging the alternative power supply, the Corporation's coal suppliers were asked in March 1955 if they would extend the coal contract on a weekly basis as from 30 June 1955.

Tenders were invited to explore the potential of additional revenue from external advertising on buses and two replies were received by mid-March 1955. At the meeting of the Transport Committee on 22 April 1955 further consideration was deferred for three months pending the receipt of more information from the tenderers as to the nature of the planned advertisements. However at its 22 July 1955 meeting it was decided not to proceed with the idea.

A further NJIC wage award and improved conditions of service, costing £23,000 pa., was notified. It should be noted here that as BCT was a full member of the NJIC for the Road Passenger Transport Industry as a result of its membership of MPTA, it was bound by its constitution to implement such awards. As applications had also been lodged for craftsmen and canteen workers, the General Manager was asked to look for possible methods of meeting this additional expenditure.

In June 1953 the Highways & Works Committee had been advised that Iford Barn near the Iford Bridge turning circle, which had been used variously in the past for storing overhead equipment and as a scout hut, was no longer required by the Transport Department. Efforts to find an alternative use for the building started in January 1954. The Town Clerk subsequently suggested that no decision be taken until plans to build a roundabout at the junction of Castle Lane East, Iford Lane and Christchurch Road had been finalised. In August 1955 the Transport Committee raised no objections to the roundabout's construction, on the understanding that the cost of altering the trolleybus overhead equipment was borne by the Highways & Works Department and with the recommendation that bus lay-bys be provided. Iford Barn was demolished.

On Whit Sunday, 20 May 1956, the southern half of the Iford roundabout came into use, and Boscombe-bound trolleybuses started following the new road layout. The eastbound (or northern) side of the roundabout came into service on 2 December 1956 and it is assumed that services 32 and 33 were cut back from Iford Bridge to the new roundabout from that date. The proposal to erect a complete circle of overhead was rejected by the MoT and a crossing in the eastbound Pokesdown

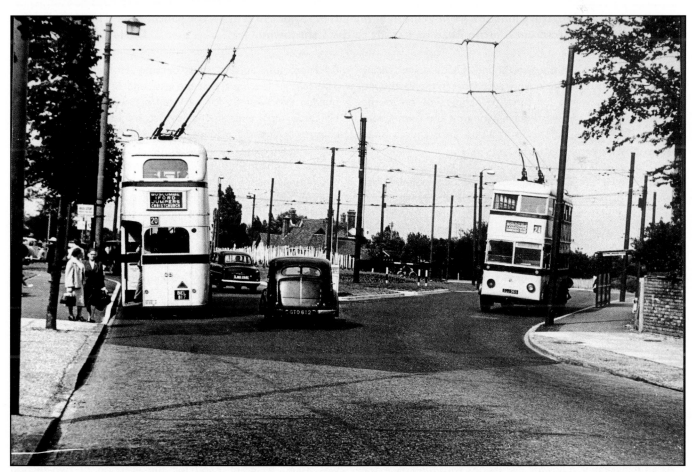

Viewed from its west side, the roundabout at the crossroads of Christchurch Road, Castle Lane East and Iford Lane, was completed in late 1956 with the trolleybus wiring coming into service on 2 December 1956. Nos. 132 (BEL817) and 91 (ALJ965), both in the 1956 livery, pass in Christchurch Road in about 1957. Interestingly no. 132 has an incomplete fleet number, only 32 being evident, whilst it has not been equipped with a rear auxiliary blind indicator. No. 91 is boarding passengers at the westbound stop moved in May 1963 due to increasing road traffic.
David Chalk collection

Having arrived at Cemetery Junction from Winton Sunbeam MS2 no. 150 crosses the southern end of Charminster Road before turning into Lansdowne Road on its way to the Lansdowne. **David Chalk collection**

to Jumpers wiring by the westbound Castle Lane wiring recommended instead. There were auto frogs in the eastbound Castle Lane East wiring for turns to Jumpers or on to the roundabout and in the westbound wiring on the roundabout itself, for turns into Castle Lane or along Christchurch Road towards Boscombe.

The MoT gave its final approval to the overhead installations at the Iford and Pit Site, Christchurch, roundabouts in September 1957. Only on 2 July 1965, however, was a frog giving access from Christchurch Road eastbound wiring direct into Castle Lane East installed to handle the increased number of depot runs to Castle Lane (Mallard Road) Depot after the closure of Central Depot, Southcote Road. Prior to this date a trolleybus travelling east along Christchurch Road had to circle Iford roundabout, with the conductor operating by hand the auto frog available to vehicles leaving Castle Lane to gain access to the westbound Castle Lane East wiring.

Application was made to the MoT in January 1955 for a further extension of time in respect of the routes authorised by the 1937 Order scheduled by the 1938 Order Confirmation Act, but which had not yet been put into operation. Consent was given on 17 May 1955. The Town Planning Committee was advised in February 1955 that, in due course, the Transport Committee proposed to acquire sufficient land for trolleybus lay-bys at Bear Cross and Tuckton Bridge.

As an experiment, following discussions with the Police, the Bournemouth Arcade stop in Old Christchurch Road, between the Bournemouth Square and Dalkeith Steps, ceased to be used except for trolleybuses on services 25 and 25A as it had become a cause of obstruction to traffic. The first stop for other services travelling towards the Lansdowne after leaving

Bournemouth Square thus became Horseshoe Common. The stop in the Square at the east end of Commercial Road outside Woolworths for services operating from Richmond Hill was also experimentally discontinued. Both of these changes became permanent in July 1955. Possibly as a result of the foregoing experiments, consideration of a renewal of the overhead equipment in the Square was deferred.

Continuing staff shortages in the summer months saw the 48-hour week reintroduced for traffic staff, with effect from 21 March 1955. Until the end of the trolleybuses in Bournemouth, the employment of university students as temporary conductors in high summer became a regular feature of operations, the annual contingent from Ireland proving particularly keen to supplement their income by working double shifts and on rest days. Some reportedly even slept on the trolleybuses in the depot between late and early shifts. However, a request for a contribution towards their travelling expenses to and from Bournemouth was refused.

On 22 April 1955 the Transport Committee learned that the MoT had authorised the Bournemouth Corporation (Trolley Vehicles) Provisional Order for the one-way system and roundabout at the Pit Site, Christchurch, and that the confirming Bill had been introduced and read a first time in the House of Commons. Royal Assent was given on 27 July 1955.

At the same 22 April 1955 meeting the Finance Committee was asked to grant £560 for the erection of two-section passenger waiting shelters during the financial year at the following trolleybus stops: Columbia Road, Ensbury Park Hotel (outward services); corner of Richmond Park and Charminster Roads (outward services); junction of Richmond Park and Holdenhurst Roads (outward services); junction of Castle

Lane and Lawford Road (inward services); Wimborne Road, top of Peter's Hill (inward services); and Wimborne Road at Moordown Depot (two shelters for inward services). In Fir Vale Road where it joined St Peter's Road, Bournemouth's sole pair of curve segments was installed in the overhead wiring soon afterwards as an experiment.

Until 1955 the Sunbeam MS2s were still being repainted with the dark earth brown roofs that they had acquired in wartime, although the BUT9641Ts had been delivered with primrose-coloured roofs and all motorbuses had, in the meantime, reverted to primrose. BUT9641T 207 received an experimental dark earth brown-coloured roof for a short period in 1954, but this was not deemed a success. Thereafter all trolleybus repaints, including the Sunbeam MS2s, featured primrose roofs.

At its meeting on 20 May 1955, the Chairman of the Transport Committee, Ald. Langton, referred to the impending retirement of Aldermen Playdon and Summerbee and thanked them both for their long service to the Transport and Tramways Committees. Both had been active on various committees since the late 1920s. Ald. Arthur Langton himself finally resigned from the position of chairman in June 1957 due to ill health. He had become a member of the then Tramways Committee in 1930 and was appointed Chairman of the Transport Committee in 1936. He served for many years on various national and regional bodies associated with municipal transport and during the period 1946-53 sat as a Traffic Commissioner and as a member of the Licensing Authority for PSVs for the South-Eastern Traffic Area. Arthur Langton had a regrettably short retirement; he died on 3 October 1958.

In July 1955 the following vehicles were listed as being in store at Castle Lane (Mallard Road) Depot:

80, 88, 137, 144, 158, 159, 163, 167, 201, 207, 209, 212, 215, 218, 220, 222

In view of the undertaking's financial position, the 22 July 1955 Transport Committee Meeting recommended an application to increase the fares.

Lightning struck the overhead wiring near Central Station at 7.05pm on 12 August 1955, putting the central area out of action until 8.50pm. Several buildings were struck by lightning, telephones were put out of action and heavy rain caused flooding throughout the town. Arcing caused a fire on the main switchboard at Southcote Road.

A suggestion that a trolleybus or motorbus should be illuminated in the 1956 summer season was referred to the Publicity Committee who, limiting their consideration to trolleybuses only, decided on no further action.

In September 1955 the undertaking stopped generating its own traction power. Thereafter the entire supply came from the SEB. On 21 October 1955 the Transport Committee invited tenders for the purchase of the generating station equipment. Having considered two quotations for the demolition of the former generating station cooling towers, the 21 December 1955 Transport Committee Meeting accepted that of Messrs James Drewitt & Son Ltd. at £372 and, having considered eight tenders for the generating station equipment, that from Messrs George Cohen, Sons & Co. Ltd. for £5,770 was accepted. The final costs of the electricity substations at Iddesleigh Road, Southcote Road and Boscombe (Pokesdown) Depot had proved lower than the contract figures.

Mr H.W. Ashby, the BCT Engineer, retired on 22 October 1955 and was replaced by Mr Thomas Marsden as Deputy General Manager and Engineer, a native of Burnley, who had

Two 1936 Sunbeam MS2s, 154 (BRU5) and 164 (BRU15) pass in Christchurch Road at Boscombe Arcade on 15 July 1955. The Savoy Cinema, once one of several in this part of Boscombe, closed in 1958.

Malcolm Pearce (G.O.P. Pearce)

On its way to Tuckton, Tuckton Road, known as Tuckton Bridge on the indicator blinds, Sunbeam MS2 165 (BRU16) exemplifies the revised livery with its primrose coloured roof as it pauses for passengers to alight at Pokesdown Fire Station on 15 July 1955. Note also that its auxiliary single-line indicator box has been moved into the upper-deck front panel. In the background is Pokesdown Station and to the left public gardens.

Malcolm Pearce (G.O.P. Pearce)

Freshly repainted into the 1955 colour scheme application (see Appendix D, Livery 6), no. 163 (BRU14) stands in Avenue Road on 14 August 1955 prior to departure service 30A to Columbia Road via Ensbury Park, and then onward to Wallisdown. Note that the half-drop front upper-deck windows have been replaced with fixed glazing and the glazed louvres above the windows replaced by metal louvres.

Malcolm Pearce (G.O.P. Pearce)

started his career with the Burnley, Colne & Nelson Joint Transport Committee. At the time of his appointment, Mr Marsden was fairly young, whereas every other senior officer had been with the undertaking for at least twenty years, and most for a lot longer. He brought with him many innovative new ideas to BCT which, with decreasing passenger figures, had to prioritise economy. It was his proposal to paint the roofs of the Sunbeam MS2s primrose rather than dark earth brown, not to improve their appearance or to standardise with the BUT9641Ts, but as an economy measure by reducing the number of colours of paint used and thus speeding up the time needed to repaint each trolleybus. He also reduced the number of coat of arms transfers applied to each vehicle, introduced smaller, less ornate fleet numbers and repainted the ancillary fleet in standard primrose and maroon livery, instead of the variety of colours that they had hitherto enjoyed. It was in no small part due to his endeavours that in the five-year period 1956-1961 the undertaking avoided any fare increases.

In December 1955 the NJIC for Craftsmen and the NJIC for the Road Passenger Transport Industry granted awards estimated to increase the undertaking's salary costs by £25,000 pa.

A new service numbering system for both motor and trolleybus services was introduced from 1 March 1956 eliminating the remaining A and B suffixes. The 22B Bournemouth Square-Tuckton via Beaufort Road and Cranleigh Road was renumbered 23. Previously, service 23 had operated Bournemouth Square-Fisherman's Walk but had disappeared as a regular daily service on 1 October 1937, when services 22 and 22A (both to and from Southbourne Cross Roads), were reintroduced, although the service number had been reintroduced on 6 May 1946 for peak hour extras. From now on vehicles terminating at Fisherman's Walk were supposed to display 37, although a

blank often sufficed. The 25A was renumbered 25. Since 2 July 1951, service number 25 had been used to denote trolleybuses terminating at Queen's Park Golf Pavilion (in principle every 30 minutes a 25A journey had simply dropped the "A"). Services 26A, 27, 28A, 29, 30A, 31, 34 and 35 were renumbered 27, 34, 29, 35, 31, 32, 36 and 38 respectively. Services 20, 21, 22, 24, 26, 28 (which had ceased to operate all day on 6 May 1946), 30 and 33 were not changed.

Trolleybus services thus became (former numbers, where applicable, are shown in brackets):

20   Bournemouth Square, Gervis Place - Lansdowne - Boscombe Gardens - Boscombe Arcade - Pokesdown Station - Iford - Jumpers Corner - Christchurch, Church Street

21   Bournemouth Square, Gervis Place - Lansdowne - Boscombe Gardens - Boscombe Arcade - Pokesdown Station - Fisherman's Walk - Southbourne Cross Roads - Tuckton Bridge - Christchurch, Church Street

22   Bournemouth Square, Gervis Place - Lansdowne - Boscombe Gardens - Boscombe Arcade - Pokesdown Station - Fisherman's Walk - Southbourne Cross Roads - Tuckton, Tuckton Road, junction with Belle Vue Road

23   Bournemouth Square, Gervis Place - Lansdowne - Boscombe Gardens - Boscombe Arcade - Pokesdown Station - Fisherman's Walk - Cranleigh Road - Beaufort Road - Tuckton, Tuckton Road, junction with Belle Vue Road (formerly service 22B)

24   Bournemouth Square, Gervis Place - Lansdowne -

A Vauxhall Cresta overtakes BUT9641T no. 215 (KLJ349) and Leyland Titan PD2/3 motorbus 253 (KEL139) as they pause at the westbound Boscombe Arcade stop on 14 August 1955. Both vehicles were part of a bulk order for Weymann bodies on motorbus and trolleybus chassis placed in 1948. The motorbus appears to be working on a service 24 journey normally operated by trolleybuses.
Malcolm Pearce (G.O.P. Pearce)

Boscombe Gardens - Boscombe Arcade - Pokesdown Station - Iford - Jumpers Corner

25   Westbourne, Seamoor Road - West Station - Bournemouth Square - Lansdowne - Central Station - Springbourne - Queen's Park Corner - Boscombe Station - Boscombe, Portman Road
or
Westbourne, Seamoor Road - West Station - Bournemouth Square - Lansdowne - Central Station - Springbourne - Queen's Park Corner - Queen's Park Golf Pavilion, Holdenhurst Road
(formerly service 25A)

26   Triangle - Bournemouth Square - Cemetery Junction - Winton - Moordown - Castle Lane West, Lawford Road

27   Triangle - Bournemouth Square - Cemetery Junction - Winton - Moordown - West Way, Castle Lane West *(formerly service 26A)*

28   Triangle - Bournemouth Square - Cemetery Junction - Five Ways - Broadway Hotel, Luckham Road

29   Triangle - Bournemouth Square - Cemetery Junction - Five Ways - Broadway Hotel - West Way, Castle Lane West *(formerly service 28A)*

30   Triangle - Bournemouth Square - Cemetery Junction - Winton - Wallisdown - Columbia Road, junction with Kinson Road

31   Triangle - Bournemouth Square - Cemetery Junction - Winton - Ensbury Park - Columbia Road, junction with Kinson Road *(formerly service 30A)*

32   Triangle - Bournemouth Square - Cemetery Junction - Five Ways - Broadway Hotel - Strouden Park - Iford Bridge *(formerly service 31)*

33   Triangle - Bournemouth Square - Cemetery Junction - Winton - Moordown - Broadway Hotel - Castle Lane - Strouden Park - Iford Bridge

34   Bournemouth Square, Gervis Place - Lansdowne - Cemetery Junction - Winton - Moordown - Lawford Road, junction with Castle Lane West *(formerly service 27)*

35   Triangle - Bournemouth Square - Cemetery Junction - Five Ways - Malvern Road, junction with Charminster Avenue *(formerly service 29)*

36   Lansdowne - Central Station - Cemetery Junction - Winton - Moordown - Ensbury Park Road - Columbia Road, junction with Kinson Road *(peak hours only) (formerly service 34)*

37   Bournemouth Square, Gervis Place - Lansdowne - Boscombe Gardens - Boscombe Arcade - Pokesdown Station - Fisherman's Walk, Wentworth Avenue *(peak hours only) (formerly service 23)*

38   Bournemouth Pier - Lansdowne - Boscombe Gardens - Boscombe Arcade - Pokesdown Station - Fisherman's Walk, Wentworth Avenue *(seasonal supplementary service) (formerly service 35)*

Less than a month later, on 26 March 1956, service 34 was extended beyond Lawford Road along Castle Lane West to West Way, replacing the 27 (which was suspended), and continuing back to Bournemouth Square and the Triangle as a circular operation interworking with service 29. Except for the period 22 July 1956-16 September 1956 when the 27 was reintroduced and again provided the paired service, the interworking of services 29 and 34 continued until 29 September 1963.

29   Triangle - Bournemouth Square - Cemetery Junction - Five Ways - Broadway Hotel - West Way, Castle Lane West

34   Bournemouth Square, Gervis Place - Lansdowne - Cemetery Junction - Winton - Moordown - West Way, Castle Lane West

The frequency of services 29 and 34 was soon reduced and a petition protesting against these reductions was presented; however, having considered the traffic receipts, the Transport Committee rejected the petition on 22 June 1956. The 26 continued to terminate at Castle Lane West, Lawford Road but on 16 September 1956 service number 27 ran for the last time (until 30 September 1963) and disappeared from timetables although it continued to be displayed by trolleybuses continuing beyond West Way to Castle Lane (Mallard Road) Depot.

On 24 June 1955, the Transport Committee considered fleet requirements and the need to purchase new trolleybuses, and agreed that the 79 remaining pre-war trolley vehicles, some over 20 years old, would need replacement over the next few years. They recommended that tenders be invited for twenty two-axle trolleybuses seating 60 or 61 passengers for delivery in 1957 and that the subject of further purchases and the most suitable time scale be considered at a later date. However, at the next Council meeting, the Transport Committee Chairman withdrew the recommendation for further consideration. The matter was deferred until 23 March 1956, when the Transport Committee again recommended that tenders be invited for the supply of twenty two-axle trolleybuses to replace vehicles dating from 1934-5, and that the Finance Committee be asked to apply for an appropriate loan sanction.

Solely trolleybus service 38 (formerly service 35) operated to Bournemouth Pier in 1956, reappearing at Easter and again for the summer season from 19 May 1956. The March 1956 service renumbering scheme had allocated 36 for supplementary seasonal services between Bournemouth Pier and Columbia Road via the Lansdowne, Cemetery Junction, Winton and Ensbury Park Road (the former 34) but this was not reintroduced for summer 1956.

Notification of an increase in the maximum demand charge was received from the SEB on 20 April 1956. The SETC approved the Corporation's application for increased fares and made positive comments as to preparation and presentation.

In June 1956, the HCC suggested that a lay-by be built on the south side of the road at Jumpers for westbound trolleybuses on services 20 and 24. This was agreed, provided that the County Council paid the cost of the necessary alterations to the overhead equipment and for repositioning the existing

It is debatable whether the nearside semaphore arm traffic indicator is really making a signal or not as no. 147 (BEL832) pulls in to the St. Swithun's Road eastbound stop in Holdenhurst Road. The pull handle for the hand-operated frog providing access to St. Swithun's Road and ultimately Central Depot, Southcote Road, can be seen on the traction pole in the foreground. A Rolls Royce is parked nonchalantly outside the Albany Commercial Hotel at 128 Holdenhurst Road.   **David Chalk collection**

Sunbeam MS2 no. 85 (ALJ61) was delivered in October 1934 and featured a quarter light followed by a 2/3-size half-drop window in the upper-deck side windows above the driver's cab. By now almost 22 years old and already repainted with a primrose coloured roof, no. 85 draws up at the westbound Boscombe Arcade stop in July 1956 on its way back to the Square on redesignated service 23 from Tuckton via Cranleigh Road and Beaufort Road (formerly the 22B).

Malcolm Pearce (G.O.P. Pearce)

Services 25 and 25A were combined for all journeys between Boscombe and Westbourne on 1 March 1956. The Boscombe terminus of both services was comprised of a "round the block" loop with a terminus at the south end of Portman Road. Having left Portman Road and turned west into Gladstone Road, no. 136 (BEL821) has just reached the crossroads with Ashley Road where it will turn north and pass Boscombe Hospital and Boscombe Station before reaching Holdenhurst Road, Springbourne at Queen's Park corner before continuing west to the Square and Westbourne on a service 25 journey (23 May 1956). No. 136 was one of the Sunbeam MS2s reconditioned by Reading's of Portsmouth. This included the removal of the auxiliary single-line indicator box from the driver's nearside windscreen and replacement by an aperture in the upper-deck front panel.

Malcolm Pearce (G.O.P. Pearce)

passenger waiting shelter.

Passenger waiting shelters were erected opposite St. Augustin's Church in Wimborne Road, southbound, i.e. on the Square side of Cemetery Junction (for services 26 and 28); at Tuckton Bridge outside Bridge House, eastbound (service 21); and Strouden Park, westbound opposite the Hotel (services 32, 33). On the Education Committee's advice, a two-section shelter was erected at the junction of Cranleigh and Beaufort Roads.

The winter 1956 timetable introduced a number of service reductions, including the withdrawal of trolleybus services 20 and 24 after the 7pm departures from Bournemouth Square. To compensate, motorbuses on limited-stop service 1 to Somerford, which paralleled the route of these services between the Lansdowne and the junction of Barrack Road with Stour Road, were diverted along Stour Road to serve Christchurch Station and Bargates in the evening, observing all intermediate stops. Alternate winter evening journeys of service 1 had already been following this route since the winter 1955 timetable.

The 23 November 1956 Transport Committee meeting considered letters from the SETC and the MPTA about oil shortages caused by the Suez Crisis. Although diesel fuel was not rationed, there were shortages and some motorbus service reductions but this did not lead to any improvement of

trolleybus frequencies or services (the economies introduced on 31 December 1956 were related to the fall in passenger numbers, particularly in winter evenings). Petrol for use in private cars was rationed for six months. Having considered a letter from Bradford's General Manager, the Town Clerk wrote to the Government expressing the Corporation's wish that every encouragement be given to the general use of electric road passenger transport.

Further wage awards by the NJIC for the Road Passenger Transport Industry and the NJIC for Craftsmen involved an additional £16,750 pa. wages bill. The Undertaking's finances, based on the Borough Treasurer's half-yearly statement and the above wage awards, combined with reduced passenger loadings after 7pm, led to a recommendation that service frequencies be reduced immediately. This included reduced daytime frequencies on trolleybus services 21, 22, 23, 25 and 35 with commensurate Sunday reductions. Having considered a reduced timetable on motorbus service 2, the full Council requested a report on the undertaking's economic position.

From 31 December 1956, all service 34 journeys were cut back from Bournemouth Square to the Lansdowne, as had been the case with its predecessor, the 27, on winter evenings since 30 March 1953, but continued to interwork with the 29 at Castle Lane West, junction with West Way, continuing to the Square and the Triangle via Charminster Road, the nominal

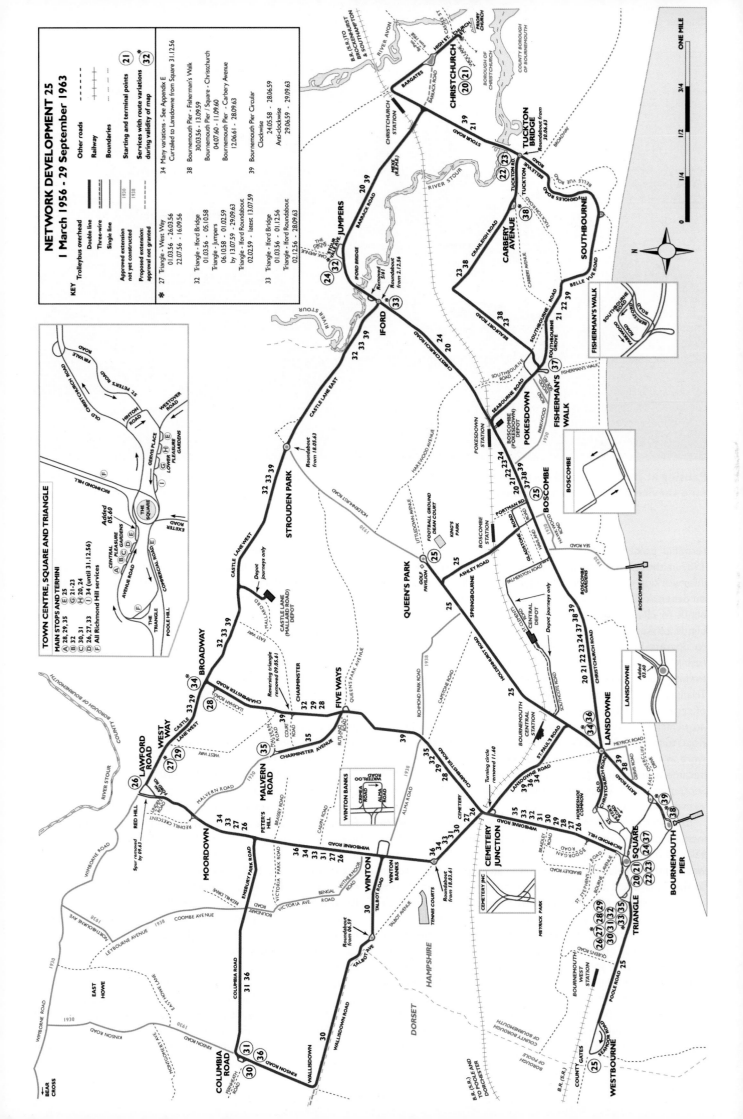

NETWORK DEVELOPMENT 25
1 March 1956 - 29 September 1963

KEY

Trolleybus overhead
- Double line
- Three-wire
- Single line

Other roads
Railway
Boundaries

Approved extension not yet constructed

Proposed extension: approval not granted

(21) Starting and terminal points

(32)* Services with route variations during validity of map

27 Triangle - West Way
01.03.56 - 26.03.56
22.07.56 - 16.09.56

32 Triangle - Iford Bridge
01.03.56 - 05.10.58
Triangle - Jumpers
06.10.58 - 01.02.59
by 13.07.59 - 29.09.63
Triangle - Iford Roundabout
02.02.59 - latest 13.07.59

33 Triangle - Iford Bridge
01.03.56 - 01.12.56
Triangle - Iford Roundabout
02.12.56 - 28.09.63

34 Many variations - See Appendix E
Curtailed to Lansdowne from Square 31.12.56

38 Bournemouth Pier - Fisherman's Walk
30.03.56 - 13.09.59
Bournemouth Pier / Square - Christchurch
04.07.60 - 11.09.60
Bournemouth Pier - Carbery Avenue
12.06.61 - 28.09.63

39 Bournemouth Pier Circular
Clockwise   24.05.58 - 28.06.59
Anti-clockwise   29.06.59 - 29.09.63

TOWN CENTRE, SQUARE AND TRIANGLE

MAIN STOPS AND TERMINI

(A) 28, 29, 35
(B) 32
(C) 30, 31
(D) 26, 27, 33
(E) 25
(G) 21-23
(H) 20, 24
(I) 34 (until 31.12.56)
(F) All Richmond Hill services

Added 05.60

Pausing at the westbound Portman Road stop in Christchurch Road, Boscombe on 23 July 1956 is no. 101 (ALJ975) on a service 20 journey to the Square. Malcolm Pearce (G.O.P. Pearce)

terminal point remaining West Way. Curiously, from 3 June 1957, although service 34 was extended to Broadway, the interworking with service 29 continued to take place, at least on paper, at West Way. In practice service 34 changed indicator blinds to 29 at Lawford Road and service 29 changed indicator blinds to service 34 at Broadway. Service 30 was curtailed to operate between Columbia Road and Winton, Alma Road (using the Winton Banks loop), except in the morning and evening peak hours when vehicles continued to and from the Triangle. The Columbia Road-Winton via Talbot Village portion of service 30 still operated in conjunction with service 31 and no vehicles on the 30 actually "shuttled" between Columbia Road turning circle and Winton Banks. Through transfer tickets were available for passengers to change at Winton Banks. This became a permanent feature of the winter timetable until 14 September 1959 when the curtailment was introduced on a year-round basis.

Trolleybuses heading south along Wimborne Road were increasingly held up by tailbacks on Richmond Hill as other vehicles made their way down to Bournemouth Square, which was still the town's prime traffic hub. In an effort to find a route to the Square less susceptible to congestion or icy conditions in winter and also offer an alternative town centre terminus for Side Route services, it was suggested that inbound trolleybuses should turn west out of Wimborne Road into Braidley Road about 450 yards north of the top of Richmond Hill. Although this route made a gentler and less exposed descent towards Bourne Avenue and the Square, it also passed beneath St. Stephen's Road, where the overbridge offered only 15ft clearance—insufficient for a trolleybus. Despite the necessity to lower the road surface beneath this bridge, the Transport Committee approved the proposal for a one-way terminal loop

running anti-clockwise along Braidley Road, past the Town Hall, and Bourne Avenue from Wimborne Road to the Square on 18 February 1955. However, they felt at that time that steps to obtain the requisite Parliamentary Powers should not be taken in isolation and that they should be included in a future wider-reaching Bill. Only in November 1956 did Braidley Road feature again in Transport Committee discussions, when the matter was deferred for a month.

On 21 December 1956 the Transport Committee reconsidered the suggested rerouting of Side Route trolleybuses down Braidley Road, and the Borough Engineer reported on pending proposals of other Committees concerning traffic routes. The report of a meeting between representatives of the Transport and Highways & Works Committees was adopted in February 1957 and, following discussions with the MoT's Divisional Road Engineer, the Braidley Road scheme was dropped. The Transport Committee's recommendation of 18 February 1955 was accordingly rescinded in April 1957, when it was recommended that the General Subcommittee consider a suggested alternative route for trolley vehicles proceeding down Richmond Hill. It is not known if this was the first reference to the idea of using Post Office Road and Yelverton Road which was minuted in early 1960.

By September 1956, six tenders had been received for twenty two-axle trolleybuses and, at its Meeting of 23 November 1956, the Transport Committee recommended that the following be accepted:

i)   for 20 trolleybus chassis with electrical equipment: the Sunbeam Trolley Bus Co. Ltd. (with electrical equipment by Crompton Parkinson Ltd.) at £3,642 each. (A lower tender was received from BUT, however it did not comply with the specification of an exit forward of the front axle.)

ii) for 20 trolleybus bodies (Bournemouth design): Metropolitan-Cammell-Weymann Ltd. (MCW) at £3,442 each. (Two lower tenders were received for bus bodies.)

The Finance Committee's application for loan sanction of £141,680 was granted in February 1957.

The *Bournemouth Evening Echo* later reported, on 16 April 1957, *"An £80,000 order for twenty, 62-seater trolleybuses has been placed with the Sunbeam Trolleybus Co. Ltd., an associate company of Guy Motors. It is for 20 double deckers to replace an equivalent number of Sunbeams supplied by the Wolverhampton company in 1935 when the Bournemouth tramway system was replaced by 103 Sunbeam trolleybuses. The old vehicles have carried millions of passengers during their 22 years of service and many of them will continue operating until the original fleet is completely replaced. Chassis for the new Sunbeams will be of the two-axle type with MCW 30ft bodies and Crompton-Parkinson electrical traction equipment".*

On 19 July 1957 the Transport Committee recommended that tenders be invited for ten more trolleybuses for delivery in 1959, to replace vehicles purchased in 1935.

The winter of 1956/57 saw the delicensing of:

Sunbeam MS2s:	80-82, 84, 111, 114, 121, 127, 128, 138, 148, 153, 168
BUT9641Ts:	200-211, 213, 214, 218, 221-223

The BUT9641Ts were 1¾ tons heavier than the Sunbeam MS2s and were equipped with 40hp more powerful traction motors with commensurately higher power consumption. Accordingly, a number of them were temporarily taken out of service at the end of the summer season and put in store for the winter. In addition, six more Sunbeam MS2s were stripped of useful parts and awaited sale for scrap: 80-82, 111, 127-128

As an economy measure, the number of borough coat of arms transfers displayed on the trolleybuses was reduced from six to two, those on the front, rear and lower-deck side panels no longer being applied. The fleet number replaced the coat of arms at the front and rear. Until now some MS2s had carried the number in the maroon band beneath the lower-deck side windows in addition to the band on the front and rear panels, whereas the BUTs had previously carried it above the offside headlight at the front and between the maroon band and the coat of arms at the rear.

By early 1957 the condition of Boscombe (Pokesdown) Depot was giving concern. Blocked drainpipes and defective glazing were allowing rainwater to accumulate on the depot floor and there were fears that it could percolate into the substation. The economics of retaining the premises as an operational depot were therefore investigated. At that time one man was employed on ticket box and cash receipt duties, whilst three cleaners and one chargehand cleaner were allocated for night cleaning work. In case of closure, Mr Marsden felt that three or four positions could be economised, saving £1,500 pa. It was difficult to operate another depot having a nightly rotation of twelve trolleybuses so close to the Central Depot, Southcote Road, without a unified control, not to mention the building maintenance costs. The savings would be minimal but, operationally, the closure was recommended. Mr W.J. Guy, Traffic Superintendent, reported that complete closure and the additional dead mileage involved until schedules were revised would increase wages by £13 6s 2d per week and mileage (ex-Central Depot, Southcote Road) by 417 miles per week.

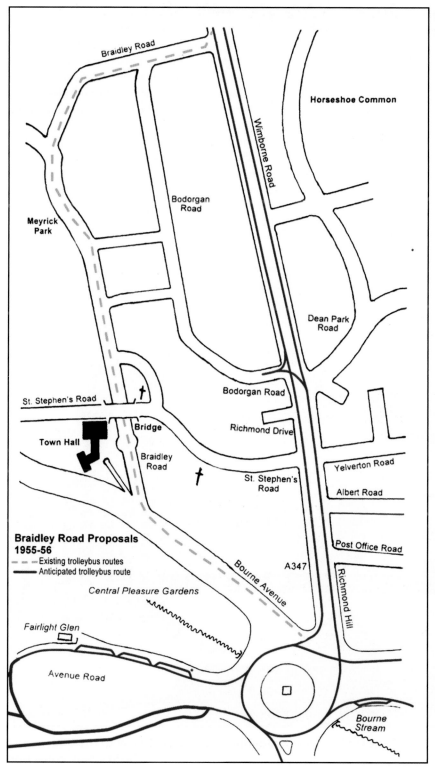

Braidley Road Proposals 1955-56
- - - Existing trolleybus routes
——— Anticipated trolleybus route

The financial year commencing 1 April 1957 brought increased charges for bulk electricity estimated to be an additional £1,848 pa.

An application was made in May 1957 for a further extension of time in respect of those trolley vehicle routes authorised by the 1937 Order, scheduled in the 1938 Order Confirmation Act, but which had not yet been put into operation. This was granted on 8 November 1957.

In August 1957, five more Sunbeam MS2 trolleybuses (83, 114, 138, 148 and 153) were noted stripped and awaiting sale for scrap, in addition to the six (80-82, 111, 127-128) previously mentioned and still awaiting disposal.

As in past years, it was decided to take a number of BUT9641Ts out of service at the end of September 1957 and them put in store for the winter. They were replaced during this period by some or all of the nine more economical MS2s which had been stored delicensed through the summer, namely trolleybuses 85, 129, 143, 147, 155, 158, 167, 171, 172.

The existing contract with Sunbeam and MCW for 20 trolleybuses was extended in September 1957 to include an additional ten vehicles at an estimated cost of £7,110 each, without calling for tenders. It was estimated that the cost would be an additional £30 per vehicle in respect of electrical equipment. Application was made for additional loan sanction.

In mid-November Messrs George & Harding commenced repairs to defective brickwork in the gable end of Boscombe Depot. Shortly thereafter, a trolleybus reversing out of the depot dewired, damaging a window at 928 Christchurch Road opposite.

The following trolleybuses were noted as de-licensed in December 1957:

Sunbeam MS2s:	80-83, 89, 90, 105, 111, 114, 116, 117, 127, 128, 131, 138, 148, 150, 153, 154, 160, 164, 166, 173.
BUT9641Ts:	200-205, 212-217

At around this time, permission was granted to Christchurch Corporation to hang flower baskets on fifteen traction poles in High Street, Christchurch.

In February 1958, the SEB announced plans to withdraw its staff from the substations at Christchurch and at Electric House, Bournemouth and indicated that it would be necessary to install automatic switching apparatus in them. Mr Reakes therefore inspected redundant automatic switchgear from Leeds Corporation's tramways and this was purchased for £400.

In the early 1950s Mr Reakes had successfully introduced both double- and single-deck open-top motorbus services along the coast, and a circular coach tour of the town and environs. Eager to build on this principle, but with a minimum investment, the idea of operating a circular tour with open-top trolleybuses, converted from vehicles which would otherwise be disposed of as life-expired, was floated. The main proponent was probably Tom Marsden, the Deputy General Manager and Engineer. Following preliminary discussions with the MoT, exploratory work started on 1936 Sunbeam MS2 160 in September 1957. The 22 November 1957 Transport Committee Meeting authorised the conversion of two trolleybuses to open-top for use during the summer on a circular tour of the town. The same

Another reconditioned Sunbeam MS2, no. 131 (BEL816) is seen in Holdenhurst Road on its way to the Square and Westbourne.
David Chalk collection

The principal unloading point at the Square for Side Route services was Albert Road at the bottom of Richmond Hill. Sunbeam MS2 no 159 (BRU10) is seen at this stop on a service 26 journey from Castle Lane West as the driver takes this opportunity to change the indicator blinds for his next trip, this time to Malvern Road. The *Bournemouth Daily Echo* newspaper offices are in the background. David Chalk collection (Roy Marshall)

meeting gave authority to dispose of ten trolleybuses purchased in 1934/35. Having considered four offers, the highest, that of James Thompson & Co. (Cardiff) Ltd., at £550, was accepted on 21 February 1958. Local newspapers announced on 4 December 1957 that two trolleybuses were to be converted to open-top for the next summer season.

The rebuilding of 160 as a prototype for the open-top trolleybuses was completed by April 1958. Following a MoT inspection on 17 April 1958, the new design was authorised for use. It was presented to the press and the public on the Pavilion forecourt on 27 May 1958, the day of the Annual Council Meeting. The front staircase and exit were removed, enabling an increase of the seating capacity from 56 to 69 (40 on the upper deck and 29 in the lower saloon). The upper deck structure above the base of the windows was cut away, and the upper deck waistband and beading removed; however, the upper deck body walls were retained and increased in height. The trolley gantry remained in place with a small section of "roof" supporting the trolley bases, whilst the trolley retaining hooks were placed on a matching single hoop at the rear. No. 157, of the same batch, was ready in May 1958. In the meantime, the conversion of a third trolleybus was approved and 112 was selected, rebuilding being completed in July 1958. The three open-top trolleybuses were renumbered: 157 (registration mark BRU 8), 160 (BRU 11) and 112 (ALJ 986) becoming 200-202 respectively, thus inaugurating a new fleet numbering system.

On Whit Saturday, 24 May 1958 an open-top trolleybus circular tour, taking one hour and operating in a clockwise direction only with no service stops, was introduced using the two rebuilt vehicles, 200 and 201, available for service at that time:

39 Bournemouth Pier - Bournemouth Square - Cemetery Junction - Broadway Hotel - Strouden Park - Iford - Jumpers - Tuckton Bridge - Southbourne - Fisherman's Walk - Pokesdown Station - Boscombe Arcade - Boscombe Gardens - Lansdowne - Bournemouth Pier

In an attempt to maximise revenue by carrying short-distance passengers in the invariably empty lower saloon whilst those making the complete circular trip travelled upstairs, and as a palliative to tour passengers who complained of the delays behind service trolleybuses loading or unloading at stops, the circular tour became a scheduled service from 7 July 1958, picking-up and setting-down passengers at intermediate stops. By this time the third conversion was also available for use, 202 being taxed from 1 July 1958 and entering service on 7 July 1958. In 1957, a proponent had commented that the 22-year-old rebuilt trolleybuses would be able to cope with a tour as this avoided the bodywork stresses of frequent starts and stops, but perhaps not with a scheduled service. This comment was not mentioned again! However, persistent staff shortages meant that seasonal services were the first to be curtailed and even during periods of fine weather, the 39 often only operated on Sundays.

Seasonal supplementary trolleybus services were reintroduced between Good Friday-Easter Monday inclusive in 1958; however, solely service 38 (Bournemouth Pier-Fisherman's Walk) was operated, this being the final year of seasonal trolleybus operations at Easter.

No. 160 (BRU11), later renumbered as 201, is seen here at Bournemouth Pier with the official sporting a de riguer Bowler hat accompanied by the General Manager, Mr. W.D. Reakes. The entrance to the Lower Pleasure Gardens which offer an attractive and relaxing floral and woodland walk along the Bourne Stream from the Pier to the Square can be seen in the background.　　　　　　　　　　　　　　　　　　　　Malcolm Pearce (G.O.P. Pearce)

On its Ministry of Transport tour of inspection, prototype open-top Sunbeam MS2 no. 160 is seen resting outside the Pier Approach Baths on 17 April 1958.　　　　　　　　　　　　　　　　　　Malcolm Pearce (G.O.P. Pearce)

Road repairs in Church Street, Christchurch, carried out in the week 12-18 May 1958, prevented trolleybuses reaching the turntable. The opportunity was taken to give the turntable its first major overhaul since installation in 1936. Initially, trolleybuses made a three-point turn at the top of Wick Lane using T-poles but later in the week the overhead wiring at the Pit Site roundabout was linked to provide a temporary terminal loop, whilst a motorbus shuttle operated to and from Church Street.

Meanwhile, the silver jubilee of trolleybus operation in the town did not go totally unrecorded. The *Bournemouth Times & Directory* of 16 May 1958 published a *"Tribute to a Trolley"*. *"It was exactly 25 years on Tuesday that trolleybuses were introduced. Ten of which have just been sold to James Thompson (Cardiff) Ltd. for £550 cost £2,100 each at the time. Two of the 1936 Sunbeams will be converted to two open-toppers this summer. The Corporation have ordered 30 trolleybuses, twenty for delivery this year and ten next. The twenty complete vehicles will cost £142,000 and the ten £71,000".*

Always with an eye for detail, Mr Marsden wrote the following memo to Foreman Dollery on 20 June 1958:

Would you make an effort, in the course of the next few days, to get hold of some of the old trolleybuses we have still running with brown tops, which appear to be particularly filthy, and give them a really good soap wash (something approaching what they get before painting in the paintshop).

Whilst I appreciate that some of them are running their last summer service I do not want to see any more similar to BEL820 and 826, which I passed on the way down this morning. It may be that the two vehicles I have mentioned are not operating directly from Central Depot, but whatever depot they are operated from would you get them tidied up as soon as possible.

The 20 June 1958 Transport Committee meeting recommended to the General Purposes Committee that powers be sought to operate trolleybus services in the newly-developed West Howe area and that the General Manager report upon the proposed routes at the next meeting. However, on 18 July 1958 these proposals were rescinded, as his report suggested that a cheaper and less cumbersome way of seeking powers for extending the trolleybus system (other than by application for each individual route) could be made in a more general Parliamentary Bill which the Corporation was then promoting.

Service 39 only ran as a Circular Tour for just over six weeks in 1958 before becoming a circular service, picking-up and setting down passengers at intermediate points, and operating in a clockwise direction (anti-clockwise operation being introduced in 1959). Open-top Sunbeam MS2 200 (BRU8), formerly no. 157, is seen heading west along Christchurch Road, Boscombe.
David Chalk collection

Those services from Bournemouth Pier that travelled along Exeter Road to the Square loaded on the west side of the Pier Approach. No. 93 (ALJ967) waits for passengers before departing to Fisherman's Walk via the Square, the Lansdowne and Boscombe on seasonal supplementary service 38. **David Chalk collection**

Sunbeam MS2 no. 152 (BRU3) leaves Gervis Place to cross the south side of the Square on its way to Westbourne. The Plummer Roddis department store is visible immediately behind the trolleybus with the Lower Pleasure Gardens to the nearside. **David Chalk collection**

CHAPTER EIGHT
INDIAN SUMMER

In the evening of 28 July 1958, the Department's Guy Arab breakdown tender FRU180 arrived at Castle Lane (Mallard Road) Depot from the Weymann factory at Addlestone, Surrey, with the first Sunbeam MF2B, fleet number 258, on tow. The 31 July 1958 edition of the *Bournemouth Evening Echo* (the Bournemouth Daily Echo had been renamed as the Evening Echo on 1 July 1958) recorded that *"Transport officials anticipate that the new buses will use less electricity. Those now in service use just over 3 units [sic] per day. The Corporation fleet is now 103. The fleet will not be increased, for as the new ones come in the old ones will be replaced. The vehicles are considerably lighter than their predecessors weighing 8 tons 19 cwt as opposed to 10 tons 6 cwt. The first one, which arrived at the beginning of the week, is expected to be in service at the weekend. Drivers are currently getting used to the front overhang"*. No doubt the reference to units per day should have read per mile. Two other points of note are that the unladen weight of 10 tons 6 cwt referred to the BUT9641Ts, not the Sunbeam MS2s which were being replaced, and the fact that the first two MF2Bs, 258 and 259, actually went into service on service 25 on Saturday 2 August 1958.

A complete Sunbeam MF2B, 260, and the chassis of 272 were exhibits at the Commercial Motor Show, held at Earl's Court, London, between 26 September and 4 October 1958, and which, as usual, was visited for a day by the General Manager and his Deputy.

An explosion in an underground cable duct in Foxholes Road on 28 July 1958 was recorded in mid-September 1958 as "being dealt with by the insurance company". Some of the cables between Pokesdown and Christchurch were from the tramway era, being simply laid in wooden troughing, which was then filled with a compound, rather than conventional armoured cables in earthenware ducts. They were thus more susceptible to water penetration and easily damaged by excavation work. Furthermore, feeder cables did not always follow the trolleybus route.

From 22 September 1958, the hourly trolleybus service 33 (Bournemouth Square - Moordown - Iford) was curtailed to weekday peak hours only, the journeys appearing as part of the service 32 timetable although the vehicles continued to display 33. To compensate for the withdrawn through service, connections at the Broadway Hotel with interworking services 29 and 34, which operated to and from Lawford Road, Moordown and Winton, were advertised. On 6 October 1958, trolleybus service 32, by now the sole service operating through Strouden Park, was extended from Iford to Jumpers Corner:

32 Triangle - Bournemouth Square - Richmond Hill - Cemetery Junction - Charminster Road - Five Ways - Broadway Hotel - Castle Lane - Strouden Park - Iford - Jumpers

Open-top Sunbeam MS2 no. 202 (ALJ986), formerly 112, makes its way towards Iford along Castle Lane East on a clockwise service 39 (31 July 1958).
Malcolm Pearce (G.O.P. Pearce)

BUT9641T no. 220 (KLJ254) circumnavigates Iford roundabout back to Castle Lane East before making its way back to the Square by way of Castle Lane and Charminster on an hourly service 32(ii) working (31 July 1958). The shops of Castle Parade are visible in the background. Malcolm Pearce (G.O.P. Pearce)

The first Sunbeam MF2B no. 258 (WRU258) with 72 seat Weymann all-metal bodywork arrives on tow at Castle Lane (Mallard Road) Depot on 28 July 1958. Malcolm Pearce (G.O.P. Pearce)

(Left) Sunbeam MF2B no. 259 (WRU259) is towed into the Castle Lane (Mallard Road) Depot complex on 29 July 1958.   Malcolm Pearce (G.O.P. Pearce)

(Below) The official handover ceremony of the first Sunbeam MF2B no. 258 at Castle Lane (Mallard Road) Depot in August 1958. It has proved possible to identify the following individuals, from left to right Norman Abbey, Assistant Engineer; unknown; Bill Biddlecombe, Deputy Chief Inspector (in uniform); Weymann's representative, possibly Norman Cook; C.F. Johnson, Sunbeam; unknown; Tom Marsden, Deputy General Manager and Engineer; W.D. Reakes, General Manager; C. Owen Silvers, Sunbeam and formerly General Manager at Wolverhampton; Councillor Lt. Col. A.L. Paris, Chairman of the Transport Committee; unknown; unknown; A. Lindsay Clegg, Town Clerk. Messrs Marsden and Reakes are standing by the front staircase.   Wolverhampton Archives (Sunbeam)

Brand new Sunbeam MF2B 258 (WRU258) is seen on driver familiarisation at Iford roundabout on 31 July 1958. Note that the trolleybus is running on BCT's trade licence registration number 094EL.

Malcolm Pearce (G.O.P. Pearce)

On its second day in service, Sunbeam MF2B no. 258 pauses to unload passengers at the Holdenhurst Road, Central Station westbound stop on 3 August 1958. Kennedy's builders' merchants at 167 Holdenhurst Road was on the north side of the railway bridge.

Malcolm Pearce (G.O.P. Pearce)

Seen on its second day in passenger service, 3 August 1958, Sunbeam MF2B no. 259 (WRU259) is loading for Queen's Park Golf Pavilion at the Square boarding point at the east end of Avenue Road for Holdenhurst Road services. No doubt, the driver standing in the road by the offside cab window is enquiring of the first impressions of no. 259's driver. On the opposite side of the road, outside Woolworth's store, one of Bournemouth's celebrated 1939 Leyland TD5 luxury motorbuses, no. 19 (FEL202), waits.   Malcolm Pearce (G.O.P. Pearce)

The driver of brand news Sunbeam MF2B no. 259 (WRU259) discusses the handling of his new steed with a fellow driver whilst passengers board at the Square loading point of service 25 in Avenue Road (2 August 1958).
                                        Wolverhampton Archives (Sunbeam)

Displaying its new 1958 fleet number, Sunbeam MS2 no. 219 (BEL814), formerly fleet no. 129, pauses at the Lansdowne eastbound stop in Christchurch Road on its way to Fisherman's Walk. The building to the nearside is the Royal London House which opened in 1958 on the site of the Metropole Hotel which was destroyed in the Second World War bombing.

David Chalk collection

Sunbeam MS2 no. 135 (BEL820) is seen at Iford on 7 August 1958.   **Malcolm Pearce (G.O.P. Pearce)**

Trolleybuses operating on service 32 normally returned to the Square on service 24 through Pokesdown and Boscombe, and vice versa.

A further twenty Sunbeam MS2 trolleybuses were advertised for sale in November 1958, three tenders being received and the highest, that of £1,200, from Messrs Scource and Son, accepted in January 1959.

Following discussions with the police, the Boscombe Library stop and the Boscombe Arcade stop, both in Christchurch Road between Heathcote Road and Sea Road on the westbound journey, were deleted and temporarily replaced by a single stop outside the Public Library. This was the principal stop in Boscombe and the name Boscombe Arcade was retained. Eastbound there had always been just one stop, but with separate boarding points for services 20, 24 and 21-23, 37, 38, the next stop being Ashley Road.

The 19 December 1958 Transport Committee Meeting received a report from Mr Reakes on the purchase of second-hand post-war trolleybuses from Brighton and authorised him to offer £1,200 for six vehicles. This was exactly the same amount as raised by the sale of 20 Sunbeam MS2s to Messrs Scource in January 1959. Thus, trolleybuses some 22 to 24 years old would be inexpensively replaced by vehicles offering the same number of seats, but just ten years old. Brighton had decided in January 1957 on a two-stage trolleybus abandonment scheme with all post-war trolleybuses being withdrawn for sale upon completion of the first stage on 24 March 1959.

Mr Reakes was interested in buying Brighton Corporation's fleet of BUT9611Ts fitted with Crompton Parkinson C422 traction motors and Allen West control equipment, Brighton

fleet numbers 45-48 and 51-52, as these were the same as those in Bournemouth's BUT9641Ts. Unfortunately, by the time that official approval had been given to the purchase 51-52 had been sold to Maidstone Corporation. As an alternative, Brighton Corporation, acting on behalf of Brighton Hove & District (BH&D) in respect of the sale of the company's trolleybuses, offered the three company vehicles, which also had Crompton Parkinson/Allen West electrical equipment (the other two post-war Brighton Corporation post-war trolleybuses, 49-50, had English Electric equipment). Accordingly, the alternative offer of seven rather than six Brighton vehicles was recommended at the 23 January 1959 meeting and Mr Reakes was authorised to increase the offer of £200 each to £250 each for seven trolleybuses.

Brighton Corporation's post-war vehicles were withdrawn in December 1958 and those of BH&D in February 1959. All seven trolleybuses destined for Bournemouth were collected from Brighton's Lewes Road Depot by Deputy Chief Inspector Biddlecombe using FRU180, the Brighton Corporation vehicles being collected in the course of February 1959 and the ex-BH&D vehicles on 4, 7 and 10 March 1959.

The *Bournemouth Evening Echo* of 4 June 1959 reported that the first two ex-Brighton vehicles, 293 and 294 (formerly BH&D 392, 393), had entered service at the beginning of the month. *"Experienced passengers will miss the second exit on the seven Brighton trolleybuses. They are 26ft long, 7ft 6in wide and seat 56 passengers. They have undergone an extensive facelift in the Corporation's workshops. First the colour had to be changed from red to yellow. Indicator boards [sic] also had to be altered. It is not yet known when all seven Brighton buses will be on Bournemouth's*

Sunbeam MF2B no. 259 (WRU259) turns briskly out of the eastbound lane of Holdenhurst Road into Ashley Road at the Queen's Park Hotel on its way to Boscombe, Portman Road on a service 25 journey (11 August 1958). Malcolm Pearce (G.O.P. Pearce)

roads. They will replace a number of old trolleybuses which are expected to run until after the summer".

The ex-Brighton BUT9611T two-axle vehicles were the smallest trolleybuses in the post-war Bournemouth fleet. Their lack of a front staircase and exit ensured that they were normally limited to peak hour operation on the Side Routes, particularly services 26, 28 and 35. Certain councillors and members of the press commented adversely on the purchase of Brighton's "cast offs", particularly as they had come from a rival seaside resort. Having the same 120hp motors as the BUT9641Ts but an unladen weight three tons less, they were the fastest trolleybuses on the system!

Still on the subject of new rolling stock, the 20 February 1959 Transport Committee meeting approved an increase in the cost of the first batch of twenty Sunbeam MF2B trolleybuses (258-277), amounting to £5 8s 3d per chassis. On 22 May 1959 it accepted MCW's final account, including increased labour costs of £66 16s and £31 13s 6d for material, per body. At its meeting on 14 July 1959 it also approved a price adjustment on the second batch of ten Sunbeam MF2B chassis (278-287) amounting to about £30 per chassis. Crompton Parkinson was granted permission to advertise that it was responsible for the electrical installations in the new trolleybuses. Subsequently, on 8 December 1959 the General Manager reported a price adjustment of £179 each to the cost of the MCW bodies fitted to 278-287 earlier in 1959. It was further recommended that the present contracts with Sunbeam and MCW be extended

again to include a further, third, batch of ten trolleybuses (to become 295-304) without calling for a new tender. Mr Reakes was asked to submit proposals for a different body design featuring interior adjustments and a platform-type staircase, together with estimates of the likely cost. The next meeting considered his report, which basically suggested the same changes subsequently introduced on the third batch of Sunbeam MF2Bs, but the ideas were dropped on grounds of cost (later, Mr Cox was more successful by substituting some metal with plastic finishes, thereby reducing the cost). The 10 November 1959 Transport Committee meeting thus recommended that the existing contracts with Sunbeam and MCW be extended to include these further ten trolleybuses at a cost of £7,546 for each vehicle (compared to £5,571 for motorbuses ordered at same time), for delivery in 1961. The Finance Committee was asked to apply for loan sanctions.

The SEB announced that traction supply charges would increase from 1 April 1959, involving an estimated annual increased cost of £500.

Lightning struck the overhead wires in Castle Lane on 22 May 1959, damaging the mercury arc rectifier in Holdenhurst substation. The equipment, covered by insurance, was replaced.

On 24 June 1959 a small roundabout came into operation at the western end of Talbot Road where it joined Talbot Avenue. No frogs were installed in the overhead wiring, only a slewing being required.

On 19 August 1958, at the north end of Ashley Road, Springbourne, BUT9641T no. 242 (KLJ342), formerly no. 208 prior to the fleet renumbering which began in May 1958, leads Sunbeam MF2B no. 258 towards Boscombe, both on service 25 workings. The Queen's Park Hotel can be seen to the nearside of no. 258. Beyond the traffic lights the east end of Soberton Road was obliterated by the construction of Wessex Way in the 1970s just as many other roads in Springbourne were cut in two.
Malcolm Pearce (G.O.P. Pearce)

On 19 August 1958, Sunbeam MF2B no. 262 (WRU262), just 17 days in passenger service, turns out of Gladstone Road, Boscombe into Ashley Road northbound towards Springbourne and thence to the Lansdowne, Central Station, the Square, the still important West Station and Westbourne. **Malcolm Pearce (G.O.P. Pearce)**

Ex-BH&D BUT9611T no. 392, Bournemouth's no. 293 (DNJ993), takes a break in Wentworth Avenue outside Portman Terrace on the Fisherman's Walk turning circle on 3 June 1959, just two days after entering service, before heading back to the Pier. The Walk itself commences behind the telephone boxes in the background and continues to the cliff lift beyond Boscombe Overcliff Drive. **Malcolm Pearce (G.O.P. Pearce)**

Ex-Brighton Corporation Transport BUT9611T no. 45, Bournemouth fleet no. 288 (HUF45) waits between journeys at the Triangle. Note that the ex-Brighton vehicles from whatever source were equipped with "orange segment" shaped flashing trafficators and Bournemouth standard indicator boxes before re-entering service.

Travel Lens

Seen in Wimborne Road at the southbound stop opposite Redhill Crescent on a service 26 journey to the Square and the Triangle is ex-BH&D BUT9611T no. 393, Bournemouth fleet no. 294 (DNJ994).

Bournemouth Transport Ltd.

On 3 June 1959, ex-BH&D BUT9611T no. 294 (DNJ994) leads open-top Sunbeam MS2 no. 201 (BRU11) on clockwise circular service 39 westwards along Christchurch Road, Boscombe.　　Malcolm Pearce (G.O.P. Pearce)

Sunbeam MF2B 258 (WRU258) rounds the Lansdowne prior to setting the auto frog for Bath Road, Westover Road and the Square on a service 21 working on 2 August 1959. Sunbeam MS2 no. 219 on service 23 is in hot pursuit. The building in the background is the Bournemouth Municipal College and Library, opened in 1913 with an impressive 150ft high tower. By the date of the photograph it was known as the College of Technology.
Photo courtesy of D. Ball, for the family of the late J.S. King

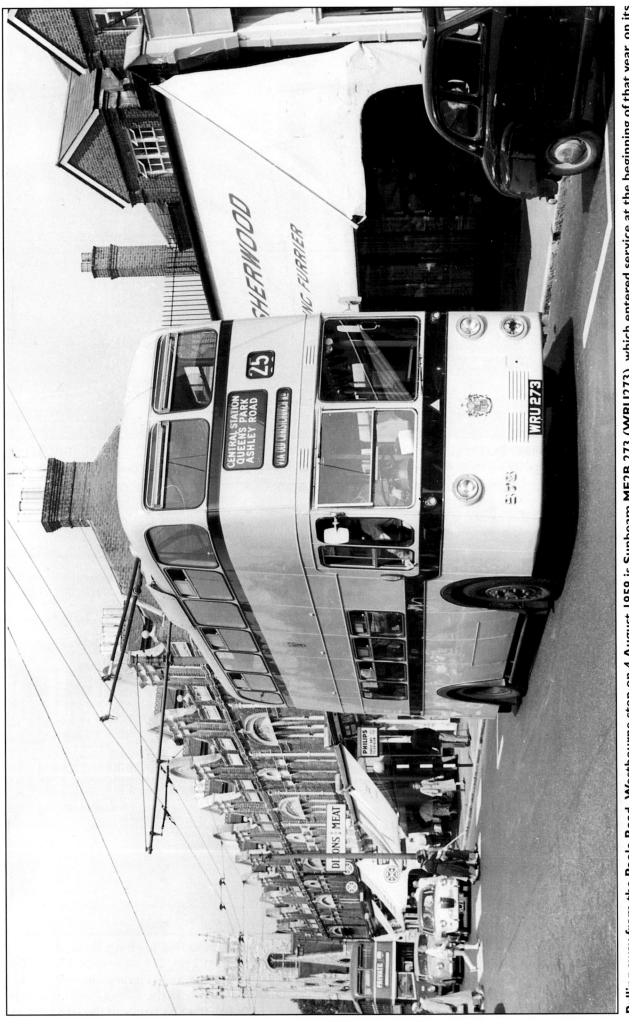

Pulling away from the Poole Road, Westbourne stop on 4 August 1959 is Sunbeam MF2B 273 (WRU273), which entered service at the beginning of that year, on its way across the town to Boscombe, Portman Road. In the background, beyond the cars waiting for pedestrians to cross the road at the zebra crossing, is an H&D AEC Regent III with Northern Counties lowbridge body delivered in the late 1940s and originally intended for Western Scottish Motor Traction Co. Ltd.
Photo courtesy of D.Ball, for the family of the late J.S. King

Sunbeam MS2 no. 209 (ALJ964), formerly fleet no. 90, enters the Square from Richmond Hill on 4 August 1959. Its next departure will be to Columbia Road as a service 31, as evidenced by the indicator blind displays which would have been set at the Albert Road stop. Photo courtesy of D.Ball, for the family of the late J.S. King

With the summer timetable, commencing on 29 June 1959, circular open-top trolleybus service 39 was modified to operate in an anti-clockwise direction in an effort not to duplicate the circular motorbus tour of the town:

39   Bournemouth Pier - Bath Road - Lansdowne - Boscombe Gardens - Boscombe Arcade - Pokesdown Station - Fisherman's Walk - Southbourne Cross Roads - Tuckton Bridge - Stour Road, Christchurch - Barrack Road - Jumpers - Iford - Strouden Park - Castle Lane - Broadway Hotel - Five Ways - Charminster Road - Cemetery Junction - St Paul's Road - Lansdowne - Bath Road - Bournemouth Pier

The absence of southbound overhead wiring in Exeter Road prevented the final portions of the journey operating through Bournemouth Square, although it was no doubt felt that the routing along Lansdowne Road and St. Paul's Road, close to Bournemouth Central Station, might increase the service's popularity. This provided an example of a rare left turn from Charminster Road into St. Paul's Road at Cemetery Junction. Mr Cunningham (General Manager from 1964) later attributed the lack of success of the open-top trolleybuses with the general public to a certain fear of dirt dropping from the trolley heads (in fact they were located behind the passenger seating) or even trolley equipment itself falling on the upper-deck passengers. In the season, the population of Bournemouth almost doubled and this brought major pressures on the undertaking. The seasonal coastal open-top motorbus service 12 and the motorbus circular tour had excellent loadings in comparison to those of the 39, and, logically, it was the open-

top trolleybus circular service which was cut first when there was a shortage of crews. This compounded the problems of making the service attractive and the thought of a totally silent open-top journey never really "took-off".

In September 1959 tenders were invited for the sale of a further twenty Sunbeam MS2 trolleybuses. There were three responses, the highest, that from Messrs Scource & Son, Chickerell near Weymouth, at £1,550 (also to include seven motorbuses) was accepted.

Trolleybus service 20 was experimentally extended from the Square to Westbourne, in company with service 25, from 14 September 1959, but it reverted to its previous town centre terminus on 14 November 1960.

The undertaking was increasingly troubled by summer traffic congestion in the town leading to delays and lost revenue. At a joint meeting of the Transport and Highways subcommittees in April 1960 it was suggested that additional "No Waiting" signs be erected in and around the Square; and a discussion took place with regard to improving the traffic flows at the Lansdowne, the delays caused by three sets of traffic lights between Boscombe Crescent and Parkwood Road, and tailbacks of traffic held up at the lights at the junction of Alma Road with Wimborne Road. Signs permitting parking on just one side of the road were fixed on various traction poles within the County Borough. They also discussed an alternative town centre terminus for the Side Routes which, like the earlier Braidley Road proposals, would have avoided the Square. It was suggested that trolleybuses descending Richmond Hill should turn left into Post Office Road, which would replace the Triangle as the terminus, then turn left again into Old Christchurch Road before turning left once more into Yelverton Road and thence back onto

Open-top Sunbeam MS2 no. 202 (ALJ986), formerly fleet no. 112, leaves Bournemouth Pier on Circular Service 39 on 3 August 1959. In the background, the impressive municipal Pavilion Theatre and Ballroom, which fronts on to Westover Road, was opened by the Duke of Gloucester in March 1929, the auditorium being enlarged in 1934. Note the white-painted traction poles in the vicinity of the Pier Approach.

Photo courtesy of D. Ball, for the family of the late J.S. King

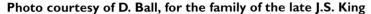

As open-top Sunbeam MS2 no. 201 (BRU11), parked in the Bournemouth Pier Approach loop, loads for another Circular Service 39 trip, Sunbeam MF2B no. 260 (WRU260) on seasonal supplementary service 38 arrives well-laden from Fisherman's Walk (4 August 1959) and makes its way across the entrance to the Pier towards the opposite (west) side of the Pier Approach which was the terminus and loading point of service 38 in the years that it operated eastbounds via Exeter Road and the Square (1956-1962). Thereafter, service 38 terminated and loaded at the same stop as the 39, i.e. in Bath Road next to the Pier Approach Baths.

Photo courtesy of D. Ball, for the family of the late J.S. King

Richmond Hill. It is believed that the proposal did not go ahead because of concerns about a loss of parking in Post Office Road which, like Yelverton Road, was relatively narrow.

Instead, a new overhead wiring layout was installed from the stops in Avenue Road around the northwest sector of Bournemouth Square to the base of Richmond Hill giving a clear run for trolleybuses proceeding up the hill and eliminating the operation of the frog at the junction of Bourne Avenue with the Square (outside Burton's premises). Trolleybuses leaving the easternmost stop in Avenue Road (service 25 and initially the extended 20) crossed those on the Richmond Hill services and followed the innermost wiring used by services 20-24 around the northwest sector of the Square roundabout. There were thus three pairs of parallel wiring around this sector of the roundabout, all Side Route services following the parallel outer wiring which gave a junction-free approach to the hill. The overhead work was completed with the removal of the facing (turnout) frog at the foot of Richmond Hill on 29 May 1960. The Transport Committee also proposed additional wiring from the bottom of Richmond Hill around the south side of the Square roundabout to a point at the start of Commercial Road, which would have eliminated the facing frog outside Bobby's store, but this was never carried out. The estimated total cost for both changes was £1,736.

A second parallel eastbound overhead line in Old Christchurch Road was brought into operation on 12 March 1960 from the corner of Stafford Road and into Holdenhurst Road, eliminating the operation of the facing frog on the north side of the Lansdowne roundabout (outside the underground public conveniences between Lansdowne Crescent and the roundabout). The frog, however, was retained for service 34 turning purposes. The new wiring continued around the outer, northern sector of the Lansdowne roundabout and gave service 25 trolleybuses a clear run into Holdenhurst Road, where a trailing frog linked up with the original eastbound overhead wiring immediately after the Lansdowne stop. Service 34 trolleybuses waiting at their Lansdowne stop did so on the inner overhead wiring, which, due to the frequency of service 25 (every 6-7 minutes in peak hours) led to occasional delays. There were three eastbound stops at the beginning of Holdenhurst Road: in sequence from the Lansdowne were trolleybus service 34, trolleybus service 25 and then motorbus services 4 and 11. It was recommended that the position of the facing frog on the south side of Lansdowne roundabout, for vehicles going down Bath Road, be altered and that the overhead equipment for those going down Old Christchurch Road be realigned, but there is no record of this ever carried being out. The estimated cost was £958.

The department's quarterly insurance records for 1 April 1960 showed the following trolleybus statistics:

Insured and available for service (total 63)

Sunbeam MS2	206, 209, 211, 215, 217, 218, 219, 221, 224, 225, 226, 228, 230, 231, 233
BUT9641T	234, 247-257
Sunbeam MF2B	258-278, 280-287
BUT9611T	288-294

Not insured (27)

Sunbeam MS2	205, 207, 208, 210, 212, 213, 214, 216, 222, 229, 232
Sunbeam open-top	200, 201, 202

BUT9641T	235-246
Sunbeam MF2B	279

Reflecting the need for additional rolling stock in commission at the height of the summer season but also the high operating costs of the BUT9641Ts, by 1 July 1960 the situation was:

Insured and available for service (82)

Sunbeam MS2	205, 206, 208, 209, 211, 213-215, 217-219, 221, 224-226, 228, 230, 231, 233
Sunbeam open-top	201, 202
BUT9641T	234-257
Sunbeam MF2B	258-287
BUT9611T	288-294

Not insured (8)

Sunbeam MS2	207, 210, 212, 216, 222, 229, 232
Sunbeam open-top	200

Ancillary vehicles allocated specifically to trolleybus operations (in both April and July)

Bedford 2-ton Overhead Department tower wagon	DEL 37
AEC Regent 661 Overhead Department tower wagon	VH6218, VH6217

(Fleet numbers for ancillary vehicles were phased out from 1950)

Mr Reakes was a speaker at the British Electrical Power Convention in early June 1960, his address being quoted in the 15 June 1960 edition of *Passenger Transport* magazine. Referring to his intention of replacing the remaining Sunbeam MS2s with new trolleybuses he added that *"It was retrograde step to abandon silent, fumeless, economical vehicles and to incur the danger of making too much transport dependent on vulnerable overseas oil. The corporation's wisdom in adopting trolleybuses in the past had been well-proven and more than justified their faith in them for the future."*

Apart from open-top circular service 39, the only other trolleybus service to reach Bournemouth Pier in the 1960 summer season was the 38, which operated alternately between the Pier or the Square and Fisherman's Walk, but with an extension between 1.30pm and 8pm to/from Christchurch via Southbourne Cross Roads and Tuckton Bridge, from 4 July 1960 until 11 September 1960. Alternate departures from Christchurch operated to Bournemouth Pier as service 38, the others going to Bournemouth Square as service 21.

Following weekend preparatory work from 22 October 1960 onwards, the remains of Cemetery Junction turning circle, accessible only by trolleybuses travelling south from Charminster Road or Wimborne Road, was removed on the night of 19/20 November 1960. It had hardly been used since Moordown Depot's closure in July 1953; the last trolleybus on service 29 (as it then was) from Malvern Road at night terminated at Cemetery Junction and then headed up Wimborne Road to Moordown.

Having considered the Finance Committee's comments about the Central Depot, and former Generating Station, Southcote Road, the General Manager had been asked to prepare estimates for the provision of additional accommodation at Castle Lane. On 12 July 1960 the Borough Architect reported on the likely cost and further consideration was deferred. In October

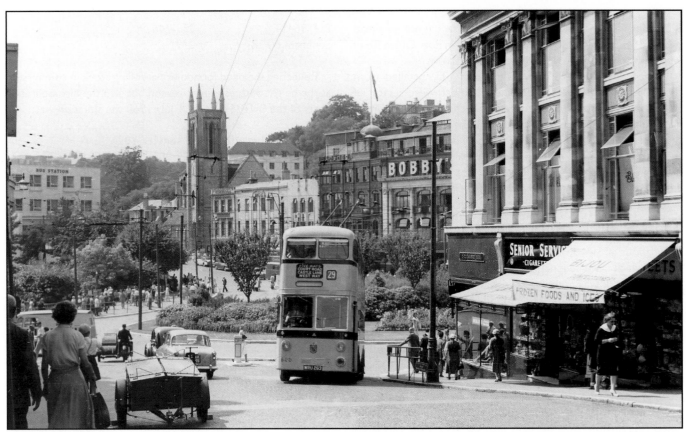

No. 263 (WRU263) prepares to tackle the 1 in 8 climb up Richmond Hill, something that it should accomplish with ease, on its way to Castle Lane West at West Way, the nominal terminus of service 29, via Charminster Road. In the left hand background is the Bus Station used by the country services of H&D and Wilts & Dorset, with the Coach Station beneath, enlarged in 1959. It was severely damaged by fire in 1976 and demolished in the early 1980s. **Photo courtesy of D.Ball, for the family of the late J.S. King**

Seen on 5 August 1959 at the westernmost stop in Columbia Road on a service 31 journey to the Square is Sunbeam MS2 96 (ALJ970) still with a smart appearance. The trolleybus retains its original fleet number and would never be renumbered, indeed, it was withdrawn in October 1959, just five months after this photograph was taken. **Photo courtesy of D.Ball, for the family of the late J.S. King**

On its way across the town centre to Westbourne, Sunbeam MS2 no. 217 (ALJ993) pauses at the westbound Lansdowne stop in Holdenhurst Road on 2 August 1959. On the ground floor of Royal London House a shop still awaits its first letting. Photo courtesy of D.Ball, for the family of the late J.S. King

BUT9641T no. 234 (KLJ334) turns south out of Holdenhurst Road into Ashley Road at the Queen's Park Hotel on its way to Boscombe as a Morris Oxford scurries across the junction.
Roger G. Funnell (courtesy Mrs. D. Funnell and Rodney Funnell)

1960 approval was given to the erection of a single-storey administration block at Castle Lane (Mallard Road) Depot to accommodate all office staff at a cost not exceeding £37,000; an extension of the garage at an estimated cost of £46,000; construction of hard standing at an estimated £3,500; and the consequent demolition of two empty farm cottages (remaining from the days when the site was a Corporation-owned farm for horses pulling municipal wagons) at an estimated cost of £300.

Boscombe (Pokesdown) Depot was still required by the Transport Department, although the Civil Defence was eager to use it for their vehicles, and enquiries were made as to the provision of doors and general improvements. Mr Reakes wrote to the Borough Architect on 30 November 1960 suggesting a meeting at the depot. He was of the opinion that, apart from a repaint and tidy-up of the mess room, little more than repairs to the leaky roof were necessary. The depot had functioned without doors throughout the trolleybus era (and it is thought that it never had them) and he was reluctant to fit them now at a cost of around £1,000.

The following statistics applied to Boscombe Depot at this time:

Number of trolleybuses parked during day: none
Number of trolleybuses parked after services cease: 10
Number of men:

cleaners	1 all night
maintenance supervisor	1 for 2 hours (checking trolleyheads)
platform staff	40 (plus an unknown number of conductors paying-in who are in the depot at night or pay in during the day).

Cost of			
maintenance	£2	19s 6d	per week
cleaning	£11	12s 2d	per week
electric light (2,425W)	£68	8s 7d	pa
water	£19	15s 0d	pa
heating—coke	£36	0s 0d	pa
heating—gas	£20	13s 9d	pa

Cost of repairs & painting building £500 in last 5 years

Fisherman's Walk, Southbourne, Cranleigh Road, Christchurch and Jumpers were noted as being the points served by trolleybuses from the depot when taking up service each morning.

The Transport Committee had, on 11 October 1960, recommended that application be made to the MoT for a further extension of time in respect of those trolley vehicle routes authorised, but which had not yet been put into operation. Accordingly, on 9 December 1960, the Town Clerk applied to the MoT to extend once more, for a period of three years, the time limited by Section 4 of the 1937 Order as confirmed by the 1938 Order Confirmation Act, 1938 (as extended in 1943 and 1946), and the consents of the MoT dated 14 May 1949, 16 May 1952, 17 May 1955, and 8 November 1957 for the commencement of the use of trolley vehicles along routes 2 (Ensbury Park Road-Wimborne Road via Coombe, Leybourne and Northbourne Avenues) and 4 (Alma Road-Holdenhurst Road via Richmond Park Road) authorised by Section 3 of the said order of 1937 (further details can be found in Appendix O).

These two extensions were now estimated to cost £22,400,

an increase of 10% since the powers were last renewed in 1957. BCT gave the following reasons for not having already implemented powers since then:

- completion of the making-up of Northbourne Avenue had only recently taken place,

- Routes 2 and 4 were intended to form a link between Kinson, East and West Howe and other parts of the Borough but the exact position of Route 2 had remained unclear until the substantial housing development already underway in that part of the town was complete,

- it would be necessary to retain a costly, parallel trolleybus and motorbus service along Alma Road at a time of financial difficulties within the undertaking.

Objections were received from almost fifty residents in Leybourne Avenue and Coombe Avenue, complaining about what they perceived as road overcrowding that would result from the introduction of trolleybuses and the detrimental visual impact of the overhead equipment. The Town Clerk responded that the roads were already licensed for 30ft-long and 8ft-wide buses; that traction poles would not spoil the area's visual amenities as they would in part be combined with street lighting standards; and that the use of trolleybuses instead of diesel buses would eliminate noise and fumes. MoT consent for a further extension of time was given on 1 May 1961.

On 30 January 1961 a minimum fare was introduced on service 32 outwards on weekdays between 4.30pm and 6.30pm. This was indicated between these hours by folding-down a wooden flap above the rear open platform entrance on all post-war trolleybuses that displayed the words "MINIMUM FARE IN OPERATION". This was the sole trolleybus service to have such a limitation (with the aim of ensuring that passengers destined for the Strouden Park area were not deprived of accommodation by short-stage passengers) and it remained in force until the end of trolleybus operation.

Further passenger waiting shelters were erected on Barrack Road, Christchurch, between the junctions with Manor Road and with Stour Road (opposite the "White Hart Hotel") westbound (service 20), and on Beaufort Road at its junction with Kimberley Road westbound (service 23). The Southbourne Ratepayers' Association's request for a service to Christchurch via Cranleigh Road was turned down at a Transport Committee Meeting on 14 February 1961.

On 11 March 1961 a roundabout was brought into use at the junction of Talbot Avenue with Wimborne Road, about a quarter of a mile south of Winton Banks junction, although the only overhead work necessary was a slewing of the conductor wires.

Fares had remained unchanged since March 1956, but by January 1961 estimates for the year ending 31 March 1962 forecast that on the basis of the existing fares and wage rates there would be a deficit of £23,934. A further wage claim for bus crews was being considered by the NJIC and it was therefore agreed that a fares revision would be considered once the result of this claim was known. Meanwhile, the SEB increased its charges with effect from 1 April 1961 involving an additional £915 pa. By mid-April 1962 it was known that the claim had been granted nationally, with effect from 16 April 1961, costing the undertaking £20,000 in a full year and that, in addition, workshop employees represented by the NJIC for Craftsmen in Municipal Passenger Transport Undertakings had also benefited from an award, costing £1,500 pa. As, combined, these would lead to a loss of £48,000 in the present financial

BUT9641T no. 239 (KLJ339) pulls forward out of Old Christchurch Road onto the Lansdowne roundabout using the kerbside overhead line that eliminated the operation of the facing frog on the north side of the roundabout.
Roger G. Funnell (courtesy Mrs. D. Funnell and Rodney Funnell)

On 7 August 1962, Sunbeam MF2B no. 296 (296LJ), in service for just three weeks, is seen rounding the south side of the Lansdowne roundabout on its way to Westbourne. The Lloyds Bank branch and row of shops in the background are in Holdenhurst Road.
Malcolm Pearce (G.O.P. Pearce)

Passing beneath the auto frog providing access from Lansdowne roundabout into the Holdenhurst Road eastbound line (the "overtaking" line from Old Christchurch Road into Holdenhurst Road is to the nearside) is Sunbeam MF2B no. 282 (YLJ282) on its way to Jumpers Corner on a service 24 journey. No. 282 will turn off the roundabout at the next exit into Christchurch Road. Roger G. Funnell (courtesy Mrs. D. Funnell and Rodney Funnell)

year, the Transport Committee recommended a fares increase and possibly new fare stages. Mr Reakes presented a report to the Transport Committee on 8 May 1961 recommending the introduction of additional fare stages. A first result was the Committee's agreement on 13 June 1961 to a new fare stage on service 25 at the British Legion Club in Ashley Road, Boscombe. The SETC granted the Corporation's request for increased fares, with effect from 11 July 1961.

In the meantime, the Transport Department was represented at the "Welcome to Citizenship" Exhibition, which opened at the Town Hall on 24 April 1961. Their stand included an auto frog assembly, a crossover assembly, sections of trolley wire and various overhead fittings.

Meanwhile, the reversing triangle on Charminster Road at its junction with Court Road was cut down on 9 May 1961. It had been little used, mainly by infrequent school specials serving Bournemouth Grammar School and Summerbee Infants' and Junior School almost opposite on East Way, and was no great distance from Five Ways turning circle or the reversing triangle at Luckham Road. On 19/20 May 1961, the original Iford turning circle on the west side of Christchurch Road between Bridle Crescent and Iford Bridge, made largely redundant by the construction of the roundabout at the junction of Castle Lane East and Christchurch Road in 1956, was also removed.

Seasonal supplementary trolleybus services 38 and 39 again served Bournemouth Pier from 12 June 1961, but this summer the 38 operated to Carbery Avenue via Fisherman's Walk, Beaufort Road and Cranleigh Road, instead of to and from Christchurch via Southbourne Cross Roads as in 1960.

There was a continuing shortage of platform staff in the 1961 summer season.

The Highways & Works Committee was informed that it was impossible to reduce the number of trolleybuses using Bournemouth Square.

A major fire, caused by an overheated pitch boiler used as part of a new venture into boat building, swept through the Weymann factory at Addlestone on the night of 4 July 1961 and reached the trimming shop, damaging three of the nine MF2B chassis already delivered by Sunbeam for bodying. On 6 July 1961, Mr G. Chesson, Weymann's Contract Manager, wrote to confirm his telephone conversations with Mr Reakes and Mr H. G. Harwood, the Sunbeam Works Manager. *"One chassis would appear to be a complete write-off, the second has sustained considerable damage and the third, although showing no sign of damage, was in fact adjacent to the fire and for this reason must be considered suspect, and will require thorough checking before it is considered fit for operation"*. Mr Chesson enquired what action was required and would be undertaken. Mr Reakes reported in October 1961 that, as a result of the fire, delivery of the new trolleybuses could only commence in July 1962.

The two damaged chassis had to be sent back to Sunbeam's Wolverhampton works for repair. Having reviewed the situation and in view of costs involved, the 14 November 1961 Transport Committee Meeting recommended that the destroyed chassis should not be replaced and Weymann be informed that only nine bodies were now required. Mr Reakes reported an increase in the cost of the new chassis had amounted to £145 14s 5d each, but pointed out that in view of the savings made

A Vanden Plas Austin Princess, one of the most luxurious cars in the BMC range at that time, overtakes BUT9641T no. 235 (KLJ335) as it heads west along Christchurch Road about 200yd past Boscombe Gardens near the Synagogue.   Roger G. Funnell (courtesy Mrs. D. Funnell and Rodney Funnell)

On 14 June 1961, Sunbeam MF2B no. 267 (WRU267) approaches the traffic lights at the cross roads of Christchurch Road with Sea Road, Boscombe, on its way to the Square. The Royal Ballrooms opened as the Grand Theatre in 1895 and traded variously as a theatre, ballroom and live music venue, being known at one time as the Hippodrome. Not visible in the photograph but immediately after Jones the Bootmaker's shop is the Boscombe Arcade. Today, this part of Christchurch Road, Boscombe, is a pedestrian precinct and the Ballroom is a listed building.

A.D. Packer

on trolley bases, jacks and batteries for the entire batch, the cost of each chassis was still about £21 below the tender price.

The other six chassis on Weymann's premises at the time of the fire, two of which carried partially-completed bodies, were towed by BCT's Guy Arab FRU180, crewed by Bill Biddlecombe and Shiftman Bertie Keeping, to Castle Lane (Mallard Road) Depot, where they were stored until Weymann's factory had been repaired sufficiently to permit normal coachbuilding to be resumed. They were returned to Weymann between April and June 1962. The tenth chassis, which had still been at Wolverhampton at the time of the fire, was brought direct to Bournemouth for storage.

The General Manager, Douglas Reakes, was due to retire on 1 December 1961 but was asked to extend his contract until 28 February 1962. Applications were invited for the post on a scale of £2,640 pa. rising by annual increments of £75 to £3,015 pa. Some 31 applications were received and six candidates selected for interview. On 10 November 1961 the Transport Committee appointed Mr Ronald Cox, then Engineer and General Manager of Rochdale Corporation Transport, to the position with effect from 1 March 1962 at a salary of £3,015 pa. Mr Cox had previously been Assistant Rolling Stock Engineer, Bradford Corporation Transport, and therefore had much trolleybus experience. Indeed, the professional magazine *The Transport World* had published his article on trolleybus starting and notching curves in their 11 March 1943 edition.

In July 1961 a quantity of surplus overhead equipment, comprising 12 traction poles at £120, 1,535yd of cadmium copper trolley wire (£250) and other miscellaneous items (£35), was purchased from Brighton Corporation, which had

abandoned its trolleybus system on 30 June 1961. These were intended for use on the anticipated extension along Holdenhurst Road from Queen's Park Golf Pavilion to Strouden Park, Castle Lane.

The highest of four tenders received for the disposal of redundant vehicles, that of Messrs W.J. Stevens & Sons, Gloucester, for the purchase of seven trolleybuses, three motorbuses and two vans at a total of £600, was accepted on 14 November 1961.

Structural defects in the main garage at Castle Lane (Mallard Road) Depot were discovered and, without prejudice to any liability between the Corporation and other parties, the work of temporary shoring at the depot was carried out by Messrs James Drewitt & Sons Ltd., who had constructed the building, at an estimated cost of £250. Subject to approval of estimates, Drewitts was authorised to proceed with the necessary repairs on a cost-plus basis without advertising for tenders, at an estimated £871 to be paid from the Reserve Fund.

The Borough Architect had inspected Boscombe (Pokesdown) Depot again in September 1961, reporting that, following repairs, brickwork and pointing were now in generally good condition, the slate roof fair (internal damp stains being due to the solid brickwork), the steel window frames and rainwater pipes corroded and oak windowsills showing signs of decay. Subsequently, the full Council recommended that the depot be transferred to the Civil Defence; however, the Transport Committee replied that it was unable to give it up because closure would involve running dead mileage of 15,250 annually at a cost of £1,500 pa. In addition, a special staff bus would have to be provided to shuttle crews to or from Castle Lane

One of Bournemouth's Sunbeam MF2B trolleybuses of the 295 - 303 batch, being fitted with its bodywork at Weymann's Addlestone factory in 1962.

David Chalk collection

Arriving at Castle Lane (Mallard Road) Depot on tow from Weymann's on 16 July 1962 is Sunbeam MF2B 296 (296LJ). No. 296 was the first of the final batch to reach Bournemouth and entered passenger service the next day. **David Chalk collection**

Complete and ready to roll, no. 295 (295LJ) awaits its tow from the Weymann factory in deepest Surrey down to Bournemouth on 26 September 1962. **David Chalk collection**

An unidentified, burned-out partially bodied Sunbeam MF2B at Weymann's Addlestone works.

David Chalk collection

One of the Sunbeam MF2B chassis with partially-completed bodies moved by BCT from Weymann's fire-damaged premises into storage at Castle Lane (Mallard Road) Depot is seen being towed through the New Forest by Guy Arab breakdown and towing vehicle FRU180 (formerly motorbus fleet no. 33).

David Chalk

Another Sunbeam MF2B chassis, this time without any form of body, arrives at Castle Lane (Mallard Road) Depot for storage towed by Guy Arab FRU180. David Chalk

or Central, Southcote Road Depots before the early shift and after the late shift with little chance of gaining any passenger revenue, whilst those conductors on early shift who lived in the Pokesdown area and paid-in there when going off-duty would be required to travel to one or other remaining depot to pay-in, for which time would have to be allowed.

At its 13 February 1962 meeting, the Transport Committee expressed their appreciation for 26 years of service to Mr Douglas Reakes on his retirement. He had been appointed Traffic Superintendent in 1935, becoming Deputy General Manager in 1944 and General Manager on 7 December 1948. An enthusiast of the trolleybus, he had become well-known throughout the industry.

With effect from 1 April 1962 the new SEB standard tariff was applied to the undertaking, involving an estimated increased annual cost of £600; however, from the same date revised meter rentals were charged, leading to an annual saving of £120.

The department's quarterly insurance records for 1 April 1962 showed the following trolleybus statistics:

Insured and available for service (total 68)

Sunbeam MS2	205-208, 210, 211, 215, 219, 221, 224, 232
BUT9641T	234-240, 244-257
Sunbeam MF2B	258-278, 280-287
BUT9611T	288-294

Not insured (15)

Sunbeam MS2	212-214, 216, 222, 229, 230, 233
Sunbeam open-top	200-202
BUT9641T	241-243
Sunbeam MF2B	279

Additional rolling stock was required to provide the enhanced services foreseen in the height of the summer season; however, the acute shortage of platform staff was to lead to summer

season service cuts. By 1 July 1962 the situation was:

Insured and available for service (total 80)

Sunbeam MS2	205-208, 210-216, 219, 221, 224, 232, 233
Sunbeam open-top	200-202
BUT9641T	234-257
Sunbeam MF2B	258-287
BUT9611T	288-294

Available for service but not insured (nil)

Sunbeam MS2s 222, 229, 232 had been withdrawn in the meantime

Ancillary vehicles allocated specifically to trolleybus operations (in both April and July)

Bedford 2-ton Overhead Department tower wagon	DEL 37
AEC Regent 661 Overhead Department tower wagon	VH6217
AEC Regent 661 Overhead Department tower wagon	VH6218
Guy Arab FD with Jones "Super 20" crane	FRU 224

On 10 April 1962, the Transport Committee considered a report on the nine Sunbeam MF2B trolleybuses on order and accepted the recommendations of the new General Manager, Mr Cox, that they be fitted with fluorescent lighting and lighter internal decor using modern finishing materials "in the Rochdale style", at an estimated additional cost of £2,215 11s 6d. In a letter to the department's insurance brokers (Messrs A.R. Stenhouse & Partners (London) Ltd.) dated 12 April 1962, Mr Cox advised that Sunbeam MF2B chassis numbers TFD 80195-197 and TFD 80200-204 were then at Castle Lane Depot until Weymann could fit the bodies. TFD 80201 was apparently missing its master controller. TFD 80198 was at Sunbeam prior

to despatch direct to Weymann. By 19 June 1962 only TFD 80200-201 and TFD 80204 were still at Castle Lane.

Commencing in July 1962 an additional display, "To and From Athletic Centre", referring to King's Park south of Dean Court Football Stadium, began to be added to the auxiliary blinds. This was presumably only used for eastbound journeys on service 25 as the choice of westbound route, by way of Bath Road or Old Christchurch Road, required the usual display.

Just £150 had been allocated to the undertaking's Diamond Jubilee celebrations on 23 July 1962. On that day, Councillor Alban Adams, Bournemouth's Mayor, drove 296, the first of the batch of nine further Sunbeam MF2B trolleybuses, accompanied by Ald. Deric Scott (Chairman of the Transport Committee), representatives of MCW, Sunbeam (by then owned by Jaguar Cars) and Mr Ronald Cox, General Manager. The Mayor commented that the town was immensely proud of its transport undertaking and said that *the new trolleybuses will certainly enhance our fleet*. The *Bournemouth Evening Echo* recorded that in 1961 the Department had carried 42 million passengers some 4.5 million miles and had taken £770,000 in revenue. Out of a fleet of 180 vehicles there were 90 trolleybuses. Other events included the publication of a commemorative brochure, prepared by Mr W.P. Ransom, Commercial Assistant to the General Manager since 1951, and special decorations to some vehicles.

At their 18 September 1962 meeting the Transport Committee gave its approval, subject to statutory consent, to the extension of the existing trolleybus route along Holdenhurst Road from Queen's Park Golf Pavilion to Strouden Park, Castle Lane (Cooper Dean). Mr Cox was authorised to make the necessary arrangements for the work to be carried out in the 1963/64 financial year at an estimated cost of £5,000. It went on to invite tenders for the disposal of a further nine Sunbeam MS2 trolleybuses and, having considered three tenders at the 10 November 1962 meeting, the highest received, that of Messrs Scource, at £46 each, was accepted.

Also in September 1962, an amended scheme for a two-storey administrative block at Castle Lane Depot (in place of plans for a larger, three-storey building of similar design) was approved, subject to the Finance Committee and Town Planning and Buildings Committee's approval, at an estimated cost of £45,000 (plus architect's fees of £5,300).

In an effort to both increase the passenger capacity and achieve operating economies with the heavy, powerful and thus expensive to run BUT9641T fleet, work started in September 1962 on experimentally removing the front staircase of 234. This was deemed a success and conversion of all the BUT9641Ts, one after the other, commenced. The rebuilding involved the removal of the front staircase (although the front exit doors were retained) and the addition of further seats using seat frames from recently-scrapped Sunbeam MS2s, increasing the seating capacity from 56 to 68 (39 in the upper saloon and 29 in the lower saloon). Flashing trafficators in replacement of semaphore arms were fitted at the sides and rear. Strip bell pushes were fitted and the original Alhambrinal ceiling linings were removed to reveal the metal above. Each rebuilt vehicle was put into service on heavily-loaded service 25 as soon as available.

What proved to be Bournemouth's last new trolleybus, Sunbeam MF2B 301, was delivered on 12 October 1962. Its delivery marked a sea change in local transport policy. The Sunbeam MF2Bs gave more maintenance problems per vehicle than any other type of Bournemouth trolleybus. The underfloor contactors were susceptible to damp and water ingress, the 24-volt lighting generator gave problems and there were excessive half-shaft (the drive from the rear axle differential to the road wheels) failures. The later General Manager, Ian Cunningham, felt that this last weakness was probably due to the influx of Guy motorbus engineers into the Sunbeam design team: the half-shafts were simply not up to the stresses of trolleybus acceleration.

In addition to the overhead equipment bought in July 1961

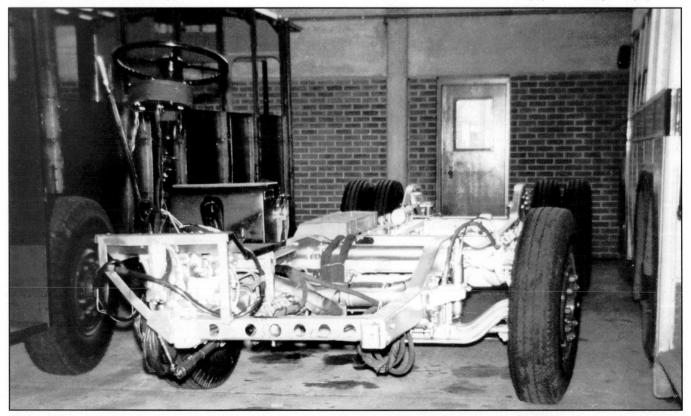

One of the unbodied Sunbeam MF2B chassis in store at Castle Lane (Mallard Road) Depot.   **David Chalk**

Approaching Jumpers Corner heading west along Barrack Road at Maundeville Road is Sunbeam MF2B no. 285 (YLJ285) on a service 20 journey to the Square. The Stourvale Hotel in the background was an Eldridge Pope house. The Dorchester brewer was known for its Huntsman Ales but ceased production in 2003. During the trolleybus era many of Bournemouth's public houses were operated by either Eldridge Pope or Strong of Romsey where brewing ceased in 1981. The scene has changed somewhat in half a century: the floral displays have disappeared but there is still an Esso petrol station next to the public house (now named simply The Stourvale).

Travel Lens

Leaving the Square roundabout past Bobby's store, Sunbeam MS2 no. 219 (BEL814) heads west up Commercial Road to the Triangle where it will take a pause before leaving on a 26 for Castle Lane West, Lawford Road.

David Chalk collection

(Left) The official handover of the final batch of Weymann bodied Sunbeam MF2Bs took place at Castle Lane (Mallard Road) Depot on 3 July 1962. Here, the Mayor of Bournemouth, Councillor Alban E. Adams, JP, shakes hands with Mr. H. A. Cook, Managing Director of Weymann, observed by the Chairman of the Transport Committee, Alderman Deric S. Scott. The General Manager of the Transport Department, Ronald Cox, accompanied by Mr. A. Whittaker, Deputy Chairman Jaguar Cars (by then owners of Sunbeam following their acquisition of Guy Motors and thus Sunbeam in October 1961) on behalf of the manufacturer look on. In the background is no. 296.   David Chalk collection
(Bournemouth Evening Echo)

(Below) One of the final batch of Sunbeam MF2Bs, no. 296 (296LJ), is seen at the Square loading point for service 25, at the east end of Avenue Road, on its way to Boscombe, Portman Road.   David Chalk collection

At the bottom of Richmond Hill Sunbeam MS2 no. 216 (ALJ991) starts its climb up to the northern suburbs of Bournemouth on "Side Route" service 31 to Columbia Road.   Barry Moore

Sunbeam MS2s no. 233 (BRU21) followed by no. 232 (BRU19) make their stately progress down Richmond Hill to the Square. Both trolleybuses already have indicator screens reset for their next departures from the Triangle.
                                                                                                            Barry Moore

from Brighton Corporation, further quantities of overhead wiring equipment and traction poles were purchased from the erstwhile Brighton and Ipswich trolleybus systems, for use in the construction of the Holdenhurst Road route extension. Until October 1962 these plans, together with the Ensbury Park-Wimborne Road via Combe, Leybourne and Northbourne Avenues (Route 2), and the Boscombe (Gladstone and Haviland Roads)-Winton via Richmond Park Road and Alma Road (Route 4) extensions, originally approved by the 1938 Order Confirmation Act, 1938 and subsequently extended several times, remained active.

Further proposals at this time (the precise course to be followed varying somewhat on each occasion the routes were discussed as suburban housing and access roads developed), never submitted for parliamentary approval, covered the route of motorbus service 7 in the Kinson area, from the junction of Columbia Road with Kinson Road (trolleybus services 30 and 31) along Fernheath Road, Maclean Road and Moore Avenue, and/or Kinson Road and Montgomery Avenue, and/or West Howe Road, to Poole Lane and then southwards along Ringwood Road to a terminus at Francis Avenue, or along Poole Lane, Holloway Avenue and then northwards along Ringwood Road to Bear Cross. Subsequent proposals were to extend trolleybuses along East Howe Lane from the junction with Leybourne Avenue instead of following Northbourne Avenue to Wimborne Road. It is understood that these were not detailed proposals, all of which would have required an additional substation and feeder cables, and, coming relatively late in the system's lifetime, none were surveyed in detail or constructed.

An accumulated deficit of almost £40,000 at the end of March 1956 had been turned into reserves of double that figure by early 1962 but, having considered the undertaking's financial position, the Transport Committee recommended on 10 November 1962 that an application for fare increases be made to the SETC.

Southbourne Ratepayers' Association again asked that Cranleigh Road trolleybus service be extended to Christchurch and Mr Cox was asked to report.

Reportedly disappointed at having failed to secure promotion to General Manager upon the retirement of Mr Reakes, the Deputy Transport Manager and Engineer, Tom Marsden, resigned in December 1962, having secured the position of General Manager at Barrow-in-Furness. He went on to manage the Aberdeen (later Grampian) undertaking and subsequently became an Executive Director of the Scottish Bus Group. Applications for his successor were invited at the prevailing salary within the scale of £1,825 to £2,085 pa.

At the end of 1962 the entrance to the bus park at the Triangle was widened at an estimated cost of £40 to enable two additional trolleybuses to be parked there.

On 19/20 December 1962 the wiring at Strouden Park turning circle, through the gorse bushes to the north east of the junction of Holdenhurst Road with Castle Lane, was cut down and the site disappeared beneath works for a new roundabout. Temporarily, trolleybuses passed through the centre of the "island" whilst other traffic followed the normal circuitous course. From 18 December 1962, those peak-hour trolleybuses terminating there, together with a single Sunday afternoon service, were extended to Iford roundabout for turning purposes.

The winter of 1962-63 proved particularly hard and Bournemouth's trolleybus services were totally suspended on 30 December 1962 for the first time in their history due to ice formation on the overhead wiring, leading to poor electrical contact and thus jerky operation on the ice-covered roads. Bodorgan Road reversing triangle was reportedly used during periods when icy weather conditions made it impossible for trolleybuses to negotiate Richmond Hill safely.

BUT9641T no. 239 (KLJ339), which re-entered service in January 1963 following the removal of its front staircase, enters the north end of Lansdowne Road at Cemetery Junction on its way from Castle Lane West, junction with West Way, and Moordown to the Lansdowne.   Roger G. Funnell (courtesy Mrs. D. Funnell and Rodney Funnell)

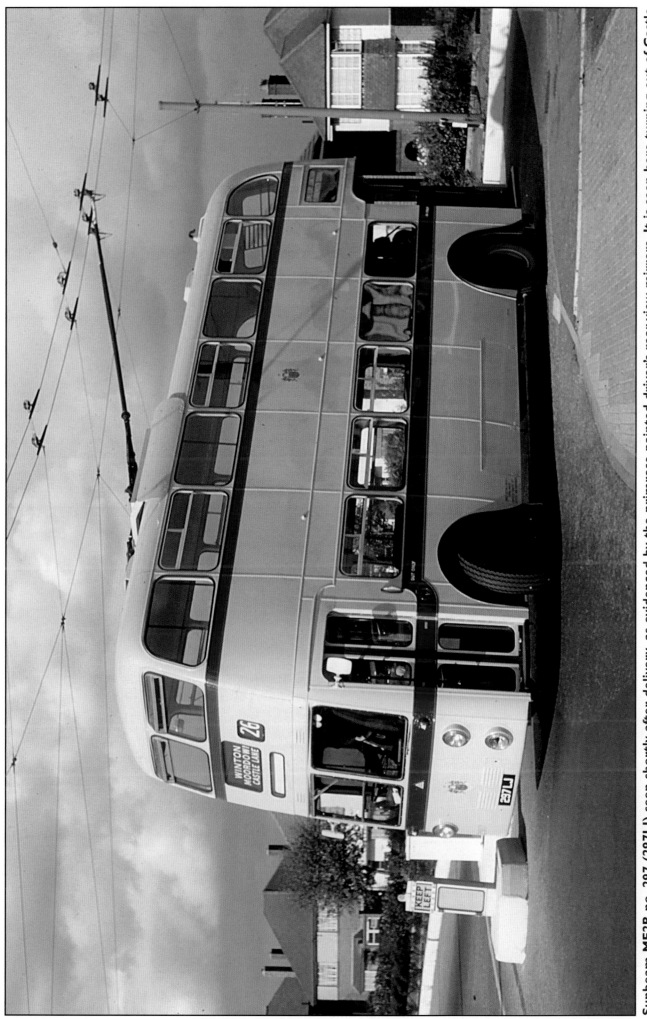

Sunbeam MF2B no. 297 (297LJ) seen shortly after delivery, as evidenced by the primrose-painted driver's rear-view mirrors. It is seen here turning out of Castle Lane West into Wimborne Road, Red Hill, Moordown, on a service 26 working to the Square (something not confirmed by the indicator blinds). Note the cherry red paintwork around the driver's cab area.

F.W. Ivey

Pulling out of St. Paul's Road into Lansdowne Road is rebuilt BUT9641T 239 (KLJ339) on its way to Castle Lane West, junction with West Way, a nominal terminal point with no turning facilities. Service 34 (ii) interworked there with the 29 (ii) and returned to Bournemouth town centre along Charminster Road. This entire area has since disappeared with the construction of the town centre by-pass, Wessex Way (A338).

Roger G. Funnell (courtesy Mrs. D. Funnell and Rodney Funnell)

Awaiting departure time is rebuilt BUT9641T no. 235 (KLJ335) in the apex of the reversing triangle at the north end of Luckham Road, the terminus for Broadway Hotel journeys along Charminster Road.

Roger G. Funnell (courtesy Mrs. D. Funnell and Rodney Funnell)

CHAPTER NINE
THE TIDE TURNS

At its first meeting of 1963, the Transport Committee instructed Mr Cox to submit a report on future trolleybus policy, including their involvement in any fleet replacement scheme. The Borough Engineer was asked to prepare a scheme for Stage II of the Castle Lane Depot development relating to the area between the workshops and the main depot building used by motorbuses and trolleybuses, upon which a second motorbus garage was built in 1965.

There were 19 applications to fill the position of Deputy General Manager and Engineer, vacated by Mr Marsden, and five applicants were invited for interview. With effect from 4 March 1963, Ian Cunningham, Assistant Rolling Stock Engineer, Edinburgh Corporation Transport, was appointed at a salary of £1,825 pa. on the scale £1,825-£2,085 pa.

On 13 February 1963, the Transport Committee approved payment, under the "rise and fall" terms of the contract, of an additional £160 per vehicle in respect of the nine new Sunbeam MF2B trolleybuses, fleet numbers 295-303, that had been delivered during July-October 1962.

An application to increase fares made in November 1962 was granted by the SETC on 12 February 1963, with effect from 21 February 1963. Their Chairman considered the increases modest, but in view of the modernity of the fleet he recommended that a reserve fund should be built up. The maximum mileage on fares above 3d was reduced. There was no increase to 2d fares, but some 4d and all other fares up to 1s were increased.

Mr Cox presented his report on the future of trolleybus operations and suggestions as to fleet replacement on 19 March 1963. In-depth research showed that British-built trolleybuses were unobtainable, except at bespoke prices, if at all. Most other British trolleybus operators had already announced a policy of trolleybus replacement, whilst spare parts and items of overhead equipment were becoming increasingly difficult to obtain. Although Bournemouth had a fleet of 39 new Sunbeam MF2Bs, none of which were more than five years old (with typically a 25-year operating life ahead of them), and an overhead wiring and power supply system in excellent condition, it must be admitted that the report accurately reflected the prevailing situation. There was no government encouragement to operate trolleybuses, no environmental lobby and nothing has subsequently shown Mr Cox's professional opinion to have been flawed.

The Transport Committee had little alternative but to recommend that:

i) No further purchases of trolleybuses be made;
ii) General Manager to report annually on the condition and suitability for continued operation of the then existing trolleybuses;
iii) As groups of trolleybuses aged and their condition became uneconomic to operate, the General Manager be requested to report as to the routes which could best continue to be served by the remaining and decreasing trolleybus fleet;

iv) The Council resolved to discontinue the use of trolley vehicles as from a date in the future, to be determined, when the then remaining fleet had been reduced to such an extent as to make its continuance uneconomic;
v) Subject to the approval of the next Finance Committee, tenders be invited for vehicle replacement for the next three years, viz. thirty double-deck motorbuses at the rate of ten per year for spring delivery in 1964, 1965 and 1966.

With respect to the proposed trolleybus extension from Queen's Park Golf Pavilion, along Holdenhurst Road to Strouden Park, Castle Lane (Cooper Dean), a further report was requested.

Having considered reports in March 1963 from the Highways & Works Committee, and from the General Manager on the cost of diverting trolleybus overhead at the junctions of Lansdowne Road and Littledown Road with St. Paul's Road to accommodate the planned town centre by-pass (now Wessex Way), the Transport Committee instructed Mr Cox to replace trolleybus services 34 and 36, which ran along the northern part of Lansdowne Road and the entire length of St. Paul's Road, with motorbuses when work started. In this connection, Mr Cox recommended in May 1963 that, in view of planned road widening along that part of Holdenhurst Road between Littledown Avenue and Castle Lane, foreseen as a continuation of the by-pass, no trolleybus route extension from Queen's Park Golf Pavilion to Strouden Park, Castle Lane should be built.

On 22 March 1963 the full Bournemouth Council decided that no further trolleybuses would be purchased and that a progressive run-down would commence as vehicles aged and the fleet contracted in size, eventually leading to route closures. It was estimated that operations would continue for another 10-15 years bearing in mind the youth of the latest Sunbeam MF2Bs, indicating final closure in 1978. History was to prove this estimate over-optimistic.

On 22 March 1963 the *Bournemouth Times & Directory* recorded:

"Trolleybuses cost more than diesel buses due to increased charges for electric current, overhead wiring and cause traffic obstruction. So, after 30 years, these 10 ton transports which so impressed the residents with their silence after the trams, are to be dispensed with by a progressive run-down of the 90 which remain of the original 103 strong fleet. It is believed that criticism of the trolleys is related to congestion in the main thoroughfares and a transformer breakdown which resulted in the centre around the Square being cluttered up with inert trolleys during a peak period, finally decided the Transport Committee.

"Mr Ronald Cox was reportedly embarrassed when the Traffic Commissioners asked him the age of the buses (some are 30 years old) when the Corporation was seeking to raise fares in February. Unhappily for Mr Cox he had been saddled with 9 new trolleys, ordered before his arrival last year. Cash price of these would have been around £75,000. They are being bought on a 14-year loan and the final cost per vehicle will be about double the price of an

Seen heading south in **Bargates**, just before **Beaconsfield Road**, Christchurch is Sunbeam MF2B no. 296 heading for the turntable terminus of service 21. Immediately behind the flats and shops to the nearside of the trolleybus was the erstwhile **BPES** traction power generating station and, later, substation.

Roger G. Funnell (courtesy Mrs D. Funnell and Rodney Funnell)

No. 299 passes the junction with the **A35 Christchurch by-pass** on the east side of the **Fountain** or **Pit Site** roundabout prior to turning into **Christchurch High Street** on a service 20 journey. In the left hand background is the tower of **Christchurch Fire Station** and behind the trolleybus is the brick-built **Conservative Club**. Note that 299 has a primrose-painted rear view mirror on the offside but a black one on the nearside!

Roger G. Funnell (courtesy Mrs D. Funnell and Rodney Funnell)

Two generations of Sunbeam MF2Bs: no. 259, the second to be delivered on 29 July 1958 and, in front, no. 299 (with its trolley booms down), which reached Bournemouth on 24 September 1962, are seen at Queen's Park Golf Pavilion terminus at the junction of Holdenhurst Road with Littledown Avenue. Both trolleybuses have their screens set for service 25 workings.

Keith Baynton collection

excellent make of diesel double-decker recently demonstrated to the Corporation. The undertaking is in fact still paying for trolleys it bought 6 years ago and will be doing so until 1975 by which time, undoubtedly, the vehicles will have disappeared from the roads. The whole trolley set-up has been an expensive one. Some people think that the Council took the wrong turning when Southcote Road power generating station came to the end of its life a few years back. That, they say, would have been an opportune time to scrap the trolleys. Instead the Council borrowed £60,000 for buildings and equipment for a switch-over of the trolleys to the grid. And the greater part of this loan was for 20 years. Now, not surprisingly, the cost of electric current is more than it cost the Corporation to generate it, and the price is always increasing.

"In the financial year ending March last year, the trolleys cost 39.92d per mile or 3.41d per passenger. The diesel buses cost 35.84d per mile or 4.73d per passenger. Trolley revenue was £389,558 and diesels £361,006. There is not, in these figures, any real indication that in working costs alone trolleys are still cheaper. For the trolleys still hold the most remunerative routes and take more money for lower mileages than do the diesels. Diesels ran more than a quarter of a million miles more than the trolleys in that year. Trolleys carried 24,557,919 passengers against 17,749,495 carried by the diesels.

"There are obvious advantages in the use of diesels—fewer hold ups, no packing in columns, nose to tail resulting from the inability of one trolley to overtake another, quicker 'taking' of roundabouts and corners, and better pace-keeping with traffic generally. The town's present traffic conditions demand that the trolleys should go. Only the older residents will mourn their passing. They will complain about fumes and noise. But the increase in these nuisances contributed by diesels can be no more than slight in face of the growing number of vehicles on all roads. And how pleasantly different the town will look with all those ugly standards and overhead wires cleared away."

On the same day the Bournemouth Evening Echo reported:

"The undertaking has had to cope with the twin problems of rising costs and dwindling passengers. The new trolleybuses bought in 1958 cost in the region of £7,000 each (in 1934 they were £2,135 each) which will give some idea of how costs have gone up and the drop of 14 million passengers carried by the trolleybuses comparing the figures for 1953 with those for 1962 certainly calls for no comment.

"As a form of urban transport in the UK the trolleybus has fallen out of favour; local councils see them—as indeed has been suggested

in Bournemouth—as causes of road congestion and managements plead that motorbuses are far more flexible in operation, although the vast majority of the travelling public who use them have great affection for the trolleybus. Whatever the decision of Bournemouth, the town can be very proud of what has been achieved in providing a silent, swift, safe and smokeless service."

On 21 April 1963, eastbound trolleybuses operating along Castle Lane started to circumnavigate the new Cooper Dean roundabout at the north end of Holdenhurst Road, Strouden Park. Westbound vehicles ceased to use the narrow track through the middle of the roundabout on 18 May 1963. The peak-hour service 32 journeys which had been temporarily extended to Iford were cut back to the new roundabout on 27 May 1963, the overhead wiring on the east side of the roundabout being equipped with an auto frog. Thereafter additional wiring on the west side to make a complete circle around the roundabout, with the then foreseen Holdenhurst Road extension in mind, was added, as planned. Frogs were included to enable westbound trolleybuses to turn and return to Iford but these were not connected up until 12 July 1963 and no services were scheduled to turn here.

The environmentally-minded Health and Watch Committee questioned the wisdom of withdrawing pollution-free trolleybuses and replacing them with noxious fume-producing diesel buses. The Transport Committee replied that it had always maintained their vehicles to the highest possible level and that it did not anticipate any difficulties as a result of the introduction of diesel buses in the place of trolleybuses!

Plans to extend service 23 from Tuckton to Christchurch during the 1963-64 winter were dropped in February 1963, but a review was promised when a scheme for a roundabout at Tuckton was completed. Although discussed by the Transport Committee on several occasions over the years, the extension was never made during the trolleybus era. Erection of traction poles on the Bournemouth side of Tuckton Bridge, at the junction of Tuckton Road with Belle Vue Road, commenced in May 1963 prior to the construction of a roundabout there. Following an overnight operation by the overhead gang, a complete circle of wiring was brought into service on Sunday 30 June 1963 enabling trolleybuses on services 22 and 23 to turn back at the roundabout, although normally the interworking of

The two most rural parts of the Bournemouth trolleybus system were Castle Lane East and Wallisdown Road. On 30 August 1964, no. 271 travels west along Wallisdown Road approaching Talbot Village Farm on a service 30 journey to Columbia Road which would potentially continue as a 31 back to the Square. Both the County Boundary between Dorset and Hampshire, and the Borough Boundary between Poole and Bournemouth followed the right hand (south) side of the road at this point. **Tim Runnacles**

these services made this unnecessary. The new wiring had been strung above the old during the preceding weeks and, after the last trolleybus had passed on the Saturday evening, the latter was cut down and the new joined up, being completed in time for the first vehicles on the Sunday morning. Sunbeam MS2 212 operating on a Reading Transport Society (RTS) tour on 7 July 1963 was the first trolleybus to run under the new wiring from Tuckton Bridge into Tuckton Road.

The 1963 summer timetable was in force from 27 May 1963 until 29 September 1963, trolleybus circular service 39 being operated by open-top Sunbeam MS2s 200 and 202, with 201 stored de-licensed at Castle Lane (Mallard Road) Depot. By now, nine of the rebuilt 3-axle BUT9641Ts (234-242) had re-entered service and 243 followed in June 1963, after which the reconstruction programme was terminated following

the decision to progressively run-down trolleybus operation. Closed-top MS2s 208, 210, 212, 213 were in service with 205, 206, 214-216, 224 also stored de-licensed at Castle Lane.

Trolleybus services in operation for the summer timetable period, the last occasion that the system was at its maximum extent, were:

20   Bournemouth Square, Gervis Place - Lansdowne - Christchurch Road - Boscombe - Pokesdown - Iford - Jumpers - Barrack Road - Christchurch, Church Street

21   Bournemouth Square, Gervis Place - Lansdowne - Christchurch Road - Boscombe - Pokesdown - Fisherman's Walk - Southbourne Cross Roads - Tuckton Bridge - Christchurch, Church Street

Sunbeam MF2B no. 269 on its way to Jumpers, passes the Midland Bank in Christchurch Road, Boscombe, with the pillars at the entrance to the Crescent Gardens visible above the Standard model Ford Anglia 105E (identifiable by the absence of a full-width chrome radiator grill) following the trolleybus.

Roger G. Funnell (courtesy Mrs D. Funnell and Rodney Funnell)

Travelling east along Christchurch Road is BUT9641T no. 257 on its way to Carbery Avenue, Tuckton on seasonal supplementary service 38 in summer 1962.   Roger G. Funnell (courtesy Mrs D. Funnell and Rodney Funnell)

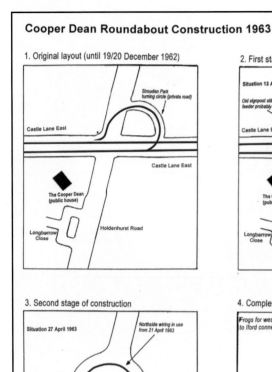

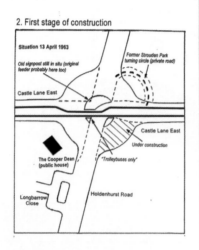

Cooper Dean Roundabout Construction 1963

1. Original layout (until 19/20 December 1962)

2. First stage of construction

3. Second stage of construction

4. Completed roundabout (from 18 May 1963)

29 Triangle - Bournemouth Square - Cemetery Junction - Five Ways - Broadway Hotel - Castle Lane West, junction with West Way
Interworking with service 34

30 Triangle - Bournemouth Square - Richmond Hill - Cemetery Junction - Winton - Wallisdown - Columbia Road

31 Triangle - Bournemouth Square - Cemetery Junction - Winton - Ensbury Park - Columbia Road

32 Triangle - Bournemouth Square - Cemetery Junction - Broadway Hotel - Strouden Park - Iford Bridge - Jumpers Corner

33 Triangle - Bournemouth Square - Cemetery Junction - Winton - Moordown - Broadway Hotel - Strouden Park - Iford
(peak hours, Monday - Saturday only)

34 Lansdowne - Central Station - Cemetery Junction - Winton - Moordown - Castle Lane West - Broadway Hotel
Interworking with service 29 at Castle Lane West, junction with West Way

35 Triangle - Bournemouth Square - Cemetery Junction - Five Ways - Malvern Road, junction with Charminster Avenue

22 Bournemouth Square, Gervis Place - Lansdowne - Christchurch Road - Boscombe - Pokesdown - Fisherman's Walk - Southbourne Cross Roads - Tuckton, Tuckton Road
Interworking with service 23

23 Bournemouth Square, Gervis Place - Lansdowne - Christchurch Road - Boscombe - Pokesdown - Fisherman's Walk - Tuckton, Tuckton Road
Interworking with service 22

24 Bournemouth Square, Gervis Place - Lansdowne - Christchurch Road - Boscombe - Pokesdown - Iford - Jumpers Corner

25 Westbourne - Bournemouth Square - Lansdowne - Central Station - Holdenhurst Road - Springbourne - Ashley Road - Boscombe, Portman Road or Westbourne, Seamoor Road - Queen's Park Golf Pavilion, Holdenhurst Road

26 Triangle - Bournemouth Square - Richmond Hill - Cemetery Junction - Wimborne Road - Winton - Moordown - Castle Lane West, Lawford Road

28 Triangle - Bournemouth Square - Richmond Hill - Cemetery Junction - Charminster Road - Five Ways - Broadway Hotel, Luckham Road

36 Lansdowne - Central Station - Cemetery Junction - Winton - Ensbury Park - Columbia Road
(peak hours, Monday - Saturday only)

37 Bournemouth Square, Gervis Place - Lansdowne - Boscombe Gardens - Boscombe Arcade - Pokesdown Station - Fisherman's Walk, Wentworth Avenue
(mainly peak hours, Monday - Saturday only)

38 Bournemouth Pier - Lansdowne - Boscombe Gardens - Boscombe - Pokesdown - Fisherman's Walk - Carbery Avenue, Tuckton

39 Bournemouth Pier - Lansdowne-Boscombe Gardens - Boscombe Arcade - Pokesdown Station - Fisherman's Walk - Southbourne - Tuckton Bridge - Jumpers - Iford - Strouden Park - Broadway Hotel - Cemetery Junction - Central Station - Lansdowne - Bournemouth Pier
Anti - clockwise circular service.

By the middle of the 1963 summer season, all the remaining Sunbeam MS2s except 224 (which had been withdrawn with an electrical fault in September 1962 and was never reinstated) were reported as licensed, many operating on all-day duties. Open-top 201, which retained its older blue-shaded fleet numbers, was also back in service.

In September 1963, orders were placed for 20 Leyland (£2,950 5s 6d each) and 10 Daimler (£3,108 each) rear-engined

No. 287 (YLJ287) is travelling east along Castle Lane East through the site of the future Cooper Dean roundabout at the junction with Holdenhurst Road. Although running on service 32 as far as Iford, the indicator blinds are already set for the journey back to the Square as a 24 via Christchurch Road.　　　　Tony Belton

Sunbeam MS2 no. 210 (ALJ967) turns back into Castle Lane at the freshly completed and wired Cooper Dean roundabout on 28 September 1963.　　　　F.W. Ivey

Having terminated as a 23 in Tuckton Road, Sunbeam MF2B no. 276 (WRU276) turns across the short stretch of Belle Vue Road between the new Tuckton roundabout and Tuckton Bridge before turning into the other section of Belle Vue Road and heading west towards Southbourne and, eventually, Bournemouth Square on a service 23 working.　　　　Tony Belton

Sunbeam MF2B no. 263 (WRU263) pulls out of the lay-by at the east end of Tuckton Road which served as the terminal point of service 22 following the reconstruction of the road layout in spring 1963 and "sets sail" along Tuckton Road, Cranleigh Road and Beaufort Road towards Fisherman's Walk and thence to the Square as a 23.
Roger G. Funnell (courtesy Mrs D. Funnell and Rodney Funnell)

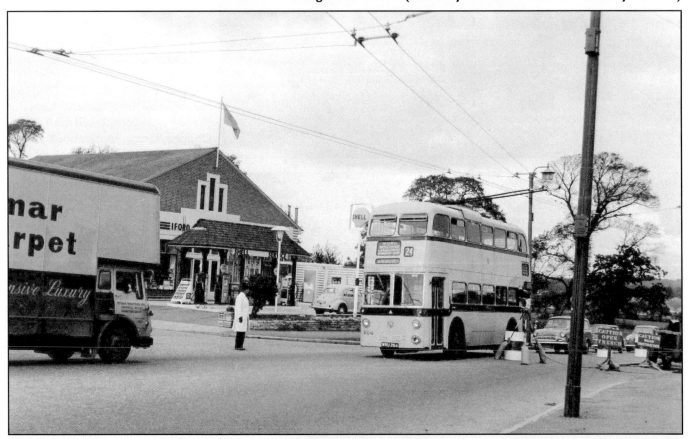

Road work has closed the westbound carriageway of Christchurch Road just east of Iford roundabout and the Overhead Department has slewed the the westbound overhead towards the centre of the road to ease the passage of trolleybuses. Sunbeam MF2B no. 264 (WRU264) passes the road work on its way from Jumpers to Bournemouth Square in October 1963.
NTA Collection (R.F. Mack)

double-deck motorbuses with MCW bodies (£4,045 10s 0d each) for trolleybus replacement purposes.

Traction units and maximum demands for the month ending 1 September 1963

Substation	Units	Maximum Demand	Simultaneous maximum demand	
			2nd Aug 1963	22 Aug 1963
Electric House	77,580	330KVA at 5pm 01.08.63	260	190
Winton	50,740	200KVA at 8am 06.08.63	150	150
Southbourne	68,570	200KVA at 5.30pm 01.08.63 & 5.30pm 13.08.63	175	180
Christchurch	50,430	175KVA at 5.30pm 23.08.63	125	125
Holdenhurst	48,840	180KVA at 5.30pm 01.08.63 & 7.30am 16.08.63	125	140
Pokesdown	74,080	235KVA at 7.30am 30.07.63 & 5pm 01.08.63	200	210
Iddesleigh Rd	88,400	280 KVA at 5pm 02.08.63 & 5pm 22.08.63	280	280
Southcote	332,500	1,020KVA at 5pm 22.08.63	980	1,020
Total	**791,320**		**2,295**	**2,295**

Tenders were invited for the sale of five of the remaining Sunbeam MS2 trolleybuses in September 1963, whilst the General Manager was authorised to negotiate with the RTS for the sale for preservation of an additional vehicle. No. 212 was selected and purchased for £30. The 20 September 1963 edition of the *Bournemouth Evening Echo* recorded the sale and interviewed the Society's Chairman, Mr M.J.C. Dare. Closed-top Sunbeam MS2s 205, 208, 210, 212, 214 and 224 were withdrawn at the end of September 1963 and, except for 212, were towed away by Scource & Son (Breakers) of Weymouth, in early November 1963. On Saturday 16 November 1963, with the press in attendance, 212 was officially handed over to the RTS. The afternoon was spent operating on the circuit around Castle Lane Depot with enthusiasts on board. At 6.15am on the Sunday, 212 left Bournemouth behind BCT lorry FRU180 for Reading, reaching its new home at 11am. The remaining MS2s, namely 206, 213, 215 and 216, together with the three open-top vehicles, were held in store for possible use in 1964, although continuing staff shortages made it unlikely that services 38 or 39 would operate.

There were rumours in the summer that work would shortly commence on the town centre by-pass; however, that was not the sole reason for the first trolleybus route closure. It had been agreed in principle that when the Transport Department moved out of Central Depot, Southcote Road, the premises would be acquired by the Borough Engineer, whose department would move from their then base, located between Holdenhurst Road, St. Paul's Road, the east end of Littledown Road and the approach to Bournemouth Central Station. This latter area would become a new bus and coach station, since named the

Travel Interchange, and it was work on the new access roads thereto which led to the early withdrawal of trolleybuses along St. Paul's Road and Lansdowne Road. Preparatory work for both the town centre by-pass, which opened in stages between 1969 and 1980, and the bus and coach station soon began, involving the demolition of many buildings as well as bisecting many of the roads leading between Charminster Road and Holdenhurst Road. The Borough Engineer's base moved in summer 1965.

Thus, the end of the summer timetable on Sunday 29 September 1963 brought the first trolleybus route closure with the withdrawal of scheduled trolleybus operation between Cemetery Junction and Holdenhurst Road along St. Paul's Road and Lansdowne Road. Trolleybus service 34 (Lansdowne-St. Paul's Road-Cemetery Junction-Winton-Moordown-Castle Lane West, Broadway Hotel) was replaced by motorbuses the next day operating an hourly clockwise route Bournemouth Square-Lansdowne-Moordown-Strouden Park-Holdenhurst Road-Lansdowne-Bournemouth Square, with redesignated service 33 operating anti-clockwise. Peak hour trolleybus services 33 (Triangle-Square-Moordown-Strouden Park-Iford) and 36 (Lansdowne-St. Paul's Road-Cemetery Junction-Winton-Ensbury Park-Columbia Road) ran for the last time on Saturday 28 September 1963. As service 34 trolleybuses had continued back to the Square down Charminster Road as service 29 and vice versa, the 29 was now linked with a reinstated service 27 operating via Moordown, Winton and Cemetery Junction to and from the Triangle. From Monday 30 September 1963 all scheduled eastbound journeys on service 25 continued along Ashley Road to Boscombe, Portman Road, leaving the Queen's Park Golf Pavilion served solely by motorbuses, although trolleybus football specials continued to turn there.

The Mains Department started removing feeder cables in St. Paul's Road on 16 December 1963 but, despite the promised early removal of the overhead wiring to permit work on another new roundabout in St. Paul's Road at Littledown Road, the redundant wiring from Cemetery Junction along Lansdowne Road and St. Paul's Road to Holdenhurst Road remained intact until 30 December 1963. All the overhead wiring and traction poles in St. Paul's Road and Lansdowne Road were removed by February 1964 except for the last 30yd at the north end of Lansdowne Road, which was retained as it included a traction power feeder point supplying Cemetery Junction. The Mains Department subsequently altered the switching to feed the area from three other feeder pillars in the vicinity so that the remaining wiring in Lansdowne Road, and redundant frogs and crossings at Cemetery Junction, could also be removed. By mid-October 1964 the Mains Department had completed its work at the north end of Lansdowne Road and the remaining service 34 wiring and junction work at Cemetery Junction had been cut down.

In November 1963, the Limmer and Trinidad Lake Asphalt Co. Ltd. resurfaced the surrounds of Christchurch turntable at a cost of £286 19s 3d. The turntable was closed, vehicles turning in Church Street by means of T-poles. The overhead in Christchurch Road each side of Iford roundabout was temporarily slewed to one side to permit one-way traffic around road works which lasted most of the winter.

The predicted date for the final abandonment of the Bournemouth trolleybus system was now given as 1973. An item in the *Daily Mail* of 11 January 1964 announced that Bournemouth's trolleybus wiring would stretch for about 100 miles and that it would fetch a scrap price of £18,000.

The first Transport Committee Meeting of 1964 considered falling revenue and the effects of the 1963 wage awards. Mr Cox was instructed to submit a report on a revised fare structure, which led to an application being made to the SETC. They granted a general increase with effect from 27 June 1964; transfer fares were abolished (although provided that a fare existed passengers could still change from a curtailed service to another service travelling to the intended destination, e.g. a Wallisdown to Square passenger could change at Winton Banks when service 30 was terminating there) and the issue of weekly tickets was limited to journeys where the single fare was 7d or more. The minimum adult fare increased to 3d and that for children to 2d. Questioned on travel concessions for Old Age Pensioners (OAPs), the Transport Committee was informed that this was illegal. Until December 1964, municipal transport undertakings were permitted by law only to provide such concessionary facilities as were in operation in 1954. The Travel Concessions Act, 1964 enabled arrangements to be made for granting concessions to "qualified persons".

In February 1964, the Highways & Works Committee advised that it did not wish to use any disused traction poles for street lighting purposes and the General Manager was authorised to dispose of any no longer required on the best possible terms. An annual charge of £1 per pole applied to the few retained and these were gradually replaced by conventional lighting standards.

Also in February 1964, the four remaining closed-top Sunbeam MS2 trolleybuses 206, 213, 215, 216 were advertised for sale and, having considered 11 tenders for a mixture of motorbuses, trolleybuses and a van, the highest, from Mr N. Stanley, Poole, at £75 each, was accepted. By 4 April 1964, 215 had been collected but the rest were still at Castle Lane Depot one week later. The final two closed-top MS2s, 206 and 216, were finally removed for scrapping in early July 1964.

The 1964 summer timetable operated as follows:
16 May 1964-7 June 1964 - Bournemouth Pier and duplicate services as required
8 June 1964-13 September 1964 - Full summer service
14 September 1964-4 October 1964 - Bournemouth Pier and duplicate services as required

The department's quarterly insurance records for 1 April 1964 showed the following trolleybus statistics:

Insured and available for service (total 70)

Sunbeam MS2	all withdrawn
BUT9641T	234-257
Sunbeam MF2B	258-287, 295-303
BUT9611T	288-294

Not insured (3)

Sunbeam open-top	200-202

By 1 July 1964 the situation was:

Insured and available for service (72)

Sunbeam open-top	200, 201
BUT9641T	234-257
Sunbeam MF2B	258-287, 295-303
BUT9611T	288-294

Trolleybuses available for service but not insured (1)

Sunbeam open-top	202

At this time, the Transport Committee received much correspondence expressing regret at the decision to discontinue trolleybuses and replace them with diesel buses.

Open-top trolleybus circular service 39 was not reintroduced with the summer 1964 timetable, perhaps due to the removal of the Cemetery Junction-Lansdowne overhead wiring and the lack of an alternative route back to Bournemouth Pier if the anti-clockwise operation was to be retained. The open-top Sunbeam MS2s 200 and 201 (BRU8 and BRU11) were relicensed from 1 June 1964 but, apart from two unconnected enthusiasts' tours using both on Sunday 14 June 1964, they did not enter service until 1 July 1964, and then only irregularly, on service 38 (Bournemouth Pier-Carbery Avenue). 202 was not relicensed. Service 38 required three vehicles, the third being a Sunbeam MF2B. The service was reduced to a 40-minute frequency after 7pm. Thereafter, the relieved vehicle operated specials between Bournemouth Square and Fisherman's Walk (in principle service 37, although no longer advertised as such), an unusual working for an open-top trolleybus if the closed-top one was not used! A shortage of seasonal staff led to the premature withdrawal of service 38, which operated for the last time on Monday 23 August 1964, this effectively being the end of normal scheduled trolleybus services to Bournemouth Pier. For much of the short season only an hourly service had been operated instead of the scheduled 20-minute service. All three open-top trolleybuses were retained in the fleet until September 1965, but solely 202 was used after the end of the 1964 summer season, and then only on enthusiasts' tours.

In March 1964 it had been announced that, subject to confirmation by Edinburgh Council, Ronald Cox, had been appointed Manager of that city's transport undertaking. The vacancy so created in Bournemouth was advertised at a salary of £3,130 pa. rising by annual increments of £90 to £3,400 pa. and ultimately to £3,490 pa.

Questioned in 1998 as to Ronald Cox being responsible for the trolleybus closure decision, Ian Cunningham was emphatic that this was not the case. Cox was then a "live wire" in the industry and although eager to change things at Bournemouth after a long period of conservative and admittedly pro-trolleybus management, he was not anti-trolleybus as such. During the first 15 months of his tenure he had sent out his deputy to secure quotations for new trolleybuses although it had proved almost impossible to obtain offers from British manufacturers or they quoted grossly inflated prices. The "pros" and "cons" of motorbus compared to trolleybus operation were tabulated; acceleration, longevity, quietness and smoothness still speaking for the trolleybus, although the cost of providing and maintaining the power supply, including switchgear, underground feeder cables and ducts, and the overhead wiring, were quantified as a disadvantage. The introduction of a diesel fuel rebate, and the frequency and cost of modifying the overhead layout and feeders to cater for roadworks, helped tip the balance against the trolleybus. Throughout Britain trolleybuses were already on the way out, although Bournemouth was in the fortunate position of having modern rolling stock and a good quantity of overhead spares, partly acquired second-hand from other operators.

Mr Cox saw the run-down of the system as a long-term aim with the Sunbeam MF2Bs lasting longer than they actually did; however, there were certain Councillors, both on the Transport Committee and in the Council generally, who unfairly blamed trolleybuses for the traffic congestion in the town centre. He ordered thirty motorbuses for delivery at the rate of ten

Sunbeam MS2 no. 214 (ALJ979) running on service 23 and BUT9641T no. 253 on a 38 to Carbery Avenue have just turned out of Beaufort Road into Cranleigh Road on 13 August 1963. The buildings behind the railings in the background accommodate Stourfield School. **Malcolm Pearce (G.O.P. Pearce)**

Also at the Stourfield School stop in Cranleigh Road, Sunbeam MS2 no. 205 is running to Tuckton, Tuckton Road on a service 23 working on 13 September 1963 **Malcolm Pearce (G.O.P. Pearce)**

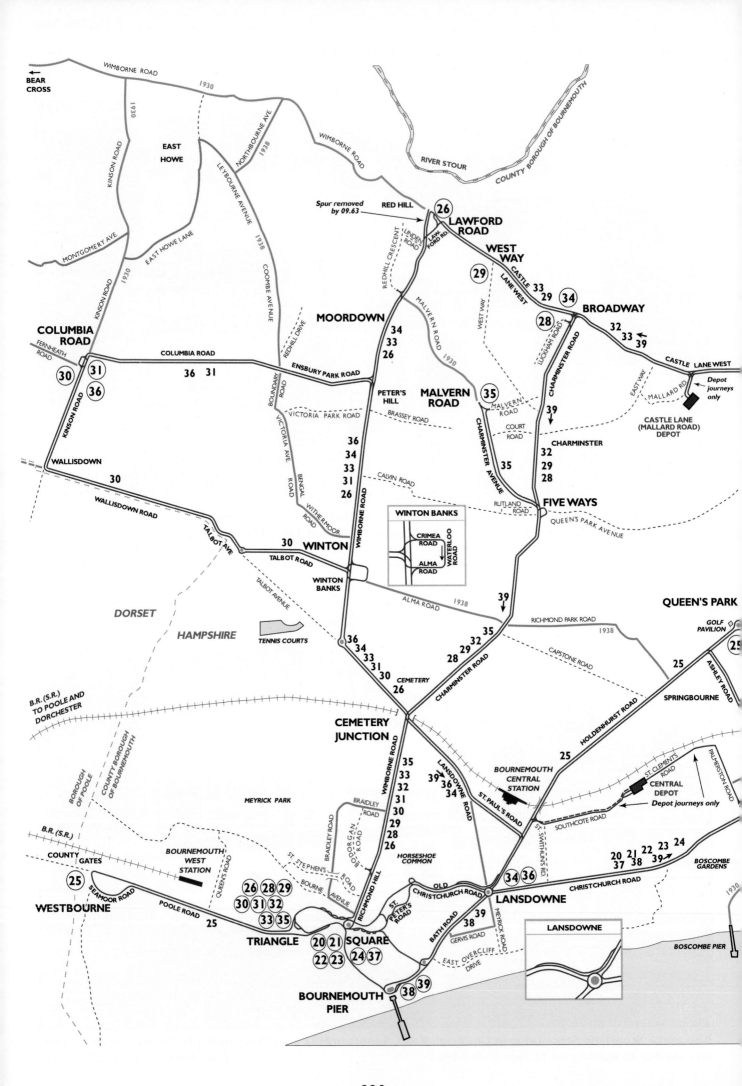

BEAR
CROSS

WIMBORNE ROAD

1930

1930

EAST
HOWE

KINSON ROAD

NORTHBOURNE AVE.

LEYBOURNE AVENUE

1938

COOMBE AVENUE

MONTGOMERY AVE.

EAST HOWE LANE

WIMBORNE ROAD

RIVER STOUR

COUNTY BOROUGH OF BOURNEMOUTH

Spur removed
by 09.63

RED HILL

㉖

LAWFORD
ROAD

WEST
WAY

㉙

CASTLE LANE WEST

33
29

㉞

BROADWAY

32
33
39

COLUMBIA
ROAD

FERNHEATH ROAD

㉚ ㉛

㊱

COLUMBIA ROAD

36 31

REDHILL DRIVE

REDHILL CRESCENT

LINDEN ROAD

LAWFORD RD.

MOORDOWN

MALVERN ROAD

1930

34
33
26

WEST WAY

LANE WEST

㉘

LUCKHAM ROAD

CHARMINSTER ROAD

CASTLE LANE WEST

EAST WAY

MALLARD RD.

Depot
journeys
only

CASTLE LANE
(MALLARD ROAD)
DEPOT

KINSON ROAD

1930

PETER'S
HILL

MALVERN
ROAD

㉟

MALVERN ROAD

COURT ROAD

39

CHARMINSTER

32
29
28

BOUNDARY ROAD

ENSBURY PARK ROAD

VICTORIA PARK ROAD

BRASSEY ROAD

WALLISDOWN

30

WALLISDOWN ROAD

VICTORIA AVE.

BENGAL ROAD

WITHERMOOR ROAD

36
34
33
31
26

CALVIN ROAD

CHARMINSTER AVENUE

35

RUTLAND ROAD

FIVE WAYS

QUEEN'S PARK AVENUE

TALBOT AVE.

30

WINTON

TALBOT ROAD

WIMBORNE ROAD

WINTON
BANKS

WINTON BANKS

CRIMEA ROAD

ALMA ROAD

WATERLOO ROAD

ALMA ROAD

1938

39

QUEEN'S PARK

GOLF
PAVILION

㉕

DORSET

HAMPSHIRE

TALBOT AVENUE

TENNIS COURTS

36
34
33
31
30
26

CEMETERY

CHARMINSTER ROAD

28 29

32 35

RICHMOND PARK ROAD

1938

CAPSTONE ROAD

25

ASHLEY ROAD

SPRINGBOURNE

B.R. (S.R.)
TO POOLE AND
DORCHESTER

CEMETERY
JUNCTION

WIMBORNE ROAD

35
33
32
31
30
29
28
26

LANSDOWNE ROAD

35

39
36
34

ST. PAUL'S ROAD

BOURNEMOUTH
CENTRAL
STATION

HOLDENHURST ROAD

25

ST. CLEMENTS ROAD

CENTRAL
DEPOT

Depot journeys only

PALMERSTON ROAD

B.R. (S.R.)

COUNTY

BOROUGH OF POOLE

COUNTY BOROUGH OF BOURNEMOUTH

MEYRICK PARK

BRAIDLEY ROAD

BODORGAN ROAD

ST. STEPHEN'S ROAD

BOURNE AVENUE

HORSESHOE COMMON

SOUTHCOTE ROAD

ST. SWITHUN'S RD.

20 21 22 23 24
37 38 39

BOSCOMBE
GARDENS

1930

GATES

㉕

WESTBOURNE

SEAMOOR ROAD

BOURNEMOUTH
WEST
STATION

QUEEN'S ROAD

POOLE ROAD

25

㉖ ㉘ ㉙
㉚ ㉛ ㉜
㉝ ㉟

RICHMOND HILL

OLD
CHRISTCHURCH ROAD

ST. PETER'S ROAD

㉞ ㊱

LANSDOWNE

CHRISTCHURCH ROAD

TRIANGLE

⑳ ㉑
㉒ ㉓

SQUARE

㉔ ㊲

BATH ROAD

GERVIS ROAD

MERRICK ROAD

38 39

LANSDOWNE

BOSCOMBE PIER

BOURNEMOUTH
PIER

㊳ ㊴

EAST OVERCLIFF DRIVE

220

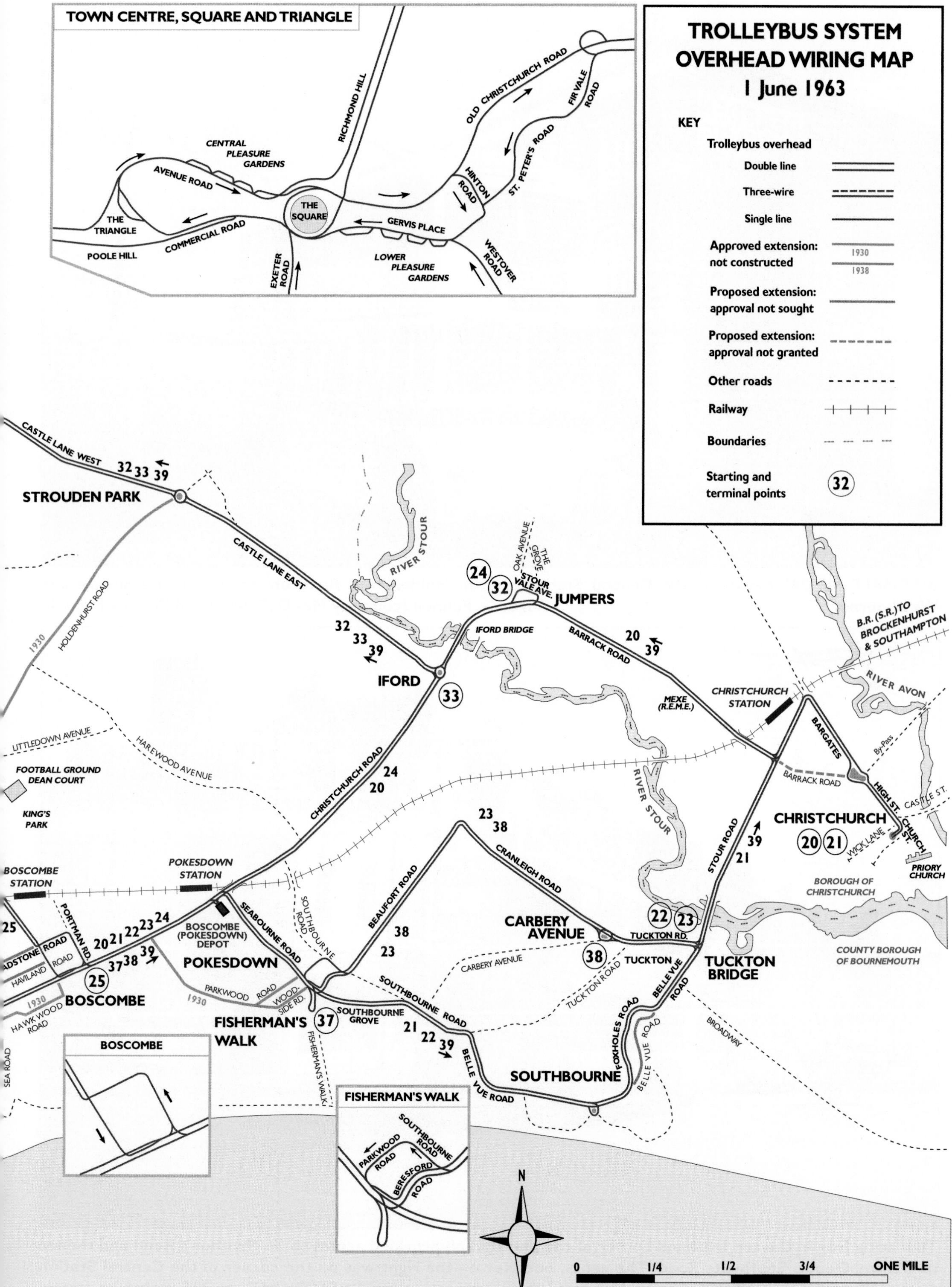
TOWN CENTRE, SQUARE AND TRIANGLE
RICHMOND HILL
OLD CHRISTCHURCH ROAD
FIR VALE ROAD
ST. PETER'S ROAD
HINTON ROAD
CENTRAL PLEASURE GARDENS
AVENUE ROAD
THE SQUARE
THE TRIANGLE
COMMERCIAL ROAD
POOLE HILL
GERVIS PLACE
LOWER PLEASURE GARDENS
EXETER ROAD
WESTOVER ROAD
TROLLEYBUS SYSTEM
OVERHEAD WIRING MAP
1 June 1963
KEY
Trolleybus overhead
Double line
Three-wire
Single line
Approved extension: not constructed
1930
1938
Proposed extension: approval not sought
Proposed extension: approval not granted
Other roads
Railway
Boundaries
Starting and terminal points
32
CASTLE LANE WEST
32 33 39
STROUDEN PARK
CASTLE LANE EAST
HOLDENHURST ROAD
1930
RIVER STOUR
OAK AVENUE
THE GROVE
STOUR VALE AVE.
24
32
JUMPERS
IFORD BRIDGE
BARRACK ROAD
20 39
32 33 39
IFORD
33
MEXE (R.E.M.E.)
CHRISTCHURCH STATION
B.R. (S.R.) TO BROCKENHURST & SOUTHAMPTON
RIVER AVON
BARGATES
By-Pass
BARRACK ROAD
HIGH ST.
CASTLE ST.
CHURCH ST.
WICK LANE
CHRISTCHURCH
20 21
PRIORY CHURCH
LITTLEDOWN AVENUE
HAREWOOD AVENUE
FOOTBALL GROUND DEAN COURT
KING'S PARK
CHRISTCHURCH ROAD
24
20
23
38
CRANLEIGH ROAD
RIVER STOUR
STOUR ROAD
39
21
BOSCOMBE STATION
POKESDOWN STATION
SOUTHBOURNE ROAD
BEAUFORT ROAD
BOROUGH OF CHRISTCHURCH
PORTMAN RD.
25
GLADSTONE ROAD
HAVILAND ROAD
20 21 22 23 24
BOSCOMBE (POKESDOWN) DEPOT
SEABOURNE ROAD
38
23
CARBERY AVENUE
22 23
TUCKTON RD.
37 38 39
POKESDOWN
CARBERY AVENUE
38
TUCKTON
TUCKTON BRIDGE
COUNTY BOROUGH OF BOURNEMOUTH
BOSCOMBE
PARKWOOD ROAD
WOODSIDE RD.
1930
HAWKWOOD ROAD
SOUTHBOURNE ROAD
TUCKTON ROAD
FOXHOLES ROAD
BELLE VUE ROAD
BROADWAY
FISHERMAN'S WALK
37
SOUTHBOURNE GROVE
21 22 39
SEA ROAD
FISHERMAN'S WALK
BELLE VUE ROAD
SOUTHBOURNE
BELLE VUE ROAD
BOSCOMBE
FISHERMAN'S WALK
SOUTHBOURNE ROAD
PARKWOOD ROAD
BERESFORD ROAD
N
0
1/4
1/2
3/4
ONE MILE

BUT9641T no. 243 pauses at the Central Station stop in Holdenhurst Road on its way to the Square and
Westbourne.   Roger G. Funnell (courtesy Mrs D. Funnell and Rodney Funnell)

The facing frog in the top left hand corner of the photograph provided access to St. Swithun's Road and thence
to Central Depot, Southcote Road. The gents outfitter on the right was on the corner of the Central Station
Approach. Holdenhurst Road rises slightly to cross the railway as rebuilt BUT9641T no. 235 makes its stately
progress east towards Springbourne, Ashley Road and Boscombe.

                                    Roger G. Funnell (courtesy Mrs D. Funnell and Rodney Funnell)

Ex-BH&D BUT9611T no. 294 is captured on film at the top of Richmond Hill on its way from Castle Lane West, Lawford Road, to the Square and onwards to the Triangle on 18 September 1963. Malcolm Pearce (G.O.P. Pearce)

Approaching the bottom of Richmond Hill another ex-BH&D BUT9611T no. 293 brakes to observe the Albert Road compulsory stop outside the Church of the Sacred Heart on 18 September 1963.

Malcolm Pearce (G.O.P. Pearce)

Sunbeam MS2 no. 224 (BEL826) unloads at the westbound Lansdowne stop in Holdenhurst Road which had, by now, become the in-town terminus of service 34 from Castle Lane West, junction with West Way. The van in the foreground was operated by Advance Laundries Ltd. - a company specialising in laundering hotel and restaurant table linen, sheets and towels - and owned by British Electric Traction Co., a major provincial bus and formerly tram operator.

Travel Lens

Having just arrived from Castle Lane West, Broadway Hotel, Sunbeam MS2 no. 215 (ALJ980) pauses at the Lansdowne terminal stop in Holdenhurst Road.

Travel Lens

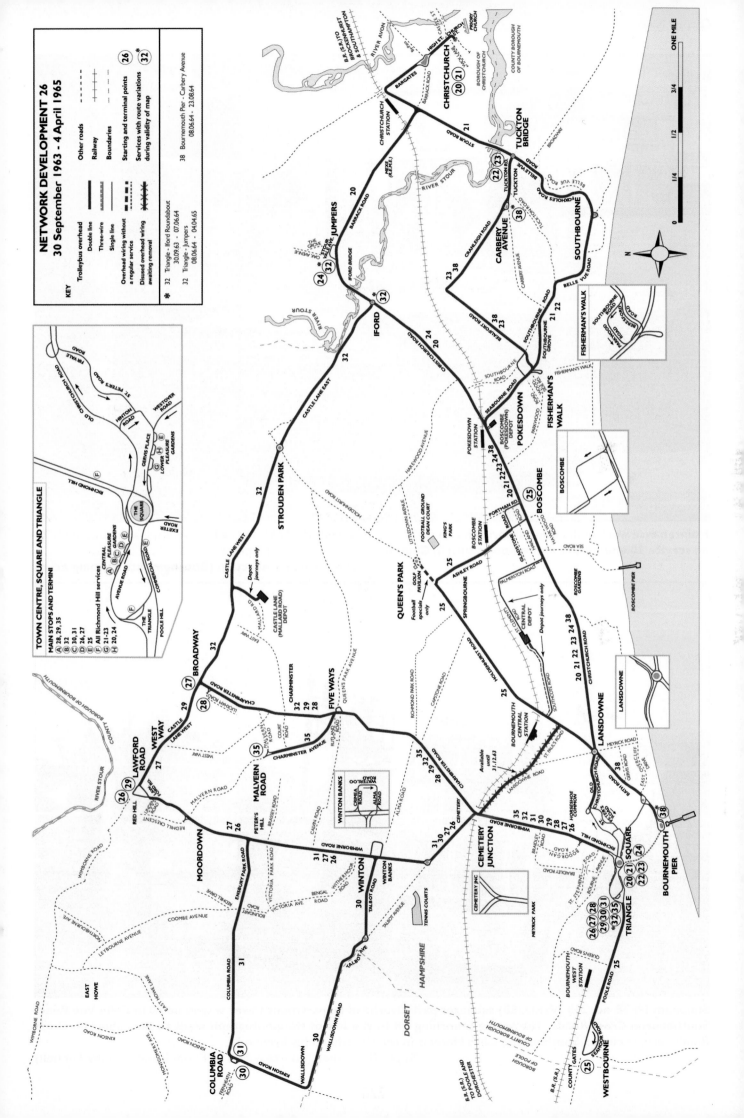

Maintenance work underway on Christchurch turntable in November 1963. In the background, a Sunbeam MF2B on service 20 undertakes a three-point turn in Church Street by means of T-poles.

David Chalk Collection (Bournemouth Evening Echo)

Sunbeam MF2B no. 258 (WRU258) squeezes past Overhead Department tower wagon no.10 in Belle Vue Road, Southbourne Cross Roads. The wiring branching off to the left of the photograph leads to Southbourne Cross Roads turning circle. Southbourne Cliffs Hotel is in the right-hand background.

Roger G. Funnell (courtesy Mrs D. Funnell and Rodney Funnell)

Having started out from Gervis Place and rounded the Square Sunbeam MF2B no. 274 (WRU274) passes the junction with Richmond Hill before starting the climb up Old Christchurch Road to the Lansdowne and then onwards to Boscombe, Southbourne and Christchurch on a service 21 journey.

Roger G. Funnell (courtesy Mrs D. Funnell and Rodney Funnell)

The reversing triangle terminus of service 35 (service 29 from 1937 to 1956) was at the junction of Charminster Avenue with Malvern Road although it was originally foreseen that overhead wiring would have continued northwestwards along Malvern Road to join Wimborne Road next to Moordown Depot. Having arrived by way of Charminster Avenue (being entered by a young cyclist in the photograph), Sunbeam MF2B no. 279 (YLJ279) prepares to reverse along Malvern Road in front of St. Walburga's School.

Roger G. Funnell (courtesy Mrs D. Funnell and Rodney Funnell)

Travelling back to the town centre on a service 35 journey, Sunbeam MF2B no. 280 (YLJ280) passes beneath the feeder wiring of Charminster Avenue switch box, a few yards beyond the junction with Charminster Road and not more than 100yd from the Five Ways turning circle. The road joining from the left is Rutland Road, the location of Royal Blue express coaches garage.   Roger G. Funnell (courtesy Mrs D. Funnell and Rodney Funnell)

There was always plenty of trolleybus traffic to the Queen's Park Golf Pavilion prior to and after matches at the Dean Court ground in King's Park during the football season. Having turned at Littledown Avenue, Sunbeam MF2B no. 268 (WRU268) is held back in Holdenhurst Road by the point duty policeman controlling traffic into the car and coach parks.
Paul Creswell

The queue of traffic has lengthened and another trolleybus is negotiating the Queen's Park Golf Pavilion turning circle whilst a third is evident on the left waiting to turn.
Paul Creswell

No. 284 (YLJ284) leads a column of three Sunbeam MF2Bs on football special duty parked in the westbound carriageway of Holdenhurst Road between Hayes Avenue and Buchanan Avenue. The motorcar overtaking the row of trolleybuses is a Hillman Minx of the early 1950s whilst a late 1950s Standard Ten heads in the opposite direction.
Paul Creswell

each year from 1964 to 1966, the first ten (together with ten delivered in autumn 1963) being used to replace the remaining pre-war motorbuses with the second and third batches being intended for the abandonment of the Side Routes in two stages, permitting the disposal of the ex-Brighton BUT9611Ts and the 14 BUT9641Ts which still retained both staircases. Finally, due to the changed circumstances, it was his successor who had no alternative but to expedite the replacement programme by doubling the 1965 and 1966 vehicle orders to twenty each year instead of ten.

Having received 29 applications for the position and selected six for interview on 20 May 1964, the Transport Committee chose Mr Ian Cunningham, BSc, AMIMechE, then Deputy General Manager of the undertaking, as the new General Manager. Mr Cunningham had been Deputy since March 1963 and was previously Assistant Rolling Stock Engineer in Edinburgh, having had responsibility for their tram fleet from 1950 to 1956. At the time of his promotion he was aged 39, married with a son and daughter, and lived in Southbourne. In 1998 he recalled how, at Transport Committee Meetings, even the General Manager could not join in the discussions unless invited to speak which, in the author's opinion, says much about the abilities of amateur local politicians in making far-reaching decisions about public transport. Fortunately, Mr Cunningham had a cordial relationship with Ald. Deric Scott, Chairman of the Transport Committee until 7 May 1964, and an unofficial discussion about the agenda normally took place prior to each Meeting. The Transport Committee themselves could only make recommendations to the full Council and not make decisions.

The position of Deputy Manager was then advertised; the 23 applications received were reduced to a short-list of seven candidates, who were interviewed on 1 July 1964. With effect from 21 July 1964, Mr Stuart Hindle, AMInstT, then Traffic Superintendent, was appointed Deputy General Manager.

The overhead wiring layout at the junction of The Grove and Barrack Road at Jumpers Corner was changed on Sunday 26 July 1964 following completion of a short portion of dual carriageway in Barrack Road. The Overhead Department worked from 11.30pm on the Saturday until 8am on the Sunday to complete the task, using all three tower wagons and Morris Commercial FG lorry 304LJ (the registration number reserved for the tenth and final Sunbeam MF2B chassis destroyed in the fire at Weymanns).

At 7.10am on 30 September 1964, a lorry skidded in Holdenhurst Road bringing down a traction pole and about fifty feet of overhead wiring, disrupting service 25. By 8am the Overhead Department had erected a new pole, adjusted the wiring and removed the old one!

The fleet had now been reduced to 70 trolleybuses, all of which were licensed for the winter season although a maximum of 60 was needed to operate services, consisting of:

200-202	Sunbeam MS2 open-top	(withdrawn but still in stock)
234-243	BUT9641T	(rebuilt without front staircase)
244-257	BUT9641T	(unrebuilt)
258-287	Sunbeam MF2B	
288-294	BUT9611T	(ex-Brighton)
295-303	Sunbeam MF2B	

The ex-Brighton BUT9611Ts could be found operating on service 25 and evening peak services along Christchurch Road. It was already evident that they would be the first batch of trolleybuses to be withdrawn, 293 having had no repaint since entering service in Bournemouth on 1 June 1959. By 20 February 1965 ex-Brighton 288 was parked in the open at Castle Lane (Mallard Road) Depot, presumed withdrawn.

From 25 October 1964 Sunday morning schedules on trolleybus services 21, 22 and 23, which each ran every 40 minutes, were revised when short workings on service 23 operating via Cranleigh Road between Fisherman's Walk and Tuckton only ceased, all journeys being extended to/from Bournemouth Square. This made the Fisherman's Walk, Southbourne Road-Parkwood Road turning circle redundant, although it remained intact.

Two Sunbeam MF2Bs emerged from the paint shop in autumn 1964 with experimental interior colour schemes, 263 being painted in coffee and 264 in grey.

At its 20 October 1964 meeting the Transport Committee authorised the sale to the National Trolleybus Association (NTA) of one of the three Sunbeam MS2 open-top trolleybuses which would become available in spring 1965. In November 1964 the *Bournemouth Evening Echo* announced that *"the world's only open-decked trolleybuses are for sale. They operated for the last time in Summer 1964 and will be on the market next spring"*. One was reportedly to go to a disused railway station at Plumtree, near Nottingham, where the NTA planned a museum. It was decided that service 38 would not operate in 1965, confirming that scheduled service trolleybus operation to Bournemouth Pier had ceased, although private hire trolleybuses operated there in October 1964, March 1965 and July 1965 at least, as well as occasional school specials from Bournemouth School for Girls in Castle Lane West, via Bournemouth Boys' School (Court Road bus stop in Charminster Road) and from Stourfield School at the junction of Beaufort Road and Cranleigh Road, to Bournemouth Symphony Orchestra concerts at the Winter Gardens in Exeter Road. These school specials continued to operate until the closure of the trolleybus routes concerned.

The Mayor, Ald. Harry Mears, was concerned how the trolleybus replacement motorbuses with their front entrance overhang would be able to negotiate corners, but added that *"Trolleys are completely out of date"*.

A fatal accident occurred between a trolleybus and an elderly lady cyclist on 8 December 1964 at the junction of Talbot Road with Sedgley Road, Winton. A verdict of accidental death was returned at the inquest.

A fault on the Elmes Road, Moordown feeder, cut traction power supplies on Wimborne Road between Winton Banks and Castle Lane West, on Columbia Road, Ensbury Park Road, Kinson Road, Talbot Road and Wallisdown Road from the start of services until about 8.30am on the morning of 10 December 1964. Services 26, 27, 30 and 31 were disrupted and replacement motorbuses brought into use.

On 2 February 1965 the full Council approved the Transport Committee's recommendations to cut costs by reducing services in an effort to prevent a deficit at the end of 1965. The possibility of another fare increase, the last having been made on 2 June 1964, was also considered.

The recommended reductions as far as trolleybus services were concerned were as follows:

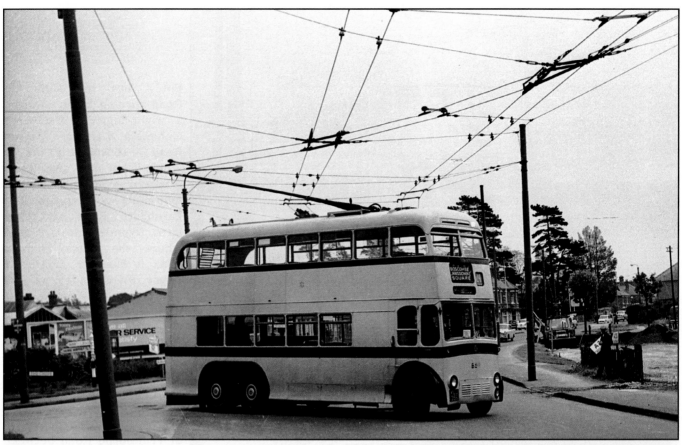

Barrack Road, Jumpers Corner, at the junction with The Grove was a two lane carriageway until July 1964 when a short portion of dual carriageway was built.Prior to the reconstruction, Weymann-bodied BUT9641T no. 256 (KLJ356) pulls out of the Jumpers turning loop to return to the Square on a service 24 working.

Roger G. Funnell (courtesy Mrs D. Funnell and Rodney Funnell)

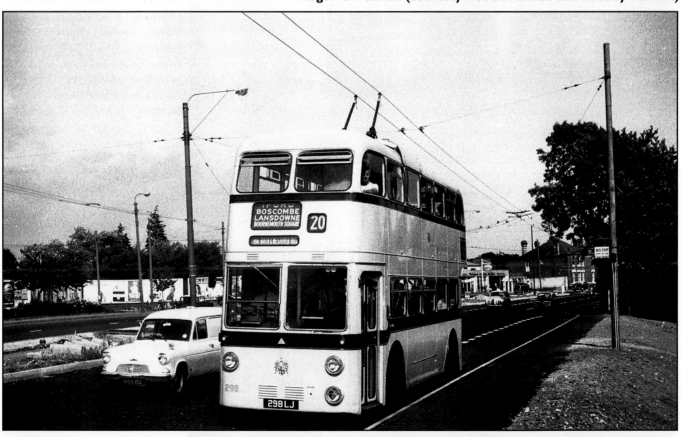

Following the construction of the dual carriageway, Sunbeam MF2B no. 298 (298LJ) pauses in the Barrack Road westbound lay-by on its way from Christchurch to the Square. The new long lay-by served both as a bus stop and provided more space for trolleybuses from The Grove to turn through the central gap onto Barrack Road. The conductor, complete with Ultimate ticket machine, stands by the front exit next to the driver.

Roger G. Funnell (courtesy Mrs D. Funnell and Rodney Funnell)

Entry into the Columbia Road turning circle involved a right-angled turn from Columbia Road into Kinson Road southbound (just visible behind the rear platform of the trolleybus) followed by a sharp turn into Fernheath Road and then into Wonderholm Parade where the black Hillman Minx is likely to cause the driver of BUT9641T no. 256 (KLJ356) some manoeuvering problems (August 1964). **D.A.P. Janes**

The broad, tree-lined expanse of Wimborne Road between Cemetery Junction and Richmond Hill provides the setting for BUT9641T no. 247 (KLJ347) heading for the town centre on a service 26 journey from Castle Lane West, Lawford Road. Note that there is no reference to the terminal point, the Triangle, on the indicator blinds, simply Square or Bournemouth Square being displayed on Side Route journeys destined for the Triangle. **D.A.P. Janes**

Sunbeam MF2B no. 263 (WRU263) comes to a halt at the west end of Columbia Road at its junction with Kinson Road. The indicator blind displays show that the trolleybus will continue south along Kinson Road to Wallisdown and Winton Banks (rather than terminate at the Wonderholm Parade turning loop) but further adjustment to show its destination and service number 30 will be required once it has rounded the corner. **D.A.P. Janes**

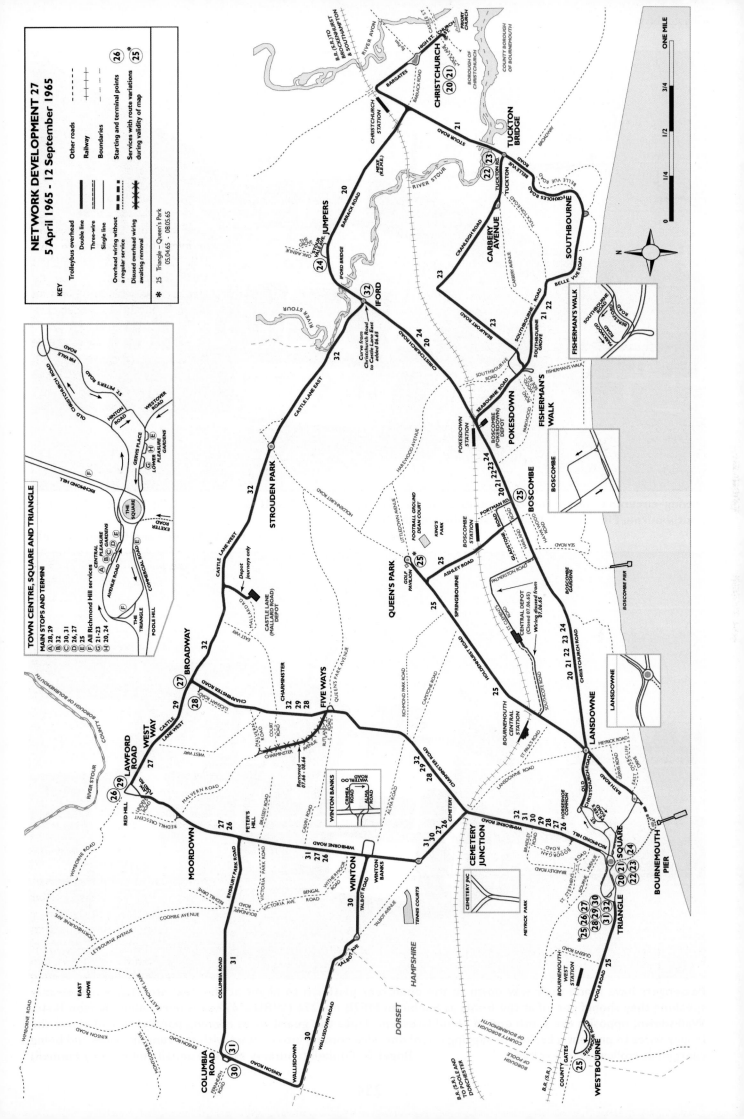

Having circumnavigated Tuckton roundabout no. 276 (WRU276) heads east along Belle Vue Road towards Southbourne, Fisherman's Walk, Boscombe and the Square.

Roger G. Funnell (courtesy Mrs D. Funnell and Rodney Funnell)

Passengers have made their way down to the open rear platform to alight at the next stop (although strictly speaking they should get off at the front) as Sunbeam MF2B no. 276 (WRU276) heads north along Kinson Road, Wallisdown, opposite the south end of Hood Crescent. Note the guard wires running parallel to and above the trolley wires to prevent a broken or sagging telephone wire coming into contact with the running wires and being charged at trolleybus line voltage. Roger G. Funnell (courtesy Mrs D. Funnell and Rodney Funnell)

20   Bournemouth Square, Gervis Place - Christchurch, Church Street
-to be withdrawn on winter Sundays.

24   Bournemouth Square, Gervis Place - Jumpers
-to be reduced from 15 minutes to a 30-minute frequency on winter Sundays.

Together giving an estimated annual saving of £4,000,

25   Westbourne, Seamoor Road - Bournemouth Square - Boscombe, Portman Road
-basic service to be reduced to 12 minutes but with additional trolleybuses operating at certain times between the Square and Queen's Park Golf Pavilion giving a 6-minute service on the common section of route.
-evening and Sunday frequency to be reduced from 10 minutes to 15 minutes.

Giving an estimated annual saving of £7,000,

26   Triangle - Bournemouth Square - Castle Lane West, Lawford Road
-to be withdrawn.

Giving an estimated annual saving of £4,000

28   Triangle - Bournemouth Square - Broadway Hotel, Luckham Road
-to be withdrawn at certain times of the day.

Together with service 35 giving an estimated annual saving of £4,000

30   Triangle - Bournemouth Square - Wallisdown - Columbia Road, junction with Kinson Road
-to be withdrawn (which would mean that the overhead wiring equipment between Winton Banks and Columbia Road would fall into disuse).

31   Triangle -   Bournemouth Square - Ensbury Park Road - Columbia Road, junction with Kinson Road
-evening and Sunday frequency to be reduced from 20 minutes to 30 minutes.

Together giving an estimated annual saving of £4,000

35   Triangle - Bournemouth Square - Malvern Road, junction with Charminster Avenue
-to be withdrawn, this being the least frequent of all trolleybus services at this time having an hourly frequency (which would mean that the overhead wiring equipment between Five Ways and Malvern Road would fall into disuse).

At the same meeting, the Council also resolved to replace trolleybuses by motorbuses "as soon as possible", with a programme of fleet replacement for the years 1966-1969. This was the first intimation of an expedited programme which would see seven-year-old trolleybuses withdrawn for scrapping.

No immediate decision was taken as to the withdrawal of trolleybus service 30; however, on 9 February 1965, Mr

Cunningham was authorised to re-route any existing services required on the withdrawal of trolleybus service 30 between Columbia Road and Winton Banks via Wallisdown.

Service 35 was withdrawn entirely after operation on Sunday 4 April 1965 and the Five Ways-Malvern Road, junction with Charminster Avenue, trolleybus route abandoned. The service on the final Sunday consisted of hourly departures from the Triangle from 2.13pm until 6.13pm, with corresponding departures from Malvern Road from 2.40pm until 6.40pm. The final vehicle to leave Malvern Road, just after 6.40pm on 4 April 1965, was Sunbeam MF2B 279. Other vehicles operating the preceding four journeys were 281, 300, 280 and 276 in that sequence. No replacement motorbus service was introduced. The overhead wiring, however, remained aloft and was only cut down in July/August 1966. To retain a 15-minute service on Sundays along Charminster Road, commencing on 11 April 1965 service 32 was strengthened from hourly to every 30 minutes during the afternoon, but all journeys henceforth terminated at Iford roundabout instead of Jumpers Corner.

On Monday 5 April 1965, in an effort to reduce unremunerative mileage run along Ashley Road and Poole Road, a 12-minute frequency on weekdays only was introduced between the Triangle and Queen's Park Golf Pavilion between approx. 8am and 9am and again between approx. 12.45pm and 6.30pm superimposed during those periods of the day on the 12-minute frequency operated between Westbourne and Boscombe (15 minutes evenings and Sundays). All journeys were part of the service 25 timetable. During the times mentioned, therefore, a combined six-minute frequency operated between the Triangle and the Queen's Park Hotel (at the north end of Ashley Road). Trolleybus service 26 was reduced to Sunday mornings and weekday peak hours only; service 28 to Sunday mornings, weekday peak hours and winter evenings only; as an interim solution service 30 ceased to run on winter evenings and Sunday mornings and afternoons; and service 31 saw its evening and Sunday service reduced to a 30-minute frequency, all commencing on 5 April 1965.

Commencing on Sunday 11 April 1965, service 20 was withdrawn entirely on winter Sundays and service 24 operations reduced to half-hourly in the afternoons, the service to Iford being reduced from six vehicles an hour to two in a single stroke. Christchurch Borough Council complained but, in view of the alternative services available, Bournemouth Council adhered to its previous decision.

With effect from 8 February 1965 an NJIC wage award led to additional costs of £5,000 for the remainder of the financial year and £33,000 in a full year. Following discussions with the TGWU, the Merit Bonus was increased from 3s to 10s per week subject to agreement with the NJIC. In March 1965 the FMPTE requested an increase of 5d per hour for craftsmen estimated to cost the undertaking £2,500 in a full year. It was planned to introduce the 40-hour week by the end of 1965.

The 1965 summer timetable operated as follows:

5-6 June 1965	Duplicate services as required.
7 June 1965-12 September 1965	Full summer service.
13 September 1965-26 September 1965	Duplicate services as required.

Municipal transport undertakings were not the only modes of public transport suffering from a fall in traffic. The railways

An inbound service 31 journey operated by Sunbeam MF2B no. 282 (YLJ282) makes its way across Cemetery Junction following Wimborne Road throughout. The cemetery was consecrated in 1878 to cater for the needs of Bournemouth's much increased population and has been enlarged twice since then to accommodate over 43,000 people.

Roger G. Funnell
(courtesy Mrs D. Funnell
and Rodney Funnell)

Seen at the roundabout at the junction of Wimborne Road with East Avenue and Talbot Avenue, ex-BH&D BUT9611T no. 292 (DNJ992) swings across the exit to East Avenue on its way to Castle Lane West, Lawford Road. The brick-built house with balcony and turreted corner is at the top of the continuation of Wimborne Road to Cemetery Junction. D.A.P. Janes

Ex-Brighton Corporation BUT9611T no. 291 (HUF48) pulls away from the Triangle boarding point to join the eastbound wiring from Westbourne and then descend towards the Square along Avenue Road before continuing up Richmond Hill and along the length of Wimborne Road through Winton and Moordown to Castle Lane West, Lawford Road on a service 26 journey.

Tony Belton

A rear view of Sunbeam MF2B no. 269 (WRU269) in the process of reversing through the spring trail frog, across the road junction with Charminster Avenue, and along Malvern Road, the terminus of service 35 and the sole terminal reversing triangle on the Bournemouth system. The metal railing to the offside of the trolleybus are those of St. Walburga's School with housing in Oakwood Road beyond. The butchers and Co-op behind the cyclist have been replaced by housing and increased foliage makes the area almost unrecognisable today.

Roger G. Funnell (courtesy Mrs D. Funnell and Rodney Funnell)

Having completed the reversal through a 25° "Y" spring trail frog, Sunbeam MF2B no. 279 (YLJ279) pulls forward beneath the frog and turns into the southbound Charminster Avenue line to await departure time back to Bournemouth Square and the Triangle. Behind the trolleybus, Malvern Road continues 1/4 mile to join Charminster Road.

Roger G. Funnell (courtesy Mrs D. Funnell and Rodney Funnell)

Now on the journey back to the Square, no. 281 (YLJ281) heads south along Charminster Avenue at Gresham Road. An Austin Cambridge saloon is in hot pursuit.

Roger G. Funnell (courtesy Mrs D. Funnell and Rodney Funnell)

The Christchurch turntable terminus was only about 80yd from the entrance to Christchurch Priory and was reached along the rather narrow Church Street in which parking was allowed. Sunbeam MF2B no. 275 (WRU275) passes Strong of Romsey's Dolphin Inn and turns into the terminus after another journey from Bournemouth Square.

Roger G. Funnell (courtesy Mrs D. Funnell and Rodney Funnell)

were incurring mounting losses due to increasing competition from road hauliers and long-distance coach services, as well as the ever-growing number of private cars. Dr. Richard Beeching's report *"The Reshaping of British Railways"* introduced proposals to abandon a number of railways in the Bournemouth area but none was more regretted than the closure of the line from Bath to Bournemouth West via the Somerset & Dorset Joint Railway (S&D), which followed a tortuous route through rural areas, but also carried many long-distance goods and passenger trains, none better known than the daily "Pines Express" to and from Manchester, with a further number of seasonal tourist trains.

A Public Enquiry into the proposed closure of Bournemouth West Station was held on 27 April 1965. Mr Cunningham attended in order to indicate any service changes that would be needed should the closure take place. The last train on the original Ringwood-Hurn-Christchurch branch line route to Bournemouth had run before the Second World War, on 28 September 1935. In 1964 services between Bournemouth and Salisbury via Wimborne, West Moors and Fordingbridge, together with those on the "old road" from West Moors through Ringwood to Lymington Junction, ceased. On 4 October 1965, Bournemouth West station was closed (Boscombe closing on the same day) and for a short time S&D trains were extended to Bournemouth Central Station but the S&D route closed in its entirety on 7 March 1966.

Apparently, at about this time the MPTA received an enquiry from Portugal for the purchase of a complete trolleybus system and Mr Cunningham was instructed to find out more. The author's researches have unfortunately brought no more information to light.

Faced with increased costs estimated to reach £136,276 in the 1965-6 financial year and a similar figure in the year thereafter, a further application to increase fares was made to the SETC in March 1965. The public hearing took place on 7 April 1965; the new fares were approved and came into effect on 15 April 1965.

The undertaking's administrative staff moved from 99-101 Southcote Road to new offices to the west of the Castle Lane Depot workshops and stores on 26 April 1965, the official opening, together with that of the second motorbus garage, located between the main garage accommodating motorbuses on one side and trolleybuses on the other, and the overhaul works, being made by the Mayor on 7 May 1965. The legal lettering at the base of each vehicle's nearside panels was changed to show "Mallard Road" as the Transport Department's Head Office. The traction poles around the depot circuit were repainted, several still standing until the complex was sold and converted into a retail park in 2006-7. Together with planned major road works at the western end of Holdenhurst Road, this led to trolleybus service 25 (Westbourne-Bournemouth Square-Holdenhurst Road-Boscombe, Portman Road), which had been operated entirely from Central Depot, being selected as the next candidate for withdrawal.

A complete timetable for trolleybus replacement was announced in May 1965:

Summer 1965: trolleybus service 25 and the six remaining ex-Brighton BUT9611T vehicles to be withdrawn and replaced by ten Daimler Fleetline motor buses.

Summer 1966: all Side Route (Richmond Hill) trolleybus services (26-32) and the 24 BUT9641T vehicles built in 1950 to be withdrawn and replaced by 20 new rear-engined, front-entrance motorbuses.

Summers 1967-69: all Main Road (Christchurch Road) trolleybus services (20-24) and the 39 Sunbeam MF2Bs to be withdrawn and replaced by 30 new rear-engined, front-entrance motorbuses.

On 7 June 1965, Central Depot, Southcote Road, was vacated and taken over as a base for the Corporation's refuse vehicles (still remaining in use, albeit with one entrance closed up, in 2018). Following the depot's closure, it was at this stage unclear if, after the planned 1966 trolleybus route closures, access to Castle Lane (Mallard Road) Depot would be retained from Iford along Castle Lane East, or whether this would be by way of Richmond Hill and Charminster Road. The former, shorter and less-obtrusive access route proved to be the case.

All trolleybus repaints now featured small black stock numerals, instead of the edged gold Gill Sans used from ca. 1960 and the larger blue-shaded gold transfers used before them. At this time all three styles of fleet number transfers could be seen, including some trolleybuses evidencing two styles as a result of accident damage repairs. Sunbeam MF2Bs 258-287 were in the course of having their front and rear staircases painted grey instead of dark brown.

Open-top MS2 202, which had last been used in September 1963, was relicensed for the period May-August 1965, but was used solely for two enthusiasts' tours, namely on Sunday 23 May 1965 by the Bournemouth Railway Club, and on 4 July 1965 by the NTA. The latter was hailed as the last open-top trolleybus tour in the world and was joined by Ian Cunningham, the General Manager. Disused open-top MS2s 200 and 201 were reportedly in poor condition by this time, and had lost many of their seats. On 30 May 1965 the RTS made another tour, something that had become an annual event, using BUT9611Ts, 290 (ex-Brighton Corporation) and 292 (ex-BH&D). This was the final enthusiasts' tour to visit Central Depot, Southcote Road.

No scheduled service trolleybuses reached Bournemouth Pier during the 1965 summer season as neither the open-top trolleybuses nor service 38 was operated (the route as far as Fisherman's Walk being covered by open-top Daimler Fleetline motorbuses on a new service 16).

On Monday 10 May 1965 the service 25 timetable, which had been introduced on 5 April 1965, was revised. A 7/8-minute frequency between Westbourne and Boscombe was reintroduced until 6.30pm after which a 15-minute service operated. The Sunday service was unchanged and continued to run every 15 minutes. The additional journeys Triangle-Queen's Park Golf Pavilion, Holdenhurst Road last operated on Saturday 8 May 1965, whilst special journeys between Bournemouth Square and Queen's Park Golf Pavilion in connection with football matches ceased.

The withdrawal of ex-Brighton BUT9611Ts continued, with 291 in May 1965 following rear-end damage, and 289, 290 and 292 in July 1965. They were stored outside at Castle Lane Depot, together with 288 and open-top Sunbeam MS2s 200 and 201, ready for disposal, leaving just 293 and 294 of the ex-Brighton fleet recorded as still in service in August 1965. The entire ex-Brighton fleet and the three open-top vehicles were offered for sale, the highest tender of £101 each for the open-toppers and £76 for the ex-Brighton trolleybuses being received from Colbro Ltd. (Dealers), Leeds. Open-top MS2 202, which had been stored inside the depot building, was sold to the NTA for preservation at the same price as tendered for its two sister vehicles.

In June 1965 a turnout and a trailing frog were inserted in

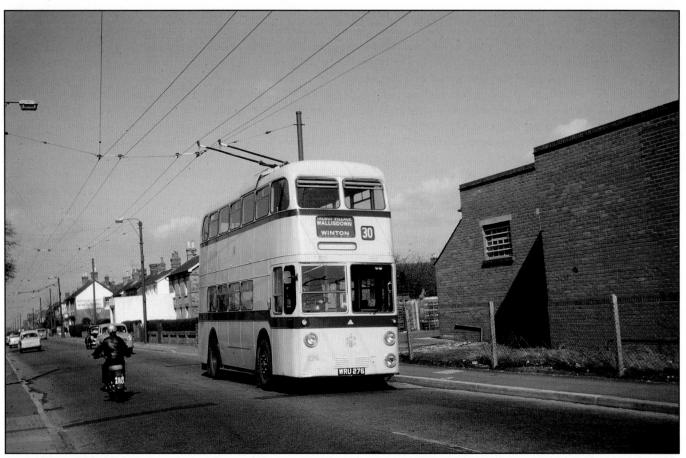

No. 276 (WRU276) is pictured in Kinson Road, three spans south of Alton Road and approaching Wallisdown Road, on its way to Winton Banks. By now, except at weekday peak hours, service 30 was curtailed to Winton, Alma Road, virtually as an extension to the 31. Roger G. Funnell (courtesy Mrs D. Funnell and Rodney Funnell)

Unrebuilt BUT9641T no. 248 (KLJ348) crosses the bottom of Richmond Hill before heading up Old Christchurch Road to the Lansdowne and then following Holdenhurst Road to Queen's Park Golf Pavilion on a service 25 working. Roger G. Funnell (courtesy Mrs D. Funnell and Rodney Funnell)

BUT9641T no. 235 (KLJ335), rebuilt in October 1962 without a front staircase, has turned out of Poole Road to follow the one-way clockwise terminal loop along Seamoor Road, Westbourne (as did all other westbound road traffic). Standing to the front nearside of no. 235 is youthful trolleybus enthusiast David Janes complete with camera. Roger G. Funnell (courtesy Mrs D. Funnell and Rodney Funnell)

The loading point at Westbourne for service 25 journeys to the Square and beyond was at the west end of Seamoor Road just before the junction with Alumhurst Road. BUT9641T no. 236 (KLJ336), rebuilt without a front staircase in December 1962, has recently arrived from the east.
Roger G. Funnell (courtesy Mrs D. Funnell and Rodney Funnell)

Almost at the opposite end of its journey, at the south end of Ashley Road, Boscombe, rebuilt BUT9641T no. 241 (KLJ341) passes beneath the crossover of the westbound wiring exiting Gladstone Road on 30 May 1965.

David Pearson

the eastbound overhead wiring at Iford roundabout to enable trolleybuses coming from the Boscombe direction to turn directly from Christchurch Road into Castle Lane East for Castle Lane Depot (Mallard Road) Depot without having to circle the roundabout. It was brought into use on 2 July 1965. By August 1965 the overhead wiring at the former Central Depot and in St. Clement's Road, the access route from Boscombe, had been dismantled, whilst the undertaking's store of copper conductor wire stored in the depot (potentially for the Holdenhurst Road extension) was disposed of to A.F. Newell & Sons Ltd., Southampton, scrap metal merchants.

The hand-operated turnout frog at the junction of Stour and Barrack Roads, Christchurch, for trolleybuses travelling from Castle Lane Depot to take up service and wishing to turn south towards Tuckton, was converted into an auto frog as from 2 August 1965.

The *Bournemouth Evening Echo* of 9 September 1965 noted that *"On Sunday the last trolleybus will operate on what was the first trolleybus route in Bournemouth. This will be the first visible indication of the change of policy which will lead to the eventual disappearance of the trolleybuses from the streets of Bournemouth by 1970. The 33 and 34 circular services around Strouden Park have been operated by motorbuses for quite some time now and the first section of overhead wire along St Paul's Road on the old 34 route has been taken down. With the change to motorbuses on the 25, wires will be taken down Triangle-County Gates and all along Holdenhurst Road and Ashley Road.*

"The next step will be in 12 months' time when the services using Richmond Hill change from trolley to motor. Target date for the withdrawal for all the remaining trolley bus services is 1968. The death knell for the trolley was in 1963 when Bournemouth Town

Council at their April meeting decided to do away with them in 5-10 years".

The end of the ex-Brighton BUT9611Ts in August 1965 and the withdrawal of trolleybuses from service 25 on Sunday 12 September 1965 signalled the completion of Stage 2 of the abandonment programme. The last service 25 journey was operated by BUT9641T 242 which left Westbourne in wet weather at 11.21pm with just three passengers on board. Trolleybuses running on the 25 on the final day were 235, 238, 242-244, 276. Thereafter ten BUT9641Ts (245, 247-250, 252, 254-57) were delicensed, leaving only 244, 246, 251, 253 (all in un-rebuilt form, with two staircases) still in service.

Further trolleybus service cuts coincided with the introduction of the winter 1965/66 timetable on 13 September 1965. Service 24 disappeared entirely apart from weekday peak-hour workings and Sunday afternoons (2.30pm-6.30pm), the latter in place of service 20 which did not operate at all on winter Sundays. During the week service 20 was increased to operate every 20 minutes.

On 14 September 1965 the Transport Committee agreed to revised timings for services 20 and 24 to give an evenly distributed service along Christchurch Road but, despite public pressure to reintroduce service 35 along Charminster Avenue, for which the wiring remained intact, no action was taken. Only in October 1965 did it agree to run, for an experimental six-month period, a weekday 35 motorbus service at 8.40am to Bournemouth Square, returning at 5.45pm.

The last of the wiring on the approach roads to the former Central Depot, Southcote Road, was removed by early September 1965. On the nights of 13/14 September 1965, the frogs and crossing at the junction of Palmerston Road and

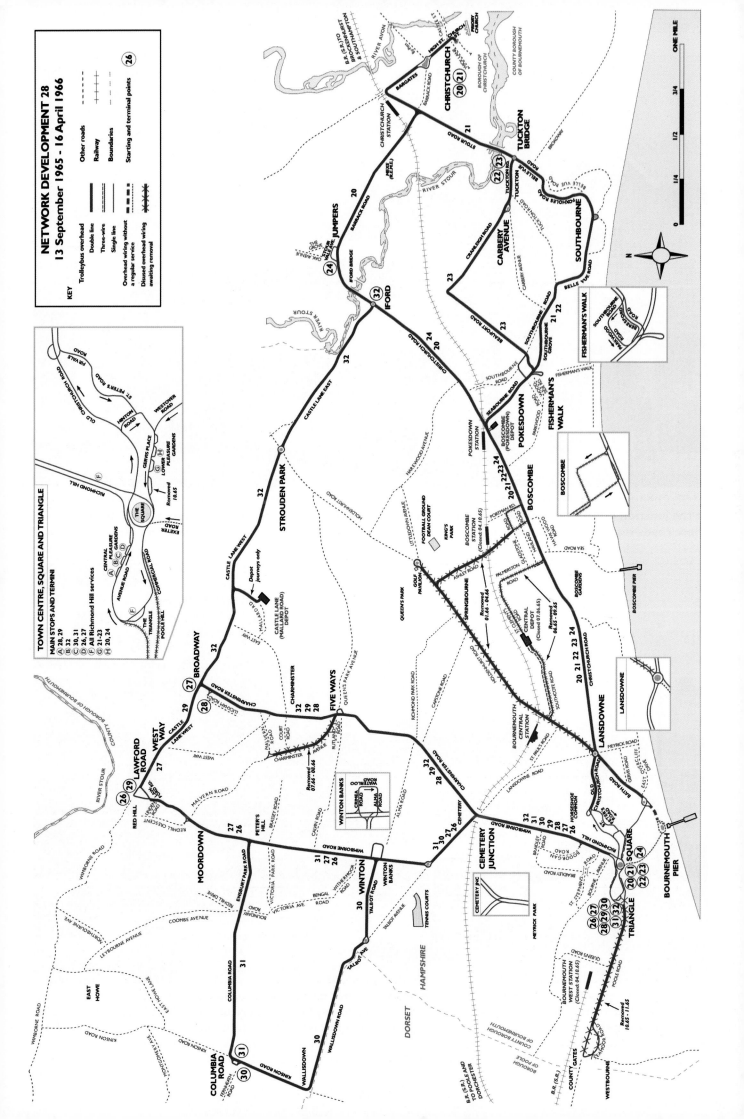

At Southbourne Cross Roads turning circle, BUT9641T 254 (KLJ354) prepares to go around the public conveniences at the junction of Southbourne Overcliff Drive and St. Catherine's Road a few yards to the south of the junction of these roads with Belle Vue Road prior to returning to the Square on an unscheduled peak hour extra (5 July 1965).
David Pearson

Upper deck passengers on any trolleybus descending Bath Road hill to Westover Road or the Pier had a wonderful view across Bournemouth Bay to the Isle of Purbeck and Old Harry Rocks. Those onboard BUT9641T 239 (KLJ339) will be enjoying the sights to maximum effect right now. On the left is the white facade of the Royal Bath Hotel with the brick-built Rothesay, Kildare and Lynwood hotels, which all backed on to the East Cliff, beyond. In an act of civic vandalism, the last three named were demolished in 1971 to make way for a car park. David Pearson

New Iford Bridge over the River Stour, which at this point was the boundary between the Boroughs of Bournemouth and Christchurch, was built in the early 1930s to replace an older, narrow structure built in 1784 (utilising even older approaches). Sunbeam MF2B no. 299 (299LJ), having turned at Jumpers Corner, heads back to Bournemouth Square with its indicator blinds not yet changed. **David Pearson**

Christchurch Road were removed. During October 1965 the traction poles in Southcote, Palmerston and St. Clement's Roads were removed, nearly 100 poles being removed in a fortnight, working just three hours every morning. The former depot exit into St. Clement's Road was sealed off and the footpath extended across it.

In October 1965 the Highways & Works Committee had white lines painted on the road at Southbourne Grove to indicate possible new traffic islands. Mr Cunningham, however, felt that they would make bus operation impossible and the idea was not pursued.

A letter dated 15 October 1965 from the FMPTE stated that, subject to completion of current negotiations with the appropriate NJICs, the 40-hour week would be introduced for craftsmen from 1 November 1965 and for drivers, semi-skilled and unskilled employees from 3 January 1966. The cost to the undertaking was estimated as £19,000 pa.

On 30 October 1965 work commenced on removing overhead wiring between Westbourne and the Triangle, i.e. Poole and Seamoor Roads, continuing through November whilst, in December 1965, those traction poles not retained for lighting purposes were burned off about 6in below ground level. This was complicated by some of the older, ex-tramway, traction poles having been filled with concrete reinforcing. Many were sold to a firm of contractors near Portsmouth for use in sea defence work. The turnout frog at the east end of Commercial Road outside Woolworths was taken out on the night of 30/31 October 1965. The turnout frog at Trinity

Church, Old Christchurch Road, for eastbound 25 trolleybuses was removed on 11 November 1965. The trolley wires that replaced the frogs at Commercial Road outside Woolworths and at Trinity Church were joined by two end fittings bolted together instead of the usual mid-span splices. Just before Christmas, all section boxes and feeder cables were removed along Ashley Road and Holdenhurst Road. After the holiday, work started on removing trolley wire in Holdenhurst Road and within a few weeks the section from the Queen's Park Hotel, at the junction with Ashley Road, to the former Roxy Cinema, about 30yd east of the junction with Cleveland Road, had been cut down.

From 6 January 1966, the Overhead Department was reorganised and for the first time since trolleybus operation commenced, no overhead crew was on duty at night. One effect of this change was that the removal of overhead equipment from defunct routes was now limited to day-time, normally Friday mornings (as two crews were on duty together) or, for more complicated work, Sunday mornings when there was, in those days, little road traffic.

Queen's Park junction and the Golf Pavilion branch were cut down by mid-January 1966. The route was tied-off between the end of Ashley Road (White House switch box) and Cleveland Road feeder by 22 January 1966. Removal of wiring was started, working outwards from the Lansdowne. By mid-March 1966 all wiring and traction poles had been removed from Holdenhurst Road, including the St. Swithun's Road junction but excluding the rest of the section between the Lansdowne and Bournemouth

Arriving in the Square ex-BH&D BUT9611T no. 293 (DNJ993), dating from 1948, has just descended the 1 in 8 (12.5%) gradient of Richmond Hill from Charminster Road and Broadway Hotel, Luckham Road. The ex-Brighton BUT9611Ts had the same 120hp traction motors as Bournemouth's own 3-axle BUT9641Ts but were almost 2 tons lighter, so they could really "go"! **Roger G. Funnell (courtesy Mrs D. Funnell and Rodney Funnell)**

Central Station, whilst half a mile in Ashley Road, up to but not including the railway bridge, had gone.

The 27 January 1966 Transport Committee meeting, having considered the financial position of the undertaking and various options, recommended an application for increased fares based on Scheme III in the General Manager's report, anticipated to increase revenue by £108,300 pa., subject to no increase in ordinary fares being greater than 1d except on summer holiday services.

It considered any deferment of the trolleybus conversion programme, to reduce costs by delaying delivery of replacement motorbuses, as impracticable, not least as overhead wiring changes would be needed. In order to limit the increases, further departmental economies were proposed, including service changes and more one-man-operated vehicles. A completely new route structure, based on main routes and feeder services with transfer ticket facilities, was proposed. It was also suggested that the weekday evening frequency be introduced on services 21-23 on winter Sundays, service 24 be withdrawn, and that the Sunday evening frequency be introduced from 1.30pm on services 26, 27 and 31 on winter Sundays.

Commencing on 6 March 1966, falling patronage provoked a further reduction in Sunday services. The Main Road trolleybus

services (21-23) and the 31 were cut to half-hourly, Richmond Hill services (27-29 and 32) were reduced to hourly with the 28 extended to Castle Lane Depot (and from 1pm to 7pm further east along Castle Lane to Strouden Park, Cooper Dean Hotel). Service 24 was reduced to weekday peak-hour only operation, and service 26, by now just a single advertised weekday journey, disappeared altogether, being regarded as a short-working of the 27. The half-hourly Sunday trolleybus service 30 was replaced by motorbuses. On 1 April 1966, the SETC approved the proposals and the increased fares were brought into operation on 8 April 1966.

A short history of the trolleybus system appeared in the February 1966 edition of the *Hampshire Magazine,* in which Ian Cunningham was quoted as saying that the main reason for the abandonment of trolleybus operation was the increasing cost of and difficulty in obtaining vehicles and spare parts. The undertaking had been making its own spares, primarily overhead wiring fittings but possibly some minor parts for vehicles, for quite some time.

Having considered Mr Cunningham's report of 31 December 1965, tenders were invited for internal and external advertising on Corporation buses, with effect from 1 August 1966 when the existing (internal advertising) contract was due to expire.

The Jumpers Corner terminus of service 24 and, from time to time, the 32, was in Stourvale Avenue which lay just to the north of Barrack Road, Christchurch, about 350yd beyond Iford Bridge. Sunbeam MF2B no.299 (299LJ) rests at the boarding point on 16 August 1964. Note the cherry red paint application in the driver's cab area and the jonquil colour of the internal window cappings giving a brighter interior finish than on the earlier Sunbeam MF2B deliveries.

David Pearson

BUT9641T no. 243 (KLJ343), rebuilt with a front staircase in May 1963 and the last of the BUT9641Ts to be so treated, pulls out of Talbot Road into Wimborne Road, Winton Banks, causing the point duty policeman to step back smartish. Although the service number blind is poorly aligned, the trolleybus is on a 30 to the Square. A Leyland Titan PD3/1 with Bournemouth's own design of radiator grill follows out of Talbot Road on motorbus service 7 to Boscombe, a motorbus service once foreseen for electrification.

Roger G. Funnell (courtesy Mrs D. Funnell and Rodney Funnell)

Advertising was also to be permitted around ten bus shelters, but not in the timetables.

The Transport Committee recommended at its 15 March 1966 meeting that, having considered four tenders for exterior advertising on Corporation buses, the highest, from Howards Publicity Ltd. (£10,660 pa. for five years plus 5% for the sixth and seventh years), be accepted as from 1 August 1966. Included in this sum was £3,496 6s plus 5% for interior advertising. However, the full Council rejected this recommendation on 12 April 1966 and tenders were re-invited for internal and external advertising on double-deck buses for periods of three, five and seven years. The existing contract with Messrs Frank Mason in respect of internal advertisements was extended for three months from 1 August 1966. In July 1966 it considered four revised tenders, the highest again coming from Howards Publicity Ltd. (£11,162 1s 6d pa. for three years commencing 1 November 1966) and this was accepted. Thus, the Council at last agreed to external advertising on the Transport Department's vehicles. Until this time, Bournemouth, Huddersfield and the Tees-side Railless Traction Board had been the only latter-day trolleybus operators not to display external advertising.

It was suggested that the passenger waiting room at the trolleybus turntable off Church Street, Christchurch, be closed and, if permitted, tenders be invited for the right to use the building, which had a flat above (previously let solely to BCT employees), as shop premises. This was agreed and the Finance Committee asked to arrange its sale.

From Saturday 16 April 1966 weekday trolleybus service 30 ceased to run and was replaced by diversions of the half-hourly motorbus service 7 (Boscombe-Kinson via Turbary Park Avenue). Trolleybus service 31 was revised between 9am and 7pm accordingly. Trolleybuses 236, a BUT9641T which had had its front staircase removed in late 1962, and 273, a seven-year-old Sunbeam MF2B, were withdrawn. The withdrawal of service 30 did not lead to any wiring being made redundant as some trolleybuses running into and out of service from Columbia Road continued to travel by way of Kinson Road, Wallisdown Road and Talbot Road to Winton Banks.

Importantly, it was agreed with the Highways & Works Committee on 19 April 1966 that all bus stops in the Borough be made "no waiting" areas.

An RTS enthusiasts' tour on Sunday 12 June 1966 used BUT9641Ts 239 (single staircase) and 244 (unrebuilt), participants changing at the half-way point, Castle Lane (Mallard Road) Depot. This tour was accordingly able to traverse the route of the erstwhile 30 through Wallisdown, in addition to little-used sections of overhead wiring in Southbourne and Bournemouth town centre.

Augmented services were introduced for the duration of the summer timetable (13 June 1966-11 September 1966). Service 20 was reintroduced on Sunday afternoons with a 20-minute frequency compared with every 30 minutes in 1965, whilst service 24 operated on Sunday mornings (10am-1pm) to and from Jumpers Corner. The last advertised peak hour journeys to and from Southbourne Cross Roads were on 11 June 1966, but unadvertised mid-day peak and Saturday trolleybuses were noted at the rarely used Southbourne Cross Roads and Five Ways, Charminster, turning circles.

Following the abandonment of service 30, the trolleybus network had contracted to:

20 Bournemouth Square, Gervis Place - Boscombe Gardens - Boscombe - Pokesdown - Iford - Jumpers - Christchurch, Church Street

21 Bournemouth Square, Gervis Place - Lansdowne - Boscombe Gardens - Boscombe - Pokesdown - Fisherman's Walk - Southbourne - Tuckton Bridge - Christchurch, Church Street

22 Bournemouth Square, Gervis Place - Lansdowne - Boscombe Gardens - Boscombe - Pokesdown - Fisherman's Walk - Southbourne Cross Roads - Tuckton Bridge, Tuckton Road

23 Bournemouth Square, Gervis Place - Lansdowne - Boscombe Gardens - Boscombe - Pokesdown - Fisherman's Walk - Beaufort Road - Cranleigh Road - Tuckton Bridge, Tuckton Road

24 Bournemouth Square, Gervis Place - Lansdowne - Boscombe Gardens - Boscombe - Pokesdown - Iford - Jumpers

27 Triangle - Bournemouth Square - Richmond Hill - Cemetery Junction - Wimborne Road - Winton - Moordown - Broadway Hotel, Castle Lane West

28 Triangle - Bournemouth Square - Richmond Hill - Cemetery Junction - Charminster Road - Five Ways - Broadway Hotel, Luckham Road

29 Triangle - Bournemouth Square - Richmond Hill - Cemetery Junction - Charminster Road - Five Ways - Broadway Hotel - Moordown, Castle Lane West, junction with Lawford Road

31 Triangle - Bournemouth Square - Richmond Hill - Cemetery Junction - Winton - Ensbury Park Road - Columbia Road, junction with Kinson Road

32 Triangle - Bournemouth Square - Richmond Hill - Cemetery Junction - Charminster Road - Five Ways - Broadway Hotel - Castle Lane - Strouden Park - Iford, junction with Christchurch Road

By April 1966 the erstwhile service 25 wiring had almost completely vanished apart from a few short stretches in Ashley Road, Boscombe, and in Holdenhurst Road, near the Lansdowne. The last portions in Ashley Road were removed on 24 April 1966, with the remains of the Holdenhurst Road equipment on 8 May 1966. It was expected that all traction poles and redundant wiring would have been removed by the end of May 1966. Redundant frogs and crossings at the Lansdowne and the junctions of Ashley Road, Christchurch Road and Portman Road, Boscombe, i.e. the former service 25 passing loop, remained in place for the time being as it was not considered worthwhile to pay overtime to overhead crews to work at night to remove them. By July 1966 only 400yd of overhead wiring remained between Central Station and the Lansdowne and all the wiring had gone from Ashley, Portman and Gladstone Roads. West of the Triangle all former service 25 wiring was down, although the trailing frog at the west end of Avenue Road, where the eastbound line from Westbourne had joined that from the Triangle and the parking area there, was still in place.

It was announced that no further trolleybus repaints would take place although 281 left the paintshop in August 1966.

Mr Cunningham submitted his proposals on 28 June 1966 for changes to the Richmond Hill services upon the withdrawal of trolleybus operation, which was now scheduled to take place in September 1966. Subject to the SETC's approval of the replacement motorbus services, his proposals to withdraw all the remaining Side Route trolleybus services were agreed by the Transport Committee, provided that transfer tickets were introduced on that part of the route previously served by motorbus services 6 and 10 and for which there would be no through bus to the Square under the proposed new arrangements.

During July and August 1966 the Overhead Department concentrated on removing the overhead equipment along the route of the former 35 service. Apart from a short stretch of plain wiring mid-way along Charminster Avenue, all the wiring, including Five Ways junction and the Malvern Road reversing triangle, was down by 22 July 1966 although the traction poles remained in situ.

During the early summer, overhead wiring was realigned and about half a dozen traction poles moved due to road works at the Tuckton and Cooper Dean roundabouts. On 22 August 1966 work started on alterations to the overhead wiring in Castle Lane West as the approach to Cooper Dean roundabout at the junction with Holdenhurst Road was converted to dual carriageway, requiring the planting of 20 new traction poles, and span wires between the roundabout and just east of the junction with Leydene Avenue. It was announced that Castle Lane East would provide the trolleybus access route to Castle Lane (Mallard Road) Depot from 26 September 1966, service trolleybuses ceasing to operate along this route from the previous day.

In tramways days there was a triangular track layout at the junction of St. Swithun's Road with Southcote Road enabling tramcars to be completely turned around ensuring equal wheel wear. Sunbeam MF2B no. 262 (WRU262) is pictured exactly there, pulling out of Southcote Road into St. Swithun's Road and thence into Holdenhurst Road on its way from Central Depot to take up service. Note the three wire overhead layout which ran between the depot area and Holdenhurst Road. **Roger G. Funnell (courtesy Mrs D. Funnell and Rodney Funnell)**

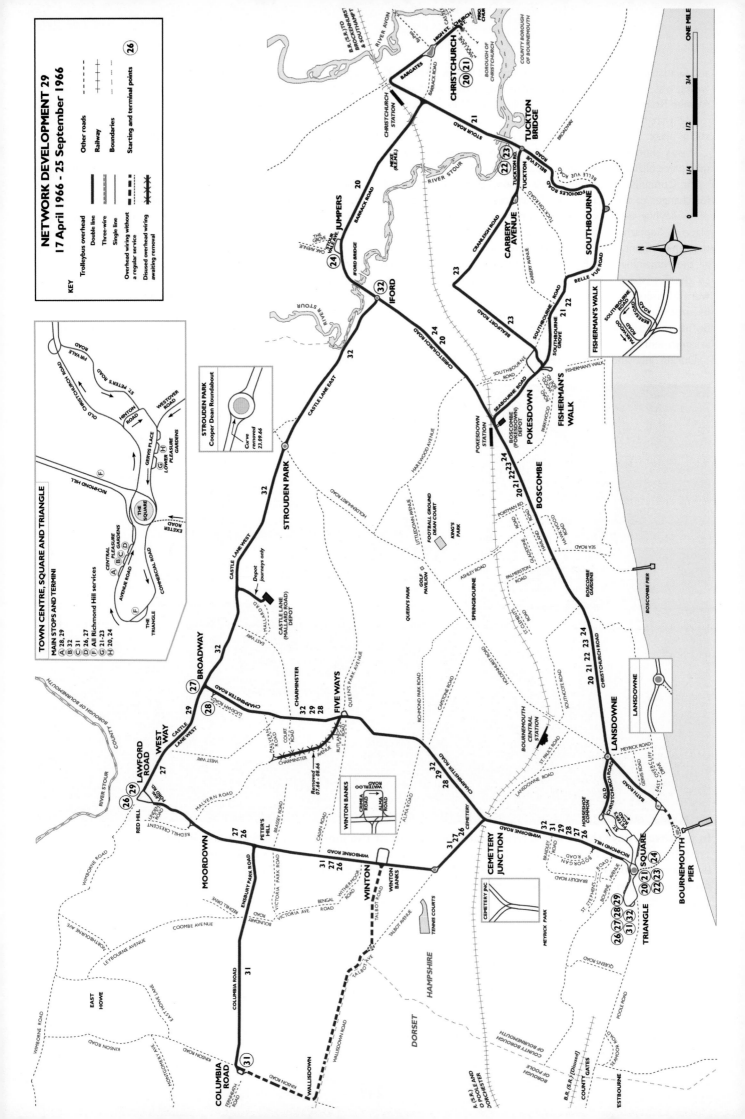

CHAPTER TEN

RUNDOWN AND FINAL CLOSURE

Tenders were invited for the disposal of 24 BUT9641T and ten Sunbeam MF2B trolleybuses, and the supply of eight single-deck motorbuses in the year 1967/68 and 20 double-deckers in the year 1968/69 to complete the trolleybus conversion programme.

At this time, BUT9641Ts 236, 246-250, 252, and 254-257 were at Castle Lane (Mallard Road) Depot awaiting sale for scrap. By arrangement, open-top MS2 202, owned by the NTA since November 1965, was also still garaged there. On the positive side Sunbeam MF2B 273, which had been withdrawn at the closure of service 30, was reinstated into the running fleet.

In July 1966 the government introduced a Prices and Income Standstill in an effort to strengthen the value of the pound. These measures, which included bus fares, also influenced the NJIC's wage award for platform staff and semi-skilled workers, which had been agreed earlier in the month. The Council agreed to honour the agreement in due course, but like other awards it was "frozen" by the government's policy, whilst an incentive bonus scheme was also put on "hold".

The trolleybus Side Routes traversing Richmond Hill (shrunken by now to services 27, 28, 29, 31 and 32) were scheduled for closure on 11 September 1966, but were given a fortnight's stay of execution due to delays in the delivery of replacement motorbuses. The summer timetable was extended accordingly. Nonetheless, on 11 September 1966, an enthusiasts' tour using two BUT9641Ts, single staircase 234 and unrebuilt 246, one of the four still retaining their original twin staircases, visited all the remaining Side Routes and the Wallisdown Road line, which had closed to service vehicles on 16 April 1966. The itinerary made 246 the last trolleybus to use the reversing triangles at Bodorgan Road (top of Richmond Hill) and at Redhill Crescent, Moordown. A foggy Sunday 25 September 1966 proved to be the final day of Side Route trolleybus operations. The Bournemouth Railway Club had hastily organised a further "farewell" tour using BUT9641T 246. On this occasion 246 became the last trolleybus to turn at Five Ways, Charminster, and also visited Bournemouth Pier, traversing the rarely-used Exeter Road line between the Pier and Bournemouth Square. The *Bournemouth Evening Echo* contained an article in its 14 October 1966 edition headed *"Enthusiasts sought to preserve old trolleybus"*.

Last vehicles were:

- last through journey on 27 (forming 29), 10pm from Triangle: 261
- last through journey on 29 (forming 27), 10.18pm from Triangle: 282
- last 28 to Broadway Hotel, Luckham Road reverser, 7.13pm from Triangle: 286
- last 31 to Columbia Road, junction with Kinson Road, 11pm from Triangle: 282
- last 32 full-working to Iford, 10.33pm from Triangle: 299

The ornate cupola on a tower was on the corner of Alma Road with Wimborne Road and belonged to the Continental Cinema, formerly the Winton Electric Palace, which by the mid-1960s was showing some rather risqué films. Sunbeam MF2B no. 298 (298LJ) travels south along Wimborne Road just past the Winton Banks junction on 8 August 1966.

David Pearson

A facing and trailing frog was added to the overhead wiring above Iford roundabout at the crossroads of Castle Lane East and Iford Lane with Christchurch Road enabling trolleybuses from the eastbound Christchurch Road line to turn left into Castle Lane East and thus reach Castle Lane (Mallard Road) Depot in July 1963. Prior to this it was necessary to circumnavigate the roundabout, although no service trolleybuses had this need. Sunbeam MF2B no. 258, having turned around the roundabout, heads back into Castle Lane East and thus through Strouden Park to Charminster Road and the Square on 8 August 1966 with a Ford Anglia in hot pursuit. **David Pearson**

Sunbeam MF2B no. 260 (WRU260) is seen heading west in Columbia Road with the traction power feeder pillar located at 191 Columbia Road just over one span behind on a damp 8 August 1966. It seems that ladies' headscarves were fashionable that summer. **David Pearson**

- last 32 short-working to Strouden Park, junction of Castle Lane West with Holdenhurst Road, 10.53pm from Triangle: 283
- last working of all from Triangle, 11.07pm to Lawford Road, Broadway and Castle Lane (Mallard Road) Depot via service 27 (but showing 26): 279
- last vehicle into Castle Lane (Mallard Road) Depot was 282 (off service 31) arriving at 11.36pm

All the remaining BUT9614Ts (234, 235, 237-244, 246, 251 and 253) were withdrawn for scrapping and ten of the initial 1958 batch of Sunbeam MF2Bs (258-267) were also withdrawn from service. They were advertised for sale and parked in two lines in the open at Castle Lane (Mallard Road) Depot.

The 18 October 1966 Transport Committee meeting considered five tenders received for the withdrawn vehicles and accepted those from a Mr R. Higgins of Christchurch for the purchase of 246 for £103, and Wombwell Diesel Co. Ltd. for the remaining BUT9641Ts at £75 each. Mr Higgins was unable to find a suitable storage site and 246 rejoined its sisters heading for the scrap yard but, at the eleventh hour, it was acquired by Mr Richard Cromwell of Effingham, Surrey, for preservation. Wombwell Diesels started collecting their purchases in December 1966, the first vehicle to leave having had its roof removed to avoid any difficulties with low bridges en route. The scrapmen then tried to move the vehicles intact but, after 244 had become wedged under Fisherton Street railway bridge, Salisbury, on 11 December 1966, the top-deck roofs of the remaining vehicles were removed at Bournemouth before towing. 250 also moved north on 11 December 1966. On 14 December 1966, 236 and 242 were collected, 251 and 254 on 15 December 1966 and 17 December 1966 respectively.

As at 18 December 1966, 234, 235, 237-240, 243, 245, 247-249, 252, 253, remained to be collected, but all had left by the end of January 1967.

It was decided to retain the ten withdrawn Sunbeam MF2Bs (258-267) stored in Castle Lane Depot yard (except for 258 which remained under cover), where they were gradually stripped of useful parts to keep the remaining MF2Bs operational.

The decimated system, with only the Christchurch Road services 20, 21, 22, 23 and weekday morning peak-hour 24, was now operated entirely by two-axle Sunbeam MF2Bs. The operating fleet now consisted of 29 trolleybuses, although the maximum schedule required just 18:

268-277 (WRU268-WRU277)	H35/28D of 1958
278-287 (YLJ278-YLJ287)	H35/28D of 1959
295-303 (295LJ-303LJ)	H37/28D of 1962

There were few changes to the routes followed by the replacement motorbus services, the 31 being extended to Moore Avenue to provide a circular working with service 3, and services 6, 9, 33 and 34 being amended somewhat to follow more closely the erstwhile trolleybus routes.

Trolley wires disappeared from Richmond Hill itself during the first week after closure, due to the pressing need to start work on a new roundabout at the top (an early stage in the construction of the town centre inner relief road, now known as Wessex Way). The connecting link on the west side of Cooper Dean roundabout, Strouden Park (at the junction of Castle Lane with Holdenhurst Road) was removed on 23 September 1966 in connection with construction of a short section of dual carriageway in Castle Lane West beyond the

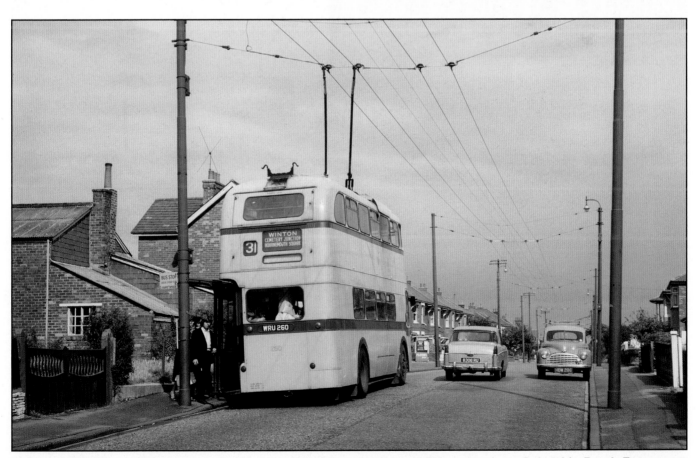

Sunbeam MF2B no. 260 stops at the Howeth Road fare stage travelling east along Columbia Road. Four spans ahead can be seen the 191 Columbia Road traction power positive feeder point.
David Pearson

The sharp turn out of the Kinson Road southbound line into Fernheath Road and thus into the turning circle in front of the shops at Wonderholme Parade often required the three axle BUT9641Ts to set-back partially through the manoeuvre, a shunt frog being included in the overhead wiring layout for this purpose. Sunbeam MF2B no. 261 has no such difficulties as it turns first into Fernheath Road and then into the Wonderholme Parade bay prior to returning to the Square and the Triangle along Columbia Road and Ensbury Park Road on 8 August 1966.

David Pearson

On 8 August 1966, Sunbeam MF2B no. 259 appears to be stopped in a column of traffic outside the Legal and General Assurance offices halfway down Richmond Hill as BUT9641T no. 243 surges past, making full use of its 120hp traction motor, with destination Columbia Road, junction with Kinson Road   David Pearson

No. 268 is climbing the slight rise in Wimborne Road at the junction with Lawford Road, service 27 (iii) having been re-introduced on 30 September 1963 in place of the 34 (ii) as the interworking partner of service of the 29 (iii). Note the remains of the facing frog in the northbound Wimborne Road line. This frog had been installed, together with northbound wiring further along Wimborne Road as far as its junction with Castle Lane West, in March 1937 to provide for the approved route extension to Ensbury, Kinson and Bear Cross which would have probably been constructed soon afterwards but for the prelude to and then the outbreak of the Second World War.   David Pearson

The north end of Charminster Road at its junction with Castle Lane West on 6 September 1966. BUT9641T no. 235 waits for another three axle BUT on service 29 to clear before turning right and heading to Castle Lane (Mallard Road) Depot. Sunbeam MF2B no. 260 is arriving from Iford on a service 32 journey.   David Pearson

The position of the parked Morris 1000 is not ideal as Sunbeam MF2B no. 264 (WRU264) pulls out of Luckham Road, having used the reversing triangle, into Charminster Road on its journey back to the Square and the Triangle on a sunny 6 September 1966. The square glasses on the lights attached to the traction poles typified Bournemouth's street lighting in the post-war trolleybus era.
David Pearson

The New Bell Inn was the next building to Boscombe (Pokesdown) Depot in Christchurch Road, Pokesdown and almost opposite Pokesdown railway station. Rebuilt BUT9641T no. 243 comes to a stop outside the Inn on its way from Tuckton to the Square (service 22) on 8 August 1966.
David Pearson

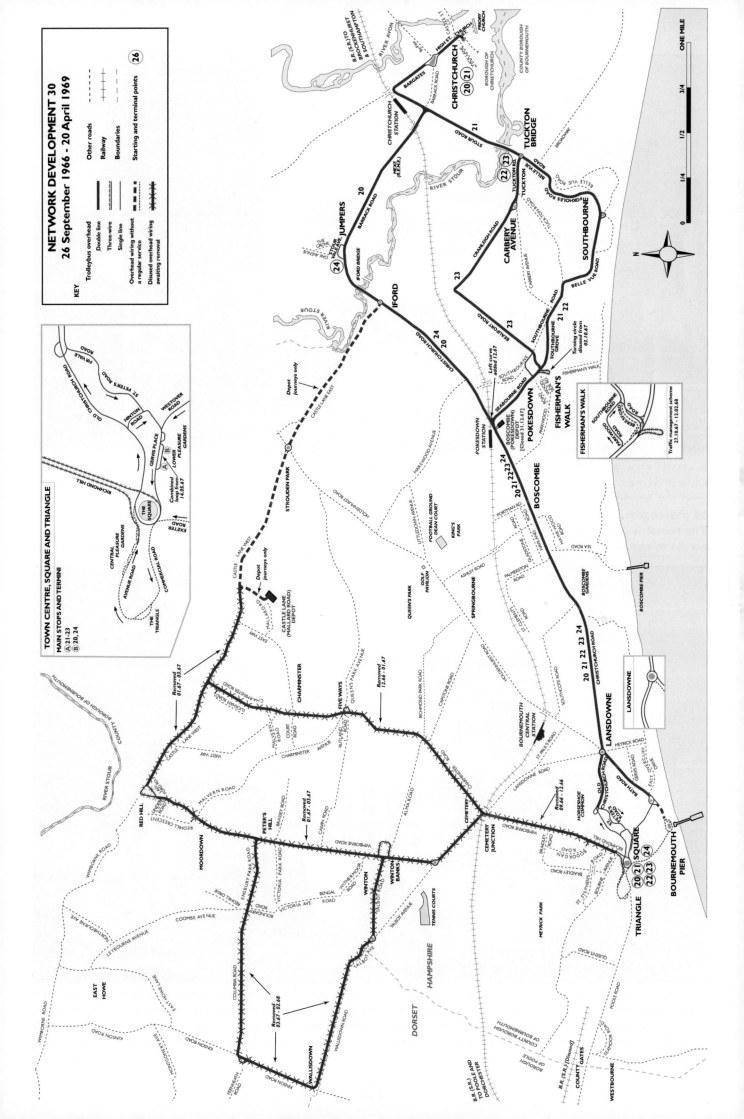

NETWORK DEVELOPMENT 30
26 September 1966 - 20 April 1969

KEY

Trolleybus overhead	Other roads
Double line	Three-wire
Single line	Railway
	Boundaries
Overhead wiring without a regular service	Starting and terminal points
Disused overhead wiring awaiting removal	26

TOWN CENTRE, SQUARE AND TRIANGLE

MAIN STOPS AND TERMINI
Ⓐ 21-23
Ⓑ 20, 24

FIR VALE ROAD
OLD CHRISTCHURCH ROAD
ST. PETER'S ROAD
WESTOVER ROAD
HINTON ROAD
GERVIS PLACE
RICHMOND HILL
THE SQUARE
EXETER ROAD
AVENUE ROAD
COMMERCIAL ROAD
THE TRIANGLE
LOWER PLEASURE GARDENS
CENTRAL PLEASURE GARDENS
Combined loop from 14.05.67

ONE MILE
0   1/4   1/2   3/4

N

FISHERMAN'S WALK
SOUTHBOURNE ROAD
BELLE VUE ROAD
PARKWOOD ROAD
Traffic management scheme 27.10.67 - 12.02.68

LANSDOWNE

CHRISTCHURCH
Borough of Christchurch
County Borough of Bournemouth
PRIORY CHURCH
RIVER AVON
HIGH ST.
CHURCH ST.
BARGATES
CHRISTCHURCH STATION
20   21
TUCKTON BRIDGE
TUCKTON ROAD
STOUR ROAD
BELLE VUE ROAD
22   23
TUCKTON
SCHOLES ROAD
SOUTHBOURNE
CARBERY AVENUE
OAK AVENUE
JUMPERS
24
IFORD BRIDGE
STOUR VALE
BARRACK ROAD
HENGISTBURY HEAD
RIVER STOUR
IFORD
20
CRANLEIGH ROAD
BEAUFORT ROAD
23
CHRISTCHURCH ROAD
24
20
BELLE VUE ROAD
SOUTHBOURNE GROVE
21   22
23
SOUTHBOURNE OVERCLIFF
SEABOURNE ROAD
POKESDOWN STATION
BOSCOMBE (POKESDOWN) DEPOT [Closed 31.12.67]
POKESDOWN
Left curve added 12.67
Turning circle disused from 03.10.67
FISHERMAN'S WALK
BOSCOMBE
20 21 22 23 24
24
HARTWOOD AVENUE
HOLDENHURST ROAD
FOOTBALL GROUND DEAN COURT
KING'S PARK
BOSCOMBE GARDENS
BOSCOMBE PIER
SEA ROAD
PORTMAN RD.
HILL ROAD
GLENROY ROAD
PALMERSTON ROAD
ASHLEY ROAD
LITTLEDOWN AVENUE
CHRISTCHURCH ROAD
20 21 22 23 24
MEYRICK ROAD
GERVIS ROAD
EAST OVERCLIFF DRIVE
EAST CLIFF
OLD CHRISTCHURCH ROAD
BATH ROAD
BOURNEMOUTH PIER
SQUARE
20 21 22 23 24
TRIANGLE
RICHMOND HILL
ST. STEPHENS ROAD
BODORGAN ROAD
BRADLEY ROAD
HORSESHOE COMMON
Removed 09.66 - 12.66
WIMBORNE ROAD
CEMETERY JUNCTION
CEMETERY
LANSDOWNE ROAD
BOURNEMOUTH CENTRAL STATION
ST. PAUL'S ROAD
SPRINGBOURNE
QUEEN'S PARK
GOLF PAVILION
QUEENS PARK AVENUE
RICHMOND PARK ROAD
CAPSTONE ROAD
ST. CLEMENTS ROAD
ST. SWITHUN'S ROAD
HAMPSHIRE
DORSET
STROUDEN PARK
Depot journeys only
CASTLE LANE EAST
CASTLE LANE (MALLARD ROAD) DEPOT
Depot journeys only
EAST WAY
CHARMINSTER ROAD
FIVE WAYS
Removed 12.66 - 01.67
CHARMINSTER
CASTLE LANE WEST
Removed 01.67 - 03.67
MALLARD ROAD
LUCERNE ROAD
MALVERN ROAD
COURT ROAD
WEST WAY
CHARMINSTER AVENUE
RUTLAND ROAD
ALMA ROAD
CAIRNS ROAD
BRASSEY ROAD
Removed 01.67 - 03.67
MOORDOWN
PETER'S HILL
ENSBURY PARK ROAD
REDHILL DRIVE
REDHILL CRESCENT
CASTLE LANE WEST
RED HILL
County Borough of Bournemouth
RIVER STOUR
WIMBORNE ROAD
WALLISDOWN ROAD
WALLISDOWN
Removed 03.67 - 02.68
COLUMBIA ROAD
KINSON ROAD
FERNHEATH ROAD
TALBOT AVENUE
TALBOT DRIVE
WINTON BANKS
WINTON
VICTORIA PARK ROAD
BOUNDARY ROAD
WITHERMOOR ROAD
BENGAL ROAD
VICTORIA AVE
TENNIS COURTS
MEYRICK PARK
COOMBE AVENUE
LETBOURNE AVENUE
NORTHBOURNE AVE.
EAST HOWE LANE
KINSON LANE
MONTROSE AVE.
B.R. (S.R.) TO POOLE AND DORCHESTER
BOROUGH OF POOLE
COUNTY BOROUGH OF POOLE
B.R. (S.R.) [Disused]
COUNTY GATES
WESTBOURNE
QUEENS ROAD
POOLE ROAD
B.R. (S.R.) TO BRANKSOME BROCKENHURST & SOUTHAMPTON

A classic view of Sunbeam MF2B no. 259 (WRU259) turning into the former coach yard of the Dolphin Hotel, Church Street, Christchurch, to terminate at the turntable on 6 September 1966. In the left foreground can be seen the handle intended to be used to rotate the trolleybus and turntable and on the right, behind the would-be passengers, is the BCT waiting room with a large board to inform visitors of Christchurch's many attractions. The remains of Christchurch Castle, built by the Normans on the site of an earlier fort to defend the harbour and access to the Rivers Avon and Stour, are visible beyond the Coffee House.   David Pearson

BUT9641T no. 251 (KLJ351), which was never rebuilt and retained its front staircase, has just arrived at the Castle Lane West, Lawford Road, terminus of service 26. The front exit doors remain open as the last alighting passengers drift away back towards the junction with Lawford Road. The tower of the brick-built Church of Holy Epiphany at the junction of Redbreast Road can be seen in the centre background behind the passenger waiting shelter.   David Pearson

(Left) BUT9641T no. 241 (KLJ341) stands at the terminal loading point of service 26 in Castle Lane West just past Lawford Road on 8 August 1966 prior to travelling back along Wimborne Road to the Square and the Triangle. The overhead wiring from Wimborne Road along Lawford Road can be seen in the background.

David Pearson

(Below) Service 32 travelled much of the length of Castle Lane (only service 33 traversed the whole of Castle Lane) from the Broadway Hotel at the junction with Charminster Road past the entrance to Castle Lane (Mallard Road) Depot through to Iford. Rebuilt BUT9641T no. 235 (KLJ335) pauses at the northernmost stop in Charminster Road, virtually opposite Luckham Road, on its way back into the town centre on 6 September 1966. The half-timbered front of the Broadway Hotel, still in business today, can be seen in the background. David Pearson

259

roundabout. The trailing and facing frogs remained in situ until March 1967, but it was accordingly no longer possible to travel all around the roundabout.

Removal of wiring along Wimborne Road now commenced with the "straight" stretches being cut down on Friday mornings, and the more complex sections and junctions on Sunday mornings, Cemetery Junction being dealt with on Sunday 30 October 1966. By 10 November 1966 the last of the traction poles in Charminster Avenue had been removed. In November 1966 the number of wired lanes inside Castle Lane (Mallard Road) Depot building was reduced from three to two.

On 22 November 1966 the NTA was granted permission to operate their preserved Portsmouth BUT9611T trolleybus 313 on the remaining system in spring 1967 at a charge of 6d per mile for traction current, subject to the legal position and appropriate insurance cover. The decision to permit "foreign" trolleybus operation was encouraged by Ian Cunningham, who saw the opportunity to create much goodwill in making Bournemouth a haven of electric street traction.

The FMPTE advised that the MoL had authorised implementation of the 9s 3d per week wage increase for drivers, conductors, semi-skilled and unskilled depot staff as from 16 January 1967. The increase to the undertaking represented £17,450 in a full year.

The first trolleybus (273) to display external advertising appeared on 11 December 1966, long after the first motorbuses had received such adornments.

On 4 December 1966, the Overhead Department managed to remove all wiring in Charminster Road from Cemetery Junction to Five Ways in just four hours. It then continued to the Broadway Hotel, where some of the junction was removed, and cut down the Five Ways complex and the Luckham Road reverser. Span wires and hangers remained from Five Ways northwards. By 5 December 1966, wiring had been removed from the foot of Richmond Hill along Wimborne Road up to, but excluding, the complex Winton Banks junction. All frogs remained at the Square. Anchor wires had been attached to the

overhead at Lawford Road at the point where the projected Bear Cross line was to have branched off and continued along Wimborne Road.

The Overhead Department concentrated on removing as much valuable copper trolley wire as possible in order that it could be sold within the 1966/1967 financial year. By early January 1967 Charminster Road was completely clear and during the rest of that month Castle Lane West from Broadway to Lawford Road was removed. From the beginning of the year both gangs worked most Sunday mornings and on 22 January 1967 they removed the complex Winton Banks "umbrella". Between 6am and 11.30am the two gangs removed five facing frogs, five trailing frogs and three crossings, a total of 13 line assemblies which had been concentrated in a distance of just 30yd. On the next two Sundays the northbound wires from Winton Banks to Ensbury Park Road junction were removed as was the southbound pair from Redhill Crescent to Ensbury Park Road junction.

By 4 February 1967 both ends of Lawford Road had been dismantled. Both wires had been cut down between Lawford Road and Broadway Hotel (inclusive), and at Ensbury Park Road junction, Redhill Crescent and Broadway Hotel, all that was left of the junctions were the parts of the frogs and crossovers which had formed the main lines. The Columbia Road-Winton route along Kinson Road, Wallisdown Road and Talbot Road was still intact, as was the Winton Banks loop, but both were anchored off and neither was connected to anything in particular. Wiring along Castle Lane West from Broadway Hotel to Mallard Road remained intact, and the hand-operated frog in the westbound wiring from Iford providing access to Mallard Road and Castle Lane Depot still appeared to be set for straight-on towards the Broadway Hotel.

In the meantime, work was proceeding on realigning the westbound wiring in Castle Lane West, retained for depot access purposes, between Cooper Dean roundabout and Strouden Park in preparation for road widening. Some new traction poles had been planted and span wires with new hangers attached,

No. 284, by now devoid of its Sunbeam manufacturer's plate enters Bath Road at the Lansdowne on its way from Tuckton to the Square. To the left of the Royal London House can be seen Holdenhurst Road with no evidence of trolleybus overhead equipment, whilst to the right of the photograph preparations for the construction of the Roundhouse Hotel on the site of the Imperial Hotel have begun. (26 July 1967) David Pearson

On 26 July 1967 Sunbeam MF2B no. 286 has reached the Carbery Avenue turning circle as it heads east along Cranleigh Road towards Tuckton roundabout at the junction of Tuckton Road with Belle Vue Road on service 23. The indicator blinds have been changed, correctly, for the return journey as an interworking service 22.

David Pearson

Although Belle Vue Road continued from Southbourne Cross Roads to Tuckton by the beginning of the 20th century, the trams followed Foxholes Road as the descent towards the River Stour was less steep with gentle bends (unlike Belle Vue Road at that time - the most curvaceous part now being known as Belle Vue Crescent) and thus the replacing trolleybuses did likewise. In April 1967 Sunbeam MF2B no. 285 (YLJ285), just seven years old, pulls out of Foxholes Road into Belle Vue Road, Southbourne, on its way west to the Square.

NTA Collection (R.F. Mack)

but elsewhere adjustable hangers were used to support the existing wiring in order that it could be slewed over when necessary. Realignment for trolleybuses heading east towards Iford took place on the night of Saturday/Sunday 11/12 March 1967, whilst that for vehicles travelling towards the depot took place in three stages: in the afternoon of 23 March 1967, on the night of 25/26 March 1967 and in the morning of 31 March 1967. This involved the first night work for some 15 months.

Craftsmen benefited from an increase previously agreed with the FMPTE from 26 December 1966 estimated to cost the undertaking £2,000 pa. The MoT wrote advising that the Government White Paper provisions for a prices and incomes standstill would end in June 1967, but that it remained important that rises in bus fares should be avoided.

In November 1966 the Transport Committee first heard of the Southbourne Traffic Management Scheme, which proposed to prohibit all traffic, except BCT buses, on a short section of Southbourne Grove, the introduction of one-way traffic in various roads nearby, parking limitations and the provision of traffic and pedestrian-operated signals. A three-month experiment was suggested, potentially extendable to six months, during which period the Council would consider further extension or permanency. Plans, announced in February 1967, for the Scheme to commence on 1 July 1967, foresaw a ban on all traffic except *"Trolley Vehicles and Public Service Vehicles belonging to the Bournemouth Corporation"*, emergency vehicles and postal delivery vans, from the north end of Southbourne Grove between a point just east of its junction with Beresford Road to the junction with Chestnut Avenue. Of greater concern were plans to make the following roads equipped for trolleybus operation one-way in the direction shown:

Beresford Road, south-westerly
Parkwood Road, north-easterly
Seabourne Road, north-westerly (from its junction with Beresford Road to its junction with Parkwood Road)
Southbourne Road, south-easterly

These proposals meant that, as a result, the Fisherman's Walk terminal loop along Southbourne Road and Parkwood Road, available to trolleybuses from Beaufort Road and Tuckton, would be wired in the opposite direction to the new traffic flow, whilst the Fisherman's Walk turning circle in Wentworth Avenue would no longer be accessible.

On 21 February 1967 the brewers, Strong & Co. of Romsey Ltd., gave notice to terminate the tenancy of the yard at the Dolphin Hotel, Christchurch, in which the trolleybus turntable was located, with effect from 30 April 1970. The agreement was subsequently extended until 10 June 1973, the turntable being used by the replacing motorbuses.

By early March 1967 all overhead wiring (including spans) had been removed from Richmond Hill, Wimborne Road, Lawford Road, Charminster Road, and Castle Lane from Wimborne Road to Charminster Road. The frogs and wires had also gone from the junction of Columbia Road with Kinson Road. The only traction poles to be removed (in late May) were on Richmond Hill and in Wimborne Road up to Cemetery Junction, whilst a few had gone in Charminster Road.

On Saturday 11 March 1967, preserved ex-Portsmouth BUT9611T trolleybus 313 (ERV938), which had last run on 27 July 1963 to close the Portsmouth system, arrived at Castle Lane (Mallard Road) Depot towed by preserved ex-Rotherham

Bristol L5G tower wagon CET440. Following a trial the next day, which included a visit to the rarely-used Horseshoe Common turning circle, it operated an NTA enthusiasts' tour on Sunday 30 April 1967 lasting eight hours and including virtually all surviving wiring, including that within Boscombe (Pokesdown) Depot.

On 14 March 1967 it was decided that 185 Setright "Shortrange" self-printing ticket machines be purchased with delivery commencing in September 1967. The hire of Bell Punch "Ultimate" machines was to be discontinued. No change in the sale of weekly return tickets was proposed, but the General Manager was asked to investigate the introduction of monthly returns, together with alternative proposals as to the method and place of sale of such tickets. Having considered the General Manager's report, the Transport Committee, at its 30 May 1967 meeting, authorised the introduction of 50-journey tickets valid for three months at a 20% discount for single fares of 9d or over, sold at Transport Department premises or through the post, and 12-journey tickets valid for two weeks at 16²/₃% discount for single fares of 9d or over, sold only on Transport Department premises. This package was introduced on 4 September 1967, replacing weekly tickets.

Paper banner advertisements for Whiteways Devon Cyder were fitted to the upper-deck side panels of Sunbeam MF2Bs 270-2, 277, 279, 295-298, 300, 302 in April 1967. Numbers 269, 282, 283 (nearside) and 272, 276, 283, 284, 296 (offside) now carried banner advertisements for Watney's Red Barrel whilst Acriflex Antiseptic Cream took space on 270 (offside) and 280 (nearside). Advertisements also increasingly appeared on the lower panels beneath the rear platform window requiring the rear fleet number transfers to reapplied at a lower level.

During the night of 13/14 May 1967, the two westernmost of the three surviving overhead loops at the stops in Gervis Place were combined into one by removing a facing frog and a trail frog to create a single loop for services 20-24. The remaining facing frog was set for all trolleybuses to enter the loop, so that only vehicles proceeding straight through Gervis Place needed to have the frog handle pulled. The third loop was retained for parking out of service trolleybuses.

A power failure from 11.45 to 12.45pm on Friday 26 May 1967 immobilised trolleybuses and cut off electricity to all other users.

On 18 May 1967 a private tour, organised by Graham Teasdill, professionally the Curator of Bournemouth's Russell-Cotes Art Gallery & Museum, but also a transport enthusiast, using preserved open-top Sunbeam MS2 202, operated Bournemouth Pier-Exeter Road-Square-Triangle-Square-Old Christchurch Road-Gervis Place-Bournemouth Square-Old Christchurch Road-Lansdowne-Bath Road-Bournemouth Pier for the South Eastern Federation of Museums and Art Galleries. The vehicle was loaned by the NTA and driven by Mr Peter Lepine-Smith.

A fatal accident took place in Seabourne Road on 5 June 1967 involving a trolleybus, a motor cycle and a pedestrian. The front of the trolleybus had to be jacked up to release the motor cyclist.

The guard wires on many sections of the erstwhile route through Wallisdown, where telephone wires crossed the trolleybus conductor wires, were removed in May/June 1967. On Sunday morning 2 July 1967, the trolley wires at Wallisdown Cross Roads were removed together with about 100yd each way along Kinson Road and Wallisdown Road. Span wires were removed the following Friday. On Fridays 21 July and 28 July

1967, the negative trolley wire was removed from Winton along Talbot Road and part of Wallisdown Road. Unlike most previous trolley wire removal, instead of being cut off at each side of every mechanical ear, the wire was first unscrewed from all the ears and then removed in one long section, presumably for reuse. In July 1967 work was resumed in burning-off redundant traction standards in Charminster Road.

During August 1967 further traction poles were burned-off in Charminster Road, and more lengths of negative trolley wire cut down in the Wallisdown area along Kinson Road, Columbia Road, part of Wallisdown Road, and part of Ensbury Park Road. Another minor alteration in August 1967 was the replacement of two traction poles at the junction of Tuckton Road with Southbourne Road, due to the original poles blocking a driveway and a road respectively, in new housing and flat development at that corner.

The winter timetable came into operation on 4 September 1967. Trolleybuses operated as in the preceding winter, i.e. no service 20 or 24 on Sundays.

At the beginning of September 1967 work commenced on overhead alterations at Fisherman's Walk in preparation for the new Southbourne Traffic Management Scheme one-way system. During the night of Saturday/Sunday 9/10 September 1967, a trailing frog was inserted in the eastbound (towards Tuckton) wiring outside the Ravenscourt Hotel at the junction of Southbourne Road with Beaufort Road, and a second trailing frog in the westbound wiring (towards Fisherman's Walk) at the junction of Beresford Road with New Park Road. A facing frog in the Southbourne Road single-line turning loop wiring (for use later) was added on Wednesday 13 September 1967 just to the west of the crossover above the junction of Southbourne Road with Beresford Road and New Park Road. From 10 September 1967, the section of single-line wiring along Parkwood Road and Southbourne Road, i.e. the Fisherman's Walk terminal loop available to trolleybuses from Beaufort Road and Tuckton, was electrically isolated by inserting a breaker at each end of the section. This enabled essential work to be carried out on this section, which eventually became one-way in the opposite direction to that previously used.

Trolleybuses from the Square terminating at Fisherman's

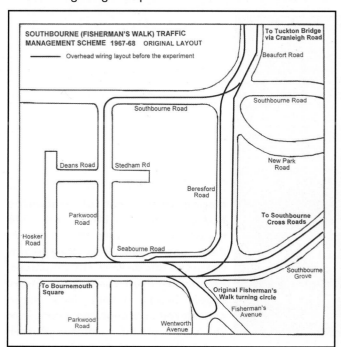

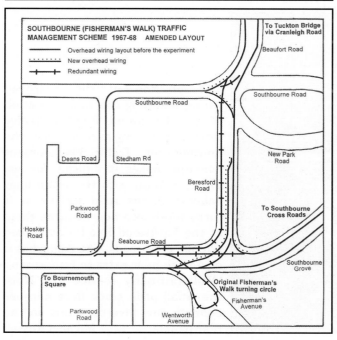

The overhead wiring layout represents that in use from the introduction of trolleybus services along Beaufort Road and Cranleigh Road on 16 August 1948 and which remained intact and in use in this form until 9 September 1967. The Parkwood Road and Southbourne Road single-line turning loop wiring was used by trolleybuses from Tuckton in an anti-clockwise direction. The original Fisherman's Walk turning circle at the east end of Wentworth Avenue came into use on 21 November 1935 whilst the overhead wiring extension along Southbourne Grove to Southbourne Cross Roads opened shortly afterwards on 23 December 1935.

The Parkwood Road and Southbourne Road single-line turning loop wiring was changed for use in a clockwise direction by all eastbound trolleybuses whether continuing along Beaufort Road to Tuckton or along Southbourne Grove to Southbourne Cross Roads and Christchurch. Trolleybuses from Tuckton could no longer terminate at Fisherman's Walk. Seabourne Road eastbound between Parkwood Road and Beresford Road was closed to trolleybuses and all eastbound journeys followed the Parkwood Road and Southbourne Road loop on 27 October 1967.

New wiring was erected in Beresford Road for both a left turn into Southbourne Grove and a right turn into Seabourne Road. Perforce the original Fisherman's Walk turning circle was no longer accessible and trolleybuses terminating at Fisherman's Walk used the Parkwood Road and Southbourne Road turning loop wiring.

In order to comply with the short-lived Southbourne Traffic Management Scheme all eastbound trolleybuses traversed Fisherman's Walk by way of Parkwood Road, Southbourne Road and Beresford Road before rejoining the previous route along Soutbourne Grove. Here Sunbeam MF2B no. 301 turns out of Seabourne Road into Parkwood Road on its way to Christchurch.   Michael Russell

Having turned out of Seabourne Road, Sunbeam MF2B no. 278 makes its way past the shops in Parkwood Road. The grey stains down the offside rear corner panels, emanating from the carbon insert slider heads, would have been considered unacceptable a couple of years beforehand.   Michael Russell

The position of the overhead wiring following the reconstruction of the Parkwood Road loop for clockwise running as required by the Southbourne Traffic Management Scheme makes it difficult for no. 278 to comply with the white lines painted on the road surface as it turns south into Southbourne Road at the Parkwood Road, Castlemain Avenue crossroads. The trolleybus is on a peak hour extra to Fisherman's Walk (formerly service 37). Note the small plain black fleet number beneath the advertisement on the rear panel.   Michael Russell

264

In September 1968, Sunbeam MF2B no. 282 (YLJ282) turns out of Seabourne Road into Beresford Road heading east towards Tuckton on service 23. The Southbourne Traffic Management Scheme is over and thus, the central pair of wires, although intact, is redundant; trolleybuses heading out of Beresford Road towards Seabourne Road, Pokesdown and the Square use the left hand pair of wires, a keep left bollard now being present at the road junction.   **NTA Collection (R.F. Mack)**

Walk began using Parkwood Road and Southbourne Road in the opposite direction to that previously used, together with Beresford Road, on Thursday 5 October, instead of the circle in Wentworth Avenue at the top of Fisherman's Walk itself (which was then disconnected).

The entire overhead wiring arrangement was aloft by 7 October 1967 and comprised:

a) a new facing frog and curve in the eastbound Seabourne Road wiring leading into Parkwood Road
b) a new auto frog and setter (intended for the future eastbound traffic flow) in the Southbourne Road wiring with new curves leading into Beaufort Road and Beresford Road for services 23 and 21/22 respectively
c) a new auto frog and setter in the Beresford Road westbound wiring with new curves leading into Seabourne Road for trolleybuses to turn both left (eastbound) towards Southbourne Cross Roads and right (westbound); trolleybuses heading for Pokesdown would, in future, pass to the right of the existing traffic island.

The complete work was tested on Sunday 15 October 1967. As the Traffic Management Scheme was envisaged for an initial six-month experimental period, the majority of the disused overhead wiring was left intact unused or strung above that actually in use, whilst only two small lengths of wiring were actually removed.

At about 6.30pm on Wednesday 18 October 1967 a sewer collapsed, resulting in a gas main burst, at the junction of Parkwood Road with Seabourne Road. Workmen found a hole twenty feet deep under the road. Due to the risk of an explosion, all trolleybus services were immediately withdrawn and replaced by motorbuses using alternative routes. The entire trolleybus fleet was housed at Castle Lane (Mallard Road) Depot for the

first time ever, whilst the replacement motorbuses were based temporarily at Boscombe. All trolleybuses were off the road until Friday 27 October 1967, except for two vehicles each day which operated morning peak hour journeys on service 20 and returned to Castle Lane in the early evening peak on service 23 by inexplicably using the new wiring at Southbourne. When full trolleybus operation resumed on 27 October 1967 vehicles immediately started to use the new wiring layout although its introduction had only been planned for 12 November 1967 to coincide with the start of the scheme. No trolleybuses at all operated on Sunday 22 October 1967, when an enthusiasts' tour on open-top Sunbeam MS2 202 and BUT9641T 246 had to be postponed until 5 November 1967.

On 16 October 1967 the Transport Committee learned that trolleybus abandonment would be completed during 1968. Mr Cunningham was authorised to make suitable commemorative arrangements provided that they were at no cost to the undertaking. The events of April 1969 were very much of his own initiative, and were to prove profitable!

From mid-October 1967, the Overhead Department resumed burning off redundant traction poles in Charminster Road about six inches below the surface of the footpath using an oxy-acetylene cutting torch, and removing wires in Columbia Road and Ensbury Park Road. The last pole in Charminster Road was burned off on Wednesday 22 November 1967. On Fridays 27 October 1967, 3 November 1967 and 10 November 1967, wiring was removed from Ensbury Park Road, followed on 17 November 1967 by that in Kinson Road. On the morning of Sunday 19 November 1967, all running and span wires were cut down by the Ensbury Park Hotel and for about 100yd along Columbia Road. More wiring along Columbia Road was removed on Friday 24 November 1967. Traction poles in Alma Road, Winton Banks, were burned off on 23 November

1967 and on the next day the Overhead Department started removing most of the remaining wiring in the Wallisdown area.

The electricity generating station with its prominent chimney at the former Central Depot, Southcote Road, was demolished in late 1967 whilst, on 1 December 1967, work started on the construction of a new roundabout at the junction of Gervis Road and Grove Road with Bath Road at the top of Bath Hill.

At the 21 November 1967 Transport Committee meeting the General Manager reported that he was proposing to discontinue use of Boscombe (Pokesdown) Depot at the earliest opportunity.

The *Bournemouth Evening Echo* reported on 30 December 1967 that *"Pokesdown Depot, the town's last link with the tram era, will close on 31 December 1967. To mark the occasion a preserved trolleybus (246) bought about a year ago by Mr Richard Cromwell of the National Trolleybus Association will make a tour. It will be visiting Pokesdown Depot throughout the day and when it makes the final departure from there at about 4pm there will be a ceremony in which a ribbon will be put across the entrance to symbolise the closure.*

"Mr Cromwell's trolleybus will be on the road again 21 January 1968 when it is being hired by the Transport Trust and during the last 8 months of trolleybus operation in Bournemouth, at least three other preserved trolleybuses will visit the town".

Pokesdown Depot (officially always known as Boscombe Depot) closed on 31 December 1967 with a special ceremony just after 4pm, the last vehicle to operate in and out of the depot (vehicles always reversed out into Christchurch Road under the guidance of an inspector) being preserved BUT9641T 246. The closure led to new overhead wiring being erected to enable westbound trolleybuses entering service from Castle Lane (Mallard Road) Depot to turn left from Christchurch Road into Seabourne Road, outside Pokesdown Fire Station. The left-hand facing frog in Christchurch Road was inserted on

the night of 5/6 December 1967, and the trail frog in Seabourne Road on 12/13 December 1967. Twin-line hangers were inserted in existing span-wires on 14 December 1967, and the conductor wire was strung up on the night of 16/17 December 1967. A trial run took place on Friday 29 December 1967. The twelve trolleybuses which had terminated at Boscombe Depot each night (vehicles were never allocated to specific depots) operated out of Castle Lane Depot as from 1 January 1968.

As at 1 January 1968, trolleybuses continued to operate on the following services:

20 Bournemouth Square, Gervis Place - Lansdowne - Boscombe Gardens - Boscombe - Pokesdown - Iford - Jumpers - Christchurch, Church Street
(weekdays and summer Sundays 2pm - 10pm only)

21 Bournemouth Square, Gervis Place - Lansdowne - Boscombe Gardens - Boscombe - Pokesdown - Fisherman's Walk - Southbourne - Tuckton Bridge - Christchurch, Church Street

22 Bournemouth Square, Gervis Place - Lansdowne - Boscombe Gardens - Boscombe - Pokesdown - Fisherman's Walk - Southbourne Cross Roads - Tuckton, Tuckton Road

23 Bournemouth Square, Gervis Place - Lansdowne - Boscombe Gardens - Boscombe - Pokesdown - Fisherman's Walk - Tuckton, Tuckton Road

24 Bournemouth Square, Gervis Place - Lansdowne - Boscombe Gardens - Boscombe - Pokesdown - Iford - Jumpers
(weekday morning peak hours and summer Sunday morning 10am-1pm only)

SOUTHBOURNE (FISHERMAN'S WALK) TRAFFIC MANAGEMENT SCHEME 1967-68 POST EXPERIMENT LAYOUT

From 12 February 1968 Seabourne Road between Parkwood Road and Beresford Road was re-opened to trolleybuses which reverted, in part, to running in the same manner as prior to 27 October 1967. The original Fisherman's Walk turning circle remained out of use and trolleybuses terminating at Fisherman's Walk continued to use the Parkwood Road and Southbourne Road turning loop wiring.

The left-hand 25° hand-operated facing frog for the turn into Parkwood Road from Seabourne Road eastbound which had been installed with a fixed bias for the turn was altered to a bias for straight on along Seabourne Road and it became necessary to pull for entry into Parkwood Road. The facing frog, auto frog setter and apparatus for the turn into Beaufort Road from Southbourne Road were removed; henceforth eastbound trolleybuses on the single-line in Southbourne Road could only turn right into Beresford Road although much of the experimental layout remained aloft at this point.

The right-hand 25° facing frog, auto frog setter and apparatus installed in Beresford Road for the turn into Seabourne Road westbound towards Pokesdown and into Southbourne Grove towards Southbourne Cross Roads and Christchurch was disconnected and the frog given a fixed bias for the original westbound wiring along Beresford Road. The central, third line fell into disuse and henceforth trolleybuses turning right into Seabourne Road reverted to the original westbound wiring. A hand-operated frog with right-hand bias was installed at the west end of Beresford Road although in practice the wiring for the left turn into Southbourne Grove became redundant. Again, the experimental layout remained aloft.

Sunbeam MF2B no. 277 (WRU277) turns out of Christchurch Road into Seabourne Road at Pokesdown Fire Station on 19 April 1969 on its way to take up service as a 23 to Carbery Avenue. The additional wiring for this turn was erected in December 1967 and enabled trolleybuses from Castle Lane (Mallard Road) Depot to operate duties previously operated by Boscombe (Pokesdown) depot.   Robin Helliar-Symons

The Southbourne Traffic Management Scheme also created a pedestrian precinct between the south end of Seabourne Road and the north end of Southbourne Grove at Fisherman's Walk with temporary kerbstones and passenger waiting shelters in the road immediately prior to Chestnut Avenue. On 31 December 1967 Boscombe (Pokesdown) Depot closed and to mark the occasion BUT9641T no. 246, by now preserved, made a tour of the remaining system. It is seen here at the Southbourne Grove stop with a branch of the National Provincial Bank, now a public house, in the background on the corner of Chestnut Avenue.   David Chalk collection

In addition, a few unusual operations survived; for instance, on weekdays two journeys from the Square turned at Fisherman's Walk (2.42pm and 5.13pm) and one at Carbery Avenue from Pokesdown at 8.28am.

Rising costs meant that the Transport Committee now anticipated a loss of £64,000 in the coming financial year. To prevent the undertaking becoming a charge on the rates it recommended an application for fare increases to cover the loss and additional running costs which would be incurred

following the then pending wage negotiations. In due course the application was approved, resulting in a completely new fare structure, based on stages approximately 0.45-mile in length being introduced from 15 June 1968. Although the SETC did not consider the application unreasonable, they "would need to be convinced that the Corporation had implemented far-reaching improvements with regard to one-man operation of its double-deck fleet" in the case of future applications. Fifty-two double-deck motorbuses were suitable for one-man operation. The

A little further around the corner at Pokesdown Fire Station Sunbeam MF2B no. 277 (WRU277) enters Seabourne Road at Pokesdown Fire Station on 19 April 1969. The additional pair of wires joined the eastbound wiring towards Fisherman's Walk just out of view to the right hand side of the photograph.

Robin Helliar-Symons

Nos. 284 and 274, both running on service 22, meet at Fisherman's Walk in the latter days of trolleybus operation. No. 284 is disfigured with paper advertisements and both trolleybuses begin to look a little tired and dishevelled. Fisherman's Walk itself runs from the east end of Wentworth Avenue (off the photograph to the right behind no. 274), where the other terminal loop was located, and follows an old track through the pines to the sea where there is a cliff lift down to the beach.   Roger G. Funnell (courtesy Mrs D. Funnell and Rodney Funnell)

Commissioners conceded that £70,000 additional revenue was needed. Even with these increases, there would be a deficiency of £11,000 by 31 March 1969, reducing the undertaking's reserves to £32,000.

On 2 January 1968 the full Council revoked the County Borough of Bournemouth (Various Roads, Southbourne) (No. 1) Experimental Traffic Order 1967. Motorbuses were substituted for trolleybuses on Sunday 11 February 1968 while workmen removed the temporary traffic signs and kerbstones which had created the pedestrian precinct. From 12 February 1968, trolleybuses reverted to the routes which had been in operation prior to 27 October 1967, with the exception of trolleybuses turning at Fisherman's Walk. These continued to use the Parkwood Road turning circle in the clockwise direction. The turning circle to the south of Seabourne Road in Wentworth Avenue at the top of Fisherman's Walk was declared permanently out of use. Sunbeam MF2B 275 was recorded as being the last to use the amended wiring in the Southbourne area, on 10 February 1968.

In January 1968 the erstwhile service 25 passing loop in Christchurch Road, Boscombe, together with the frogs leading to and from the disused Boscombe Depot, were replaced with normal overhead, resulting in an uninterrupted run from the Lansdowne to Pokesdown junction. At the junction of Portman Road with Christchurch Road, Boscombe sections of running wire replacing the frogs were joined by two end fittings bolted together instead of the usual mid-span splices. All that now remained of the service 25 wiring was a frog at the west end of Avenue Road where the eastbound wiring from Poole Hill had joined that on the north side of the Triangle, and frogs at the Lansdowne (the redundant facing frog for service 25 at the Lansdowne roundabout was subsequently removed

on Sunday 26 May 1968). The last wiring in Wallisdown was removed on 19 February 1968. On 1 March 1968 the positive, and on 8 March 1968 the negative, trolley wire was cut down in Castle Lane West eastwards from Broadway to Mallard Road. Dismantling of span wire on this stretch started on 12 March and, by 15 March 1968, all wiring had gone. In the period 25-28 March 1968 traction poles in Wimborne Road, Winton and Moordown were burned off.

At lunchtime on 16 April 1968, a service 23 trolleybus dewired at a trailing frog at Fisherman's Walk, causing a 30-minute power failure. At one time 16 trolleybuses were caught on either side of the section and, to restore the timetable, one vehicle was turned at Southbourne Cross Roads, two at Fisherman's Walk and two were terminated short at Jumpers, displaying service 24, instead of continuing to Christchurch as service 20s.

Trolleybus 286 re-entered service on 9 May 1968 after a 39-day "rest" for no known reason. 274, which had been involved in an accident on 8 December 1967, was under repair, although a repaint was not planned. "Whiteway's Devon Cyder" advertisements were now displayed by 13 vehicles, namely 268, 271, 273, 277, 280, 282, 283, 285, 286, 295, 296, 301 and 302.

Even at this late stage in the trolleybus system's history, there were occasions when it was necessary to erect new traction poles: one at the site of the new roundabout at the top of Bath Hill (junction of Bath Road with Gervis Road and Grove Road) at Easter 1968, one in Castle Lane West, Strouden Park, in May 1968 to permit construction of an access road to a new shopping centre ("The Hampshire Centre") and one in Stour Road, Christchurch, in June 1968, where a new road was built. On the other hand, redundant poles in Kinson Road, Wallisdown, were burned off in May 1968 for pavement resurfacing, while in mid-July 1968 work resumed in burning off traction poles in

Sunbeam MF2B no. 296 (296LJ) climbs up Boscombe Hill from the stop at Boscombe Gardens and the Linden Hall Hydro Hotel heading east towards central Boscombe, Iford and Christchurch. The feeder pillar at the base of the traction pole P100 in the foreground was known as Boscombe Hill and provided traction power to the section of Christchurch Road from Derby Road to Palmerston Hotel.

Roger G. Funnell (courtesy Mrs D. Funnell and Rodney Funnell)

Wimborne Road at Moordown.

The summer timetable came into operation on 2 June 1968 and the trolleybus short working to Carbery Avenue (referred to above) ceased, although vehicles continued to turn there on Sundays at 12.30pm and 2.15pm. It became noticeable that more motorbuses were running as extras on trolleybus routes.

In an article which appeared in the 15 June 1968 issue of the *Bournemouth Times*, Leslie Amos wrote: *"The fleet of trolleybuses was doomed by the nationalisation of public transport. The town council, expecting to have its buses taken over, transferred financial reserves to the rate fund and created a debt in the building of Castle Lane Depot for the government of the day to take over. But Bournemouth was left holding its transport undertaking and a crippling loan liability. The electrical generating station was the worse for wear after the war and with reserve funds long spent by the ratepayers and the repayments on Castle Lane Depot already taking the cream off the fares receipts, the council had again to cut itself a huge chunk of humble pie. Following a lightning strike at the power station arrangements were made to take current from the electricity board and soon Bournemouth and the other towns which were also no longer generating their own power had their former cheapest-running trolleybuses costing more than motorbuses.*

"And as town after town got rid of its trolleys, the manufacturers cut down production and raised prices. Then spares became short and expensive, and overhead wires and other gear also became special-supply equipment with matching price tags. 17 years ago Bournemouth had 127 trolleybuses. It dropped the fleet to 93 when facing up to the problem of the old power station, then bought 20 brand new replacements between July 1958 and January 1959, to make the fleet 113. In 1959 it bought 7 which Brighton had redundant and 10 more new ones at the end of 1959. In fact 9 new trolleys were delivered between August and September 1962. Now presumably the fleet of trolleys is the 19 bought since September 1959. And after 10 of them have done 9 years' service and the rest 6 years—built to last 20 years at least, they say—these, too, will be towed away for breaking up.

"Only the Boscombe-Southbourne-Tuckton areas still enjoy the trolleys. The people there have had the luck of the last of the silent, smokeless, gasless, most civilised of conveyances for a few years longer than most of us. Very soon they too must close their windows and, if they travel by bus, take the bruises suffered by the initiates of the rough ride".

On 2 July 1968 the contract with MCW for the supply of 17 double-deck motorbus bodies during 1968 was terminated by mutual agreement and a substitute agreed with Walter Alexander & Co. (Coachbuilders) Ltd. for delivery in December 1968/January 1969. This provided a "stay of execution" for the remaining trolleybuses and as a consequence it was announced that electric operations would continue until spring 1969. The *Bournemouth Evening Echo* asked on 23 August 1968 if one trolleybus route could be kept as a tourist attraction and drew a comparison with Blackpool electric trams and Douglas horse trams.

The winter timetable, with effect from 8 September 1968, depicted Sunbeam MF2B 270 on the cover together with the statement "Last Trolleybus Year—the trolleybuses will be replaced by motorbuses in 1969". Various historical snippets were included and service 20-24 timings were titled "Trolleybus Service", on the initiative of the Assistant Traffic Superintendent, David Chalk.

Boscombe (Pokesdown) Depot is empty and devoid of overhead wiring as Sunbeam MF2B no. 285 (YLJ285), a September 1959 delivery, passes heading east along Christchurch Road. In just a few yards the trolleybus will turn into Seabourne Road and continue through Fisherman's Walk and Southbourne before crossing Tuckton Bridge and terminating on Christchurch turntable on a service 21 working.

Roger G. Funnell (courtesy Mrs D. Funnell and Rodney Funnell)

At about 9.30am on 14 September 1968, Sunbeam MF2B 275 suffered electrical damage in Pokesdown due to a lightning strike nearby and was withdrawn from service, thus providing replacement half-shafts for 276, which was reinstated after a period in storage. Following an accident, 279 received front panels from withdrawn 258. In the period 15-17 October 1968, six of the nine vehicles (272, 275, 277, 280, 281, 283, 295, 300 and 301) which had retained their triangular Sunbeam maker's badge had them removed. The Corporation had previously sold the badges to enthusiasts at the princely sum of 2s 6d each (the author has one and the official receipt!).

The 17 September 1968 Transport Committee meeting authorised the General Manager to handle an application to purchase five redundant Sunbeam MF2B trolleybuses without advertising for tenders. The application came from Teesside Municipal Transport which had taken on responsibility for the Tees-side Railless Traction Board's compact trolleybus network on the south bank of the River Tees downstream from Middlesbrough. However, they had already committed to purchase five of Reading's front-entrance Sunbeam F4As. It is known that Reading Council put Teesside under pressure to honour their contract and Bournemouth heard no more.

The last redundant traction poles in Wimborne Road were burned off on 18 September 1968. Those in Lawford Road were removed on 4 October 1968 with those in Castle Lane West between Mallard Road and Wimborne Road coming next.

In November 1968, trolleybuses 269, 281 (the last to be repainted) and 302 were withdrawn due to the lack of replacement half-shafts. The first ten Sunbeam MF2Bs and 275 were increasingly cannibalised for minor parts such as driver's rear view mirrors, windscreen wipers, seats and window frames.

The *Bournemouth Times* of 28 December 1968 recorded that *"Bournemouth trolleybuses were expected to go off the road for all time in September 1968 but were reprieved due to the late delivery of diesel buses to replace them. They will finally enter Mallard Road Depot next spring and electric current over the last 12 miles of wiring Square-Christchurch will be switched off. Thousands of people are sad at the end of the era of silent, fumeless, smooth-running electric cars. The Corporation is arranging a decent 'funeral'. There will be a final parade on the last-run day, special tickets to become souvenirs for passengers, and some sort of civic 'requiem'."*

Mr Peter Lepine-Smith, an enthusiast in possession of a trolley vehicle driver's licence and who operated a $^1/_3$-scale miniature Reading trolleybus in his Great Bookham, Surrey, garden, volunteered to work as a trolleybus driver in Bournemouth. In agreement with the TGWU this was permitted for five weeks in autumn 1968, as he drove only on middle/late shifts which were never popular with the regular drivers. The same gentleman, trading as the Maypine Trolleybus Company, used his Scammell lorry to tow the RTS's preserved Sunbeam MS2 212 from its storage in Walsall to Reading on 19 January 1969, and, on 25 January 1969, onwards to Bournemouth, to operate tours over the remains of its home system in February 1969.

During the course of the winter there were two further enthusiasts' tours. Rotherham Daimler CTE6 44 (FET618) operated in December 1968, whilst on 26 January 1969 Bournemouth BUT9641T 246 and Reading Sunbeam S7 174 (ERD145), two of the trolleybus exhibits at the 1950 Commercial Motor Transport Exhibition, were reunited after 18 years for a joint tour of the system.

Looking back, Ian Cunningham was adamant that there was never a conscious decision to cut back on vehicle maintenance

On 26 March 1969, a rather careworn Sunbeam MF2B, no. 285 (YLJ285), turns out of Bath Road into Westover Road in front of the Royal Bath Hotel. Although bereft of its Sunbeam manufacturer's badge, the trolleybus is without advertisements and still retains its Bournemouth coat of arms on the upper deck side panels and straw coloured plain Gill Sans fleet numbers with gold edges beneath the offside headlamp. The Bath Hotel was the first hotel, albeit smaller than today, to open in the new resort of Bournemouth on 28 June 1838, the day of Queen Victoria's Coronation. The "Royal" was added to the title after the Prince of Wales, later King Edward VII, stayed there in 1856. Other illustrious guests have included David Lloyd George, Benjamin Disraeli and Oscar Wilde.

David Pearson

271

(Above) Although following the rule of the road, westbound no. 274's trolley heads are attached to the eastbound running wires as it pulls out of Church Street into High Street, Christchurch during road repairs on 26 March 1969.

David Pearson

(Left) Having passed the road works using the "wrong" pair of running wires, two inspectors prepare to transfer the trolley booms of no. 274 to the correct pair of wires for the westbound journey along High Street, Christchurch and then onwards to Bournemouth Square on service 20 (26 March 1969). David Pearson

and no short-cuts were taken; indeed, he was proud that there was never a serious accident or fatality which could be attributed to poor maintenance or technical inadequacy. Nonetheless, by now maintenance of the remaining 25 trolleybuses (268, 270-274, 276-280, 282-287, 295-301, 303) had become minimal, many vehicles having defective destination blind illumination and dewirement indicators. An overview of the fleet indicated:

268 unused (reason unknown)

271, 278, 286, 296 remained respectable

271, 279, 280, 282, 286, 295, 296, 300, 301, 303 in the best mechanical order

271, 296 were noted for their rapid acceleration

273 had an exceptionally leaky windscreen

274, 296 were sluggish

280, 282, 300 were speedy

280 the only trolleybus retaining olive green lining (with a black appearance)

287, 297 suffering from worn shock absorbers

297 noted for various different hues of primrose due to accident repairs

298 the only member of the final batch to have been repainted (in 1966)

The last of the redundant traction poles in Castle Lane West, between Mallard Road and Lawford Road, were removed on 7 January 1969. From 8 January 1969, the Overhead Department was busy, almost daily, removing traction poles in the Wallisdown area. Talbot Road and Wallisdown Road were cleared by the

end of January 1969 and it was expected that Columbia Road and Ensbury Park Road would be cleared by early March 1969.

On 26 March 1969 road resurfacing in Christchurch High Street led to "wrong-wire" running by trolleybuses leaving the turntable and returning to Bournemouth using the eastbound wiring.

The end was, indeed, approaching. On 3 April 1969, workshop staff decorated the upper deck side panels of Sunbeam MF2B 278 with boards carrying the wording "LAST WEEK OF BOURNEMOUTH TROLLEYBUSES", the upper deck rear panels with "LAST SERVICE SATURDAY 19TH APRIL 1969" and, at the front encroaching into the window area "BCT" beneath which appeared the Borough coat of arms and then the dates "1933-1969". All the boards were festooned with coloured lights borrowed from Blackpool Corporation Transport, where they were normally used to illuminate trams. The vehicle operated in normal service throughout the Last Trolleybus Week, making an impressive sight in the evenings.

The Last Trolleybus Week (14-19 April 1969) featured a trolleybus-operated special service from Bournemouth Pier to Castle Lane (Mallard Road) Depot via Boscombe, Iford and Castle Lane East, outbound via Exeter Road, Bournemouth Square and Old Christchurch Road, and inbound via Bath Road. Departing from a separately signed stop outside the Pier Approach Baths (starting point of the 39 in better days), trolleybuses operated an hourly service leaving Bournemouth Pier at 30 minutes past the hour (except 1.30pm) between 10.30am and 4.30pm, and leaving Castle Lane Depot on the hour between 10am and 4pm (except 1pm). Passengers could

Sunbeam MF2B no. 296 (296LJ) passes over the pedestrian "Zebra" crossing, complete with flashing Belisha beacon, in Gervis Place at The Arcade immediately prior to the junction with Westover Road. In the background is St. Peter's Church. The Arcade, originally known as the Gervis Arcade, runs between Old Christchurch Road and Gervis Place, and was built between 1866 and 1872, by the businessman Henry Joy.

Roger G. Funnell (courtesy Mrs D. Funnell and Rodney Funnell)

board or alight at any intermediate stop, the single fare being 1s 6d adults and 9d children. Destinations displayed were (outbound):

VIA
LANSDOWNE
CASTLE LANE DEPOT

or just

CASTLE LANE DEPOT

and (inbound):

BOURNEMOUTH PIER
VIA
LANSDOWNE

in both cases with the auxiliary blind displaying:

TO AND FROM SHOW

It the depot canteen, a free exhibition of trolleybus memorabilia, photographs and models had been assembled, which included extracts from Council Minutes, tenders for trolleybuses and large photographs of every type of vehicle operated, as well as one of a wartime loan in Wolverhampton. Scale drawings of Sunbeam MS2s 202 and 216 were on show,

together with a number of models, including two Sunbeam MF2Bs and a larger model of a 1950 BUT9641T chassis, with a portion of the lower deck bodywork mounted, which had been loaned by MCW.

A collection of different types of ticket issuing machines was displayed, together with souvenir tickets, including examples of the special issues for the 1937 and 1953 Coronations, sundry relevant brochures and a complete series of timetables. There was also a display of overhead wiring and underground equipment, including sections of feeder cable, a complete frog, a section box, power station units and vehicle-mounted items, including the control gear of an MF2B and a sectionalised demonstration BTH motor. Three trolleybuses already in preservation—open-top Sunbeam MS2 202, closed-top Sunbeam MS2 212 and BUT9641T 246—were parked outside the canteen from Monday until Friday.

A commemorative brochure outlining the history and development of trolleybuses in Bournemouth and including details of the vehicles operated, photographs and route map, had been prepared by BCT's David Chalk, and sold fast at 2s 6d a copy. Even Bobby's department store in Bournemouth Square had a special display in their ladies' fashions window whilst announcements about the Last Week were made on several local news or current affairs bulletins on radio and television.

On Monday 14 April 1969 trouble was experienced with the facing frog at Bournemouth Square for Commercial Road and a tower wagon was in attendance all morning. The frog was permanently fixed for Old Christchurch Road on the last day meaning that trolleybuses could no longer access the Triangle

Preparing for its next departure on service 22 to Tuckton, especially spruced-up and decorated Sunbeam MF2B no. 278 (YLJ278) is seen at the loading point in Gervis Place.
David Chalk collection

Sunbeam MF2B no. 297 (297LJ) leaves the west side of Bournemouth Pier Approach and heads up Exeter Road on its way to the Square and thence Castle Lane (Mallard Road) Depot on the special service to the exhibition.

David Chalk collection

The three Bournemouth trolleybuses already in preservation at that time, 246, 202 and 212, together with a Sunbeam MF2B (potentially from the special service to/from Bournemouth Pier) are seen parked outside the staff canteen at the rear of Castle Lane (Mallard Road) Depot. The large letters "G" and "J" in the nearside driver's cab windscreen of 202 and 212 are their individual identification letters for the closure procession on 20 April 1969.

Malcolm Pearce (G.O.P. Pearce)

or Avenue Road.

Saturday 19 April 1969 was the last day of normal service and it became necessary to operate duplicates on the special service to the Castle Lane Depot Exhibition. It was stressed, however, that any duplicates required for normal services, particularly last journeys, would be operated by motorbuses. Sunbeam MF2B 271 was the last normal service trolleybus to leave Bournemouth Square for Castle Lane Depot. Operating as the 11.25pm service 20 to Iford only, it left the Square 10 minutes late at 11.35pm, having accommodated the large queue which had accumulated at Gervis Place to board it. The penultimate departure was the delayed 11.10pm service 23 to Tuckton operated by 286. Determined to be the last scheduled trolleybus to operate in Bournemouth, the driver used the Carbery Avenue turning circle as a delaying tactic before operating via Stour Road, Barrack Road, Iford (with a dewirement at the roundabout) and Castle Lane East to Castle Lane Depot, which was reached some 10 minutes after 271. There was a considerable police presence to deter souvenir collectors.

The final day, Sunday 20 April 1969, dawned clear but bitterly cold. The first enthusiasts' tour of the day to take to the streets was the RTS's Sunbeam MS2, 212, with Driver A. Hayward of 44 years' service at the controls, which departed from Castle Lane (Mallard Road) Depot at 8.05am. No. 212 had the system to herself for an hour. Open-top MS2 202 (Driver P. Lepine-Smith) and BUT9641T 246 (driven by former Deputy Chief Inspector W. Biddlecombe) set out at 9am, whilst a special quarter-hourly tour was operated by the Corporation for the general public between Bournemouth Pier and Christchurch, from 10am until 1pm, eastbound via Iford and westbound via Southbourne, at a special return fare of 3s (children 1s 6d). Vehicles did not pick up after leaving the Pier, and business was brisk.

Vehicles in the closure procession were given black identification letters on a white card, which was displayed in the lower nearside corner of the windscreen. From 1pm trolleybuses began to make their way down to the Pier and were parked in alphabetical order, with chocks under the wheels, between the Royal Bath Hotel roundabout and the Pier Approach Baths. The identification letters were carried by:

A: 301, B: 298, C: 297, D: 303, E: 278, F: 285, G: 202, H: 246, J: 212, K: 295, L: 273, M: 274, N: 279, P: 283, Q: 280, R: 282, S: 284.

By 2pm a considerable crowd had assembled, and the Mayor of Bournemouth, Ald. Michael W. Green, JP, despatched the trolleybuses, which travelled up Exeter Road at some distance apart and not exceeding 20mph to avoid overloading the power supply. The author was in the cab of J (212) which still managed to blow out a circuit breaker on the initial ascent from the Pier! Trolleybuses P-S departed at 2.20pm, followed by K-N, F-J and finally A-E serenaded by the local Air Training Corps (ATC) band. The Mayor and the Transport Committee travelled in 301, crewed by Driver "Crash" Adams and Conductress Grace Dearmer, and accompanied for the first part of the journey by local celebrity Ken Bailey (who later achieved fame in a Yellow Buses advertising campaign), dressed in a red long-tailed coat, Union Flag waistcoat and top hat, riding a bicycle. The first three groups of trolleybuses travelled via the Square-Lansdowne-Boscombe-Pokesdown-Fisherman's Walk-Tuckton Bridge-Stour Road (Christchurch) junction-Jumpers-Iford-Castle Lane

East-Castle Lane (Mallard Road) Depot. The passengers had to alight at the depot area entrance, where a crowd had assembled. Trolleybuses K-N were marshalled under cover, whilst F-J were lined up across the front of the depot building to show the various stages in the fleet's development.

Trolleybuses A-E followed the same route to Stour Road (Christchurch) junction under police escort, and then proceeded past Christchurch Railway Station to the terminus. C and D waited outside Christchurch Town Hall whilst E was on the turntable and A and B waited in Bargates, moving forward to the terminus one after the other under the direction of an Inspector. Once off the turntable B-E waited in Bargates until rejoined by trolleybus A (301), which had been turned by the Mayor of Bournemouth. The convoy then re-formed and returned to Stour Road junction before running along Barrack Road to Jumpers, Iford, Castle Lane East and Castle Lane (Mallard Road) Depot, where they were met by the ATC band and a large crowd of well-wishers.

Trolleybus E disembarked its passengers at the depot entrance and was held temporarily on the loop running through the bus wash whilst B, C and D travelled with passengers to the rear of the depot and were immediately depoled just beyond the canteen. Trolleybus A with passengers still onboard followed and the Mayor took the controls for a circuit of the depot wiring. E was then reversed out of the bus wash and followed A around, parking outside the canteen. There followed a handover ceremony for the 17 Leyland Atlantean Alexander-bodied replacement motorbuses, followed by tea for the invited guests in the canteen.

After the final procession on 20 April 1969, most of the vehicles were left outside the depot, but they were all moved inside under their own power on Monday 21 April 1969, in the forlorn hope of sale to another operator. The last to be driven in was 278, which was moved from the bodyshop into the main garage after the removal of its special decorations on Tuesday 22 April 1969.

The 21 April 1969 edition of the *Bournemouth Evening Echo* carried the following report:

"One of the drivers in yesterday's procession was 65-year-old William Biddlecombe who in May 1933 drove LJ7701 on the opening of the first experimental route. Until last year he was Deputy Chief Inspector and Driving Instructor/Examiner of the Corporation Transport Department. In the 33 years up to his retirement he was responsible for training 1,671 trolley drivers.

"Today work will start on removing the 40 miles of overhead wires that still exist.

"Because of the difficulty in obtaining spares—one of the reasons for the death of the trolleys—the Corporation have been using 10 trolleys as spare parts donors to keep the trolley fleet alive. Apart from the difficulty in obtaining spares, the trolleys have proved uneconomic to run. New road schemes, the high cost of wiring, and the increase of privately owned cars have also contributed to the down fall of the trolley".

The *Bournemouth Evening Echo's* 26 April 1969 edition continued: *"Bournemouth Passenger Transport Association is negotiating for the purchase of 301, the last trolleybus built for use in the UK. A spokesman said that the fate of 301 and the other trolleybuses still at Mallard Road would be decided within four weeks pending the results of an experiment with one of Bournemouth's trolleys in Walsall to see if it was suitable for their requirements. Walsall were reportedly interested in purchasing the entire fleet but had yet to make an offer".*

The General Manager reported to the Transport Committee on 6 May 1969 about the final day of trolleybus operation. The Committee thanked Mr Cunningham and his staff for the arrangements, Mr D.L. Chalk for the preparation of the souvenir booklet and Mr G. Teasdill, the Curator of the Bournemouth Museums, for his assistance with the exhibition of trolleybus relics. A trolleybus was offered to the Montagu Motor Museum on permanent loan and Mr Cunningham was authorised to invite tenders for the purchase of the remainder of the fleet.

Prematurely withdrawn 269, 270 and 281 were stored in the open with 258-267 on abandonment. The final withdrawal dates for the rest of the fleet were:

19 April 1969:   268, 271, 272, 276, 277, 286, 287, 296, 299
20 April 1969:   273, 274, 278, 279, 280, 282, 283, 284, 285, 295, 297, 301, 303

A four-page leaflet advertising the Sunbeam MF2Bs accompanied by a personal letter from Ian Cunningham, was sent to all known trolleybus operators worldwide, based on their entries in the Road Passenger Transport Directory, known as the Little Red Book, but produced no replies. There had been informal contact with both Reading and Teesside, but nothing transpired, whilst the mounting of the MCW bodies on motorbus chassis had also been considered, but was discounted due to the necessity of one-man-operation. A Bradford newspaper suggested that Bradford should buy Bournemouth's bargain fleet for £150-£250 per vehicle.

Ian Cunningham later confirmed that the conversion of the Sunbeam MF2B fleet to one-man operation was never considered at Bournemouth, although Walsall's Manager, Mr R. Edgley Cox, reportedly planned this in his prototype conversion of 300 into a bimodal diesel/trolleybus (see Appendix A).

In the first two weeks after abandonment, the Overhead Department started anchoring-off various sections of wiring ready for cutting down. All the running wires in Beaufort Road and some in Castle Lane were unscrewed from the ears to facilitate the easy removal of ¼-mile lengths for sale to Teesside Municipal Transport. On 23 April 1969 wiring was removed in Mallard Road from the depot entrance to Castle Lane West to permit the removal of a single traction pole which was in the way of road construction, whilst in Pokesdown a pole was removed to provide access to the forecourt of a new filling station.

Reading had reportedly received an offer of just £20,000 for dismantling its trolleybus overhead network for its scrap value. Ian Cunningham felt that it would be more remunerative for the undertaking's own Overhead Department to carry out the task and there was no great rush as copper prices were increasing. The sole remaining overhead gang and their Superintendent, Bill Pearce, consisted of mainly long-service employees close to retirement age, and who would be unable to obtain alternative employment in the event of redundancy. It was thus agreed that the remaining overhead installation would be dismantled by the Transport Department's staff and that tenders would subsequently be invited for the disposal of redundant substation equipment, overhead wiring and underground supply cables. Ian Cunningham studied the *Financial Times* newspaper in order to sell the scrap copper running wire at the right moment: over a seven-year period £250,000 was raised from the sale of redundant trolleybus equipment and, at the same time, the undertaking had proved its social responsibility. This went a long way to meeting the costs of the replacement motorbuses, and no additional cost was put on the local ratepayers, all in an era when municipal transport undertakings were expected to make neither a profit nor a loss, but always "break-even" in their operations. As no better offers were expected, the sales of 600 and 200 traction poles respectively, and three miles

The column of trolleybuses to be used in the closure procession begin to assemble in Bath Road between the Pier Approach Baths and the Royal Bath Hotel at lunchtime on 20 April 1969.   **David Chalk collection**

of overhead wiring, to preservation societies without inviting tenders was agreed. The Finance Committee were to dispose of the Transport Department's substations and substation sites on the most satisfactory terms.

On 25 July 1969 the Works & Transportation (General) Subcommittee considered eleven tenders for the withdrawn trolleybuses and accepted those of the Transport Museum Society of Ireland for one vehicle (299) at £200; Bournemouth Passenger Transport Association (BPTA) for 301 at £150; and the tender of Wombwell Diesels Co. Ltd. for the purchase of the remaining 36 vehicles (258-287, 295, 296, 298, 300, 302, 303) for £150 each. No response had been received from the Montagu Motor Museum and the offer to loan a vehicle was accordingly withdrawn. Sunbeam MF2B 297 was offered on permanent loan to the Russell-Cotes Art Gallery and Museum with authority to loan it to the Portsmouth Transport Museum, on the condition that the vehicle was displayed indoors.

Wombwell Diesels started towing away the Sunbeam MF2Bs as follows:

11 August	270, 281	13 August	264, 269
15 August	258, 267	18 August	265, 266
29 August	261, 262	2 September	285
3 September	259, 260	5 September	263, 275, 278

In March 1998 Ian Cunningham reminisced to the author about the trolleybuses and stressed how it was the major road works in the centre of Bournemouth, specifically today's Wessex Way, which had influenced their premature withdrawal.

It was felt impracticable to make frequent overhead changes, reroute underground services and resite deeply-imbedded traction poles around the underpass excavations beneath the current roundabouts at the top of Richmond Hill and on St. Paul's Road. When challenged as to the ability of foreign operators to cope with similar upheavals, he pointed out that such temporary solutions were expensive and no grants would have been forthcoming, all costs having to be met from revenue.

Although motorbuses permitted more flexible scheduling, direct comparison showed the trolleybus to be no more expensive to operate than motorbuses on heavily-trafficked, profitable routes. It should also be remembered that, by the 1960s, motorbus operations benefited from fuel tax rebates whereas the nationalised electricity boards were not prepared to offer any further discounts on supplies used for DC traction current making it subsequently easy for motorbuses to earn the same revenue at less cost. In retrospect, had Bournemouth continued to operate trolleybuses, Mr Cunningham would have seriously considered equipping them with traction batteries to permit easier rerouting around diversions or road works, and unscheduled turning manoeuvres. Despite an occasional complaint of trolley booms dewiring, for example at the top of Fir Vale Road (a location for which a complete solution was never found), and crashing through first floor windows or dirt falling from the trolley heads on to cars behind, damaging their paintwork, the people of Bournemouth did not want to lose their "Silent Service" and he remained convinced that electric traction, perhaps including trolleybuses on reserved track, could survive even in post-deregulation Britain.

The column of waiting trolleybuses progressively lengthened. Amongst the Sunbeam MF2Bs the preserved Sunbeam MS2 no. 212 and BUT9641T no. 246, as well as the decorated no. 278, can be identified.

David Chalk collection

The column of parked trolleybuses from the rear. By now open-top Sunbeam MS2 no. 202 has joined the queue.
David Chalk collection

The trolleybuses in the closure procession parked in front of the Pier Approach Baths begin to fill up with passengers as a Charlie's Cars Harrington-bodied coach in that firm's well known plum and cream livery begins its climb up Bath Hill past the Pavilion.
David Chalk collection

Decorated Sunbeam MF2B no. 278 (YLJ278) pulls away past the entrance to the Pier Approach Baths at the head of the final group of five trolleybuses and heads off towards Exeter Road, the Square, Christchurch, Castle Lane (Mallard Road) Depot and, finally, oblivion (20 April 1969)

David Chalk collection

(Left) The Mayor of Bournemouth, Ald. Michael W. Green, JP, sits in the driver's seat of Sunbeam MF2B no. 301, with the crew, Conductress Dearmer and Driver Adams standing smartly by the cab window (20 April 1969).   David Chalk collection

(Below) Decorated Sunbeam MF2B no. 278 (YLJ278) pulls off Christchurch turntable into Church Street with the Priory Church tower clearly visible. The parish church is particularly long with portions having their origins in the 11th Century. The German Kaiser Wilhelm II (Kaiser Bill) worshipped here in November 1907.

David Chalk collection

Decorated trolleybus no. 278 heads the column of Sunbeam MF2Bs A-E in east end of Bargates, Christchurch, a few yards from the by-pass roundabout, prior to departure under police escort along Barrack Road and Castle Lane to Castle Lane (Mallard Road) Depot for the final time.   David Chalk collection (Rowland Adams)

There were a total of 19 vehicles - 16 of which were Sunbeam MF2Bs - in the final trolleybus procession. Here no. 280, one of the first group to leave Bournemouth Pier, turns out of Mallard Road into the Castle Lane Depot complex.   Malcolm Pearce (G.O.P. Pearce)

In the closing minutes of the ceremonial procession, decorated Sunbeam MF2B no. 278 pulls off Castle Lane West into Mallard Road prior to entering the depot complex.　　　　　Malcolm Pearce (G.O.P. Pearce)

No. 298, the penultimate vehicle in the final group of trolleybuses in the ceremonial procession, pulls into Mallard Road from Castle Lane West.　　　　　Malcolm Pearce (G.O.P. Pearce)

CHAPTER ELEVEN
LIFE AFTER DEATH

Since 1969 there have been several projects to establish an operating museum for preserved Bournemouth trolleybuses or British trolleybuses in general, in the immediate Bournemouth area. To date, all have failed.

Following the successful rescue of a representative collection of vehicles from the fleet in the years leading up to the system closure and immediately thereafter, attention turned towards preserved trolleybus operation. Although the Transport Department had disposed of redundant overhead equipment to both the NTA and RTS for their museum projects, these were not specifically aimed at the Bournemouth vehicles. Some fifty traction poles in good condition were stored at Castle Lane (Mallard Road) Depot from 1972 until 15 June 1973 for the NTA's museum scheme at Matchams Park near Ringwood, Hampshire, when they were moved to the intended museum site. The BPTA was also involved in this project, which was later abandoned.

At a later date, the BPTA purchased 46 traction poles from Talbot Road from the Lighting Department for use in another museum project, this time at Muscliffe Farm, but this project was also abandoned.

In the early 1990s, a project to operate preserved trolleybuses on a one-way circular route in the town centre, commencing at the Square, south along Exeter Road to the Pier, up Bath Road as far as the Royal Bath Hotel roundabout then west along Westover Road and Gervis Place back to the Square, almost became reality. In a report prepared by consultants Merz & McLellan and quoted in the *Bournemouth Evening Echo* of 27 March 1991 and 3 April 1991, it was stated that such a route, potentially with extensions to a proposed retail development at the Triangle or east to the Travel Interchange, would be entirely feasible and environmentally welcome. A number of local councillors, led by Mr M. Peters, who had had the opportunity to see preserved Bournemouth trolleybuses in operation at the Black Country Museum in Dudley, lobbied for the project. There seemed to be support from the local authority, which envisaged a tourist attraction similar to Blackpool's trams, and from Bournemouth Transport Ltd., by now trading as Yellow Buses Bournemouth, subject to the trolleybuses not running in competition with their own scheduled services. Having agreed on the route and legal requirements, Bournemouth Borough Council's Engineer and Surveyor's Department put out the provision, installation, operation and maintenance of a heritage trolleybus route to tender in November 1992, attracting six expressions of interest which developed into three responses.

On 2 February 1993, the Borough Engineer and Surveyor gave details of the proposed Bournemouth Town Centre Heritage Trolleybus Route to the Policy & Resources Committee. Tenders had been received from Bournemouth Heritage Transport, i.e. the BPTA; the Electric Trolley Vehicle Co. Ltd.; and Bournemouth Transport Ltd., i.e. Yellow Buses. The tender documentation of Electric Trolley Vehicle Co. Ltd., a company created specifically for this project, had been prepared jointly by officers of the NTA and BTS, Mr Michael Russell and Mr Francis Whitehead respectively, through the offices of Peter Brett Associates, Consulting Engineers. Except for the BPTA,

the tenderers had requested exemption from "Local Service" under the Transport Act 1985 for what was considered a unique tourist venture.

The lowest tender received, at no cost whatsoever or alternately with payment of 5% of gross revenue to the Council (if lawful), was presumably from Bournemouth Heritage Transport. It offered to provide at least one vehicle, and a more frequent peak service when trolleybuses would run after 10pm. Theme events using other operators' vehicles were also foreseen. Stops were proposed on Exeter Road (at its northern end and also opposite the Bournemouth International Centre); on Bath Road (opposite Bath Road South Car Park) and Gervis Place (outside the Pavilion, the layover timing point). It planned to use its own preserved vehicles (including an open-top trolleybus) which would be garaged and maintained at the former Central Depot, Southcote Road. The proposed fare structure was £1.00 adult, 40p children, 60p OAPs, subject to periodic review and valid all day. The tenderer would extend the service to Westbourne or Boscombe if it was commercially attractive to both parties.

The Electric Trolley Vehicle Co. Ltd. tender was in the sum of £276,001.04 (including a provisional £142,110.50 for equipment, administration and Order-making procedures) covering setting up the system. These figures would have been reduced if possible Department of Transport sponsorship for a demonstration trolleybus project was forthcoming. Operations would have been self-financing and at no cost to the Council. The Borough Engineer and Surveyor commented that the provisional figures would have to be confirmed to avoid invalidating this offer.

They proposed to use five different vehicles, including open-top trolleybuses and one modified for disabled users, on a rotating basis, with special events when other vehicles might be operated. The tenderer requested permission to use the route for test and demonstration purposes to pursue trolleybus research, subject to no adverse effect on services. Stops were proposed at Gervis Place (timing point); Exeter Road near Exeter Crescent; Bath Road opposite the Bournemouth International Centre (timing point) and opposite Bath Road South Car Park; and Westover Road outside Pavilion. The service would run a 15-minute frequency to 11pm during the peak season, with one-person-operation in the low season. The proposed fare structure was 70p adults and 40p children for the round trip, with 40p adults and 20p children for point-to-point, subject to periodic revision.

Bournemouth Transport Ltd. tendered £2,040,000, qualified by a link to the Retail Price Index (RPI) and requiring the Council to commit £290,000 in year 1, £175,000 in year 2 and £1,575,000, payable monthly in arrears, for years 3 to 11. It planned to hire preserved vehicles and would operate a ten-minute frequency May to mid-June and mid-September to May, with a five-minute frequency mid-June to mid-September. The proposed fare structure was 50p (year 2), adjusted by RPI for years 3–11. Stops at Gervis Place (near Old Christchurch Road); Exeter Road, (near Exeter Crescent); Exeter Road (opposite the Bournemouth International Centre); Bath Road (opposite Bath Road South Car Park); and Westover Road (between the

Pavilion and the Tourist Office) were suggested.

The Borough Engineer and Surveyor drew attention to the recent legislative changes affecting the Order-making procedure for setting up a trolleybus system, for which there was no precedent. Any statutory objections, perhaps provoked by Council proposals to make points on the route Conservation Areas, might lead to a Public Inquiry, thereby delaying the procedure. He went on to note that reports on the financial standing of two of the tenderers was still outstanding but that, in principle, the nil tender (No.2) offered the most attractive proposition, subject to appropriate financial and insurance cover being provided. On this basis, authority was sought to proceed with the project as quickly as possible.

In late April 1993 the Council advised all tenderers that it had been decided not to proceed with the project. It is understood that this decision was taken as a result of its interpretation of the 1992 change in the official approval process whereby a Ministerial Order instead of a Private Bill sufficed for trolley vehicle installations. Although intended as a cheaper and less cumbersome procedure, promotion of the Order for the Bournemouth Heritage Trolley Bus Route would have been a test case, with no clear financial precedent. Under these circumstances the Council got "cold feet", whilst a local election shortly afterwards bringing a different party into the majority and voting Mr Peters out of office led to the project's final collapse.

Disappointed local enthusiasts then prompted discussions aimed at restoring the circuit of overhead wiring around the premises of Castle Lane Depot for trolleybus demonstration purposes. This would have been modelled on the access circuit used during the trolleybus era and would have been aided by the continued existence of a number of wall-mounted rosettes and traction poles. There were, reportedly, objections from neighbouring residents fearing increased noise in the immediate depot area and damaged property from flying trolley heads. At this time the BPTA was involved in Routemaster Bournemouth, which ran motorbuses on key services in direct competition with Yellow Buses, and the author believes that this situation contributed to a breakdown in discussions.

The following Bournemouth trolleybuses have been preserved:

Sunbeam MS2 202 (112) (ALJ986)

202 was withdrawn by BCT in July 1965, its final use being for a NTA tour on 4 July 1965. After purchase by the NTA in December 1965, open-top 202 was initially stored at BCT's Castle Lane (Mallard Road) Depot, being used on enthusiasts' tours of Bournemouth (including participation in the closing procession on 20 April 1969), Cardiff (5 & 19 October 1969) and Reading (28 July 1968). Due to a lack of space at Castle Lane Depot, 202 was taken to Bournemouth (Hurn) Airport for open-air storage on 28 November 1970. Between 5 July 1972 and 30 May 1973, 202 was again stored at Castle Lane Depot on loan to the Russell-Cotes Art Gallery & Museum, Bournemouth, before returning to Bournemouth Airport where it was housed in hangar 102. During its stay at Castle Lane restoration work was carried out to the upper-deck seating, internal side panels and trolley gantry.

Coinciding with the move of the BPTA collection from Bournemouth Airport to Poole, on 19 September 1998, 202 was moved to premises near Fifield, Maidenhead, Berkshire, where it underwent further restoration, including completion of

a major overhaul of its braking system. The vehicle participated in the "Trolleys Galore" event at the Black Country Museum, Dudley, between 28 May and 9 July 2000, following which almost six weeks were spent running at the Trolleybus Museum at Sandtoft.

On 20 August 2000, 202 was moved to the East Anglia Transport Museum, Carlton Colville near Lowestoft, on a renewable loan agreement, where it has operated in fine weather during most seasons. The current loan agreement extends to December 2025.

Sunbeam MS2 212 (99) (ALJ973)

212 was withdrawn together with the remaining pre-war closed-top trolleybuses, after several years of summer-only use, on 29 September 1963 following 28½ years of service. In anticipation of the demise of the MS2s, the RTS had hired 212 for a tour of the system on 7 July 1963. At about the same time the Society had begun negotiations with the Transport Department for its purchase for preservation. Although 210 was a possible candidate, 212 was chosen as it appeared to be in the best structural condition and because it had been repainted in 1959. A price of £60 plus £2 each for the "slave" tyres was agreed. The trolleybus was formally handed over on 16 November 1963 to the Society's Secretary at a ceremony reported by the local press at Castle Lane (Mallard Road) Depot during which 212 made several circuits of the depot wiring. The following day 212 made the 5½-hour journey on tow behind BCT's Guy Arab breakdown lorry and towing tender FRU180 to its new home at Smith's Coaches garage in Reading. It was stored in the open with a tarpaulin slung across the open back platform and the trolley booms de-tensioned.

On 19th July 1964, 212 attended the Bean Car Club's rally at Bracknell, where it won second prize for being "prettiest vehicle"!

In March 1965, Mr R. Edgley Cox, General Manager and Engineer, Walsall Corporation Transport, and Vice-President of the RTS, granted permission for 212 to be stored under cover at Walsall Corporation Transport's Birchills Depot. 212 arrived there on 28 March 1965.

As the final trolleybus abandonment loomed closer in Bournemouth, arrangements were made for 212 to return to the South Coast to perform enthusiasts' tours. Walsall Corporation kindly prepared 212 for the tow south, in two stages again via Reading on 19 and 25 January 1969, and loaned a set of new tyres. Once back at Castle Lane Depot, RTS members cleaned the trolleybus internally and externally, made minor body repairs and touched up the paintwork. 212 was tested, taxed as "private" and insured by the Maypine Trolleybus Company (an enthusiast organisation) ready for three special tours of the remnants of the Bournemouth system on 16 February 1969 (separate morning and afternoon RTS tours) and 23 February 1969 (BPTA). A trial run was also made during the late afternoon of 15 February 1969. These were the first preserved trolleybus tours operated by the RTS.

On 20 April 1969 and taxed as "Hackney", 212 left Castle Lane (Mallard Road) Depot at 8.15am for its final tour of the system (RTS) before making its way to Bournemouth Pier (Bath Road) to take its place in the closure procession with RTS members on board and the author in the driver's cab.

Soon after the system closure, 212 was towed to Pound Hill, Crawley, for storage, remaining there until October 1969 when it was moved north to Belton near Sandtoft in North

Lincolnshire, prior to being moved to the new museum venture at Sandtoft, in which the RTS was a major participant, on 8 November 1969 as one of the first vehicles on the site. Since 212's arrival at the Trolleybus Museum at Sandtoft (formerly known as the Sandtoft Transport Centre), it has continuously been stored under cover. It is understood that it was used in passenger-carrying service around the demonstration circuit for several seasons. In 1979, the trolleybus was repanelled where necessary, the destination indicator boxes rebuilt to original standards and flatted down or stripped. The body's wooden structure proved to be in excellent condition. It was July 1982 before 212 entered Sandtoft's workshops for a cosmetic external repaint into the original 1935 lined-out livery, reappearing with its original pre-1958 fleet number, 99. Electrical tests were carried out in the hope of bringing the vehicle up to operating standards but showed a major fault in the main cabling, probably due to the rubber insulation breaking down. Re-cabling was carried out at the "Transperience" transport museum in Bradford in December 1996, but 99 was then found to have a defective traction motor and resistors needing refurbishment. Once sufficient funds are available, the electrical work, final signwriting, interior redecoration, rejuvenation of the leather seats and the refitting of glass louvres above the side windows and upper-deck front windows will be carried out in order that 99 can return to passenger-carrying duties.

BUT 9641T 246 (212) (KLJ346)

Initially reserved for a Mr R. Higgings, Christchurch, for preservation, when the sale fell through, 246 joined the batch of BUT9641Ts sold to Wombwell Diesels Co. Ltd. for scrap. It was purchased almost immediately from the breakers, having never left Bournemouth, by Mr Richard Cromwell, Effingham, Surrey, for preservation (at £125). 246 was initially stored at BCT's Castle Lane (Mallard Road) Depot and used on a number of local enthusiasts' tours as well as participating in the closure procession on 20 April 1969. It was transferred to storage at Epsom, Surrey, on 15 June 1969 and then to Weybridge in spring 1970, being used on an enthusiasts' tour of the Cardiff system on 7 September 1969.

In August 1971, 246 was sold to the BPTA for £400 and initially transferred to storage at Bournemouth (Hurn) Airport on 12 September 1971. It was then stored at the airport until under-cover storage became available at Castle Lane (Mallard Road) Depot in May 1973. In the winter of 1974/75 246 was repainted into 1950s livery. Whilst in BPTA ownership, 246 was stored under cover variously at Castle Lane Depot; Bournemouth Airport; Christchurch Buses' premises (formerly Norton's timber yard) in West Quay Road, Poole; and Shamrock Buses' premises in Newtown and Holton Heath, Poole.

In 2011 ownership of 246 passed from the BPTA to the West of England Transport Collection where it was stored undercover at Winkleigh, Devon.

In 2015 it was acquired by two enthusiasts, David Lawrence and David Pearson, who intend to restore the trolleybus to operating condition; 246 is currently in temporary storage at the NTA's depot in Suffolk.

Sunbeam MF2B 286 (YLJ286)

Bournemouth's last service trolleybus was sold in August 1969 to Wombwell Diesels Co. Ltd. for scrap. That same month it was purchased by the London Trolleybus Preservation Society but it remained in store at Castle Lane (Mallard Road) Depot until March 1973, when it was taken to the East Anglia Transport Museum, Carlton Colville near Lowestoft, where it is used in passenger-carrying service.

Sunbeam MF2B 297 (297LJ)

297 was offered on permanent loan to the Russell-Cotes Art Gallery and Museum in July 1969, having probably been initially the Sunbeam MF2B set aside for free loan to the Montagu Motor Museum, Beaulieu. It was also offered to Portsmouth Transport Museum but none of these bodies was able to store the trolleybus under cover (a condition of the loan) at the time it was offered to them. It was then sold to the BPTA in December 1971 for £250 and subsequently stored variously at BCT's Castle Lane (Mallard Road) Depot; Bournemouth (Hurn) Airport; Christchurch Buses' premises in West Quay Road, Poole; and Shamrock Buses' premises in Newtown, Poole.

Restored to operating condition, on 23/24 July 1977 it ran with a generator trailer loaned by London-based enthusiasts around Castle Lane Depot's perimeter road in connection with the 75th anniversary celebrations of Bournemouth Corporation Transport. In June 1989, following a second refurbishment, 297 operated on test at the Black Country Museum, Dudley, prior to a July 1989 appearance at the Sandtoft Transport Centre (now known as the Trolleybus Museum at Sandtoft) before returning to Dudley for their fortnight-long "Trolleydays" event later in the month. In a more adventurous excursion 297 ran under power between Westbourne and (the post-trolleybus) St. Michael's roundabout on Saturday 28 September 1991 again using the generator trailer. It made a number of round trips and, towards the end of the afternoon, ventured into Branksome, well off the former trolleybus route.

In 1999, following an extended period in passenger-carrying service at the Black Country Museum, 297 returned to Castle Lane Depot where it was prepared for a trip to the trolleybus-operating city of Ústí nad Labem in the Czech Republic which would be celebrating its public transport centenary in June 1999. Enthusiasts from all over Europe, together with their preserved vehicles, were invited to participate and the BPTA resolved to send 297 to operate in the event. Professional hauliers were engaged to take 297, on suspended tow, to Ústí nad Labem by way of a "high vehicle" route, but with instructions to halt and check bridges with restricted clearance. Unfortunately, the trolleybus struck a bridge in Luxembourg at speed, which devastated the roof as far back as the trolley gantry. The hauliers returned immediately to Britain and accepted full responsibility for the accident. Following a period in storage at Poole, temporary roof repairs were carried out and in 2007 the trolleybus was taken to the Trolleybus Museum at Sandtoft, where the damaged upper deck was repaired, the trolley gantry replaced and the bodywork, mechanical parts and electrics refurbished. 297 then took up residence at the Black Country Museum in 2008, remaining there until 2011, when it returned to Sandtoft.

In May 2016, the Trolleybus Museum at Sandtoft acquired 297, where it remains in passenger-carrying service.

Sunbeam MF2B 299 (299LJ)

Although acquired for preservation at a cost of £200 by the Transport Museum Society of Ireland (TMSI) in August 1969 (tender accepted in July 1969), 299 remained inside Castle Lane (Mallard Road) Depot until 10 December 1971, when it was towed away to Birkenhead for shipment to Dublin. There are no details of the vehicle's whereabouts until 24 June 1972 when 299 arrived on the TMSI's museum premises at Howth, near Dublin.

299 was taken to the Irish Transport Museum at Castleruddery, County Wicklow, and was stored there, latterly in the open and in a fairly dilapidated condition, until late 2016. In 2015 the TMSI decided to rationalise their collection of vehicles and offered 299 to the BTS. Having considered the likely cost of transport back to Britain, restoration and depot accommodation, the offer could not be countenanced. Accordingly 299 was offered for disposal, it being made clear that options for the trolleybus reluctantly included scrapping, potentially for spares, if no enthusiast was interested. By now, acquisition of 297 by the Trolleybus Museum at Sandtoft and 301 by the BTS in May 2016 tended to rule out 299's survival.

In late 2016, enthusiast Keith Baynton acquired 299 for preservation and on 9 February 2017, 299 was taken on suspended tow to await a ferry crossing back to the UK. The vehicle is now under cover in Ellesmere Port, Cheshire, undergoing a comprehensive restoration to operating condition.

Sunbeam MF2B 301 (301LJ)

The last trolleybus to be delivered to Bournemouth, the BPTA purchased 301 from BCT in August 1969 (tender accepted in July 1969) for £150, but it remained stored under cover at Castle Lane (Mallard Road) Depot, although appearing at various local public events. In 1976 the vehicle was given

its first external repaint since delivery prior to joining the procession to celebrate the 75th anniversary of Bournemouth Corporation Transport in 1977 and being displayed at the BTS 25th anniversary rally to Didcot Railway Centre in 1986.

301 benefited from a second repaint in 1990 before being taken to join 297 at the Black Country Museum, Dudley, where both Bournemouth trolleybuses ran in passenger-carrying service. In 1991 it was loaned to the Museum of Land Transport, Leyland, Lancashire, remaining on static display there until returning to Bournemouth in 2010.

In 2011 the BPTA loaned 301 to the West of England Transport Collection where it was stored under cover at Winkleigh, Devon.

In May 2016, the BTS acquired 301 for a token amount and placed it in temporary storage at a site near Reading, Berkshire, until it was moved on suspended tow to the Trolleybus Museum at Sandtoft in October 2018.

When urban bus services were deregulated, the BPTA endeavoured to generate funds to support its collection of preserved Bournemouth trolleybuses and motorbuses through arm's length involvement in a variety of financially-independent commercial bus operations. These have included Routemaster Bournemouth (1993–4), Vintage Yellow Buses, which also traded as Christchurch Buses, the "low cost" contract arm of Yellow Buses (1994–2000), and Shamrock (2001–11). When Shamrock ceased trading, trolleybus 246 and the BPTA's motorbus collection passed to the West of England Transport Collection.

Over the 2019 Spring Bank Holiday weekend the Trolleybus Museum at Sandtoft staged a special event to commemorate fifty years since the closure of the Bournemouth trolleybus system. Here the Museum's three Bournemouth trolleybuses, Sunbeam MF2B no. 301, Sunbeam MS2 no. 99, and Sunbeam MF2B no. 297, in the company of Keith Burbidge's miniature trolleybus are seen lined up for photographers on 25 May 2019.

David Bowler

APPENDIX A
TROLLEYBUS FLEET DETAILS

It was common practice in the 1930s for the general managers of municipal transport undertakings both to seek the optimum solution for their operational needs and also display a certain individuality. This was normally achieved by a review of the trolleybuses used by similarly-sized municipalities faced with comparable topography followed by a call for tenders for a small initial fleet of vehicles having the characteristics that the general manager found appropriate.

Bournemouth approached this in a slightly different manner. The Tramways Committee had visited Hastings and Maidstone prior to the inclusion of power to operate trackless trolleys in the Bournemouth Corporation Act, 1930. They subsequently visited Wolverhampton and built up a close rapport with the undertaking there. Thus, it was not surprising that a Sunbeam product, both built and operated in that town, was selected as one of the four prototype trolleybuses to be tested on Bournemouth's experimental route between the Square and County Gates. The trialled Sunbeam MS2 (LJ7701) excelled in all respects and resulted in follow-on orders for a further 102 trolleybuses of the same type and with virtually identical bodywork over a period of just ten months. That such vehicles were still in service 28 and 29 years later illustrates the wisdom of this decision.

This appendix details the electrical and mechanical equipment, the bodywork and alterations subsequently made to each vehicle, for each batch of trolleybuses bought by the undertaking and is accompanied by tabular details of fleet number, chassis and body number, dates of delivery, entry into service, withdrawal, etc.

The information that follows, as with much of the content of this book, is an amalgam of material sought out in Bournemouth Corporation Transport's official records, the Transport Committee Minutes, internal BCT memoranda and reports, articles in the professional trade press of the time, and manufacturers' catalogues and press releases.

The original vehicle records listing specific dates such as delivery, entry into service, reconstruction, withdrawal, etc., no longer survive. They were incinerated, together with much of the undertaking's early written records, in the 1970s when the Mallard Road Works Stores were reorganised. That the salient details still survive is due to the dedication of David Chalk.

BCT's vehicle records were maintained by the Works Office, which, from 1953, was located on the ground floor of the Mallard Road workshop block. On the first floor, within the main stores, there was a locked room which contained old vehicle and other records dating back to the start of tramway operation (although full details of the trams were disposed of during the paper salvage drive of World War Two). Records from the mid-1930s were a mixture of typed and written details on separate sheets of paper. Prior to that, records were handwritten in large, thick ledgers.

When the Head Office moved from Southcote Road to Mallard Road in 1965, David Chalk's place of work was similarly transferred and he used this as an opportunity over a period of time to inspect the various records for each vehicle, e.g. one for tyres, one for maintenance (overhauls, repaints, etc.), one holding the basic details of each vehicle such as chassis number, delivery date, etc., and eventually copy the salient details into a standard format requiring just one or two pages for each batch of vehicles. This information has been the prime source for the tabular details shown for each batch of trolleybuses and I am most grateful to David Chalk for putting his files at my disposal.

288

68 Sunbeam-BTH MS2

Fleet No.	Reg.Mark	Chassis Number	Body Number	Date of Delivery	Date into Service	Date of Withdrawal	Date of Disposal
68	LJ7701	12077	C560	10.05.1933	13.05.1933	30.09.1950	.05.1952

Chassis: Three-axle Sunbeam type MS2 manufactured by Sunbeam Motor Car Co. Ltd., Moorfield Road Works, Blakenhall, Wolverhampton, Staffordshire.

Motor: British Thomson-Houston Co. Ltd. (BTH), Rugby, Warwickshire, Type 201 compound-wound (80hp) for regenerative control.

Electrical equipment: British Thomson-Houston (BTH); scissors-type controller, 12 notches (1-6, resistance; 7, full power; 8-12, field weakening).

Dewirement indicators: neon line-lights and buzzer.

Brakes: Regenerative and Lockheed vacuum-assisted hydraulic brakes, with Reavill vacuum exhauster, and handbrake, mechanical to all rear wheels.

Body: Highbridge double-deck composite six-bay construction with single rear staircase, and conventional rear, semi-vestibuled open platform entrance and exit.

Built by Weymann Motor Bodies (1925) Ltd., Station Road, Addlestone, Surrey. H32/28R.

Length: 27ft 6in   Width: 7ft 6in

Wheelbase: 17ft to centre of rear bogie with a rear bogie wheelbase of 3ft 11¼in giving a turning circle on either lock of less than 60 ft.

Unladen weight: 7 tons 19 cwt 3 qtrs

Tyres: 36 X 8 high-pressure pneumatic singles to all wheels according to the pre-war system of measuring tyre sizes (the first number being the overall diameter of the tread in inches and the second being the height of the tread above the wheel rim).

Until 1928 the Sunbeam Motor Car Co. Ltd., together with its partners Talbot and Darracq (STD Group) concentrated on producing prestigious cars and motor racing; however a slump in sales reflecting the world economic depression encouraged them to branch out into motor buses. In 1931 a marketing organisation, Sunbeam Commercial Vehicles, was set up. An unsold three-axle motor bus chassis was adapted as a prototype trolleybus chassis, the MS1, fitted with a Weymann body and passed to Wolverhampton Corporation transport for evaluation in mid-1931. The result was an order for three Sunbeam trolleybuses, the improved chassis being designated the MS2, delivered in June 1932, and a single example for Derby in October 1932 before the Company was successful in placing one on hire to Bournemouth for use on their experimental trolleybus route.

The vehicle was delivered to Bournemouth on 10 May 1933 as one of the first four experimental vehicles, participated in the official opening ceremony of 13 May 1933 and together with the AEC 661T entered service that same day on the Bournemouth Square-Westbourne trial route.

Chassis: The Sunbeam MS2 was substantially similar to its predecessor the MS1, but fitted with a compound wound regenerative motor and braking. The axles and rear bogie were based on the Sunbeam "Sikh" motorbus chassis.

Reversed Elliott pattern front axle based on an "I"-section beam, 4in deep and 3in wide, with taper roller bearings to take the load thrust on the king pins. The rear axle comprised a Kirkstall 100-ton tensile heat-treated steel dropped forging main axle casting and DB worm gear, forged with driving flanges bolted to the wheel hubs.

Channel section alloy steel frame, with a maximum depth of 11in which increases to 15½in at the wheel arches to permit attachment of the spring swivel brackets.

Pressed steel cross-channels, one of which supporting one

An offside view of LJ7701 on test.
Keith Baynton collection

Sunbeam-BTH MS2 LJ7701 seen in Wolverhampton prior to delivery to Bournemouth for trials. Note the original curved trolley booms and the primrose rear dome. With the success of the trials, the vehicle was purchased and became no. 68 in the Bournemouth fleet. LJ7701 proved to be the basic protoype for 102 similar Sunbeam-BTH MS2s.

David Chalk collection

end of the traction motor sub-frame. Flanged tubes riveted to the channel webs joined the fore and aft ends of the wheel arches.

Bogie wheelbase:	3ft 11¼in
Chassis weight:	4tons 8cwt 1qtr
Chassis length:	27ft 5½in
Chassis width:	7ft 5½in
Chassis frame width:	3ft 6⁵/₁₆in

Front springs: Woodhead divided backplate springs semi-elliptical above axle 44in centres, 3½in wide.
Rear springs: twin Woodhead centrally pivoted 47¼in centres, 3½in wide.

Marles V5 cam and lever steering, requiring 4¼ turns for full lock (8½ from lock to lock).

By removing eleven bolts holding the swivel brackets to the frame and disconnecting the propeller shaft and brakes, the bogie could be removed from the chassis frame and wheeled out from underneath the vehicle for overhaul purposes.

Underslung worm-type rear axles were used with fully-floating axle shafts to back wheel hubs. There was a one-piece tubular propeller shaft 4in diameter with Hardy-Spicer universal joints. Standard ratio 9⅔ to 1.

Steel disc wheels on taper roller bearings.

Grouped grease nipples at various points provided lubrication to the chassis.

Electrics: The British Thomson-Houston Type 201 (80nhp) compound-wound traction motor was resiliently mounted at four points in a sub-frame amidships within the chassis frame between the front and the leading rear axle. The single turn armature winding motor had a one-hour rating of 80hp at 500v drawing 130 amps. In order to reduce its height, the motor was of square section 2ft 7in long and 1ft 4⅝in high, only projecting 4in above the top of the chassis frame at the front. It tilted somewhat towards the rear and had an 11in ground clearance. By releasing the forward Silentbloc mounting pins the motor and its sub-frame could be hinged downwards, after which the rear pins could also be removed and the motor lowered.

The series resistances were mounted on the exterior face of the nearside chassis frame and the shunt resistances on the offside. Steel stone guards in front and louvred under-shields protected them from damage. The contactors for the shunt field resistance were on a panel mounted on an aluminium dashboard in front of the driver whilst those for the line circuit and starting resistance were either on the dashboard or at the nearside of the driver. The reverser was mounted on the latter. BTH "scissors-type" pedal-operated master controller, controlling BTH solenoid-operated contactors fitted with magnetic blow out coils, located immediately alongside the pedal.

Brecknell Willis & Co. Ltd., Bristol, 18ft-long taper trolley booms mounted on a squat base incorporating Timken roller bearings permitting a deviation of up to 15ft from the centre line of the overhead wires, equipped with wheel collectors.

The change-over switch for operation on tram tracks was located on the rear platform and a skate intended to run in the groove of the tram rail was provided.

Brakes: The vehicle was fitted with regenerative braking for conventional stopping. The driver reduced foot pressure on the control pedal so that the controller returned towards the full field position, the braking effect increasing as the pedal rose and strengthened the shunt field. Until the controller reached the off position, the starting resistance was held out of circuit so that full regeneration down to about 10mph was provided. The trolleybus was brought to a halt with the vacuum-assisted hydraulic footbrake which operated on all wheels.

The Sunbeam patent hydraulic brake control gear comprised a master-cylinder box with three cylinders, each 1½in in diameter, in a single casting which actuated the brakes on one axle, whilst an outer casing acted as a reserve tank by which each system was kept full of fluid. A compensating and sealing device together with the multiple master cylinder ensured safe braking in the case of a fracture in the pipelines as only one of the three systems would be affected.

The front brake drums were 16¾in diameter and the shoes 3¾in wide, the rear brake drums of malleable cast iron were 19¾in diameter and the shoes 4in wide, all shoes being equipped with ⁷/₈in thick Ferodo linings, giving 884 sq in lining area for the foot brake. The Lockheed brake shoe actuators employed pressure cylinders 2in in diameter mounted on brake shoe carrier brackets which expanded the shoes by means of short push-rods connected to the master-cylinders by copper tubing and flexible hoses.

The pull-on handbrake was linked mechanically by rods acting on the rear bogie wheels; the handbrake lever was to the offside of the driver's steering column.

Bodywork: Composite six-bay highbridge double-deck construction, equipped with conventional, enclosed forwards-ascending half-turn (90°) staircase with semi-vestibuled open platform entrance and exit at the rear, marketed by Metropolitan-Cammell-Weymann Motor Bodies Ltd. and built by Weymann Motor Bodies (1925) Ltd., Addlestone, Surrey. The body had an English oak timber frame and the roof structure was in best white ash. External panelling was in 18G aluminium, the shaped panels being in 20G steel, an additional skin being evident at the rear of the upper-deck.

The exposed trolley gantry was constructed of three externally-mounted steel channels carried down to the top of the lower-deck pillars of bays 2 and 3 which linked at upper-deck floor level with a horizontal steel channel running along each side from the front pillar of the driver's cab to a few inches behind the central grab rail on the rear platform. The gantry was not in direct contact with the roof.

Half-drop windows were fitted to bays 2-4 (both sides) of the lower deck and bays 1, 3, 5 (both sides) of the upper deck. The upper pane dropped outside the fixed lower pane. In the vent panel immediately above the lower-deck windows in bays 2, 4 and 6 on both sides, ten-vane ventilation vents slanting rearwards somewhat from the vertical at the top were fitted. There was a roof-mounted ventilator on each side of bay 6.

The upper deck single-pane front windows were fixed. There was a non-standard-length window with radiused corners on the offside of the rear platform through which the staircase was visible. The rear elevation was particularly upright with a single window having radiused corners at the top on the platform and on the upper-deck an emergency exit door divided centrally into two panes with radiused top outer corners and bottom hinges.

The emergency exit door could be opened by an external handle mounted on the rear dome to the offside immediately above the door, or from the inside by a comparable handle attached to a horizontal locking bar mounted on the cantrail immediately above the door. The horizontal bar was equipped with four prongs that engaged with brackets on the top of the door. It is not known how, with the door opened, access to the roof catwalk and trolley gear was achieved. There was metal bracing running forward of each of the trolley boom retention hooks.

Metal louvres were fitted above the upper- and lower-deck saloon side windows and the front upper-deck windows, as well as the non-standard offside window of the rear platform and the "D" windows above the rear platform both sides, the louvres protruding at about 20° from the sides of the vehicle in bays 2 and 3 due to the steel channels supporting the trolley gantry.

The front registration plate was mounted centrally about one-third of the way up the front panel. The rear registration details were painted centrally at the top of the rear platform window.

The front panel protruded some 6in forward of the driver's cab windscreen with a flat front and bulbous nose. The rest of the front profile continued with a gentle rake and an almost imperceptible "V"-shaped upper-deck front panels and windows. The triangular Sunbeam chassis maker's badge was fitted in the waistband centrally beneath the driver's windscreen.

The offside windscreen was divided horizontally into two; the upper two-thirds being top-hinged and opening outwards. This upper pane was equipped with an external rectangular frame within which a windscreen wiper blade moved transversely backwards and forwards. The lower pane and its full depth nearside counterpart deepened a little in a gentle curve progressively towards their extremities, the front waistband matching this somewhat at its extremities on the front panels beneath. The driver's cab was equipped with a front-hinged door (three hinges) on the offside with an opening handle in a triangular-shaped recess in the waistband.

The window of the door was divided horizontally, the upper portion having a single fixed pane which deepened in a curve towards the front of the vehicle, and the lower portion having two panes, the rear pane sliding forwards behind the front pane for signalling purposes. There was a matching window layout on the nearside. There was a tall narrow fixed side window, almost triangular in shape but with a curved base as it rose to align with the windscreen, between the window in the cab door and its counterpart on the nearside, and the front corner pillar on both sides. The base of the cab door was horizontal immediately above the offside front wheel arch.

A rectangular driver's rear-view mirror was mounted externally on the front offside cab pillar only, there originally being none on the nearside.

There was a three-piece metal "fairing" mudguard over the rear wheels. Individual mud flaps hung behind each wheel of the front and third axles.

A single wooden lifeguard ran beneath the side panels between the first and second axles.

A bamboo trolley retrieval pole was carried in a tube suspended below axle level from the frame cross-members and was accessible from the rear of the vehicle.

Lighting: External lighting comprised two headlights mounted on plinths on the front panel. The lighting arrangements at the rear are not known due to an absence of photographic evidence, however, it is likely that there was a single rear light mounted at the top of the offside lower-deck corner panel.

Internal lighting not known.

Lighting from motor generator.

Seating: Details not known. Squabs and backs were upholstered in Connolly Brothers pleated brown hide.

In the lower saloon there were four rows of forward-facing double seats and a six-person bench seat over the rear bogie on both sides. In the upper saloon there were seven rows of forward-facing double seats on the offside and nine rows on the nearside.

The driver's seat was in pleated brown hide.

Destination equipment: A single-line final-destination indicator box was fitted in the upper-deck front panelling centred above the driver's windscreen with a square service number indicator box immediately above centred above the final-destination box. It is assumed that there was a single-line final-destination indicator box surmounted by a square service number indicator box at the rear but no photographic evidence has been found. No indicator boxes were mounted inside the lower saloon.

External Livery: Delivered in the manufacturer's interpretation of Livery 1 (see Appendix D).

Internal Livery: Cream scratchproof Rexine leathercloth-covered ceilings. Side panels covered in brown-grained scratchproof Rexine leathercloth. All windows were surrounded internally by varnished wood frames and mouldings. Primrose yellow paint to rear platform and staircase. All handrails and stanchions covered in black Doverite. Cab area painted brown below the waist and primrose yellow above.

Notes: LJ7701 was originally on hire from Sunbeam at a cost of 3d per mile. In November 1933, the Transport Committee recommended its purchase for £2,000 and this was subsequently agreed (invoiced 20 December 1933), whereupon it was allocated the Bournemouth fleet number 68. The vehicle's performance ensured that the Sunbeam MS2, but combined with a Park Royal body, was selected as being the most appropriate for Bournemouth's needs.

The vehicle spent most of its life on the Westbourne-Holdenhurst Road-Boscombe service and was only very occasionally to be seen in other parts of the town.

Subsequent alterations: Diffused glass soon replaced the transparent glazing in the non-standard-length window on the offside of the rear platform.

In 1935 number 68 was fitted with coasting and run-back brakes as required by a MoT instruction related to trolleybus operation on Richmond Hill. Sunbeam fitted this equipment as a "follow-on" to similar work being carried out on the second batch of MS2s then being delivered, at a charge of £25.

Wooden "slip-boards" indicating the principal intermediate and terminal points, similar to those already used on BCT motor buses, were mounted above the lower saloon waist-rail level running from halfway along bay 3 to halfway along bay 5 on both sides.

Reconstructed in September 1936 with a forward-descending

front staircase and a front exit equipped with a two-leaf folding door manually controlled from the driver's cab by means of a lever coupled to an interlock to break the controller circuit, thus preventing the trolleybus from starting off with the door open. Diffused glass replaced the transparent glazing in bay 1 offside as this now backed on to the front staircase.

This reduced the seating capacity to H31/25D. The fixed front windows to the upper deck were replaced with half-drop openers surmounted by glass louvres in addition to metal louvres above. Front side lights of identical style to those on the main Sunbeam MS2 fleet were fitted to the waistband. A rectangular driver's rear-view mirror was added to the front nearside pillar.

From November 1935 BCT adopted a revised layout for the indicator boxes in the front and rear upper-deck panels, trolleybuses delivered beforehand being progressively rebuilt accordingly. In September 1936, when number 68 was reconstructed, a rectangular indicator box, 2ft 6in wide and 1ft 3in deep, able to display up to four lines of information (intermediate points and the final destination), was built into the front panel at the same position as the single-line final-

destination and service number indicator boxes it replaced. Somewhat larger, 10in by 10in, service number boxes were built into the front panel to the nearside of the rectangular box. At the rear, the single-line final-destination and service number indicators were removed from the panelling and a rectangular indicator, 2ft 6in wide and 1ft 3in deep, able to display up to four lines of information (intermediate points and the final destination) inserted in its place. A rear service number box, 10in by 10in, was built into the nearside of the (vent) panel immediately above the platform window.

Auxiliary single-line indicator boxes to show the alternative in-town route options and journeys via special events were never fitted.

In 1938 or early 1939 the trolley wheel collectors were replaced by Anti-Attrition Metal Co. OB type slipper heads with carbon inserts.

Later, a larger rectangular driver's rear-view mirror replaced the circular one on the front offside cab pillar

Disposal: 68 to James Thompson & Co. (Cardiff) Ltd., Dumballs Road, Cardiff, breakers, in May 1952.

A postwar view of no. 68 at the Square loading point at the east end of Avenue Road.

Omnibus Society (R.T. Wilson)

69 AEC-EE 663T

Fleet No.	Reg.Mark	Chassis Number	Body Number	Date of Delivery	Date into Service	Date of Withdrawal	Date of Disposal
69	LJ7702	663T003		20.05.1933	23.051933	30.06.1950	24.12.1950

Chassis: Three-axle type AEC-EE 663T manufactured by the Associated Equipment Company Ltd. (AEC) at the AEC works, Windmill Lane, Southall, Middlesex.
Motor: English Electric Co. Ltd. (EE), Phoenix Works, Bradford, Yorkshire.
Type DK 130/2F series-wound (80hp) augmented field equipment, non-regenerative.
Electrical equipment: D701B controller.
Dewirement indicator: single neon line-light.
Brakes: Rheostatic; Lockheed hydraulic actuated by Westinghouse compressed air; and handbrake, mechanical to all rear wheels.
Body: Highbridge double-deck composite six-bay construction with single rear staircase, and conventional rear, semi-vestibuled open platform entrance and exit.
Built by English Electric Co. Ltd., Dick, Kerr Works, Preston, Lancashire. H32/28R
Length: 27ft 5½in   Width 7ft 6in over pillars
Wheelbase: 16ft 6in (from front axle to centre of rear bogie), giving a turning circle of 59ft 3in.
Unladen weight: 8tons 3cwt.
Tyres: 36 X 8 high-pressure pneumatic singles to all wheels

according to the pre-war system of measuring tyre sizes.

There are indications that the chassis of this trolleybus was one of three AEC-EE prototypes (001-3) built between April and September 1930 for demonstration purposes and equipped with flimsy-looking highbridge but low-height English Electric bodies. The original full-fronted bodies proved structurally weak, access to the traction motor for maintenance was difficult and they proved non-compliant with the February 1931 MoT Revised Conditions of Fitness Regulations and the July 1932 MoT Memorandum on the Form, Construction, Dimensions and Weight of Trolley Vehicles and their Electrical Equipment. It is understood that all three original bodies were scrapped.

New half-cab bodies were placed on chassis 001 and 003. Chassis 001 with new half-cab body incorporating front and rear staircases and front exit doors entered service with Southend-on-Sea Corporation in May 1932 who purchased it in November 1932 with local registration mark JN2086 (fleet number 116). It was rebuilt later with a full-front but with the front staircase and exit removed. Chassis 002 was rebuilt into chassis 663T070 and in 1932 became one of Birmingham Corporation's five AEC trolleybuses (registration marks OJ1012-16, fleet numbers 12-16) equipped with a Brush body.

AEC-EE 663T LJ7702 operating on the experimental trolleybus service to County Gates, Westbourne, photographed at the loading point on the south side of the Square outside Bobby's store where Exeter Road joins the Square.
David Chalk collection (Bournemouth Transport Ltd.)

LJ7702 was delivered to Bournemouth on 20 May 1933 as the last of the four experimental vehicles to arrive, equipped with a half-cab, bonnet and imitation AEC motorbus-style radiator. The vehicle entered service on the Bournemouth Square-Westbourne trial route on 23 May 1933.

Chassis: Conventional cranked chassis frame over rear bogie based on the AEC Regent 663 motorbus chassis and axles. The side members were pressed out of 5/16in steel with a maximum depth of 11^{1}/$_{8}$in having 3in-wide flanges with a "kick up" swept over the front and rear axles to permit the mounting of a low floor level body. The arches over the rear bogie were reinforced by inserted channels of the same thickness. The frame level under load was 1ft 10^{1}/$_{2}$in. The frame was held rigid by channel section and tubular cross-members to eliminate distortion.

Wheel track: front 6ft 5^{3}/$_{8}$in, rear 6ft 2^{3}/$_{4}$in.
Chassis weight: 4 tons 4cwt

Frame overall length: 26ft 9in
Frame maximum width: 5ft
Height of frame laden: 22^{1}/$_{2}$in
Chassis overall width: 7ft 6in over rear tyres.
Road clearance under rear axle 7^{1}/$_{2}$in.

Bogie wheelbase: 4ft

Semi-elliptic springs:
Front: above axle, 4ft 2in long between centres
Rear: below axle, 4ft 9in long between centres.

The axles were made from 100-ton steel 3in in diameter and mounted on adjustable taper roller bearings. A chrome vanadium spring steel torque blade was used permitting freedom of motion of each axle.

The socket attachments of this cross-member formed a rigid assembly with the front end of the front axle spring anchorages and, on the offside, the steering box. The rear ends of the front axle spring were shackled by a similar arrangement to the second chassis cross-member. The 57in-long cantilever springs of the rear axles were centrally pivoted upon needle-roller trunnion bearings carried by cast-steel brackets mounted beneath the wheel arches, to which they were riveted and joined by a large cross-tube. The ends of the springs had solid eyes and were anchored to brackets under the axle tubes. Hydraulic shock absorbers on all axles.

The rear axle bogie was supported by two springs carried in the centre by chairs swinging in GM bushes in the bogie brackets, which were riveted to the frame and further stiffened by a 4in tubular cross-member brazed in the brackets to resist torsion.

Semi-floating under-slung worm drive rear axles. The rear axle casings were one-piece nickel steel forgings carrying the worm gearing in separate casings. The 8^{1}/$_{2}$in worm gear was offset to the nearside to avoid any obstruction of the gangway, and the worms and traction motor were skewed at an angle of 3° to maintain a straight drive line. Ratio 9.33 to 1.

There was a three-piece tubular propeller shaft, fitted with Hardy-Spicer needle-roller self-aligning bearing universal joints, connecting the traction motor with the third differential which was offset to the nearside of the leading rear axle. A further

shaft connected with the differential on the second rear axle to ensure an even distribution of the driving torque between the two rear axles.

AEC roller bearing front axle equipped with AEC Marles worm and nut steering.

Forged alloy steel disc hubs on taper roller bearings.

Electrics: The front-mounted English Electric DK 130/2F traction motor was on a sub-frame offset to the nearside and angled downwards to provide a straight transmission line to the leading rear axle differential. The motor had a one-hour rating of 80hp at 500v. It was accessible by opening the bonnet as with a conventional front-engine half-cab motorbus. This location was considered beneficial for motor ventilation purposes whilst giving a better weight distribution over the front axle. The claimed advantage of easier maintenance or removal, compared to a motor mounted amidships underfloor in the chassis frame, proved over-optimistic and was not pursued.

The master controller and reverser were mounted forwards of the traction motor beneath the bonnet to the nearside of the driver's cab and accessible behind the imitation radiator.

The contactors were carried in two asbestos-lined steel cases mounted on the external face of the offside chassis frame member.

The jointless, unbreakable and non-rusting resistance grid was carried on chassis cross-members to the rear of the frame in front of the rear axle and offset to the offside leaving space for the propeller shaft, itself offset to the nearside. They were shielded from road dirt, but otherwise well-ventilated. There were four main cable runs carried within the frame channel sheathed in rubber ply tubing.

Brecknell, Willis & Co. Ltd., Bristol, lightweight trolley equipment, and trolley bases, the booms being equipped with current collecting wheels.

A "skate" could be fitted to allow current return via the tramway track.

Traction batteries for manoeuvring purposes were not fitted.

Brakes: Rheostatic; Lockheed compressed air-actuated hydraulic, activated by the brake pedal and operating on all wheels, controlled through a Westinghouse valve operated by the foot pedal. A small motor-driven compressor supplied air to a reservoir at 100 lbs per square inch. The brake drums, 17in diameter, were made of hard pressed steel, fitted with renewable liners ^{1}/$_{2}$in thick, and all the brake shoes were 3^{1}/$_{4}$in wide and interchangeable.

Automatic adjustment was provided on the rear wheels.

The mechanical handbrake operated on separate single shoes in the rear brake drums.

The handbrake lever was to the offside of the driver's steering column.

Bodywork: Highbridge double-deck composite six-bay construction with conventional, enclosed forwards-ascending half-turn (90°) staircase with semi-vestibuled open platform entrance and exit at the rear, built by English Electric Co. Ltd. at Preston. In virtually all respects the body was a longer version of that on the AEC-EE661T (LJ7703).

The upper-deck body pillars slotted into the wooden rail of the framework above the upper saloon windows i.e. the cantrail. There were curved steel brackets bolted to the metal roof (inside the roof there was a steel strengthening plate on each side) and each end of the three transverse pressed steel girders, above the forward pillar of bay 1, the pillar between bays 1 and 2, the pillar between bays 2 and 3, and above the rear pillar of bay 3, supporting the exposed trolley gantry, which was not in direct contact with the roof, resting on these brackets. The whole was masked from view by large bulbous fairings on the roof extending over bays 1-3.

The front of the top deck featured a curvaceous almost bulbous roof line with V-shaped fixed windows and a semi-piano front upper-deck panel which overhung the driver's cab. On the lower deck, the side windows in bays 2 and 4, and on the upper deck bays 1, 3 and 5, were equipped with half-drop openers. The upper pane dropped outside the fixed lower pane. Glazed louvres, which were deeper above the centre of each pane, were individually fitted in stainless steel frames above each half-drop opener.

Top-hinged access doors were fitted at the base of the lower-deck nearside panel bays 1 and 2, and on the offside panel bays 1, 2 and 3 providing access to the equipment mounted on the exterior face of the chassis members.

There was a metal "fairing" mudguard over the rear wheels, this being swept particularly low behind the rearmost wheel. Individual mud flaps hung behind the front wheels.

The upper-deck rear emergency exit door was divided centrally into two panes with radiused top outer corners and had four hinges at its base. The emergency exit door could be opened by an external handle mounted centrally on the rear dome immediately above the rain strip above the door, or from the inside by a comparable handle attached to a horizontal locking bar mounted on the cantrail immediately above the door. It is not known how, with the door opened, access to the roof catwalk and trolley gear was achieved.

Despite the protruding rear indicator box, small protruding rubber bumpers a quarter of the way up the frame on the nearside and offside of the emergency exit door aligned with similar bumpers at the base of the waistrail on each side of the rear indicator box. When the emergency exit door was opened to its fullest extent, the emergency exit door hung down and rested on these bumpers.

There were two windows of unequal width to the rear of the platform. The rear registration mark was affixed to the top of the wider, nearside pane. The front registration plate was mounted to the base of the imitation radiator.

The vehicle was equipped with an offside half-cab, bonnet and short imitation AEC motor bus- style radiator (similar to the Nottinghamshire & Derbyshire Traction Co.'s AEC661Ts) which was mounted particularly high. The chassis and equipment maker's badge, AEC in an inverted triangle surmounted by the winged EE symbol, was fitted centrally at the top of the radiator. The front of the driver's cab had a rake, tilting back considerably beneath the upper-deck overhang to accommodate the protruding bonnet. It was equipped with a single opening windscreen, divided into two panes of equal depth, equipped with a central top-mounted windscreen wiper and painted frame. There was a front-hinged (three hinges) cab door with an opening handle in a triangular-shaped recess in the waistband. The window of the door was divided horizontally, the upper portion having a single fixed pane deeper at the front, the top of which slanted downwards to a radiused corner at the rear, and the lower portion having two panes, the rear pane sliding forwards behind the front pane, for signalling purposes.

There was a fixed side window, almost triangular in shape but with a vertical section at its leading edge to align with the base of the windscreen and a slant to the rear to align with the upper pane in the cab door, between the cab door and the front offside corner pillar. There were matching windows on the nearside of the cab alongside the bonnet, the foremost almost triangular window being fixed and the larger window being divided vertically into two sliding panes to provide ventilation to the cab.

The base of the cab door was curved over the wheel arch to a position about 9in from the rear of the door thereafter the base, beneath the cab door handle, was horizontal, parallel to the waistband and about 1ft 6in below it.

A rectangular step protruded somewhat from the offside lower-deck panels between the front wheel and the first access door at the same height as the top of these doors.

All wheels were fitted with chromed hub bosses and wheel nut guard rings

A rectangular driver's rear-view mirror was mounted externally on the front offside cab pillar only.

The trolley boom retention hooks were attached to each side of a single stanchion at the rear of the roof.

A single tubular lifeguard, held by protruding attachments or outriggers beneath the body panels, ran beneath the tumblehome of the lower-deck side panels between the front and leading rear axles.

A tube, mounted externally at the base of the nearside vent panel and extending from just forward of the lower-deck front nearside pillar to the rear nearside pillar with the open end adjoining the rear platform vestibule, accommodated a bamboo trolley retrieval pole. This required a short extension of the vent panel above the open area to the nearside of the bonnet to provide the necessary support.

Lighting: External lighting comprised two headlights positioned in motorbus style, the nearside one was mounted on an outrigger from the chassis between the mudguard and the bonnet, and the offside one partially inset into the driver's cab front panel. The sidelights were mounted on stems above the nearside mudguard and protruding from the lower-deck offside panel at the front beneath the corner pillar.

There were two rear lights located in the extremity of the rear offside corner panels, one at the level of the vent panels and the other at the base of the corner panels.

A brake light was mounted in the extremity of the rear offside corner panels, in the waistband.

Internal lighting arrangements are not known.

Seating: Not known.

Destination equipment: A single-line final-destination indicator box was fitted in the centre of the upper-deck front panelling above the driver's windscreen and imitation radiator with a square service number indicator box immediately above centred above the final-destination box. At the rear there was a rectangular box centred above the rear platform windows protruding from the upper-deck panelling for its entire depth which contained a single-line final-destination indicator box surmounted by a square service number indicator box.

External Livery: Delivered in the manufacturer's interpretation of Livery 1 (see Appendix D).

Internal Livery: Not known.

Notes: LJ7702 was originally on hire from AEC-EE at a cost of 3d per mile. In November 1933, the Transport Committee recommended its purchase for £2,042 and this was subsequently agreed, whereupon it was allocated the Bournemouth fleet number 69.

Subsequent alterations: Following the decision to place major orders for Sunbeam MS2s the AEC663T became non-standard and in 1934 (commencing on 8 October 1934) 69 was rebuilt by BCT with separate forwards-descending half-turn front staircase and front exit equipped with a two-leaf folding door manually controlled from the driver's cab thereby reducing the seating to H28/24R. Straight-backed seats were fitted and the longitudinal seats in the lower saloon were lowered. All windows were re-bedded. The rear differential was taken down and examined. The propeller shafts were overhauled and fitted with new centre bearings, cases and splices. A Sunbeam 24V

lighting set was fitted and the vehicle rewired to suit. Following a complete overhaul 69 entered the paint shop on 16 January 1935.

From September to November 1936 the vehicle was converted to a motor bus by removing the electrical control equipment and substituting an AEC six-cylinder petrol engine, "crash" gearbox and working radiator and bonnet with a rebuilt half-cab. The unladen weight became 7 tons 17cwt. 69 re-entered service as a motor bus on 10 November 1936.

Disposal: 69 was stored at Christchurch substation yard from 27 September 1950 and sold to Sherwood Car Sales, Ringwood Road, Parkstone, Poole, Dorset, dealer, on 24 December 1950. Re-sold to Southend-on-Sea Corporation in early 1951 for conversion into a mobile convenience. The vehicle was disposed of in early 1967 and went to Kirby, Rochford, Essex, breakers in May 1967.

Between September and November 1936 AEC-EE 663T, no. 69 (LJ7702) was rebuilt as a motorbus by removing the electrical control equipment and substituting an AEC six cylinder petrol engine, "crash" gearbox and working radiator and bonnet. It is seen here at Boscombe Pier in November 1936 shortly after re-entering service in its new form.   **Malcolm Pearce (G.O.P. Pearce)**

70 AEC-EE 661T

Fleet No.	Reg.Mark	Chassis Number	Body Number	Date of Delivery	Date into Service	Date of Withdrawal	Date of Disposal
70	LJ7703	661T007		11.05.1933	13.051933	30.06.1950	12.1950

Chassis: Two axle type AEC-EE 661T manufactured by the Associated Equipment Company Ltd. (AEC) at the AEC works, Windmill Lane, Southall, Middlesex.
Motor: English Electric Co. Ltd. (EE), Phoenix Works, Bradford, Yorkshire.
Type DE 403A series-wound (80nhp) augmented field equipment, non-regenerative.
Electrical equipment: D487B controller, 8 notches including 2 weak field.
Dewirement indicator: single neon line-light.
Brakes: Rheostatic; Lockheed hydraulic actuated by Westinghouse compressed air; and handbrake, mechanical to all rear wheels.
Body: Highbridge double-deck composite six-bay construction with single rear staircase, and conventional rear, semi-vestibuled open platform entrance and exit.
Built by English Electric Co. Ltd., Dick, Kerr Works, Preston, Lancashire. H26/24R
Length: 25ft 8in   Width: 7ft 6in
Wheelbase: 15ft 6½in, giving a turning circle of 57ft 8in.
Unladen weight: 6 tons 0 cwt 8 qtrs.
Tyres: 36 X 8 high-pressure front, 38 X 9 high-pressure rear (twins), according to the pre-war system of measuring tyre sizes.

Delivered on 11 May 1933 as one of the four experimental vehicles, LJ7703 participated in the official opening ceremony of 13 May 1933 and together with the Sunbeam MS2 (LJ7701) entered service that same day on the Bournemouth Square-Westbourne trial route.

Chassis: based on the AEC Regent 661 motorbus chassis and axles. Chassis 007 was built in November 1932.
See 69 AEC-EE 663T for chassis frame construction details (these being identical).

Track: front 6ft 3¹⁄₁₆in, rear 5ft 10³⁄₄in
Chassis weight: 3 tons 5cwt

Frame overall length 24ft 10½in
Frame maximum width: 3ft 11⁵⁄₈in
Chassis overall width: 7ft 5⁵⁄₈in over rear tyres.
Road clearance under rear axle 7½in.

The axles were made from 100-ton steel 3in in diameter and mounted on adjustable taper roller bearings. A chrome vanadium spring steel torque blade was used permitting freedom of motion of each axle.

Semi-elliptic springs:
Front: above axle, 4ft 2in long between centres
Rear: below axle, 5ft 2in long between centres.

See 69 AEC-EE 663T for further chassis details, these being

identical except for references to the rear bogie.

Electrics: The front-mounted English Electric DE 403A traction motor was on a sub-frame offset to the nearside and angled downwards to provide a straight transmission line to the rear axle differential. The motor had a one-hour rating of 80hp at 500v.
See Appendix A, 69 AEC-EE 663T for further electrical details, these being identical.

Brakes: See Appendix A, 69 AEC-EE 663T for details, these being identical.

Bodywork: Highbridge double-deck composite six-bay construction with conventional, enclosed forwards-ascending half-turn (90°) staircase with semi-vestibuled open platform entrance and exit at the rear, built by English Electric Co. Ltd. at Preston. In virtually all respects the body was a shorter version of that on the AEC-EE663T (LJ7702).
See 69 AEC-EE 663T for further bodywork details, these being identical except for the following:
Top-hinged access doors were fitted at the base of the lower deck offside panel bays 1, 2 and 3 providing access to the equipment mounted on the exterior face of the offside chassis member.
The mudguard over the rear wheels was swept particularly low. Individual mud flaps hung behind the front wheels.
Both front wheels were fitted with chromed hub bosses and wheel nut guard rings.
A single tubular lifeguard, held by protruding attachments or outriggers beneath the body panels, ran beneath the tumblehome of the lower-deck side panels between the front and rear axles. A tube, mounted externally at the base of the nearside vent panel and extending from just forward of the lower-deck front nearside pillar to the rear nearside pillar with the open end adjoining the rear platform vestibule, accommodated a bamboo trolley retrieval pole. The vent panel extended forwards above the open area to the nearside of the bonnet and was aligned with the top of the driver's windscreen in order to provide the necessary support.

Lighting: See 69 AEC-EE 663T for details (these being identical).

Seating: Not known.

Destination equipment: See 69 AEC-EE 663T for details (these being identical).

External Livery: Delivered in the manufacturer's interpretation of Livery 1 (see Appendix D).

Internal Livery: Not known.

The crowds admire AEC-EE 661T LJ7703 as it departs once more for County Gates, Westbourne on the experimental service on 13 May 1933. David Chalk collection (Bournemouth Transport Ltd.)

Notes: LJ7703 was initially on hire from AEC-EE at a cost of 3d per mile. In November 1933, the Transport Committee recommended its purchase for £1,853 and this was subsequently agreed, whereupon it was allocated the Bournemouth fleet number 70.

Subsequent alterations: Following the decision to place major orders for Sunbeam MS2s the AEC661T became non-standard and in 1934 (commencing on 11 October 1934), 70 was rebuilt by BCT with separate forwards-descending half-turn front staircase and front exit equipped with a two-leaf folding door manually controlled from the driver's cab thereby reducing the seating to H24/22D.

From March to June 1936 the vehicle was converted to a motorbus by removing the electrical control equipment and substituting an AEC six-cylinder petrol engine, "crash" gearbox and working radiator and bonnet with a rebuilt half-cab. The unladen weight became 6 tons 14cwt. 70 re-entered service as a motorbus on 1 July 1936.

Disposal: 70 was stored at Christchurch substation yard from 2 August 1950 and sold to Sherwood Car Sales, Ringwood Road, Parkstone, Poole, Dorset, dealer, on 24 December 1950.

AEC-EE 661T LJ7703 looked very similar to its three-axle sister LJ7702, but was shorter and had only two axles. It is seen here descending the west side of the Triangle on its way to the Square. The vehicle was subsequently given Bournemouth fleet number 70.   **David Chalk collection (Bournemouth Transport Ltd.)**

71 Thornycroft

Fleet No.	Reg.Mark	Chassis Number	Body Number	Date of Delivery	Date into Service	Date of Withdrawal	Date of Disposal
71	LJ7704	BD10269		11.05.1933	15.051933	01.10.1941	01.1942

Chassis: Two-axle type BD manufactured by John I. Thornycroft & Co. Ltd., Basingstoke, Hampshire.

Motor: Brush Electrical Engineering Co. Ltd., Falcon Works, Nottingham Road, Loughborough, Leicestershire. Compound-wound for regenerative control. Further details not known.

Electrical equipment: British Thomson-Houston Co. Ltd., Rugby. Type not known.

Brakes: Regenerative, achieved by releasing the power pedal; vacuum servo-assisted activated by the brake pedal and operating on all wheels; and handbrake, mechanical to the rear wheels.

Body: Single-deck with combined centre entrance and exit built by Brush Electrical Engineering Co. Ltd., Falcon Works, Nottingham Road, Loughborough, Leicestershire. B32C.

Length: 26ft   Width 7ft 6in

Unladen weight: 5 tons 19cwt 3qtr

Tyres: 22 X 8.25 high-pressure to all wheels (twins at rear) according to the pre-war system of measuring tyre sizes.

The established steam and motorbus manufacturer Thornycroft never seriously entered the trolleybus market. In the period 1922-1933 they built 5 trolleybus chassis; that supplied to Bournemouth for demonstration purposes being the last but one and the only single-deck Thornycroft trolleybus to enter regular service in Britain. The vehicle was delivered by rail to Bournemouth on 11 May 1933 as the third of the four experimental vehicles to arrive and entered service on the Bournemouth Square-Westbourne trial route on 15 May 1933. The original Hampshire registration mark, CG4313, was replaced with the Bournemouth Borough LJ7704 prior to entering service.

Chassis: Not known.

Electrics: Not known.

Brakes: Regenerative on power pedal. Vacuum servo-assisted, activated by the brake pedal and operating on all wheels.
The pull-on handbrake was to the offside of the driver's steering column.

Bodywork: Composite six-bay single-deck construction, equipped with a central entrance and exit built by Brush Electrical Engineering Co. Ltd., Loughborough, Leicestershire. The bodywork narrowed in the driver's cab area to give pronounced front wheel mudguards.

Half-drop openers equipped with a single "pinch fastener" at the top of each pane were fitted to the side windows in bays 1, 4, 5 on the nearside, and to bays 1, 2, 4, 5 on the offside. The upper pane dropped outside the fixed lower pane. At the rear there was a single large oval window.

Glazed louvres in chromium-plated steel frames were fitted above the side windows in bays 1, 2, 4-6 nearside, and 1-6 offside thus including the rear panes which were radiused at

the rear, top and bottom. The side windows were surmounted by a rainstrip which continued along the edge of the "peaked" roof above the driver's windscreen. Additional ventilation was provided by two roof-mounted ventilators to the rear of the entrance and exit door. There was a single top-hinged access door or valence panel at the base of the offside panels in bay 3 giving access to equipment mounted on the external face of the chassis frame.

There was a broad entrance and exit on the nearside equipped with a manually-operated door which slid forwards into bay 2 when open. Entry involved a step up from the kerb followed by a single step up to the saloon floor with a curved-top handrail covered in Doverite in front of the first forwards-facing double seat to the rear of the door and a used ticket box behind the double seat to the front of the step. There was a single chromium-plated stanchion behind this latter seat on the nearside of the gangway. No platform as such was evident. In addition to the stanchion, two ceiling-mounted chromium-plated handrails extended above the gangway above the longitudinal seats

Extensions were bolted to the roof rail immediately above the body pillars of bay 1 and curved steel brackets bolted to the roof supported the exposed trolley gantry which was not in direct contact with the roof. Radio interference suppressors were mounted on the roof of the driver's cab forward of the trolley gantry. The trolley gantry was masked from view by large, somewhat square, fairings built around it.

The driver's cab had front-hinged doors (three hinges) on both sides each equipped with a backwards sliding "signalling" window in the lower portion, and a black centrally-mounted opening handle mounted in a black-moulded circular inset. The window of the offside cab door was divided horizontally, the upper portion having a single fixed pane and the lower portion having two panes, the rear pane sliding forwards behind the front pane, for signalling purposes. Forwards of the opening doors there was a wedge-shaped side window which narrowed towards the top to allow for the swept-back front windscreen. The front panel beneath the driver's windscreen had a centrally-mounted, blank "radiator" outline which initially carried the two symbols of the manufacturers and a circular access hole for towing purposes. The front registration plate was attached to the base of the "radiator" outline. The offside driver's windscreen was divided horizontally into two panes of equal depth, all in a chromium-plated frame. The top-hinged upper pane could be opened outwards and was equipped with a windscreen wiper mounted centrally at the top. A rectangular driver's rear-view mirror was mounted externally on the front offside cab pillar only, there being none on the nearside.

There were three windows in the bulkhead behind the driver, those on the nearside and offside having the same depth as the saloon side windows, and that in the middle being shorter and equipped with two panes which could be opened for communication purposes. Inside the cab the circuit breakers and other electrical equipment were mounted on a panel

The **Brush-Thornycroft** demonstrator, probably photographed near the Thornycroft factory in Basingstoke, carrying its original Hampshire registration mark CG4313. The "legal lettering" at the base of the nearside panels to the rear of the front axle is interesting and fully correct, viz.: Brush Thornycroft Vehicle. On Hire To Bournemouth Corporation. I. Bulfin, Engineer & General Manager.   **David Chalk collection**

The trolley wheels and bamboo retriever pole (above the nearside windows) are clearly visible in the above photograph.
                                                                                    David Chalk collection

An interior view of the **Brush Thornycroft** single deck trolleybus looking forwards to the driver's cab. Note the manner in which the ceiling-mounted lamps were angled to throw light over the central entrance/exit, and the excellent forwards view for passengers through the cab. **David Chalk collection**

Another interior view of the **Brush Thornycroft** demonstrator looking towards the rear. **David Chalk collection**

303

above the middle bulkhead window. Attached to the bulkhead above each window inside the saloon was a fold-down blind to prevent reflections from the lower saloon on to the driver's windscreen during the hours of darkness.

The base of the cab door was curved over the wheel arch to a position about 9in from the rear of the door thereafter the base, beneath the cab door handle, was horizontal, parallel to the waistband and about 1ft 6in below it.

A rectangular step protruded somewhat from the side panels on each side immediately behind the front mudguard providing access to the cab.

Two wooden lifeguards ran beneath the side panels between the first and second axles on both sides. Individual mud flaps hung behind each wheel of the front and rear axles.

The rear registration plate was inset into the rear panels at about two-thirds of the depth between the waistband and the base of the panels. There was a rectangular access door to the offside of the inset and a broad, narrow access door at the base of panels beneath the inset.

Metal trolley boom retention hooks with cross bracing were mounted at the rear of the roof but there seems to have been no catwalk. On the nearside along the roofline above the rainstrip, hooks above the pillar between bays 1 and 2, 3 and 4, and 5 and 6 (total three) supported a bamboo trolley retriever pole.

Both front wheels were equipped with hubs engraved with the Thornycroft "T" manufacturer's badges, and wheel nut protector rings.

Lighting: In addition to rather prominent chromed headlights, large and somewhat dated sidelights were mounted on stems at the base of the nearside and offside cab corner pillars. Single rear light mounted at the top of the offside corner panel, the top aligned with the highest point of the oval rear window, and incorporating a hook from which an oil lamp could be hung in an emergency. A lens in the corner panel permitting the saloon interior lighting to shine through seems to have been the source of illumination to the rear light.

Internally there were nine oval lamps with diffused, patterned glass covers and chromium-plated surrounds mounted on plinths in the cove panels. There were two each side in the front compartment, two each side in the rear compartment and a single lamp on the offside opposite the nearside door.

Seating: Semi-bucket type seats with quilted, possibly artificial, crocodile leather curved backs and plain leather squabs based on concealed interior frames with exposed pressed steel supports. The rear of each seat was finished in a plain material. At the rear of each forwards-facing double seat there was a curved grab handle adjacent to the aisle and a centrally-mounted cigarette stubber. The broad sliding door, entrance steps and central platform area dictated the seating layout. On the nearside there were three rows of forwards-facing double seats forward of the door, then to the rear of the door came a double seat, a longitudinal seat on a raised plinth over the rear axle for two passengers and then a further forwards-

facing double seat. On the offside, from the front, there were five rows of forwards-facing double seats, a longitudinal seat on a raised plinth over the rear axle for three passengers and then a further forwards-facing double seat. At the rear was a bench seat for five passengers. Due to position of the door, all the double seats forward of the rear axle were staggered. The driver's seat was upholstered in plain leather.

Destination equipment: There was a single-line final-destination indicator box with external illumination at the front, mounted centrally on the pronounced roof "peak" over the windscreen but none at the rear.

External livery: The demonstrator was painted in a two-tone blue livery with dark blue lower panels, pale blue window surrounds and roof, separated by a white waistband which narrowed above the "radiator" outline apex beneath the pillar dividing the driver's cab windscreen into two. The dark blue panels had a single gold line immediately below the central white band and carried the legend BRUSH-THORNYCROFT in gold-block lettering on the lower panels in bays 1 and 2. For subsequent changes see Appendix D.

Internal Livery: Cream ceilings. The bay 1 and 2 pillars on both sides and bay 3 pillars on the nearside continued into the ceiling to provide additional support to the trolley gantry and sliding door. These pillars and the window surrounds were varnished/polished wood. Side panels covered in dark leathercloth. There were five bell-pushes, one each in the surround above the window in bay 4 nearside, in bay 2 on both sides, and above the pillar between bays 5 and 6 on both sides. The saloon floor was covered with linoleum and included a number of metal-edged hatches on the nearside and along the central aisle.

Notes: LJ7704 was initially on hire from Brush at a cost of 3d per mile. In November 1933, the Transport Committee recommended its purchase for £1,450 and this was subsequently agreed, whereupon it was allocated the Bournemouth fleet number 71. Following the decision to standardise on the Sunbeam MS2, Bluebird became very much an "odd man out".

Subsequent alterations: No. 71 was out of service from 24 November 1934 until 23 December 1936 during which time the motor was returned to Brush for overhaul and the vehicle, which initially retained its blue colour scheme, was repainted in standard Bournemouth primrose livery.

Disposal: 71 was sold to Derry & Co., dealers, on 14 January 1942 and passed to South Shields Corporation Transport where it was also the only single-deck trolleybus on the system, as their fleet number 236. Due to wartime conditions it entered service in South Shields in primrose livery with the maroon bands repainted blue. Withdrawn from service in 1950, it had become a caravan at the local Golden City amusement park by August 1953.

72 - 89 Sunbeam-BTH MS2

Original Fleet No.	New 1958 Fleet No.	Registration Mark	Chassis Number	Body Number	Date of Delivery	Date into Service	Date of Withdrawal	Date of Disposal
72		AEL400	12031S	3477	08.06.1934	13.06.1934	.03.1953	.07.1953
73		AEL401	12032S	3478	13.06.1934	22.06.1934	.03.1953	.07.1953
74		AEL402	12034S	3479	15.06.1934	22.06.1934	.12.1950	.05.1952
75		AEL403	12036S	3480	17.06.1934	22.06.1934	.12.1952	.07.1953
76		AEL404	12038S	3481	20.06.1937	22.06.1934	.12.1952	.07.1953
77		AEL405	12037S	3482	20.06.1934	22.06.1934	.12.1952	.07.1953
78		AEL406	12030S		14.06.1934	22.06.1934	.12.1952	.05.1952
79		AEL407	12033S		01.07.1934	04.07.1934	.09.1952	.07.1953
80		AEL408	12035S		03.07.1934	05.07.1934	.12.1954	.03.1958
81		AEL409	12039S		20.07.1934	22.07.1934	.03.1955	.03.1958
82		AEL410	12040S		22.07.1934	24.07.1934	.03.1955	.03.1958
83		AEL411	12041S		24.07.1934	28.07.1934	.01.1957	.03.1958
84	205	ALJ60	12047S	3611	02.10.1934	03.10.1934	.09.1963	.10.1963
85	206	ALJ61	12048S	3612	18.10.1934	22.10.1934	.09.1963	.03.1964
86	207	ALJ62	12049S	3613	07.10.1934	09.10.1934	.08.1962	.01.1963
87		ALJ63	12050S	3614	09.10.1934	12.10.1934	.12.1958	.01.1959
88	208	ALJ64	12051S	3615	11.10.1934	13.10.1934	.09.1963	.10.1963
89		ALJ65	12052S	3616	13.10.1934	20.10.1934	.10.1957	.01.1959

Chassis: Three axle Sunbeam type MS2 manufactured by Sunbeam Motor Car Co. Ltd., Moorfield Road Works, Blakenhall, Wolverhampton, Staffordshire.

Motor: British Thomson-Houston Co. Ltd., Rugby, Warwickshire, Type 201 compound-wound (80 nhp) for regenerative control. Electrical equipment: British Thomson-Houston (BTH); scissors-type controller, 12 notches (1-6, resistance; 7, full power; 8-12, field weakening).

Dewirement indicator: neon line-lights and buzzer.

Brakes: Regenerative, achieved by releasing the power pedal; Lockheed vacuum-assisted hydraulic, activated by the brake pedal and operating on all wheels; and handbrake, mechanical to all rear wheels.

Body: Highbridge double-deck composite six-bay construction with twin staircases, conventional rear, semi-vestibuled open platform entrance and front exit, the latter equipped with a manually-operated, two-leaf folding door controlled from the driver's cab.

Built by:

72-77 Park Royal Vehicles Ltd., Abbey Road, Park Royal, London NW10 — H31/25D

78 - 83 English Electric Co. Ltd., Dick Kerr Works, Preston, Lancashire (Park Royal Design) — H31/25D

84 - 89 Park Royal Vehicles Ltd., Abbey Road, Park Royal, London, NW10 — H31/25D

Length: 28ft 7$\frac{1}{4}$in   Width: 7ft 6in   Height: 15ft 7$\frac{1}{2}$in (laden, measured over retaining hooks).

Wheelbase: 17ft 0in (from front axle to centre of rear bogie), giving a turning circle of 59ft.

Unladen weight: 72-83   8 tons 7cwt 2qtr

84-89   8 tons 12cwt

Tyres: 36 X 8 high-pressure to all wheels according to the pre-war system of measuring tyre sizes, as previously described.

Sunbeam's efforts to develop a new less prestigious car proved unsuccessful and an unrepaid loan led the Sunbeam Motor Car Co. Ltd. to the verge of bankruptcy and a Receiver was appointed. On 17 November 1934 Sunbeam Commercial Vehicles became a limited company.

Chassis: The main frame was constructed from high tensile steel with channel-section side members, the webs being 11in deep amidships with diagonal channel and tubular cross members to give maximum rigidity. To the rear of the traction motor was a deep box-section girder, the short 4in-diameter propeller shaft passing through a tunnel formed at the junction of a semi-cruciform structure in the centre. The shaft was fitted with a needle roller universal joint at each end, connecting the traction motor with a differential on the leading rear axle ensuring a distribution of torque between the two rear axles.

Chassis length: 27ft 5$\frac{1}{2}$in
Chassis width: 7ft 5$\frac{1}{2}$in
Chassis weight less traction equipment and cabling: 4tons 8cwt 1qtr
Height of frame laden: 25in

Woodhead semi-elliptic divided backplate springs with solid eyes to all axles:
Front: 3$\frac{1}{2}$in wide, 3ft 8in long
Rear: 3$\frac{1}{2}$in wide, 3ft 11$\frac{1}{4}$in long.

Twin springs located on swivel brackets with large diameter

Sunbeam MS2 no. 85 (ALJ61) was one of the Park Royal Vehicles bodied examples delivered in October 1934. It is seen at the body-builder's factory prior to delivery. Note the triangular quarter light (which did not open) and the ⅔-size half-drop pane above the driver's cab and the over-optimistic destination Poole Park on the offside lower saloon indicator blind (visble through the lower saloon windows).

David Chalk collection

Rear nearside view of Sunbeam MS2 no. 85 (ALJ61) photographed at Park Royal Coachworks factory in October 1934.

David Chalk collection

The upper saloon of Park Royal bodied Sunbeam MS2 no. 72 (AEL400) looking towards the rear. Note the single seat on the nearside, opposite the front exit stairwell, and the torpedo shaped grab handle attached to the top of the seat backs adjacent to the aisle. Bournemouth Transport Ltd.

The lower saloon of Park Royal bodied Sunbeam MS2 no. 72 (AEL400) looking towards the driver's cab. Bournemouth Transport Ltd.

phosphor bronze bearings were fitted to each side of the rear bogie providing transverse rigidity. By removing the bolts on the spring brackets and disconnecting the propeller shaft and brakes, the bogie could be removed from the chassis frame and wheeled out from underneath the vehicle for overhaul purposes.

Underslung worm-type rear axles were used, the main axle casing being made from a steel drop forging. The differentials each having four planets and two sun wheels, contained in a steel cage to which was also mounted the worm and wheel (ratio 91/3 to 1). There was a third differential.

Grouped grease nipples at various points provided lubrication to the chassis. A box in the driver's cab equipped with ten nipples lubricated the shackle pins, spring pins, the foot brake pedal, the hand brake lever, steering wheel, etc.

Sunbeam invoice value £2,135 each Sunbeam serial order Bournemouth 1-18.

Electrics: The British Thomson-Houston Type 201 (80nhp) compound-wound traction motor was resiliently mounted at four points in a sub-frame amidships within the chassis frame between the front and the leading rear axle. The single turn armature winding motor had a one-hour rating of 80hp at 500V drawing 130 amps. Maximum safe motor speed was 3,000rpm, whilst the speed corresponding to a road speed of 30mph on a level road was 2,646rpm.

By releasing the forward Silentbloc mounting pins the motor and its sub-frame could be hinged downwards, after which the rear pins could also be removed and the motor lowered.

The reverser handle was detachable.

The self-cleaning contactors were mounted in the driver's cab on the offside and front offside, the line and resistance contactors being on one panel with the auxiliary contactors and relays, such as the shunt field contactors and over-voltage relay, on a second panel. Both panels were of lightweight insulating material. The BTH electromagnetic switches operating coils were energised through the master controller. In the case of regenerative voltage exceeding line voltage, a relay in the shunt field inserted a resistance in the lighting circuit to prevent a lamp burn-out.

All power and control wiring was shrouded in metallic tube sheathing to prevent interference in radio reception. Filters were also incorporated in the control circuits avoiding the necessity of using mains choke coils.

BTH rustless and jointless unbreakable grid main resistances were mounted on the nearside external face of the chassis frame with steel shielding from the lower saloon bodywork and a steel stone guard beneath. Shunt resistance wire wound on porcelain tubes and embedded in porcelain. Sunbeam quoted power consumption as being from 1.65 units per mile.

Regeneration was obtained by releasing the foot pedal and allowing the master controller to return towards the full field notch, thus strengthening the shunt field, the braking effect increasing as the field strengthened. Should the driver have brought back his controller to one of the starting resistance notches this would not affect regeneration, as the starting resistance, having once been shorted out, remained so until the controller was brought into the "off" position when all the contactors opened. This avoided any possibility of inefficient

An English Electric bodied Sunbeam MS2, no. 80 (AEL408), seen in the Triangle parking area on 11 July 1954 just five months before its withdrawal.
Malcolm Pearce (G.O.P. Pearce)

regeneration with series resistance in circuit. It was estimated that energy savings in the region of 5-20%, dependent on gradients and the number of stops per mile, etc., could be attained in comparison to a trolleybus equipped with a normal series-wound motor.

The motor generator set comprised two insulated machines with a continuous rated capacity of 1,000 watts at 24V. The high voltage portion of the unit was resiliently insulated from the main chassis frame and body. The main load for the interior lights was taken from the generator unit whilst only the current required for the legally-required external lights and accessories, e.g. horn, bells, windscreen wiper, etc., was taken from the small 40 amp hour battery and the dynamo was only in operation when the interior lamp load was taken.

Brecknell, Willis & Co. Ltd., Bristol, lightweight trolley equipment, and trolley bases, the booms being equipped with trolley wheels.

A "skate" could be fitted to allow current return via the tramway track.

Traction batteries for manoeuvring purposes were not fitted.

Brakes: The vehicles were fitted with regenerative braking for conventional stopping. The driver released the control pedal until speed was reduced to about 10 mph and then brought the trolleybus to a halt with the vacuum-assisted hydraulic footbrake which operated on all wheels.

The Sunbeam patent hydraulic brake control gear comprised a master-cylinder box with three cylinders, each $1\frac{1}{2}$ in in diameter, which actuated the brakes on one axle, whilst an outer casing acted as a reserve tank by which each system was kept full of fluid. A compensating and sealing device together with multiple master cylinder ensured safe braking in the case of a fracture in the pipelines as only one of the three systems would be affected.

A Dewandre vacuum servo between the brake pedal and the master cylinders amplified the driver's foot pressure reducing the physical effort required in braking. The vacuum supply tank for the servo system was exhausted by a rotary exhauster driven from the forward end of the traction motor.

The front brake drums were $16\frac{3}{4}$in diameter and the shoes $3\frac{3}{8}$in wide, the rear brake drums of malleable cast iron were $19\frac{3}{4}$in diameter and the shoes 4in wide, all shoes being equipped with $7/8$in thick Ferodo linings, giving 884 sq in lining area for the foot brake. The Lockheed brake shoe actuators employed pressure cylinders 2in in diameter mounted on brake shoe carrier brackets which expanded the shoes by means of short push-rods connected to the master-cylinders by copper tubing and flexible hoses.

As the footbrake had purely a hydraulic action, it was possible for a driver to draw power to change automatic frogs by depressing the power and brake pedals together thus avoiding the tiring and potentially dangerous arrangement of pulling hard on the handbrake lever whilst taking power and steering at the same time. This was necessary on trolleybuses equipped with electric braking on the footbrake pedal whereby engaging the electric brake cut off the power pedal circuits.

The pull-on handbrake was linked mechanically by rods acting on the rear bogie wheels; the handbrake lever was to the offside of the driver's steering column.

Bodywork: Composite six-bay highbridge double-deck construction, equipped with forward-ascending half-turn (90°) rear staircase and forward-descending half-turn front staircase, built to a Park Royal Vehicles design by both Park Royal Vehicles Ltd., London NW10 and English Electric Co. Ltd., Preston, Lancashire. The body had an English oak timber frame and the roof structure was in best white ash. External panelling was in 18G aluminium, the shaped panels being in 20G steel.

The ash roof sticks were strengthened in both saloons with single steel carlines bolted to the cantrails. The roof of the lower saloon was pine boards covered with cotton duck roofing canvas laid in thick white lead paint and having a further floor covering of pine boards, the space between the decks being ventilated.

The exposed trolley gantry was constructed of three externally-mounted steel channels carried down to the top of the lower-deck pillars of bays 2 and 3 which linked at upper-deck floor level with a horizontal steel channel running along each side from the front pillar of the driver's cab to a few inches behind the central grab rail on the rear platform. The gantry was not in direct contact with the roof.

The vehicles featured twin staircases with a conventional rear, semi-vestibuled open platform entrance and a front exit equipped with a two-leaf folding door manually controlled from the driver's cab by means of a slide-handle, immediately above the nearside bulkhead window, coupled to an interlock to break the controller circuit thus preventing the trolleybus from starting off with the door open. To open the door, the driver flipped over the safety catch and pulled the slide towards him. The main power cable made its way forward from the platform supporting the trolley bases along the centre line of the roof before entering the roof panels at the rear of the front dome and making its way down to the switches in the driver's cab. Access to the trolley gear was by means of a removable wooden slatted platform with gaps in its frame to fit over the protective rail to the rear window pane, stored securely on the rear platform beneath the staircase when not required and which could be fitted across the upper saloon emergency exit to cover the glass, thence to the roof catwalk.

The upper-deck rear emergency exit door contained a single large window with radiused top outer corners and bottom hinges (three hinges for 72-77 and 84-89, four for 78-83). The emergency exit door could be opened by an external handle mounted on the rear dome immediately above the rain strip and to the offside for 72-77 and 84-89 (centrally for 78-83) above the door, or from the inside by a comparable handle attached to a horizontal locking bar mounted on the cantrail immediately above the door. The horizontal bar was equipped with three prongs that engaged with brackets on the top of the door. When opened, it was retained at 90° to the upper-deck rear panels by leather covered chains on each side.

There were a number of other detail differences between the English Electric and Park Royal-built bodies:

72-77 Widney Stuart "Aero" pattern half-drop openers equipped with a single "pinch fastener" at the top of each pane were fitted to the side windows in bays 2-4 (both sides) of the lower deck and to bays 1, 3, 5 on the nearside and to bays 3, 4, 5 on the offside of the upper deck. The upper pane dropped outside the fixed lower pane. The upper deck single-pane front windows were fixed. Plate glass $3/16$in thick was used for the side windows in both saloons. There were four rotating Flettner Extractor ventilators on the roof and four large side ventilators in the vent panel above the bay 2-4 (both sides) lower deck windows. The side ventilators were almost as deep as the vent panel. Those in bays 2-4 were located at the rear of each bay whilst that in bay 6 was located at the front.

Glazed louvres in stainless steel frames were fitted above the side windows on the lower deck bays 2-6 nearside, 1-6 offside (thus including the diffused glass pane behind the front staircase), and on the upper deck bays 1-6 both sides.

A single top-hinged access door or valence panel was fitted at the base of the lower-deck offside panels in bays 3 and 4, taking up the rear two-thirds of bay 3 and the front half of bay 4 (up to the leading rear axle).

Despite the protruding rear indicator box, small protruding rubber bumpers half way up the frame on the nearside and offside of the emergency exit door aligned with similar bumpers on the panel beneath just above the rear indicator box. When the retaining chains were removed and the emergency exit door opened to its fullest extent the door hung down and rested on these bumpers. Cross-bracing between the trolley boom retention hooks.

78-83 Widney Stuart "Aero" pattern half-drop openers equipped with a single "pinch fastener" at the top of each pane were fitted to the side windows in bays 2-4 (both sides) of the lower deck and to bays 1, 3, 5 on the nearside and to bays 3, 4, 5 on the offside of the upper deck. The upper pane dropped outside the fixed lower pane. The upper-deck front windows were fixed. Plate glass $^3/_{16}$in thick was used for the side windows in both saloons. There were four large rotating extractor ventilators on the roof above bays 3, 5 on both sides, which protruded noticeably more from the roof than those on the Park Royal-bodied vehicles, and four side ventilators in the vent panel above the bays 2, 3, 5, 6 (both sides) lower deck windows. The side ventilators were much smaller than those on 72-77. Those in bays 2, 5 were located at the front of each bay whilst those in bays 3, 6 were located at the rear.

Glazed louvres in stainless steel frames were fitted above the side windows on the lower deck bays 2-6 nearside, 1-6 offside (thus including the diffused glass pane behind the front staircase), and on the upper deck bays 1-6 and the "D" window above the rear platform both sides.

A step was let into the base of the offside bay 1 side panel without any form of protection to the bodywork, immediately behind the front axle.

Top-hinged access doors or valence panels were fitted at the base of the lower-deck offside panels in bays 2, 3 and 4, taking up the rear two-thirds of bay 2, all bay 3 and the front half of bay 4 (up to the leading rear axle).

There were small protruding rubber bumpers in the top corners of the frame of the emergency exit door but no equivalent bumpers on the rear panels. It is unclear how these bumpers would have prevented the emergency exit door resting on the protruding rear indicator box if opened to its fullest extent. The trolley boom retention hooks were attached to each side of a single "Y"-shaped stanchion at the rear of the roof.

84-89 The upper deck side windows on both sides immediately above the driver's cab featured a non-opening quarter light, followed by a Widney Stuart "Aero" pattern half-drop window using a $^2/_3$-size pane of glass. Further half-drop openers equipped with a single "pinch fastener" at the top of each pane were fitted to the side windows in bays 2-4 (both sides) of the lower deck and to bays 2, 3, 5, 6 (both sides) of the upper deck. The upper pane dropped outside the fixed lower pane. The front upper deck windows had bottom-hinged,

"pull-in" opening top hopper ventilators, surmounted by glazed louvres in stainless steel frames. Plate glass 3/16in thick was used for the side windows in both saloons. There was a single rotating Flettner Extractor ventilator mounted centrally in the front dome and three on the offside mounted centrally above bays 1, 3, 4. There were four side ventilators in the vent panel above the bays 2-5 (both sides) lower deck windows, these being much smaller than those on 72-77, and located at the rear of each bay.

All saloon side windows, including the upper deck quarter light and the "D" window above the rear platform, were equipped with glazed louvres in stainless steel frames.

A single top-hinged access door or valence panel was fitted at the base of the lower-deck offside panels in bays 3 and 4, taking up the rear two-thirds of bay 3 and the front half of bay 4 (up to the leading rear axle).

Despite the protruding rear indicator box, small protruding rubber bumpers half way up the frame on the nearside and offside of the emergency exit door aligned with similar bumpers on the panel beneath just above the rear indicator box. When the retaining chains were removed and the emergency exit door opened to its fullest extent the door hung down and rested on these bumpers. Cross-bracing between the trolley boom retention hooks.

All bodies had a single rear platform window with radiused upper corners. The front registration plate was mounted centrally on the front panel, the top of the plate aligned with the base of the headlamps. The rear registration plate was to the offside of the rear panel beneath the triangular power brake light.

The driver's cab was equipped with an offside opening windscreen and single offside front hinged door. The window of the door was divided horizontally, the upper portion having a single fixed pane and the lower portion having two panes, the rear pane sliding forwards behind the front pane, for signalling purposes. The windscreen and all glass at the front of the lower deck was Triplex toughened safety glass.

A rectangular driver's rear-view mirror was mounted externally on the front offside cab pillar only, there originally being none on the nearside.

There was a three-piece metal "fairing" mudguard over the rear wheels. Individual mud flaps hung behind each wheel of the front and rear axles whilst a flap mudguard hung at an angle beneath the rear platform.

The ceiling of each saloon was 3-ply birch, weatherproofed and with aluminium side eaves panelled out with mouldings and enamelled white.

There were four bell pushes on each deck and a single one on the rear platform. Card advertisements could be displayed internally in varnished wood retaining channels in the cove panels between the lighting installations. In addition to the stanchions in both saloons, two ceiling-mounted handrails extended above the gangway, those in the lower saloon equipped with sliding leather-hung grab handles above the longitudinal seats. The offside handrail in the upper saloon was shorter than that on the nearside to avoid a rail being immediately above the top of each staircase. Used-ticket boxes were fitted on the rear panel at the top of the front staircase, immediately below the nearside cab rear window by the front exit and on the rear platform.

The offside windscreen was stainless steel and divided

horizontally at approximately two-thirds depth into two panes (half depth on English Electric-bodied 78-83). The upper top-hinged pane opened outwards and was equipped centrally with a top-mounted wiper.

A single tubular metal lifeguard ran beneath the side panels between the first and second axles. A bamboo trolley retrieval pole was carried in a tube mounted 9in to the nearside of the centreline under the chassis and was accessible from the rear of the vehicle.

Lighting: External lighting comprised two headlights mounted on plinths on the front panel, two front side lights on the lower-deck waistband and a single rear light mounted at the top of the offside lower-deck corner panel, the top aligned with the top of the rear platform window. A red power brake light in a red triangular frame was mounted on the offside of the rear panel immediately above the registration plate.

Lighting circuits were supplied from a Sunbeam patent motor generator set made up of a CAV Bosch dynamo and a $2\frac{1}{2}$ hp Newton Motor with a 24V 1,000 watt output. There were 32 open reflector-type interior lights 24V 20 watt with four fuses (separate fuses for accessories). The small circular light fittings were in white Bakelite with GEC lamp holders.

The 11 bells were fed from a 24V battery 48 amps hour capacity.

Seating: Based on Accles & Pollock painted tubular light alloy steel frames with chromium-plating to the rounded corners of the seat backs and Birmabright torpedo-shaped grab handles attached to the top of the seat backs adjacent to the aisle.

Squabs and backs were upholstered in Connolly Brothers brown hide leather (pleated squabs and plain backs) with brown scratchproof Rexine leathercloth seat-backs. Due to the position of the offside front staircase, seats in both the upper and lower saloons were staggered which gave more space for moving along the gangways. Accordingly the lower deck had a four-person bench seat over the rear bogie on the offside and a five-person bench seat on the nearside.

The upper saloon had two rows of single seats on the front nearside and a bench seat for three passengers on the offside immediately in front of the front exit staircase well. At the rear of the upper saloon there was a double seat on the nearside at the rear above the open platform adjacent to the rear staircase. The other double seats were staggered, there being five on the offside and seven on the nearside.

The driver's seat was in brown hide leather.

Destination equipment: A single-line final-destination indicator box was fitted in the upper-deck front panelling centred above the driver's windscreen with a square service number indicator box immediately above centred above the final-destination box. At the rear there was a rectangular box with an arched top centred above the rear platform window protruding from the upper-deck panelling for its entire depth and projecting more at its top than at its base due to the upwards curve of the panel to meet the rear dome. In the rear panel of this box was a single-line final-destination indicator box surmounted by a square service number indicator box.

Additional single-line final-destination indicator boxes were mounted inside the lower saloon at the top of the lower saloon bay 6 side window on both sides (behind the longitudinal seat).

External Livery: Delivered in Livery 1 (see Appendix D).

Internal Livery: Side panels were plywood covered with brown-grained scratchproof Rexine leathercloth. The internal roof skin was in plywood and the ceilings were covered with cream scratchproof Rexine leathercloth with varnished/polished wooden mouldings. The window frames were varnished wood. Brown paint to staircases and seat frames. All handrails and stanchions covered in black Doverite. Cab area painted brown to the waistline and primrose yellow above.

The saloon side windows in bays 1-6 were equipped with internal spring roller blinds with metal casings over the rollers. The floors of both decks were fitted with oak slatting.

Notes: No. 73 was used prior to 22 June 1934 for driver-training purposes.

Nos. 86 and 87 were reconditioned by Reading & Co. Ltd., London Road, Hillsea, Portsmouth:

86: 1 August 1950 - 17 October 1950
87: 2 June 1950 - 31 August 1950

All of this class, except 88, as the oldest trolleybuses in the fleet were loaned to other operators during the Second World War. Nos. 84, 85, 86 and 88 survived long enough to be renumbered in 1959/1960 in the 1958 fleet numbering scheme.

Subsequent alterations: In 1935 this first batch of MS2s were fitted with coasting and run-back brakes as required by a MoT instruction related to trolleybus operation on Richmond Hill. Sunbeam fitted this equipment as a "follow-on" to similar work being carried out on the second batch then being delivered, at a charge of £25 per vehicle. As delivered, these vehicles had a controller (or reverser as it was known in Bournemouth) with three positions, "off", "forward" and "reverse"; a further position "brake" was added. The vehicle had to be brought to a definite stop at the top of a hill and by selecting the "brake" position on the controller the driver could limit the speed of the descending trolleybus to about 8mph. The vehicle had to be stopped again at the bottom of the hill to disengage the coasting brake. The run-back brake was for emergencies only and in the event of a complete brake and power failure when ascending any hill, the driver placed one circuit breaker in the "off" position which then limited the run-back speed to about 2mph.

From the end of May 1935, wooden "slip-boards" indicating the principal intermediate and terminal points, similar to those already used on BCT motorbuses, were mounted above the lower saloon waist-rail level running from halfway along bay 3 to halfway along bay 5 on both sides.

From November 1935 BCT adopted a revised layout for the indicator boxes in the front and rear upper-deck panels, trolleybuses delivered beforehand being progressively rebuilt accordingly. A rectangular indicator box, 2ft 6in wide and 1ft 3in deep, able to display up to four lines of information (intermediate points and the final destination), was built into the front panel at the same position as the single-line final-destination and service number indicator boxes it replaced.

Somewhat larger, 10in by 10in, service number boxes were built into the front panel to the nearside of the rectangular box. At the rear, the single-line final-destination and service number indicators were removed from the protruding rectangular box which was then glazed to accommodate a rectangular indicator, 2ft 6in wide and 1ft 3in deep, able to display up to four lines of information (intermediate points and the final destination). A rear service number box, 10in by 10in, was built into the nearside of the (vent) panel immediately above the platform window.

The opening of an alternative route from the Lansdowne to the Square in May 1937 led to the progressive addition of an auxiliary single-line indicator box to show the alternative in-town route options and journeys via special events. A wooden-cased auxiliary indicator box was added at the top of the nearside driver's cab windscreen and in the (vent) panel immediately above the rear platform window. Photographic evidence shows that many members of the first batch of MS2s did not receive auxiliary indicators until after the Second World War.

From an early date, as a result of accident damage and standardisation, the offside rectangular driver's rear-view mirror were successively replaced by round equivalents as fitted to nos. 90-173.

From 1937 trolley wheel collectors were progressively replaced by Anti-Attrition Metal Co. OB type slipper heads with carbon inserts.

From 1938-9 semaphore arm illuminated traffic indicators in black protective boxes began to be fitted externally on the leading side pillar to the driver's cab on both sides. This exercise was not completed when the Second World War broke out. After reconditioning 165 and potentially other MS2s had semaphore arm indicators mounted in the base of the lower-deck pillar forwards of the front exit on the nearside and immediately behind the driver's cab door on the offside. From the same dates, fitment of rectangular driver's rear view mirror to the front nearside cab pillar began.

Post-war 9.00in×20.00in tyres were fitted.

Post-war a fog light hanging beneath the front panel on the nearside, aligned with the nearside headlamp, was added.

Post-war the front rectangular intermediate points and final destination indicator was moved up to lower beading of the upper deck waistrail and the single-line auxiliary indicator added immediately below, the separate box in the driver's cab windscreen being removed. It is unlikely that all members of the first batch of MS2s received this alteration.

Post-war bodywork changes included the panelling over of the diffused glass lower-deck window behind the front (exit) staircase; the glass louvres above the upper-deck front windows and the side windows of both saloons were replaced with metal rainshields, those over the side windows sometimes surviving longer than those at the front; and on 84-89 the quarter light and ⅔-size half-drop window towards the front of the upper saloon were removed and replaced by a single fixed pane. This original window layout on 84-89 possibly provided additional body strength which could explain their relatively late survival when compared to other members of the initial batch of MS2s. The number and position of roof-mounted extractor ventilators seems to have varied indiscriminately. The original driver's

offside rear-view mirror was replaced with a larger rectangular mirror and a matching external mirror was mounted on the nearside front cab pillar. Semaphore arm illuminated traffic indicators were fitted to the leading side pillar of the driver's cab on both sides.

From 1950, commencing with those vehicles reconditioned by Reading & Co. Ltd. in Portsmouth, the auxiliary single-line indicator box in the driver's nearside windscreen was removed and replaced by an aperture in the upper-deck front panel beneath the rectangular box which displayed intermediate points and the final destination. This was achieved by moving the rectangular box up to border on the lower beading of upper deck waistrail. The position of the rear auxiliary indicator box was unchanged. The trolleybuses involved were:

Altered by Reading: 86, 87 (2).
Altered by BCT: 80-82, 84, 85, 88 (6).

Those vehicles reconditioned by BCT or Reading had their half-drop front upper-deck windows replaced with fixed glazing. The glazed louvres fitted above the side windows on the lower deck, and the front and side windows of the upper deck, were progressively removed and replaced by metal louvres. Some vehicles operated with a mixture of glass and metal louvres.

205, 206, 208 were fitted with flashing "orange segment"-shaped trafficators mounted in the lower-deck waistband in bay 1 a few inches to the rear of the leading pillar on the nearside, and behind the driver's cab door on the offside. Possibly in the same exercise, red reflectors were added to the base of the rear panel on the nearside and offside, aligned with the top of the registration plate.

Disposal:

72, 73, 75, 76, 77, 79	to James Thompson & Co. (Cardiff) Ltd., Dumballs Road, Cardiff, breakers, in July 1953
74, 78	to James Thompson & Co. (Cardiff) Ltd., Dumballs Road, Cardiff, breakers, in May 1952
80, 81, 82, 83	to James Thompson & Co. (Cardiff) Ltd., Dumballs Road, Cardiff, breakers, in March 1958 (at £55 each plus £2 each for reinstating the handbrake for towing).
87, 89	to Scource & Sons, breakers, Pulton Lane, Chickerell, Dorset, in January 1959
207	to Scource & Sons, breakers, Pulton Lane, Chickerell, Dorset, in January 1963
205, 208	to Scource & Sons, breakers, Pulton Lane, Chickerell, Dorset, in October 1963 (at £46 each), the front registration plate of 205 being retained for a local resident.
206	to N. Stanley, breakers, Alder Road, Poole, in March 1964

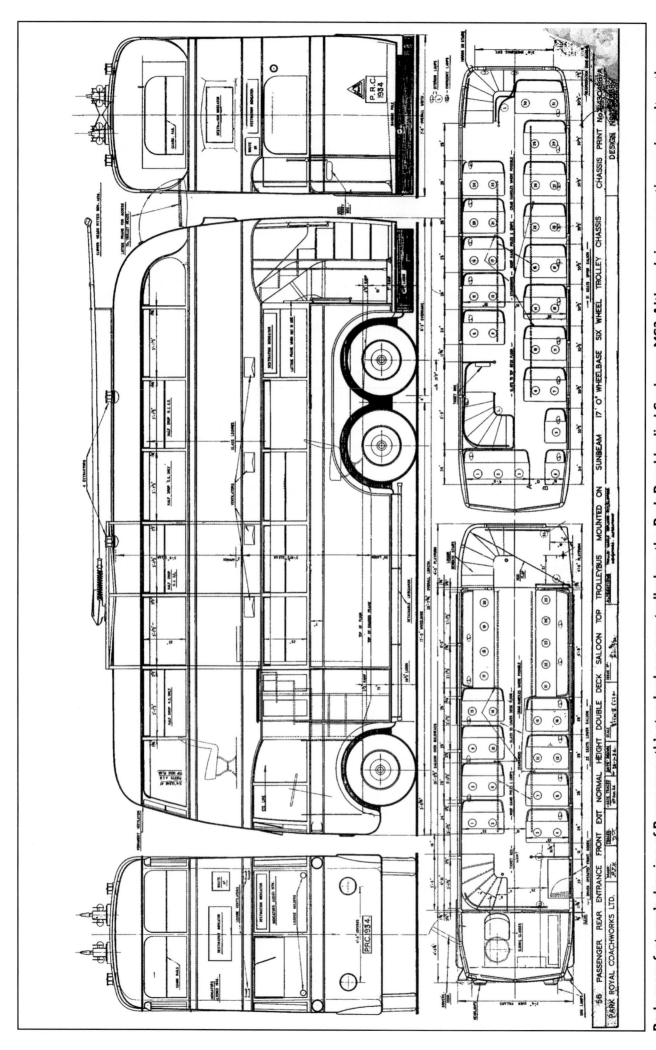

Body manufacturer's drawing of Bournemouth's standard pre-war trolleybus, the Park Royal bodied Sunbeam MS2. Although incorporating various alterations, e.g. revised indicator boxes, introduced prior to 1934 (the date of the traced drawing), the original drawing dates from 1934 and has a number of discrepancies with the vehicles "as built", including the sidelights being too far apart and a spurious licence holder in the driver's offside windscreen.

90-173 Sunbeam-BTH MS2

Original Fleet No.	New 1958 Fleet No.	Registration Mark	Chassis Number	Body Number	Date of Delivery	Date into Service	Date of Withdrawal	Date of Disposal
90	209	ALJ 964	12053T	3627	11.02.1935	25.03.1935	04.1960	12.196
91		ALJ 965	12054T	3628	13.02.1935	23.03.1935	08.1958	01.1959
92		ALJ 966	12055T	3629	15.02.1935	25.03.1935	10.1958	01.1959
93	210	ALJ 967	12056T	3630	18.02.1935	25.03.1935	09.1963	10.1963
94		ALJ 968	12057T	3631	20.02.1935	25.03.1935	12.1950	05.1952
95		ALJ 969	12058T	3632	22.02.1935	25.03.1935	07.1959	12.1959
96		ALJ 970	12065T	3633	25.02.1935	25.03.1935	10.1959	12.1959
97	211	ALJ 971	12066T	3634	27.02.1935	25.03.1935	09.1962	01.1963
98		ALJ 972	12067T	3635	01.03.1935	25.03.1935	12.1950	05.1952
99	212	ALJ 973	12068T	3636	04.03.1935	25.03.1935	09.1963	11.1963
100		ALJ 974	12069T	3637	06.03.1935	17.04.1935	09.1959	12.1959
101	213	ALJ 975	12070T	3638	08.03.1935	17.04.1935	09.1963	03.1964
102		ALJ 976	12071T	3639	11.03.1935	28.03.1935	12.1950	05.1952
103		ALJ 977	12072T	3640	13.03.1935	25.03.1935	12.1950	05.1952
104		ALJ 978	12073T	3641	15.03.1935	25.03.1935	12.1950	05.1952
105	214	ALJ 979	12074T	3642	18.03.1935	06.06.1935	09.1963	10.1963
106	215	ALJ 980	12075T	3643	20.03.1935	06.06.1935	09.1963	03.1964
107		ALJ 981	12076T	3644	20.03.1935	06.06.1935	12.1950	05.1952
108		ALJ 982	12077T	3645	25.03.1935	06.06.1935	12.1950	05.1952
109		ALJ 983	12078T	3646	27.03.1935	07.06.1935	12.1957	01.1959
110		ALJ 984	12079T	3647	29.03.1935	07.06.1935	12.1950	05.1952
111		ALJ 985	12080T	3648	01.04.1935	07.06.1935	12.1955	03.1958
112	202	ALJ 986	12081T	3649	03.04.1935	06.06.1935	07.1965	12.1965
113		ALJ 987	12082T	3650	05.04.1935	06.06.1935	12.1950	05.1952
114		ALJ 988	12083T	3651	08.04.1935	07.07.1935	09.1956	03.1958
115		ALJ 989	12084T	3652	11.04.1935	03.07.1935	12.1959	12.1959
116		ALJ 990	12085T	3653	26.04.1935	02.07.1935	09.1959	12.1959
117	216	ALJ 991	12086T	3654	29.04.1935	04.07.1935	09.1963	03.1964
118		ALJ 992	12087T	3655	01.05.1935	02.07.1935	01.1959	01.1959
119	217	ALJ 993	12088T	3656	03.05.1935	04.07.1935	07.1960	12.1961
120		ALJ 994	12089T	3657	08.05.1935	03.07.1935	12.1950	05.1952
121	218	ALJ 995	12090T	3658	13.05.1935	07.07.1935	07.1960	12.1961
122		ALJ 996	12091T	3659	15.05.1935	07.07.1935	05.1959	12.1959
123		ALJ 997	12092T	3660	17.05.1935	07.07.1935	11.1958	01.1959
124		ALJ 998	12093T	3661	20.05.1935	07.07.1935	12.1950	05.1952
125		ALJ 999	12094T	3662	18.06.1935	07.07.1935	09.1959	12.1959
126		BEL 811	12095T	3663	08.08.1935	10.08.1935	12.1950	05.1952
127		BEL 812	12096T	3664	10.08.1935	14.08.1935	12.1955	03.1958
128		BEL 813	12097T	3665	13.08.1935	17.08.1935	12.1955	03.1958
129	219	BEL 814	12098T	3666	15.08.1935	18.08.1935	08.1962	01.1963
130		BEL 815	12099T	3667	17.08.1935	22.08.1935	09.1958	12.1959
131	221	BEL 816	12100T	3668	20.08.1935	24.08.1935	09.1962	01.1963
132	222	BEL 817	12101T	3669	22.08.1935	04.09.1935	10.1959	01.1963

315

Original Fleet No.	New 1958 Fleet No.	Registration Mark	Chassis Number	Body Number	Date of Delivery	Date into Service	Date of Withdrawal	Date of Disposal
133		BEL 818	12102T	3670	26.08.1935	04.09.1935	12.1950	05.1952
134		BEL 819	12103T	3671	28.08.1935	04.09.1935	08.1958	01.1959
135		BEL 820	12104T	3672	30.08.1935	06.09.1935	11.1958	12.1959
136		BEL 821	12105T	3673	03.09.1935	10.09.1935	07.1959	12.1959
137		BEL 822	12106T	3674	05.09.1935	14.09.1935	09.1959	12.1959
138		BEL 823	12107T	3675	15.10.1935	01.06.1936	09.1956	03.1958
139		BEL 824	12108T	3676	17.10.1935	01.06.1936	08.1959	12.1959
140		BEL 825	12109T	3677	19.10.1935	01.06.1936	01.1959	12.1959
141	224	BEL 826	12110T	3678	22.10.1935	01.06.1936	09.1962	10.1963
142		BEL 827	12111T	3679	24.10.1935	01.06.1936	12.1959	12.1959
143		BEL 828	12112T	3680	05.12.1935	01.06.1936	07.1959	12.1959
144	225	BEL 829	12113T	3681	26.10.1935	01.06.1936	08.1960	12.1961
145		BEL 830	12114T	3682	04.12.1935	01.06.1936	01.1959	01.1959
146		BEL 831	12115T	3683	07.12.1935	01.06.1936	01.1959	01.1959
147	226	BEL 832	12116T	3684	09.12.1935	01.06.1936	09.1960	12.1961
148		BEL 833	12117T	3685	11.12.1935	01.06.1936	09.1956	03.1958
149		BEL 834	12118T	3686	14.12.1935	01.06.1936	12.1959	12.1959
150		BRU 1	12119T	3687	17.12.1935	09.04.1936	08.1957	01.1959
151		BRU 2	12120T	3688	19.12.1935	08.04.1936	12.1950	05.1952
152		BRU 3	12121T	3689	21.12.1935	07.04.1936	12.1958	01.1959
153		BRU 4	12122T	3690	07.01.1936	09.04.1936	09.1956	01.1959
154		BRU 5	12123T	3691	08.01.1936	09.04.1936	09.1957	01.1959
155		BRU 6	12124T	3692	10.01.1936	08.04.1936	11.1958	01.1959
156		BRU 7	12125T	3693	13.01.1936	09.04.1936	12.1959	12.1959
157	200	BRU 8	12126T	3694	20.01.1936	09.04.1936	08.1964	11.1965
158		BRU 9	12127T	3695	22.01.1936	09.04.1936	11.1958	01.1959
159	228	BRU 10	12128T	3696	24.01.1936	09.04.1936	10.1960	12.1961
160	201	BRU 11	12129T	3697	25.01.1936	01.06.1936	08.1964	11.1965
161		BRU 12	12130T	3698	27.01.1936	01.06.1936	12.1959	12.1959
162	229	BRU 13	12131T	3699	14.02.1936	01.06.1936	10.1959	01.1963
163	230	BRU 14	12132T	3700	22.02.1936	01.06.1936	08.1960	01.1963
164		BRU 15	12133T	3701	15.02.1936	01.06.1936	09.1957	01.1959
165		BRU 16	12134T	3702	18.02.1936	01.06.1936	01.1959	12.1959
166		BRU 17	12135T	3703	20.02.1936	01.06.1936	09.1957	01.1959
167	231	BRU 18	12136T	3704	25.02.1936	01.06.1936	06.1960	12.1961
168	232	BRU 19	12137T	3705	27.02.1936	01.06.1936	08.1962	01.1963
169		BRU 20	12138T	3706	29.02.1936	01.06.1936	12.1950	05.1952
170	233	BRU 21	12139T	3707	04.03.1936	01.06.1936	09.1962	01.1963
171		BRU 22	12140T	3708	06.03.1936	02.06.1936	12.1959	12.1959
172		BRU 23	12141T	3709	11.03.1936	01.06.1936	12.1959	12.1959
173		BRU 24	12142T	3710	13.03.1936	01.06.1936	08.1957	01.1959

Chassis: Three axle Sunbeam type MS2 manufactured by Sunbeam Commercial Vehicles Ltd., Moorfield Road Works, Blakenhall, Wolverhampton, Staffordshire.

Motor: British Thomson-Houston Co. Ltd., Rugby, Warwickshire, Type 201 compound-wound (80 nhp) for regenerative control.

Electrical equipment: British Thomson-Houston (BTH); scissors-type controller, 12 notches (1-6, resistance; 7, full power; 8-12, field weakening).

Dewirement indicator: neon line-lights and buzzer.

Brakes: Regenerative, achieved by releasing the power pedal; Sunbeam-Lockheed vacuum assisted hydraulic, activated by the brake pedal and operating on all wheels; electrical coasting brake selected at master controller; handbrake, mechanical to all rear wheels; and emergency electrical run-back brakes.

Body: Highbridge double-deck composite six-bay construction with twin staircases, conventional rear, semi-vestibuled open platform entrance and front exit, the latter equipped with a manually-operated, two-leaf folding door controlled from the driver's cab.

Built by Park Royal Vehicles Ltd., Abbey Road, Park Royal, London NW10   H31/25D

Length: 28ft 7$\frac{1}{4}$in   Width: 7ft 6in   Height: 15ft 7$\frac{1}{2}$in (laden, measured over retaining hooks).

Wheelbase: 17ft (from front axle to centre of rear bogie), giving a turning circle of 59ft.

Unladen weight: 8 tons 12cwt

Tyres: 36 X 8 high-pressure to all wheels according to the pre-war system of measuring tyre sizes.

Sunbeam's financial situation had not improved in the meantime and the Company went into liquidation. In July 1935 the STD Group and Sunbeam Commercial Vehicles Ltd. was purchased by Rootes Securities Ltd. This partially explains Sunbeam's flexibility in the contractual negotiations in autumn 1934.

Sunbeam invoice value £2,198 each. Sunbeam serial order Bournemouth 20-103

Order for 36 completed on 04.09.34 valued at £79,794. Order for 48 completed on 05.10.34 valued at £102,192, together totalling £181, 986.

They were guaranteed for 50,000 miles and were able to maintain a speed of 26$\frac{1}{2}$mph fully loaded.

Chassis: See 72-89 Sunbeam-BTH MS2 for details (these being identical).

Electrics: See 72-89 Sunbeam-BTH MS2 for details, these being identical except—

There was no provision for a "skate" to allow current return through tram track.

Brecknell Willis lightweight collector gear with adjustable spring tension and buffers, roller bearings on hinge pins and base swivel pins. The trolley poles were 18ft-long and equipped with trolley wheels.

Sunbeam MS2/Park Royal no. 134 (BEL819), an example from the follow-on order placed in October 1934 for a further 48 identical vehicles delivered in 1935-1936 but prior to the introduction of Duncan Morrison's larger indicator boxes at front and rear. Note the wooden "tramcar-style" side slipboards, mounted on both sides of the trolleybus above the lower maroon band at lower saloon window level and showing up to four intermediate points in black lettering on a white background. The photograph appears to have been taken in Poole Road.
Wolverhampton Archives (Sunbeam BTH)

Brakes: See 72-89 Sunbeam-BTH MS2 for details, these being identical except—

Coasting and run-back brakes as required by an MoT instruction related to trolleybus operation on Richmond Hill. The BTH equipment cost £18 10s for each trolleybus. The controller (or reverser as it was known in Bournemouth) had four positions, "off", "forward", "reverse" and "brake". The vehicle had to be brought to a definite stop at the top of a hill and by selecting the "brake" position on the controller the driver could limit the speed of the descending trolleybus to about 8mph. The vehicle had to be stopped again at the bottom of the hill to disengage the coasting brake. The run-back brake was for emergencies only and in the event of a complete brake and power failure when ascending any hill, the driver placed one circuit breaker in the "off" position which then limited the run-back speed to about 2mph.

Bodywork: See 72-77 Sunbeam-BTH MS2 for details, these being identical except—

Widney Stuart "Aero" pattern half-drop openers equipped with a single "pinch fastener" at the top of each pane were fitted to the side windows in bays 2-4 (both sides) of the lower deck and to bays 1-6 on the nearside and to bays 2-5 on the offside of the upper deck. Half-drop openers were also fitted to the upper-deck front windows. The upper pane dropped outside the fixed lower pane. Plate glass 3/16in thick was used for the side windows in both saloons. There was a total of

five rotating Flettner Extractor ventilators on the roof: one mounted centrally in the front dome and four on the offside mounted towards the rear of bays 1, 4, and towards the front of bays 3, 6. There were four small side ventilators (as 84-89) in the vent panel above the bays 2-5 (both sides) lower deck windows, located at the rear of each bay.

Glazed louvres in stainless steel frames were fitted above the side windows on the lower deck bays 2-6 nearside, 1-6 offside (thus including the diffused glass pane behind the front staircase); on the upper deck bays 1-6 and the "D" window above the rear platform both sides; and above the upper deck front windows.

Despite the protruding rear indicator box, small protruding rubber bumpers half way up the frame on the nearside and offside of the emergency exit door aligned with similar bumpers on the panel beneath just above the rear indicator box. When the retaining chains were removed and the emergency exit door opened to its fullest extent the door hung down and rested on these bumpers. Each trolley boom retention hook was braced towards the front of the vehicle.

The driver's cab was equipped with an offside opening windscreen and single offside front-hinged door. The window of the door was divided horizontally, both portions having two panes, the rear pane sliding forwards behind the front pane. The upper portion was for ventilation and lower for signalling purposes.

A round driver's rear-view mirror with chromium-plated

Another view of Sunbeam MS2 no. 134 also taken for the manufacturer's publicity purposes.
Wolverhampton Archives (Sunbeam BTH)

back was mounted externally on the front offside cab pillar only, there originally being none on the nearside.

The instrument panel had the following gauges and instruments: Jaeger speedometer 0-60mph, Smith's vacuum gauge, BTH audible indicator, illuminated by metal filament lamps.

Lighting: See 72-77 Sunbeam-BTH MS2 for details (these being identical).

Seating: See 72-77 Sunbeam-BTH MS2 for details (these being identical).

Destination equipment: 90-142, 144: A single-line final-destination indicator box was fitted in the upper-deck front panelling centred above the driver's windscreen with a square service number indicator box immediately above centred above the final-destination box. At the rear there was a rectangular box with an arched top centred above the rear platform window protruding from the upper-deck panelling for its entire depth and projecting more at its top than at its base due to the upwards curve of the panel to meet the rear dome. In the rear panel of this box was a single-line final-destination indicator box surmounted by a square service number indicator box.

Additional single-line final-destination indicator boxes were mounted inside the lower saloon at the top of the lower saloon

bay 6 side window on both sides (behind the longitudinal seat).

143, 145-173: A rectangular indicator box, 2ft 6in wide and 1ft 3in deep, able to display up to four lines of information (intermediate points and the final destination), was built into the front panel at the same position as the single-line final-destination and service number indicator boxes it replaced.

Somewhat larger, 10in by 10in, service number boxes were built into the front panel to the nearside of the rectangular box. At the rear, the single-line final-destination and service number indicators were removed from the protruding rectangular box which was then glazed to accommodate a rectangular indicator, 2ft 6in wide and 1ft 3in deep, able to display up to four lines of information (intermediate points and the final destination). A rear service number box, 10in by 10in, was built into the nearside of the (vent) panel immediately above the platform window.

Delivery: The August 1934 tender of Sunbeam Commercial Vehicles Ltd. at £79,128 for 36 trolleybuses was accepted by Bournemouth Council on 4 September 1934 and although there were two lower tenders, the Transport Committee in making their recommendation took heed of Mr Bulfin's advice "on the advantages of having uniform vehicles and equipment throughout the undertaking". A month later another order, the fifth within 12 months, was placed for a further 48 trolleybuses. This brought the total number of Sunbeam vehicles already

Sunbeam MS2 BEL830 was exhibited at the 12th Commercial Motor Transport Exhibition held at Olympia, London, 7 - 16 November 1935 but incorrectly displaying fleet number 143 instead of 145. It was BEL830 that introduced the enlarged indicator boxes, able to display up to four lines of information (intermediate points and the final destination), although its number indicator apertures were smaller than the subsequent standard. It is seen at the Park Royal factory prior to the Exhibition.
David Chalk collection

supplied or on order up to 103, which was at that time the largest trolleybus fleet of one manufacture to be purchased by a British municipality.

By special arrangement with Sunbeam the two orders (90-173) were delivered consecutively at a rate of one or two vehicles per week between February 1935 and March 1936 thus ensuring continuity of work on the production line. Between the placing of the orders and the start of production the Sunbeam Motor Car Co. Ltd. formed a subsidiary company, Sunbeam Commercial Vehicles Ltd., to manufacture trolleybuses and heavy commercial vehicles.

The first ten vehicles of the batch, 90-99, entered service together on 25 March 1935, opening the new route 24 (Bournemouth Square-Iford Bridge) and its westward extension 24A (Westbourne-Bournemouth Square-Iford Bridge).

External Livery: Delivered in Livery 1 (see Appendix D)

Internal Livery: See 72-89 Sunbeam-BTH MS2 for details (these being identical).

Subsequent alterations: See 72-89 Sunbeam-BTH MS2 for details, these being identical except—

113 was fitted with a G.D. Peters vacuum-operated front exit door on 10 December 1935, followed by 116 and possibly others in the late 1930s.

From 1936 the indicator boxes in the front and rear upper-deck panels of 90-142, 144 were progressively rebuilt to the layout introduced with 143. A rectangular indicator box, 2ft 6in wide and 1ft 3in deep, able to display up to four lines of information (intermediate points and the final destination), was built into the front panel at the same position as the single-line final-destination and service number indicator boxes it replaced.

Somewhat larger, 10in by 10in, service number boxes were built into the front panel to the nearside of the rectangular box. At the rear, the single-line final-destination and service number indicators were removed from the protruding rectangular box which was then glazed to accommodate a rectangular indicator, 2ft 6in wide and 1ft 3in deep, able to display up to four lines of information (intermediate points and the final destination). A rear service number box, 10in by 10in, was built into the nearside of the (vent) panel immediately above the platform window.

From 1938-9 semaphore arm illuminated traffic indicators in black protective boxes began to be fitted externally on the leading side pillar to the driver's cab on both sides. This exercise was not completed when the Second World War broke out. After reconditioning 165 and potentially other MS2s had semaphore arm indicators mounted in the base of the lower-deck pillar forwards of the front exit on the nearside and immediately behind the driver's cab door on the offside. From the same dates, fitment of rectangular driver's rear-view mirror to the front nearside cab pillar began.

From 1950, commencing with those vehicles reconditioned by Reading & Co. Ltd. in Portsmouth, the auxiliary single-line indicator box in the driver's nearside windscreen was removed and replaced by an aperture in the upper-deck front panel beneath the rectangular box which displayed intermediate points and the final destination. This was achieved by moving the rectangular box up to border on the lower beading of upper-deck waistrail. The position of the rear auxiliary indicator

box was unchanged. The trolleybuses involved were:

Altered by Reading: 92, 96, 106, 112, 135, 136, 139, 148, 167, 173 (10).

BCT continued to recondition Sunbeam MS2s until 1956-7 when the Sunbeam MF2Bs were ordered.

Altered by BCT: 90, 93, 97, 99, 101, 105, 117-19, 121-3, 125, 127, 129, 130, 131, 132, 137, 140-7, 150, 152, 153, 156-9, 160, 163, 165, 167, 168, 170, 172 (41).

The following vehicles are known to have not been reconditioned: 72-9, 94, 98, 100, 102-4, 107-9, 110, 111, 113, 115, 116, 120, 124, 126, 133, 134, 149, 151, 161, 164, 169, 171 (33).

This leaves 12 vehicles which were probably altered but for which no photographic confirmation has been found: 83, 89, 91, 95, 114, 128, 138, 154, 155, 162, 163, 166

Those vehicles reconditioned by BCT or Reading had their half-drop front upper deck windows replaced with fixed glazing. The glazed louvres fitted above the side windows on the lower deck, and the front and side windows of the upper deck, were progressively removed and replaced by metal louvres. Some vehicles operated with a mixture of glass and metal louvres.

From the late 1950s flashing "orange segment"-shaped indicators mounted in the lower deck waistband in bay 1 a few inches to the rear of the leading pillar on the nearside, and behind the driver's cab door on the offside, replaced semaphore arm indicators. These were fitted to at least 205, 206, 208, 210-16, 219, 221, 232, 233. Possibly in the same exercise, red reflectors were added to the base of the rear panel on the nearside and offside, aligned with the top of the registration plate.

Notes: The Sunbeam order book shows all chassis numbers with a "T" suffix and body numbers with a "B" prefix, presumably indicating "Bournemouth".

Chassis 12132T (later to carry trolleybus 163) and complete trolleybus BEL830, incorrectly displaying fleet number 143 instead of 145, were exhibits at the 12th Commercial Motor Transport Exhibition held at Olympia, London, 7-16 November 1935. It was BEL830 that introduced the enlarged indicator boxes, although its number indicator apertures were smaller than the subsequent 10in by 10in standard. It will be noted that the delivery of 163 was delayed in relation to preceding and following vehicles probably due to the appearance of its chassis at the Commercial Motor Transport Exhibition.

130, 137, 152 were allocated new fleet numbers 220, 223, 227 respectively in the 1958 renumbering scheme but were withdrawn before the numbers were displayed.

The following vehicles were reconditioned by Reading & Co. Ltd., London Road, Hillsea, Portsmouth:

92: 29 August 1950-20 October 1950
96: 13 June 1950-28 September 1950
106: 28 September 1950-7 December 1950
112: 31 August 1950-6 November 1950
135: 17 October 1950-1 January 1951
136: 2 September 1950-23 November 1950
139: 1 June 1950-1 August 1950
148: 12 June 1950-29 August 1950

167: 20 October 1950-9 January 1951
173: 6 November 1950-7 February 1951

The following vehicles were rebuilt as open-top trolleybuses by the Transport Department:

112: re-entered service 7 July 1958 renumbered as 202
157: re-entered service 24 May 1958 renumbered as 200
160: following an MoT inspection on 17 April 1958, re-entered service 24 May 1958 renumbered as 201.

On 4 December 1957, a press announcement advised that two trolleybuses (and six motorbuses) would be converted to open-top in time for the 1958 summer season. Trolleybus 160 was taken as a prototype for the conversion and in the period September 1957-April 1958 the front staircase and exit door were removed (and replaced by standard near and offside glazed panels), and seating added in the space thereby created increasing the passenger capacity from 56 to 69 (OT40/29R). The roof and upper-deck window area were removed entirely whilst the upper-deck side panels were increased in height and a curved elipse added to the front panels above the indicator boxes. The trolley gantry was retained and a matching, externally mounted, steel channel linked to the horizontal steel channel, was added at the rear of bay 7 to support the trolleyboom retaining hooks. The vertical channels, trolley gantry (sides and top) and trolley bases were painted aluminium. The upper beading of the upper-deck waistband was removed and the band area, previously painted maroon, and the lower beading were painted primrose yellow. The internal upper-deck side panels, which had no lining panels behind bay 1, the pillars strengthening the vertical channels supporting the trolley gantry, and the underside of the small roof section supporting the trolleybases, were painted cream. The floor was waterproofed and painted brown, a longitudinal rain water outlet being added behind the horizontal steel channel along both sides. Metal anti-slip ridging was added to the floor. There was no lighting on the open upper deck. Varnished slatted wooden seats replaced the previous leather seats on the upper deck, the original tubular metal frames being retained. Internally there was little change but for the addition of two forward-facing double seats, one on each side of the gangway. The rear staircase floor area was painted light grey, and the panels cream. The additional comment CIRCULAR SERVICE was added in white letters on a red background to the blind in the auxiliary single line indicator box and 39 added to the service number blind (on 202 the service number 39 was printed in white on a pale green background). The prototype, by now renumbered 201, was presented to the public on 18 April 1958 following a MoT inspection the day before. The second conversion was ready for service in May in time for the introduction of the circular tour service 39 on 24 May 1958. The rebuilt open-top trolleybuses introduced a new fleet numbering system whereby fleet number and registration number coincided as far as possible.

After reconstruction 202, at least, had battery boxes under the front nearside and offside seats in the lower saloon.

Disposals:

94, 98, 102, 103, 104, 108, 110, 113, 120, 124, 126, 133, 151, 169	to James Thompson & Co. (Cardiff) Ltd., Dumballs Road, Cardiff, breakers, in May 1952
111, 114, 127, 128, 138, 148	to James Thompson & Co. (Cardiff) Ltd., Dumballs Road, Cardiff, breakers, in March 1958 (at £55 each plus £2 each for reinstating the handbrake for towing)
91, 92, 109, 118, 123, 134, 140, 145, 146, 150, 152, 153, 154, 155, 158, 164, 166, 173	to Scource & Sons, Pulton Lane, Chickerell, Dorset, breakers, in January 1959
95, 96, 100, 115, 116, 122, 125, 130, 135, 136, 137, 139, 142, 143, 149, 156, 161, 165, 171, 172	to Scource & Sons, Pulton Lane, Dorset, breakers, in December 1959 (at £70 each)
209, 217, 218, 225, 226, 228, 231	to W.J. Stevens & Sons, 59 Alvin Street, Gloucester, breakers, in December 1961 (for £600 together with 3 Leyland motor buses and 2 vans).
211, 219, 221, 222, 229, 230, 232, 233	to Scource & Sons, Pulton Lane, Chickerell, Dorset, breakers, in January 1963 (at £46 each).
210, 214, 224	to Scource & Sons, Pulton Lane, Chickerell, Dorset, breakers, in October 1963 (at £46 each).
213, 215, 216	to N. Stanley, Alder Road, Poole, breakers, in March 1964 (at £75 each).
200, 201	to Colbro Ltd., Jaw Bone Works, Rothwell Haigh, Leeds, dealers, in November 1965 (at £101 each).
212	to the RTS for preservation on 17 November 1963 (at £30).
202	to to the NTA for preservation in December 1965 (at £101).

200-223 BUT9641T

Original Fleet No.	New 1958 Fleet No.	Registra-tion Mark	Chassis Number	Body Number	Date of Delivery	Date into Service	Date of Withdrawal	Date of Disposal
200	234	KLJ 334	9641T.426	M4300	23.08.1950	01.10.1950	25.09.1966	.12.1966
201	235	KLJ 335	9641T.427	M4298	23.07.1950	01.10.1950	25.09.1966	.12.1966
202	236	KLJ 336	9641T.428	M4295	21.07.1950	01.10.1950	.04.1966	.12.1966
203	237	KLJ 337	9641T.429	M4294	08.07.1950	01.10.1950	25.09.1966	.12.1966
204	238	KLJ 338	9641T.430	M4301	25.08.1950	01.10.1950	25.09.1966	.12.1966
205	239	KLJ 339	9641T.431	M4296	25.07.1950	01.10.1950	25.09.1966	.12.1966
206	240	KLJ 340	9641T.432	M4297	21.08.1950	01.10.1950	25.09.1966	.12.1966
207	241	KLJ 341	9641T.433	M4299	28.07.1950	01.10.1950	25.09.1966	.12.1966
208	242	KLJ 342	9641T.434	M4302	30.08.1950	01.10.1950	25.09.1966	.12.1966
209	243	KLJ 343	9641T.435	M4303	07.09.1950	01.10.1950	25.09.1966	.12.1966
210	244	KLJ 344	9641T.436	M4304	12.09.1950	01.10.1950	25.09.1966	.12.1966
211	245	KLJ 345	9641T.437	M4305	14.09.1950	01.11.1950	.09.1965	.12.1966
212	246	KLJ 346	9641T.438	M4306	19.10.1950	01.11.1950	25.09.1966	.01.1967
213	247	KLJ 347	9641T.439	M4308	25.09.1950	01.11.1950	.09.1965	.12.1966
214	248	KLJ 348	9641T.440	M4307	22.09.1950	01.11.1950	.09.1965	.12.1966
215	249	KLJ 349	9641T.441	M4310	06.10.1950	01.11.1950	.09.1965	.12.1966
216	250	KLJ 350	9641T.442	M4309	04.10.1950	11.11.1950	.09.1965	.12.1966
217	251	KLJ 351	9641T.443	M4312	13.10.1950	01.11.1950	25.09.1966	.12.1966
218	252	KLJ 352	9641T.444	M4314	06.12.1950	01.01.1951	.1965	.12.1966
219	253	KLJ 353	9641T.445	M4311	10.10.1950	01.11.1950	25.09.1966	.12.1966
220	254	KLJ 354	9641T.446	M4317	14.11.1950	01.01.1951	.09.1965	.12.1966
221	255	KLJ 355	9641T.447	M4313	26.10.1950	01.01.1951	.09.1965	.12.1966
222	256	KLJ 356	9641T.448	M4315	08.11.1950	01.01.1951	.09.1965	.12.1966
223	257	KLJ 357	9641T.449	M4316	10.11.1950	01.01.1951	.09.1965	.12.1966

Chassis: Three-axle type BUT9641T manufactured by the British United Traction Ltd., 14 Hanover House, Hanover Square, London W1 at the AEC works, Windmill Lane, Southall, Middlesex.

Motor: Crompton Parkinson Ltd., Chelmsford, Essex, Type C422 (120hp) four-pole, with a light compound winding incapable of regeneration (known as "controlled rheostatic").

Electrical equipment: Allen West & Co. Ltd., Brighton, 13 notches, PA control panel mounted alongside the driver's seat. Dewirement indicators: 2 orange line-lights and buzzer.

Brakes: Westinghouse compressed air on all wheels, 2-stage rheostatic, coasting and run-back brakes. Handbrake on rear wheels

Body: Highbridge double-deck all metal six-bay construction with twin staircases, conventional rear, semi-vestibuled open platform entrance and front exit, the latter equipped with an air-operated, two-leaf folding door controlled from the driver's cab.

Built by Weymann's Ltd., Station Road, Addlestone, Surrey. Seating H31/25D.

Length: 30ft   Width 8ft 0in

Wheelbase: 18ft 5in to centre of rear bogie with a rear bogie wheelbase of 4ft giving a turning circle on either lock of 63 ft.

Wheel track: front 6ft 815/16in, rear 6ft 815/16in.

Unladen weight: 10 tons 6cwt 0qtr   Laden weight: 14 tons 10cwt

Tyres: Single 11.00in×20in single all round.

In late 1946 AEC and Leyland Motors combined their trolleybus activities with the formation of British United Traction Ltd. (BUT), manufacture being initially based at the Leyland factory at Ham, just north of Kingston upon Thames, Surrey. Falling demand for new trolleybuses following the nationalisation of the power supply industry led to the construction of chassis for double-deck trolleybuses being transferred to the AEC factory at Southall, Middlesex from 1948. Single-deck trolleybuses, principally for the export market, were built at Leyland and the Ham factory sold.

Chassis: The BUT9641T used a number of components from the AEC Regent III motorbus chassis such as front axle and steering gear. The rear bogie was, in fact, an improved version of that used on the pre-war AEC664T trolleybus.

Channel section alloy steel frame, varying in depth up to 11¼in with 3in flanges and a thickness of 5/16in, braced by tubular cross members which carry the electrical equipment and provide rigidity to the frame. Strengthening flitches of alloy steel further stiffened the frame where it rises over the front and rear axles. Front axle beam (reversed Elliot type) of alloy steel stamping with taper-fit swivel pins and taper-roller thrust bearings to take vertical loads. The front axle incorporated a high degree of centre point effect, making for easier steering.

Bournemouth BUT9641T, fleet no. 203 (KL337) was delivered on 8 July 1950 and was snapped by the Weymann official photographer before leaving Addlestone. Note the original livery style featuring olive green painted beading to the vent panels above the lower deck windows, the large coat of arms at front, rear and on the side panels of both decks, and the illuminated semaphore arm traffic indicators. Indicator blinds have yet to be fitted.
Transport Museum Wythall (Metro-Cammell-Weymann)

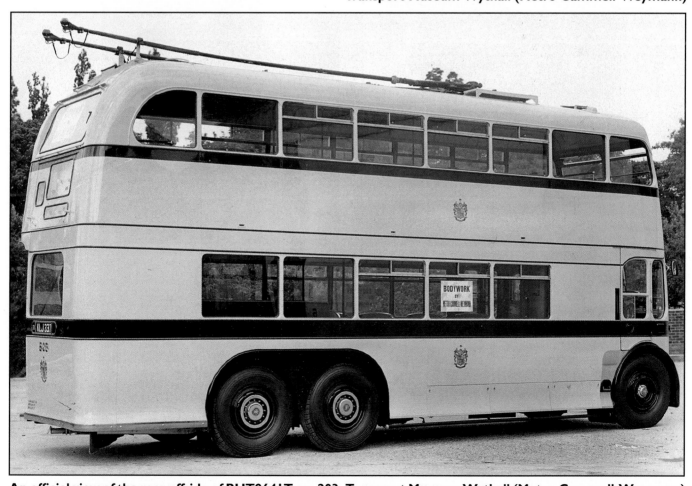

An official view of the rear offside of BUT9641T no. 203. Transport Museum Wythall (Metro-Cammell-Weymann)

The fully floating rear axles had a ratio of 10¹/₃ to 1 at 8in centres and incorporated a third differential. The axle casings were nickel steel stampings on to which the spring and brake shoe carriers and the torque arms were pressed. The worm casings, carrying the final drives, were bolted beneath the axle casings. The rear axle hubs rotated on taper roller bearings fitted with bellows-type packless glands retaining the lubricant. The worm wheel and four-star bevel differential gear units were carried on taper roller bearings in screwed adjustable housings, the worm wheels being pressed on to multi-toothed registers on the differential casings, ensuring a positive drive apart from the securing bolts.

The underslung worm drive to the leading rear axle was by a short large-diameter propeller shaft, offset to the nearside, equipped with Layrub coupling at the front end and Hardy Spicer wide angle coupling at the rear. Inter-axle drive used a Hardy Spicer wide angle jointed propeller shaft. The 2¹/₈in-diameter nickel-chrome molybdenum steel drive shafts had a 56-tooth drive in the wheel hubs and 20 involute sided splines on the differential ends. All differential bevel pinions were bushed and fitted with renewable phosphor bronze thrust washers.

The suspension featured reversed camber, semi-elliptic springs with solid eyes:

Front: 11 leaves 3¹/₂in wide, 4ft 2in long
Rear: 14 leaves 4¹/₄in wide, 4ft 9¹/₄in long.
Worm and nut steering, requiring 6⁷/₈ turns from lock to lock.

Chassis length: 29ft 11¹/₂in
Chassis frame width: 3ft 3¹³/₁₆in front; 5ft 4¹/₁₆in rear.
Chassis width: 7ft 9¹/₁₆in front axle; 7ft 9⁵/₁₆in rear axle.
Chassis weight less traction equipment and cabling 4 tons 1cwt 2qtr

The rear bogie incorporated radius arms transmitting the axle torque reaction directly to the frame thus equalising axle loading and providing greater acceleration without wheel spin and smoother, more efficient braking designed to offer upwards of 20% increase in tyre life. The single inverted semi-elliptic springs at each side were pinned at their ends to the rear axles and pivoted to the frame through large-diameter plain bearing trunnions, automatically lubricated, and cast steel brackets bolted to the side members. Horizontal radius links fitted with phosphor-bronze self-aligning bearings transmitted the torque reactions directly from torque arms on the axle casings to a bracket bolted to the frame.

Ventilated three-piece disc wheels.

A mileage-operated mechanical pump driven from the propeller shaft coupling provided automatic Tecalemit lubrication to 40 points on the chassis.

Electrics: The Crompton Parkinson C422 self-ventilating flood-proof traction motor was resiliently mounted between the chassis frames offset to the nearside ahead of the leading rear axle and behind the statutory 10in ground clearance limit.

Rear entrance, platform and staircase detail of Bournemouth's BUT9641Ts.
Transport Museum Wythall (Metro-Cammell-Weymann)

Front exit and staircase detail of Bournemouth's BUT9641Ts.
Transport Museum Wythall (Metro-Cammell-Weymann)

The air-filtered motor had a one-hour rating of 120hp at 550V drawing 185 amps. Access to the brush gear and commutator was obtained through large openings at the top and bottom of the motor frame, protected in service by screened air inlets and commutator inspection covers.

The main Allen West control gear was of unit construction. It featured the assembly of all electrical control items including the master controller on one insulating base, mounted on rubber blocks to the nearside of the driver's seat, adjacent to the cab bulkhead.

Provision was made for battery manoeuvring equipment but it was not fitted. Mounted in the chassis frame forward of the traction motor, the Allen West main resistance had stainless steel grids and spot welding throughout to prevent rust and corrosion. The lightweight shunt resistance was of non-corrodible resistance material having a negligible temperature coefficient. The compound field was used for acceleration, the shunt field being a sufficiently small proportion of the whole to avoid generating high voltages. Protection from severe overload was given by two main circuit breakers situated in the driver's cab. The 13 steps in the electrical control equipment comprised 9 resistance (1-9), a full power (10) and 3 field weakening (11-13) notches. During braking the shunt excitation was increased and part of the series field was used as a decompounding winding which effectively limited the braking characteristics to

the desired value.

Brecknell Willis & Co. Ltd. lightweight trolley bases and collector gear with BICC Edinburgh-type slipper heads using renewable carbon inserts, supplied with radio interference suppression to meet MoT requirements. The 15ft-long one-piece trolley booms, when restrained by their retaining hooks, extended 1ft 3in beyond the rearmost part of the bodywork. They had a slightly greater diameter than those on the Sunbeam MS2s. Dewirements or loss of traction power were indicated by audible and visible warning instruments.

Oldham batteries supplied a 24-volt power source for auxiliaries such as the dewirement indicators, trafficators, windscreen wipers and lighting. 12 of the vehicles had Metropolitan-Vickers/CAV motor generator sets and the other 12 Metropolitan-Vickers/Simms sets bolted directly to the offside internal face of the chassis frame.

Brakes: Rheostatic braking was used down to 4mph, further pressure on the brake pedal at this speed bringing the compressed air brake into use.

The air compressor (with rubber insulating supports to absorb vibration) and two reservoirs, one for the brakes and the other for the front door, were bolted directly to the offside external face of the chassis frame and accessible behind three valence panels. The compressor had a 5 cu ft per min capacity powered by a ³/₄ hp 600 volt motor maintaining a pressure of 70-

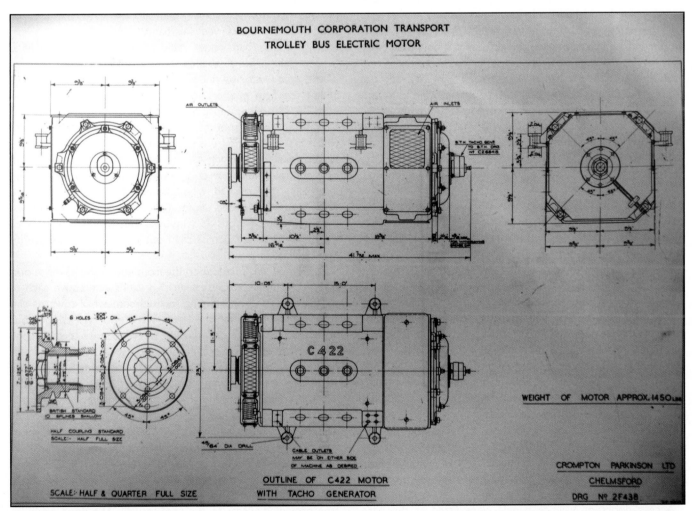

Crompton Parkinson C422 traction motor as used on Bournemouth's BUT9641T vehicles and the ex-Brighton BUT9611Ts.

Bournemouth Transport Ltd.

90lb per sq in in the reservoirs. The Westinghouse compressed air brakes operated on all wheels with a separate cylinder to each wheel, one being on top of each king pin with four cylinders on the rear bogies (instead of the customary two) mounted on the axles in order to eliminate the effects of spring deflection on the brake linkage. The compressor governor was mounted on the front nearside of the driver's cab.

The control valve, actuated by rod from the driver's brake pedal, governed the admission of air to the six brake cylinders, each of which operated a brake camshaft directly through a lever. The front brake cylinders were mounted vertically above the hollow swivel pins, and the rear cylinders horizontally below the axle casings. Seamless steel piping was used throughout, with cone and nut unions and 7-ply rubber hoses where required. The coasting brake limited speed to 7mph down a 1 in 9 gradient and the emergency run-back brake restricting speed backwards to less than ½ mph.

The handbrake operated eight shoes on the rear bogie axles; the pull-on handbrake lever was to the offside of the driver's steering column.

Drums 16¾in diameter, linings ⅝in thick, front shoes 3in wide, rear shoes 6in wide, giving 810 sq in lining area for the foot brake and 648 sq in for the handbrake.

A low pressure alarm provided an audible and visual warning to the driver if air pressure should fall enough to affect efficient braking.

The BUT9641Ts were inspected by the MoT on 21 November 1951. The roads were slippery at the time and Col. C.A. Langley found it difficult to get satisfactory brake tests with the Tapley recorder. He noted that the rheostatic/air brake on the first vehicle was not as powerful as it should have been, and that from a speed of 30mph the Tapley recordings varied from 45% to 55%; the handbrake however gave 25%. On the second vehicle the power brake was satisfactory and gave a reading of 61%, but the maximum recording with the handbrake was only 15%. Recordings of 60% with the power brake and 25% with the handbrake should have been obtainable with new vehicles, and Col. Langley considered that the brakes on the BUTs should be adjusted so as to give these minimum readings.

Bodywork: All metal, six-bay highbridge double-deck construction with integral trolley gantry, equipped with forwards-ascending half-turn (90°) rear staircase and forwards-descending half-turn front staircase, both having a landing at their midpoint, built by Weymann's Ltd. Addlestone, Surrey, and marketed by Metropolitan-Cammell-Weymann Ltd. The body pillars were secured to the cross members with self-lubricating bushes and stainless steel pins to relieve the body of strains caused by chassis distortion. There was a conventional semi-vestibuled open platform entrance at the rear and a front exit with a G.D. Peters air-operated two-leaf folding door controlled from the driver's cab by means of a lever coupled to an interlock to break the controller circuit, thus preventing the trolleybus from starting off with the doors open.

The bodywork featured Weymann characteristics of the period such as the gently curving front and rear elevations, a rounded roof, splayed out skirting panels to sides and rear, low-set front headlamps and curved tops to the rear platform window.

Access doors or valence panels were fitted at the base of the lower-deck offside panels in bays 1 (behind the step giving access to the driver's cab), 2 and 3, giving access to the compressor and air reservoirs.

The base of the lower-deck panelling at the rear and along the offside as far forward as the rear axle was finished with a protective aluminium strip.

There was a three-piece metal "fairing" mudguard over the rear wheels with mud flaps behind the rearmost tyre.

The integral trolley gantry was above bay 2. The main power cable made its way forward from the exposed platform supporting the trolley bases along the centre line of the roof before turning to the offside and entering the roof panels above the first offside pillar (which was slightly wider than the other) inside which it made its way down to the switches in the driver's cab. Access to the trolley gear was by means of a removable wooden slatted platform with gaps in its frame to fit over the protective rail to the rear window pane, stored securely on the rear platform beneath the staircase when not required and which could be fitted across the upper saloon emergency exit to cover the glass, thence to the roof catwalk.

Small rubber bumpers half way up the frame on the nearside and offside of the emergency exit door aligned with similar bumpers on the panel beneath to the nearside and offside of the rear indicator boxes.

A large removable panel with curved upper corners and three columns of six ventilation vanes extended across the base of the front panels between the headlamps, the top of the panel aligned with the centre of the headlights. The rectangular front registration plate was located beneath the offside headlamp between the panel and the front offside mudguard. The BUT maker's symbol was fitted centrally beneath the driver's windscreen on the curved waistband.

All windows had gently radiused almost square corners, however, the driver's cab side windows and the upper corners of the rear platform window were noticeably more rounded. Sliding top light openers were fitted to the side windows in bays 1-5 (nearside) and 2-5 (offside) of the upper saloon and bays 2-4 (both sides) of the lower saloon. The front portion slid towards the rear. The front upper-saloon windows had bottom-hinged, "pull-in" opening top hopper ventilators, surmounted by metal rainshield louvres. The windows were all surrounded internally by varnished wood frames. Protective rails were fitted across the glazed panes of the two fixed front windows, the two rearmost offside windows and the rear window of the upper deck, and across the front vestibule window on the lower deck.

Ventilation was provided to the front end of the lower saloon and in the driver's cab through two vanes, one above each of the driver's cab windscreens, located somewhat towards the centre line of the vehicle. There were also two deeper but shorter vanes above the opening top ventilators to the upper saloon front windows, again located towards the centre line of the vehicle, and linked through concealed trunking to extractor ventilators. A covered vent was positioned on both sides of the cab in the waistband beneath the leading side window.

The rear upper-deck emergency exit door had three hinges at its base and a single, deep window with radiused corners. There was an external door opening handle, painted red, halfway up the offside of the door frame, with an equivalent handle inside. There was a rain strip immediately above the door and above that, centrally in the rear dome, there was a grab handle and step providing access to the roof catwalk. The door could be retained open in the horizontal position by leather-covered chains on each side inside the upper saloon.

**BUT9641T/Weymann driver's cab from the nearside.
BaMMOT Archive (Metro-Cammell-Weymann)**

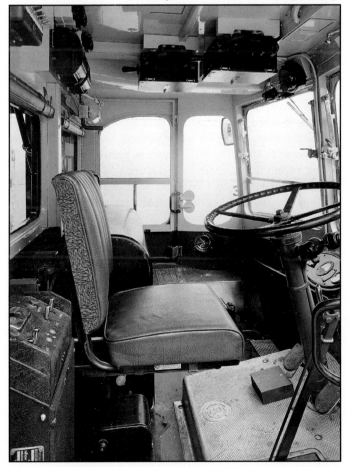

**BUT9641T/Weymann driver's cab from the offside.
BaMMOT Archive (Metro-Cammell-Weymann)**

The rear staircase had three steps (four risers) from the platform to the landing and then a further three steps (four risers) to the upper deck; the front staircase had two steps (three risers) from the upper deck to the landing and then a further three steps (four risers) to the lower deck, each riser equipped with aluminium kicking plates and each step with metal-edged canvas treads and nosings. The front exit was equipped with a glazed vestibule panel. There were two steps (two risers) prior to the drop down to the ground.

The driver's cab had front-hinged doors (3 hinges) on both sides, each equipped with a backwards sliding "signalling" window in the lower portion, and a black-painted downwards opening handle mounted in a black-painted shield-shaped inset. The fixed upper window pane and the door deepened progressively in a curve towards the front of the vehicle to align with the foremost offside cab window. Inside the driver's cab there was an adjustable sun visor above both windscreens. There were two windows in the bulkhead behind the driver, separated by a wide central pillar upon which was mounted, at driver's shoulder height, the control handle for the air-operated front exit door. Attached to the bulkhead above each window inside the driver's cab was a fold-down blind to prevent reflections from the lower saloon on to the driver's windscreen during the hours of darkness.

A step with protective black rubber surrounds was let into the base of the offside bay 1 side panel, with an aluminium "kicking plate" from the base of the offside cab door to the bottom of the panel, immediately behind the front axle. There was a smaller, almost triangular, aluminium plate beneath the nearside cab door between the front axle and the front exit, but no equivalent step.

Both windscreens were chromium-plated and divided horizontally at approximately two-thirds depth into two panes, the upper top-hinged pane on both sides opening outwards and equipped centrally with a top-mounted wiper. The lower panes deepened in a gentle curve progressively towards their extremities matching the curved waistband across the front panels beneath.

Small rectangular driver's rear-view mirrors were mounted externally on outriggers, painted black, towards the top of the front cab pillars on both sides.

There were used ticket boxes on the offside panel at the top of the front staircase, below the nearside front bulkhead window by the front exit and below the nearside vestibule window on the rear open platform. Internal advertisement frames were mounted in the upper saloon on the coving around the front staircase behind the front offside bench seat and visible to those descending the stairs, and on the outside of the coving aligned with the central gangway. In the lower saloon frames were mounted on the front bulkhead at the bottom of the front staircase, aligned with the central panel between the windows at the rear of the driver's cab, and on the panelling around the front staircase aligned with offside seats. In addition, advertisement cards could be secured along the cove panels above the side windows in both saloons.

The rear bulkhead had a vestibule window with radiused corners on the nearside, beneath which there was a used tickets box, an unpaid fares box and a curved handrail to assist boarding passengers. On the offside, at cove panel height, there was a holder for the conductor's waybill and a copy of the byelaws. Diagonally-ribbed rubber rear platform floor covering. The conductor had a locker on the rear platform under the stairs.

All six wheels were equipped with chromed hubs, complete with BUT manufacturer's badges, and wheel nut protector rings.

All platform, saloon and staircase handrails and stanchions were coated with black Doverite.

A circular conductor's mirror was fixed in the upper deck rear offside dome at the head of the stairs.

Diamond-shaped bell pushes with chromed circular bases were located in the ceiling of the upper (five) and lower (two) saloons, on the rear platform on the staircase stringer, and on the ceiling above the nearside front bulkhead window to the driver's cab.

A single tubular metal lifeguard ran beneath the side panels between the first and second axles. There were individual mud flaps behind each wheel of the front and rear axle whilst a flap mudguard hung at an angle beneath the rear platform. A bamboo trolley retrieval pole was carried in a tube mounted centrally under the chassis and was accessible from the rear of the vehicle.

Lighting: External lighting comprised two low-set headlights on the front panel, two front side lights with chromed surrounds on plinths aligned with the extremities of the windscreens in the down-swept waistband beneath the driver's windscreen, and in the lower-deck waistband, centrally beneath the rear platform window, an illuminated rear registration plate in the centre of a glass panel with semi-circular ends with a braking light, featuring white STOP lettering, to the nearside and a rear light to the offside.

A spot light was fitted below the nearside headlight.

Semaphore arm illuminated traffic indicators were fitted to the side pillars immediately to the rear of the driver's cab doors, the top of the arm aligned with the base of the upper pane of glass in the door.

Internal lighting in each saloon was provided by tungsten bulbs behind square diffused glasses with angled corners mounted on chrome fittings in the coves between the patterned Alhambrinal panels and space for advertisement cards. There were nine lamps on the nearside and ten lamps on the offside of the upper saloon, the second and third lamps on the offside were above the front staircase and the rearmost two were above the top of the stairs and the staircase itself. There were five lamps each side in the lower saloon with an additional lamp just forward of the front exit doors and another above the rear platform.

Seating: Based on painted tubular steel frames with chromium-plated top and built-in "orange segment"-shaped grab facility adjacent to the aisle. Squabs and backs were upholstered in beige, brown and orange patterned moquette, having pleated squabs but plain backs, on Dunlopillo cushions. The moquette upholstered seat backs had brown hide panelling to the tops and sides. Brown scratchproof patterned rear to the seat backs. There were upright stanchions covered in black Doverite in both saloons attached to the ceiling, rear of the seat and floor. Lower saloon: behind seat 3 nearside; seats 1, 4 offside. Upper saloon: behind seats 4, 6 nearside; seat 5 offside; and at both stairheads.

In the lower saloon ceiling-mounted handrails covered in black Doverite extended from the rear platform entrance to the front staircase.

Due to the position of the offside front staircase, seats in both the upper and lower saloons were staggered, which gave more space for moving along the gangways and resulted in a slightly greater seat pitch on the offside of both saloons.

Accordingly the lower-deck had a four-person bench seat over the rear bogie on the offside and a five-person bench seat on the nearside, both with hide tops to the armrests at their forwards end. The upper saloon had three rows of single seats on the front nearside and a bench seat for three passengers on the offside immediately in front of the front exit staircase well. At the rear of the upper saloon a bench seat above the open platform could accommodate three passengers. The other double seats were staggered, there being five on the offside and six on the nearside.

The driver's seat was in brown hide with a plain squab and pleated back.

Destination equipment: Rectangular off-centre indicator box 30in X 15in capable of displaying up to three lines of intermediate points and the final destination, i.e. a total of up to four lines, with an auxiliary (in-town "via" or special event) indicator 30in X 5in immediately below and a separate square service number indicator box 10in X 10in to the nearside at front and rear. A further rectangular indicator box repeating up to four lines of intermediate points and the final destination was fitted immediately above the rear open platform entrance.

The ECO blind-winding equipment at the front was carried out by the driver using handles and viewing panels in the cab ceiling immediately behind the windscreen.

Some, if not all, vehicles were fitted later with a wooden fold-down flap indicating when the minimum fare used on service 32 was in operation. This was mounted on hinges immediately above the rear platform entrance.

External Livery: Delivered in Livery 5 (see Appendix D).

Internal Livery: Ceilings and coves were covered with cream-coloured Alhambrinal panels with maroon and primrose insets, and varnished/polished wooden mouldings. Window frames were also varnished/polished wood. Side panels below the waist rail were brown Alhambrinal. Marble-effect material applied to the lower deck front bulkhead and upper deck front panels (incorporating access doors to the indicator boxes) and flooring forward of the front staircase. Brown paint to staircases and seat frames. Handrails and stanchions were chromed steel or covered in black Doverite. Cab area painted primrose.

The saloon floors, apart from the upper deck front flooring, were covered in brown linoleum with brown-painted metal, anti-slip transverse strips in the upper deck gangway at the rear and top of the entrance staircase.

Subsequent alterations: Red reflectors were fitted towards the base of the rear panel above the outward curve of the skirting in 1954.

The semaphore arm illuminated traffic indicators fitted on the side pillars immediately to the rear of the driver's cab doors were replaced by flashing "orange segment"-shaped trafficators mounted immediately above the lower maroon band.

234-243 had their front staircase removed and seating increased to H39/29D by adding two double seats on the offside of the lower saloon, and in the upper saloon by replacing the original three rows of single seats on the nearside with three rows of double seats and the front offside bench seat and staircase with four rows of double seats. This alteration was facilitated by the slightly greater seat pitch on the offside of both saloons. One vehicle, probably 234, was stripped of all the original seating and fitted with noticeably narrower re-

The lower saloon of Bournemouth BUT9641T no. 203 looking towards the rear platform.
BaMMOT Archive (Metro-Cammell-Weymann)

Lower saloon of Bournemouth BUT9641T fleet no. 203 looking towards the front of the vehicle.
BaMMOT Archive (Metro-Cammell-Weymann)

Upper saloon of a Bournemouth BUT9641T (no. 203) as delivered, looking towards the rear of the vehicle.
BaMMOT Archive (Metro-Cammell-Weymann)

Bournemouth BUT9641T upper saloon of no. 203 as delivered looking towards the front of the vehicle.
BaMMOT Archive (Metro-Cammell-Weymann)

trimmed seating removed from withdrawn Sunbeam MS2s. This provided a float of standard BUT9641T Deans "Dapta" seats for the subsequent rebuilds. Most vehicles retained their bell-push buttons, although one or two benefited from strip bell-pushes. Most rebuilt vehicles additionally gained rear flashing trafficator globes mounted on the extremities of the lower-deck waistband below the rear platform window. The rebuilding increased the unladen weight to 10 tons 9cwt 2qtr.

On 13 November 1962, the new General Manager, Ronald Cox, wrote to Col W.P. Reed, MoT, advising him of the alterations being carried out to all 24 (sic) of the BUT 9641Ts involving the removal of the front staircase and increasing the seating capacity from 56 to 68 seats. The spacing of the new seats conformed with the then current PSV regulations and all work was to be carried out in accordance with the current MoT regulations, i.e. the Trolley Vehicles Memorandum. Satisfactory tilt tests had been carried out at London Transport's Aldenham works. Referring to their 1951 figures, the MoT queried the braking. Tapley readings were taken that same month, unloaded at 20mph, and recorded handbrake 34%, footbrake 57.5%. Loaded the figures were: footbrake 49%, handbrake 24%. The MoT would have preferred higher results and commented that they would be relying on the Department's workshops to ensure that these figures were maintained. The staircases of the rebuilt BUT9641Ts were repainted dove grey in a similar manner to some members of the 1958-9 Sunbeam MF2Bs (258-287).

	Date of rebuilding	Re-entered Service
234	September 1962	November 1962
235	October 1962	November 1962
236	December 1962	December 1962
237	December 1962	December 1962
238	December 1962	January 1963
239	January 1963	February 1963
240	February 1963	February 1963
241	March 1963	March 1963
242	April 1963	May 1963
243	May 1963	June 1963

The chromed wheel nut protector rings were removed from the front offside wheel from some vehicles in the early 1960s. In some cases these were replaced with step rings.

Notes: The Weymann bodies on the 24 BUT9641Ts were part of a larger order encompassing 30 Leyland PD2/3 motorbuses 224-253, the largest single bodywork order placed by the department. Delivery brought the trolleybus fleet up to its maximum strength of 127 vehicles - beyond the undercover storage capabilities of the undertaking - and thus 18 Sunbeam MS2s were withdrawn and stored at the Castle Lane Depot site until being sold for scrap in May 1952.

203 was used from 24 July 1950 for driver training.

212 was exhibited on the Weymann stand at the 15th International Commercial Motor Transport Exhibition at Earl's Court, London, 22 September 1950-30 September 1950. The chassis of 218 was exhibited at the same exhibition which explains why it was the last to be delivered to BCT.

212 returned to Weymann 5 February 1951-11 April 1951 following a collision with 141 on 18 December 1950 and re-entered service on 1 August 1951.

200-223 were renumbered to 234-257 between June 1958 and February 1959.

207 was repainted with a chocolate roof in 1954.

All the BUT9641Ts withdrawn in 1965 were last used on 12 September 1965, i.e. the last date of trolleybus operation on service 25.

Disposal: 234-245, 247-257 all sold to Wombwell Diesels Co. Ltd., breakers, in December 1966 (at £75 each).

246 was reserved for a Mr R. Higgins, Christchurch, for preservation. When the sale fell through it joined the batch sold to Wombwell Diesels Co. Ltd. from whom it was purchased for preservation by Mr Richard Cromwell.

A latter-day view of BUT9641T no. 251 (KLJ351) at the west end of the central Depot, Southcote Road. Note the composite 3-wire frog, which could be run through in either direction, and 2-wire branch (9 June 1963).

Tim Runnacles

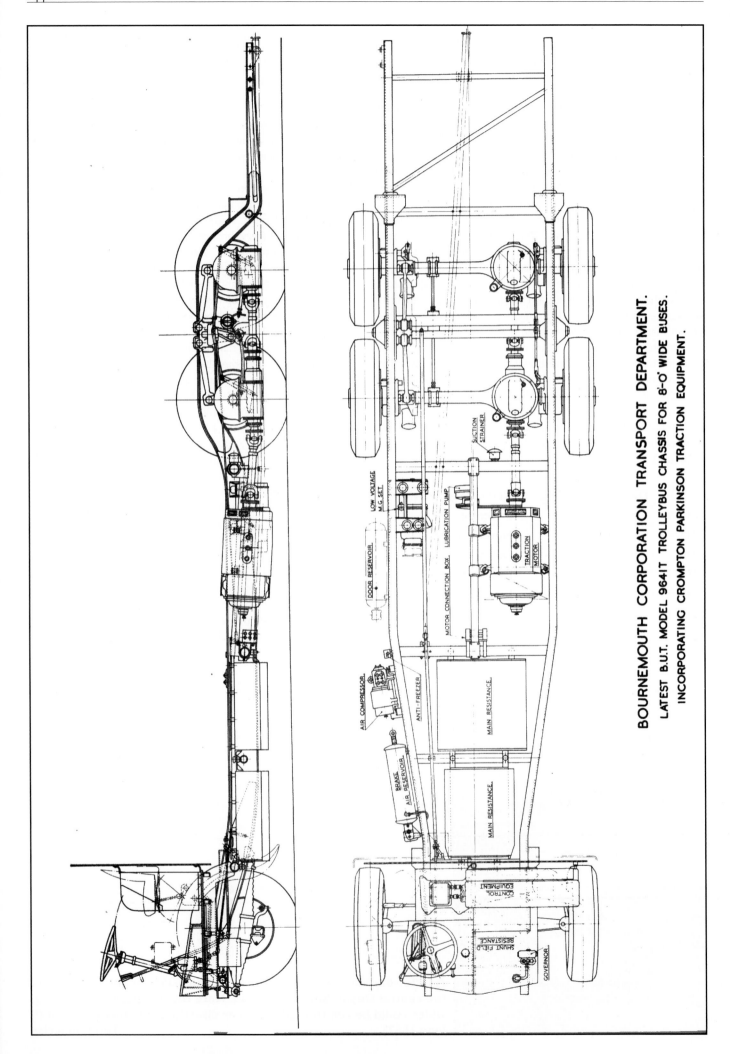

BOURNEMOUTH CORPORATION TRANSPORT DEPARTMENT.

LATEST B.U.T. MODEL 9641T TROLLEYBUS CHASSIS FOR 8-0' WIDE BUSES.

INCORPORATING CROMPTON PARKINSON TRACTION EQUIPMENT.

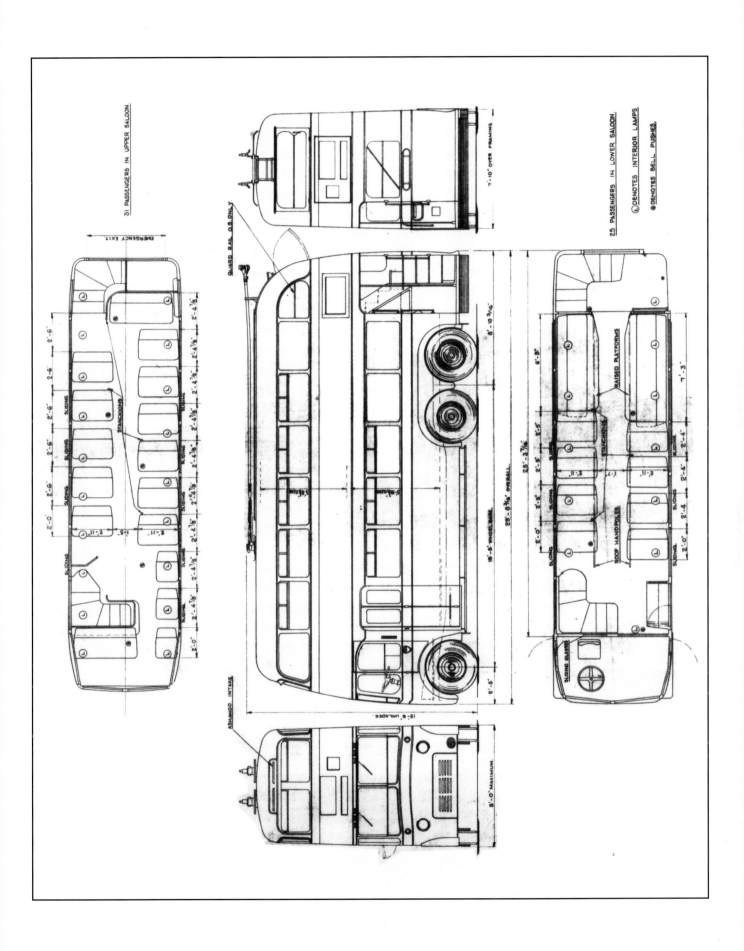

258-287 Sunbeam MF2B

Fleet No.	Registration Mark	Chassis Number	Body Number	Date of Delivery	Date into Service	Date of Withdrawal	Date of Disposal
258	WRU 258	STB80157	M8233	28.07.1958	02.08.1958	25.09.1966	15.08.1969
259	WRU 259	STB80158	M8234	29.07.1958	02.08.1958	25.09.1966	03.09.1969
260	WRU 260	STB80159	M8235	13.10.1958	01.11.1958	25.09.1966	03.09.1969
261	WRU 261	STB80160	M8237	05.08.1958	01.09.1958	25.09.1966	29.08.1969
262	WRU 262	STB80161	M8236	01.08.1958	02.08.1958	25.09.1966	29.08.1969
263	WRU 263	STB80162	M8238	07.08.1958	01.09.1958	25.09.1966	05.09.1969
264	WRU 264	STB80163	M8239	11.08.1958	01.09.1958	25.09.1966	13.08.1969
265	WRU 265	STB80164	M8240	29.08.1958	01.09.1958	25.09.1966	18.08.1969
266	WRU 266	STB80165	M8241	03.09.1958	03.11.1958	25.09.1966	18.08.1969
267	WRU 267	STB80166	M8242	09.09.1958	01.12.1958	25.09.1966	15.08.1969
268	WRU 268	STB80167	M8244	18.09.1958	01.12.1958	19.04.1968	14.10.1969
269	WRU 269	STB80168	M8243	15.09.1958	01.12.1958	30.11.1968	13.08.1969
270	WRU 270	STB80169	M8245	08.10.1958	01.01.1959	28.02.1969	11.08.1969
271	WRU 271	STB80170	M8246	16.10.1958	01.01.1959	19.04.1969	17.09.1969
272	WRU 272	STB80171	M8251	15.12.1958	01.02.1959	19.04.1969	11.09.1969
273	WRU 273	STB80172	M8247	04.11.1958	01.01.1959	20.04.1969	09.09.1969
274	WRU 274	STB80173	M8248	13.11.1958	01.01.1959	20.04.1969	09.09.1969
275	WRU 275	STB80174	M8250	03.12.1958	01.02.1959	14.09.1968	05.09.1969
276	WRU 276	STB80175	M8249	25.11.1958	01.02.1959	19.04.1969	01.10.1969
277	WRU 277	STB80176	M8252	07.01.1959	01.02.1959	19.04.1969	11.09.1969
278	YLJ 278	STB80177	M8582	15.09.1959	01.11.1959	20.04.1969	05.09.1969
279	YLJ 279	STB80178	M8583	21.09.1959	01.10.1959	20.04.1969	11.09.1969
280	YLJ 280	STB80179	M8580	07.09.1959	01.10.1959	20.04.1969	25.09.1969
281	YLJ 281	STB80180	M8577	07.08.1959	01.09.1959	30.11.1969	11.08.1969
282	YLJ 282	STB80181	M8578	27.08.1959	01.09.1959	20.04.1969	16.09.1969
283	YLJ 283	STB80182	M8575	21.07.1959	01.08.1959	20.04.1969	23.09.1969
284	YLJ 284	STB80183	M8581	12.09.1959	01.11.1959	20.04.1969	23.09.1969
285	YLJ 285	STB80184	M8579	02.09.1959	01.10.1959	20.04.1969	02.09.1969
286	YLJ 286	STB80185	M8574	16.07.1959	01.08.1959	19.04.1969	.08.1969
287	YLJ 287	STB80186	M8576	23.07.1959	01.08.1959	19.04.1969	16.09.1969

Sunbeam MF2B chassis
Wolverhampton Archives
(Sunbeam collection)

Chassis: Two axle "transit" type Sunbeam MF2B, primarily foreseen for export markets, manufactured by Sunbeam Trolleybus Co. Ltd., Fallings Park, Wolverhampton, Staffordshire.

Motor: Crompton Parkinson Ltd., Chelmsford, Essex, Type: C423 (95nhp), with a light compound winding incapable of regeneration (known as "controlled rheostatic").

Electrical equipment: Allen West & Co. Ltd., Brighton, incorporating automatic acceleration with 13 power notches, the master controller and reverser was beneath the driver's seat.

Dewirement indicators: 2 green line-lights and buzzer

Brakes: Westinghouse compressed air on all wheels, 2-stage rheostatic, coasting and run-back brakes. Handbrake on rear wheels

Body: Highbridge double-deck all metal five bay construction with twin staircases, conventional rear, semi-vestibuled open platform entrance and separate front exit with air-operated folding doors controlled from the driver's cab placed forward of the leading axle.

Built by Weymann's Ltd., Station Road, Addlestone, Surrey.

Seating: 258/259 and 261-269 H34/28D
260 and 270-287 H35/28D

Length: 30ft   Width: 7ft 11¾ in   Height: 15ft 7in unladen (over trolley base)

Wheelbase: 15ft 10in giving a turning circle over the full body on either lock of 58ft.

Unladen weight: 8 tons 19 cwts 2 qtrs
Wheel track: front 6ft 11½ in, rear 6ft.
Tyres: front 11.00in X 20in 14-ply, double rear 10.00in X 20in 12-ply.

The original tender specifying 20 two-axle 8ft-wide double-deck rear entrance, front exit trolleybuses capable of carrying 62 seated passengers was issued in July 1956

Chassis: The frame was built of high tensile steel channel side-members with pressed steel centre cross-members for torsional rigidity and other tubular cross-members, the whole assembly being bolted together. "I" section carbon alloy steel front axle. The rear axle had an underslung worm-driven unit on the nearside with fully floating axle shafts, the casing being a one-piece alloy steel drop forging. The hardened steel worm had 8½ in centres and an axle ratio of 10.33 to 1.

Chassis length: 29ft 7½ in
Chassis width: 7ft 10in
Minimum ground clearance: 7in

Semi-elliptic leaf springs to all axles:
Front: 4in wide, 4ft 6in long
Rear: 4in wide, 5ft 2in long.

Sunbeam MF2B fleet no. 260 (WRU260) immediately prior to delivery. Note the centrally mounted rectangular ventilator in the upper-deck front dome to 258-269, this being a standard fitment to MCW motorbus bodies of the time. There was, unfortunately, never a trolleybus service 42! BaMMOT Archive (Metro-Cammell-Weymann)

Conventional suspension used semi-elliptic Silico Manganese leaf-type springs. The individual leaves were shot peening for fatigue resistance, fitted with anti-roll clips and supplemented by overload rubber buffers. Telescopic shock absorbers were fitted to both axles. A 24-point Tecalemit belt-driven lubricator provided automatic chassis lubrication. Normal ventilated disc-type wheels. The 21in diameter driver's wheel with a ratio of $5\frac{1}{2}$ turns lock to lock connected with Marles cam and double roller type steering gear mounted in a cast-iron casing on the chassis frame.

Electrics: The "controlled rheostatic" Crompton Parkinson C423 self-ventilating, flood-proof traction motor was angled towards the nearside and resiliently supported on four rubber anti-vibration mountings between the chassis frames ahead of the rear axle. The motor had a one-hour rating of 95hp at 550V. It could be easily removed from the chassis for overhaul. The drive to the rear axle was by a short tubular shaft with Hardy Spicer universal joints at each end, the differential being offset to the nearside in alignment with the traction motor.

A 24V CAV overhung auxiliary generator together with control board charged the battery when the traction motor was running; the Crompton Parkinson battery supplying power for the control systems, accessories and internal and external lighting. Allen West control gear was used with the master controller and reverser placed under the driver's seat in the cab. The main resistors were mounted between the chassis side members in front of the traction motor, fully shielded against splashing from the road, with a further steel and asbestos shield mounted over them to protect the body from undue heat. The contactor panel was mounted in a waterproof steel case on the offside external face of the chassis frame and accessible behind two valence panels. Pre-adjusted automatic acceleration and coasting and run-back brakes were provided. Shielded R.P. resistors were mounted between the frame side members.

The automatic acceleration device was an entirely electro-mechanical, compact unit located in the position normally used by the over-current relay. The master controller was driven through a pre-compressed spring incorporated in the drive. An eddy-current drag unit was driven from the master controller, thus delaying the controller so that the spring was wound up if the speed of power pedal depression exceeded a certain rate. Provided this rate was not exceeded, the controller remained under the driver's direct control and the trolleybus could be driven in a similar manner to one equipped with normal equipment. A ratchet allowed the master controller to be returned instantaneously to the "off" position.

The drag unit consisted of an eddy-current disc rotating in a magnetic field. This field was created by a coil connected across the main motor series field, so that the drag field strength varied according to the current being taken by the motor, and regulated the speed of progression of the controller according to grade and load conditions. A resistance was incorporated in series with the drag coil. Part of this resistance was provided with accessible tappings, enabling the operator to pre-set the acceleration rate required by changing one connection. Up to four tappings could be provided for selected acceleration rates on the level.

The drag coil series resistance was cut out until the B1 contactor closed by means of an interlock on this contactor. This reduced the rate of controller progression over the first three notches, ensuring smooth, uniform acceleration under all conditions. A current limit relay in the main motor circuit cut out the drag coil series resistance when the accelerating current exceeded a pre-determined figure and reduced the rate of controller progression to a crawl until the current had fallen to a safe figure.

The drag device did not come into action until the first notch had been obtained, so that there was no delay in obtaining power. When the trolleybus was travelling at speed and the pedal was rapidly depressed to its full extent, such as after a section insulator, controller progression from the "off" position to the last notch took place in less than one second. The drag unit construction was robust; the $\frac{1}{2}$in pinions driving the eddy drag disc ran in ball-bearings, whilst the ratchet was also $\frac{1}{2}$in wide and made from lubricant-free materials. The parts were intended to have the same life-expectancy as the vehicle. The entire unit was totally enclosed and required no maintenance, excluding lubrication at each major vehicle overhaul.

Brecknell Willis & Co. Ltd., slipper-type trolley collector gear equipped with Anti-Attrition OB-type heads and renewable carbon inserts with radio interference suppression to meet MoT requirements. The lightweight Accles & Pollock trolley booms, insulated at the sockets by means of Bakelite sleeves, allowed 15ft deviation to either side of the overhead line. The 16ft-long booms, when restrained by their retaining hooks, extended 6in beyond the rearmost part of the bodywork. To control the vertical movement of the trolley poles a hydraulic damping device was fitted and a brake restricted the swing of the poles in case of dewirement. They were made up of two tubes of different diameter; the larger diameter of the two running from the trolley base and being about two feet shorter than normal. The smaller-diameter tube inserted into the end of the larger one and reached to the trolley head, and was covered with rubber tubing painted white which made the reduced diameter less obvious. It is believed that this arrangement added spring and flexibility at the boom end and so helped to minimise dewirements.

There was a concealed trolley gantry above bay 2.

The 13 steps in the electrical control equipment comprised 10 resistance (1-10), a full power (11) and 2 field weakening (12-13) notches and rheostatic braking (two notches).

Traction batteries for manoeuvring purposes were not fitted.

Brakes: Rheostatic braking was used down to 4mph, further pressure on the brake pedal at this speed bringing the compressed air brake into use.

The air compressor (with rubber insulating supports to absorb vibration) and the front door reservoir were bolted directly to the nearside external face of the chassis frame and accessible behind two top-hinged access doors or valence panels in bays 2, 3. The brake reservoir was bolted to the offside external face of the chassis frame forward of the contactor panel, accessible behind the top-hinged access door in bay 2.

The foot braking system was operated by Westinghouse air-pressure equipment with separate cylinders for each wheel, the air compressor delivering 4.8 cu ft actual swept volume per minute driven by a $\frac{3}{4}$hp electric motor. A pull-on handbrake was linked to the rear shoes; the pull-on handbrake lever was to the offside of the driver's steering column.

The front brake drums were $16\frac{1}{2}$in diameter with brake linings 4in wide and $\frac{1}{2}$in thick giving 208 sq in lining area. The rear brake drums were made of chromidium iron alloy, manufactured by the Midland Motor Cylinder Co. Ltd., and had

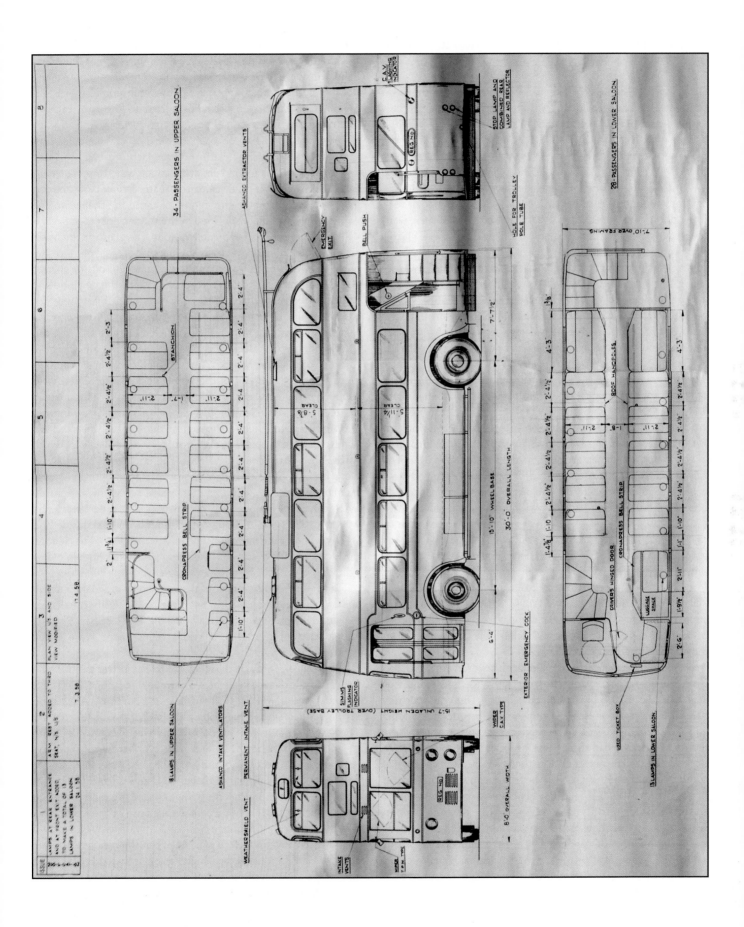

a diameter of 16¼in with brake linings 6½in wide and ½in thick giving 364 sq in lining area. Two notches of rheostatic braking were available before the air brakes came into operation. Coasting and run-back (equipment type CT/MP.2.) brakes were fitted as required by an MoT instruction related to trolleybus operation on Richmond Hill.

Bodywork: All-metal five-bay construction with twin staircases, rear open platform entrance and separate front exit with air-operated two-leaf folding doors placed forward of the leading axle, based on a detailed proposal and drawing from BCT and incorporating some Weymann "Aurora" features, built by Weymann's Ltd., Addlestone, Surrey, and marketed by Metropolitan-Cammell-Weymann Ltd. A standard MCW centrally-mounted rectangular ventilator in the upper-deck front dome was fitted to the early deliveries, 258-269. Both the upper and lower portions of the folding doors were glazed. The rear staircase was forward-ascending and that at the front of the vehicle forward-descending. There were three forwards-facing single seats on the front nearside of the upper saloon and a forwards-facing triple bench (originally a double bench on 258, 259, 261-269) on the offside immediately in front of the front exit staircase well. Rectangular driver's rear-view mirrors were mounted on the front offside and nearside front pillars.

Channel steel floor bearers were connected to the tubular steel lower saloon pillars (which had timber inserts) by means of steel brackets, the upper saloon pillars being of aluminium alloy section. The saloon floors were of ¾in tongue and groove softwood covered in brown linoleum with conventional Pyramid floor treading. Structural lining panels were provided in both saloons and alloy roof hoopsticks and purlins used. The carlines supporting the upper-deck floor were of flanged steel channel section connected to the pillars by means of fabricated brackets. The exterior panelling was 18-gauge aluminium with the exception of the front and rear domes which were in 16-gauge and the lower offside rear corner panel which was glass fibre. The panels were butt jointed and covered with alloy mouldings, secured to the timber inserts by wood screws. The front exit door forward of the front axle was of the Deans "Glider" pattern, air-operated via a separate air reservoir supplied by the Westinghouse compressor. An interlock to break the controller circuit prevented the trolleybus from moving with the door open.

Hand rails and sockets were Doverite covered and insulated from the metal structure. The rear entrance and front exit staircases were 20-gauge steel construction. The rear staircase had three steps (four risers) from the platform to the landing and then a further three steps (four risers) to the upper deck; the front staircase had three steps (four risers) from the upper deck to the landing and then a further two steps (three risers) to the lower deck, each step being equipped with Ferodo nosings to the treads. There were two steps (two risers) prior to the drop down to the ground. The front exit was equipped with a glazed vestibule panel forward of the luggage space and nearside longitudinal seat which were opposite the front staircase. The rear platform was covered with aluminium-cased Ferodo tread, 1¾in wide, and the platform edge was fitted with Ferodo nosings. A Desmo staircase mirror located in the offside rear dome enabled the conductor to watch the upper deck.

The main power cables made their way forward on planking from the exposed platform supporting the trolley bases along the centre line of the roof before turning to the offside and entering the roof panels above the first offside pillar inside which it made its way down to the switches in the driver's cab.

The rear upper-deck emergency exit door had three hinges at its base and a single, deep window with radiused corners. There was an external door opening handle, painted red, halfway up the offside of the door frame, with an equivalent handle inside. There was a rain strip immediately above the door and above that, centrally in the rear dome, there was a grab handle and step providing access to the roof catwalk. The door could be retained open in the horizontal position by leather-covered chains on each side inside the upper saloon. There was a lightweight platform manufactured by Deans and looking like a small aluminium step-ladder, which was normally fixed over the protective rail to the rear window pane and ran from top to bottom, in the centre of the door, thence to the roof catwalk. Although specified in the tender documents, early deliveries appear to have run without the platform in place. Small rubber bumpers near to the upper outer corners of the emergency exit door frame on the nearside and offside aligned with similar bumpers on the panel beneath to the nearside and offside of the rear indicator boxes.

Three pairs of single slide Rawling's "Streamlight" windows in polished aluminium frames were fitted to bays 1, 3, 5 (both sides) of the upper deck, and bays 1-3 (nearside) and bays 2-4 (offside) of the lower-deck. Auster "pull-in" opening windows were fitted to the front of the upper deck. Direct Claytonrite rubber glazing as used in Weymann's "Orion" bodies, instead of steel pans, was used for the saloon windows. The windows were of 26oz toughened sheet glass but for the deep driver's windscreen, rear platform and vestibule windows, etc, which were 3/16in toughened plate glass. The corners of all windows were radiused. The driver's cab was equipped with an offside opening windscreen and a fixed nearside screen manufactured by British Steel Frames Ltd., both with electric demisters and wipers (a TPM wiper being top-mounted on the offside and a CAV wiper bottom-mounted on the nearside). The second offside cab window was equipped with a Rawlings double sliding light, the lower light forming a driver's "signalling" window.

There were two Ashanco intake ventilators in the roof above and a little forward of midway above bay 1 and two Ashanco extractor vents above and towards the front of bay 5 whilst above each of the driver's windscreens there were three centrally-located ventilator louvres.

The front exit staircase backed on to the driver's cab, which had a small glazed draught screen behind the driver's left shoulder and a waist-high front-hinged door on the nearside in the style of a one-man-operated motorbus of the period. There was no external cab door. The driver was provided with an adjustable Chapman 32 H.B. seat with brown Vynide and Rexine cushion and squab, and an electric heater.

In the front waistband there was a triangular Sunbeam maker's symbol mounted centrally beneath the pillar between the two driver's cab windscreens. At the base of the front panel was the registration number plate and, immediately above, two columns of six ventilation vanes. Between the nearside column and the fog light a small top-hinged door provided access to an anchorage for a screw-in towing eye.

Cronapress strip bell pushes were attached to the nearside ceilings of both saloons, that in the lower saloon running from bay 1 to bay 5, and that in the upper saloon from bay 2 to 5, with an additional bell push placed in the rear staircase stringer for use by the conductor when standing on the rear entrance

Sunbeam MF2B upper saloon looking towards the rear. The thirty 1958-59 deliveries, nos. 258-287, could be easily identified by the three single seats on the front nearside.

Transport Museum Wythall (Metro-Cammell-Weymann)

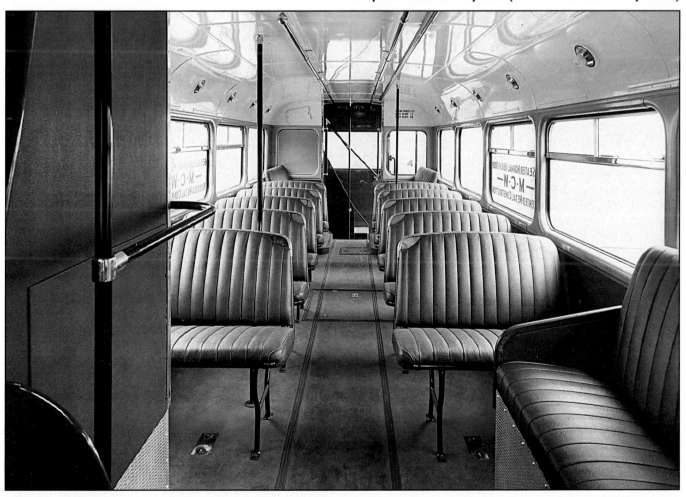

Sunbeam MF2B lower saloon looking towards the rear. Transport Museum Wythall (Metro-Cammell-Weymann)

platform. Card advertisements could be displayed internally in retaining channels between the lighting installations in the cove panels of both saloons, and in display cases on the front staircase and on the offside rear bulkhead of the lower saloon. A double-compartment ticket-box locker was built into the rear staircase stringer. Used-ticket boxes were fitted on the rear panel at the top of the front staircase, immediately below the nearside cab windscreen by the front exit and on the rear platform vestibule beneath the window. A bamboo trolley retrieval pole was carried centrally under the chassis.

Lighting: Externally at the front there were two headlights mounted on slight protrusions to accommodate the curved near and offside of the front panel, and two sidelights mounted similarly on the lower-deck waist band. At the rear there was a glass panel with semi-circular ends in the waistband beneath the rear window containing the rear registration number and, to either side, red braking lights. Circular rear lights were fitted to 258-277 two-thirds of the way down the rear lower-deck panel. That on the nearside was fitted in a separate plinth at the base of the rear platform window nearside pillar, which also provided the base for a rear passenger grab rail. On 278-287 combined BMAC rear lights and reflectors were used in the same locations instead of circular units.

A fog light was fitted below the nearside headlight. All lights were of the Simms flush type and controlled by a Simms 6.B.100 switchboard. A Simms Flasher unit controlled flashing "orange segment"-shaped LE10 trafficators mounted immediately above the lower-deck maroon-painted waistband between the front exit doors and the lower-deck bay 1 side windows on the nearside, and behind the driver's cab "signalling" window on the offside. Circular CAV 556 units were fitted on the lower-deck waist band at the rear.

Internally, exposed bulb tungsten lighting was fitted in the cove panels of both saloons, the rear platform entrance and destination boxes. There were eight lamps mounted in metal protrusions with stainless steel reflectors in the cove panels on each side of the upper saloon with a ninth in the rear dome (that on the offside being above the rear staircase). There were five lamps mounted in metal protrusions with stainless steel reflectors in the cove panels on the offside of the lower saloon, six on the nearside, one in the ceiling above the front exit door which only illuminated when the door was open and thus the vehicle at a standstill, and one in the ceiling above the rear platform.

Seating: Deans "Dapta" lightweight frames painted brown with stainless steel top rail and built-in "orange segment"-shaped grab facility adjacent to the aisle. Dunlopillo cushions and polyether squabs covered in brown coloured Vynide and Rexine, both seat and squab being fully fluted. Brown scratchproof patterned rear to the seat backs. In the lower saloon, a bench seat having space for two passengers was fitted on the nearside behind the front exit door over the front wheel arch. At the rear, bench seats over the rear wheel arch on both the near and offsides each accommodated three passengers. There were also five rows of forward-facing double seats. The upper saloon had three rows of single seats (the third seat opposite the stairhead equipped with a tubular armrest) on the front nearside and a bench seat for three passengers on the offside immediately in front of the front exit staircase well.

At the rear of the upper saloon a bench seat above the open platform could both accommodate two passengers on 258, 259, 261-269 and three passengers on 260, 270-287. A larger rear bench seat for three passengers was fitted to 258, 259, 261-269 in October 1958. There were seven rows of forward-facing double seats on the nearside and six on the offside.

There were upright stanchions covered in black Doverite in both saloons attached to the ceiling, rear of the seat and floor. Lower saloon: behind seat 4 nearside; seat 1 offside. Upper saloon: behind seat 2 nearside; seat 5 offside; and at both stairheads.

In the lower saloon ceiling-mounted handrails covered in black Doverite extended from the rear platform entrance to the front exit above the gangway edge of the aisle seats on the nearside and from the entrance to above seat 1 (bay 2) above the gangway edge of the aisle seats on the offside.

Destination equipment: Rectangular off-centre indicator box 30in X 15in capable of displaying up to three lines of intermediate points and the final destination, i.e. a total of up to four lines, with an auxiliary (in-town "via" or special event) indicator 30in X 5in immediately below and a separate square service number indicator box 10in X 10in to the nearside at front and rear. A further rectangular indicator box repeating up to three lines of intermediate points and the final destination was fitted immediately above the rear open platform entrance. The destination equipment gearing was manufactured by Equipment & Engineering Co.

External Livery: Delivered in Livery 6 (see Appendix D)

Internal Livery: The side panels below the waistrail were lined in brown Rexine leather-cloth with the ceilings cellulosed in broken white. Window cappings were stove enamelled in a gold metallic colour. Brown paint was used for the front and rear staircases, the driver's cab and the seat frames. The upper saloon front panels between the waist and the floor were covered with black fluted rubber. All handrails and stanchions were covered in black Doverite.

The saloon floors were covered in brown linoleum with brown-painted metal, anti-slip transverse strips in the upper-deck gangway at the rear and top of the entrance staircase.

Subsequent alterations: 258, 259, 261-269 re-seated October 1958 to H35/28D by replacing the upper saloon rear double bench seat above the open platform with a larger bench seat for three passengers.

A wooden fold-down flap indicating when the minimum fare used on service 32 was in operation was mounted on hinges immediately above the rear open platform entrance at the beginning of 1961.

Scheduled maintenance saw many of the earlier deliveries repainted externally to the same standards as the second batch of MF2Bs (295-303) but this work came to an end in early-1964 with the decision to "run down" the system. A handful of trolleybuses, including 269, 278, 279, 286, benefited from a repaint in the then current livery style in 1966.

Plain gold Gill Sans stock numerals gradually replaced the more traditional shaded version from 1963 and from 1966, often as a result of accident damage, several of these trolleybuses received plain black stock numerals. These were mounted slightly higher than the gold numerals at the front below the offside headlight and lower on the rear panel below the platform window (to accommodate an advertisement). From September 1967 exterior advertising was carried on the upper-deck side panels (obliterating the Bournemouth coat of arms) and below the rear platform window. Additional coats of arms were accordingly added to the lower deck side panels centred on bay 3. From 1966 onwards the triangular Sunbeam manufacturer's plate was removed from the front lower waistband.

All vehicles had the upper and lower saloon metallic gold window surrounds repainted in clonquite (light primrose) and some had their staircases and cabs repainted in dove grey (varying treatments) in an effort to brighten their interiors. As an experiment, one of the low-numbered vehicles appeared in 1962 with a light peppermint green ceiling on one deck and light salmon pink on the other.

The primrose driver's external rear-view mirrors were repainted black during routine maintenance.

Notes: The Commercial Motor Show held at Earl's Court, London, 26 September 1958-4 October 1958, featured 260 (bodied and complete) and the chassis of 272 on the Sunbeam stand (stand 63). 260 was fitted with a non-standard pressed registration number plate for the Exhibition and retained this until withdrawal.

It is understood that 278-287, which were always intended for delivery in 1959, were originally allocated registration marks WRU278-87; however, these were issued to a variety of private cars, motor cycles and commercial vehicles during the summer of 1958.

These ten trolleybuses were ordered while 258-277 were under construction and the 30 chassis were produced as one batch. The chassis of 278-285 were delivered to Mallard Road Depot for storage on the following dates:

278	18 December 1958;	279	10December1958;
280	16 December 1958;	281	7 January 1959;
282	3 February 1959;	283	7 February 1959;
284	26 February 1959;	285	10 March 1959

The chassis were delivered by BCT to Weymann's on 29, 30, 31 May and 3, 10, 19, 23, 25 June 1959.

Disposals: 258-287 all sold to Wombwell Diesels Co. Ltd., breakers, August 1969 for £150 each (258-267 having been withdrawn on 25 September 1966 and stored and cannibalised in the open at the rear of the Mallard Road Workshops). 286 was sold by Wombwell Diesels the same month to the London Trolleybus Preservation Society. Initially stored at Mallard Road Depot, 286 was transferred to the East Anglia Transport Museum, Carlton Colville, on 16 November 1972, where it has been restored to working order.

288 - 294 BUT9611T

Original Fleet No.	Registration Mark	Chassis Number	Body Number	Brighton Fleet & Fleet No.	Brighton Date into Service	Bournemouth Date of Delivery	Bournemouth Date into Service	Date of Withdrawal	Date of Disposal
288	HUF 45	9611T.027	M3399	45 (BCT)	.05.1948	28.02.1959	02.11.1959	28.02.65	.11.1965
289	HUF 46	9611T.028	M3398	46 (BCT)	.05.1948	24.02.1959	01.10.1959	31.07.65	.11.1965
290	HUF 47	9611T.029	M3396	47 (BCT)	.06.1948	21.02.1959	01.12.1959	31.07.65	.11.1965
291	HUF 48	9611T.030	M3397	48 (BCT)	.06.1948	19.02.1959	01.01.1960	30.05.65	.11.1965
292	DNJ 992	9611T.047	M3403	391 (BH&D)	.03.1948	10.03.1959	02.11.1959	31.07.65	.11.1965
293	DNJ 993	9611T.048	M3402	392 (BH&D)	.03.1948	04.03.1959	01.06.1959	31.08.65	.11.1965
294	DNJ 994	9611T.049	M3404	393 (BH&D)	.03.1948	07.03.1959	01.06.1959	31.08.65	.11.1965

Note: Bournemouth Corporation Transport records quote body numbers M3403 and M3404 for DNJ992 and DNJ994 respectively, whereas a number of enthusiast publications quoting BH&D records show M3404 and M3403 for these two vehicles.

Chassis: Two-axle type BUT9611T manufactured by the British United Traction Ltd., Hanover House, 14 Hanover Square, London W1 at Leyland Motors' Ham Works, Kingston upon Thames, Surrey.
Motor: Crompton Parkinson Ltd., Chelmsford, Essex, Type C422 (120hp) four pole, with a light compound winding incapable of regeneration (known as "controlled rheostatic").
Electrical equipment: Allen West & Co. Ltd., Brighton, 9 notches, (1-5, resistance; 6, full power; 7-9, field weakening). Control equipment mounted at the front of the chassis and in the cab

to the nearside of the driver's seat.
Dewirement indicators: orange line-light and buzzer.
Brakes: Westinghouse compressed air on all wheels, two-stage rheostatic series dynamic, coasting brake set for 14 mph and run-back brake set for 1 mph. Handbrake on rear wheels
Body: Highbridge double-deck all metal five bay construction with conventional rear, semi-vestibuled open platform entrance and exit.
Built by Weymann's Ltd., Station Road, Addlestone, Surrey.
Seating H30/26R.

Weymann-bodied BUT9611T as delivered to Brighton Corporation as their no. 50 (HUF50) in 1948. Following withdrawal in Brighton in December 1958, this example was sold to Bradford Corporation, receiving their fleet no. 803, and remained in service in Yorkshire until November 1963.   Transport Museum Wythall (Weymann)

Length: 26ft   Width: 7ft 6in   Height 15ft 6in
Wheelbase: 16ft 4in giving a turning circle on either lock of 59ft.
Wheel track: front 6ft 5½in, rear 5ft 9 ³/₁₆ in.
Unladen weight: 7 tons 6 cwt on delivery to Brighton, Bournemouth recorded 8 tons 10 cwt.
Tyres: front 11.00in X 20in, double rear 9.00in X 20in.

Purchased from Brighton Corporation Transport 45-48 (Bournemouth 288-291) and Brighton, Hove & District Omnibus Company Limited (BH&D) 391-393 (292-294) these were the only second-hand trolleybuses to be operated by Bournemouth.

The Corporation vehicles had been delivered to Brighton in March 1948 entering service in May and June 1948. At the time they were advertised for sale their relatively low total mileage was recorded as 45 - 280,000, 46 - 291,000, 47 - 316,000, 48 - 310,000. The three BH&D vehicles, the Company's only post-war trolleybuses, had entered service in March 1948 and were used primarily on Brighton's service 44 between Seven Dials and Black Rock, operating out of the Company's Whitehawk garage. They were almost identical to Brighton Corporation's 45-52. The BH&D vehicles were renumbered as follows: 6391 as 391 in August 1957, 6392 and 6393 as 392 and 393 in February 1956.

The post-war Corporation trolleybuses were withdrawn from service in December 1958 and the BH&D vehicles in early February 1959 (392 was delicensed and stored from 30

September 1958, while 391 and 392 were delicensed and stored from 28 February 1959) although the first Brighton route withdrawals (41, 42, 43A, 44 and 48) only took place on 24 March 1959. In February 1959 Bournemouth purchased four of Brighton Corporation Transport's eight post-war trolleybuses, the others (49-50) going to Bradford (their 802-803) and the remaining two (51-52) to Maidstone (their 51-52 also), and all three BH&D post-war vehicles.

Chassis: The BUT9611T chassis was based on the AEC Regent III motorbus chassis and was thus a development of the pre-war AEC661T. The chassis also incorporated most of the modifications introduced with the 3-axle BUT9641T. The chassis cost £2,277 each.

Chassis length: 26ft
Chassis frame width: front 3ft 3⁷/₈in, rear 3ft 9¹¹/₃₂in
Overall width (over tyres): 7ft 5½in front; 7ft 5⁵/₈in rear.
Chassis weight less traction equipment and cabling: 3 tons

When compared with the pre-war AEC661T the chassis featured a re-designed rear axle with underslung worm drive, improved shaft and worm-wheel bearings. Conventional transmission. The propeller shaft, equipped with Layrub bushes, improved commutation by preventing transmission vibrations from reaching the traction motor.

Channel section shallow steel frame, braced by tubular cross

Rear offside view of Weymann bodies BUT9611T as delivered to Brighton Corporation as their no. 50 in spring 1948.
Transport Museum Wythall (Weymann)

members. The front axle beam was an alloy steel stamping with taper fit swivel pins and taper roller thrust bearings to take vertical loads.

Fully floating axles, both axles being equipped with stabiliser bars. Newton telescopic shock absorbers were fitted on the front axles only. The front axle and steering gear were common components with the AEC Regent III.

On the rear axle renewable strip-type thrust bearings were fitted behind the differential pinions and the axle shaft bevel wheels. Involute splines were used on the axle shafts with detachable cast inserts carrying the oil seals at the splined ends of the shafts.

Tecalemit slide-on individual nipples were used for lubrication.

Electrics: The Crompton Parkinson C422 self-ventilating, flood-proof traction motor was resiliently mounted between the chassis frames offset to the nearside just ahead of the rear axle. The resistances were placed between the chassis frame in front of the traction motor with the shunt field resistance located under the cab.

Brecknell Willis & Co. Ltd. lightweight trolley bases and collector gear with Anti-Attrition OB-type slipper heads using renewable carbon inserts, supplied with radio interference suppression to meet MoT requirements. The 15ft-long trolley booms, when restrained by their retaining hooks, extended 2ft 3in beyond the rearmost part of the bodywork. Dewirements or loss of traction power were indicated by audible and visible warning instruments.

Lighting from CAV D13 TB 24V overhung motor generator. Equipped with battery manoeuvring equipment and Exide 24V 80Ah traction batteries mounted on the exterior of the chassis frame. The batteries were connected in parallel for lighting (24V 160Ah) and in series for traction (48V 80Ah).

Brakes: Westinghouse compressed air on all wheels, two-stage rheostatic series dynamic, coasting brake set for 14mph and run-back brake set for 1mph (both on 1 in 9 gradients). Handbrake on rear wheels; the pull-on handbrake lever was to the offside of the driver's steering column.

Bodywork: All metal, five-bay highbridge double-deck construction with integral trolley gantry, forwards-ascending half-turn (90°) rear staircase with conventional semi-vestibuled open platform entrance and exit at the rear, built by Weymann's Ltd. Addlestone, Surrey, and marketed by Metropolitan-Cammell-Weymann Ltd. The body pillars were secured to the cross members with self-lubricating bushes and stainless steel pins to relieve the body of strains caused by chassis distortion.

The bodywork featured Weymann characteristics of the period such as the gently curving front and rear elevations, a rounded roof, splayed out skirting panels to sides and rear, low-set front headlamps and curved tops to the rear platform window. The order cost of the bodies was £2,400 each.

Access doors or valence panels were fitted at the base of the lower-deck offside panels in bays 1 (behind the step giving access to the driver's cab), and 2, giving access to the compressor and air reservoir.

The base of the lower-deck panelling at the rear and along the offside as far forward as the rear axle was finished with a protective aluminium strip. There was also a narrower aluminium edging strip along the base of the side panels between the wheel arches.

The mudguards above all four wheels were swept back at the rear.

The integral trolley gantry was above bay 2. The main power cables made their way forward from the platform supporting the trolley bases along the centre line of the roof before entering the front dome at a point aligned fractionally to the rear of the front corner pillar. The cables continued forwards in a conduit inside the central pillar of the upper-deck front windows down to the switches in the driver's cab. Access to the trolley gear was by means of a removable wooden slatted platform with gaps in its frame to fit over the protective rail to the rear window panes, stored securely on the rear platform beneath the staircase when not required and which could be fitted across the upper saloon emergency exit to cover the glass, thence to the roof catwalk.

Immediately above the rearmost upper saloon side window (above the rear platform) on each side, at the rear end of the roof-mounted catwalk, a transverse rod attached to the trolley boom restraining hooks, extended across much of the width of the vehicle to avoid roof damage when pulling down the trolley booms and stowing them beneath the retraining hooks.

There were four roof-mounted Ashanco extractors above bays 1 and 4 on each side with rectangular grills in the upper saloon cove panels.

There was a large removable panel with curved upper corners, in which there were three columns of six ventilation vanes, extending across the base of the front panels between the headlamps, with the registration plate immediately above. The depth of the panel extended to about three quarters of the depth of the headlamps. The BUT maker's symbol was fitted centrally beneath the driver's windscreen at the top of the front panel. The windows were all surrounded internally by varnished wood frames. Protective rails were fitted across the glazed panes of the two rearmost offside windows and the rear window of the upper-deck, and across the rear platform window.

All windows had gently radiused almost square corners, however, the driver's cab side windows and the upper corners of the rear platform window were noticeably more rounded. Wind-down half-drop openers were fitted to the tops of the Widney "Aero" side windows in bays 1, 3, 5 of the upper saloon and bays 1, 3 of the lower saloon on both sides; the winding handle in the top of the fixed lower pane was placed variously at one third or halfway along the top rail. Turning the handle actuated a mechanism that caused the upper pane to move up or down. The upper pane dropped outside the fixed lower pane.

The front upper-deck windows had bottom-hinged, "pull-in" opening top hopper ventilators, surmounted by metal rainshield louvres. The rear upper-deck window/emergency exit was centrally divided with a grab handle and pronounced "step" end to the roof-mounted trolley access planks. Metal rainshields were fitted above all side windows and the front upper-deck windows. Both nearside and offside driver's cab windscreens were divided horizontally into two; the upper two-thirds being top-hinged and opening outwards. Opening cab door on offside only with curved rearward top corner (matching nearside) and sliding signalling window. Originally equipped with front and rear destination boxes of two-blind rectangular type with ultimate destination box, that at the front being flush with the between-decks panel but that at the rear projecting beyond the curve of the body. A large single-blind rectangular side destination box

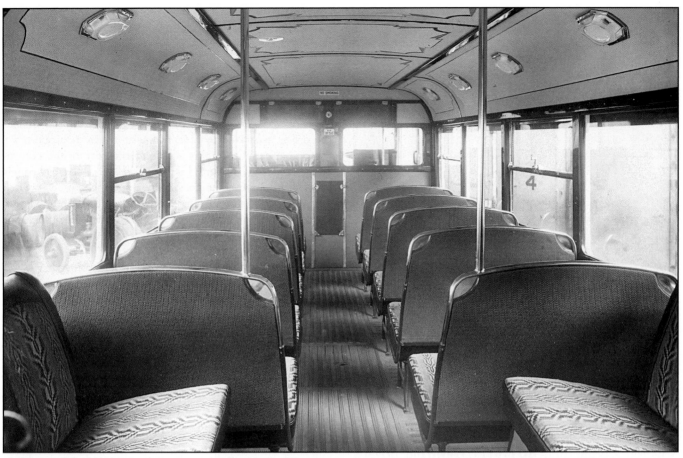

Brighton Corporation BUT9611T/Weymann lower saloon looking forwards prior to delivery to Brighton.
Transport Museum Wythall (Weymann)

Brighton Corporation BUT9611T/Weymann upper-saloon looking towards the rear, prior to delivery to Brighton
in 1948. **Transport Museum Wythall (Weymann)**

Brighton Corporation BUT9611T/Weymann driver's cab from the offside.

Transport Museum Wythall (Weymann)

was mounted over doorway. There was a used ticket box below the nearside vestibule window on the platform. A glass panel containing the rear registration mark was located in the vent panel above the rear platform window.

The rear upper deck emergency exit door had three hinges at its base and two oblong windows with radiused outer corners. There was a chromed external door opening handle in the top of the door frame, above and just to the offside of the pillar between the two windows, with an equivalent handle inside.

There was a rain strip immediately above the door and above that, centrally in the rear dome, there was a grab handle and step providing access to the roof catwalk. The door could be retained open in the horizontal position by leather-covered chains on each side inside the upper saloon

The rear staircase had three steps (four risers) from the platform across the width of the vehicle to the two corner steps and then a further two steps (three risers) to the upper deck, each riser equipped with painted kicking plates and each step with metal-edged canvas treads and nosings.

The driver's cab had a front-hinged door (three hinges) on the offside equipped with a sliding "signalling" window in the lower portion, and a black-painted downwards-opening handle mounted in a black-painted shield-shaped inset. The fixed upper window pane and the door deepened progressively in a curve towards the front of the vehicle to align with the foremost offside cab window. There was no door in the nearside cab panelling but the window arrangement, including a sliding widow in the lower portion of the second window, matched that on the offside.

Both windscreens were chromium-plated and divided horizontally at approximately two-thirds depth into two panes, the upper top-hinged pane on both sides opening outwards and

equipped centrally with a top-mounted wiper. Ventilation to the driver's cab was provided by two rows of six horizontal vents above each windscreen.

Small unpainted rectangular driver's rear-view mirrors were mounted externally towards the top of the front cab pillars on both sides.

There were two windows in the front bulkhead behind the driver, separated by a central pillar which incorporated a removable panel providing access to the rear of the control panel inside the driver's cab. Two similar removable panels were located above the bulkhead windows with a bell push in between. Attached to the bulkhead above each window inside the driver's cab was a fold-down blind to prevent reflections from the lower saloon on to the driver's windscreen during the hours of darkness.

The front wheels were equipped with chromed hubs and wheel nut protector rings. The hubs of all wheels were stamped with the BUT manufacturer's symbol.

The rear bulkhead had a vestibule window with radiused corners on the nearside, beneath which there was a used tickets box and a curved handrail to assist passengers boarding and alighting, whilst on the offside there was a glass-fronted panel for official notices. The rear platform floor was covered with wooden slats laid diagonally to which there was a rubber edge.

The main platform handrails and stanchions were coated with black Doverite. Those in the saloons and on the staircase were chromed.

Round buzzer bell pushes with chromed circular bases marked PUSH ONCE were located in the upper saloon on the ceiling of bay 2 above the nearside aisle seats and on a matching wooden plinth mounted on the wooden surrounds above the offside window bay 5; in the lower saloon in the front bulkhead centrally above the windows to the driver's cab and on the ceiling of bay 3 above the nearside aisle seats; and on the rear platform on the staircase riser and on the vestibule panel, just above the top right hand corner of the window.

A single wooden lifeguard ran beneath the side panels between the front and rear axles. There were individual mud flaps behind each wheel whilst a flap mudguard hung at an angle beneath the rear platform. A bamboo trolley retrieval pole was carried in a tube mounted centrally under the chassis and was accessible from the rear of the vehicle.

The ex-Brighton trolleybuses were virtually smaller, two-axle, versions of Bournemouth's own BUT9641Ts (200-223).

Delivered with chromed front wheel rings and spot lights, the spot lamps were removed prior to 1956. In 1954, Brighton Corporation Transport increased the seating capacity of their 45-48 (and 49-52) from the original H30/24R to H30/26R. The BH&D vehicles had been delivered with this seating capacity. Rear reflectors were added in 1954.

Lighting: External lighting comprised two low-set headlights on the front panel, two front side lights with black surrounds on plinths in the curved extremities of the front panels beneath the windscreen corner pillars, a single rear light mounted at the top of the offside lower-deck corner panel, the top aligned with the top of the glass panel containing the rear registration details, and centrally immediately beneath the rear platform window, a glass panel with semi-circular ends with a braking light, featuring red STOPPING lettering, and on each side an arrow to indicate a left or right turn.

A spot light was fitted below the nearside headlight.

Semaphore arm illuminated traffic indicators were fitted to the side pillars immediately to the rear of the driver's cab door on the offside and the cab side windows on the nearside, the top of the arm aligned with the base of the upper pane of glass.

Internal lighting in each saloon was provided by tungsten bulbs behind square diffused glasses with angled corners mounted on chrome fittings in the Alhambrinal cove panels and surrounded by painted embellishments. There were five lamps each side of the upper saloon, with another centrally in the rear dome mounted on a wood plinth to fit the curvature of the dome. There were five lamps each side in the lower saloon with another, smaller one with a glass diffuser, above the rear platform

Seating: Based on green-painted tubular steel frames with chromium-plated top and built-in "orange segment"-shaped grab facility adjacent to both the aisle and side panels. Squabs and backs were upholstered in a green/brown/beige zig-zag banded Lister moquette (Brighton Corporation), or a red/green/beige semi-random (BH&D) patterned moquette, on Dunlopillo cushions. The moquette upholstered seat backs were individually "framed" with green (Brighton Corporation) or dark red (BH&D), hide panelling to the tops and sides. Scratchproof patterned rear to the seat backs. There were upright chromed stanchions in both saloons attached to the ceiling and the top rail of the seat close to the grab facility, located at:

Lower saloon: seat 5 both sides.

Upper saloon: seat 3 nearside; seat 4 offside; and at the stairhead.

The lower saloon had five rows of double seats and a three-person bench seat over the rear axle on both sides. The upper saloon had six rows of double seats and two single seats (opposite the stairhead giving more space) on the nearside and a double seat, inset somewhat due to indicator box in the adjacent exterior upper-deck side panels, above the rear platform, on the offside there were seven rows of double seats.

The driver's seat was in hide with a plain squab and pleated back.

Internal Livery: Brighton Corporation Transport's internal livery featured green lower panels, except platform and stairs which were red, the cab interior which was red and cream, varnished wood window frames and patterned Alhambrinal coverings to the ceilings and cove panels with the straps covering the joints the same dark brown varnish as the window frames. The Alhambrinal covering featured a different pattern on the ceiling to that on the cove panels. Chromed stanchions and grab rails in the saloons and staircase, black plastic stanchions and grab rails on the platform. BH&D vehicles had an identical colour scheme except that the ceilings and cove panels had a plain glossy white covering instead of Alhambrinal.

The saloon floors were covered in linoleum with painted metal, anti-slip strips lengthwise along the gangways (9 abreast on the upper deck, 10 on the lower deck) and 6 transverse strips in front of each forward-facing seat.

External Livery: Red lower-deck and upper-deck panels, cream lower and upper-deck window surrounds and roof. The two fleets were not finished in the same shades of red: it is assumed that BH&D used the standard Tilling Group red whereas the Brighton Corporation Transport red was slightly darker. Black mudguards and wings. Red wheels. Both Brighton

Corporation and BH&D vehicles carried the fleet name "Brighton Hove & District Transport". Corporation vehicles also carried the Brighton coat-of-arms beneath the name.

Alterations upon purchase: The front indicator box and equipment was removed and the front upper-deck panels replaced with the standard Bournemouth three aperture boxes, namely a rectangular off-centre indicator box 30in X 15in capable of displaying up to three lines of intermediate points and the final destination, i.e. a total of up to four lines, with an auxiliary (in-town "via" or special event) indicator 30in X 5in immediately below and a separate square service number indicator box 10in×10in to the nearside. The equipment in the protruding indicator box at the rear was removed; the box was retained but widened to accommodate the three aperture boxes, as above. The size of the aperture of the side indicator box above the rear open platform entrance was reduced to 30in X 15in, reglazed with rubber and was capable of displaying up to four lines of intermediate points and the final destination.

Upper and lower-deck waistbands were created by adding a second, lower line of beading.

Flashing "orange segment"-shaped trafficators mounted above the lower-deck waistband in bay 1 a few inches to the rear of the leading pillar on the nearside, and behind the driver's cab door on the offside replaced the semaphore arm indicators used in Brighton. In addition, flashing globes were mounted on the extremities of the lower-deck waistband below the rear platform window. Red reflectors were added one-third of the way up the rear panel on the nearside and offside.

The glass panel containing the rear registration mark was removed from its position in the vent panel above the rear platform window and relocated to the glass panel with semi-circular ends beneath the rear window, replacing the braking light. The arrows to indicate a left or right turn in this same panel were replaced by two red lenses, one being the rear light and the other indicating braking, and the original red tail light at the top of the offside lower-deck corner panel was removed.

A spotlight was reinstalled below the nearside headlamp.

The coasting brake was reset for 8mph and the battery traction equipment was removed reducing the unladen weight to 8 tons 7cwt.

External Livery: Repainted into BCT Livery 6 (see Appendix D)

Internal changes: Not known.

Subsequent alterations: Some, if not all, vehicles were fitted with a wooden fold-down flap indicating when the minimum fare used on service 32 was in operation. This was mounted on hinges immediately above the rear platform entrance.

Notes: BH&D allocated stock numbers to the bodies of vehicles and these were carried in the driver's cab. This numbering policy originated at an early date with BH&D's predecessor Thomas Tilling when bodies were exchanged between chassis. The stock numbers of the BH&D trolleybuses sold to Bournemouth were: BH&D 391-393 (Bournemouth 292-294), stock numbers 7075-7077 respectively.

Disposal: 288-294 to Colbro (Dealer), Rothwell, Yorkshire, in November 1965 (at £76 each) for scrap.

(Left) Brighton Corporation BUT9611T/ Weymann rear platform and staircase. Transport Museum Wythall (Weymann)

(Below) Starting its descent of Richmond Hill southbound to the Square and the Triangle on 30 July 1963 is BUT9611T no. 291 (HUF48), formerly Brighton Corporation Transport no. 48. The indicator blinds are already set for its next northbound journey. F.W. Ivey

295-303 Sunbeam MF2B

Fleet No.	Registration Mark	Chassis Number	Body	Date of Delivery	Date into Service	Date of Withdrawal	Date of Disposal
295	295 LJ	TFD80195	M9524	26.09.1962	02.10.1962	20.04.69	17.09.1969
296	296 LJ	TFD80196	M9518	16.07.1962	24.07.1962	19.04.69	23.09.1969
297	297 LJ	TFD80197	M9519	18.08.1962	01.09.1962	20.04.69	.12.1971
298	298 LJ	TFD80198	M9522	17.09.1962	02.10.1962	20.04.69	09.10.1969
299	299 LJ	TFD80200	M9523	24.09.1962	02.10.1962	19.04.69	.08.1969
300	300 LJ	TFD80201	M9521	31.08.1962	01.09.1962	15.01.69	26.01.1969
301	301 LJ	TFD80202	M9516	12.10.1962	01.11.1962	20.04.69	.08.1969
302	302 LJ	TFD80203	M9525	05.10.1962	01.11.1962	06.02.69	07.10.1969
303	303 LJ	TFD80204	M9520	24.08.1962	01.09.1962	20.04.69	01.10.1969

Chassis: Two axle "transit" type Sunbeam MF2B, primarily foreseen for export markets, manufactured by Sunbeam Trolleybus Co. Ltd., Fallings Park, Wolverhampton, Staffordshire.
Motor: Crompton Parkinson Ltd., Chelmsford, Essex, Type: C423 (95 nhp), with a light compound winding incapable of regeneration (known as "controlled rheostatic").
Electrical equipment: Allen West & Co. Ltd., Brighton, incorporating automatic acceleration with 13 power notches, the master controller and reverser was beneath the driver's seat.
Dewirement indicators: 2 green line-lights and buzzer
Brakes: Westinghouse compressed air on all wheels, 2-stage rheostatic, coasting and run-back brakes. Handbrake on rear wheels
Body: Highbridge double-deck all metal five bay construction with twin staircases, conventional rear, semi-vestibuled open platform entrance and separate front exit with air-operated folding doors controlled from the driver's cab placed forward of the leading axle.
Built by Weymann's Ltd., Station Road, Addlestone, Surrey.
Seating: H37/28D
Length: 30ft   Width: 7ft 11 3/4in   Height: 15ft 7in unladen
(over trolley base)
Wheelbase: 15ft 10in giving a turning circle over the full body on either lock of 58ft.
Unladen weight: 8 tons 19 cwts 2 qtrs
Wheel track: front 6ft 11 1/2in, rear 6ft.
Tyres: front 11.00in X 20in 14-ply, double rear 10.00in X 20in 12-ply.

The final batch of Sunbeam MF2B trolleybuses conformed in general dimensions and chassis details with the earlier batches purchased by the undertaking in 1958 and 1959. There were a number of changes to the internal decor, seat covering and lighting, giving a brighter interior finish which was to become the standard for future BCT motorbus orders well into the 1980s.

Chassis: See 258-287 Sunbeam MF2B for details (these being identical).

Electrics: See 258-287 Sunbeam MF2B for details (these being identical).

Brakes: See 258-287 Sunbeam MF2B for details (these being identical).

Bodywork: See 258-287 Sunbeam MF2B for details, these being identical except—
The rear entrance and front exit staircases were fitted with light steel Pneustrip treads and nosings with the centre gangway in both saloons covered in brown Multislat Treadmaster. Fluted aluminium treads were added between the seats.
The draught screen behind the driver's left shoulder incorporated two glazed panels: a curved one facing the passenger gangway and a second flat pane facing the staircase.

Lighting: See 258-287 Sunbeam MF2B for details, these being identical except—
The rear lighting comprised two combined BMAC rear lights and reflectors mounted two-thirds of the way down the rear lower-deck panel. That on the nearside was fitted in a separate plinth at the base of the rear platform window nearside pillar, which also provided the base for a rear passenger grab rail.
Internal Philips fluorescent lighting was fitted in both saloons, the rear platform entrance and destination boxes.

Seating: Deans "Dapta" lightweight frames painted cherry red with stainless steel top rail. Latex foam-filled cushions and polyether squabs were trimmed in a maroon-coloured Connolly hide, both seat and squab being fully fluted. The seat backs were "Yellow Snug" shade Warerite. The seating layout of the lower saloon was identical to that in the earlier Sunbeam MF2B deliveries (258-287).
A modification to the front exit stairhead in relation to 258-287 permitted use of three rows of double seats (the third seat opposite the stairhead equipped with a tubular armrest) in place of single seats on the front nearside of the upper saloon and a single double seat on the offside instead of a triple seat immediately in front of the front exit staircase well. As a result, the leading three nearside seats were narrower than the other double seats. At the rear of the upper saloon a bench seat above the open platform could accommodate three passengers. There were seven rows of forward-facing double seats on the nearside and six on the offside.

Destination equipment: See 258-287 Sunbeam MF2B for details (these being identical).

Sunbeam MF2B chassis from the final batch. The master controller (known as the "reverser" in Bournemouth) is beneath the driver's seat. The main resistances are under the floor, within the chassis frame, as is the traction motor. The contactor cabinet and the batteries for auxiliary electrical equipment are mounted on the offside of the chassis frame. The comparative simplicity of a trolleybus is evident.

David Chalk collection (Crompton Parkinson)

Numerically the last Bournemouth trolleybus, Sunbeam MF2B/Weymann no. 303 (303LJ) awaits collection from the body-builder's Addlestone works in August 1962.

David Chalk collection (Weymann)

Internal Livery: The saloon ceilings on both decks were finished in off-white plastic-coated Darvic panels, and the single-skin domes and lower saloon front bulkheads painted to match. The pressed aluminium window cappings were stove enamelled in a jonquil colour. Interior lining panels were covered with "Red Relief" Warerite and a matching cherry red finishing line was added at cant rail level. Cherry red paint was also used for the front and rear staircases, the driver's cab and the seat frames. All handrails and stanchions covered in black Doverite. The interior colour scheme had been developed by the newly-appointed General Manager, Ronald Cox, during his time at Rochdale and was closely related to that undertaking's specifications.

External Livery: Delivered in Livery 7 (see Appendix D)

Subsequent alterations: From 1966 and often as a result of accident damage, several of these trolleybuses received plain black fleet numbers. These were mounted slightly higher than the gold numerals at the front below the offside headlight and lower on the primrose lower panel below the rear platform window (to accommodate an advertisement). From September 1967 exterior advertising was carried on the upper-deck side panels (obliterating the Bournemouth coat of arms) and below the rear platform window. Additional coats of arms were accordingly added to the lower deck side panels centred on bay 3. From 1966 onwards the triangular Sunbeam manufacturer's plate was removed from the waist band on the front panels. Solely 298 ever received a full external repaint.

Notes: These vehicles were scheduled for delivery in 1961 but were delayed by a fire at Weymann's factory at the beginning of July 1961 in which chassis TFD80199 was destroyed, TFD80198 severely damaged and TFD80201, due to its proximity to the fire and water damage, considered suspect. One chassis, TFD80204, had not left Sunbeam at the time of the fire and upon completion was towed direct to Bournemouth. The two damaged chassis were returned to Sunbeam for repair and eventually eight out of the nine remaining chassis were stored at Castle Lane (Mallard Road) Depot, two with the lower-deck framing mounted. They were towed back to Addlestone between April and June 1962. Body M9517 was never built, £3,932 16s 8d being the insurance valuation of the chassis destroyed in the fire. This was insufficient to cover the cost of building a replacement whilst BCT was not prepared to pay the difference between the insurance settlement and what Sunbeam would have charged for what would have been a single bespoke trolleybus chassis. By this time Sunbeam had virtually ceased building trolleybuses (they only built six more, for Coimbra, Portugal, in 1966). The registration mark 304LJ, which was rendered surplus by the fire, was subsequently allocated to a departmental van.

These nine vehicles were the only trolleybuses in England, Scotland and Wales with "reversed" registration marks and were the last trolleybuses to be built for scheduled service use in the UK. Number 301 was the last trolleybus to enter scheduled service in the UK and was the last trolleybus to operate in Bournemouth.

On 23 July 1962, to celebrate the undertaking's Diamond Jubilee, 296 was driven around the Castle Lane (Mallard Road) Depot site by the Mayor.

Disposals: 300 was towed from Bournemouth to Walsall by the Maypine Trolleybus Company on 26 January 1969 and loaned to Walsall Corporation Transport for experimental rebuilding as a one-man-operated, bimodal diesel/trolleybus based on the design of the Walsall General Manager and Engineer, Mr R. Edgley Cox. The vehicle was to feature a single front staircase, a widened (combined) front entrance and exit, increased seating capacity on both decks and a diesel engine at the rear of the vehicle in the space provided by the former open platform and rear staircase. 300 would have been a prototype for a possible purchase of the entire Bournemouth MF2B fleet but Walsall's plans were given up when the Corporation transport undertaking was merged into the West Midlands Passenger Transport Executive in October 1969.

295, 296, 298, 300, 302, 303, sold to Wombwell Diesels Co. Ltd., breakers, in August 1969, for £150. They were collected on the following dates:

295	17 September 1969;
296	23 September 1969;
298	9 October 1969;
302	7 October 1969;
303	1 October 1969.

297 was offered on permanent loan to the Russell-Cotes Art Gallery and Museum in July 1969, having probably been initially the Sunbeam MF2B set aside for free loan to the Montagu Motor Museum, Beaulieu. It was also offered to Portsmouth Transport Museum but none of these bodies was able to store the trolleybus under cover (a condition of the loan) at the time it was offered to them. It was then sold to the BPTA in December 1971 for £250.

299 was sold to the Transport Museum Society of Ireland, in August 1969 for £200 but remained inside Castle Lane (Mallard Road) Depot until 10 December 1971.

300 was collected from Walsall in February 1970 and went to Hoyle, breaker, Wombwell, in July 1970.

301 was sold to the BPTA in August 1969, for £150.

Within days of entering service in July 1962, brand-new Sunbeam MF2B no. 296 takes on passengers at the eastbound Square boarding point in Avenue Road prior to departure on a service 25 journey to Boscombe.
David Chalk collection

The first of the final batch of Sunbeam MF2Bs to reach Bournemouth was no. 296, seen here arriving at Castle Lane (Mallard Road) Depot on tow from Weymann's works at Addlestone, Surrey on 16 July 1962.   **David Chalk**

APPENDIX B
DEMONSTRATORS

The four prototype trolleybuses used on Bournemouth's experimental route between the Square and County Gates were selected and hired by the undertaking. Apart from a number of initial route-proving tests, the vast majority of their involvement in the experiment was carrying fare-paying passengers and all four were subsequently purchased and joined the BCT fleet. Full details of these four prototypes, both as delivered and subsequently, are shown in Appendix A.

Solely those vehicles demonstrated in Bournemouth to transport professionals and which did not carry fare-paying passengers, are detailed below.

AEC-EE 691T

Chassis: Three axle type AEC-EE 691T manufactured by the Associated Equipment Company Ltd. (AEC) at the AEC works, Windmill Lane, Southall, Middlesex.
Motor: English Electric Co. Ltd. (EE), Phoenix Works, Bradford, Yorkshire.
Type DK404 compound-wound (80hp) augmented field equipment, regenerative.
Electrical equipment: English Electric DK.23 Form 6 controller.
Brakes: Regenerative; rheostatic; compressed air activated by the brake pedal and operating on all wheels; handbrake, mechanical to all rear wheels.
Body: Highbridge double-deck all-metal five bay construction with single central staircase, and central, enclosed entrance and exit.
Built by London General Omnibus Co. Ltd., Chiswick Works, Chiswick High Road, Chiswick, Middlesex.   H40/34C
Length: 30ft   Width 7ft 6in
Wheelbase: 18ft 7 $^{5}/_{16}$in (from front axle to centre of rear bogie).
Unladen weight: 7 tons 18 cwt 1 qtr.
Tyres: assumed to have been 36 X 8 high-pressure pneumatic singles to all wheels.

Following the successful conversion, in the course of 1931, of their lightly-trafficked tramways in the Hampton Court, Kingston upon Thames, Twickenham and Wimbledon areas of southwest London using a fleet of 56-seater AEC-EE663T trolleybuses, the London United Tramways (LUT) looked for means of emulating the higher passenger carrying capacity of the capital's bogie tramcars with a trolleybus. From January 1932, the LUT General Manager, Mr C.J. Spencer, an early enthusiast of railless electric traction who had introduced trolley vehicles to Bradford in 1911, and his staff worked closely with AEC engineers to design a trolleybus capable of carrying in excess of 70 passengers. The result was designated as an AEC-EE691T having 3-axles, registered AHX801, finished in the LUT livery and displaying fleet number 61, and which was presented to the press at the AEC works in Southall on 23 February 1933.
This was followed by extensive trials on the LUT system prior to its display and operation in Bournemouth on behalf of AEC-EE during the 38th annual convention of the Incorporated Municipal Electrical Association, 12-17 June 1933. No. 61 was never owned

by the LUT but only purchased by London Transport following its formation on 1 July 1933. It was subsequently demonstrated by AEC-EE to Brighton Corporation Transport in January 1936 when that undertaking was considering converting its tramways to trolleybus operation.
In many respects 61 set the standard for the British trolleybus era with its underfloor or chassis-side equipment and high capacity, and was the prototype for many of the features of the future standard London trolleybus design.

Chassis: Cranked chassis frame over rear bogie based on the AEC Regent 663 motorbus chassis and axles, but with a set-back front axle. The side members were pressed out of 5/16in steel with a maximum depth of 111/8in having 3in wide flanges with a "kick up" swept over the front and rear axles to permit the mounting of a low floor level body. The arches over the rear bogie were reinforced by inserted channels of the same thickness. There was a drop in the nearside of the chassis frame between the front nearside wheel and the leading rear nearside wheel to accommodate the door well. The frame was held rigid by channel section and tubular cross-members to eliminate distortion.

Chassis weight: 4 tons 5 cwts 3 qtrs including electrical equipment.

The axles were made from 100-ton steel 3ins in diameter and mounted on adjustable taper roller bearings. A chrome vanadium spring steel torque blade was used permitting freedom of motion of each axle. The socket attachments of this cross-member formed a rigid assembly with the front end of the front axle spring anchorages and, on the offside, the steering box. The rear ends of the front axle spring were shackled by a similar arrangement to the second chassis cross-member. The rear axle springs were centrally pivoted upon needle-roller trunnion bearings carried by cast-steel brackets mounted beneath the wheel arches, to which they were riveted and joined by a large cross-tube. The ends of the springs had solid eyes and were anchored to brackets under the axle tubes. Hydraulic shock absorbers on all axles.
The rear axle bogie was supported by two springs carried in the centre by two chairs swinging in GM bushes in the bogie brackets, which were riveted to the frame and further stiffened by a 4in tubular cross-member brazed in the brackets to resist torsion.
Semi-floating under-slung worm drive rear axles. The rear axle casings were one-piece nickel steel forgings carrying the worm gearing in separate casings. The worm gear was offset to the nearside to avoid any obstruction of the gangway.
There was a tubular propeller shaft, fitted with Hardy-Spicer needle-roller self-aligning bearing universal joints, connecting the traction motor with the third differential which was offset to the nearside of the leading rear axle. A further shaft connected with the differential on second rear axle to ensure an even distribution of the driving torque between the two rear axles.
AEC roller bearing front axle equipped with AEC Marles

London United Tramways no. 61 (AHX801), the sole **AEC-EE 691T** chassis built, was fitted with a 30ft long all-metal centre entrance entrance/exit body constructed by the London General Omnibus Co. Ltd. (LGOC), a sister company, at their Chiswick works.

Peter Smith collection

London United Tramways no. 61 (AHX801). Both views appear to have been taken at the LGOC's Chiswick works

Peter Smith collection

worm and nut steering.

Forged alloy steel disc hubs on taper roller bearings.

Electrics: The English Electric DK404 compound-wound traction motor was resiliently mounted in a sub-frame amidships to the nearside of the chassis frame and connected by a short propeller shaft to the leading rear axle differential. A DK403 motor had originally been foreseen.

The master controller and reverser were mounted within the chassis frame beneath the driver's cab floor. The contactors were carried in two asbestos-lined steel cases mounted on the external face of the offside chassis frame member.

Brecknell, Willis & Co. Ltd., Bristol, lightweight trolley equipment, and trolley bases, the booms being equipped with current collecting wheels.

Brakes: The vehicle was fitted with regenerative braking for conventional stopping. The driver released the control pedal until speed was reduced to 15 mph. Speed was further reduced by the rheostatic brake and then brought to a halt with the compressed air brake, both of which were operated by the foot brake pedal.

Braking was on all six wheels and of the internal expanding type, assisted by Lockheed hydraulic mechanism. There was also a mechanical handbrake, the operating lever was to the offside of the driver's steering column.

Bodywork: All metal highbridge double-deck five bay construction with central backwards-ascending staircase with centre entrance and exit equipped with double sliding doors, built by the London General Omnibus Co. Ltd., at their Chiswick Works. The body design had much in common with the AEC-EE Q-type double-deck trolleybus of the period.

The all metal body construction was based on a steel frame with light alloy panelling in an effort to achieve the lowest possible weight consistent with safety, smooth running and speed. The bodywork introduced characteristics of the mid-1930s such as the slightly raked front elevation, an almost vertical rear elevation, gently curved lower deck panelling, a rounded roof, and splayed out skirting panels at the rear.

The upper-deck body pillars slotted into the steel rail of the framework above the upper saloon windows, i.e. the cantrail. There were curved steel brackets bolted to the metal roof (inside the roof there was a steel strengthening plate on each side) and each end of the two transverse pressed steel girders, above the forward and rear pillars of bay 2, supporting the exposed trolley gantry, which was not in direct contact with the roof and rested on these brackets. The bay 2 pillars on both sides of the upper deck were broader than the other pillars and also equipped with strengthening plates at the top. Lightening holes were made in the transverse girders to reduce the vehicle's weight. Cross-bracing between the trolley boom retention hooks.

The main power cable made its way along the forwards edge of the leading girder supporting the trolley gantry to the nearside of the roof which it entered above the forward pillar of bay 2 and thence down to the switches in the driver's cab.

The upper deck rear emergency exit door contained a single large trapezoid-shaped window with radiused top outer corners and three bottom hinges. The emergency exit door could be opened by an external handle mounted centrally in upper part of the door frame, or from the inside by a comparable handle

attached to a horizontal locking bar mounted on the cantrail immediately above the door. It is not known how, with the door opened, access to the roof catwalk and trolley gear was achieved.

Two small protruding rubber bumpers in the top of the upper deck emergency exit door frame aligned with similar bumpers on the panel each side of and towards the base of the rear indicator box. When the retaining chains were removed and opened to its fullest extent the emergency exit door hung down and rested on these bumpers.

Half-drop openers were fitted to the side windows in bays 4, 5 (both sides) of the lower-deck and to bays 1, 3, 5 (both sides) of the upper-deck. The upper pane dropped outside the fixed lower pane. All other side windows and the upper-deck single pane front windows were fixed. The upper rear corners of the rearmost side "D" windows on both decks were deeply radiused.

A single top-hinged access door or valence panel was fitted at the base of the lower-deck offside panels in bays 1 and 2.

The centre entrance/exit was equipped with double sliding doors of the style used on Underground trains of the period operated by Peters pneumatic engines and controlled from the driver's cab. They were interlocked with the traction control circuit thus preventing the trolleybus from starting off with the doors open. A conductor's valve for emergency use was positioned on the staircase panelling. The leading door slid forwards into the bay 1 panelling and the other door slid backwards into the bay 3 panelling leaving a step-free entrance 4ft 3in wide.

Due to the absence of an open platform, an emergency exit door incorporating a single rectangular window and an opening handle inset into the waistband was built into the centre of the lower deck rear panels. There was a narrower, matching rectangular window on each side of the door each surmounted by two ventilator vanes.

A large rectangular removable panel with two mesh-covered openings for ventilation purposes extended across the base of the front panels between the headlamps, the top of the panel aligned with the bottom of the chrome headlight plinths and its outer edges aligned with inner edge of the headlight plinths. The rectangular front registration number plate was located centrally at base of the removable panel.

The rear registration plate was inset on the offside of the rear panel, its base aligned with the bottom of the lower deck emergency door.

The driver's cab was located on the offside of the trolleybus forward of the front axle, surrounded by a rear and side bulkhead, and with a bench seat for three passengers on the nearside. Both windscreens were chromium-plated and divided horizontally at approximately two-thirds depth into two panes, the upper top-hinged pane on both sides was equipped centrally with a top-mounted wiper whilst the upper pane on the offside opened outwards. On the nearside there was a single window which broadened towards the front of the cab whilst on the offside there was a rear hinged door with a vertically-divided window for signalling purposes and a small, slanted window between the door and the offside corner pillar. The base of the cab door was curved over the wheel arch. Towards the front of the door there was an opening handle inset into the waistband. An entrance step was let into the base of the offside side panel without any form of protection to the bodywork, immediately in front of the front axle.

A rectangular driver's rear view mirror was mounted externally on the front offside cab pillar only.

There was a metal "fairing" mudguard over the rear wheels. Individual mud flaps hung behind each wheel of the front and leading rear axles.

A single tubular lifeguard, held by protruding attachments or outriggers beneath the body panels, ran beneath the "tumble-under" of the lower-deck side panels between the front and leading rear axles on both sides. It is not known if a trolley retrieval pole was carried on the vehicle.

All wheels were fitted with chromed hub bosses and wheel nut guard rings

Lighting: External lighting comprised two headlights mounted on plinths halfway up the front panel, two protruding "bicycle-style" front side lights on the lower deck waistband aligned with the cab front pillar and a single rear light mounted in the offside lower deck corner panel above the inset registration plate. The nearside headlight had a darkened lens and was potentially for use as a fog light.

A red brake light was mounted on the offside of the rear panel beneath the waistband.

Internal lighting arrangements are not known.

Seating: There was a bench seat for 4 persons on the front nearside of the lower saloon and a bench seat for 3 persons on the nearside of the upper saloon above the central entrance/exit facing the staircase. All other seats were forward facing double seats.

The upholstered seats had Dunlop rubber-filled squabs and backs.

In addition, there was accommodation for five standing passengers.

Destination equipment: Rectangular indicator boxes with radiused corners were fitted in the centre of the upper deck front panelling above the driver's windscreen, in the nearside upper deck side panels immediately above the entrance/exit doors and at the rear in the upper deck panels above the lower deck emergency exit door. In LUT service, these boxes displayed blinds giving service number, final destination and intermediate point information. Whilst demonstrated at Bournemouth solely SPECIAL was displayed.

External Livery: The main lower and upper deck body panels, and the lower deck and upper deck window surrounds were painted in the standard red of the Underground Group of Companies. The cantrail, lower and upper deck waistband, the front dome and main roof area including the trolley gantry were finished in light cream. At the time 61 was demonstrated in Bournemouth the rear dome and wheels were grey, and full LUT fleetname and ownership details were evident as well as commercial advertising of the period.

Internal Livery: Not known.

Notes: AHX801 was the sole AEC-EE 691T to be built. At an unknown pre-war date, the livery application was amended to the London Transport standard of red upper deck waistband and silver roof. In early 1945 the vehicle was rebuilt with a full-width front bulkhead behind the driver's cab, the nearside bench seat was removed and placed rearwards-facing

against the bulkhead, a raised floor was added in the entrance/exit area from which a number of seats were removed and a conductor's desk placed beneath the staircase, reducing the seating capacity to 69, as part of a Pay As You Board experiment carried out on service 604 from March to October 1945. At the end of the experiment the conductor's desk was removed and the capacity increased to 71.

Until April 1948, London Transport 61 was based at Fulwell Depot and operated primarily on ex-LUT services 604, 605 and 667. From 13 April 1948, 61 was based at Hounslow Depot (known as Isleworth after 1 October 1950). It was withdrawn from passenger service in 1951 and then transferred to Fulwell Depot where it was used for driver training purposes until June 1952.

Disposal: Following a period in store at Fulwell Depot 61 was sold to Thompson & Co. (Cardiff) Ltd., Dumballs Road, Cardiff, breakers, in February 1954.

71 Trackless Cars

Chassis: Two axle type manufactured by Trackless Cars Ltd. Hepworth Chambers, 148 Briggate, Leeds, Yorkshire.
Motors: English Electric Co. Ltd. (EE), Phoenix Works, Bradford, Yorkshire.
Two Type DK26B (20hp) traction motors (other sources suggest 25hp)
Electrical equipment: English Electric Type D controller.
Brakes: foot pedal operated and handbrake, mechanical to the front wheels.
Body: Double-deck with combined centre entrance and exit. Built by Blackburn Aeroplane and Motor Co. Ltd. at their Olympia Works, Roundhay Road, Leeds, Yorkshire (one of the shareholders of Trackless Cars).
Seating H34/30C.
Length: 24ft 11in   Width: 7ft 6in   Height (unloaded):
                                                13ft 10ins (to roof)
Wheel base 15ft
Unladen weight: 8 tons 6 cwt
Tyres: solid rubber on spoked wheels.

Little is known of Trackless Cars Ltd. and its associated suppliers (Tramway Supplies Ltd., the Blackburn Aeroplane and Motor Co. Ltd., etc.). Trackless Cars Ltd. was registered on 21 February 1922 with a nominal capital of £10,000. The company had been known earlier as Electric Traction Co. There was an agreement with Messrs Bishop and Chadwick (referred to below) to manufacture and deal with electric trackless and railless cars. The registered address was Hepworth Chambers, 148 Briggate, Leeds. Other businesses registered at the same address included ABC Tramway Appliances Co. Ltd. and the Electric Traction Co. (Bishop System) Ltd.

Tramway Supplies Ltd. had a works between nos. 433 and 505 Meanwood Road, Leeds, and the Blackburn Aeroplane and Motor Co. Ltd. assembled their products in their Olympia Works, which occupied a site between Gledhow Wood Road and Ravenscar Avenue on Roundhay Road, Leeds; G.A. Bishop had a house at 337 Roundhay Road.

Trackless Cars Ltd. demonstrated the vehicle on trade plates to delegates at the Tramways and Light Railways Congress held in Bournemouth on 22 and 23 June 1922.

After the Congress, it was taken to the London United

Tramways' Fulwell Depot, where it was inspected by senior staff of the London & Suburban Traction Co. Ltd. (the holding company behind the London United Tramways (LUT), the Metropolitan Electric Tramways and the South Metropolitan Electric Tramways). The vehicle was also demonstrated to the LUT, possibly in Haydon's Road, Merton, where an experimental route existed 1922-1923, in July 1922. It was purchased by Leeds Corporation Tramways, who already operated Trackless Cars' vehicles, in December 1923 for £950, a fraction of its original cost. Here it was registered NW5550 on 4 January 1924, given fleet number 513 and entered service on 10 January 1924, only to be withdrawn by 1 January 1926 and sold for scrap to A. Allen, 143 New Road Side, Horsforth for £12 10s (less equipment) on 12 January 1927.

Trackless Cars Ltd. went into voluntary liquidation in June 1924.

Chassis: The chassis was built in two sections, according to a patent held by Messrs G.A. Bishop and R.A. Chadwick, there being a fore-carriage beneath the driver's cab containing the two motors, one in front of the front axle and one behind. The frame was built from channel-section steel, the "bend" where the lower level of frame member commenced being in one piece strengthened with steel plates. The frame was braced by transverse members riveted to the side members.

Each motor drove one of the front road wheels direct by a pinion on the motor shaft and an internal ring gear fixed in the wheels thus increasing mechanical efficiency and removing the noise associated with cardan shafts, differentials and gear chains. By having the power unit in a separate fore-carriage it was possible to fit a dropped rear axle thereby lowering the chassis beneath the body and reduce the ground clearance to 11in. The front axle was turned from 3% nickel steel, the rear axle was cranked to allow for the low-floor of the body and also made of 3% nickel steel.

The fore-carriage was designed to be easily interchangeable and by removing eight bolts could be removed and replaced within two hours. The lower portion or under-carriage of the fore-carriage was connected to the upper or fixed portion, i.e. the driver's cab, by a ball-race turntable.

The under-carriage was connected to the rotating turntable by clamping the inverted semi-elliptic springs to seatings on the turntable. The springs were also attached by links to the torque arms on the under-carriage frame. The rear axle was also equipped with long, resilient steel semi-elliptic springs with additional support. All bearings were easily accessible for lubrication purposes.

It was claimed that the three-point suspension of the front drive unit absorbed the entire starting torque before the reaction was transmitted through the chassis frame.

All gears were totally enclosed in oil baths.

Low-geared worm and worm rack steering rotated the entire turntable and fore-carriage.

Electrics: The two DK26B interpole traction motors were mounted fore and aft of the front axle being supported at the outer ends by shock absorbers bearing on the under-carriage frame. Separate suspension ensured self-alignment of the motors. The transmission gear was simple: a pinion at the end of each motor shaft engaged directly with an internal gear ring fixed in the front road wheels.

English Electric Type D hand-operated series parallel master controller located on the floor of the driver's cab. Maley resistances. Twin circuit breakers having blow-out coil and simple trip mechanism. The breaker could be reset by means of a moulded insulated handle. All electrical equipment was ordered through Tramway Supplies Co. Ltd., Leeds, and located in the self-contained drive unit in the fore-carriage.

Brakes: Internal expanding brakes with renewable linings of frictional fabric, on all wheels. There were two different foot pedal-operated brakes acting on the rear wheels: the "service" brake controlled by the right foot and the other having attached to the foot pedal a ratchet device primarily to hold the vehicle on an incline. The front wheel brakes were considered as primarily for emergency purposes and were operated by a pull-on handbrake lever on the offside of the driver's steering column. Further details remain unknown.

Bodywork: Composite five-bay double-deck construction, equipped with a rearwards-ascending full-turn (180°) central staircase, central entrance and exit fitted with platform doors built by the Blackburn Aeroplane and Motor Co. Ltd., Leeds, Yorkshire. The design of the driver's cab area was typical of early British railless trolley vehicles of the period however the main, passenger carrying, portion of the body, although showing its tramcar origins, was almost streamlined. Bournemouth's trams were all open-top and at a time when top-covered motorbuses were a rarity (they were not even permitted in London until 1925), the low-built chassis made it possible to add a roof to the upper deck and remain within the maximum height limitations of the period.

Lower saloon headroom: 6ft
Upper saloon headroom: 5ft 9¾in

The centre of gravity was 3ft 11in above the road surface when empty and 4ft 9in when fully loaded, meaning that the tilting angle was 43° and 38° respectively

The underframe and end sills consisted of ash suitably strengthened with steel plates, held together by steel angle brackets, attached to the chassis frame. Corner and side posts were ash with interior panels of polished walnut sheathed on the outside by steel sheet. The curvaceous body had broad corner pillars to both the lower and upper decks. All side windows were equipped with tramcar-style top-light bottom-hinged pull-in glass ventilators above the main panes. The lower-deck side windows in bay 1 both sides had a curved lower corner towards the front of the vehicle extending half way up the depth of the main pane, those in bay 5 had a curved lower corner towards the rear. The upper-deck side windows in bay 1 both sides had a curved upper corner towards the front of the vehicles descending halfway down the depth of the top light and main pane combined, those in bay 5 had a curved upper corner towards the rear. All other corners in these and the other bays were not radiused.

There was a two-leaf inwards-opening hand-operated folding door, the leaf towards the front of the vehicle turned and slid to a position at 90° to bay 1 and that towards the rear turned and slid to a position at 90° to bay 3. When open to their fullest extent there was a 2ft 9in wide doorway and a single step up from the pavement to the platform.

There was a single narrow front window to the upper-deck located above the roof of the driver's cab which curved

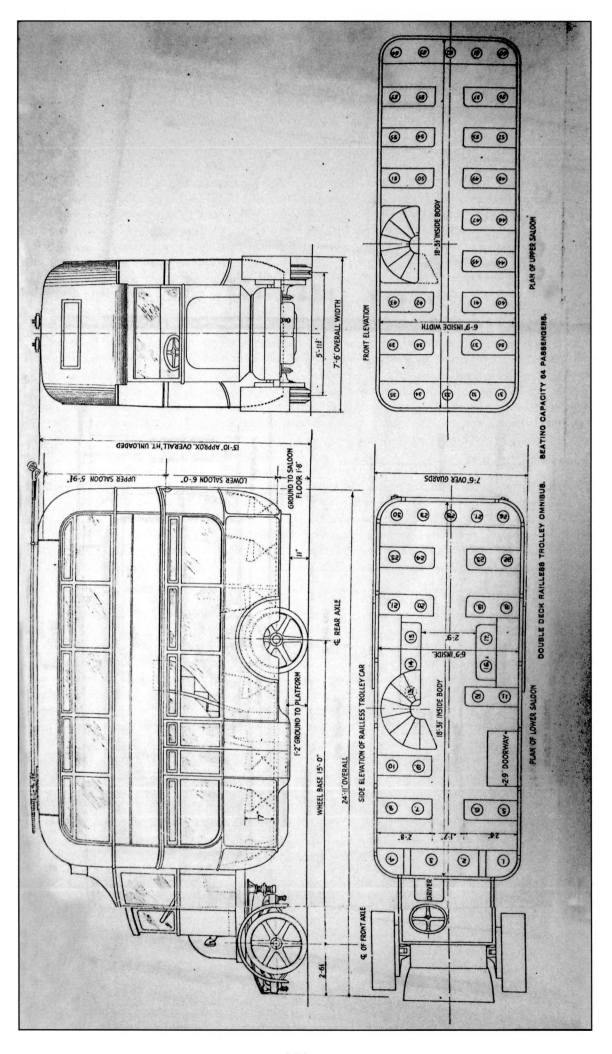

upwards to the rear. Larger, centrally-divided windows were fitted at the rear of upper and lower decks.

There were deep mudguards, descending almost to the hubs, above the rear wheels.

The driver's cab was a part of the main passenger-carrying body but located above the fore-carriage behind the hub of the front axle. Located partially between the front wheels and the pronounced front wheel mudguards it was, at 4ft 8in wide, considerably narrower than the main body. There was a curved protective sheet in line with the dumb irons and forward of the front wheels and a bulbous front panel above the front wheels beneath the driver's windscreen. The offside driver's windscreen was divided horizontally at approximately two-thirds depth into two panes. The top hinged upper pane could be opened outwards. Each side of the driver's cab had two windows which lowered progressively towards the front beneath the cab roof which also curved down towards the front. The larger nearside cab window was built into a door, complete with ornate carriage door handle, which provided the sole access to the driver's cab. There was a noticeable roof "peak" to the cab roof above the windscreen.

A bamboo trolley retrieval pole was carried between two brackets mounted on the offside pillar beneath the top lights between bays 1 and 2, and between bays 4 and 5, 9 ins to the nearside of the centreline under the chassis and was accessible from the rear of the vehicle.

The trolley booms were of the top-covered tramcar type with their springs forward of the twin trolley bases.

Lighting: Prominent headlights were attached to front and side of the driver's cab front corner pillar. It is assumed that there was single rear light at cantrail height in the rear panels. Internal lighting not known.

Seating: Spring cushion seating with padded backs.

On the lower deck there was a row of four rearwards-facing seats backing on to the front bulkhead, a double rearwards-facing seat behind each rear axle wheel arch, longitudinal bench seats for two above the nearside rear axle wheel arch and for three above the offside wheel arch and staircase, a row of five forwards-facing seats backing on to the rear panels, and three further double forwards-facing seats each side. The double forwards-facing seats were located in bay 1 (nearside and offside), bay 2 (opposite the entrance) offside, bay 3 nearside (opposite the staircase) and bay 5 (nearside and offside). The total lower-deck seating capacity was 30 passengers.

On the upper deck there was a row of five rearwards-facing seats backing on to the front bulkhead, a row of five forwards-facing seats backing on to the rear panels, seven rows of forward-facing seats on the nearside, two rows of double forwards-facing seats on the offside forward of the staircase and three rows of double forwards-facing sets on the offside to the rear of the staircase. The total upper-deck seating capacity was 34 passengers.

Destination equipment: None at the time of its appearance in Bournemouth. Subsequently a single-line final-destination indicator box was fitted centrally at the front of the driver's cab roof.

External livery: The demonstrator was painted in an approximation of the Leeds City Tramways livery of the period, namely pale primrose lower deck window area, upper-deck and roof, with deep chocolate brown lower panels. The chocolate brown application was swept up to the height of the upper-deck floor line around the broad curved corner pillars.

Internal Livery: Not known.

Disposal: Leeds Corporation Tramways withdrew 513 by 1 January 1926 and it was sold for scrap to A. Allen, 143 New Road Side, Horsforth for £12 10s (less equipment) on 12 January 1927.

APPENDIX C
WARTIME LOANS

Upon the outbreak of the Second World War the number of BCT passengers initially fell considerably due to a combination of concerns about operating in the "black-out", the absence of evening entertainment and the end of holiday-making "for the duration" which led to the reduction or withdrawal of evening frequencies and the suspension of several all-day services. Bournemouth found itself with a surplus of over 30 trolleybuses and these were placed in store. As defence manufacturing increased, so Britain's industrial cities and towns experienced major growths in traffic demand and thus undertakings having too many vehicles began to loan or sell their surplus to the harder-pressed operators. Few trolleybus operators had spare vehicles available and these were predominantly in seaside towns, specifically Bournemouth, Brighton and Hastings, although at various stages in the conflict Bradford and Kingston upon Hull were able to loan or sell trolleybuses to other undertakings.

The loans or sales appear to have been coordinated by the MoT/MoWT and/or RTC, but there is much to suggest that the first loan of Bournemouth trolleybuses, to Wolverhampton Corporation Transport was facilitated by the existing friendly relationship between the two transport departments dating back to the start of trolleybus operation in Bournemouth.

Llanelly

The start of production at Morris Motors' new Nuffield factory in Llethri Road, Felinfoel, (where Spitfire radiators were manufactured) in 1943 presented Llanelly District Traction with an immediate need for additional trolleybuses. Bournemouth 77 (which had returned from loan in Newcastle upon Tyne in February 1943) and 123 (which had returned in May 1943 having spent 3 months in South Shields) were despatched to Llanelly. There have been reports, which cannot be corroborated, of a Bournemouth trolleybus being sighted in Llanelly in summer 1943, some six months before they entered service there, so it is possible that one or both vehicles travelled from the north-east by way of Llanelly for inspection or testing purposes prior to returning to Bournemouth for attention.

They were towed there (and back) by BCT. They were never fitted with local destination blinds and displayed service numbers only. The front exit doors were locked shut with a metal bar. The Bournemouth MS2s introduced carbon skid trolleyhead inserts to the Llanelly system. After arrival in Llanelly, a change of bogie springs was needed due to damage sustained in Newcastle, and a Bournemouth engineer was on hand at Llanelly for a time after their introduction to put right any minor defects. They were used on all Llanelly routes without restriction and were highly thought-of by the drivers. Both trolleybuses are known to have suffered frontal damage during their stay in Llanelly. The hire cost of the Bournemouth trolleybuses was recorded in December 1944 as £840 12s 6d for the year end. They were returned to their home town on 29 June 1945, after a loan period of 18 months.

London

In the early part of the war London Transport found itself short of all types of passenger vehicles, due to wartime losses and increased passenger demand. New vehicles were not available. Bournemouth loaned 18 trolleybuses to London Transport which paid BCT to tow them to the capital, presumably using the three Thornycroft BC/FC lorries converted earlier in 1940 from motorbuses, three at a time on six days within an eleven day period. All the loaned trolleybuses were based at Ilford Depot in East London and used exclusively on local routes 691 Barkingside - Barking and 693 Chadwell Heath - Barking, which operated entirely in suburbia where the lower than normal seating capacity caused no hardship. Special destination blinds were made. The front exit doors were not used in London and locked shut.

These were the only Sunbeam trolleybuses ever to operate in London. 86 was repaired at London Transport's Charlton Works following war damage. The Ilford staff nicknamed them "Yellow Perils", reportedly due to the doubtful performance of their brakes. The Bournemouth vehicles carried Metropolitan Stage Carriage Licence plates on the open rear platform during their stay in London (number 77 carrying MSC plate 10946N). Half of the loaned trolleybuses were released in November 1941 and towed back to Bournemouth, again by BCT three at a time, the others were released in September 1942 (as the SA class, intended for Durban and Johannesburg, South Africa, entered service with London Transport) and passed to Newcastle upon Tyne.

Newcastle upon Tyne

The remaining nine Bournemouth trolleybuses on loan to London Transport were released in September 1942, by which time sufficient AEC and Leyland vehicles of the SA class, intended for export to South Africa, had become available. They travelled direct to Newcastle upon Tyne. Both Bournemouth and the Newcastle upon Tyne Corporation Transport and Electricity Department operated a rear entrance, front exit policy at this time (although their doors were motorised), and the loaned vehicles fitted in well with the local fleet. Four Bournemouth vehicles became surplus to requirements in March/April 1943 when Newcastle put into service six of the ten second-hand English Electric E11 trolleybuses dating from 1929-1932 which they had acquired from Bradford in October 1942. One (77) of the Bournemouth vehicles returned to Bournemouth in early February 1943 and three others were passed to South Shields at the beginning of March 1943. The other five Bournemouth trolleybuses remained in Newcastle until May 1945.

They were used predominantly on the 4 group of services operating across the city, Denton - Westgate Road - Walker - Wallsend. One vehicle reportedly fell into the pits at Wingrove Depot.

South Shields

Severe bombing of the town, home to many busy Tyneside shipyards, ensured that the 36 trolleybuses in the fleet (which by 1942 also included ex-Bournemouth Thornycroft LJ7704, South Shields 236) were hard-pressed, although no route served the

Fleet Number	Registration Number	Loaned to	Date Delivered	Date Into Service	Date Withdrawn	Date Departed	Destination
72	AEL400	London	21/12/40			01/09/42	Newcastle
		Newcastle	11/09/42	19/10/42	23/05/45	29/05/45	Bournemouth
73	AEL401	London	13/12/40			01/09/42	Newcastle
		Newcastle	12/09/42	19/10/42	30/04/45	30/04/45	Bournemouth
74	AEL 402	London	23/12/40			11/11/41	Bournemouth
75	AEL 403	London	21/12/40			04/11/41	Bournemouth
76	AEL 404	Wolverhampton	04/09/40			27/10/48	Bournemouth
77	AEL 405	London	17/12/40			01/09/42	Newcastle
		Newcastle	17/09/42	19/10/42		05/02/43	Bournemouth
		Llanelly	28/12/43			29/06/45	Bournemouth
78	AEL 406	London	15/12/40			01/09/42	Newcastle
		Newcastle	28/09/42	02/12/42	26/02/43	02/03/43	South Shields
		South Shields	02/03/43			31/05/43	Walsall
		Walsall	01/06/43			22/08/45	Bournemouth
79	AEL 407	London	19/12/40			01/09/42	Newcastle
		Newcastle	22/09/42	19/10/42	26/02/43	02/03/43	South Shields
		South Shields	02/03/43			31/05/43	Walsall
		Walsall	01/06/43			17/07/45	Bournemouth
80	AEL 408	London	15/12/40			07/11/41	Bournemouth
81	AEL 409	London	19/12/40			11/11/41	Bournemouth
82	AEL 410	London	15/12/40			01/09/42	Newcastle
		Newcastle	03/10/42	04/12/42	12/05/45	24/05/45	Bournemouth
83	AEL 411	London	19/12/40			07/11/41	Bournemouth
84	ALJ 60	Wolverhampton	07/09/40			04/06/46	Bournemouth
85	ALJ 61	London	17/12/40			11/11/41	Bournemouth
86	ALJ 62	London	13/12/40			04/11/41	Bournemouth
87	ALJ 63	London	23/12/40			01/09/42	Newcastle
		Newcastle	27/09/42	19/10/42	12/05/45	15/05/45	Bournemouth
89	ALJ 65	London	23/12/40			07/11/41	Bournemouth
105	ALJ 979	Wolverhampton	09/09/40			08/06/46	Bournemouth
107	ALJ 981	Wolverhampton	13/09/40			29/06/48	Bournemouth
117	ALJ 991	London	21/12/40			04/11/41	Bournemouth
123	ALJ 997	London	13/12/40			01/09/42	Bournemouth
		Newcastle	06/10/42	02/12/42	22/01/43	02/03/43	South Shields
		South Shields	02/03/43			31.05.43	Bournemouth
		Llanelly	28/12/43			29/06/45	Bournemouth
129	BEL814	Wolverhampton	17/09/40			08/12/48	Bournemouth
130	BEL815	Wolverhampton	20/09/40			20/07/48	Bournemouth
131	BEL816	Wolverhampton	24/09/40			30/05/46	Bournemouth
132	BEL817	Wolverhampton	27/09/40			06/07/48	Bournemouth
137	BEL822	Wolverhampton	03/10/40			04/11/48	Bournemouth
145	BEL830	London	17/12/40			01/09/42	Newcastle
		Newcastle	09/10/42	01/12/42	30/04/45	05/05/45	Bournemouth
156	BRU7	Wolverhampton	16/10/40			23/05/46	Bournemouth
161	BRU12	Wolverhampton	24/10/40			20/05/46	Bournemouth
168	BRU19	Wolverhampton	10/10/40			27/07/48	Bournemouth

Sunbeam MS2 no. 72 (AEL400) heading for Barking Broadway on London Transport route 691 from Barkingside
David Chalk collection (photographer's name not recorded)

A rear view of MS2 no. 87 (ALJ63) whilst on loan to London Transport travelling north towards Barkingside in February 1941.   David Chalk collection (photographer's name not recorded)

shipyards themselves. In addition, an air raid on 30 September 1941 had seen three trolleybuses burnt out in the Market Place. Trolleybus wiring was strung along Centenary Avenue under the 1939 Defence Regulations enabling the introduction of a new trolleybus service Tyne Dock - Horsley Hill (South Shields only introduced a service numbering system in 1950) further increasing the demand for trolleybuses. It was opened by the ex-Bournemouth Thornycroft on 28 September 1942.

The Bournemouth Sunbeam MS2 trolleybuses 78, 79 and 123, despatched direct from Newcastle upon Tyne, worked on the Prince Edward Road service, Market - Fremantle Road (journeys beyond to Marsden Bay being suspended for much of the war). They were known locally as "Newcastle Trolleys" due to their livery and rear entrance, front exit layout despite the internal advertising panels being full of cards extolling the virtues of Bournemouth. The three trolleybuses stayed until the end of May 1943 after which they were towed to Bournemouth.

Bournemouth's official records state that only three Sunbeam MS2s (78, 79 and 123, despatched from Newcastle upon Tyne) were loaned to South Shields. It has been suggested that a fourth, 77, also operated in the town in February – October 1943. This suggestion is based on an incomplete hand-written entry in the Newcastle records (which contains a number of transposed dates) and enthusiast recollections that the Market – Freemantle Road service was operated entirely by Bournemouth trolleybuses and South Shields' own Daimler CTM4 234, five vehicles being required to maintain the service.

Walsall

At the end of their stay in South Shields, Bournemouth 78 and 79 were despatched direct to Walsall for a further two years' service there. A number of motorbuses had been destroyed when an incendiary bomb hit the depot and the undertaking welcomed the opportunity of additional trolleybus capacity, not least as the Sunbeam MS2s were technically similar to 21 of its own fleet. The MS2s were based at Walsall's Birchills Depot and operated on service 30 (The Bridge – Leamore – Bloxwich), not venturing onto the Wolverhampton service, Walsall's only other trolleybus route at that time. Throughout their stay the Bournemouth vehicles had their front exit locked out of use. The delivery of new utility vehicles in June 1945 permitted their return to Bournemouth and they were collected by a BCT towing vehicle driven by Bill Biddlecombe.

Wolverhampton

The news that ten new trolleybuses ordered in 1939 were unlikely to be delivered for a considerable period of time and wartime traffic growth in the industrial Black Country led Wolverhampton's Manager, Mr Charles Owen Silvers, to approach Bournemouth for the loan of 12 trolleybuses. Not surprisingly, Wolverhampton also operated MS2s from the local Sunbeam works. The town's newest MS2s (223-226 and 245), featuring BTH equipment and Park Royal bodywork, were, but for the front exit, virtually identical to the vehicles loaned by Bournemouth.

Arrangements were made for Sunbeam to collect the trolleybuses from Bournemouth and tow them to Wolverhampton at the cost of £21 per vehicle and these arrived in Wolverhampton between 4 September 1940 and 24 October 1940. The hire cost was £240 each pa. Mr Silvers also endeavoured to negotiate the hire of twenty Bournemouth drivers and twenty conductors to crew them, but only 23 staff in all were prepared to transfer. They were paid their normal wages plus 3s 6d per night subsistence and subsidised travel to their home town, but some soon returned due to their inability to find suitable accommodation and the lack of opportunities to visit Bournemouth. The transferred crews retained their dark blue uniforms with red piping.

No. 123 (ALJ997) is seen loading in South Shields Market Place prior to departure to Prince Edward Road in April 1943. Due to the livery similarities, the loaned vehicles were known in South Shields as "Newcastle buses" despite clearly showing their South Coast origins.

South Tyneside Libraries

Bournemouth vehicles were also loaned to Walsall Corporation Transport. Sunbeam MS2 no. 78 (AEL406) is seen with its crew posing for the camera at the High Street, Bloxwich terminus alongside the ornamental gardens just south of the Lichfield Road crossroads. Note that the **BOURNEMOUTH CORPORATION** legend on the lower-deck waistband remains although other "blackout" and security measures, such as the white paint applied to the front and rear of the mudguards and the matt chocolate applied to the roof (but not the window surrounds), are evident.
                                                                                      Deryk Vernon collection

Towards the end of the war, Bournemouth Sunbeam MS2 no. 79 (AEL407) was photographed at the High Street, Bloxwich terminus. At this time Walsall operated but two trolleybus routes, that through Willenhall to Wolverhampton, jointly operated with Wolverhampton Corporation Transport, and the 3 mile long line between The Bridge and Bloxwich.
                                                David Chalk collection (photographer's name not recorded)

Upon arrival, the Bournemouth trolleybuses were fitted with wheel-type trolley heads. In principle, the front exit doors were not used in Wolverhampton, but drivers, whether from Bournemouth or not, are known to have used this means of unloading packed vehicles.

The first ten (76, 84, 105, 107, 129-132, 137, 156), based at Park Lane Depot which had been built in 1938 to serve Wolverhampton's northern routes, operated daily on service 13 (Pear Tree – Merry Hill) and from 1946 on cross-town service 12 (Pear Tree – Finchfield). They were used irregularly on all other Park Lane Depot services. The other two, Bournemouth 161 and 168, operated from Cleveland Road

Depot on service 9 (Amos Lane – Jeffcock Road). When 161 returned to Bournemouth in 1946, 168 joined the others at Park Lane Depot. Very occasionally, odd vehicles operated on other Cleveland Road workings for a day or two permitting easier supervision following repairs. Numbers 76 and 84 were renumbered 176 and 184 respectively to avoid confusion with vehicles having the same numbers in the native fleet.

The vehicles loaned to Wolverhampton operated in no other towns and, before being returned to Bournemouth, were given a full overhaul and repaint as the Black Country atmosphere and wartime lack of attention had made them shabby. It is not known who towed them back to Bournemouth.

Bournemouth Sunbeam MS2 no. 105 (ALJ979) was photographed approaching the crossroads of Darlington Street with School Street and Waterloo Road, Wolverhampton heading for the town centre on service 13 (Merry Hill – Pear Tree). David Chalk collection (photographer's name not recorded)

(Above) The conductor eyes the photographer suspiciously as Bournemouth no. 130 (BEL815) stands at the boarding point in Stafford Street, Wolverhampton prior to departure westwards to Bradmore and Finchfield.

David Chalk collection
(photographer's name not recorded)

(Left) No. 129 (BEL814) heading west in Darlington Street, Wolverhampton.

David Chalk collection
(photographer's name not recorded)

APPENDIX D

LIVERY

Throughout the tramway era, Bournemouth's tramcars appeared in a livery of maroon and primrose, applied in the traditional manner of maroon waist panel, dashes and upper deck decency boards, and primrose rocker panels and window surrounds. This same colour scheme was used on the undertaking's experimental motor buses before the First World War, but it was the appearance of the first "proper" motor buses, as distinct from the lightweight semi-open vehicles used on tourist-orientated services, in 1927 that introduced a "reversed" livery in which primrose predominated.

It was basically this livery that appeared on three of the four trolleybus demonstrators and on Bournemouth's initial trolleybus fleet. There were only minor differences to the style of application, relating primarily to the colour of the roof, lining and location of transferred lettering, etc., to these vehicles and subsequent deliveries throughout the trolleybus era. Indeed, the scheme survived unchanged until 1973 when the maroon bands were abandoned, although the use of primrose survived until 2006 when it was replaced by a different shade of yellow following sale of the undertaking to RATP Transdev on 16 December 2005.

Trolleybuses were repainted every two years before the Second World War. During the war there were no full repaints, but vehicles continued to be 'touched up', as required. Post-war repaints were initially approximately every three years, but around 1960 this changed to about every four years. Solely 298 of the final batch of Sunbeam MF2Bs ever received a full external repaint.

It is important to note that the vehicles circulating on the streets did not necessarily all appear in the then current livery application at the same time. The numerical codes for the successive styles of livery application have been given for reasons of clarity and were not official BCT classifications.

1) 1933-1938
Applied to the following vehicles upon delivery:

68	Sunbeam MS2/Weymann
69	AEC663T/English Electric
70	AEC661T/English Electric
72 – 77	Sunbeam MS2/Park Royal
78 – 83	Sunbeam MS2/English Electric
84 – 89	Sunbeam MS2/Park Royal
90 – 173	Sunbeam MS2/Park Royal

All over primrose, with two maroon bands painted at the lower deck waistband, that is below the lower deck windows, and the upper deck waistband, that is below the upper deck windows. The vent panel, that is above the lower deck windows, was yellow. The lower and upper deck waistband beadings, and vent panel beadings were picked out in olive green. The roof and front domes were painted white (the rear dome being primrose).

The primrose panels were lined with a tramcar-style single red line, 1/8in broad, with simple square corners. The lining was applied to divide the upper deck panels into separate front, side,

rear corner, and rear portions, and the lower deck panels into cab nearside (whole side on the offside), front exit doors, side panels, rear platform and offside corner. Narrower lining was applied to the panels at lower deck window level between the driver's cab and the front exits doors on the nearside and the diffused bay 1 window on the offside. Mudguards and lifeguard rails were painted black, and wheels maroon with chromed wheel hubs.

Possibly to reduce wear to the paintwork, dark coloured reinforcing was applied to the edges to lower deck nearside rear pillar extending as high as the upper line of beading of the waistband and on the edge of the rear panels facing the open entrance platform extending as high as the lower line of beading of the vent panel.

Trolley gantry, roof catwalk and related equipment above the upper deck window-line, and trolley boom restraining hooks were painted white. Trolley poles were black. Drivers' rectangular rear view mirrors were black and the circular mirrors were chrome (later black).

Large Bournemouth coat of arms was displayed on both sides of the lower and upper deck side panels, centred beneath the bay 3 side windows, on the front panel beneath the driver's cab windscreen centrally between the headlamps, and centrally on the rear panel beneath the platform window. A small coat of arms was additional affixed centrally to the vent panel above the rear platform window. The lower deck maroon band was emblazoned with 5in high plain and unlined gold sans serif upper-case lettering BOURNEMOUTH CORPORATION running from bay 2 to bay 6.

Ownership details with the General Manager's name and title in 3/4in high black serif upper-case lettering, and the head office address beneath in somewhat smaller black sans serif upper-case lettering were applied to the base of the nearside lower deck panels, bay 2, immediately to the rear of the front exit, and at the base of the offside lower deck panels, bay 2, immediately to the rear of the front axle, viz:

I. BULFIN, ENGINEER & GENERAL MANAGER
TRANSPORT OFFICES, WOOTTON GARDENS,
BOURNEMOUTH.

Following the May 1935 decision to appoint Mr. Morrison as General Manager upon Mr. Bulfin's retirement, these details were amended in black lower-case lettering to reflect the new name:

Duncan P. Morrison, General Manager,
TRANSPORT OFFICES, WOOTTON GARDENS,
BOURNEMOUTH.

Those vehicles with Park Royal bodywork had a small manufacturer's transfer at the base of the nearside panel immediately in front of the front axle.

The unladen weight was shown in upper-case sans serif black typeface at the base of the offside lower deck panels to the rear of the second rear axle with the maximum permitted speed beneath.

(Above) Livery I (1933 - 1938): an unidentified Sunbeam MS2 is seen broadside on at Christchurch turntable.

Omnibus Society (C.F. Klapper)

(Left) Livery I (1933 - 1938): a rear offside view of Sunbeam MS2 no. 140 (BEL825) outside the Power Station Generator Room at Central Depot, Southcote Road. Note the shape of the rear indicator box which was to prove entirely suitable for the deeper screens introduced in November 1935, as well as the lined out rear offside corner panel.

Omnibus Society (R.T. Wilson)

Livery I (1933 - 1938): Sunbeam MS2 no. 158 (BRU9) unloads following its arrival at Christchurch. No. 158 has already been equipped with a semaphore arm illuminated traffic indicator (in a black box on the leading side pillar), first introduced in 1938. Omnibus Society (C.F. Klapper)

The seating capacity was indicated in upper-case sans serif black typeface at the nearside base of the rear platform panel.

Small gold numerals, edged in black, were mounted on the nearside base of the front panel beneath and a little to the nearside of the nearside headlamp, at the rear at the base of the lower deck rear platform corner panel to show the individual vehicle's fleet number.

Small upper-case sans serif red lettering appeared centrally above the window in the upper-deck rear emergency exit door, reading EMERGENCY DOOR. Centrally in the yellow-painted vent panel, the same style of lettering showed ENTRANCE above the open rear platform and EXIT ONLY above the front exit doors.

Detail differences by vehicle type:

68 Sunbeam MS2: Both the primrose and yellow panels were lined with a tramcar-style single red line, 1/8in broad, with simple square corners. The lining was not divided into panels but continued around the entire vehicle. Large Bournemouth coat of arms was displayed on both sides of the lower deck side panels, towards the rear of bay 2, on the front panel beneath the driver's cab windscreen centrally between the headlamps, and,

it is assumed, centrally on the rear panel beneath the platform window. There were no coats of arms on the upper deck side panels.

The Bournemouth coat of arms was carried on both sides of the lower deck immediately below the 3rd side pillar, also front and rear lower deck panels with additional small coat of arms positioned centrally on yellow band of rear elevation.

Following reconstruction in September 1936 with a front staircase and exit door, the livery application and all transfers was adapted to that of the main fleet of Sunbeam MS2s. The lining in the yellow vent panel area was removed and the lining on the upper-deck primrose panels was divided into separate front, side, rear corner, and rear portions, and on the lower-deck panels into cab nearside (whole side on the offside), front exit doors, side panels, rear platform and offside corner. The position of the lower-deck coat of arms was moved backwards and located centrally on bay 3 with an additional pair of transfers in the same location on the upper deck side panels.

Gold sans serif upper-case lettering BOURNEMOUTH CORPORATION some 5in tall was applied to the lower deck waistband running from immediately behind the driver's cab to above the front of the rear bogie. Following reconstruction with a front exit, this legend was moved somewhat to the rear, running between the front of bay 2 and the middle of the rear bogie.

69 AEC-EE 663T: Both front and rear domes were painted primrose, the white roof extending over bays 1 - 6, including the fairings around the trolley gantry. The upper-deck waistband was broader than that on the lower-deck and covered the top of the semi-piano front upper-deck front panel. No Bournemouth Corporation insignia was originally carried.

There was a single red line around the top and bottom of the upper-deck panels. On the lower-deck panels the lining was applied as a portion from on the nearside from the front pillar to the rear pillar curving above the rear bogie, a separate almost square portion surrounding the headlamp on the front offside beneath the driver's cab windscreen, and on the offside as a portion from the front pillar of the driver's cab round to the nearside of the rear panel.

Black trolleyboom retaining hooks, wheels, mudguards and lifeguard rails. Using upper-case sans serif black typeface, legal lettering-ownership details were applied at the bottom of the bay 1 lower-deck side panel on both sides, the unladen weight was shown at the base of the offside lower deck panels to the rear of the second rear axle with the maximum permitted speed beneath and the seating capacity was indicated at the nearside base of the rear platform panel.

Later Bournemouth coat of arms on both sides, upper and lower deck, bay 3, also rear lower deck panels with additional small coat of arms positioned centrally on the vent panel above the platform rear windows were added. The narrowness of the lower-deck waistband prevented the legend BOURNEMOUTH CORPORATION being added to the sides (when rebuilt as a motorbus this legend was applied to the side vent panel).

Following the 1934 reconstruction with front exit and staircase, small upper-case sans serif red lettering was added centrally to the vent panel, showing ENTRANCE above the open rear platform and EXIT ONLY above the front exit doors.

70 AEC-EE 661T: Both front and rear domes were painted primrose, the white roof extending over bays 1 - 6, including the fairings around the trolley gantry. The upper-deck waistband was broader than that on the lower-deck and covered the top of the semi-piano front upper-deck font panel. No Bournemouth Corporation insignia was originally carried.

There was a single red line around the top and bottom of the upper-deck panels. On the lower-deck panels the lining was applied as a portion from on the nearside from the front pillar to the rear pillar curving above the rear bogie, a separate almost square portion surrounding the headlamp on the front offside beneath the driver's cab windscreen, and on the offside as a portion from the front pillar of the driver's cab round to the nearside of the rear panel.

Black trolleyboom retaining hooks, wheels, mudguards and lifeguard rails. Using upper-case sans serif black typeface, legal lettering-ownership details were applied at the bottom of the bay 1 lower-deck side panel on both sides, the unladen weight was shown at the base of the offside lower deck panels to the rear of the rear axle with the maximum permitted speed beneath and the seating capacity was indicated at the nearside base of the rear platform panel.

Later Bournemouth coat of arms on both sides, upper and lower deck, bay 3, also rear lower deck panels with additional

small coat of arms positioned centrally on the vent panel above the platform rear windows were added. The narrowness of the lower-deck waistband prevented the legend BOURNEMOUTH CORPORATION being added to the sides (when rebuilt as a motorbus this legend was applied to the side vent panel).

Following the 1934 reconstruction with front exit and staircase, small upper-case sans serif red lettering was added centrally to the vent panel, showing ENTRANCE above the open rear platform and EXIT ONLY above the front exit doors.

Thornycroft BD 71: The blue livery was initially retained but with the BRUSH - THORNYCROFT lettering removed.

In late 1936 no. 71 was repainted into a single-deck version of the standard Bournemouth livery, namely all over primrose, with a single maroon band painted at the lower deck waistband, the beadings of which were picked out in olive green. The maroon waistband narrowed above the "radiator" outline apex. The body panels were unlined. Mudguards and lifeguard rails were painted black, and wheels maroon.

Large Bournemouth coat of arms were displayed on the side panels, beneath the window pillar between bays 1 and 2, centred beneath the bay 3 side window on the offside, within the centrally-mounted, blank "radiator" outline on the front panel beneath the driver's cab windscreen, and on the rear panel between the window and the rear registration number plate.

The maroon waistband was emblazoned with ornate 5in high gold serif upper-case lettering BOURNEMOUTH CORPORATION, shaded in blue, "Bournemouth" being applied in bays 1 and 2, and "Corporation" in bays 4 and 5 to allow for the central entrance and exit.

Ownership details with the General Manager's name and title in $3/4$in high black serif upper-case lettering, and the head office address beneath in somewhat smaller black sans serif upper-case lettering were applied to the base of the nearside lower deck panels, bay 1, immediately to the rear of the front axle. The unladen weight was shown in upper-case sans serif black typeface at the base of the nearside lower deck panels forwards of the rear axle with the maximum permitted speed beneath.

2)   1938 - 1940
By spring 1938 the livery application was altered as follows:

All over primrose, with two maroon bands painted at the lower deck waistband, that is below the lower deck windows, and the upper deck waistband, that is below the upper deck windows. Primrose paint was applied to the vent panel, that is above the lower deck windows, in place of yellow and to the entire roof (the previous white having proved impractical). The lower and upper deck waistband beadings, and vent panel beadings were picked out in olive green.

The body panels were unlined. Mudguards and lifeguard rails were painted black, and wheels maroon with chromed wheel hubs.

The dark coloured reinforcing applied to the upright edges of the open entrance platform was removed.

Trolley gantry, roof catwalk and related equipment above the upper deck window-line, and trolley boom restraining hooks were painted primrose. Trolley poles were black.

Large Bournemouth coat of arms was displayed on both sides of the lower and upper deck side panels, but somewhat lower than previously on the lower deck side panels, centred

Livery 2 (1938 - 1940): no. 102 (ALJ976) was photographed in Kinson Road opposite the Columbia Road turning loop on 15 April 1938 in the revised livery which incorporated a primrose roof and vent panel, and large ornate gold fleet numbers, shaded in blue, on the front, rear and side panels Malcolm Pearce (G.O.P. Pearce).

beneath the bay 3 side windows, on the front panel beneath the driver's cab windscreen centrally between the headlamps, and centrally on the rear panel beneath the platform window.

The introduction of a square service number and an auxiliary in-town "via" indicator boxes to the vent panel above the rear platform window resulted in the deletion of the small coat of arms in this location. The lower deck maroon band was emblazoned with ornate 5in high gold serif upper-case lettering BOURNEMOUTH CORPORATION, shaded in blue, running from bay 2 to bay 6 (matching the style of the fleet numbers).

Ownership details with the General Manager's name and title in ³/₄in high black script lettering, and the head office address beneath in black sans serif upper-case lettering were applied to the base of the nearside lower deck panels, bay 2, immediately to the rear of the front exit, and at the base of the offside lower deck panels, bay 2, immediately to the rear of the front axle, viz:

Duncan P. Morrison, General Manager,
TRANSPORT OFFICES, WOOTTON GARDENS,
BOURNEMOUTH.

The small manufacturer's transfer at the base of the nearside panel immediately in front of the front axle originally applied to those vehicles with Park Royal bodywork was not replaced.

The unladen weight was shown in upper-case sans serif black typeface at the base of the offside lower deck panels to the rear of the second rear axle with the maximum permitted speed beneath.

The seating capacity was indicated in upper-case sans serif black typeface at the nearside base of the rear platform panel.

Large ornate gold numerals, shaded in blue, were mounted on the lower-deck waistband centrally at the front replacing the triangular Sunbeam manufacturer's badge and at the rear beneath the platform window to show the individual vehicle's fleet number. Further numerals of the same style were placed on the lower-deck side panels, between the waistband and the coat of arms in bay 3.

Small upper-case sans serif red lettering appeared centrally above the window in the upper-deck rear emergency exit door, reading EMERGENCY DOOR. The lettering indicating ENTRANCE above the open rear platform and EXIT ONLY above the front exit doors was removed and replaced by upper-case sans serif black lettering indicating OUT ONLY preceded by an arrow pointing forwards in bay 2, and IN ONLY followed by an arrow pointing to the rear in bay 6, located centrally in the vent panel.

3) 1940 – 1945

In October 1940 the livery application was altered to provide a measure of camouflage to the fleet although it is assumed that some "black-out" and security measures had been introduced prior to this date:

Primrose below the upper deck waistband, with two maroon bands painted at the lower deck waistband, that is below the lower deck windows, and the upper deck waistband, that is below the upper deck windows. Everything above the upper-deck waistband, that is the upper deck window surrounds, roof and domes, trolley gantry, roof catwalk and related equipment, and trolley boom restraining hooks were painted a matt chocolate colour. Trolley poles remained black.

Livery 3 (1940 - 1945): no. 148 (BEL833) displays the wartime livery with its bodywork above the upper-deck waistband painted in a matt chocolate colour, all references to the ownership and town name removed, and the application of white paint to the mudguards, etc., to fulfil wartime "black-out" restrictions. It is seen in St. Clement's Road in June 1943. **Malcolm Pearce (G.O.P. Pearce)**

Large Bournemouth coat of arms were displayed on both sides of the lower and upper deck side panels centred beneath the bay 3 side windows (those on the lower deck side panels retaining their lower position), on the front panel beneath the driver's cab windscreen centrally between the headlamps, and centrally on the rear panel beneath the platform window. The ornate shaded lettering BOURNEMOUTH CORPORATION was removed from the lower deck waistband, except apparently for those trolleybuses loaned to other undertakings, and replaced by the large ornate gold numerals, shaded in blue, indicating the fleet number of the individual vehicle, previously located between the waistband and the coat of arms, on both sides in bay 3.

The lower and upper deck waistband beadings, and vent panel beadings were picked out in olive green.

Front and rear portions of the mudguards above the first and second axles wheel arches were painted white, other portions remaining black. The base of the offside rear corner panel and the lifeguard rails were painted white to fulfil wartime "black-out" restrictions. Wheels and the formerly-chromed wheel hubs were maroon.

Ownership details with the General Manager's name and title in ³/₄in high black script lettering, and the head office address beneath in black sans serif upper-case lettering were applied to the base of the nearside lower deck panels, bay 2, immediately to the rear of the front exit, and at the base of the offside lower deck panels, bay 2, immediately to the rear of the front axle, viz:

Duncan P. Morrison, General Manager,
TRANSPORT OFFICES, WOOTTON GARDENS,
BOURNEMOUTH.

The unladen weight was shown in upper-case sans serif black typeface at the base of the nearside lower deck panels immediately in front of the second rear axle with the maximum permitted speed beneath, instead of on the offside.

The seating capacity was indicated in upper-case sans serif black typeface at the nearside base of the rear platform panel.

Large ornate gold numerals, shaded in blue, were mounted on the lower-deck waistband centrally at the front replacing the triangular Sunbeam manufacturer's badge and at the rear beneath the platform window to show the individual vehicle's fleet number. Further numerals of the same style were placed on the lower-deck side panels, between the waistband and the coat of arms in bay 3.

4)   1945 – 1948
During May 1945 the livery application was altered as follows:

Primrose below the top of upper deck windows (cantrail), with two maroon bands painted at the lower deck waistband, that is below the lower deck windows, and the upper deck waistband, that is below the upper deck windows. Roof and domes, trolley gantry, roof catwalk and related equipment, and trolley boom restraining hooks were painted a gloss chocolate colour. Trolley poles were black but for approximately the last 3ft which were white (the addition of this feature had begun in the later years of the war).

Mudguards and lifeguard rails were painted black, and wheels maroon with chromed wheel hubs.

The lower and upper deck waistband beadings, and vent panel beadings were picked out in olive green.

Ownership details with the head office address in black old fashioned script lettering, and the General Manager's name and title beneath in somewhat smaller black old fashioned script

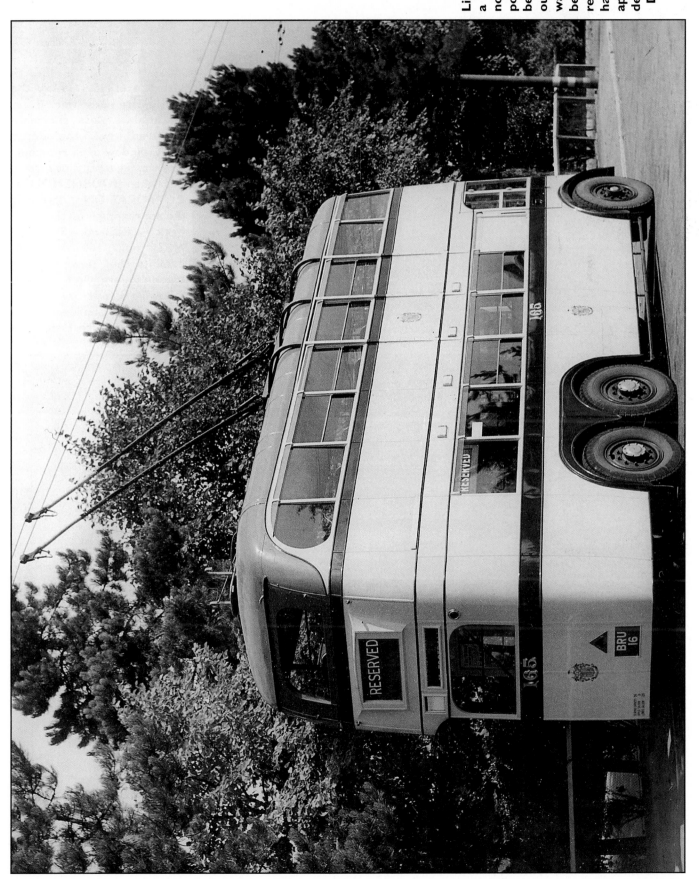

Livery 4 (1945 - 1948): a rear offside view of no. 165 in the first post-war livery. It will be noted that lining out of the main panels was not reinstated. It is believed that the first repaints into Livery 4 had no fleet number applied to the lower deck side waist band. David Chalk collection (Bournemouth Transport)

Livery 4 (1945 - 1948): the immediate post-war livery featured a gloss chocolate coloured roof, the upper deck window area returning to the earlier primrose, but the **BOURNEMOUTH CORPORATION** lettering did not reappear on the lower deck waistband. Sunbeam MS2 no. 165 (BRU16) exhibits the "new look" at Queen's Park Golf Pavilion, following reconditioning.

David Chalk collection (Bournemouth Transport)

Livery 5 (1948 - 1956): Sunbeam MS2 no. 152 (BRU3) and no. 168 (BRU19) standing in the Triangle parking area on 21 July 1954 exempify the application of this style of livery.
Malcolm Pearce (G.O.P. Pearce)

lettering were applied to the base of the nearside lower deck panels, bay 2, immediately to the rear of the front exit. No information was applied to the offside lower deck panels.

Corporation Transport Dept.
Southcote Road
Bournemouth

Duncan P. Morrison   General Manager,

It is believed that the first repaints after the war had a plain maroon band with no fleet number applied.

Large ornate gold numerals, shaded in blue, were mounted on the lower-deck waistband centrally at the front and at the rear beneath the platform window to show the individual vehicle's fleet number. Further numerals were placed on the lower-deck side panels, between the waistband and the coat of arms in bay 3.

The unladen weight was shown in upper-case sans serif black typeface at the base of the nearside lower deck panels immediately in front of the second rear axle with the maximum permitted speed beneath, instead of on the offside.

The seating capacity was indicated in upper-case sans serif black typeface at the nearside base of the rear platform panel.

5)   1948 – 1956
The livery application was altered, being applied to the following trolleybuses upon delivery or purchase and to earlier vehicles upon repaint:

200 - 223   BUT9641T/Weymann (with several
                 noticeable differences)

Primrose below the top of the upper deck windows (cantrail),

with two maroon bands painted at the lower deck waistband, that is below the lower deck windows, and the upper deck waistband, that is below the upper deck windows. Except on the BUT9641Ts, roof and domes, trolley gantry, roof catwalk and related equipment, and trolley boom restraining hooks were painted a gloss chocolate colour. Trolley poles were black but for approximately the last 3ft which were white.

The lower and upper deck waistband beadings, and vent panel beadings were picked out in olive green.

Large Bournemouth coat of arms were displayed on both sides of the lower and upper deck side panels centred beneath the bay 3 side windows (those on the lower deck side panels being again applied at a higher level), on the front panel beneath the driver's cab windscreen centrally between the headlamps, and centrally on the rear panel beneath the platform window.

The large ornate gold numerals, shaded in blue, indicating the fleet number of the individual vehicle, were removed from the lower-deck side panels but retained on the lower-deck waistband at front and rear.

Mudguards and lifeguard rails were painted black, and wheels maroon with chromed wheel hubs.

Full ownership details with the General Manager's name and title beneath were applied in ¾in high black elongated sans-serif upper-case condensed lettering at the base of the nearside lower deck panels, bay 1, immediately to the rear of the front axle, viz:

CORPORATION TRANSPORT DEPT
SOUTHCOTE ROAD, BOURNEMOUTH
W.D. REAKES M.INST.T., GENERAL MANAGER

The unladen weight was shown in ¾in high black elongated sans-serif upper-case condensed typeface at the base of the nearside lower deck panels forward of the leading rear axle

Livery 5 (1948 - 1956): the colour scheme of the BUT9641Ts reintroduced a primrose roof, something that would subsequently be universally introduced to the trolleybus fleet. No. 204 (KLJ338) is seen at the loading point in Portman Road, Boscombe.   **Omnibus Society (R.T. Wilson)**

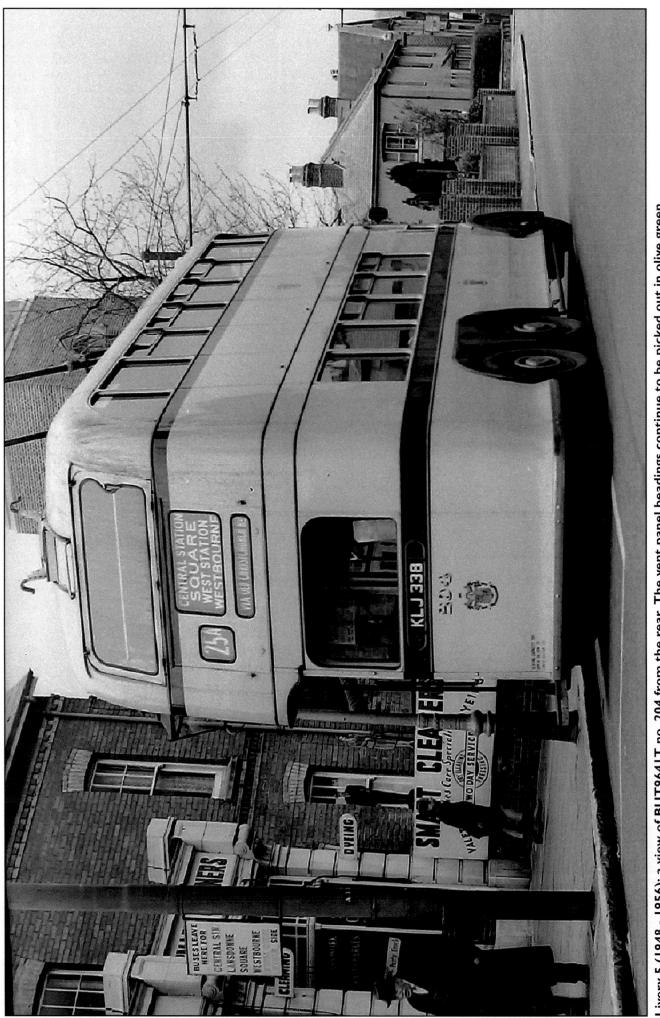

Livery 5 (1948 - 1956): a view of BUT9641T no. 204 from the rear. The vent panel beadings continue to be picked out in olive green.

Omnibus Society (R.T. Wilson)

(Left) Livery 5 (1948 - 1956): the ornate County Borough Arms as applied to the BUT9641Ts upon delivery.

Malcolm Pearce (G.O.P. Pearce)

(Below) Livery 5 (1948 - 1956): experimentally, BUT9641T no. 207 (KLJ341) appeared for a short time with a chocolate brown painted roof as retained on the Sunbeam MS2s. It was not deemed a success. No. 207 was photographed in Avenue Road at the 25A stop.

David Chalk collection

with the maximum permitted speed beneath.

The seating capacity was indicated in ¾in high black elongated sans-serif upper-case condensed typeface at the nearside base of the rear platform panel.

Detail differences by vehicle type:

BUT9641T: All over primrose including the roof, domes and trolley gantry, with two maroon bands painted at the lower deck waistband, that is below the lower deck windows, and the upper deck waistband, that is below the upper deck windows. The lower deck waistband was arched to the centre of the driver's cab windscreen.

Large ornate gold numerals, shaded in blue, indicating the fleet number of the individual vehicle, were carried on the front panel between the offside headlight and sidelight, and centrally mounted on the primrose lower panel below the rear platform window.

241 appeared with its roof experimentally painted chocolate brown in 1954.

6). 1956-1962

The livery application was altered once again, being applied to the following trolleybuses upon delivery or purchase and to earlier vehicles upon repaint:

258 – 287	Sunbeam MF2B/Weymann
288 – 294	BUT9611T/Weymann

All over primrose, with two maroon bands painted at the lower deck waistband, that is below the lower deck windows, and the upper deck waistband, that is below the upper deck windows. The lower and upper deck waistband beadings were picked out in olive green. Roof and domes, trolley gantry and trolley boom restraining hooks were painted primrose. Roof catwalk and related equipment were grey or black. Trolley poles were black but for approximately the last 2ft which were white.

The number of Bournemouth coat of arms was reduced. These were now displayed only on both sides of the upper decks, bay 3, and were smaller than those previously applied.

The vent panel beadings were no longer picked out in olive green but were finished in primrose.

Small upper-case sans serif red lettering appeared centrally above the window in the upper-deck rear emergency exit door, reading EMERGENCY DOOR.

The lettering in the vent panel indicating OUT ONLY preceded by an arrow pointing forwards in bay 2 and IN ONLY followed by an arrow pointing to the rear in bay 6 was removed and replaced by the same wording in small white lettering but without arrows located in the lower-deck waistband to the rear of the front exit and forward of the rear entrance, i.e. for the BUT9641Ts and Sunbeam MS2s beneath the bay 2 nearside lower-deck window and the bay 6 nearside lower-deck window.

The large ornate gold fleet numbers were replaced by slightly smaller blue shaded gold numbers. These were now located centrally on the front panels beneath the driver's windscreen and centrally on the rear lower deck panels beneath the platform window.

Livery 6 (1956 - 1962): a primrose painted roof and deletion of olive green from the vent panel beadings became the new standard for the fleet, as shown by this photograph of Sunbeam MF2B no. 269 (WRU269) heading east along Poole Road on 4 August 1959.   **Photo courtesy of D.Ball, for the family of the late J.S. King**

(Above) Livery 6 (1956 - 1962): BUT9641T no. 247 (KLJ347) is seen at the Square, Avenue Road boarding point in Avenue Road.
Photo courtesy of D.Ball, for the family of the late J.S. King

(Left) Livery 6 (1956 - 1962): ex-BH&D BUT9611T no. 294 (DNJ994) exemplifies the simplified livery as it poses outside Garage No.1 at Castle Lane (Mallard Road) Depot Works on 9 June 1963.   Tim Runnacles

(Above) Livery 7 (1962 - 1966): the most noticeable change was the introduction of smaller straw coloured plain fleet numbers in place of the blue shaded gold fleet numbers, as seen on BUT9641T no. 243 (KLJ343) climbing Poole Hill where Commercial Road branches off to join Durley Road heading west towards Poole Road and Westbourne.

Roger G. Funnell (courtesy Mrs D. Funnell and Rodney Funnell)

(Left) Livery 7 (1962 - 1966): Sunbeam MF2B no. 298 (298LJ) stands in Gervis Place awaiting its next journey on service 24 to Iford and Jumpers on 19 April 1964.   Tim Runnacles

Livery 8 (1966 - 1969): the most noticeable change was the introduction of paper advertisements on the upper deck side panels and on the rear panel beneath the rear platform window leading to the application of additional coat of arms on the lower deck side panels. Fleet numerals were changed to small black transfers. Application of this livery was far from universal. Sunbeam MF2B no. 297 (297LJ) is seen resting on Christchurch turntable.

F.W. Ivey

Detail differences by vehicle type:

BUT9611T: due to the absence of a front exit, no boarding or exiting instructions were applied to the lower-deck waistband. Sunbeam MF2B: the lower-deck waistband curved down from the height of the side windows to that of the front windscreen immediately behind the front exit on the nearside and the driver's cab "signalling" window on the offside.

The white lettering IN ONLY and OUT ONLY in the lower-deck waistband was located beneath the bay 5 lower-deck side window and the bay 1 lower-deck side window respectively.

An additional coat of arms of the previous, larger style, was displayed centrally on the front lower deck panels beneath the driver's windscreen. The front fleet number was positioned beneath the front offside headlight. The driver's rear view mirrors were painted primrose.

7). 1962-1966

The livery application was altered once again, being applied to the following trolleybuses upon delivery or purchase and to earlier vehicles upon repaint:

295 – 303　　　Sunbeam MF2B/Weymann

All over primrose, with two maroon bands applied as before, the maroon being of a slightly darker shade that that previously used. The lower-deck waistband curved down from the height of the side windows to that of the front windscreen immediately behind the front exit on the nearside and the driver's cab "signalling" window on the offside.

The beading to the lower and upper deck waistbands was bright Buckingham green in place of the olive green previously used.

Mudguards and lifeguard rails were painted black, and wheels maroon.

Smaller straw coloured plain Gill Sans numbers with gold edges were applied in place of the small blue shaded gold fleet numbers.

Detail differences by vehicle type:

Sunbeam MF2B 295 – 303: Docker Bros. Ltd. paint was used throughout.

8). 1966-1969

The livery application was altered minimally:

Small plain black fleet numbers replaced the straw coloured plain Gill Sans numbers with gold edges.

These were mounted slightly higher than the gold numerals at the front beneath the offside headlight and lower on the panel beneath the rear platform window (to allow sufficient space to accommodate an advertisement). On occasion, as a result of accident damage, black fleet numbers appeared at one end of a trolleybus but earlier designs at the other.

From September 1967, by which time the fleet consisted solely of Sunbeam MF2Bs, exterior advertising was carried on the upper deck side panels (obliterating the Bournemouth coat of arms) and beneath the rear platform window. Additional coats of arms were accordingly added to the lower deck side panels centred on bay 3. From 1966 onwards the triangular

Livery 8 (1966 - 1969): displaying its black fleet numbers beneath the advertisement at the rear, Sunbeam MF2B no. 277 (WRU277) signals its intention to leave the Lansdowne roundabout and turn into Bath Road. Note how the left lens of the auto frog indicator has illuminated to confirm that the frog has been correctly set (19 April 1969). **Robin Helliar-Symons**

Sunbeam manufacturer's plate was removed from the front lower maroon band. Most of the final batch of Sunbeam MF2Bs (280, 295, 296, 297, 299, 300, 301, 302, 303) never received a full external repaint.

To reflect the new head office address the ownership details with the General Manager's name and title beneath were applied in ¾in high black elongated sans-serif upper-case condensed lettering at the base of the nearside lower deck panels, bay 2, immediately to the rear of the front axle, viz:

IAN CUNNINGHAM B.Sc., A.M.I.Mech.E.,
GENERAL MANAGER
CORPORATION TRANSPORT
MALLARD ROAD, BOURNEMOUTH

Internal Livery, Lettering and Numerals
Until 1962 the lower- and upper-saloons of Bournemouth's trolleybuses were painted in varying applications of brown and cream, accompanied by varnished woodwork and brown scratchproof leather cloth (Rexine or similar) coverings to waistrail height. The only known exceptions are the ex-Brighton vehicles for which internal livery information is shown in the Trolleybus Fleet Details and the four experimental trolleybuses for which internal livery information is incompletely known.

All seat fittings were painted brown. The floors were normally finished in brown linoleum, brown or dark grey waterproof paint being applied to the open rear platform area. Handrails were covered in black Doverite.

The platform area, excluding the nearside lower saloon rear bulkhead, and the staircase were finished in brown.

Cards with red typeface were placed on available spaces or glass-fronted panels with the exhortation WHEN ALIGHTING PLEASE USE THE FRONT EXIT.

Paper advertisements, normally referring to local events or traffic notices, were applied to the lower- and upper-saloon side windows throughout the trolleybus era. Card advertisements were also held in retaining channels in the lower- and upper-saloon cove panels.

Upper Saloon
On the Sunbeam MS2s as delivered EMERGENCY DOOR (in two lines) was applied to the inside of the dome above the rear emergency exit door with PULL TO OPEN and an arrow indicating to the offside on the top offside corner of the door itself.

The open-top MS2s additionally displayed the warning MIND YOUR HEAD on both sides of the trolley gantry above the upper-deck gangway.

On the BUT9641Ts the fleet number preceded by No was applied centrally in ornate gold numerals to the inside of the front dome, e.g. No255, above the central window pillar. Some if not all ex-Brighton BUT9611Ts carried these transfers above the nearside front window (with a lost property notice above the offside window).

On the BUT9641Ts as delivered EMERGENCY EXIT was applied to the top of the rear emergency exit door with PULL TO OPEN and an arrow indicating to the offside at the base of the offside rear corner pillar.

On the Sunbeam MF2Bs the fleet number preceded by No was applied centrally in ornate gold numerals to the inside of the front dome, e.g. No300 with NO STANDING in smaller plain lettering beneath. These were replaced by equivalent but smaller black transfers upon repaint.

On the Sunbeam MF2Bs as delivered EMERGENCY EXIT was applied to the cantrail centrally above the rear emergency exit door with PULL TO OPEN and an arrow indicating to the offside in the offside lower portion of the door. EMERGENCY DOOR was applied in some cases upon repaint.

Lower Saloon

On both the Sunbeam MS2s and the BUT9641Ts the fleet number preceded by No was applied above the nearside saloon window in the driver's cab rear bulkhead in ornate gold typeset, e.g No210 with NO SMOKING in smaller similar typeset beneath. Beneath the NO SMOKING applied to the front bulkhead, BUT9641Ts also displayed the following instruction:

NO PERSON MAY ENTER BOARD OR LEAVE OR
ATTEMPT TO ENTER, BOARD OR LEAVE ANY BUS
WHILST IN MOTION

This same instruction was also applied to the waistband on the nearside of the rear platform bulkhead behind the handrail.

There was a used ticket box attached to the driver's cab rear bulkhead beneath the nearside saloon window labelled USED TICKET BOX (in two lines with BOX centrally beneath) and with arrows pointing upwards to the opening. On the BUT9641Ts identical wording with arrows appeared at the stairhead on the upper-saloon offside and on the used ticket box in the nearside platform bulkhead.

At the top of the BUT9641T folding front exit doors was displayed a white notice with red upper case lettering:

CAUTION
DOOR OPENS INWARDS
STAND CLEAR

The seating capacity was indicated in upper case gold (Sunbeam MS2 and BUT9641T) black (Sunbeam MF2B) typeface at the top of the nearside rear bulkhead inside the lower saloon above the platform window:

Sunbeam MS2:

TO CARRY
25 LOWER DECK
31 UPPER DECK

BUT9641T:

TO SEAT
25 LOWER SALOON
31 UPPER SALOON

Sunbeam MF2B:

SEATING CAPACITY 63
UPPER SALOON 35
LOWER SALOON 28

BUT9641Ts and Sunbeam MF2Bs had an undesignated single metal pouch in the lower saloon at cove panel height on the offside rear bulkhead, possibly for storing the BCT Bye-laws or the conductor's waybill, but latterly always empty.

Appearance of a Sunbeam MS2 (no. 210) lower saloon in the early 1960s. F.W. Ivey

Appearance of a Sunbeam MS2 (no. 210) upper saloon in the early 1960s. F.W. Ivey

Appearance of an unrebuilt
BUT9641T (no. 255) lower saloon in
the early 1960s.   **Tony Belton**

Appearance of an unrebuilt
BUT9641T (no. 255) upper saloon in
the early 1960s.   **Tony Belton**

Appearance of a final batch Sunbeam
MF2B (no. 303) upper saloon in the
early 1960s.   **Tony Belton**

SERVICES AND SERVICE ALTERATIONS

Service intervals shown refer to weekdays, i.e. Monday-Saturday inclusive during the trolleybus era, daytime unless otherwise stated. They do not reflect weekday evening or Sunday frequencies. There may be minor omissions prior to 1939.

In addition to the interworking referred to under specific services, there were many examples of trolleybuses arriving in the town centre on one service but leaving again on a different one. The running timetables do not show any regular pattern. In summary, it can be stated that Main Road services (20 to 24) interworked with each other at Gervis Place and Side Route services (26 to 35) interworked with each other at the Triangle.

Pre-war the weekday service intervals applied all day, every day, including Sundays. From September 1939, reduced frequencies applied on Sundays and weekday evenings and this continued until the end of the system, except in the late 1940s and early 1950s, when in the summer months the same frequency applied all day, every day, on the majority of routes.

There were no Sunday services at all, whether tram, trolleybus or motorbus-operated, prior to 9am until 25 September 1938 when one special early Sunday morning journey was introduced at the request of hotel workers and other shift workers. Thereafter, disregarding wartime special journeys and curtailments, a very limited number of special early Sunday

morning services ran along non-standard routes, which could include a combination of different motorbus and trolleybus routes or even include roads not normally served, before 9am, but none were operated by trolleybuses.

Throughout the trolleybus era, services on public holidays (including Boxing Day) were advertised as "curtailed services from approximately 7am to 10am and then normal weekday services, augmented as required". No trolleybuses ever operated on Christmas Day. Trams had operated on Christmas Day from 1902 to 1914 (inclusive) and some motorbus works services ran on Christmas Day during 1942-4.

No timetables were published during the Second World War and few details survive; however, it is known that most services had reduced frequencies for various periods.

Service 20

22.07.43 Trolleybus service commenced Bournemouth Square, Gervis Place - Lansdowne - Boscombe Gardens - Boscombe Arcade - Pokesdown Station - Iford - Jumpers Corner - Christchurch, Church Street via Old Christchurch Road, Lansdowne, Christchurch Road, Barrack Road, Stour Road, Bargates, High Street and Church Street.

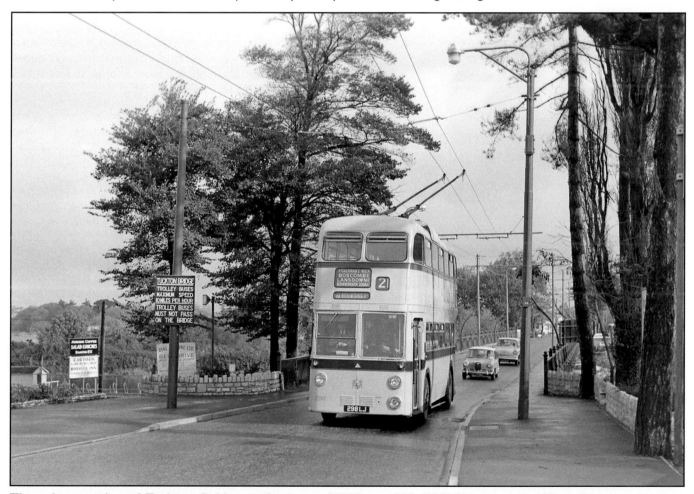

The sylvan setting of Tuckton Bridge as Sunbeam MF2B no. 298 (298LJ) crosses the River Stour and enters Bournemouth in September 1965. The car behind the trolleybus is a Riley Elf based on the BMC Mini and marketed 1961-1969 as a small luxury car.
NTA Collection (R.F. Mack)

Sunbeam MS2 no. 146 (BEL831) is seen at the Pokesdown Station stop in Christchurch Road heading east towards the Square on a service 21 working (16 August 1954). Malcolm Pearce (G.O.P. Pearce)

Between the Lansdowne and Gervis Place westbound journeys to Bournemouth Square operated alternately by way of either Old Christchurch Road, Fir Vale Road and St. Peter's Road, or via Bath Road and Westover Road.

Service interval: 20 mins.

29.09.52   *Winter service interval: 30 mins.*

21.09.53   *Winter service interval: 24 mins*

17.09.56   *Service interval: 30 mins all the year.*

14.09.59   Extension from Bournemouth Square to Westbourne, Seamoor Road via Poole Hill and Poole Road.

Between Bournemouth Square and the junction of Poole Hill with Norwich Road, eastbound journeys followed the west side of The Triangle and then Avenue Road, and westbound journeys followed Commercial Road.

Service interval: 30 mins all the year.

14.11.60   Curtailed to Bournemouth Square, Gervis Place.

11.04.65   Winter Sunday service withdrawn.

13.06.65   Sunday service re-introduced for peak summer months. Thereafter a Sunday service operated only during the peak summer months.
Service interval: 30 mins Sundays.

13.09.65   *Service interval: 20 mins weekdays (Summer Sundays 30 mins 2pm-7pm; 1966-1968 20 mins 2pm-10pm).*

18.10.67   Trolleybuses temporarily replaced by motorbuses but for two weekday morning peak journeys, due to a burst gas main and road collapse at Fisherman's Walk, Seabourne Road.

27.10.67   Trolleybus operation resumed.

Service interval: 20 mins.

19.04.69   Last day of operation by trolleybus. Replaced by motorbus service 20.

Service 21

08.04.36   Trolleybus service commenced Bournemouth Square, Gervis Place - Lansdowne - Boscombe Gardens - Boscombe Arcade - Pokesdown Station - Fisherman's Walk - Southbourne - Tuckton Bridge - Christchurch, Church Street via Old Christchurch Road, Lansdowne, Christchurch Road, Seabourne Road, Southbourne Grove, Southbourne Road, Belle Vue Road, Foxholes Road, Belle Vue Road, Stour Road, Bargates, High Street and Church Street.

Between the junction of Dean Park Crescent with Old Christchurch Road and Bournemouth Square westbound journeys followed Fir Vale Road, St. Peter's Road and Gervis Place.

Trolleybuses terminated at Christchurch by making a "three-point turn" from Church Street into the former coach yard of the Dolphin Hotel using a

T-pole and connecting cables.

Service interval: 10 mins (including service 21A).

19.06.36 Purpose-built turntable in the former coach yard of the Dolphin Hotel, Church Street, Christchurch came into use. Henceforth journeys commenced and terminated at this turntable.

01.07.36 *Service interval: 5 mins.*

01.10.36 *Service interval: 10 mins (including service 21A).*

08.05.37 Alternate westbound journeys to Bournemouth Square diverted between the Lansdowne and Gervis Place along Bath Road and Westover Road instead of Old Christchurch Road, Fir Vale Road, St. Peter's Road.

Service interval: 10 mins (including service 21A).

06.05.46 *Service interval: 10 mins.*

04.10.48 Some weekday morning peak journeys extended to Westbourne, Seamoor Road, via Poole Hill and Poole Road.

Between Bournemouth Square and the junction of Poole Hill with Norwich Road, eastbound journeys followed the west side of The Triangle and then Avenue Road, and westbound journeys followed Commercial Road.

03.10.49 *Service interval 12 mins.*

27.05.50 *Service interval 10 mins.*

02.10.50 *Service interval: 12 mins all the year.*

15.10.51 *Service interval: 15 mins all the year.*

13.07.53 *Summer service (until 20.09.53) interval: 12 mins.*

19.09.53 Weekday morning peak extensions to Westbourne: last day of operation.

21.09.53 *Service interval: 15 mins.*

12.07.54 *Summer service (until 19.09.54) interval: 12 mins.*

11.07.55 *Summer service (until 18.09.55) interval: 12 mins.*

16.07.56 *Summer service (until 16.09.56) interval: 12 mins.*

31.12.56 *Service interval: 20 mins.*

03.06.57 *Service interval: 15 mins.*

15.07.57 *Summer service (until 15.09.57) interval: 12 mins.*

16.09.57 *Winter service interval: 20 mins.*

24.05.58 *Summer service interval: 15 mins.*

22.09.58 *Service interval: 20 mins.*

13.07.59 *Summer service (until 13.09.59) interval: 15 mins.*

18.10.67 Trolleybuses temporarily replaced by motorbuses due to a burst gas main and road collapse at Fisherman's Walk, Seabourne Road.

Eastbound journeys to Christchurch temporarily diverted at Fisherman's Walk via Parkwood Road, Southbourne Road and Beresford Road, instead of Seabourne Road, returning to the normal route at Southbourne Grove. Westbound journeys were unaffected.

27.10.67 Trolleybus operation resumed.

Introduction of the Southbourne Traffic Management Scheme. Eastbound journeys to Christchurch continue to follow the previous diversion at Fisherman's Walk via Parkwood Road, Southbourne Road and Beresford Road, instead of Seabourne Road, returning to the normal route at Southbourne Grove.

11.02.68 Southbourne Traffic Management Scheme ceased. Motorbuses operated on this day only reverting to the direct route through Seaborne Road.

12.02.68 Trolleybus operation resumed. Eastbound journeys revert to Seabourne Road between the crossroads with Parkwood Road and the junction with Beresford Road.

19.04.69 Last day of operation by trolleybus. Replaced by motorbus service 21.

Service 21A
08.04.36 Trolleybus service commenced Westbourne, Seamoor Road - Bournemouth Square - Lansdowne - Boscombe Gardens - Boscombe Arcade - Pokesdown Station - Fisherman's Walk - Southbourne - Tuckton Bridge - Christchurch, Church Street via Poole Road, Poole Hill, Bournemouth Square, Old Christchurch Road, Lansdowne, Christchurch Road, Seabourne Road, Southbourne Grove, Southbourne Road, Belle Vue Road, Foxholes Road, Belle Vue Road, Stour Road, Bargates, High Street and Church Street.

Between Bournemouth Square and the junction of Poole Hill with Norwich Road, eastbound journeys followed the west side of The Triangle and then Avenue Road, and westbound journeys followed Commercial Road.

Between the junction of Dean Park Crescent with Old Christchurch Road and Bournemouth Square westbound journeys followed Fir Vale Road, St. Peter's Road and Gervis Place.

Trolleybuses terminated at Christchurch by making a "three-point turn" from Church Street into the former coach yard of the Dolphin Hotel using a T-pole and connecting cables.

Service interval: 30 mins.

19.06.36 Purpose-built turntable in the former coach yard of the Dolphin Hotel, Church Street, Christchurch came into use. Henceforth journeys commenced and terminated at this turntable.

31.05.36 Last day of operation: service suspended.

01.10.36 Service reintroduced.

08.05.37 Alternate westbound journeys between the Lansdowne and Gervis Place along Bath Road and Westover Road instead of Old Christchurch Road, Fir Vale Road and St. Peter's Road.

Service interval: 30 mins.

24.02.40 Last day of operation: service suspended.

10.04.47 Service reintroduced Westbourne, Seamoor Road to Christchurch via original route.

Weekday morning peak-hours only.

Service interval: irregular; 4 journeys from Westbourne (none from Christchurch).

02.10.48 Last day of operation. No direct replacement.

Service 22
23.12.35 Trolleybus service commenced Bournemouth Square, Gervis Place - Lansdowne - Boscombe Gardens - Boscombe Arcade - Pokesdown Station - Fisherman's Walk - Southbourne Cross Roads, junction with St Catherine's Road and Southbourne Overcliff Drive via Old Christchurch Road, Lansdowne, Christchurch Road, Seabourne Road, Southbourne Grove, Southbourne Road and Belle Vue Road.

Between the junction of Dean Park Crescent with Old Christchurch Road and Bournemouth Square westbound journeys followed Fir Vale Road, St. Peter's Road and Gervis Place.

Service interval: 10 mins (including service 22A from 01.01.36).

08.04.36 Last day of operation: service suspended.

01.10.37 Service reintroduced with alternate westbound journeys diverted between the Lansdowne and Gervis Place along Bath Road and Westover Road instead of Old Christchurch Road, Fir Vale Road, St. Peter's Road.

Service interval: 10 mins (including service 22A).

By 06.38 *Summer service interval: 10 mins.*

08.11.43 Some unadvertised peak-hour journeys extended beyond Southbourne Cross Roads to Tuckton, Tuckton Road, junction with Belle Vue Road via Belle Vue Road, Foxholes Road and Belle Vue Road.

06.05.46 *Service interval: 10 mins.*

01.08.46 Most daytime (10am-5pm) journeys extended beyond Southbourne Cross Roads to Christchurch, junction of Stour Road with Barrack Road, via Tuckton Bridge and Stour Road.

Interworking with service 24 at Christchurch, junction of Stour Road with Barrack Road.

10.46 All journeys curtailed to Southbourne Cross Roads. Interworking with service 24 ceased.

By 07.47 All weekday daytime journeys extended beyond Southbourne Cross Roads to Tuckton, Tuckton Road, junction with Belle Vue Road; evening and Sunday journeys continued to terminate at Southbourne Cross Roads.

01.08.47 Most daytime (10am-5pm) journeys extended beyond Tuckton, Tuckton Road, junction with Belle Vue Road to Christchurch, junction of Stour Road with Barrack Road, via Tuckton Bridge and Stour Road.

Interworking with service 24 at Christchurch, junction of Stour Road with Barrack Road.

16.09.47 All journeys curtailed to Southbourne Cross Roads or Tuckton, Tuckton Road, junction with Belle Vue Road.

Interworking with service 24 ceased.

05.10.47 Most journeys extended from Tuckton, Tuckton Road, junction with Belle Vue Road to Tuckton, Carbery Avenue via Tuckton Road.

As the reversing triangle at Tuckton, Tuckton Road, had been removed, it is assumed that journeys advertised as terminating and starting at Tuckton actually continued to Carbery Avenue for turning purposes.

16.08.48 All journeys curtailed to Tuckton, Tuckton Road, junction with Belle Vue Road.

Interworking with service 22B.

Service interval: 10 mins.

04.10.48 Some weekday morning peak journeys extended to Westbourne, Seamoor Road, via Poole Hill and Poole Road.

01.08.49 *Service interval: 10 mins*

03.10.49 *Service interval 12 mins*

27.05.50 *Service interval 10 mins.*

02.10.50 *Service interval 12 mins all the year.*

15.10.51 *Service interval: 15 mins all the year.*

13.07.53 *Summer service (until 20.09.53) interval: 12 mins.*

19.09.53 Weekday morning peak extensions to Westbourne: last day of operation.

21.09.53 *Service interval: 15 mins.*

12.07.54 *Summer service (until 19.09.54) interval: 12 mins.*

11.07.55 *Summer service (until 18.09.55) interval: 12 mins.*
01.03.56 Interworking with service 23 commenced.

16.07.56 *Summer service (until 16.09.56) interval: 12 mins.*

17.09.56 *Service interval: 15 mins*

31.12.56 *Service interval: 20 mins.*

03.06.57 *Service interval: 15 mins.*

15.07.57 *Summer service interval: 12 mins.*

16.09.57 *Winter service interval: 20 mins.*

24.05.58 *Summer service interval: 15 mins.*

22.09.58 *Winter service interval 20 mins.*

13.07.59 *Summer service interval: 15 mins.*

14.09.59 *Service interval: 20 mins*

18.10.67 Trolleybuses temporarily replaced by motorbuses due to a burst gas main and road collapse at Fisherman's Walk, Seabourne Road.

Eastbound journeys to Christchurch temporarily diverted at Fisherman's Walk via Parkwood Road, Southbourne Road and Beresford Road, instead of Seabourne Road, returning to the normal route at Southbourne Grove. Westbound journeys were unaffected.

27.10.67 Trolleybus operation resumed.

Introduction of the Southbourne Traffic Management Scheme. Eastbound journeys to Christchurch continue to follow the previous diversion at Fisherman's Walk via Parkwood Road, Southbourne Road and Beresford Road, instead of Seabourne Road, returning to the normal route at Southbourne Grove.

11.02.68 Southbourne Traffic Management Scheme ceased. Motorbuses operated on this day only reverting to the direct route through Seaborne Road.

12.02.68 Trolleybus operation resumed. Eastbound journeys revert to Seabourne Road between the crossroads with Parkwood Road and the junction with Beresford Road.

19.04.69 Last day of operation by trolleybus. Replaced by motorbus service 22.

Service 22A

01.01.36 Trolleybus service commenced Westbourne, Seamoor Road - Bournemouth Square - Lansdowne - Boscombe Gardens - Boscombe Arcade - Pokesdown Station - Fisherman's Walk - Southbourne - Southbourne Cross Roads, junction with St Catherine's Road and Southbourne Overcliff Drive via Poole Road, Poole Hill, Bournemouth Square, Old Christchurch Road, Lansdowne, Christchurch Road, Seabourne Road, Southbourne Grove, Southbourne Road and Belle Vue Road.

Between Bournemouth Square and the junction of Poole Hill with Norwich Road, eastbound journeys followed the west side of The Triangle and then Avenue Road, and westbound journeys followed Commercial Road.

Between the junction of Dean Park Crescent with Old Christchurch Road and Bournemouth Square westbound journeys followed Fir Vale Road, St. Peter's Road and Gervis Place.

Service interval: 30 mins.

08.04.36 Last day of operation: service suspended.

01.10.37 Service reintroduced with alternate westbound journeys diverted between the Lansdowne and Gervis Place along Bath Road and Westover Road instead of Old Christchurch Road, Fir Vale Road, St. Peter's Road

Service interval: 30 mins.

24.02.40 Last day of operation: service suspended.

10.04.47 Service reintroduced and extended Westbourne, Seamoor Road - Bournemouth Square - Lansdowne - Boscombe Gardens - Boscombe Arcade - Pokesdown Station - Fisherman's Walk - Southbourne Cross Roads - Tuckton, Tuckton Road, junction with Belle Vue Road via Poole Road, Poole Hill, Bournemouth Square, Old Christchurch Road, Lansdowne, Christchurch Road, Seabourne Road, Southbourne Grove, Southbourne Road, Belle Vue Road, Foxholes Road and Belle Vue Road.

Service interval: 20 mins during the daytime (from 8 am). No evening service.

15.09.47 *Service interval: 15 mins.*

05.10.47 Some journeys extended from Tuckton, Tuckton Road, junction with Belle Vue Road to Carbery Avenue via Tuckton Road.

Service interval: 20 mins.

16.08.48 All journeys curtailed to Tuckton, Tuckton Road, junction with Belle Vue Road.

As the reversing triangle at Tuckton, Tuckton Road, had been removed, it is assumed that journeys advertised as terminating and starting at Tuckton actually continued to Carbery Avenue for turning purposes.

03.10.48 Last day of operation. No direct replacement.

Service 22B

16.08.48 Trolleybus service commenced Bournemouth Square, Gervis Place - Lansdowne - Boscombe Gardens - Boscombe Arcade - Pokesdown Station - Fisherman's Walk - Tuckton, Tuckton Road, junction with Belle Vue Road via Old Christchurch Road, Lansdowne, Christchurch Road, Seabourne Road, Beresford Road, Beaufort Road, Cranleigh Road and Tuckton Road.

Between the Lansdowne and Gervis Place westbound journeys to Bournemouth Square operated alternately by way of either Old Christchurch Road, Fir Vale Road and St. Peter's Road, or via Bath Road and Westover Road.

Interworking with service 22 at Tuckton, Tuckton Road, junction with Belle Vue Road.

Service interval: 10 mins.

04.10.48 Main service extended from Bournemouth Square to Westbourne, Seamoor Road via Poole Hill and Poole Road.

Interworking with service 22 at Tuckton, Tuckton Road, junction with Belle Vue Road.

Service interval: 20 mins between Westbourne and Tuckton, 10 mins between Fisherman's Walk and Tuckton.

Travelling west in Tuckton Road, some 50yd from the junction with Belle Vue Road, on 14 August 1954 is Sunbeam MS2 no 140 (BEL825) on a 22B working. The symbol of Mercury's head on the signs outside Elford's garage is that of National Benzole, a petroleum mixture. The brand name was changed to simply National from 1959 and phased out completely in the 1990s.
Malcolm Pearce (G.O.P. Pearce)

The Fisherman's Walk - Tuckton service was enhanced to a 10-min service interval in both directions by a "shuttle service" every 20 mins between these two points.

Between Bournemouth Square and the junction of Poole Hill with Norwich Road, eastbound journeys followed the west side of The Triangle and then Avenue Road, and westbound journeys followed Commercial Road.

Fisherman's Walk terminal loop: from the junction of Beresford Road with Beaufort Road, shuttle journeys followed Southbourne Road, Parkwood Road, Seabourne Road and Beresford Road in an anti-clockwise direction.

By 08.49 *Service interval: 20 mins between Westbourne and Tuckton, 10 mins between Bournemouth Square and Tuckton.*

03.10.49 *Service interval: 24 mins between Westbourne and Tuckton, 12 mins between Fisherman's Walk and Tuckton.*

The Fisherman's Walk - Tuckton service was enhanced to a 12-min service interval in both directions by a "shuttle service" every 24 mins between these two points.

27.05.50 Main service curtailed to Bournemouth Square - Tuckton, Tuckton Road, junction with Belle Vue Road.

Service interval: 20 mins.

The Fisherman's Walk - Tuckton service was enhanced to a 10-min service interval in both directions by a "shuttle service" every 20 mins between these two points.

02.10.50 *Service interval: 24 mins between Bournemouth Square and Tuckton, 12 mins between Fisherman's Walk and Tuckton.*

The Fisherman's Walk - Tuckton service was enhanced to a 12-min service interval in both directions by a "shuttle service" every 24 mins between these two points.

18.06.51 Main service extended from Bournemouth Square to Westbourne, Seamoor Road via Poole Hill and Poole Road.

Interworking with service 22 at Tuckton, Tuckton Road, junction with Belle Vue Road.

Service interval: 24 mins between Bournemouth Square and Tuckton, 12 mins between Fisherman's Walk and Tuckton.

The Fisherman's Walk - Tuckton service was enhanced to a 12-min service interval in both directions by a

"shuttle service" every 24 mins between these two points.

14.10.51 Last day of service to Westbourne, Seamoor Road.

15.10.51 Main service curtailed to Bournemouth Square - Tuckton, Tuckton Road, junction with Belle Vue Road.

Interworking with service 22 at Tuckton, Tuckton Road, junction with Belle Vue Road.

Service interval: 30 mins between Bournemouth Square and Tuckton, 15 mins between Fisherman's Walk and Tuckton.

The Fisherman's Walk - Tuckton service was enhanced to a 15-min service interval in both directions by a "shuttle service" every 30 mins between these two points.

13.07.53 All journeys operate Bournemouth Square, Gervis Place - Tuckton, Tuckton Road, junction with Belle Vue Road.

Interworking with service 22 at Tuckton, Tuckton Road, junction with Belle Vue Road.

Summer service (until 20.09.53) interval: 12 mins.

21.09.53 *Service interval: 15 mins.*

12.07.54 *Summer service (until 19.09.54) interval: 12 mins*

20.09.54 *Service interval: 15 mins.*

11.07.55 *Summer service (until 18.09.55) interval: 12 mins*

19.09.54 *Service interval: 15 mins.*

29.02.56 Last day of operation. Service renumbered 23 (iii).

Service 23 (i)
21.11.35 Trolleybus service commenced Bournemouth Square, Gervis Place - Lansdowne - Boscombe Gardens - Boscombe Arcade - Pokesdown Station - Fisherman's Walk, Wentworth Avenue via Old Christchurch Road, Lansdowne, Christchurch Road and Seabourne Road.

Between the junction of Dean Park Crescent with Old Christchurch Road and Bournemouth Square westbound journeys followed Fir Vale Road, St. Peter's Road and Gervis Place.

Service interval: 5 mins (including service 23A from 01.01.36).

23.12.35 *Service interval: 10 mins.*

01.07.36 *Service interval: peak hours only.*

30.09.36 Last day of peak hour only service.

Passing the bottom of Richmond Hill is BUT9641T no. 252 (KLJ352) on its way to Tuckton, Tuckton Road. This photograph shows the auto frog for accessing the hill located on the roundabout itself (above the Standard Vanguard estate following no. 252) which was replaced by a new overhead wiring arrangement in May 1960.

Photo courtesy of D.Ball, for the family of the late J.S. King

01.10.36   *Service interval: 10 mins (including service 23A).*

08.05.37   Alternate westbound journeys to Bournemouth Square diverted between the Lansdowne and Gervis Place along Bath Road and Westover Road instead of Old Christchurch Road, Fir Vale Road, St. Peter's Road.

30.09.37   Last day of operation: service suspended.

06.05.46   Service reintroduced at peak-hours only Westbourne, Seamoor Road or Bournemouth Square, Gervis Place-Fisherman's Walk, Wentworth Avenue via original route.

19.09.53   All journeys (weekday morning peak-hour only) curtailed to Bournemouth Square, Gervis Place.

29.02.56   Service renumbered 37.

Service 23 (ii)

07.04.50   Seasonal supplementary trolleybus service commenced Bournemouth Pier - Lansdowne - Boscombe Gardens - Boscombe Arcade - Pokesdown Station - Fisherman's Walk, Wentworth Avenue via Bath Road, Lansdowne, Christchurch Road and Seabourne Road

Service interval: 20 mins.

11.04.50   Last day of operation: seasonal supplementary service, i.e. Good Friday-Easter Tuesday inclusive.

27.05.50   Seasonal supplementary service reinstated for the summer.

Service interval: 20 mins.

01.10.50   Last day of operation; seasonal supplementary service suspended.

23.03.51   Seasonal supplementary service reinstated for Easter.

Between Bournemouth Pier and the Lansdowne eastbound journeys followed Exeter Road, Bournemouth Square and Old Christchurch Road; westbound journeys followed Bath Road.

27.03.51   Last day of operation; seasonal supplementary service suspended, i.e. Good Friday-Easter Tuesday inclusive.

12.05.51   Seasonal supplementary service reinstated for Whitsun.

15.05.51   Last day of operation; seasonal supplementary service suspended.

04.06.51   Seasonal supplementary service reinstated for the summer.

30.09.51   Last day of operation; seasonal supplementary service suspended.

11.04.52   Seasonal supplementary service reinstated for Easter.

14.04.52 Last day of operation; seasonal supplementary service suspended, i.e. Good Friday-Easter Monday inclusive.

31.05.52 Seasonal supplementary service reinstated for the summer.

28.09.52 Last day of operation; seasonal supplementary service suspended.

03.04.53 Seasonal supplementary service reinstated for Easter.

06.04.53 Last day of operation; seasonal supplementary service suspended, i.e. Good Friday-Easter Monday inclusive.

23.05.53 Seasonal supplementary service reinstated for the summer.

20.09.53 Last day of operation; seasonal supplementary service suspended.

16.04.54 Service renumbered 35 (i).

Service 23 (iii)

01.03.56 Redesignated trolleybus service (formerly trolleybus service 22B) commenced Bournemouth Square, Gervis Place - Lansdowne - Boscombe Gardens - Boscombe Arcade - Pokesdown Station - Fisherman's Walk - Tuckton, Tuckton Road, junction with Belle Vue Road via Old Christchurch Road, Lansdowne, Christchurch Road, Seabourne Road, Beresford Road, Beaufort Road, Cranleigh Road and Tuckton Road.
Between the Lansdowne and Gervis Place westbound journeys to Bournemouth Square operated alternately by way of either Old Christchurch Road, Fir Vale Road and St. Peter's Road, or via Bath Road and Westover Road.

Interworking with service 22 at Tuckton, Tuckton Road, junction with Belle Vue Road.

Service interval: 15 mins.

16.07.56 *Summer service (until 16.09.56) interval: 12 mins.*

17.09.56 *Service interval: 15 mins.*

31.12.56 *Service interval: 20 mins.*

03.06.57 *Service interval: 15 mins.*

15.07.57 *Summer service interval: 12 mins.*

14.09.57 *Service interval: 20 mins.*

24.05.58 *Summer service interval: 15 mins.*

22.09.58 *Winter service interval: 20 mins.*

13.07.59 *Summer service interval: 15 mins.*

Having passed beneath the auto frog giving access to Beresford Road, Sunbeam MS2 no. 214 (ALJ979) loads at the service 23 stop at the south end of Seabourne Road, Fisherman's Walk, on its way to Tuckton by way of Beaufort Road and Cranleigh Road on 13 August 1963.
Malcolm Pearce (G.O.P. Pearce)

14.09.59   *Winter service interval: 20 mins.*

25.10.64   Sunday morning short-workings between Fisherman's Walk and Tuckton only ceased, all journeys being extended to/from Bournemouth Square.

18.10.67   Trolleybuses temporarily replaced by motorbuses due to a burst gas main and road collapse at Fisherman's Walk, Seabourne Road.

   Eastbound journeys to Tuckton, Tuckton Road, junction with Belle Vue Road temporarily diverted at Fisherman's Walk via Parkwood Road and Southbourne Road, instead of Seabourne Road and Beresford Road, returning to the normal route at the junction of Beresford Road with Beaufort Road. Westbound journeys were unaffected.

27.10.67   Trolleybus operation resumed.

   Introduction of the Southbourne Traffic Management Scheme. Eastbound journeys to Tuckton, Tuckton Road, junction with Belle Vue Road continue to follow the previous diversion at Fisherman's Walk via Parkwood Road and Southbourne Road, instead of Seabourne Road and Beresford Road, returning to the normal route at the junction of Beresford Road with Beaufort Road.

11.02.68   Southbourne Traffic Management Scheme ceased. Motorbuses operated on this day only reverting to the direct route through Seabourne Road and Beresford Road.

12.02.68   Trolleybus operation resumed. Eastbound journeys revert to Seabourne Road and Beresford Road between the crossroads with Parkwood Road and the junction of Beresford Road with Beresford Road.

19.04.69   Last day of operation by trolleybus. Replaced by motorbus service 23.

Service 23A

01.01.36   Trolleybus service commenced Westbourne, Seamoor Road - Bournemouth Square - Lansdowne - Boscombe Gardens - Boscombe Arcade - Pokesdown Station - Fisherman's Walk, Wentworth Avenue via Poole Road, Poole Hill, Old Christchurch Road, Lansdowne, Christchurch Road and Seabourne Road.

   Between Bournemouth Square and the junction of Poole Hill with Norwich Road, eastbound journeys followed the west side of The Triangle and then Avenue Road, and westbound journeys followed Commercial Road.

   Between the junction of Dean Park Crescent with Old Christchurch Road and Bournemouth Square westbound journeys followed Fir Vale Road, St. Peter's Road and Gervis Place

   Service interval: 30 mins (shown in the service 23 timetable).

01.06.36   *Summer (until 29.09.36) service interval: 15 mins.*

30.09.36   *Service interval: 30 mins.*

08.05.37   Alternate westbound journeys to Bournemouth Square diverted between the Lansdowne and Gervis Place along Bath Road and Westover Road instead of Old Christchurch Road, Fir Vale Road, St. Peter's Road.

30.09.37   Last day of operation. No direct replacement.

Service 24 (i)

25.03.35   Trolleybus service commenced Westbourne, Seamoor Road - West Station - Bournemouth Square - Lansdowne - Boscombe Gardens - Boscombe Arcade - Pokesdown Station - Iford Bridge via Poole Road, Poole Hill, Bournemouth Square, Old Christchurch Road, Lansdowne and Christchurch Road.

   Between Bournemouth Square and the junction of Poole Hill with Norwich Road, eastbound journeys followed the west side of The Triangle and then Avenue Road, and westbound journeys followed Commercial Road.

   Between the junction of Dean Park Crescent with Old Christchurch Road and Bournemouth Square westbound journeys followed Fir Vale Road, St. Peter's Road and Gervis Place.

   Service interval: 8 mins.

01.01.36   Curtailed to Bournemouth Square, Gervis Place (replaced west thereof by service 24A).

   Service interval: 7-8 mins.

01.07.36   Service curtailed to operate morning peaks and all evening only (service 24A timetable enhanced at other times of the day).

01.10.36   Service reinstated all-day daily.

08.05.37   Alternate westbound journeys to Bournemouth Square diverted between the Lansdowne and Gervis Place along Bath Road and Westover Road instead of Old Christchurch Road, Fir Vale Road, St. Peter's Road

   Service interval: 15 mins.

01.11.37   *Service interval: 8 mins.*

07.08.44   Extended Iford Bridge - Jumpers Corner via Christchurch Road, Barrack Road, Oak Avenue and Stourvale Avenue.

Jumpers terminal loop: from the junction of Oak Avenue with Christchurch Road, all journeys followed Oak Avenue, Stourvale Avenue (terminal point) and The Grove to its junction with Barrack Road.

06.05.46 *Service interval: every few minutes.*

01.08.46 Alternate journeys extended beyond Jumpers Corner to Christchurch, junction of Stour Road with Barrack Road, via Barrack Road.

Interworking with service 22 at Christchurch, junction of Stour Road with Barrack Road

Service interval: 5 mins to/from Jumpers Corner, 10 mins to/from Christchurch, junction of Stour Road with Barrack Road.

10.46 All journeys curtailed to Jumpers Corner.

Interworking with service 22 ceased.

01.08.47 Alternate journeys extended beyond Jumpers Corner to Christchurch, junction of Stour Road with Barrack Road, via Barrack Road.

Interworking with service 22 at Christchurch, junction of Stour Road with Barrack Road.

Service interval: 5 mins to/from Jumpers Corner, 10 mins to/from Christchurch, junction of Stour Road with Barrack Road.

16.09.47 All journeys curtailed to Jumpers Corner.

Interworking with service 22 ceased.

Service interval: 5 mins

21.09.53 *Service interval: 20 mins summer, 24 mins winter.*

17.09.56 *Service interval: 4 journeys per hour throughout the year.*

22.09.58 Interworking with service 32 (ii) at Jumpers Corner (this interworking at Jumpers continued until 30 September 1963 regardless of whether service 32 was terminating at Iford or Jumpers Corner).

29.09.63 Interworking with service 32 (ii) ceased.

11.04.65 *Winter Sunday afternoon service interval reduced to 30 mins (2.20pm-6.50pm).*

07.06.65 *Service interval: 3 journeys per hour throughout the year.*

13.09.65 Reduced to weekday morning peak hours and Sunday afternoon only operation.

28.02.66 Reduced to weekday morning peak hours only operation.

On 20 June 1952, Sunbeam MS2 no. 117 (ALJ991) awaits departure time at Iford Bridge turning circle. This was the final summer that seasonal supplementary service 24 (ii) between Bournemouth Pier and Iford Bridge operated. Note former tramcar no. 1 still in use as a passenger waiting room in the background.   **A.D. Packer**

13.06.66 Increased to weekday morning peak hours and Sunday morning (10am-1pm) only operation.

12.09.66 Reduced to weekday morning peak hours only operation.

11.06.67 Increased to weekday morning peak hours and Sunday morning (10am-1pm) only operation.

04.09.67 Reduced to weekday morning peak hours only operation.

18.10.67 Trolleybuses temporarily replaced by motorbuses due to a burst gas main and road collapse at Fisherman's Walk, Seabourne Road.

27.10.67 Trolleybus operation resumed.

02.06.68 Increased to weekday morning peak hours and Sunday morning (10am-1pm) only operation.

09.09.68 Reduced to weekday morning peak hours only operation.

19.04.69 Last day of operation by trolleybus. Replaced by motorbus service 24.

Service 24 (ii)

07.04.50 Seasonal supplementary service commenced for Easter, Bournemouth Pier - Lansdowne - Boscombe Gardens - Boscombe - Pokesdown - Iford Bridge via Bath Road, Lansdowne and Christchurch Road.

11.04.50 Last day of operation; seasonal supplementary service suspended, i.e. Good Friday - Easter Tuesday inclusive.

27.05.50 Seasonal supplementary service reinstated for the summer.

Service interval: 20 mins.

01.10.50 Last day of operation; seasonal supplementary service suspended.

23.03.51 Seasonal supplementary service reinstated for Easter.

Between Bournemouth Pier and the Lansdowne eastbound journeys followed Exeter Road, Bournemouth Square and Old Christchurch Road; westbound journeys followed Bath Road.

27.03.51 Last day of operation; seasonal supplementary service suspended, i.e. Good Friday - Easter Tuesday inclusive.

12.05.51 Seasonal supplementary service reinstated for Whitsun.

15.05.51 Last day of operation; seasonal supplementary service suspended.

04.06.51 Seasonal supplementary service reinstated for the summer.

30.09.51 Last day of operation; seasonal supplementary service suspended.

11.04.52 Seasonal supplementary service reinstated for Easter.

14.04.52 Last day of operation; seasonal supplementary service suspended, i.e. Good Friday - Easter Monday inclusive.

31.05.52 Seasonal supplementary service reinstated for the summer.

28.09.52 Last day of operation. No direct replacement.

Service 24A

01.01.36 Trolleybus service commenced Westbourne, Seamoor Road - Bournemouth Square - Lansdowne - Boscombe Gardens - Boscombe Arcade - Pokesdown Station - Iford Bridge via Poole Road, Poole Hill, Bournemouth Square, Old Christchurch Road, Lansdowne, and Christchurch Road.

Between Bournemouth Square and the junction of Poole Hill with Norwich Road, eastbound journeys followed the west side of The Triangle and then Avenue Road, and westbound journeys followed Commercial Road.

Between the junction of Dean Park Crescent with Old Christchurch Road and Bournemouth Square westbound journeys followed Fir Vale Road, St. Peter's Road and Gervis Place.

Service interval: 15 mins (8 mins 01.07.36-30.09.36)

08.05.37 Alternate westbound journeys to Westbourne diverted between the Lansdowne and Gervis Place along Bath Road and Westover Road instead of Old Christchurch Road, Fir Vale Road, St. Peter's Road.

31.10.37 Last day of operation. No direct replacement.

Service 25 (i)

13.05.33 Experimental (unnumbered) trolleybus service commenced Bournemouth Square - West Station - Westbourne, Seamoor Road via Poole Hill and Poole Road.

Between Bournemouth Square and the junction of Poole Hill with Norwich Road, eastbound journeys followed the west side of The Triangle and then Avenue Road, and westbound journeys followed Commercial Road.

Service interval: every few minutes.

27.02.34 Service number 25 allocated for use with trial of a new design of ticket machine.

22.06.34 Extended eastwards Bournemouth Square to Boscombe, Portman Road thus operating Westbourne, Seamoor Road - West Station - Bournemouth Square - Lansdowne - Central Station - Springbourne - Queen's Park Corner - Boscombe Station - Boscombe, Portman Road via Poole Road, Poole Hill, Old Christchurch Road, Lansdowne, Holdenhurst Road, Ashley Road and Christchurch Road.

Between the junction of Dean Park Crescent with Old Christchurch Road and Bournemouth Square westbound journeys followed Fir Vale Road, St. Peter's Road and Gervis Place.

Boscombe terminal loop: from the junction of Ashley Road with Gladstone Road, all journeys followed Ashley Road, Christchurch Road, Portman Road and Gladstone Road.

Service interval: 5 mins.

20.10.34 Football special journeys commenced between Westbourne and Queen's Park Golf Pavilion, Holdenhurst Road instead of Boscombe, Portman Road, branching from the main service at Queen's Park Corner.

01.03.36 Curtailed to operate between Bournemouth Square and Boscombe, Portman Road or Queen's Park Golf Pavilion, Holdenhurst Road (that part of the route between Westbourne and Bournemouth Square being replaced by service 25A)

Service interval: Square-Boscombe: 5 mins.

Service interval: Square-Queen's Park: football specials.

08.05.37 Alternate westbound journeys to Bournemouth Square diverted between the Lansdowne and Gervis Place along Bath Road and Westover Road instead of Old Christchurch Road, Fir Vale Road, St. Peter's Road.

31.10.37 Last day of operation. Replaced by enhanced service 25A.

Service 25 (ii)

07.04.50 Seasonal supplementary service commenced for Easter, Bournemouth Pier - Lansdowne - Central Station - Springbourne - Queen's Park Corner - Queen's Park Golf Pavilion, Holdenhurst Road via Bath Road and Holdenhurst Road.

Service interval: 20 mins.

11.04.50 Last day of operation; seasonal supplementary service, i.e. Good Friday-Easter Tuesday inclusive.

27.05.50 Seasonal supplementary service reinstated for the summer.

01.10.50 Last day of operation. No direct replacement.

Service 25 (iii)

02.07.51 Revised trolleybus service commenced Westbourne, Seamoor Road - West Station - Bournemouth Square - Lansdowne - Central Station - Springbourne - Queen's Park Corner - Queen's Park Golf Pavilion, Holdenhurst Road via Poole Road, Poole Hill, Old Christchurch Road, Lansdowne and Holdenhurst Road.

Between Bournemouth Square and the junction of Poole Hill with Norwich Road, eastbound journeys followed the west side of The Triangle and then Avenue Road, and westbound journeys followed Commercial Road.

Between the Lansdowne and Gervis Place westbound journeys to Bournemouth Square operated alternately by way of either Old Christchurch Road, Fir Vale Road and St. Peter's Road, or via Bath Road and Westover Road.

Service interval: 30 mins.

01.03.56 Services 25 and 25A combined for all journeys Westbourne, Seamoor Road - West Station - Bournemouth Square - Lansdowne - Central Station - Springbourne - Queen's Park Corner - Boscombe Station - Boscombe, Portman Road, or Westbourne, Seamoor Road - Queen's Park Golf Pavilion, Holdenhurst Road via Poole Road, Poole Hill, Old Christchurch Road, Lansdowne, Holdenhurst Road and Ashley Road (for journeys terminating at Boscombe).

Service interval: Westbourne-Boscombe: every few minutes.

Service interval: Westbourne-Queen's Park: 30 mins.

31.12.56 *Service interval: Westbourne-Boscombe: every 6 mins.*

Service interval: Westbourne-Queen's Park: 5 or 6 journeys daily.

15.07.57 *Service interval: Westbourne-Boscombe: every 5 mins.*

Service interval: Westbourne-Queen's Park: 5 or 6 journeys daily.

16.09.57 *Service interval: Westbourne-Boscombe: winter 7 mins, summer 5 mins.*

Service interval: Westbourne-Queen's Park: 5 or 6 journeys daily.

24.05.58 *Service interval: Westbourne-Boscombe: 6 mins.*

Service interval: Westbourne-Queen's Park: 5 or 6 journeys daily.

397

14.07.58   Service interval: Westbourne-Boscombe: 5 mins.

Service interval: Westbourne-Queen's Park: 5 or 6 journeys daily.

22.09.58   Service interval: Westbourne-Boscombe: winter 7 mins.

Service interval: Westbourne-Queen's Park: 5 or 6 journeys daily.

13.07.59   Service interval: Westbourne-Boscombe: 5 mins.

Service interval: Westbourne-Queen's Park: 5 or 6 journeys daily.

16.05.59   Service interval: Westbourne-Boscombe: 6 mins.

Service interval: Westbourne-Queen's Park: 5 or 6 journeys daily.

14.09.59   Service interval: Westbourne-Boscombe: winter 8 mins.

Service interval: Westbourne-Queen's Park: 5 or 6 journeys daily.

04.06.60   Service interval: Westbourne-Boscombe: 7mins, all year.

Service interval: Westbourne-Queen's Park: 5 or 6 journeys daily.

28.09.63   Last day of operation: Westbourne, Seamoor Road-Queen's Park Golf Pavilion, Holdenhurst Road service withdrawn (football specials to/from Queen's Park Golf Pavilion continue to operate).

05.04.65   Additional journeys introduced Triangle-Queen's Park Golf Pavilion, Holdenhurst Road weekdays, morning peaks and afternoons only.

Service interval: Westbourne-Boscombe: 12 mins (15 mins evenings and Sundays).

Service interval: Triangle-Queen's Park: 12 mins.

08.05.65   Last day of operation: additional journeys Triangle-Queen's Park Golf Pavilion, Holdenhurst Road withdrawn.

10.05.65   Service interval: Westbourne-Boscombe: 7-8 mins.

12.09.65   Last day of operation by trolleybus. Replaced by motorbus service 25.

Service 25A

01.03.36   Trolleybus service commenced Westbourne, Seamoor Road - West Station - Bournemouth Square - Lansdowne - Central Station - Springbourne - Boscombe Station - Boscombe, Portman Road or Queen's Park Golf Pavilion, Holdenhurst Road (football specials only) via Poole Road, Poole Hill, Bournemouth Square, Old Christchurch Road, Lansdowne, Holdenhurst Road and Ashley Road.

Between Bournemouth Square and the junction of Poole Hill with Norwich Road, eastbound journeys followed the west side of The Triangle and then Avenue Road, and westbound journeys followed Commercial Road.

Between the junction of Dean Park Crescent with Old Christchurch Road and Bournemouth Square westbound journeys followed Fir Vale Road, St. Peter's Road and Gervis Place.

Boscombe terminal loop: from the junction of Ashley Road with Gladstone Road, all journeys followed Ashley Road, Christchurch Road, Portman Road and Gladstone Road.

Service interval: Westbourne-Boscombe: 15 mins.

Service interval: Westbourne-Queen's Park: football specials.

08.05.37   Alternate westbound journeys to Bournemouth Square diverted between the Lansdowne and Gervis Place along Bath Road and Westover Road instead of Old Christchurch Road, Fir Vale Road, St Peter's Road.

01.11.37   Service interval: Westbourne-Boscombe: 5 mins.

Service interval: Westbourne-Queen's Park: football specials.

06.38   Alternate journeys from Westbourne, Seamoor Road diverted to Queen's Park Golf Pavilion, Holdenhurst Road, and vice versa.

28.07.38   Seasonal supplementary service commenced for the summer Bournemouth Square - Queen's Park Golf Pavilion, Holdenhurst Road, Old Christchurch Road, Lansdowne and Holdenhurst Road.

Service interval: Westbourne-Boscombe: 5 mins (including service 25B).

Service interval: Square-Queen's Park: 10 mins (summer only).

Service interval: Westbourne-Queen's Park: hourly (winter only).

30.09.38   Seasonal supplementary service suspended.

07.39   Seasonal supplementary service commenced.

30.09.39   Seasonal supplementary service suspended.

25.02.40   All journeys to/from Queen's Park Golf Pavilion, Holdenhurst Road, withdrawn.

Service interval: Westbourne-Boscombe: every few minutes.

01.11.48 Trolleybus service Westbourne, Seamoor Road-Queen's Park Golf Pavilion, Holdenhurst Road reintroduced.

Service interval: Westbourne-Boscombe: every few minutes.

Service interval: Westbourne-Queen's Park: 30 mins.

01.08.49 *Service interval: Westbourne-Boscombe: every 5 mins.*

Service interval: Westbourne-Queen's Park: 30 mins.

01.07.51 Service 25A journeys Westbourne, Seamoor Road-Queen's Park Golf Pavilion, Holdenhurst Road renumbered 25 (iii).

29.02.56 Last day of operation. Service 25A journeys Westbourne, Seamoor Road-Boscombe, Portman Road renumbered 25 (iii) and combined with Westbourne, Seamoor Road-Queen's Park Golf Pavilion, Holdenhurst Road service 25 (iii).

Service 25B

28.07.38 Trolleybus service commenced Westbourne, Seamoor Road - West Station - Bournemouth Square - Lansdowne - Central Station - Springbourne - Boscombe Station - Boscombe - Pokesdown Station - Fisherman's Walk, Wentworth Avenue via Poole Road, Poole Hill, Bournemouth Square, Old Christchurch Road, Lansdowne, Holdenhurst Road, Ashley Road, Christchurch Road and Seabourne Road.

Between Bournemouth Square and the junction of Poole Hill with Norwich Road, eastbound journeys followed the west side of The Triangle and then Avenue Road, and westbound journeys followed Commercial Road.

Between the junction of Dean Park Crescent with Old Christchurch Road and Bournemouth Square westbound journeys followed Fir Vale Road, St. Peter's Road and Gervis Place.

Between the junction of Ashley Road with Gladstone Road and the junction of Portman Road with Christchurch Road, Boscombe, eastbound journeys followed Ashley Road and Christchurch Road, and westbound journeys followed Portman Road and Gladstone Road.

Service interval: 15 mins (shown in timetables as service 25A).

08.05.37 Alternate westbound journeys to Bournemouth Square diverted between the Lansdowne and Gervis Place along Bath Road and Westover Road instead of Old Christchurch Road, Fir Vale Road, St. Peter's Road.

24.02.40 Last day of operation. No direct replacement.

Service 26

07.06.35 Trolleybus service commenced Bournemouth Square - Cemetery Junction - Winton - Moordown Depot via Richmond Hill and Wimborne Road.

Service interval: summer 5 mins, winter 6 mins.

28.06.35 Moordown terminus extended to Wimborne Road, Redhill Crescent.

15.04.37 Alternate journeys extended to Castle Lane West, Lawford Road via Wimborne Road.

Service interval: 6 mins all year (12 mins to/from Castle Lane West, Lawford Road).

Between the junction of Wimborne Road with Lawford Road and Castle Lane West, northbound journeys followed Lawford Road and southbound journeys followed Castle Lane West and Wimborne Road.

19.10.38 Curtailed to Moordown, Wimborne Road, Redhill Crescent except at weekday morning peak hours.

01.10.39 Weekday morning peak hour journeys curtailed to Moordown, Wimborne Road, Redhill Crescent.

Service interval: 7-8 mins (including service 26A).

06.05.46 *Service interval: every few minutes (including service 26A).*

30.03.47 Town Centre terminus extended to Triangle.

Between Bournemouth Square and the Triangle, eastbound journeys followed Avenue Road, and westbound journeys followed Commercial Road.

14.08.50 Curtailed to Moordown Depot, turning in the depot premises.

26.07.53 Service extended to Moordown, Wimborne Road, junction with Redhill Crescent, due to closure of Moordown Depot.

12.10.53 Extended to Castle Lane West, Lawford Road.

Between the junction of Wimborne Road with Lawford Road and Castle Lane West, northbound journeys followed Lawford Road and southbound journeys followed Castle Lane West and Wimborne Road.

Service interval: two journeys per hour (every 10 mins with services 26A and 33).

26.03.56 *Service interval: three journeys per hour (every 15 mins with service 33).*

22.07.56 *Service interval: three journeys per hour (every 20 mins with service 27).*

399

17.09.56   *Service interval: three journeys per hour (every 15 mins with service 33).*

22.09.58   *Service interval: 15 mins.*

30.09.63   *Service interval: 30 mins (every 15 mins with service 27).*

05.04.65   Service reduced to Sunday mornings and weekday peak hours only.

05.03.66   Last day of trolleybus operation. No direct replacement.

Service 26A (i)

19.10.38   Trolleybus service commenced Bournemouth Square - Cemetery Junction - Winton - Moordown - Castle Lane West - Broadway Hotel - Five Ways - Cemetery Junction - Bournemouth Square via Richmond Hill, Wimborne Road, Lawford Road, Castle Lane West, Charminster Road, Wimborne Road and Richmond Hill.

         Unidirectional circular service (clockwise) worked in conjunction with service 28A.

         Service interval: 30 mins.

05.05.46   Unidirectional circular service withdrawn. Replaced by service 26A (ii) and 28A (ii).

Service 26A (ii)

06.05.46   Revised trolleybus service commenced Bournemouth Square - Cemetery Junction - Winton - Moordown - Castle Lane West, junction with West Way via Richmond Hill, Wimborne Road, Lawford Road and Castle Lane West.

         Between the junction of Wimborne Road with Lawford Road and Castle Lane West, northbound journeys followed Lawford Road and southbound journeys followed Castle Lane West and Wimborne Road.

         Interworking with service 28A at Castle Lane West, junction with West Way.

         Service interval: 15 mins.

30.03.47   Town Centre terminus extended to Triangle. Between Bournemouth Square and the Triangle, eastbound journeys followed Avenue Road, and westbound journeys followed Commercial Road

         Service interval: 15 mins.

15.10.51   *Service interval: 20 mins.*

29.02.56   Last day of operation. Service 26A (ii) renumbered 27 (iii).

The driver of no. 100 (ALJ974) on a service 27 (i) journey to Castle Lane West, junction with Lawford Road, chats briefly with his counterpart in no. 167 prior to departure from the Lansdowne stop at the west end of Holdenhurst Road in the early 1950s.
Omnibus Society (R.T. Wilson)

Service 27 (i)

28.06.35 Trolleybus service commenced Bournemouth Square, Gervis Place - Lansdowne - Central Station - Cemetery Junction - Winton - Moordown, Wimborne Road, Redhill Crescent via Old Christchurch Road, Lansdowne, Holdenhurst Road, St. Paul's Road, Lansdowne Road and Wimborne Road.

Between the junction of Dean Park Crescent with Old Christchurch Road and Bournemouth Square westbound journeys followed Fir Vale Road, St. Peter's Road and Gervis Place.

Service interval: summer 6 mins, winter 8 mins.

11.03.37 Extended to Castle Lane West, junction with Lawford Road via Wimborne Road.

Between the junction of Wimborne Road with Lawford Road and Castle Lane West, northbound journeys followed Lawford Road and southbound journeys followed Castle Lane West and Wimborne Road.

15.04.37 Curtailed to Moordown, Wimborne Road, Redhill Crescent.

Service interval: 8 mins all year.

08.05.37 Alternate southbound journeys to Bournemouth Square diverted between the Lansdowne and Gervis Place along Bath Road and Westover Road instead of Old Christchurch Road, Fir Vale Road, St. Peter's Road.

06.05.46 Extended to Castle Lane West, junction with Lawford Road via Wimborne Road.

Service interval: every few minutes.

08.48 *Service interval: every few minutes.*

By 03.49 *Service interval: every 10 mins.*

30.03.53 Weekday daytime service curtailed to Moordown Depot extended during peak hours to Castle Lane West, junction with Lawford Road. Evening service curtailed to Lansdowne - Moordown Depot only except in peak summer period.

Service interval: 15 mins weekday daytime, 10 mins peak hours; 30 mins evenings, 15 mins summer peak evenings. 30 mins, winter evenings and Sunday mornings between Lansdowne and Moordown Depot.

26.07.53 Journeys to/from Moordown Depot extended to Moordown, Wimborne Road, junction with Redhill Crescent, in connection with the closure of Moordown Depot.

29.02.56 Last day of operation. Service 27 (i) renumbered 34.

Service 27 (ii)

23.03.51 Seasonal supplementary service commenced for Easter, Bournemouth Pier - Lansdowne - Central Station - Cemetery Junction - Winton - Moordown Depot via Bath Road, Lansdowne, Holdenhurst Road, St. Paul's Road, Lansdowne Road and Wimborne Road.

27.03.51 Last day of operation; seasonal supplementary service suspended, i.e. Good Friday-Easter Tuesday inclusive.

12.05.51 Seasonal supplementary service reinstated for Whitsun.

15.05.51 Last day of operation; seasonal supplementary service suspended.

04.06.51 Seasonal supplementary service reinstated for the summer.

30.09.51 Last day of operation. No direct replacement.

Service 27 (iii)

01.03.56 Revised trolleybus service (formerly service 26A (ii)) commenced Triangle - Bournemouth Square - Cemetery Junction - Winton - Moordown - Castle Lane West, junction with West Way, via Richmond Hill, Wimborne Road and Castle Lane West.

Between the junction of Wimborne Road with Lawford Road and Castle Lane West, northbound journeys followed Lawford Road and southbound journeys followed Castle Lane West and Wimborne Road.

Between Bournemouth Square and the Triangle, eastbound journeys followed Avenue Road, and westbound journeys followed Commercial Road.

Interworking with service 29 at Castle Lane West, junction with West Way.

Service interval: 20 mins

26.03.56 Last day of operation; service suspended.

22.07.56 Service reintroduced Triangle-Castle Lane West, junction with West Way, via previous route.

Interworking with service 29 at Castle Lane West, junction with West Way.

Service interval: 20 mins

16.09.56 Last day of operation; service suspended.

Waiting at the service 27 terminal stop in Castle Lane West at the north end of Lawford Road is BUT9641T no. 214 (KLJ348) in its original livery.
Omnibus Society (R.T. Wilson)

Still in fine fettle, Sunbeam MS2 no. 206 (ALJ61) dating from October 1934 crosses Cemetery Junction from Charminster Road into Wimborne Road on its way to the Square.
Photographer's name not recorded

30.09.63 Service reintroduced and extended along Castle Lane West to Broadway Hotel.

Interworking with service 29 (ii) at Castle Lane West, junction with West Way.

Service interval: 30 mins.

25.09.66 Last day of trolleybus operation. Replaced by motorbus service 27.

Service 28 (i)

23.08.35 Trolleybus service commenced Bournemouth Square - Cemetery Junction - Five Ways - Broadway Hotel, Luckham Road via Richmond Hill, Wimborne Road and Charminster Road.

Service interval: summer 4 mins to Five Ways, 8 mins to Broadway Hotel, Luckham Road; winter 6 mins to Five Ways, 12 mins to Broadway Hotel.

01.05.36 *Service interval: 5 mins to Five Ways, 10 mins to Broadway Hotel, Luckham Road.*

05.04.37 *Service interval: all year 10 mins to Broadway Hotel, Luckham Road (from 19.10.38 including service 28A).*

06.05.46 Service reduced to weekday peak hours only.

30.03.47 Town Centre terminus extended to Triangle.

Between Bournemouth Square and the Triangle, eastbound journeys followed Avenue Road, and westbound journeys followed Commercial Road.

29.09.52 Service operating weekday peak hours, winter evenings and Sunday mornings.

Service interval: 30 mins.

26.03.56 *Service interval: increased to hourly all day*

22.07.56 Service reduced to weekday peak hours only and first/last journeys from/to Castle Lane (Mallard Road) Depot.

17.09.56 *Service interval: increased to hourly with additional journeys during weekday morning peak hours and at other times.*

31.12.56 *Service interval: two journeys per hour (not exactly every 30 mins) with additional journeys during weekday peak hours and at other times. Sunday mornings and winter evenings hourly.*

22.09.58 *Service interval: hourly with additional journeys during weekday morning peak hours and at other times. Sunday mornings hourly.*

05.04.65 Service reduced to weekday peak hours, winter evenings and Sunday mornings.

13.06.65 *Service interval: 30 mins.*

06.03.66 Sunday service: mornings and evening only.

13.06.66 Sunday service: increased to full weekday service.

25.09.66 Last day of trolleybus operation. Replaced by motorbus service 28.

Service 28 (ii)

07.04.50 Seasonal supplementary service commenced for Easter, Bournemouth Pier - Bournemouth Square - Cemetery Junction - Five Ways via Exeter Road, Richmond Hill, Wimborne Road and Charminster Road.

Between Bournemouth Pier and Cemetery Junction, northbound journeys followed Exeter Road and Richmond Hill, and southbound journeys followed Lansdowne Road, St. Paul's Road, Holdenhurst Road and Bath Road.

11.04.50 Last day of operation; seasonal supplementary service suspended, i.e. Good Friday-Easter Tuesday inclusive.

27.05.50 Seasonal supplementary service reinstated for the summer.

Service interval: 20 mins.

01.10.50 Last day of operation. No direct replacement.

Service 28A (i)

19.10.38 Trolleybus service commenced Bournemouth Square - Cemetery Junction - Five Ways - Broadway Hotel - Castle Lane West - Moordown - Winton - Cemetery Junction - Bournemouth Square via Richmond Hill, Wimborne Road, Charminster Road, Castle Lane West, Wimborne Road and Richmond Hill.

Unidirectional circular service (anti-clockwise) worked in conjunction with service 26A.

Service interval: 30 mins.

05.05.46 Unidirectional circular service withdrawn. Replaced by service 26A (ii) and 28A (ii).

Service 28A (ii)

06.05.46 Revised trolleybus service commenced Bournemouth Square - Cemetery Junction - Five Ways - Broadway Hotel - Castle Lane West, junction with West Way via Richmond Hill, Wimborne Road, Charminster Road and Castle Lane West.

Interworking with service 26A at Castle Lane West, junction with West Way.

Service interval: 15 mins.

30.03.47 Town Centre terminus extended to Triangle. Between Bournemouth Square and the Triangle, eastbound journeys followed Avenue Road, and westbound journeys followed Commercial Road.

Service interval: 15 mins.

15.10.51 *Service interval: 20 mins.*

29.02.56 Last day of operation. Service 28A (ii) renumbered 29 (ii).

Service 29 (i)

05.04.37 Trolleybus service commenced Bournemouth Square - Cemetery Junction - Five Ways - Malvern Road, junction with Charminster Avenue, via Richmond Hill, Wimborne Road, Charminster Road and Charminster Avenue

Service interval: 10 mins.

06.05.46 *Service interval: 15 mins.*

30.03.47 Town Centre terminus extended to Triangle.

Between Bournemouth Square and the Triangle, eastbound journeys followed Avenue Road, and westbound journeys followed Commercial Road.

Service interval: 15 mins.

15.10.51 *Service interval: 20 mins.*

29.02.56 Last day of operation. Service 29 (i) renumbered 35 (ii).

Service 29 (ii)

01.03.56 Revised trolleybus service (formerly service 28A (ii)) commenced Triangle - Bournemouth Square - Cemetery Junction - Five Ways - Broadway Hotel - Castle Lane West, junction with West Way via Richmond Hill, Wimborne Road, Charminster Road and Castle Lane West.

Between Bournemouth Square and the Triangle, eastbound journeys followed Avenue Road, and westbound journeys followed Commercial Road.

Interworking with service 27 (ii) at Castle Lane West, junction with West Way.

Service interval: 20 mins.

25.03.56 Interworking with service 27 (ii) ceased.

26.03.56 Interworking with service 34 (ii) at Castle Lane West, junction with West Way.

Service interval: 30 mins.

21.07.56 Interworking with service 34 (ii) ceased.

22.07.56 Interworking with service 27 (ii) at Castle Lane West, junction with West Way.

Service interval: 20 mins.

16.09.56 Interworking with service 27 (ii) ceased.

17.09.56 Interworking with service 34 (ii) at Castle Lane West, junction with West Way.

Service interval: 30 mins.

29.09.63 Interworking with service 34 (ii) ceased.

30.09.63 Extended to Moordown, Castle Lane West junction with Lawford Road via Castle Lane West.

Interworking with service 27 (iii) at Castle Lane West, junction with West Way.

25.09.66 Last day of trolleybus operation. Replaced by motorbus service 29.

Service 30 (i)

15.04.38 Trolleybus service commenced Bournemouth Square - Cemetery Junction - Winton - Wallisdown - Columbia Road, junction with Kinson Road via Richmond Hill, Wimborne Road, Talbot Road, Talbot Avenue, Wallisdown Road and Kinson Road.

Service interval: 20 mins.

08.04.39 Extended from Columbia Road, junction with Kinson Road to Bournemouth Square via Columbia Road, Ensbury Park Road, Wimborne Road and Richmond Hill.

Unidirectional circular service (clockwise) worked in conjunction with service 30A (i).

Service interval: 20 mins.

05.05.46 Unidirectional circular service withdrawn. Replaced by services 30 (ii) and 30A (ii).

Service 30 (ii)

06.05.46 Revised trolleybus service commenced Bournemouth Square - Cemetery Junction - Winton - Wallisdown - Columbia Road, junction with Kinson Road via Richmond Hill, Wimborne Road, Talbot Road, Talbot Avenue, Wallisdown Road and Kinson Road

Service interval: 15 mins (12 mins 2pm-7pm)

30.03.47 Town Centre terminus extended to Triangle

Between Bournemouth Square and the Triangle, eastbound journeys followed Avenue Road, and westbound journeys followed Commercial Road

Service interval: 15 mins

Turning out of Lawford Road into the eastbound carriageway of Castle Lane West is Sunbeam MF2B no. 273 (WRU273) with its indicator blinds already changed for the journey back to the Square and the Triangle as an interworking 29. In the background, another Sunbeam MF2B awaits departure time of a 26 journey to the Square. The auxiliary indicator display for all Side Routes was normally a blank white. **Paul Creswell**

15.10.51 *Service interval: 20 mins.*

26.03.56 *Service interval: 30 mins.*

31.12.56 Curtailed to operate Winton, Alma Road - Columbia Road, junction with Kinson Road via Talbot Road, Talbot Avenue, Wallisdown Road and Kinson Road except at weekday peak hours when services continued to operate to/from Triangle via Bournemouth Square.

Winton terminal loop: from the junction of Talbot Road with Wimborne Road, all journeys crossed Wimborne Road into Crimea Road and followed Crimea Road, Waterloo Road and Alma Road before crossing Wimborne Road back into Talbot Road.

Service interval: 30 mins.

15.07.57 All journeys extended to Triangle.

16.09.57 Curtailed to operate Winton, Alma Road - Columbia Road, junction with Kinson Road via Talbot Road, Talbot Avenue, Wallisdown Road and Kinson Road except at weekday peak hours when services continued to operate to/from Triangle via Bournemouth Square.

14.07.58 All journeys extended to Triangle.

22.09.58 Curtailed to operate Winton, Alma Road - Columbia Road, junction with Kinson Road via Talbot Road, Talbot Avenue, Wallisdown Road and Kinson Road except at weekday peak hours when services continued to operate to/from Triangle via Bournemouth Square.

13.07.59 All journeys extended to Triangle.

14.09.59 Curtailed to operate Winton, Alma Road - Columbia Road, junction with Kinson Road via Talbot Road, Talbot Avenue, Wallisdown Road and Kinson Road except at weekday peak hours when services continued to operate to/from Triangle via Bournemouth Square.

Service interval: 30 mins

05.04.65 Winter evening and Sunday morning and afternoon service withdrawn.

06.03.66 Motorbuses take over Sunday service.

16.04.66 Last day of trolleybus operation. Replaced by motorbus service 30.

Service 30A (i)

08.04.39 Trolleybus service commenced Bournemouth Square - Cemetery Junction - Winton - Ensbury Park - Columbia Road - Wallisdown - Winton - Cemetery Junction - Bournemouth Square, via Richmond Hill, Wimborne Road, Ensbury Park Road, Columbia Road, Kinson Road, Wallisdown Road, Talbot Avenue,

When service 30 was running between Winton and Columbia Road - where it interconnected with the 31- its Winton Banks terminus was in Crimea Road. It is there that we see 1959 Sunbeam MF2B no. 287 (YLJ287) awaiting departure to Wallisdown and Columbia Road.   Paul Creswell

Talbot Road, Wimborne Road and Richmond Hill.

Unidirectional circular service (anti-clockwise) worked in conjunction with service 30 (i).

Service interval: 20 mins.

05.05.46   Unidirectional circular service withdrawn. Replaced by services 30 (ii) and 30A (ii).

Service 30A (ii)

06.05.46   Revised trolleybus service commenced Bournemouth Square - Cemetery Junction - Winton - Ensbury Park - Columbia Road, junction with Kinson Road, via Richmond Hill, Wimborne Road, Ensbury Park Road and Columbia Road

Service interval: 15 mins (12 mins 2pm-7pm).

30.03.47   Town Centre terminus extended to Triangle.

Between Bournemouth Square and the Triangle, eastbound journeys followed Avenue Road, and westbound journeys followed Commercial Road.

Service interval: 15 mins.

15.10.51   *Service interval: 20 mins.*

29.02.56   Last day of operation. Service 30A (ii) renumbered 31(iii).

Service 30A (iii)

07.04.50   Seasonal supplementary trolleybus service commenced for Easter, Bournemouth Pier - Cemetery Junction - Winton - Columbia Road, junction with Kinson Road via Wimborne Road, Ensbury Park Road and Columbia Road.
Between Bournemouth Pier and Cemetery Junction, northbound journeys followed Exeter Road and Richmond Hill, and southbound journeys followed Lansdowne Road, St. Paul's Road, Holdenhurst Road and Bath Road.

11.04.50   Last day of operation; seasonal supplementary service suspended, i.e. Good Friday-Easter Tuesday inclusive.

27.05.50   Seasonal supplementary service reinstated for the summer.

Service interval: 20 mins.

01.10.50   Last day of operation; seasonal supplementary service suspended.

11.04.52   Seasonal supplementary service reinstated for Easter.

14.04.52   Last day of operation; seasonal supplementary service suspended, i.e. Good Friday-Easter Monday inclusive.

31.05.52 Seasonal supplementary service reinstated for the summer.

28.09.52 Last day of operation; seasonal supplementary service suspended.

Service interval: according to requirements.

03.04.53 Seasonal supplementary service reinstated for Easter.

06.04.53 Last day of operation; seasonal supplementary service suspended, i.e. Good Friday-Easter Monday inclusive.

23.05.53 Seasonal supplementary service reinstated for the summer.

20.09.53 Last day of operation; seasonal supplementary service suspended and renumbered 34 (i).

Service 31 (i)

15.10.51 Trolleybus service commenced Triangle - Bournemouth Square - Cemetery Junction - Broadway Hotel - Strouden Park - Iford - Pokesdown Station - Boscombe Arcade - Boscombe Gardens - Lansdowne - Bournemouth Square, Gervis Place via Avenue Road, Richmond Hill, Wimborne Road, Charminster Road, Castle Lane West, Castle Lane East, Christchurch Road, Old Christchurch Road, Fir Vale Road and St. Peter's Road.

Unidirectional circular service (clockwise) worked in conjunction with service 32 (i).

Service interval: irregular but approximately hourly.

01.04.52 *Service interval: regular hourly.*

23.05.53 Additional hourly journeys Triangle - Bournemouth Square - Cemetery Junction - Broadway Hotel - Strouden Park, junction of Castle Lane West with Holdenhurst Road introduced.

11.10.53 Last day of operation. Replaced by service 31 (ii) and 24 (although not an advertised interworking).

Service 31 (ii)

12.10.53 Trolleybus service commenced Triangle - Bournemouth Square - Cemetery Junction - Broadway Hotel - Strouden Park - Iford Bridge via Richmond Hill, Wimborne Road, Charminster Road, Castle Lane West, Castle Lane East and Christchurch Road.

Between Bournemouth Square and the Triangle, eastbound journeys followed Avenue Road, and westbound journeys followed Commercial Road.

Interworking with service 33 at Iford Bridge.

Service interval: hourly with extra PM journeys to Strouden Park, junction with Holdenhurst Road.

On the first day of operation of unidirectional circular services 31 and 32, 15 October 1951, BUT9641T no. 216 (KLJ350), is seen travelling south along Charminster Road opposite Luckham Road reversing triangle. In the heat of the moment, the indicator blind displays 31 - the clockwise service - although the anti-clockwise service shown was the 32. Castle Lane West is in the background.
Malcolm Pearce (G.O.P. Pearce)

29.02.56 Last day of operation. Service 31(ii) renumbered 32(ii).

Service 31 (iii)

01.03.56 Trolleybus service (formerly service 30A (ii)) commenced Triangle - Bournemouth Square - Cemetery Junction - Winton - Ensbury Park - Columbia Road, junction with Kinson Road via Richmond Hill, Wimborne Road, Ensbury Park Road and Columbia Road.

Between Bournemouth Square and the Triangle, eastbound journeys followed Avenue Road, and westbound journeys followed Commercial Road.

Service interval: 20 mins

26.03.56 *Service interval: 15 mins*

05.04.65 *Service interval: evening and Sunday service reduced to 30 mins*

25.09.66 Last day of trolleybus operation. Replaced by motorbus service 31.

Service 32 (i)

15.10.51 Trolleybus service commenced Bournemouth Square, Gervis Place - Lansdowne - Boscombe Gardens - Boscombe Arcade - Pokesdown Station - Iford - Strouden Park - Broadway Hotel - Cemetery Junction - Bournemouth Square - Triangle via Old Christchurch Road, Christchurch Road, Castle Lane East, Castle Lane West, Charminster Road, Wimborne Road, Richmond Hill and Commercial Road.

Unidirectional circular service (anti-clockwise) worked in conjunction with service 31 (i).

Service interval: irregular but approximately hourly.

01.04.52 *Service interval: regular hourly.*

23.05.53 Additional hourly journeys Strouden Park, junction of Castle Lane West with Holdenhurst Road - Broadway Hotel - Cemetery Junction - Bournemouth Square - Triangle introduced.

11.10.53 Last day of operation. Replaced by services 24 (although not an advertised interworking) and 31 (ii).

Despite the flexibility offered by Bournemouth's indicator blinds, those for service 32 (ii) were unable to display IFORD, STROUDEN PARK and SQUARE in the correct geographical sequence when returning to the town centre. Sunbeam MF2B no. 303 (303LJ) heads west along Castle Lane West at the junction with Mallard Road (the depot access line) in August 1965.
NTA Collection (R.F. Mack)

Turning back at Iford roundabout, the junction of Castle Lane East with Christchurch Road, is Sunbeam MF2B no. 296 (296LJ). In the foreground above no. 296 is the additional frog and wiring added in July 1965 to enable trolleybuses to turn from Christchurch Road eastbound into Castle Lane East westbound following the closure of Central Depot, Southcote Road.   Roger G. Funnell (courtesy Mrs D. Funnell and Rodney Funnell)

BUT9641T no. 246 (KLJ346) is seen heading south along Charminster Road at the junction with Capstone Road, the sole tram route in Bournemouth not to be converted to trolleybus opertion. The branch of the National Provincial Bank (a High Street bank that merged with the Westminster Bank in 1968) on the corner of King's Road is now a betting office.   Travel Lens

Service 32 (ii)

01.03.56 Redesignated trolleybus service (formerly service 31 (ii)) commenced Triangle - Bournemouth Square - Cemetery Junction - Broadway Hotel - Strouden Park - Iford Bridge via Richmond Hill, Wimborne Road, Charminster Road, Castle Lane East, Castle Lane West and Christchurch Road.

Between Bournemouth Square and the Triangle, eastbound journeys followed Avenue Road, and westbound journeys followed Commercial Road.

Interworking with service 33 at Iford Bridge.

Service interval: hourly.

02.12.56 Service curtailed to new Iford roundabout, Christchurch Road junction with Castle Lane East.

21.09.58 Interworking with service 33 ceased.

22.09.58 Additional hourly journeys Triangle - Bournemouth Square - Cemetery Junction - Broadway Hotel - Strouden Park, junction of Castle Lane West with Holdenhurst Road introduced.

22.09.58 Interworking with service 24 at Jumpers Corner (this interworking at Jumpers continued until 30 September 1963 and trolleybuses always ran through to Jumpers Corner despite service 32 public timetables to the contrary).

06.10.58 Iford journeys extended to Jumpers Corner via Christchurch Road, Barrack Road, Oak Avenue and Stourvale Avenue.

Jumpers terminal loop: from the junction of Oak Avenue with Christchurch Road, all journeys followed Oak Avenue, Stourvale Avenue (terminal point) and The Grove to its junction with Barrack Road.

Sunday service to Iford only.

02.02.59 Curtailed to Iford roundabout, junction with Christchurch Road.

Interworking with service 24 at Jumpers Corner.

**By
13.07.59** Extended Iford roundabout - Jumpers Corner via Christchurch Road, Barrack Road, Oak Avenue and Stourvale Avenue.

Interworking with service 24 at Jumpers Corner.

03.06.60 Additional hourly journeys Triangle - Strouden Park, junction of Castle Lane West with Holdenhurst Road ceased, although some peak hour journeys continued to run until 25.09.66.

04.06.60 *Service interval: weekdays 30 mins to Jumpers.*
Service interval: Sundays hourly to Iford.

30.01.61 Minimum fare introduced, outwards on weekdays 4.30pm-6.30pm.

12.06.61 *Service interval: Sundays (until 10.09.61) 30 mins to Iford.*

09.06.62 *Service interval: Sundays (until 09.09.62) 30 mins to Iford.*

18.12.62 Peak-hour journeys terminating at Strouden Park, junction of Castle Lane West with Holdenhurst Road extended to Iford to facilitate the construction of Cooper Dean roundabout

27.05.63 Peak-hour journeys cut back from Iford to Strouden Park, junction of Castle Lane West with Holdenhurst Road upon completion of Cooper Dean roundabout

Service interval: Sundays (until 29.09.63) 30 mins to Iford.

29.09.63 Interworking with service 24 ceased.

30.09.63 Curtailed to Iford roundabout, junction with Christchurch Road.

Service interval: weekdays 30 mins.

Service interval: Sundays hourly.

08.06.64 Extended Iford roundabout-Jumpers Corner via Christchurch Road, Barrack Road, Oak Avenue and Stourvale Avenue.

05.04.65 Curtailed to Iford roundabout, junction with Christchurch Road.

11.04.65 *Service interval: Sunday afternoons 30 mins to Iford.*

25.09.66 Last day of trolleybus operation. Replaced by motorbus service 32

Service 33

23.05.53 Trolleybus service commenced Winton, Crimea Road - Moordown - Broadway Hotel - Strouden Park, Castle Lane East, junction with Holdenhurst Road, via Wimborne Road and Castle Lane West.

Between the junction of Wimborne Road with Lawford Road and Castle Lane West, northbound journeys followed Lawford Road and southbound journeys followed Castle Lane West and Wimborne Road.

Winton terminal loop: from the junction of Wimborne Road with Crimea Road, all journeys followed Crimea Road, Waterloo Road and Alma Road to its junction with Wimborne Road.

Service interval: hourly.

12.10.53 Extended to operate between Triangle and Iford Bridge, via Bournemouth Square, Richmond Hill, Wimborne Road, Moordown, Castle Lane West, Castle Lane East and Christchurch Road.

Between Bournemouth Square and the Triangle, eastbound journeys followed Avenue Road, and westbound journeys followed Commercial Road.

Interworking with service 31 (ii) at Iford Bridge.

Service interval: hourly.

29.02.56 Interworking with service 31 (ii) ceased.

01.03.56 Interworking with 32 (ii) at Iford Bridge.

02.12.56 Service curtailed to new Iford roundabout, Christchurch Road junction with Castle Lane East.

21.09.58 Interworking with service 31 (ii) ceased.

22.09.58 Service reduced to operate at weekday peak hours only.

28.09.63 Last day of operation. Replaced by circular motorbus service 33.

Service 34 (i)
05.06.54 Redesignated supplementary seasonal service (formerly service 30A (iii)) commenced for the summer, Bournemouth Pier - Lansdowne - Central Station - Cemetery Junction - Winton - Ensbury Park - Columbia Road, junction with Kinson Road via Bath Road, Holdenhurst Road, St. Paul's Road, Lansdowne Road, Wimborne Road, Ensbury Park Road and Columbia Road

Service interval: up to 8 journeys each way daily.

20.09.54 Last day of operation; seasonal supplementary service suspended.

One morning peak hour journey (Monday-Saturday), shown in the service 30A timetable, continued to operate between Lansdowne and Columbia Road, junction with Kinson Road.

28.05.55 Seasonal supplementary service reinstated for the summer between Bournemouth Pier and Columbia Road, junction with Kinson Road.

18.09.55 Last day of seasonal supplementary service operation.

29.02.56 Last day of morning peak hour operation between Lansdowne and Columbia Road, junction with Kinson Road. Service 34 (i) renumbered as service 36, but journeys to/from Bournemouth Pier never reintroduced.

Service 34 (ii)
01.03.56 Redesignated trolleybus service (formerly service 27 (i)) commenced Bournemouth Square, Gervis Place - Lansdowne - Central Station - Cemetery Junction - Winton - Moordown - Castle Lane West, junction with Lawford Road via Old Christchurch Road, Holdenhurst Road, St. Paul's Road, Lansdowne Road and Wimborne Road.

Between the junction of Dean Park Crescent with Old Christchurch Road and Bournemouth Square westbound journeys followed Fir Vale Road, St. Peter's Road and Gervis Place.

Alternate westbound journeys to Bournemouth Square diverted at the Lansdowne via Bath Road and Westover Road instead of via Old Christchurch Road, Fir Vale Road and St. Peter's Road.

Between the junction of Wimborne Road with Lawford Road and Castle Lane West, northbound journeys followed Lawford Road and southbound journeys followed Castle Lane West and Wimborne Road.

**The driver of no. 111 (ALJ985) has full lock on the steering in preparation for turning at Fisherman's Walk, Wentworth Avenue, on 6 May 1954, the first day of summer operation of seasonal supplementary service 35 to and from Bournemouth Pier.
Malcolm Pearce (G.O.P. Pearce)**

Service interval: 15 mins, off-peak to Moordown, Redhill Crescent, extended to Castle Lane West, Lawford Road at peak hours.
30 mins, winter evenings and Sunday mornings between Lansdowne and Moordown, Redhill Crescent.

26.03.56 Extended to Castle Lane West, junction with West Way via Castle Lane West.

Interworking with service 29 (ii) at Castle Lane West, junction with West Way.

Service interval: 30 mins

21.07.56 Interworking with service 29 (ii) ceased.

22.07.56 Curtailed to Castle Lane West, Lawford Road.

Service interval: 20 mins

17.09.56 Extended to Broadway Hotel via Castle Lane West.

Interworking with service 29 (ii) at Castle Lane West, junction with West Way.

Service interval: 30 mins

31.12.56 Curtailed to Lansdowne (instead of Bournemouth Square) - Castle Lane West, junction with West Way. Interworking with service 29 (ii) at Castle Lane West, junction with West Way.

Service interval: 30 mins

03.06.57 Extended to Broadway Hotel via Castle Lane West.

Interworking with service 29 (ii) at Castle Lane West, junction with West Way.

Service interval: 30 mins

29.09.63 Last day of operation. Replaced by circular motorbus services 33 and 34.

Service 35 (i)

16.04.54 Redesignated seasonal supplementary trolleybus service (formerly service 23 (ii)) commenced for Easter, Bournemouth Pier - Lansdowne - Boscombe Gardens - Boscome Arcade - Pokesdown Station - Fisherman's Walk, Wentworth Avenue via Christchurch Road and Seabourne Road.

Between Bournemouth Pier and the Lansdowne eastbound journeys followed Exeter Road, Bournemouth Square and Old Christchurch Road; westbound journeys followed Bath Road.

Service interval: 15 mins

Sunbeam MF2B no. 262 (WRU262) turns at Fisherman's Walk, Wentworth Avenue, on peak hour service 37 (11 August 1958).
Malcolm Pearce (G.O.P. Pearce)

19.04.54   Last day of operation: seasonal supplementary service suspended, i.e. Good Friday-Easter Monday inclusive.

05.06.54   Seasonal supplementary service reinstated for the summer.

19.09.54   Last day of operation: seasonal supplementary service suspended.

08.04.55   Season supplementary service reinstated for Easter.

11.04.55   Last day of operation: seasonal supplementary service suspended, i.e. Good Friday-Easter Monday inclusive.

28.05.55   Seasonal supplementary service reinstated for the summer.

18.09.55   Last day of operation: seasonal supplementary service suspended.

29.02.56   Season supplementary service 35 (i) renumbered 38.

Service 35 (ii)
01.03.56   Redesignated trolleybus service (formerly service 29 (i)) commenced Triangle - Bournemouth Square - Cemetery Junction - Five Ways - Malvern Road, junction with Charminster Avenue, via Richmond Hill, Wimborne Road, Charminster Road and Charminster Avenue.

Between Bournemouth Square and the Triangle, eastbound journeys followed Avenue Road, and westbound journeys followed Commercial Road.

Service interval: 20 mins

26.03.56   *Service interval: 30 mins*

31.12.56   *Service interval: hourly*

04.04.65   Last day of trolleybus operation. Initially no replacement motorbus service.

Service 36
01.03.56   Redesignated trolleybus service (formerly service 34 (i)) commenced Lansdowne - Central Station - Cemetery Junction - Winton - Ensbury Park - Columbia Road, junction with Kinson Road, via Holdenhurst Road, St. Paul's Road, Lansdowne Road, Wimborne Road, Ensbury Park Road and Columbia Road.

Service interval: one morning peak hour journey from Columbia Road to Lansdowne (shown under service 31 timetable), Monday-Saturday only.

17.09.56   Additional journeys now operating but shown in the service 30 and 31 timetables.

Service interval: two morning peak journeys (one via Talbot Village) from Columbia Road to Lansdowne and

three afternoon peak journeys from Lansdowne to Columbia Road, Monday-Saturday only.

16.09.57   Afternoon peak journeys now shown in both service 31 and 34 timetables.

14.09.59   Afternoon peak journeys curtailed to Monday-Friday only.

28.09.63   Last day of trolleybus operation. Replaced by motorbus service 36.

Service 37
01.03.56   Redesignated trolleybus service (formerly trolleybus service 23 (i)) commenced Bournemouth Square, Gervis Place - Lansdowne - Boscombe Gardens - Boscombe Arcade - Pokesdown Station - Fisherman's Walk, Wentworth Avenue, via Old Christchurch Road, Lansdowne, Christchurch Road and Seabourne Road.

Weekday peak hours only and occasionally at other times.

Between the junction of Dean Park Crescent with Old Christchurch Road and Bournemouth Square westbound journeys followed Fir Vale Road, St. Peter's Road and Gervis Place.

Alternate westbound journeys to Bournemouth Square diverted between the Lansdowne and Gervis Place along Bath Road and Westover Road instead of Old Christchurch Road, Fir Vale Road, St. Peter's Road.

30.09.63   Service 37 ceased to be advertised although peak-hour extras between Bournemouth Square and Fisherman's Walk continued to operate displaying service 22 until 19.04.69.

Service 38
30.03.56   Redesignated seasonal supplementary trolleybus service (formerly trolleybus service 35 (i)) commenced for Easter, Bournemouth Pier - Lansdowne - Boscombe Gardens - Boscombe Arcade - Pokesdown Station - Fisherman's Walk, Wentworth Avenue via Lansdowne, Christchurch Road and Seabourne Road.

Between Bournemouth Pier and the Lansdowne eastbound journeys followed Exeter Road, Bournemouth Square and Old Christchurch Road; westbound journeys followed Bath Road.

02.04.56   Last day of operation; seasonal supplementary service suspended, i.e. Good Friday-Easter Monday inclusive.

19.05.56   Seasonal supplementary service reinstated for the summer.

Service interval: 15 mins

Standing in Carbery Avenue on the turning loop prior to returning to the Pier along Cranleigh Road is BUT9641T no. 235 (KLJ335) on a service 38 working. Roger G. Funnell (courtesy Mrs D. Funnell and Rodney Funnell)

16.09.56 Last day of operation; seasonal supplementary service suspended.

19.04.57 Seasonal supplementary service reinstated for Easter.

22.04.57 Last day of operation; seasonal supplementary service suspended, i.e. Good Friday-Easter Monday inclusive.

03.06.57 Seasonal supplementary service reinstated for the summer.

Service interval: 15 mins

15.09.57 Last day of operation; seasonal supplementary service suspended.

04.04.58 Seasonal supplementary service reinstated for Easter.

07.04.58 Last day of operation; seasonal supplementary service suspended, i.e. Good Friday - Easter Monday inclusive. Last year of Easter operations.

24.05.58 Seasonal supplementary service reinstated for the summer.

Service interval: 15 mins

21.09.58 Last day of operation; seasonal supplementary service suspended.

16.05.59 Seasonal supplementary service reinstated for the summer.

13.09.59 Last day of operation; seasonal supplementary service suspended.

04.07.60 Seasonal supplementary service reinstated for the summer and extended to operate Bournemouth Pier or Bournemouth Square - Lansdowne - Boscombe Gardens - Boscombe - Pokesdown - Fisherman's Walk - Southbourne -Tuckton Bridge - Christchurch via Lansdowne, Christchurch Road, Seabourne Road, Southbourne Grove, Southbourne Road, Belle Vue Road, Foxholes Road, Belle Vue Road, Stour Road, Bargates, High Street and Church Street.

Between Bournemouth Pier and the Lansdowne eastbound journeys followed Exeter Road, Bournemouth Square and Old Christchurch Road, and westbound journeys followed Bath Road.

Journeys commence and terminate alternately at Bournemouth Pier and Bournemouth Square to/from Fisherman's Walk only

Journeys from both Bournemouth Pier and Bournemouth Square extended to/from Christchurch between 1.30pm and 8pm.

Service interval: 15 mins, afternoon extensions to/from Christchurch approximately every 30 mins.

11.09.60 Last day of operation; seasonal supplementary service suspended.

12.06.61 Seasonal supplementary service reinstated for the summer and curtailed to operate Bournemouth Pier - Lansdowne - Boscombe Gardens - Boscombe - Pokesdown - Fisherman's Walk - Carbery Avenue, Tuckton, via Lansdowne, Christchurch Road, Seabourne Road, Beresford Road, Beaufort Road and Cranleigh Road.

Between Bournemouth Pier and the Lansdowne eastbound journeys followed Exeter Road, Bournemouth Square and Old Christchurch Road, and westbound journeys followed Bath Road.

Service interval: 20 mins

10.09.61 Last day of operation; seasonal supplementary service suspended.

09.06.62 Seasonal supplementary service reinstated for the summer, operating eastbound from Bournemouth Pier to the Lansdowne via Bath Road instead of via Exeter Road, Bournemouth Square and Old Christchurch Road.

Service interval: 20 mins

09.09.62 Last day of operation; seasonal supplementary service suspended.

27.05.63 Seasonal supplementary service reinstated for the summer.

Service interval: 20 mins

29.09.63 Last day of operation; seasonal supplementary service suspended.

08.06.64 Seasonal supplementary service reinstated for the summer using open-top trolleybuses.

23.08.64 Last day of trolleybus operation. Replaced by motorbus service 16.

A school special operated by Sunbeam MF2B no. 279 (YLJ279) descends Charminster Road at its junction with Malvern Road on a damp day in September 1966. On the summit of the hill is the tower of the St. Francis of Assisi Church opposite the junction of Charminster Road with West Way. NTA Collection (R.F. Mack)

Service 39

24.05.58 Summer season open-top trolleybus circular tour commenced Bournemouth Pier - Bournemouth Square - Cemetery Junction - Broadway Hotel - Strouden Park - Iford - Jumpers - Tuckton Bridge - Southbourne - Fisherman's Walk - Pokesdown Station - Boscombe Arcade - Boscombe Gardens - Lansdowne - Bournemouth Pier via Exeter Road, Richmond Hill, Wimborne Road, Charminster Road, Castle Lane West, Castle Lane East, Christchurch Road, Barrack Road, Stour Road, Belle Vue Road, Foxholes Road, Belle Vue Road, Southbourne Road, Southbourne Grove, Seabourne Road, Christchurch Road and Bath Road.

Unidirectional circular tour (clockwise). No scheduled stops at intermediate points.

Service interval: up to 10 departures daily with a round-trip journey time of 1 hour.

07.07.58 Tour revised to operate as a circular service, picking-up and setting down passengers at intermediate points.

21.09.58 Last day of operation, summer season service suspended.

16.05.59 Summer season service reinstated.

29.06.59 Summer season open-top trolleybus circular service rerouted to operate anti-clockwise Bournemouth Pier - Lansdowne - Boscombe Gardens - Boscombe Arcade - Pokesdown Station - Fisherman's Walk - Southbourne - Tuckton Bridge - Jumpers - Iford - Strouden Park - Broadway Hotel - Cemetery Junction - Central Station - Lansdowne - Bournemouth Pier via Bath Road, Christchurch Road, Seabourne Road, Southbourne Grove, Southbourne Road, Belle Vue Road, Foxholes Road, Belle Vue Road, Stour Road, Barrack Road, Christchurch Road, Castle Lane East, Castle Lane West, Charminster Road, Lansdowne Road, St. Paul's Road, Holdenhurst Road and Bath Road.

Service interval: up to 10 departures daily.

13.09.59 Last day of operation, summer season circular service suspended.

04.06.60 Summer season circular service reinstated.

Service interval: up to 8 departures daily.

11.09.60 Last day of operation, summer season circular service suspended.

12.06.61 Summer season circular service reinstated.

Service interval: up to 8 departures daily.

10.09.61 Last day of operation, summer season circular service suspended.

09.06.62 Summer season circular service reinstated.

09.09.62 Last day of operation, summer season circular service suspended.

27.05.63 Summer season circular service reinstated.

Service interval: up to 8 departures daily.

29.09.63 Last day of trolleybus operation. No direct replacement.

Passengers could travel on trolleybuses travelling out of service to or from depots. This facility included Central Depot, Southcote Road, although neither access route was used by scheduled trolleybus services, and Castle Lane (Mallard Road) Depot after 25 September 1966 when scheduled trolleybus services along Castle Lane ceased, but such journeys were not advertised. In the case of Central Depot conductors were instructed to charge the minimum fare from Boscombe or Central Station to or from the depot, plus the normal fare to or from any further point. By the late 1950s, if not earlier, all run-outs from Central Depot to scheduled Main Road service journey were by way of St. Clement's Road and Palmerston Road, although there were never any bus stops in either road during the trolleybus era. Run-outs along Southcote Road seemed to be limited to service 25 vehicles as well as a variety of specials and Pier services. Vehicles running in to Central Depot generally showed either Boscombe or Central Station on the main blind.

APPENDIX F

DESTINATION AND SERVICE NUMBER DISPLAYS

The hired trolleybuses, except the single-deck Thornycroft (LJ7704), used on the first experimental route and the first Sunbeam MS2s (72-142 and 144) displayed roller blinds showing solely the final destination in an aperture built into the upper-deck panels at the front and rear, with a service number roller blind in a second aperture immediately above. LJ 7704 had solely an aperture above the windscreen displaying a roller blind showing the single-line final destination; there was no rear aperture and no number blinds. The Sunbeam MS2s were delivered with single-line final destination boxes mounted at the top of the rearmost lower saloon window on each side. From spring 1935 wooden "tramcar-style" side slipboards, as used on BCT motorbuses since the mid-1920s, mounted on both sides of the trolleybus above the lower maroon band at lower saloon window level and showing up to four intermediate points in black lettering on a white background, were also carried.

No. 145 appeared at the 1935 Commercial Motor Show with larger destination screens and these were adopted as standard in November 1935 using a display of up to four lines of information (intermediate points and the final destination) which accommodated short workings by the judicious placing of black blank lines so that only a reduced number of lines were visible in the aperture. The screens were approximately 2ft 6in wide and 1ft 3in deep, and the lettering on the new blinds (which latterly were up to 40ft long) was to a common height of $2^{7}/_{8}$in at $3^{3}/_{8}$in centres, but varied in width according to the length of the word concerned. However, photographs show that at first some destinations continued to be shown by means of a single large name; when trolleybuses started to operate on service 30 between Bournemouth Square and Columbia Road via Winton and Talbot Village, some blinds showed the single destination **WALLISDOWN** in large letters. The displaced single-line destination blinds were remounted in the side destination boxes. The gradual reconstruction of earlier trolleybus deliveries with four-line main indicator boxes superseded the slip-boards, which were found to be illegal because they extended the effective width of the trolleybus to more than the prevailing 7ft 6in maximum, but the holders

remained in place well into the 1940s.

The place names were printed on the blinds in groups: the Bournemouth Square-Christchurch via Southbourne route for example having three blank black lines followed by:

BOSCOMBE
FISHERMANS WALK
SOUTHBOURNE
TUCKTON BRIDGE
CHRISTCHURCH

A trolleybus operating from the Square to Christchurch would display:

FISHERMANS WALK
SOUTHBOURNE
TUCKTON BRIDGE
CHRISTCHURCH

whereas one going only as far as Southbourne Cross Roads would show one of the blank black lines followed by:

BOSCOMBE
FISHERMANS WALK
SOUTHBOURNE

Judicious use of the blank black lines before and after the place name groups permitted the display of any logical combination of intermediate points and final destination.

The post-war BUTs and Sunbeam MF2Bs were not equipped with single-line side indicator boxes inside the lower saloon but, unlike the Sunbeam MS2s, had a third rectangular indicator box

Sunbeam MS2 no. 171 (BRU22) delivered in March 1936 and seen in Wimborne Road outside Moordown Depot shows the larger destination screens able to display up to four lines of information (intermediate points and the final destination) with a service number blind box to the nearside (in the vent panel above the platform window at the rear) which became standard in November 1935

A.D. Packer

This view of Sunbeam MS2 no. 72 (AEL400) at the Park Royal Works illustrates the original indicator aperture layout with a single-line final-destination box surmounted by a service number box centrally located immediately above at front and rear. The destination shown proved over-optimistic whilst the indicator boxes inside the lower saloon and the trolley heads have yet to be fitted.   **David Chalk collection**

30in X 15in capable of displaying up to three lines of intermediate points and the final destination, i.e. a total of up to four lines, built into the nearside upper-deck panelling immediately above the rear open platform entrance. The only legend borne by trolleybuses not in public service was **RESERVED** although the Sunbeam MS2 side indicator box blinds also included **DEPOT ONLY** and **SPECIAL**. All motorbus blinds from 1930 onwards, included tram and, later, trolleybus destinations and service numbers so that motorbuses could operate over these routes in an emergency or on the limited number of early Sunday morning services which were gradually introduced from 1938. There were no special displays for the various terminal points in the town centre such as Gervis Place or the Triangle, only **SQUARE** or later **BOURNEMOUTH SQUARE** being included on the blinds.

The service number boxes originally used on the pre-December 1935 Sunbeam MS2 deliveries were even smaller than those used latterly at the rear immediately above the platform rear window. They featured suitably-sized number blinds. Once the service number indicator box had been moved to the nearside of the front destination display and increased in size to 10 X 10in, 10³/₈ in-wide blinds using 8in-high numerals and 6in-high alphabetical suffixes were used front and rear. On the MS2s sans-serif characters were used except for the number 1. As the aperture at the rear was smaller than that at the front, the rear number display appeared as a rather tight fit. The BUTs and Sunbeam MF2Bs used the same size of aperture and blind but apparently a different style of characters.

There is photographic evidence that, once the rectangular apertures were in use, the original Sunbeam MS2 blinds, whilst apparently using the same style of lettering throughout, certainly used a variety of sizes, e.g. **RESERVED** or **WALLISDOWN**.

Their service number blinds featured "tails" on the ends of each number in an undefinable style of script.

A limited number of Sunbeam MS2s were fitted with new final destination and intermediate point blinds in 1942. These can be identified by the absence of any reference to Jumpers or Christchurch after Iford, as the Barrack Road extension only opened in July 1943, and the absence of West Way, as until May 1946, services 26A and 28A operated as circular services and did not show West Way as a destination. Wallisdown was also shown as part of a standard four-line display rather than as a large single-line destination.

A further batch of final destination and intermediate point blinds was produced in 1954 to re-equip those Sunbeam MS2s that remained in the fleet. It is believed that they were made by Norbury & Co. The blind content was similar to those used in the 1958 Sunbeam MF2Bs and included **BOURNEMOUTH SQUARE** rather than **SQUARE**.

There appear to have been two batches of replacement number blinds, the first supplied around 1954 and the second in the late 1950s. The former, having a content similar to BCT's BUT9641Ts, i.e. service numbers 20-35 with 36-38 added later, also included **A** and **B** suffix options, e.g. 21A, 22B, etc., and was fitted in the front number displays of the surviving Sunbeam MS2s (including preserved 202 (112) and 212 (99)). The figure **2** had a swan neck, and the **3** was flat-topped. Similar style inserts were used to add the service number **24** to some early Sunbeam MF2B number blinds, added between **31** and **32**, and to add service numbers **36-38** to the original BUT9641T blinds. The ex-Brighton BUT9611Ts were fitted with 1954 number blinds removed from Sunbeam MS2s withdrawn in the meantime. Only very occasionally was this type of blind found in a Sunbeam MF2B, although a handful of BUT9641Ts gained them in later life. The second batch of replacement number blinds, whilst otherwise identical in font style (flat-topped 3s, etc.), contained solely service numbers 20-38 with no suffix options, and was used as replacements in some BUT9641Ts and latterly in at least one Sunbeam MF2B, namely the front display on 274 (at the rear, by 1968, the rear display of 274 had an earlier blind complete with suffixes).

The BUT9641Ts and Sunbeam MF2Bs used the same size of aperture and indicator blinds, but their original final destination and intermediate point blinds, and auxiliary blinds, apparently used a different style of characters, perhaps of Gill Sans style, whilst their service number blinds were identifiable by their "straight-necked" **2** and "round-topped" **3**.

It is important to point out that, during the trolleybus era, commercial indicator blind manufacturers for provincial transport undertakings tended to use their own styles and not a particular style of character. Additions, exchanges and repairs meant that individual vehicles of the same type frequently contained different styles of character on a single blind.

The introduction of services along Bath and Westover Roads in 1937 brought with it the use of auxiliary (in-town "via" or special event) single-line indicators with a 30in X 5in aperture to denote which of the two alternative routes to the Square the trolleybus was taking. On the Sunbeam MS2s these boxes were initially located at the top of the driver's nearside windscreen and in the (vent) panel immediately above the rear platform window. From 1950 the auxiliary single-line indicator box in the driver's nearside windscreen was removed and replaced by an aperture in the upper-deck front panel beneath the rectangular box which displayed intermediate points and the final destination. The BUTs and Sunbeam MF2Bs had the auxiliary indicator box built into the front and rear upper-deck panels beneath the main intermediate points and final destination box. Lettering on the auxiliary blinds was generally 4in high. The idea of a coloured blind (at first a paper sticker or board in the driver's cab windscreen) was perpetuated from tramway days when trams to Poole via Upper Parkstone carried a red destination board whilst those via Lower Parkstone did not. The size of the lettering was in principle unimportant, the coloured background providing the identifying feature. The **VIA BRASSEY ROAD** display presumably distinguished trolleybuses going to Wallisdown via Ensbury Park, as opposed to **VIA TALBOT VILLAGE**, or to West Way via Moordown, as opposed to the post-war **VIA CHARMINSTER ROAD** and corresponding to the **VIA PETERS HILL** on the Sunbeam MF2B blinds. **ALBERT ROAD ONLY** was used by trolleybuses operating via Richmond Hill and destined for the Triangle parking area following the deletion of the Commercial Road stop for Side Route services. Yellow-painted boards lettered in black were carried in the driver's cab windscreen of those earlier trolleybuses not equipped with this display on their blinds.

The Sunbeam MS2s appear to have retained their original auxiliary blinds at front and rear until withdrawal and this was, presumably, the case with the BUT9641Ts. The ex-Brighton BUT9611Ts were equipped with new auxiliary blinds having an almost identical content to the 1958-1958 Sunbeam MF2B (258-287) deliveries (those fitted to the 1962 Sunbeam MF2Bs (295-303) were slightly different). Unlike the original auxiliary blinds fitted to all new Sunbeam MF2Bs, those in the BUT9611Ts evidently included a black blank display whereas those in the Sunbeam MF2Bs had a white blank and those in the

BUT9641Ts had a black blank followed by the words EKO (the manufacturer) enclosed within a diamond and STOP.

Indicator blind displays were normally changed for the next journey before reaching the actual terminus, so that the trolleybus was displaying its new destination as it arrived there. These changes were sometimes made prematurely and it became common practice to change indicator blinds on vehicles proceeding from the east to the Square once the Lansdowne had been reached. On service 32, which in Summer 1963 interworked with service **24**, Bournemouth Square-Charminster-Iford-Bournemouth Square, creating a circular route, it was officially laid down that vehicles on service 32 would change their service number blinds to 24 upon reaching the Broadway Hotel and on service 24 the 32 blind would be displayed from Iford. On other circular routings (interworking), e.g. 22/23 and 29/34, the displays were changed at the nominal terminus of the outward journey, although in all cases passengers could be conveyed through and this was indicated in the respective fare tables. Until the 1950s, the conductor was responsible for changing the blinds in readiness for each trip, going upstairs to open the access doors in the front interior panels for this purpose, but after that the driver took charge of the front blinds and new vehicles were equipped with handles at the front of the driver's cab ceiling.

The Sunbeam MF2Bs featured number blinds running from **20** to **42** with no **A** suffixes but the number **24** appeared twice, once after **23** and again after **31**, to accommodate circular routings along Castle Lane. This facilitated a minimum of blind changing when services 24 and 32 interworked. The BUT 9641Ts brought with them a simplification in the coloured auxiliary (in-town "via" or special event) blinds, **VIA BATH AND WESTOVER ROADS** appearing on a red background, **VIA OLD CHRISTCHURCH ROAD** on a blue background and all others on black. The Sunbeam MF2Bs retained solely **VIA BATH AND WESTOVER ROADS** on a coloured (red) background, all other displays being printed on black, but blind changes with the motorbus fleet ensured that a few vehicles still had blue **VIA OLD CHRISTCHURCH ROAD** blinds, in some cases only in one display. In general, less use was made of the auxiliary blinds on the trolleybuses than on the motorbuses, those on the Main Road and Ashley Road services being restricted to **VIA BATH AND WESTOVER ROADS** or **VIA OLD CHRISTCHURCH ROAD,** while those on the Side Routes displayed a blank black screen (white on the Sunbeam MF2Bs). Special indications were used as appropriate.

The ex-Brighton BUT9611Ts were equipped with main final-destination and intermediate point blinds from Sunbeam MS2s (potentially from those withdrawn in in 1957 and 1958), the blinds probably having only been supplied in 1954.

Service number **39** was added to the blinds of the three open-top Sunbeam MS2 conversions whilst initially the main screen showed **CIRCULAR TOUR** in large letters, however, when in July 1958 the service started to pick-up and set-down at intermediate points standard blind displays were used. On No. 202 the service number **39** was added on a length of pale green material used for the open-top motorbus coastal service.

Although there were detail differences over the years and, on occasion, individual intermediate points and the final destination blinds received additional, sewn-in sections, typical blind displays for the various types of Bournemouth trolleybuses are shown below:

Appendix F

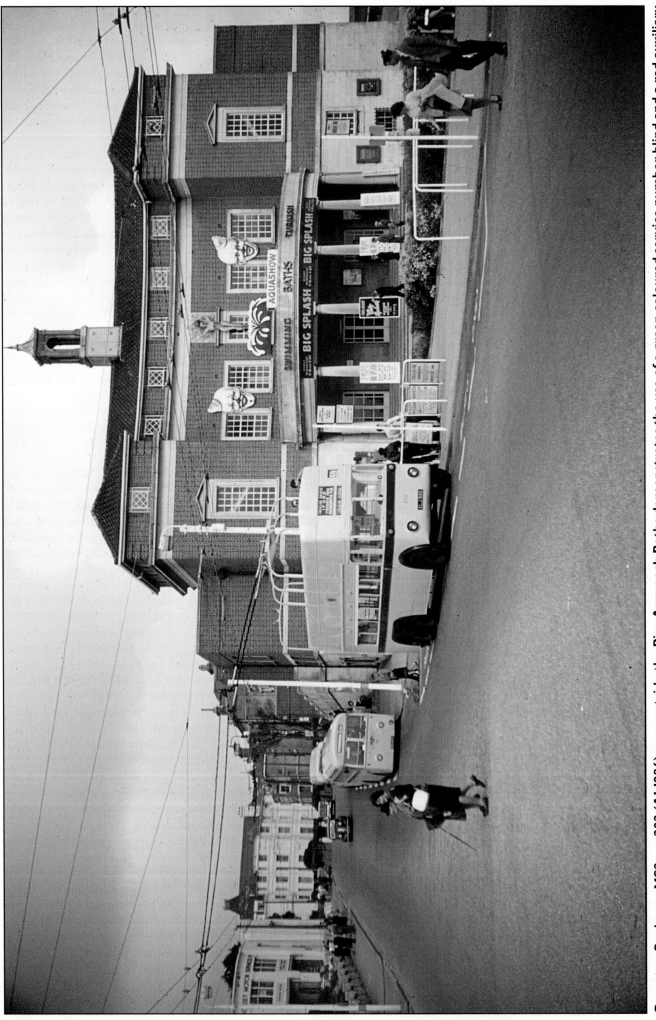

Open top Sunbeam MS2 no. 202 (ALJ986) seen outside the Pier Approach Baths demonstrates the use of a green coloured service number blind and a red auxiliary blind in its front indicator boxes. The layout as such is that introduced in November 1935 with the 1950 repositioning of the auxiliary indicator box.   Paul Creswell

420

From 1950, the auxiliary single-line indicator box in the driver's nearside windscreen on Sunbeam MS2s was removed and replaced by an aperture in the upper-deck front panel beneath the main indicator box, as seen on no. 96 (ALJ970) at the Square. No change was made to the auxiliary display at the rear.   David Chalk collection

The rear indicator box layout on open top Sunbeam MS2s was identical to that on the "closed top" vehicles of the same type although coloured service number blinds were definitely non-standard.
Paul Creswell

As can be seen from this view of Sunbeam MF2B no. 274 (WRU274) passing BUT9641T no. 252 (KLJ352) in Gervis Place, the post-war trolleybus deliveries, including the ex-Brighton BUT9611Ts, adopted the 1935 standard indicator aperture layout with an auxiliary indicator beneath in the upper deck front panels whilst all apertures at the rear were located in the upper deck panels.

Roger G. Funnell (courtesy Mrs D. Funnell and Rodney Funnell)

The standard appearance of the rear indicator boxes on the post-war trolleybus deliveries can be seen fom this view of Sunbeam MF2B no. 278 (YLJ278) leaving the Christchurch terminus. The Sunbeam MF2Bs, the BUT9641Ts and the ex-Brighton BUT9611Ts all had indicator boxes in the upper deck panels above the open rear plaform. Christchurch still retains its nautical flavour!   Roger G. Funnell (courtesy Mrs D. Funnell and Rodney Funnell)

TROLLEYBUS INDICATOR BLINDS
A) Front, platform and rear screens BUT9641Ts

A

POKESDOWN

STROUDEN PARK
IFORD

CEMETERY JUNCTION
SQUARE

LANSDOWNE
BOSCOMBE
IFORD
JUMPERS
CHRISTCHURCH

IFORD
BOSCOMBE
LANSDOWNE
SQUARE

BOSCOMBE
FISHERMANS WALK
SOUTHBOURNE
TUCKTON BRIDGE
CHRISTCHURCH

BOSCOMBE
FISHERMANS WALK
CRANLEIGH ROAD
TUCKTON BRIDGE
CARBERY AVENUE

FISHERMANS WALK
BOSCOMBE
LANSDOWNE
SQUARE
WESTBOURNE

BOURNEMOUTH SQUARE
CENTRAL STATION
QUEENS PARK
ASHLEY ROAD

BOURNEMOUTH PIER B
VIA
LANSDOWNE
CASTLE LANE DEPOT

continued ↑

WINTON
MOORDOWN
CASTLE LANE
WEST WAY
CEMETERY JUNCTION
SQUARE

RESERVED

FIVE WAYS
COURT ROAD
CASTLE LANE
WEST WAY

FIVE WAYS
MALVERN ROAD

CENTRAL STATION
WINTON
MOORDOWN
CASTLE LANE

CENTRAL STATION
LANSDOWNE
SQUARE

WINTON
TALBOT VILLAGE
WALLISDOWN

WINTON
ENSBURY PARK
COLUMBIA ROAD
WALLISDOWN
WINTON
CEMETERY JUNCTION
SQUARE

WINTON
MOORDOWN
STROUDEN PARK

MOORDOWN
WINTON
SQUARE

Notes to BUT9611T and BUT 9641T main screens:

A   The maker's name, Norbury & Co., Statham Street, Pendlebury, appeared here.

B   BOURNEMOUTH PIER was written in deep letters across two lines

Latterly, some BUT9641Ts had their blinds replaced with 1954 blinds from withdrawn Sunbeam MS2s as evidenced by some photographs showing blind displays with BOURNEMOUTH SQUARE rather than simply SQUARE. It is believed that this appeared in larger lettering in the display for service 25.

B) Front, platform and rear blinds Sunbeam MF2Bs

Notes to Sunbeam MF2B front, platform and rear screens:

A   The maker's name, Norbury & Co., Statham Street, Pendlebury, appeared here.

B   BOURNEMOUTH PIER was written in deep letters across 2 lines

A

POKESDOWN

STROUDEN PARK
IFORD

CEMETERY JUNCTION
BOURNEMOUTH SQUARE

LANSDOWNE
BOSCOMBE
IFORD
JUMPERS
CHRISTCHURCH

IFORD
BOSCOMBE
LANSDOWNE
BOURNEMOUTH SQUARE

BOSCOMBE
FISHERMANS WALK
SOUTHBOURNE
TUCKTON BRIDGE
CHRISTCHURCH

BOSCOMBE
FISHERMANS WALK
CRANLEIGH ROAD
TUCKTON BRIDGE
CARBERY AVENUE

FISHERMANS WALK
BOSCOMBE
LANSDOWNE
BOURNEMOUTH SQUARE
WESTBOURNE

BOURNEMOUTH SQUARE
CENTRAL STATION
QUEENS PARK
ASHLEY ROAD

CENTRAL STATION
BOURNEMOUTH SQUARE
WEST STATION
WESTBOURNE

A

continued ↑

B

BOURNEMOUTH PIER
VIA
LANSDOWNE
CASTLE LANE DEPOT

WINTON
MOORDOWN
CASTLE LANE
WEST WAY
CEMETERY JUNCTION
BOURNEMOUTH SQUARE

RESERVED

FIVE WAYS
COURT ROAD
CASTLE LANE
WEST WAY

FIVE WAYS
MALVERN ROAD

CENTRAL STATION
WINTON
MOORDOWN
CASTLE LANE

CENTRAL STATION
LANSDOWNE
BOURNEMOUTH SQUARE

WINTON
TALBOT VILLAGE
WALLISDOWN

WINTON
ENSBURY PARK
COLUMBIA ROAD
WALLISDOWN
WINTON
CEMETERY JUNCTION
BOURNEMOUTH SQUARE

WINTON
MOORDOWN
STROUDEN PARK
IFORD
BOURNEMOUTH SQUARE

BOSCOME
IFORD
STROUDEN PARK

MOORDOWN
WINTON

B

C) Front and rear blinds (31 October 1942) Sunbeam MS2s

D) Front and rear blinds (final style or pre-1954 with the addition of "Pokesdown") Sunbeam MS2s

SQUARE
LANSDOWNE
BOSCOMBE
IFORD

BOSCOMBE
LANSDOWNE
SQUARE
WESTBOURNE

FISHERMANS WALK
BOSCOMBE
LANSDOWNE
SQUARE

BOSCOMBE
FISHERMANS WALK
SOUTHBOURNE
CHRISTCHURCH

LANSDOWNE
CENTRAL ST<u>N</u>
QUEEN'S PARK
ASHLEY ROAD

CENTRAL ST<u>N</u>
LANSDOWNE
SQUARE
WESTBOURNE

GARAGE ONLY

CEMETERY JT<u>N</u>
WINTON
WALLISDOWN
COLUMBIA ROAD

continued ↑

CEMETERY JT<u>N</u>
WINTON
COLUMBIA ROAD
WALLISDOWN

CEMETERY JT<u>N</u>
WINTON
BRASSEY ROAD
MOORDOWN
CASTLE LANE JT<u>N</u>

WINTON
CEMETERY JT<u>N</u>
SQUARE

LANSDOWNE
CEMETERY JT<u>N</u>
WINTON
MOORDOWN
CASTLE LANE JT<u>N</u>

CEMETERY JT<u>N</u>
CENTRAL ST<u>N</u>
LANSDOWNE
SQUARE

KING'S ROAD
FIVE WAYS
COURT ROAD
CASTLE LANE

KINGS ROAD
CEMETERY JT<u>N</u>
SQUARE

GARAGE ONLY

RESERVED

CEMETERY JT<u>N</u>

KING'S ROAD
FIVE WAYS
MALVERN R<u>D</u> JT<u>N</u>

POKESDOWN   A

LANSDOWNE
BOSCOMBE
IFORD
JUMPERS
CHRISTCHURCH

IFORD
BOSCOMBE
LANSDOWNE
SQUARE

BOSCOMBE
FISHERMANS WALK
SOUTHBOURNE
TUCKON BRIDGE
CARBERY AVENUE

FISHERMANS WALK
BOSCOMBE
LANSDOWNE
SQUARE
WESTBOURNE

CENTRAL STATION
QUEENS PARK
ASHLEY ROAD

CENTRAL STATION
SQUARE
WEST STATION
WESTBOURNE

BOURNEMOUTH PIER   B
VIA
LANSDOWNE
CASTLE LANE DEPOT

WINTON
MOORDOWN
CASTLE LANE
WEST WAY
CEMETERY JUNCTION

continued ↑

SQUARE

RESERVED

FIVE WAYS
COURT ROAD
CASTLE LANE
WEST WAY

FIVE WAYS
MALVERN ROAD

CENTRAL STATION
WINTON
MOORDOWN
CASTLE LANE

CENTRAL STATION
LANSDOWNE
SQUARE

WINTON
TALBOT VILLAGE
WALLISDOWN

WINTON
ENSBURY PARK
COLUMBIA ROAD
WALLISDOWN
WINTON

CEMETERY JUNCTION
SQUARE

WINTON
MOORDOWN
STROUDEN PARK
IFORD
SQUARE

BOSCOMBE
IFORD
STROUDEN PARK

MOORDOWN
WINTON
SQUARE

Notes to MS2 main screens:

A   The maker's name, Norbury & Co., Statham Street, Pendlebury, appeared here.

B   BOURNEMOUTH PIER was written in deep letters across 2 lines

C   Open top MS2s 200-202 also had:
CIRCULAR TOUR written in deep letters on 2 lines taking up the entire screen

D) Auxiliary screens Sunbeam MS2

TO AND FROM FETE	
TO AND FROM FLOWER SHOW	
TO AND FROM REGATTA	
HORSESHOE COMMON	A
VIA IFORD	
VIA SOUTHBOURNE	
CIRCULAR SERVICE	B
VIA OLD CHRISTCHURCH ROAD	C
VIA BATH AND WESTOVER ROADS FOR BOURNEMOUTH PIER AND PAVILION	D
VIA ASHLEY ROAD	E
VIA CENTRAL STATION	E
VIA BRASSEY ROAD	F
VIA TALBOT VILLAGE	I
TO AND FROM FOOTBALL	I, H
TO AND FROM CRICKET	I, H
TO AND FROM TENNIS	I, H
TO AND FROM HOCKEY & RUGBY FESTIVAL	G, I, H
TO AND FROM CIRCUS	I, H
TO AND FROM CARNIVAL	I, H
TO AND FROM SHOW	I, H
TO AND FROM PAGEANT	I, H
TO AND FROM BAND CONTEST	I, H
TO AND FROM EXHIBITION	I, H

Notes to Sunbeam MS2 auxiliary screens:

A   This display was on an additional piece of blind sewn in.

B   Open top MS2 202 (at least) had a dark red background to this display. This was possibly an older display intended for use on services 26A, 28A, 30 and 30A when they first commenced.

C   White letters on blue blind.

D   White letters (two lines of text) on red blind.

E   White letters on green blind.

F   White letters on orange blind.

G   "Hockey & Rugby" were printed in a curve thicker at the ends of the line with "Festival" centred below and increasing in depth towards the centre of the word.

H   "To and From" were printed in 3 lines of block capitals preceding the event name.

I   White letters on black blind.

E) Auxiliary screens Sunbeam MF2Bs

VIA BATH AND WESTOVER RDS	A
VIA OLD CHRISTCHURCH ROAD	B
VIA IFORD	B
VIA SOUTHBOURNE	B
VIA HOLDENHURST ROAD	B
VIA CHARMINSTER ROAD	B
VIA PETERS HILL	B
ALBERT ROAD ONLY	B
SCHOOL SPECIAL	B
TO AND FROM FOOTBALL	B, C
TO AND FROM CRICKET	B, C
TO AND FROM TENNIS	B, C
TO AND FROM SHOW	B, C
TO AND FROM CIRCUS	B, C
TO AND FROM REGATTA	B, C
TO AND FROM CARNIVAL	B, C
TO AND FROM ATHLETIC CENTRE	B, C

Notes to Sunbeam MF2B auxiliary screens:

A.   White letters on red blind

B.   White letters on black blind

C.   "To and From" were printed in 3 lines of block capitals preceding the event name.

D.   This display was included on the blinds fitted to 295-303 when new but added to 258-287 after delivery.

F) Side destination screens (rearmost nearside and offside lower saloon windows) Sunbeam MS2

G) Service number blinds BUT 9611T, BUT 9641T

MALVERN ROAD JN
COLUMBIA ROAD
WALLISDOWN
FOOTBALL GROUND
COURT ROAD
CASTLE LANE JN   A
BRASSEY ROAD
TUCKTON BRIDGE
CRANLEIGH ROAD
CHRISTCHURCH   B
VIA SOUTHBOURNE
CHRISTCHURCH   B
VIA IFORD
CROSS ROADS SOUTHBOURNE
FISHERMANS WALK
IFORD
SQUARE
COUNTY GATES   C
SPECIAL
RESERVED
DEPOT ONLY
CEMETERY JUNCTION
WINTON
LANSDOWNE
FIVE WAYS
CASTLE LANE
MOORDOWN
WESTBOURNE
WEST STATION
SQUARE
ASHLEY ROAD
CENTRAL STATION
QUEENS PARK
CAPSTONE ROAD

20	25	30A
24	25A	31
24A	26	24
21	26A	32
21A	27	33
22	27A	34
22A	28	35
22B	28A	36
23	29	37
23A	30	38

continued ↑   continued ↑

Notes to side destination screens:

A.   Castle Lane Junction referred to Lawford Road
B.   Printed on 2 lines.
C.   Blacked-out on the vehicle inspected (206), a move carried out in autumn 1947 (see main text).

These blinds did not consider points on trolleybus routes opened after 1950.

H) Service number blinds Sunbeam MS2

20	25A	24
24	26	32
24A	26A	33
21	27	34
21A	28A	35
22	29	36
23	30	37
23A	30A	38
25	31	

A (next to 23)
B (next to 38 column)

continued ↑   continued ↑

I) Service number blinds Sunbeam MF2B

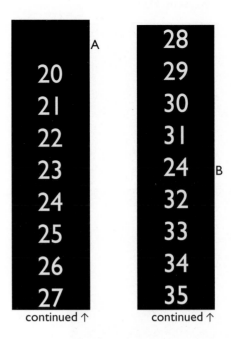

20	28	36
21	29	37
22	30	38
23	31	39
24	24	40
25	32	41
26	33	42
27	34	
	35	

A (top of first MF2B column)
B (next to 24)
C (next to 40, 41, 42)
A (bottom right)

continued ↑   continued ↑

Notes to Sunbeam MS2 number blinds:

A   An MS2 was recorded in March 1954 as having numbers 22A and 22B between 22 and 23. After 30A, numbers 31 to 35 had been added, presumably in the mid-1950s. Only on completely new blinds was 24 repeated after 31. Originally such numbers as 22B, 25B and so on brought into use during the lifetime of the trolleybus were added by sewing on additional lengths, sometimes at the end of the blind and out of numerical sequence.

B   Open-top MS2s 200-202 had the number 39 added and in the case of 202 this was printed on a piece of green material.

Notes to Sunbeam MF2B number blinds:

A   Indicates a blank (black) line prior to and after individual displays.

B   The second number 24 was to accommodate circular routings along Castle Lane when services 24 and 32 interworked.

C   Intended for any additional services.

Travelling west along Holdenhurst Road, just past the Central Station and the junction with St. Swithun's Road, on 4 July 1965 is **BUT9641T no. 243 (KLJ343), rebuilt in May-June 1963 without a front staircase, on its way to Westbourne. Could the gentleman staning in the road, apparently with a camera in his hands, be a trolleybus enthusiast?**
Robin Helliar-Symons

APPENDIX G
DEPOTS AND WORKSHOPS

Until about 1950 those Sunbeam MS2 trolleybuses delivered in 1935 having ALJ or BEL registration mark letters and even registration numbers (BCT referring to vehicles primarily by their registration numbers rather than fleet numbers) were allocated permanently to Moordown Depot, all other vehicles were based at Central Depot, Southcote Road. In this respect, when Boscombe (Pokesdown) Depot later became an operating base, no trolleybuses were based there and a vehicle starting from Boscombe one morning could return to Central Depot, Southcote Road that evening and operate on any of the workings from there the next day. When the BUT 9641Ts were delivered, they were initially all allocated to Central Depot, but some were transferred to Boscombe or Moordown depots from 1951. Thereafter, it seems that the policy of allocating trolleybuses to a specific depot was abandoned, perhaps with the opening of Castle Lane (Mallard Road) Depot in 1953. The three open-top Sunbeam MS2s, however, were allocated to Central Depot whilst they were in operation.

When the fleet was at its maximum extent it was impossible to store all trolleybuses under cover.

Boscombe (Pokesdown) Depot

A brick building with stone facings in the same style as that in Southcote Road, the small Boscombe Depot was set back about 20ft from the south side of Christchurch Road next to the New Bell Inn public house about 100yds west of its junction with Seabourne Road and close to Pokesdown Station. Overall width was 57ft 7in, incorporating a 33ft 7in entrance, with an internal depth of 126ft. The structure featured a single circular window centred above the entrance with matching circular embellishments and arches each side of the entrance which was surmounted by a deep girder. Internal natural illumination was by roof lights supplemented by whitewashed walls. Entrance doors were apparently never fitted to the depot building. A small low-walled yard brought the property in line with the shops on the south side of Christchurch Road. The yard entrance was equipped with metal gates until removal during the wartime salvage drive. The depot opened for trams on 12 April 1906.

The trams accessed the depot building by a trailing junction from the outbound line of the Pokesdown Station passing loop. There were four short terminal tram tracks, the easternmost having a siding towards the front of the building; the floor space taken up by this siding being built over in 1955 when a BCT-owned traction power substation 12ft wide and about 50ft deep was built alongside the eastern boundary wall. There was an office and crew mess-room at the rear of the building in the left hand (eastern) corner, looking from the road. The facilities were always very basic, as no crews used the premises during the day, and comprised just a table, chairs, kettle, washbasin and telephone, initially Boscombe 410, but changed to Bournemouth

Boscombe (Pokesdown) Depot in the early 1950s, giving an impression of the original overhead wiring access - namely a facing frog in both the east and westbound lines in Christchurch Road. Sunbeam MS2 no. 150 (BRU1) rests at the entrance and other vehicles are parked inside. On the pavement outside, the crew room's empties await the milkman.
Omnibus Society (R.T. Wilson)

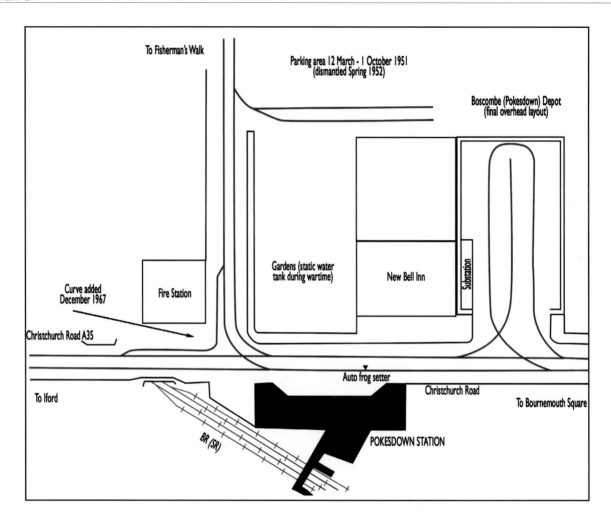

43028 in 1964. No other structural alterations were ever made. From 23 December 1935, all remaining operational trams were housed at Boscombe.

Trams were operated until services to Christchurch ceased on 8 April 1936 and once the trams had been removed, the building was used as a store for both motorbuses and trolleybuses. Construction of an air raid shelter inside the depot building at an early date in the Second World War prevented any vehicles being stored there until April 1941 when some space was made available for storage purposes. It is not known when trolleybus overhead wiring access was erected but as the depot became operational for trolleybuses only in the second half of 1945 following the removal of the air raid shelter in July 1945, it is likely to have been around that date. The original trolleybus overhead wiring layout inside the depot building had just two lines with access by a facing frog in the eastbound Christchurch Road wiring and a facing frog in the westbound wiring. Trolleybuses entered the depot nose-in and had to reverse out into the main road under the guidance of an inspector.

At some later date the wiring layout was altered to three lines of trolleybus overhead wiring inside the depot building. The central line was entered over a facing frog from the westbound Christchurch Road wiring. The line on the eastern side of the depot, closest to the New Bell Inn, was entered by a facing frog in the eastbound Christchurch Road wiring, made a tight loop at the rear of the building, which could not be negotiated by trolleybuses, and exited into a trail frog in the westbound Christchurch Road wiring. Trolleybuses continued to drive in to the depot nose-in and reverse out into the main road.

Boscombe Depot offered cramped overnight accommodation

for up to 16 trolleybuses, although 17 were garaged there in the winter of 1950-51, but once the substation had been added, capacity fell to 12 vehicles. Between November 1950 and October 1951, when the fleet was at its maximum size, the limited depot space was supplemented by overnight parking accommodation for 16 trolleybuses on the west side of Seabourne Road near its junction with Christchurch Road, Pokesdown, adjacent to the depot. Boscombe never garaged motorbuses.

After closure on 31 December 1967 the depot was used as an indoor market for the sale of second-hand goods. It was demolished in the mid-1990s and the site has since been redeveloped as an apartment block, set back from the road with a large garden at the front.

Moordown Depot

This depot in the then northernmost suburbs of Bournemouth was opened on 25 May 1906 to provide a practical operating base at the end of the line for the Side Route trams which, in any case, could not easily access Central Depot due to the track layout. Constructed in brick it was built on a plot of land on Wimborne Road opposite the present-day Barrie Road just south of the Malvern Road/Redhill Crescent crossroads. The car shed had two bays: the narrower one to the north was partitioned off in January 1923 to accommodate a three-road paint shop (which was moved from Central Depot) and crew rooms at the rear, whilst the wider second bay had six roads accessed by two three-line fans. Trams entered and left the building from the inbound line of the Moordown terminal loop.

The Moordown Depot property was extended twice prior to the trolleybus era. In 1921 a small, shallower building with

The overhead wiring layout at Boscombe (Pokesdown) Depot was changed, presumably at some time in the 1950s, to provide three lines as shown. Sunbeam MF2B nos. 299 (299LJ) and 298 (298LJ) display the final livery style on 30 April 1967.

David Pearson

four shorter roads, set back further from Wimborne Road, was added to the south and angled from the original main shed to accommodate a new batch of bogie trams (Nos. 93-112). Prior to this, some single-truck tramcars were housed at Central Depot; however, it now became possible to base the majority of the single-truck cars at Moordown. The remainder, primarily ex-PDET cars, had by then been withdrawn and were stored off the tracks at Central Depot.

The side and end walls of this building were built of brick, and were windowless but for a circular window in the upper portion of the rear wall. The front entrance was left open with vertical wooden planking extending to the apex of the roof. Old tram rails were used for the building's girder work. Later, in 1930, the original main shed was extended forwards to within about six feet of the pavement along Wimborne Road. It was equipped with a brick and stone "public building" front typical of the period, and roller-shutter doors, which were seldom used with the exception of those at the front of the paint shop. The paint shop continued to be used as such until the depot complex was closed and vacated. From 1931, Moordown's capacity was 30 trams and six motorbuses. In late 1938, the main building was re-roofed with corrugated iron sheets.

On 28 June 1935 trams ceased using Moordown Depot after a three-week period of combined tram and trolleybus

operation along Wimborne Road north of Cemetery Junction. Initially trolleybuses turned at Moordown by driving into the depot forecourt and then reversed into Wimborne Road, but on 28 June 1935 terminating trolleybuses were extended to a reversing triangle at the junction of Redhill Crescent with Wimborne Road about 50yds north of the depot. Increasing road traffic led to use of the triangle being discontinued on 14 August 1950 and trolleybuses started to use a turning circle which had been erected through the depot yard and a side wall in the original shed. The nominal capacity of Moordown Depot was 36 trolleybuses achieved by parking six rows of four vehicles in the main shed and a further four rows of three in the later separate extension. However, normally only 30 trolleybuses were accommodated as six motorbuses were garaged there from 1931. Up to a further seven vehicles were parked in the open when the fleet was at its maximum. Moordown served the Side Routes of the system. The telephone number was Winton 945.

There was a mess room above the crew rooms at the rear of the paint shop and this was extended in August 1943 to form a canteen serving meals.

An ex-driver recalls: "Moordown based crews were in many ways a breed of their own and we (Central Depot crews) didn't mix a lot. In fact if you had to take a bus into Moordown Depot for

431

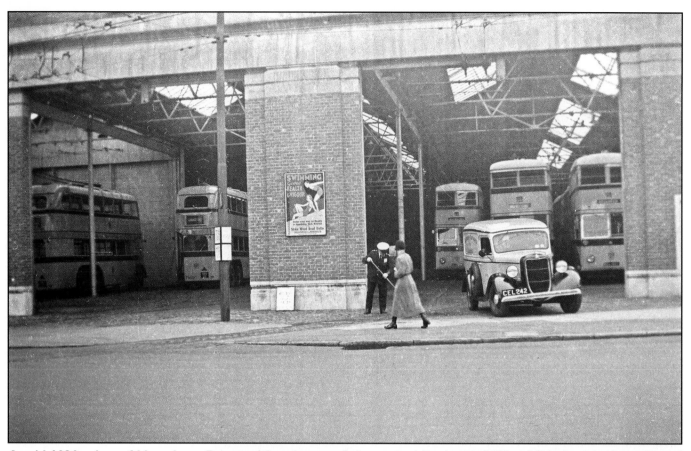

A mid-1930s view of Moordown Depot with only two of the several Sunbeam MS2s visible having the enlarged indicator box introduced in 1935. Tram tracks into Wimborne Road are still evident as the undertaking's Fordson 15cwt van no. 5 (CEL242) departs.   Omnibus Society (R.T. Wilson)

Sunbeam MS2 nos. 155 (BRU6) and 163 (BRU14) are parked in Moordown Depot's annexe shed of 1921 as BUT9641T no. 213 (KLJ347) branches off the access wiring to use the turning circle erected above the depot yard and through the south side wall of the main shed in summer 1950. Judging by the number of spectators this photograph must have been taken soon after the turning circle's inauguration.   Omnibus Society (R.T. Wilson)

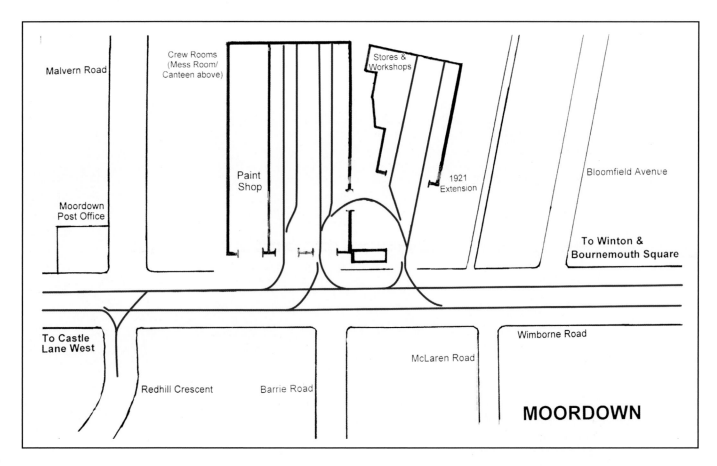

Map labels: Malvern Road · Crew Rooms (Mess Room/Canteen above) · Stores & Workshops · Moordown Post Office · Paint Shop · 1921 Extension · Bloomfield Avenue · To Winton & Bournemouth Square · To Castle Lane West · Redhill Crescent · Barrie Road · McLaren Road · Wimborne Road · **MOORDOWN**

any reason and went into their canteen for a cup of tea, you were regarded with suspicion".

The growing need of public transport and thus a larger fleet of vehicles prompted the undertaking to consider enlarging its depot accommodation. Plans had been shelved in October 1939 due to the outbreak of war. Architects visited London Transport's Chiswick works, various trolleybus depots and the H&D maintenance facilities at Southampton. In an effort to look ahead some 35 years they anticipated that Bournemouth, Christchurch and Poole Boroughs might come under unified control and that all transport services could be nationalised. Whatever the future might bring, Bournemouth would retain its prominent position and a much larger fleet of vehicles was anticipated. Their plans were based on the need to accommodate 240 vehicles, but they felt that 350 might be required to serve just Bournemouth and Christchurch in the not too distant future. Should Poole also be considered the figure could reach 500. The alternative sites considered were Boscombe (Pokesdown); the Central Depot, Southcote Road; Moordown; and Strouden Farm, Castle Lane. The architects felt that the existing depots at Boscombe (Pokesdown) and Moordown should be closed; the Central Depot, Southcote Road, should be enlarged to accommodate 100 vehicles and a new depot built off Castle Lane to accommodate an additional 200 vehicles.

On 13 March 1945 a Transport Subcommittee recommended the compulsory purchase of property in Rose Gardens (numbers 5, 7, 9, 13, 15, 17), at the rear of Moordown Depot to permit an extension, increased maintenance facilities there and an alternative depot exit into Rose Gardens and Malvern Road. This would have enabled all vehicles in the fleet to be housed under cover. At that time, the proposal was simply to buy the necessary land and houses, but not to demolish the buildings. The MoT pointed out that such a Compulsory Purchase Order would not be confirmed unless recommended on the grounds

of public safety. The Finance (Negotiating) Subcommittee were instructed to acquire 5, 7, 9 Rose Gardens, together with the allotment ground at the rear, at an estimated cost of £2,500 each, and the rear of numbers 13, 15, 17 Rose Gardens at £1,500. Ultimately the houses at 13, 15, and 17 would be required. The initial plans for an extension to Moordown Depot were available in June 1948 and sent to Mr Lindsay Clegg, Town Clerk.

Despite their intention of retaining Moordown Depot to serve as the operating base for services to the northern part of Bournemouth, the 18 January 1946 decision to build new facilities off Castle Lane ultimately made Moordown redundant. Negotiations to acquire housing and land at the rear of the depot were halted on 26 November 1948 and given up entirely on 20 May 1949. On Saturday 25 July 1953, coinciding with the opening of Castle Lane (Mallard Road) Depot, the Moordown depot complex and turning circle ceased to be used, last journeys terminating at Castle Lane rather than Moordown Depot. The site was vacated completely by 26 July 1953. It was leased to Post Office Telephones as a vehicle depot and subsequently demolished in 1984. A supermarket and related car park has since been built on the site.

Central Depot, Southcote Road

The tramcar sheds at Southcote Road constituted just a portion of a complex which originally embraced an electricity generating station, cooling towers, stores and workshops, and later the Transport Department offices and motorbus garage. The original buildings were in brick with stone facings and round-topped windows. The main car shed comprised six long "run-through" stabling roads in two bays featuring roof lights and Doric pediments above each doorway. Built on to the southern wall of the shed was a shorter two-road workshop. The depot came into use for the opening of Bournemouth's first tram route, Lansdowne-Pokesdown, on 23 July 1902.

Moordown Depot on its final day of use, 25 July 1953, showing a range of Sunbeam MS2s including nos. 92, 165 and 152, and a single BUT9641T no. 215 (KLJ349). The tram track depot fan is still intact whilst it will be noted that trolleybuses drove into the shed but reversed out, before using the circle of wiring through the main shed to exit on to Wimborne Road (no. 92 seems to be following this circle). **David Chalk collection**

In 1921, an additional car shed serving as an overhaul works and containing pits, a body shop and paint shop, was built to the south of the eastern end of the main depot with six short roads accessible from the west only. It replaced the two-road workshop which was converted into staff rooms for platform staff, the depot inspector and garage foreman. A canteen, mess or recreation room and stores were located above. The paint shop was transferred to Moordown in January 1923 and the space created became part of the overhaul works. When tramway operation ceased, the building that had served as the overhaul works was unused and became derelict, being occasionally used for motorbus storage purposes and only being demolished after the Transport Department had vacated the premises. The open yard to the west of the building was roofed over in 1930-31 to become a motorbus garage.

Henceforth, trolleybus overhauls were carried out in the main car shed (by now the trolleybus garage) whilst there were pits in the motorbus garage which also accommodated a body shop and workshop at its western end.

As the main operating depot and workshops, Central Depot, Southcote Road was able to accommodate a maximum of 54 trolleybuses by parking them in six rows of nine vehicles each, although official reports indicate that it was planned for just 36. Roller-shutter doors, possibly with "drawbridge" sections in the overhead wiring, were installed before tramway operations ceased, but fell into disuse. In later years they tended to be shut solely on Christmas Day when no trolleybus services operated.

The depot building and yard featured a number of unusual overhead wiring installations in conjunction with the three-wire layout along the Southcote Road western access route. This layout probably dated back to the period of time in the mid-1930s when both trams and trolleybuses were using the

access routes to get to and from the depot, with minimal alterations being made once the tramways had been completely abandoned. During the tramway era there were two short sections of (single, positive) overhead wire on each side of the single through wire in each of the two bays of the depot building. These four sections were limited to the inside of the building, thereby giving each of the six tramway sidings its own overhead wire but avoiding the use of frogs. It would seem that these four single positive overhead wires were left in place following tramway abandonment, one each side of the through trolleybus wiring in each bay of the building, for testing purposes. Rewiring trolleybuses inside the depot building in the hours of darkness must have been something of a nightmare!

Initially, the undertaking's head office had been at 5 Lansdowne Crescent, moving to 6 Wootton Gardens, off Old Christchurch Road, on 22 March 1920, where it remained until 1940 when the building's dilapidated state prompted a move to Southcote Road. In May 1926, 101 Southcote Road, a semi-detached house on the north side of the road adjoining the generating station was purchased, and in December 1933, the other part of the house, 99 Southcote Road was bought for £240 12s. Both houses were used to house generating station shift employees until 1 April 1940 when the undertaking's headquarters moved to 99/101 Southcote Road, the new headquarters being created by knocking the two houses (99 and 101) into one. The original telephone number was Bournemouth 77, but this changed to Bournemouth 20077 in 1959.

In a letter to the Transport Committee, dated 6 December 1957, the General Manager, Mr W.D. Reakes, revisited the subject of expanded and improved depot and workshop accommodation. Considering the Southcote Road facilities, he detailed the following alternative solutions:

The east end of the Central Depot complex viewed from St. Clement's Road on 16 June 1934 with Sunbeam MS2 no. 72 (AEL400), just eight days after delivery, parked outside the main tramcar shed.

Malcolm Pearce (G.O.P. Pearce)

A youngster watches the latest form of public transport in Bournemouth manoeuvering at the east end of the Central Depot yard on 16 June 1934. Once again it's Sunbeam MS2 no. 72 (AEL400).

Malcolm Pearce (G.O.P. Pearce)

435

CENTRAL DEPOT, SOUTHCOTE ROAD

A	trolleybus garage (formerly tram shed)	M	garage	Depot layout immediately before its vacation on 6 June 1965
B	motorbus garage (a roofed-over yard)	N	cable store	
C	Overhead Department store	P	Dawson washing machine	Courtesy: John Mawson (extract from an original plan prepared in 1965)
D	Overhead Department office and workshop	Q	store	
E	two-storey office block	R	scrap metal compound	
F	Head Office building (99 Southcote Road)	S	private houses and shops	
G	power house - boiler room	T	workshops and offices, including Conductors', Inspectors' and Depot Foreman's Rooms; Canteen and recreation room above	
H	power house – generator room			
I	Mains Department office	U	position of former cooling towers	
J	railway siding			
K	SEB substation (transformer and switch yard at rear)			
L	BCT substation			

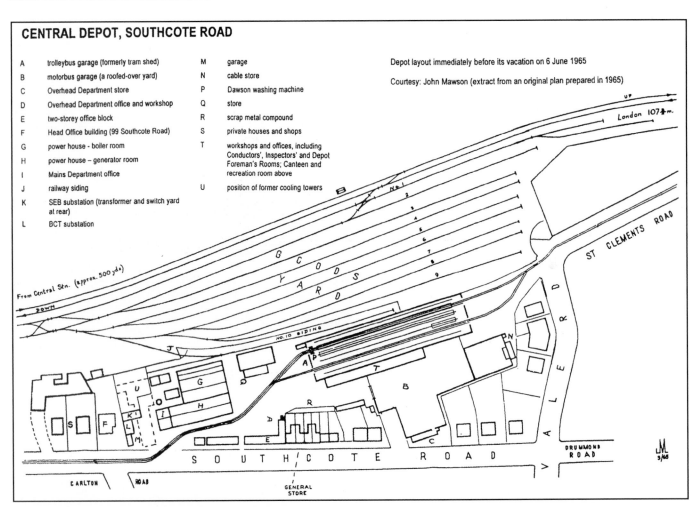

Some thirty years after the preceding photograph, **BUT9641T no. 253 (KLJ353)** and an unidentified Sunbeam **MF2B of the 258 - 262 series**, are seen outside the west end of the main shed. Note the three-wire overhead line leading to the north entrance. Roger G. Funnell (courtesy Mrs D. Funnell and Rodney Funnell)

Sunbeam MF2B no. 283 (YLJ283) and an unidentified but rebuilt BUT 9641T are seen inside the main shed at Central Depot, Southcote Road.   Roger G. Funnell (courtesy Mrs D. Funnell and Rodney Funnell)

The BCT Head Office at 99 Southcote Road with the cooling towers, chimney and power house of the electricity generating station. The brick-built structure in the right foreground with a clerestory roof and corrugated covering is the new electricity substation erected in 1955 to replace BCT's own generating station. It's construction necessitated the demolition of one of the cooling towers.   David Chalk collection

Former Generating Station: The option of retaining the whole or part of the present building had been reviewed, but so many structural alterations would have had to be made that he recommended the demolition of the shell and its replacement with a new structure.

To convert the former generating station into a workshop would have required much work to the front portion, e.g. removal of pillars and switchboard platform, dismantling of gantry and filling-in of pits. The rear, lower level, portion would have had to be built up to the height of the front portion. The chimney would have been demolished, thus providing hard core. The front and dividing walls, together with the low wall at the rear of the building bordering on the railway line would have had to be removed, leaving the side and rear walls. The heating of a 40ft-high building would have proved costly.

A new steel-framed structure was considered for the Southcote Road site, having asbestos cement sheeting some 20ft high at the front, for maintenance pits and on the east side to provide paint and body shops, and to allow sufficient space at the point where these two shops would join the engine shop for two storeys, having offices and stores on the first floor, and ablutions, toilet and heating boiler on the ground floor. The remainder of the building was foreseen as comprising machine, electrical, engine, panel beaters', welders' and smiths' shops, tyre stores and saw mills. This would need to be 15ft high. The construction would have provided 23,660 sq ft of accommodation compared to 34,250 at Castle Lane.

Central Depot: By now, the depot was deemed able to accommodate a maximum of 50 trolleybuses and 46 motorbuses tightly packed. This was considered undesirable for manoeuvring and fire-risk reasons. The end of the leaseholds on 143, 145, 147, 149, 151 Southcote Road (immediately to the west of the cross-roads with Vale Road) in 1964 would have provided an opportunity to extend the depot offering accommodation for up to 36 more vehicles. The floor would have had to be supported on pillars due to the fall of the land at the rear of the houses, the existing garage floor being 10ft higher than the gardens at the rear of the then existing houses. Single-deck motorbuses could have been accommodated below the main garage with ramped access from Vale Road. If the entire site under the houses was excavated to allow for a 12ft headroom it would have proved possible to accommodate the entire single-deck fleet (then 23 motorbuses) and construct a two-floor depot accommodating about 155 vehicles. In 1957, BCT had 191 vehicles in their fleet, thus even allowing for 14 trolleybuses at Boscombe (Pokesdown) Depot, 22 vehicles would still have had to be housed elsewhere.

In early 1962 it was decided to build a second garage, enabling the entire fleet to be stabled at one place, and a new administration block at the Mallard Road site. On 26 April 1965 the Transport Department's headquarters moved to new office accommodation at Mallard Road, Castle Lane, and on 7 June 1965 the depot was vacated, to be taken over by the Sanitary Department as a base for its waste disposal vehicles. The main shed was still intact in 2018 albeit with the eastern entrances sealed off.

Castle Lane (Mallard Road) Depot

History and Development: In early 1945 the Transport Committee considered requirements for post-war developments and visited the Castle Lane area in November 1945, the Town Planning Committee favouring the Corporation Farm, Strouden Park site (measuring about 10 acres) for a new depot. Strouden Farm had been used to keep the horses used to haul municipal refuse carts, etc., mechanisation of which had been deferred due to the Second World War. An alternative site at Sheepwash bordered by Castle Lane East and Riverside Avenue was felt unsuitable. On 13 December 1945, Mr Morrison wrote to the Town Planning Committee that, in selecting the most suitable position for a new depot, the Transport Committee had services in the east of Bournemouth particularly in mind. He anticipated the following situation would result:

Boscombe (Pokesdown)—to be disposed of as soon as alternative accommodation available.

Castle Lane—a new depot to be built housing and servicing vehicles in the eastern parts of the Borough.

Central Depot, Southcote Road—the existing depot, maintenance and workshop facilities to be retained as the Department's operational hub.

Moordown—to be retained and expanded as a running depot to cater for the northern parts of the Borough.

Sufficient land would be required off Castle Lane to provide a main building initially able to accommodate 70 trolleybuses (or motorbuses). Ideally the depot would be open at both ends to ease trolleybus operations and, in design and construction, it would be free from obstructions such as roof columns, i.e. ideally a single span building. Provision for future extension was to be allowed for. There should be space for the long-planned staff recreational facilities. Shell concrete construction was preferred to economise in the use of steel which would have been required in a framed structure and which was subject to supply restrictions.

The first plan showed an area of ca. 300 X 750ft for an initial 300 X 100ft depot on part of the Strouden Farm and a proposed housing development around this, fronting Strouden Lane and Broad Avenue. There was also an area intended for use as an open space. This was passed to Messrs Jackson & Greenen, Chartered Architects, Bournemouth, to prepare a scheme and to coordinate with town planning officials.

On 4 June 1946 the land was transferred to the Transport Committee at a figure agreed by the District Valuer. In May 1948, it was discovered that a space marked on an old map of the proposed site was in fact a house which had not been conveyanced to the Transport Department and which accordingly remained under the control of the Housing Committee!

Shortage of under-cover garage accommodation prompted the examination of a temporary building at Beales, Old Christchurch Road, in September 1948, but the 'eaves' height of 10ft 7in was totally unsuitable for trolleybuses which would have required an additional 8ft 6in in height. At that time, Central Depot had parking space under reasonable conditions for 32 motorbuses, but was home for 40. The trolleybus garage, planned for 36 vehicles, was accommodating 45, whilst six departmental lorries were parked in the open. There was thus a lack of accommodation for 23 vehicles. At Moordown Depot, seven vehicles were regularly parked in the open and there were three others which needed to be moved from the new shed to ease congestion. At Boscombe there was reasonable space for 12 trolleybuses, but 17 were in fact garaged there.

Jackson & Greenen presented their plans and estimates on 30 October 1948, offering alternative methods of construction featuring reinforced concrete, an aluminium frame and a steel frame. Shell concrete construction (the second most expensive option) was recommended due to the economies in steel (which was then in short supply), consisting of an 81-vehicle garage (£47,238) and workshops (£116,833). In view of structural and wind pressure constraints, any form of temporary building was not recommended. If instructed within a month, the architects felt that they could go to tender at the end of January 1949, allowing construction to commence in March and with the hope of some accommodation being available by end 1949.

There was much correspondence with the MoT and RTC with respect to securing approval, leading to a Mr Ralfs of the MoT, Southampton, visiting Bournemouth to inspect the situation. This resulted in a suggestion that the Castle Lane trolleybus extension and thus access to any new depot be reconsidered in view of the nation's economy. However, by spring 1949, the construction of the new depot off Castle Lane had become formal policy and tenders were invited.

The start of site works for Castle Lane Depot was delayed when Trevor Construction withdrew their tender. The next lowest tender, of £16,392 8s 7d from Messrs Grounds & Newton, Ltd., was accepted and, on 29 August 1949, the Transport Committee requested the Finance Committee to approve an estimated £151,216 for the first section of the scheme, including road works, garage overhead wiring and ancillary equipment. In September, it was recommended that the widening and reconstruction of part of Mallard Road, at an estimated £2,885, also be included in the cost of the new depot. By October 1949, 14 tenders had been received for the new maintenance works and garage. The lowest, from Messrs James Drewitt & Son Ltd. for £97,948 was accepted subject to Finance Committee and MoT approval, and to satisfactory sureties being submitted.

By October 1951 construction work was well underway at the Mallard Road site (but not without the customary trials and tribulations related to any building project, large or small) and the garage was made available by the builders for vehicle storage purposes. However, it was not in a finished state, whilst construction of the workshops had only just commenced. Overhead wiring access from Castle Lane to Mallard Road was installed at the same time as the Castle Lane trolleybus route extension, between Broadway Hotel and Iford, was constructed and comprised of a double-line junction to/from both east and west. Although trolleybuses could reach the site entrance by 15 October 1951, manoeuvring to a parking position for storage could initially only be accomplished on tow as the wiring in the depot area was only completed in stages during early 1952.

There was a circuit of overhead wiring, followed in a clockwise manner, around the site. Only a single garage, No. 1 and the only one equipped for trolleybuses, was constructed in this first phase of the development. It provided for 11 lines of nine vehicles, from Road 1 on the west side to Road 11 on the east. Three pairs of trolleybus wires ran through the building serving Roads 1-6 so that 54 trolleybuses could be accommodated, plus any parked elsewhere out of reach of the overhead such as the open-top Sunbeam MS2s in winter. Trolleybuses were parked according to type, i.e. BUTs together on one road, Sunbeam MS2s on the next and so on.

Construction Details: On 24 July 1953 the new Castle Lane (Mallard Road) Depot came into use following the official opening by the Mayor, Councillor H.P.E. Mears, OBE, JP, the previous day. Last journeys to Moordown Depot ran into Castle Lane on Saturday 25 July 1953 and first journey left Castle Lane Depot on Sunday 26 July 1953. The souvenir brochure produced for the opening of the depot and workshop

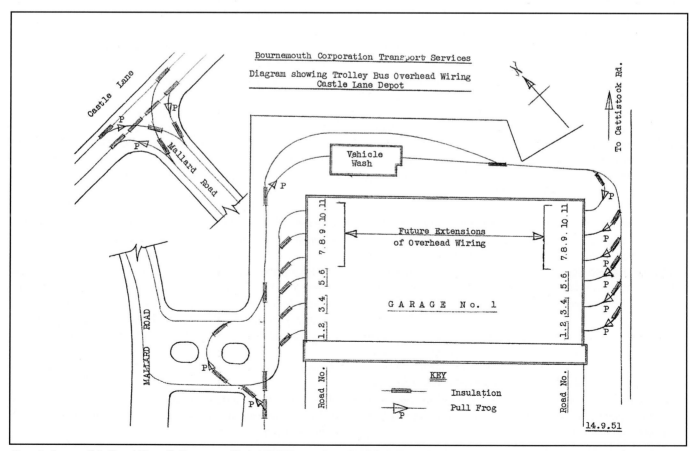

Castle Lane (Mallard Road) Depot official BCT overhead wiring layout.   **Bournemouth Transport Ltd.**

facilities recorded (with the author's additions or explanations shown in square brackets):

"In 1946 Mr Morrison's proposal to build a new depot off Castle Lane was approved by the Transport Committee and full Council, and under his direction plans for the buildings were put in hand. The Government ban on capital expenditure in 1947 caused preparatory work to be deferred and it was c. 12 months later that approval to go forward was received from the Ministry of Transport. There was a condition that the general construction must be such as to economise in the use of steel. So far the proposed buildings had been designed as steel framed with an estimated steel requirement of 634 tons but after research work it was finally decided to use a combination of reinforced and pre-stressed concrete, saving 416 tons of steel. The 24 acre Strouden Farm site had previously been used for the stabling and grazing of the Corporation's cart horses. The plans were prepared with a view to the work being carried out in sections spread over a number of years and to be readily extended with the growth of the fleet. The Maintenance Workshops so far constructed are capable of dealing with 240 buses but the plans have been prepared so that this section may eventually be enlarged to deal with up to 500 buses. James Drewitt & Son Ltd. were the building contractors and Phorpres bricks were used (600,000 common, 150,000 rustics, 150,000 Saxon facings).

"Description of the buildings

"Garage: 300ft long X 150ft wide offering a column-free covered space of 45,000 square feet. The 150ft span is the largest then constructed in the UK with pre-stressed beams and shell roof. The roof consisted of nine reinforced concrete shells of 2½in thickness, pressure sprayed on the "Gunite" system, with a span of 33ft, the intermediate beams are alike 10in wide and 5ft 6in deep. The external beams are slightly larger. The beams were cast in-situ and post-tensioned by the Magnel-Blaton system. An extractable rubber core was used to form the ducts through which the completed cables were threaded. [In fact when No. 2 Garage was eventually opened in 1965, it was of a different construction from No. 1.]

"The wire used was 0.276in in diameter and during stressing were extended 7¾in inducing a compressive force in the concrete of 507 tons. With the exception of the outside walls the building was constructed entirely of concrete thus eliminating all maintenance work which would be needed in a steel roofed building. An inspection pit with glazed tiles and fluorescent lighting is provided and at one section gallery pits are formed on either side for the easy inspection of electrical equipment of vehicles.

"Administration Block: constructed on the south-west side of the garage and designed to accommodate the second similar garage when required. It consists of workshops, tyre store, drying rooms, conductors' and inspectors' rooms, washing rooms and toilets, a first aid room, mess room and accompanying kitchen. A sprinkler system with 583 heads is provided.

"Drive-through vehicle wash: designed for two vehicles one behind the other. [A pair of trolley wires ran through the vehicle wash.] Each vehicle as it passes through is vacuumed inside and all rubbish conveyed directly to an incinerator. The bus then moved forward to the second position where it was sprayed over with water from sparge pipes attached to side gantries, outside cleaning being completed with a brush.

"Workshop & maintenance works: a concrete building divided into maintenance, machine, body and stores sections. The maintenance block contains repair pits. There is a series of 10 pits connected to a master pit and two isolated pits. Two pits are provided with hydraulic jacks to accommodate the various wheel bases of vehicles for the purpose of hoisting for the removal of wheels. The pits were lined with glazed tiles and equipped with fluorescent lighting. The machine block contains a machine shop, engine room, electrical shop, timber store, timber mill, smiths' shop, panel beaters' shop, tyre store and repair shop. Foundations were laid for a paint shop but this work was deferred for economic reasons. Ample storage space was provided for the needs of a large and growing undertaking. Just inside the main entrance on the south-west side of the building is a loading platform over which a travelling crane operates to convey heavy items to the first floor. Also on the first floor is a records room, paint store and clothing store.

"In general the roof consisted of 45 half shells with north lights with the exception of the stores block which has a flat roof. Pre-stressing is also used here on the Freyssinet system whereby four cables are used in each shell, each cable containing 12 wires 0.20in in diameter encased in a plastic sheath and placed in position before the concrete was pressure sprayed. The wires in this case were extended 3¼in to 3½in in a length of 54 feet. Runways with travelling cranes are provided to carry heavy equipment to such parts of the building as required. Hot air heating is diffused through thermostatically controlled electric fans. Fire precautions similar to the garage comprise 734 automatic sprinkler heads.

"Canteen: a steel-framed building with brick infilling walls capable of seating 150. An up-to-date kitchen with spacious serving hatch provided with a tray sliding counter where meals could be provided on the cafeteria system. Provision was made for future developments such as an Assembly Hall, Sports Pavilion and a billiards and games room above the canteen.

"Boiler house: a mechanically-fed boiler is installed, this being sufficient to supply then then needs of the workshops. There is space for a second boiler should the workshops be extended.

"Substation: A two-section building, part containing the transformer and thus under the control of the SEB and from which the main cable is extended to supply the school on the adjoining site, and the other containing the Transport Department's main switches. [Note that the substation did not supply traction current.]

"Garage lighting: angle type parabolic reflectors with 300-watt lamps mounted 22ft above the ground and spaced 27ft apart, the average illumination at ground level being 3-4½ lumens per sq ft.

"Pit lighting: the 300ft long pit was lit with 41, 4ft 40-watt Sieray fluorescent lamps in a staggered arrangement, the lamps being set 16in below ground level providing c. 20 lumens per sq ft and providing good illumination to the underside of trolleybuses, minimal glare and visibility even when working immediately above the tube.

"Esavian shutter doors

"The entire site is surrounded by a concrete road with one-way trolleybus overhead wiring. There is a fire hydrant ring main with hydrants at convenient intervals".

The trolleybus depot featured a white-tiled and illuminated access pit with removable metal gratings at floor surface level on one side to make wheel changes easier. It was kept particularly clean, aided by a large number of "home-made" racks, stands and tables for spare parts and replacement items.

Expansion: In his review of the options for expanded and improved depot and workshop accommodation, sent to the Transport Committee on 6 December 1957, Mr Reakes wrote of the alternative of centralising everything, including the administrative offices but excluding Boscombe (Pokesdown) Depot, under one roof, at Castle Lane (Mallard Road) Depot. A portion of land lying between the workshops and the already existing garage could be treated with cement, offering sufficient accommodation in total for the Department's entire fleet. Half would be under cover and half on a hard-standing.

A rearrangement of the stores in the workshops could provide office accommodation for the entire administration and the offices at Central Depot, Southcote Road, would be available for alternative use. However, the traction substation at Central Depot would have been retained.

Having deliberated for several years, in early 1962 it was decided to build a second garage of similar size to the initial structure at the Mallard Road site, limited to motorbuses, located to the west of the existing garage enabling the entire fleet to be stabled at one place. At the same time a new two-storey administrative block was constructed on the west side of the depot loop road, opposite the workshops and stores, to replace the "temporary" solution existing at Southcote Road since the move from Wootton Gardens on 1 April 1940. On 26 April 1965 the Transport Department headquarters relocated to Mallard Road, an official opening by the Mayor of the new offices and second garage taking place on 7 May 1965. The garage and office accommodation at Central Depot, Southcote

Road was vacated completely by 7 June 1965.

Mallard Road was officially referred to as Castle Lane Depot until the Head Office moved there in April 1965 whereupon it became known as Mallard Road Depot. Although Castle Lane was in operation from July 1953, garage No. 1 was completed by 1 October 1951 and was used for storing vehicles out of service. These included vehicles that were, or would be shortly, up for sale, together with vehicles delicensed for the winter. The use of the premises from 1951 enabled the temporary parking space off Seabourne Road, adjacent to Boscombe (Pokesdown) Depot, to be discontinued.

Following abandonment of trolleybus operation Mallard Road Depot continued as BCT's sole operating base, workshops and head office. This situation continued after the Transport Act 1985 forced the undertaking to become an "arm's length company", Bournemouth Transport Ltd., owned by Bournemouth Council and trading as "Yellow Buses Bournemouth", a title which BCT had formally adopted in May 1982 although it had been colloquially known as "yellow buses" for many years. The company began to seek a more economical headquarters with the aim of vacating Mallard Road; however, their plans were thwarted in 1999, when English Heritage recommended No. 1 Garage building for listing as of architectural significance due to its innovative single-span concrete roof. It subsequently received Grade 2 listing. In late 2005, Bournemouth Council decided to sell Yellow Buses to Transdev, a public transport company owned predominantly by Caisse des Dépôts et Consignations, an investment company of the French State. The company left its Mallard Road home and moved into a new facility on Yeomans Way, which lies somewhat to the north of Castle Lane West, almost opposite Mallard Road, on 1 March 2006. Mallard Road Depot was remodelled as a retail park in 2007, retaining the listed garage building which became a do-it-yourself superstore.

On the occasion of the 15 April 1965 enthusiasts' tour BUT9611Ts no. 294 (DNJ994) ex-BH&D and no. 291 (HUF48) ex-Brighton Corporation Transport are seen outside the vehicle wash facility on the north side of the Castle Lane (Mallard Road) Depot complex. Roger G. Funnell (courtesy Mrs D. Funnell and Rodney Funnell)

Trolleybus Maintenance

The trolleybuses received intermediate servicing every 75,000 miles and major overhauls every 150,000 miles based on individual vehicle records. Except in the system's closing years, trolleybuses received an external repaint every three years, resulting in a very smart turn out. Electrical equipment required little maintenance apart from cleaning, lubrication, the checking of wiring and connections, and the renewal of worn contacts. Such items were covered on a time-interval rota system. Every seven weeks each trolleybus was checked for electrical and mechanical faults, including adjustment of the traction motor brush pressure, motor generator sets, greasing of the control equipment and trolley heads, testing all high voltage cabling and checking the upward pressure of the trolley heads. This pressure had to be 30lbs at 21ft above the ground and was checked by hanging a 21ft long bamboo trolley rewiring pole, with a 30lb weight attached to the end, to the trolley head. The spring tension was correct if the weight just touched the ground. The trolley pole itself was a steel tube, 15ft long and weighing 40lbs, extended by a further 3ft by the trolley base itself.

Drivers wrote down any faults noted in service on vehicle report sheets which were entered in a book by the night staff for attention the next day. No trolleybus was allowed to return to service until reported brake or steering faults had been rectified. Each month, all recorded faults were cumulated into a monthly defect report on squared paper which showed brake, dewirement and steering faults by date and vehicle, thus providing an easy way of tracing the cause of recurrent defects. Faults were shown as crosses in the appropriate squares, and their frequent repetition indicated a need to investigate their cause, e.g. poor driving skills, the overhead wiring, etc.

Coloured pins on a progressive mileage chart indicated the total mileage recorded by each vehicle and the dates at which intermediate servicing and major overhauls had been given or were due. Each vehicle's maintenance history was recorded in a Kardex file; major and minor repairs were shown in red and green ink respectively, together with the chassis number and the dates of last overhaul, servicing, body overhaul and painting. Another Kardex file recorded to which trolleybus all the main chassis units were fitted in order that their location could be quickly identified. A card index was also used to record the maintenance history of main units; on a separate card for each unit were entered details of work done, time spent on it, and material used.

The MoT required that a daily leakage test be made, each vehicle being equipped with "test sockets" attached to half-a-dozen points into which a tester could be plugged. If leakage exceeded three milliamps the trolleybus was taken out of service. Trolleyheads were examined nightly and the carbon inserts changed when required, wear being greatest in icy or wet weather. The night foreman recorded E (examined), A (adjusted) or G (greased), as appropriate, against the fleet number. In latter years, when the fleet had fallen to around 70 trolleybuses, the three depots were using between 6-12 carbon inserts per night, but this figure rose to about 20 in periods of wet weather. To ensure good electrical conductivity and smooth running, a cast iron slipper was fitted to the trolleyheads of special empty "ghost" trolleybuses, which operated throughout the night (see Appendix O for details), and to the first service vehicles each morning, to clear ice and sleet from the running wires during periods of very frosty weather.

As each trolleybus ran into Castle Lane (Mallard Road) Depot after service it passed through a carefully isolated washing bay built alongside the east wall of the main garage before being parked under cover until next required for service.

The workshops themselves were accessible through wooden doors on the north side of the building leading directly on to 12 white-tiled pits, a number of which – possibly as many as every second – were equipped with short lengths of trolleybus overhead wiring above for vehicle testing purposes. These wires ran from the door lintel to the first lateral roof beam with insulators at each end and could only be energised from the external perimeter overhead wiring by the use of T-poles. As there was no connection to the external overhead wiring, T-poles were also used to move trolleybuses in and out of the workshops. At a later date, possibly in connection with the closure of Central Depot, Southcote Road in April 1965, two hand-operated frogs were inserted into the external perimeter wiring with spurs connected to the internal wires above two of the pits.

Ten of these pits continued into a sunken area from which dismantled components could be hoisted and carried by runway through a degreasing plant into the adjoining units assembly and machine shop. This runway passed above a line of workbenches to an enclosed store of reconditioned parts, and components were issued direct for replacements without passing through the main stores. Current for the motor-driven machinery in the unit assembly and machine shop was taken from overhead bus-bars from which short leads could be dropped directly to the machines wherever they were placed.

Many worn parts were reconditioned for further service by welding, the worn surfaces being built up with new metal and machined to the original dimensions. This included the splined ends of half-shafts, differential casings, broken hub flanges and the hollow trunnion shafts that carried the rear springs of the BUT9641T chassis. When the outer ends of these shafts were worn, the shaft was cut into halves which were then reversed and joined in the centre over a tight-fitting inner shaft. The new outer ends, when worn, were cut off and replaced by new additions, again using the same method of jointing. The amount of reconditioning work increased as it became difficult to obtain replacement spares from the manufacturers.

One of the workshop pits was divided by a broad central trench extending to the pits on either side to ease the work of dismantling heavy chassis components, such as the offset Crompton Parkinson motors used in the BUT9611Ts and BUT9641Ts. When a trolleybus was positioned over this pit, the front wheels were run across two steel channel girders that bridged the trench; the girders were then removed until needed again for the vehicle's departure. A mobile hydraulic jack was used to lower the components and take them away from the pit.

The workshops made up a number of assembly benches consisting of used lathe faceplates rotatably mounted on tramcar trolleybases cut down to a convenient height. Once a traction motor armature had been dismantled and removed, annular steel plates were bolted to the end flanges of the housing so that, when supported by these and engaged with free-running flanged wheels on one of the special assembly benches, the housing could be turned over to any suitable position for checking or repair.

(Above) **By the standards of the time Castle Lane (Mallard Road) Depot and Workshops were the most modern and well-equipped of any municipal transport undertaking in the UK. In this early 1960s view four Sunbeam MF2Bs, including nos. 277 and 278, and a sole BUT9641T, as well as five motorbuses, including two open-top Leyland TD5s, are in for docking over the white tile-lined maintenance pits.**
David Chalk collection
(Bournemouth Transport Ltd.)

(Left) **A further view of the docking facilities with two BUT9641Ts nos. 240 (KLJ340) and 235 (KLJ335), and a single ex-BH&D BUT9611T no.293 (DNJ993) over the pits. The tall pale blue painted Esavian building entrance doors are to the rear of the vehicles.** **Bournemouth Transport Ltd.**

The main workshops with a variety of heavy machinery and axles in the foregoround, and the pits in the background

Bournemouth Transport Ltd.

APPENDIX H
POWER SUPPLY AND GENERATING STATION

The Mains Department was formed in 1935 with responsibility for the operation and maintenance of the Southcote Road generating station, section boxes and underground feeder cables. Prior to that, the generating station had been the direct responsibility of the General Manager, Mr Bulfin, who had previously overseen its construction and operation in his capacity as Resident Engineer and then Borough Electrical Engineer. Day to day operation was carried out by a number of Assistant Electrical Engineers, including Henry Andrews, who was appointed Chief Assistant to Mr Bulfin in October 1905.

Following Mr Bulfin's retirement in September 1935 responsibility passed to a Mains Superintendent and his Assistant. By the 1950s, the Mains Superintendent was Mr A. Stevenson and his Assistant, Harold Mount. When Mr Stevenson retired in March 1954 he was succeeded by Mr Mount, but in view of the pending closure of the generating station the position of Assistant Mains Superintendent was not filled. Once the Generating Station closed in September 1955, the Mains Superintendent became responsible for the three BCT-owned substations at Iddesleigh Road, Pokesdown Depot and Southcote Road.

Harold Mount retired in the early 1960s and in the knowledge that the trolleybus system would be rundown and eventually closed, he was not directly replaced. An electrical engineer, Bert Weedon, took over the tasks until the trolleybus abandonment and carried on as a general electrician until his retirement in the 1970s.

One of the claimed economies of converting life-expired electric tramways to trolleybus operation was the continued use of the existing traction power supply system with limited additional investment and Bournemouth Corporation's trolleybus network was no exception, the current supply arrangements being closely based on that built up in the first five years of the twentieth century for the electric tramways. The trolleybuses like the trams before them received Direct Current (DC) electric power through overhead wires suspended above the route and supplied by underground cables from the power station and through local substations. A trolleybus system required two overhead wires, one of positive potential carrying current to the vehicle, and the other of negative potential returning the current and completing the connection. The trolley wire closest to the centre of the road was the positive wire. A tramway uses the running rails for its return connection.

Legislation required that the positive wire was interrupted every half mile, the sections each side of the insulating break being entirely separate from each other but connectable through switchgear placed in a cast iron roadside section pillar or a box mounted on a traction pole. Identical feeder pillars housed the cables from which the mains power supply was connected to the overhead wiring. Equipment in either pillar could be used to cut off power entirely in an emergency. The negative trolley wire was continuous but at points where negative feeder cables were connected the negative feed came either from a separate pole-mounted switch box or feeder pillar (which to the onlooker, was identical to a positive equivalent) and exceptionally from the same feeder pillar as the positive cables.

A typical trolleybus drawing away from rest will draw about 200 amps of current, which at a line voltage of 550 volts DC equates to 110 kW, but this drops off rapidly as the vehicle overcomes the initial rolling resistance and gains speed. In comparison a typical domestic electric heater element will use 1 kW or a 60-100 watt lamp bulb 0.06-0.1 kW, wattage being the amount of energy used, calculated by multiplying the voltage by the current flowing (in amperes). This is of course variable dependent on the rate of acceleration, any gradient and the passenger load. The average consumption of electricity per trolleybus was thus reckoned as 3 kWh per mile as opposed to less than 2 kWh for a tram.

Traction power needs increased considerably from the end of 1950 with the arrival of the fleet of 24 BUT 9641Ts having 120 hp motors and weighing in at over 10 tons (compared to the Sunbeam MS2 of the mid 1930s with 80 hp motors and an unladen weight of 8 tons 12 cwt) whilst passenger loadings soared. Peak traction power requirements often occurred on summer Saturdays, still a working or half working day in many businesses during the trolleybus era, when there would be a combination of holidaymakers travelling to or from the railway stations or coach departure points, and residents going home, to the shops or to a major sporting event.

Power generation during the tramway and trolleybus era

The first electricity supplies in Bournemouth and the surrounding area were provided by the Bournemouth and Poole Electricity Supply Co. Ltd. (BPES) from their generating station in Bourne Valley Road, Branksome, conveniently bordering on the gas works and LSWR mainline at Gasworks Junction. Bournemouth was one of the few municipalities having a population in excess of 60,000 inhabitants that did not have its own electricity undertaking.

After the First World War the government made a review of the nation's electric power industry consisting of over 600 separate undertakings, most of which were too small to operate economically. This led to the Electricity (Supply) Act 1919 which created Electricity Commissioners who could set up voluntary Joint Electricity Authorities for areas with the agreement of the undertakings concerned. It was foreseen that the Authorities would be able to produce electricity more economically by building new larger power stations and that, by linking the various stations, power could be transmitted around their area as supply and demand varied.

Few Joint Authorities were created however and as a natural corollary, the Electricity (Supply) Act 1926 foresaw a standardisation of the electricity supply throughout the UK through the creation of a synchronised 132 kV/50 Hz Alternating Current (AC) regional grid initially involving a collection of local networks, with emergency interlinks, covering most of the country and later through a national grid. The implementation was entrusted to the Central Electricity Board who began to construct a network of large generating plants and a network of trunk transmission lines linking the largest plants throughout Britain and supplying bulk power to the existing undertakings. The first portion of this network, the National Grid, opened in 1935.

On 1 April 1948 the electricity supply industry was nationalised, the British Electricity Authority taking over responsibility for the operation of the nation's power stations and the "Grid", and the supply of electrical energy to the Area Boards. The BPES became the main constituent of the Bournemouth Sub-area, one of four making up the Southern Electricity Board (SEB). Under the Electricity Act, 1957 the Central Electricity Generating Board took over the British Electricity Authority's responsibilities.

Power Station

The infant tramways department was eager to generate its own traction power and built its own generating station, as part of its depot and workshop facilities, in 1902 on a plot of land behind private housing on the north side of Southcote Road and bordered by the LSWR mainline railway and associated sidings to the north and Vale Road to the east. The power station was built to the west of and adjoining the main car shed. It supplied tramway traction power within the county borough boundaries and, initially, current for street lighting and cliff lifts, all domestic and industrial electricity needs were supplied by the BPES. Those trams running in the boroughs of Christchurch and Poole were supplied by the BPES from the company's generating stations at Bargates in Christchurch, which opened in 1903 primarily to supply the tramway extension into the Priory town, and from their main plant in Branksome respectively.

Bournemouth Tramways' Southcote Road generating station building was 150ft wide, 100ft deep and 40ft high. It was constructed in two sections with a dividing wall. The front portion, which contained the generators, was not level throughout but had a number of pits accommodating ancillary equipment, whereas the rear portion was 6-8 ft lower and housed the boilers. There were also a number of auxiliary buildings, including the coal bunkers, electrical workshops, switchboard, offices, stores, toilets and bathrooms, cooling towers and chimney, making up an integral part of the Central Depot facilities, situated between the main car shed and the private houses that later became the undertaking's head office building.

The original plant comprised four 3-crank Bellis & Morcom triple expansion engines, 450bhp, having 12in, 18½in and 28in X 12in cylinders, running at 360rpm, taking steam at 175psi and exhausting to condensers. Each engine was coupled direct to a multi-polar British Thomson-Houston compound-wound generator exhausting to condensers having a capacity of 1,168kW with a constant potential of 550 volts DC. The condensing plant comprised two 2-crank Bellis and Morcom compound engines, having cylinders 5½in and 9in X 5in, running at 500rpm, which were used to drive the condensing pumps. Steam was raised by five Lancashire boilers supplied with coal by railway using a private siding off the LSWR mainline at the rear of the property and taking water from an artesian well. The main J.G. Stather switchboard had seventeen panels, comprising six generator and one motor generator panel on the right-hand side, and seven feeder panels, two Board of Trade panels and one main panel on the left.

In 1926, two 750 kW turbo-generators and associated Babcock & Wilcox boilers were installed to replace the original

reciprocating motors (although all four were retained for use in an emergency), necessitating the construction of a gantry to accommodate these sets. After the General Strike the plant was rebuilt to burn either coal or oil. These were augmented in 1942 by a 1,500kW Daniel Adamson steam turbo set coupled to a Mather & Platt generator, dating from 1928 and bought from the Bristol Tramways & Carriage Co. who had been forced to abandon tramway operation on 11 April 1941 when an air raid severed feeder cables across St. Philip's Bridge from their Counterslip generating station. The purchase required an extension to the gantry referred to above and an increase in the number of supporting pillars. The Bellis & Morcom triple expansion engines were then scrapped.

In 1926 the BPES gave up generating electricity at Christchurch and the facilities there became a substation supplied through the grid primarily from the Bourne Valley plant and, from 1950, the new Hamworthy, Poole power station. Also by 1926 Southcote Road had ceased to supply street lighting power or the cliff lifts. Trolleybuses have a greater rolling resistance than a tramcar due to their use of rubber tyres on an asphalt surface rather than a steel wheel or a steel rail, and combined with increased passenger traffic, traction current demands rose. In order to cope, the BPES added traction supply substation equipment to the existing domestic/industrial substations at Electric House, Yelverton Road (actually located in Verulam Place, a cul-de-sac off Yelverton Road); Carbery Avenue, Southbourne; and Green Road, Winton, in the second half of 1936 to supplement Southcote Road's output.

It is not known how it was possible for Bournemouth Corporation Transport to continue generating its own electrical supply at Southcote Road following the nationalisation of the power industry in 1948. One can only surmise that both Bournemouth, Glasgow (Pinkston) and various London Transport power stations (Greenwich; Lots Road, Chelsea; Neasden) were allowed to continue as production was limited to DC power for traction purposes only. In the early post-war period when capacity-related (rather than strike-related) load-shedding was a relatively common event, the SEB was probably relieved not to have an additional peak-hour demand from the trolleybuses when their own domestic and industrial needs were at their height. By 1953, Southcote Road had a maximum generating capacity of 3,000kW.

When operational, Southcote Road generating station consumed about 200 tons of coal per week in summer. This all arrived by train on the Transport Department's own siding (No.10), which led off the railway goods yard on the south side of the mainline about 500 yards east of Bournemouth Central Station.

Although no trolleybuses operated on Christmas Day at any time during the trolleybus era, it remained necessary for some employees to be on duty at the generating station.

In late August 1955, shortly before the generating station closed down, a lightning strike to the overhead wiring near Central Station managed to negotiate the various safety devices and reached the Southcote Road switchboard, setting it on fire and causing serious damage. The strike found a path to the Mather & Platt generator, which was destroyed. The incident took place at 7.05 pm and brought trolleybus services to a standstill in the central area for about two hours until alternative supplies and temporary repairs could be effected. As the changeover to SEB supplies was about to take place, the generator was never repaired. Until then, the undertaking

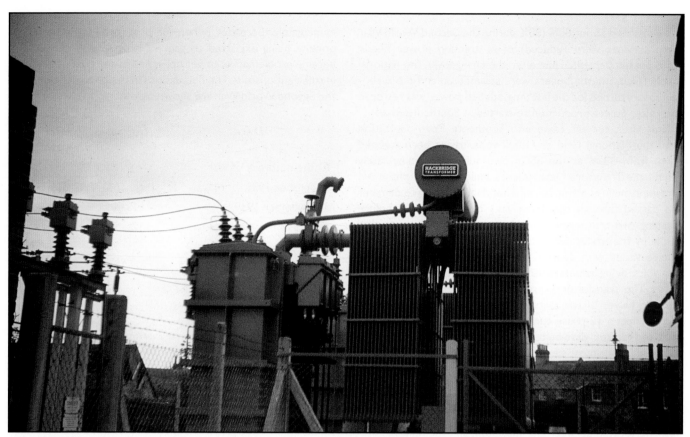

The Southern Electricity Board substation was erected behind the BCT substation towards the rear of the BCT Southcote Road complex, partially on the site of the former cooling towers. This view of the switch yard shows a standard three phase transformer and associated cooling system radiator manufactured by Hackbridge Transformers, as could be found in many substations unrelated to traction power or trolleybuses throughout the country (28 June 1964).
Paul Creswell

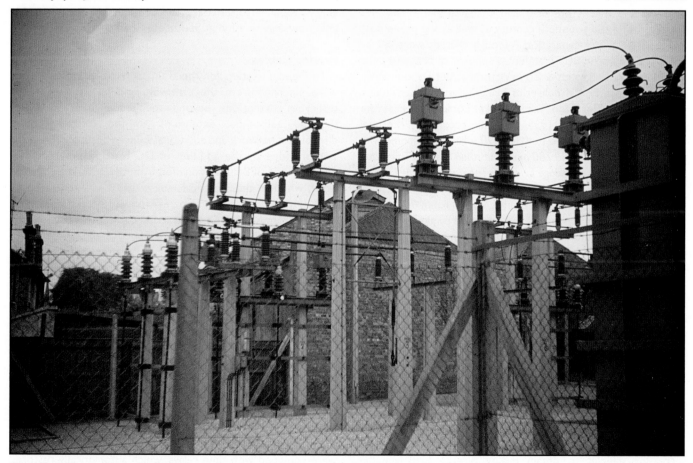

The Southern Electricity Board substation behind the BCT substation was equipped with conventional three phase high voltage switchgear of the period as could be found in thousands of installations throughout the UK (28 June 1964).
Paul Creswell

had generated about 60% (80% during the Second World War when services were reduced) of its traction power needs. On 6 September 1955, just after the changeover, the national supply failed, and the boilers were steamed up and the turbo-generators turned for the last time, but SEB power was restored soon after power production re-started at Southcote Road.

Thereafter, current came into Southcote Road substation from the National Grid at 11,000 volts, having been stepped down from 33kV at the SEB's own substation immediately behind the Transport Department's building. Three-phase AC current came in at about 20 amps, varying according to demand, and passed through two heavy-duty circuit breakers, before reaching two transformers which reduced the voltage to that usable by the trolleybuses, nominally 565 volts DC. The actual voltage varied with demand but was not permitted to reach 600 volts, being counterbalanced by subsequent transmission losses. The transformers produced a six-phase AC current, the two halves of the system being slightly out of phase so that in effect a 12-phase current resulted. This was fed to two pairs of Hewittic glass-bulb rectifiers, from which the current emerged as an almost steady DC supply. The engines were sold to George Cohen Sons & Co. Ltd. for £5,770

Part of Southcote Road substation was leased to the SEB for their own purposes until 1967 when it was replaced by a large transformer, serving the newly-electrified third rail DC mainline, located between the substation and the railway.

Fuel

BCT's Southcote Road generating station, as well as the BPES stations (until Hamworthy was converted to oil in 1955) burnt coal to raise steam and thereby generate electricity. Indeed, coal was the leading domestic and industrial fuel in the first six decades of the twentieth century, as well as the prime cost factor in electricity generation. Although charges were set by national agreement, BCT's preferred supplier of coal and coke was Messrs W. D. Barnett & Co. of Victoria Street, London SW1, under contract, typical deliveries being Elliott Washed Beans, Seaborne Screenings and furnace coke. Looking back at the year ending 31st March 1935, Mr Bulfin recorded: *"The total output of current amounted to 4,548,390 units, as compared with 4,362,110 units, some 186,280 more units than last year. This is due to increased trolleybus mileage being run. The coal consumed during the year was 5,629 tons, as against 5,335 tons last year. The total cost per unit, including all capital charges, worked out at 0.70d".* Just over one year later, coal prices had increased by almost 10% or 2s per ton due to increasing industrial demand.

	Increase	Price per ton
During 1934 and 1935		29s 3d
January 1936	1s	30s 3d
July 1936	1s	31s 3d
July 1937	5s 6d	36s 9d
July 1938	10d	35s 11d

Wartime inflation, and dramatically increased demand, led to coal rationing, supply being co-ordinated by the Ministries of Mines, and Fuel and Power. Prices rocketed, whilst it became increasing difficult to obtain quality furnace fuels suitable for power generation, as public transport usage rose to unprecedented levels. In the closing months of the war and

immediately thereafter (when the best grade coals were, as a priority, being exported to gain valuable foreign currency) it became problematical to get deliveries of any type of solid fuel in sufficient quantity. The fluctuations in the price of coal during the Second World War are shown below:

Date	Increase	Price per ton
At the outbreak of war		35s 11d
1 October 1939	6d	36s 5d
3 November 1939	1s 4d	37s 9d
May 1940	2s 1d	39s 10d
1 November 1940	2s 9d	42s 7d
1 December 1940	11d	43s 6d
1 January 1941	8d	44s 2d
June 1941	10d	45s
19 July 1941	10d	45s 10d
1 July 1943	1s	46s 10d
1 February 1944	3s	49s 10d
1 August 1944	4s	53s 10d
1 April 1945	8d	54s 6d
1 May 1945	3s 6d	58s

The post-war recovery fuelled general inflation, which varied between 3% and over 9% in the decade 1945 - 1955, and industry's need for coal saw prices continue to increase reaching 65s 9d in July 1948, 79s 8d in May 1950 and 106s 7d in July 1953. Thereafter coal prices continued to rise inexorably until power generation at Southcote Road ceased.

Feeder Cables

The feeder system for the tram to trolleybus conversions were inherited from the tramways and by the late 1930s trolleybus extensions beyond the erstwhile tram routes required substantial extensions to the traction power distribution network and additional sources of supply. The latter was provided by the addition of DC traction power supply equipment to SEB substations fed from the grid. At Southcote Road, whether the electrical energy had been generated by BCT or taken in bulk from the SEB (in which case it was first rectified from AC to DC), the traction current was taken to the switchboard busbars (bars of solid copper running the length of the rear of the board, their heavy rectangular section offering virtually no resistance to the current and enabling connections to the various switches to be solidly bolted to them). From the busbars, feeder cables in ducts went out underground to various parts of the system, each being connected to the busbars through a heavy-duty circuit breaker and isolating switch.

If the current exceeded a set value, its magnetic effect opened the automatic circuit breaker, preventing excessive current from entering a cable and damaging it. Current would be cut off by a broken trolley wire if the live ends made a good contact with earth; a dewired trolley head might create a short circuit across the insulators of a frog or crossover, etc. The circuit breakers were equipped with time relays, which automatically restored current after a pre-set period. If the fault was still present, they reopened. If this cycle of events occurred three times, on the fourth occasion the circuit breakers stayed open and an alarm sounded in the Mains Superintendent's office. It was then necessary to locate the fault and isolate the feeder concerned until it was safe to restore current.

As a "fail safe" feature, each feeder cable was equipped with indicator lights which illuminated only when power was off. When it was necessary to switch off the current from a particular feeder, for example to inspect a broken wire, the automatic circuit breaker was made to function by pressing a switch and the isolating switch was then quickly opened before the restoring device on the breaker had time to operate. The isolating switches were of the "knife" pattern, which could not be opened when under load as this would have caused arcing which could potentially burn the entire switch out.

At the BCT-owned substations at Iddesleigh Road and Boscombe (Pokesdown) Depot, red exterior warning lamps illuminated if a circuit breaker opened and stayed open. Drivers of passing trolleybuses were instructed to report any lamp seen illuminated.

Nineteen feeder cables left the Southcote Road main switchboard. From left to right these were:

Cable	Name	Cross-sectional area of copper conductor		Note
1	Southcote Road	0.183		
2	St. Clement's Road	0.183	including Central Depot	
3	Ashley Road	0.183		
4	Holdenhurst Road	0.31		
5	Winton	0.31		A
6	Cemetery	0.243		A
7	Lansdowne No.1	0.31	fed Lansdowne (exclusive) to the Royal Bath Hotel Junction and Bournemouth Pier	
8	Cleveland Road	0.183	fed part of the Ashley Road route.	B
9	St. Peter's	0.31	fed the Square.	C
10	Lansdowne No.2	0.31	fed Lansdowne (exclusive) to Derby Road	
11	Richmond Hill No.1	0.31	fed Lansdowne (inclusive) to Trinity Church	
12	Richmond Hill No.2	0.31	live cable to Beales mains pillar.	D
13	Beales	0.31	fed Albert Road to Trinity Church	
14	Poole Hill	0.31	coupled to Grosvenor Road	
15	Grosvenor Road	0.243	coupled to Poole Hill	
16	Meyrick Park Crescent	0.31	part of a Southcote Road - Moordown & Winton link	
17	Charminster	0.5		E
18	Parkwood Road 1 in	0.5	fed Boscombe Hill - Pokesdown substation	
19	Parkwood Road 1/2 in	1.00	fed route "P" Palmerston Hotel-Warwick Road. F	F

Notes

A   Both cables were connected to the overhead at St. Paul's Road and Lansdowne Road to feed Route "O" but, beyond, were disconnected by normally open switches. The Cemetery Junction cable ended at St. Augustin's feeder pillar where it was live but not connected to the overhead line. The substation at Electric House fed the overhead up to this point and the 0.243 sq in Cemetery cable was thus merely an alternative source of supply for emergency purposes. The rest of the 0.31 sq in Winton cable was again divided into two by an open switch in Ensbury Mains Pillar; the part from Cemetery Junction to Peter's Hill feeder pillar was fed from Iddesleigh Road substation which fed the overhead on this part of route "M". The final section of the cable was live and connected to a 0.5 sq in cable fed by both Green Road and Southcote Road substations.

B   Coupled to the Ashley Road cable by virtue of the fact that they both fed the same overhead wire, adjacent half mile sections being connected by normally closed switches at the White House pole switch box.

C   The St. Peter's cable continued to Bobby's feeder pillar where it was live but not normally connected to the overhead.

D   Alternative supply for any section in an emergency.

E   The part immediately connected to Southcote Road was coupled to Iddesleigh Road substation at Cemetery Junction and served as an equaliser between the two substations. The next section was used to join Iddesleigh Road substation to the overhead at Alma Road. It divided again, the next section connecting Green Road substation to the line at Five Ways and Luckham Road feeder pillars. The final section was connected to Holdenhurst substation and fed the Castle Lane route including Mallard Road Depot.

F   Cables 18 and 19 were coupled to feed Boscombe Hill and were then isolated by open switches. The third and final section of cable 19 was a connection to Carbery substation.

Each of the outgoing cables was connected to an ammeter which showed the current passing, the meters being of the centre zero type as, due to the inter-connections, some cables were feeding back current to the substation. For example, the cables which connected Southcote Road to sections also fed by other substations (such as Electric House, Green Road, Iddesleigh Road, etc.), fed current to Southcote Road when traffic in the sections concerned was light. On sections not connected to any other cables it was possible to judge how many trolleybuses were moving in the section. At night the trolleybuses returned to depot and the various meters reached zero indicating when the last trolleybus was "home".

The actual route of the cable runs, together with their cross-sections, was carefully mapped for both departmental use and to guide the public utilities in their excavating activities. Their position could also be identified from the unique style of manhole covers every few hundred yards along the pavement. These covers incorporated a rectangular metal grid ventilator (until it filled up with dirt and dust), making them very different from those used by the GPO or, latterly, the SEB. Cable runs were installed parallel to all the former tram routes, but did not always contain power supply cables. The Derby Road-Lansdowne and Bournemouth Square-Poole Hill via Avenue Road runs contained only telephone cables. Underground cables did not always follow the trolleybus routes; the 0.5 sq in Parkwood Road cable ran from Southcote Road via Derby Road to Christchurch Road; the Cleveland Road and Ashley Road feeders ran via Cleveland and Tower Roads respectively, and at Southbourne the cables deviated via Tuckton and Seafield Roads, whilst the trolleybuses ran along Belle Vue Road. The 1 sq in Parkwood Road cable ran via Parkwood Road, hence its name, and did not go via Boscombe (Pokesdown) Depot and Seabourne Road.

Substations

Around the end of the 19th century DC was preferred for electric traction purposes because the speed of direct current motors and thus that of the vehicle could be simply controlled by varying the voltage applied to them. Alternating Current (AC) however was preferable to DC for power distribution and generation because power loss in transmission lines decreases significantly with higher voltages and during the tram and trolleybus era only AC could efficiently be transformed between voltages. Nonetheless traction power for Bournemouth's electric tramways within the county borough boundary was entirely generated and distributed as DC by feeder cables to strategic locations along the routes throughout the town, and this principle applied initially to the trolleybuses too.

As mentioned above, AC substations had been opened at Electric House, Yelverton Road; Carbery Avenue, Southbourne;

and Green Road, Winton, in 1936, whilst traction power equipment was added to an existing BPES substation at Throop Road, Holdenhurst in 1951. Further substations were built by BCT at Southcote Road, Iddesleigh Road and Pokesdown in 1955 to replace the Southcote Road generating station. These power supply arrangements would have sufficed for any subsequent trolleybus route extensions, such as Alma Road, Holdenhurst Road and Richmond Park Road, but any routes along Kinson Road or into West Howe would have required a further substation in the north western suburbs.

Once the BPES had commenced AC power distribution for traction purposes to their substations it was necessary to find a means of converting this energy for use by tramcar and later trolleybus motors which operated with DC electricity. Elsewhere, in the early days of AC distribution, this had been done with a rotary converter, a large, rotating electromechanical device and basically a hybrid of a single winding AC motor and a DC generator (dynamo).

The complexity and size of rotary converters required regular attention and maintenance by skilled staff, and any loss of the incoming supply would cause protective switchgear to "drop out" requiring a manual restart. Thus from the late 1920s the needs for additional or replacement equipment was met by the new technology of the mercury arc rectifier. In a rectifier substation, the incoming high voltage AC supply was first reduced by transforming to the correct input voltage of approximately 400 volts AC, and thence converted to a nominal 550 volts DC for the overhead line, whereas a rotary converter was an AC motor driving a DC generator that produced a DC current. A mercury arc rectifier had an efficiency of about 93-95%, dependent on load, compared to a rotary converter's efficiency of just over 90%.

The operation of mercury arc rectifiers (also known as Cooper-Hewitt or Hewittic rectifiers after their inventor, the American Peter Cooper Hewitt) was based on the discovery that an electric spark (arc) vaporises mercury contained in a steel tank into a vapour that can only conduct electric current in a single direction between the pool of mercury and a metal anode. AC was fed to the anodes of the octopus-like glass bulbs and an arc was set up between the anodes and a pool of mercury in the bottom of the bulb. Incoming current, alternating at a frequency of 50 cycles a second (the standard frequency of the National Grid supply) flashed 50 times per second between the anodes and the mercury-covered cathodes forming a virtually continuous arc. Multiple anodes were used, fed from a multiple-phase transformer, the arc jumping from the cathode pool to each anode in sequence. The arc glow changed in intensity as the number of trolleybuses moving increased or reduced, or even changed speed. There were three, six or even twelve transformer phases, each feeding one anode. Six

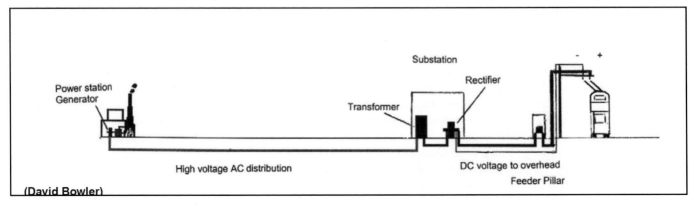

(David Bowler)

and twelve-phase systems used star-connected three-phase transformers with inter-phase transformers between the star common connections. In a six-phase rectifier there were 6 arms on each bulb, each connected to a phase of the supply, and thus the output was close to being a continuous current but with a slight ripple, that is, the actual voltage waxed and waned by about 20% of the nominal 550 volts DC at a frequency of 300 cycles (hertz).

Construction was either a glass bulb cooled by an external fan or a steel tank of water for very large units with capacities above about 500 amps. To initiate the arc, an igniting electrode was dipped into the pool of mercury using an external electromagnet thereby drawing a small spark to ionise the mercury vapour, initiating the main arc. These substations had virtually no moving parts and made it practicable to open small substations along the route wherever power was needed. Control circuits within the mercury arc rectifier ensured that if no current at all was being taken from the overhead, the arc within the rectifier did not die out. Mercury arc rectifiers were used until the end of trolleybus operation.

The traction current was taken from the rectifiers to the switchboard busbars. From the busbars, feeder cables went out to various parts of the system, each being connected to the busbars through a heavy-duty circuit breaker and isolating switch.

If the current exceeded a set value, its magnetic effect opened the automatic circuit breaker preventing excessive current from entering a cable and damaging it. A broken positive trolley wire would cut off current if the live ends made a good contact with earth; a dewired trolley head might create a short circuit across the insulators of a frog or crossover, etc. The circuit breakers were equipped with time relays that automatically restored current after a pre-set period. If the fault was still present they reopened. If this cycle of events occurred 3 times, on the fourth occasion the circuit breakers stayed open and an alarm sounded. It was then necessary to locate the fault and isolate the feeder concerned until it was safe to restore current.

The conversion equipment in the SEB substations comprised glass bulb mercury arc rectifiers, belonging to SEB and was housed in buildings owned by them and containing distribution equipment for the general power supply.

Carbery

Traction power equipment was added to the existing BPES substation on the west side of Watcombe Road, Southbourne, at its junction with Paisley Road, to serve the increased traction current needs of the trolleybuses in 1936. Now swathed in trees, the substation remains in use for domestic and industrial supply purposes and the building is extant (2017) although the main window spaces have been bricked-up.

The traction substation was owned and maintained by the BPES (later the SEB). Maximum capacity 500kW.

Traction power was supplied to the following feeders (cable cross-sectional area shown where known):

- Carbery, Southbourne Road (0.6 sq in)
- Clifton Road, Belle Vue Road (0.5 sq in)
- Fisherman's Walk, Southbourne Grove (0.5 sq in)
- Parkwood Road (0.6 sq in)

All in conjunction with Pokesdown Substation through Parkwood Road MP.

Christchurch

The BPES constructed an ornate two-storey brick building partially surmounted by ventilator lights which opened in 1903 as an electricity generating station to serve the Christchurch part of the company's area. Located behind housing on the north side of Beaconsfield Road, it was accessible from Bargates, and backed on to the River Avon at its confluence with the Mill Stream. When Bournemouth's trams reached Christchurch in October 1905 they were also supplied by the station.

Generation ceased in 1926 when the regional grid came into operation and substations providing both an AC domestic and industrial supply and DC traction current opened. The traction substation was owned and maintained by the BPES (later the SEB). Maximum capacity 400kW. In late 1958 the DC circuit breakers were replaced by new panels equipped with Bertram Thomas high-speed breakers, the other newer substations, i.e. excluding Electric House, being already similarly equipped with more modern switchgear. The AC substation became redundant in the late 1970s and the high voltage switchgear serving Christchurch was moved outside the building, which then became the Museum of Electricity, finally closing in 2012. The Grade II listed building remains as one of the most complete Edwardian power stations to survive.

Traction power was supplied to the following feeders (cable cross-sectional area shown where known):

- Bargates (0.4 sq in)
- Foxholes, Belle Vue Road (0.4 sq in)
- Red House, Belle Vue Road (0.4 sq in)
- Stour Road (0.4 sq in)

All in conjunction with Pokesdown Substation (0.4 sq in).

Electric House

In 1930 the BPES built a new headquarters and showrooms on the north side of Yelverton Road in the centre of the town, the traction power substation was added to existing transmission and supply equipment, located behind the building off Verulam Place, in 1936. The traction substation was owned and maintained by the BPES (later the SEB). Maximum capacity 600kW. In late 1958 the DC circuit breakers were replaced by new panels equipped with Bertram Thomas high-speed breakers, the other newer substations, i.e. excluding Christchurch, being already similarly equipped with more modern switchgear.

Traction power was supplied to the following feeders (cable cross-sectional area shown where known):

Via Beales MP (0.5 sq in)

- Richmond Hill (0.4 sq in)
- St. Augustin's, Wimborne Road
- Trinity Church, Old Christchurch Road (0.31 sq in)
- Yelverton Road, Richmond Hill opposite the junction with Yelverton Road (0.4 sq in)

Via Hinton Road MP (0.5 sq in)
- Bobby's (0.4 sq in)
- Grosvenor Road (0.31 sq in)
- Poole Hill (0.31 sq in)
- Square Office (0.31 sq in)
- St. Peter's (0.31 sq in)

Green Road

In order to serve the increased demand from the trolleybuses, traction power equipment was added to the existing BPES substation, a two storey brick building on the north side of Green Road, Winton, in 1936. Maximum capacity 500kW. The building remains in use (2017) for electricity supply purposes but the main window areas have been bricked up and the entire area surrounded by a security wall, fencing and trees.

Traction power was supplied to the following feeders (cable cross-sectional area shown where known):

- Bryanstone Road, Wimborne Road opposite the junction with Bryanstone Road (0.31 sq in)
- Cemetery Junction, Wimborne Road (0.31 sq in)
- Elmes Road Wimborne Road, Moordown at its junction with Elmes Road (0.31 sq in)
- Ensbury MP
- Linden Road, Wimborne Road at its junction with Linden Road (0.25 sq in)
- Meyrick Park Crescent, Wimborne Road (0.31 sq in)
- Peters Hill, Wimborne Road (0.31 sq in)
- St. Augustin's, Wimborne Road at its junction with St. Augustin's Road (0.31 sq in)

Holdenhurst

An SEB substation was already in existence on the south side of Throop Road on the southwest corner of its crossroad with Holdenhurst Road about 100 yards north of Castle Lane West when trolleybuses were extended from Broadway to Iford in 1951. Maximum capacity 500kW. It supplied traction current henceforth, but was presumably demolished in connection with the construction of the A338 spur road into Bournemouth and associated flyover above the Castle Lane roundabout.

Traction power was supplied to the following feeders (cable cross-sectional area shown where known):

Via Cattistock Road MP (0.5 sq in)

- Broadway Hotel (0.5 sq in) in conjunction with Green Road and Iddesleigh Road

- Castle Lane Depot (0.25 sq in)
- East Way (0.5 sq in)

- Crantock Grove, Castle Lane West (0.5 sq in)
- Holdenhurst Junction, Castle Lane East (0.5 sq in)

Iddesleigh Road

As a result of the decision to cease generating its own traction power at Southcote Road, in 1955 BCT built an additional substation on a portion of Wimborne Road Cemetery at the east end of Iddesleigh Road just prior to its junction with Charminster Road. A single story, windowless brick building 60ft X 15ft, it was owned and maintained by BCT, but parts of the substation were leased to the SEB. Maximum capacity 500kW. The building remains extant.

The equipment comprised an Oil-filled Circuit Breaker (OCB) transformer, an outdoor rectifier transformer, a 500 kW glass bulb mercury arc rectifier unit and auxiliary equipment with four high speed DC circuit breakers.

Traction power was supplied to the following feeders (cable cross-sectional area shown where known):

- Alma Road (0.5 sq in)
- Broadway Hotel (0.5 sq in) in conjunction with Holdenhurst
- Cemetery MP (0.5 sq in) in conjunction with Southcote Road substation
- Five Ways (0.5 sq in)
- Green Road MP (0.5 sq in) in conjunction with Green Road substation
- Luckham Road (0.5 sq in)
- Wellington Road (0.5 sq in)

Pokesdown

Also as a result of the decision to cease generating its own traction power, a substation was installed in a walled-off area 20ft X 15ft in size along the eastern boundary wall, and towards the front of, Boscombe (Pokesdown) Depot. The equipment comprised an OCB transformer, an outdoor rectifier transformer, a 500 kW glass bulb mercury arc rectifier unit and auxiliary equipment with four high speed DC circuit breakers. It was owned and maintained by BCT. Maximum capacity 500kW.

Traction power was supplied to the following feeders (cable cross-sectional area shown where known):
- Bargates, Christchurch *
- Boscombe depot (0.31 sq in) ++
- Carbery Avenue, Southbourne Road **
- Clifton Road, Belle Vue Road (0.5 sq in) **
- Exton Road, Christchurch Road (0.5 sq in)
- Foxholes, Belle Vue Road (0.4 sq in) *
- Harewood Avenue, Christchurch Road (0.5 sq in)
- Parkwood Road MP
- Red House, Belle Vue Road (0.4 sq in) *
- Stour Road (0.4 sq in) *
- Warwick Road (0.5 sq in)

* In conjunction with Christchurch Substation
** In conjunction with Carbery Substation.
++ Via Parkwood Road MP

Southcote Road

A new substation building 60ft X 35ft was built on BCT premises. The new equipment comprised three OCB transformers, three outdoor rectifier transformers, three 500 kW glass bulb mercury arc rectifier units and auxiliary equipment with 20 high speed DC circuit breakers it was owned and maintained by BCT, but parts of the substation were leased to the SEB. Maximum capacity 1,500kW.

Traction power was supplied to the following feeders (cable cross-sectional area shown where known):

- Ashley Road (0.183 sq in)
- Cemetery MP (0.5 sq in)
- Central Depot, Southcote Road (0.183 sq in)
- Cleveland Road, Holdenhurst Road (0.183 sq in)
- Holdenhurst Road (0.31 sq in)
- Lansdowne, Holdenhurst Road (0.31 sq in)
- Meyrick Park Crescent
- Southcote Road (0.183 sq in)

The power supplied by the five SEB substations was metered at the outgoing DC busbars, except in the case of Holdenhurst where it was metered at the incoming high voltage AC supply.

The Sunbeam MS2 trolleybuses had compound-wound traction motors for regenerative control which was considered to reduce power-consumption and wear on brake linings, particularly on hilly systems. During regenerative braking the traction motor acted as a generator and the electric power produced was fed back into the overhead wires and subsequently to the substations. A rotary converter could absorb regenerated energy but a mercury arc rectifier presented, in effect, an open circuit. This resulted in an over-voltage in the traction current supply which could damage other equipment connected to the supply (such as burning-out the high tension bulbs on adjacent trolleybuses) and much reduced braking on the trolleybus concerned if no other vehicles were drawing current in the section at the time. Bournemouth's subsequent trolleybus deliveries were equipped with rheostatic braking whereby the traction motor again acted as a generator, but the electric power produced was dissipated as heat in a brake grid resistance.

As the overhead line was divided into sections connected at substations, it sufficed to install banks of ballast resistances (simulating the presence of another trolleybus) in the Christchurch, Pokesdown and Southcote Road substations, with Allen West over-voltage relays to absorb any over-voltage created by vehicles regenerating. If no current at all was being taken from the overhead line, the arc within the mercury arc rectifier could die out. To prevent this, bleeder resistances

between the positive and negative busbars of each substation ensured that current was always flowing. At Southcote Road the bleeder resistance was provided by two electric fire elements, connected in series, which also served to keep the substation warm and dry.

The overhead remained live 24 hours a day with the sole exception of the Bournemouth Pier section (Royal Bath Hotel to the Square) which was switched out during the winter season, requiring attention by the Overhead Department whenever a school special to the Winter Gardens or an enthusiasts' tour was planned. At the substations there were metering devices to record the state of the system. Voltmeters and ammeters recorded the incoming current, and further meters recorded the output from the rectifiers. During the mid-1960s the maximum output from both pairs of rectifiers at Southcote Road was 600 volts at 500 amps, totalling 300 kW. Two recording meters in the circuit, at the point where the feeds from the rectifiers were connected to the busbars, traced a continuous graph on recording paper so that the maximum output at any given time could be seen. At the height of the morning rush hour, 8.45 am, output typically reached 1,850 amps. In the peak of the summer season, maximum system demand rose to 2,175 kW (July 1963) and 2,295 kW (August 1963). Demand was, of course, related to the size of the fleet, but in 1960, when the number of trolleybuses available for service averaged 63 in winter and 82 in summer, Mr W.D. Reakes, writing in the *Electrical Review* gave

Circuit breakers and other traction power supply equipment inside the 1955 BCT substation at Southcote Road.
Bournemouth Transport

Traction power supply equipment inside the 1955 BCT substation at Southcote Road.   Bournemouth Transport

BCT's Iddesleigh Road substation as constructed: both the substation building (which is still in use by the local electricity company) and the glazed-over area towards Charminster Road remain unaltered in 2018.
David Chalk collection (Hackbridge + Hewittic Electric Co. Ltd.)

the following figures: maximum winter system demand 2,000 kW; in summer 2,700 kW. Traction current consumption for an average week: winter 130,000 kW, summer 200,000 kW, giving an annual consumption approaching 7,200,000kWh.

Meters in each of the eight substations recorded the amount of AC current consumed. The basis for payment was a contract with the SEB for the supply of current over a given period at a rate per unit based on the quantity used. This special rate was based on the maximum demand figures taken from the above mentioned recording meters.

Under normal conditions the overhead system was divided into 21 electrical sections and was broken into 93 half-mile lengths of running wire plus the seasonal Bournemouth Pier section, Central Depot constituting three separate sections, the Mallard Road complex and its bus wash, all of which could also be isolated separately, making a total of 28 sections. The electrical sections were frequently linked. For example, the lines from Bournemouth Square (exclusive) to Westbourne formed one section fed by Electric House and Southcote Road substations, although the line could have been divided up into four sub-sections by the use of feeder pillar switching.

Dead ends in the feeder cables at Columbia Road and at the junction of Castle Lane East with Holdenhurst Road, together with the tied-off overhead line at Lawford Road, Redhill, gave evidence of planned extensions which never came to fruition. Before the Castle Lane/Holdenhurst Road roundabout was built, there was a supplementary mid-section feeder to the overhead at Holdenhurst Mains Pillar, the intention being to link up with Route "Q" which would have had breakers at the junction. A live tail which would have gone off to Route "Q" was connected to Holdenhurst Switch Box, was left standing in isolation in the middle of the new roundabout, making it a Mains Pillar. As Route "F" eastward from this point was linked via the overhead to Pokesdown substation, the two substations were coupled.

Two sections, Moordown and Westbourne, were fed jointly by Southcote Road and Green Road or Electric House substations respectively, whilst the ten sections making up the outlying parts of the system were fed by five other unattended substations independent of Southcote Road. The connections between the power supply feeder cables and the overhead wiring were installed in cast iron feeder pillars or switch boxes, every half-mile along the line of route and elsewhere as electrically necessary. Within each pillar, knife switches could be opened to interrupt the supply to the overhead line or link sections as required. Fuses were also fitted in the cables leading to the overhead, although the automatic circuit breakers within the substations were the first line of defence against excessive

Many of the pillars, whether feeder or mains, used for the trolleybus network had originally supplied powers to the trams and were identifiable as such by the title cast on the front door. This example still survives outside the Head Office of Yellow Buses in Yeomans Way, Bournemouth.
David Bowler

current passing into the line. A further piece of equipment was the lightning arrester, a coil and spark gap, to "choke" the very high voltage current and impede its progress in the hope that it would find it easier to pass to earth. Each trolleybus was also equipped with a lightning arrester; on the Sunbeam MS2s the "choke" coil was wound into the positive cable and could be seen mounted over the centre pillar of the driver's cab windscreen, immediately next to the positive circuit breaker.

In each feeder pillar a card diagram showed the normal connections and position of each switch, in addition to showing to which cables the pillar was connected. Nine (ten following the addition of one at Cooper Dean roundabout) of these roadside boxes, known as Mains Pillars, were not connected to the overhead at all, but contained junctions between various mains, enabling the current supply to be varied. Twenty four switch boxes were connected to the overhead wiring only and served to link a section with its neighbour. Six of these were smaller boxes containing just one or two knife switches and were often mounted on the traction poles themselves (pole switch boxes).

The boxes were kept securely locked. Originally, Inspectors and other officials were supplied with keys so that they could open the boxes in an emergency and cut off the current to a section, but at a later date their issue was restricted to employees of the Mains and Overhead Department, who better understood the implications of their actions.

The strategically important layout at Bournemouth Square could be supplied from any one of five feeder pillars or pole switch boxes, Albert Road, Bobby's (outside the department store on the Square which then bore that name), St. Peter's (the one normally used), Square Office or Yelverton Road. It could also be fed from the Lansdowne cables by closing the switches

at the Royal Bath Hotel switch box or a combination of those in the Bobby's feeder pillar and the Bournemouth Pier switch box. In an emergency it would also have been practical to link the Square wiring to the Richmond Hill, Old Christchurch Road or Poole Hill sections.

Most of the ducts which had carried the underground feeder cables were sold to the SEB or to the Post Office Telephones once trolleybus operation had been abandoned and the valuable cables removed.

Electrical Feeders

There were 53 positive feeder pillars at the following locations:

Albert Road (pole mounted)	on the north side of Old Christchurch Road opposite its junction with Hinton Road
Alma Road	on the west side of Charminster Road to the north of its junction with Alma Road
Ashley Road	on the east side of Ashley Road immediately to the south of its junction with North Road
Bargates	on the east side of Bargates south of its junction with Avon Buildings
Bobby's	on the south side of Bournemouth Square outside Bobby's department store
Boscombe Hill	on the north side of Christchurch Road opposite and a little to the east of Boscombe Spa Road
Boscombe Depot	inside Boscombe (Pokesdown) Depot building

Bryanstone Road positive feeder pillar in Wimborne Road, Winton, showing the cast iron box on the kerb at the base of the traction pole (on the right hand side of the photograph) which housed the switchgear required for this particular location and the four cables to the two positive overhead lines (one cable to the supply to south section and the other for the supply to the north section). Sunbeam MF2B no. 264 (WRU264) heads south towards the town centre in September 1966.
NTA collection (R.F. Mack)

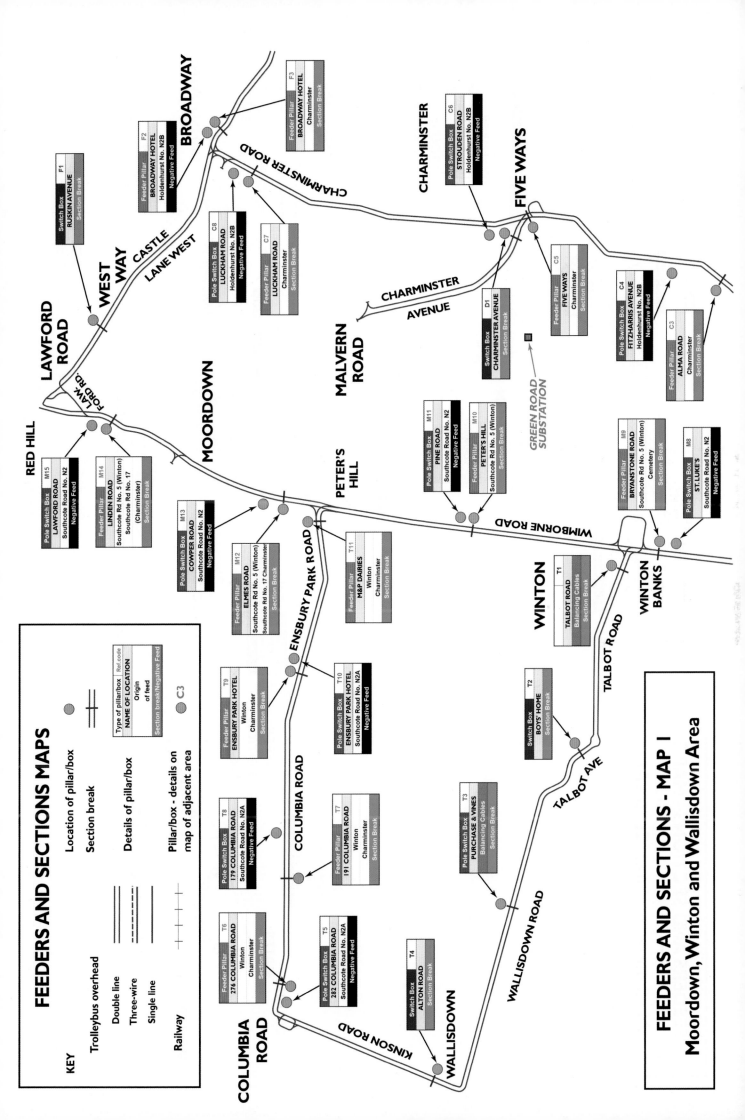

FEEDERS AND SECTIONS MAPS

KEY

● Location of pillar/box

╫ Section break

Trolleybus overhead

Double line

Three-wire

Single line

Railway

Details of pillar/box

Type of pillar/box	Ref.code
NAME OF LOCATION	
Origin of feed	
Section break/Negative Feed	

● C3 Pillar/box - details on map of adjacent area

FEEDERS AND SECTIONS - MAP I

Moordown, Winton and Wallisdown Area

Pillar/box details:

- **F1** Switch Box — RUSKIN AVENUE — Section Break
- **F2** Feeder Pillar — BROADWAY HOTEL — Holdenhurst No. N2B — Negative Feed
- **F3** Feeder Pillar — BROADWAY HOTEL — Charminster — Section Break
- **C8** Pole Switch Box — LUCKHAM ROAD — Holdenhurst No. N2B — Negative Feed
- **C7** Feeder Pillar — LUCKHAM ROAD — Charminster — Section Break
- **C6** Pole Switch Box — STROUDEN ROAD — Holdenhurst No. N2B — Negative Feed
- **C5** Feeder Pillar — FIVE WAYS — Charminster — Section Break
- **C4** Pole Switch Box — FITZHARRIS AVENUE — Holdenhurst No. N2B — Negative Feed
- **C3** Feeder Pillar — ALMA ROAD — Charminster — Section Break
- **D1** Switch Box — CHARMINSTER AVENUE — Section Break
- **M15** Pole Switch Box — LAWFORD ROAD — Southcote Road No. N2 — Negative Feed
- **M14** Feeder Pillar — LINDEN ROAD — Southcote Rd No. 5 (Winton) — Southcote Rd No. 17 (Charminster) — Section Break
- **M13** Pole Switch Box — COWPER ROAD — Southcote Road No. N2 — Negative Feed
- **M12** Feeder Pillar — ELMES ROAD — Southcote Rd No. 5 (Winton) — Southcote Rd No. 17 Charminster — Section Break
- **M11** Pole Switch Box — PINE ROAD — Southcote Road No. N2 — Negative Feed
- **M10** Feeder Pillar — PETER'S HILL — Southcote Rd No. 5 (Winton) — Section Break
- **M9** Feeder Pillar — BRYANSTONE ROAD — Southcote Rd No. 5 (Winton) Cemetery — Section Break
- **M8** Pole Switch Box — ST. LUKE'S — Southcote Road No. N2 — Negative Feed
- **T11** Feeder Pillar — M&P DAIRIES — Winton — Charminster — Section Break
- **T10** Pole Switch Box — ENSBURY PARK HOTEL — Southcote Road No. N2A — Negative Feed
- **T9** Feeder Pillar — ENSBURY PARK HOTEL — Winton — Charminster — Section Break
- **T8** Pole Switch Box — 179 COLUMBIA ROAD — Southcote Road No. N2A — Negative Feed
- **T7** Feeder Pillar — 191 COLUMBIA ROAD — Winton — Charminster — Section Break
- **T6** Feeder Pillar — 276 COLUMBIA ROAD — Winton — Charminster — Section Break
- **T5** Pole Switch Box — 282 COLUMBIA ROAD — Southcote Road No. N2A — Negative Feed
- **T4** Switch Box — ALTON ROAD — Section Break
- **T3** Pole Switch Box — PURCHASE & VINES — Balancing Cables — Section Break
- **T2** Switch Box — BOYS' HOME — Section Break
- **T1** — TALBOT ROAD — Balancing Cables — Section Break

GREEN ROAD SUBSTATION

Place names: BROADWAY, CHARMINSTER, FIVE WAYS, WEST WAY, CASTLE LANE WEST, LAWFORD ROAD, RED HILL, MOORDOWN, PETER'S HILL, MALVERN ROAD, WINTON, WINTON BANKS, COLUMBIA ROAD, WALLISDOWN

Roads: CHARMINSTER ROAD, CHARMINSTER AVENUE, WIMBORNE ROAD, ENSBURY PARK ROAD, COLUMBIA ROAD, TALBOT ROAD, TALBOT AVE, WALLISDOWN ROAD, KINSON ROAD, LAWFORD RD

FEEDERS AND SECTIONS - MAP 2

Westbourne and Town Centre Area

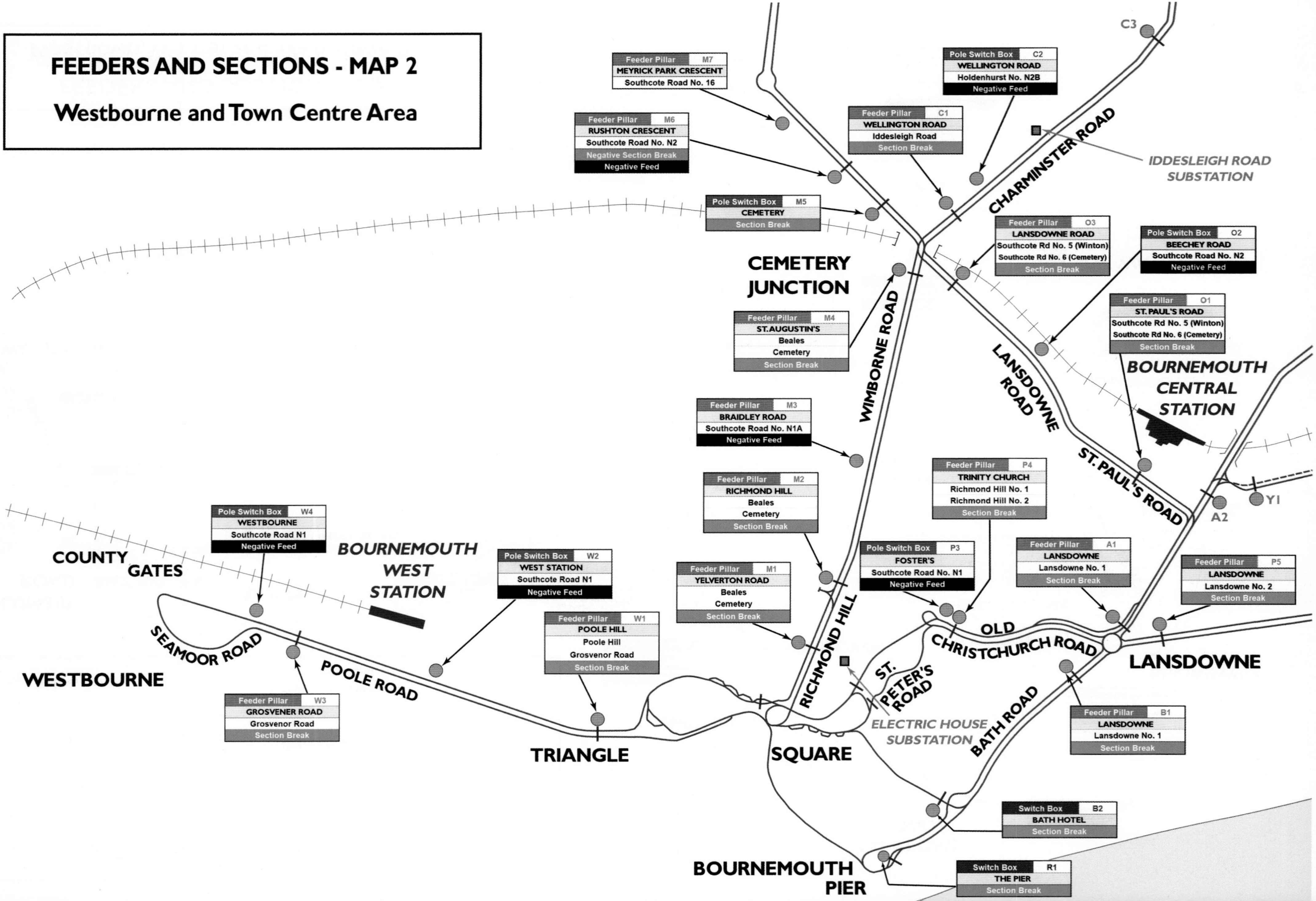

C3

IDDESLEIGH ROAD SUBSTATION

CHARMINSTER ROAD

Pole Switch Box	O2
BEECHEY ROAD	
Southcote Road No. N2	
Negative Feed	

Feeder Pillar	O1
ST. PAUL'S ROAD	
Southcote Rd No. 5 (Winton)	
Southcote Rd No. 6 (Cemetery)	
Section Break	

BOURNEMOUTH CENTRAL STATION

Y1

A2

Feeder Pillar	P5
LANSDOWNE	
Lansdowne No. 2	
Section Break	

LANSDOWNE

Feeder Pillar	B1
LANSDOWNE	
Lansdowne No. 1	
Section Break	

Feeder Pillar	O3
LANSDOWNE ROAD	
Southcote Rd No. 5 (Winton)	
Southcote Rd No. 6 (Cemetery)	
Section Break	

ST. PAUL'S ROAD

LANSDOWNE ROAD

Pole Switch Box	C2
WELLINGTON ROAD	
Holdenhurst No. N2B	
Negative Feed	

Feeder Pillar	A1
LANSDOWNE	
Lansdowne No. 1	
Section Break	

OLD CHRISTCHURCH ROAD

BATH ROAD

Switch Box	B2
BATH HOTEL	
Section Break	

Feeder Pillar	C1
WELLINGTON ROAD	
Iddesleigh Road	
Section Break	

Feeder Pillar	P4
TRINITY CHURCH	
Richmond Hill No. 1	
Richmond Hill No. 2	
Section Break	

Switch Box	R1
THE PIER	
Section Break	

Pole Switch Box	P3
FOSTER'S	
Southcote Road No. N1	
Negative Feed	

ST. PETER'S ROAD

ELECTRIC HOUSE SUBSTATION

WIMBORNE ROAD

CEMETERY JUNCTION

Feeder Pillar	M4
ST.AUGUSTIN'S	
Beales	
Cemetery	
Section Break	

Pole Switch Box	M5
CEMETERY	
Section Break	

Feeder Pillar	M3
BRAIDLEY ROAD	
Southcote Road No. N1A	
Negative Feed	

Feeder Pillar	M2
RICHMOND HILL	
Beales	
Cemetery	
Section Break	

RICHMOND HILL

SQUARE

BOURNEMOUTH PIER

Feeder Pillar	M1
YELVERTON ROAD	
Beales	
Cemetery	
Section Break	

Feeder Pillar	M7
MEYRICK PARK CRESCENT	
Southcote Road No. 16	

Feeder Pillar	M6
RUSHTON CRESCENT	
Southcote Road No. N2	
Negative Section Break	
Negative Feed	

Feeder Pillar	W1
POOLE HILL	
Grosvenor Road	
Section Break	

TRIANGLE

Pole Switch Box	W2
WEST STATION	
Southcote Road N1	
Negative Feed	

BOURNEMOUTH WEST STATION

POOLE ROAD

COUNTY GATES

SEAMOOR ROAD

WESTBOURNE

Pole Switch Box	W4
WESTBOURNE	
Southcote Road N1	
Negative Feed	

Feeder Pillar	W3
GROSVENER ROAD	
Grosvenor Road	
Section Break	

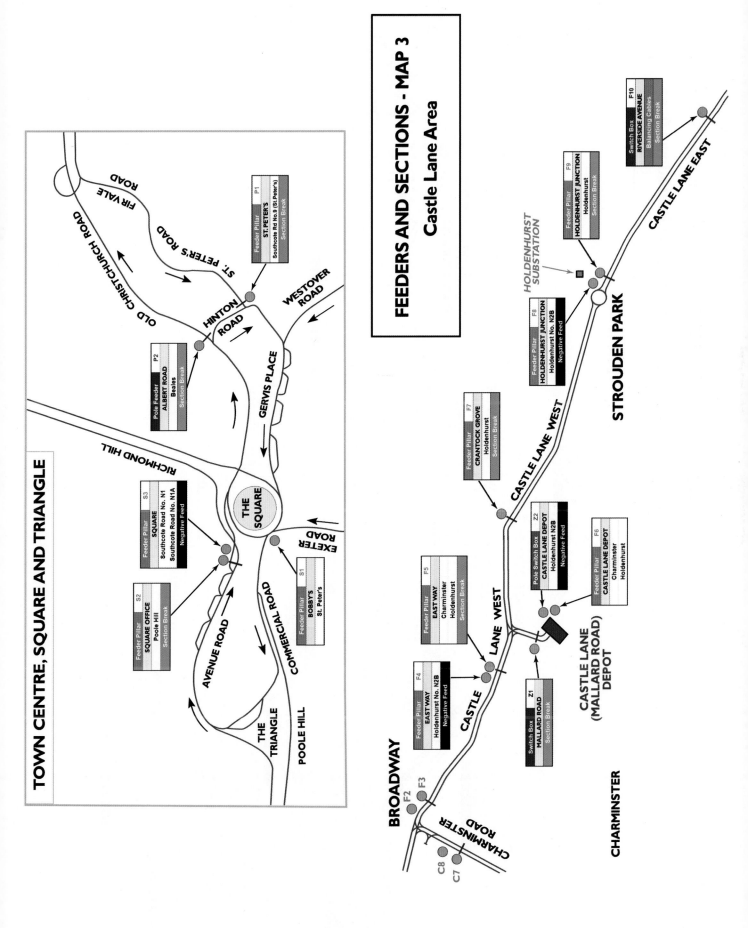

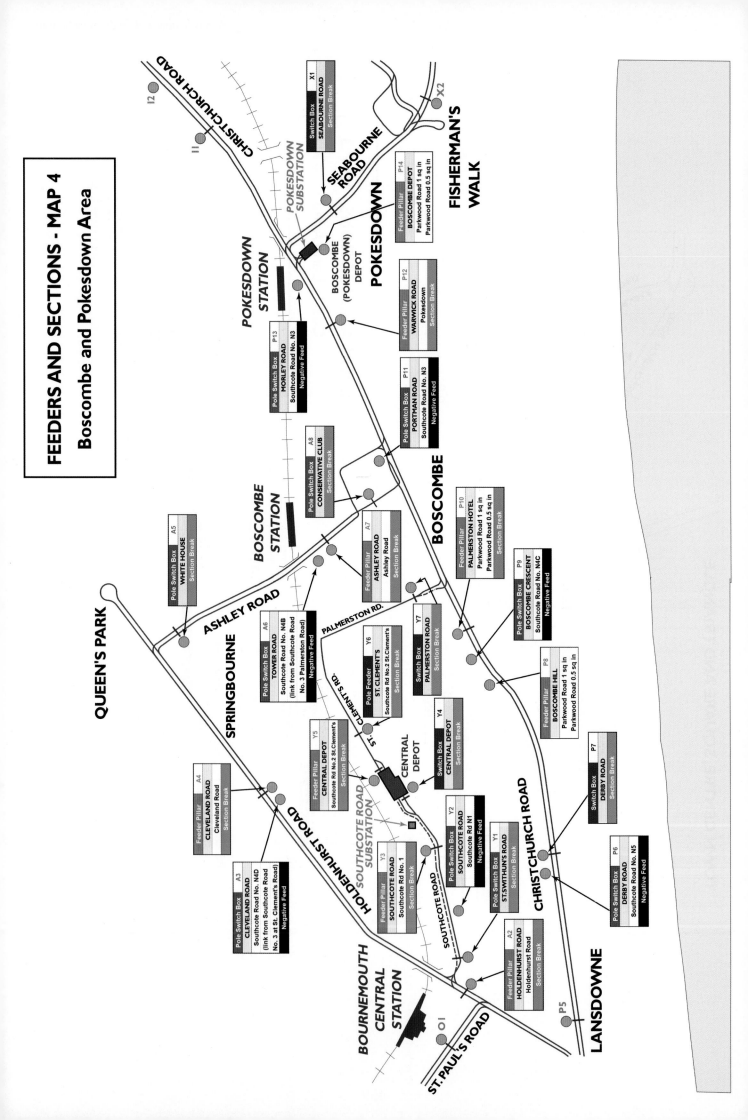

FEEDERS AND SECTIONS - MAP 4
Boscombe and Pokesdown Area

QUEEN'S PARK

CHRISTCHURCH ROAD

I2

I1

Switch Box X1
SEABOURNE ROAD
Section Break

X2

SEABOURNE ROAD

POKESDOWN STATION

POKESDOWN SUBSTATION

BOSCOMBE (POKESDOWN) DEPOT

POKESDOWN

Feeder Pillar P14
BOSCOMBE DEPOT
Parkwood Road 1 sq in
Parkwood Road 0.5 sq in

FISHERMAN'S WALK

Feeder Pillar P12
WARWICK ROAD
Pokesdown
Section Break

Pole Switch Box P13
MORLEY ROAD
Southcote Road No. N3
Negative Feed

Pole Switch Box P11
PORTMAN ROAD
Southcote Road No. N3
Negative Feed

Pole Switch Box A8
CONSERVATIVE CLUB
Section Break

BOSCOMBE STATION

BOSCOMBE

Pole Switch Box A5
WHITE HOUSE
Section Break

ASHLEY ROAD

Feeder Pillar A7
ASHLEY ROAD
Ashley Road
Section Break

Feeder Pillar P10
PALMERSTON HOTEL
Parkwood Road 1 sq in
Parkwood Road 0.5 sq in
Section Break

SPRINGBOURNE

Pole Switch Box A6
TOWER ROAD
Southcote Road No. N4B
(link from Southcote Road
No. 3 Palmerston Road)
Negative Feed

PALMERSTON RD.

Pole Feeder Y6
ST. CLEMENT'S
Southcote Rd No.2 St.Clement's
Section Break

Switch Box Y7
PALMERSTON ROAD
Section Break

Pole Switch Box P9
BOSCOMBE CRESCENT
Southcote Road No. N4C
Negative Feed

ST. CLEMENT'S RD.

Feeder Pillar Y5
CENTRAL DEPOT
Southcote Rd No.2 St.Clement's
Section Break

CENTRAL DEPOT

Switch Box Y4
CENTRAL DEPOT
Section Break

Feeder Pillar P8
BOSCOMBE HILL
Parkwood Road 1 sq in
Parkwood Road 0.5 sq in

CHRISTCHURCH ROAD

Feeder Pillar A4
CLEVELAND ROAD
Cleveland Road
Section Break

HOLDENHURST ROAD

SOUTHCOTE ROAD SUBSTATION

Pole Switch Box A3
CLEVELAND ROAD
Southcote Road No. N4D
(link from Southcote Road
No. 3 at St. Clement's Road)
Negative Feed

Pole Switch Box Y2
SOUTHCOTE ROAD
Southcote Rd N1
Negative Feed

Switch Box P7
DERBY ROAD
Section Break

Feeder Pillar Y3
SOUTHCOTE ROAD
Southcote Rd No. 1
Section Break

Pole Switch Box Y1
ST.SWITHUN'S ROAD
Section Break

SOUTHCOTE ROAD

Feeder Pillar A2
HOLDENHURST ROAD
Holdenhurst Road
Section Break

Pole Switch Box P6
DERBY ROAD
Southcote Road No. N5
Negative Feed

BOURNEMOUTH CENTRAL STATION

O1

P5

ST.PAUL'S ROAD

LANSDOWNE

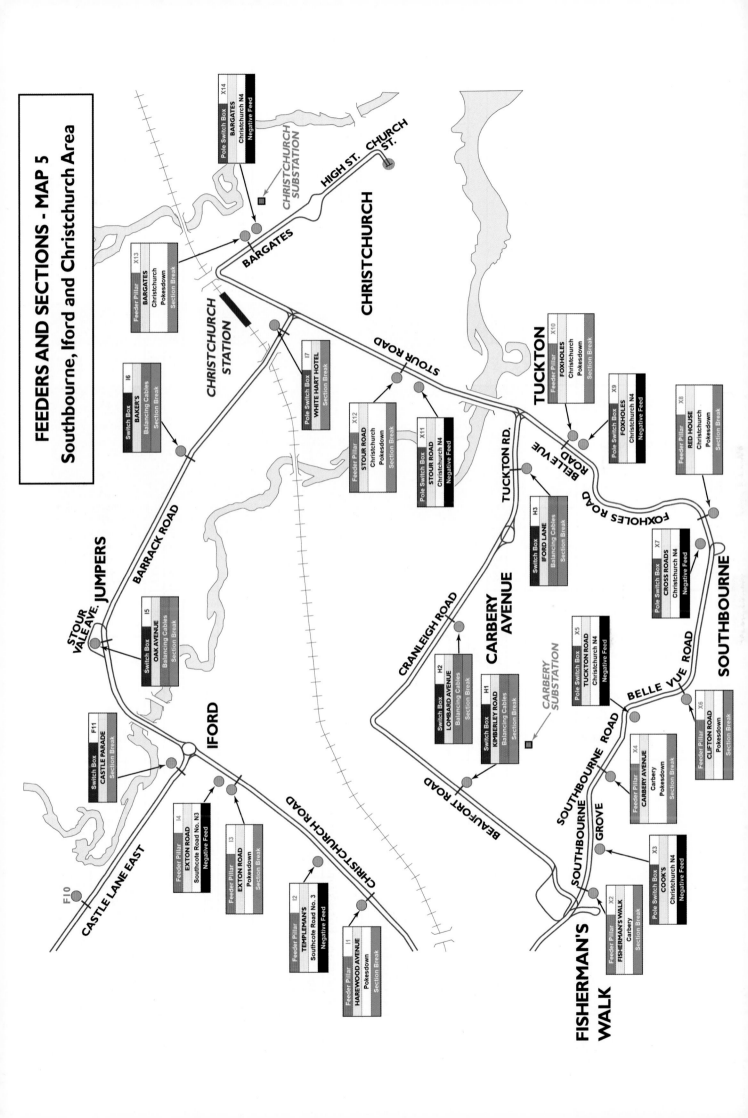

FEEDERS AND SECTIONS - MAP 5
Southbourne, Iford and Christchurch Area

CASTLE LANE EAST

F10

IFORD

JUMPERS

STOUR VALE AVE.

BARRACK ROAD

CHRISTCHURCH ROAD

CHRISTCHURCH STATION

HIGH ST. CHURCH ST.

CHRISTCHURCH SUBSTATION

BARGATES

CHRISTCHURCH

STOUR ROAD

TUCKTON RD.

TUCKTON

BELLE VUE ROAD

FOXHOLES ROAD

CRANLEIGH ROAD

BEAUFORT ROAD

CARBERY AVENUE

CARBERY SUBSTATION

SOUTHBOURNE ROAD

GROVE

BELLE VUE ROAD

SOUTHBOURNE

FISHERMAN'S WALK

Pole Switch Box	X14	
BARGATES		
Christchurch N4		
Negative Feed		

Feeder Pillar	X13	
BARGATES		
Christchurch		
Pokesdown		
Section Break		

Switch Box	I6	
BAKER'S		
Balancing Cables		
Section Break		

Pole Switch Box	I7	
WHITE HART HOTEL		
Section Break		

Feeder Pillar	X12	
STOUR ROAD		
Christchurch		
Pokesdown		
Section Break		

Pole Switch Box	X11	
STOUR ROAD		
Christchurch N4		
Negative Feed		

Feeder Pillar	X10	
FOXHOLES		
Christchurch		
Pokesdown		
Section Break		

Pole Switch Box	X9	
FOXHOLES		
Christchurch N4		
Negative Feed		

Feeder Pillar	X8	
RED HOUSE		
Christchurch		
Pokesdown		
Section Break		

Switch Box	H3	
IFORD LANE		
Balancing Cables		
Section Break		

Pole Switch Box	X7	
CROSS ROADS		
Christchurch N4		
Negative Feed		

Switch Box	I5	
OAK AVENUE		
Balancing Cables		
Section Break		

Switch Box	H2	
LOMBARD AVENUE		
Balancing Cables		
Section Break		

Switch Box	H1	
KIMBERLEY ROAD		
Balancing Cables		
Section Break		

Pole Switch Box	X5	
TUCKTON ROAD		
Christchurch N4		
Negative Feed		

Feeder Pillar	X6	
CLIFTON ROAD		
Pokesdown		
Section Break		

Switch Box	F11	
CASTLE PARADE		
Section Break		

Feeder Pillar	I4	
EXTON ROAD		
Southcote Road No. N3		
Negative Feed		

Feeder Pillar	I3	
EXTON ROAD		
Pokesdown		
Section Break		

Feeder Pillar	I2	
TEMPLEMAN'S		
Southcote Road No. 3		
Negative Feed		

Feeder Pillar	I1	
HAREWOOD AVENUE		
Pokesdown		
Section Break		

Feeder Pillar	X4	
CARBERY AVENUE		
Carbery		
Pokesdown		
Section Break		

Pole Switch Box	X3	
COOK'S		
Christchurch N4		
Negative Feed		

Feeder Pillar	X2	
FISHERMAN'S WALK		
Carbery		
Section Break		

Key to Reference Codes used on Feeders and Sections Map

Ref. on map	Name and location	Side of road	Traction Pole No.	Feeder Pillar +/-, +	Fed from	Direction(s) of Feed	Switch Box +	Pole Switch Box	Negative Feed -	Section Pillar +/-	Section Break	Balancing Cable	Notes
See footnote 1	See Footnote 2	See Footnote 3			See Footnote 4	See Footnote 5					See Footnote 6		
P 2	Albert Road, Old Christchurch Road	N	P5J	Yes	13	E&W					Yes		Pole mounted. 0.25 feed from Beales MP.
C 3	Alma Road, Charminster Road	W	C26	Yes	17	N&S					Yes		
A 7	Ashley Road	E	A87	Yes	3	N&S					Yes		
X 13	Bargates, Christchurch	E	X172	Yes	21+25	N&S					Yes		
S 1	Bobby's, Bournemouth Square	S	S ?	Yes	9	E&W							Fed from Square 0.4. Fed WB Avenue Road line and The Square roundabout.
P 8	Boscombe Hill, Christchurch Road	N	P100	Yes	18+19	E&W							Located inside the depot building. Fed depot wiring only.
P 14	Boscombe Depot	N/A	N/A	Yes	18+19	N/A							
F 3	Broadway Hotel, Castle Lane West	N	F48	Yes	17	E&W					Yes		Negative at same point, feeding W only.
M 9	Bryanstone Road, Wimborne Road	E	M74	Yes	5	N&S					Yes		
X 4	Carbery Avenue, Southbourne Road	W	X43	Yes	20+25	E&W					Yes		
F 6	Castle Lane Depot, Mallard Road	N/A	N/A	Yes	17+23	N/A							Located at the east corner of the depot complex perimeter line. Disconnected before final closure.
M	Cemetery Junction, Wimborne Road	S	M46	Yes	5	N&S					Yes		BCT plans show as feeder (earlier) and pole switch box (later)
Y 5	Central Depot (Southcote Road)	N/A	N/A	Yes	2	E&W					Yes		Inside the depot building connected to both lines
A 4	Cleveland Road, Holdenhurst Road	S	A47	Yes	8	E&W					Yes		
X 6	Clifton Road, Belle Vue Road	W	X56	Yes	25	E&W					Yes		
T 7	191 Columbia Road	S	T127	Yes	5+17	E&W					Yes		Fed by 0.5 from Ensbury Park MP
T 6	276 Columbia Road	S	T110	Yes	5+17	E&W					Yes		Fed by 0.5 from Ensbury Park MP. Live tail for route extension.
F 7	Crantock Road, Castle Lane West	N	F96	Yes	23	E&W					Yes		
F 5	East Way, Castle Lane West	N	F70	Yes	17+23	E&W					Yes		

Ref. on map	Name and location	Side of road	Traction Pole No.	Feeder Pillar +/-, +	Fed from	Direction(s) of Feed	Switch Box +	Pole Switch Box	Negative Feed -	Section Pillar +/-	Section Break	Balancing Cable	Notes
See footnote 1	See Footnote 2	See Foot-note 3			See Foot-note 4	See Foot-note 5					See Foot-note 6		
M 12	Elmes Road, Wimborne Road	W	M122	Yes	5+17	N&S					Yes		
T 9	Ensbury Park Hotel, Ensbury Park Road	N	T153	Yes	5+17	E&W					Yes		Fed by 0.5 from Ensbury Park MP
13	Exton Road, Christchurch Road	N	136	Yes	25	E&W					Yes		
X 2	Fisherman's Walk, Southbourne Grove	S	X24	Yes	20	N&S					Yes		
C 5	Five Ways, Charminster Road	W	C57J	Yes	17	N&S					Yes		Section break SB in Charminster Avenue trailing frog
X 10	Foxholes, Belle Vue Road	S	X120	Yes	21+25	E&W					Yes		
W 3	Grosvenor Road, Poole Road	S	W44	Yes	15	E&W					Yes		
11	Harewood Avenue, Christchurch Road	N	115	Yes	25	E&W					Yes		
F 9	Holdenhurst Junction, Castle Lane East	N	F124	Yes	23	E&W			Yes		Yes		
A 2	Holdenhurst Road (east of St. Paul's Road)	S	A18	Yes	4	E&W					Yes		
B 1	Lansdowne, Bath Road	N	B7	Yes	7	E&W					Yes		
P 5	Lansdowne, Christchurch Road	N	P60	Yes	10	E&W					Yes		
A 1	Lansdowne, Holdenhurst Road	S	A2	Yes	7	E&W					Yes		
O 3	Lansdowne Road	N	O4	Yes	5+6	E&W					Yes		
M 14	Linden Road, Wimborne Road	W	M151	Yes	5	N&S					Yes		
C 7	Luckham Road, Charminster Road	W	C85	Yes	17	N&S					Yes		
T 11	M & P Dairies, Ensbury Park Road	N	T170	Yes	5+17	E&W					Yes		
M 7	Meyrick Park Crescent, Wimborne Road	S	M54	Yes	16	N&S							
P 10	Palmerston Hotel, Christchurch Road	N	P112	Yes	18+19	E&W					Yes		
M 10	Peter's Hill, Wimborne Road	E	M98	Yes	5	N&S					Yes		
M 10	Peter's Hill, Wimborne Road	E	M98	Yes	5	N&S					Yes		
W 1	Poole Hill	N	W22	Yes	14+15	E&W					Yes		
X 8	Red House, Belle Vue Road	S	X85	Yes	21+25	E&W					Yes		
M 2	Richmond Hill	W	M11	Yes	6+13	N&S					Yes		

Ref. on map (See footnote 1)	Name and location (See Footnote 2)	Side of road (See Footnote 3)	Traction Pole No.	Feeder Pillar +/-, +	Fed from (See Footnote 4)	Direction(s) of Feed (See Footnote 5)	Switch Box +	Pole Switch Box	Negative Feed -	Section Pillar +/-	Section Break (See Footnote 6)	Balancing Cable	Notes
Y 3	Southcote Road	N	Y17	Yes	1	E&W					Yes		
S 2	Square Office, Avenue Road	N	S ?	Yes	14	E&W			Yes		Yes		
M 4	St. Augustin's, Wimborne Road	W	M35	Yes	6	N&S					Yes		
Y 6	St. Clement's	S ?	Y35A	Yes	2	E&W					Yes		Pole mounted
O 1	St. Paul's Road	E	O30	Yes	5+6	N&S					Yes		
P 1	St. Peter's, St. Peter's Road	E	PZ-4ZL	Yes	9	N&S					Yes		Fed Hinton Road and St. Peter's Road.
X 12	Stour Road	W	X148	Yes	21+25	N&S					Yes		
T 1	Talbot Road	N/A	T7								Yes	Yes	Section break in negative wire only.
P 4	Trinity Church, Old Christchurch Road	N	P42	Yes	11+12	E&W					Yes		Coupled to Beales MP
P 12	Warwick Road, Christchurch Road	S	P143	Yes	25	E&W					Yes		
C 1	Wellington Road, Charminster Road	W	C4	Yes	24	N&S					Yes		
M 1	Yelverton Road, Richmond Hill	W	M6	Yes	13	N&S					Yes*		Fed from Richmond Hill 0.4 FP. *Section break only on SB line.
Switch Boxes													
T 4	Alton Road, Kinson Road	E	T83			N&S	Yes				Yes		
I 6	Baker's, Barrack Road, Christchurch	N	I86			E&W	Yes				Yes	Yes	Balancing Cable at I87
B 2	Bath Hotel, Westover Road	S	B ?			E,S,W	Yes				Yes		
T 2	Boy's Home, Talbot Avenue	N	T30			E&W	Yes				Yes		
F 11	Castle Parade, Castle Lane East, Iford	N	F173			E&W	Yes				Yes		
Y 4	Central Depot (Southcote Road)	N/A	N/A			N/A	Yes				Yes		Inside the depot building connected to the southern of the two lines.
D 1	Charminster Avenue	E	D1			N&S	Yes				Yes		
P 7	Derby Road, Christchurch Road	N	P82			E&W	Yes				Yes		
H 3	Iford Lane, Tuckton Road	S	H81			E&W	Yes				Yes	Yes	Balancing cable at H80

464

Ref. on map	Name and location	Side of road	Traction Pole No.	Feeder Pillar +/-, +	Fed from	Direction(s) of Feed	Switch Box +	Pole Switch Box	Negative Feed -	Section Pillar +/-	Section Break	Balancing Cable	Notes
See footnote 1	See Footnote 2	See Foot-note 3			See Foot-note 4	See Foot-note 5					See Foot-note 6		
H 1	**Kimberley Road**, Beaufort Road	E	H27			E&W	Yes				Yes	Yes	Balancing cable at H26
H 2	**Lombard Avenue**, Cranleigh Road	S	H55			E&W	Yes				Yes	Yes	Balancing cable at H54
Z 1	**Mallard Road**	N	Z ?			N&S	Yes				Yes		
I 5	**Oak Avenue**, Barrack Road, Jumpers	N	I60			E&W	Yes				Yes	Yes	Balancing cable at I61
Y 7	**Palmerston Road**	E	Y63			N&S	Yes				Yes		
F 10	**Riverside Avenue**, Castle Lane East	N	F150			E&W	Yes				Yes	Yes	Balancing cable at F149
F 1	**Ruskin Avenue**, Castle Lane West	N	F19			E&W	Yes				Yes		
X 1	**Seabourne Road**	E	X6			N&S	Yes				Yes		
R 1	**The Pier**, Bath Road	N	R18			E&W	Yes				Yes		
	Pole Mounted Switch Boxes												
M 5	**Cemetery**, Wimborne Road	S	M46			N&S		Yes			Yes		BCT plans show as feeder (earlier) and pole switch box (later)
A 8	**Conservative Club**, Ashley Road, Boscombe	E	A97			N&S		Yes			Yes		
T 3	**Purchase & Vines**, Wallisdown Road	N	T56			E&W		Yes			Yes	Yes	Balancing cable at T58
Y 1	**St. Swithun's Road**, Southcote Road	S	Y2			E&W		Yes			Yes		
17	**White Hart Hotel**, Barrack Road, Christchurch	N	1108			E&W		Yes			Yes		Section break in both negative and positive wire.
A 5	**White House**, Ashley Road, Springbourne	W	A70			N&S		Yes			Yes		
	Mains Pillar												
-	**Beales**	-	??		13								Located in the vicinity of Hinton Road and Old Christchurch Road
-	**Carbery**, Southbourne Road	-	X43		20								Near X43
-	**Cattistock Road**, Castle Lane West	N	F81		23								Near F81
-	Cemetery	-	??		6+17								

Ref. on map	Name and location	Side of road	Traction Pole No.	Feeder Pillar +/-, +	Fed from	Direction(s) of Feed	Switch Box +	Pole Switch Box	Negative Feed -	Section Pillar +/-	Section Break	Balancing Cable	Notes
See footnote 1	See Footnote 2	See Footnote 3			See Foot-note 4	See Foot-note 5					See Foot-note 6		
-	**Ensbury Park Road**	-	??		5+17				Yes				Sometimes referred to as simply "Ensbury"
-	**Green Road**	-	??		26				Yes				
-	**Hinton Road**	-	??		22								
-	**Holdenhurst**	-	??		22								Located in the centre of Cooper Dean roundabout. Live tail for route extension.
-	**Luther Road**	-	??		26								
-	**Parkwood Road**	-	??		20+25								
	Negative Return 7												
X 14	**Bargates**, Christchurch	W	X173		N4	N&S		Yes	Yes				
-	**Beales**	N/A	N/A		N1 & N1B				Yes				T-joint in cable pit to cable N1B.
O 2	**Beechey Road**, Lansdowne Road	N	O13		N2	E&W		Yes	Yes				
P 9	**Boscombe Crescent**, Christchurch Road	N	P106		N4C	E&W		Yes	Yes				
M 3	**Braidley Road**, Wimborne Road	W	M22		N1A	N&S			Yes				
F 2	**Broadway Hotel**, Castle Lane West	N	F48		N2B	W		Yes	Yes				
-	**Carbery**, Southbourne Road	N/A	X47		N4	E&W			Yes				Link in Mains Pillar to Carbery substation (1 sq in).
Z 2	**Castle Lane Depot**, Mallard Road	N/A	Z ?		N2B	N/A		Yes	Yes				Located at the east corner of the depot complex perimeter line. Disconnected before final closure.
	Cattistock, Castle Lane West	N	F81		N2B				Yes				Link in Mains Pillar to Castle Lane Depot (0.25 sq in).
-	**Cemetery**	N/A	N/A		N1A				Yes				T-joint in cable pit and link to cables N2 & N2B.
A 3	Cleveland Road, Holdenhurst Road	S	A46		N4D	E&W		Yes	Yes				

466

Ref. on map (See footnote 1)	Name and location (See Footnote 2)	Side of road (See Footnote 3)	Traction Pole No.	Feeder Pillar +/-, +	Fed from (See Footnote 4)	Direction(s) of Feed (See Footnote 5)	Switch Box +	Pole Switch Box	Negative Feed -	Section Pillar +/-	Section Break (See Footnote 6)	Balancing Cable	Notes
T 8	179 Columbia Road	N	T128		N2A	E&W		Yes	Yes				
T 5	282 Columbia Road	S	T109		N2A	E,S,W		Yes	Yes				
X 3	Cook's, Southbourne Grove	W	X27		N4	N&S		Yes	Yes				
M 13	Cowper Road, Wimborne Road	W	M124		N2	N&S		Yes	Yes				
-	Crantock Road, Castle Lane West	N	F96		N2B	W			Yes		Yes		Link in Mains Pillar.
X 7	Cross Roads, Belle Vue Road, Southbourne	N	X80		N4	E&W		Yes	Yes				
P 6	Derby Road, Christchurch Road	N	P80		N5	E&W		Yes	Yes				
F 4	East Way, Castle Lane West	N	F70		N2B	W			Yes				
T 10	Ensbury Park Hotel, Ensbury Park Road	N	T154		N2A			Yes	Yes				Link in Mains Pillar to cable N2A.
-	Ensbury Park Road	N/A	N/A		N2			Yes	Yes				
1 4	Exton Road, Christchurch Road	N	137		N3	E&W		Yes	Yes				
C 4	Fitzharris Avenue, Charminster Road	W	C31		N2B	N&S		Yes	Yes				
-	Five Ways, Charminster Road	N/A	N/A		N2B				Yes				T-joint in cable pit and link to Green Road substation (0.75 sq in).
P 3	Foster's, Old Christchurch Road	N	P41		N1	E&W		Yes	Yes				
X 9	Foxholes, Belle Vue Road	S	X118		N4	E&W		Yes	Yes				
F 8	Holdenhurst Junction, Castle Lane East	N	F124	Yes	23	E&W		Yes	Yes		Yes		
-	Holdenhurst Road (east of St. Paul's Road)	N/A	N/A	Yes	N2				Yes		Yes		Link in Mains Pillar to cable N2.
M 15	Lawford Road, Wimborne Road	W	M152		N2	N&S		Yes	Yes				
C 8	Luckham Road, Charminster Road	E	C86		N2B	N&S		Yes	Yes				
P 13	Morley Road, Christchurch Road, Boscombe	N	P151		N3	E&W		Yes	Yes				
-	Palmerston Road	N/A	N/A		N3				Yes				T-joint in cable pit and links to cables N4B & N4C.
M 11	Pine Road, Wimborne Road, Moordown	E	M99		N2	N&S		Yes	Yes				T-joint in cable pit and 0.75 sq in cable to Green Road substation.

Ref. on map	Name and location	Side of road	Traction Pole No.	Feeder Pillar +/-, +	Fed from	Direction(s) of Feed	Switch Box +	Pole Switch Box	Negative Feed -	Section Pillar +/-	Section Break	Balancing Cable	Notes
See footnote 1	See Footnote 2	See Footnote 3			See Footnote 4	See Footnote 5					See Footnote 6		
P 11	Portman Road, Christchurch Road, Boscombe	N	P130		N3	E&W		Yes	Yes				
M 6	Rushton Crescent, Wimborne Road	S	M49		N2	E&W		Yes	Yes		Yes		Section break in both negative and positive wire.
Y 2	Southcote Road	N	Y6	Yes	N1	E&W		Yes	Yes				
S 3	Square Office, Avenue Road	N	S ?		N1 & N1A	E&W			Yes		Yes		T-joint in cable pit and link to cable N1A.
-	St. Clement's Road	S	Y45A		N3				Yes				T-joint in cable pit and link to cable N4D.
M 8	St. Luke's, Wimborne Road	W	M73		N2	S		Yes	Yes				
X 11	Stour Road	W	X145		N4	N&S		Yes	Yes				
C 6	Strouden Road, Charminster Road	W	C65		N2B	N&S		Yes	Yes				
I 2	Templeman's, Christchurch Road, Iford	N	119		N3	E&W		Yes	Yes				
A 6	Tower Road, Ashley Road	W	A85		N4B	N&S		Yes	Yes				
-	Tuckton Bridge	N/A	N/A		N4				Yes				Link in cable pit.
X 5	Tuckton Road	W	X52		N4	N&S		Yes	Yes				
-	Warwick Road, Christchurch Road	N/A	N/A		N3	N&S			Yes				T-joint in cable pit and 0.75 sq in link to cable N4A.
C 2	Wellington Road, Charminster Road	W	C8		N2B	N&S		Yes	Yes				
W 4	Westbourne, Poole Road	N	W70		N1	E&W		Yes	Yes				0.5 sq in cable from West Station. Single connection to the loop.
W 2	West Station, Poole Road	N	W34		N1	E&W		Yes	Yes				0.5 sq in cable to Westbourne.

468

Footnotes

▮ Shading indicates "No"

1 The alpha codes relate to the BCT traction pole numbering system. The reference numbers relate solely to the accompanying Feeders and Sections Map. They do not represent pole numbers and were not used in any official capacity.

2 Names shown in Bold were used within BCT to locate and map equipment. The precise wording on BCT plans has been used where known. Additional information shown in normal font is included to aid location on the maps.

3 Location of Piller on pavement or Box on pole:
N = North, E = East, W = West, S = South, ? = Not known

4 Feeder cable number:

From Southcote Road main switchoard:
1. Southcote Road
2. St. Clement's Road
3. Ashley Road
4. Holdenhurst Road
5. Winton
6. Cemetery
7. Lansdowne No.1
8. Cleveland Road
9. St. Peter's
10. Lansdowne No.2
11. Richmond Hill No.1
12. Richmond Hill No.2
13. Beales
14. Poole Hill
15. Grosvenor Road
16. Meyrick Park Crescent
17. Charminster
18. Parkwood Road 1 ins
19. Parkwood Road 1/2 ins

From Substations:
20. Carbery
21. Christchurch
22. Electric House
23. Holdenhurst
24. Iddesleigh Road
25. Pokesdown
26. Winton, Green Road

Negative Return cable number:
Cable sizes shown are the cross-sectional area of copper conductor, not the diameter. A cable shown as 1 sq in has a diameter of 0.56 inches.
From Southcote Road main switchoard:
N1. 1 sq in (0.5 sq in from West Station to Westbourne)
N1A. 0.5 sq in
N1B. 1 sq in
N2. 1 sq in
N2A. 0.5 sq in
N3. 1 sq in
N4A. 1 sq in (0.75 sq in from Christchurch substation to Tuckton Bridge)
N4B. 0.5sq in (link from cable 3 at Palmerston Road).
N4C. 0.5 sq in (link from cable 3 at Palmerston Road).
N4D. 0.5 sq in (link from cable 3 at St. Clements Road).
N4E. 1 sq in (link from Carbery substation to cable N4).
N5. 1 sq in

From Substations:
N2B. 0.75 sq in (from Holdenhurst substation)
N4. 1 sq in (from Christchurch substation)

5 For each Feeder Pillar, the direction for which power was provided is shown by a letter / letters (Where a Section Break was included this might not be for both directions): N = North, E = East, W = West, S = South, ? = Not known

6 Feeder Pillars were also Section Breaks (Section Insulators) except where there was a nearby Switch Box.

7 Names in italics are underground cable joints not connected to the overhead wiring.

Broadway Hotel	on the north side of Castle Lane West to the east of the junction with Charminster Road and to the east of the Broadway Hotel building
Bryanstone Road	on the east side of Wimborne Road two spans south of the junction with Alma Road and opposite the junction with Bryanstone Road
Carbery Avenue	on the south side of Southbourne Road opposite its junction with Carbery Avenue
Castle Lane Depot	on the east side of the Transport Department's property on the peripheral wiring between the trailing frog leading from the washer and the depot building entrance frog
Cemetery Junction	on the south side of Wimborne Road immediately after Cemetery Junction (Note: shown on later BCT plans as a Pole Switch Box)
Central Depot	inside Central Depot (Southcote Road) building on the northern of the two lines
Cleveland Road	on the south side of Holdenhurst Road on the west side of its junction with Cleveland Road opposite Springbourne Library
Clifton Road	on the west side of Belle Vue Road just to the south of its junction with Clifton Road
191 Columbia Road	on the south side of Columbia Road, some 150 yards east of its junction with Talbot Rise (opposite the house with that number)
276 Columbia Road	on the south side of Columbia Road, some 50 yards east of its junction with Kinson Road
Crantock Grove	on the north side of Castle Lane West at the junction with Crantock Grove
East Way	on the north side of Castle Lane West between the junctions with East Way and Mallard Road (opposite)
Elmes Road	on the west side of Wimborne Road, Moordown at its junction with Elmes Road
Ensbury Park Hotel	on the north side of Ensbury Park Road one span east of the crossroads with Boundary Road, Columbia Road and Redhill Avenue
Exton Road	on the north side of Christchurch Road on the east corner of its junction with Colemore Road
Fisherman's Walk	on the south side of Southbourne Grove south of the junction with Beresford Road
Five Ways	on the west side of Charminster Road immediately to the south of the junction with Charminster Avenue
Foxholes	on the south side of Belle Vue Road immediately to the south of its junction with Broadway
Grosvenor Road	on the south side of Poole Road on the east side of its junction with Grosvenor Road
Harewood Avenue	on the north side of Christchurch Road immediately to the east of its junction with Harewood Avenue
Holdenhurst Junction	on the north side of Castle Lane East immediately to the east of the Cooper Dean roundabout (junction with Holdenhurst Road)
Holdenhurst Road	on the south side of Holdenhurst Road one span south of the junction with St. Swithun's Road
Lansdowne (Bath Road)	on the north side of Bath Road one span west of the Lansdowne roundabout
Lansdowne (Christchurch Road)	on the north side of Christchurch Road two spans to the east of the Lansdowne roundabout
Lansdowne (Holdenhurst Road)	on the south side of Holdenhurst Road immediately to the north of Lansdowne roundabout
Lansdowne Road	on the north side of Lansdowne Road a little to the east of Cemetery Junction
Linden Road	on the west side of Wimborne Road on the southern corner of its junction with Linden Road.
Luckham Road	on the west side of Charminster Road to the north of its junction with Charminster Place
M & P Dairies	on the north side of Ensbury Park Road immediately prior to its junction with Wimborne Road, Moordown
Meyrick Park Crescent	on the south side of Wimborne Road to the east of its junction with the western end of Meyrick Park Crescent
Palmerston Hotel	on the north side of Christchurch Road to the east of its junction with the east end of The Crescent
Peter's Hill	on the east side of Wimborne Road on the south corner of its junction with Pine Road
Poole Hill	on the north side of Poole Hill two spans east of its junction with West Hill Road
Red House	on the south side of Bell Vue Road to the west of its junction with Church Road
Richmond Hill	on the west side of Richmond Hill at its junction with Bodorgan Road and between the entrance and exit to the reversing triangle at this point
Southcote Road	on the north side of Southcote Road opposite the junction with Carlton Road (to the west of the entrance to/exit from Central Depot)
Square Office	on the north side of Avenue Road immediately prior to its egress into the Square
St. Augustin's	on the west side of Wimborne Road on the southern corner of its junction with St. Augustin's Road
St. Clement's (pole mounted)	on the south side of St. Clement's Road in the vicinity of Cleveland Road
St. Paul's Road	on the east side of St. Paul's Road opposite its junction with Oxford Road
St. Peter's	on the east side of St. Peter's Road at its junction with Hinton Road
Stour Road	on the west side of Stour Road on the north corner of its junction with Douglas Avenue

Trinity Church	on the north side of Old Christchurch Road immediately to the east of Holy Trinity Church
Warwick Road	on the south side of Christchurch Road, Boscombe opposite its junction with Warwick Road
Wellington Road	on the west side of Charminster Road immediately to the north of its junction with Wellington Road
Yelverton Road	on the west side of Richmond Hill on the northern corner of its junction with St. Stephen's Road and opposite the junction with Yelverton Road

Switch Boxes

Externally identical to mains and feeder pillars, and their pole mounted equivalents, switch boxes contained the necessary switches to connect or disconnect in various permutations the overhead trolley wires of adjacent sections fed from different sources. There was no connection to the underground feeder cables.

Switch Boxes were located at the following places:

Alton Road	on the east side of Kinson Road immediately to the south of its junction with Alton Road
Baker's	on the north side of Barrack Road, Christchurch on the east side of its junction with Elizabeth Avenue
Bath Hotel	on the south side of Westover Road immediately to the west of its junction with Bath Road
Boys' Home	on the north side of Talbot Avenue opposite the Talbot Manor Home for Boys
Castle Parade	on the north side of Castle Lane East, Iford at its junction with the western end of Castle Parade
Central Depot	inside Central Depot (Southcote Road) building on the southern of the two lines
Charminster Avenue	on the east side of Charminster Avenue at its south end opposite Rutland Road
Derby Road	on the north side of Christchurch Road on the east corner of its junction with Derby Road
Iford Lane	on the south side of Tuckton Road opposite its junction with Iford Lane
Kimberley Road	on the east side of Beaufort Road one span north of the crossroads with Kimberley Road
Lombard Avenue	on the south side of Cranleigh Road on the west corner of its junction with Lombard Avenue
Mallard Road	on the north side of Mallard Road opposite the entrance to Castle Lane (Mallard Road) Depot complex
Oak Avenue	on the north side of Barrack Road, Jumpers, about a quarter of the way between the junction with Oak Avenue and the junction with Stourvale Avenue
Palmerston Road	on the east side of Palmerston Road on the north side of its junction with Haviland Road

Riverside Avenue	on the north side of Castle Lane East a little to the west of its junction with Riverside Avenue
Ruskin Avenue	on the north side of Castle Lane West immediately to the west of its junction with Ruskin Avenue
Seabourne Road	on the east side of Seabourne Road opposite Harcourt Road
The Pier	on the north side of Bath Road outside the Pavilion and opposite the Pier Approach Baths

Pole Mounted Switch Boxes

Pole Mounted Switch Boxes were located at the following places:

Cemetery	on the south side of Wimborne Road immediately to the north of Cemetery Junction (Note: shown on earlier BCT plans as a Feeder Pillar)
Conservative Club	on the east side of Ashley Road, Boscombe at its crossroads with Haviland Road
Purchase & Vines	on the north side of Wallisdown Road opposite Talbot Village Farm
St. Swithun's Road	on the south side of Southcote Road immediately to the east of its junction with St. Swithun's Road
White Hart Hotel	on the north side of Barrack Road, Christchurch at the southeast corner of the hotel building and to the west of Belvedere Road
White House	on the west side of Ashley Road, Springbourne, a little to the north of Grant's Avenue.

Mains Pillars

Mains Pillars were located at the following places:

Beales	Old Christchurch Road (assumed)
Carbery	Southbourne Road
Cattistock Road	Castle Lane West, Strouden Park near traction pole F81
Cemetery	Not known
Ensbury	Wimborne Road (assumed)
Green Road	Not known
Hinton Road	Not known
Holdenhurst	Added after spring 1963 in the middle of the Cooper Dean roundabout at the junction of Castle Lane East with Holdenhurst Road
Luther Road	Not known
Parkwood Road	Not known

Negative Return

Negative Return feeders were located at the following places:

Bargates	on the east side of Bargates to the north of its junction with Beaconsfield Road
Beechey Road	on the north side of Lansdowne Road on the west corner of its junction with Beechey Road
Boscombe Crescent	on the north side of Christchurch Road, Boscombe immediately before the junction with the west end of The Crescent

The cast metal container with the Bournemouth coat of arms on its door is a pole switch box, this one being the **White House PSB** attached to traction pole A70 in Ashley Road, Springbourne. **BUT9641T** no. 246 (KLJ346) passes on its way south to Boscombe in August 1964. In the background another **BUT** 6-wheeler turns into Holdenhurst Road heading for the Square. **NTA collection (R.F. Mack)**

Braidley Road	on the west side of Wimborne Road at its junction with Braidley Road	Derby Road	on the north side of Christchurch Road one span to the west of the Derby Road crossroads
Broadway	on the north side of Castle Lane West to the east of the junction with Charminster Road and to the east of the Broadway Hotel building one span east of the Broadway Hotel positive feeder	East Way	on the north side of Castle Lane West between the junctions with East Way and Mallard Road (opposite)
Castle Lane Depot	on the east side of the Transport Department Department's property on the peripheral wiring between the trailing frog leading from the washer and the depot building entrance frog	Ensbury Park Hotel	on the north side of Ensbury Park Road two spans east of the crossroads with Boundary Road, Columbia Road and Redhill Avenue
Cleveland Road	on the south side of Holdenhurst Road one span to the west of its junction with Cleveland Road	Exton Road	on the north side of Christchurch Road on the east corner of its junction with Colemore Road
179 Columbia Road	on the north side of Columbia Road, some 120 yards east of its junction with Howeth Road	Fitzharris Avenue	on the west side of Charminster Road at its junction with Fitzharris Avenue
282 Columbia Road	on the south side of Columbia Road, one span east of its junction with Kinson Road	Foster's	on the north side of Old Christchurch Road immediately to the east of Holy Trinity Church
Cook's	on the west side of Southbourne Grove in the vicinity of Grand Avenue	Foxholes	on the south side of Belle Vue Road to the south of its junction with Broadway
Cowper Road	on the west side of Wimborne Road, Moordown at its junction with Cowper Road	Holdenhurst Junction	on the north side of Castle Lane East immediately to the east of the Cooper Dean roundabout (junction with Holdenhurst Road)
Crantock Grove	on the north side of Castle Lane West at the junction with Crantock Grove	Lawford Road	on the west side of Wimborne Road south of its junction with Lawford Road and one span north of Linden Road feeder pillar
Cross Roads	on the north side of Belle Vue Road at Southbourne Crossroads immediately to the east of the junction with Seafield Road	Luckham Road	on the west side of Charminster Road to the north of its junction with Charminster Place

Morley Road	on the north side of Christchurch Road, Pokesdown, two spans west of the entrance frog to Boscombe (Pokesdown) Depot
Pine Road	on the east side of Wimborne Road on the north corner of its junction with Pine Road
Portman Road	on the north side of Christchurch Road, Boscombe, immediately after the trailing frog from Ashley Road
Rushton Crescent	on the south side of Wimborne Road to the west of its junction with the western end of Rushton Crescent
Southcote Road	on Southcote Road to the east of its junction with St. Swithun's Road
Square Office	on the north side of Avenue Road immediately prior to its egress into the Square
St. Clement's	on the south side of St. Clement's Road to the east of Walpole Road
St. Luke's	on the east side of Wimborne Road three spans south of the junction with Alma Road and in the vicinity of the junction with St. Luke's Road
Stour Road	on the west side of Stour Road opposite the junction with South View Road
Strouden Road	on the west side of Charminster Road in the vicinity of the junction with Strouden Road
Templeman's	on the north side of Christchurch Road, just east of its junction with Waltham Road
Tower Road	on the west side of Ashley Road on the corner of its junction with Tower Road
Tuckton Road	on the west side of Belle Vue Road opposite its junction with Tuckton Road
Wellington Road	on the west side of Charminster Road 4 spans north of its junction with Wellington Road
Westbourne	on the north side of Poole Road on the east corner of its junction with Surrey Road South
West Station	on the north side of Poole Road on the west corner of its junction with Queens Road
Yelverton Road	on the west side of Richmond Hill on the northern corner of its junction with St. Stephen's Road and opposite the junction with Yelverton Road. (Note: removed by the early 1960s)

Negative Return and Earthing

The Bournemouth system was all-insulated, with the continuous negative wire earthed at one point - the Generating Station, and later the substation at Southcote Road. This could be identified by the apparently continuous negative wire, devoid of the half mile gaps evident in the positive wire. In fact, the negative wire was broken by section insulators at Castle Lane West, near the Broadway Hotel (replaced latterly); Oak Avenue, Iford (installed when those at the Broadway Hotel were removed); Roslin Road, Winton; Rushton Crescent in Wimborne Road just north of Cemetery Junction; the Triangle (a jumpered-over "breaker") and the White Hart Hotel, in Barrack Road, Christchurch. The negative insulators were inserted for line testing purposes and were normally bridged over by jumper cables, Meyrick Park Crescent being an exception.

There was a relatively simple network of five main negative return cables, indicating its tramway origins, each with various branches and links, which brought the return current back from the overhead line to a busbar connected to electrodes buried in coke breeze in the Central Depot, Southcote Road yard where the entire system was earthed.

The negative return cables were connected to the overhead by means of pole-mounted switch boxes, although at six places (Broadway, Crantock Grove, East Way, Holdenhurst, Square Office and Yelverton Road) they were connected at positive feeder pillars from which six cables, instead of the usual four, led out to the overhead wiring. Each was identifiable by name although in some cases the naming logic, e.g. Cooks or Templemans, which presumably had their origins in a company or shop name, had ceased to exist by the final years of the trolleybus system. The negative return connections were usually adjacent to the positive feeders and thus also at approximately half mile intervals, but the two were normally given separate names, e.g. the positive feeder at pole M98 was named Peter's Hill whereas the negative at pole M99 was named Pine Road (for an explanation of pole and wiring route numbering, see Appendix J).

Neither the positive mains nor the negative returns always ran parallel to an actual trolleybus route, e.g. negative cable 5 to Derby Road ran via Drummond Road rather than following Southcote Road as its positive equivalents along the western part of Christchurch Road, whilst negative cable 1 to Westbourne followed Commercial Road rather than Avenue Road. Both negative and positive cables followed Parkwood Road between the junction of Christchurch Road with Parkwood Road and the junction of Seabourne Road with Parkwood Road rather than Christchurch Road and Seabourne Road; both negative and positive cables followed Seafield Road and Tuckton Road between Southbourne Cross Roads and the junction of Belle Vue Road with Tuckton Road; and both negative and positive cables followed Cleveland Road between Southcote Road and Holdenhurst Road rather than a trolleybus route.

There were even sections of overhead not connected to the underground network, where the overhead itself carried the return current. A mile-long section, Seabourne Road to Kimberley Road, was created in 1948 when the Cranleigh Road route opened. Where there was double-track overhead and thus two negative wires, these were cross-connected to equalise the current in them and reduce resistance to a minimum. The two negative wires were normally connected through the switch boxes, by which they were coupled to their underground return cables, but where there were no cables along the route, equalisers consisting of short lengths of cable connected at either end to the negative wires and running along a convenient span wire (usually the one next to a half-mile section insulator) could be seen. Equalisers or balancing cables could be found linking the two positive trolley wires or the two negative trolley wires could be found at many points throughout the system. Mallard Road switch box had both positive and negative switches connected to the outward line to enable the depot wiring to be fed from Castle Lane in an emergency (the inward line had insulators in both wires with jumpers omitted). Under normal circumstances, the depot was fed by its own cables running along Cattistock Road to the east of the property from Cattistock mains pillar on Castle Lane, which was not connected to the overhead and which had both positive and negative cable connections. The negative feeder was removed well before 1969.

High-voltage tests were made to check the insulation on all positive feeder and negative return cables periodically. Leakage from the positive system was checked every Friday night after the last trolleybus had run into depot and when any current passing was clearly leaking to earth. The MoT's 1936 Regulations for Bournemouth stipulated a maximum permissible leakage current of 1/100 amp per mile of route, and required that operations had to cease if the fault could not be located and corrected within 24 hours.

No limit was placed on the number of trolleybuses which could operate on a given section at any one time but, if several vehicles were all starting away at the same time, the line voltage fell. The vehicles' controls were designed to function at half the normal line voltage, but problems developed if this fell below 400 volts. At times when few trolleybuses were operating, line voltage was accordingly high and high speeds could be obtained.

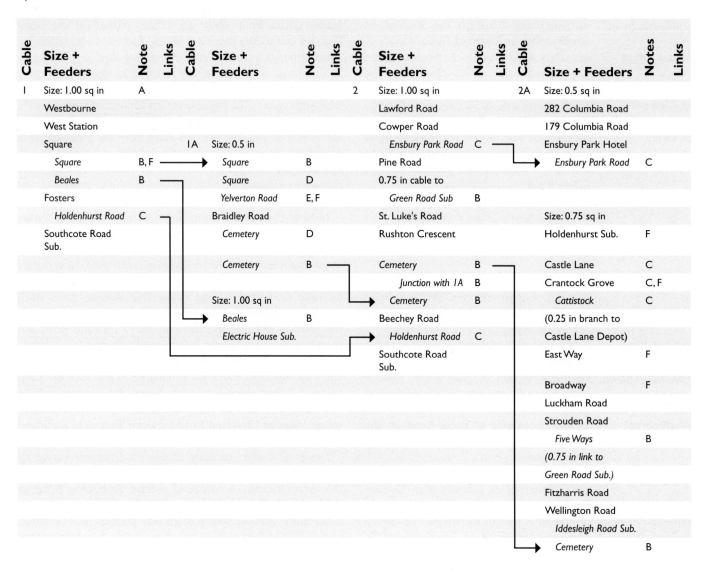

Cable	Size + Feeders	Note	Links	Cable	Size + Feeders	Note	Links	Cable	Size + Feeders	Note	Links	Cable	Size + Feeders	Notes	Links
1	Size: 1.00 sq in	A						2	Size: 1.00 sq in			2A	Size: 0.5 sq in		
	Westbourne								Lawford Road				282 Columbia Road		
	West Station								Cowper Road				179 Columbia Road		
	Square			1A	Size: 0.5 in				*Ensbury Park Road*	C			Ensbury Park Hotel		
	Square	B, F			*Square*	B			Pine Road				*Ensbury Park Road*	C	
	Beales	B			*Square*	D			0.75 in cable to						
	Fosters				*Yelverton Road*	E, F			*Green Road Sub*	B			Size: 0.75 sq in		
	Holdenhurst Road	C			Braidley Road				St. Luke's Road				Holdenhurst Sub.	F	
	Southcote Road Sub.				*Cemetery*	D			Rushton Crescent						
					Cemetery	B			*Cemetery*	B			Castle Lane	C	
									Junction with 1A	B			Crantock Grove	C, F	
	Size: 1.00 sq in				Size: 1.00 sq in				*Cemetery*	B			*Cattistock*	C	
	Beales	B							Beechey Road				(0.25 in branch to		
	Electric House Sub.								*Holdenhurst Road*	C			Castle Lane Depot)		
									Southcote Road Sub.				East Way	F	
													Broadway	F	
													Luckham Road		
													Strouden Road		
													Five Ways	B	
													(0.75 in link to		
													Green Road Sub.)		
													Fitzharris Road		
													Wellington Road		
													Iddesleigh Road Sub.		
													Cemetery	B	

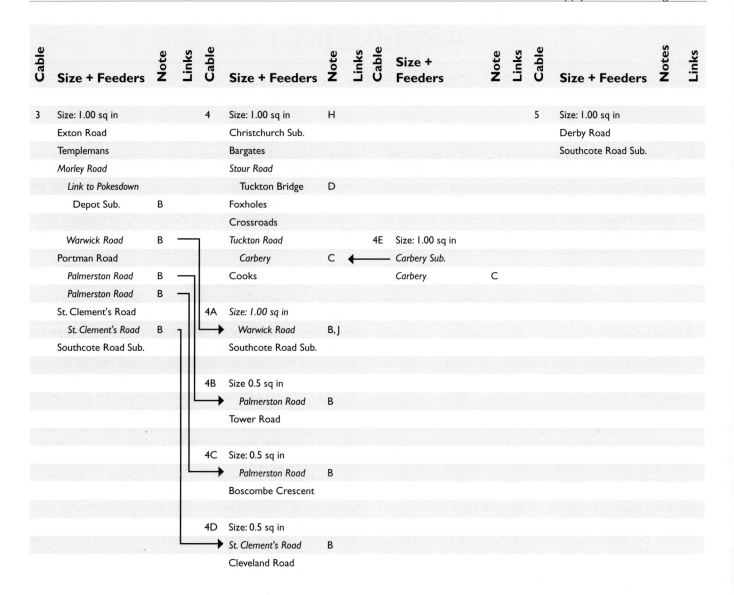

Cable	Size + Feeders	Note	Links	Cable	Size + Feeders	Note	Links	Cable	Size + Feeders	Note	Links	Cable	Size + Feeders	Notes	Links
3	Size: 1.00 sq in			4	Size: 1.00 sq in	H						5	Size: 1.00 sq in		
	Exton Road				Christchurch Sub.								Derby Road		
	Templemans				Bargates								Southcote Road Sub.		
	Morley Road				*Stour Road*										
	Link to Pokesdown				Tuckton Bridge	D									
	Depot Sub.	B			Foxholes										
					Crossroads										
	Warwick Road	B			*Tuckton Road*			4E	Size: 1.00 sq in						
	Portman Road				*Carbery*	C			*Carbery Sub.*						
	Palmerston Road	B			Cooks				*Carbery*		C				
	Palmerston Road	B													
	St. Clement's Road			4A	Size: 1.00 sq in										
	St. Clement's Road	B			*Warwick Road*	B, J									
	Southcote Road Sub.				Southcote Road Sub.										
				4B	Size 0.5 sq in										
					Palmerston Road	B									
					Tower Road										
				4C	Size: 0.5 sq in										
					Palmerston Road	B									
					Boscombe Crescent										
				4D	Size: 0.5 sq in										
					St. Clement's Road	B									
					Cleveland Road										

Notes:

Names in italics were underground cable connections <u>not</u> connected to the overhead wiring.

Unless otherwise shown, all connections to the overhead wire were by pole-mounted switch box.

Cable sizes shown are the cross-sectional area of copper conductor, not the diameter, viz. cables shown as 1 sq in had a diameter of 0.56 in.

A   0.5 sq in from West Station to Westbourne

B   T-joint in cable pit, i.e. a chamber beneath a manhole cover.

C   Link in Mains Pillar.

D   Link in cable pit, i.e. a chamber beneath a manhole cover.

E   Link in Feeder Pillar.

F   Feeder Pillar.

G   Two 0.75 sq in cables between Holdenhurts Road Substation and Castle Lane Mains Pillar.

H   0.75 sq in Christchurch Substation to Tuckton Bridge; 1.00 sq in from Tuckton Bridge to Southcote Road.

J   Link between 3 and 4A at Warwick Road was 0.75 sq in.

Sub.   Substation.

Based on the BCT Mains Superintendent's official drawing F10B.

APPENDIX I
OVERHEAD WIRING

Installation

The trolleybus overhead equipment installed in spring 1933 for the initial, experimental route between Bournemouth Square and County Gates, Westbourne, about 1 mile and 260 yards long, was erected by the Transport Department's own overhead department. Trams also continued to operate along the route, which was an integral part of the Poole - Christchurch tramway. Once it had been decided to adopt trolleybuses in place of tramways, the erection of the more complex overhead equipment for the conversion of each tram route and all subsequent extensions beyond the former tramways were carried out entirely by the undertaking's own Overhead Department.

As the trolleybuses started to replace the tramways, entirely new wiring was installed. Wherever both trams and trolleybuses were likely to work together, e.g. along Christchurch Road between the Lansdowne and Pokesdown Station, separate trolleybus wiring was hung between the kerb and the tram overhead enabling trolley vehicles to "undertake" the trams. On occasion the trolleybus wires were hung from the tramway side bracket poles whilst the tramway positive wire was rehung on short span wires running between the ends of opposite bracket arms. Much of the Bournemouth system was constructed with single-line hangers as used on the tramways but new material was used throughout.

During the conversion period, the Overhead Department engaged additional staff on a temporary basis to excavate holes for new traction poles and generally assist the linesmen. These men came from the tramway permanent way gang, which had an ever-decreasing workload, and employees rendered surplus to requirements due to the withdrawal of Bournemouth's trams from the Poole area.

The trolleybuses were indeed the direct successors of their rail-bound predecessors in that they continued to use many items of tramway overhead equipment; in fact this was one of the economic arguments in favour of replacing the trams with railless electric traction. The first electric tramway overhead equipment, together with the permanent way and conduit system, had been supplied and erected by Messrs. J.G. White & Co. Ltd., of London EC4.

The trolley wire suspension was arranged to suit tramcars with swivel trolley heads, i.e. the wire was not always placed centrally over the track, and employed bracket arms, predominantly of the single-arm type on one side or, on occasion, both sides of the road, e.g. Poole Road. Many of these bracket arms retained ornate scrollwork until the conversion to trolleybus operation whilst the ornate cast bases bearing the Bournemouth coat of arms remained in use until the end of the trolleybus era. The initial electric tramway overhead work featured double trolley wire throughout, despite many sections of single track, using 0.384in hard drawn figure eight section copper wire supplied in half mile sections and supported by galvanised steel span wires. However, by the early 1930s British Standard 23 trolley wire, size 3/0 or 4/0 was in use.

Large scale route diagrams showing the proposed line, together with plans and profiles of the roads over which the trolleybuses would operate, were prepared to accompany the application for MoT approval. Once granted, details of the individual pole positions, plans of junctions, etc., were drawn up. On the electrical side, requirements were prepared for the provision of section insulators, feeder cables, etc. Actual construction commenced with the planting of traction poles in their appointed positions, after which the span wires would be placed in position and tightened up so as to pull the tops of the backwards-slanting poles slightly together. The span wires were immersed in Stockholm tar for one week before use, to provide a lifetime's corrosion protection. Before the span wires were slackened off, the hangers were inserted. A half mile cod line (a thin rope) would be attached to the span wires as if it were the first of the trolley wires. Its position represented the position of the negative wire of the first pair and its location was carefully adjusted so that straight sections were really straight and curved sections smoothly curved. The route of the trolley wires was kept as straight as possible, minor deviations and irregularities of the kerb line being ignored to obtain a smooth run. It was assumed that the trolleybus would normally be running more or less beneath the route of the trolley wires and to avoid running with the trolley booms continually at a sideways angle the negative trolley wire was normally not strung more than 7ft from the kerb on roads up to 26ft wide, increasing to 11ft for roads between 39 and 45ft in width. A distance of 13ft was never exceeded. Wherever possible, curves were aligned so that the radius of the trolley wire was less than the route of the vehicle beneath thereby minimising the risk of a dewirement.

The position of the negative wire for either the outbound or inbound pair of wires was then marked on each of the span wires, the procedure being repeated for the position of the second pair before the cod line was moved to the next half mile section. The span wires were then cut, a turnbuckle being used to keep the two parts of the span wire taunt during this operation, and the hangers placed in position. The trolley wire would then be run out and simply tied to each span wire alongside the hangers, the ends of each half mile length being temporarily fastened to a suitable traction pole.

The conductor wires used by the trolleybuses were supported by 12in long cast metal ears consisting of two side plates which, by tightening clamping screws, gripped the lobe on top of the grooved wire. The positive wire was hung on the right in the direction of travel and the negative wire on the left for safety reasons. A supporting boss located midway along the length of the ear retained a screw-in moulded compound insulator, widely known as an "insulated bolt", which was itself retained in the hanger.

By the mid-1930s a range of pre-assembled overhead fittings and in particular a single unit supporting both trolley wires (twin line hanger), an insulated spacer keeping the two wires the designated distance apart ensuring triple insulation between the wires, came onto the market. All trolleybus routes were equipped with trolley wires 24in (2ft) apart, but for a few spans at the Square during the experimental period, Bournemouth never employing the 18in spacing used by many earlier trolleybus operators, and the trolley vehicles were initially equipped with under-running swivel head wheel collectors. Double-eye globe strain insulators, made of brown glazed porcelain, were placed in the span wires to ensure triple insulation between positive and earth, and double insulation between negative and earth.

The linesmen then worked along the length, fitting the trolley wire to each hanger and screwing the ears up tight, riveting the ends of the screws over to prevent them working loose at any time. The half-mile section breakers were fitted and the battered ends of the trolley wire which had been fastened to the traction poles were trimmed off. As every new route was connected to an existing line at one or both ends, the final connecting up could be done at the last moment after the route itself was complete, usually in a single overnight operation when traffic on the existing route had ceased. If the ends of the trolley wire which had been tied off to traction poles could not be made long enough to allow for trimming later, new undamaged lengths were spliced in or, alternately, the wire could be straightened by using special rollers to iron out any kinks.

When two lengths of trolley wire were ready to be joined, they were pulled together by the use of clamps and a screw tensioner, a dynamometer or heavy-duty spring balance being used to adjust the tension in the wires to the correct figure of 2,000lbs. This would indicate where the new wire should be cut. Both ends were then cleaned, straightened and joined, adjustments being made to the hangers along the whole line if any had been pulled slightly out of position by the tensioning. After a number of trial runs, the overhead wiring was ready for official inspection.

In the early days of operation, the majority of urban telephone wires were still hung in the air rather than being installed underground and guard wires were hung above and parallel to the trolleybus overhead where telephone wires crossed the road to prevent a broken or sagging telephone wire coming into contact with the running wires and being charged at trolleybus line voltage. The guard wires consisted of a second pair of thinner wires attached to span wires of the same material, the whole network being suspended about 3 feet above the trolley wires themselves. At intervals the guard wires were earthed through a connection to the negative trolley wire. Examples could be seen on in Charminster Avenue, Columbia Road and Kinson Road until the mid-1960s.

Protective netting hanging between the traction poles some 15-20ft above the ground and parallel to the actual running wires immediately above the footpath was installed at points where dewirements were more frequent, despite the high standard of overhead wiring work, and where a swinging trolley pole could cause damage. Installations could be found until the end of trolleybus operation at the beginning of the eastbound overtaking wiring in Old Christchurch Road preceding Lansdowne roundabout and on the entry curves to Fir Vale Road travelling towards Bournemouth Square.

Pre-war the overhead wiring layout, including crossings and junctions, was constructed on an individual basis from single line hangers and tramway style components, e.g. a left hand 25° facing junction would be made up of two single 25° left hand frogs and a 25° left hand insulated crossing with plain trolley wire in between. There appears to have been no preferred supplier of overhead equipment, although it may be noted that Estler Bros. was the UK agent for Ohio Brass Co., Mansfield, USA, fittings at one time. In the mid-1930s British Insulated

Cables Ltd. (BIC), whose equipment was manufactured at Prescot, Lancashire, began to introduce a range of pre-assembled overhead fittings in which rigid spacer bars linked the various parts and post-war they became the favoured supplier although The Anti-Attrition Metal Co., London SE15, by then licensed manufacturer and distributor of Ohio Brass fittings, continued to supply specific items and angles. In May 1945 BIC amalgamated with Callender's Cable & Construction Co. Ltd. of Belvedere, Erith, Kent, to become British Insulated Callender's Cables Ltd. (BICC).

In the case of span wire overhead construction, the galvanised steel supporting wire ran between traction poles planted, normally at the kerb, on each side of the road, and attached to the upper section of the pole by a galvanised mild steel pole strap. MoT regulations required that the height of the trolley wire should not be less than 20ft above the surface of the road, but to allow for sagging of the wires during hot weather a figure of 21ft was used in practice. Double insulation between the positive and negative trolley wires was provided by the hangers supporting the trolley wire (the primary insulation) and between the trolley wire and earth by the insulated bolt into the hanger and an insulator located either in the span wire or between the span wire and the retaining bracket (the secondary insulation). Wall-mounted rosettes, anchored in roadside buildings, could replace one or both traction poles. Span wire construction provided a flexible support to the trolley wire.

Where side bracket traction poles were employed the insulators supporting the trolley wire were carried by short lengths of span wire known as bowstrings thus providing the required double insulation between the positive trolley wire and earth, and also providing a degree of elasticity to the trolley wire support thereby increasing trolley wire life (rigid suspension inevitably caused wire fractures). Part of the weight of the arm, which normally would not exceed the recommended maximum length of 16ft, was taken by a tie-rod or rods.

Simple span wire suspension inevitably sagged towards the centre of the road, which meant that the negative trolley wire hung slightly higher than the positive one; however, this did not create an evident problem for the later slider trolley heads (also known as slipper heads). The difference in heights could be ameliorated by the availability of single line hangers in three forms, downwards, level and upwards. Use of an "up" and "down" hanger to support a pair of wires would bring a span wire incline of 1:10 into the horizontal. Latterly, a range of L-shaped twin-line hanger end fittings was introduced whereby the two trolley wires could be brought into uniform vertical alignment.

The initial cost of overhead equipment, excluding special work such as junctions, varied considerably according to the planned operating speed and geography of the route, a heavily curved section requiring proportionately more traction poles and bridle or pull-off span wires.

Unlike some other trolleybus systems Bournemouth did not employ any kind of markings or signs, whether at the side of the road, on the road surface or hanging from a span wire, to denote a frog, section breaker or other special work. Neither were strings of strategically placed "fairy lights" hung from the span wires to guide drivers through junctions or wide bends in fog.

There were overtaking or passing loops at a number of points on the system post-war, specifically Avenue Road eastbound, Boscombe (in Christchurch Road from Ashley Road towards

Portman Road) eastbound, Bournemouth Pier, Gervis Place westbound, and at the Lansdowne (from Old Christchurch Road into Holdenhurst Road) eastbound. But for the last named, all remained in use until the final closure of the system.

Trolley Wire

In 1933, the Joint Committee on Overhead Line Equipment made up of specialists from members of the Municipal Tramways & Transport Association and the Tramways and Light Railways Association (the trade association of private tramways operators), recommended standardisation on a single profile of grooved trolley wire, British Standard (BS) 23 Revision 1, to gradually replace the various types then in use. In 1919 it had recommended a total of eight forms, four round and four grooved, each using 0 (1/0), 00 (2/0), 000 (3/0) and 0000 (4/0) wire, the suspension lobes being different in each case. The BS 23 Revision 1 profile accommodated suspensions that were not exactly vertical even when suspension ears projected beyond the wire diameter and did not disrupt the passage of V-shaped bronze trolley wheels, whether attached to fixed or swivel trolleyheads.

Fortunately, BCT made the decision to use new standard 4/0 SWG grooved trolley wire (presumed to be hard drawn copper or copper cadmium) as each tram route was converted to trolleybus operation. This type of trolley wire ensured that a mechanical suspension ear did not protrude beyond the diameter of the wire, and reduced noise and sparks from trolley wheels, thereby removing any interference with wireless reception so far as the ears were concerned. Worn trolley wheels were able to operate through ears on an even path, avoiding wear of the ears or the dishing of the trolley wire where it left the ear. A further advantage lay in the fact that grooved trolley wire had a greater collecting diameter than round wire, providing a valuable increase as laden trolleybuses of this period, weighing 12-13 tons, took starting currents in excess of 300 amps. Conductivity improved further when Bournemouth trialled the use of swivelling sliding heads employing carbon inserts and standardised on by the end of the 1938-39 financial year, as sliding heads provided a larger wire contact area than a trolley wheel. By the late 1950s the vast majority of positive section insulators, splicing ears (under normal circumstances, these were not used on curves), frogs and insulated crossings were of the BIC/BICC type.

BIC/BICC referred to the standard sections used by most trolleybus operators as SG (Standard Groove) or NS (New Standard) and these identifying codes appeared on the cast bronze end fittings for frogs, crossings and section insulators.

BICC issued the BS23 Revision 3 New Standard, which retained the principal groove dimensions but revised the cross-section to a circular profile, in April 1949. The special work

end fittings were interchangeable with earlier products. At the same time the company withdrew all but 4/0 grooved wire for tramways and trolleybuses, and formalised the reduced lobe width that many undertakings had been using for more than a decade, in effect, placing undertakings still running under SG wire in the position of using a non-preferred section.

Maintenance

Although the original tramway network had been installed by specialist contractors, subsequent maintenance, repairs, renewals and alterations to the tramway overhead equipment were carried out by BCT's own linesmen. Official returns show that there were just two linesmen and as annual reports refer to "several miles of trolley wire being renewed", it is unclear how this was carried out. If it was at night, the linesmen would not have been available during the day whilst if it had been in the day the tram service would have been interrupted. They had the use of a horse-drawn tower wagon with the horse being hired from the Borough Engineer or a local contractor. A horse and cart was also frequently hired from a Mr F.H. Welch.

The horse-drawn tower wagon was replaced by converting a former Tilling-Stevens TS3 motorbus in 1920 but the horse-drawn wagon was retained for some years thereafter as a reserve. At some stage, additional gangs were employed, probably after World War One when many single line sections of the tramways were doubled, and by 1930 there was linesman coverage 24 hours per day, seven days a week.

The previous in-house policy in respect of overhead equipment continued with the wiring of the trial route, the subsequent conversions of tramway overhead equipment for trolleybus operation through to the demise of the trolleybus system.

The Overhead Department was based at Central Depot, Southcote Road, where there was a small store, however, in 1935 a barn at Iford Bridge turning circle was acquired and this became the main store for overhead equipment. From 1934 each overhead gang was made up of two linesmen and a driver/handyman under the control of a Foreman and the Superintendent. There were four overhead gangs working seven days a week in three eight hour shifts to provide 24 hours coverage per day and who followed a four-week rota consisting of an early shift (6am - 2pm), a late shift (2pm - 10pm) and a night shift (10pm - 6am) with the fourth gang covering rest days, holidays and illness. Their whereabouts at any given time was shown on a special board at Central Depot. There was a scheduled maintenance programme, normally carried out by the night shift, and each route was inspected on a regular basis. Occasional work such as layout alterations, the renewal of fittings and rewiring was also dealt with by the night shift, assisted by the fourth gang working their rest day where necessary for

large projects, e.g. the installation of wiring at a new roundabout. The preferred opportunity for carrying out major installation or layout alterations was between midnight Saturday and 8am (or later) on Sunday when two or more gangs would work.

By the late 1940s, the Superintendent was Fred W. Harris and the Foreman was William (Bill) Pearce. When Fred Harris retired about 1960 due to ill health, Bill Pearce (who had had to cover long periods of Fred Harris' illness) was promoted to Superintendent but the position of Foreman was not filled.

The barn at Iford Bridge ceased to be used as a

store from June 1953 when sufficient space became available at Castle Lane (Mallard Road) Depot, and the Overhead Department moved there in its entirety in June 1965 when Central Depot, Southcote Road was vacated.

The regular maintenance programme had to consider that normal wear and tear made the trolley wire thin where it led in and out of any rigid fitting. In order to remove and replace a worn or broken length of trolley wire, "come-along" clamps would be attached to the trolley wire, one each side of the section needing repair or replacement, and an unscrewed turnbuckle, i.e. an expanding screw with hooks at each end, would be hooked onto the rings attached to each clamp. The turnbuckle was progressively tightened thereby increasing the tension in the trolley wire on the "outer" side of the "come-along" clamps but creating looseness or sag between them. The section to be removed could then be cut out and a new length, with a joining or splicing ear at each end, inserted to a fixing clamp fastened to the trolley wire ends protruding from the "inner" side of the "come-along" clamps. Once the clamping screws within each splicing ear had been securely tightened to ensure mechanical and electrical connection and any kinks removed by the use of special straightening rollers, the tension in the wires would be adjusted to the appropriate figure for that location with a dynamometer or heavy duty spring balance. The turnbuckle would then be gradually opened, allowing the overhead wiring layout to return to its normal position, and the "come-along" clamps removed.

A similar procedure was followed to handle or remove longer distances of trolley wire or frogs. Dependent on the weight, the turnbuckle(s) would be tied off and secured to a traction pole(s) thereby retaining the length under tension. When the overhead wiring network was being dismantled, trolley wire could be dropped in 40-yard lengths and the span wires would either be taken down at the same time or left in situ and removed at a later date.

Span wires suffered no mechanical wear and tear, and were normally only replaced in conjunction with changes to the road layout or when they were life-expired, the biggest enemy being corrosion.

Following the March 1963 announcement that the trolleybus system would be rundown and eventually closed, several Overhead Department employees (mostly the younger ones) decided to leave for alternative employment and it became increasingly common for an overhead gang to consist of only two men. Eventually, from 6 January 1966, the night shift was deleted and the number of gangs reduced from four to three. Henceforth they worked nine hours per day in a five-day week made up of an early shift (6am - 3pm) and a late shift (3pm - midnight) with the third gang covering rest days, holidays and illness. Two gangs worked together on a Friday early shift, but one gang usually worked their rest day on a Sunday early shift in order to provide enough men to remove the more complex parts of the overhead line when road traffic was light.

Although there was no longer a night shift, it was still necessary, on occasion, to carry out some work at night to deal with on-going alterations to the remains of the system, e.g. widening of Castle Lane West in the vicinity of Cooper Dean roundabout and the Southbourne Traffic Management Scheme. In most cases this was achieved by the late shift working two or three hours of overtime but on rare occasions a complete night shift was worked by one gang on their rest day.

In connection with the abandonment of trolleybus operation, the Overhead Department was reduced to just four employees: Bill Pearce (Superintendent), H. Tunnicliffe and Les Watts (linesmen), and Bernard Mabe (driver/handyman). During the closure procession on 20 April 1969 they were stationed with their tower wagon at Fisherman's Walk close to a BCT private telephone in case of any emergencies. From 21 April 1969 they worked a permanent early shift (6am - 2pm) with Saturday as a rest day. After a few months Bernard Mabe transferred to the vehicle workshops leaving just Bill Pearce and the two linesmen to remove all the remaining overhead wiring, traction poles and underground feeder cables. Bill Pearce was very much a "hands-on" Superintendent and was frequently to be seen on top of the tower wagon closely involved with the linesmen's work. The final items of equipment were removed in December 1971 and the two linesmen were retired being of pensionable age. Bill Pearce, being slightly younger, was retained to head a newly created Street Works section dealing with bus stop poles and signs, passenger waiting shelters, etc., and he finally retired in December 1974.

Some worn parts of the overhead wiring equipment such as crossings, frogs and trolleyheads, were reconditioned by the Department by building up using sifbronze. Maintenance work included an examination of all bracket poles, one pole being thoroughly overhauled each week, every bolt being inspected and the whole painted with protective paint.

Linesmen were despatched to the correct location for their duties by reference to the alpha-numeric code painted on each traction pole. Simple diagrams were drawn to complement instructions given for work at junctions or other points where there were many line fittings needing attention. Crossovers, frogs and insulators received an annual coat of Kalbitum paint; in addition automatic frogs were stripped down, cleaned and lubricated every three months. All renewals were recorded in a book, compiled from inspection reports, showing the condition of the entire system which had a trolley wire length of over 107 miles (24.8 miles of double line wiring, 4.24 miles of single line wiring) at its maximum extent in summer 1963. Also recorded were the particulars and times of emergency calls to remedy defects and the times that these were cleared.

Some statistics from 1963, provided by John Mawson, are of interest:

Line miles	107
Route miles	29
Turnouts:	92
of which, auto frogs	27
Junctions	80
Crossovers	55
Section insulators:	
Anti-Attrition	36
BICC	94
Traction poles	3237

The life of trolley wire was between 13 and 15 years. The totals for section insulators do not include insulator units incorporated into turnouts, junctions and crossovers.

An oddity was the turnout used by trolleybuses from Tuckton Bridge to turn at Carbery Avenue which had its operating handle on the right-hand side of the road.

During the trolleybus era, the Overhead Department operated the following tower wagons:

Fleet No.	Reg No.	Type	Into Service	Withdrawn	Note
	EL2105	Tilling-Stevens TS3 petrol-electric	1915	June 1936	1
	EL2103	Tilling-Stevens TS3 petrol-electric	August 1917	March 1937	2
	EL2106	Tilling-Stevens TS3 petrol-electric (tower transferred to RU 2012)	July 1933	January 1936	3
1	RU2012	Tilling-Stevens TS6 petrol-electric	January 1936	May 1945	4
2	RU2013	Tilling-Stevens TS6 petrol-electric	June 1936	September 1950	5
6	RU2014	Tilling-Stevens TS6 petrol-electric	May 1937	October 1948	6
3	DEL37	Bedford 2-ton lorry, Rawlins tower	June 1937	December 1965	7
10	VH6218	AEC Regent 661, Lee Motors	Feb. 1947	May 1967	8
12	VH6217	AEC Regent 661, Lee Motors	Nov. 1948	Post 1969	8

Note

1	Converted c. 1930 from a single deck motorbus (constructed in April 1915 from a new TS3 chassis and a second-hand body) and withdrawn in 1929.
2	Converted in August 1920 from an open-top double deck motorbus (dating from April 1914) to a lorry and again to a tower wagon in August 1920.
3	Converted in July 1933 from a single deck motorbus (constructed in May 1915 from a new TS3 chassis and a second-hand body) and withdrawn in 1930.
4	Converted from single deck motorbus 13 dating from October 1925. Prior to conversion, it is recorded that the chassis was used from December 1935 for several months to convey tram bodies from Central Depot, Southcote Road to Kings Park dump. Equipped with the tower formerly used on EL2106.
5	Converted from single deck motorbus 14 dating from October 1925. After conversion there was a crew compartment immediately behind the driver, then a tower (that formerly used on EL2105). It is believed that there was also a crane mounted at the rear of the chassis. It was replaced by TF 447.
6	Converted from single deck motorbus 15 dating from October 1925. After conversion there was a space behind the driver to carry drums of wire, then a crew compartment in the centre and a tower (that formerly used on EL2103) at the rear.
7	Purchased new. Used mainly for painting traction poles after 1948 and accordingly given a green livery in June 1963.
8	Ex-Huddersfield motorbuses, first registered in March 1934 and purchased by Bournemouth 11 January 1945. They were not used in public service in Bournemouth. BCT removed the body from No. 10 (VH6218) in February 1945. It was then rebuilt with shortened chassis and a crew/workshop behind the driver's cab by Lee Motors. BCT then fitted a double-lift tower. An identical conversion was made to No. 12 (VH6217) but all work was carried out by BCT. Originally in scarlet livery with maroon bands. The petrol engine in VH6217 was replaced by a diesel engine from a withdrawn motorbus in July 1965. After removal of the last overhead wiring on 18 January 1971 (within Mallard Road depot), the vehicle was used to pull out lengths of underground feeder cable. That work was completed by the end of 1971 and VH 6217 was finally withdrawn and de-licensed on 31 December 1971. It subsequently returned to service as a temporary recovery vehicle on trade plate 256EL from 31 January to 9 February 1972 before being sold to the BPTA in April 1972. In 2011 ownership passed from the BPTA to the West of England Transport Collection where it was stored undercover at Winkleigh, Devon. VH6217 was acquired by the Dundee Museum of Transport on 22 March 2015 and has been repainted in the green livery of the former Dundee Corporation Transport. (6218 retained petrol engine until withdrawal).

The Overhead Department also had a hand-pushed tower wagon which may originally have been horse-drawn and could have been the one which toppled over at the crossroads of Holdenhurst Road with St. Paul's Road and Waverley Road in spring 1935. It was used for painting traction poles until at least the 1940s and remained in stock at Central Depot, Southcote Road, unused, until 1965 when it was disposed of.

Tilling-Stevens TS3 petrol-electric EL2103 was rebuilt as a tower wagon in 1920.   **Bournemouth Transport**

In addition, amongst the ancillary vehicles the Overhead Department was responsible for TF 447 and FRU 224 but also made use of the others shown below, as and when required:

Fleet No.	Reg No.	Type	Into Service	Withdrawn	Note
	LJ1608	Thornycroft BC/FC	August 1940	March 1957	9
	TF447	Leyland SQ2 crane	September 1950	September 1962	10
	FRU 224	Guy Arab FD crane	Dec 1962	September 2003	10, 11
	DEL36	Bedford WH tipper	April 1937	December 1962	12
	304LJ	Morris Commercial FG tipper	Nov 1962	June 1979	12
	EL9749	Shelvoke & Drewry van	July 1924	mid-1941	13

Note

9   Converted from motorbus 44 in August 1940 and fitted with trolley booms in January 1941. The booms had interchangeable heads used to either lubricate the overhead wires or to cut ice from the wires, the idea being to eliminate sparks showing at night. The booms were removed in 1946 when the lorry was rebuilt, fitted with the engine from ex-Huddersfield AEC Regent 661 motorbus (VH6189) and thereafter was used mainly as a breakdown recovery vehicle. It was used to tow some of the Sunbeam MS2 trolleybuses to London on loan in 1940 and later to deliver the BUT9641Ts in 1950.

10   Originally on hire from Brighton Corporation (not necessarily the Transport Department) and purchased October 1950 for £500, including the £50 hire charge. In 1962 the crane was transferred to FRU224.

11   Converted from 1944 double deck motorbus 40 in March 1962.

12   Replaced by 304LJ.

12   Carried the registration number of what would have been the tenth 1962 Sunbeam MF2B trolleybus

13   Delivered with a Tramocar-style body having a single door, this vehicle was initially used as an office van, one of its tasks being to take each day's takings from the Head Office to the bank daily. It was possibly converted into a lorry, in which case probably in 1932, following the sale of Tilling-Stevens TS3 lorry (EL5341), formerly a bus new in 1920.

No. 3, a Bedford 2 ton lorry was delivered on 4 June 1937 and equipped with a Rawlins tower. It is seen here at Castle Lane (Mallard Road) Depot in its latterday green livery.
David Bowler collection (photographer's name not recorded)

No. 12 was an AEC Regent 661 double deck motorbus first registered by Huddersfield Corporation Transport on 16 March 1934 which was bought by Bournemouth on 11 January 1945 and converted into a tower wagon. It is seen at Castle Lane (Mallard Road) Depot. **David Bowler collection (photographer's name not recorded)**

In the untroubled times of the trolleybus era, the simple pull handle hanging down a traction pole to operate a frog and thus change the direction of the trolley heads and booms was not a great attraction to vandals. Ex-BH&D BUT9611T no. 292 (DNJ992) waits in the easternmost of the Avenue Road loops at the 26 stop in 1965. The frog pull on pole S14 gave access to the boarding point for Holdenhurst Road services and Old Christchurch Road.

NTA Collection (R.F.Mack)

The conductor holds the operating pull down and correctly watches the trolley heads until they have completely cleared the hand-operated facing frog leading from the southbound Kinson Road line into the Columbia Road turning circle at Wonderholme Parade as BUT9641T 256 (KLJ356) completes its 31 journey from the Triangle and Square. Both the pulley wheel and operating cable are evident.

Roger G. Funnell (courtesy Mrs D. Funnell and Rodney Funnell)

Frogs

Strictly speaking a "frog" is an item of overhead equipment where a trolleybus trolley wheel or slider head diverged from a single conductor wire to two, or converged from two conductor wires into one, in the same manner as points or a switch on a railway. More generally a frog is considered to refer to all the items necessary to provide points or switches in the overhead wiring for a pair of trolley wires. Frogs were built up from metal castings with wooden beam insulation and runners instead of trolley wire, but to the same profile, where the positive and negative wires crossed. A pair of single line switch frogs, a leader and a companion; a centre crossing, where the wires crossed; extruded runners and insulating spacers, were needed to build up what is more commonly known as a frog. The insulating spacers that kept the trolley wires the required 24in apart were either wood or two pairs of galvanised steel links, secured by pins, appearing like a large rivet, with a double-eye globe insulator between them to ensure the necessary triple insulation between positive and negative trolley wires, and between the positive trolley wire and earth.

The experimental trolleybus route between Bournemouth Square and County Gates, Westbourne, required no facing or trailing junction and thus frogs only became necessary when the first tram to trolleybus conversion took place and trolleybus overhead wiring was installed along Holdenhurst Road and Ashley Road to Boscombe, and along the access route to Central Depot. Hand-operated facing or turnout frogs were installed at the Square to allow vehicles from the east to turn back without continuing to Westbourne, at the junction of Holdenhurst Road with St. Swithun's Road, and at Christchurch Road, Boscombe (the latter two for depot access purposes). Operation of such frogs required the conductor to leave the rear platform and pull a handle, attached at a convenient height to a nearby traction pole, and connected by a wire cable to the frog mechanism when the trolleybus needed to follow a branch line or secondary route.

Once the tramway conversion programme was complete and the trolleybus system began to expand, acknowledgement that the conductor's first priorities were to collect fares and ensure his passengers' safety, as well as increasing trolleybus and other traffic, encouraged BCT to adopt electrically-operated frogs at frequently-used locations. Hand-operated frogs were installed or retained at places where a bus stop was located close to the frog, e.g. Avenue Road, Gervis Place; at lesser-used junctions, e.g. from Lawford Road into Castle Lane West eastbound, Stour Road northbound into Barrack Road, and at terminal loops, e.g. Five Ways, Southbourne Cross Roads. The hand-operated frogs installed in Bournemouth were of the pull and hold variety. There is no evidence that Bournemouth employed mechanically re-set hand-operated turnout frogs, where once pulled the handle could be released immediately, the frog remaining set for the branch line until the trolley head struck a small rubber roller at the side of the frog which unlatched the mechanism and allowed springs to return the frog to its normal position, set for the main line.

The trolley heads ran on their flanges through the pre-war frogs and crossing (rather than the later, "profile running") leading to vertical movement, resulting in the term "ramp-end". This both restricted speed and broke the carbon inserts when slider heads were adopted. In the late 1930s a range of standard assemblies for double-tongued switch frogs with crossings employing less obtrusive "wire profile" fittings having reversible insulated running strips matching the profile of the trolley wire and retained by a "dumb-bell" insulator unit, became available. BIC produced switch frogs in angles of 15° and 25° and crossings in fifteen varieties of between 17½° and 90°, whilst Anti-Attrition also produced a variety of switch frogs including angles of 12° and 17° and crossings of 17° and 23°. Combined with the use of slider heads these permitted higher speeds with little risk of dewirement, 30mph being achieved in tests when following the main line beneath turnout frogs, although legislation limited speeds at junctions and crossings to initially 5mph and later to 8mph. Trailing (junction) frogs were usually simple castings with no moving components, the heads running through on their flanges, however they were also available with moving tongues for installation at locations where it was not easy to coast.

One or two frogs on the Bournemouth system were made up of a mixture of Anti-Attrition and BICC parts, e.g. frog no. 27 on the accompanying table. When a completely new route was constructed, complete frog sets would be ordered from the suppliers, but where just one or two frogs were involved they would be "home-made" from what was on the shelf in the store.

Electrically-operated point turners were in widespread use on British tramways although Bournemouth only installed one, at the Lansdowne for either Christchurch Road or Holdenhurst Road. However, they only operated the points in the tram track and the frog in the overhead line was set mechanically as required by a hanging lever or "poker" (due to its appearance) which was prised by the tramcar's trolley pole when following one route, but not the other. Thus, electrically-operated frogs for trolleybus overhead lines, known as "auto frogs", using similar technology to that employed by tramways, were introduced into the UK in about 1930.

Bournemouth's first auto frog came into use on 6 March 1936 at the Lansdowne junction (eastbound) and simply replaced the tramway point turner at this location. By 5 May 1938 there was an auto frog on the south side of the Square between the tramways waiting room and Bobby's department store enabling trolleybuses from Gervis Place to turn back towards Old Christchurch Road whilst those destined for Westbourne continued towards Commercial Road, whilst another was installed at Pokesdown by 28 May 1939. Thereafter their use was progressively extended. The Overhead Department standardised on the Forest City automatic frog setter devised by the Forest City Electric Co., Illinois, USA, and manufactured in the UK at that company's Stretford, Manchester works. This required a break in either the negative or, normally in Bournemouth, positive wire and the installation of a transfer contact ahead of the frog with a restoring contact skate hung about half an inch above the positive wire just beyond the frog to return it to the normal route.

Bournemouth's auto frog installation policy was "power on for the branch" and "coast for straight on", i.e. power off at the foot pedal operated controller for the main route, and normally coinciding with the insulated route along which a driver was required to coast with power off. Some 10-15 yards before the frog, a transfer or setting contact and appearing to the pedestrian rather like a bulky hanger, was fixed immediately above the positive trolley wire to energise the auto frog. As the trolleybus approached the transfer contact, a driver wishing to take the branch line would keep his foot on the power pedal, simultaneously controlling the vehicle's speed with the

Sunbeam MF2B no. 299 (299LJ) passes the egress of Meyrick Road on to the Lansdowne roundabout. Careful observation of the overhead line above the third spacer after the junction or trailing frog for the egress from the Christchurch Road westbound line shows the auto frog setter with the electrical wiring to the operating solenoid following the span wire to the traction pole located on the island in Meyrick Road. As no. 299 is routing down Old Christchurch Road, its driver will not need to operate the auto frog and will simply coast, i.e. not draw power, as his trolley heads pass underneath the setting contact. **NTA collection (R.F. Mack)**

On the same roundabout, the auto frog setter for continuing around the north side of the roundabout (the frog had Old Christchurch Road as its default setting) can be seen, again in the negative conductor wire, just above the front of the trolleybus and aligned with the side of Royal London House in this photograph. Traction poles to left and right support confirming indicator boxes. **NTA collection (R.F. Mack)**

An example of an auto frog confirming or signal indicator box can be seen on the traction pole on the left hand pavement above the cast iron base. This one was located in Old Christchurch Road at the start of the "overtaking" wiring for eastbound Holdenhurst Road trolleybuses around the north side of the Lansdowne roundabout. Sunbeam MF2B no. 260 (WRU260) is destined for the Square.   **NTA collection (R.F. Mack)**

hand brake. The trolley wheel or slider head touched the transfer contact thereby bringing the frog operating solenoid momentarily into the traction motor circuit. If the trolleybus was drawing power, current passed from the positive wire, through the traction motor to the transfer contact, thence through the connecting cable to the frog setter operating relay installed in a traction pole mounted box about 8ft above the ground which then sent current to the operating solenoid further up the pole and back to the overhead. If the driver wished to remain on the main (default) line, he would coast under the transfer contact with his foot off the power pedal to ensure that no current was taken through the setter. Bournemouth became particularly adept at installing the transfer contact and frog prior to a road junction where the vehicle's reduced speed passing beneath a frog might prove a disruption to other vehicles, e.g. at Trinity Church, Old Christchurch Road, heading east towards the Lansdowne, and in Commercial Road heading west to the Triangle. This had a further advantage of ensuring that there was a reduced amount of complicated overhead wiring immediately above busy road junctions or roundabouts, thereby reducing the risk of dewirements.

Exceptionally, the transfer or setting contact in the Belle Vue Road eastbound line at Tuckton roundabout (23), in Christchurch Road eastbound line at Pokesdown (7) and on Lansdowne roundabout (43) giving access to Bath Road (and potentially other locations) was above the negative wire. Use of the negative line depended on the location being fairly near to a negative feeder point so that the negative line was almost at earth potential otherwise there would not be sufficient current flowing to operate the series coil in the frog setter operating relay.

The Forest City setter employed a powerful solenoid, contained in a somewhat smaller oblong metal box mounted on the traction pole adjacent to the overhead frog, exerting a pull of ca. 80 lbs (betraying its tramway origins) and working a normal hand operated frog, which could be operated or reset manually in case of failure. It also lit an indicator lamp which confirmed to the trolleybus driver that the frog switch tongues had moved to the required position both before and after the trolley heads had passed beneath the frog.

Confirming indicator lights were built into the front panel of the auto frog setter operating relay, an aluminium painted oblong metal box with a gently curved top to provide some protection against the elements, normally attached to the nearside traction pole closest to the frog. There was a sun visor, immediately above the indicator lens. Although BICC and Forest City offered their own indicator light systems, Bournemouth developed its own simplified version. The indicator box had two separate lenses and lamps, but in many cases the second lens was blanked off. No light was illuminated when a trolleybus coasted beneath the transfer contact to follow the main line thereby confirming that the frog had not been inadvertently set; the other lamp, normally equipped with an orange lens, gave the "branch" line indication. Exceptionally both lamps illuminated to confirm the "branch" line had been set. There appeared to be no system to the colours used in the relay boxes, whether related to route or junction (left or right) frog used. The auto frog at Bournemouth Square proceeding from Gervis Place back into Old Christchurch Road had red and green lenses probably to distinguish its indication from that of the second auto frog controlling the divergence of the Triangle and Westbourne lines, which had white lenses, a short way ahead. The signal indicator box at Westbourne acted as a headway regulator by displaying both a red and white light when an eastbound trolleybus was on the section of Poole Road between the two ends of Seamoor Road. That at the south end of Christchurch High Street showed if a trolleybus was occupying narrow Church Street or the turntable beyond.

The setting contact and, towards the top of the nearby traction pole, light signal in High Street, Christchurch. Sunbeam MS2 no. 212 (ALJ973), by this date preserved by the RTS, passes on an enthusiast's tour on 16 February 1969.   **NTA collection (R.F. Mack)**

Surrounded by H&D Bristol Lokekka motorbuses, BUT9641T no. 239 (KLJ339) on a service 26 working to Castle Lane West, Lawford Road, has reached the junction with Ensbury Park Road. The auto frog setter can be seen in the positive conductor wire just prior to the hanger spacer preceding the frog itself whilst the restoring contact is in the positive wire leading into Ensbury Park Road immediately after the frog. NTA collection (R.F. Mack)

In High Street, Christchurch, Sunbeam MF2B no. 295 (295LJ) passes beneath the setting contact in the postive conductor wire which operated a light signal showing if a trolleybus was occupying narrow Church Street or the turntable beyond. Identical contacts were located shortly after a turnout to reset auto frogs to their normal route (26 July 1967).
David Pearson

All auto frogs could also be worked as hand-operated frogs and were equipped with a grab handle for manual operation. Each relay box was equipped with a pull cord attached to the armature of the relay to allow it to be reversed, break the circuit to the operating solenoid and thus allow the frog to return to normal cancelling an illuminated lamp after an erroneous setting by the driver. If, when taking the branch line, the light went out before the trolley heads had cleared the frog or if the light did not go out after they had cleared the frog, the driver would stop and send his conductor back to pull the frog manually or pull the reset cord if the frog had not restored.

Further evidence of whether or not the trolleys had taken the correct route was provided by the driver's dewirement indicator, which would give a momentary audible signal when the trolley heads followed the "main line" or insulated route and passed under the insulated section of the frog.

The skate used as a restoring contact with the Forest City machine had a lightly-sprung contact strip suspended about half an inch above the positive wire of the branch line just beyond the frog. As the trolley head passed beneath, it came into contact with the contact strip thus sending a current at line voltage back to the frog setter relay. This reversed the relay

and cut off current to the operating solenoid thus allowing the position of the frog to reset to the normal main line route. The same skates were used for signalling purposes at Christchurch and Westbourne.

Drivers were required to learn which auto frogs needed operating for each route as a part of their training, nonetheless it should be remembered that the driver was some 30ft in front of the trolley heads. The position of the transfer contact provided sufficient distance to stop the trolleybus if a driver had failed to operate the frog or operated it in error. The conductor would then alight to set or re-set the frog manually for the appropriate direction, using the hand-operated cable pull. As road traffic continued to increase and turning lanes started to be painted on the road surface, it was surprising, in view of the Overhead Department's forwards approach, that a policy of installing the transfer contact and frog further back from the road junction, where the trolleybus' reduced speed passing beneath a frog might prove a disruption to other vehicles, was not adopted. In such case the setter or transfer contact could be conveniently located at a point where the vehicle was travelling slowly just before or immediately after a trolleybus stop. This would have been a useful development at, for example,

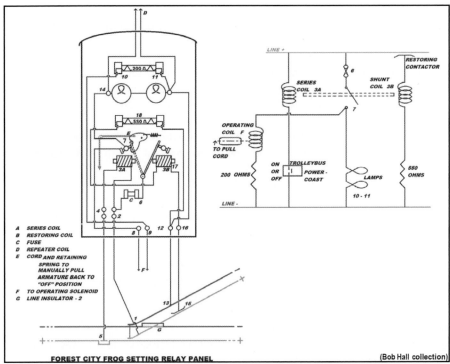

A SERIES COIL
B RESTORING COIL
C FUSE
D REPEATER COIL
E CORD AND RETAINING
SPRING TO
MANUALLY PULL
ARMATURE BACK TO
"OFF" POSITION
F TO OPERATING SOLENOID
G LINE INSULATOR - 2

FOREST CITY FROG SETTING RELAY PANEL   (Bob Hall collection)

Cemetery Junction or Pokesdown Station, but was adopted solely in Commercial Road westbound for the facing frog for the Triangle where two parallel pairs of wires continued up to the turn itself allowing the trolleybus driver to concentrate on the surrounding traffic conditions and select the correct traffic lane on the climb up from the Square. It also allowed other trolleybuses to overtake in another traffic lane. This layout also gave the driver a last chance to avoid dewirement should he or she have incorrectly gained the wrong wiring after the frog by manually transferring the trolley poles using the bamboo pole carried by every trolleybus, from one pair of trolley wires to the other.

No indication, such as a sign hanging from the span wires or a marking on the road surface, was ever provided to give trolleybus drivers warning that they were approaching special overhead work.

Frogs would normally not freeze due to the heating effect of current flowing in the wires however, despite liberal applications of an anti-freeze and glycerine mixture, early morning journeys could suffer and auto frogs might require manual operation.

In normal use the solenoid would only be energised for a short while from when a trolleybus passed the setting contact to when it activated the restoring skate. Coils burned out from time to time, perhaps due to a trolleybus having been forced to stop between the two contacts leaving the solenoid energised and heating up, or a malfunction of the reset contactor or circuit, and had to be replaced.

The frog setter comprised a rather crude "stick" relay (so called because when operated it stuck in that position until reversed by another electric current). It relied upon balance either side of vertical equilibrium to remain in place, rather than a continuous current, and hence the box had to be mounted vertically. The armature was actually shaped like a sector of a circle and not as shown diagrammatically. Giving it added weight would result in a good contact at 7.

The restoring circuit included a 200Ω resistance and was presumably left in place. It may be that whereas the operating circuit included the pole-mounted solenoid there was no corresponding resistance in the restore circuit which therefore

required one on the relay panel.

There was no resistor in the operating circuit, the resistance of coil A was enough to suit the situation bearing in mind that normally a current would only flow briefly in the circuit and because the resistance of the trolleybus circuitry provided limitation to the current flow.

The operation of the frog setter was as follows:-

When a trolleybus passed under the setting contact 5 with power on, current at line voltage was drawn through the circuit in the order 1 - 2 - 3 - 4 - 5 and thence through the traction motor of the vehicle to the negative line. As the trolleybus could be drawing some power all the time, e.g. for a motor generator or an air compressor, the resistance of coil A was presumably high enough to ensure that it only operated at the appropriate voltage.

The setting coil A, or 3, pulled the armature over, making contact at 7. Current flowed 1 - 2 - 6 - 7 - 8 and thus to the operating solenoid, returning 9 - 10 - 11 - 12 - 13. Although current would no longer be flowing through the operating circuit the armature stayed in the operating position simply by its own weight.

At the same time current flowed 7 - 14 - 11 - 12 - 13 causing the lamp(s) to illuminate, thus indicating that the armature has been pulled over by coil A (or 3) and that (presumably) the frog has been operated. This type of auto frog did not prove the position of the frog tongues.

When a trolleybus operated the restoring contact skate current at line voltage passed 15 - 16 - 17 - 18 - 12 - 13. This operated the restoring coil B, pulling armature over to its normal position and opening contact 7.

The cord dangling from the bottom of the box and fixed to a cam made of insulating material was used to pull the live armature over manually should the frog fail to restore (or be switched in error). Whether there was any insulation or whether this relied on the cord keeping dry is not known. If the frog did not respond correctly and the route was not set for the branch the frog was worked as a normal pull frog as the operating handle and wire had nothing to do with the frog setter, passing behind the relay box.

Experimental installations of other types of auto frogs were made from time to time. The Webster and the Wiseman (Alfred Wiseman & Co. Ltd., Glover Street, Birmingham) types both resembled the BICC product, which had small operating solenoids mounted on the frog itself. It is known that Bournemouth investigated the driver-controlled radio operated frogs with which London Transport experimented in the Croydon and Sutton areas in the late 1940s.

Sprung trail or shunt frogs were used at reversing triangles, on the Columbia Road turning circle; in the Central Depot, Southcote Road, access route; and in the Castle Lane (Mallard Road) Depot wiring.

Auto frog locations and operating direction

The figure in brackets on the first line in each case relates to the reference numbers on the accompanying map and table. Several of the auto frogs listed below were removed in connection with the installation of roundabouts, the introduction of one-way systems, etc.

Christchurch Road, Boscombe, eastbound, junction with Portman Road (3)
Operate for Portman Road

Christchurch Road eastbound at Pokesdown Station, junction with Seabourne Road (7)
Operate for Seabourne Road

Castle Lane East eastbound at Iford roundabout, junction with Christchurch Road (10)
Operate for roundabout

Christchurch Road eastbound at Iford roundabout, junction with Castle Lane East (11)
Operate for Castle Lane East westbound

Barrack Road eastbound, junction with Oak Avenue (16)
Operate for Oak Avenue and Jumpers turning circle

Stour Road, Christchurch westbound, junction with Barrack Road (18)
Operate for Barrack Road and Iford

Belle Vue Road eastbound at Tuckton prior the installation of the roundabout, junction with Tuckton Road (20)
Operate for Tuckton Bridge and Christchurch

Belle Vue Road westbound at Tuckton prior the installation of the roundabout, junction with Tuckton Road (21)
Operate for Tuckton Road

Tuckton Road eastbound at Tuckton prior the installation of the roundabout, junction with Belle Vue Road (22)
Operate for Tuckton Bridge and Christchurch

Belle Vue Road eastbound at Tuckton roundabout, junction with Tuckton Road (23)
Operate for Tuckton Bridge and Christchurch

Belle Vue Road westbound at Tuckton roundabout, junction with Tuckton Road (24)
Operate for roundabout and Tuckton Road

Tuckton Road eastbound at Tuckton roundabout, junction with Belle Vue Road (25)
Operate for roundabout and Southbourne

Seabourne Road eastbound at Fisherman's Walk, junction with Beresford Road (32)
Operate for Beresford Road

Southbourne Road eastbound at Fisherman's Walk, junction with Beresford Road (35)

Operate for Beresford Road (Southbourne Traffic Management Scheme)

Beresford Road westbound at Fisherman's Walk, junction with Southbourne Grove (36)

Operate for Seabourne Road and Pokesdown (Southbourne Traffic Management Scheme)

Old Christchurch Road eastbound set-back frog prior to the installation of Lansdowne roundabout (37)
Operate for Holdenhurst Road

Old Christchurch Road eastbound later set-back frog for additional pair of wires around north side Lansdowne roundabout (38)
Operate for Holdenhurst Road

Holdenhurst Road westbound prior to the installation of Lansdowne roundabout (41)
Operate for Bath Road

Christchurch Road westbound prior to the installation of Lansdowne roundabout (42)
Operate for Bath Road

Christchurch Road and Holdenhurst Road westbound at Lansdowne roundabout (43)
Operate for Bath Road

Christchurch Road and Holdenhurst Road westbound at Lansdowne roundabout west side (44)
Operate for roundabout (default was Old Christchurch Road westbound)

Lansdowne roundabout north side (46)
Operate for Holdenhurst Road eastbound (default was Christchurch Road eastbound)

Holdenhurst Road westbound at Lansdowne roundabout (47)
Operate for roundabout (default was Christchurch Road eastbound)

Bath Road westbound at the Royal Bath Hotel, junction with Westover Road (48)
Operate for Bournemouth Pier

Bournemouth Pier (50)
Operate for Exeter Road and Square (default was Bath Road eastbound)

Commercial Road westbound (52)
Operate for Poole Road and Westbourne

Bournemouth Square prior to the installation of a roundabout, outside Bobby's (58)
Operate for Commercial Road westbound

Bournemouth Square roundabout north side at bottom of Richmond Hill (61)
Operate for Richmond Hill

Bournemouth Square roundabout, outside Bobby's department store (62)
Operate for Commercial Road westbound

Holdenhurst Road eastbound, junction with St. Paul's Road (71)
Operate for Cemetery Junction

Between October 1947 and December 1950, the junction of Belle Vue Road with Tuckton Road only permitted turns from or towards the Southbourne direction. At some date during this period Sunbeam MS2 no. 131 (BEL816) approaches the junction from Tuckton Road. Omnibus Society (R.T. Wilson)

Wimborne Road northbound at Cemetery Junction, junction with Charminster Road (76)
Operate for Charminster Road northbound

Wimborne Road southbound at Cemetery Junction, junction with Lansdowne Road (77)
Operate for Lansdowne Road southbound

Wimborne Road northbound at Winton Banks, junction with Talbot Road (79)
Operate for Talbot Road westbound
Wimborne Road northbound at Moordown, junction with Ensbury Park Road (84)
Operate for Ensbury Park Road westbound

Charminster Road northbound at Five Ways, junction with Charminster Avenue (96)
Operate for Charminster Avenue northbound

Castle Lane West eastbound at Broadway Hotel, junction with Charminster Road (98)
Operate for Charminster Road southbound

Castle Lane West eastbound, junction with Mallard Road (100)
Operate for Mallard Road

Castle Lane West eastbound at Cooper Dean roundabout, Strouden Park, junction Holdenhurst Road (105)
Operate for roundabout

Castle Lane (Mallard Road) Depot, on the south side of the loop around the premises (103)
Auto frog setter not connected to any frog, for driver training purposes

Reversers (reversing triangles)

Reversing triangles installed at the terminal point of a route were built up using two spring-reset trailing frogs also known as shunt frogs, making reversal, in respect of the trolley booms, entirely automatic. There was a sole example on the Bournemouth system at Malvern Road in the road junction with Charminster Avenue. All other reversing triangles were installed at an intermediate point and these required, in addition, a crossover and a trail (junction) frog to re-join the through wiring.

As a vehicle entered the reversing triangle, the trolley wheels or sliding heads passing in the normal, "trailing" direction, pushed the frog tongues aside. Once the vehicle began its reversing manoeuvre, the wheels or heads reversing through the frog on to the triangle were automatically routed on to the "branch" and pushed through another spring trail frog at the apex. On leaving, again in the "trailing" position, they were automatically routed to the exit from the reversing triangle.

Reversing triangles were installed at:

Bodorgan Road: An emergency installation off Wimborne Road at the top of Richmond Hill had a switch frog in place of the normal spring trail frog at the entrance, thus providing an example of a facing frog being run through in the wrong direction. This triangle was only used when severe weather conditions made it unsafe for trolleybuses to use the hill. Southbound trolleybuses reversed into Bodorgan Road through a 25° left hand switch frog suspended at pole M10, through a 25° "Y" shunt or spring trail frog and returned to the Wimborne Road northbound line at M12 through a 25° right hand trail frog. Bodorgan Road reverser was installed in 30 June 1945 and it remained available for use until the closure of the Side Routes on 25 September 1966.

Just east of the overhead wiring "T" junction with Tuckton Road visible in the background, BUT9641T 248 (KLJ348) drifts the 130yd to Tuckton Bridge prior to continuing over the River Stour into Christchurch on 6 May 1961.
Barry Moore

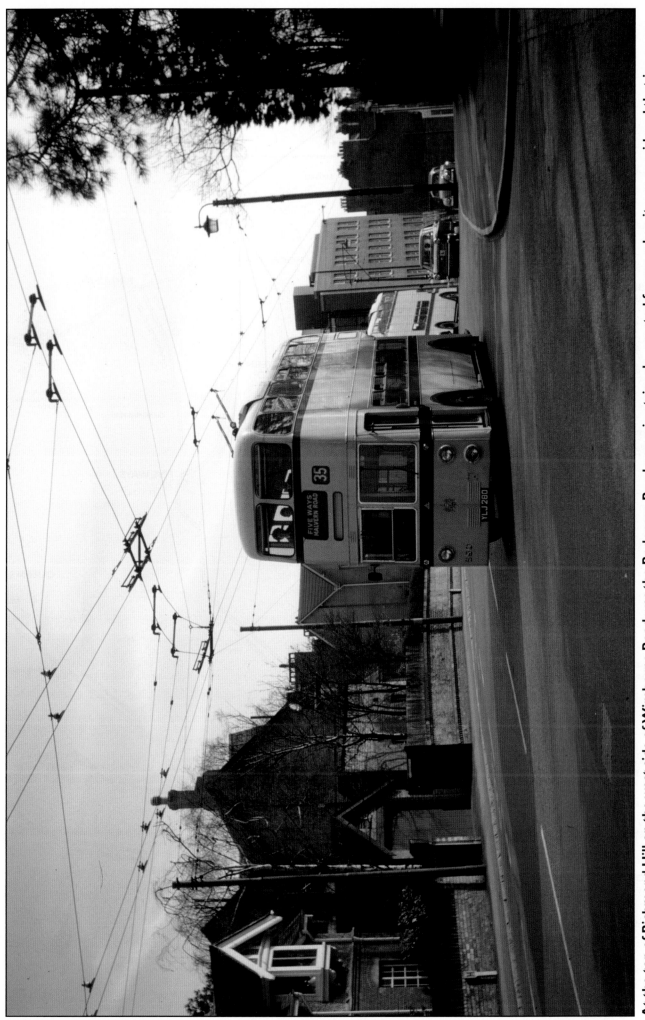

At the top of **Richmond Hill** on the west side of **Wimborne Road** was the **Bodorgan Road** reversing triangle, erected for use when it was considered that ice or snow made it unsafe to use **Richmond Hill**. Sunbeam **MF2B** no. 280 (**YLJ280**) has just crested the hill on a service 35 working to **Malvern Road**.
Roger G. Funnell (courtesy Mrs D. Funnell and Rodney Funnell)

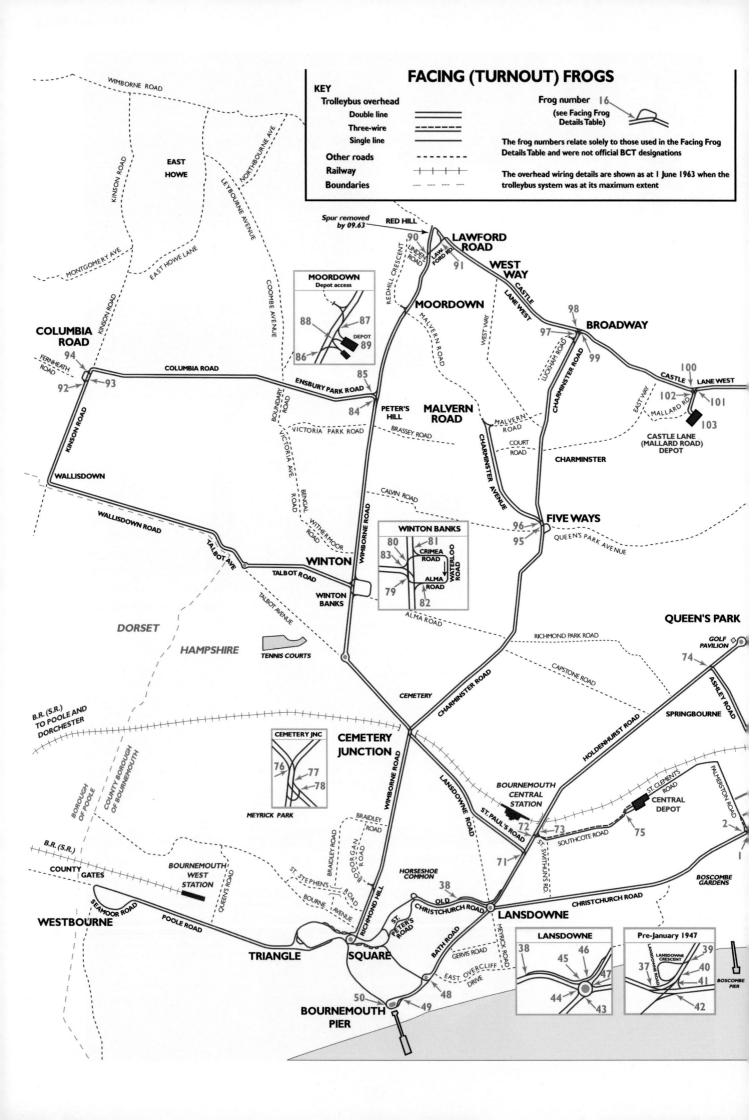

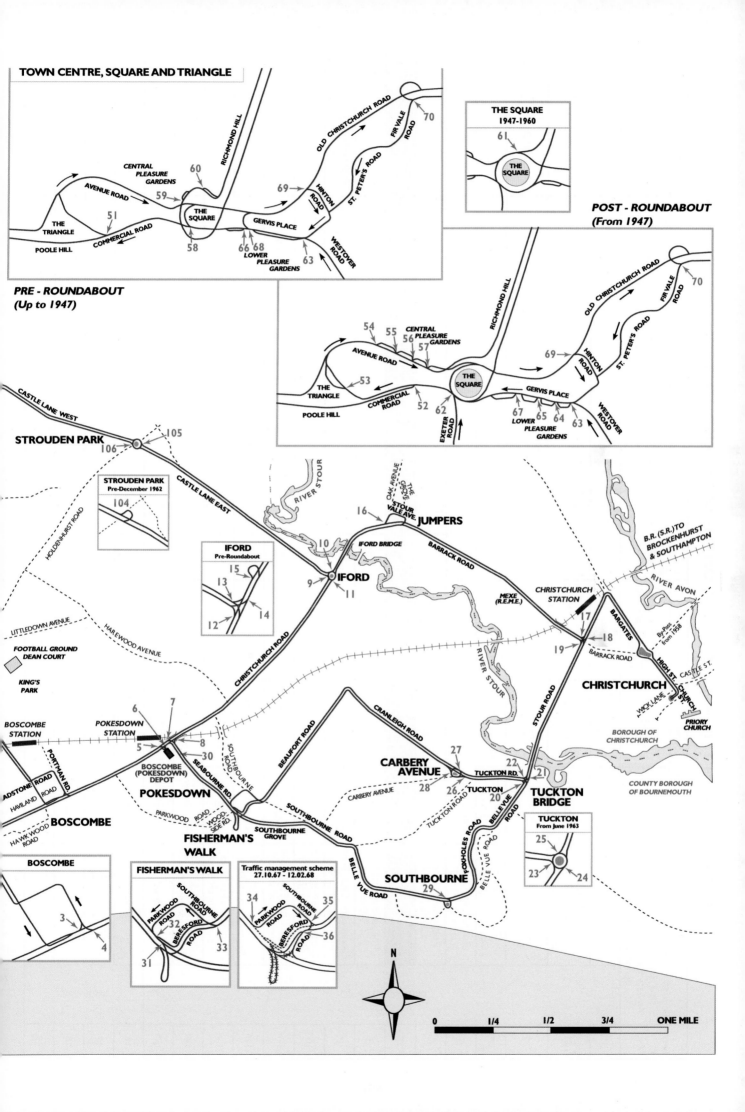

TOWN CENTRE, SQUARE AND TRIANGLE

PRE - ROUNDABOUT
(Up to 1947)

THE SQUARE
1947-1960

POST - ROUNDABOUT
(From 1947)

DETAILS OF FACING (TURNOUT) FROGS ON THE BOURNEMOUTH TROLLEYBUS SYSTEM

Key to Map	Location (Sequence is Main Road Route then side Routes from West to East. An asterisk (*) by the Key number denotes a Note below)	Route Options — Left	Route Options — Right	Default Left or Right	Auto or Manual	Angle (°) and direction of frogs		Make	Wording on pole, setter box, etc. (where definitely known)	Pole Code	Frog installed	Frog into scheduled use	Frog removed
1*	Palmerston Road, Boscombe (Wbnd)	Lansdowne	Palmerston Road	L	M	25	R	BI		P 114	1934	22 Jun 1934	Jun 1965 - Mar 1966
2*	Palmerston Road, Boscombe (South end), Depot access	Tied off	Central Depot	L	M	12	R	AA		Y 64	1935	25 Mar 1935	Jun 1965 - Mar 1966
3*	Portman Road, Boscombe (Ebnd)	Portman Road	Christchurch Road	R	A	12 / 17	L	BI	Green metal plate on pole lettered "Pull and release" (hand operation of auto frog)	P 131	Mar 1935	25 Mar 1935	Dec 1965 - June 1966
4*	Portman Road, Boscombe (Wbnd)	Christchurch Road	Portman Road	L	M	12 / 17	R	AA		P 132	Jul 1938	28 Jul 1938	Dec 1965 - June 1966
5	Pokesdown Depot access (Ebnd)	Christchurch Road	Depot	L	M	25	R	BI		P 153 ?	Mid-1945	2nd half 1945	21 Jan 1968
6	Pokesdown Depot access (Wbnd)	Depot	Christchurch Road	R	M	25	L	BI		P 154	Mid-1945	2nd half 1945	21 Jan 1968
7*	Pokesdown Station (Ebnd)	Iford	Seabourne Road	L	A	15/ 17½	R	BI		P 157	Autumn 1935	21 Nov 1935	5 Sept 1969
8	Pokesdown Station (Wbnd)	Seabourne Road	Boscombe	R	M	25	L			11 ?	22 Dec 1967	No scheduled use	5 Sept 1969
9*	Castle Lane East, Iford Roundabout (Ebnd)	Castle Lane	Iford Bridge	R	M	17/ 25	L	AA		IR	July 1965	No scheduled use	Jun 1969
10*	Castle Lane East, Iford Roundabout (Ebnd)	Iford Bridge	Pokesdown	L	A	15/ 17½	R	BI		IR	Nov 1956	2 Dec 1956	Jun 1969
11*	Castle Lane East, Iford Roundabout (Wbnd)	Pokesdown	Castle Lane	L	A	15/ 17½	R	BI		IR	May 1956	20 May 1956	Jun 1969
12*	Castle Lane East, Iford Pre-roundabout (Ebnd)	Castle Lane	Iford Bridge	R	M	25	L			I 43	Oct 1951	15 Oct 1951	1 Dec 1956
13*	Castle Lane East, Iford Pre-roundabout (Ebnd)	Iford Bridge	Pokesdown	R	M	25	R			F 173	Oct 1951	15 Oct 1951	1 Dec 1956
14*	Castle Lane East, Iford Pre-roundabout (Wbnd)	Pokesdown	Castle Lane	L	M	25	R	BI		I 46	Oct 1951	15 Oct 1951	19 May 1956
15*	Iford Bridge	Turning Circle	Christchurch Road	R	M	25	L	BI		I 49	1943	22 July 1943	19-20 May 1961
16	Jumpers	Oak Avenue	Barrack Road	R	A	25	L	BI		I 59	1944	7 Aug 1944	Apr-Sep 1969
17	Barrack Road, Christchurch (Ebnd)	Stour Road (Nbnd)	Tuckton Bridge	L	M	25	Y	BI		I 111	1943	22 July 1943	Apr-Sep
18	Stour Road, Christchurch (Wbnd)	Tuckton Bridge	Barrack Road (Wbnd)	L	A	15/ 25	R	BI		X 157	1943	22 July 1943	Apr-Sep 1969
19	Stour Road, Christchurch (Ebnd)	Barrack Road (Wbnd)	Stour Road	R	M	15/ 17½	L	BI		X 156	1946	1 August 1946	Apr-Sep 1969

Main road groupings (far left): Rows 1–15 "Christchurch Road"; Rows 16–19 "Stour Road".

Key to Map	Location (Sequence is Main Road Route then side Routes from West to East. An asterisk (*) by the Key number denotes a Note below)	Route Options Left	Route Options Right	Operation Default Left or Right	Operation Auto or Manual	Angle (°) and direction of frogs		Make	Traction Pole Wording on pole, setter box, etc. (where definitely known)	Pole Code	Dates Frog installed	Dates Frog into scheduled use	Dates Frog removed
20*	Belle Vue Road Pre-roundabout (Ebnd)	Tuckton Road	Tuckton Bridge	L	A	25	Y			X 125	1947	5 Oct 1947	Jun 1963
21*	Belle Vue Road Pre-roundabout (Wbnd)	Southbourne	Tuckton Road	L	A	15/17½	Y	BI		X ??	1950	No scheduled use	Jun 1963
22*	Tuckton Road Pre-roundabout (Ebnd)	Tuckton Bridge	Belle Vue Road	R	A	15/17½	R	BI		H 88	1950	No scheduled use	Jun 1963
23*	Belle Vue Road (Ebnd)	Tuckton Road	Roundabout	L	A	25	Y	BI		XHR	1963	30 Jun 1963	Jun-Sep 1969
24	Belle Vue Road (Wbnd)	Southbourne	Roundabout	L	A	15/17½	R	BI		XHR	1963	30 Jun 1963	Jun-Sep 1969
25	Tuckton Road (Ebnd)	Tuckton Bridge	Roundabout	L	A	15/17½	R	BI		XHR	1963	30 Jun 1963	Jun-Sep 1969
26*	Cranleigh Road (Nbnd) at Carbery Avenue	Turning Circle	Fishermans Walk	R	M	15/17½	R	BI/AA		H 76	1948	16 Aug 1948	Jun-Sep 1969
27	Cranleigh Road (Sbnd) at Carbery Avenue	Tuckton	Turning Circle	L	M	25	R	BI		H 74	1948	26 Sep 1948	Jun-Sep 1969
28	Carbery Avenue turning circle	Fishermans Walk	Cranleigh Road (Sbnd)	L	M	25	Y	BI		HL ??	1948	26 Sep 1948	Jun-Sep 1969
29*	Southbourne Cross Roads	Tuckton	Turning Circle	L	M	25	Y	BI		X 80	Apr 1936	1 Oct 1937	Jun-Sep 1969
30	Pokesdown, Seabourne Road (Nbnd) Overnight Parking Area	Parking Area	Pokesdown Station	R	M	25	L			X 3	Mar 1951	No scheduled use	Spring 1952
31*	Seabourne Road (Sbnd) at Wentworth Avenue	Southbourne	Turning Circle	L	M	25	R	BI		X 21	Nov 1935	23 Dec 1935	Jun-Sep1969
32	Seabourne Road (Ebnd) at Beresford Road	Beresford Road	Southbourne	R	A	15/17½	L	BI		X 20	Aug 1948	16 Aug 1948	Jun-Sep 1969
33*	Southbourne Road (Wbnd) at Beresford Road	Fishermans Walk	Parkwood Road	L	A/M	25	R	BI		H 8	Aug 1948	16 Aug 1948	3 Sep 1969
34*	Seabourne Road (Sbnd) One-way system	Parkwood Road	Seabourne Road (redundant)	L	M	25	L	BI		X 17 ?	Sep 1967	5 Oct 1967	3 Sep 1969
35*	Southbourne Road (Ebnd) One-way system	Beaufort Road	Beresford Road	L	A	25	Y	BI		E 1 ?	Sep 1967	5 Oct 1967	3 Sep 1969

Group labels (left margin): Tuckton (rows 22–23); Carbery Avenue (rows 26–28); Fisherman's Walk (rows 31–34)

Key to Map	Location — Sequence is Main Road Route then side Routes from West to East. An asterisk (*) by the Key number denotes a Note below	Route Options: Left	Route Options: Right	Operation: Default Left or Right	Operation: Auto or Manual	Angle (°) and direction of frogs (angle)	Angle (°) and direction of frogs (direction)	Make	Traction Pole: Wording on pole, setter box etc. (where definitely known)	Pole Code	Dates: Frog installed	Dates: Frog into scheduled use	Dates: Frog removed
36*	Beresford Road (Wbnd) One-way system	Southbourne Grove	Seabourne Road (Ebnd)	L	A	25	R	BI		H ??	13 Sep 1967	5 Oct 1967	3 Sep 1969
37	Old Christchurch Road Pre-roundabout (Ebnd)	Holdenhurst Road	Christchurch Road	R	A		L	BI		P 44 J	Mar 1945	18 Mar 1945	27 Jan 1947
38*	Old Christchurch Road (Ebnd)	Holdenhurst Road	Christchurch Road	R	A	15/17½	L	BI	Round white target with red centre on pole supporting auto frog setter	P 44 J	Mar 1960	12 Mar 1960	11 Nov 1965
39*	Holdenhurst Road Pre-roundabout (Wbnd)	Lansdowne	Lansdowne Crescent	R	M	25	R			A 2 ?	Mar 1935	No scheduled use	26 Jan 1947
40*	Holdenhurst Road Pre-roundabout (Wbnd)	Christchurch Road	Lansdowne	R	M	25	L			A 1 ?	Mar 1935	No scheduled use	26 Jan 1947
41*	Holdenhurst Road Pre-roundabout (Wbnd)	Bath Road	Old Christchurch Road	R	A	25	R			A ??	Apr 1937	8 May 1937	26 Jan 1947
42*	Christchurch Road Pre-roundabout (Wbnd)	Bath Road	Old Christchurch Road	R	A	25	Y	BI		P 60 ?	Apr 1937	8 May 1937	26 Jan 1947
43	Lansdowne Roundabout	Bath Road	Old Christchurch Road	R	A	25	Y	BI		L	26 Jan 1947	27 Jan 1947	Jul 1969
44	Lansdowne Roundabout	Old Christchurch Road (Westb)	Roundabout	L	A	25	Y	BI		L	26 Jan 1947	27 Jan 1947	Jul 1969
45*	Lansdowne Roundabout	Lansdowne Road	Roundabout	R	fixed	25	Y	BI		L	26 Jan 1947	No scheduled use	1947
46	Lansdowne Roundabout	Holdenhurst Road (Ebnd)	Christchurch Road (Ebnd)	R	A	25	Y	BI		L	26 Jan 1947	27 Jan 1947	Jul 1969
47	Lansdowne Roundabout	Christchurch Road (Ebnd)	Roundabout	L	A	25	L	BI		L	26 Jan 1947	27 Jan 1947	Jul 1969
48	Royal Bath Hotel, Bath Road (Wbnd)	Bournemouth Pier	Westover Road	R	A	15/17½	R	BI		BHJ 2	Mar 1950	7 Apr 1950	10 Aug 1969
49	Bournemouth Pier, Bath Road	Loading bay	Turning Circle & Square	R	M	12/17	R	AA		R ??	Mar 1950	7 Apr 1950	13 Jul 1969
50	Bournemouth Pier	Exeter Road & Square	Bath Road & Lansdowne	R	A	15/17	R	BI		R ??	Mar 1950	7 Apr 1950	13 Jul 1969

Location grouping labels: rows 39–47 grouped as "Lansdowne"; row 49 grouped as "Pier".

Key to Map	Location — Sequence is Main Road Route then side Routes from West to East. An asterisk (*) by the Key number denotes a Note below	Group	Route Options Left	Route Options Right	Operation Default Left or Right	Operation Auto or Manual	Angle (°) and direction of frogs		Make	Traction Pole Wording on pole, setter box, etc. (where definitely known)	Traction Pole Pole Code	Dates Frog installed	Dates Frog into scheduled use	Dates Frog removed
51*	Commercial Road (Wbnd)	Triangle	Poole Hill & Westbourne	Triangle	L	M		R			W ??	Jul 1936	No scheduled use	Mar 1947
52*	Commercial Road (Wbnd)	Triangle	Poole Hill & Westbourne	Triangle	R	A	15/17	L	BI/AA		W ??	Mar 1947	6 Apr 1947	30/31 Oct 1965
53	Triangle	Avenue Road	Parking Area	Avenue Road	R	M	2/17	L	AA		WEL ??	15 May 1948	23 May 1948	Jun 1969
54	First (Fairlight Glen) loop	Avenue Road	Loading bay	Square	R	M	25	L	BI		W 90 ALJ	1947	30 Mar 1947	22 Jun 1969
55	Second loop	Avenue Road	Loading bay	Square	R	M	25	L	BI		W 93 ALJ	1947	30 Mar 1947	22 Jun 1969
56	Third (Square) loop	Avenue Road	Loading bay	Square	R	M	25	L	BI		W 95 ALJ	1947	30 Mar 1947	22 Jun 1969
57	Service 25 (Ebnd) Boarding Point		Old Christchurch Road	Richmond Hill	R	M	25	L	BI		S 14 J	May 1960	29 May 1960	Sep 1966
58*	Tramway Waiting Rooms (Wbnd) Pre-roundabout outside Bobby's store	Square	Commercial Road	Old Christchurch Road	R	M/A	25	R			S ??	Spring 1934	22 Jun 1934	29 Mar 1947
59*	Central Pleasure Gardens Pre-roundabout	Square	Loading bay	Richmond Hill	R	M	25	L			S ??	1937	1937	29 Mar 1947
60*	North side between Bourne Avenue & Richmond Hill Pre-roundabout	Square	Loading bay	Richmond Hill	R	M	25	L			S ??	1938 or 1939	1938 or 1939	29 Mar 1947
61*	Roundabout, bottom of Richmond Hill		Richmond Hill	Old Christchurch Road	R	A	??/17½	L	BI		S ??	Mar 1947	30 Mar 1947	29 May 1960
62*	Roundabout, Bobbys		Commercial Road	Roundabout	R	A	25	Y	BI		S 11	Mar 1947	30 Mar 1947	by 15 Jun 1969
63*	Original single long loop, later first (easternmost) loop	Gervis Place	Loading bay	Square	R	M	25	L	BI		B 35 L	Dec 1935	Dec 1935	4 May 1969
64*	Second loop	Gervis Place	Loading bay	Square	R	M	25	L	BI		B 36 L	Mar 1947	30 Mar 1947	4 May 1969
65	Third loop	Gervis Place	Loading bay	Square	R	M	25	L	BI		B 38 L	Mar 1947	10 Aug 1947	14 May 1967
66	Fourth (westernmost) loop	Gervis Place	Loading bay	Square	R	M	12/17	L	AA		B 40 L	Apr 1941	Apr 1941	Mar 1947

Key to Map	Location — Sequence is Main Road Route then side Routes from West to East (An asterisk (*) by the Key number denotes a Note below)	Route Options — Left	Route Options — Right	Default Left or Right	Auto or Manual	Angle (°)	Direction of frogs	Make	Pole Code	Frog installed	Frog into scheduled use	Frog removed
67	Fourth (westernmost) loop	Loading bay	Square	R	M	12/17	L	AA	B 40 L	Jun 1953	28 Jun 1953	Oct 1965
68	Emergency turn-back	Square	Old Christchurch Road	L	M	25	R		B 39 ?	12 Apr 1941	12 Apr 1941	2-3 May 1953
69	Hinton Road	Old Christchurch Road	Gervis Place	L	M	25	R		PLZ	1 Aug 1946	No scheduled use	21 Oct 1969
70	Horseshoe Common	Gervis Place	Turning Circle	L	M	25	R		PZ	May 1942	No scheduled use	3 Oct 1969
71*	St. Paul's Road	Cemetery Junction	Holdenhurst Road	R	A	25	L	BI	A 14 J	Spring 1935	28 Jun 1935	Jan - Feb 1964
72	St. Swithun's Road (Nbnd)	Springbourne	Southcote Road	L	M	25	R	BI	A 19	Spring 1934	22 Jun 1934	Jun 1965 - Mar 1966
73*	St. Swithun's Road (Sbnd)	Southcote Road	Lansdowne	R	M	25	L	BI	A 21	Spring 1934	22 Jun 1934	Jun 1965 - Mar 1966
74*	Queen's Park Hotel	Queen's Park Golf Pavilion	Ashley Road	R	M	12/17	R	AA	A 66 J	Post Mar 1935	Post Mar 1935	Mar 1967
75*	Central Depot, Southcote Road	There was one BI RH 25° hand-operated (M) frog with Default L at the western entrance to the shed and one Bonsor LH hand-operated shunt frog at the eastern entrance. See Appendix I text for details of the complex access layout.										Jun 1965 - Mar 1966
76	Cemetery Junction (Nbnd)	Wimborne Road	Charminster Road	L	A	25	R	BI	M 40 J	1935	23 Aug 1935	30 Oct 1966
77	Cemetery Junction (Sbnd)	Lansdowne Road	Richmond Hill	R	A	25	L	BI	M 39 J	Jun 1935	28 Jun 1935	By mid-Oct 1964
78*	Cemetery Junction (Sbnd)	Lansdowne Road	Turning Circle	L	M	25	R		O 1	Jun 1935	7 June 1935	20 Nov 1960
79*	Winton Banks (Nbnd)	Talbot Road	Wimborne Road	R	A	25	L	BI	M 78	Apr 1938	15 Apr 1938	22 Jan 1967
80	Winton Banks (Nbnd)	Wimborne Road	Crimea Road	L	M	25	R	BI	M 80 ?	7 Jun 1935	15 Apr 1938	22 Jan 1967
81	Winton Banks (Sbnd)	Crimea Road	Cemetery Junction	R	M	25	L	BI	M 82 J ?	7 Jun 1935	15 Apr 1938	22 Jan 1967
82	Winton Banks Loop, Alma Road	Cemetery Junction	Wimborne Road (Nbnd)	R	M	25	Y	BI	M 77	7 Jun 1935	15 Apr 1938	22 Jan 1967
83	Talbot Road (Ebnd)	Moordown	Cemetery Junction	R	M	25	L	BI	T 1	Apr 1938	15 Apr 1938	Mar 1967 - Feb 1968
84	Moordown, Ensbury Park Road	Ensbury Park Road	Moordown	R	A	25	L	BI	M 116	Early 1939	8 Apr 1939	Feb 1967

Main Road Route sections (left margin groupings): Gervis Place · Old Christchurch Road · Holdenhurst Road · Central Depot · Wimborne Road

Key to Map	Road	Location (Sequence is Main Road Route then side Routes from West to East; An asterisk (*) by the Key number denotes a Note below)	Route Options — Left	Route Options — Right	Operation — Default Left or Right	Operation — Auto or Manual	Angle (°) and direction of frogs		Make	Traction Pole — Wording on pole, setter box, etc. (where definitely known)	Traction Pole — Pole Code	Dates — Frog installed	Dates — Frog into scheduled use	Dates — Frog removed
85	Wimborne Road	Ensbury Park Road (Ebnd)	Moordown	Winton Banks	R	M	25	Y	BI		T 170	Early 1939	8 Apr 1939	Feb 1967
86*	Wimborne Road	Moordown Depot access (Nbnd)	Lawford Road	South shed & turning circle	L	M		R			M 133	1936	1936	Summer 1953
87*	Wimborne Road	Moordown Depot access (Sbnd)	Main shed	Wimborne Road	R	M		L			M 136	1936	1936	Summer 1953
88*	Wimborne Road	Moordown Depot access (Sbnd)	South shed & turning circle	Winton Banks	R	M		L			M 134	1936	1936	Summer 1953
89	Wimborne Road	Moordown Depot	There were three RH and two LH facing frogs in the final depot complex									May - Jun 1935	7 Jun 1935	Summer 1953
90*	Kinson Road	Moordown	Wimborne Road	Lawford Road	R	fixed	25	R	BI		M 154 J	Early 1937	11 Mar 1937	Jan - Feb 1967
91	Kinson Road	Lawford Road	Castle Lane	Broadway Hotel	L	M	25	Y	BI		MFL	Early 1937	11 Mar 1937	Jan - Feb 1967
92	Kinson Road	Kinson Road (Nbnd), Wonderholme Parade access	Turning Circle	Columbia Road	R	M	25	L	BI		T 85	Early 1939	8 Apr 1939	By Mar 1967
93	Kinson Road	Kinson Road (Sbnd), Wonderholme Parade access	Kinson Road	Turning Circle	L	M	25	R	BI		T 102 J	Early 1939	8 Apr 1939	By Mar 1967
94	Kinson Road	Wonderholme Parade	Columbia Road	Kinson Road	L	M	25	R	BI		TL ??	Early 1939	8 Apr 1939	By Mar 1967
95*	Charminster Road	Five Ways	Charminster Road	Queen's Avenue	L	M	25	R	BI		C 52 J	Summer 1935	23 Aug 1935	4 Dec 1966
96*	Charminster Road	Five Ways	Charminster Avenue	Charminster Road	R	A	25	L	BI		C 57	Apr 1937	5 Apr 1937	22 Jul 1966
97	Castle Lane	Broadway Hotel	Moordown	Strouden Park	L	M	12/23	R	AA		C 100 J	Sep - Oct 1951	15 Oct 1951	Jan - Mar 1967
98	Castle Lane	Broadway Hotel (Ebnd)	Strouden Park	Charminster Road	L	A	12/17	R	AA		F 4X J	Sep - Oct 1951	15 Oct 1951	Jan - Mar 1967
99	Castle Lane	Broadway Hotel (Wbnd)	Charminster Road	Moordown	R	M	12/17	L	AA		F 46 J	Sep - Oct 1951	15 Oct 1951	Jan - Mar 1967
100*	Castle Lane	Castle Lane West (Ebnd), depot access	Strouden Park	Mallard Road	L	A	12/17	R	AA		F 73	Sep - Oct 1951	24 Jul 1953	12-16 May 1968
101*	Castle Lane	Castle Lane West (Wbnd), depot access	Mallard Road	Broadway Hotel	R	M	12/23	L	AA		F	Sep - Oct 1951	24 Jul 1953	27 May 1969
102*	Castle Lane	Mallard Road, depot egress	Broadway Hotel	Strouden Park	L	M	12/23	R	AA		F	Sep - Oct 1951	24 Jul 1953	12-16 May 1968

Key to Map	Location: Sequence is Main Road Route then side Routes from West to East. An asterisk (*) by the Key number denotes a Note below	Route Options – Left	Route Options – Right	Operation – Default Left or Right	Operation – Auto or Manual	Operation – Angle (°) and direction of frogs		Traction Pole – Make	Traction Pole – Wording on pole, setter box, etc. (where definitely known)	Traction Pole – Pole Code	Dates – Frog installed	Dates – Frog into scheduled use	Dates – Frog removed
103	Castle Lane (Mallard Road) Depot	There were eight AA hand-operated (P) facing frogs (four 12/23° and four 12/17°) and one auto frog setter not connected to any frog (for driver training purposes) in the depot complex.									Early 1952	*24 Jul 1953*	*12-18 Jan 1971*
104	Strouden Park, Cooper Dean	Turning Circle	Iford	R	M	??	L			**F 120**	Mar-Apr 1953	23 May 1953	19-20 Dec 1962
105	Cooper Dean Roundabout (Ebnd)	Iford	Roundabout	L	A	15/17½	R	BI		*FR ??*	Apr 1963	18 May 1963	*Mar - Aug 1970*
106	Cooper Dean Roundabout (Wbnd)	Broadway Hotel	Roundabout	L	M	25	R	BI		*FR ??*	12 Jul 1963	*No scheduled use*	*26 Mar 1967*

(Rows 103–106 grouped under: Castle Lane)

General

Not all of the frogs detailed above were in situ at the same time. Generally the 1962-63 situation is listed (including pole numbers where known) unless specifically shown otherwise.

Dates shown in italics are assumed dates considering all available evidence.

During the early post-war years many of the original (ramp-end) frogs and crossings incorporating wooden beams were progressively replaced with less obtrusive pre-assembled "wire section" equivalents.

The maximum number of facing frogs on the system at any one time , including those within depots, was 92 of which 27 were auto-frogs (1963 figures).

Where two frog angles are shown, e.g. 15/25, the first figure refers to the angle at the switch tongues and the second figure refers to the angle of the crossing. The second figure will always be the bigger of the two. The angle of both the positive and negative switch tongues was the same, the runner connecting one switch to the crossing being bent.

An automatic tramway point controller was installed at the east end of Old Christchurch Road to control the junction for Christchurch Road or Holdenhurst Road at the Lansdowne in the 1920s. It was supplied by Forest City Company who also supplied the trolleybus "auto frog" setters from early 1936. All auto frogs (skate operation) also had a pull facility for emergencies, including a reset option.

Each pole had a white-painted alpha-numeric code stencilled on it 6-8 feet above ground level (dependent on whether road signs were also affixed to the same pole). White-painted poles in the vicinity of Bournemouth Pier and grey-painted poles in Christchurch were identified by black-painted alpha-numeric codes.

Where a Pole Numeric Code is uncertain it is shown in the above table in italics with a single question mark; where unknown it is shown in italics with two question marks.

Poles which were removed, stored and, later, reused in another part of the system were renumbered accordingly.

Notes to specific frogs or junctions

1   Ramp-end frog

2   Spring-loaded trailing frog, i.e. a shunt frog, in positive wire and a little further south a spring-loaded trailing frog in the negative wire. There is some evidence that a three-wire layout along Palmerston Road and St. Clement's Road to Central Depot, as employed on the St. Swithun's Road and Southcote Road access line, existed pre-war.

3   The left turn out of Christchurch Road (Ebnd) into Portman Road (Nbnd) provided a part of the Ashley Road, Boscombe terminal turning loop for service 25. The Ashley Road and Christchurch Road wiring joined at a Wiseman 25° Y trail frog, located at pole **P 129 J**, a little to the west, providing a link for service 25B (Ebnd).

4   Enabled vehicles on service 25B from Fisherman's Walk to turn from Christchurch Road into Portman Road before continuing to Holdenhurst Road and Central Station.

7   Exceptionally the setter was above the negative line. Auto frog equipment installed by 28 May 1939.

9   Provided access for vehicles from Boscombe to reach Castle Lane (Mallard Road) Depot following the closure of Central Depot, Southcote Road.

10   Auto-frog setter was located in Castle Lane East near Castle Parade.

11   Auto-frog setter was located on south side of roundabout, opposite the junction with Iford Lane.

12-14   These frogs were installed at the "T" junction replaced by Iford roundabout.

20-22   These frogs were installed at the "T" junction replaced by Tuckton roundabout.

23   The auto frog setter in Belle Vue Road (Ebnd) was supplemented by a further setter on the west side of Tuckton roundabout between the exit and entrance wiring for Belle Vue Road on 23 April 1967. Exceptionally the setter in Belle Vue Road (Ebnd) was above the negative line.

26   Pulled from right hand/opposite side of road. Hybrid with B1 15° switches and 17½° AA crossing.

29   Ramp-end frog

31   This frog was out of use from 4 October 1967. In the Southbourne experimental one-way system, Parkwood Road, Southbourne Road, Beresford Road and Seabourne Road became one-way. Traffic turning north from Beresford Road into Seabourne Road, i.e. service 23, used the right-hand lane for which purpose additional overhead wiring was provided. These crossed the existing wires leasing into Wentworth Avenue and the Fisherman's Walk turning circle but a crossover was not provided. The loop wires were simply carried over the top of the wires leading to the turning circle which could not therefore be used. The original configuration at that point was never restored.

33   The original anti-clockwise turning loop along Southbourne Road and Parkwood Road was installed to serve as the northern terminus of the 22B Fisherman's Walk - Tuckton "shuttle service" which commenced on 16 August 1948. It is known to have had an auto frog in the mid-1950s but this was subsequently removed.

34-   Frogs installed in order for trolleybuses to be able to comply with the Southbourne (Fisherman's Walk) Traffic Management Scheme which operated 27 October 1967 - 11

36   February 1968. The turning loop along Southbourne Road and Parkwood Road was incorporated into the one-way system, vehicles now running in clockwise direction. It was used by all Ebnd trolleybuses on services 21-23 as well as serving as the Fisherman's Walk terminal loop. When the Management Scheme was prematurely terminated the turning loop continued to be used in a clockwise direction although all through services returned to the direct Ebnd wiring in Beresford Road and Seabourne Road.

37   Frog for the junction of Christchurch Road and Holdenhurst Road set back from the Lansdowne with second, parallel, Ebnd overhead line at the east end of Old Christchurch Road.

38   Provided entry to the second, parallel, Ebnd overhead line at the east end of Old Christchurch Road outside Trinity Church around the north side of the Lansdowne roundabout into the west end of Holdenhurst Road where it ended in a trail frog immediately after the service 34 Lansdowne stop. It provided the frequent service 25 with an uninterrupted run around the busy and often congested Lansdowne roundabout.

39   Provided entry to an anti-clockwise turning loop from Holdenhurst Road Wbnd along Lansdowne Crescent and the south end of Lansdowne Road (Sbnd) to rejoin the Holdenhurst Road Ebnd wiring opposite the Metropole Hotel. Served as the terminal point for short workings from the northern suburbs until the Lansdown roundabout was built.

40-42   These frogs were installed at the Lansdowne junction prior to the construction of the roundabout in January 1947.

45   This frog provided a turnout from the roundabout into Lansdowne Road (Nbnd) and together with a trail frog installed at the same time, were intended to offer an alternative route to St. Paul's Road between Cemetery Junction and the Lansdowne as well as a turning loop for vehicles to/from the northern suburbs. No overhead wiring was ever installed in Lansdowne Lansdowne Road and the frog was never used as it led nowhere.

51   Located at the junction of Commercial Road with the Triangle, this frog provided access to the Triangle loop.

52   Hybrid with B1 15° switches and 17° AA crossing. Frog set back towards Square with parallel second pair of wires in Commercial Road 6 April 1947.

58   This frog was installed at the Square for trolleybuses turning back to Old Christchurch Road and equipped with an auto-frog setter by 5 May 1938.

59   Served the Central Pleasure Gardens loading bay used by services 28, 28A and 29.

60   Seved the loading bay outside Henlys' motor showroom and Burtons located between Bourne Avenue and the bottom of Richmond Hill used by services 26, 26A, 30 and 30A.

61   Located at the junction of Bourne Avenue, this frog was removed on 29 May 1960. In principle it was replaced by the frog (57) at the eastern end of Avenue Road (pole **S 14J**) and a B1 12¹/₁₂° crossover on the Square roundabout thereby providing an uninterrupted run for trolleybuses proceeding up Richmond Hill or along Old Christchurch Road. The location

of the auto-frog setters is unknown (service vehicles ascended Richmond Hill from both Avenue Road and Exeter Road).

62 Could be set from both the setter at the north end of Exeter Road and the setter on the south side of the Square roundabout after the junction with the Gervis Place wiring. This was the sole facing or turnout frog in the final layout at the Square.

63 A single long loop for vehicle loading purposes, running from just after the junction with Westover Road to the east side of the Square at pole **B 35 L**, was installed in Gervis Place in December 1935. This loop was divided into two retaining the original facing and trailing frogs in their original positions (the additional switch frog being inserted at **B 40 L** just west of the traffic signals where Gervis Place and Old Christchurch Road merge), with a short length of single track overhead wiring in between that incorporated the frog for the emergency turn-back into Old Christchurch Road, in April 1941. This westernmost loop was removed in March 1947 but reinstated in June 1953.

The easternmost loop in Gervis Place was divided into two in March 1947 in conjunction with the construction of the Square roundabout. The first loop retained the original 25° facing frog just after the junction with Westover Road (**B 35 L**) and the second loop retained the 15o trail frog prior to the emergency turn-back into Old Christchurch Road.

64 The second loop commencing at pole **B 36 L** was further divided into two loops in 1954 creating a total of four loops in Gervis Place. The new loops started at **B 36 L**, for Iford services 20 and 24, and at pole **B 38 L** for Fisherman's Walk services 21-23. These two loops were again combined into one on 14 May 1967.

71 Ramp-end frog

73 Ramp-end frog

74 No frog was installed in the Ebnd wiring at Ashley Road, Springbourne, when the Queen's Park Gold Pavilion branch opened on 20 October 1934. Parallel wiring was installed for one span and it was necessary to transfer the trolley booms from one set of wires to the other during a stop at this point. A frog was installed at a later date, possibly in May/June 1938 when regular services were first introduced to/from Queen's Park Golf Pavilion.

75 No scheduled services operated along Southcote Road or Palmerston Road and St. Clement's Road however fare-paying passengers were carried on depot journeys.

78 Provided entry to the turning circle accessible from the north and erected above the apex of the junction between Lansdowne Road and Wimborne Road at Cemetery Junction.

79 From April 1965 this auto frog could be set from both the setter in Wimborne Road (Nbnd) and a new, additional setter at the west end of Alma Road.

86-8 Facing frog access to Moordown depot was not provided immediately due to high demands on the Overhead Department in 1935. It is assumed that they were added in the second half of 1936 as photographic evidence shows that they had still not been installed in June 1936.

90 Ramp-end frog. This frog provided a turnout into Lawford Road, it being intended in 1937 that the Wimborne Road (Nbnd) wiring would continue to the junction with Castle Lane West and thence to Ensbury, Kinson and Bear Cross. Only a few spans of Nbnd overhead wiring was installed beyond the junction with Lawford Road and no further extension along Wimborne Road was ever built. The frog was never used as it led nowhere.

95 Ramp-end frog

96 Ramp-end frog

100-02 All Castle Lane (Mallard Road) Depot access and egress wiring was installed at the same time as the wiring along Castle Lane between Broadway Hotel and Iford, however, no overhead wiring was erected in the depot complex itself until early 1952. Trolleybuses stored there prior to this date would have been towed to their parking location.

102 Default changed from L (towards Broadway Hotel) to R (towards Strouden Park and Iford) c. 1963.

Key Nbnd = Northbound
Sbnd = Southbound

Ebnd = Eastbound
Wbnd = Westbound

G 5 ?   Information in italics followed by ? is assumed correct but remains uncertain
??   Solely ?? in italics indicates unknown

Brassey Road: The reversing triangle was located in Victoria Park Road, which ran almost due west from Wimborne Road just under 200 yards south of Ensbury Park Road, and opposite Brassey Road. It is assumed that it was erected as part of the conversion of the Moordown tram route to trolleybus operation and that it thus became available for service on 7 June 1935, probably as the turning point for a potential short-working in place of the Lansdowne - Brassey Road short-working trams which had terminated there. As it was only ½ mile south of Moordown Depot and Redhill Crescent there seems to have been little purpose in its installation. No overhead wiring details survive and there is no record of Brassey Road reverser being regularly used. Instructions were given that it was no longer to be used from 5 September 1946 due to increasing road traffic and it was dismantled on 29 May 1948.

Capstone Road: Located on the north side of Holdenhurst Road at its junction with Capstone Road was the location of a tramway junction and terminus of the line from Charminster Road, a reverser was included in the tram to trolleybus conversion of the Holdenhurst Road route which opened on 22 June 1934. Some trams on short-workings had terminated here (although there was never any intention of converting the tramway along Capstone Road to trolleybus operation) and it is assumed that this is the reason why a reversing triangle was erected here. Nothing is known of the overhead wiring details, other than that trolleybuses could reverse from the Holdenhurst Road eastbound wiring into Capstone Road. There is no record of the reversing triangle being regularly used whilst from 20 October 1934 there was a more easily

negotiated turning circle at Queen's Park Golf Pavilion just 700 yards further east along Holdenhurst Road. It is understood that it was removed in the late 1930s.

Court Road: Northbound trolleybuses in Charminster Road reversed into Court Road which was almost opposite two schools, occasional school specials being the purpose of this reverser, beneath a 25° right hand spring trail frog, then beneath another 25° right hand shunt and returned to the Charminster Road southbound line beneath a 25° left hand trail frog. It is not known when the reverser at Court Road was installed, but as there is no reference to it in the documents handling the route opening, it is likely that it was put in place prior to Bournemouth Grammar School moving to East Way immediately opposite in September 1939. It was removed on 9 May 1961.

Luckham Road: Until overhead wiring was extended into Castle Lane West at Broadway Hotel and beyond to Moordown, Luckham Road reverser was the northernmost terminus of Charminster Road services, coming into operation on 23 August 1935. It remained in regular daily use until the withdrawal of Side Route trolleybuses on 25 September 1966. Northbound trolleybuses reversed out of Charminster Road into Luckham Road (an early Bournemouth Council housing estate) beneath a 25° right hand spring trail frog, then came another 25° right hand spring trail frog and finally, from 19 October 1938 when the Castle Lane West link opened, trolleybuses pulled-out beneath the southbound Charminster Road wiring beneath a 25° left hand trail frog. All the frogs in the assembly were of BIC manufacture in the early ramp end style

Malvern Road: Erected in early spring 1937, this reverser came

After 25 March 1956, the reversing triangle at Redhill Crescent, Moordown, was rarely used, however, this was just the sort of location that enthusiasts wished to visit on their tours. BUT9641T no. 246 (KLJ346) pulls out of Redhill Crescent into the southbound Wimborne Road line in just such a tour in September 1966. **Paul Creswell**

into service on 5 April 1937 for the opening of the Charminster Avenue route. Although an extension along Malvern Avenue to Moordown was authorised, it was never constructed, and the Malvern Road reverser became the longest serving terminal reversing triangle (as opposed to ones at intermediate points along a route) on the Bournemouth system. Trolleybuses heading north along Charminster Avenue turned west into Malvern Road beneath a 25° right hand spring trail frog and then reversed along Malvern Road across the junction with Charminster Avenue beneath a 25° "Y" spring trail frog by St. Walburga's School before turning into the southbound Charminster Avenue line. The reversing triangle remained in regular daily use by service 29 and replacement service 35 until 4 April 1966 when the route was closed.

Redhill Crescent: Located on the west side of Wimborne Road opposite the northern egress of Malvern Road (a proposed trolleybus route) and 50 yards north of Moordown Depot, this reversing triangle came into use on 28 June 1935 as the northern terminus of trolleybus services to Moordown. Trolleybus operation along Wimborne Road had commenced on 7 June 1935 and during this brief, intervening period during which trams continued to run between the Lansdowne and Moordown, trolleybuses reversed in Moordown depot forecourt. Although trolleybuses were extended further north along Wimborne Road, the Redhill Crescent reverser remained in use by services 26 or 27 until 14 August 1950 when, following representations from Bournemouth Trades Council, it was locked out of use and replaced by a turning loop in the Moordown Depot premises. All of the overhead (including frogs and crossover) were taken down on the night of 11/12 November 1950 and the supporting traction poles were removed shortly afterwards.

The reverser was re-installed in July 1953 to provide a turning point at Moordown after the forthcoming closure of Moordown Depot and came into operation on 26 July 1953 once again for services 26 and 27. As then installed, northbound trolleybuses reversed from Wimborne Road into Redhill Crescent beneath a 25° right hand spring trail frog, then under a 25° "Y" spring trail frog and then turned into the Wimborne Road southbound line beneath a 25° left hand trail frog unusually made up of 15° switch tongues but with a 17½° crossing. Service changes saw the end of scheduled use on 25 March 1956. Thereafter, the reversing triangle was retained until the closure of the Side Routes on 25 September 1966 seeing occasional use primarily for enthusiasts' tours.

Tuckton: A spring trail frog was installed in the eastbound Belle Vue Road wiring at the crossroads with Tuckton Road and Wick Lane, about 100 yards west of Tuckton Bridge, to enable trolleybuses to reverse into the east end of Tuckton Road with a second trail (junction) frog for vehicles to return to the westbound Belle Vue Road wires. It is understood that, probably due to the unavailability of overhead equipment caused by wartime conditions, a second trail frog at the apex of the "branch" into Tuckton Road was not installed and that there were two parallel pairs of wires above Tuckton Road requiring a transfer of trolley booms from one pair to the other to complete the reversing manoeuvre. Some weekday peak-hour unadvertised journeys terminating at Southbourne Cross Roads were extended to Tuckton Road from 8 November 1943.

There is no evidence of any timetabled journeys using the Tuckton reversing arrangements until 1947. All timetabled journeys continued to terminate at Southbourne Cross Roads

(service 22) or Christchurch (21) until late 1946 or spring 1947 except for the summer season 1 August 1946 - October 1946 during which services 22 and 24 were extended to interwork at the junction of Stour Road with Barrack Road, Christchurch.

In December 1946 it was agreed to improve the layout of the reversing arrangements to avoid the necessity of having to re-pole trolleybuses. This involved the installation of a second frog on the "branch" in Tuckton Road to create a complete reversing triangle and it is assumed that this work was carried out in spring 1947 (although no corroborating evidence of a reconstruction has been discovered) with service 22A being extended to Tuckton from 10 April 1947. The July 1947 timetable also showed all weekday daytime journeys on service 22 extended to Tuckton, but it is not known precisely when these started to operate.

From 5 October 1947, all trolleybuses terminating at Tuckton were extended about 600 yards westwards along Tuckton Road to a turning circle at the junction of Carbery Avenue and Cranleigh Road, the reversing arrangements being absorbed into the new overhead wiring layout at the junction of Tuckton Road with Belle Vue Road.

By June 1961 only four reversers remained, namely Luckham Road and Malvern Road for normal service trolleybuses, and Bodorgan Road and Redhill Crescent for emergency use. There is no indication that additional reversing triangles were proposed at any other points, apart from early discussions concerning the Strouden Park terminus at the junction of Castle Lane and Holdenhurst Road, including authorised and proposed routes, on the Bournemouth system at any time.

Traffic islands or roundabouts were installed at the following locations after the construction of trolleybus equipment at the junctions concerned:

Location	Date
Christchurch Road, Iford, at the junction with Castle Lane East	December 1956
Bargates, Christchurch, at the junction with Barrack Road, High Street and Sopers Lane (and Christchurch by-pass from May 1958)	August 1955
Holdenhurst Road, Strouden Park (Cooper Dean), at the junction with Castle Lane East and Castle Lane West	May 1963
Lansdowne, at the junction with Bath Road, Christchurch Road, Holdenhurst Road, Lansdowne Road, Meyrick Road and Old Christchurch Road	January 1947
Square, at the junction with Avenue Road, Commercial Road, Exeter Road, Gervis Place, Old Christchurch Road and Richmond Hill	March 1947
Talbot Road, at the junction with Talbot Avenue	June 1959
Tuckton, at the junction with Belle Vue Road, Tuckton Road and Wick Lane	June 1963
Wimborne Road, at the junction with East Avenue and Talbot Avenue	March 1961

Little used or unusual sections of overhead wiring

Trolleybuses did not regularly operate along the following stretches of overhead wiring (BCT alpha route code shown in parenthesis):

Exeter Road (R): Notwithstanding the fact that operations to and from Bournemouth Pier were seasonal, the single line along Exeter Road from the Pier to the Square was infrequently used after the end of the 1961 summer season. Exceptions were special journeys with school children to and from the Winter Gardens, a little to the west of the junction with Cranborne Road, for performances of the Bournemouth Symphony Orchestra or as an essential part of any trolleybus enthusiast tour itinerary.

Seasonal supplementary services using Exeter Road at various times in the 1950-61 period were the 23(ii), 24(ii), 28(ii), 30A(iii), 35(i), 38 and 39.

Southcote Road (Y): At the south (Boscombe) end of Palmerston Road there was a unique arrangement whereby the four running wires leading to and from the double junction with Christchurch Road, immediately past the Palmerston Hotel, were reduced to two.

Trolleybuses travelling south along Palmerston Road first encountered a spring trail frog which routed both negative and positive trolley heads left in order to join the Christchurch Road eastbound line. A little further south the positive wire divided into two at an ordinary spring reset trail frog which was also normally set for the left-hand line.

Until 1954, trolleybuses travelling north along Palmerston Road, i.e. from Christchurch Road westbound towards Central Depot, were required to stop on the three-wire section to the north of the spring reset trail frog in the positive wire for the booms to be transferred, the negative nearside boom to the positive central wire and the positive offside boom to the

negative offside wire. The northbound negative wire was tied-off at two traction poles provided for this purpose. In 1954 a crossover was made up from spare ramp-end fittings, enabling northbound trolleybuses to run through without re-poling, but it was considered advisable for trolleybuses to come to a complete standstill at the junction, and thus the frogs at the Boscombe end of the crossover were hand-operated, although those at the Central Depot end were spring trail frogs enabling a trolleybus to run straight through towards Christchurch Road.

Whether before or after 1954, trolleybuses heading north towards the depot were thus running as if on the "wrong" set of wires. This required no special electrical switching arrangements on the vehicle or at the roadside as a trolleybus motor, being compound wound, rotates in the same direction as usual if the polarity of the supply is reversed, i.e. to reverse, either the direction of current through the field coils or through the armature, but not both, must be reversed. However, a depot-bound trolleybus meeting one taking up service would have to hook down a trolley pole to enable the vehicles to pass.

At the other end of the same route, between Central Depot and Holdenhurst Road, there was a much longer section of three-wire overhead (two negative wires either side of a single central positive wire). It was rumoured that this was a remnant from the last days of the trams, which avoided unnecessary overhead wiring reconstruction when both trolleybuses and trams were operating to and from Central Depot. Indeed, photographs taken in the early years of trolleybus operation at the east entrance to Central Depot suggest that there could have originally been three-wire overhead along St. Clement's Road and Palmerston Road too. At the junction with Holdenhurst Road, a spring reset frog led the positive trolley onto the left-hand line of the conventional "twin track" overhead layout.

None of Route Y was used by scheduled trolleybus services,

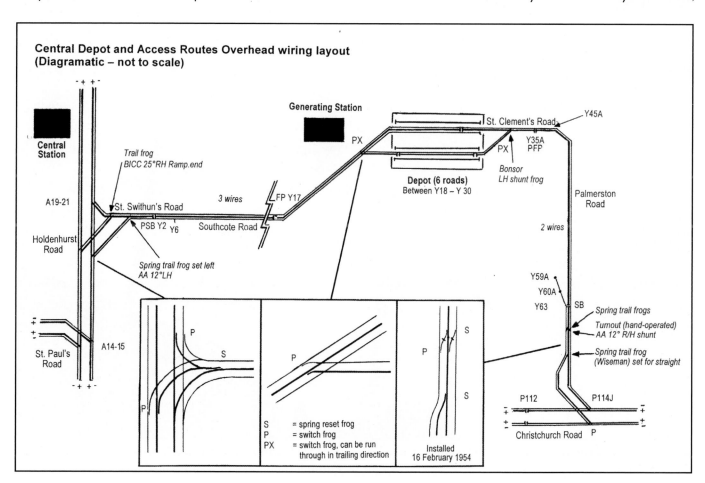

Central Depot and Access Routes Overhead wiring layout (Diagramatic – not to scale)

Re-built **BUT9641T** no. 236 (KLJ336) is seen at the north end of St. Swithun's Road heading for Central Depot, Southcote Road, in 1963 or 1964. The photograph well shows how the lines out of Holdenhurst Road contracted into a three-wire layout. The overall roof of Bournemouth Central Station is visible in the background.

Roger G. Funnell (courtesy Mrs D. Funnell and Rodney Funnell)

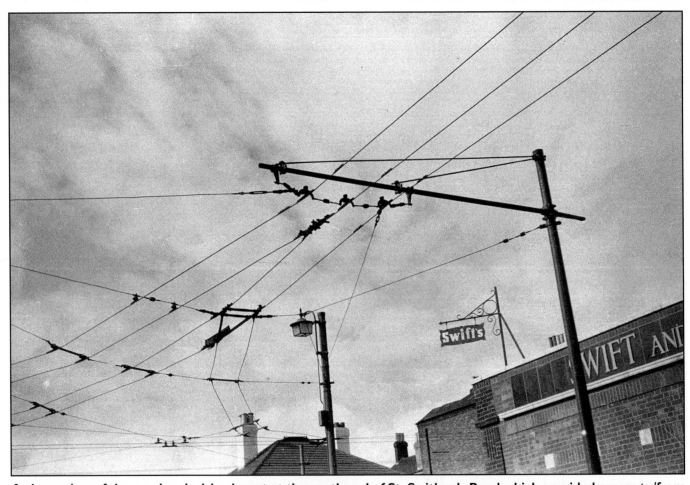

A closer view of the overhead wiring layout at the north end of St. Swithun's Road which provided access to/from Central Depot, Southcote Road.   Roger G. Funnell (courtesy Mrs D. Funnell and Rodney Funnell)

The conductor pulls the operating handle for the frogs in the crossover at the south end of Palmerston Road, Boscombe, so that Sunbeam MF2B no. 268 (WRU268) can proceed to Central Depot, Southcote Road.
Roger G. Funnell (courtesy Mrs D. Funnell and Rodney Funnell)

but passengers could travel on trolleybuses travelling to or from Central Depot, although such journeys were not advertised.

Termini

Trolleybus terminal arrangements can be conveniently categorised as follows (it will be noted that Bournemouth trolleybuses were not equipped with traction batteries for emergency manoeuvring or terminating purposes):

Those on BCT private property

Christchurch turntable (XT): The Christchurch tram terminus was in the narrow Church Street (the main access to Christchurch Priory Church) and which, together with the lanes in the vicinity, offered no suitable solution for a trolleybus terminus. Thus, after debate, it was agreed with Christchurch Council that a trolleybus turning circle could be built in Christchurch High Street in the width of the road outside the Town Hall. However, BCT continued to investigate alternative options and in November 1935 entered into negotiations with the brewers Strong & Co. of Romsey Ltd. to lease the coach yard, off Church Street, adjoining their Dolphin Hotel public house. This location was finally selected for the unusual solution

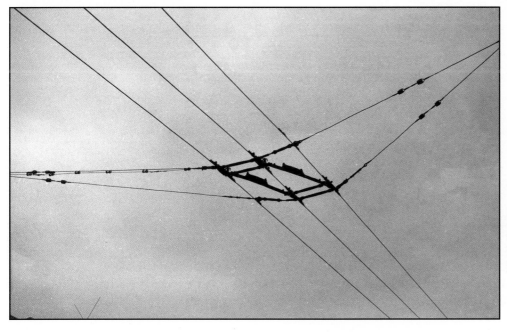

The crossover at the south end of Palmerston Road, Boscombe, whereby three lines became two.
Roger G. Funnell (courtesy Mrs D. Funnell and Rodney Funnell)

509

of a hand-operated turntable upon which a trolleybus could be rotated by 180° following its arrival and then prepared for its return to Bournemouth. This solution was one of just two such turntables at a terminal point in the UK, the other being at Longwood, Huddersfield. The yard was not owned by BCT but leased from Strong & Co. initially for twenty years at £150 pa.

Work on the turntable was not complete when, on 8 April 1936, the ceremonial last tram and first trolleybus to Christchurch ran. Trolleybuses terminated at Christchurch by making a "three-point turn" from Church Street into the yard using a T-pole and connecting cables until 19 June 1936 when the turntable was deemed ready for use.

There was no special overhead wiring; eastbound and westbound pairs of wires were tied off at an insulated span wire supported by two traction poles immediately after the turntable backing on the surrounding wall to the yard. The yard was illuminated in the hours of darkness by lamps, fed from the normal electricity supply, attached to these poles. An arriving trolleybus turned into the yard from Church Street and stopped for the passengers to alight before continuing onto the turntable. The conductor hauled down the trolley booms using one of the bamboo retrieval poles hanging from one of the traction poles beyond the turntable and secured the booms beneath the vehicle's retaining hooks. The crew then rotated the turntable using the handle provided, the conductor returned the trolley booms to the westbound pair of wires and the driver drove the trolleybus off the turntable. Only then could waiting passengers board the trolleybus.

The above relates the official operating procedure. It became accepted practice to simply lean against the bodywork or even pull on the rear platform handrail (rather than use the handle

provided) to rotate the turntable, however a small minority of latter-day drivers developed the habit of turning the steering wheel abruptly as the trolleybus pulled on to the turntable, putting it in motion. There were never plans to electrify the operation of the turntable: the latter-day equipment box and cabling were provided for the T-poles used when the turntable was lifted for maintenance purposes in about 1946-47, in May 1958 and in November 1963.

A skate in the overhead line at the south end of High Street, where the road was comparatively wide, illuminated signal lamps indicating that the narrow section of road beyond and the turntable was occupied. At busy periods trolleybuses would wait briefly here until the departing trolleybus had pulled out of Church Street. A second contact in the overhead wiring above the exit from the yard extinguished the signal lamps as the trolleybus departed.

The turntable functioned without problems until the abandonment of trolleybus operation and continued to serve the replacing motorbuses until 10 June 1973 when services were rerouted away from Church Street. The area has since been redeveloped and a complex of shops with flats above built over the former Dolphin Hotel and yard but the turntable remains in situ as a means of turning residents' private cars.

Iford Bridge (I): A single line clockwise turning circle was installed above a new and well-illuminated road surface on the north side of Christchurch Road just past Bridle Crescent about 70 yards from the Borough Boundary with Christchurch and on the Bournemouth side of the River Stour. The land, previously occupied by the farmhouse of Clingan's Farm, was purchased from Bournemouth Council by the undertaking at a cost of £2,250. The circle came into service on 25 March 1935

Sunbeam MS2 no. 127 (BEL812) stands amongst the bushes in the Strouden Park turning circle on Castle Lane East at the junction with Holdenhurst Road prior to returning to the Square on a service 31 afternoon extra (21 September 1955).

Malcolm Pearce (G.O.P. Pearce)

At the westernmost end of Christchurch Road, Bournemouth - after Iford Bridge the road continues as Barrack Road, Christchurch - **BUT9641T no. 216 (KLJ350)** travels west towards the Square prior to construction of a roundabout at the junction with Castle Lane East in 1956. Iford Bridge turning circle is visible to the left of the black car receding into the distance.   **Omnibus Society (S.E. Letts)**

At the junction of Christchurch Road with Castle Lane East on 15 October 1951, the first day of trolleybus services between the Broadway Hotel and Iford, **BUT9641T no. 219 (KLJ353)** turns into Christchurch Road on unidirectional circular service 32.   **Malcolm Pearce (G.O.P. Pearce)**

as the terminus of service 24 and was provided with the body of single-deck tram no. 1, located to the west of the barn used as an overhead equipment store, prior to the opening to serve as a passenger waiting room.

When trolleybuses were extended across the river into Christchurch on 22 July 1943, access to Iford Bridge turning circle from the eastbound line was provided by a 25° left hand hand-operated facing frog. There were no changes to the layout of the turning circle in its lifetime although service 24 was subsequently extended to Jumpers whilst Castle Lane services terminated there between 1953 and 1956.

On 2 December 1956 a new roundabout was opened at the crossroads of Christchurch Road, Castle Lane East and Iford Lane, some 120 yards west of the turning circle, and it is assumed that all journeys that, until then, terminated at Iford Bridge turning circle were curtailed to Iford roundabout. The redundant turning was removed on 19/20 May 1961.

Moordown Depot (T): An anti-clockwise turning circle, which could be accessed from both the northbound and southbound Wimborne Road lines, was constructed through the yard of the extension building on the south side of the main depot building by linking up existing stabling wiring in the summer of 1950. Trolleybuses from the northbound line entered through the gateway in front of the extension building, swung to the left in the yard and drove through a specially-made doorway in the south wall of the main depot building and out again through the front entrance into the southbound line. Those from the southbound line followed the same procedure but, having pulled the hand-operated "Y" frog which was set for southbound departures, turned north on leaving the front entrance of the main building.

From 15 August 1950 it was used as the terminus for all services to Moordown in place of the Redhill Crescent reverser. This situation continued until the closure of Moordown Depot on 25 July 1953 whereupon all services terminating there were extended to the reinstated Redhill Crescent reversing triangle.

Strouden Park (FQR): It was planned to terminate the route extension along Castle Lane West, foreseen primarily as an access route to Castle Lane (Mallard Road) Depot, at the junction of Castle Lane with Holdenhurst Road in a developing area known as Strouden Park. A piece of land in the Meyrick Estate to the north east of the junction was purchased and a clockwise turning circle was erected there above a gravelled road surface and brought into use on 23 May 1953 as the terminus of extra journeys on services 31(ii) and 32. By then overhead wiring had been hung along the length of Castle Lane East to Iford and access to the turning circle was by left hand hand-operated facing frog.

From 18 December 1962 all journeys scheduled to terminate at Strouden Park were extended to Iford roundabout and on 19/20 December 1962 the Strouden Park turning circle was cut down to make way for a new roundabout.

Around traffic islands or at wide road junctions:

Cemetery Junction (M): a tight turning circle was constructed above the junction of the north end of Lansdowne Road with Wimborne Road. A hand-operated right-hand 25° facing frog, located in front of the tramway passenger waiting shelter and public lavatories, gave access to the loop which swung around above the junction and rejoined the Wimborne Road northbound wiring outside St. Augustin's Church a short distance before the auto frog setter for Charminster Road.

The turning circle remained in regular use until 26 March 1956, but was only cut-down in 1960.

Columbia Road, Kinson Road (Wonderholme Parade) (TL): A narrow island between a service road running between Acres Road and Fernheath Road (now known as Turbary Park Road) and Kinson Road was selected as the location for a turning circle to serve trolleybuses from both Kinson Road and Columbia Road. A row of shops, Wonderholme Parade, built in the early 1930s fronted on to the service road. Service 30 began to turn there on 15 April 1938, however, when the trolleybus route along Columbia Road opened on 8 April 1939, the main service was reorganised to provide unidirectional circular services around the Moordown - Ensbury Park - Wallisdown - Winton loop in a clockwise (30) and anticlockwise (30A) direction. Thus initially, few journeys actually turned here. This changed post-war when services 34(i) and 36 as well as seasonal supplementary services 30A(iii) and 34(i) terminated here, in addition to any 30 or 31 journeys which did not interwork.

Access was by means of a 25° left hand hand-operated frog from the northbound Kinson Road line and by a 25° right hand hand-operated frog from the southbound Kinson Road line. When leaving the north end of the circle there was a 25° right hand frog leading into the southbound Kinson Road line (straight on for the northbound line and thus Columbia Road). A shunt frog was included in the trailing frog where the wires from the southbound Kinson Road line joined the access wires from the northbound line above Fernheath Road as BUT9641Ts terminating on workings from Columbia Road had some difficulties in swinging round in one go. This frog enabled trolleybuses to reverse back towards Fernheath Road for a second attempt.

The turning circle was not altered upon conversion of service 30 to motorbus operation on 16 April 1966 and remained intact as the terminus of service 31 journeys along Columbia Road until 25 September 1966. The complex was removed, together with all wiring along Columbia Road, Ensbury Park Road, Kinson Road, Talbot Avenue, Talbot Road, Wallisdown Road, between March 1967 and 19 February 1968.

Fisherman's Walk, Wentworth Avenue (XFL): A terminal loop was installed at the north end of Fisherman's Walk in the width of the road at the junction of Wentworth Avenue with Fisherman's Avenue to serve journeys from the Square when the first stage of the trolleybus route extension towards Christchurch opened on 20 November 1935. When the route was extended to Southbourne on 23 December 1935 the Fisherman's Walk loop, some 30 yards south of the mainline in Seabourne Road, was retained as a turning circle. Access was by a 25° right hand hand-operated frog which, after August 1948, was located just south of the Beresford Road access frog.

The circle remained in use until 4 October 1967 when work on the Southbourne Traffic Management Scheme, which included the introduction of one-way traffic in various roads nearby, made access impractical and henceforth trolleybuses from Pokesdown and the Square terminating at Fisherman's Walk began using the Parkwood Road loop in the opposite direction to that previously used. The turning circle in Wentworth Avenue at the top of Fisherman's Walk was then disconnected but remained intact until after trolleybus operation in Bournemouth was abandoned.

Fisherman's Walk, Parkwood Road (E): A single line anti-clockwise loop was installed in summer 1948 running north along Southbourne Road from a 25° right hand hand-operated switch frog above the junction with Beresford Road, and then into Parkwood Road as far as Seabourne Road where it trailed into the southbound line. Access was solely from the Carbery Avenue and Tuckton direction, the 22B and, later 23, Tuckton - Fisherman's Walk "shuttle service" terminating here. By the mid-1950s an auto frog had replaced the hand-operated switch frog although this was subsequently removed at an unknown date.

The introduction of the Southbourne Traffic Management Scheme involved, amongst other changes, the entire loop being reconstructed for clockwise operation. This involved a 25° left hand facing frog, locked for the turn into Parkwood Road, inserted in the eastbound Seabourne Road wiring; a 25° "Y" auto frog above Southbourne Road just prior to the junction with Beresford Road and New Park Road with a 25° right hand trailing frog into the eastbound (towards Tuckton) wiring and a 25° left hand trailing frog into the westbound wiring (towards Fisherman's Walk); and a 25° right hand auto frog and setter in the Beresford Road westbound wiring with new curves leading into Seabourne Road for trolleybuses to turn both left (eastbound) towards Southbourne Cross Roads and right (westbound) towards Pokesdown.

Trolleybus operation under the new layout commenced on 27 October 1967, however, within a month it was evident that the Scheme had done nothing to reduce general traffic problems whilst local traders complained at a fall in business. It was decided to abandon the experiment in January 1968. From 12 February 1968, trolleybuses reverted to the routes which had been in operation prior to 12 November 1967, but for journeys from the Square and Pokesdown terminating at Fisherman's Walk which continued to use the Parkwood Road turning circle in the clockwise direction.

Horseshoe Common: As a result of the 12 April 1941 wartime bombing raid on the town centre, on 19 September 1941 the Transport Committee instructed the General Manager to investigate construction of an emergency trolleybus turning point at Horseshoe Common to avoid the network being paralysed by future raids. On 24 October 1941 he was told to erect a turning circle as soon as possible around an island at the junction of Dean Park Road with Old Christchurch Road opposite the turn into Fir Vale Road. It was available for use by late March or early April 1942. Access was by 25° "Y" hand-operated switch frog. The tight turning circle was used for some time following the 23 May 1943 air raid, but there is no record of its use subsequently except for enthusiasts' tour and possibly for driver training. The turning circle remained aloft and available for use until the system's abandonment.

Lansdowne: Although the General Manager was instructed on 22 May 1936 to erect a turning circle at the Lansdowne for trolleybuses arriving there on the westbound Holdenhurst Road line to turn back along Holdenhurst Road, it is not known precisely when it was constructed and opened. An anti-clockwise turning circle around the island made up by Lansdowne Crescent between Holdenhurst Road and Lansdowne Road was installed in the 1936-37 financial year, but no timetabled services were scheduled to turn there until 31 December 1956 (when service 34(ii) was curtailed to the Lansdowne) by which time the turning circle had been removed and the roundabout built (January 1947).

Queen's Park Golf Pavilion (Q): a turning circle was opened on 20 October 1934 at the junction of Holdenhurst Road with Littledown Road, opposite the Golf Pavilion, to serve as the terminus of the short branch along Holdenhurst Road beyond Ashley Road. Post-war a small circular island was constructed in the apex of the junction.

Southbourne Cross Roads (XSL): A terminal loop was installed around the public conveniences constructed at the junction of Southbourne Overcliff Drive and St. Catherine's Road a few yards to the south of the junction of these roads with Belle Vue Road to serve journeys from the Square when the second stage of the trolleybus route extension (the first stage being to Fisherman's Walk) towards Christchurch opened on 23 December 1935. When the route was extended to Christchurch on 8 April 1936 the Southbourne Cross Roads loop was retained as a turning circle. Access was by a 25° right hand hand-operated frog in the eastbound wires. It was served by service 22 and variations thereof throughout the era of trolleybus operation in Southbourne. The turning circle remained in regular use until 19 April 1969, the last day of normal scheduled trolleybus operation in Bournemouth.

Square (S): the experimental trolleybus route from Westbourne terminated with a single line clockwise turning circle around the tramway loading points, waiting room and offices in the middle of the Square. Trolleybuses departing for Westbourne loaded at the northern (orange-segment shaped) of the two traffic islands between the tramway and the junction with Exeter Road on the south side of the Square. When, on 22 June 1934, overhead wiring was extended further east into Old Christchurch Road and Gervis Place, the turning circle wiring at the bottom of Richmond Hill was removed and a facing frog and a trailing frog installed in the through wiring so that a clockwise turning circle, again around the tramway loading points, waiting room and offices but at the opposite end, accessible from the east could be installed. The facing frog, located in front of Bobby's department store on the south side of the Square, was converted to auto operation by 5 May 1938.

On 7 June 1935 trolleybus operation on Richmond Hill commenced necessitating a second single line clockwise turning circle around the tramway loading points, waiting room and offices in the middle of the Square which crossed the existing east-west wiring without any connection and continued towards the junction with Bourne Avenue before turning back onto Richmond Hill. On the south, west and north sides of the Square, this new turning circle was "outside" the existing wiring. Initially this loop served solely the Moordown service (26) along Wimborne Road which had a loading point on the north side of the Square between Bourne Avenue and Richmond Hill outside Henlys' car showrooms and Burton the tailors. On 23 August 1935 trolleybus service 28 along Charminster Road to Broadway was introduced, the loading point for this service being on the west side of the Square outside the entrance to the Central Pleasure Gardens. The alighting point for these services was Albert Road near the bottom of Richmond Hill (a compulsory stop to deselect the electrical coasting brake) although passengers could also travel round to the boarding point in the Square. As these two services each operated every five minutes and their timetabled layover or waiting time was not more than one or two minutes, there was no necessity for a service 28 departure to pass a loading 26 or an arriving 26 to pass a loading 28.

A loop was added at the boarding point outside the entrance to the Central Pleasure Gardens at some date in 1937, however, this was not necessarily due to the introduction of service 29 to/from Malvern Road on 5 April 1937 as the five minute frequency along Charminster Road was unchanged but shared between services 28 and 29. It is assumed that entry to the loop was by hand-operated left-hand 25° facing frog and exit by an equivalent trailing frog.

The introduction of service 30 on 15 April 1938 and service 30A on 8 April 1939 resulted in an additional six Side Route journeys per hour using the second, outer turning circle (the introduction of services 26A and 28A in the meantime had not increased the frequencies along Charminster Road and Wimborne Road). This meant that a total of 16 trolleybuses an hour (one every four minutes) would be using the loading point outside Henlys' car showrooms and Burton the tailors, resulting in there almost always being a vehicle loading there, precluding a Charminster Road departure from passing. Thus, although despite exhaustive effort no photographic evidence has been found of the existence of a second loop here, it is likely that a passing loop was installed at this stop either in 1938 or 1939. Due to the road layout and sharp corner prior to the ascent of Richmond Hill, it would appear that entry to the loop would have been by hand-operated left-hand 25° facing frog and exit by a right-hand trailing frog.

A roundabout came into operation on 30 March 1947 whereupon the Square ceased to be a terminal point as such, Side Route trolleybuses using the eastern and southern portions of the roundabout to reach Commercial Road and the Triangle before turning back into Avenue Road and thus the Square. The Triangle effectively became the terminal and point of origin for these services, and the timetabled layover or waiting time was taken at the Triangle or Avenue Road. Passengers for the Square continued to alight at Albert Road although there was a further stop before the Triangle until about 1960, outside Woolworth's store just off the south side of the Square at the eastern end of Commercial Road. Services from and to the Lansdowne terminating at the Square continued to terminate and start from Gervis Place whereupon they would circumnavigate the Square prior to heading east along Old Christchurch Road. In all cases the indicator blinds continued to show SQUARE or, later, BOURNEMOUTH SQUARE as the destination.

Circular routing around a number of streets:

Boscombe (AL): An anti-clockwise terminal turning loop along the south end of Ashley Road to its junction with Christchurch Road, eastbound along Christchurch Road to its junction with Portman Road, northbound along Portman Road and then westbound along Gladstone Road to its junction with Ashley Road was installed for the conversion of the Holdenhurst Road tram route to trolleybus operation, coming into service on 22 June 1934. There were no special features until trolleybuses were extended along the length of Christchurch Road necessitating the insertion of a trail frog out of Ashley Road and a left hand facing frog in the eastbound wiring to provide access into Portman Road. The latter was equipped with a setter and auto frog operation subsequently, probably at an early date due to the high number of trolleybuses passing beneath this junction.

A right hand frog providing access to Portman Road from the westbound Christchurch Road wires was installed prior to the introduction of service 25B Westbourne - Fisherman's Walk via Holdenhurst Road and Ashley Road on 28 July 1938. Although this service ceased in February 1940, this link remained in place until 1966. The trail frog out of Ashley Road was replaced by

Heading south along Wimborne Road at the complex Winton Banks is Sunbeam MF2B no. 300 (300LJ) on its way to the Square and Triangle on a service 31 working. Talbot Road is to the left between the National Provincial Bank and Lloyds Bank, and Alma Road is to the right in front of the branch of Boots the Chemists.

NTA collection (R.F. Mack)

a crossing, a short section of wiring parallel to the eastbound Christchurch Road wiring and a Wiseman "Y" trail frog on 26 April 1953.

Jumpers (IL): A 25° left hand auto frog from the eastbound Barrack Road wiring provided access to an anti-clockwise turning loop along Oak Avenue, Stourvale Avenue and the southern end of The Grove from whence it joined the Barrack Road westbound wiring which opened to service trolleybuses on 7 August 1944. Service 24 was extended from Iford Bridge to this point paralleling service 20 to/from Christchurch which had commenced on 22 July 1943. Apart from minor changes to the overhead wiring to adapt to a changed road layout due to the construction of a short length of dual carriageway in Barrack Road at its junction with The Grove, there were no alterations to the loop. It served as the terminal point of service 24 throughout its life and for service 32 at various periods 1958 - 1964. The loop remained in regular use until trolleybus operation in Bournemouth ceased.

Triangle (WEL): A hand-operated facing frog, assumed to have been right hand, was inserted into the Commercial Road westbound line at its junction with the Triangle in July 1936 as the Transport Committee already had thoughts of running all trolleybuses terminating in the Square through to the Triangle. There was a trailing frog into the Avenue Road eastbound wiring on the north side of the Triangle. It is understood that this connecting line was little used prior to 1947. In conjunction with the revised layout at the Square and the extension of the Richmond Hill Side Route services to the Triangle, access to the Triangle was set back towards Square to a location about 30yd west of Bobby's department store, with parallel second pair of wires in Commercial Road on 6 April 1947 and the right hand frog replaced by a left hand auto frog.

In spring 1948 a parking area was constructed in the grassed area of the Triangle with a single trolleybus line being erected on 15 May 1948, access being by a hybrid 12°/17° left hand hand-operated frog with a 25° left hand trailing frog at the exit. The parking area was used by both motorbuses and trolleybuses.

The line through the Triangle remained busy until the withdrawal of the Richmond Hill trolleybus services on 25 September 1965 and with space for a maximum of three vehicles at the passenger loading point, there was frequently a tailback of vehicles. Thereafter it remained intact to provide access to the parking area and for turning trolleybuses until the final abandonment of trolleybus operation.

Westbourne (WL): A clockwise turning loop along Seamoor Road and Poole Road following the route followed by the trams and all other road traffic was wired to serve as the terminus of the experimental Square - Westbourne trolleybus route which opened on 13 May 1933. There were no special wiring features but for a skate in the wiring which was installed at the stop preceding entry into Seamoor Road and operated a warning lamp intended to prevent trolleybuses bunching up in Poole Road eastbound prior to returning to Bournemouth Square.

Winton (ML): It is assumed that the clockwise turning loop along Alma Road, Waterloo Road and Crimea Road was installed in conjunction with opening of the trolleybus route along Wimborne Road to Moordown on 7 June 1935 although MoT approval was only received in January 1937 (it was common practice during the years of rapid trolleybus route expansion in the UK for the MoT to permit trolleybus operation of short routes pending a future visit to inspect longer routes). The loop was probably initially intended to replace a tramway short-working to Alma Road, the area being widely known as Winton Banks due to the presence of a branch of a "High Street Bank" on each corner of the junction of Wimborne Road with Talbot Road.

Access to Alma Road was possible from the northbound Wimborne Road line by a 25° right hand hand-operated frog or from the southbound Wimborne Road line by a 25° left hand hand-operated frog. Upon leaving Crimea Road there was a 25° "Y" hand-operated frog for the turn into the Wimborne Road northbound and southbound lines.

Amongst the 13 frog sets and crossovers making up the Winton Banks layout there was just one auto frog, the left hand facing frog from Wimborne Road into Talbot Road westbound. This was operated by a setter in the Wimborne Road northbound line and, from April 1965, a second setter in the Alma Road line, both setters being wired into the relay box in Wimborne Road. The reason for this late change to the overhead equipment was, no doubt, the winter curtailment of service 30 journeys to Winton, Alma Road, and increased motor traffic on Wimborne Road making hand operation of the frog into Talbot Road at the busy, traffic light controlled junction hazardous.

Unfulfilled proposals

A number of trolleybus route extensions, for which approval had been received, were never constructed:

Bournemouth Corporation Act 1930

The relevant paragraph numbers in this Act are shown in parenthesis.

(3) Meyrick Road from its junction with Bath Road at the Lansdowne, along Meyrick Road and Gervis Road to the junction of Gervis Road with Bath Road

(5) Sea Road, Boscombe from its junction with Christchurch Road to the Boscombe Pier Approach

(6) Hawkwood Road, Boscombe, from its junction with Sea Road to Heathcote Road, and then along Heathcote Road to its junction with Christchurch Road

(7) Parkwood Road from its junction with Christchurch Road, Pokesdown, to its junction with Seabourne Road, Fisherman's Walk

(8) Woodside Road from its junction with Seabourne Road, Fisherman's Walk, to its junction with Parkwood Road

(10) (part of) Holdenhurst Road from its junction with Littledown Avenue (Queen's Park Golf Pavilion) to its junction with Castle Lane East (then and until 1931 the Borough Boundary)

(12) (part of) Malvern Road from its junction with Charminster Avenue to its junction with Wimborne Road, Moordown.

(13) (part of) Wimborne Road from its junction with Castle Lane West, Red Hill, Moordown, to its junction with Ringwood Road, Bear Cross (then and until 1931 in the Rural District of Poole)

(14) (part of) Kinson Road from its junction with Columbia Road to its junction with Wimborne Road, Kinson.

Bournemouth Corporation (Trolley Vehicles) Order Confirmation Act 1938

The relevant Route numbers in this Act are shown in parenthesis.

(2) Redhill Drive from its junction with Ensbury Park Road to its junction with Coombe Avenue, along Coombe Avenue, Leybourne Avenue and Northbourne Avenue to its junction with Wimborne Road, Ensbury

(4) Alma Road, Winton, from its junction with Wimborne Road, then along Richmond Park Road to its junction with Holdenhurst Road, Springbourne.

In addition, a number of further extensions were proposed (although official approval was not sought) at various times until 1957, the actual routes to be followed varying on occasion as Bournemouth's suburbs continued to expand:

Ringwood Road from its junction with Wimborne Road, Bear Cross, along Ringwood Road to its junction with Wallisdown Road and then along Wallisdown Road to its junction with Kinson Road (proposal abandoned due to objections from Dorset County Council, Poole Corporation and H&D).

Fernheath Road from its junction with Columbia Road and Kinson Road, along Coleman Road and Moore Avenue to its junction with Poole Lane, then along Poole Lane to its junction with Ringwood Road, West Howe.

Leybourne Avenue from its junction with Northbourne Avenue, along East Howe Lane to its junction with Kinson Road, thence along Montgomery Avenue, Cunningham Crescent and

Cunningham Place to its junction with Moore Avenue.

None of the above reached the stage at which drawings of traction pole location and overhead wiring layout proposals for routes or terminal arrangements were prepared.

Vehicle Equipment

The two current collectors on the roof of each trolleybus consisted of three main parts: the trolley base carrying the trolley boom and allowing the boom to swing in a horizontal plane and to rise under spring tension; the boom itself and, at the extreme end of the boom, the trolley head, which made contact with the undersurface of the power conducting trolley wire. All three parts were insulated from each other, and the base was also insulated from the trolley gantry by bonded-rubber mountings provided to minimise the transmission of noise to the roof. Unlike other trolleybus systems, it was noticeable how in Bournemouth there was minimal noise in the upper saloon whenever the vehicle passed beneath special work! Radio suppressor coils were mounted on the roof forward of the base on all Bournemouth's pre-war trolley vehicles. The trolley wheels were about 4in in diameter.

The current was carried from the trolley head by a flexible cable running through the hollow trolley boom which narrowed to 1in diameter at the trolley head end. The boom, a tapering steel tube was wrapped in black bitumen-impregnated insulating tape to minimise the chance of it shorting the trolley wires in the event of a dewirement. Approximately the last 3ft of the trolley boom at the restraining hook end was painted white post-war. There is nothing to indicate that this was a wartime measure to aid re-wiring in the "black- out". All vehicles were equipped with Brecknell Willis trolley bases having paired springs lying alongside the trolley boom. The vertical upward pressure of the trolley heads on the wire could be measured by

Crossing beneath the northbound wiring leading into Lawford Road on a southbound service 26 working is Sunbeam MF2B no. 266 (WRU266) on 7 August 1959. The turnout frog and northbound running wires as far as the junction with Castle Lane West, intended for an extension to Bear Cross, are still aloft above Wimborne Road. Photo courtesy of D. Ball, for the family of the late J.S. King

hanging a scale from each boom and could be adjusted at the springs on the trolley base, Bournemouth applying an upward pressure of 30lb.

The Sunbeam MS2s, BUT9641Ts and BUT9611Ts were delivered with one piece 15ft long trolley booms, their total length being extended by the trolley base and trolley head. The Sunbeam MF2Bs were supplied with lightweight trolley booms made up of two tubes of different diameter totalling 16ft in length; the larger diameter of the two running from the trolley base and being about two feet shorter than normal. The smaller diameter tube inserted into the end of the larger one and reached to the trolley head, and was covered with rubber tubing painted white which made the reduced diameter less obvious. In all cases the booms permitted the trolleybus to deviate considerably either side of the overhead line; in the case of the Sunbeam MF2B by up to 15ft.

During the course of the 1938-1939 financial year the wheel collector swivel trolley heads were replaced throughout the fleet with slider heads, the entire unit comprising a steel "harp" (which fitted on to the end of the boom and was retained by two bolts) into which sat a swivelling gunmetal globe. On top of the globe there was a phosphor bronze (BICC) or steel (AA) slipper into which fitted a preformed carbon insert skid. The self-lubricating carbon inserts dramatically reduced trolley wire wear, in some cases almost doubling the "wire life", virtually removed the necessity to apply a conductive grease to the trolley wires, reduced the risk of dewirements, permitted higher operating speeds and eliminated the noise (particularly when wet) from the trolley wheels rotating at high speed.

The carbon inserts were inspected for damage and wear daily, an average life being around 800 miles but considerably less in wet or frosty weather conditions. Frost or ice on the trolley wires interrupted conductivity resulting in control difficulties and a jerky ride as well as intense arcing which quickly damaged and wore the carbon insert.

Instructions issued in September 1953 highlighted the importance of running the first bus on all routes on schedule and that, in the event of frost, the Night Superintendent at Central Depot was to ascertain the conditions in the Boscombe Depot and Castle Lane Depot areas. If defrosting was deemed necessary, key staff, then including Deputy Chief Inspector Biddlecombe and Inspector Forscey, were to be called in and the Engineer at Christchurch substation asked to make traction power available in the Christchurch section. The slipper trolley heads of the early service vehicles were equipped with cast-iron inserts, so-called "Frost Heads", instead of the conventional carbon inserts whilst in severe frost special trolleybuses or "Ghost Buses", equipped with "Frost Heads", were run prior to the start of services. Progress would be accompanied by considerable flashing and a shower of sparks, to remove frost and ice from the trolley wires. The cast-iron inserts were replaced with a normal carbon insert as soon as possible as their prolonged use would not only remove the frost but would also "shave" the trolley wire.

When "Ghost Buses" were operated, they were crewed by an experienced driver and by a second man from the depot staff equipped with a spare trolley head, spanners and torch. The trap doors over the resistances were taken up to enable them to cool as much as possible: BUT9641Ts were not to be used and Sunbeam MS2s 72-89 avoided unless no others were available as they had no trap doors. The routes to be taken, quoted verbatim from the 14 September 1953 instructions, were:

Boscombe (Pokesdown) Depot

1. Leave Boscombe Depot via the route of service 21. Proceed to Christchurch, return to Boscombe Depot via the 20 route. Repeat until wires are cleared.

2. Leave Boscombe Depot via the route of service 20. Proceed to Stour Road, return to Boscombe Depot via the 21 route. Repeat until wires are cleared.

3. Leave Boscombe Depot via the route of service 22 for Tuckton Bridge. Proceed to Fisherman's Walk via Cranleigh Road. Return via Cranleigh Road to Tuckton Bridge, then to Boscombe Depot via the 22 route. Repeat until wires are cleared.

Central Depot, Southcote Road

1. Leave Central Depot and proceed to Portman Road, then via the route of service 25 to the Square via Old Christchurch Road then to Westbourne and return to Ashley Road via the 25 route. Return to Square by 25 route unless different instructions are received.

2. Leave Central Depot for Castle Lane via Portman Road and Pokesdown; turn at Mallard Road and return to Iford (Bridge) and repeat journey to Mallard Road from Iford until wires are clear or other instructions are received from the Inspector at Iford

Castle Lane (Mallard Road) Depot.

1. Leave Castle Lane Depot for (Winton) Banks via Moordown, go up Talbot Road to Wallisdown, and return to Banks via Ensbury Park Road. Turn at Banks and run in reverse direction, via Ensbury Park Road and Talbot Road to Banks, then to Square via 26 route and return to Castle Lane Depot via 26 route unless otherwise instructed.

2. Castle Lane Depot to Iford, turn at Iford (Bridge) turning circle and return along Castle Lane to Cemetery Junction via Charminster; turn at Cemetery Junction and go to Luckham Road and back to Cemetery Junction; turn at Cemetery Junction and go to Malvern Road and from there go to Square via Lansdowne (27 route) and return to Castle Lane Depot via Charminster unless otherwise instructed by Inspector on duty.

(Author's clarifications are shown in italics).

The collecting equipment on the vehicles themselves was not the responsibility of the Overhead Department and fell under the jurisdiction of the Engineering Department, effectively by the early 1960s, Mr. N. Abbey, Assistant Engineer.

APPENDIX J
TRACTION POLES

On those routes where trolleybuses directly replaced trams it was usually possible to retain the tramway traction poles having first established the extent of any corrosion. It was recognised that the size of pole and rake at each location had originally been selected to support one or two tramway trolley wires, whereas with the conversion a minimum of four trolleybus trolley wires and potentially temporarily two tram trolley wires, now needed to be supported. In some cases the tramway poles were re-raked and internally reinforced with concrete.

Where additional support was required, principally on the outside of curves, at junctions, at crossings and at terminal loops, or along roads not previously served by trams, new BS traction poles were planted. The standard pole used on the Bournemouth system was a 31ft heavy steel pole, 9½in in diameter at the base, tapering initially to 8½in and then again to 7½in at the top, but those manufactured after the early 1940s had fractionally larger dimensions of 9⅝in, 8⅝in and 7⅝in respectively. They were manufactured by a variety of steel tube manufacturers, e.g. Stewarts & Lloyds, and were not a specialist item. About 6½ft of the pole was buried in the ground, with a backwards rake to compensate for the weight of the overhead equipment, and the sunken portion embedded in concrete. Once the overhead wiring was complete its weight pulled that part of the pole above the surface into the vertical.

Longer, 33ft or 35ft, and heavier poles were used on curves, junctions and turning circles to support the greater weight and sag of the overhead wiring, again some being filled with concrete for further strengthening or to extend their lives. Finally, each pole position, classified according to length and weight, was plotted on detailed route plans.

On straight sections of road there was a traction pole at least every 40yd but along curved sections of road where the trolley wire had to be pulled into a series of straights approximating to the desired curves these were more frequent. In such cases of stepped curvature the angle did not exceed 10° to reduce the risk of dewirements. There was a considerable weight of equipment aloft: as an example the two pairs of trolley wires on a straight section between two traction poles, together with the supporting hangers and span wires, weighed about 235lb whilst a post-war BICC electrically-operated turnout frog weighed in excess of 80lb.

Statutory regulations stipulated a maximum longitudinal span of 120ft with a minimum conductor height of 20ft above the surface of the road except under bridges and this separation was retained where existing tramway traction poles were reused. Along routes not previously traversed by trams shorter spans of 105ft became general to compensate for the increased weight aloft.

Poles were planted or removed using the Transport Department's own crane. To remove a pole, a chain attached to the crane was secured to the top. A heavy cast iron collar was bolted around it near the base and steel wedges driven in to secure the collar. Hydraulic jacks were then placed under the collar and by the use of a hand pump, a single employee could force the pole up out of the ground. The crane could then lift the pole up completely and place it at the side of the road or onto a waiting lorry. Poles filled with concrete were more difficult to remove and in many cases were cut off at footpath level. The heavy cast-iron base featuring the Bournemouth Borough coat-of-arms was a relic of tramway days intended to protect the traction pole from damage by other road vehicles. They were added and removed by lifting over the top of the pole although in latter days a well-aimed sledge hammer sufficed for their final removal.

The traction poles, some 3,200 poles by Summer 1963 when the system was at its maximum extent, supporting the overhead wiring along each trolleybus route were individually identified by alpha-numeric code. Each route had a unique alphabetic code and every traction pole was numbered consecutively along the line of route commencing at the Bournemouth Square "end". The purpose was to allow accurate identification of the location of any incident or of any work that needed to be done. Traction poles on the left hand side of the road (looking outwards from Bournemouth Square) were stencilled with a white-painted alpha-numeric code e.g. B1, C70, about 6ft above ground level, whilst the counterpart on the right hand side received the same code plus an "A" suffix e.g. B1A, C70A. On sections having bracket arm traction poles or additional poles for bridles supporting pull-offs on the outside of bends, the alpha-numeric sequence continued but without the matching partner on the opposite side of the road. A similar coding system had been used in tramway days, but there were detail differences. The entire system was renumbered once the trams had gone and the trolleybus network well established.

Code	Location (pole numbering as in the sequence of streets shown)	Highest No.
A	Lansdowne - Holdenhurst Road - Ashley Road - Boscombe	93
B	Lansdowne - Bath Road - Westover Road - Bournemouth Square	40
C	Cemetery Junction - Charminster - Castle Lane West (Broadway Hotel)	100
D	Five Ways - Charminster Avenue-Malvern Road	25
E	Fisherman's Walk loop (Southbourne Road and Parkwood Road)	11
F	Castle Lane West (Broadway Hotel) - Castle Lane East (Iford)	173
H	Fisherman's Walk - Beaufort Road - Cranleigh Road - Tuckton	88
I	Pokesdown Station - Christchurch Road- Barrack Road - Stour Road, Christchurch	111
L	Lansdowne Roundabout	Not known
M	Bournemouth Square - Winton - Moordown - Castle Lane West (Red Hill)	161

O	Cemetery Junction - Lansdowne Road-St. Paul's Road - Holdenhurst Road	32
P	Bournemouth Square - Christchurch Road - Pokesdown Station	157
Q	Ashley Road, Springbourne - Holdenhurst Road - Queen's Park Golf Pavilion	8
R	Bournemouth Square - Exeter Road - Bournemouth Pier - Royal Bath Hotel	28
S	Bournemouth Square	Not known
T	Wimborne Road (Winton Banks) - Wallisdown - Kinson Road - Columbia	170
W	Bournemouth Square - Poole Road - Westbourne, Seamoor Road	46
X	Pokesdown Station - Fisherman's Walk - Southbourne - Belle Vue Road - Tuckton - Stour Road - Christchurch Priory	191
Y	Holdenhurst Road - Central Depot, Southcote Road-Boscombe	65
Z	Castle Lane (Mallard Road) Depot	Not known

Poles supporting crossovers, junctions and turnouts had "J" suffixes, e.g. W86J. Turning circles and loops were distinguished by the addition of an "L" suffix to the normal route alpha-numeric code. The bracket arm traction poles along the left hand side of Oak Avenue and Stourvale Avenue making up the service 24 terminal loop at Jumper's Corner were accordingly coded 11L-118L. The prefix "T" was used to denote the Christchurch turntable, e.g. XT1.

There were exceptions in the vicinity of Bournemouth Square. The additional traction poles supporting the emergency turning circle at Horseshoe Common were given the same alpha-numeric codes as the adjacent poles on the main ("P") route plus a "Z" suffix. The circle was thus poled with P14Z, P31Z and P31ZA. The Hinton Road (The Quadrant) line which enabled trolleybuses from Avenue Road or Bournemouth Pier to turn back into Gervis Place to take up service from there was installed in August 1946 prior to the construction of the Bournemouth Square roundabout. It had only 2 or 3 poles and branched off Old Christchurch Road at P5 where the insulation at the frog also served as a section breaker and thus had no jumper bridging the gap. The first pole on the loop was P6A paired with P6 on the main line, then followed P6Z. The only other pole was "jointly" owned by route PL and carried the code P277AL, instead of P27ZAL, as presumably the painter left the bottom bar off the "Z".

The additional traction poles planted at roundabouts added to existing trolleybus routes upset the coding system. An "R" suffix was added rather than recode the entire route, e.g. at Iford the normal sequence between 143 and 146 was broken into by IR1-IR20 inclusive. The major roundabouts at Bournemouth Square (some 40 poles) and the Lansdowne had their own coding using the letters "S" and "L" respectively. The Bodorgan Road reversing triangle at the top of Richmond Hill employed poles M10B-M10G to avoid interrupting the existing numbering sequence all the way to Moordown.

The Strouden Park turning circle on Castle Lane prior to the roundabout was coded "FQ" instead of the more logical "FL" in preparation for the extension of wiring along Holdenhurst Road from Queen's Park to Castle Lane, Route "Q". On Route

On an unknown date in the late 1950s, Sunbeam MS2 no. 93 (ALJ967) joins the Lansdowne roundabout from Old Christchurch Road on its way to Tuckton Bridge with a service 23 working. Note the ornamental scrollwork on the strap holding the span wire to the traction pole behind the front dome of the trolleybus.

Photographer's name not recorded

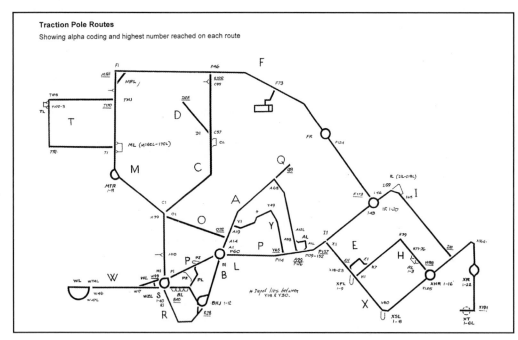

Traction Pole Routes
Showing alpha coding and highest number reached on each route

The finials were originally orange. Exceptionally the poles immediately in front of the Royal Bath Hotel (Route "B") and in the vicinity of Bournemouth Pier (Route "R") were painted white. In 1962 the poles in High Street, Christchurch, between the Pit Site roundabout and just past the Town Hall (XR7-X183 inclusive) were repainted grey to better blend with the character of the street. Also in the system's latter days a number of traction poles on the west side of Westover Road immediately in front of the Pavilion (B25, B26) were painted black relieved in orange to make them less obtrusive when the illuminated fountains in the Pavilion forecourt were operating.

"H", the Fisherman's Walk loop also received the non-standard pole route coding "E" as "HL" had already been used for the Carbery Avenue turning circle. This code would have been used for the Boscombe via Parkwood Road route authorised in the Bournemouth Corporation Act 1930, but it was never constructed.

Traction poles and bracket arms were painted leaf green which weathered down to a paler, almost olive grey, shade over the years. Repainting took place at regular intervals one route at a time, the work being recorded on a running list which the foreman painter entered when the work was complete.

Before European standard street signs were introduced those traction poles supporting notices or traffic lights received yellow or black and white bands up to a height of ca. 10ft. Poles A6A and A7A flanking the Central Fire Station on the south side of Holdenhurst Road were painted red from 6-11ft above the ground as a warning to traffic. In the war traction pole bases were painted white as an aid to black-out driving.

The narrow approach and sharp turn on to the Christchurch turntable and the lack of space in the yard itself for more than one vehicle at a time required the installation of a special signal

Sunbeam MS2 no. 215 (ALJ980) takes the sharp turn out of the Square roundabout and commences the steep climb up Richmond Hill

D.A.P. Janes

to show approaching trolleybuses if the terminal was already occupied. A skate on the overhead at pole X188 illuminated lamps on poles X189 and X190 indicating that the turntable section was occupied. When the trolleybus turned out of the yard, a second overhead contact extinguished the signal lamps. The original plans for this signalling arrangement included a set of breakers and switch to cut off power to a short section of line ensuring that no following trolleybus could reach the occupied turntable but this was subsequently deemed "overkill".

A similar signal facility was installed at the stop preceding the junction of Poole Road and Seamoor Road, Westbourne, to prevent trolleybuses bunching up in Poole Road prior to returning to Bournemouth Square in the years that many services were extended to Westbourne. This signal was removed in early 1964.

The conversion of the Bournemouth Square-Christchurch and the Cemetery Junction-Moordown routes from tram to trolleybus operation required the provision of separate trolleybus conductor wires along roads which would continue to be served by trams, albeit for just three weeks in the case of the Moordown route. Bournemouth's trams were equipped with swivel trolley heads which would have enabled their trolley poles to follow the trolleybus positive trolley wire located closer to the kerb, however, this was deemed impractical as a trolleybus would have rapidly caught up a slower-moving tram and been unable to pass it. This meant that it was necessary to suspend and maintain up to six trolley wires along much of these routes, i.e. two tram positive conductor wires and two pairs of trolleybus conductor wires, which together with fittings

imposed a weight of more than 350lb on each suspension point located every 40yd.

The successful interface of a trolleybus trolley wheel or slider head with the conductor wire was primarily dependent upon maintaining the suspension ears vertical to the trolley head. It was accordingly decided that on the wider portions of the route each pair of trolleybus trolley wires would be suspended from bracket arms fixed to traction poles on each side of the road and to terminate the span wires supporting the single tramway trolley wires at bolts fixed into the ends of the bracket arms. This resulted in the trolleybus conductor wire ears being maintained in a vertical position by the bracket arm bowstrings although the tramway conductor wires were fractionally higher above the top of the rails. On occasion this meant that either bracket arms had to be attached to existing traction poles where span wires were employed for the trams or that a second traction pole, equipped with a bracket arm, had to be planted on the opposite side of the road where a single pole with a bracket arm supporting both tram conductor wires was used. Where this occurred, once tramway operation had been abandoned, the bracket arms were progressively removed and the trolleybus conductor wires were supported by span wires.

Other than the above, single bracket arms were infrequently used on the Bournemouth system and primarily along roads having one-way wiring only, e.g. Stourvale Avenue, or in the few streets deemed too narrow for span wires, e.g. the west end of Old Christchurch Road. There were no examples of single bracket arms supporting two pairs of trolleybus conductor wires, i.e. both inbound and outbound, although single bracket

The unique gantry suspension arrangement on Tuckton Bridge provide a frame around Sunbeam MS2 no. 217 (ALJ993) as it crosses the River Stour into Bournemouth and onwards to the Square on 7 August 1959.
Photo courtesy of D.Ball, for the family of the late J.S. King

arms did support three wires in Southcote Road and the south end of Palmerston Road.

Once tramway overhead wiring had been cut down, single bracket arms were used on:

Charminster Road (poles supporting single bracket arms were planted on both sides of the road; they were replaced by span wire suspension later)

Christchurch Road, Pokesdown Station-Iford Bridge (poles supporting single bracket arms were planted on both sides of the road; they were replaced by span wire suspension later)

Crimea Road

Fir Vale Road

Gervis Place, north of Westover Road

Gladstone Road

Oak Avenue

Old Christchurch Road

Palmerston Road

Poole Road, Westbourne

Portman Road

St. Clement's Road

St. Peter's Road

St. Swithun's Road

Southcote Road

Square (at isolated locations prior to the construction of the roundabout)

Stourvale Avenue

Triangle

Westover Road

Wimborne Road, Winton (poles supporting single bracket arms were planted on both sides of the road; they were replaced by span wire suspension later)

Unlike Portsmouth, the closest neighbouring trolleybus system, Bournemouth did not use gantries or double bracket arms, where a steel tube was substituted for a span wire, the sole example being on Tuckton Bridge.

Bournemouth never used the catenary suspension system, pioneered by Nottingham, for its span wire construction as by 1934 it had been found that when several trolleybuses were running close together the combined upward pressure from the trolley poles could raise the trolley wires sufficiently to touch the span wires above and cause a short circuit. However, there were isolated examples of a supplementary span wire, strung at a higher level above the main span wire and equipped with a short dropper, being used to support the additional weight of insulated crossings, etc., e.g. at the Broadway Hotel junction of Castle Lane West with Charminster Road.

Wall-mounted rosettes were infrequently used, the only known locations being:

Castle Lane (Mallard Road) Depot, attached to the depot building

Central Depot, Southcote Road, attached to the Generating Station and possibly other buildings

Old Christchurch Road, attached to Beales store (still in place in 2016)

The chronology below shows the main dates for the erection, modification and removal of trolleybus overhead equipment in traction pole route code order. The dates when sections of line were anchored off, prior to removal; dates of removal of pole straps and other pole fitting; and dates of removal of section boxes, feeder cables and other ancillary equipment, are not included. Where it has proved possible to quote distances, these are based on average out/inwards distances calculated by the Department on 19 March 1959. On this date total route mileage was considered to be 29.04 miles plus 1 mile of depot wiring.

The use of David Chalk's records in the compilation of the Overhead Equipment: Route Chronology that follows is gratefully acknowledged.

BUT9641T no. 246 (KLJ346), which was subsequently preserved, reverses gingerly into Luckham Road at the Broadway Hotel, CharminsterRoad reversing triangle, terminus of service 28.

Roger G. Funnell (courtesy Mrs D. Funnell and Rodney Funnell)

At the junction of Columbia Road with Kinson Road, Sunbeam MF2B no. 263 (WRU263) reaches the nominal terminus of services 30 and 31. Having arrived here as a 31 working, no. 263 will continue through Wallisdown as a service 30 to Winton and potentially onwards to the Square and Triangle.

Roger G. Funnell (courtesy Mrs D. Funnell and Rodney Funnell)

Sunbeam MF2B no. 278 (YLJ278) pulls away from the Jumpers terminus in Stourvale Avenue before turning into the westbound carriageway of Barrack Road and crossing Iford Bridge back into Bournemouth on a service 24 journey to the Square.

Roger G. Funnell (courtesy Mrs D. Funnell and Rodney Funnell)

Overhead Equipment: Route Chronology

Dates in italics are assumed dates but cannot be confirmed

Route Code	Route	Opened to traffic	Dates of removal	
			Wiring	Poles
A	**Lansdowne - Boscombe**			
	via Holdenhurst Road, Ashley Road (1.98 miles)	22.06.1934		
	Reversing triangle at Capstone Road junction with Holdenhurst Road	22.06.1934	1946	1946
	Old Christchurch Road at Lansdowne, EB frog set-back to Old	18.03.1945	27.01.1947	
	Christchurch Road, junction with Stafford Road (services 25 & 25A)			
	Second pair of EB wires around north side of roundabout from Old	12.03.1960	27.03.1966	
	Christchurch Road, junction with Stafford Road, around the Lansdowne and into Holdenhurst Road (service 25) introduced			
	Holdenhurst Road turnout frog and crossover St. Paul's Road		21.01.1964	
	Holdenhurst Road trail frog St. Paul's Road		23.01.1964	
	Route A last used 12.09.1965			
	Holdenhurst Road (Lansdowne - Ashley Road)		01.1966 - 24.04.1966	02.1966 - 07.1966
	Ashley Road (entire length)		01.1966 - 04.1966	02.1966 - 07.1966
AL	Christchurch Road - Ashley Road, Boscombe, one-way loop	22.06.1934	01.1966 - 04.1966	02.1966 - 07.1966
	Portman Road and Gladstone Road			
B	**Lansdowne - Bournemouth Square**			
	One-way WB via Bath Road, Westover Road, Gervis Place (0.64 miles)	08.05.1937		
	Emergency link from Gervis Place into Old Christchurch Road	13.04.1941	03.05.1953	
	EB wiring Royal Bath Hotel to Lansdowne	07.04.1950		
	Route B last used 20.04.1969			
	Bath Road (Lansdowne to Westover Road)		20 - 30.08.1969	07 - 21.10.1969
	Westover Road (entire length)		27.04.1969	02.01.1970

Route Code	Route	Opened to traffic	Dates of removal	
			Wiring	Poles
BHJ	Bath Road junction with Westover Road at Royal Bath Hotel	07.04.1950	03.08.1969	20.05.1970 & 22.05.1970
BL	Gervis Place, single loop at loading point	23.12.1935		
	Single loop divided into two at western end	04.1941	10.1965	
	Gervis Place loops modified to provide three loops	30.03.1947		
	Second (middle) loop further divided into two (totalling four)	1954		
	Second and third loops combined again into one (totalling two)	13.- 14.05.1967	04.05.1969	09.01.1970 - 23.01.1970
C	**Cemetery Junction - Castle Lane West, Broadway Hotel**			
	via Charminster Road (2 miles)	23.08.1935	12.1966 - 01.1967	05.1967 - 22.11.1967
	Reversing triangle at Luckham Road junction with Charminster Road	23.08.1935	12.1966 - 01.1967	05.1967 - 22.11.1967
	Reversing triangle at Court Road junction with Charminster Road		09.05.1961	05.1961
	Route C last used 25.09.1966			
CL	Five Ways, junction with Queen's Park Avenue, one-way loop	23.08.1935	12.1966 - 01.1967	05.1967 - 22.11.1967
D	**Five Ways - Malvern Road**			
	via Charminster Avenue (0.46 miles) with a reversing triangle at the	05.04.1937	07.1966 & 08.1966	10.1966 & 11.1966
	junction of Charminster Avenue with Malvern Road			
	Route D last used 03.04.1965			
E	**Fisherman's Walk**, Southbourne Road and Parkwood Road, one-way	16.08.1948		
	loop NB from the junction with Beaufort Road to the junction with			
	Seabourne Road (0.07 miles)			
	Last used by service trolleybuses in original form 27 September 1967			
	Reconstructed for vehicles travelling in the opposite direction, i.e. SB,	05.10.1967	03.09.1969	05.03.1970 & 06.03.1970
	as part of the Southbourne Traffic Management Scheme			
	Route E last used 20.04.1969			

Route Code	Route	Opened to traffic	Dates of removal — Wiring	Dates of removal — Poles
F	**Castle Lane**			
	Castle Lane West, junction with Wimborne Road, Moordown to junction	19.10.1938	01.1967 - 03.1967	10.1968 - 01.1969
	with Charminster Road, Broadway Hotel (0.67 miles)			
	Castle Lane West, junction with Charminster Road, Broadway Hotel to	15.10.1951		
	Castle Lane East, junction with Christchurch Road, Iford (2.36 miles)			
	Castle Lane West, junction with Charminster Road, Broadway Hotel to		01.03. - 15.03.1968 &	10.1968 - 07.01.1970
	Castle Lane West, junction with Mallard Road		12.05. - 16.05.1968	
	Castle Lane West, junction with Mallard Road to Castle Lane East,		27.05.1969 &	17.08. - 14.09.1970 &
	junction with Christchurch Road, Iford		17.03.1970 - 28.08.1970	16.04.1971 - 20.06.1971
	Route F Castle Lane West, junction with Wimborne Road, Moordown to junction with Mallard Road last used 25.09.1966			
	Route F Castle Lane West, junction with Mallard Road to Castle Lane East, junction with Christchurch Road, Iford last used 20.04.1969			
FQR	Strouden Park turning circle, junction of Castle Lane West with	23.05.1953	19.12.1962 & 20.12.1962	
	Holdenhurst Road (0.13 miles)			
FR	Strouden Park, Cooper Dean roundabout, junction of Castle Lane West	27.05.1963		04.1971 - 06.1971
	with Holdenhurst Road			
	Connecting link on west side of roundabout	12.07.1963	23.09.1966	
	West side trail frog		12.03.1967	
	West side facing frog		26.03.1967	
	Remainder of roundabout		03.1970 - 08.1970	
G	Not used			
H	**Fisherman's Walk - Tuckton**	On the following dates:	On the following dates:	On the following dates:
	Tuckton, Tuckton Road junction with Belle Vue Road to Cranleigh Road,	05.10.1947	}	}
	junction with Carbery Avenue, via Tuckton Road		}	}
			} 3 September 1969	}

Route Code	Route	Opened to traffic	Dates of removal	
			Wiring	Poles
	Fisherman's Walk to Cranleigh Road, junction with Carbery Avenue	16.08.1948	} 1-9 May 1969	} 5 - 27 April 1970
	via Beresford Road, Beaufort Road and Cranleigh Road (1.56 miles)		} 8 - 28 August 1969	} 2 - 30 April 1971
	Additional frogs inserted at Tuckton, Tuckton Road junction with Belle	05.12.1950	} 1 -24 August 1969	} 4 - 16 May 1971
	Vue Road, to enable trolleybuses to proceed to/from Stour Road and		} 8 - 17 October 1969	}
	Christchurch		}	}
	Various changes at both ends of Beresford Road, Fisherman's Walk to	10.1967	}	}
	accommodate the Southbourne Traffic Management Scheme		}	}
	Route H last used 20.04.1969			
HL	Cranleigh Road, junction with Carbery Avenue one-way loop	05.10.1947		
	Additional frogs at turning circle to enable trolleybuses from the east, i.e.	26.09.1948		
	Fisherman's Walk, to turn			
I	**Pokesdown - Iford Bridge**			
	via Christchurch Road, from its junction with Seabourne Road to Iford	25.03.1935	27.05.1969 &	21.- 30.09.1970
	Bridge (1 mile)		24.04.- 12.06.1970	
	Iford Bridge turning circle	25.03.1935	20.05.1961	05. & 06.1961
	Iford Bridge to Stour Road, Christchurch	22.07.1943	22.05. - 26.06.1969	01.- 24.07.1969
	via Christchurch Road and Barrack Road			
	Additional frogs and wiring installed at the junction of Stour Road EB	01.08.1946		
	with Barrack Road WB and vice versa			
	Additional frogs and wiring installed at the junction of Christchurch Road	29.12.1967		
	WB with Seabourne Road EB, Pokesdown			
	Left hand facing frog in Christchurch Road WB installed 05./06.12.1967			
	Used by special party trolleybus	31.12.1967		
	Regular use by empty trolleybuses from Castle Lane (Mallard Road)	01.01.1968		
	Depot taking up service at Fisherman's Walk			
	Route I last used 20 April 1969			

Route Code	Route	Opened to traffic	Dates of removal Wiring	Poles
IL	Jumpers terminal loop, one-way clockwise from junction of Christchurch	07.08.1944	20.06.1969	01. - 04.07.1969
	Road with Oak Avenue, along Oak Avenue and Stourvale Avenue to			
	junction with Christchurch Road (0.19 miles)			
IR	Iford roundabout, junction of Christchurch Road with Castle Lane East		30.08.1970	04. - 15.09.1970
	South side for WB trolleybuses	20.05.1956		
	Entire roundabout	02.12.1956		
	Additional frogs and wiring to enable trolleybuses to turn from			
	Christchurch Road EB into Castle Lane East WB	02.07.1965		
J	Not used			
K	Not used			
L	**Lansdowne roundabout,** junction of Bath Road, Christchurch Road,			
	Holdenhurst Road, Old Christchurch Road and Lansdowne Road	27.01.1947	20.07.1969	21.12.1969 & 11.01.1970
	Second pair of EB wires around north side of roundabout from Old	12.03.1960	27.03.1966	
	Christchurch Road, junction with Stafford Road, around the Lansdowne			
	and into Holdenhurst Road (service 25) introduced			
	Facing (switch) frogs in Old Christchurch Road, junction with Stafford			
	Road (Trinity Church) removed		11.11.1965	
	Facing (switch) frog on roundabout for Holdenhurst Road removed		26.05.1968	
	Route L last used 20.04.1969			
M	**Richmond Hill - Moordown**			
	via Wimborne Road from bottom of Richmond Hill to Moordown Depot	07.06.1935		
	Turning circle at Cemetery Junction	23.08.1935	23.10.1960 & 6/10.11.1960	
	Reversing triangle at Victoria Park Road (Brassey Road)	07.06.1935	29.05.1948	06.1948
	Moordown Depot	1935	07.1953	07.1953
	Frogs and crossings outside Moordown Depot	1935	08.1953	08.1953

Route Code	Route	Opened to traffic	Dates of removal	
			Wiring	Poles
	Extension along Wimborne Road from Moordown Depot to Wimborne Road, junction with Redhill Crescent (reversing triangle)	28.06.1935	01-03.1967	10.1966 - 18.09.1968
	Richmond Hill	07.06.1935	09.1966 - 05.12.1966	05.1967
	Cemetery Junction, Wimborne Road/Lansdowne Road facing frog and crossover	28.06.1935	07.10.1964	
	Cemetery Junction, Wimborne Road/Lansdowne Road trail frog	28.06.1935	08.10.1964	
	Wimborne Road, Richmond Hill - St. Luke's Church, Winton	07.06.1935	} 10.1966 - 12.1966,	10.1966 - 18.09.1968
	Cemetery Junction	28.06.1935	} 30.10.1966 &	10.1966 - 18.09.1968
	Winton Banks junction (Alma Road, Crimea Road, Talbot Road, Wimborne Road)	07.06.1935	} 22.01.1967	10.1966 - 18.09.1968
	Reversing triangle at Wimborne Road, junction with Redhill Crescent	28.06.1935	11.11.1950	11.1950
	Reversing triangle replaced by loop inside Moordown Depot	14.08.1950	07.1953	07.1953
	Reversing triangle at Wimborne Road, junction with Redhill Crescent reinstalled	26.07.1953	01-03.1967	10.1966 - 18.09.1968
	Extension along Wimborne Road from Wimborne Road, junction with Redhill Crescent to Castle Lane West (including frog for Bear Cross extension)	11.03.1937	01-03.1967	10.1966 - 18.09.1968
	Emergency reversing triangle, top of Richmond Hill at Bodorgan Road	30.06.1945	10.1966 - 12.1966	10.1966 - 18.09.1968
	Route M last used 25 September 1966			
MFL	Lawford Road, one-way from Wimborne Road to Castle Lane West as part of an anti-clockwise terminal loop (0.2 miles)	11.03.1937	05.1967	04.10.1968
	Route MFL last used 25 September 1966			
ML	Winton (Winton Banks), one-way clockwise loop from Wimborne Road via Crimea Road, Waterloo Road and Alma Road	07.06.1935	03.1967	23.11.1967

Route Code	Route	Opened to traffic	Dates of removal Wiring	Dates of removal Poles
	Route ML last used 25 September 1966			
MTR	Roundabout at junction of Wimborne Road with Talbot Avenue	11.03.1961	10.1966 - 12.1966	10.1966 - 18.09.1968
	(wiring realignment)			
N	Not used			
O	**Holdenhurst Road - Cemetery Junction**			
	via St. Paul's Road, Lansdowne Road (0.7 miles)	28.06.1935		
	St.Paul's Road except for c. 50yd short of Cemetery Junction and	28.06.1935	30.12.1963 - 02.1964	01.1964 - 02.1964
	Lansdowne Road retained for traction power feeder purposes			
	Remaining 50yd in Lansdowne Road	28.06.1935	10.1964	11.1964
	Route O last used 29.09.1963			
P	**Bournemouth Square - Horseshoe Common - Lansdowne**	22.06.1934	14.09.1969 - 01.10.1969	} 24.06.1970; 18.11.1970 -
	via Old Christchurch Road one-way EB to Horseshoe Common;			} 29.11.1970; 02.03.1971 -
	Horseshoe Common - Lansdowne via Old Christchurch Road in both			} 21.03.1971
	directions			
	One-way emergency loop line Gervis Place to Old Christchurch Road	12.04.1941	02-03.05.1953	
	Extension Lansdowne - Pokesdown Station via Christchurch Road	25.03.1935	18.01.1970 - 28.01.1970 &	22.03.1971 - 29.03.1971 &
			04.02.1970 - 27.02.1970	02.04.1971 - 21.04.1971
	Boscombe (Pokesdown) Depot	1945	01.1968	
	Depot wiring, access and interior, last used 31.12.1967			
	Frogs and crossover outside Boscombe (Pokesdown) Depot	1945	21.01.1968	
	Christchurch Road, junction with Palmerston Road facing frog WB	25.03.1935	14.09.1965	
	Christchurch Road, junction with Palmerston Road, trail frog and	22.06.1934	15.09.1965	
	crossover			
	Old Christchurch Road at Lansdowne, EB frog set-back to Old	18.03.1945	27.01.1947	

Route Code	Route	Opened to traffic	Dates of removal	
			Wiring	Poles
	Christchurch Road, junction with Stafford Road (services 25 & 25A)			
	Second pair of EB wires around north side of roundabout from Old	12.03.1960	27.03.1966	
	Christchurch Road, junction with Stafford Road, around the Lansdowne and into Holdenhurst Road (service 25) introduced			
	Second pair of EB wires last used 12.09.1965			
	Switch frog in Old Christchurch Road removed	12.03.1960	11.11.1965	
	Parallel EB wiring introduced in Christchurch Road, Boscombe, to enable service 25 vehicles to pass those waiting at "Main Road" stop	26.04.1953	28.01.1968	
	Christchurch Road, junction with Portman Road, frog and crossing	25.03.1935	14.01.1968	
	Route P last used 20.04.1969			
PL	Horseshoe Common - Gervis Place, junction with Westover Road one-way WB via Fir Vale Road and St. Peter's Road	22.06.1934	02.11.1969 - 08.07.1970	} 04.09.1970. - 15.09.1970
	St. Peter's Road, junction with Hinton Road		29.10.1969	} 04.09.1970. - 15.09.1970
PLZ	One-way loop in Hinton Road (The Quadrant) from Old Christchurch Road into Gervis Place (0.04 miles)	01.08.1946	21.10.1969	01.07.1970 & 03.07.1970
PZ	Emergency turning circle at Horseshoe Common, Old Christchurch Road	01.05.1942	12.09.1969	22.11.1970
	Horseshoe Common frogs and crossover	01.05.1942	03.10.1969	22.11.1970
Q	Holdenhurst Road, Ashley Road - Queen's Park Golf Pavilion			
	via Holdenhurst Road from its junction with Ashley Road to its junction with Littledown Avenue including a turning circle at Littledown Avenue (0.18 miles)	20.10.1934	01.1966 - 07.1966	02.1966 - 07.1966
	Route Q last used 12.09.1965			

Route Code	Route	Opened to traffic	Dates of removal	
			Wiring	Poles
R	**Bath Road, Royal Bath Hotel - Bournemouth Square**			
	via Bath Road, Bournemouth Pier Approach, Exeter Road from the junction with Westover Road to Bournemouth Pier in both directions, one-way WB from Bournemouth Pier to the Square (0.55 miles)	07.04.1950		
	Bournemouth Pier Approach	07.04.1950	13.07.1969	25.-26.09.1969
	Bournemouth Pier to Square via Exeter Road running wires	07.04.1950	27.07.1969	01.-05.10.1969
	Bournemouth Pier to Square via Exeter Road span wires	07.04.1950	01.08.1969	15.-16.12.1969
	Westover Road - Bournemouth Pier via Bath Road	07.04.1950	10.08.1969	01.01.1970
	Route R last used 20.04.1969			
S	**Bournemouth Square**			
	Basic layout, turning circle from west for experimental trolleybus route	13.05.1933	21.06.1934	
	Through wiring EB to Old Christchurch Road and WB from Gervis Place with a turn back loop from the east added	22.06.1934	29.03.1947	
	Wiring to/from Richmond Hill with turning circle around shelter added	07.06.1935	29.03.1947	
	Loop added at loading point outside entrance to Upper Pleasure Gardens	1937	29.03.1947	
	Loop added at loading point on northside of Square (Bourne Avenue)	1938 or 1939	29.03.1947	
	Existing wiring layout replaced by traffic roundabout thereby linking Main Road and Side Route wiring at the Square for the first time	30.03.1947		14.- 22.01.1970
	Additional line for NB Side Route services added on west side (Central Pleasure Gardens) side of the roundabout eliminating the switch frog at the bottom of Richmond Hill	29.05.1960	09.1966	14.- 22.01.1970
	Wiring on east, south and west sides		15.06.1969	}
	North side pull-offs		02.07.1969	}
	All remaining wiring at Bournemouth Square		06.07.1969	} 14.- 22.01.1970
	Poles on the roundabout island itself removed by Borough Engineer			30.11.1969
	Route S last used 20.04.1969			

Route Code	Route	Opened to traffic	Dates of removal	
			Wiring	Poles
T	**Wimborne Road, Winton (Winton Banks) - Columbia Road**			
	via Talbot Road, Talbot Avenue, Wallisdown Road, Kinson Road,	15.04.1938	03.1967 - 19.02.1968	05.1968 - 03.1969
	including a turning circle at the junction of Kinson Road with Columbia			
	Road (Wonderholme Parade) (1.9 miles)			
	Extension junction of Kinson Road with Columbia Road - junction	08.04.1939	03.1967 - 19.02.1968	05.1968 - 03.1969
	of Ensbury Park Road with Wimborne Road, Moordown			
	via Columbia Road, Ensbury Park Road (1.15 miles)			
TL	with additional switch frogs giving access to the turning circle at the			
	junction of Kinson Road with Columbia Road (Wonderholme Parade)			
	Route T last used 25.09.1966			
TMJ	Junction Ensbury Park Road with Wimborne Road, Moordown	08.04.1939	03.1967 - 19.02.1968	05.1968 - 03.1969
U	Not used			
V	Not used			
W	**Bournemouth Square - Westbourne**			
	via Commercial Road one-way WB to Poole Hill	13.05.1933		
	via Triangle (west side) and Avenue Road one-way EB			
	Poole Hill - Seamoor Road, Westbourne via Poole Road in both			
	directions (1.15 miles);			
	Second pair of WB wires in Commercial Road to Triangle (east side)	06.04.1947		
	Route W wiring in Poole Hill, Poole Road, Seamoor Road, Triangle			
	(west side) and nearside line in Commercial Road last used 12.09.1965			
	Triangle - Westbourne via Commercial Road, Poole Hill and Poole Road	13.05.1933	30.10.1965 - 11.1965	12.1965
	Triangle (west side)	13.05.1933	11.1965	12.1965
	Commercial Road WB facing frog (Triangle or Westbourne)	07.1936	31.10.1965	

Route Code	Route	Opened to traffic	Dates of removal	
			Wiring	Poles
	Commercial Road WB nearside line	13.05.1933	11.1965	
	Avenue Road and remaining equipment in Commercial Road between	13.05.1933	} 11.05.1969;	} 21.08.1969;
	the Square and the Triangle		} 01 - 22.06 1969;	} 26-29.04.1970
			} 25.07.1969	} 26-29.05.; 15-16.06.1970
WEL	Triangle (east side) loop between Commercial Road and Avenue Road	07.1936	06.1969	04.1970 - 06.1970
	with switch frog in Commercial Road and trail frog in Avenue Road			
	Loop through Triangle parking area added with frogs on Triangle east	23.05.1948	06.1969	04.1970 - 06.1970
	side			
	Route WEL last used 12.09.1965			
WL	Seamoor Road, Westbourne			
	One-way clockwise terminal loop from Poole Road, junction with	13.05.1933	11.1965	12.1965
	Surrey Road South to Poole Road, junction with Seamoor Road (one-			
	way road system used by all traffic)			
WL	Three loops added at loading points in Avenue Road EB	30.03.1947		
X	Pokesdown Station - Fisherman's Walk			
	via Seabourne Road (0.5 miles)	21.11.1935		
	Extension Fisherman's Walk to Southbourne Cross Roads	23.12.1935		
	via Southbourne Grove, Southbourne Road, Belle Vue Road			
XSL	Turning circle at the junction of Southbourne Overcliff Drive and	23.12.1935	30.10.1969	04.-06.01.1970
	St. Catherine's Road with Belle Vue Road (1 mile)			
	Extension Southbourne Cross Roads to Christchurch, Church	08.04.1936		
	Street via Belle Vue Road, Foxholes Road, Belle Vue Road, Stour Road,			
	Bargates, High Street, Church Street (2 miles)			
	Pokesdown - Tuckton: Seabourne Road, Southbourne Grove,		} 23-29.10.1969; 05-28.11.	} 02. & 12.09.1970; 22-29.
	Southbourne Road, Belle Vue Road, Foxholes Road, Belle Vue Road		} 1969; 03-30.12.1969	} 11.1970; 28.03.1971
			} 07-30.01.1970; 12.03.	}

Route Code	Route	Opened to traffic	Dates of removal — Wiring	Poles
	Christchurch, High Street		} 1970; 01-17.04.1970	}
	Christchurch, Bargates	08.04.1936	18.05.1969	04.-31.08.1969
	Christchurch, Stour Road (Bargates to Barrack Road)	08.04.1936	06.06.1969	04.-31.08.1969
	Christchurch, Stour Road (Barrack Road to Tuckton Bridge)	08.04.1936	05.06.1969	30.-31.07.1969
	Tuckton Bridge (last wiring in Christchurch)	08.04.1936	19-30.06.1969 / 06. & 08.08.1969	01.-02.09.1969
	Reversing triangle added at Tuckton, Tuckton Road, junction with Belle Vue Road	08.11.1943	05.10.1947	
	Trolleybus parking area added in Seabourne Road at rear of Boscombe (Pokesdown) Depot. Parking area last used 30.09.1951	12.03.1951	03.1952	03.1952
	Trolleybuses adopted the one-way system used by all other traffic at the Pit Site, Barrack Road, Christchurch	28.08.1955		
	Pit Site wiring modified to conform with roundabout changes for the new A35 Christchurch by-pass road	09.08.1959	18.05.1969 & 08.06.1969	08.1969
	Additional frogs and wiring installed at the junction of Christchurch Road WB with Seabourne Road EB, Pokesdown. Trail frog in Seabourne Road EB installed 12./13.12.1967	29.12.1967		
	Regular use by empty trolleybuses from Castle Lane (Mallard Road) Depot taking up service at Fisherman's Walk	01.01.1968		
	Southbourne Traffic Management Scheme. Wiring changes in Fisherman's Walk area for experimental one-way system completed by 08.10.1967. Experimental traffic management scheme introduced 12.11.1967. Experimental traffic management scheme discontinued 10.02.1968. Trolleybuses reverted to two-way working in Seabourne Road 12.02.1968	27.10.1967		
	Route X last used 20.04.1969			

Route Code	Route	Opened to traffic	Dates of removal	
			Wiring	Poles
XFL	Fisherman's Walk, Wentworth Avenue turning circle	21.11.1935	} 19.09.1969; 31.10.1969;	} 08 - 22.04.1970; 16 - 28.
			} 16.11.1969	} 07.1970; 10 - 13.08.1970
	Route XFL last used 04.10.1967			
XHR	Tuckton roundabout			
	Roundabout at junction of Belle Vue Road, Stour Road and Tuckton Road	30.06.1963	06.09.1970	04.04.1971
	on west side of Tuckton Bridge replacing conventional three-way junction			
	Route XHR last used 20.04.1969			
XTL	Turntable in the former coach yard of the Dolphin Hotel, Church Street,	19.06.1936	06.06.1969	04 - 31.08.1969
	Christchurch			
Y	**Holdenhurst Road - Christchurch Road**			
	via St. Swithun's Road, Southcote Road, through Central Depot, St.	22.06.1934	06.1965 - 09.1965	10.1965
	Clement's Road, Palmerston Road, using a common positive wire			
	between Holdenhurst Road and the east entrance of Central Depot and			
	for a short distance at the south end of Palmerston Road, and single bi-			
	directional wiring in St. Clement's Road and the remainder of Palmerston			
	Road (1 mile), including depot wiring (0.43 miles)			
	Route Y last used 07.06.1965			
Z	**Castle Lane West - Castle Lane (Mallard Road) Depot**			
	via Mallard Road (0.1 miles)	26.07.1953	23.04.1969 & 24.08.1970	01 - 03.09.1970
	All depot and workshop wiring (0.48 miles)	26.07.1953		
	Note: traction poles on this route never received alpha-numeric codes			
	Castle Lane (Mallard Road) Depot lines reduced from three to two	26.07.1953	11.1966	
	Castle Lane (Mallard Road) Depot remainder of lines	26.07.1953	12 - 18.01.1971	12.05.1971 - 08.08.1971
	Route Z last used 22.04.1969			

APPENDIX K

FARES, FARE TABLES AND TICKETS

Fares

The electric tramways introduced a system of overlapping penny stages, averaging just under one mile in length, supplemented by a range of reduced workmen's and discounted return fares. The trolleybuses adopted a similar stage structure whilst, in principle, the trolleybus fare stages were the same as those on the tram services they replaced. The first proper fare tables only appeared in the January 1937 public timetable. Thereafter detailed fare tables were included in each issue of a combined fare and timetable, which later developed into two separate booklets, separate sheets and notices on the vehicles being used for immediate amendments.

Fares applicable on Bournemouth's trams and trolleybuses were stipulated in the appropriate parliamentary legislation, namely the Bournemouth Corporation Tramways Order, 1900 and the Bournemouth Corporation Act, 1930. They could be amended upon application to the MoT, subject to the MoT's approval. Motor bus fares and licensing were the responsibility of the County Borough Council until the Road Traffic Act, 1930 came into force. Thereafter motor bus fares and time tables, amongst many other features of passenger road transport operation, were subject to the approval of the MoT's Traffic Commissioner for the South-Eastern Area. As many of BCT's motor bus and trolleybus services operated along a common route, the Transport Committee adopted a policy of standardising fare scales whichever mode was employed. Later, in 1954, further legislation enabled area Traffic Commissioners, when considering fare applications from motor bus operators, to ensure that any discrepancies between fares and charges on an undertaking's motorbus and trolleybus services were reduced or eliminated. This had no effect on fare protection agreements, e.g. between BCT and H&D.

At their meeting of 22 February 1935, the Transport Committee considered fares and fare stages for the further trolleybus services proposed at that time, recommending that the time up to which return fares could be issued should be extended from 8.30am to 8.45am. However, as far as is known the time remained unchanged at 8.30am. Service numbers had clearly already been assigned.

In the majority of cases, the fares were the same or somewhat less than those charged on the trams but considerably cheaper than the motorbus fare applicable between the same two points.

21 Bournemouth Square-Christchurch

Ordinary Fares:-

Sqaure and Lansdowne	Id
Lansdsowne and Boscombe Arcade	Id
Boscombe Arcade and Parkwood Road	Id
Parkwood Road and Fisherman's Walk	Id
Fisherman's Walk and Cross Roads	Id
Cross Roads and Tuckton Bridge West	Id
Tuckton Bridge West and Tuckton Bridge East	Id
Tuckton Bridge East and Christchurch	Id

Workmen's Fares and Returns:-	Workmen's	Returns
Square and Boscombe Arcade	Id	2d
Boscombe Arcade and Parkwood Road	Id	2d
Parkwood Road and Fisherman's Walk	Id	2d
Fisherman's Walk and Cross Roads	Id	2d
Cross Roads and Tuckton Bridge West	Id	2d
Tuckton Bridge West and Tuckton Bridge East	-	-
Tuckton Bridge East and Christchurch and vice versa	I¹/₂d	2d

25 Westbourne-Boscombe, Ashley Road via Bournemouth Square and Holdenhurst Road

Ordinary Fares:-

Westbourne and Square	Id
Square and Lansdowne	Id
Lansdowne and Capstone Road	Id
Capstone Road and Ashley Road Terminus	Id

537

Square and Capstone Road	1¹/₂d
Lansdowne and Queen's Park Corner	1¹/₂d
Central Station and Ashley Road Terminus	1¹/₂d
Westbourne and Lansdowne	2d
Square and Queen's Park Corner	2d
Lansdowne and Ashley Road Terminus	2d
Westbourne and Capstone Road	2¹/₂d
Square and Ashley Road Terminus	2¹/₂d
Westbourne and Queen's Park Corner	3d
Westbourne and Ashley Road Terminus and vice versa	3¹/₂d

Workmen's Fares and Returns:-	Workmen's	Returns
Westbourne and Lansdowne	1d	
Square and Capstone Road	1d	
Lansdowne and Ashley Road Terminus	1d	
Westbourne and Capstone Road	1¹/₂d	
Square and Ashley Road Terminus	1¹/₂d	
Westbourne and Ashley Road Terminus and vice versa	2d	

26 Bournemouth Square-Moordown via Wimborne Road

Ordinary Fares:-

Square and Cemetery Junction	1d
Top of Richmond Hill and Talbot Avenue	1d
Cemetery Junction and Peter's Hill	1d
Talbot Avenue and Brassey Road	1d
Peter's Hill and Moordown Post Office or Depot	1d
Brassey Road and Moordown (Castle Lane Jn.)	1d
Square and Peter's Hill	1¹/₂d
Cemetery Junction and Moordown PO or Depot	1¹/₂d
Talbot Avenue and Moordown (Castle Lane Jn)	1¹/₂d
Square and Brassey Road	2d
Cemetery Junction and Moordown (Castle Lane)	2d
Square and Moordown Post Office or Depot and vice versa	2¹/₂d

Workmen's Fares and Returns:-	Workmen's	Returns
Cemetery Junction and Moordown PO or Depot	1d	2d
Square and Brassey Road	1d	2d
Talbot Avenue and Moordown (Castle Lane Jn.)	1d	2d
Square and Moordown Post Office or Depot	1¹/₂d	3d
Top of Richmond Hill and Moordown (Castle Lane)	1¹/₂d	3d
Square and Moordown (Castle Lane Junction) and vice versa	2d	4d

28 Bournemouth Square-Castle Lane (Broadway Hotel) via Charminster Road

Ordinary Fares:-

Square and Cemetery Junction	1d
Top of Richmond Hill and King's Road	1d
Cemetery Junction and Five Ways	1d
King's Road and Court Road	1d
Five Ways and Castle Lane	1d
Square and King's Road	1¹/₂d
Top of Richmond Hill and Five Ways	1¹/₂d
Cemetery Junction and Castle Lane	1¹/₂d
Square and Court Road	2d
Square and Castle Lane	2¹/₂d
Special Transfer:	
King's Road and Holdenhurst Road Junction and vice versa	1d

Workmen's Fares and Returns:-	Workmen's	Returns
Square and Five Ways	1d	2d
Top of Richmond Hill and Court Road	1d	2d
Cemetery Junction and Castle Lane	1d	2d
Square and Castle Lane and vice versa	1¹/₂d	3d

27 Lansdowne-Moordown via St. Paul's Road and Wimborne Road

Ordinary Fares:-

Lansdowne and Cemetery Junction	1d
Cemetery Junction and Peter's Hill	1d
Peter's Hill and Moordown Post Office or Depot	1d
Talbot Avenue and Brassey Road	1d

Holdenhurst Road Junction and Talbot Avenue	1d	
Brassey Road and Moordown (Castle Lane Jn)	1d	
Lansdowne and Peter's Hill	1½d	
Cemetery Junction and Moordown PO or Depot	1½d	
Talbot Avenue and Moordown (Castle Lane Jn.)	1½d	
Cemetery Junction and Moordown (Castle Lane)	2d	
Lansdowne and Brassey Road	2d	
Lansdowne and Moordown Post Office or Depot	2½d	
Lansdowne and Moordown (Castle Lane Jn.) and vice versa	3d	

Workmen's Fares and Returns:-	Workmen's	Returns
Lansdowne and Brassey Road	1d	2d
Cemetery Junction and Moordown PO or Depot	1d	2d
Talbot Avenue and Moordown (Castle Lane Jn.)	1d	2d
Lansdowne and Moordown Post Office or Depot	1½d	3d
Holdenhurst Road Junction and Moordown (Castle Lane Junction) and vice versa	2d	4d

Return Fares

Return tickets at reduced fares were issued to any passenger on request boarding any trolleybus at any place at which the trolleybus should be according to the timetable in force before and including 8.45am on any day, excepting Sundays, Christmas Day, Good Friday and Bank Holidays.

Return tickets were available for return journeys at any time on day of issue only, within the same stage only.

Fares: 2d for any 1d workmen's stage
3d for any 1½d workmen's stage
4d for any 2d workmen's stage

Conditions:
The tickets were not transferable.
The tickets were issued subject to the Corporation Bye-laws.
Through tickets only issued and accepted on trolleybuses.
Return tickets if mutilated were not accepted on the return journey.

Workmen's Fares

Workmen's hours: On weekdays, but not on Sundays, Christmas Day, Good Friday or Bank Holidays, before 8am; between 12 noon and 2pm, Saturdays only; other days between 4.30pm and 6pm from 1 November to 28 February, and between 5pm and 6.30pm from 1 March to 31 October.

The Bournemouth Corporation Act 1930 required that the Corporation continued to offer "cheap fares for the labouring classes", as required by section 33 of the Bournemouth Corporation Tramways Order 1900, on the trolleybus services replacing trams. Periodic reviews of these workmen's fares were permitted, the maximum applicable fare being subject to approval by the MoT. Reduced workmen's fares were available to all passengers, there being no discrimination between those wearing overalls and others despite the wording of the Act, but from April 1935 only for single journeys. Thus, return fares at double the workmen's fare became the practical solution for the daily journey to and from work. Workmen's fares were abolished on 30 November 1952.

Weekly Return Fares

Weekly return fares were introduced on 1 December 1952 replacing Workmen's fares, and continued in use throughout the remaining years of trolleybus operation. Five-day (10-journey) and six-day (12-journey) weekly return tickets were available on Mondays only of each week, with three- and four-day tickets being issued when a week contained public holidays, e.g. Christmas, Boxing Day. Such tickets were valid for travel at any time during the week, except Sundays. Based on the range of single fares in force at the time, as single fares increased so higher values were added and lower ones discontinued.
The applicable weekly fare was calculated as 10 or 12 times the adult single fare, less 16⅔% calculated to the nearest 3d (1½d to be considered as 3d). By June 1964, weekly tickets were only issued when the adult single fare was 7d or above.

Weekly return fares were abolished on 3 September 1967 and replaced by 50-journey tickets valid for three months and 12-journey tickets valid for two weeks, offering a 20% reduction on the applicable fare.

Transfer Fares

In the tramway era, Transfer Tickets were issued over certain stages, e.g. Ashley Road to Pokesdown Station, Capstone Road-Boscombe Arcade, but generally through tickets were only issued on through cars. Certain of these fares survived into the trolleybus era, for example transfer fares continued to be available from service 25 to services 21-23 and vice versa, changing at Boscombe. Following the curtailment of service 30 to run between Winton, Alma Road (rather than the Square) and Columbia Road at off-peak times or in the winter, Transfer Tickets were available for all points to/from the Triangle changing to/from services 26 and 31 at Winton Banks.

A broader selection of 5-day and 6-day Transfer Fares was available.

These transfer options were deleted from the June 1964 Fare Tables and did not reappear.

All-Day

In 1953 (only) All-Day tickets, valid on all motorbus and trolleybus services except the motorbus summer pleasure services were offered.

Fare Tables

The trolleybuses adopted a staged fares list, in principle 1d per stage of equal distance and ½d for a half stage, similar to that used on the tramways, but it was only with appearance of the January 1937 timetable that the first proper fare tables were issued. The express motorbus services paralleling the tram route had operated at premium fares which had led to

Sunbeam MS2 no. 172 (BRU23) stands at the Seamoor Road, Westbourne loading point in 1949 prior to departure on a service 22B journey across the town centre to Tuckton, Tuckton Road (Tuckton Bridge).

David Chalk collection

discrepancies as the trolleybuses were introduced. On 8 August 1935 fares between any two points were unified whether made by motorbus, tram or trolleybus. Fares were charged for a stage or portion of a stage.

Fares were included in the timetable booklet from January 1937 until September 1939; then from April 1947 until September 1951 (except February 1951 when a fare increase was pending) and then again from August 1954 to March 1955. Separate fare table booklets were issued from 1 December 1952 and thereafter whenever there was a fare increase (which became increasingly frequent) or major service revision, duplicated sheets being used for intermediate amendments. Fare table booklets were produced in-house using an office duplicating machine.

Although passengers could be carried, on request, on journeys to/from Central Depot, Southcote Road, this was not advertised and no through fares were published, at least not in post-war years. Although there were bus stops in Southcote Road for motorbus service 5, there were no stops in Palmerston Road or St. Clements Road on the access route to/from Boscombe.

Tickets

The three ticketing systems employed by Bournemouth Corporation Transport Services on the trolleybuses are reviewed below; however, it must be stressed that this is not an exhaustive study of a complex topic and that the details of paper ticket colour and denomination are incomplete. The undertaking changed these details frequently whilst only incomplete uncatalogued records survive.

Bell Punch

Until 1954 trolleybus tickets were of the same Bell Punch fare stage colour-coded type as used on the trams. Initially, the name of the fare stages applicable to the service or services, e.g. Square, Top of Richmond Hill, Cemetery Junction, etc. were printed in sequence of travel along the edges of the paper ticket with the title "Bournemouth Corporation Transport Services" and other information in a central column. The fare value of the ticket was denoted by the amount printed upon it and the colour of the paper. Although motorbuses also used the Bell Punch system, the tickets were in entirely different series whilst the fare values and paper colours did not correspond to those used on the trolleybuses.

The conductor was equipped with a wooden rack holding pre-printed paper tickets, divided by value, under a spring and cancelling punch. The cancelling punch was used by the conductor to make a small round hole against the fare stage, indicated by geographical name or, from 1939, number, where the passenger had started the journey whilst the fare paid indicated how far the passenger could travel. The Bell Punch recorded the number of holes punched on a secure register inside the machine whilst the small coloured circle of paper punched out of the ticket was retained in the machine (for accounting purposes if required). It also made an audible ring thus ensuring that a fraudulent conductor was not selling a used ticket. At the terminus and specified "booking-up points" the conductor would record the serial number of the first ticket of each denomination on the rack and enter this on the waybill. This would be checked by inspectors, who would board vehicles at random, to ensure that the conductor was issuing tickets correctly and that passengers had paid the appropriate fare.

The tramway period ticket colours were retained but overprinted with the fare value and a "TB" overprint in green

Corporation Transport Services.

Electric Trolley 'Bus Fares.

WESTBOURNE and ASHLEY ROAD, BOSCOMBE (via Holdenhurst Road).   Route No. 25.

ORDINARY FARES:

Westbourne and Square ...	
Square and Lansdowne	1d
Lansdowne and Capstone Road ...	
Capstone Road and Ashley Road Terminus ...	
Square and Capstone Road ...	
Lansdowne and Queen's Park Corner ...	1½d.
Central Station and Ashley Road Terminus ...	
Westbourne and Lansdowne	
Square and Queen's Park Corner	2d
Lansdowne and Ashley Road Terminus ...	
Westbourne and Capstone Road ...	2½d
Square and Ashley Road Terminus ...	
Westbourne and Queen's Park Corner ...	3d
Westbourne and Ashley Road Terminus and Vice Versa	3½d

WORKMEN'S FARES:

Westbourne and Lansdowne	
Square and Capstone Road	1d
Lansdowne and Ashley Road Terminus ...	
Westbourne and Capstone Road ...	1½d
Square and Ashley Road Terminus ...	
Westbourne and Ashley Road Terminus and Vice Versa	2d

PREPAID TICKETS:

Prepaid Tickets in Packets of **24** Penny for 2/- are sold at the Transport Offices between the hours of 9 a.m. and 5 p.m.

DOG TICKETS—NO LARGE DOGS ARE ALLOWED IN, OR UPON, THE CARS OR TROLLEY 'BUSES.

A charge of 1d. each is made for small dogs. Any dog taken inside a car must be carried on the lap, and if outside must be kept on a leash and under control. Tickets only available upon car on which issued.

PASSENGERS' TICKETS.

Any passenger unable to deliver up his or her ticket on demand will be required to pay the fare for the distance travelled.

PARCELS, LUGGAGE, ARTICLES. etc., will be conveyed under the following conditions :—

1.—Any package or article deposited on the platform of cars will be charged for at the rate of 1d. per package.
2.—A passenger may take with him personal luggage not exceeding 28lbs. in weight free of charge, provided the same is carried by hand and does not occupy any part of a car (seat, platform, etc.) and not be of a form or description to annoy or inconvenience other passengers.
3.—Where the personal luggage exceeds 28lbs., a charge of 1d. will be made.
4.—No parcels over 56lbs. in weight or exceeding a maximum girth measurement of 6ft. will be accepted on a car.
5.—No parcel will be accepted on a car unless accompanied by a passenger.
6.—All parcels, luggage, or articles are carried at the responsibility of the passenger.

LOST PROPERTY.

Any property found in or upon any tramcar or omnibus of the Corporation, or in any shelter or room used in connection with the tramways or omnibuses of the Corporation shall forthwith be handed to the conductor of the tramcar or omnibus, or to an official of the department.

Application for Lost Property can be made at the Transport Offices, Wootton Gardens, weekdays between the hours of 9 a.m. and 5 p.m. (9 a.m. and 1 p.m. on Saturdays).

TRAMWAYS AND TROLLEY 'BUSES— WORKMEN'S TICKETS:

Any Two 1d. "Ordinary" Stages for 1d.
Any Three 1d. "Ordinary" Stages for 1½d. and so on.

"Workmen's" Hours: On Week-days, but not on Sundays, Christmas Day, Good Friday or Bank Holidays before 8 a.m.; between 12.0 noon and 2 p.m. Saturdays only; other days between 4.30 p.m. and 6 p.m. from 1st November to 28th February, and between 5 p.m. and 6.30 p.m. from 1st March to 31st October.

RETURN TICKETS AT REDUCED RATES.

A "Return" Ticket will be issued to any passenger on request boarding any service car or trolley 'bus at at any place at which the vehicle should be according to the time table in force before and including 8.30 a.m. on any day excepting Sundays, Christmas Day, Good Friday and Bank Holidays.

"Return" Tickets are available for return journey at any time on day of issue only within the same stage only.

FARES : 2d. for any 1d. Workmen's Stage.
         3d. ,,   1½d.   ,,   ,,
         4d. ,,   2d.   ,,   ,,
and so on.

No Penny Return Tickets.

CONDITIONS :—
The Tickets are not transferable.
The Tickets are issued subject to the Corporation Bye-Laws.
Through Tickets only issued and accepted in Through Vehicles.
Return Tickets if mutilated not accepted on the Return Journey.

Passengers travelling across Tuckton Bridge will be charged ½d. Toll in addition to the above Fares.

CHILDREN'S FARES ON TRAMS AND TROLLEY 'BUSES.

A child sitting on lap of a passenger is carried free if under 5 years of age but half Ordinary Fare is charged for any additional child, irrespective of age, accompanying such passenger.
Children between the age of 5 and 14 travel at Half Ordinary Fare with a minimum fare of 1d.

22

541

```
                    SERVICE 25
WESTBOURNE (1)                              SPECIAL FARE
                                 Pavilion or Horseshoe Common - Westbourne : 4d.
2    WEST STATION (2)
3  2   SQUARE (4)
5  3  2   LANSDOWNE (5)
5  4  3  2   CENTRAL STATION (6)
6  5  4  3  2   CAPSTONE ROAD (7)
7  6  5  3  3  2   QUEEN'S PARK CORNER (8)
7  6  5  4  3  2  2   GOLF PAVILION or KING'S PARK GATES (9)
8  7  6  5  4  3  2  2   ASHLEY ROAD and PORTMAN ROAD (10)
```

TRANSFER FARES			
JOURNEY	5-DAY	6-DAY	CHANGING AT
Maclean Road (7) - Lansdowne	5/6d	6/9d	Banks to 2,3,6,34
- Barracks	8/3d	10/-d	Boscombe to 1, 20
Columbia Road (7) - Lansdowne	4/9d	5/9d	Banks to 2,3,6,34
- Barracks	7/9d	9/3d	Boscombe to 1, 20
- Somerford	8/3d	10/-d	Boscombe to 1
Winton Banks (7) - Barracks	6/3d	7/6d	Boscombe to 1, 20
- Somerford	7/9d	9/3d	Boscombe to 1
King's Road (7) - Barracks	5/6d	6/9d	Boscombe to 1, 20
Central Station (25) - Pokesdown	4/3d	5/-d	Boscombe to 1,20-24
- Fisherman's Walk	4/3d	5/-d	Boscombe to 21,22,23
- Tuckton Corner	4/9d	5/9d	Boscombe to 21,22
- Cross Roads	5/6d	6/9d	Boscombe to 21,22
- Tuckton Bridge	6/3d	7/6d	Boscombe to 21,22,23
Broadway (28,29,32) - Lansdowne	4/3d	5/-d	Cemetery to 2,3,6,34
West Way (29) - Boscombe	4/9d	5/9d	King's Road to 7, 8
Columbia Road (30,31) - Lansdowne	4/9d	5/9d	Banks to 2,3,6,34
Wallisdown (30) - Lansdowne	4/9d	5/9d	Banks to 2,3,6,34
Talbot Village (30) - Lansdowne	4/3d	5/-d	Banks to 2,3,6,34
Howeth Road (31) - Lansdowne	4/9d	5/9d	Banks to 2,3,6,34
SERVICES 18, 33 to SERVICES 28, 29	As Ser. 32 P.21		Broadway
SERVICE 8 to SERVICE 2	As Ser. 6 P.7		Ensbury Park Hotel

```
SQUARE (4)                  SERVICE 30 (via LANSDOWNE)
2    LANSDOWNE (5)                          SPECIAL FARES
4  2   CEMETERY JUNCTION (7)         Square - Park Road (6)      : 3d.
5  4  2   WINTON BANKS or OSBORNE ROAD (9)   Lansdowne - East Avenue (8) : 3d.
6  5  3  2   BOYS' HOME (10)
7  6  4  2  2   TALBOT VILLAGE SCHOOL (11) (Slades Lane)
8  7  5  4  3  2   WALLISDOWN CROSS ROADS (12)
8  7  6  4  4  3  2   COLUMBIA ROAD (13)
```

```
LANSDOWNE (5)               SERVICE 36
2    CEMETERY JUNCTION (7)                  SPECIAL FARE
4  2   WINTON BANKS or WYCLIFFE ROAD (9)  Lansdowne - East Avenue (8) : 3d.
5  3  2   BRASSEY ROAD (10)
6  4  3  2   ENSBURY PARK HOTEL (11)
7  5  4  3  2   HOWETH ROAD (14)
7  6  4  2  2   COLUMBIA ROAD (13)
```

```
BOURNEMOUTH PIER (2)        SERVICE 39
2    LANSDOWNE (5)                          SPECIAL FARES
4    2   CEMETERY JUNCTION (7)        Pier - Derby Road            : 3d.
5    3   2   KING'S ROAD (8)          Cooper-Dean - Mallard Road   : 3d.
5    5   3       FIVE WAYS (11)       Strouden Park - Court Road   : 3d.
7    6   4   3   2   BROADWAY (15)    Park Road (6) - Pier         : 3d.
8    7   6   5   4   2   STROUDEN PARK HOTEL (16)
8    8   7   6   5   4   2   COOPER-DEAN (17)       FARES NOT SHOWN
9    9   8   7   6   5   3   2   RIVERSIDE AVENUE (18)   ARE AS SERVICE
10   9   8   8   7   5   4   3   2   IFORD (19)         38, PAGE 18
10   10  9   8   7   6   5   3   2   2   JUMPERS (20)
1/-  11  11  10  8   7   5   3   2   2   BARRACKS (16)
1/2  1/2 1/1 1/1 1/- 10  9   8   6   3   2   STOUR ROAD (15)
1/4  1/4 1/3 1/2 1/1 11  10  9   7   5   4   3   TUCKTON BRIDGE (14)
1/5  1/5 1/4 1/3 1/2 1/- 11  10  8   6   5   4   CROSS ROADS (13)
1/6  1/6 1/5 1/4 1/3 1/1 1/- 11  9   7   6   5   TUCKTON CORNER (12)
1/7  1/7 1/6 1/5 1/4 1/2 1/1 1/- 10  8   7   6   FISHERMAN'S WALK (11)
1/8  1/8 1/7 1/6 1/5 1/3 1/2 1/1 11  9   8   7   POKESDOWN (9)
1/9  1/9 1/8 1/7 1/6 1/4 1/3 1/2 1/- 10  9   8   BOSCOMBE ARCADE (7)
1/10 1/10 1/9 1/8 1/7 1/5 1/4 1/3 1/1 11 10  9   BOSCOMBE GARDENS (6)
1/11 1/11 1/10 1/9 1/8 1/6 1/5 1/4 1/2 1/- 11   LANSDOWNE (5)
2/-  2/-  2/11 1/10 1/9 1/7 1/6 1/5 1/3 1/1 1/-  10   BOURNEMOUTH PIER (2)
```

```
SQUARE (4) or PIER (2)      SERVICES 21, 22, 37, 38
2ᵈ   LANSDOWNE (5)                          SPECIAL FARES
4  2   BOSCOMBE GARDENS (6)          Square - Derby Road : 3d.
5  3  2   BOSCOMBE ARCADE or ASHLEY ROAD (7)   Pier - Derby Road : 3d.
6  5  3  2   POKESDOWN (9)
7  5  4  3  2   FISHERMAN'S WALK (11)
7  6  5  4  3  2   TUCKTON CORNER (12)
8  7  6  5  4  3  2   CROSS ROADS (13)
9  8  7  6  5  4  3  2   TUCKTON BRIDGE (14)
9  8  7  6  5  5  4  3  2   STOUR ROAD or STOURBANK ROAD (15)
10 9  8  6  6  5  4  3  2   CHRISTCHURCH PRIORY (16)


     N.B.  PIER - LANSDOWNE via SQUARE : 3d.
           LANSDOWNE - SQUARE via PIER : 3d.
```

```
SQUARE (4) or PIER (2)      SERVICES 23, 38
2ᵈ   LANSDOWNE (5)                          SPECIAL FARES
4  2   BOSCOMBE GARDENS (6)          Square - Derby Road : 3d.
5  3  2   BOSCOMBE ARCADE or ASHLEY ROAD (7)   Pier - Derby Road : 3d.
6  5  3  2   POKESDOWN (9)                 TRANSFER FARE
7  5  4  3  2   FISHERMAN'S WALK (11)   Seafield Rd. - Christchurch : 4d.
7  6  5  4  3  2   CRANLEIGH ROAD (18)    Changing at Tuckton Bridge to
8  7  6  5  4  3  2   SEAFIELD ROAD (17)   Service 21.
9  8  7  6  5  4  3  2   TUCKTON BRIDGE (14)
* See Note on Facing   5  4  3  2   CROSS ROADS (13)
  Page                 6  5  4  3  2   TUCKTON CORNER (12)
                       7  6  5  4  3  2   FISHERMAN'S WALK (11)
```

NOTE: When Service 23 is operating between Tuckton Bridge and Fisherman's Walk
only, passengers may purchase transfer tickets to all points to the Square,
changing to Services 21 or 22 at Fisherman's Walk, and vice versa.

```
TRIANGLE (3)                SERVICES 26, 28, 29, 35
2    SQUARE or ALBERT ROAD (4)              SPECIAL FARE
3  2   CEMETERY JUNCTION (7)         Square - East Avenue (8) : 3d.
4  4  2   WINTON BANKS or WYCLIFFE ROAD (9)
6  5  3  2   BRASSEY ROAD (10)
6  6  4  3  2   MOORDOWN or MACLAREN ROAD (12)
7  6  5  4  3  2   LANFORD ROAD (13)
7  7  6  4  3  2  2   WEST WAY (14)
8  7  6  5  4  3  2  2   BROADWAY or MALVERN ROAD (15)
9  9  7  6  5  4  4  3  2   FIVE WAYS (11)
9  9  8  7  6  5  5  4  3  2   KING'S ROAD or RICHMOND PARK ROAD (8)
10 10 9  8  7  6  6  5  4  2   CEMETERY JUNCTION (7)
11 10 10 9  8  7  7  6  5  3  2   SQUARE or ALBERT ROAD (4)
11 11 10 9  9  8  7  6  5  4  3  2   TRIANGLE (3)
```

```
TRIANGLE (3)                SERVICES 30, 31
2    SQUARE or ALBERT ROAD (4)              SPECIAL FARE
3  2   CEMETERY JUNCTION (7)         Square - East Avenue (8) : 3d.
4  4  2   WINTON BANKS or OSBORNE ROAD (9)
5  5  3  2   BOYS' HOME (10)
6  6  4  2  2   TALBOT VILLAGE SCHOOL (11) (Slades Lane)
7  7  5  4  3  2   WALLISDOWN CROSS ROADS (12)
8  7  6  4  4  3  2   COLUMBIA ROAD (13)
8  8  7  6  5  4  2  2   HOWETH ROAD (14)
9  9  8  7  6  5  4  3  2   ENSBURY PARK HOTEL (11)
9  9  8  7  6  5  4  3  2   BRASSEY ROAD (10)
10 10 9  8  7  6  4  4  3  2   WINTON BANKS or WYCLIFFE ROAD (9)
11 10 10 9  8  7  6  5  4  3  2   CEMETERY JUNCTION (7)
11 11 10 9  8  7  6  5  4  3  2  2   SQUARE or ALBERT ROAD (4)
11 11 11 10 9  9  8  7  6  5  4  3  2   TRIANGLE (3)
```

NOTE: WHEN SERVICE 30 IS OPERATING BETWEEN COLUMBIA ROAD and WINTON BANKS ONLY,
PASSENGERS MAY PURCHASE THROUGH TRANSFER TICKETS FOR ALL POINTS TO THE
TRIANGLE, CHANGING AT WINTON BANKS TO SERVICES 26 and 31, OR VICE VERSA.

Awaiting departure time at Jumpers Corner are Sunbeam MF2Bs nos. 266 (WRU266) on service 32, and 276 (YLJ276) on service 24.   Roger G. Funnell (courtesy Mrs D. Funnell and Rodney Funnell)

(or orange or blue for high values). Nearly forty different Bell Punch tickets with the "TB" overprint are known to have been issued. Prior to the introduction of trolleybuses, motorbus tickets had been overprinted with a "B" overprint to distinguish them from those issued on trams. Towards the end of the geographical-stage period (1939), oversized geographical 1½d, on tramway-standard pink paper, and 2½d, on motorbus-standard red paper, tickets appeared including both motorbus and trolleybus stages. These lacked the overprinted "TB". In early 1939 there was a change to numerical-stage tickets, the "TB" overprint ceased and a single set of colours was used for both motorbus and trolleybus services. Issuance of separate ½d Tuckton Bridge toll tickets ceased at this time although the toll continued to be charged until 1 December 1942. The ½d was added to the applicable fare and a single ticket, now with a "TB", i.e. Tuckton Bridge, overprint, issued for the combined amount.

The first generation of numerical-stage tickets had stages 1-20 reading from top left to top right but this was reversed later, the stages reading from bottom right to bottom left. In general the tramway period colours were retained but red was used for the 2½d and 3½d tickets in accordance with the above precedent. During the Second World War, Bell Punch stopped supplying grey tickets and the grey 6d became primrose. There were certain colour changes in higher values, and some new high values were added.

Although efficient and successful, the ticketing system was "administration heavy", slow, required considerable manual dexterity and was labour-intensive. BCT carried out experiments with ticket issuing machines during the 1930s, but the Bell Punch remained the undertaking's standard until the Ultimate system was progressively adopted in the winter of 1953-54. In the 1930s trials took place with both TIM and Verometer machines, the TIM being used on the experimental County Gates, Westbourne-Bournemouth Square trolleybus service from 27 February 1934. Similar trials using two Gibson and two Ultimate machines were carried out in 1953. There had been a trial with a forerunner of the Ultimate in 1946 but details are not known.

During the trolleybus era the undertaking purchased tickets for its Bell Punch machines solely from the Bell Punch Co. Ltd., London rather than other specialist printers.

During the trolleybus era, the return journey on the greatly discounted return fares was handled by issuing an exchange ticket of the same value as the original one to avoid misuse. From early 1939 until 1942 a single universal exchange ticket was used with fare values instead of stages printed down the sides which was then punched to show the return ticket value to which it corresponded. On 10 July 1942 exchange tickets were discontinued as an economy measure and conductors used nippers which made a square hole in the originally issued return ticket. Normal return fares were abolished in 1952.

Tuckton Bridge toll house.　　　　　　　　　　　　　　**Malcolm Pearce (G.O.P. Pearce)**

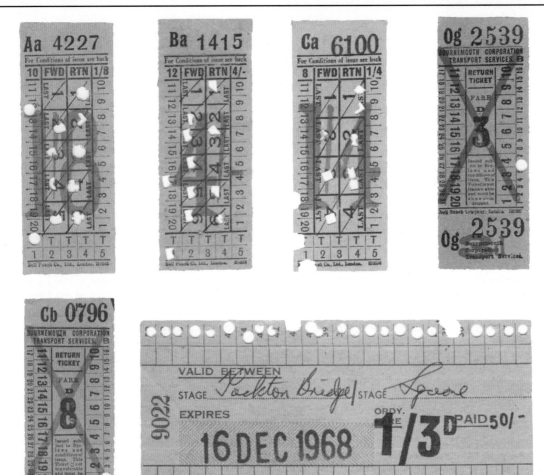

Bell Punch Weekly tickets　　　　　　　　　　　　　　**Malcolm Pearce (G.O.P. Pearce)**

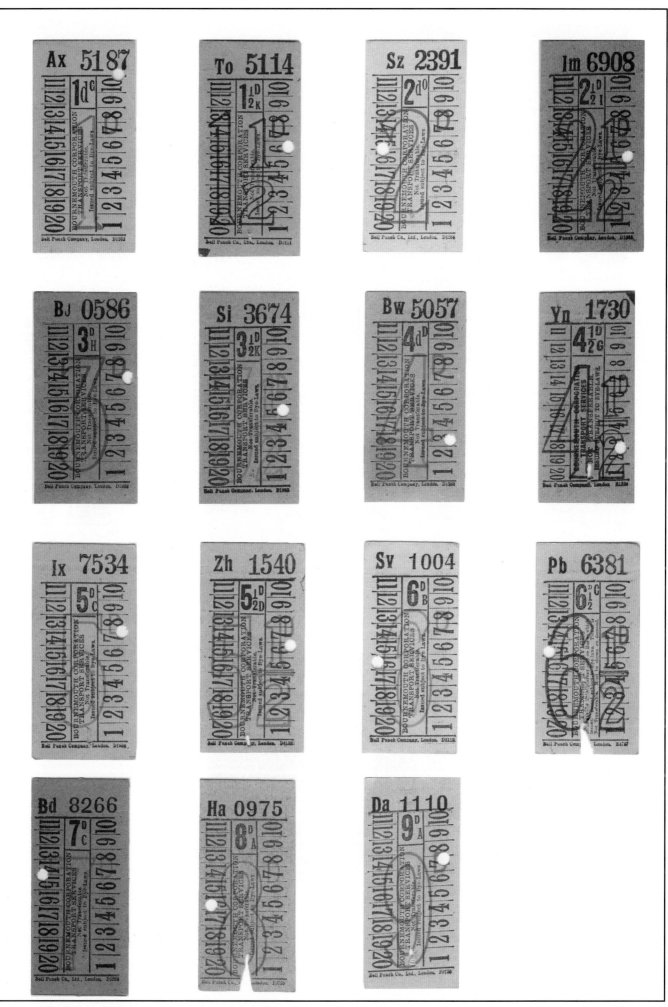

Range of Bell Punch tickets with values 1d to 9d.

Malcolm Pearce (G.O.P. Pearce)

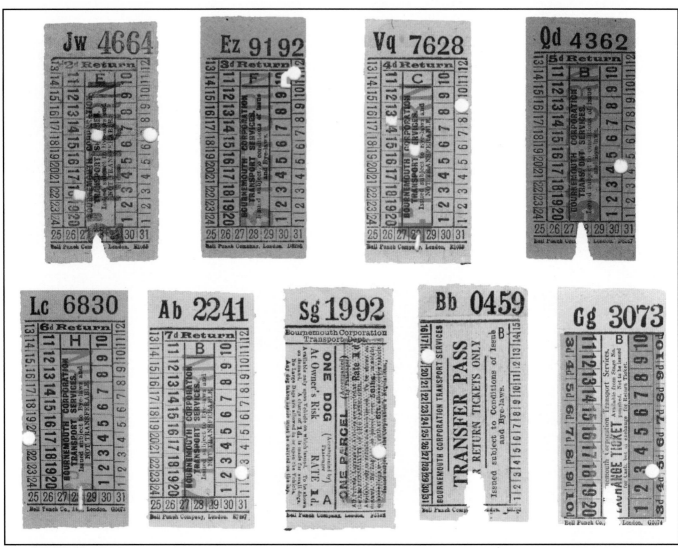

Bell Punch Dog, Return, Exchange and Transfer tickets   **Malcolm Pearce (G.O.P. Pearce)**

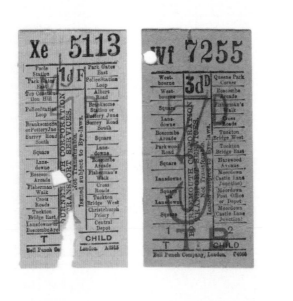

Bell Punch tickets with "T" and "TB" overprint   **Malcolm Pearce (G.O.P. Pearce)**

Ticket colours and styles

a) Pre-war

Title "Bournemouth Corporation Transport Services". Geographical or numerical fare stages. All printing in black.

Colour	Denomination	Comment
Singles:		
Beige/buff with green value overprint	1d	
Pink with blue value overprint	1½d	
White with green value overprint	2d	
Sage with blue value overprint	2½d	
Orange with green value overprint	3d	
Salmon with blue value overprint	3½d	
Light blue with orange value overprint	4d	
Yellow with orange value overprint	5d	
Grey	6d	
Lilac	7d	
White/red	1d	Parcel
Mauve	1d	Dog
Pink	½d	Tuckton Bridge Toll

b) Post-war

Title "Bournemouth Corporation Transport Services". Numerical fare stages. All printing in black.

Colour	Denomination	Comment
Singles:		
Beige/buff with green value overprint	1d	
Pink with blue value overprint	1½d	
White with green value overprint	2d	
Orange with green value overprint	3d	
Mauve with orange value overprint	4d	
Yellow with orange value overprint	5d	
Beige/buff with orange value overprint	6d	
Purple with orange value overprint	7d	
Pale brown with green value overprint	8d	
Pale(r) brown with green value overprint	9d	
Bright orange with green value overprint	10d	
Pink with blue value overprint	11d	
Pale purple with blue value overprint	1s	
Light olive with orange value overprint	1s 2d	
Beige/buff with blue value overprint	1s 3d	
Returns:		
Beige/buff with orange value overprint	1½d	school child only
Purple with orange value overprint	1½d	school child only
Pale green with blue value overprint	2d	blue "X" across ticket
Pink with green value overprint	3d	
Beige with green value overprint	4d	
White with black value overprint	6d	orange "X" across ticket
Blue with orange value overprint	1s 3d	
Pink with green value overprint	1s 9d	
Beige/buff with orange value overprint	2s 6d	blue stripe across ticket
Beige/buff overprinted "Parcel" or "Dog"	1d	orange stripe across ticket
Beige/buff transfer pass for return ticket holders	No value	
Pale blue black print	3s 4d	combined road and river trip return
Purple black print	3s 9d	combined road and river trip return
Beige/buff black print	1s 10d	combined road and river trip child return
Orange black over-print	2s	combined road and river trip child return
Pale green black	2s	All day except motorbus services12, 14, 15
Blue black	1s	All day Child
Weekly returns:		

Bell Punch tickets with numerical fare stages were issued although Ultimate tickets were in use for other fares. The paper colour indicated the days of validity and number of journeys, e.g. three days for six journeys, with the value being shown by an overprint. For this reason only a limited number of examples from the large number of weekly return fares offered are listed below.

Orange with black print orange value overprint	9d	for three days, i.e. in the week including Christmas Day and Boxing Day
Purple with black print green value overprint	3s 8d	for four days, i.e. in a week including a Bank Holiday
Pale green with black print orange value	1s 8d	for five days overprint
Pink with black print green value overprint	8s	for six days

All-day (1953 only):

Sage with black print and black value overprint	2s	Adult
Bright Blue with black print and black value overprint	1s	Child

Ultimate

A trial with two Bell Punch "Ultimate" ticket issuing machines, which basically offered an automated version of the manufacturer's traditional pre-printed ticket system, began on 12 March 1953. Their speed of operation and the continued colour coding of tickets according to their value was deemed ideal for the BCT network. It was decided to progressively introduce the Bell Punch Ultimate ticketing system and the changeover was completed by 22 March 1954, the entire stock of machines being hired from the manufacturers.

The majority (360) of the Ultimate machines used in Bournemouth accommodated six, instead of the more customary five, fare denominations, pre-printed on rolls of either 500 or later 1,000 (when thin manilla paper was used), colour-coded, 1¼ in-square paper tickets. The blank tickets were printed in black with three "fare type" boxes or squares across the base of the ticket headed "SINGLE" on the left, "JOINT" in the centre and "RETURN", with a red herringbone background grid effect, and titled "Bournemouth Corp. Trans. S." or later "Bournemouth Corp. Transport". They were used on both motorbus and trolleybus services. Each pre-printed ticket had a unique alpha-numeric identification also printed in black and made up of two serial letters (upper case followed by lower case, progressing in a Ba, Bb, Bc respectively Ca, Cb, Cc sequence) followed or preceded by a 5-digit serial number. Commercial advertisements appeared on the reverse of the ticket. Each new ticket roll had a piece of gummed tape to join it to the end of the old one thus avoiding the conductor having to change rolls mid-journey.

Four different typefaces appeared during the period that BCT was using Ultimate tickets on its trolleybuses, involving successively a change to the type layout, the overprinting of the fare value usually in blue in a serif style, and finally a sans-serif style overprint.

The number of the fare stage at which a passenger had boarded the vehicle was set by turning a knurled wheel on the right hand side of the Ultimate machine. Each ticket compartment had its own operating lever which, when depressed, printed the fare stage boarded number from 00 to 99 in purple ink in one of three possible "fare type" boxes or squares, "SINGLE", "JOINT" and "RETURN", of the ticket. When the lever was released, the ticket was ejected, torn off against a serrated cutter by the conductor and given to the passenger as a receipt for his fare paid. The number of tickets of each value issued was recorded from the printed serial numbers on the ticket roll and visible through a transparent "window" on the top of the machine. When a button below the operating lever was depressed in the same issuing operation a double length ticket of the required denomination was ejected, in which case the fare stage number was printed in the appropriate square of the first ticket only whilst an inked cancellation mark was made across the serial

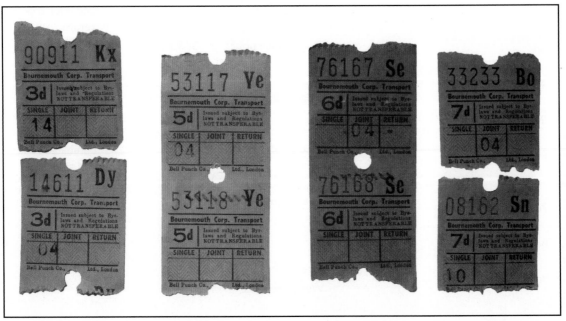

Utimate 3d, 5d, 6d and 7d tickets. The 3d tickets were issued for a 3d fare, the 5d and 6d tickets show how two tickets in each case were issued to make up a 10d and a 1s fare, and the first 7d ticket is part of an 11d "joint issue".

David Bowler

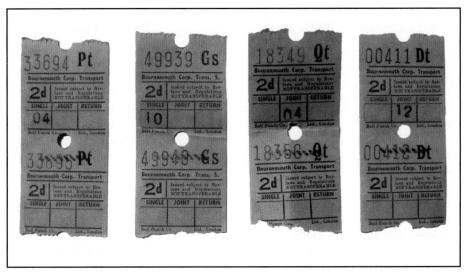

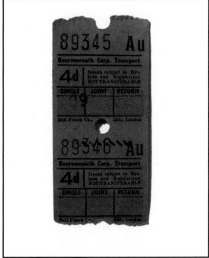

Ultimate 2d tickets

UltimateTwo 4d tickets issued for an 8d fare.   David Bowler

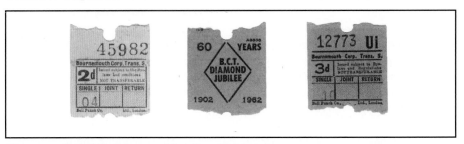

Ultimate 3d BCT Diamond Jubilee 1962 ticket.

Malcolm Pearce (G.O.P. Pearce)

number of the second ticket. A return ticket requiring a double length ticket to reach the required denomination was issued by pulling out the knurled wheel entirely allowing the first ticket to be imprinted with the stage number in the "RETURN" box whilst a cancellation was made across the serial number of the second ticket. As before, the conductor continued to record the number of tickets of each denomination that had been issued and entered this on the waybill at the journey's specified "booking-up points".

The following ticket colours and denominations limited to a maximum of six at any one time were used during the period that Ultimate ticket machines were used in Bournemouth:

Colour	Type	Denomination	Period	Comment
Beige	Single	1d	1953-1964	
Pink	Single	1½d	1953-1956	
White	Single	2d	1953-1968	
Orange	Single	3d	1953-1968	
Purple	Single	4d	1953-1968	
Yellow	Single	5d	1953-1968	
Pink	Single	6d	1964-1968	
Pale green	Single	7d	1956-1968	
Green	Return	1s 9d	1953-1956	overprinted "return"
Pale green	Single	2s	1958-1964	overprinted "single"
Mauve	Single	2s 6d	1950-1964	
Green	Circular tour	3s	1964-1965	
Purple	Circular tour	3s 6d	1965-1968	

In order to make up additional fare values, "joint issues" of more than one ticket, so called "married tickets", were made in a defined combination. This was originally as follows:

1d	single 1d ticket
2d	single 2d ticket
3d	single 3d ticket
4d	single 4d ticket
5d	single 5d ticket
6d	two 3d tickets
7d	single 7d ticket
8d	two 4d tickets
9d	one 7d ticket and two 1d tickets
10d	two 5d tickets
11d	one 7d and two 2d tickets joint issue
1s	one single and one double 4d tickets
1s 2d	two 7d tickets
1s 3d	one single and one double 5d tickets
1s 6d	three double 3d tickets
1s 9d	one single and one double 7d tickets

From 27 June 1964, the minimum adult fare became 3d and that of a child 2d, making the 1d compartment of the Ultimate ticket machine redundant. This was used for a new 6d ticket instead of a double 3d and all fares over 1s were thereafter made up from a double 6d ticket plus a second ticket of the necessary value.

The reason for a "defined combination" was to enable more different fare values to be issued than there were actual tickets

549

and which by the very ingenious mechanism of the Ultimate machine could be individually recorded. A counter, known as a "numerator", was located on the front of the machine and fitted to each of the six ticket compartments between the operating lever and the button for issuing double-length tickets. It was connected to the mechanism for issuing these and thus the number of double-length issues made was recorded, the numerator moving on by one number for each double issue. For example, as a double 1d ticket was only issued when a 9d fare was taken, the number of double 1d tickets issued represented the number of passengers travelling at that fare. Then more statistical data could be derived by reference to the "defined combination". If, say, the waybill noted that nine 1d tickets had been issued and the corresponding numerator had recorded two double issues of 1d tickets then the accounts department would know that 5 fares at 1d and two fares at 9d had been issued (as the conductor had given two passengers a 7d and a double 1d ticket for their 9d fare). The "numerator" beneath the right-hand end ticket compartment, as worn by the conductor, recorded the total number of tickets sold (the "total numerator") and double-issue tickets could not be issued from this compartment. This effectively meant that Bournemouth's Ultimate machines initially could issue tickets to cover a maximum of eleven different fares during any one period of time.

Throughout the trolleybus era, the undertaking purchased tickets for its Ultimate machines solely from Bell Punch, the printer's name "Bell Punch Co. Ltd. London" appearing across the base of the ticket.

The undertaking offered a large number of transfer fares between points not linked by direct services at the beginning of the trolleybus era, e.g. Iford Bridge to Fisherman's Walk. By the time the Ultimate machines were in use these were basically limited to fares between points in Winton or Moordown and points beyond Strouden Park on service 32 to compensate for the infrequent operation and subsequent withdrawal of services 33 and 34, and points on the outer portions of services 23 (Fisherman's Walk-Tuckton Bridge) and 30 (Winton Banks-Columbia Road) which did not work their full length throughout the day.

As with the Bell Punch, it was necessary for the conductor to complete a waybill at specified "booking-up points". In November 1957, those in operation on trolleybus services were as follows:

20, 24
Bournemouth Square
Boscombe
Warnford Road
Jumpers Christchurch

21, 22, 23
Bournemouth Square
Boscombe
Fisherman's Walk
Seafield Road
Southbourne Cross Roads

25
Boscombe
Queen's Park
Lansdowne
Bournemouth Square

30
Triangle
Cemetery Junction
Boys' Home
Columbia Road

31
Triangle
Cemetery Junction
Brassey Road
Columbia Road

32
Triangle
Cemetery Junction
Five Ways
Castle Lane

Westbourne
Strouden Hotel
Iford

26
Triangle
Cemetery Junction
Brassey Road
Lawford Road

28
Triangle
Cemetery Junction
Five Ways
Castle Lane, Broadway

29
Triangle
Cemetery Junction
Five Ways
Castle Lane, Broadway
West Way

33
Triangle
Cemetery Junction
Brassey Road
Lawford Road
Castle Lane, Broadway
Strouden Hotel
Iford

34
Lansdowne
Cemetery Junction
Brassey Road
Lawford Road
West Way

When a vehicle operated a short-working, the terminal was considered the "booking-up point".

Setright Speed

Increasingly frequent fare increases and consequently changed denominations in the last few years of trolleybus operation encouraged the undertaking to evaluate a more flexible ticketing solution. In 1968 the Setright Speed ticket issuing machine, manufactured by Setright Registers Ltd., Fairfield Works, Fairfield Road, Bow, London E3, was introduced.

The machine had a box-like structure with a superimposed boss on the top and a semi-circular magazine containing a blank paper roll beneath. There were a series of numbered and lettered metal rings around the boss upon which the conductor "dialled" the issuance details required for each ticket. The upper ring had two concentric dials: the inner dial set the fare stage at which the passenger boarded, and the outer dial set the fare value. The lower ring had dials for the day and month. Lastly came a lever, almost on the main body of the machine, which had settings for the type of ticket: "C" (child), "O" (ordinary), "CON" (concession), "T" (transfer), "CT" (child transfer), "SP" (special). The Bournemouth machines added in purple ink (in sequence from left to right) stage boarded, from 00 to 99; the fare value, up to 19s 11d; date of issue; serial number of the ticket; machine identity; and type of ticket, e.g. ORD (ordinary), on to a blank roll of buff or off-white paper with the printed heading "BOURNEMOUTH CORP. TRANSPORT" and "issued subject to Bye-laws & Regs." at the base. Commercial advertisements appeared on the reverse of the ticket.

The paper ticket was printed and ejected by releasing a small safety catch trigger on the base of the machine (to avoid unnecessary issues) and by rotating a crank handle on the side by one turn for each ticket.

The machines contained counters showing the total value of fares issued in units of 1d and 1s together with the total number of tickets sold. A statistical counter recorded the number of tickets sold at one predetermined value.

Hants & Dorset and Wilts & Dorset

The Bournemouth Corporation Act, 1930, granted H&D the right to continue carrying local passengers within the Bournemouth area on their country services which paralleled urban trolleybus and motorbus services but all revenue less operating costs passed to Bournemouth. From 1930, BCT provided H&D with special H&D tickets which were over-stamped BCT for such local passengers. The same conditions applied to the jointly-operated H&D and Wilts & Dorset Salisbury service 38 to and from Christchurch. A special issue of Bournemouth Corporation Bell Punch tickets using a colour system approximating to that used pre-1939 for Corporation motorbus tickets, cancelled latterly using the Setright Speed return ticket punch, was printed for use on a journey which could also be made by trolleybus.

The Bournemouth Corporation Act 1930 contained an agreement that H&D buses running over BCT routes to and from points outside Bournemouth would charge 50% higher fares for local passengers that they carried between any points between the Square and Bear Cross and Purewell.

A different agreement was contained in the Poole Road Transport Act 1935, whereby all revenue taken on H&D buses from passengers travelling wholly within the BCT area would pass to BCT, less the cost of carrying those passengers. BCT provided the company with special H&D tickets which were over-stamped BCT and BCT Inspectors had the right to board H&D buses to make occasional checks. The agreement lasted for 40 years. Certain H&D journeys were exempt from this agreement and did not carry local passengers, this restriction being displayed by white lettering on a maroon background on a wooden board carried across the motorbus radiator or by a coloured indicator blind showing "NOT ON SERVICE FOR BOURNEMOUTH CORPORATION PASSENGERS".

Setright Speed A variety of tickets issued for different values, including a single child (C) ticket.   **David Bowler**

At the north end of Lawford Road Sunbeam MS2 no. 212 (ALJ973) turns into the eastbound lane of Castle Lane East with its indicator blinds already prepared for its return to the Square and the Triangle on interworking service 29 whilst Sunbeam MF2B no. 276 (WRU276) follows on its way to Castle Lane (Mallard Road) Depot.
Travel Lens

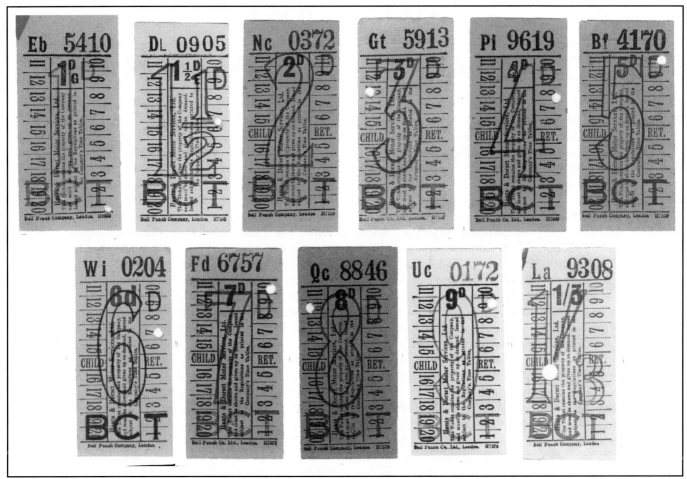

H&D Bell Punch tickets issued on H&D motorbuses for use when carrying local passengers within the BCT area.
Malcolm Pearce (G.O.P. Pearce)

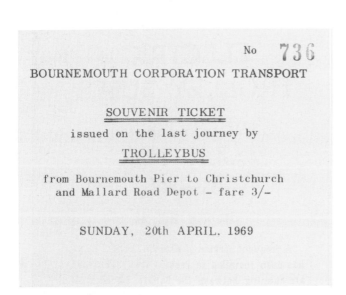

No 736

BOURNEMOUTH CORPORATION TRANSPORT

SOUVENIR TICKET

issued on the last journey by

TROLLEYBUS

from Bournemouth Pier to Christchurch
and Mallard Road Depot - fare 3/-

SUNDAY, 20th APRIL. 1969

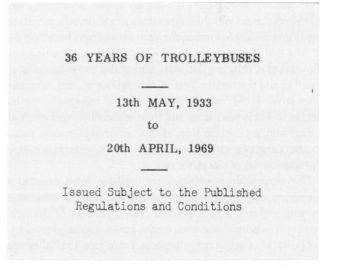

36 YEARS OF TROLLEYBUSES

————

13th MAY, 1933

to

20th APRIL, 1969

————

Issued Subject to the Published
Regulations and Conditions

APPENDIX L

TIME TABLES AND PUBLIC INFORMATION

Throughout the electric tramway era the times of first and last journeys to and from key points on the route of travel, and the frequency or frequencies throughout the day, or the departure times from each terminal, were, as in many other places, included in commercially-produced town or city guides. BCT did not publish its own public time or fare "tables" as such but provided the necessary information to independent publishers, such as Sydney J. Mate who produced the "Official Time Table of the Bournemouth Corporation Tramways & Route Guide" and Russell's "Bournemouth Pocket ABC Railway Guide", which, despite its name, also included bus and tram services of BCT and H&D. This procedure, to the same format, continued unchanged until around the end of 1930, the booklets including brief information on places of interest, parks, theatres, etc., and the motorbus or tram services that reached them, often with the journey time to intermediate points and the applicable fare. Early issues in the tramway era even included an illustrated description of the route!

Bournemouth Corporation Transport Services began to publish its own public time tables (always shown as two words) in January 1931, although prior to this a number of leaflets had been produced, mainly for motorbus services as and when they were introduced, e.g. in April 1930 for the Express Bus services. BCT time tables were issued monthly from January 1931 until September 1939 although the actual times were usually the same, just varying between summer and winter. The first five years showed a volume number and an issue number, i.e. January 1931 was Volume 1, Number 1 and December 1935 was Volume 5, Number 12. This system was dropped from January 1936, when the slightly larger dimensions were introduced, and from then timetables just showed a month and year. Time table information for each service was based on a list of first and last departures from each origin or starting point on weekdays (Monday-Saturday during the trolleybus era) and Sundays, and the service interval throughout the day. In addition from January 1937 the booklet contained relevant fare tables, details of workmen's fares and their availability, regulations and a diagrammatic system map, as well as advertisements related to the Council's various attractions. There was, however, no alphabetical list of places served.

The time table booklets were available from conductors, transport enquiry offices and from the Tourist Information Bureau, whilst in a period when many members of the public read newspapers in libraries, copies could also be viewed in all public libraries in the operating area. From June 1957, they were also sold by a selected number of newsagents throughout the area, these being supplied to the retailer on a sale or return basis. Conductors were no longer forced to sell them, but were encouraged to do so by buying a number of copies at a discount and selling them at the normal price, thus making a small profit for themselves. However, every conductor had to carry a copy when on duty in order to comply with regulations made under the Road Traffic Act, 1930.

Until September 1939, when more than one trolleybus service operated along a single common route, such as the 21 and 21A between the Square and Christchurch or the 25 and 25A between the Square and Boscombe, the service frequency to and from the Square was combined in that of the main service. For example, from 8 April 1936, service 21 was shown with a 10 minutes frequency, but this included service 21A with a 30 minutes frequency to Westbourne. This was not confined to Main Road services. The 28 from Five Ways to the Square showed a frequency of 5 minutes, but this included service 29, there being a 10 minutes frequency on each service. The first pre-war time tables to be set out in a detailed tabular format were those for services 26A, 28A, 30 and 30A, as and when they were introduced in the late 1930s. When time tables began to be published again after the Second World War they all appeared in detailed tabular format.

Fares were included in the time table booklet until September 1939; then from April 1947 until September 1951 (except February 1951) and then again from August 1954 to March 1955. Separate fare table booklets were issued from 1 December 1952 and thereafter whenever there was a fare increase. Fare table booklets were all were produced in-house using an office duplicating machine.

No time table booklets were published following the outbreak of the Second World War and although, in principle, the existing timings continued there were timetable changes, service curtailments and service extensions. In all cases, information was published in the local newspapers a few days

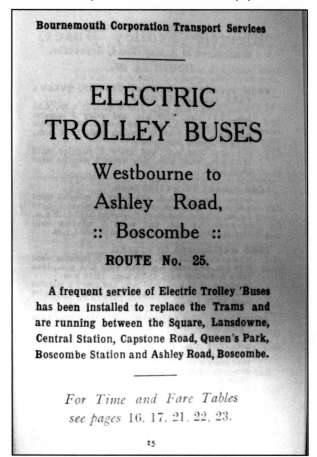

Bournemouth Corporation Transport Services

ELECTRIC TROLLEY BUSES

Westbourne to
Ashley Road,
:: Boscombe ::

ROUTE No. 25.

A frequent service of Electric Trolley 'Buses has been installed to replace the **Trams** and are running between the Square, Lansdowne, Central Station, Capstone Road, Queen's Park, Boscombe Station and Ashley Road, Boscombe.

*For Time and Fare Tables
see pages 16. 17. 21. 22. 23.*

15

1934 BCT time table featuring "Electric Trolley Buses" between Westbourne and Ashley Road, Boscombe. David Bowler collection

Electric Trolley Buses.
Westbourne to Ashley Road, Boscombe.
ROUTE No. 25.

FROM SQUARE TO CENTRAL STATION, QUEEN'S PARK and ASHLEY ROAD.

WEEK DAYS—5.51 a.m., 6.11 a.m., 6.31 a.m., 6.51 a.m., 7.11 a.m., 7.30 a.m. and every 8 minutes until 10.2 a.m., 10.7 a.m. and every 5 minutes until 8.22 p.m., then every 8 minutes until 11.18 p.m., 11.24 to Central Station only.

SUNDAYS—9.46 a.m. and every 8 minutes until 12.18 p.m., 12.22 p.m., then every 5 minutes until 10.42 p.m.

FROM SQUARE TO WESTBOURNE.

WEEKDAYS—7.28 a.m. and every 8 minutes until 9.44 a.m., 9.50 a.m. and every 5 minutes until 8 p.m., 8.6 p.m. and every 8 minutes until 11.8 p.m.

SUNDAYS—9.8 a.m. and every 8 minutes until 12 p.m., then every 5 minutes until 10.40 p.m.

FROM WESTBOURNE TO SQUARE.

WEEKDAYS—7.38 a.m. and every 8 minutes until 9.54 a.m. and every 5 minutes until 8.14 p.m., then every 8 minutes until 11.10 p.m., 11.16 p.m.

SUNDAYS—9.15 a.m., 9.22 a.m. and every 8 minutes until 12.10 p.m., 12.14 p.m. and every 5 minutes until 10.49 p.m.

FROM LANSDOWNE TO CENTRAL STATION, QUEEN'S PARK and ASHLEY ROAD.

WEEKDAYS—5.56 a.m., 6.16 a.m., 6.36 a.m., 6.56 a.m., 7.16 a.m., 7.36 a.m. and every 8 minutes until 10.8 a.m. and every 5 minutes until 8.28 p.m., then every 8 minutes until 11.24 p.m.

SUNDAYS—9.52 a.m. and every 8 minutes until 12.24 p.m., 12.28 p.m., then every 5 minutes until 10.48 p.m.

FROM BOSCOMBE (Junction of Ashley & Christchurch Roads) TO SQUARE (via Ashley and Holdenhurst Roads).

WEEKDAYS—5.30 a.m., 5.50 a.m., 6.10 a.m., 6.30 a.m., 6.50 a.m., 7.8 a.m. and every 8 minutes until

16

Boscombe to Square.—continued.

9.24 a.m., 9.30 a.m., then every 5 minutes until 7.40 p.m., 7.46 p.m., 7.54 p.m., 8.0 p.m., then every 8 minutes until 10.48 p.m., 10.56 p.m.*, 11.4 p.m.* (*) to Central Station only.

SUNDAYS—9.32 a.m. and every 8 minutes until 11.40 a.m., then every 5 minutes until 10.20 p.m., 10.30 p.m*, 10.35 p.m.* (*) to Central Station only

FROM CAPSTONE ROAD (Junction Holdenhurst Rd. TO CENTRAL STATION and SQUARE.

WEEKDAYS—5.37 a.m., 5.57 a.m., 6.17 a.m., 6.37 a.m., 6.57 a.m., 7.15 a.m. and every 8 minutes until 9.31 a.m., 9.37 a.m., then every 5 minutes until 7.47 p.m., 7.53 p.m., 8.1 p.m., 8.7 p.m., then every 8 minutes until 10.55 p.m., 11.3 p.m.*, 11.11 p.m.* (*) to Central Station only.

SUNDAYS—9.39 a.m. and every 8 minutes until 11.47 a.m., then every 5 minutes until 10.27 p.m., 10.37 p.m.*, 10.42 p.m. (*) to Central Station only.

FROM CAPSTONE ROAD (Junction Holdenhurst Rd.) TO ASHLEY ROAD (Junction Christchurch Road).

WEEKDAYS—6.2 a.m., 6.22 a.m., 6.42 a.m., 7.2 a.m., 7.22 a.m., 7.42 a.m. and every 8 minutes until 10.14 a.m., then every 5 minutes until 8.34 p.m. then every 8 minutes until 11.30 p.m.

SUNDAYS—9.58 a.m. and every 8 minutes until 12.22 p.m., 12.30 p.m., 12.34 p.m., then every 5 minutes until 10.54 p.m.

FROM CENTRAL STATION TO SQUARE.

WEEKDAYS—5.40 a.m., 6.0 a.m., 6.20 a.m., 6.40 a.m., 7.0 a.m., 7.18 a.m. and every 8 minutes until 9.34 a.m., 9.39 a.m., then every 5 minutes until 7.50 p.m., 7.56 p.m., 8.4 p.m., 8.9 p.m., then every 8 minutes until 10.58 p.m.

SUNDAYS—9.42 a.m. and every 8 minutes until 11.50 a.m., then every 5 minutes until 10.30 p.m.

FROM CENTRAL STATION TO ASHLEY ROAD (Junction Christchurch Road).

WEEKDAYS—5.58 a.m., 6.18 a.m., 6.38 a.m., 6.58 a.m., 7.18 a.m., 7.38 a.m. and every 8 minutes until 10.10 a.m., then every 5 minutes until 8.30 p.m., then every 8 minutes until 11.26 p.m.

SUNDAYS—9.54 a.m. and every 8 minutes until 12.26 p.m., 12.30 p.m., then every 5 minutes until 10.50 p.m.

17

Timings of route (sic) 25 in 1934.

David Bowler collection

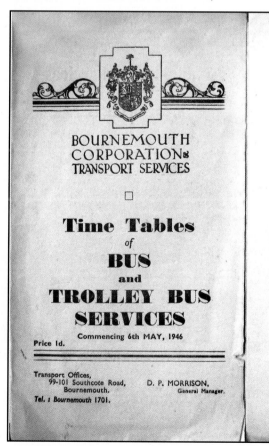

TROLLEY BUSES

SERVICES 20 & 24
SQUARE—JUMPERS—CHRISTCHURCH.

From Square. 6X56 a.m., 7.10 a.m., 7.25 a.m., 7.40 a.m., 7X53 a.m., 8.3 a.m., then every 10 minutes to Jumpers and every 20 mins. to Christchurch until 9.3 p.m., 9X13 p.m., 9.25 p.m., 9.37 p.m., 9.52 p.m., 10X7 p.m., 10.22 p.m., 10X37 p.m., 10.50 p.m. 11X10 p.m., 11X25 p.m. SUNDAYS—8X30 a.m., 9.50 a.m., then every 30 minutes until 12.20 p.m., 12X33 p.m., 12.43 p.m., then every 10 minutes to Jumpers and every 20 minutes to Christchurch until 9.3 p.m., 9X13 p.m., 9.25 p.m., 9.37 p.m., 9.52 p.m., 10X7 p.m., 10.22 p.m., 10X37 p.m., 10.50 p.m., 11X10 p.m., 11X25 p.m.

(X denotes to Jumpers only).

From Christchurch. 7.17 a.m., 7.40 a.m., then every 20 minutes until 9.20 p.m., 9.46 p.m., 10.1 p.m., 10.16 p.m., 10.31 p.m., 10.55 p.m. SUNDAYS—10.23 a.m. then every 30 minutes until 12.53 p.m., 1.20 p.m. then every 20 minutes until 9.20 p.m., 9.46 p.m., 10.1 p.m., 10.16 p.m., 10.31 p.m., 10.55 p.m.

From Jumpers. 6.34 a.m., 6.49 a.m., 7.2 a.m., 7.17 a.m., 7.30 a.m., then every 10 minutes until 9.10 p.m., 9.30 p.m., 9.40 p.m., 9.55 p.m., 10.10 p.m., 10.25 p.m., 10.40 p.m., 11.3 p.m. SUNDAYS—7.30 a.m., 10 a.m., then every 30 minutes until 1 p.m., then every 10 minutes until 9.10 p.m., 9.30 p.m., 9.40 p.m., 9.55 p.m., 10.10 p.m., 10.25 p.m., 10.40 p.m., 11.3 p.m.

SERVICE 21
SQUARE — BOSCOMBE — SOUTHBOURNE — TUCKTON — CHRISTCHURCH.

From Square. 6.28 a.m., 6.48 a.m., 7.8 a.m., 7.30 a.m., 7.35 a.m., then every 10 minutes until 6.55 p.m., 7.7 p.m., 7.15 p.m., then every 15 minutes until 9.30 p.m., 10 p.m., 10.30 p.m., 11 p.m., 11.30 p.m. SUNDAYS—9.57 a.m. then every 30 minutes until 12.27 p.m., 12.50 p.m., 1.10 p.m., 1.35 p.m., then every 10 minutes until 6.55 p.m., 7.7 p.m., 7.15 p.m., then every 15 minutes until 9.30 p.m., 10 p.m., 10.30 p.m., 11 p.m., 11.30 p.m.

From Christchurch. 7.10 a.m., 7.30 a.m., 7.45 a.m., then every 10 minutes until 7.15 p.m., 7.30 p.m., 7.37 p.m., then every 15 minutes until 10.7 p.m., 10.37 p.m., 11X7 p.m. SUNDAYS—9.41 a.m., then every 30 minutes until 12.41 p.m., 1.10 p.m., 1.30 p.m., 1.50 p.m., 2.5 p.m., then every 10 minutes until 7.15 p.m., 7.30 p.m., 7.37 p.m., then every 15 minutes until 10.7 p.m., 10.37 p.m. 11X7 p.m.

(X—To Pokesdown Station only).

Time Table leaflet of 6 May 1946
Bournemouth Libraries

555

TROLLEY BUSES

SERVICES 20 & 24

SQUARE—JUMPERS—CHRISTCHURCH.

From Square. 6X56 a.m., 7.10 a.m., 7.25 a.m., 7.40 a.m., 7X53 a.m., 8.3 a.m., then every 10 minutes to Jumpers and every 20 mins. to Christchurch until 9.3 p.m., 9X13 p.m., 9.25 p.m., 9.37 p.m., 9.52 p.m., 10X7 p.m., 10.22 p.m., 10X37 p.m., 10.50 p.m. 11X10 p.m., 11X25 p.m. SUNDAYS—8X30 a.m., 9.50 a.m., then every 30 minutes until 12.20 p.m., 12X33 p.m., 12.43 p.m., then every 10 minutes to Jumpers and every 20 minutes to Christchurch until 9.3 p.m., 9X13 p.m., 9.25 p.m., 9.37 p.m., 9.52 p.m., 10X7 p.m., 10.22 p.m., 10X37 p.m., 10.50 p.m., 11X10 p.m., 11X25 p.m.

(X denotes to Jumpers only).

From Christchurch. 7.17 a.m., 7.40 a.m., then every 20 minutes until 9.20 p.m., 9.46 p.m., 10.1 p.m., 10.16 p.m., 10.31 p.m., 10.55 p.m. SUNDAYS—10.23 a.m. then every 30 minutes until 12.53 p.m., 1.20 p.m. then every 20 minutes until 9.20 p.m., 9.46 p.m., 10.1 p.m., 10.16 p.m., 10.31 p.m., 10.55 p.m.

From Jumpers. 6.34 a.m., 6.49 a.m., 7.2 a.m., 7.17 a.m., 7.30 a.m., then every 10 minutes until 9.10 p.m., 9.30 p.m., 9.40 p.m., 9.55 p.m. 10.10 p.m., 10.25 p.m., 10.40 p.m., 11.3 p.m. SUNDAYS—7.30 a.m., 10 a.m., then every 30 minutes until 1 p.m., then every 10 minutes until 9.10 p.m., 9.30 p.m., 9.40 p.m., 9.55 p.m., 10.10 p.m., 10.25 p.m., 10.40 p.m., 11,3 p.m.

SERVICE 21

SQUARE — BOSCOMBE — SOUTHBOURNE — TUCKTON — CHRISTCHURCH.

From Square. 6.28 a.m., 6.48 a.m., 7.8 a.m., 7.30 a.m., 7.35 a.m., then every 10 minutes until 6.55 p.m., 7.7 p.m., 7.15 p.m., then every 15 minutes until 9.30 p.m., 10 p.m., 10.30 p.m., 11 p.m., 11.30 p.m. SUNDAYS—9.57 a.m. then every 30 minutes until 12.27 p.m., 12.50 p.m., 1.10 p.m., 1.35 p.m., then every 10 minutes until 6.55 p.m., 7.7 p.m., 7.15 p.m., then every 15 minutes until 9.30 p.m., 10 p.m., 10.30 p.m., 11 p.m., 11.30 p.m.

From Christchurch. 7.10 a.m., 7.30 a.m., 7.45 a.m., then every 10 minutes until 7.15 p.m., 7.30 p.m., 7.37 p.m., then every 15 minutes until 10.7 p.m., 10.37 p.m., 11X7 p.m. SUNDAYS—9.41 a.m., then every 30 minutes until 12.41 p.m., 1.10 p.m., 1.30 p.m., 1.50 p.m., 2.5 p.m., then every 10 minutes until 7.15 p.m., 7.30 p.m., 7.37 p.m., then every 15 minutes until 10.7 p.m., 10.37 p.m., 11X7 p.m.

(X—To Pokesdown Station only).

SERVICE 28

SQUARE—FIVE WAYS—CASTLE LANE.

From Square. 6.30 a.m., 7.5 a.m., 7.24 a.m., 7.36 a.m , 7 52 a m., 8.6 a.m., 8.15 a.m., 8.25 a.m., 8.38 a.m., then every 15 minutes until 10.23 p.m , 10.38 p.m., 10.46 p.m., 10.53 p.m., 11.8 p.m., 11.23 p.m., 11.35 p.m. SUNDAYS—9 a.m., 9.54 a.m., then every 15 minutes until 12.24 p.m., 12.38 p.m., 12.45 p.m., 1.5 p.m., 1.25 p.m., 1.45 p.m., 2.8 p.m., then every 15 minutes until 10.23 p.m., 10.38 p.m., 10.46 p.m., 10.53 p.m., 11.8 p.m., 11.23 p.m., 11.35 p.m.

From Castle Lane. 6.5 a.m., 6.45 a.m., 7 a.m., 7.14 a.m., 7.36 a.m., 7.44 a.m., 7.59 a.m., 8.7 a.m., 8.14 a.m., 8.22 a.m., 8.29 a.m., 8.37 a.m., 8.44 a.m., then every 15 minutes until 9.14 p.m., 9.22 p.m., then every 15 minutes until 11.7 p.m., 11.19 p.m. SUNDAYS—8.45 a.m., 9.37 a.m., then every 15 minutes until 12.52 p.m., 1.2 p.m., 1.20p.m., 1.40 p.m., 1.59 p.m., then every 15 minutes until 9.14 p.m., 9.22 p.m., then every 15 minutes until 11.7 p.m., 11.19 p.m.

SERVICE 28a

SQUARE—FIVE WAYS—CASTLE LANE—WEST WAY.

From Square. 7.5 a.m., 7.24 a.m., 7.52 a.m., 8.6 a.m., 8.15 a.m., 8.25 a.m., 8.53 a.m., then every 30 minutes until 1.53 p.m., 2.9 p.m., then every 15 minutes until 9.9 p.m., 9.23 p.m., then every 15 minutes until 11.8 p.m. SUNDAYS—9 a.m., 9.54 a.m., then every 15 minutes until 12.24 p.m., 12.38 p.m., 1.5 p.m., 1.25 p.m., 1.45 p.m., 2.9 p m., then every 15 minutes until 9.9 p.m., 9.23 p.m., then every 15 minutes until 11.8 p.m.

From West Way. 6.3 a.m., 6.58 a.m., 7.12 a.m., 7.32 a.m., 7.42 a.m., 8.5 a.m., 8.12 a.m., 8.20 a.m., 8.27 a.m., 8.35 a.m., 8.41 a.m., then every 30minutes until 2.11 p.m., then every 15 minutes until 9.11 p.m., 9.20 p.m., then every 15 minutes until 11.5 p.m., 11.17p.m., SUNDAYS—9.35 a.m., then every 15 minutes until 12.50 p.m., 1.18 p.m., 1.38 p.m., 1.57 p.m., 2.11 p.m., then every 15 minutes until 9.11 p.m., 9.20 p.m., then every 15 minutes until 11.5 p.m., 11.17 p.m.

SERVICE 29

SQUARE—FIVE WAYS—MALVERN ROAD.

From Square. 6.57 a.m., 7.16 a.m., 7.30 a.m., 7.45 a.m., 7.56a.m., 8.2 a.m., 8.19 a.m., 8.27 a.m., 8.34 a.m., 8.44 a.m., 9 a.m., then every 15 minutes until 10.15 p.m., 10.31 p.m. SUNDAYS—12.55 p.m., 1.15 p.m., 1.35 p.m., 1.55 p.m., 2.0 p.m., then every 15 minutes until 10.15 p.m., 10.31 p.m.

From Malvern Road. 7.10 a.m., 7.30 a.m., 7.52 a.m., 8.4 a.m., 8.11 a.m., 8.19 a.m., 8.33 a.m., 8.41 a.m., 8.50 a.m., 9.8 a.m., then every 15 minutes until 9.8 p.m., 9.20 p.m., 9.31 p.m., 9.46 p.m., 10.1 p.m., 10.16 p.m., 10.31 p.m., 10X45 p.m. SUNDAYS—7.18 a.m., 1.10 p.m., 1.30 p.m., 1.53 p.m., then every 15 minutes until 9.8 p.m., 9.20 p.m., 9.31 p.m., 9.46 p.m., 10.1 p.m., 10.16 p.m. 10.31 p.m., 10X45 p.m.

(X—To Cemetery Junction only).

SERVICE 30

SQUARE—WINTON—WALLISDOWN via Talbot Road.

From Square. 6.10 a.m., 6.50 a.m., 7.27 a.m., then every 20 minutes until 1.47 p.m., 2.5 p.m., then every 15 minutes until 7.5 p.m., then every 20 minutes until 10.25 p.m., 10.50 p.m., 11.30 p.m. SUNDAYS—9.5 a.m., 9.50 a.m., 11.10 a.m., 12.30 p.m., 1.7 p.m., 1.27 p m., 1.47 p.m., 2.5 p.m., then every 15 minutes until 7.5 p.m. then every 20 minutes until 10.25 p.m., 10.50 p.m. 11.30 p.m.

From Wallisdown. 7.17 a.m., then every 20 minutes until 1.37 p.m., then every 15 minutes until 6.37 p.m., 6.55 p.m., then every 20 minutes until 10.15 p.m., 10.34 p.m., 10.54 p.m., 11X28 p.m. SUNDAYS—8.45 a.m., 9.30 a.m., 10.50 a.m., 12.10 p.m., 1.17 p.m., 1.37 p.m., then every 15 minutes until 6.37 p.m., 6.55 p.m., then every 20 minutes until 10.15 p.m., 10.34 p.m., 10.54 p.m., 11X28 p.m.

(X—To Winton only).

For additional buses to Wallisdown via Ensbury Park Road see timetable for Service 30a.

SERVICE 30a

SQUARE — WINTON — WALLISDOWN (via Ensbury Park Road).

From Square. 7.37 a.m., then every 20 minutes until 1.57 p.m. then every 15 minutes until 6.57 p.m., 7.15 p.m., then every 20 minutes until 10.35 p.m., 11.10 p.m., SUNDAYS — 10.30 a.m. 11.50 a.m., 1.17 p.m., 1.37 p.m., 1.57 p.m., then every 15 minutes until 6.57 p.m., 7.15 p.m., then every 20 minutes until 10.35 p.m., 11.10 p.m.,

From Wallisdown. 5.30 a.m., 6.30 a.m., 7.7 a.m., then every 20 minutes until 1.27 p.m., 1.45 p.m., then every 15 minutes until 6.45 p.m., 6.52 p.m., 7.15 p.m., 7.25 p.m., then every 20 minutes until 10.5 p.m. 10.30 p.m., 10.50 p.m., 11.10 p.m., SUNDAYS—5.30 a.m., 6.25 a.m., 10.10 a.m., 11.30 a.m., 12.50 p.m., 1.27 p.m., 1.45 p.m., then every 15 minutes until 6.45 p.m., 6.52 p.m., 7.15 p.m., 7.25 p.m., then every 20 minutes until 10.5 p.m., 10.30 p.m., 10.50 p.m., 11.10 p.m.

For additional buses to Wallisdown via Talbot Road see timetable for Service 30.

Suttons, Printers, Boscombe

SERVICES 21 & 22

SQUARE — BOSCOMBE — FISHERMAN'S WALK — SOUTHBOURNE.

From Square. 6.28 a.m., 6.48 a.m., 7.8 a.m., 7.30 a.m., then every few minutes until 9.30 p.m., then every 15 minutes until 11.30 p.m. SUNDAYS—7.30 a.m., 8 a.m., 9.42 a.m., then every 15 minutes until 12.42 p.m., 12.50 p.m., then every few minutes until 9.30 p.m., then every 15 minutes until 11.30 p.m.

From Southbourne. 6.45 a.m., 7.20 a.m., 7.25 a.m., 7.40 a.m., 7.55 a.m., then every few minutes until 9.17 p.m., then every 15 minutes until 10.47 p.m., 11X17 p.m. SUNDAYS—7.50 a.m., 8.50 a.m., 9.35 a.m., then every 15 minutes until 12.50 p.m., 1.10 p.m., then every few minutes until 9.17 p.m., then every 15 minutes until 10.47 p.m., 11X17 p.m. ("X" to Pokesdown Station only.)

SERVICES 21, 22 & 23

SQUARE — BOSCOMBE — FISHERMAN'S WALK.

From Square. 6.8 a.m., 6.28 a.m., 6.48 a.m., 7.8 a.m., 7.20 a.m., 7.30 a.m., then every few minutes until 9.30 p.m., then every 15 minutes until 11.30 p.m. SUNDAYS—7.30 a.m., 8 a.m., 9.42 a.m., then every 15 minutes until 12.27 p.m., then every few minutes until 9.30 p.m., then every 15 minutes until 11.30 p.m.

From Fisherman's Walk. 5.35 a.m., 5.53 a.m., 6.13 a.m., 6.33 a.m., 6.50 a.m., 7.15 a.m., then every few minutes until 9.22 p.m., 9.37 p.m., 9.52 p.m., 10.7 p.m., 10.22 p.m., 10.52 p.m. SUNDAYS—7 a.m., 7.55 a.m., 8.55 a.m., 9.25 a.m., then every 15 minutes until 12.55 p.m., 1.10 p.m., then every few minutes until 9.22 p.m., 9.37 p.m., 9.52 p.m., 10.7 p.m., 10.22 p.m., 10.52 p.m.

SERVICE 25a

WESTBOURNE—SQUARE—CENTRAL STN.—ASHLEY ROAD BOSCOMBE.

From Westbourne. 7.10 a.m., 7.22 a.m., then every few minutes until 10.40 p.m., 10.55 p.m., 11.10 p.m., 11.25 p.m. SUNDAYS—9.10 a.m., 9.42 a.m., then every 15 minutes until 1.12 p.m. 1.24 p.m., then every few minutes until 10.40 p.m., 10.55 p.m., 11.10 p.m., 11.25 p.m.

From Square. 5.51 a.m., 6.11 a.m., 6.31 a.m., 6.51 a.m., 7.15 a.m., 7.30 a.m., then every few minutes until 10.48 p.m., 11.3 p.m. 11.18 p.m., 11.33 p.m. SUNDAYS—7.30 a.m., 8.15 a.m., 9.15 a.m., 9.35 a.m., then every 15 minutes until 1.20 p.m., then every few minutes until 10.48 p.m., 11.3 p.m., 11.18 p.m., 11.33 p.m.

From Ashley Road. 5.30 a.m., 5.50 a.m., 6.10 a.m., 6.30 a.m., 6.50 a.m., 7.10 a.m., then every few minutes until 10.14 p.m., 10.29 p.m., 10.44 p.m., 10.59 p.m., 11.14 p.m. SUNDAYS—7.40 a.m., 8 a.m., 8.45 a.m., 9.30 a.m., then every 15 minutes until 12.45 p.m., 12.58 p.m., then every few minutes until 10.14 p.m., 10.29 p.m., 10.44 p.m., 10.59 p.m., 11.14 p.m.,

SERVICE 26

SQUARE — WINTON — MOORDOWN.

From Square. 6.20 a.m., 6.40 a.m., 7.2 a.m., 7.18 a.m., 7.32 a.m., 7.42 a.m., 7.51 a.m., 8 a.m., 8.12 a.m., 8.23 a.m., then every few minutes until 9.45 p.m., then every 15 minutes until 11.30 p.m. SUNDAYS—6 a.m., 6.55 a.m., 7.2 a.m., 9 a.m., 9.46 a.m., then every 15 minutes until 12.31 p.m., 12.51 p.m., 1.2 p.m., then every few minutes until 9.45 p.m., then every 15 minutes until 11.30 p.m.

From Moordown. 6 a.m., 6.20 a.m., 6.40 a.m., 6.50 a.m., 7 a.m., 7.16 a.m., then every few minutes until 9.14 p.m., then every 15 minutes until 11.14 p.m. SUNDAYS—6.15 a.m., 7 a.m., 7.13 a.m., 8.45 a.m., 9.30 a.m., then every 15 minutes until 1 p.m., 1.16 p.m., then every few minutes until 9.14 p.m., then every 15 minutes until 11.14 p.m.

SERVICE 26a

SQUARE—WINTON—MOODOWN—WEST WAY.

From Square. 7.18 a.m., 7.51 a.m., 8.52 a.m., then every 30 minutes until 1.52 p.m., then every 15 minutes until 8.52 p.m., 9 p.m., then every 15 minutes until 11 p.m. SUNDAYS—9.46 a.m. then every 15 minutes until 12.31 p.m., 1.1 p.m., 1.21 p.m., 1.52 p.m. then every 15 minutes until 8.52 p.m., 9 p.m., then every 15 minutes until 11 p.m.

From West Way. 7.23 a.m., 7.42 a.m., 8.12 a.m., 8.22 a.m. 8.32 a.m, 8.42 a.m., then every 30 minutes until 1.42 p.m., 2.11 p.m., then every 15 minutes until 9.11 p.m., 9.25 p.m., then every 15 minutes until 11.10 p.m. SUNDAYS—10.12 a.m., then every 15 minutes until 12.57 p.m., 1.22 p.m., 1.42 p.m., 2.11 p.m., then every 15 minutes until 9.11 p.m., 9.25 p.m., then every 15 minutes until 11.10 p.m.

SERVICE 27

SQUARE—LANSDOWNE—CENTRAL STN—WINTON —MOORDOWN—CASTLE LANE JUNC.

From Square. 7.12 a.m., 7.22 a.m., 7.37 a.m., 7.52 a.m., then every few minutes until 9.28 p.m., 9.41 p.m., 9.56 p.m., 10.11 p.m., 10.26 p.m., 10.35 p.m., 10.50 p.m., 11.10 p.m., 11.30 p.m.
SUNDAYS—7.30 a.m., 8 a.m., 12.50 p.m., 1.5 p.m., 1.20 p.m., 1.35 p.m., 1.48 p.m., then every few minutes until 9.28 p.m., 9.41 p.m., 9.56 p.m., 10.11 p.m., 10.26p.m., 10.35 p.m., 10.50 p.m., 11.10 p.m., 11,30 p.m.

From Moordown. 6.5 a.m., 6.35 a.m., 6.47 a.m., 7 a.m., then every few minutes until 9.8 p.m., 9.21 p.m., 9.35 p.m., 9.50 p.m., 10.5 p.m., 10.14 p.m., 10.21 p.m. 10.49 p.m., 11.9 p.m. SUNDAYS—7.35 a.m., 9X35 a.m., 10X20 a.m., 11X0 a.m., 11X50 a.m., 12X31 p.m., 12.46 p.m., 1.1 p.m., 1.16 p.m., 1.28 p.m., then every few minutes until 9.8 p.m.,[9.21 p.m., 9.35 p.m.,9.50 p.m., 10.5 p.m., 10.14 p.m. 10.21 p.m., 10.49 p.m., 11.9 p.m. (X—to Lansdowne only).

SERVICE 28

SQUARE—FIVE WAYS—CASTLE LANE.

From Square. 6.30 a.m., 7.5 a.m., 7.24 a.m., 7.36 a.m , 7 52 a m., 8.6 a.m., 8.15 a.m., 8.25 a.m., 8.38 a.m., then every 15 minutes until 10.23 p.m , 10.38 p.m., 10.46 p.m., 10.53 p.m., 11.8 p.m., 11.23 p.m., 11.35 p.m. SUNDAYS—9 a.m., 9.54 a.m., then every 15 minutes until 12.24 p.m., 12.38 p.m., 12.45 p.m., 1.5 p.m., 1.25 p.m., 1.45 p.m., 2.8 p.m., then every 15 minutes until 10.23 p.m., 10.38 p.m., 10.46 p.m., 10.53 p.m., 11.8 p.m., 11.23 p.m., 11.35 p.m.

From Castle Lane. 6.5 a.m., 6.45 a.m., 7 a.m., 7.14 a.m., 7.36 a.m., 7.44 a.m., 7.59 a.m., 8.7 a.m., 8.14 a.m., 8.22 a.m., 8.29 a.m., 8.37 a.m., 8.44 a.m., then every 15 minutes until 9.14 p.m., 9.22 p.m., then every 15 minutes until 11.7 p.m., 11.19 p.m. SUNDAYS—8.45 a.m., 9.37 a.m., then every 15 minutes until 12.52 p.m., 1.2 p.m., 1.20p.m., 1.40 p.m., 1.59 p.m., then every 15 minutes until 9.14 p.m., 9.22 p.m., then every 15 minutes until 11.7 p.m., 11.19 p.m.

SERVICE 28a

SQUARE—FIVE WAYS—CASTLE LANE—WEST WAY.

From Square. 7.5 a.m., 7.24 a.m., 7.52 a.m., 8.6 a.m., 8.15 a.m., 8.25 a.m., 8.53 a.m., then every 30 minutes until 1.53 p.m., 2.9 p.m., then every 15 minutes until 9.9 p.m., 9.23 p.m., then every 15 minutes until 11.8 p.m. SUNDAYS—9 a.m., 9.54 a.m., then every 15 minutes until 12.24 p.m., 12.38 p.m., 1.5 p.m., 1.25 p.m., 1.45 p.m., 2.9 p m., then every 15 minutes until 9.9 p.m., 9.23 p.m., then every 15 minutes until 11.8 p.m.

From West Way. 6.3 a.m., 6.58 a.m., 7.12 a.m., 7.32 a.m., 7.42 a.m., 8.5 a.m., 8.12 a.m., 8.20 a.m., 8.27 a.m., 8.35 a.m., 8.41 a.m., then every 30minutes until 2.11 p.m., then every 15 minutes until 9.11 p.m., 9.20 p.m., then every 15 minutes until 11.5 p.m., 11.17p.m., SUNDAYS—9.35 a.m., then every 15 minutes until 12.50 p.m., 1.18 p.m., 1.38 p.m., 1.57 p.m., 2.11 p.m., then every 15 minutes until 9.11 p.m., 9.20 p.m., then every 15 minutes until 11.5 p.m., 11.17 p.m.

SERVICE 29

SQUARE—FIVE WAYS—MALVERN ROAD.

From Square. 6.57 a.m., 7.16 a.m., 7.30 a.m., 7.45 a.m., 7.56a.m., 8.2 a.m., 8.19 a.m., 8.27 a.m., 8.34 a.m., 8.44 a.m., 9 a.m., then every 15 minutes until 10.15 p.m., 10.31 p.m. SUNDAYS—12.55 p.m., 1.15 p.m., 1.35 p.m., 1.55 p.m., 2.0 p.m., then every 15 minutes until 10.15 p.m., 10.31 p.m.

From Malvern Road. 7.10 a.m., 7.30 a.m., 7.52 a.m., 8.4 a.m., 8.11 a.m., 8.19 a.m., 8.33 a.m., 8.41 a.m., 8.50 a.m., 9.8 a.m., then every 15 minutes until 9.8 p.m., 9.20 p.m., 9.31 p.m., 9.46 p.m.,

Time Table leaflet of 6 May 1946 (continued). **Bournemouth Libraries**

beforehand with appropriate traffic notices appearing on the vehicles whilst on occasion leaflets were produced using an office duplicating machine.

A more detailed leaflet was produced for 6 May 1946 (when further trolleybus services were introduced) and monthly booklets were reintroduced from October 1946 and continued until September 1951, except that the July 1951 time table also covered August. These booklets all used the revised format showing the timings of each individual journey on each service from its starting point to its destination as well as the timings at various intermediate points, with separate tables for weekdays and Sundays. They also included an index of services, a map of the system and abbreviated conditions of carriage, a limited number of commercial advertisements, as well as details of various tourist attractions. Later issues contained an alphabetical index to places served accompanied by the relevant service numbers. In the winter of 1951/52, folded leaflets were produced dated 15 October 1951, 1 November 1951, 1 January 1952 and 1 April 1952. The use of booklets resumed in July 1952, initially on a quarterly basis, but monthly publication was reintroduced from April 1953 to March 1957. From June 1957 they were produced four times per year but from September 1959 this became twice per year until the end of the trolleybus era. By 1965 the winter time table although commencing on a specific date (13 September 1965) was published "until further notice" whereas previously the expiry date had been shown (the day prior to the start of the summer time table).

BCT published its own time tables, except for:

July 1952-June 1954	Henbest Publicity Services Ltd., Bournemouth.
July 1954-March 1957	Starsons (Publishers) Ltd., Risca, Monmouthshire.

Printers

October 1946-March 1947	Suttons, Boscombe.
April 1947-September 1951	Edwards & Bryning Ltd., Rochdale.
October 1951-June 1954	Henbest Publicity Services Ltd., Bournemouth.
July 1954-March 1957	The Starling Press Ltd., Risca, Monmouthshire.
June 1957-September 1967	Sydenhams Ltd., Bournemouth.
June and September 1968	Sydenham Millsons, Bournemouth.

Prices

January 1931-September 1939	1d.
May 1946-June 1949	2d.
July 1949-September 1951	3d.
October 1951-April 1952	2d.
July 1952-September 1962	3d.
May 1963-June 1964	4d.
September 1964-September 1968	6d.

Series of time tables of different dates showing post-war frequency developments of Holdenhurst Road service:

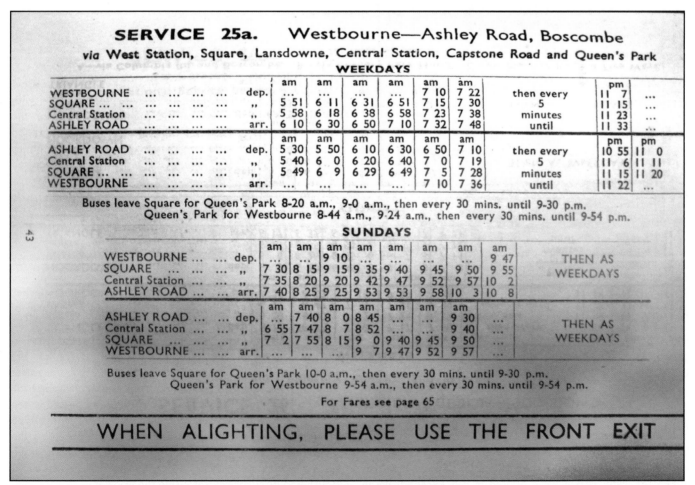

25A time table August 1949. Observe how the frequencies slowly reduce!

557

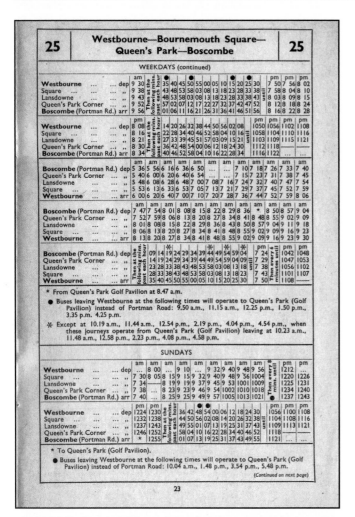

25 time table valid 14 July 1958 - 21 September 1958
David Bowler collection

25 time table valid 30 September 1963 - 7 June 1964
David Bowler collection

PLEASE TENDER THE CORRECT FARE

Dimensions (approximate)

January 1931 to December 1935	3⅛in wide X 4¾in high
January 1936 to September 1939	3⅝in wide X 6in high
October 1946 to June 1954	3⅞in wide X 6in high
July 1954 to March 1957	4⅜in wide X 5⅝in high
June 1957 to April 1969	5½in wide X 8½in high

The colour of the time table booklet cover was matt buff until December 1935 and then yellow from January 1936 until September 1939. From October 1946 until March 1957, the colour varied with each issue, except for winter 1951/52 (leaflets) and March 1957 which were white. Printing was mainly in black, but from April 1947 to June 1954 the words OFFICIAL TIME TABLE were printed in red. Exceptionally in March 1957 all printing on the cover was in blue. Matt yellow covers were used from June 1957 to September 1964 with the printing being in red for the summer and blue for the winter. From June 1965 until the end of trolleybus operation the covers were printed on glossy white paper with a photo added from June 1968. Colours still varied from summer red to winter blue.

The pages of every timetable were printed on white paper, but after some years this would change to a pale yellow with age. The text was always in black, except from June 1957 to September 1965 when it was blue.

Post-war, the print run was usually 10,000 but in some years a reprint was required. The figure gradually increased over the years and the two issues during the final year of trolleybus operation, June and September 1968, each had a print run of 18,000.

The preparation of the BCT schedules that appeared in the public timetables throughout the trolleybus era was the responsibility of the Traffic Office until June 1957, thereafter Mr R. Davies, Personal Assistant to the General Manager, took over timetable production. From 1963 this work passed to the Senior Schedules Clerk, David Chalk, who following his 1968 promotion to Assistant Traffic Superintendent, produced the Winter 1968/1969 Time Table featuring a trolleybus photograph on the front cover and a variety of facts and figures about Bournemouth's trolleybuses inside the booklet.

Stop Signs

All "standard" bus stops served by Bournemouth's trolleybuses displayed rectangular flags or signs attached at right angles to traction poles or separate supporting tubular poles painted the same leaf green as the traction poles. At important boarding points, additional information such as service number(s) serving the stop, and a list of the most important stops served by each service, was added, making the flags correspondingly deeper and larger. Latterly, a dozen stainless steel bus stop poles were placed at main stops around the Square and Bournemouth Pier (an innovation of Ronald Cox).

The flags or signs were originally wooden with white lettering on a brown background (a similar brown to that used for the vehicle roofs during the Second World War). An example is shown in the photograph of a lightweight steel passenger waiting shelter in Chapter 6 (page 116).

```
FARE STAGE
BUS STOP

SERVICE 25
FARE STAGE
FORM QUEUE
```

From the mid-1930s yellow metal plate flags with the appropriate information painted on to them in black began to appear, primarily at important boarding points. Examples are known to have been placed at Boscombe Gardens by 1937 and Queen's Park Corner by 1935, and others were evident at Christchurch terminus, Bournemouth Pier and in Bournemouth town centre by the early 1950s. In the mid-1950s it became policy to replace the brown signs with yellow ones having black lettering, the change from wooden signs to metal plates being spread over several years. Standard signs such as BUS STOP and REQUEST BUS STOP were purchased from a specialist manufacturer, those at terminal and major loading points were prepared individually in-house. At first they were simply screwed onto the wooden boards, but eventually they replaced the wooden boards with just a single metal plate. The signs were also fixed to lamp posts in some cases.

Early deliveries of metal plates included flags displaying BUS STOP with FORM QUEUE THIS SIDE or FORM QUEUE OTHER SIDE beneath, again lettered in black on a yellow background, priority probably being given to placing them along the busiest (trolleybus) routes. More important stops were equipped with larger and deeper rectangular stop flags prepared by BCT displaying BUS STOP, FORM QUEUE THIS SIDE or FORM QUEUE OTHER SIDE, with SERVICE (some had no heading at all) indicating the service number(s) serving the stop, and a list of the most important stops served by each service, beneath, on occasion in parallel columns, lettered and numbered in black on a yellow background. A separate sign above or beneath the main flag indicating FARE STAGE, lettered in black capitals on a yellow background, was added where required. Town centre and terminal stop flags were accompanied by a metal disc at the side, indicating the service number or numbers, and illuminated from above.

Latterly the small double-sided metal flags used all over the UK in this period appeared at less-important stops again with black printing on a yellow background or yellow printing on a black band.

```
BUS STOP
QUEUE THIS SIDE
FARE STAGE
```

```
REQUEST
BUS STOP
```

```
TROLLEY
BUS STOP
ONLY
```

```
SERVICE 24

BOSCOMBE
IFORD
JUMPERS

QUEUE OTHER SIDE
ALL BUSES FROM
THIS STOP GO TO
BOSCOMBE
```

```
BUSES LEAVE
HERE FOR
CENTRAL STN
LANSDOWNE
SQUARE
WESTBOURNE
FORM QUEUE
OTHER SIDE
```

```
30   31
BUS STOP
QUEUE THIS SIDE
```

(Left) Amidst decorations for the 1937 Coronation, a new **TROLLEY BUSES STOP HERE BY REQUEST** yellow plate metal flag has been planted at the westbound Boscombe Garden stop. A Sunbeam MS2 is approaching from the direction of the Lansdowne. **David Chalk collection**

(Below) The westbound stop in Poole Road opposite the **Grand Cinema** which opened in 1922 and still survives, albeit as a bingo hall. BUT9641T no. 202 (KLJ336) waits at the stop outside the cinema as a **Charlie's Cars Albion** coach overtakes. **Photographer's name not recorded.**

David Chalk collection

Sunbeam MS2 no.129 (BEL814) and BUT9641T no. 219 (KLJ353) rest off-duty at the Triangle parking area in the early 1950s.

OPERATIONS

In order to run the public timetable of the Bournemouth trolleybus system three separate internal documents were required: the Running Timetables which indicated which vehicle operated each departure, Duty Sheets which listed the crew signing-on, break and signing-off times together with service and vehicle to be operated, and the Rotas or Rosters which showed each individual crew member their duty numbers for the week.

The following information relates to the situation existing around 1963.

Running Timetables

Three Running Timetables sufficed for the entire trolleybus network (there was a fourth for all motorbus services), namely the Bournemouth Square-Christchurch services (20-24, 37) known as the Main Road group, those passing Cemetery Junction (26-36) known as the Side Routes, and, lastly, the Ashley Road service (25) which was the busiest and most frequent of all. Separate timetables were issued each summer for seasonal services 38 and 39. The Side Routes Running Timetable included the actual service number to be displayed due to the existence of "ghost" numbers 27, 33 and 36 for vehicles running to and from Castle Lane (Mallard Road) Depot or operating short-workings. Running Timetables were duplicated on foolscap sheets (double foolscap for the Main Road and Side Route groups), corresponding to today's A4 and A3 sizes, and printed in black (blue during Ronnie Cox's tenure as General Manager).

Running Timetables were read horizontally across the page, only the minutes past each hour being shown. Each journey was marked with a Bus Letter denoting the vehicle working it. The first trolleybus to run out of the depot on the Main Road services each morning was allocated Bus Letter A, each successive run-out receiving the next letter in the alphabet. By following the Bus Letter through the table, an individual vehicle's duties throughout the day could be seen. The trolleybuses themselves did not carry any physical indication of their Bus Letter unlike the "running numbers" used by other larger operators.

The "Leave Depot" column contained an alphabetical code for the respective depot: B for Boscombe (Pokesdown), C for Central, Southcote Road, and MR for Castle Lane (Mallard Road). The former Moordown Depot used the code M. No code was used for the service 25 Running Timetable as all vehicles used ran-out from Central Depot.

During the day, although trolleybuses operated different services within each Running Timetable they rarely changed group. An exception involved the Main Road group, where two of the four buses each hour on service 24 were in fact Side Route vehicles which had worked along Castle Lane to Jumpers and which, having completed a return trip, to Bournemouth Square rejoined service 32.

A dash (-) next to the Bus Letter indicated a service operating from the Lansdowne to Bournemouth Square ran via Bath Road. On the Main Road, alternate trolleybuses passing through Boscombe, but not alternate vehicles on each individual service, took the Bath Road, Westover Road route.

The same rule applied to the Holdenhurst Road services: alternate 25 and 34 (earlier 27) trolleybuses operated via Bath and Westover Roads. The lack of alternative eastbound wiring ensured that all trolleybuses on all services from Bournemouth Square to the Lansdowne operated via Old Christchurch Road. The alternative routes were not advertised in public timetables, although trolleybuses displayed the appropriate blue or red "in town via" auxiliary screen at front and rear. Exceptionally the October 1949 timetable showed all westbound 22B services operating via Bath and Westover Roads.

Two positive symbols (++) indicated that the trolleybus ran out of service, not necessarily to the depot. The destination would be shown on the Duty Sheet.

A continuous shortage of crews during the period that open-top service 39 operated led to its frequent cancellation, staff only being released for seasonal services when all normal services had been fully crewed, with motorbus coastal service 12 taking priority. A gap between the return of the 3.40pm and the 7.20pm departure enabled the crews to be used on other services and meal break reliefs.

SUMMARY OF VEHICLES REQUIRED
Monday-Saturday

Depot	Central	Boscombe	Mallard Road	No. of vehicles
Main Road	8*	10	2	20
Side Routes	-	-	26	26
Ashley Road	9*	-	-	9
Service 38	3†	-	-	3
Service 39 (o/t)	2	-	-	2
Specials	7	-	-	7
Total vehicles	29	10	28	67++

* included 1 trolleybus after working an early morning special duty which may have been one of the 7 Specials listed below
† these 3 trolleybuses could all be allocated after having worked early morning specials
++ allowing for notes * and † the total could be reduced to 62 vehicles, the number of dedicated specials then being only 2, but this did not include any specials starting from Mallard Road (details unknown). Total requirement on a full day was probably in the order of 70 trolleybuses

Based on summer 1963 time tables when the system was at its maximum extent.

Duty Sheets

There were also three crew duty sheets for the trolleybus system (with a fourth for the motorbuses) referring to the drivers and conductors rather than the trolleybuses themselves and these were divided into Mondays to Fridays (printed on white paper), Saturdays (pink), Sundays and Public Holidays (blue). One copy was typed and kept in the Traffic Office, but carbon paper was used to print other copies for display in the depots and the Square. Duty sheets were separate for Mondays

27

Bournemouth Corporation Transport

Comm. 27th May, 1963
Page 1.

SERVICES 20, 21, 22, 23 & 24

WEEKDAYS

Bus Let	Lve. Dpot dep.	X'ch ton.	Tuck Road	Cran Rds.	Crss Walk	Fish ers.	Jump are.	Squ- are.	Bus Lot	Squ- are.	Jump ers.	Fish Walk	Crss Rds.	Cran Road	Tuck ton.	X'ch arr.
A-	5.31B	—	—	—	5.35	—	5.50	5.55	A	—	6.10	6.10	—	—	—	6.50
D-	5.51B	—	—	—	55	—	6.10	6.15	D	6.43	30	56	—	—	6.54	59
C-	6.28C	—	—	6.15	—	6.20	30	—	C	—	—	—	—	—	7.00	—
A	—	6.45	—	—	—	—	42	—	A	7.05	45	6.50	—	6.50	14	6.54
B-	6.36C	7.00	—	—	—	—	50	47	B	15	51	56	—	—	20	—
E-	6.50C	7.04	—	—	—	—	—	50	E	—	—	7.10	—	7.05	—	7.10
G-	7.00B	—	—	35	—	—	—	55	G	—	7.05	11	7.42	—	30	7.13
F-	6.14B	—	—	—	—	6.20	—	56	F	15	11	16	—	—	34	25
D	—	—	18	—	—	—	—	7.05	D	—	22	—	—	—	40	—
Z-	6.42C via Lans & Cen. Station	14	—	—	—	—	7.10	Z	—	29	25	30	—	—	46	36
I-	6.25C	—	—	6.54	—	—	—	10	I	—	—	30	37	—	—	50	39
X-	6.37B	—	—	—	—	—	—	20	X	—	20	32	—	—	—	—
J-	7.23B	—	—	—	—	—	—	27	J	47	37	37	—	—	—	—
K-	7.09C	—	—	—	—	—	24	34	K	—	42	47	—	50	—	55
L-	7.38B	—	—	—	—	—	28	39	L	—	27	56	—	—	59	—
C-	—	—	—	—	—	—	—	43	C	—	34	57	—	—	8.01	8.06
M-	7.47B	—	7.04	—	—	—	39	44	M	8.05	39	—	—	—	06	—
B	—	—	—	—	—	—	42	53	B	—	43	57	—	—	—	12
N-	7.28C	—	—	—	—	17	45	54	N	—	44	8.02	8.02	8.07	10	—
D	—	—	—	—	—	—	—	59	D	—	53	11	—	—	16	—
E-	—	—	—	—	—	—	47	8.04	E	15	54	12	—	8.07	17	26
A-	8.07B	—	—	—	24	—	53	07	A	—	59	17	—	—	19	—
O	—	7.12	—	—	27	—	58	10	O	30	07	22	—	—	21	38
G-	7.21B	7.22	—	30	—	25	8.03	12	G	—	10	27	—	—	26	—
P	—	—	—	—	35	—	03	13	P	—	12	29	— —	—	30	—
Z	—	—	—	—	40	—	08	18	Z	35	13	32	—	—	34	47
R-	7.32MR	—	31	—	45	40	11	22	R	—	18	37	—	—	37	—
F	—	—	—	—	50	—	13	24	F	45	22	42	42	—	41	58
J	—	—	—	—	55	48	18	27	J	—	24	47	—	—	46	—
I	—	—	44	—	8.00	—	21	33	I	50	27	52	—	—	50	9.07
K-	—	—	—	—	05	—	23	36	K	—	33	57	—	—	9.01	—
L	—	—	—	—	10	53	28	38	L	—	36	—	—	—	—	—
S	—	7.50MR	—	54	—	—	31	—	S	59	38	—	—	9.02	9.01	58
X	—	8.00	8.04	—	15	8.08	34	—	X	—	—	—	—	—	—	—
M-	7.50MR	8.00	—	—	—	—	—	—	M	—	—	—	—	—	—	—
C-	8.00	—	56	—	—	—	—	—	C	—	57	—	—	9.02	—	9.07
N	—	—	06	—	—	—	—	—	N	—	—	—	—	—	06	—

Bournemouth Corporation Transport

Page 1.

SERVICES 25   WEEKDAYS   Comm. 27th June 1963

Bus Let	Lve. Dpot	Ashl Road dep.	Q'ns Park dep.	Caps Road	Squ-are.	West brne arr.	West brne dep.	Squ-are.	Caps Road	Q'ns Park arr.	Ashl Road arr.
A	5.39	-		-	-	-	-	5.50	6.01	-	6.06
B	5.28	5.36	-	5.42	5.53	6.00	6.07	6.15	26	-	31
C	5.48	56	-	6.02	6.13	20	20	28	39	-	44
A-		6.16	-	22	33	40	40	48	59	-	7.04
B		36	-	42	53	7.00	7.00	7.08	7.19	-	24
C		50	-	56	7.05	10	10	18	29	-	34
D	7.02	-		-	13	20	20	28	39	-	44
E	7.10	-		-	21	28	28	36	47	-	52
A		7.10	-	7.17	29	36	36	44	55	-	8.00
F-	7.10	18	-	25	37	44	44	52	8.03	-	08
B		26	-	33	45	52	52	8.00	11	-	15
G	7.25	33	-	40	52	59	59	07	19	-	24
C-		40	-	47	59	8.06	8.06	14	26	-	31
D		47	-	54	8.06	13	13	21	33	8.35	-
E-		54	-	8.01	13	20	20	28	40	-	46
A		8.01	-	08	20	27	27	35	47	-	53
F-		08	-	15	27	34	34	42	54	-	9.00
H	8.07	15	-	22	34	41	41	49	9.01	-	07
B-		22	-	29	41	48	48	56	08	-	14
G		29	-	36	48	55	55	9.03	15	-	21
I	from Special			-	-	-	-	07	19	-	25
C-		36	-	43	55	9.02	9.03	11	23	-	29
D		-	8.46	50	9.02	09	11	19	31	-	37
E		50	-	57	09	16	18	25	37	-	43
A-		56	-	9.03	15	22	24	32	44	-	50
F	9.03	-		10	22	29	31	39	51	-	57
H-		09	-	16	28	35	37	45	57	-	10.3
B		16	-	23	35	42	44	52	10.4	-	10
G-		22	-	29	41	48	50	58	10	1013	-
I		29	-	36	48	55	57	10.5	17	-	23
C-		35	-	42	54	10.1	10.3	11	23	-	29
D		42	-	49	10.1	03	10	18	30	-	36
E-		48	-	55	07	14	16	24	36	-	42
A		55	-	10.2	14	21	23	31	43	-	49
F	10.1	-		08	20	27	29	37	49	-	55
H		08	-	15	27	34	36	44	56	-	11.2
B-		14	-	21	33	40	42	50	11.2	-	08
G		-	1025	28	40	47	49	57	09	-	15
I-		27	-	34	46	53	55	11.3	15	-	21
C		34	-	41	53	11.0	11.2	10	22	-	28
D-		40	-	47	59	06	08	16	28	-	34
E		47	-	54	11.6	13	15	23	35	1138	-
A-		53	-	11.0	12	19	21	29	41	-	47
F	11.0	-		07	19	26	28	36	48	-	54
H-		06	-	13	25	32	34	42	54	-	1200
B		13	-	20	32	39	41	49	12.1	-	12.7
G-		19	-	26	38	45	47	55	07	-	13
I		26	-	33	45	52	54	12.2	14	-	20
C-		32	-	39	51	58	12.0	08	20	-	26
D		39	-	46	58	12.5	07	15	27	-	33
E-		-	1149	52	12.4	11	13	21	33	-	39
A		52	-	59	11	18	20	28	40	12 43	-
F-		58	-	12.5	17	24	26	34	46	-	52
H	12.5	-		12	24	31	33	41	53	-	59
B-		11	-	18	30	37	39	47	59	-	1.05
G		18	-	25	37	44	46	54	1.06	-	12
I-		24	-	31	43	50	52	1.00	12	-	18
C		31	-	38	50	57	59	07	19	-	25
D-		37	-	44	56	1.03	1.05	13	25	-	31
E		44	-	51	1.03	10	12	20	32	-	38
A-		-	1254	57	09	16	18	26	38	-	44
F		57	-	1.04	16	23	25	33	45	-	51
H-	1.03	-		10	22	29	31	39	51	-	57
B		10	-	17	29	36	38	46	58	-	2.04
G-		16	-	23	35	42	44	52	2.04	-	10
I		23	-	30	42	49	51	59	11	2.14	-

to Fridays and Saturdays, because, although the basic timetable may have been the same, there were a number of specials which operated on Mondays to Fridays, but not on Saturdays. A crew (driver and conductor) always stayed together so that each duty applied to both drivers and conductors.

The Duty Sheets listed all the duties required to provide crew coverage for all trolleybuses in service from the time they left the depot until the time they returned. Each individual duty showed the reporting time, where to report, the service number and Bus Letter to be operated, and the finishing time. Early duties always started at a depot and finished in the Square whilst late duties started in the Square and finished in a depot. Spreadover duties usually started and finished at a depot.

Crews were granted ten minutes to sign-on and ten minutes to sign-off. In addition, at the Square, they were allowed three minutes "walking time" from Gervis Place to the Avenue Road crew room.

A typical duty, somewhat simplified, would appear something like this:

```
123   0700MR   22B 0710 to 1120   4.10
               23D 1215 to 3.45   3.30   20   6   8.06   8
```

123 was the duty number; 0700 the signing-on time at Mallard Road; 22 the service to be operated; B the Bus Letter; 0710 to 1120 the period of the first part of the shift; 4.10 the number of paid hours in the first part of the shift; 23 the service to be operated after the break (11.20-12.15); D the Bus Letter; 1215 to 3.45 the period of the second part of the shift; 3.30 the number of paid hours in the second part of the shift; 20 the minutes allowed for signing-on and signing-off; 6 the minutes allowed for walking time; 8.06 the total number of hours and minutes worked and 8 the hours paid. The time of 11.20 would be the arrival time at Gervis Place and 3.45 would also be the arrival time. Crews always took over a vehicle at its scheduled arrival time, not at its departure time.

A duty had a nominal duration of eight hours (the amount paid in wages) but in practice could be up to 8 hours and 7 minutes. Duties were divided into early duties, late duties and the unpopular spreadover duties which involved a start time of approximately 7am and an end time of about 7pm, but with a long break in between. Early and late duties usually had a break of about one hour. All breaks, including the long one in a spreadover duty, were unpaid. Crews never returned to the same bus after their break, as this would not have been practical. Usually crews worked a six day week with the same duty as far as possible. Other crews would then do a week of different duties each day, covering the days off of the other crews.

Trolleybuses were not allocated to crews all day; for example a crew might operate Main Road bus letter B for approximately four hours and then, after their break, operate letter M. Crews were always allocated to the same duty rosters so that Main Road crews always worked Main Road journeys and Side Route crews always worked Side Routes, etc. This was in part so that trolleybus drivers only had to learn the overhead wiring specialities for a particular section of route. When services 24 and 32 interworked, they were always operated by Side Route crews as the drivers were already familiar with the overhead wiring layout between the Square and Lansdowne from their service 27 journeys, and the section between Lansdowne and Iford was straightforward with no special training required.

There were, however, about a dozen specially-trained drivers who could work the whole trolleybus system and this was useful when service 39 was introduced.

There was a sheet posted in the depot and compiled by the night staff which allocated a vehicle number, in fact the registration number and not the fleet number, to each duty so that crews knew which number vehicle they were to take out. However, drivers did not have a copy of the list showing which vehicle had been allocated to each Bus Letter. Crews coming off duty at the Square were supposed to change the indicator blinds for the next journey at the stop prior to the Square, so that the relieving crew would know which vehicle to look out for. The relieving crew would refer to the Running Timetable to establish the arrival of the vehicle which they were scheduled to take over, e.g. referring to the Main Road extract above, a crew taking on Bus Letter P at 7.53am would see that it arrived as a service 22 from Tuckton and would leave again as a service 23 for Tuckton via Cranleigh Road at 7.59am. They would also, of course, be looking for a crew leaving the vehicle for their break.

Rotas or Rosters

Rotas or rosters were separate for drivers and conductors and would show the duty numbers to be worked in a week, again divided, as far as trolleybuses were concerned, into the Main Road group, the Side Routes, and service 25. Latterly a week started on a Sunday, although in earlier years it seems to have varied. Pre-war a week started on a Thursday for some reason.

A typical duty sheet for a driver or conductor would look like this:

J. Gilmour   345   123   123   123   off   123   278
where 345 was Sunday, 278 was Saturday and Thursday was the rest day.

These sheets were posted each week on a Friday so that crews could see their duties for the following week. There was, however, a master rota showing all the duties needed to cover all operations. This was set out in weekly lines of duties and crews dropped down a line each week so that they knew in advance which duties they would be working and could always swop duties, provided they completed a prescribed form which had to be signed by both parties swopping. There were some "spare" drivers and conductors (usually the newest recruits) who would work the duties of crews who were on holiday or were off sick. They, of course, would not know their workings until the Friday prior to the week concerned. Motorbus and trolleybus workings were never mixed.

Once a driver or conductor was allocated to a particular rota, they normally stayed on that rota, unless they requested a change. Any driver or conductor could change specific duties on a particular day with someone on another rota by submitting the appropriate application form, but changes between staff tended to be on the same rota.

In addition to the three rotas mentioned above, there was a fourth trolleybus rota, namely "Rush Conductors". The name originated from the pre-war practice of putting an extra conductor on some journeys during busy periods, especially in the summer months. Post-war, although the name survived, the duties were completely different. The rota consisted of about eight long-serving and reliable employees who could drive or conduct any vehicle (motorbus or trolleybus) on any route. They were basically spare staff who reported at various times in case any driver or conductor failed to report. They were mostly on very early starts, with one late duty, and also covered early and late special staff buses to bring crews in and take them home when normal services were not operating. They also assisted the Depot Inspector if they were not required to work.

Communications

Throughout the trolleybus era and possibly earlier, BCT had its own private internal telephone system (in addition to the GPO lines) with the telephone lines laid in the ducts used for the feeder cables. There was a master set in the Inspector's Control Office at the Square and other telephones were located in the Traffic Office; in the Charminster Road mess room (used

by crews on the Boscombe to West Howe motorbus services and where crew reliefs took place); and in steel boxes attached to traction poles at Christchurch turntable, Fisherman's Walk westbound stop, and at Boscombe and Winton. Keys to the boxes were held by all Inspectors and by the Overhead and Mains Departments.

Even by the standards of the day, the internal telephone system was old-fashioned, calls having to be signalled by turning a handle on the handset half a dozen times which would ring a bell in the Square Control Office. The Square office could ring any of the other phones, but the other phones could only ring the Square and not each other. On the last trolleybus day (20 April 1969) the tower wagon was stationed by the Fisherman's Walk telephone in case any problems arose.

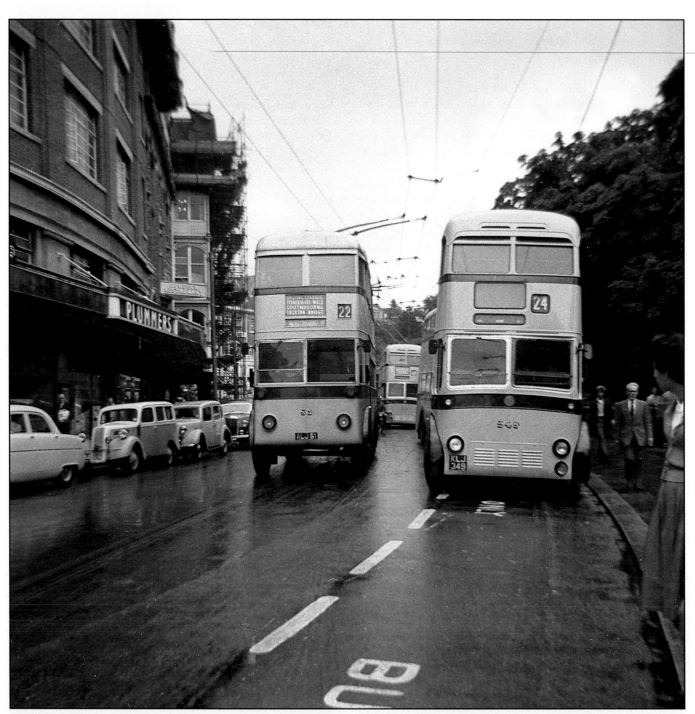

Sunbeam MS2 no. 85 (ALJ61), as yet without its new fleet number, passes BUT9641T no. 249 (KLJ349) in Gervis Place in 1959-1960. No. 85 is already running beneath the overhead wiring of the third loop for the service 22 boarding point.

Tony Belton

ENTHUSIASTS' TOURS

Private hire of trolleybuses was never a major activity. The Southern Counties Touring Society was a regular client during the 1950s and many other enthusiast societies hired trolleybuses during the 1960s. Bournemouth Education Department also was a regular client from the late 1950s to the end of operations taking schoolchildren to the Winter Gardens for concerts by the Bournemouth Symphony Orchestra. These usually involved Bournemouth School with children picked

up and set down in Charminster Road at East Way bus stop, and Stourfield School with children picked up and set down at the junction of Beaufort Road with Cranleigh Road. As these concerts were always during the winter period, the power for the lines to Bournemouth Pier had to be specially switched on.

The following tours by public transport and trolleybus enthusiasts are known to have taken place (there may have been more):

(Above) Open-top Sunbeam MS2 no. 202 (ALJ986) enters the Square from Richmond Hill on the 4 July 1965 NTA tour of the system. No. 202 was purchased by the NTA some six months after the tour and remains in preservation to this day.   F.W. Ivey

(Right) A typical enthusiasts' tour itinerary, interestingly prepared by David Chalk who was the undertaking's Assistant Traffic Superintendent at the time, encompassing all the unusual and little used parts of the system in addition to the main routes. On 7 July 1963, the RTS visited Bournemouth and toured in Sunbeam MS2 212 (ALJ973). Just three months later this trolleybus was also purchased by the enthusiasts who had hired her. It too remains in preservation, at the Trolleybus Museum at Sandtoft, currently in its original pre-war livery as no. 99.

David Chalk collection

Bournemouth Corporation Transport

READING TRANSPORT SOCIETY - PROPOSED TROLLEYBUS TOUR

Sunday, 7th July, 1963.

1.00pm	Central Station
1.02pm	Lansdowne
1.07pm	Bournemouth Pier
1.10pm	Bournemouth Square
1.17pm	Westbourne
1.25pm	Bournemouth Square
1.33pm	Winton (via Richmond Hill)
1.40pm	Ensbury Park Hotel (via Ensbury Park Road)
1.44pm	Columbia Road/Kinson Road
1.54pm	Winton (via Talbot Village)
2.00pm	Moordown (Old tram depot)
2.06pm	Broadway Hotel
2.10pm	Five Ways
2.18pm	Cemetery Junction
2.22pm	Lansdowne (via St. Paul's Road)
2.27pm	Bournemouth Square (via Westover Road)
2.28pm	Triangle
2.30pm	Bournemouth Square
2.35pm	Lansdowne (via Old Christchurch Road)
2.42pm	Boscombe Arcade
2.48pm	Queen's Park Hotel (via Ashley Road)
2.55pm	Central Station
2.58pm	Central Depot arrive.
3.20pm	Depart.
3.25pm	Boscombe Arcade
3.30pm	Pokesdown Station
3.54pm	Iford roundabout
3.41pm	Mallard Road Depot arrive.
4.00pm	Depart.
4.07pm	Iford roundabout
4.09pm	Jumpers Corner (Tea at Jumpers Cafe)
4.30pm	Depart.
4.38pm	Christchurch turntable arrive.
4.42pm	Depart
4.48pm	Tuckton Bridge
4.59pm	Fisherman's Walk (via Cranleigh Road)
5.08pm	Tuckton Bridge (via Southbourne)
5.19pm	Fisherman's Walk (via Cranleigh Road)
5.23pm	Pokesdown Depot arrive.
5.30pm	Depart.
5.35pm	Boscombe
5.40pm	Queen's Park Hotel (via Ashley Road)
5.47pm	Central Station.

The trolleybus used for this tour will be ALJ 973, a 1935 Sunbeam MS2/Park Royal - subject to service availability.

Arrangements have been made for a visit to the various depots, by kind permission of the General Manager, Mr Ronald Cox, M.Inst.T., M.I.R. All members visit the depots at their own risk, and the Bournemouth Corporation take no responsibility for injury, damage, etc.

DLC/NM,

Date	Vehicle	Organiser (where known) and Comments
4 July 1948	Sunbeam MS2	Southern Counties Touring Society
24 June 1956	Not known	PSV Circle, possibly limited to Castle Lane (Mallard Road) Depot only
March 1957	Sunbeam MS2	Southern Counties Touring Society
21 July 1957	Not known	Southern Counties Touring Society
3 June 1962	Not known	Tramway Museum Society
22 July 1962	Not known	Southern Counties Touring Society
7 July 1963	212	RTS, including Tuckton Bridge roundabout
16 November 1963	212	Handover to RTS at Castle Lane (Mallard Road) Depot
14 June 1964	200	Southern Counties Touring Society
28 June 1964	200	RTS
23 May 1965	202	Bournemouth Railway Club
30 May 1965	290/292	RTS
4 July 1965	202	National Trolleybus Association
12 June 1966	239/244	RTS, including closed Wallisdown route
11 September 1966	234/246	Farewell tour of Richmond Hill routes
25 September 1966	246	Bournemouth Railway Club, including Richmond Hill
12 March 1967	Portsmouth 313	Trials, including Horseshoe Common
30 April 1967	Portsmouth 313	NTA
18 May 1967	202	South Eastern Federation of Museums & Art Galleries
17 September 1967	268	RTS
17 September 1967	303	Southern Counties Touring Society
22 October 1967	202/246	Mallard Road Depot confines only
5 November 1967	202/246	NTA & Maypine Trolleybus Company
5 November 1967	202/246	NTA & Maypine Trolleybus Company
31 December 1967	246	Boscombe (Pokesdown) Depot closure
21 January 1968	246	Transport Trust
19 May 1968	Glasgow TBS21	Arrived Mallard Road 9 May 1968
23 June 1968	London 260	London Trolleybus Preservation Society
30 June 1968	London 260	London Trolleybus Preservation Society
28 July 1968	202	NTA, operated in Reading.
17 September 1968	268	
24 November 1968	Huddersfield 631	Huddersfield Trolleybus Preservation Society
8 December 1968	Rotherham 44	NTA
29 December 1968	301	RTS
29 December 1968	246	BPTA
5 January 1969	246	
5 January 1969	Maidstone 56	
26 January 1969	246	) NTA & Maypine Trolleybus Co., Messrs
26 January 1969	Reading 174	) Cromwell & Russell (1950 show vehicles)
26 January 1969	Maidstone 56	
16 February 1969	212	RTS preserved vehicle
23 February 1969	212	BPTA
20 April 1969	202	NTA preserved vehicle, last day of system
20 April 1969	212	RTS preserved vehicle, last day of system
20 April 1969	246	Preserved vehicle, last day of system
29 December 1968	301	RTS
29 December 1968	246	BPTA
5 January 1969	246	
5 January 1969	Maidstone 56	
26 January 1969	246	) NTA & Maypine Trolleybus Co., Messrs
26 January 1969	Reading 174	) Cromwell & Russell (1950 show vehicles)
26 January 1969	Maidstone 56	
16 February 1969	212	RTS preserved vehicle
23 February 1969	212	BPTA
20 April 1969	202	NTA preserved vehicle, last day of system
20 April 1969	212	RTS preserved vehicle, last day of system
20 April 1969	246	Preserved vehicle, last day of system

On 11 September 1966 BUT9641T 246 (KLJ346) was used on a tour of the Side Routes which closed a fortnight later. No. 246 passes the main entrance to Bournemouth Pier. **David Pearson**

Turning back up Bath Road at Bournemouth Pier, preserved Sunbeam MS2 212 (ALJ973) is seen on the 16 February 1969 RTS tour of the remains of the system. **NTA collection (R.F. Mack)**

A former Portsmouth Corporation Transport trolleybus, BUT9611T no. 313 (ERV938), pauses in Stourvale Avenue, the Jumpers Corner terminus on the 30 April 1967 NTA tour. This trolleybus is preserved at the East Anglia Transport Museum.   David Pearson

Former London Transport 1936 C2 class AEC-EE 664T no. 260 (CUL260), is seen in Belle Vue Road, just a few yards beyond Southbourne Cross Roads with Sunbeam MF2B no. 301 (301LJ) on service 21 to the Square immediately behind (23 June 1968). Tony Belton

APPENDIX O

LEGISLATION RELATING TO TROLLEYBUSES IN BOURNEMOUTH

Trolleybuses in the UK were essentially regulated in the same manner as their predecessors, the trams, and treated as light railways. This necessitated that a Bill be promoted in Parliament and an Act secured for the construction of a new trolleybus system or the conversion of an existing tramway to trolleybus operation.

This Appendix contains the relevant paragraphs of the:

    1) Bills and Acts of Parliament
    2) Statutory Rules and Orders
    3) Bournemouth Corporation Byelaws
    4) Transport Department Internal Instructions

relating to trolleybus operation in Bournemouth. Part IV of the Bournemouth Corporation Act, 1930 which provided the foundation for all other legislation is quoted in its entirety and includes both interesting indications of how political and social norms have changed since 1930, e.g. prohibition on competition, as well as little known facts, for example that Bournemouth Corporation was permitted to introduce and operate trolleybuses between Christchurch and Purewell.

Note: These extracts use the same grammar, spelling and style as the original documents. In view of the complex and dated terminology used in the original text, some explanatory additions have been made by the Author. These are shown in italics.

1) Bills and Acts of Parliament

The authorisation of a new trolleybus route normally required the presentation and confirmation of a Provisional Order as laid down under the Tramways Act, 1870. In 1945 a more flexible solution became available based on the Statutory Orders (Special Procedure) Act, 1945. Where this Act applied there was no fixed timetable for the Parliamentary stages; if an Order was unopposed, the introduction of a confirming Bill and the need for consideration of the Order and Bill on the floor of, or in Committee of, either House of Parliament was avoided; and if an Order was opposed the procedure was expedited. An example was Section 59 (2) of the Bournemouth Corporation Act, 1960.

Since the withdrawal of the trolleybuses, the Tramways Act, 1870, has been rescinded and replaced by the Transport & Works Act, 1992, which provides for new tramway, trolley vehicle and guided transport installations.

Although there are several references in the local press of the period to the planned presentation of the Bournemouth District Railless Traction Bill and the Poole, Sandbanks & Westbourne Railless Traction Bill in the January 1914 Session of Parliament, no details are available at the Public Records Office nor has the full text of the draft Bills been discovered.

1.1) Poole, Sandbanks & Westbourne Railless Traction Bill

Sponsored by Clough, Smith & Co, Spencer House, South Place, London EC. Deposited 30 November 1913 by S. Whittlestone (Wyatts, Parliamentary Agents). Solicitor: Messrs Wyatt & Co., Victoria Embankment, London. Published Maps and Diagram only.

First Reading (House of Lords) 19 February 1914. Objections noted from Bournemouth Corporation and from owners on or in the neighbourhood of the proposed trolley vehicle routes.

Second Reading 3rd March 1914.

Select Committee appointed on 31 March 1914 to look at the Bill and to hear witnesses. Bill examined on 1 and 4 May 1914.

Stephen Sellon, Consulting Engineer (formerly consulting engineer to the British Electric Traction Co.) gave most evidence, including the following details of the scheme:

- Winter timetable would be a thirty minute service (route 1) for 12 hours a day, with an hourly service for 4 hours. Much more intensive service in summer
- Average of five passengers a journey would be expected in winter
- Likely operational costs of under 6d a mile (including contribution to wear and tear); average fares would be around 2d per passenger
- Maximum size of cars would be 28 passengers; five required for service, one for spare
- The routes would use the Cedes Stoll overhead collection system; route 1 would probably have separate sets of wires for each direction, but route 2 would probably only have one set of wires
  (passing vehicles would exchange trolley carriages)
- County Gates to Haven Hotel would be a 4d fare, with only 2d to Canford Cliffs.

It was conceded that there would possibly be congestion in the County Gates area, but much was made of the ease of turning Cedes vehicles.

Harry Webber (General Manager of Keighley Corporation) gave strong evidence for the compatibility of trolley vehicles with rural areas with expensive houses. However, Sellon was unable to convince their Lordships that his own experience at Aberdare was in any real way relevant to the character of the proposed route. Evidence from several prosperous landowners was against having trolley vehicles, and the Bill was not received favourably.

Bill not proceeded further with on 5 May 1914.

Route No. 1: County Gates, The Avenue, Western Road, Haven Road, Flaghead Road and West Road, to the Haven Hotel (Banks Road) Sandbanks (4 miles 4.23 chains).

Route No. 1A: Ravine Road (south) from Western Road (3.78 chains).

Route No. 2: from the junction with route 1 (West Road Sandbanks) via Shore Road, Lilliput Hill Road, Sandbanks Road to the junction with the existing tramways of Bournemouth Corporation at Parkstone Road (2 miles 3 furlongs 4.9 chains).

Route No. 2A: connection from Shore Road to West Road to allow access to route 1 northbound (1.82 chains).

1.2) The Bournemouth District Railless Traction Bill

Deposited 30 November 1913 by A. Locke of Bakers (Parliamentary Agents). Solicitor: Messrs Baker & Sons,

Westminster, London. Published maps a diagram and a copy of the Gazette Notice were provided.

The Gazette Notice included:

"To incorporate a Company to provide, equip and maintain, work and run mechanically propelled vehicles (hereinafter called trolley vehicles) ...."

"Also to run omnibuses in connection with or substitution for the trolley vehicles upon the said routes, or in prolongation thereof".

Powers were to include the building of a generating station at the rear of the west side of Charminster Avenue.

Route No. 1: From Kings Road (Winton) via Charminster Road to Charminster Avenue (Junction with Malvern Road) (7 furlongs, 9.5 chains).

Route No. 2: From Crescent Road via Malvern Road to Moordown Tramway Depot (Wimborne Road) (4 furlongs, 9 chains).

1.3) Bournemouth Corporation Act, 1930 (Ch. clxxxi.), (20 & 21 Geo. 5.)

As stated above, Part IV of the 1930 Act referred specifically to trolley vehicles whilst other parts referred to a variety of other topics, not least extensions to the County Borough boundaries:

"And whereas by the Bournemouth Corporation Act 1904 the Corporation were empowered to construct maintain and work the tramways therein referred to.

And whereas it is expedient to empower the Corporation to provide and work mechanically propelled vehicles adapted for use along roads without rails and moved by electrical power transmitted thereto from some external source (in this Act called "trolley vehicles").

Part IV.
Trolley Vehicle Omnibuses and Tramways

90.

(1) The Corporation may provide maintain and equip (but shall not manufacture) trolley vehicles and may work the same along any street or road in the borough or in the county of Southampton i.e. excluding Poole, Dorset, along which tramways have been constructed by the Corporation.

(2) The Corporation may also work trolley vehicles along the following routes:-

In the borough-

(1) Commencing in Bath Road at its junction with Christchurch Road i.e. the Lansdowne proceeding along Bath Road, Bournemouth Pier Approach and Exeter Road to and terminating in the Square on the south side at its junction with Exeter Road;

(2) Commencing in Westover Road at its junction with Bath Road proceeding along Westover Road to and terminating at Bournemouth Arcade i.e. Gervis Place by a junction with the Corporation tramway route at that point;

(3) Commencing in Meyrick Road at its junction with Bath Road i.e. the Lansdowne proceeding along Meyrick Road and Gervis Road and terminating in Gervis Road at its junction with Bath Road;

(4) Along Gervis Place from its junction with Hinton Road to the junction of Old Christchurch Road and Gervis Place;

(5) Along Sea Road from its junction with Christchurch Road to the Boscombe Pier Approach;

(6) Commencing at the junction of Sea Road and Hawkwood Road proceeding along Hawkwood Road to Heathcote Road and along that road to its junction with Christchurch Road;

(7) Along Parkwood Road from its junction with Christchurch Road to the junction of Parkwood Road with Seabourne Road;

(8) Along Woodside Road from its junction with Seabourne Road to the junction of Woodside Road with Parkwood Road, *i.e. presumably a one-way system was envisaged with Route 7 above with inward trolleybuses travelling via Woodside Road and outward via Parkwood Road.*

In the borough and rural district of Christchurch in the county of Southampton, *i.e. Hampshire-*

(9) Commencing in the borough in Christchurch Road by a junction with the existing Corporation tramway in that road at Pokesdown Station proceeding along Christchurch Road to and terminating at Iford Bridge at the boundary of the borough of Christchurch:

In that borough-

(10) Commencing in Holdenhurst Road at the junction of that road with Ashley Road and proceeding along Holdenhurst Road to and terminating at the borough boundary in that road, *i.e. Castle Lane East;*

(11) Commencing in Charminster Road at its junction with Capstone Road proceeding along Charminster Road to and terminating at the borough boundary in that road, *i.e. at the Broadway Hotel, Castle Lane West;*

(12) Commencing at the junction of Charminster Road and Charminster Avenue, *i.e. Five Ways,* proceeding along Charminster Avenue and Malvern Road to and terminating at the junction of Malvern Road with Wimborne Road, *i.e. Moordown:*

In the borough and the rural district of Poole in the county of Dorset-

(13) Commencing in the borough at the termination of the existing tramway in Wimborne Road proceeding along that road to and terminating at Bear Cross in the parish of Kinson in the rural district of Poole;

(14) Commencing in the borough in Talbot Road at its junction with Wimborne Road proceeding along Talbot Road and Talbot Village Road (later named Wallisdown Road) to and along Kinson Road and terminating therein at its junction with Wimborne Road in the parish of Kinson in the rural district of Poole;

and with the consent of the Minister of Transport along any other street or road in the borough or the said parishes of Holdenhurst and Kinson which the Corporation think it necessary or convenient to use for the purpose of providing a turning point or of connecting trolley vehicle routes or of obtaining access thereto from any depot garage building or work of the Corporation.

(3) Before equipping any trolley vehicle route to include a

turning point or before arranging for a new turning point on any route the Corporation shall submit plans of the turning point to the Minister of Transport for approval.

(4) No turning point shall be provided upon any street or road belonging to or maintained by a railway company without the consent in writing of such company.

91.

(1)

(a) Before the Corporation commence to run trolley vehicles over any road or part of a road it shall be determined by agreement between the Corporation and the road authority (where it is not the Corporation) or failing agreement by the Minister of Transport whether it is necessary (in order to provide for the running under the powers of this Act of a trolley vehicle service over any such road or part of a road) to adapt alter or reconstruct such road or part of a road or to strengthen any bridge and if so what sum of money per mile of road so to be adapted altered or reconstructed or what sum of money in respect of any such bridge shall be payable by the Corporation to the road authority by way of contribution towards the cost incurred in such adaptation alteration reconstruction or strengthening.

(b) Within six months after the date upon which all questions to be agreed or determined in pursuance of paragraph (a) of this subsection have been so agreed or determined the Corporation shall give notice in writing to the road authority as to whether they intend to run trolley vehicles over the road or part of a road or bridge in question.

(c) If the Corporation give notice in writing to the road authority that they intend to run trolley vehicles over the road or part of a road or bridge in question and if it shall have been agreed or determined that the Corporation are to make any payment to the road authority under the provisions of paragraph (a) of this subsection the Corporation shall on receipt of any certificate which may from time to time be issued by the engineer in charge of the work of adaptation alteration or reconstruction of such road or part of a road or of strengthening such bridge pay to the road authority such proportion of the total amount of the contribution agreed or determined to be payable by the Corporation as the amount so certified to have been expended upon such work bears to the total amount estimated to be expended by the road authority on such work Provided that the aggregate amount to be so paid by the Corporation shall not exceed the amount of the contribution agreed or determined to be payable by them as aforesaid.

(d) Notwithstanding anything in this subsection the Corporation shall not be required to pay any sum in respect of any work towards or in respect of the adaptation alteration or reconstruction of any such road or part of a road or the strengthening of any bridge which is not executed within three years from the date on which the Corporation shall commence to run trolley vehicles over the road or part of a road to be adapted altered or reconstructed or over the bridge to be strengthened.

(e) Not more than one payment or (in the case of a payment by instalments in accordance with paragraph (c) of this subsection) one series of payments shall be made in

respect of any such road or part of a road so adapted altered or reconstructed or of any such bridge so strengthened.

(2) Any payment made to a road authority under this section in respect of any county road maintained and repaired by them under section 32 of the Act of 1929 shall be credited to the county council in ascertaining the amount payable by them under section 33 of the said Act and any such payment made to a road authority in respect of an unclassified road in respect of which an agreement exists under section 34 of the said Act shall be credited to the council of the urban district in ascertaining the amount payable by them to the county council under the said Act.

(3) If any such adaptation alteration reconstruction or strengthening as aforesaid shall involve an alteration of any telegraphic line belonging to or used by the Postmaster-General the enactments contained in section 7 of the Telegraph Act 1878 shall apply to any such alteration and the road authority shall be deemed to be "undertakers" within the meaning of the said Act.

(4) The road authority shall not under section 23 of the Highways and Locomotives (Amendment) Act 1878 as amended by section 12 of the Locomotives Act 1898 or otherwise make any claim against the Corporation in respect of extraordinary traffic by reason of the user of any highway by the trolley vehicles of the Corporation.

(5) An agreement under this section with respect to any county road maintained by a local authority at the expense of any county council shall not be made except with the concurrence of that county council.

(6) Nothing in this Act shall impose any obligation upon any canal company to strengthen adapt alter or reconstruct any bridge maintainable by them or enlarge any existing obligation.

92.

(1) The Corporation may in under or over the surface of the streets or roads along or adjoining those along which they are authorised to work trolley vehicles or in which it may be necessary so to do in order to connect the apparatus and equipment for working such vehicles with any generating station place erect and maintain all necessary and proper standards brackets conductors mains cables wires posts poles and any other necessary or convenient apparatus and equipment for the purpose of working trolley vehicles by electrical power and may for that purpose subject to such of the provisions of Part II of the Tramways Act 1870 as are incorporated in this Act and to the provisions of this Act open and break up any such street or road and any sewers drains water or gas pipes tubes wires telephonic and telegraphic apparatus therein or thereunder and may supply electrical energy for the purpose of working the trolley vehicles:

Provided that no post or other apparatus shall be erected on the carriageway except with the consent of the Minister of Transport.

(2) Nothing in this section shall extend to or authorise any interference with any works of any undertakers within the meaning of the Electricity (Supply) Acts 1882 to 1928 to which the provisions of section 15 of the Electric Lighting Act 1882 apply except in accordance with and subject to the provisions of that section.

(3) The Corporation may also adapt and use for the purpose of working trolley vehicles any apparatus and equipment already provided by them for working tramways.

(4) In this section the expression "generating station" has the meaning assigned to it by section 25 of the Electric Lighting Act 1909.

93.

Subject to the provisions of this Act the Corporation shall have the exclusive right of using any apparatus provided erected or maintained by them for the purpose of working trolley vehicles and any person (except by agreement with the Corporation) using the said apparatus shall for every offence be liable to a penalty not exceeding twenty pounds.

94.

(1) The trolley vehicles authorised by this Act shall not be deemed to be light locomotives within the meaning of the Locomotives on Highways Act 1896 nor shall they be deemed to be motor cars within the meaning of any provisions of the Motor Car Act 1903 (except sub-section (1) of section 1 and the provisions necessary for enforcing that subsection section 6 and the provisions as amended by the Roads Act 1920 relating to the licensing and licences of drivers) and subject to those exceptions neither the Motor Car Acts 1896 and 1903 nor any bye-laws or regulations made thereunder nor the enactments mentioned in the schedule to the Locomotives on Highways Act 1896 nor the Locomotives Act 1898 shall apply to the said trolley vehicles.

(2) The trolley vehicles authorised by this Act shall not be deemed to be omnibuses within the meaning of the Town Police Clauses Act 1889.

95.

Nothing in this Act shall in any way affect the duties of excise now payable by law on licences to be taken out for trolley vehicles authorised by this Act as hackney carriages.

96.

(1) The trolley vehicles and the electrical equipment thereof used under the authority of this Act shall be of such form construction weight and dimensions as the Minister of Transport may approve and no trolley vehicle shall be used by the Corporation which does not comply with the requirements of the Minister of Transport.

(2) Before applying to the Minister of Transport for his approval of the weight of any trolley vehicle to be used upon any road which crosses a bridge belonging to or repairable by a railway company the Corporation shall give to such railway company notice of the weight of the trolley vehicle proposed to be used by them upon such road and the Minister of Transport shall consider and determine after such inquiry as he may think fit any objections which may be submitted by the railway company to him on the ground that the strength of such bridge is insufficient to carry trolley vehicles of such weight Provided that such objections shall be forwarded by such railway company to the Corporation at the same time as they are submitted to the Minister of Transport.

97.

No trolley vehicle route shall be opened for public traffic until it has been inspected and certified to be fit for traffic by an officer appointed by the Minister of Transport.

98.

(1) The following provisions of the Tramways Act 1870 (so far as the same are applicable for the purposes and are not inconsistent with the provisions of this Act) are hereby incorporated with this Act and shall apply to the trolley vehicles authorised by this Act and such provisions shall be read and have effect as if the works to be constructed in the streets or roads for moving the trolley vehicles by electrical power were tramways and as if the said trolley vehicles were carriages used on tramways :—

Part II.
(Relating to the construction of tramways) except sections 25 28 and 29;

Section 41	(Tramways to be removed in certain cases);
Section 46	(Byelaws by local authority);
	(Penalties may be imposed in. bye-laws);
Section 48	(Power to local authority to license drivers conductors &c.);
Section 49	(Penalty for obstruction of promoters in laying out tramway);
Section 51	(Penalty on passengers practising frauds on the promoters);
Section 53	(Penalty for bringing dangerous goods on the tramway);
Section 55	(Promoters or lessees to be responsible for all damages);
Section 57	(Right of user only);
Section 60	(Reserving powers of street authorities to widen &c. roads); and
Section 61	(Power for local or police authorities to regulate traffic in roads).

(2) Nothing in this section shall be deemed to exclude a trolley vehicle from the provisions of section 78 of the Highways Act 1835 as to the side of the road on which any wagon cart or other carriage is to be kept.

99.

(1) The following provisions of the Bournemouth Corporation Tramways Order 1900 the Bournemouth Corporation Act 1901 and the Bournemouth Corporation Tramways Act 1903 shall subject as hereinafter provided extend and apply to the trolley vehicles and the trolley vehicle undertaking as authorised by this Act or as authorised within or outside the borough by any Provisional Order made under the powers of the section of this Act of which the marginal note is "Minister of Transport may authorise new routes" as if those provisions were with all necessary modifications re-enacted in this Act (namely):—
The Bournemouth Corporation Tramways Order 1900—

Section 19	(Provisions as to motive power);
Section 20	(Mechanical power works);
Section 22	(Byelaws);
Section 23	(Amendment of the Tramways Act 1870 as to byelaws by local authority);

Section 24   (Special provisions as to use of electrical power);

Section 26   (Traffic upon tramways);

Section 30   (Passengers' fares);

Section 31   (As to fares on Sundays and holidays);

Section 33   (Cheap fares for labouring classes);

Section 35   (Payment of rates);

Section 36   (Periodical revision of rates and charges).

The Bournemouth Corporation Act 1901—

Section 12   (Power to attach brackets &c. to buildings);

Section 15   (Penalty for malicious damage).

The Bournemouth Corporation Tramways Act 1903—

Section 9   (Power to accept lease of tramways outside borough);

Section 10   (Working agreements):

Provided that in the application of such provisions the same shall be read and have effect as if the apparatus and equipment for working the trolley vehicles and the trolley vehicle routes (together or separately as the context may require) were "tramways" within the meaning of the said Order and Acts and as if trolley vehicles were engines or carriages used on such tramways and as if the undertaking authorised by and the purposes of the said Orders and Acts including the trolley vehicle undertaking.

(2) In the application of the above-mentioned provisions any matter or thing to be determined by arbitration shall be so determined under and subject to the provisions of the Tramways Act 1870.

100.

(1) Notwithstanding anything in this Act contained if any of the works authorised to be executed by this Act involves or is likely to involve any alteration of any telegraphic line belonging to or used by the Postmaster-General the provisions of section 7 of the Telegraph Act 1878 shall apply (instead of the provisions of section 30 of the Tramways Act 1870) to any such alteration.

(2) In the event of any tramways or trolley vehicles of the Corporation being worked by electricity the following provisions shall have effect:—

(a) The Corporation shall construct their electric lines and other works of all descriptions and shall work their undertaking in all respects with due regard to the telegraphic lines from time to time used or intended to be used by His Majesty's Postmaster-General and the currents in such telegraphic lines and shall use every reasonable means in the construction of their electric lines and other works of all descriptions and the working of their undertaking to prevent injurious affection whether by induction or otherwise to such telegraphic lines or the currents therein Any difference which arises between the Postmaster-General and the Corporation as to compliance with this subsection shall be determined by arbitration;

(b) If any telegraphic line of the Postmaster-General is injuriously affected by the construction by the Corporation of their electric lines and works or by the working of the undertaking of the Corporation the Corporation shall pay the expense of all such alterations in the tele-graphic lines of the Postmaster-General as may be necessary to remedy such injurious affection;

(c) Before any electric line is laid down or any act or work for working the tramways or trolley vehicles by electricity is done within ten yards of any part of a telegraphic line of the Postmaster-General (other than repairs) the Corporation or their agents not more than twenty-eight nor less than fourteen days before commencing the work shall give the Postmaster-General written notice specifying the course of the line and the nature of the work including the gauge of any wire and the Corporation and their agents shall conform with such reasonable requirements (either general or special) as may from time to time be made by the Postmaster-General for the purpose of preventing any telegraphic line of the Postmaster-General from being injuriously affected by the said act or work. Any difference which arises between the Postmaster-General and the Corporation as to any requirement so made shall be determined by arbitration;

(d) If any telegraphic line of the Postmaster-General situate within one mile of any portion of the works of the Corporation is injuriously affected and he is of opinion that such injurious affection is or may be due to the construction of the Corporation's works or to the working of their undertaking the engineer-in-chief of the Post Office or any person appointed in writing by him may at all times when electrical energy is being generated or used by or supplied to the Corporation enter any of the Corporation's works for the purpose of inspecting the Corporation's plant and the working of the same and the Corporation shall in the presence of such engineer-in-chief or such appointed person as aforesaid make any electrical tests required by the Postmaster-General and shall produce for the inspection of the Postmaster-General the records kept by the Corporation pursuant to the Ministry of Transport regulations;

(e) In the event of any contravention of or wilful non-compliance with this section by the Corporation or their agents the Corporation shall be liable to a fine not exceeding twenty pounds and to a further fine not exceeding ten pounds for every day during which such contravention or non-compliance continues after conviction thereof or if the telegraphic communication is wilfully interrupted to a fine not exceeding fifty pounds and to a further fine not exceeding fifty pounds for every day on which such interruption continues after conviction thereof;

(f) Provided that nothing in this section shall subject the Corporation or their agents to a fine under this section if they satisfy the court having cognisance of the case that the immediate doing of any act or the execution of any work in respect of which the penalty is claimed was required to avoid an accident or otherwise was a work of emergency and that they forthwith served on the postmaster or sub-postmaster of the postal telegraph office nearest to the place where the act or work was done a notice of the execution thereof stating the reason for doing or executing the same without previous notice;

(g) For the purposes of this section a telegraphic line of the Postmaster-General shall be deemed to be injuriously affected by an act or work if telegraphic communication by means of such line is whether through induction or otherwise in any manner affected by such act or work or by any use made of such work;

(h) For the purposes of this section and subject as therein provided sections 2 10 11 and 12 of the Telegraph Act 1878 shall be deemed to be incorporated with this Act;

(i) The expression "electric line" has the same meaning in this section as in the Electric Lighting Act 1882;

(j) Any question or difference arising. under this section which is directed to be determined by arbitration shall be determined by an arbitrator appointed by the Minister of Transport on the application of either party whose decision shall be final and sections 30 to 32 both inclusive of the Regulation of Railways Act 1868 shall apply in like manner as if the Corporation or their agents were a company within the meaning of that Act;

(k) Nothing in this section contained shall be held to deprive the Postmaster General of any existing right to proceed against the Corporation by indictment action or otherwise in relation to any of the matters aforesaid;

(l) In this section the expression "the Corporation" includes their lessees and any person owning working or running carriages on any of the tramways or trolley vehicles on the trolley vehicle routes of the Corporation;

(m) Section 25 (For protection of Postmaster-General) of the Bournemouth Corporation Tramways Order 1900 section 43 (For the protection of the Postmaster-General) of the Christchurch and Bournemouth Tramways Act 1900 section 3 (For protection of Postmaster-General) of the Bournemouth Corporation Tramways Act 1903 and section 13 (For protection of Postmaster-General) of the Bournemouth Corporation Act 1904 are hereby repealed.

101.

(1) It shall be lawful for the Postmaster-General in any street or public road or part of a street or public road in which he is authorised to place a telegraph to use for the support of such telegraph any posts and standards (with the brackets connected therewith) erected in any such street or public road by the Corporation in connection with the tramways or trolley vehicles of the Corporation and to lengthen adapt, alter and replace such posts standards and brackets for the purpose of supporting any telegraph and from time to time to alter any telegraph so supported subject to the following conditions:-

(a) In placing maintaining or altering such telegraph no obstruction shall he caused to the traffic along or the working or user of the tramways or trolley vehicles;

(b) The Postmaster-General shall give to the Corporation not less than twenty-eight days' notice in writing of his intention to exercise any of the powers of his section and shall in such notice specify the streets or public roads or parts of streets or public roads along which it is proposed to exercise such powers and the manner in which it is proposed to use the posts standards and brackets and also the maximum strain and the nature and direction of such strain. Any difference as to any matter referred to in such notice shall be determined as hereinafter provided;

(c) Unless otherwise agreed between the Postmaster-General and the Corporation the Postmaster-General shall pay the expense of lengthening adapting altering or replacing under the provisions of this section any post

standard or bracket and the expenses of providing and maintaining any appliances or making any alteration rendered necessary in consequence of the exercise of the powers of this section for the protection of the public or the unobstructed working or user of the tramways or trolley vehicle routes or to prevent injurious affection of the Postmaster-General's telegraphs or any telegraphic or telephonic line or electrical apparatus of the Corporation or by any regulations which may from time to time be made by the Ministry of Transport arising through the exercise by the Postmaster-General of the powers conferred by this section;

(d) Unless otherwise agreed or in case of difference determined as hereinafter provided all telegraphs shall be attached to the posts standards or brackets below the level of the trolley wires and on the side of such posts or standards farthest from the trolley wires. Any difference as to the conditions of attachment shall be determined as hereinafter provided;

(e) Unless otherwise agreed no telegraph shall he attached to any post or standard placed in or near the centre of any street or public road;

(f) The Postmaster-General shall cause all attachments to posts standards or brackets used by him under the powers of this section to be from time to time inspected so as to satisfy himself that the said attachments are in a proper condition and state of repair;

(g) The Postmaster-General shall make good to the Corporation and shall indemnify them against any loss damage or expense which may be incurred by them through or in consequence of the exercise by the Postmaster-General of the powers conferred upon him by this section unless such loss damage or expense be caused by or arise from gross negligence on the part of the Corporation their officers or servants;

(h) The Postmaster-General shall make such reasonable contribution to the original cost of providing and placing any post standard or bracket used by him and also to the annual cost of the maintenance and renewal of any such post standard or bracket as having regard to the respective interests of the Corporation and the Postmaster-General in the use of the post standard or bracket and to all the circumstances of each case may be agreed upon between the Postmaster-General and the Corporation or failing agreement determined as hereinafter provided;

(i) The Corporation shall not be liable for any interference with or damage or injury to the telegraphs of the Postmaster-General arising through the exercise by the Postmaster-General of the powers conferred by this section and caused by the maintaining and working of the tramways or the trolley vehicle routes or by any accident arising thereon or by the authorised use by the Corporation of electrical energy unless such interference damage or injury be caused by gross negligence on the part of the Corporation their officers or servants;

(j) If it shall become necessary or expedient to alter the position of or remove any post standard or bracket the Postmaster-General shall upon receiving twenty-eight days' notice thereof at his own expense alter or remove the telegraph supported thereby or at his option retain the post standard or bracket and pay the Corporation the value of the same Provided that if the Corporation or the body having the control of the street or public road object to the retention of the post standard or bracket by the Postmaster-General a difference shall be deemed to have arisen and shall be determined as hereinafter provided.

(2) Nothing in this section contained shall prevent the Corporation from using their posts standards or brackets for the support of any of their electric wires and apparatus whether in connection with their tramways trolley vehicles or other municipal undertakings or shall take away any existing right of the Corporation of permitting the use by any company or person of their posts standards or brackets in connection with the lighting of the streets or otherwise Provided that any difference between the Postmaster-General and such company or person in relation to the use of the posts standards or brackets by the Postmaster-General and such company or person respectively shall be determined as hereinafter provided.

(3) All differences arising under this section shall be determined in manner provided by sections 4 and 5 of the Telegraph Act 1878 for the settlement of differences relating to a street or public road.

(4) In this section—
the expression "the Corporation" includes their lessees;
the expression "telegraph" has the same meaning as in the Telegraph Act 1869;
other expressions have the same meaning as in the Telegraph Act 1878.

102.
(1)
  (a) If at any time hereafter the Corporation desire to provide maintain equip and work trolley vehicles upon any road as defined by the Tramways Act 1870 (other than the streets and roads in this Act hereinbefore referred to), they may make application to the Minister of Transport and the Minister of Transport is hereby empowered to make a Provisional Order authorising the working and use by the Corporation of trolley vehicles subject to such conditions and restrictions (if any) as he may think fit upon any road or roads to which such application relates and containing such incidental provisions as the said Minister may deem expedient and subject to the terms of the' Provisional Order the provisions of this Act shall apply as if the working and use of trolley vehicles upon such road were authorised by this Act.
  (b) The Minister of Transport shall not make any Provisional Order under this section relating to any road outside the borough except with the consent of the local authority and (where the local authority is not the road authority) of the road authority of the district in which such road is situate but such consent or consents shall in no case be unreasonably withheld and any question arising as to whether any such consent is unreasonably withheld shall be determined by the said Minister.

(2) No such application.shall be entertained by the Minister of Transport unless the Corporation shall—
  (a) have published once in each of two successive weeks in the months of October or November notice of their intention to make such application in some newspaper or newspapers circulating in the area to which the application relates;
  (b) have also published such notice once in the months of October or November in the London Gazette;
  (c) have posted for fourteen consecutive days in the months of October or November in conspicuous positions in each of the roads to which such application relates a notice of their intention to make such application;
and each such notice shall state the time for and method of bringing before the Minister of Transport any objections to the grant of such application.

(3) The Minister of Transport may and he is hereby empowered to prescribe the procedure with respect to any application for a Provisional Order under this section.

(4) The Minister of Transport shall consider any such application and may if he thinks fit direct an inquiry to be held in relation thereto or may otherwise inquire as to the propriety of proceeding upon such application and he shall consider any objection to such application that may be lodged with him in accordance with the prescribed procedure and shall determine whether or not it is expedient and proper that the application be granted with or without addition or modification or subject or not to any restriction or condition.

(5) In any case where it shall appear to the Minister of Transport expedient that the application be granted he may settle and make a Provisional Order authorising the same and shall as soon as conveniently may be thereafter procure a Bill to be introduced into either House of Parliament for an Act to confirm the Provisional Order which shall be set out at length in the schedule to the Bill and until confirmation with or without amendment by such Act of Parliament a Provisional Order under this Act shall not have any operation.

(6) If while any such Bill is pending in either House of Parliament a petition is presented against any Provisional Order comprised therein the Bill so far as it relates to the Order petitioned against may be referred to a select Committee and the petitioner shall be allowed to appear and oppose as in the case of a Bill for a special Act.

(7) The Act of Parliament confirming a Provisional Order under this Act shall be deemed a public general Act.

(8) The making of a Provisional Order under this section shall be prima facie evidence that all the requirements of this section in respect of proceedings required to be taken previously to the making of such Provisional Order have been complied with.

(9) Any expenses incurred by the Minister of Transport in connection with the preparation and making of any such Provisional Order and any expenses incurred by the Minister of Transport in connection with any inquiry under this section shall be paid by the Corporation.

103.
Notwithstanding anything in this Act or any provisions of the Tramways Act 1870 incorporated with this Act the following provisions shall (unless otherwise agreed between the

Corporation on the one hand and the mayor aldermen and burgesses of the borough of Christchurch (in this section referred to as "the Christchurch Corporation") on the other hand) have effect with reference to the purchase by the Christchurch Corporation of the trolley vehicle undertaking of the Corporation authorised by this Act within the borough of Christchurch (in this section referred to as "the Christchurch undertaking"): —

(1) Subject as hereinafter provided it shall be lawful for the Christchurch Corporation if by resolution passed at a special meeting they so decide to purchase the Christchurch undertaking on the thirty-first day of December nineteen hundred and fifty-five or the thirty-first day of December in every subsequent seventh year upon terms of paying—

   (a) if the purchase is effected on the thirty-first day of December nineteen hundred and fifty-five the fair market value of the Christchurch undertaking as a going concern but without any addition in respect of compulsory purchase;

   (b) if the purchase is effected on or after the thirty-first day of December nineteen hundred and sixty-two upon the terms of paying the then value (exclusive of any allowance for past or future profits of the Christchurch undertaking or any compensation for compulsory sale or other consideration whatsoever) of the Christchurch undertaking and of all lands buildings works materials and plant of the Corporation suit-able to and used by them for the purposes of the Christchurch undertaking;
   which values respectively shall be determined in case of difference by arbitration in manner provided by section 43 of the Tramways Act 1870:

(2) The power of compulsory purchase conferred on the Christchurch Corporation by this section shall be exerciseable only upon and subject to the following terms and conditions (that is to say):—

   (a) if the Christchurch Corporation decide to purchase the Christchurch undertaking they shall give to the Corporation notice in writing of such their decision not later than the thirty-first day of December in the year preceding the date of purchase;

   (b) the sum to be paid to the Corporation in respect of such purchase shall if not agreed be determined by a referee nominated under the said section 43 of the .Tramways Act 1870:

(3) Subject to the foregoing provisions of this section the said section 43 of the Tramways Act 1870 including the provisions of that section with regard to the transfer to and vesting in and exercise by the purchasing authority of the rights powers and authorities of the promoters in respect of the undertaking sold the payment of the purchase money and all expenses incurred in the purchase and the borrowing of money for the purposes thereof shall apply to the purchase of the undertaking by the Christchurch Corporation under this section as if the said section 43 with any necessary modifications were re-enacted in this Act:

(4) On the sale to the Christchurch Corporation such arrangements as may be approved by the Minister of Transport shall be made for vesting in the Christchurch Corporation and the sale shall not take effect until an instrument has been properly executed in a form approved by the Minister for carrying such arrangements into effect.

104.

(1) Subject to the provisions of this Act the Corporation may provide and maintain (but shall not manufacture) and may run omnibuses within the borough and with the consent of the Minister of Transport and the local authority of the district within the borough of Poole and the areas which on the appointed day will be added to the borough under Part II (Extension of boundaries) of this Act and along the following routes:—

   (i)   the route of the existing tramways of the Corporation between the boundary of the borough and Church Street in the borough of Christchurch:

   (ii) from the boundary of the borough of Christchurch at Iford Bridge along Barrack Road High Street Castle Street Bridge Street Waterloo Place and Rotten Row to Purewell in the borough of Christchurch, i.e. ¾ mile further east beyond the tram and later trolleybus terminus.

Provided that the consent of a local authority shall not be unreasonably withheld and any question whether or not such consent has been unreasonably withheld shall be determined by the Minister of Transport.

(2) In the case of any application under the provisions of this section for the consent of the Minister of Transport the Corporation shall give notice in writing of their proposals to the road authority (where it is not also the local authority) and shall publish notice of such proposals in the London Gazette and in such other manner as the Minister of Transport shall direct stating the manner in which and the time within which any persons affected by such proposals may object thereto.

(3) The Corporation may purchase by agreement take on lease and hold lands and buildings and may erect on any lands acquired by or belonging to them omnibus carriage and motor-houses buildings and sheds and may provide such plant appliances and conveniences as may be requisite or expedient for the establishment running equipment maintenance and repair of such omnibuses but the Corporation shall not create or permit any nuisance on any lands upon which they erect any such houses buildings or sheds.

(4) Every omnibus moved by electrical power shall be so equipped and worked as to prevent any interference with telegraphic communication by means of any telegraphic line of the Postmaster-General.

(5) The provisions of section 51 (Penalty on passengers practising frauds on the promoters) and section 56 (Recovery of tolls penalties &c,) of the Tramways Act 1870 shall apply to and in relation to the omnibuses of the Corporation as if they were carriages used on tramways.

(6) The Corporation may make byelaws for regulating the travelling in or upon their omnibuses and for the prevention of nuisances in or upon the same or in or against any premises held by the Corporation in connection therewith.

(7) Section 20 (Corporation may run omnibuses) of the Bournemouth Corporation Act 1904 is hereby repealed.

105.

The Corporation shall perform in respect of the trolley vehicles and omnibuses provided under this Act such services in regard to the conveyance of mails as are prescribed by the Conveyance of Mails Act 1893 in the case of a tramway to which that Act applies.

106.

(1) The powers of running omnibuses under the provisions of this Act on any road or part of a road outside the borough may at the expiration of ten years from the date on which such running commences and at the expiration of any subsequent period of ten years be determined by the Minister of Transport on the application of the local authority of the borough or district in which such road or part of a road is situate upon such terms as the said Minister may determine.

(2) Before issuing an order to determine the said powers the Minister of Transport shall hold a local inquiry at which opportunity shall be afforded to any person interested to object to the continuance or cesser of such powers.

107.

If the Corporation do not within three years from the giving of the consent of the Minister of Trans-port to the running by the Corporation of omnibuses on any route outside the borough provide a service of omnibuses on such route or having provided shall discontinue any such service the said Minister may on the application of any local authority within whose borough or district the route or any part of the route is situate and after considering any representation which may be made on behalf of the Corporation by order declare that unless a service of omnibuses be provided within such period as the said Minister may by such order prescribe the powers of the Corporation under this Act in respect of the pro-vision and running of omnibuses on such route or part of such route shall determine and if within the prescribed period such service be not provided as from the expiration of such period the powers of the Corporation under this Act in relation to the provision and running of omnibuses on such route or part of such route shall cease Provided that this section shall not apply or have effect in the event of the failure of the Corporation to provide a service of omnibuses on any route being due to strikes unforeseen accident or circumstances beyond the control of the Corporation nor if the Corporation are providing an adequate service of tramways or trolley vehicles on such route.

108.

Subject to the provisions of this section the Corporation may demand and take for passengers and parcels carried on the omnibuses of the Corporation fares and charges not exceeding such maximum fares and charges as may from time to time be approved by the Minister of Transport in connection with such omnibuses Any application for a revision of such maximum fares or charges may be made by the Corporation or by the local authority of any borough or district in which such omnibuses are run.

109.

(1) Every passenger travelling upon the trolley vehicles or omnibuses of the Corporation may take with him personal luggage not exceeding twenty-eight pounds in weight without extra charge but all such luggage shall be carried by hand and at the responsibility of the passenger and shall not occupy any part of a seat required for a passenger nor be of a form or description to annoy or inconvenience other passengers.

(2) The Corporation may if they think fit convey—
  (a) on the trolley vehicles or omnibuses small parcels not exceeding fifty-six pounds in weight and dogs in the care of passengers;
  (b) on the trolley vehicles materials for the construction and repair of roads of or by the Corporation and materials for the purposes of the Corporation or for or in connection with the several undertakings of the Corporation

(3) The Corporation may make such charges for small parcels as the Minister of Transport may from time to time approve and such a charge for a dog as shall not exceed the fare payable by the passenger having the care of the dog.

110.

The Corporation may for the purpose of regulating and facilitating the traffic on market or fair days or for the execution of any works by the Corporation or their lessees or during the time of any public meeting procession or demonstration or for any other purpose which the Corporation having regard to the good government of the borough or the safety of the public may deem necessary order that the working of the tramways of the Corporation or any part thereof or the running of trolley vehicles or omnibuses on any trolley vehicle or omnibus route of the Corporation or part thereof respectively shall be stopped delayed or suspended but so that such stoppage delay or suspension shall continue only so long as may reasonably be necessary for the purposes aforesaid or any of them and the Corporation shall not be liable to pay compensation for damages in respect thereof.

111.

(1) The Corporation and any local authority empowered to run omnibuses in any borough or urban or rural district adjacent to the borough or adjacent to any borough or urban or rural district in which any route over which the Corporation are for the time being empowered to run omnibuses is situate may enter into and carry into effect agreements for the working user management and maintenance of all or any of the omnibus services which the contracting parties are empowered to provide subject to the provisions of the respective Acts under which such omnibus services are authorised.

(2) The Corporation and any company body or person may enter into and carry into effect agreements for the working user management and maintenance subject to the provisions of this Act of any omnibus services within the borough or on any route over which the Corporation are for the time being empowered to run omnibuses.

(3) The Corporation and any such local authority company body or person as aforesaid may also enter into and carry into effect agreements for all or any of the following purposes (that is to say):—

(a) The working user management and maintenance of any omnibuses lands depots buildings sheds and property provided in connection with any such omnibus services as aforesaid by either of the contracting parties and the right to provide and use the same and to demand and take the fares and charges authorised in respect of such services;

(b) The supply by any of the contracting parties under and during the continuance of any such agreement under this section of omnibuses and conveniences in connection therewith necessary for the purposes of such agreement and the employment of officers and servants;

(c) The interchange accommodation conveyance transmission and delivery of traffic arising on or .coming from or destined for any omnibus service of the contracting parties;

(d) The payment collection and apportionment of the fares and charges and other receipts arising from any such omnibus service as aforesaid.

(4) The Corporation shall not enter into or carry into effect any agreement under the provisions of this section in relation to any omnibus service lands depots buildings sheds or property beyond the borough otherwise than with the consent of the local authority of the borough or district within which such omnibus service lands depots buildings sheds or property are situate Provided that on complaint being made to the Minister of Transport that such consent is unreasonably withheld the said Minister may if he thinks fit by order dispense with such consent.

112.
The Corporation may run through cars along any of the routes of the tramways of the Corporation or any specified portion thereof and through trolley vehicles or omnibuses along any route on which the Corporation are for the time being authorised to run trolley vehicles or omnibuses and such cars trolley vehicles and omnibuses shall be distinguished from other cars trolley vehicles and omnibuses in such manner as may be directed by the Corporation and they may demand and take for every passenger carried on such cars trolley vehicles and omnibuses a fare or charge not exceeding the maximum fare or charge authorised or chargeable for and in respect of the whole of such route or the whole of the portion thereof traversed by any such car trolley vehicle or omnibus Provided that during the running of such through cars trolley vehicles or omnibuses the Corporation shall maintain a reasonably sufficient ordinary service of cars trolley vehicles or omnibuses as the case may be.

113.
The Corporation may appoint the stations and places from which cars on their tramways and their trolley vehicles and omnibuses shall start or at which they may stop for the purpose of taking up or setting down passengers and may fix the time during which such cars trolley vehicles and omnibuses shall be allowed to remain at any such place but any such appointment and regulations shall (as respects any station or place outside the borough) be subject to the consent of the local authority

of the borough or district within which that station or place is appointed which consent shall not be unreasonably withheld and any question as to whether or not any such consent is unreasonably withheld shall be determined by the Minister of Transport.

114.
(1) Notwithstanding anything contained in this or any other Act or Order to the contrary the Corporation may on any occasion run and reserve cars on any of the tramways of the Corporation and trolley vehicles and omnibuses on any route on which the Corporation are for the time being authorised to run trolley vehicles or omnibuses for any special purpose which the Corporation may consider necessary or desirable provided that such special cars trolley vehicles and omnibuses shall be distinguished from other cars trolley vehicles and omnibuses in such manner as the Corporation may direct and that during the running of such special cars trolley vehicles or omnibuses the Corporation shall maintain a reasonably sufficient ordinary service of cars trolley vehicles or omnibuses as the case may be.

(2) The Corporation may make byelaws and regulations for prohibiting the use of any such cars trolley vehicles or omnibuses by any persons other than those for whose conveyance the same are reserved.

(3) The restrictions contained in this or any other Act or Order of the Corporation as to fares rates or charges for passengers shall not extend to any special cars run upon the tramways of the Corporation or trolley vehicles or omnibuses run for such special services as aforesaid and in respect thereof the Corporation may demand and take such fares rates or charges as they shall think fit.

115.
(1) The Corporation may erect and maintain sheds shelters and waiting-rooms for the accommodation of passengers on any tramways or trolley vehicle or omnibus routes and may with the consent of the local authority and road authority use for that purpose portions of the public streets or roads due regard being given to the convenience of the general traffic along any such street or road but shall not use for the purpose any part of the highway outside the borough without the consent of the local and road authorities.

(2) Section 17 (Waiting-rooms) of the Bournemouth Corporation Act 1904 is hereby repealed.

116.
The Corporation may provide cloakrooms and rooms or sheds for the storage of bicycles tricycles and other vehicles at any depot or building used by them in connection with their tramway trolley vehicle and omnibus undertakings and at suitable places on the routes of the tramways and trolley vehicle and omnibus routes of the Corporation and the Corporation may make charges for the use of such cloakrooms rooms and sheds and for the deposit of articles and things and bicycles tricycles and other vehicles therein but shall not use for the purpose any part of the highway without the consent of the road authority.

117.

The following provisions for the protection and benefit of railway companies shall apply and have effect except in so far as may be otherwise agreed in writing between the Corporation and the railway company affected:—

Notwithstanding anything contained in this Act no shed shelter waiting-room cloakroom or room shall be erected maintained or provided or starting or stopping place appointed nor shall the Corporation require persons waiting at any stopping place or any terminus to wait in any line or queue so as to cause interference with or to render less convenient the access to or exit from any station depot or property belonging to any railway company nor shall any such shed shelter waiting-room or cloakroom be erected maintained or provided on any bridge carrying any street or road over the railway of any railway company.

118.

Any property found in any tramcar trolley vehicle or omnibus of the Corporation or in any shelter or room used in connection with the tramways trolley vehicles or omnibuses of the Corporation shall forthwith be handed to the conductor of the tramcar trolley vehicle or omnibus or be taken to the tramway offices of the Corporation and if the same be not claimed within six months after the finding thereof it may be sold as unclaimed property by public auction after notice by advertisement in one or more local newspapers once in each of two successive weeks and the proceeds thereof carried to the revenue account of the tramway undertaking of the Corporation.

The Corporation may make byelaws for securing the safe custody and redelivery of any property accidentally left in tramcars trolley vehicles or omnibuses of the Corporation or in any shelter or room used in connection with such tramcars trolley vehicles or omnibuses and fixing the charges to be made in respect thereof.

119.

(1) The Corporation may attach to any lamppost pole standard or other similar erection erected on or in the highway on or near to the route of any of the tramways trolley vehicles or omnibuses of the Corporation signs or directions indicating the position of stopping places for tramcars trolley vehicles and omnibuses Provided that in cases where the Corporation are not the owners of such lamp-post pole standard or similar erection they shall give notice in writing of their intention to attach thereto any such sign or direction and shall make compensation to the said owner for any damage or injury occasioned to such lamp-post pole standard or similar erection by such attachment and the Corporation shall indemnify the said owner against any claim for damage occasioned to any person or property by or by reason of such attachment.

(2) Nothing in this section shall be deemed to require the said owner to retain any such lamp-post pole standard or similar erection when no longer required for his purposes.

(3) The Corporation shall not attach any such sign or direction to any pole post or standard belonging to the Postmaster-General except with his consent in writing.

(4) The Corporation shall not attach any such sign or direction to any lamp-post pole standard or any similar erection belonging to any railway company without the consent of such company in writing.

(5) The Corporation shall not attach any such sign or direction to any pole post or standard belonging to the mayor aldermen and burgesses of the borough of Poole without their consent in writing.

120.

Any byelaws and regulations made by the Corporation under the provisions contained in this Part of this Act shall be made subject and according to the provisions of the Tramways Act 1870 with respect to the making of byelaws.

121.

Subject to the provisions of this Act the trolley vehicle and omnibus undertakings authorised by this Act shall be deemed to form part of the tramway undertaking of the Corporation Provided that in the accounts of the Corporation relative to their tramway undertaking the receipts and expenditure upon and in connection with trolley vehicles and omnibuses respectively shall (so far as may be reasonably practicable) be distinguished from the receipts and expenditure upon or in connection with the remainder of such undertaking and in such accounts capital shall be distinguished from revenue.

122.

The Corporation shall in every year within three months after the close of their financial year or such longer period as the Minister of Transport may allow furnish to the Minister of Transport a copy of the annual accounts of their tramway undertaking.

123.

(1) The tramways of the Corporation on any trolley vehicle or omnibus route of the Corporation may be abandoned or discontinued either temporarily or permanently Provided that no such tramway shall be so abandoned or discontinued by the Corporation until they shall have provided trolley vehicles or omnibuses on the route of such tramway or on the portion thereof so proposed to be abandoned or discontinued or along such other route (in lieu of the route of such tramway or portion thereof as aforesaid) as shall be approved by the Minister of Transport.

(2) The Corporation may take up and remove and use or dispose of the rails of any such tramway or part of a tramway and the posts poles wires and other works and apparatus provided in connection therewith and in the case of any road outside the borough shall make good the surface thereof to the reasonable satisfaction of the road authority.

(3) Nothing in this section shall relieve the Corporation of any liability imposed upon them by section 41 (Tramways to be removed in certain cases) of the Tramways Act 1870 in relation to any tramway in the event of the Corporation discontinuing the working of such tramway otherwise than in accordance with the provisions of this Act.

(4) As from the date upon which a service of trolley vehicles or omnibuses is provided by the Corporation in lieu of a tramway

service within the borough the revenue of the tramway undertaking of the Corporation shall (to such extent as the Corporation may from time to time by resolution determine) cease to be charged under any statutory enactment relating to that undertaking with expenses incurred by the Corporation upon or in connection with the maintenance and repair of the streets in which such service was run but nothing in this section shall relieve the Corporation from any liability attaching to them in respect of such maintenance and repair.

(5) As from the date on which the Corporation shall have restored and made good the roads on which the existing tramways outside the borough are laid in pursuance of the provisions of this Act they shall cease to be under any obligation to maintain or repair any part of the roadway in which the said tramways are situate.

(6) The provisions of section 33 (Cheap fares for labouring classes) and section 36 (Periodical revision of rates and charges) of the Bournemouth Corporation Tramways Order 1900 shall apply to any service of omnibuses provided under the powers of this Act in substitution for a service of tramcars to the same extent as the said provisions applied to the tramways replaced by such service.

124.

(1) If and so long as the Corporation provide a service of tramcars trolley vehicles or omnibuses or a service of tramcars trolley vehicles and omnibuses along any protected route or part thereof and such service adequately meets the requirements of such protected route or part thereof it shall not be lawful except as in this section provided or except in pursuance of any agreement entered into by the Corporation under the provisions of the section of this Act of which the marginal note is "Working and other agreements with regard to omnibuses" for any company (except the Southern Railway Company in pursuance of their statutory powers) or for any other local authority body or person to run omnibuses along such protected route or along any other route in competition with such service or services of the Corporation along the protected route.

(2) Any failure on the part of the Corporation to afford an adequate service along any protected route which is due to strikes unforeseen accidents or circumstances beyond the control of the Corporation shall not entitle any such company authority body or person to run omnibuses along such protected route or along any other route in competition therewith.

(3) The Corporation as the licensing authority for the borough may in order to give effect to the foregoing provisions of this section when licensing an omnibus to ply for hire grant such licence subject to conditions as to the routes upon which such omnibus shall or shall not ply for hire Provided that—

(a) if any question arises between the Corporation and any company authority body or person as to whether any route in respect of which a licence may be applied for or may be granted to any such company authority body or person is competitive such question shall on the application of either of the parties be determined as in this section provided;

(b) the right of the applicant for the licence of appeal to the Minister of Transport from the decision of the Corporation under section 14 (3) of the Roads Act 1920 shall not be affected but the said Minister in making any order under that section shall have regard to the provisions of this section;

(c) omnibuses belonging to the same proprietor may be transferred by him from one route to another route on which he is for the time being licensed to run omnibuses so long as he does not at one and the same time allow a greater number of his omnibuses to ply for hire on any protected route or any route in competition therewith than the number of licences which he holds for such route.

(4)

(a) The licensing authority of any area outside the borough in which any protected route or part thereof is situate shall on receiving any application (otherwise than from the Southern Railway Company acting under their statutory powers) for a licence for an omnibus to ply for hire on any protected route or a route in competition therewith in that area forthwith give notice in writing to the Corporation of the application and the Corporation shall be entitled to submit to the licensing authority any objections to or representations on the grant of the licence which they may think fit.

(b) The licensing authority when considering such an application as aforesaid shall have regard to the, provisions of subsection (1) of this section and shall also consider any objections or representations submitted by the Corporation with reference to the application and if the licensing authority decide to grant the licence they shall attach thereto such conditions as to the routes along which the omnibus to which the licence relates shall or shall not ply for hire and such other conditions as may be necessary or desirable to protect the services (whether of tramcars trolley vehicles or omnibuses or any combined service of any of such vehicles) for the time being provided by the Corporation on the protected route Provided that the right of the applicant for the licence of appeal to the said Minister from the decision of the licensing authority under section 14 (3) of the Roads Act 1920 shall not be affected but the said Minister in making any order under that section shall have regard to the provisions of this section.

(c) The licensing authority shall on making their decision with respect to any application for such a licence as is referred to in this subsection forthwith give notice in writing to the Corporation of their decision.

(d) If the Corporation object to the decision of the licensing authority or to any conditions attached or to the non-attachment of any conditions to the licence the Corporation shall have a right of appeal to the said Minister within a period of fourteen days after receiving notice of the decision of the licensing authority and if the Corporation so appeal to the said Minister with respect to any such licence as aforesaid the licence shall not come into force until the matter has been determined by the said Minister under subsection (5) of this section.

(5) Any question at any time arising as to whether or not the Corporation are providing an adequate service along any protected route or whether there is or would be any such competition as aforesaid shall be determined by the Minister of Transport on the application of any interested party and the said Minister shall have power to make such order thereon as he thinks fit Any order made by the said Minister under this section shall be final and binding on the parties affected thereby and not subject to appeal to any court and shall on the application of the said Minister or the Corporation or the applicant for a licence be enforceable by writ of mandamus.

(6) Nothing in this section shall be deemed—
  (a) to restrict the running of any omnibus by any such company authority body or person along any protected route or a particular part of a protected route or any other route in competition therewith if such omnibus serves a district or districts beyond the protected route and no passenger conveyed by such omnibus is both taken up and set down on any one journey on any protected route or any route in com petition therewith; or
  (b) to entitle the Corporation or other licensing authority to refuse the renewal of a licence to ply for hire with an omnibus along a protected route or a particular part of a protected route or a route in competition with a protected route if the omnibus was on the thirtieth day of November nineteen hundred and twenty-nine in use in connection with a service which was on that date being operated on and has since that date been regularly in operation on any protected route (or part thereof) or any route in competition therewith or to entitle the Corporation or other licensing authority to refuse the renewal of a licence to ply for hire with an omnibus substituted by the licensee for any omnibus to which the protection of this paragraph applies or to restrict the running of any such last-mentioned omnibus or substituted omnibus along any protected route or part of a protected route or other route in competition therewith; or
  (c) to prevent the grant or renewal by the Corporation or any licensing authority of any licence to ply for hire with an omnibus on the condition that no passenger conveyed by the omnibus to which the licence relates shall be both taken up and set down on any one journey on any protected route or any route in competition therewith except as regards an omnibus running on any service on the thirtieth day   of November nineteen hundred and twenty-nine which was not on that date subject to such a condition.

7) In this section the expression "protected route" means any existing tramway or trolley vehicle route of the Corporation or any part of any such existing tramway or trolley vehicle route and any of the trolley vehicle routes authorised by this Act or routes along which the Corporation may be running omnibuses under the powers of this Act.

(8) Nothing in this section shall apply to any omnibuses run by the Hants and Dorset Motor Services Limited along any route commencing within the borough and terminating at any point outside the borough not being a point on either of the routes described in subsection (1) of the section of this Act of which the marginal note is "Power to provide and run omnibuses" or along any route commencing at any such point and terminating in the borough.

125.
The agreement made the twenty-fourth day of March nineteen hundred and thirty between the Corporation of the one part and the Hants and Dorset Motor Services Limited of the other part and set out in the Second Schedule to this Act is hereby confirmed and made binding upon the parties thereto.

126.
(1) Where the Corporation consider that any tree hedge or shrub overhangs any street outside the borough so as to be likely to obstruct or interfere with the passage of their tramcars trolley vehicles or omnibuses or to obstruct the view of drivers thereof the Corporation may require the authority by whom powers may be exercised under section 23 of the Public Health Act 1925 to exercise those powers in respect of the trees hedges or shrubs to which the requisition refers.

(2) If the said authority have not adopted the said section or having adopted the said section or being a county council the said authority refuse or neglect to exercise those powers in accordance with the said requisition the Corporation may apply to the Minister for and the Minister may make an order conferring on the Corporation all or any of the powers with reference to such street of a local authority under the said section in respect of the street or streets in which the said trees hedges or shrubs are situated.

(3) On the making of such order any authority having powers under section 23 of the Public Health Act 1925 shall during the continuance of the order cease to exercise such powers in respect of the said street or streets to the extent to which they have been conferred on the Corporation.

127.
The Corporation may by resolution declare that any byelaws for the time being in force on the tramways of the Corporation shall with such modifications as they may deem necessary apply to and be enforceable with respect to their trolley vehicles or omnibuses and the premises held in connection therewith and the persons travelling in or upon the same Provided that any modifications as aforesaid shall be subject to the approval of the Minister of Transport.

128.
If any obstruction to the traffic on any of the tramways or trolley vehicle routes of the Corporation is caused by any vehicle breaking or any load falling from a vehicle the person in charge of the vehicle shall forthwith remove the vehicle or load so as to prevent the continuance of the obstruction and if he fail to do so the Corporation may so remove the vehicle or load and may remove any other obstruction of the like character to such traffic and may provide and use all necessary plant and apparatus and take all necessary steps to remove any such obstruction and may recover the reasonable cost of so doing from the owner of the vehicle.

129.

Notwithstanding anything contained in this Act the following provisions for the protection of the mayor aldermen and burgesses of the borough of Poole (in this section called "the Poole Corporation") shall unless otherwise agreed in writing between the Corporation and the Poole Corporation apply and have effect (that is to say):—

The Corporation shall not under or by virtue of the powers conferred upon them by the sections of this Act of which the marginal notes respectively are "Power to provide and run omnibuses" and "Working and other agreements with regard to omnibuses" provide or run or enter into any agreement authorising any other authority company or person to provide or run omnibuses within the borough of Poole except with the consent of the Poole Corporation which consent may be given upon such terms and subject to such conditions as the Poole Corporation in their absolute discretion may think fit.

130.

Notwithstanding anything contained in this Act the following provisions for the protection of the mayor aldermen and burgesses of the borough of Christ-church (in this section referred to as "the Christchurch Corporation") shall (unless otherwise agreed in writing between the Corporation and the Christchurch Corporation) apply and have effect (that is to say):

(1) If and when the Corporation shall have ceased for a period of six consecutive months to operate a regular tramway service along any portion of the existing main tramway between the junction of Christchurch Road with Ashley Road in the borough and the existing tramway terminus in Christchurch the whole of such tramway shall for the purposes of this section be deemed to have been permanently abandoned and discontinued:

(2) The Corporation shall give to the Christchurch Corporation not less than one month's previous notice in writing of their intention (whether in pursuance of subsection (1) of this section or otherwise) permanently to abandon and discontinue the tramways in the borough of Christchurch:

(3) The Corporation shall within six months after the abandonment and discontinuance of the existing tramways in the borough of Christchurch take up and remove the rails paving and paving setts of the said tramways and (if trolley vehicles are not substituted) the overhead and other equipment of the said tramways and shall make good the surface of such portions of the roads in which such tramways are laid as are repairable by the Corporation under the pro-visions of section 28 of the Tramways Act 1870 in accordance with the provisions of this Act and clear away all surplus paving and metalling material and rubbish and properly fence watch and light the roads during the execution of such works:

(4) The restoration of such portions as are repairable by the Corporation under the provisions of section 28 of the Tramways Act 1870 of such of the roads in which the tramways are laid as are vested in the Christchurch Corporation shall be carried out in accordance with specifications and particulars to be previously submitted to the Christchurch Corporation and reasonably approved by them prior to the commencement of the work If within one month after the service on the Christchurch Corporation of the notice referred to in subsection (2) of this section the Christchurch Corporation give notice to the Corporation that they desire themselves to do the works necessary for the restoration of such portions of such roads as aforesaid the Corporation shall in lieu of carrying out the said works pay to the Christchurch Corporation in respect thereof such sum per superficial yard of the portions of the said roads so to be restored as may be agreed between the Corporation and the Christchurch Corporation or as in case of difference may be settled by arbitration under this section which sum shall be taken to represent the cost of the restoration of such portions of such roads as aforesaid to the reasonable satis-faction of the road authority as required by this Act:

(5) The obligations and liabilities of the Corpora-tion under the Tramways Act 1870 in relation to the maintenance of the portions of the roads vested in the Christchurch Corporation in which the tramways are laid shall continue until the Corporation shall have complied with their obligations under subsection (3) of this section:

(6) If in pursuance of the provisions of the section of this Act of which the marginal note is "Power to use trolley vehicles" the Corporation provide maintain and equip trolley vehicles on any portion of the main tramway route in the borough between the junction of Christchurch Road with Ashley Road and Tuckton Bridge they shall simultaneously provide maintain and equip trolley vehicles on the route of the tramways in the borough of Christchurch from Tuckton Bridge along Stour Road Bargates and High Street to the junction of High Street with Castle Street and along Church Street:

(7) No advertisement (other than time-tables and notices relating to the Corporation's tramways trolley vehicle or omnibus undertaking) shall be displayed on any apparatus erected or used on any road or bridge in the borough of Christchurch under the powers of this Act without the consent of the Christchurch Corporation:

(8) The Christchurch Corporation with the consent of the Corporation may use free of cost for the purpose of fixing thereto street lamps lighting brackets street names fire alarm plates or direction signs any posts or standards provided or used by the Corporation in the borough of Christchurch under or by virtue of the pro-visions of this Act but not so as to interfere with the use of such posts or standards for the purposes of the Corporation or to make the same unfit for such purposes or dangerous to persons or traffic in or passing through the adjoining streets or roads and the Christchurch Corporation shall pay the cost where necessary of insulating the posts or standards so used and shall make compensation to the Corporation for any damage which may be caused to the said posts or standards by reason of the exercise of the powers contained in this subsection and shall indemnify the Corporation against any claim or demand which may be occasioned by such user. Any consent of the Corporation under this subsection shall not be unreasonably withheld:

(9) If it is reasonably necessary to alter the position of any post bracket or overhead wire erected or used for the purposes of the trolley vehicles of the Corporation in the borough of Christchurch owing to the widening or improvement of any

road by the Christchurch Corporation the Corporation shall at the expense of the Christchurch Corporation alter the position of such post bracket or overhead wire in such manner as the Christchurch Corporation may direct:

(10) All posts and apparatus to be erected by the Corporation under the powers of the section of this Act of which the marginal note is "As to electrical works" in any street or road in the borough of Christchurch shall be of such design as the Christchurch Corporation may approve and such posts and apparatus and all such apparatus placed or laid under any such street or road shall be placed in such position as the Christchurch Corporation may approve:

(11) The Corporation shall not under the powers of the section of this Act of which the marginal note is "As to electrical works" place or erect any apparatus in under or over the surface of any street or road vested in the Christchurch Corporation for the purpose of connecting a trolley vehicle route with a generating station without the consent of the Christchurch Corporation:

(12) The trolley vehicles run by the Corporation in the borough of Christchurch shall be of the same type as those used in the borough for services similar to those given in the borough or Christchurch:

(13) The Corporation shall not exercise the powers of the section of this Act of which the marginal note is "Attachment of signs indicating stopping places to lamp posts &c." in respect of any posts poles standards or other similar erections belonging to the Christchurch Corporation nor the powers of the section of this Act, of which the marginal note is "Cloakrooms &c." in respect of any highway in the borough of Christchurch without the consent of the Christchurch Corporation:

(14) The Corporation shall in every year within a reasonable period after the close of their financial year furnish to the Christchurch Corporation a copy of the annual accounts of the Corporation so far as they relate to any service of trolley vehicles or omnibuses which the Corporation may operate:

(15) Any consent or approval of the Christchurch Corporation under any of the subsections of this section shall not be unreasonably withheld:

(16) Any difference which may arise between the Corporation and the Christchurch Corporation with regard to any of the matters referred to in this section or as to whether or not any consent has been unreasonably withheld shall be settled by an engineer to be appointed in default of agreement on the application (after notice in writing to the other of them) of the Corporation or the Christchurch Corporation by the Minister of Transport and subject as aforesaid the provisions of the Arbitration Act 1889 or of any statutory modification or re-enactment thereof shall apply to any such arbitration.

131.

The following provisions for the protection of the Southern Railway Company (in this section referred to as "the company") shall unless otherwise agreed in writing between the Corporation and the company apply and have effect in relation to the trolley vehicles (that is to say):-

(1) In this section the word "apparatus" means standards brackets conductors mains cables wires posts poles and any other apparatus and equipment for the purpose of working trolley vehicles under or in pursuance of this Act:

(2) All apparatus where the same shall be placed or erected upon across under or over any bridge or the approaches thereto or other work belonging to or maintainable by the company or which will otherwise affect the same shall be placed or erected and maintained according to plans and particulars to be previously submitted to and reasonably approved by the company or in case of difference between them and the Corporation by an arbitrator to he appointed as hereinafter provided. Provided that if the company shall not within twenty-eight days from the delivery of such plans and particulars signify their disapproval thereof they shall be deemed to have approved thereof

(3) All apparatus shall be placed or erected under the superintendence (if such superintendence be given) and to the reasonable satisfaction of the company. The Corporation shall place erect maintain and use the apparatus so as not injuriously to affect any such bridge or approaches or other work and in the event of any injury being occasioned to such bridge or approaches or work by the placing erection maintenance user or removal of the apparatus upon across under or over the same the company may make good the injury and may recover from the Corporation the reasonable expenses of so doing:

(4) The Corporation shall bear and on demand pay to the company the reasonable expense (if any) incurred by the company of and in connection with the employment by the company during the placing erection maintenance or removal by the Corporation of any apparatus affecting any railway bridge or other work belonging to or maintainable by the company of such inspectors signalmen and watchmen as may be reasonably necessary for inspecting watching and protecting such railway bridge or work and the conduct of the traffic on such railway with reference to and during the placing erection maintenance or removal of any apparatus of the Corporation and for preventing all interference obstruction danger and accident from any of the operations or from the acts or defaults of the Corporation or their contractors or any person in the employ of either of them while engaged upon work of the Corporation:

(5) The Corporation shall not in any manner in the placing erection maintenance or removal of any apparatus obstruct or interfere with the free uninterrupted and safe user of any railway belonging to or maintainable by the company or any traffic thereon:

(6) The Corporation shall be responsible for and make good to the company all losses damages and expenses which may be occasioned to the company or any of their works or property or to any works or property which they may be liable to maintain or to the traffic on their railways or to any company or person using the same by or by reason of the placing erection maintenance user or failure of any apparatus or by reason of any act default or omission of the Corporation or of any person in their employ or of their contractors while engaged upon work of the Corporation and the Corporation shall effectually indemnify and hold harmless the company from

all claims and demands upon or against them by reason of such placing erection maintenance user or failure or of any such act default or omission:

(7) If the company shall hereafter require under statutory powers existing at the passing of this Act to widen lengthen strengthen reconstruct alter or repair any of their bridges approaches or other works under or upon which the apparatus is laid or to widen or alter any railway thereunder or thereover the Corporation shall afford to the company all reasonable and proper facilities for the purpose and if it shall be necessary for such purpose that the apparatus be taken up diverted or removed and if the company accordingly give to the Corporation twenty-eight days' notice in writing (or in easy of emergency such notice as mav be reasonably practicable) requiring such taking up diversion or removal then the working or user of such part of the apparatus shall be stopped or delayed or such part of the apparatus shall be taken up diverted or removed as stated in such notice at the reasonable expense of the Corporation and under their superintendence (if they shall give such superintendence) but no such working or user shall be stopped or delayed for a longer period than may be necessary for effecting such purpose as aforesaid and such part of the apparatus shall be restored with all practicable dispatch and the company shall not be liable to pay compensation in respect of such stoppage delay or taking up diversion or removal:

(8) The Corporation shall from time to time pay to the company any additional expense which the company may reasonably incur in effecting such widening lengthening strengthening reconstruction alteration or repairing as is mentioned in the last preceding subsection or in the maintenance of any bridge approach or other work of the company constructed under statutory powers existing at the passing of this Act by reason of the existence or user of the works or apparatus:

(9) If and when the company shall require to reconstruct alter repair or paint any bridge constructed under statutory powers existing at the passing of this Act under which any electric wire of the company has been placed the Corporation shall in order to ensure the safety of the workmen employed in such reconstruction alteration repairing or painting cut off the electric current from the trolley wires under such bridge at such time as shall be agreed between the Corporation and the engineer of the company or failing agreement as shall he determined by arbitration under this section unless the Corporation shall have previously adopted some other means of protection to workmen approved by the said engineer Provided that the Corporation shall not be required to cut off the electric current at any time for a longer period than shall be necessary for effecting the purpose of the company:

(10) If having regard of the proposed position of any apparatus of the Corporation when considered in relation to the position of the works of the company at any point where any apparatus will be constructed over or under any railway or other works of the company constructed under statutory powers existing at the passing of this Act it becomes necessary in order to avoid injurious affection or danger from the breaking or falling of wires that any electric telegraphic telephonic or signal wires or apparatus or electrical works or apparatus for traction purposes of the company shall be altered or protected the company may execute any works reasonably necessary for such protection or alteration and the reasonable expense of so doing shall be repaid to the company by the Corporation:

(11) Any difference which may arise under this section between the Corporation and the company shall be settled by an arbitrator to be appointed on the application of either party by the President of the Institution of Civil Engineers and subject as aforesaid the provisions of the Arbitration Act 1889 shall apply to any such arbitration.

132.
The following provisions for the protection of the Southern Railway Company (in this section referred to as "the company") shall unless otherwise agreed between the Corporation and the company apply and have effect (that is to say):—

(1) On the taking up or removal by the Corporation under the section of this Act of which the marginal note is "As to abandonment of tramways" of any rails posts poles wires or other works and apparatus situate on or attached to any bridge or bridge approaches or property belonging to or maintainable by the' company the Corporation shall to the reasonable satisfaction of the company restore the surface of any road on such bridge or bridge approaches or any property disturbed by such taking up or removal and make good all damage thereto:

(2) The. Corporation shall give to the company not less than seven days' previous notice in writing of their intention to carry out any such works as are referred to in subsection (1) of this section and shall state in such notice the place and time at which they propose to commence those works and the company may where reasonably necessary employ watchmen or inspectors to watch any of such works and operations of the Corporation and the reasonable cost thereof together with any expense to which the company may reasonably be pit in consequence of such works and operations shall be borne by the Corporation:

(3) Any difference which may arise under this section between the Corporation and the company shall be settled by an arbitrator to be appointed on the application of either party by the President of the Institution of Civil Engineers and the provisions of the Arbitration Act 1889 shall aplly to any such arbitration.

133.
Nothing in the Act shall impose any obligation on any railway company to strengthen adapt alter or reconstruct any bridge or road belonging to or maintainable by or at the expense of a railway company or enlarge any existing obligation.

1.4) Bournemouth Corporation Bill, 1935 (not presented)

This was a late Bill promoted in March 1935 with the same intent as the Bournemouth Corporation (Trolley Vehicles) Provisional Order, deposited in January 1935.

An Act to authorise the Mayor Aldermen and Burgesses of the borough of Bournemouth to use trolley vehicles upon a route in the borough of Poole in the county of Dorset and for other purposes.

3.

(1) The Corporation may use trolley vehicles upon the following route in the borough of Poole in addition to any routes upon which they are already authorised to use trolley vehicles (that is to say):-

A route (3 miles 5 furlongs 5 chains or thereabouts in length) commencing at County Gates and proceeding along Poole Road Ashley Road View Road St. Peter's Road North Road Parkstone Road Longfleet Road High Street an terminating on the eastern side of the level crossing in Towngate Street on the Southern Railway, *i.e. the Upper Parkstone tram route.*

(2) Before equipping the said route to include a turning point or before arranging for a new turning point thereon the Corporation shall submit plans of the turning point to the Ministry of Transport for approval.

4.

(1) The provisions of Part IV (Trolley Vehicles Omnibuses and Tramways) of the Act of 1930 shall so far as they are applicable and have not been modified by the Road Traffic Act 1930 extend and apply to the trolley vehicles and route referred to in and authorised by this Act in like manner as they apply to the trolley vehicles and routes authorised by the said Part IV.

(2) The trolley vehicle undertaking authorised by this Act shall be deemed to form part of the tramway undertaking of the Corporation.

5.

(1) The Corporation shall have power in addition and without prejudice to their power of borrowing under the Local Government Act 1933 from time to time to borrow without the consent of any sanctioning authority for and in connection with the purposes mentioned in the first column of the following table the respective sums mentioned in the second column of the said column and they shall pay of all moneys so borrowed within such periods as the Corporation may determine not exceeding those respectively mentioned in the third column of the said table (namely):-

(1) Purpose	(2) Amount	(3) Period for repayment
(a) The provision of trolley vehicles.	£45,000	Ten years from the date or dates of borrowing.
(b) The provision of equipment and the construction of other works necessary for working trolley vehicles on the trolley vehicle route authorise by the Act.	£35,000	Twenty years from the date or dates of borrowing.
(c) The payment of any sum payable by the Corporation under the provisions of the section of this Act of which the marginal note is "As to abandonment of light railways".	The sum requisite	Twenty years from the date or dates of borrowing.
(d) The payment of the costs charges and expenses of the Act.	The sum requisite	Five years from the passing of this Act.

1.5) Poole Road Transport Act, 1935 (Ch. cxv), (25 & 26 Geo. 5.)

An Act to make better provision with respect to road transport services in the borough of Poole; and for other purposes.

Whereas under powers conferred by the Poole and District Light Railway Order 1899 (hereinafter referred to as "the order of 1899") the Poole and District Electric Traction Company Limited (hereinafter referred to as "the Poole Company") constructed certain light railways which are situate in the borough of Poole as now constituted:

And whereas under or by virtue of the following Agreements Orders and Conveyance (all of which are mentioned in the recitals to the Agreement scheduled to this Act)-

(1) The Agreements dated the 11th March 1903 and the 5th May 1903 scheduled to and confirmed by the Bournemouth Corporation Tramways Act 1903;

(2) The Poole (Extension) Order 1905;

(3) A Conveyance dated the 19th April 1909; and

(4) The Agreement dated the 14th December 1927 scheduled to and confirmed by the Poole Corporation Act 1928,

The said light railways are now vested in the Mayor Aldermen and Burgesses of the borough of Poole (hereinafter referred to as "the Poole Corporation") as the owners thereof and are being worked by the Mayor Aldermen and Burgesses of Bournemouth (hereinafter referred to as "the Bournemouth Corporation") as lessees thereof for a term of years which will expire on the 7th June 1935:

And whereas the said light railways have been constructed in the public roads and constitute a continuous line of tramway extending from the level crossing of the railway of the Southern railway Company over Towngate Street in the borough of Poole to County Gates on the boundary between the borough of Poole and the county borough of Bournemouth and are being worked by electricity on the overhead system:

And whereas by the Poole and District Light Railway (Extension) Order 1903 the Poole Company were authorised to construct a further light railway in the borough of Poole as now constituted and in pursuance of the aforesaid Agreements Order and Conveyance or some of them this further light railway was constructed by the Bournemouth Corporation and conveyed to the Poole Corporation and for a period of years worked by Bournemouth Corporation as lessees thereof but in pursuance of the said agreement of the 14th December 1927 it has been abandoned and the rails track and equipment thereof have been removed:

And whereas by the Poole Corporation Act 1928 the Poole Corporation are authorised to run omnibuses within the borough of Poole and with the consent of the Minister of Transport and the local authority of the district (such consent of the local authority not to be unreasonably withheld) along any route outside that borough within a distance of ten miles from Poole Railway Station but by an Agreement made before the passing of that Act (i.e. on the 3rd July 1928) between the Poole Corporation of the first part the Bournemouth Corporation of the second part and Hants and Dorset Motor Services Limited (hereinafter referred to as "the Company") of the third part it was provided (inter alia) that for a period of seven years from the date of the passing of that Act (which period will expire on the 3rd August 1935) the Poole Corporation should not themselves exercise any of the power of running omnibuses conferred upon them by that Act and that the Company and the Poole Corporation should enter into a working agreement with respect to operating of omnibuses in the borough of Poole:

And whereas the Company are operating an extensive system of public service vehicles within the borough of Poole and the county borough of Bournemouth and surrounding districts (including services of stage carriages within the borough of Poole in pursuance of the Heads of Agreement of the 15th March 1928 mentioned in the recitals to the Agreement scheduled to this Act) and some of these services traverse the route of the said light railways,

And whereas it would be to the public advantage if the said light railways were acquired by the Company and the Company were empowered (subject to the provisions of this Act) to abandon them and if the Company were to run services of stage carriages in substitution for services of cars on the route thereof.

And whereas the Poole Corporation and the Company have entered into the Agreement set forth in the Schedule to this Act and it is expedient that the said Agreement be confirmed and that other provision consequential on or ancillary to carrying out of the Agreement be enacted as in this Act contained:

And whereas it is expedient that the other provisions of this Act be enacted:

And whereas the purpose of this Act cannot be effected without the authority of Parliament:

10.
(1) The Poole and District Light Railway (Extension) Order 1903 is hereby repealed.

(2) Subsection (5) of section 6 (Purchase and leasing of Poole undertaking) of the Bournemouth Corporation Tramways Act 1903 is hereby repealed.

The schedule to the Act:

The existing stage carriage services of the Company between Bournemouth and Poole via Lower Parkstone shall be rearranged so adequate and sufficient services of stage carriages shall be operated on the following routes (hereinafter referred to as "the specified routes") that is to say:-

No 1. From a point at or near the existing light railway terminus in High Street Poole to Bournemouth via High Street Parkstone Road Commercial Road Castle Hill Saint Osmund's Road Penn Hill Avenue North Lodge Road Lindsay Road County Gates to the Square Bournemouth.

No 2. From a point at or near the existing light railway terminus in High Street Poole to Bournemouth via High Street Longfleet Road Fernside Road Commercial Road Castle Hill Bournemouth Road Pottery Junction and Poole Road to the Square Bournemouth.

No 3. From a point at or near the existing light railway terminus in High Street Poole to Bournemouth via High Street Parkstone Road North Road Saint Peter's Road View Road Ashley Road and Poole Road to the Square Bournemouth.

No 4. From a point at or near the existing light railway terminus in High Street Poole to Bournemouth via High Street Longfleet Road Fernside Road North Road Saint Peter's Road View Road Ashley Road and Poole Road to the Square Bournemouth.

No. 5. From a point in Ashley Road near the top of Sea View Road along Ashley Road and Poole Road to the Square Bournemouth.

The agreement to remain in force until 31 December 1975 unless sought on 31 December 1957 or any subsequent year by not less than 12 months notice in writing.

1.6) Bournemouth Corporation (Trolley Vehicles) Order Confirmation Act, 1938 (Ch. xxi.), (1 & 2 Geo. 6.)
Order authorising the mayor aldermen and burgesses of the borough of Bournemouth to work and use trolley vehicles upon additional routes in the borough of Bournemouth and in the borough of Christchurch.

1.
(1) This Order may be cited as the Bournemouth Corporation (Trolley Vehicles) Order 1937.
(2) The Bournemouth Corporation Act 1930 and this Order may be cited together as the Bournemouth Corporation (Trolley Vehicles) Act and Order 1930 and 1937.

2. In this Order the following expressions have the meanings hereby respectively assigned to them (that is to say):-
"The borough" means the county borough of Bournemouth;
"The Corporation" means the mayor, aldermen and burgesses of the borough;
"The Act of 1930" means the Bournemouth Corporation Act 1930;
"Trolley vehicle" has the meaning assigned to it by section 4 (Interpretation) of the Act of 1930;
"The Minister" means the Minister of Transport.

3.
(1) Subject to the provisions of this Order and of the Act of 1930 so far as such provisions relate to trolley vehicles and trolley vehicle routes and are applicable to this Order the Corporation may work and use trolley vehicles upon the following routes (in the borough except where otherwise stated) in addition to any routes upon which they are already authorised to use trolley vehicles (that is to say):-

Route No. 1 (1 mile 1 furlong 9.5 chains or thereabouts in length) commencing in Columbia Road at its junction with Kinson Road proceeding along Columbia Road and Ensbury Park Road and terminating therein at its junction with Wimborne Road, *i.e. Moordown;*

Route No. 2 (1 mile 1 furlong 4.7 chains or thereabouts in

length) commencing in Redhill Drive at its junction with Ensbury Park Road proceeding along Redhill Drive to and along Coombe Avenue and along Leybourne Avenue and Northbourne Avenue and terminating in the last-mentioned road at its junction with Wimborne Road;

Route No. 3 (3 miles 0 furlong 3.7 chains or thereabouts in length) commencing in Castle Lane at its junction with Lawford Road proceeding along Castle Lane and terminating therein at its junction with Christchurch Road, *i.e. Iford;*

Route No. 4 (1 mile 4 furlongs or thereabouts in length) commencing in Alma Road at its junction with Wimborne Road, Road with Wimborne Road, *i.e. Moordown:*
. Winton Banks, proceeding along Alma Road and along Richmond Park Road and terminating therein at its junction with Holdenhurst Road, *i.e. Springbourne;*

Route No. 5 (1 mile 4 furlongs 4.8 chains or thereabouts in length) commencing in Tuckton Road at its junction with Bellevue Road, *i.e. Tuckton,* proceeding along Tuckton Road and Cranleigh Road to and along Beaufort Road and Beresford Road and terminating in that road at its junction with Southbourne Grove, *i.e. Fisherman's Walk;*

Route No. 6 (1 furlong 3 chains or thereabouts in length) commencing in Parkwood Road at its junction with Seabourne Road proceeding in a north-easterly direction along Parkwood Road to and along Southbourne Road in a south-easterly direction and terminating in that road at its junction with Beresford Road;

Route No. 8 (1 mile 2 furlongs 6.5 chains or thereabouts in length to be situate in the borough and in the borough of Christchurch) commencing in Christchurch Road at its junction with Iford Lane proceeding along Christchurch Road and along Barrack Road and terminating therein at its junction with Stour Road Christchurch.

Note: Route 7 of the Provisional Order became Route 8 in the Confirmation Act, and Route 8 Bear Cross – Wallisdown via Ringwood Road and Wallisdown Road of the Provisional Order was deleted, thus the Confirmation Act contained no Route 7.

Provided that-
(a) Before equipping any route to include a turning point or arranging for a new turning point on any route the Corporation shall submit plans of the turning point to the Minister for approval and shall also submit a copy of such plans to the chief constable of Hampshire and before approving any such plans the Minister shall give to the chief constable an opportunity for making representations with reference thereto and shall consider any such representations which may be made to him;
(b) Section 124 (Restricting running of omnibuses in competition) of the Act of 1930 shall not apply to any route authorised by this Order which was not before the confirmation of this Order a protected Route within the meaning of that section.

(2) The application of the provisions of the Act of 1930 as amended by the Road Traffic Act 1930 of this Order in accordance with subsection (1) of section 102 of the Act of 1930 shall have effect with any necessary modification and so far only as the same are applicable for the purpose and for the purpose of such application the expressions "trolley vehicles" and "trolley vehicle route" where used in the Act of 1930 shall be deemed to include the trolley vehicles and the routes

authorised by the Order and the expression "trolley vehicle undertaking" where used in the Act of 1930 shall include the trolley vehicles and trolley vehicle routes authorised by this Order.

4. If the Corporation shall not have commenced to use trolley vehicles upon each of the routes authorised by this Order within five years from the passing of the Act confirming this Order or such extended time as the Minister may upon the application of the Corporation (and in the case of a route outside the borough after considering the representations of the local authority and the highway authority concerned) allow the powers conferred by this Order shall so far as they relate to the use of trolley vehicles upon any route upon which the Corporation shall not have commenced to use trolley vehicles cease to be exercisable.

5. The Corporation shall not exercise the powers of section 90 (Power to use trolley vehicles) of the Act of 1930 for the purpose of providing a turning point or of connecting the trolley vehicle routes or of obtaining access thereto from any depot garage building or work of the Corporation in relation to any road or street in the borough of Christchurch without the consent of the mayor aldermen and burgesses of the borough of Christchurch which consent shall not be unreasonably withheld and any question as to whether such consent has been unreasonably withheld shall be determined by the Minister of Transport.

6. Notwithstanding anything contained in this Order the following provisions for the protection of the mayor aldermen and burgesses of the borough of Christchurch (in this section referred to as "the Christchurch Corporation") shall unless otherwise agreed in writing between the Corporation and the Christchurch Corporation apply and have effect (that is to say):-
(1) No advertisement (other than time tables and notices relating to the Corporation's trolley vehicle undertaking) shall be displayed on any apparatus erected or used on any road or bridge in the borough of Christchurch under the powers of this Order without the consent of the Christchurch Corporation which consent shall not be unreasonably withheld:
(2) The Christchurch Corporation with the consent of the Corporation may use free of cost for the purpose of fixing thereto street lamps lighting brackets street names fire alarm plates or direction signs any posts or standards provided or used by the Corporation in the borough of Christchurch under or by virtue of the provisions of this Order but not so as to interfere with the use of such posts or standards for the purposes of the Corporation or to make the same unfit for such purposes or dangerous to persons or traffic in or passing through the adjoining streets or roads and the Christchurch Corporation shall pay the cost where necessary of insulating the posts or standards so used and shall make compensation to the Corporation for any damage which may be caused to said posts or standards by reason of the exercise of the power contained in this subsection and shall indemnify the Corporation against any claim or demand which may be occasioned by such user. Any consent of the Corporation under this subsection shall not be unreasonably withheld:
(3) Any difference which may arise between the Corporation

and the Christchurch Corporation with regard to any of the matters referred to in this section or as to whether or not any consent has been unreasonably withheld shall be settled by an engineer to be appointed in default of agreement on the application (after notice in writing to the other of them) of the Corporation or the Christchurch Corporation by the Minister of Transport and subject as aforesaid the provisions of the Arbitration Acts 1889 to 1934 or of any statutory modification or re-enactment thereof shall apply to any such application.

7. The following provisions apply for the protection of the Bournemouth and Poole Electricity Supply Company Limited (in this section called "the company" shall unless otherwise agreed in writing between the Corporation and the company apply and have effect:-

(1)   In this section the expression "works" where used with reference to works of the company has the meaning assigned to that expression in the Electric Lighting Act 1882:

(2)   Nothing in this Order or in any Act or any other Order in the application of such Act or Order to the working of trolley vehicles and trolley vehicles routes authorised by this Order shall extend to or authorise any interference with any works of the company except in accordance with and subject to the provisions of section 15 of the Electric Lighting Act 1882 and of section 17 of the schedule to the Electric Lighting (Clauses) Act 1899:

(3)   Before placing or erecting any apparatus or equipment for or in connection with the working of trolley vehicles on any of the routes authorised by this Order in any road in under or over which any works of the company are situate the Corporation shall (unless they contemplate altering the position of any such works) give seven days' notice to the company of their intention to place or erect such apparatus or equipment and shall at the same time deliver a plan and section of the proposed work. If it should appear to the company that the placing or erection of such apparatus would interfere with or endanger any such works of the company or interfere with or impede the supply of electricity by the company the company may give notice to the Corporation to lower or otherwise alter the position of such works or to support the same or to substitute temporarily or otherwise other works in such manner as may be considered necessary and any difference as to the necessity of such lowering alteration support or substitution shall be settled by arbitration in manner provided by section 28 of the Electric Lighting (Clauses) Act 1899:

(4)   (a) If any structure which shall hereafter be erected by the Corporation under the powers of section 115 or section 116 of the Act of 1930 is situate in any highway forming part of any of the routes authorised by this Order over any works of the company laid or placed before the erection of the structure and the company give to the Corporation notice in writing of their desire to obtain access to such works the Corporation shall either remove temporarily the structure or so much thereof as shall require to be so removed in order to afford such access or (if the Corporation determine not to remove the structure or part thereof) bear any additional expense due to the existence of the structure which may be reasonably incurred by the company in obtaining such access:

(c)   Any difference between the company and the Corporation arising under this subsection shall be referred to and settled by a single arbitrator to be agreed upon between the Corporation and the company or failing agreement to be appointed on the application of either party (after notice in writing to the other) by the President of the Institution of Civil Engineers and subject as aforesaid the provisions of the Arbitration Act 1889 and the Arbitration Act 1934 shall apply to the arbitration.

8.

(1) The Corporation shall have power in addition and without prejudice to their powers of borrowing under the Local Government Act 1933 from time to time to borrow without the consent of any sanctioning authority for an in connection with the purposes mentioned in the first column of the following table the respective sums mentioned in the second column of the said table and they shall pay off all moneys so borrowed within such periods as the Corporation may determine not exceeding those respectively mentioned in the third column of the said table (namely):-

(1) Purpose	(2) Amount	(3) Period for repayment
(a) The provision of trolley vehicles.	£54,000	Period for repayment calculated (except where otherwise stated) from the date or dates of borrowing.
(b) The provision of electrical equipment and the construction of other works necessary for working trolley vehicles along the routes authorise by this Order.	£44,000	Twenty years.
(c) The payment of the costs charges and expenses of this Order.	The sum requisite	Five years from the confirmation of this Order.

(2) The provisions of Part IX of the Local Government Act 1933 so far as they are not inconsistent with this Order or the provisions of any scheme made under section 244 (Consolidated loans fund) of the Act of 1930 shall extend and apply to money borrowed under this section as if it were borrowed under Part IX of that Act and the period fixed for the repayment of any money borrowed under this section shall as respects that money be the fixed period for the purpose of the said Part IX.

(3) In the application of the said provisions of the Local Government Act 1933 to the borrowing of any further money for the purposes of this Order the Minister shall be the sanctioning authority.

9. All regulations and byelaws relating to the trolley vehicles authorised by the Act of 1930 and made in pursuance of that Act or any other statutory enactment shall with any necessary modifications apply to the trolley vehicles used by the Corporation in pursuance of this Order.

10. The provisions of section 250 of the Local Government Act 1933 shall not apply in respect of byelaws to be made by the Corporation in pursuance Part IV (Trolley vehicles omnibuses and tramways) of the Act of 1930.

11. The Minister may hold such inquiries as he may consider necessary in regard to the exercise of any powers conferred upon him or the giving of consents under this Order and section 290 of the Local Government Act 1933 shall apply accordingly.

12. All costs charges and expenses of and incidental to the preparing and obtaining and confirming of this Order or otherwise incurred in relation thereto as taxed by the taxing officer of the House of Lords or of the House of Commons shall be paid by the Corporation.

1.7) Bournemouth Corporation (Trolley Vehicles) Order Confirmation Act, 1955 (Ch. v.), (4 Eliz. 2)

An Act to confirm a Provisional Order made by the Minister of Transport and Civil Aviation under the Bournemouth Corporation Act 1930 relating to Bournemouth Corporation trolley vehicles.

[27th July 1955]

Whereas under the authority of section one hundred and two of the Bournemouth Corporation Act 1930 the Minister of Transport and Civil Aviation has made the Provisional Order set out in the schedule to this Act annexed:

And whereas a Provisional Order made by the Minister of Transport and Civil Aviation under the authority of the said section is not of any validity or force whatever until the confirmation thereof by Act of Parliament:

And whereas it is expedient that the Provisional Order made by the Minister of Transport and Civil Aviation under the authority of the said section and set out in the schedule to this Act annexed be confirmed by Act of Parliament:

Be it therefore enacted by the Queen's most Excellent Majesty by and with the advice and consent of the Lords Spiritual and Temporal and Commons in this present Parliament assembled and by the authority of the same as follows:-

1.   The Order set out in the schedule to this Act annexed shall be and the same is hereby confirmed and all the provisions thereof in the manner and form as they are set out in the said schedule shall from and after the passing of this Act have full force and validity and the date of the same shall be the date of the passing of this Act.

2.   This act may be cited as the Bournemouth Corporation (Trolley Vehicles) Order Confirmation Act 1955.

SCHEDULE

Provisional Order authorising the mayor aldermen and burgesses of the borough of Bournemouth to use trolley vehicles upon an additional route in the borough of Christchurch.

1.

(1) This Order may be cited as the Bournemouth Corporation (Trolley Vehicles) Order 1955.

(2) The Bournemouth Corporation (Trolley Vehicles) Act and Order 1930 and 1937 and this Order may be cited together as the Bournemouth Corporation (trolley Vehicles) Act and Orders 1930 to 1955.

2. In this Order the following expressions have the respective meanings hereby assigned to them namely:-

"the Act of 1930" means the Bournemouth Corporation Act 1930;

"the Act of 1933" means the Local Government Act 1933;

"the Corporation" means the mayor, aldermen and burgesses of the borough of Bournemouth;

"the Minister" means the Minister of Transport and Civil Aviation;

"trolley vehicle" has the meaning assigned to it by section 4 (Interpretation) of the Act of 1930.

3.

(1) The Corporation may work and use trolley vehicles upon the following route in the borough of Christchurch in addition to any routes upon which they are already authorised to use trolley vehicles (namely):-

A route (9.1 chains or thereabouts in length) commencing at the junction of Barrack Road with High Street passing along Barrack Road to its junction with the reconstructed road connecting Barrack Road with Bargates and passing along the reconstructed road and terminating at its junction with Bargates,

(2) The application of the provisions of the Act of 1930 as amended by the Road Traffic Act 1930 to this Order in accordance with subsection (1) of section 102 of the Act of 1930 shall have effect with any necessary modification and so far only as the same are applicable for the purpose and for the purpose of such application the expressions "trolley vehicles" and "trolley vehicle route" where used in the Act of 1930 shall be deemed to include the trolley vehicles and the routes authorised by this Order and the expression "trolley vehicle undertaking" where used in the Act of 1930 shall include the trolley vehicles and trolley vehicle routes authorised by this Order:

Provided that in such application to this Order:

(a) section 94 (Vehicles not to be deemed light locomotives or motor cars) of the Act of 1930 shall have effect as if subsection (1) was omitted therefrom;

(b) section 124 (Restricting of omnibuses running in competition) of the Act of 1930 shall not apply to the Route authorised by this Order.

4. If the Corporation shall not have commenced to use trolley vehicles upon the route authorised by this Order within five years from the passing of the Act confirming this Order or such extended time as the Minister may upon the application of the Corporation allow the powers conferred by this Order shall so far as they relate to the use of trolley vehicles upon that route cease to be exercisable.

5. All regulations and byelaws relating to the trolley vehicles of the Corporation and made in pursuance of the Act of 1930 or any other statutory enactment shall with any necessary modifications apply to the trolley vehicles used by the

Corporation in pursuance of this Order.

6. The Minister may hold such inquiries as he may consider necessary in regard to the exercise of any powers conferred upon him or the giving of consents under this Order and section 290 of the Act of 1933 shall apply accordingly.

7. This Order shall be deemed to be an enactment passed before and in force at the passing of the Town and Country Planning Act 1947 and for the purposes of subsection (4) of section 13 and subsection (1) of section 118 of that Act.

8. All costs charges and expenses of and incidental to the preparing and obtaining and confirming of this Order or otherwise incurred in relation thereto as taxed by the taxing officer of the House of Lords or of the House of Commons shall be paid by the Corporation.

1.8) Extensions of time

On 9 December 1960 the Town Clerk applied to the MoT to extend for a further period of 3 years the time limited by Section 4 of the Bournemouth Corporation (Trolley Vehicles) Order, 1937 confirmed by the Bournemouth Corporation (Trolley Vehicles) Order Confirmation Act, 1938 as extended in 1943 and 1946, and the consents of the MoT dated 14 May 1949, 16 May 1952, 17 May 1955, and 8 November 1957 for the commencement of the use of trolley vehicles along routes 2 & 4 authorised by Section 3 of the said order of 1937, namely:

Route No. 2 (1 mile, 1 furlong 4.7 chains or thereabouts in length) commencing in Redhill Drive at its junction with Ensbury Park Road proceeding along Redhill Drive to and along Coombe Avenue and along Leybourne Avenue and Northbourne Avenue and terminating in the last mentioned road at its junction with Wimborne Road;

Route 4 (1 mile, 4 furlongs or thereabouts in length) commencing in Alma Road at its junction with Wimborne Road proceding along Alma Road and along Richmond Park Road and terminating therein at its junction with Holdenhurst Road.

Formal consent was given on 1 May 1961. This was the last occasion that Bournemouth Corporation approached the legislative authorities in connection with their trolley vehicle system apart from the formal abandonment procedure.

2) Statutory Rules and Orders

2.1) 1933, No. 676

TROLLEY VEHICLE
Bournemouth Corporation System

ADDITIONAL REGULATIONS, DATED JULY 7, 1933, MADE BY THE MINISTER OF TRANSPORT AS REGARDS ELECTRICAL POWER ON THE BOURNEMOUTH CORPORATION TROLLEY VEHICLE SYSTEM

The Minister of Transport, under and by virtue of the powers conferred upon him in this behalf, does hereby make the following regulations for securing to the public reasonable protection against danger in the exercise of the powers conferred by Parliament with respect to the use of electrical power on the trolley vehicle system on all or any of the routes on which the use of such power has been authorised by the provisions of the Bournemouth Corporation Act 1930 (2-1 G.5c. clxxxi) and the applied provisions of the Bournemouth Corporation Tramways Order 1900 ((63-4 V.c. ccviii.) (hereinafter called "the routes"):

And the Minister of Transport does also hereby make the following byelaws with regard to the use of electrical power on the routes.

REGULATIONS

I.   Every trolley vehicle used on the routes shall comply with the following requirements, that is to say:-

(a) It shall be fitted with an apparatus to indicate to the driver the speed at which it is running.

(b) It shall be fitted with at least two independent brakes each capable of stopping and holding the vehicle on any gradient on the routes. One of the brakes at least must be applied by pedal.

(c) It shall be conspicuously numbered inside and outside.

(d) It shall be fitted with a bell, horn, gong, or other approved means for giving warning when necessary.

(e) It shall be so constructed as to enable the driver to command the fullest possible view of the road.

(f) It shall be equipped with an efficient fire extinguisher of a type suitable for dealing with electrical fires, and also a pair of rubber gloves.

II.   No trailer vehicle shall be used on the routes except in case of the removal of a disabled trolley vehicle.

III. No passenger shall be allowed to travel standing on the steps, platform, staircase or upper deck of a trolley vehicle.

IV. During the hours of darkness, which expression means in summer time the time between one hour after sunset and one hour before sunrise and during the remainder of the year the time between half-an-hour after sunset and half-an-hour before sunrise, and at any time during fog, every trolley vehicle on the routes shall carry a lamp so constructed and placed as to exhibit white lights visible within a reasonable distance to the front and every such vehicle shall carry a lamp so constructed and placed as to exhibit a red light visible within a reasonable distance to the rear. The front lamps shall be fixed on opposite sides of the vehicle, be as nearly as possible of the same power and be fixed at the same height from the ground in such position that no part of the vehicle or its equipment extends laterally on the same side as the lamp more than

12 inches beyond the centre of the lamp. The rear lamp shall be fixed either on the centre line or on the off-side of the vehicle.

V.   The speed at which the trolley vehicles may be driven or propelled along the routes shall not exceed the rate of
Thirty miles an hour-
> In Poole Road, between St. Michael's Church and the eastern end of Seamoor Road

Twenty miles an hour-
> a) In Seamoor Road
> b) In Poole Road, between its two junctions with Seamoor Road

Fifteen miles an hour-
> a) When descending Poole Hill
> b) In The Triangle
> c) In Avenue Road

Ten miles an hour-
> a) When rounding the curve from The Triangle into Avenue Road

Five miles an hour-
> a) When turning from Poole Road into Seamoor Road
> b) When turning from Seamoor Road into Poole Road
> c) In The Square

At all other places not specifically mentioned the speed shall not exceed the rate of twenty-five miles an hour.

VI.   The electrical pressure or difference of potential between the two overhead conductors used in connection with the working of the routes shall in no case exceed 600 volts. the electrical energy supplied through feeders shall not be generated at or transformed to a higher pressure than 650 volts, except with the written consent of the Minister of Transport, and subject to such regulations and conditions as he may prescribe.

VII.   The interval between the supports to which the overhead conductors used in connection with the working of the routes are attached shall not, except with the approval of the Minister of Transport, exceed 120 feet, and as a general rule the overhead conductors shall in no part be at a less height than 20 feet from the surface of the street, except where they pass under railway or other bridges or at curves.

VIII.   Each positive overhead conductor shall be divided up into sections not exceeding (except with the special approval of the Minister of Transport) one-half of a mile in length, between every two of which shall be inserted an emergency switch so enclosed as to be inaccessible to pedestrians.

IX.   Each separate insulator on the overhead conductors shall be tested not less frequently than once in a month, and any insulator found to be defective shall at once be removed and an efficient insulator substituted.

X.   All electrical conductors fixed upon the trolley vehicles in connection with the trolley wheels shall be formed of flexible cables protected by india-rubber insulation of the highest quality, and additionally protected wherever they are adjacent to any metal so as to avoid risk of the metal becoming charged.

XI.   The insulation of the electrical conductors from the metal work of each trolley vehicle shall be tested and recorded daily before the vehicle is used for passenger traffic with a testing pressure not less than 500 volts. No trolley vehicle shall be taken out for use if the leakage current exceeds 3 milliamperes.

XII.   The hand-rails used by passengers on entering or leaving a trolley vehicle shall either be constructed of some non-conducting substance or be covered with a suitable insulating material.

XIII.   An emergency cut-off switch shall be provided and fixed so as to be conveniently reached by the driver in case of any failure of action of the controller switch.

XIV.   If and whenever telegraph, telephone, or other wires, unprotected with a permanent insulating covering, cross above, or are liable to fall upon, or to be blown on to, the overhead conductors of the routes, efficient guard wires shall be erected and maintained at all places. Provided that this regulation shall not apply to Post Office over-road stay wires or other uncovered wires which are not electrical conductors where they are connected at each end to the negative conductor.

XV.   The guard wires shall be connected to the negative overhead conductor at intervals of not more than two spans.

XVI.   The poles carrying section switch boxes shall be efficiently connected with earth.

XVII.   Where on the routes there are two negative trolley wires these shall be cross-connected at intervals of not more than half a mile.

XVIII.   No gas or electric lamp bracket shall be attached to any pole unless triple insulation is provided between the pole and the positive overhead conductors.

In the case of any lamp suspended from the span wire carrying the overhead conductors that portion of the span wire from which the lamp is suspended shall be separated from that portion or portions on which the trolley wire or wires are carried by a suitable insulator.

(NOTE.-The above-mentioned provisions with regard to triple insulation will not apply to the erection of lamp brackets in particular cases where the Minister of Transport is satisfied that adequate protection is attained by other methods of insulation an/or earthing approved by him).

Penalty

NOTE.-The Bournemouth Corporation or any company or person using electrical power on the routes contrary to any of the above regulations is, for every such offence, subject to a penalty not exceeding £10; and also in the case of a continuing offence, to a further penalty not exceeding £5 for every day during which offence continues after conviction thereof.

BYELAWS

I.   The bell, horn, gong, or other approved apparatus shall be sounded by the driver of the trolley vehicle whenever necessary as a warning.

II.   The trolley vehicles on the routes shall be brought to a standstill as soon as possible whenever it is necessary to avoid impending danger and on all occasions immediately before commencing to descend Poole Hill.

III.   A printed copy of these regulations and byelaws shall be kept in a conspicuous position inside of each trolley vehicle in use on the routes.

Penalty

NOTE.-Any person offending against or committing a breach of any of these byelaws is liable to a penalty not exceeding forty shillings.

The provisions of the Summary Jurisdiction Acts, with respect to the recovery of penalties, are applicable to penalties for the breach of these regulations or byelaws.

Signed this 7th day of July, 1933.

E.W. Rowntree
Assistant Secretary, Ministry of Transport.

There was a glimpse of countryside on Barrack Road, Christchurch, once Iford Bridge into the Priory Town had been crossed. Sunbeam MF2B no. 302 (302LJ) heads east approaching Jumpers Corner and Stourvale Avenue en route to Christchurch, Church Street.
Roger G. Funnell
(courtesy Mrs D. Funnell and Rodney Funnell)

2.2) 1934 No. 909

TROLLEY VEHICLE
Bournemouth Corporation System

ADDITIONAL REGULATIONS, DATED AUGUST 16, 1934, MADE BY THE MINISTER OF TRANSPORT AS REGARDS ELECTRICAL POWER ON THE BOURNEMOUTH CORPORATION TROLLEY VEHICLE SYSTEM

The Minister of Transport, under and by virtue of the powers conferred upon him in this behalf, does hereby make the following regulations for securing to the public reasonable protection against danger in the exercise of the powers conferred by Parliament with respect to the use of electrical power on the trolley vehicle system on all or any of the routes on which the use of such power has been authorised by the provisions of the Bournemouth Corporation Act 1930 (2-1 G.5c. clxxxi) and the applied provisions of the Bournemouth Corporation Tramways Order 1900 (63-4 V.c. ccviii.) (hereinafter called "the routes"):

REGULATIONS

I. The speed at which trolley vehicles shall be driven or propelled along the routes shall not exceed the rate of:-

1. TWENTY miles an hour:
   (a) in Old Christchurch Road
   (b) in Ashley Road, between the southern approach to the bridge over the Southern
       Railway at Boscombe Station and Christchurch Road
   (c) in Portman Road
   (d) in Gladstone Road
   (e) in St. Swithun's Road, Southcote Road, St. Clement's Road and Palmerston Road

2. FIFTEEN miles an hour
   (a) in Fir Vale Road and St. Peter's Road
   (b) in Gervis Place, between Hinton Road and Westover Road

3. TEN miles an hour
   When passing over the bridge over the Southern Railway at Boscombe Station and the approaches thereto.

4. FIVE miles an hour
   (a) when traversing all turning circles and triangles
   (b) when passing through all trolley wire junctions and crossings
   (c) when turning from Palmerston Road into Christchurch Road
   (d) when turning from Ashley Road into Christchurch Road
   (e) when turning from Christchurch Road into Portman Road
   (f) when turning from Portman Road into Gladstone Road
   (g) when turning from Gladstone Road into Ashley Road
   (e) when turning from Holdenhurst Road into Ashley Road and vice versa.

II. The insulation of the electrical conductors from the metal work of each trolley vehicle shall be tested and the leakage current recorded daily before the vehicle is used for passenger traffic with a testing pressure of not less than 500 volts. The arrangements for this test shall be such as to ensure that the whole of the high tension circuits of the vehicle, including any compressor or similar motor circuit, are subjected to the test pressure. If a high resistance instrument is used for the test, the scale shall be suitably calibrated to ensure that the resistance of the instrument itself does not affect the accuracy of the indication of the true leakage from conductors to chassis. No trolley vehicle shall be taken out for use if the leakage current exceeds 3 milliamperes.

III. Regulation XI of the Regulations and Byelaws made on the 7th day of July 1933 (S.R. & O. 1933, No. 676) is hereby rescinded.

These regulations shall be read with the Regulations and Byelaws made in this behalf by the Minister of Transport on the 7th day of July 1933 for the Bournemouth Corporation Trolley Vehicle System.

Signed this 16th day of August 1934.

E.W. Rowntree
Assistant Secretary, Ministry of Transport.

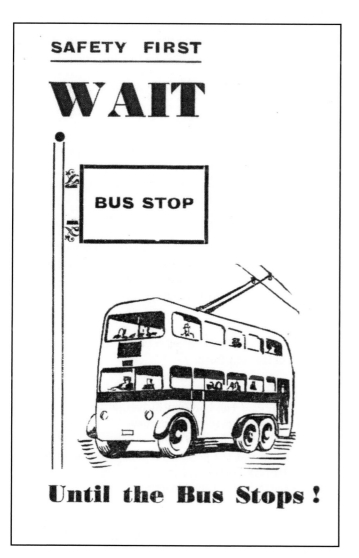

SAFETY FIRST

WAIT

BUS STOP

Until the Bus Stops !

2.3) 1936, No. 1353

TROLLEY VEHICLE
Bournemouth Corporation System

REGULATIONS, DATED DECEMBER 21, 1936, MADE BY THE MINISTER OF TRANSPORT UNDER THE PROVISIONS OF SECTIONS 19 AND 24 OF THE BOURNEMOUTH CORPORATION TRAMWAYS ORDER, 1900, (confirmed by 63 & 64 Vict. c. ccviii) AND SECTION 99 OF THE BOURNEMOUTH CORPORATION ACT, 1930, 20 & 21 Geo. 5. c. clxxxi.) FOR REGULATING THE USE OF ELECTRICAL POWER; FOR PREVENTING FUSION OR INJURIOUS ELECTROLYTIC ACTION OF OR ON DAS OR WATER PIPES OR OTHER METALLIC PIPES, STRUCTURES, OR SUBSTANCES; AND FOR MINIMISING AS FAR AS IS REASONABLY PRACTICABLE INJURIOUS INTERFERENCE WITH THE ELECTRIC WIRES, LINES, AND APPARATUS OF PARTIES OTHER THAN THE BOURNEMOUTH CORPORATION, AND THE CURRENTS THEREIN, WHETHER SUCH LINES DO OR DO NOT USE THE EARTH AS A RETURN.

Definitions
In the following regulations-

The expression "energy" means electrical energy.

The expression "generator" means the dynamo or dynamos or other electrical apparatus used for the generation or conversion of energy.

The expression "motor" means any electric motor carried on a trolley vehicle and used for the conversion of energy.

The expression "wire" means any wire or apparatus used for telegraphic, telephonic, electrical signalling or similar purposes.

The expression "current" means an electric current exceeding one-thousandth part of an ampere.

The expression "the Corporation" means the Bournemouth Corporation, and includes their lessees, and any person owning, working or running trolley vehicles over the trolley vehicle system of the Corporation.

REGULATIONS
1. Any generator shall be of such pattern and construction as to be capable of producing a continuous current without appreciable pulsation.
2.
  (1) The positive conductor used for transmitting energy from the generator to the motors shall be insulated from earth.
  (2) The negative conductor shall be connected to earth at one point only, namely, at a generating station or at a sub-station, but shall elsewhere be insulated.

3. The insulation of the said positive and negative conductors, and of all feeders and other conductors, shall be so maintained that the leakage current shall not exceed one-hundredth of an ampere per mile of route. The leakage current shall be ascertained not less frequently than once in every week before or after the hours of running when the said conductors are fully charged. If at any time it should be found that the leakage current exceeds one-half of an ampere per mile of route, the leak shall be localised and the cause thereof removed as soon as practicable, and the running of the trolley vehicles shall be stopped unless the leak is localised and the cause thereof

removed within 24 hours.

4. In the disposition, connections, and workings of feeders the Corporation shall take all reasonable precautions to avoid injurious interference with any existing wires.

5. The Corporation shall so construct and maintain their trolley vehicle system as to secure good contact between the motors and the said conductors.

6. The Corporation shall adopt the best means available to prevent the occurrence of undue sparking at the rubbing or rolling contacts in any place and in the construction and use of their generators and motors.

7. The Corporation shall, so far as may be applicable to their system of working, keep records of the matters specified below. These records shall, if and when required, be forwarded for the information of the Minister of Transport.

Number of trolley vehicles running.

Length of routes.

Daily Records
   Maximum working pressure.
   Maximum working current.

Weekly Records
   Leakage current (vide Regulation 3).

Occasional Records
   Localisation and removal of leakages, stating time occupied.
   Particulars of any abnormal occurrence affecting the electric working of the routes.

8. The Regulations made by the Minister of Transport in this behalf, dated the 7th day of July, 1933, (S.R.&O.1933, No. 675) are hereby rescinded.

Signed this 21st day of December, 1936.

F. Gordon Tucker,
Assistant Secretary, Ministry of Transport.

2.4) 1936, No. 1354

TROLLEY VEHICLE
Bournemouth Corporation System

ADDITIONAL REGULATION AND BYELAW, DATED DECEMBER 21, 1936, MADE BY THE MINISTER OF TRANSPORT AS REGARDS ELECTRICAL POWER ON THE BOURNEMOUTH CORPORATION TROLLEY VEHICLE SYSTEM

The Minister of Transport, under and by virtue of the powers conferred upon him in this behalf, does hereby make the following regulations for securing to the public reasonable protection against danger in the exercise of the powers conferred by Parliament with respect to the use of electrical power on the trolley vehicle system on all or any of the routes on which the use of such power has been authorised by the provisions of the Bournemouth Corporation Act 1930 (2-1 G.5c. clxxxi) and the applied provisions of the Bournemouth Corporation Tramways Order 1900 ((63-4 V.c. ccviii.) (hereinafter called "the routes"):

And the Minister of Transport does also hereby make the following byelaw with regard to the use of electrical power on the routes.

REGULATIONS

I. The speed at which trolley vehicles shall be driven or propelled along the routes shall not exceed the rate of:-
1. Thirty miles an hour-
   In Stour Road between Tuckton Bridge and Barrack Road, Christchurch.

2. Twenty miles an hour-
   (a) In Charminster Road, between Heron Court Road and Queen's Park Avenue.
   (b) When traversing the bend at the junction of Lansdowne Road and St. Pauls Road.
   (c) In Belle Vue Road, Southbourne, between Cross Roads and Foxholes Road.
   (d) In Foxholes Road, Southbourne, except when descending the hill east of Guild Hill Road where the speed shall not exceed the rate of ten miles an hour.
   (e) In High Street, Christchurch.

3. Fifteen miles an hour-
   In Lansdowne Road between points ten yards on either side of Beechey Road.

4. Ten miles an hour-
   (a) In Richmond Hill between Richmond Gardens and The Square on the descending journey.
   (b) When crossing Tuckton Bridge.
   (c) When passing the junction of High Street, Christchurch, and Barrack Road.
   (d) In Church Street, Christchurch.

5. Five miles an hour-
   (a) When turning from St. Pauls Road into Holdenhurst Road and vice versa.
   (b) When turning from Stour Road, Christchurch into Bargates and vice versa.

(c) When passing the traffic island at the junction of High Street, Christchurch Road, and Castle Street on the outward journey.

BYELAW

The trolley vehicles on the routes shall be brought to a standstill on all occasions at the following points:-
(a) On Richmond Hill, at Richmond Gardens on the descending journey.
(b) On Richmond Hill, at the Church of the Sacred Heart, *i.e. Albert Road,* on the descending journey.
(c) In St. Pauls Road, before crossing Littledown Road.

These regulations and this byelaw shall be read with the Regulations and Byelaws made in this behalf by the Minister of Transport, on the 7th day of July 1933 (as amended) and the 16th day of August 1934 for the Bournemouth Corporation Trolley Vehicle System.

Signed this 21st day of December 1936.

F. Gordon Tucker,
Assistant Secretary, Ministry of Transport.

On 4 July 1965 Sunbeam MF2b no. 276 (WRU276) crests the summit of Richmond Hill on its way north to Winton and Columbia Road. It is no exaggeration to write that trolleybuses could outpace family cars on the hill. **Robin Helliar-Symons**

3) Bournemouth Byelaws

MADE ON THE THIRD DAY OF APRIL, 1951, BY THE MAYOR, ALDERMEN AND BURGESSES OF THE COUNTY BOROUGH OF BOURNEMOUTH, ACTING BY THE COUNCIL UNDER THE POWERS CONFERRED ON THEM BY SECTIONS 46 AND 47 OF THE TRAMWAYS ACT, 1870, SECTIONS 98, 118 AND 120 OF THE BOURNEMOUTH CORPORATION ACT, 1930, AND THE BORNEMOUTH CORPORATION (TROLLEY VEHICLES) ORDER CONFIRMATION ACT, 1938, WITH RESPECT TO THEIR TROLLEY VEHICLES AND CERTAIN PREMISES

1. In these Byelaws unless the context otherwise requires the following expressions have the meanings hereby respectively assigned to them, that is to say:-
"Corporation" means the Mayor, Aldermen and Burgesses of the County Borough of Bournemouth, acting by the Council.
"Trolley Vehicle" means any trolley vehicle owned and used by the Corporation for the conveyance of passengers.
"Trolley Vehicle system" means the system of trolley vehicles worked by the Corporation.
"Passenger" means any person other than an authorised person who has entered a trolley vehicle and travels thereon.
"Intending passenger" means any person waiting at a stopping place on a trolley vehicle route for the purpose of becoming a passenger on a trolley vehicle or who is about to enter a trolley vehicle for that purpose.
"Conductor" includes any officer or servant of the Corporation having the charge of or helping in the charge of a trolley vehicle.
"Driver" means any officer of servant of the Corporation driving or helping to drive a trolley vehicle. "Authorised person" means any officer or servant of the Corporation (including the conductor) on duty upon or in connection with the trolley vehicle.
"Premises" means a cloakroom room or shed for the storage of bicycles tricycles　　　and other vehicles or any shelter or other accommodation provided in connection with any service of trolley vehicles of the Corporation.
"General Manager" means the General Manager for the time being of the trolley vehicle system.

2. The Interpretation Act, 1889 shall apply to the interpretation of these Byelaws as it applies to the interpretation of an Act of Parliament.

3. When a trolley vehicle is carrying passengers or waiting to pick up passengers a passenger or intending passenger shall not -
(i) use obscene or offensive language or conduct himself in a riotous or disorderly manner
(ii) enter or alight from the trolley vehicle otherwise than by the doors or openings provided for the purpose
(iii) when entering or attempting to enter the trolley vehicle wilfully and unreasonably impede passengers seeking to enter the trolley vehicle or to alight therefrom;
(iv) enter or remain in or on the trolley vehicle when requested not to do so by an authorised person on the ground that the trolley vehicle is carrying its full

complement of passengers;

(v) travel in or on the upper deck of the trolley vehicle unless he occupies a seat provided for that purpose, or in or on any part of the trolley vehicle not provided for the conveyance of passengers;

(vi) wilfully do or cause to be done with respect to any part of the trolley vehicle or its equipment anything which is calculated to obstruct or interfere with the working of the trolley vehicle or to cause injury or discomfort to any person;

(vii) when the trolley vehicle is in motion distract the driver's attention without reasonable cause or speak to him unless it is necessary to do so in order to give directions as to the stopping of the trolley vehicle;

(viii) give any signal which might be interpreted by the driver as a signal from theconductor to start;

(ix) spit upon or from or wilfully damage, soil or defile any part of the trolley vehicle;

(x) when in or on the trolley vehicle distribute printed or similar matter of any description or distribute any article for the purpose of advertising;

(xi) wilfully remove, displace, deface or alter any number plate, notice board, fare table, route indicator or destination board or any printed or other notice or advertisement in or on the trolley vehicle;

(xii) when in or on the trolley vehicle to the annoyance of other persons use or operate any noisy instrument or make or combine with any other person or persons to make excessive noise by singing, shouting or otherwise;

(xiii) when in or on the trolley vehicle throw any money to be scrambled for by any person on the road or footway; or throw out of the trolley vehicle any bottle liquid or litter or any article or thing likely to annoy persons or to cause damage or injury to any person or property;

(xiv) throw any article from the trolley vehicle or attach to or trail from the trolley vehicle any streamer, balloon, flag or other article in such manner as to overhang the road;

(xv) wilfully obstruct or impede any authorised person;

(xvi) smoke or carry a lighted pipe, cigar or cigarette in or on any part of the trolley vehicle in or on which a notice is exhibited that smoking is prohibited;

(xvii) when in or on the trolley vehicle beg, sell or offer for sale any article;

(xviii) if his condition is such as to be offensive to passengers, or the condition of his dress or clothing is such that it may reasonably be expected to soil or injure the linings or cushions of the trolley vehicle or the clothing of other passengers, enter or remain in or on the trolley vehicle after an authorised person shall have requested him either not to enter or to leave the trolley vehicle and in such latter case shall have tendered to him the amount of any fare previously paid; provided that on trolley vehicles specially run for artisans, mechanics or daily labourers no passenger shall be prevented from entering or remaining in or on the trolley vehicle under the provisions of this Byelaw, on the grounds of the condition of his dress or clothing, if such condition is due solely due to the nature of his employment;

(xix) enter or travel in or on a trolley vehicle with loaded firearms, or any dangerous or offensive article or, except with the consent of an authorised person, bring into or on to the trolley vehicle any bulky or cumbersome article

or place any such article elsewhere in or on the trolley vehicle than as directed by an authorised person;

(xx) bring any animal into or on to the trolley vehicle without the consent of an authorised person or retain any animal in or on the trolley vehicle after being requested by an authorised person to remove it or place any animal elsewhere in or on the trolley vehicle than as directed by an authorised person.

4.

(a) No passenger shall use or attempt to use:-

(i) any ticket which has been altered or defaced, with intent to avoid payment of a fare; or

(ii) any ticket which has been issued to another person if such ticket bears thereon an indication that it is not transferable; or

(iii) any period or season ticket which has expired, with intent to avoid payment of a fare.

(b) Every passenger shall-

(i) unless he is the holder of a ticket in respect of that journey, immediately upon demand, declare the journey he intends to take or has taken and pay the conductor the fare for the whole of such journey and accept the ticket provided therefor;

(ii) if requested by the conductor, leave the trolley vehicle on completion of the journey the fare for which he has paid;

(iii) show his ticket, if any, when required to do so by any authorised person, or, if he fails so to show his ticket, pay the fare for the journey taken or to be taken by him;

(iv) if required to do so surrender his ticket to any authorised person at the end of the journey covered by that ticket;

(v) if required to do so surrender any period or season ticket held by him at the expiry of the period for which it was issued to him;

(vi) if required to do so surrender any ticket held by him either on completion of the journey or journeys covered by that ticket or in exchange for a new ticket covering the journey or journeys he is still entitled to take.

5. Byelaw 3 (i) (ix) (x) (xi) and (xii) of these Byelaws shall extend and apply to the premises of the Corporation as if the words "when a trolley vehicle is carrying passengers or waiting to pick up passengers" were omitted therefrom and as if references to a trolley vehicle and to an intending passenger included references to those premises and to a person waiting on those premises respectively.

6. A passenger not being an artisan, mechanic or daily labourer, with the true intent and meaning of the statutory provisions relating to the Corporation shall not use or attempt to use any ticket intended only for artisans, or mechanics, or daily labourers.

7. No person except with the leave of an authorised person shall board or attempt to board a trolley vehicle which is disabled or otherwise not in service for the carriage of passengers.

8. No person shall commit any nuisance in, on, or against any trolley vehicle or premises used in connection with the trolley vehicle system.

9.

(i) Immediately before or on the termination of any journey, the conductor shall so far as practicable search the vehicle for any property accidentally left therein, and shall as soon as may be and in any case within twenty-four hours, hand such property together with any property found in the vehicle and handed to him by any other person, in the state in which it came into his possession, to the General Manager or his representative, who shall give the conductor a receipt for the property.

Provided that any property found by or handed to a conductor, may, if he goes off duty before the completion of the journey, either be dealt with by him in accordance with the provisions of this byelaw or be handed by him in the state in which it came into his possession, to the conductor who comes on duty in his place who shall give him a receipt therefor and deal with it in accordance with the provisions of this byelaw.

Provided also that if before such property has been handed to the General Manager or his representative, it is claimed by a person who satisfies the conductor that he is the owner, it shall be returned to that person forthwith without fee or reward on giving his name and address to the conductor who shall as soon as may be report the facts and give the claimant's name and address and a description of the property to the General Manager or his representative.

(ii) Any property found in the vehicle which is not handed to the conductor in pursuance of sub-section (i) hereof and any property found in any shelter, or room used in connection with the trolley vehicle system shall be taken by the person finding the property in the state in which it came into his possession to the tramway office of the Corporation, and the General Manager or his representative shall give him a receipt for the property.

(iii) The General Manager or his representative having the custody of property in pursuance of this byelaw shall retain the property in safe keeping for a period of at least six months, unless the property is previously claimed by the owner thereof.

Provided that official documents, including licences, passports and aliens' identity books, shall be returned forthwith to the appropriate Government Departments, local authority or other body or person by whom they were issued.

Provided also that where the name and address of the owner of any property, other than documents referred to in the preceding proviso, are readily ascertainable the General Manager or his representative shall forthwith notify him that the property is in his possession any may be claimed in accordance with this byelaw.

(iv) If any property which has been handed to the General Manager or his representative be claimed and the claimant proves to the satisfaction of the General Manager or his representative that it belongs to him, it shall thereupon be delivered to him upon payment to the Corporation of a sum not exceeding 3d and in the case of property of a value exceeding 2/- an additional sum (up to an amount not exceeding £2) of 1/12th of the value of the property, any fraction of a penny being reckoned as a penny. For the purpose of this byelaw the value of the property shall be deemed to be such sum as may be agreed between the claimant and the General Manager or his representative, or failing agreement, such sum may be fixed by an appraiser. Any fee payable to such appraiser shall be paid by the claimant.

(v) If any property which has been handed to the General Manager or his representative appears to him to be of a perishable nature and it be not claimed and proved to his satisfaction to belong to the claimant within 48 hours from the time when it was found he may thereupon destroy or otherwise dispose of it as he sees fit.

Provided that any property which is or becomes objectionable may be destroyed or disposed of at any time at the discretion of the General Manager or his representative.

(vi) Where any property is forwarded to a claimant all costs of packing and carriage reasonably incurred shall be paid to the Corporation by the claimant.

(vii) Where any property is contained in a package, bag or other receptacle the General Manager or his representative may cause such receptacle to be opened and the contents examined if he deems it necessary to do so for the purpose either (a) of identifying and tracing the owner of the property, or (b) of ascertaining the nature of the contents.

(viii) Where any property is claimed by any person the General Manager or his representative may require the claimant to open any receptacle in which it may be contained and to submit the contents to examination for the purpose of establishing his claim to ownership.

10. A conductor shall to the best of his ability take steps whenever necessary to enforce these Byelaws and to prevent the breach thereof.

11. Any person contravening these Byelaws shall be liable to a penalty not exceeding forty shillings and may be removed from the trolley vehicle or premises as the case may be by an authorised person, or on the request of an authorised person, by any police constable.

12. There shall be placed and kept placed in a conspicuous position inside of each trolley vehicle and premises in use a printed copy of these Byelaws.

13. These Byelaws shall come into force on the first day of August 1951.

Given under the Common Seal of the County Borough of Bournemouth this third day of April One Thousand Nine Hundred and Fifty-one.

THE COMMON SEAL OF THE MAYOR   )
ALDERMEN AND BURGESSES OF THE   )
BOROUGH OF BOURNEMOUTH was   )
hereunto affixed in the presence of   )

"A. LINDSAY CLEGG", Town Clerk.

I hereby certify that a true copy of the foregoing Bye-laws has, in accordance with the provisions of Section 46 of the Tramways Act, 1870, been laid before the Minister of Transport not less than two calendar months before such Bye-laws come into operation, and that such Bye-laws have not been disallowed by the Minister of Transport within the said two calendar months. Signed this twenty-third day of July, 1951.

"G.F. STEDMAN"
An Under Secretary of the Ministry of Transport.

4) Transport Department Internal Instructions

4.1) Speed Limits

BOURNEMOUTH CORPORATION TRANSPORT SERVICES

Speed restrictions - The speed at which the trolley vehicles may be driven or propelled along the routes shall not exceed the rate of 30 m.p.h. or such lower rate of speed as hereinafter specified

1) Twenty five miles per hour:-
a) In Beresford Road
b) In Tuckton Road between Belle Vue Road and Cranleigh Road
c) In Southbourne Grove
d) In Southbourne Road between Southbourne Grove and Belle Vue Road
e) In Belle Vue Road between Southbourne Road and Cross Roads
f) When ascending Commercial Road and Poole Hill
g) In Castle Lane between Ibbertson Road and Throop Road

2) Twenty miles per hour:-
a) In Exeter Road between its junction with Pier Approach and Terrace Road
b) In Castle Lane between Holmfield Avenue and Christchurch Road
c) In Belle Vue Road, Southbourne, between Cross Roads and Foxholes Road
d) In Foxholes Road, Southbourne
e) In Seamoor Road
f) In Old Christchurch Road
g) In St. Swithun's Road
h) In Southcote Road
i) In Wallisdown Road between its junction with Firs Glen Road and Talbot Road
j) In Wimborne Road when rounding the curve at its junction with Talbot Avenue
k) In Charminster Road from its junction with Alma Road to its junction with Richmond Wood Road
l) In Charminster Road when rounding the corner at its junction with Maxwell and Hankinson Roads
m) In Bath Road when descending the hill between Parsonage Road and the east side of Bournemouth Pier Approach

3) Fifteen miles per hour:-
a) In Gervis Place
b) When rounding the bend in Lansdowne Road at its junction with St. Paul's Road
c) In The Triangle
d) When descending Poole Hill
e) In Avenue Road
f) In Ensbury Park Road when rounding the curve at its junction with Highfield Road
g) In Fir Vale Road
h) In St. Peter's Road
i) In Mallard Road
j) When rounding the bend between Barrack Road and High Street, Christchurch
k) In Ashley Road when passing over the railway bridge and its approach at Boscombe Station

l) In Exeter Road between its junction with Terrace Road and The Square

m) In The Square

4) Eight miles per hour:-
   a) When descending Richmond Hill
   b) When turning from The Triangle into Avenue Road
   c) When passing over Tuckton Bridge
   d) When rounding Pier Approach
   e) In High Street, Christchurch, when passing the traffic island at its junction with Castle Street (outward journey only)
   f) When turning at either junction of Poole Road and Seamoor Road
   g) When passing through all trolley wire junctions and crossings
   h) When rounding all turning circles and right-angled turns
   i) At all reversing triangles

The above list represents the proposed new speed limits (abolition of 5 mph speed limits with restriction increased to 8 mph, and abolition of 10 mph speed limit with restrictions distributed to 8 and 15 mph) sent to Brigadier C.A. Langley, MoT, on 22 November 1956.

BYELAWS

The trolley vehicles on the routes shall be brought to a standstill as soon as possible whenever it is necessary to avoid impending danger, and on all occasions immediately before reaching the following points:-

a) Richmond Hill (descending vehicles only) at (i) Richmond Gardens and (ii) The Church of the Sacred Heart

b) Outside No. 23 Poole Hill (descending vehicles only)

4.2) Instructions for Frosty Weather

BOURNEMOUTH CORPORATION TRANSPORT SERVICES
ARRANGEMENTS FOR DEALING WITH FROST ON TROLLEY WIRES

It is most important that the first bus on all routes should run to time and in the event of frost, Night Superintendent Lacey, or his Deputy, must contact Castle Lane and Boscombe Depots, to ascertain what conditions prevail and, if necessary, will give instructions for the undermentioned staff to be called in for defrosting.

Should this be done, he must also contact the Engineer at the Christchurch Sub-Station, and ask him to make power available on the Christchurch Section.

Instructions must also be given for "Frost Heads" to be fitted on the early service vehicles, and in severe cases a special bus must be run before the services commence to clear the wires so that no delay is caused. The numbers of the vehicles so fitted, must be noted and a change over to normal heads made as soon as possible.

CENTRAL SECTION
Deputy Chief Inspector W. Biddlecombe
35 Athelstan Road
Southbourne
Telephone: Southbourne 1332

who will be in charge of this section.

Inspector C. Forscey
3 Swanmore Road
Boscombe East
Telephone: Southbourne 3344

The second man on all vehicles to be supplied from the Depot Staffs.

All vehicles to carry a spare head, spanners and a torch.

Trap doors over resistances must be taken up to allow resistances to cool as much as possible.

400 i.e. AEL400-AEL411 (72-83) and 60 i.e. ALJ60-ALJ65 (84-89) class buses have no trap doors and should not be used if others are available.

B.U.T. vehicles NOT TO BE USED UNDER ANY CIRCUMSTANCES

Separate sheets will be issued showing the routes to be taken, but these may be varied according to conditions.

14.9.53
E/L

BOURNEMOUTH CORPORATION TRANSPORT SERVICES

BOSCOMBE DEPOT
ROUTE NO. 1

Leave Boscombe Depot via No. 21 route. Proceed to Christchurch, return to Boscombe Depot via No. 20 route. Repeat until wires are cleared.

ROUTE NO. 2

Leave Boscombe Depot via No. 20 route. Proceed to Stour Road, return to Boscombe Depot via No. 21 route. Repeat until wires are cleared.

ROUTE NO. 3

Leave Boscombe Depot via No. 22 route for Tuckton Bridge. Proceed to Fisherman's Walk, via Cranleigh Road. Return via Cranleigh Road to Tuckton Bridge, then to Boscombe Depot via No. 22 route. Repeat until wires are cleared.

CENTRAL DEPOT
ROUTE NO. 1

Leave Central Depot and proceed to Portman Road, then No. 25 route to the Square via Old Christchurch Road then to Westbourne and return to Ashley Road, via 25 route. Return to Square by 25 Route unless different instructions are received.

ROUTE NO. 2

Leave Central Depot for Castle Lane via Portman Road and Pokesdown; turn at Mallard Road and return to Iford and repeat journey to Mallard Road from Iford until wires are clear, or other instructions are received from the Inspector at Iford.

CASTLE LANE DEPOT
ROUTE NO. 1

Leave Castle Lane Depot for Banks via Moordown, go up Talbot Road to Wallisdown and return to Banks via Ensbury Park Road. Turn at Banks and run in reverse direction, i.e. via Ensbury Park Road and Talbot Road to Banks, then to Square via 26 Route and return to Castle Lane Depot via 26 Route unless otherwise instructed.

ROUTE NO. 2

Castle Lane Depot to Iford, turn at Iford circle and return along Castle Lane to Cemetery Junction via Charminster; turn at Cemetery Junction and go to Luckham Road and back to Cemetery Junction; turn at Cemetery Junction and go to Malvern Road and from there go to Square via Lansdowne (No. 27 Route) and return to Castle Lane Depot via Charminster unless otherwise instructed by Inspector on duty.

4.3) Trolleybus Driving Instructions

BOURNEMOUTH CORPORATION TRANSPORT SERVICES

In issuing these instructions, I do so realising that they are far from complete but as I wish them to be as short and concise as possible, much must be left to the discretion of the driver of the vehicle, at the same time they should serve as a useful guide to all the Traffic Staff.

IN THE DEPOT

Before starting from Depot, the following routine must be observed.

1. See that the trolleys are on the proper wire.
2. Test main lighting by turning on the main switch (Important) Main lights must be switched off when in use, if trolleys are taken off or replaced on the overhead.
3. See that trolley dewirement buzzer buzzer is in the "on" position.
4. Set Circuit Breakers in "on" position, and bring reverser handle to "forward" position.
5. Test windscreen wiper and electric horn, and see that driving mirrors are in position.
6. The front exit door must be closed and locked before attempting to move.
7. On returning to Depot, place circuit breakers, all switches and reverser in "off" position. Open front door.
8. When leaving the vehicle, the handbrake must be firmly applied.
9. On commencing and completion of a duty, drivers and conductors must examine their vehicle and report on the form provided, all defects and damage, no matter how small, in order that it may receive immediate attention.

OPERATING TROLLEY BUSES IN SERVICE

All trolley buses are equipped with four forward brakes and one run-back electric brake. These consist of: Hand, foot, regenerative, electric and run-back brakes.

(IMPORTANT) The electric brake must be used in the following manner:

Stop the bus at top of hill, place reverser handle in "brake", position as marked, and allow the bus to drift away. When changing to forward position the bus must be brought to a definite stop, otherwise serious damage will be caused to the electrical equipment.

RUN-BACK BRAKE

In the event of a complete brake and power failure, whilst ascending any hill, place one circuit breaker in the "off" position. This will check your speed to 2 mph.

The handbrake is for parking and emergency stopping, and should be firmly applied when leaving vehicle, and a scotch placed under a wheel. This especially applies when on inclines or declines.

The foot brake is vacuum assisted, n.b. this refers to Sunbeam MS2s vehicles, the BUTs and Sunbeam MF2Bs having compressed air brakes, and the gauge on the dash will show the amount in inches created.

The vacuum builds up when the bus is in motion, the usual

amount being 23 ins.

When the foot pedal is depressed a certain amount of vacuum is used at each application: about 1 1/2 ins. It is, therefore, wrong to ride with the foot on the brake pedal. When the vacuum gauge shows less than 10 inches the driver should drive with great care, using the hand brake to assist in bringing the vehicle to a stop, and arrange for the vehicle to be sent into the Depot for attention.

POWER CONTROL OPERATION

There are 12 notches on the control panel, and when using the power pedal, the first five notches must be definitely felt for, but you should not dwell on numbers 1 to 5, as these are Resistance Notches and will quickly cause overheating of resistances. The following notches automatically come in as the pedal is depressed and full power is obtained.

For regenerative braking, n.b. again this refers to Sunbeam MS2 vehicles only, release the pressure on the control pedal slowly, until speed is reduced as required. For a smooth stop regenerate to 10 mph, when regeneration ceased, then fully release the power pedal, the bus can then be brought to a stop by means of the foot brake.

FROGS, CROSSINGS AND SECTION INSULATORS

The speed of trolley buses under ALL Frogs and Crossings must not exceed 5 m.p.h.

Drivers must pass under all Breakers and Insulated Crossings with the Power Pedal in the "off" position. Failure to observe this instruction will cause flashing and damage to the overhead fittings.

DEWIREMENTS

If the trolley head leaves the wire, the driver must immediately bring the vehicle to a standstill, and must not apply power until the trolley head has been replaced and the proper signal to proceed received from the Conductor.

If the trolley head appears to have been damaged, the driver should use his own discretion as to whether he considers it advisable to proceed on his journey or wait until repairs have been carried out. If he does proceed, however, he should take steps to have the head inspected at the earliest possible opportunity.

Dewirements must be reported to the first Official on duty, also the exact time, place and pole number, and whether on the inward or outward journey.

In order to avoid dewirements at curves, the trolley bus must be driven so as to follow a curve greater that the curve of the overhead wires. Where this is impossible for traffic reasons, the speed must be further reduced.

When the driver of a trolley bus observes the Overhead Department's Lorry standing under the wires, he must not pass same until notified by the man working on the top of the lorry that everything is in order for him to proceed. (PASS WITH CARE)

* A special form must be made out for all dewirements*

FLOODED ROADWAY

Trolleybuses must not be driven upon flooded roads at a speed exceeding 8 mph and must be kept as far as possible to the crown of the road.

TYRE PUNCTURES

In the event of a tyre being punctured the trolleybus must be parked immediately at the side of the road, in such a position as to cause as little inconvenience as possible to other road users. The conductor must then arrange for the transfer of passengers to other vehicles, and the driver must notify the Square Inspector (Phone Bournemouth 404).

ACCIDENT PROCEDURE

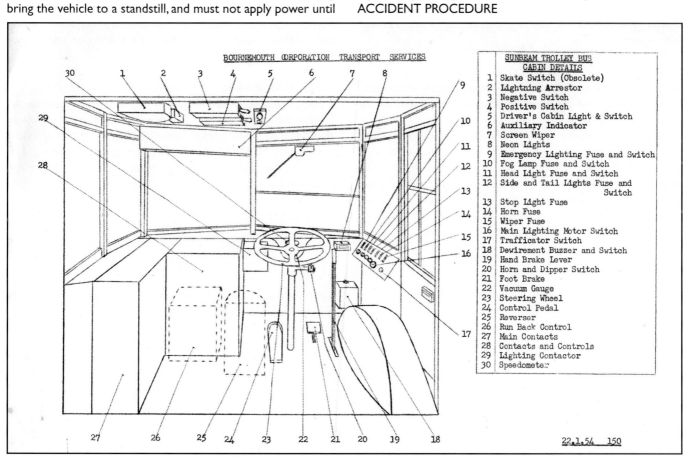

BOURNEMOUTH CORPORATION TRANSPORT SERVICES

SUNBEAM TROLLEY BUS
CABIN DETAILS

1 Skate Switch (Obsolete)
2 Lightning Arrestor
3 Negative Switch
4 Positive Switch
5 Driver's Cabin Light & Switch
6 Auxiliary Indicator
7 Screen Wiper
8 Neon Lights
9 Emergency Lighting Fuse and Switch
10 Fog Lamp Fuse and Switch
11 Head Light Fuse and Switch
12 Side and Tail Lights Fuse and Switch
13 Stop Light Fuse
14 Horn Fuse
15 Wiper Fuse
16 Main Lighting Motor Switch
17 Trafficator Switch
18 Dewirement Buzzer and Switch
19 Hand Brake Lever
20 Horn and Dipper Switch
21 Foot Brake
22 Vacuum Gauge
23 Steering Wheel
24 Control Pedal
25 Reverser
26 Run Back Control
27 Main Contacts
28 Contacts and Controls
29 Lighting Contactor
30 Speedometer

22.1.54   150

603

In the event of being involved in an accident causing injury to passengers or other personnel, obtain medical attention for the injured first, then the Inspector in the Square must be notified.

If involved in any accident, however slight or trivial it may appear to you, the following procedure is necessary at the time of the accident.

1. Under no circumstances admit liability or make a statement unless in the presence of the General Manager, Traffic Superintendent or an Inspector.
2. Obtain full particulars of all persons and property involved.
3. Names and addresses of witnesses.
4. Make a rough sketch of the scene of the accident.

REPORTING DEFECTS

Defects connected with the vehicle, body or fittings, are to be reported at the completion of duty on the driver's report sheet provided. Under no circumstances are drivers or conductors to give any information to the public regarding defects which may arise in their vehicles and they should be careful not to make any statement likely to be detrimental to themselves or the Department.

SERVICE RUNNING

When on service DO NOT DRIVE CLOSE BEHIND ANOTHER BUS and avoid grouping of vehicles which should be at least 200 yards apart.

UNATTENDED VEHICLES

Drivers and conductors are not to leave their vehicles unattended at terminal points or any particular stop if it is essential for one to leave the other must be left in charge.

REVERSING

The driver must not reverse the vehicle until the "All Clear" signal is given. Reversing handle must not be moved until bus is stationary.

HIGHWAY CODE AND ROAD TRAFFIC ACTS

The Highway Code is a code of behaviour, based on courtesy, common sense and the Road Traffic Acts, laid down for the guidance of all users of the road.

Its strict observance at all times would greatly reduce the number of accidents. It is your duty to make yourself familiar with the Highway Code and such parts of the Road Traffic Acts as concern you and strictly conform to the regulations and advice contained in them. You, as a PSV (sic) driver, are conspicuous and should therefore, at all times, act in such a manner as to set an example to other road users.

4.4 BUT 9641T Additional Driving Instructions

BOURNEMOUTH CORPORATION TRANSPORT SERVICES

Instructions to drivers of BUT Trolleybuses which will be in service as and from Sunday, 1st October 1950

WHEN TAKING VEHICLE FROM DEPOT

1. Set circuit breaker in the 'ON' position.
2. Close compressor control switch and wait for low pressure alarm to indicate that there is sufficient air pressure to proceed.

RHEOSTATIC BRAKING

The brake is actuated by the right pedal. A slight depression of the pedal brings in the first rheostatic brake notch, further depression of the pedal the second notch, and still further depression brings in the air brake with an intensity proportional to the amount depressed. (Please use with care to avoid passengers being thrown off balance).

It will be realised that however the brakes are applied to the vehicle, whether for normal service stop or under emergency conditions, the rheostatic brake is always brought into operation first. It is maintained in operation until the vehicle's speed falls to the low speed of 2 to 3 mph after which the vehicle is brought to rest by the air brake.

If at any time it is necessary to make an emergency brake application, the depression of the brake pedal, whilst the power pedal is also depressed, immediately cuts off the power. Under no circumstances is it possible to feed power from the line and at the same time apply the footbrake to the vehicle.

AIR PRESSURE ALARM

If the air pressure falls below a certain level, the low pressure alarm in the driver's cabin operates, a red signal arm is raised and a buzzer sounds. If this happens the driver should not proceed.

COASTING BRAKE

The coasting brake must be used in the following manner:-

Stop the bus at the top of the hill, place control handle in 'BRAKE' position as marked, and allow bus to drift away. When changing to 'FORWARD' position, the bus must be brought to a definite stop, otherwise serious damage will be caused to the electrical equipment.

WHEN LEAVING VEHICLE

When leaving the vehicle in Depot or Bus Park, make sure the circuit breakers are in the 'OFF' position and that the compressor control is switched off.

ABOVE ALL, PLEASE REMEMBER YOU ARE DRIVING AN EIGHT FOOT WIDE VEHICLE.

W.D.REAKES
GENERAL MANAGER

WJG/BJB
1.1.57

APPENDIX P
PERSONALITIES

Ignatius Mary Bulfin, BA, MIMunE, MIEE, AMICE, MIME

Born on 6 February 1870 in Dublin, Ignatius Bulfin was the son of Col. Patrick Bulfin and brother of Lt. Gen Sir E.S. Bulfin (who subsequently also retired to Bournemouth).

After graduating in higher mathematics and science at the Royal University of Ireland, he received his practical training with W. H. Allen and Co., Bedford, and at the same time attended classes at Finsbury Technical College. He joined the staff of Bournemouth Corporation in 1895 where he entered the office of the Borough Surveyor as a Surveyor's Assistant. In 1901 he was appointed Resident Engineer overseeing the construction of the Tramway Department's Southcote Road Generating Station. In February 1903 he became the Borough Electrical Engineer with responsibility for the electrical aspects of the new and growing tramways system, and in 1909 he was promoted to the position of Chief Assistant and Electrical Engineer of the tramways undertaking with responsibility for the Generating Station and permanent way.

Mr Bulfin joined the Institution of Electrical Engineers as an Associate in 1898 and was elected an Associate Member in 1899 and a Member in 1907. He was also an Associate Member of The Institution of Civil Engineers and a Member of The Institution of Mechanical Engineers. On 28 July 1911 he was appointed General Manager as successor to Charles Hill, however, he always regarded himself as more of an engineer than a manager and in 1926 he persuaded the Tramways Committee to change his title to "Engineer and General Manager" with the word "engineer" coming before "general manager". This took effect from 22 October 1926 and this title subsequently appeared on the trams, trolleybuses and motorbuses in his charge until his retirement.

He developed a manganese steel lip inserted on to the guard rail at all sharp curves to successfully avoid derailments and reduce wear. Noted for his strong character and disciplinarian attitudes, he insisted on keeping his tramcar fleet in immaculate condition and was known to have sent dirty trams back into the depot to be cleaned on several occasions. After some twenty years of effective management, during the years 1930-35 he was responsible for the evaluation of railless traction and the subsequent change-over from trams to trolleybuses.

A slightly built man, he was extremely superstitious and would never introduce new routes on a Friday or on the 13th of a month. It is said that when the Transport Committee wished to start the experimental trolleybus service on Saturday 13 May 1933, he was very much against the idea. Despite being under great pressure, he only agreed provided that the service should not start before midday!

On his retirement in September 1935 Mr Bulfin received glowing tributes for 40 years of service to the Borough and was granted an allowance of one month's salary in lieu of holidays for the current year. He continued to live in Southbourne until his death in a nursing home on 19 February 1954.

Duncan Paterson Morrison, BSc, MInstT

Born in 1886, Duncan Morrison was one of the two sons of William Morrison, Manager of the Sunderland Tramways Co. from 1882 until its takeover by the Corporation in 1900 (whereupon he became the Traffic Manager), then from 1901 Traffic Manager and from 1904 General Manager of the BET's Gateshead & District Tramways Co.

Mr D.P. Morrison photographed in 1934 whilst still General Manager and Engineer at Kingston upon Hull.
Malcolm Wells collection

Duncan Morrison graduated from Durham University with a BSc in mechanical and civil engineering, joining Dick, Kerr and Co. as an apprentice in 1909 and then until 1912 as an assistant engineer. He moved on to his father's Gateshead company as Assistant Engineer and later as Chief Engineer and Assistant Manager.

In 1926 he was appointed General Manager and Engineer of Dundee Corporation Tramways, where he introduced municipal motorbus services and centralised the Corporation's transport services, prior to taking up the same position at Kingston upon Hull in 1931. As his predecessor, Mr Morrison experienced problems with the Hull Transport Committee and decided to leave for Bournemouth in 1935 where he was appointed Engineer and General Manager on 7 May 1935 as successor to Mr Bulfin. At the time of his appointment to Bournemouth he was 50 years old and had a reputation at Hull, where tramway replacement was being actively discussed, of being motorbus-orientated. He took up his new duties on 1 August 1935.

Alderman Langton, Chairman of the Transport Committee, considered Mr Morrison a most efficient manager. In addition to his managerial skills, he drove the extension of the trolleybus system forward and was much involved in planning the post-war layouts of the Lansdowne and Square. At some stage in his career, he was also Engineer and General Manager to the British Electrical Federation of Tramway and Bus Operators. After several years of recurring illness and absences, Mr Morrison died in post on 1 November 1948, aged 61 years, leaving a widow and three daughters. He lived in Roslin Road South, Winton.

Wifried Douglas Reakes, MInstT

Wilfried Reakes was born in Axbridge, Somerset, on 1 December 1896 to Alfred Ernest Reakes and Sarah Newman.

He received his early training with the Bristol Tramways & Carriage Co. Ltd., under Sidney Smith, leaving that company in 1926 to join United Automobile Services at Norwich as the District Manager's Assistant. In 1928 he was appointed Traffic Manager to East Midlands Motor Services, returning to Norwich as District Manager the

Despite spending his formative years with motor bus operators, Mr W. D. Reakes was a committed protagonist of the trolleybus and Bournemouth's "Silent Service".
Transport World

following year (at that time United and East Midlands shared a common Managing Director). When United centralised their activities in the north, he took over the Yorkshire area as District Manager and then the Durham District holding the position of Area Traffic Superintendent.

Mr Reakes joined Bournemouth Corporation Transport Department in September 1935 as Traffic Superintendent, being promoted to Deputy General Manager and Traffic Superintendent on 21 April 1944. Having effectively run the undertaking through Mr Morrison's long periods of illness, he was appointed General Manager, without the position being advertised, in late 1948. He retired on 28 February 1962

He was married to Muriel Bessie Tolley and had a son. He passed away on 30 June 1980 in Glenroy Gardens, Southbourne.

Ronald Cox, MInstT, MIRTE

Ronald Cox was born at St. Helens on 3 February 1916, joining the local Corporation Transport undertaking in 1935 as a trainee. Both his father and grandfather had been railwaymen.

Following six years' war service, latterly with the Royal Air Force Transport Command as a Flight Lieutenant, in 1946 he returned to St. Helens as Senior Traffic Officer. Two years later he moved to Salford as Traffic Superintendent. In 1953 he joined Rochdale Corporation Transport as Deputy General Manager and Engineer, being promoted in 1954 at the age of 38 to be the undertaking's General Manager and Engineer. Here he instigated a modernisation policy in the administration, maintenance and operating fleet.

He joined Bournemouth Corporation Transport on 1 March 1962 and, less than a year later, in January 1963 was instructed to prepare a report on future trolleybus operations. This review was unbiased and conducted professionally; nonetheless it was Ronnie Cox (as he was widely known) who was tasked with implementing Bournemouth Council's 22 March 1963 decision to progressively abandon the trolleybus system. During his short tenure at Bournemouth, where his predecessor had been very

careful with the undertaking's finances, Mr Cox was considered by some members of staff as having invested in projects which generated no additional revenue such as the introduction of stainless steel bus stop poles and increased frequencies on some services with falling passenger numbers. On 1 July 1964, he was designated General Manager of Edinburgh Corporation Transport.

In January 1973 the Greater Glasgow Passenger Transport Authority appointed Mr Cox as Director General of its Passenger Transport Executive which at that time was responsible for public transport operations in an area of 700 square miles containing nearly two million people. At this time he was also a Council Member of the Association of Public Passenger Transport Operators.

Innovation was a hallmark of his managerial career and he did not shy away from pressing the case for public transport in the press. He retired at 60 in 1976 from being Director General of Greater Glasgow PTE and, being a keen dinghy sailor, went to live in Salcombe, Devon, but suffered a heart attack in the late 1980s.

The ambitious Ronald Cox rather broke the pattern of long service, spending less than two and a half years with Bournemouth.
Bournemouth Transport

Ian Cunningham, MBE, BSc, CEng, FCIT, MIMechE

Born and bred in Scotland, Ian Cunningham studied engineering at the University of Edinburgh and following National Service with REME joined Edinburgh Corporation Transport Department in 1948 as a student apprentice. He associated his own professional enthusiasm for electric traction to his time in Edinburgh and engineering responsibility for the Royal Burgh's tram fleet. He subsequently rose to the position of Assistant Rolling Stock Engineer.

In March 1963 he was appointed Deputy General Manager and Engineer at Bournemouth reporting to Ronald Cox who had only moved to Bournemouth from Rochdale the year before. The Bournemouth Transport Committee had requested a report on future trolleybus policy, including fleet replacement, and thus one of Ian's first tasks was to identify potential suppliers of affordable trolleybus chassis. By 1963 British manufacturers saw these as bespoke products and no suitable source was identified. This situation, combined with an increasing differential between trolleybus and diesel bus operating costs, and plans for a town centre by-pass all led to Bournemouth Council deciding in March 1963 that no more trolleybuses would be purchased and that a progressive run-down of the system would commence as vehicles aged and the fleet contracted in size, eventually leading to route closures. Just over a year later Ronnie Cox

Ian Cunningham served BCT and its successor organisation Bournemouth Transport Ltd., from March 1963 until October 1989, a total of twenty six years and seven months of which twenty two years and three months were as General Manager (followed by three years in the equivalent position as the Managing Director of the privatised limited Company). Bournemouth Transport

moved to Edinburgh and Ian Cunningham was appointed General Manager.

Mr Cunningham oversaw the staged withdrawal of trolleybuses from the St. Paul's Road services, Holdenhurst Road, Richmond Hill and finally Christchurch Road, culminating in a series of special events for the Last Trolleybus Week (14-19 April 1969) including an illuminated trolleybus, an exhibition at the Mallard Road Head Office and a closure procession. He also ensured that both the events and the subsequent sale of copper trolley wire were profitable for the undertaking!

Despite the system's closure, he always retained his view that from engineering and environmental perspectives electric traction provided the best solution for urban street passenger transport but that it was unattainable in Britain due to government policy and public attitudes. He proved a willing source of information when the first edition of "Bournemouth Trolleybuses" was prepared and invited the author into his home on a number of occasions.

Faced with a continuing fall in passenger numbers followed by arms-length privatisation Ian Cunningham worked hard and successfully to re-integrate bus services in the local community by promoting the "Yellows" and their services in the social scene and for charity events. Professionally he was a Member of the Institute of Mechanical Engineers, the Public Road Transport Association and the Association of Public Passenger Transport. In 1978 he was elected President of the Confederation of British Road Passenger Transport.

Upon his retirement in 1990 he was awarded an MBE for his services to the community. Thereafter he continued to follow his life-long interest in music, being an accomplished cellist, church organist, singer and conductor, and gave presentations on the history of public transport in Bournemouth.

Ian Cunningham, General Manager of Bournemouth Corporation Transport and Managing Director of its successor organisation Bournemouth Transport Ltd. from 1964 until his retirement in 1990, passed away on 16 March 2014. He was 89 years old and had been ill for some time. A widower he left two children from his first marriage, two stepchildren and four grandchildren. He is remembered by older trolleybus enthusiasts for the unique way in which he permitted preserved vehicles from many systems to operate in Bournemouth and his commitment to giving the Bournemouth trolleybuses a fitting send off.

William George Biddlecombe

William (Bill) Biddlecombe joined Bournemouth Corporation Tramways as a Conductor in the early 1920s and was promoted to Motorman prior to the demise of the tramways. He was also a motorbus Driver. As a great enthusiast of the trolleybus and, indeed, anything modern, he soon became an accomplished trolleybus and motorbus driver, being selected as one of the drivers entrusted with 152 when it was especially decorated and illuminated for King George VI's Coronation festivities in 1937.

During the Second World War Bill Biddlecombe was responsible for towing the majority of those Bournemouth trolleybuses loaned to other operators.

Early in 1948 his title was changed from Instructor Inspector to Inspector Examiner and it is understood that he was thus authorised to carry out trolleybus driving tests and in July 1948 he was promoted Deputy Chief Inspector "in addition to his other duties". In September 1952 the South Eastern Licensing Authority appointed him as driving test examiner for motorbuses. When not examining, instructing or standing-in for the Chief Inspector, Bill Biddlecome frequently worked as Inspector during Easter, Whitsun and the summer season at Bournemouth Pier where his excellent inter-personal skills were of value.

Bill Biddlecombe delivered the majority of Bournemouth's vehicles from the manufacturers between 1939 and 1968. He also drove on any special jobs, including the official handing-over ceremonies from vehicle manufacturers and the MoT inspection of the initial Sunbeam MS2 open-top conversion. Several of his relations also worked for BCT at various times and his youngest son was an apprentice engineer in the BCT workshops prior to starting his own business.

He retired in 1968, but reappeared to drive preserved BUT9641T trolleybus 246 on the final day of trolleybus operation, 20 April 1969.

On Good Friday, 7 April 1950, Bill Biddlecombe (foreground) was on duty as the first trolleybuses reached Bournemouth Pier.

Malcolm Pearce (G.O.P. Pearce)

607

APPENDIX Q
STATISTICS

1) Capital Expenditure (major items)

Year	Expenditure Item	Amount £	s	d	Incomes (write-offs) Item	Amount £	s	d	Comments
1934	Trolleybuses and equipment	10,008	8	5		---			
1935	Trolleybuses	63,691	11	3		---			
	Overhead equipment	28,369	17	11					
	Iford turning circle	2,250							
1936	Trolleybuses	)177,448	16	1		---			
	Overhead equipment	)							
1937	Trolleybuses	17,097	14	1		---			
	Overhead equipment	7,165	5	0					
	Cables	4,236	12	5					
	Christchurch turntable	829	18	6					
	Parliamentary expenses	1,330	0	8					
1938	Trolleybuses	37	12	3		---			
	Overhead equipment	7,912	11	3					
	Cables	1	10	0					
	Christchurch turntable	45	13	8					
1939	Overhead equipment	6,314	3	6		---			
	Street improvements	5,838							
	Vehicles	154	19	10					
	Parliamentary expenses	1,103	17	6					
1940	Overhead equipment	3,547	8	0		---			
1941	Overhead equipment	136	17	0		---			
1942	Generating station	29,466	5	5	Trolleybus	1,450			single decker
1943	Electric coal conveyor	187	5	0		---			
	Superheaters (3)	516							
	Overhead equipment								
	Barrack Road extension	2,923	7	11					from reserve fund
1944	Turbo generator	3,123	11	6		---			
	Overhead equipment								
	Barrack Road extension	63	14	3					
1945	Turbo generator	1,755	14	2		---			
	Extension of								
	overhead equipment	710	9	2					
1946	Turbo generator	288	9	3		---			
	Extension of								
	overhead equipment	7	11	0					
1947	Overhead equipment	293	9	9		---			
1948	Overhead equipment	1,941	11	1		---			
1949	Overhead equipment	5,819	0	2		---			
1950	Overhead equipment:					---			
	Pier Approach	4,753	16	0					

Year	Expenditure Item	Amount £	s	d	Incomes (write-offs) Item	Amount £	s	d	Comments
1951	Trolleybuses	147,599	19	3		---			
	Trolleybus equipment:								
	Fisherman's Walk to Pier								
	Approach extension	35	2	1					
	Castle Lane extension	7,731	13	10					
1952	Trolleybuses	860				---			
	Trolleybus equipment:								
	Fisherman's Walk to Tuckton								
	Bridge extension	583	5	9					
	Castle Lane extension	13,283	17	9					
1953	Trolleybus	257	7	11	Trolleybuses scrapped	39,680	10	0	
	Equipment Castle Lane								
	extension	737	16	1					
1954	Trolleybus equipment	3,448	17	6	Trolleybuses scrapped	13,299			
	Castle Lane extension	31,417	2	2					
1955	Electrical and cabling work at new	1,200				---			
	substations								
1956	Electrical and cabling work at new	39,136			Power station plant	67,431			
	substations				scrapped				
1957	Electrical and cabling work at new	10,804				---			
	substations								
1958		---			Trolleybuses scrapped	22,165			
1959	Trolleybuses	137,963			Trolleybuses scrapped	44,330			
	Trolleybus equipment	400							
1960	Trolleybuses	73,772			Trolleybuses scrapped	44,330			
1961	Trolleybuses	3,784				---			
1962	Trolleybuses	37,376				---			
1963	Trolleybuses	32,230			Trolleybuses scrapped	35,664			
1964	Trolleybuses	1,438			Trolleybuses scrapped	13,110			
1965		---				8,616			
1966		---				8,249			
1967		---				148,710			
1968		---				---			
1969		---				---			
1970	Abandonment: removal of system	7,045			Trolleybuses scrapped	284,858			
1971	Abandonment: removal of system	8,333			Abandonment	15,378			
					Equipment	221,058			
1972	Abandonment: removal of system	6,305			Abandonment	6,305			

2) Statement of Borrowing Powers, Advances and Itemised Expenditure

PURPOSE	Date of Act or Sanction	Period for repayment (years)	Amount (£)	Advances made in the following years
Vehicles	Bournemouth Corporation Act 1930	10	300,000	1934, 1935, 1936, 1950, 1951, 1954, 1955
Equipment	Bournemouth Corporation Act 1930	20	157,000	1935, 1936, 1938, 1940
Iford, Land for Turning Circle	6 July 1936	20	2,250	1935
Road works	Bournemouth Corporation Act 1930	20	47,000	1936, 1937, 1938, 1939
Parliamentary expenses	Bournemouth Corporation Act 1930	5	1,061	1938
Parliamentary expenses	Local Government Act 1931	5	227	1938
Parliamentary expenses	Bournemouth Corporation Act 1930	5	1,120	1939
Vehicles	Bournemouth Corporation Confirm. Act 1938	10	54,000	1951
Vehicles	21 October 1949	10	30,621	1951
Equipment (Castle Lane)	15 May 1950	25	31,296	1951, 1952
Equipment	15 July 1950	25	6,635	1951
Vehicles	20 March 1951	10	5,126	1951, 1952
Holdenhurst Substation	Bournemouth Corporation Act 1930	15	2,000	1953
Turning Circle	Bournemouth Corporation Act 1930	25	500	1954
Electric Cabling	23 April 1954	20	50,702	1955, 1956, 1957
Vehicles	11 February 1957	14	141,680	1959, 1960
Vehicles	14 January 1958	14	71,110	1960, 1961
Vehicles	24 February 1960	14	75,470	1962, 1963, 1964

3) Operating Statistics

Year	Number of passengers per mile	Fare per passenger (d)	Traffic revenue per mile	Working expenses per mile	Working expenses per passenger	Net revenue charges per mile	Net revenue charges per passenger
1934	8.70	1.72	14.99	11.83	} See Notes below		
1935	8.58	1.72	15.17	11.76	} See Notes below		
1936	7.86	1.60	12.60	10.90	} See Notes below		
1937	10.24	1.51	15.45	10.78	1.05		
1938	9.70	1.59	15.27	10.74	1.11		
1939	9.39	1.58	14.78	10.91	1.16		
1940	10.20	1.58	16.32	11.78	1.16		
1941	11.09	1.55	17.20	13.24	1.19		
1942	13.47	1.58	21.22	14.19	1.06		
1943	14.48	1.55	22.43	15.24	1.05		
1944	13.95	1.71	23.86	16.86	1.21	2.99	0.21
1945	15.33	1.75	26.91	18.77	1.22	2.62	0.17
1946	15.80	1.80	28.46	20.33	1.28	1.76	0.11
1947	14.32	1.82	26.04	20.41	1.42	0.64	0.04
1948	13.61	1.84	25.05	21.45	1.57	0.60	0.04
1949	13.42	1.79	24.16	22.29	1.66	0.58	0.04
1950	13.82	1.72	23.83	23.23	1.68	0.59	0.04
1951	13.63	1.75	23.84	23.82	1.75	0.87	0.06
1952	13.40	2.31	31.01	27.30	2.04	2.52	0.19
1953	12.96	2.45	31.81	29.84	2.30	2.98	0.23
1954	12.46	2.80	34.89	30.56	2.45	3.47	0.28
1955	12.23	2.84	34.78	32.40	2.65	3.51	0.29
1956	11.85	2.99	35.50	33.55	2.83	3.68	0.31
1957	11.92	3.53	42.03	34.57	2.90	4.11	0.35
1958	12.11	3.51	42.49	37.14	3.07	4.22	0.35
1959	11.83	3.53	41.81	37.23	3.15	4.39	0.37
1960	11.74	3.54	41.58	36.85	3.14	5.96	0.51
1961	11.83	3.54	41.92	36.87	3.12	6.42	0.54
1962	11.70	3.81	44.53	39.92	3.41	5.00	0.43
1963	11.46	3.96	45.35	42.24	3.69	5.09	0.44
1964	11.24	4.29	48.18	44.25	3.93	5.36	0.51
1965	10.71	4.99	53.51	47.33	4.42	5.85	0.55
1966	10.02	6.42	64.42	49.17	4.90	7.82	0.78
1967	9.66	6.46	62.37	48.83	5.06	9.55	0.99
1968	11.02	6.50	71.60	56.21	5.10	5.53	1.15
1969	8.73	7.70	67.88	53.65	6.14	10.02	5.10

Notes:

The statistics for 1934 - 1936 relate to the undertaking as a whole, i.e. tram, trolleybus and motor bus. Full separate trolleybus statistics are not available for these years.

4) Abstracts of Accounts (In each case for year ending 31 March)

Year	Total Revenue	Working Expenses	Gross Balance (Excluding bank interest)	Net Rev Charges (Loan & interest charges)	Net Balance Profit (loss)	Capital Expenditure	Sales (+) and write-offs (-)	Note	Cumul. capital Expenditure	Miles run	Passengers carried	Nbr veh.
1934						10,008 8 5			10,008 8 5			4
1935						84,303 0 9			94,311 9 2			37
1936	114,871 2 5	77,653 2 2	37,218 0 3	23,455 0 0	13,763 0 3	177,448 16 1	34,000 0 1	1	305,760 5 3	1,857,984	18,973,849	106
1937	168,362 2 11	115,506 5 0	53,470 18 9	39,411 19 0	14,058 19 9	30,659 10 8	0 0		336,419 15 11	2,570,421	26,324,803	104
1938	180,018 11 7	124,586 10 11	55,432 0 8	41,145 0 0	14,404 0 1	7,997 7 2			344,417 3 1	2,785,462	26,994,490	104
1939	182,617 19 5	132,628 14 0	49,989 5 5	41,885 0 0	8,104 5 5	13,411 0 10	119,012 0 2	2	476,840 10 11	2,917,087	27,390,558	104
1940	190,071 3 7	137,145 0 0	52,926 3 7	41,929 6 11	10,996 6 8	1,321 8 0			478,161 18 11	2,794,812	28,494,985	104
1941	171,640 18 8	127,882 1 11	43,758 16 9	39,540 0 0	4,218 16 9	136 17 0			478,298 15 11	2,316,843	25,709,253	104
1942	252,016 17 1	161,906 13 10	90,110 4 3	67,487 0 0	22,623 4 3		1,450 0 3	3	476,848 15 11	2,738,982	36,775,895	104
1943	272,910 5 11	179,594 6 5	93,315 19 6	33,342 0 0	59,973 19 6	2,923 7 6	67,270 11 11	4	412,500 16 11	2,827,512	40,951,696	104
1944	261,063 2 7	178,160 0 5	82,903 2 2	31,901 0 0	51,002 2 2	63 14 3			412,564 11 2	2,535,435	35,361,965	103
1945	289,462 9 8	195,852 12 1	93,609 17 7	27,339 0 0	66,984 4 3	710 9 2			413,275 0 4	2,504,769	38,395,486	103
1946	311,980 7 6	218,010 16 5	93,969 11 1	18,932 0 0	75,037 11 1	7 11 0			413,282 11 4	2,573,489	40,665,391	103
1947	328,719 8 9	253,757 17 5	74,961 11 4	7,955 0 0	67,006 11 4	293 9 9	5,167 14 11	4	418,743 16 0	2,983,757	42,735,741	103
1948	338,650 10 9	285,823 9 2	52,827 1 7	8,031 0 0	44,796 1 7	1,941 11 1			420,685 7 1	3,197,703	43,512,250	103
1949	350,214 5 7	319,143 19 1	31,070 6 6	8,372 0 0	22,698 6 6	5,819 0 2			426,504 7 3	3,435,851	46,131,073	103
1950	342,816 7 9	330,719 7 0	12,097 0 9	8,457 0 0	3,640 0 9	4,753 16 0			431,258 3 3	3,417,963	47,255,913	103
1951	333,445 4 8	329,410 10 7	4,034 14 1	9,447 0 6	-5,412 5 11	155,366 15 2			586,624 18 5	3,319,141	45,235,606	127
1952	396,458 19 0	345,782 12 4	50,676 6 8	31,938 4 11	18,738 1 9	22,507 2 10			609,132 1 3	3,040,327	40,740,388	127
1953	399,507 19 4	370,907 11 6	28,600 7 10	34,280 0 6	-5,679 12 8	40,675 13 0	79,360 19 0	5	570,446 15 3	2,983,688	38,660,146	109
1954	406,547 12 0	351,422 8 10	55,125 3 2	39,949 4 6	15,175 18 8	3,448 17 6	13,299 0 0	5	560,596 12 9	2,759,805	34,390,263	103
1955	401,940 0 0	369,168 0 0	32,772 0 0	40,202 0 0	-7,272 0 0	1,200 0 0			561,797 0 0	2,734,333	33,441,804	103
1956	409,299 0 0	378,851 0 0	30,448 0 0	38,947 0 0	-8,499 0 0	39,136 0 0	67,431 0 0	6	533,502 0 0	2,709,685	32,114,997	103
1957	436,155 0 0	351,417 0 0	84,738 0 0	40,166 0 0	44,572 0 0	10,804 0 0			544,306 0 0	2,439,872	29,086,555	103
1958	404,932 0 0	345,784 0 0	59,148 0 0	39,812 0 0	19,336 0 0		22,165 0 5	5	522,141 0 0	2,234,470	27,053,030	93
1959	397,853 0 0	346,434 0 0	51,419 0 0	40,770 0 0	10,649 0 0	138,363 0 0	44,330 0 5	5	616,174 0 0	2,233,197	26,427,978	100
1960	392,326 0 0	339,686 0 0	52,640 0 0	54,954 0 0	-2,314 0 0	73,772 0 0	44,330 0 5	5	645,616 0 0	2,212,402	25,974,738	90
1961	382,160 0 0	327,160 0 0	55,000 0 0	57,685 0 0	-2,685 0 0	3,784 0 0			649,400 0 0	2,129,572	25,196,802	90
1962	398,928 0 0	349,421 0 0	49,507 0 0	42,042 0 0	7,465 0 0				686,776 0 0	2,099,573	24,557,919	83
1963	402,434 0 0	366,716 0 0	35,718 0 0	44,406 0 0	-8,688 0 0	37,376 0 0	3,414 0 5	5	683,362 0 0	2,083,612	23,875,422	83

Year	Total Revenue	Working Expenses	Gross Balance (Excluding bank interest)	Net Rev Charges (Loan & interest charges)	Net Balance Profit (loss)	Capital Expenditure	Sales (+) and write-offs (-)	Note	Cumul. capital Expenditure	Miles run	Passengers carried	Nbr veh.
1964	429,090 0 0	382,507 0 0	46,583 0 0	46,818 0 0	-235 0 0		11,671 0 0	5	671,691 0 0	2,074,431	23,319,122	77
1965	447,673 0 0	387,817 0 0	59,856 0 0	50,259 0 0	9,597 0 0		8,866 0 0	5	662,825 0 0	1,966,430	21,057,307	73
1966	424,088 0 0	313,196 0 0	110,892 0 0	51,356 0 0	59,356 0 0		8,199 0 0	5	654,626 0 0	1,529,852	15,332,449	63
1967	317,014 0 0	241,359 0 0	75,655 0 0	48,746 0 0	26,909 0 0		148,710 0 0	7	505,916 0 0	1,186,210	11,456,601	29
1968	228,202 0 0	168,748 0 0	59,454 0 0	38,662 0 0	20,792 0 0				505,916 0 0	720,493	7,997,929	29
1969	232,674 0 0	176,615 0 0	56,059 0 0	33,703 0 0	22,356 0 0				505,916 0 0	790,037	6,899,945	29
1970							284,858 0 0	6	221,058 0 0	0		
1971							221,058 0 0	7	0 0 0	0		

Notes:

1 Tramway equipment sales
2 Power station and tramway equipment sales
3 Trolleybus withdrawn (single-decker)
4 Believed to apply to the write-off of the remaining tramway debts
5 Trolleybuses scrapped
6 Power station plant scrapped
7 Overhead equipment abandonment

Comments:

The amounts shown above are extracted from a variety of different official statistics prepared by Bournemouth Corporation Transport Services for the Transport Committee and do not necessarily exactly reflect the final Annual Accounts produced by the Bournemouth Borough Council Treasurer's Office. Any discrepancies are due to delayed credits or debits, bank interest earned, etc.

The above figures relate solely to the trolleybus operations of Bournemouth Corporation Transport Services. Trolleybuses ran primarily on the most heavily-laden and thus most profitable services. That trolleybus operations always made a trading profit, and that they made a net profit in all but eight years of their 35 year tenure is thus not solely related to their passenger appeal and economic running costs. Pre-war the undertaking as a whole made a net loss due to the outstanding loan charges from the tramway system, the tram to trolleybus conversion programme and the new trolleybus fleet. Profits from trolleybus operations were used to subsidise the less profitable motorbus services, as funding for the Department's reserves and as contributions towards the rates (totalling £113,00 in the immediate post-war period).

5) Traction Current used

Year	Units generated for traction	Units bought	Traction Units	Units per mile	Cost per mile (d)	Cost per Unit (d)	Notes
1934	3,876,530	1,466,405	5,342,935	2.35			Tram/Trolleybus
1935	4,019,640	1,437,631	5,457,271	2.39			Tram/Trolleybus
1936	5,512,110	634,152	6,146.262	2.38			Tram/Trolleybus
1937	4,841,420	1,389,530	6,230,950	2.42	1.85	0.764	Trolleybus only
1938	4,747,350	1,860,240	6,607,590	2.37	1.99	0.840	
1939	5,115,710	1,924,345	7,040,055	2.41	2.04	0.846	
1940	4,748,900	2,058,541	6,807,441	2.43	2.14	0.880	
1941	3,857,820	1,833,000	5,690,820	2.46	2.55	1.037	
1942	5,025,690	1,808,030	6,833,720	2.49	3.41	1.369	
1943	5,455,100	1,901,565	7,356,665	2.60	3.38	1.300	
1944	5,206,150	1,619,910	6,826,060	2.69	3.15	1.171	
1945	4,693,990	2,268,890	6,962,880	2.78	3.56	1.281	
1946	5,044,420	2,319,575	7,363,995	2.86	4.03	1.409	
1947	5,084,110	3,362,015	8,446,125	2.83	3.83	1.353	
1948	5,918,030	2,683,225	8,601,255	2.70	4.05	1.500	
1949	6,161,860	2,947,105	9,108,965	2.65	4.02	1.517	
1950	6,077,500	2,813,255	8,890,755	2.60	4.15	1.596	
1951	6,341,206	2,879,485	9,220,691	2.78	4.55	1.637	
1952	6,038,105	2,826,600	8,864,705	2.92	5.35	1.832	
1953	5,699,671	3,166,390	8,866,061	2.97	6.11	2.057	
1954	5,024,290	2,884,500	7,908,790	2.86	6.2	2.168	
1955	4,733,110	3,142,830	7,875,940	2.89	6.6	2.284	
1956	1,286,980	7,208,150	8,495,130	3.13	5.44	1.738	Generating station closed 31AUG55
1957		7,679,150	7,679,150	3.15	4.45	1.413	
1958		7,190,670	7,190,670	3.22	4.69	1.456	
1959		7,350,483	7,350,483	3.29	4.77	1.450	
1960		7,081,660	7,081,660	3.20	4.51	1.409	
1961		7,046,280	7,046,280	3.31	4.65	1.406	
1962		7,120,885	7,120,885	3.39	5.02	1.479	
1963		6,918,690	6,918,690	3.32	5.08	1.529	
1964		6,998,480	6,998,480	3.34	5.19	1.538	
1965		6,546,670	6,546,670	3.33	5.23	1.572	
1966		4,910,862	4,910,862	3.21	6.06	1.887	
1967		3,205,967	3,205,967	2.70	7.72	2.118	
1968		2,334,350	2,334,350	3.24	6.43	1.986	
1969		2,297,900	2,297,900	2.90	5.72	1.96	

Notes:

The statistics for 1934 - 1936 relate to the undertaking's combined electric traction, i.e. tram and trolleybus.
Full separate trolleybus statistics are not available for these years.

BIBLIOGRAPHY

Title	Author	Publisher	Date	ISBN number
Books, Brochures and Pamphlets				
Book of Bournemouth	David & Rita Popham			
Bournemouth and the Second World War	M.A. Edgington	Bournemouth Local Studies Publications	1994	ISBN 1-873887-03-5
Bournemouth Corporation Transport, Vol. 1	John Mawson	Advertiser Press	1967	
Bournemouth Corporation Transport, Parts 1 & 2	W.P. Ransom	Bournemouth Local Studies Publications	1982	ISBN 0 96287 40 5 & 41 5
Bournemouth Trams and Buses	C.G. Roberts	Locomotion Papers	1972	
Bournemouth Trolleybuses 1933-1969	David L. Chalk	Bournemouth Corporation Transport	1969	
The Tramways of Bournemouth and Poole	R.C. Anderson	Light Railway Transport League	1964	
Bournemouth and Poole Tramways	R.C. Anderson	Middleton Press	1995	
85th Anniversary Bournemouth Transport	David L. Chalk	Bournemouth Transport	1987	
Bournemouth Transport 75 years	David L. Chalk	Bournemouth Transport	1977	
Transport Department Diamond Jubilee 1902-1962		Bournemouth Corporation Transport	1962	
Brighton Corporation Transport - Fleet History	R. Knight	E.L.P.G. Enterprises	1971	
History of the British Trolleybus	Nicholas Owen	David & Charles	1974	ISBN 0 7153 6370 0
Llanelly Trolleybuses	Geoff Griffiths	Trolleybooks	1992	ISBN 0 904235 15 7
Silent Service	David L. Chalk	Omnibus Society	1962	
Trolleybus Trails	J. Joyce	Ian Allan	1963	
The Trolleybuses of Brighton and Hove	David Kaye & Martin Nimmo	Reading Transport Society	1967	
The Trolleybuses of Newcastle upon Tyne	T.P. Cannaux & N.H. Hanson	Trolleybooks	1974	ISBN 0 904235 02 5
The Trolleybuses of South Shields	Geoff Burrows	Trolleybooks	1976	ISBN 0 904235 04 1
Under Two Liveries	H. Brearley & D.T. Beach	West Riding Transport Society	1970	
Newspapers				
The Bournemouth Daily Echo		Copies held at Bournemouth Reference Library	1900-1958	(30 June 1958)
Bournemouth Evening Echo		Copies held at Bournemouth Reference Library	1958-1972	(1 July 1958)
Bournemouth Visitors' Directory		Copies held at Bournemouth Reference Library	1861-	
Bournemouth Times & Directory		Copies held at Bournemouth Reference Library		
Professional Periodicals				
Bus & Coach		Particularly September 1958 issue		
Electrical Review	W.D. Reakes	27 May 1960 issue		
Passenger Transport		Particularly 16 August 1950, 4 May 1955 issues		
The Commercial Motor		Particularly 19 March 1937, 24 May 1946 issues		
The Tramway & Railway World				
The Transport World		Particularly 19 July 1934, 7 November 1935, 14 May 1936, 18 June 1936 issues		

Title	Author	Publisher	Date	ISBN number
Enthusiast's Periodicals				
Buese Illustrated (issues 30, 88,147 including Bournemouth trolleybus related articles)		Ian Allan	1949-70	
National Trolleybus Association Newssheet		National Trolleybus Association	1963-	
Reading Transport Society Newssheet		Reading Transport Society	1961-1966	
Journal of the Bournemouth Passenger Transport Association (known variously as Journal of the Bournemouth Heritage Transport Collection, Transbourne News, Trolley)		Bournemouth Passenger Transport Association	1969-1995	
Trolleybus (Journal of the Reading Transport Society until April 1971 and of the British Trolleybus Society thereafter)		British Trolleybus Society Particularly Vol. 46, No. 551, June 2007 issue	1967-date	
Trolleybus Society Newssheet		Trolleybus Society	1954-55	
Trolleybus Magazine		National Trolleybus Association	1963-date	
Others				
Bournemouth Council Minutes			1912-1972	
Transport Committee Minutes			1912-1972	